The Huainanzi

TRANSLATIONS FROM THE ASIAN CLASSICS

The Huainanzi

A GUIDE TO THE THEORY AND PRACTICE OF GOVERNMENT IN EARLY HAN CHINA

Liu An, King of Huainan

Translated and edited by
John S. Major, Sarah A. Queen, Andrew Seth Meyer, and Harold D. Roth, with additional contributions by Michael Puett and Judson Murray

COLUMBIA UNIVERSITY PRESS
NEW YORK

Columbia University Press
Publishers Since 1893
New York Chichester, West Sussex

Library of Congress Cataloging-in-Publication Data
Huainan zi. English
The Huainanzi : a guide to the theory and practice of government in early Han China / Liu An, King of Huainan [. . . [et al.]] ; translated and edited by John S. Major . . . [et al.], with additional contributions by Michael Puett and Judson Murray.
p. cm. — (Translations from the Asian classics)
Includes bibliographical references and index.
ISBN 978-0-231-14204-5 (cloth : alk. paper)
I. Liu, An, 179–122 B.C. II. Major, John S. III. Title. IV. Title: Guide to the theory and practice of government in early Han China. V. Series.
BL1900.H822E5 2010
181'.114—dc22

2009019565

Columbia University Press books are printed on permanent and durable acid-free paper.
This book is printed on paper with recycled content.
Printed in the United States of America

c 10 9 8 7 6 5

For our children

CONTENTS

ACKNOWLEDGMENTS

WE OWE a particular debt of gratitude to three colleagues who participated actively in this translation project. Michael Puett and Judson Murray served as cotranslators of chapters 13 and 21, respectively, and they also participated in many of our team meetings and online conversations and made many valuable contributions. Jay Sailey's active and enthusiastic participation in the early stages of our work helped get the project off to a good start, and his continuing interest in our work provided welcome moral support.

William Boltz's work of determining the ending rhymes for sentences enabled us to proceed with our method of formatting the translations so as to preserve such distinctive features as parallel prose and verse. Jung-Ping Yuan and Bo Lawergren provided much-appreciated advice about ancient Chinese stringed instruments. Similarly, we thank Scott Cook and Dan Lusthaus for lending us their expertise on musical matters. We thank Martin Kern of Princeton University for sharing with us his penetrating insights into the structure and rhetoric of chapter 21 of the *Huainanzi*, and Michael Nylan of the University of California at Berkeley for her comments on the structure of chapter 7. We are grateful also to Charles Le Blanc, Rémi Mathieu, and their co-workers on the complete French translation of the *Huainanzi* for their collegiality and goodwill. Our work has also benefited enormously from the textual labors of several modern scholars; we would like to express our gratitude to Zhang Shuangdi, Chen Yiping, and He Ning for their critical editions; to Kusuyama Haruki for his critical edition and Japanese translation; and to D. C. Lau and his associates in the ICS Ancient Chinese Text Concordance Series project at the Chinese

University of Hong Kong for the splendid concordance edition that we have used as the basic text for our translation.

Anne Holmes prepared this book's index with her customary effortless-seeming expertise. Sara Hodges did similarly excellent work on the book's maps. Matthew Duperon at Brown University did yeoman's work on the book's bibliographical appendix, as well as helping check the notes and other tasks in the final stages of manuscript preparation. Gail Tetreault, Kathleen Pappas, and Melina Packer at Brown University and Nancy Lewandowski at Connecticut College provided invaluable staff support for the project, for which we are very grateful.

We are deeply indebted to our editor at Columbia University Press, Jennifer Crewe, for her expert and supportive work on this volume. We also wish to thank the project editor, Irene Pavitt; the copy editor, Margaret B. Yamashita; and the book's designer, Lisa Hamm. In addition, we want to express our appreciation for the careful reading of our manuscript by the press's peer reviewers, who made many valuable suggestions for improving our work.

We acknowledge with deep gratitude the support of the Chiang Ching-kuo Foundation for International Scholarly Exchange, which provided a two-year grant to launch this translation project. Without that initial funding, this book very likely would not exist. Some of Harold Roth's later work on the project was supported by a grant from the National Endowment for the Humanities. Additional funding from the trustees of Brown University for the Richard B. Salomon Faculty Research Awards, and the Brown University Departmental Research Funds for Arts, Humanities, and Social Sciences enabled our translation team to meet at Brown several times a year for a period of more than a decade. Those meetings were the key to making this project a truly collaborative effort.

For the members of the translation team, the writing of this book involved not only difficult challenges and sustained hard labor over a period of years but also steadily strengthening feelings of collegiality, friendship, and pleasure in one another's company. Accordingly, each of us thanks the others for making this project a rich and deeply gratifying experience.

In addition, John Major wishes to thank Professors Nathan Sivin and Ying-shih Yü for first guiding his steps onto the path of *Huainanzi* studies, and to acknowledge with grateful memory several scholars of an older generation, including Derk Bodde, Wing-tsit Chan, H. G. Creel, Benjamin I. Schwartz, and Joseph Needham, for their kind encouragement and support. He feels a great debt of gratitude to many colleagues in the field of Early China studies, too numerous to mention individually, for their friendship and generosity over the course of a long and rewarding career. He also thanks his wife, Valerie Steele, and his brother, David C. Major, both of whom read large sections of the manuscript and made many valuable suggestions for its improvement. He is grateful as well to his son Steve Major for his understanding and enthusiasm, and to his nephew Graham Majorhart for invaluable last-minute assistance.

Sarah Queen wishes to thank her mentors who inspired, encouraged, and guided her in her initial forays into Han intellectual history: Benjamin I. Schwartz, Tu Wei-ming, Michael Loewe, and Nathan Sivin. She would also like to thank John Major and Harold Roth for inviting her to participate in the most gratifying project of her academic career and for all the years of guidance, expertise, and support that each has offered her as she sought to expand the depth and breadth of her expertise in Han intellectual history. In addition, she would like to thank her colleagues in the field of Early China who shared their knowledge, offered their encouragement, and gave generously of their time as she developed various interpretive arguments for this project: Paul Goldin, Martin Kern, Michael Nylan, Michael Puett, and David Schaberg. Finally, on a more personal note, Sarah Queen would like to thank her family and friends for their endless reserves of love and support. She offers a special thanks to Thomas and Benjamin for understanding their mother's seemingly insatiable penchant to get lost in early Chinese texts.

Andrew Meyer first encountered the *Huainanzi* in Hal Roth's undergraduate seminar, an experience that changed his life. He thanks his mentors in classical Chinese here and overseas and his instructors in Chinese history, especially Peter Bol, whose teaching has indelibly shaped his approach to intellectual history. He thanks his colleagues and administrators at Brooklyn College for their support, and the Whiting Foundation which provided generous financial support during part of his work on this project. Finally, he thanks his wife, Emilie, who assisted in the editing of early drafts, and his daughter, Ada, who was very patient while Mommy and Daddy peered at rows of Chinese writing.

Harold Roth wishes to thank his early mentors, Frederick Mote and Tu Wei-ming, for initiating him into the long and winding path of Chinese studies; Wayne Schlepp for his patient demonstration of careful scholarship; Angus Graham for his brilliant work, his always interesting eccentricities, and his kindly teaching; and Joshu Sasaki for his deep insight and encouragement. Many other colleagues in the field have given him support at critical moments in his career, and he would like to take this opportunity to acknowledge several of them: Fred Ward, Benjamin Wallacker, Roger Ames, Paul Thompson, Sarah Allan, and Henry Rosemont Jr. He gratefully acknowledges the support, over the years, of the chairs of the Departments of Religious Studies and East Asian Studies at Brown University. He also wants to thank his sons, Zach and Gus, and his wife, Lis, for their support and understanding through the fourteen years of this project.

Collectively, we thank our predecessors in the study of the *Huainanzi*. Only by standing on their capacious shoulders have we been able to accomplish our own work in the field. Above all, we thank Liu An and his long-ago circle of thinkers at the court of Huainan for bequeathing to posterity his marvelous book, which we now have the privilege of presenting for the first time in its entirety to the English-speaking world.

The Huainanzi

INTRODUCTION

THIS BOOK is the first complete English translation of the *Huainanzi,* a work from the early Han dynasty that is of fundamental importance to the intellectual history of early China. With this translation, we hope to acquaint specialists and general readers alike, to a degree that heretofore was not possible, with the philosophical richness of the text, its careful and deliberate organization and presentation of a great range of material, and the sophistication of its literary style and rhetorical techniques.

In 139 B.C.E., the imperial kinsman Liu An, king of Huainan, presented to the young Emperor Wu of the Han dynasty a book in twenty-one chapters, today known as the *Huainanzi* (*Master of Huainan*). Concise but encyclopedic and drawing on a wide range of sources, this book was designed to survey the entire body of knowledge required for a contemporary monarch to rule successfully and well. Organized in a "root and branch" structure, the work's early chapters set out the fundamental nature of the world and of human society, while the later chapters deal with the application of that knowledge to various practical concerns. Taken as a whole, the work is in effect a model curriculum for a monarch-in-training.

In this introduction, we give an overview of the *Huainanzi,* its historical context, and our principles and methods of translation. We also discuss the *Huainanzi*'s content, organization, and sources; the place of the text in early Han history; and the various ways in which the *Huainanzi* has been viewed by scholars. In addition, we also provide a substantial introduction to each chapter.[1] The translated chapters themselves are the heart of the book.

We believe that most of the *Huainanzi* was written during the reign of Emperor Jing (157–141 B.C.E.), several decades and three imperial generations into the Han era. During those decades, a controversy raged over the proper organization and structure of the imperial realm: Was it to be centralized, decentralized, or a mixture of the two? Although the *Huainanzi* deals much more with fundamental philosophical issues and their application than it does with nuts-and-bolts questions of state organization and administration, this controversy is an essential part of the background for understanding the work as a whole. Indeed, this controversy bore directly on the hopes and aspirations of the work's patron, editor, and coauthor, Liu An. Accordingly, it is with this background that we begin.

The Early Han Background to the *Huainanzi*: The History, Politics, and Competing Images of Empire

When the rebel leader Liu Bang proclaimed himself the king of Han in 206 B.C.E., he had to confront the causes of the Qin dynasty's collapse and its mixed legacy. Although the Qin had succeeded in unifying the empire by defeating or forcing the capitulation of the independent polities of the late Warring States period, the Qin Empire had proved ephemeral, dissolving in rebellion after the death of the First Emperor. As Liu Bang triumphed over his rival Xiang Yu in the post-Qin struggle, taking the title of emperor in 202, he was perhaps already thinking about how to perpetuate the unification of the empire while avoiding the causes of Qin's rapid collapse. What vision of empire, form of governance, and techniques of statecraft would be most efficacious in the quest to establish a more enduring dynasty? How would the newly founded Han dynasty build on the administrative successes of the Qin but at the same time avoid its catastrophic policy failures?

The answers to these questions were not at all clear. Indeed, they were to be worked out only slowly in the ensuing decades, during the reigns of Liu Bang himself (Emperor Gaozu) and his successors Liu Ying (Emperor Hui), the Empress Dowager Lü Zhi (whose disputed reign lasted from 188 to 180 B.C.E.), Liu Heng (Emperor Wen), Liu Qi (Emperor Jing), and Liu Che (Emperor Wu). During that period, lasting slightly more than a century, numerous scholars, officials, and members of the imperial household made competing claims and offered various responses concerning these vital questions.

The founder of the Han and his immediate successors did not lack for advice. Liu Bang himself was an unlettered man of action, scornful of scholarly long-windedness,

1. These introductory materials in themselves amount to a "book-within-a-book" about the *Huainanzi*, and some readers might find it helpful to read them consecutively as a way of gaining an overview of the entire text before reading the translated chapters themselves.

but he was willing to listen to the advice of Lu Jia (ca. 228–140 B.C.E.) on the merits of (possibly imagined) Zhou-style court rituals, as well as the maintenance in milder form of many Qin administrative policies and on techniques for recruiting able officials. Shusun Tong (d. after 188 B.C.E.) played a central role in designing Liu Bang's imperial rituals.[2] Emperors Hui and Wen benefited from the advice of the courtier Jia Yi (201–169 B.C.E.), whose literary works are seen as being in the tradition of Confucius and who attacked the statist policies of Qin (associated with such thinkers as Lord Shang and Li Si) as excessively zealous. Chao Cuo (d. 154 B.C.E.) grounded much of his political advice in his understanding of the classic *Documents* (*Shang shu*) but nevertheless was a proponent of increasing the power of the central government against that of the neofeudal kingdoms. During the reign of Emperors Wen and Jing, and especially under the influence of their mother, Empress Dowager Dou, prominence was given to the advice of a number of scholars who proposed an ideal of state policies based on the model of the sage-emperor embodied in the *Laozi* and the centralizing tendencies and cosmological empowerment associated with the supposed teachings of the Yellow Emperor. (As we note later, all these advisers seem to have based their arguments on their interpretations of specific texts, and all drew on diverse traditions. Thus subsequent efforts to assign these early Han figures to "schools" are, in our view, anachronistic and unhelpful.)

Despite six decades' worth of conflicting advice, what was true for Liu Bang, the founding father of the Han, remained true for his great-grandson and successor Liu Che. Various models of how to organize and govern an empire, drawn from the collective experience of China's past with their attendant forms of governance and policies, contended for supremacy. At one extreme was the highly centralized model of the Qin, which, as the Qin implemented it, must have seemed to many Han observers to have been a serious mistake. At the other extreme was, reaching back further to the Western Zhou era, the decentralized model of the preimperial age sanctified by its association with the sage-rulers Kings Wen and Wu and the Duke of Zhou. Liu Bang's reign, as Michael Puett has argued, reflects an ambivalence toward these competing models of empire,[3] and this ambivalence gave rise to a third model that contained both centralized and decentralized elements and was the de facto sociopolitical arrangement of the Han Empire at the time of Liu Che's accession. On the one hand, in adopting the Qin title of emperor and instituting the commandery system of the Qin in about one-third of the empire, Liu Bang demonstrated his inclinations toward a highly centralized vision of empire. On the other hand, he also engaged in a number of acts expressly meant to distance himself from the Qin. He lowered taxes, a measure that proved to be immediately popular; however, proposals to reduce the strictness of the Qin legal code were made but not

2. Martin Kern, *The Stele Inscriptions of Ch'in Shih-huang: Text and Ritual in Early Chinese Imperial Representation*, American Oriental Series, vol. 85 (New Haven, Conn.: American Oriental Society, 2000), 170, 172–73, 176–79, 184–87.

3. Michael J. Puett, *The Ambivalence of Creation: Debates Concerning Innovation and Artifice in Early China* (Stanford, Calif.: Stanford University Press, 2001), 150–52.

implemented. To administer the remaining two-thirds of his empire, he revived the traditional practice of establishing regional kingdoms, parceling out large tracts of land, first to the military allies who aided him in his victory over Xiang Yu and later to his own kinsmen. Both groups were awarded the title of king, and they were granted extensive autonomy and authority in their respective local kingdoms. During the early decades of the Han period, Gaozu's integrative approach was debated among scholars and statesmen, especially given its association with the dynasty's founder and because it was the sociopolitical status quo at the start of Liu Che's reign.

Emperor Gaozu's commitment to Western Zhou ideals of governance also is apparent in the court rituals he chose to follow and his choice to rule with the Potency of Water (in the political application of the Five Phases theory, according to which each dynasty was believed to rule, in succession, through the Potency of Earth, Wood, Metal, Fire, or Water). Those symbolic acts marked the Han as the legitimate successor to the Western Zhou.[4] But the dangers of enfeoffment became increasingly clear to the emperor as a number of his regional kings revolted against the central court. In an effort to stave off the crisis, the emperor replaced the renegade rulers with members of his own family, but the potential danger was only diminished, not avoided entirely, as the history of the following decades would prove. Gaozu himself is said to have died from a wound received while fighting against Liu An's earliest predecessor, Ying Bu, the first king of Huainan, who had revolted against the emperor.[5]

Following Gaozu's death, the dynasty was plagued by a number of problems concerning dynastic succession. These included an attempted coup by Empress Dowager Lü, who seized power on the death of Emperor Hui in 188 B.C.E. and wielded de facto control during a confused interregnum until her own death in 180. As central power waned in the years after Gaozu's death, the power of the kingdoms grew proportionately. By the time of Emperor Wen's reign (180–157 B.C.E.), the kingdoms had become so powerful that a number of ministers began to advocate increased centralization to remedy the challenges posed by the fiefs. Thus began the policy of gradually reducing the size of the largest kingdoms.

The history of Huainan is an instructive example. The fief was first granted to Ying Bu (who was not a blood relative of the Liu clan) in 203 B.C.E. It was bestowed on Liu Chang, the seventh son of Emperor Gaozu (and, later, Liu An's father), in 196, after Ying Bu's rebellion and death; Liu Chang was still an infant when he became king of Huainan. Liu Chang's brother Liu Ying (Emperor Hui) ascended the throne in 193 and ruled until 188. He was succeeded (after the Empress Dowager Lü's interregnum) in 180 by another brother, Liu Heng (Emperor Wen). Unwilling to

4. Puett, *Ambivalence of Creation*, 151.

5. Ying Bu (also known as Qing Bu) was an ally of Xiang Yu in the wars of the Qin downfall; he later came over to the side of Liu Bang and was enfeoffed in 203 B.C.E. as the king of Huainan. After the failure of his revolt in 196 B.C.E., Ying was executed and his family exterminated. See Michael Loewe, *A Biographical Dictionary of the Qin, Han, and Xin Periods (221 BC–AD 24)* (Leiden: Brill, 2000), 651–52.

accept that he had been passed over as a potential heir of the throne and apparently dissatisfied with being only a territorial king, Liu Chang rebelled against Emperor Wen in 174, soon after reaching his majority. When the plot failed, Liu Chang was indicted and died on the road to exile. Many of his co-conspirators were executed, and the kingdom of Huainan was temporarily abolished, replaced by centrally administered commanderies. In 172, perhaps remorseful about the miserable death of his brother, Emperor Wen conferred fiefs on four of Liu Chang's sons, with Liu An, then about seven years old, becoming lord of Fuling. In 164, the emperor reestablished kingdoms in what had been Liu Chang's kingdom of Huainan but reduced their power by dividing the formerly massive realm into three: a smaller kingdom of Huainan plus the kingdoms of Hengshan and Lujiang. Liu An was then named the king of Huainan, succeeding at last to his father's title. This development must have been bittersweet: on the one hand, Liu An was elevated to the status of king, but on the other hand, the territory over which he ruled was drastically reduced from what his father had administered in the heyday of his career.

The settlement of 164 B.C.E., moreover, seemed to stem only temporarily the tide of unrest within the imperial clan, and the situation of the unruly kingdoms grew to crisis proportions during the reign of Emperor Jing. Seven of the enfeoffed kings launched a revolt against the central court in 154. Significantly, Liu An did not join the revolt, opting instead to demonstrate his support of and loyalty toward the central court. Emperor Jing was successful in quelling the revolt and further reduced the power of the kingdoms by expanding the commandery system. Nevertheless, the tensions between the two most polarized competing visions of empire—the exclusively centralized and the largely decentralized models—were anything but resolved, leaving some room for the development of a third model that negotiated a middle ground. Liu An's interest in making his influence felt at court during the reign of Emperor Jing was no doubt shaped by the complicated court politics and policies of that era. The *Huainanzi*, embodying Liu An's own understanding of how an empire should be organized and ruled, was most likely written during those years and probably in response to current affairs.

When Liu Che (Emperor Wu) assumed the throne at about fifteen years of age (sixteen *sui*, in Chinese reckoning) in 141 B.C.E., much of the empire remained under the control of the enfeoffed kings, and it was not clear whether the young emperor (still dominated by his grandmother, Empress Dowager Dou) would continue the centralizing efforts of his predecessor or resort to the earlier policies of Emperor Gaozu. Liu An, by then known as both a patron of learning and an imperial kinsman, presented a book—the work in twenty-one chapters that we now know as the *Huainanzi*—to Liu Che shortly after he ascended the throne. The gift apparently was intended to impress the young emperor with Liu An's particular vision of empire. The work reflects the interests of a royal relative whose primary concern was to preserve both the independence of his kingdom and his authority as its lord. The ideal empire was imagined in the *Huainanzi* as consisting of, first and foremost, a Zhou-style realm in which royal relatives administered semiautonomous local kingdoms

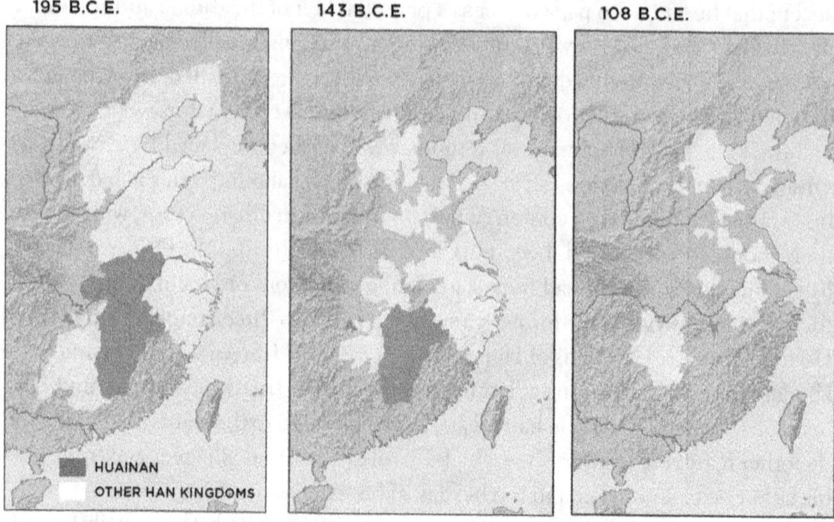

At the beginning of the Han era, the eastern half of the empire was divided into semiautonomous kingdoms ruled by members of the Liu clan; the western half of the empire was under the direct rule of the emperor. At the time the *Huainanzi* was written (during the reign of Emperor Jing), many of the kingdoms had been extinguished and their territory converted into commanderies, governed by appointed officials who reported to the imperial administration. The kingdom of Huainan was abolished in 122 B.C.E. By the end of the second century B.C.E., the kingdoms had almost entirely disappeared; the most prominent exceptions were Changsha, south of the middle reaches of the Yangzi River; Guangling, in the lower Yangzi valley; and Yan, in the eastern Yellow River Plain. (Map by Sara Hodges, with data from the China Historical Geographic Information service [CHGIS], version 4, Harvard Yenching Institute, Cambridge, Mass., January 2007)

while giving their ultimate allegiance to the benevolent rule of an enlightened sage-emperor. Using the model of Emperor Gaozu's integrative approach, Liu An and the authors of the *Huainanzi* also incorporated, on a more limited basis, different policies, techniques, and institutions characteristic of centralized as well as decentralized rule.

How to get the ruler to act on the vigorous arguments that the book made in defense of that vision, and the implicit and explicit claims concerning Liu An and his kingdom in this imagined realm, must have been Liu An's most pressing concern during his time in Chang'an. As the emperor (relying, Liu An must have hoped, on his avuncular advice) struggled to find a secure footing from which to challenge and eclipse the power and influence of Empress Dowager Dou, it was unclear what the future would hold, which court factions would emerge victorious, and in what policy direction the central court would head. The time was ripe for Liu An to stake his claim to political and intellectual authority.

Liu An and the *Huainanzi*

When Liu An succeeded to his father's throne in the kingdom of Huainan, he would have had two overriding policy goals and perhaps one covert ambition. The first goal would have been to remain in the good graces of his uncle Emperor Wen and later his cousin Emperor Jing, along with the latter's mother, Empress Dowager Dou. (A formidable figure, she had become a junior consort of Liu Heng, the future Emperor Wen, in 188 B.C.E. and was a dominant presence behind the throne from the time of her husband's accession in 180. She continued to wield power through the reign of her son Emperor Jing and into the reign of her grandson Emperor Wu, until her own death in 135.) The second goal would have been to promote policies, in whatever way Liu An could, that would preserve and expand the power of the Han kingdoms against the centralizing tendencies of the imperial throne. A possible covert ambition—one he could neither express nor pursue openly for fear of being accused of treason—might have been to position and promote himself as a possible heir to the throne during the reign of Emperor Jing. It would not have been implausible for another member of that generation (the grandsons of the founder, Liu Bang) to be considered in line for the throne.

Pursuing the first objective (and the third, if Liu An did indeed see himself as a potential heir to Emperor Jing) was in large part a matter of lying low and biding his time and of not risking all on desperate adventures. Thus we see Liu An declining to be a part of the Revolt of the Seven Kings in 154 B.C.E. The second objective would have demanded the use of the arts of political persuasion, an area in which Liu An proved to be adept as he grew into manhood.

Liu An was an enthusiastic man of letters, whose interests ranged from administrative matters to cosmology, from rhetoric to poetry, from natural philosophy to the occult. He was a great patron of scholarship, and he attracted to his court and lent support to a large number of men of learning. He was known as a quick, adept, and prolific writer and is credited with having produced many original works, including more than eighty *fu* (poetic expressions); treatises on alchemy, music, and natural philosophy; and a commentary on the *Chuci* poem "Li sao" (Encountering Sorrow). He is also known as the author of the work that bears the name *Huainanzi* (*Master of Huainan*),[6] although nowadays we would be more likely to use the term "general editor."

The earliest description of the *Huainanzi*, from the "Biography of Liu An" in Ban Gu's (32–92 C.E.) *Han shu* (*History of the* [*Former*] *Han Dynasty*), indicates that the

6. An alternative rendering of this title popularized by Mark Csikszentmihalyi is *Masters of Huainan*. Such a translation underscores the fact of multiple authorship. See Csikszentmihalyi, *Readings in Han Chinese Thought* (Indianapolis: Hackett, 2006), 63. However, we adhere to the traditional understanding of the titles of Chinese classics, which typically took the name of their putative author or patron (even when that author [e.g., Laozi] may have been a mythical figure). We believe that "Huainanzi" refers specifically to Liu An as the "Master of Huainan."

work was the product of many hands. According to Ban Gu, Liu An summoned no fewer than "several thousand guests and visitors" to his court, including a group of men called "masters of esoteric techniques" (*fangshushi*), presumably to contribute to the work. Ban Gu also describes the work as having a tripartite organization: an "inner book" consisting of twenty-one chapters; an "outer book" with more chapters than the inner book but an unspecified total number; and a "middle book" consisting of eight sections (*zhuan*) comprising an unknown number of chapters. This last book, said to consist of more than 200,000 words, discussed alchemical techniques relating to the quest to become a spirit immortal (*shen xian*).[7] Fragments of this lost work were compiled into reconstituted redactions by a number of Qing-dynasty scholars and show it to have been filled with the lore and recipes of the esoteric masters.[8]

In his preface to the *Huainanzi* (ca. 212 C.E.), the early commentator Gao You provides more detail:

> Many of the empire's masters of esoteric techniques journeyed [to Huainan] and made their home [at Liu An's court]. Subsequently [Liu An], with the following eight men, Su Fei, Li Shang, Zuo Wu, Tian You, Lei Bei, Mao Bei, Wu Bei, and Jin Chang, and various Confucians [*ru*][9] who were disciples of the Greater and Lesser Mountain [traditions], together discoursed upon the Way and its Potency and synthesized and unified Humaneness and Rightness to compose this work.[10]

Ban Gu emphasizes the rich discussions and debates that animated Liu An's court and likely engendered the content of some of the *Huainanzi*'s chapters. Chapter 13, "Fan lun" (Boundless Discourses), is an apt description of the essays that probably

7. *Han shu* 44/2145. For a list of works attributed to Liu An and his retainers, see Le Blanc 1985, 41–52. (For these and other abbreviated citations, see the section "Conventions Used in This Work" near the end of this introduction.)

8. Roth 1992, 432–34, lists eight such works.

9. In recent years, the word *ru* 儒 has occasioned a certain amount of scholarly controversy. It is often translated as "Confucian," and we follow that practice. Some scholars prefer to leave the term untranslated, pointing out that "Confucianism" as a coherent doctrine did not take shape until late in the Western Han period. We are not satisfied with that practice, as the actual meaning of *ru* is obscure, and the term as such is unfamiliar and potentially confusing or simply not informative to English-language readers except for specialists in early Chinese studies. Some other scholars have begun to translate *ru* as "classicists," but in our view that term is too broad. Many Han intellectuals who were not *ru* (such as Daoists and Mohists) appealed to the texts of their own traditions for classical authority; indeed, the *Huainanzi* itself takes the *Laozi* to be a canonical work. In our view, the most important feature of the early *ru* is that they invested canonical authority in texts (the *Odes*, the *Documents*, the *Spring and Autumn Annals*, etc.) that were closely associated with the tradition of Confucius. Thus we translate *ru* as "Confucian" or "Confucians."

For discussions of the word *ru*, see Nicolas Zufferey, *To the Origins of Confucianism: The Ru in Pre-Qin Times and During the Early Han Dynasty* (Bern: Peter Lang, 2003); Michael Nylan, "Han Classicists Writing in Dialogue About Their Own Tradition," *Philosophy East and West* 47, no. 2 (1997): 133–88; and Anne Cheng, "What Did It Mean to Be a *Ru* in Han Times?" *Asia Major*, 3rd ser., 14, no. 2 (2001): 101–18.

10. Gao You's preface in Zhang Shuangdi 1997, 1:1–2. For a discussion of key terms such as the Way, Potency, Humaneness, and Rightness, see app. A.

emerged from court discussions moderated by Liu An. On the basis of its content and formal characteristics, chapter 19, "Xiu wu" (Cultivating Effort), might be construed as a model of how to construct a successful debate or disputation. Still other chapters (for example, chapters 14, 16, and 17) appear to be collections of various types of performative literature and gnomic verse. Progress reports and chapter summaries also may have been presented orally and debated at court from time to time. The literary content and form of the majority of chapters, however, strongly suggest that the *Huainanzi* is predominantly the product of extensive compilation and composition from written sources. This observation tallies with Liu An's reputation, as he is said to have had a splendid library at his palace.

Regardless of exactly how the chapters were written, it is impossible to say whether or not the men named by Gao You were really the authors of any of them. Likewise, Liu An's exact role in compiling the book is unclear; it is possible that he was the author of some of the essays. Benjamin Wallacker suggests that he may have posed topics or prepared outlines on the basis of which his scholars studied, debated, and composed essays.[11] It is at least probable that Liu An exercised some sort of editorial supervision and approved the essays in their final form. Even a casual reading of several chapters is enough to indicate that not all the essays were written by the same hand, although the book as a whole does have thematic coherence (as we discuss more fully later).

In the end, any discussion of authorship of the *Huainanzi* is necessarily inconclusive, so we are left with the already well-known fact that the *Huainanzi* as a whole is the product of a group of scholars working under the supervision and the patronage of Liu An. Nonetheless, what is clear from Ban Gu's statements is that the text is a collaborative work that included Liu An in some manner and a number of men who were identified with differing areas of expertise and diverse specialties. Even though they drew on a wide range of sources and represented disparate points of view, the authors were chiefly concerned with forging a synthesis between the paired concepts of Way and Potency, on the one hand, and Humaneness and Rightness, on the other.

As noted previously, Liu An paid his respects at the court of Emperor Wu in 139 B.C.E., in the second year after the latter's enthronement. On that occasion, he presented a book to the emperor, described in the *History of the* [*Former*] *Han Dynasty*[12] as a work in twenty-one chapters (*pian*) entitled the *Nei shu* (*Inner Book*), which was duly added to the imperial library. Although some scholars have raised questions about exactly what Liu An presented to the emperor during his visit, most accept that it was something substantially identical to, or at least closely resembling, the work we now know as the *Huainanzi*.

That being so, we must ask again: For whom was the *Huainanzi* written? Many scholars have made the natural assumption that because the *Huainanzi* (or some version thereof) was presented *to* Emperor Wu, it must have been written *for* him.

---

11. Benjamin Wallacker, "Liu An, Second King of Huai-nan," *Journal of the American Oriental Society* 92 (1973): 36–49.

12. *Han shu* 44/2146.

But on reflection, that seems improbable. First, before the year 141 B.C.E., there was no reason for anyone to think that Liu Che would succeed to the throne. His accession was a result of a complicated and bloody struggle at court waged on his behalf by his mother and Empress Dowager Dou, and no one could have seen it coming a long way off. But with that in mind, it also seems improbable that a work as long, complicated, and sophisticated as the *Huainanzi* could have been written and edited by Liu An and his court scholars between the time the news of Liu Che's enthronement reached Huainan in 141 and the time Liu An left to make his respectful visit to the imperial court at Chang'an in 139. (It is possible that some of the work's chapters were written earlier by the Huainan scholars as independent texts; if many chapters were already to hand, it might have been possible to compile what we know as the *Huainanzi* on a tight schedule between 141 and 139. But even if that were so, it would not contradict our view that most of the content of the *Huainanzi* predates 141. It also seems to us unlikely that a work as organizationally coherent as the *Huainanzi* could have been assembled quickly from preexisting components.)

We believe it is much more likely that the *Huainanzi* was written during the reign of Emperor Jing, when Liu An was a talented and ambitious young man with a case to make for his own importance as a member of the imperial family and the ruler of a territorial kingdom. The strong indebtedness to the *Laozi* that characterizes parts of the work, including very conspicuously chapter 1, supports this interpretation, as the *Laozi* enjoyed substantial imperial patronage at the time. If that is so, who was the intended audience? Perhaps Emperor Jing, Liu An's cousin, in whose hands Liu An's future as a potential heir to the throne principally rested. Perhaps the intellectual world of the Han imperial court, broadly conceived. Perhaps Liu An himself, who could have used the work as a manual for his own ambitions. Perhaps Liu An's sons, who could inherit their father's imperial ambitions if circumstances proved propitious.

We will return to the question of the *Huainanzi*'s intended audience. For the moment, we rest our discussion by noting that it seems most unlikely that the work was written specifically for Emperor Wu. Rather, we think that in presenting his work to the imperial throne, Liu An was responding to changed circumstances and making the best of things. The young Liu Che had become emperor; Liu An had not. It therefore was in Liu An's interest to try to cultivate political and family influence over his young nephew[13] and to persuade him, if possible, of the importance of governing an empire composed in large part of feudal kingdoms such as Huainan, rather than of bureaucratic commanderies. The presentation of the *Huainanzi* to Emperor Wu was an important event, and it is easy to surmise why Han historians and bibliographers would make a special effort to record, retrospectively, the circumstances of that event. That is all the more true given the pivotal role of this emperor and his reign

13. Liu An's father and Emperor Jing's father were brothers; Liu An and Emperor Jing were thus cousins, and Emperor Wu, Emperor Jing's son, was (in modern genealogical terms) Liu An's first cousin once removed. But as a member of Emperor Wu's father's generation, Liu An's effective status with respect to the young emperor would have been that of an uncle.

not only in the changing relationship between the emperor and his royal relatives in the remaining local kingdoms but also in the related debates about centralized, decentralized, and mixed models of empire and competing theories of rulership.

A second question of interest is: Was the work presented to Emperor Wu the same as the received version of the *Huainanzi*? We agree with most scholars in believing that it was, although absolute proof is lacking. Records indicate that the work presented to Emperor Wu was a book in twenty-one chapters, and the present *Huainanzi* has exactly that number. The fact that the *Huainanzi* has been preserved (when all other works of Liu An have been lost except for scattered quotations in other texts) may be because it was added to the Han imperial library after Liu An's visit in 139 B.C.E. As we argue at greater length later, chapter 21, which serves as a postface summarizing and integrating the content of the first twenty chapters,[14] may well have been written especially for the occasion of presenting the text to Emperor Wu, to explain clearly to him what he was getting. The literary form of that chapter suggests that it was written for oral performance at the imperial court, as a poetic oration delivered, presumably, by Liu An himself. The reference in chapter 21 to "this book of the Liu clan" reinforces this view. It is also quite possible that the specific content of the work's chapters was modified for the purpose of making a presentation to the emperor—for example, adding material showing the benefits of relying on loyal and talented subordinates, or warning against the perils of centralized despotism. Our view, then, is that the work presented to Emperor Wu was substantially the same as the *Huainanzi* as we know it.

Other scholars, however, Michael Loewe prominent among them,[15] contend that while portions of the work as it now exists date from the period between 164 and 139 B.C.E., work on the compendium continued until Liu An's death seventeen years later.[16] Liu An's books and papers were confiscated by Emperor Wu's officials after his suicide, so any works written by Liu An or at his direction between the years 139 and 122 could easily have been incorporated into (or used to replace) the copy of the *Huainanzi* already in the imperial library. We have not encountered convincing arguments in favor of this position, however, which seems to rest primarily on the fact that it could have been so. But the notion that chapters may have been added to the text after it was presented to the throne in 139 requires rejecting the idea that chapter 21 was written exactly for that occasion. This argument also implicitly endorses the idea that the *Huainanzi* is at best a minimally organized text to which material could be added indiscriminately from time to time. In contrast, in our view, the chapters of the *Huainanzi* correspond to the *Nei shu* as described by Ban Gu[17] and were arranged in a deliberate and conscious order, all of a piece. This

14. In this way *Huainanzi*, chap. 21, resembles the final chapter (chap. 33) of the *Zhuangzi*, which similarly serves as a postface to and summary of the entire work.

15. Loewe, *Biographical Dictionary*, 244; Loewe's views in private correspondence with Aihe Wang, *Cosmology and Political Culture in Early China* (Cambridge: Cambridge University Press, 2000), 112.

16. These issues are explored in Roth 1992, 55–58.

17. *Han shu* 44/2145.

sense of conscious order is powerfully reinforced by the fact that the chapter titles themselves form a rhymed set.[18] As we will see, the text's structure and organization are purposeful and coherent, and the author's viewpoints on the key issues of the day are informed, reasoned, and readily discernable through careful consideration of its contents. Moreover, the work's systematic arrangement and the rhetorical and polemical arguments are summarized and described by the person most intimately associated with the text, Liu An, the putative author of chapter 21.

Of course, when the *Huainanzi* was entered into the imperial library collection in the late second century B.C.E., it embarked on a journey of its own. The text as we now know it undoubtedly reflects the work of later redactors and editors. One of us has written extensively on the textual history of the *Huainanzi*,[19] and the complex evolution of the text in the centuries after it was written is summarized in appendix C.

Having considered the questions of when and by whom the *Huainanzi* was written and what the original content of the work may have been, we will return to the questions of the book's intended audience and its intended effect on that audience. First, however, we need to say more about the life of Liu An.

During the early years of Emperor Wu's reign, Liu An's political ambitions did not meet with much success. Despite the cordial reception given him by the emperor in 139 B.C.E., he seems to have acquired little actual influence at court. In 139 and on subsequent visits, he apparently tried to win (or buy) the favor of influential court figures but never gained entry into the emperor's inner circle. Then with the death of Empress Dowager Dou in 135, Liu An's ambitions suffered a serious setback. Emperor Wu, now a strong-minded young man, set about purging the court of figures favored by the late Empress Dowager and her son Emperor Jing, men whose views, like Liu An's *Huainanzi*, privileged the canonical status of the *Laozi*. Liu An now found his position shifting from that of a would-be uncle/adviser to the emperor, to the compiler of a potentially seditious political work informed by a disfavored point of view. His gamble in presenting the *Huainanzi* to the throne had not succeeded, and he himself was in a dangerous position.

Back in Huainan, Liu An may have occupied his time by working with his court scholars on the middle book and the outer book of the *Huainanzi*; we do not know when those now-lost portions of the work were written.[20] But literary and scholarly efforts were not enough for him. Perhaps feeling frustrated and resentful, he was accused (how justly, it is now difficult to say) of harboring imperial ambitions and

---

18. We are indebted to Martin Kern for calling this important fact to our attention. See his "Language, Argument, and Southern Culture in the *Huainanzi*: A Look at the 'Yaolüe'" (paper presented at the conference "Liu An's Vision of Empire: New Perspectives on the *Huainanzi*," Harvard University, Cambridge, Mass., May 31, 2008), and "Western Han Aesthetics and the Genesis of the *Fu*," *Harvard Journal of Asiatic Studies* 63 (2003): 383–437.

19. Roth 1992.

20. Almost the entire middle book (also known as *Huainan zhongpian* 淮南中篇) has been lost, although some fragments have been preserved. The Tang- and Song-dynasty encyclopedias and commentaries often quote it, and these passages were collected by a number of Ming and Qing scholars under the title *Huainan wanbi shu* 淮南萬畢術. See also Roth 1992, 432–34.

having engaged in treasonous plotting. If he was a conspirator, he was an inept one. Even as he was said to have plotted, reports of his growing disloyalty reached the imperial court. In 123 B.C.E., an imperial commission concluded that Liu An was guilty of gross impropriety. Some later scholars have questioned that verdict, in part because the principal testimony against him came from an accused co-conspirator, Wu Bei (one of the scholars identified by Gao You as having shared in the writing of the *Huainanzi*), who was trying to save his own neck. But some of the evidence was damning; for example, Liu An had ordered an imperial seal carved for his own use. As officials made their way to Huainan to arrest Liu An and bring him to Chang'an, the last king of Huainan committed suicide in 122. His principal wife and his heir were executed, along with some other family members; his goods (including his extensive library) were confiscated by the throne; and the kingdom of Huainan was once again, and permanently, abolished. According to a later legend, recorded in the Tang Daoist hagiographical collection called the *Shenxianzhuan* (*Accounts of Spirit Immortals*), at the moment of his death Liu An and the members of his household, including even his domestic animals, were transformed into immortals and rose bodily into the heavens in broad daylight. Thus while Liu An might be accounted a political failure in his own era, he was not only esteemed as a thinker and a writer but also revered as an actual immortal, by at least some people in later times.

The Content and Organization of the *Huainanzi*

The Organization of the Text

In seeking to understand the principles that guided Liu An and his court scholars in arranging the twenty-one chapters of the text, we relied first on the *Huainanzi*'s chapter 21, "An Overview of the Essentials" (Yao lüe). Such an approach assumes that the postface was likely written by Liu An himself when the text was nearing completion or had just been completed, but before its presentation to Emperor Wu in 139 B.C.E. Most probably the postface, which has the literary form of a *fu* 賦 (poetic expression), was recited orally by Liu An when he presented the *Huainanzi* to the throne. We believe this to be a plausible assumption based on both internal and external evidence: the form and content of the postface itself, the biographical details of Liu An, and the bibliographical descriptions of the *Huainanzi*. As the preceding discussion indicates, "An Overview of the Essentials" is invaluable in providing an emic or internal understanding of the content, organization, and aims of the text. This chapter claims that the *Huainanzi* is (1) a comprehensive text containing all the theoretical knowledge a ruler needs to govern his empire successfully; (2) an eminently practical text, chiefly concerned with elucidating the interconnections between the Way as an abstract entity and its manifestations in concrete affairs; (3) a programmatic text providing the ruler with the requisite techniques to act efficaciously in any circumstance he might confront, whether looking outward to the world at large or focusing inward on the self; and (4) an unprecedented landmark text that both continues the pioneering work of the ancient sages and sage-kings of China's antiquity and, more important, innovatively expands on the legacy of the sages. The intended result was an unparalleled synthesis of early Chinese thought and political philosophy that subsumed and surpassed all that had come before it.

To appreciate these and other features of the work, a good procedure is for readers to read chapter 21 first, to familiarize themselves with the content, organization, and aims of both the text as a whole and its individual chapters, treating the postface as a preface written to help them navigate this long and complex compendium. There, readers will see that they are intended to proceed from the beginning of the work to its end, reading its chapters successively and reaping the benefits that each offers. Thus the *Huainanzi* constitutes a coherent work, following a purposeful organization that is anything but haphazard. The authors' vision of the text is one of interlinked and overarching coherence built on a cumulative reading of its individual chapters.

Looking across the twenty chapters that constitute the work, excluding the concluding postface, the text appears to fall into two parts that correspond roughly to the first and the second half of the text. Charles Le Blanc has argued that the first part of the text is devoted to "Basic Principles" (chapters 1–8) and that the second half is concerned with "Applications and Illustrations" (chapters 9–20).[21] We agree with Le Blanc's description of the structure of the text and his argument that the text shifts from basic principles to applications and illustrations. It is supported by a consideration of the chapter titles. The titles of the first twenty chapters of the text rhyme; the first rhyme sequence ends with the title of chapter 8, and the title of chapter 9 begins a new rhyme sequence.[22] It is further supported by the explicit language of the postface, which characterizes the change in emphasis in accordance with two complementary claims: that the work moves from explicating principles of the Way (*dao* 道) to illustrating its various applications in affairs (*shi* 事; that is, the ordinary tasks and concerns of humans), and from roots (*ben* 本) to branches (*mo* 末). Such a reading of the text also is supported by the summary of chapter 9 found in chapter 21, which equates "techniques" (*shu*) and "affairs" (*shi*): "'The Ruler's Techniques' [addresses] the affairs [*shi*] of the ruler of humankind."

The Structure of the Work: Roots and Branches

Roots: Theoretical Principles of the Way

We propose that this two-part division has even more profound significance than has heretofore been realized. The division between the Way and affairs, its content understood as signifying principles and applications, is a powerful guide to understanding the overall meaning of the text as well as a manifestation of the still

21. Charles Le Blanc, "*Huai nan tzu*," in *Early Chinese Texts: A Bibliographical Guide*, ed. Michael Loewe, Early China Special Monograph, no. 2 (Berkeley: Society for the Study of Early China and the Institute of East Asian Studies, University of California, 1993), 189.

22. Kern, "Language, Argument, and Southern Culture in the *Huainanzi*."

more fundamental metaphor of "roots and branches" that operates on many levels throughout the entire work. Perhaps the author of the postface puts it best in his attempt to give an overview:

> Thus,
> numerous are the words we have composed
> and extensive are the illustrations we have provided,
> yet we still fear that people will depart from the root and follow the branches.
> Thus,
> if we speak of the Way but do not speak of affairs,
> there would be no means to shift with[23] the times.
> [Conversely,]
> if we speak of affairs but do not speak of the Way,
> there would be no means to move with [the processes of] transformation. (21.1)

And furthermore,

> . . . if we spoke exclusively of the Way, there would be nothing that is not contained in it. Nevertheless, only sages are capable of grasping its root and thereby knowing its branches. At this time, scholars lack the capabilities of sages, and if we do not provide them with detailed explanations,
> then to the end of their days they will flounder in the midst of darkness and obscurity
> without knowing the great awakening brought about by these writings' luminous and brilliant techniques. (21.3)

For the author of the postface, the text was composed to incorporate both the root of the Way and the branches as expressed in human affairs. Moreover, the text is organized in close accordance with the root–branch metaphor that structures its discussion of cosmology, cosmogony, human history, and self-development at many points. Chapter 1, "Originating in the Way," is the root of the entire text, and the text moves through increasingly ramified and posterior realms until it lands in the "current day" of the Han in chapter 20.

The theoretical coherence of the text is most obvious in the first eight chapters, which can be seen as providing the foundational principles or "root" of the entire work. Chapter 1 is the root of these chapters and these chapters are the roots of the work, and within each chapter is found the same "root–branch" structure. We propose that this root–branch principle is operative at many ontological and existential levels throughout the *Huainanzi*. At the cosmic level, it may be perceived in the process of cosmogenesis: the universe began as a unitary, undifferentiated mass of energy that then coalesced by stages into yin and yang, the Five Phases, and the

23. Literally, "float and sink."

increasingly complex and differentiated world of space-time and matter (see the various cosmogonies laid out in 2.1).[24] At the level of human development, the root–branch process can be seen in the progress of the prenascent human being from "corporeal mass" to embryo to the progressive incorporation of distinct elements such as flesh, muscle, and bone (see 7.2). At the historical level, the principle is evident in the evolution of human society from the totally unstructured spontaneity of the age of Fuxi and Nüwa[25] through the ever-increasingly diversified and sophisticated forms of social and political organization in subsequent eras (this process is laid out at many points in the text, especially 6.7, 8.1, and 9.3).

The many levels (cosmic, personal, historicopolitical) at which the root–branch structure is conceptualized operate both synchronically and diachronically throughout the *Huainanzi*. An excellent example of this is found in 8.7:

> The thearch embodies the Grand One;
> the king emulates yin and yang;
> the hegemon follows the four seasons;
> the prince uses the six pitch pipes.[26]

The succession from thearchs to kings, hegemons, and princes is on one level a historical one: earlier rulers such as the Yellow Emperor were traditionally accorded the title *di* (emperor or thearch), while later rulers like the Zhou dynasts went by the title *wang* (king). During the Spring and Autumn period, some powerful aristocrats are said to have served as "hegemons," exercising authority over other rulers of territorial states; during the Warring States period, some rulers reigned as princes essentially independently of the Zhou monarchy. Thus in historical terms, each of these types of rulers modeled themselves on the cosmic principle most suited to the time in which each lived. Because the *di* lived in a simpler time, they embodied the cosmogonically prior and monistic Grand One; because the kings lived in a later and more complex era, they modeled themselves on the cosmogonically "younger" and structurally dualistic yin and yang; and so on. This digression may also be read synchronically. Han elites lived in an era that simultaneously possessed both emperors (for example, Emperor Wu, the ruler to whom the *Huainanzi* was presented) and kings (for example, Liu An, the patron of the text itself). The cosmogonic root–branch model provides not only a structural map of earlier eras in human history but also a normative guide to the prioritized stations of the "present-day" political matrix. Emperors must continue to embody the superior Grand One (which persists in and pervades the ramified reality of latter days), and kings must continue to model themselves on the subordinate phenomenon of yin and yang.[27] These simultaneous

24. See "Chapters and Chapter Sections" near the end of this introduction.

25. Serpent-bodied brother and sister deities portrayed in some Chinese myths both as fashioners of Heaven and Earth and as early rulers.

26. *Liu lü* (六律) means both "six pitch pipes" and "six standards."

27. "Hegemon" and "prince" would obviously have been anachronisms in the Han but would have had structural analogues in the officials and magistrates of the Han state bureaucracy.

synchronic and diachronic valences are operative throughout the text of the *Huainanzi* and are key to understanding its overall structure.

Branches: Applications and Illustrations of the Way in Human Affairs

The coherence of the second half of the text is somewhat less obvious. This has led some scholars to conclude that the organization and coherence of the text tend to break down after chapter 9.[28] In this regard, we would confirm with some qualifications the position of Charles Le Blanc, who has argued that the later chapters are chiefly concerned with illustrations and applications and that such concern is borne out by their literary form, content, and titles. These chapters are generally compilations of materials from different literary genres meant to illustrate broader principles of the Way introduced in chapters 1 through 8 as specific kinds of human affairs, often accompanied by editorializing comments provided by the *Huainanzi* compilers.[29] Accordingly, chapters in this half of the text carry titles containing terms such as "precepts" (*cheng* 稱), "responses" (*ying* 應), "overviews" (*lüe* 略), "discourses" (*lun* 論), "sayings" (*yan* 言), and "persuasions" (*shui* 說).[30]

Thus we would argue that there is a purposeful shift in focus between the first and second parts of the text that corresponds to the claims of the *Huainanzi* postface that the text aims to clarify the relationship between the Way and its affairs. So conceived, the relationship between the first and the second half of the text becomes eminently transparent; it is one of roots and branches. It also explains why the coherence and logical progression of the text might appear to break down. In the second half of the text, the reader encounters a bewildering stream of illustrations and applications. Such a panoply bespeaks the authors' stated intent to present a comprehensive account of the root that is the Way and its branches that are the applications to human affairs, an account that will stand the test of time and bring honor and glory to the Liu clan and prosperity and longevity to its reigning dynasty.

Both the Way-and-affairs and the roots-and-branches approaches to the text can be summarized in table 1, in which we hope to demonstrate that content and form are

---

28. For example, Mark Edward Lewis argues,

> Having ascended the primal unity, through first divisions, the structure of space and time, and the origins of man, to the highest forms of men in the sage and the ruler, the text, like the *Lü shi chun qiu*, loses a clear sense of structure. Nevertheless, the passage in the early chapters from primal unity to the sage provides a natural model for the ideal of an all-encompassing textual unity incorporating all philosophical and technical traditions. (*Writing and Authority in Early China* [Albany: State University of New York Press, 1999], 307)

29. A very good example of this approach is *Huainanzi*, chap. 14, "Sayings Explained" (Quan yan 詮言). Although not usually recognized as such, the chapter is a collection of nearly seventy maxims or brief sayings (*yan* 言) whose illustrative points are typically unpacked and explicated by the *Huainanzi* compilers at the end of each saying.

30. See, for example, chap. 10, "Profound Precepts" (Mou cheng 繆稱); chap. 13, "Boundless Discourses" (Fan lun 氾論); chap. 14, "Sayings Explained" (Quan yan 詮言); chap. 15, "An Overview of the Military" (Bing lue 兵略); and chaps. 16 and 17, "A Mountain of Persuasions" and "A Forest of Persuasions" (Shui shan 說山 and Shui lin 說林).

TABLE 1 Structure of the *Huainanzi*

Chapter Title	*Dao* 道: The Way	*Ben* 本: Roots
1. Originating in the Way	The principle of universality: the Way as the origin of all things and the source of comprehensiveness	The Way (*dao* 道)
2. Activating the Genuine	Cosmogonic principles of nondifferentiation, differentiation, division, transformation, and change	Potency (*de* 德)
3. Celestial Patterns	Principles of astronomy, astrology, and mathematical harmonics	Heaven (*tian* 天)
4. Terrestrial Forms	Principles of geography, topography, and ecology	Earth (*di* 地)
5. Seasonal Rules	Integration of time and space: annual cycles of yin and yang and the Five Phases	Cyclical time (*shi* 時)
6. Surveying Obscurities	Things respond resonantly to one another: a great mystery	Resonance (*ganying* 感應)
7. Quintessential Spirit	The origins and nature of human consciousness and physiology, principles of self-cultivation, and characteristics of the sage	Humankind (*ren* 人)
8. The Basic Warp	The distinguishing principles of sagely virtue, the authority of the ancient Five Emperors and Three Kings	Morality (*renyi* 仁義)
	***Shi* 事: Affairs**	***Mo* 末: Branches**
9. The Ruler's Techniques	The distinguishing techniques of the sagely ruler	Techniques (*shu* 術)
10. Profound Precepts	Illustrations of correct deportment toward the populace by means of Quintessential Sincerity	Precepts (*cheng* 稱)
11. Integrating Customs	Illustrations of how to integrate diverse customs and ritual practices broadly conceived	Records (*ji* 記)
12. Responses of the Way	Illustrations of how to respond to diverse circumstances by means of the Way, as the *Laozi* does	Exegesis (*jie* 解)
13. Boundless Discourses	Illustrations of how to assess and adjust to change as a sage does	Discourses (*lun* 論)
14. Sayings Explained	Demonstrations of how to compare by means of analogies and to elucidate the main tenets of human affairs through illustrations from gnomic verse	Sayings (*yan* 言)

Chapter Title	*Shi* 事: Affairs	*Mo* 末: Branches
15. An Overview of the Military	Explanations of which military methods should be employed and under what circumstances	Overview (*lüe* 略)
16. A Mountain of Persuasions	Demonstrations of how to construct persuasive arguments through the use of talking points	Persuasions (*shui* 說)
17. A Forest of Persuasions	Demonstrations of how to construct persuasive arguments through the use of talking points	Persuasions (*shui* 說)
18. Among Others	Explications of paradoxes to illustrate the workings of the Way in various life situations	Dialectics (*bian* 辯)
19. Cultivating Effort	Illustrations of why a ruler must devote effort to the task of rulership and how to assert or refute a particular proposition in the course of oral debate or discussion	Refutations (*nan* 難)
20. The Exalted Lineage	Demonstrations of how the current ruler can continue the illustrious "lineage" of the Five Emperors and Three Kings and bring honor and prosperity to the Liu clan	Genealogy (*zong* 宗)
21. An Overview of the Essentials	Explanations of why the *Huainanzi* was written and how it is intended to be understood	Overview (*lüe* 略) and poetic exposition (*fu* 賦)

inextricably linked. In both the Way-and-affairs and the roots-and-branches perspectives, chapter 9 serves as the fulcrum linking and balancing the two parts of the work. Each of chapters 9 to 19 deals with an affair (*shi*) and how it naturally gives rise to a genre form of literature (*wen*), with the chapter itself illustrating the genre it surveys.

Table 1 dramatically validates the claim made in chapter 21 that the work should be read sequentially, from beginning to end; to that extent, the *Huainanzi* can be seen to constitute a carefully constructed curriculum for a would-be sage-ruler. We stress that this root–branch structure may be (indeed, must be) read both diachronically and synchronically. While progressing from chapter 1 through chapter 20, the reader moves through ever-later realms in the progressive history of cosmogenesis and human society, beginning with the origins of the universe in the undifferentiated Way and ending in the diverse and complex world of the Han dynasty. At the same time, the reader moves normatively through realms of descending priority toward the endeavor of universal rule: from the Way that pervades and directs all things to the minute contingencies of interpersonal politics and individual duty.

Using this method, the *Huainanzi* proposes to present a structure within which all human knowledge and effort may be prioritized and integrated.

The Claims the *Huainanzi* Makes for Itself

In formal terms, chapter 21, "An Overview of the Essentials," is the final chapter of the *Huainanzi*, but as noted previously, it effectively serves as an introduction to the work as a whole.[31] It orients the reader and provides a navigational guide for the long and complex journey through the text. It is particularly noteworthy that through the "Overview" the reader is introduced to the rhetorical strategy of the text and comes to appreciate the grand design extending to each successive chapter. The "Overview" itself, written in a combination of prose and tetrasyllabic verse in the *fu* style, is organized into four parts that introduce the text in a progressive and ever-widening purview. It elucidates the theoretical goals of the work, the content of its individual chapters, the progressive organizational flow of the chapters from one to the next, and the contributions of the work within a comparative and historical framework.

In the first paragraph of chapter 21, the author lays out his broad philosophical claims about the text and introduces the chapter titles that identify the content of each chapter. The opening lines explain that the *Huainanzi* is an account of the Way and its Potency, clarifies their relationship to human beings and their affairs, and encompasses all the knowledge one needs to govern successfully. Implying that previous and contemporaneous works have failed to make these connections adequately, the author defines his task as explicating the critical link between cosmic and political order. The introduction emphasizes the interrelationship between the Way and human affairs and asserts that such knowledge will empower the ruler to be both efficacious and adaptable to the times. At the end of this section, the twenty chapter titles are named in rhymed verse that serves to emphasize the careful and deliberate ordering of the book's contents.

The second section of chapter 21, summaries of the previous twenty chapters with their respective titles, introduces the main topics of each chapter and familiarizes the reader with the categories, concepts, and vocabulary pertinent to each of them. Most important, it outlines the different practical applications and benefits of the knowledge derived from each chapter. This link between the theoretical and practical or the descriptive and prescriptive aspects of the chapters is evident in both the semantic and the syntactic structure of the chapter summaries. Whereas the first section of the "Overview" discusses the relationship between the Way and human affairs, this second section is a concerted effort to harmonize the theoretical and the

31. For two studies conducted by team members on the important topic of the claims that the *Huainanzi* makes for itself, see Sarah A. Queen, "Inventories of the Past: Rethinking the 'School' Affiliation of the *Huainanzi*," *Asia Major*, 3rd ser., 14, no. 1 (2001): 51–72; and Judson Murray, "A Study of 'Yao lue' 要略, 'A Summary of the Essentials': Understanding the *Huainanzi* Through the Point of View of the Author of the Postface," *Early China* 29 (2004): 45–108.

practical, the cosmological and the political—a process that the author claims to be a distinctive contribution of the twenty chapters of this text.

The third section takes a different look at the chapters. Rather than describing them one by one in sequence, this section shows how the chapters relate to and build on one another, implying that they have been arranged in a deliberate and coherent fashion. The text, we are shown, is to be read and studied from beginning to end and demonstrates how comprehending the content of any one chapter is predicated on successfully mastering the principles presented in the preceding one. Reflecting the text itself, this section moves from cosmogony to cosmology to ontology; from the meta-phenomenal Way as utter nondifferentiation to the phenomenal world of differentiated things that it generates; from the Way's macrocosmic aspects visible in Heaven, Earth, and the four seasons to its microcosmic manifestations in human beings; from cosmogony to human genesis; from the motions of the celestial bodies to the movements of human history; and from the cultivation of oneself to the governance of the world. This section thus outlines the text's demonstration of its authority as a compendium encapsulating everything worth knowing and utilizing in governing the world.

The fourth and final section of chapter 21 deepens the author's claim for uniquely valid comprehensiveness, by situating the *Huainanzi* within a (partly legendary) evolution of practices and texts stretching from the exemplary King Wen of the Zhou, through innovations in the Warring States era, to the Qin dynasty, and beyond to Liu An's time. This taxonomy or inventory of the past summarizes the noteworthy events of nearly a thousand years by recounting both their particular historical circumstances and the specific contributions made by key people and texts that figured prominently in each era. The high points mentioned include the strategies of the Grand Duke in advancing the affairs of King Wen, the teachings of the Confucians, the writings of Master Guan, the admonitions of Master Yan, the reliance on Vertical and Horizontal Alliances and Long- and Short-Term Coalitions, writings on performance and title, and the laws devised by Shang Yang. The creation of the *Huainanzi* is contrasted with the time- and context-bound nature of all those policies and teachings. The *Huainanzi* itself is presented as being both timeless and utterly comprehensive, because it is said to have both subsumed and surpassed all these important historical innovations. This claim is reinforced in the concluding passage of this section, which speaks of "the book of the Liu clan" itself in terms quite unlike those used in describing all the earlier developments and characterizes the work as an exhaustive repository of theoretical and practical knowledge.

One of the main rhetorical purposes of the final section's historical digression is showing how in each era, some figures stood apart from the throne or even from the royal court itself. Such personages as Guan Zhong, Confucius, and the Grand Duke were not rulers themselves, but they laid down the basic principles by which kingship was conducted in their era. This embodies a special plea by Liu An and his court: although their presentation of a comprehensive summa that could (and should, according to the text's own claims) serve as the ideological blueprint of the Han Empire may seem like an unforgivable act of *lèse majesté*, there is in fact ample historical precedent for it. Note that this claim somewhat attenuates the "threat" posed by the *Huainanzi* but is still quite audacious; Liu An is claiming for himself and his court a role of "partnership in rule" comparable to that perceived to have been played by Guan Zhong, Confucius, and other towering figures of the past. To use a classical allusion that would have been clear to his contemporaries, Liu An is setting up Huainan to be the "Zou 鄒 and Lu 魯"—the home of high-minded sage-advisers—of the Han era.

The Place of the *Huainanzi* in Early Han History

We return to the questions posed earlier: For whom was the *Huainanzi* written, and with what intended effect?

After years of relative neglect by Western scholars, there was an upsurge of interest in the *Huainanzi* beginning with the publication in 1962 of Benjamin Wallacker's translation of chapter 11.[32] A main strategy for trying to understand the *Huainanzi* was trying to locate the text in one or another "school" of early Chinese thought, and over a period of many years, the intellectual affiliation of the *Huainanzi* became the topic of considerable debate and disputation. During that time, almost every major *Huainanzi* scholar (including some of us) weighed in with views on whether the *Huainanzi* was a "miscellaneous" or an "eclectic" work, a Daoist or a Huang-Lao text, or an example of syncretism. We do not propose to prolong that debate in these pages. We take note of the voluminous literature on the subject,[33] but even more of the consensus that has begun to emerge in very recent years that the whole question is neither as unproblematical nor as useful as was once thought. Many scholars now feel that there may be little to be gained from arguments that "the *Huainanzi* is a text of the 'X' (or 'Y' or 'Z') school."

The essence of this position can perhaps be summed up in this way: writers of the Warring States and early Han periods spoke often of the *bai jia*, the "Hundred Traditions" (or "Hundred [Intellectual] Lineages" or "Hundred Specialists").[34] The term appears three times (in this sense) in the *Huainanzi* itself. Even granted that in this context, "hundred" just means "many," the implication of the term is great variety, fluidity, and diversity of thought. But that means that in writing his famous essay on Han intellectual life,[35] the "Liu jia yao zhi" (Essential Tenets of the Six Lineages), Sima Tan at the very least conflated a great deal.

From this perspective, another problem is that while Sima Tan was writing as a historian with the aim of giving a schematic account of the major intellectual tradi-

32. Wallacker 1962.

33. See "The Debate over the Intellectual Affiliation of the *Huainanzi*."

34. The translation "hundred schools" for *bai jia* is sanctified by long usage, but we associate ourselves with scholars who have argued that the term *school* implies more organizational structure and more doctrinal unity and discipline than was true of the era, and therefore we avoid that term.

35. *Shiji*, chap. 130.

tions up to his time, his essay seems to prefigure the work of the bibliographers Liu Xiang and his son Liu Xin in classifying and cataloging the Han imperial library. Their scheme, in turn, was incorporated by Ban Gu into the "Monograph on Arts and Literature" of the *Han shu* (*History of the* [Former] *Han Dynasty*),[36] a source on which so much of the debate on texts and their filiation turns. In the view of some scholars, the categories thus created are basically designed to answer the question of where any given book should be placed on the shelves of a library rather than being attempts to comprehend and analyze the complexities of contemporary intellectual life. Applied retrospectively to the thinkers of the Warring States and early Han periods, these "school" categories can be seen as true Procrustean beds; within each school, one size fits all. From this perspective, therefore, the classification of Warring States and Han texts on the basis of what are essentially mid-Han bibliographical categories obscures as much as it clarifies. Early Chinese intellectual life was more dynamic than the classificatory rubrics would imply. Intellectuals created texts not only as contributions to and within particular lineage traditions but also in response to new, complex, and shifting social, political, economic, and cultural circumstances.

A narrow reliance on bibliographic categories also obscures the role of praxis in constructing intellectuals' group identity during the Warring States and early Han. To early thinkers, the shared performance of common rituals or methods of personal cultivation was ample cause for affinity. Furthermore, it is clear that Sima Tan was aware of the importance of praxis in the intellectual lineages he identifies. For example, he mentions the Confucian emphasis on ritual and hierarchy, and the Daoist practices of self-cultivation. Hence his categories were neither arbitrary nor unprecedented. They bear a direct relationship not only to the content of the texts from which he drew to develop his classifications but also to the distinctive practices associated with them. Thus, used judiciously, Sima Tan's classificatory scheme is one source of useful insights into Han and pre-Han intellectual life. It becomes problematic when developed into—and applied as—"one size fits all" bibliographical categories, as did the later Han bibliographers and those who rely on their scheme. In our analytical comments on the *Huainanzi* in the chapters' introductions and footnotes, we have taken pains to identify links between the text and both written sources and specific techniques, and to point out their intellectual affiliation where appropriate. At the same time, we have been mindful of the *Huainanzi*'s own claim that it draws on a great number of traditions but transcends all of them.

From this perspective, the starting point for any discussion of the place of the *Huainanzi* in the intellectual history of the Han should be to remember that the *Huainanzi* was the product of a particular group of intellectuals clustered in a particular place in a singular geopolitical context. Accordingly, we begin with the text itself, asking what explicit and implicit claims this particular group of intellectuals is articulating. In this regard, chapter 21 is germane, as it describes the specific concerns that inspired the production of this text, its goals, and its structure and organization.

36. *Han shu*, chap. 30.

It also situates the *Huainanzi* in a long history of textual production beginning with the *Strategies of the Grand Duke* attributed to King Wen.

Our discussion thus turns on the issue of what messages the text may be perceived to encode, how those messages would be understood by a Han readership, and what pragmatic effects would have been if the program of the text had been adopted.

The immediate milieu within which the *Huainanzi* was created was one of political turmoil over whether the empire was to be a centralized bureaucratic state or a relatively decentralized neofeudal one. This explains why the *Huainanzi* is best understood as the conceptual blueprint for a vision of a decentralized empire that aspired to a diffuse or shared form of governance in which the central court worked out an accommodation with local sources of power and authority, particularly the royal relatives enfeoffed as kings throughout much of the empire. The numerous references to the seemingly historical narratives of the Three Kings and the Three Dynasties[37] are a thinly veiled commentary on the contemporary scene and call on the imperial regime to reinstitute the decentralized governance that the Three Kings represent.

One such illustrative historiographical narrative found in "Surveying Obscurities" (chapter 6) attributes the sociopolitical and cosmic degeneration of the world from the Three Dynasties period to late Warring States and Qin times to the disruption of blood ties (that is, kinship relations) between the "Son of Heaven" and his "flesh and bone" residing in the feudatories. The author blames the multitude of meddling, conniving, and obsequious scholar-officials, who had interposed themselves between the ruler and his royal relatives, for this estrangement between them and, ultimately, for the decline of the world. Not surprisingly, scholar-officials like the infamous Qin statesman Li Si and key Former Han figures such as Gongsun Hong, Zhang Tang, and Dong Zhongshu all viewed the deterioration from Western Zhou to Warring States times as having been caused by the disenchantment and disloyalty of the royal relatives to their own family members, most notably the ruler, or the "Son of Heaven." The authors of the *Huainanzi* obviously view the problem from the other direction, and in "Surveying Obscurities" they praise the Han emperorship for reestablishing kinship relations and thereby reuniting the world as one family. This emphasis on the importance of kinship relations and the contributions of the emperor's own "flesh and bone" to the cause of empire appears repeatedly throughout the text.

Whereas some scholars have seen the decentralized form of governance praised throughout the *Huainanzi* as reflecting an eclectic acceptance of diverse perspectives in the text,[38] we dissent from this interpretation. Rather than seeing the *Huainanzi* as arguing that a multiperspectival view is a requisite for successful rule, we observe that the text argues consistently that its own perspective is correct, precisely because its root–branch configuration contains the key to reconciling all the seemingly multifarious forms of knowledge and practice that human civilization had

37. For these terms, see app. A.
38. Vankeerberghen 2001, 4.

heretofore generated. The text that the *Huainanzi* claims is "sacrosanct for all time" is itself, because it alone demonstrates how every text that has ever been generated may be made to work as part of an integral unity. This is different from a "multiperspectival view." The *Huainanzi* does not claim that every viewpoint is right but that a person's or a text's perspective (and the action that follows from it) becomes right when it is correctly placed within the *Huainanzi*'s developmental rubric. Advocates of ritual, for example, have a place in the empire, but their concerns have a lower priority than the study of the fundamental patterns of Heaven or the apophatic self-cultivation of the ruler. The message of the *Huainanzi* is not one of open-ended pluralism but of the integration of ramified elements within an intrinsically hierarchical structure.

By providing this forceful and empirically plausible structure within which the interrelationship of all realms of human knowledge and endeavor could be understood, the *Huainanzi* demonstrates how seemingly irreconcilable diversity can be made to work as part of an integral unity, a problem that neatly mirrored the fundamental challenge of governing the Han Empire.

This posed a clear threat to many firmly entrenched interests at the Han court, because the *Huainanzi* authors had accomplished (or could plausibly claim to have done so) that for which many others had striven without success. For example, the Confucians[39] at the imperial court had reached a rough consensus on which ancient texts should be accorded canonical status[40] but still disagreed over how they should be interpreted (which explains the development of several different exegetical traditions per classic) and ranked in order of importance. The *Huainanzi* schematic demonstrates how the five basic realms represented by the five classics may be both ordered relative to one another and fit into a larger context incorporating endeavors and forms of knowledge exterior to the Confucian canon:

1. The *Changes* (chapter 6, "Surveying Obscurities")
2. The *Spring and Autumn Annals* (chapter 8, "The Basic Warp")
3. The *Rites* (chapter 11, "Integrating Customs")
4. The *Odes* (chapter 12, "Responses of the Way")
5. The *Documents* (chapter 14, "Sayings Explained")

The reasoning underlying these correlations[41] is too lengthy and complex to be explained in detail here, but the gist of the argument is as follows:

---

39. For the term *ru* as "Confucians," see n. 9.

40. This is true even though some of the Confucian classics did not assume their final form and content until later in the Western Han period. For a discussion of the formation of the classical canon, see Michael Nylan, *The Five "Confucian" Classics* (New Haven, Conn.: Yale University Press, 2001).

41. In saying that these chapters "correspond" to the Confucian classics, we are not implying that they parallel those classics or duplicate their content but simply that they play roles in the organizational and intellectual scheme of the *Huainanzi* analogous to the roles played by the classics for the *ru* Confucians.

1. The *Changes* links to "Surveying Obscurities" because both deal with correlative connections between seemingly unconnected phenomena, connections that are dark, mysterious, and difficult to explain.

2. The *Spring and Autumn Annals* corresponds to "The Basic Warp" because both examine the moral dimensions of human history and ascribe "praise and blame" to events in the past.

3. The *Rites* corresponds to "Integrating Customs" because both deal with the theory and practice of ritual in all its forms, including not only such matters as religious observances and mourning customs but also clothing, food, music, and other manifestations of culture.

4. The *Odes* corresponds to "Responses of the Way" because the latter employs the *Laozi* as a source of exegetical and explanatory authority in exactly the same way as the *Odes* was used in such texts as the *Hanshi waizhuan* (*Master Han's Supplementary Disquisitions on the Book of Odes*).

5. The *Documents* links with "Sayings Explained" because the latter uses brief apothegms and their exegeses to understand the norms of human behavior, in ways analogous to how the former uses historical documents to illuminate successful and unsuccessful actions of past rulers.

This "hijacking" (as so it would have seemed) of the classics would have made intellectuals like Dong Zhongshu furious. It achieves what Confucians could not accomplish among themselves (show how the five classics relate to one another in a coherent order) and implies that the entire Confucian canon accounts for only a quarter of a truly comprehensive enumeration of the fundaments of rulership. (This in turn evokes the image of "one corner of a square," a term that occurs several times in the *Huainanzi* as a metaphor for limited learning.) Perhaps this was an additional element that led to the decision of Han court scholars, deeply invested in politics, that Liu An and his entire intellectual enterprise were too dangerous a threat to be allowed to survive.

Sources of the *Huainanzi*

Our present understanding of the place of the *Huainanzi* in Han intellectual life rests on a number of important points. First, the *Huainanzi* draws on the foundational classic of Daoism, the *Laozi;* borrows extensively from the *Zhuangzi;* and urges on the would-be sage-ruler techniques of self-cultivation closely associated with the Daoist tradition. It is equally true that the text draws heavily on non-Daoist works, including the *Odes*, the *Changes*, and the *Documents;* the *Hanfeizi*, the *Guanzi*, and the *Lüshi chunqiu;* the *Chuci* and the *Shanhaijing;* the *Zisizi* and the *Mozi;* and undoubtedly other texts that have not been transmitted as part of the received corpus of early literature. The text contains much material from a body of historical, quasi-historical, and legendary anecdotal lore and gnomic verse that was widely known from oral and written transmissions in the Warring States, Qin, and Han times. Despite such a disparity of sources, however, the *Huainanzi* is much more than just a collection of unconnected chapters; rather, it is a work characterized by a strong degree of organizational and philosophical coherence that reflects the intentions of its authors and editors.

As we argued earlier, although the *Huainanzi*'s overall structure and content is coherent and consciously organized, it is easy to demonstrate that a great deal of its content was quoted or paraphrased directly from preexisting sources. It is equally easy, and more pertinent to an understanding of the work, to show that often the original quotation is subtly changed or placed in a new context, altering the original meaning to advance the new arguments made by the Huainan masters.[42] (We return to this point in several of the individual chapter introductions.) Scholars have identified more than eight hundred direct quotations or close paraphrases of Zhou and very early Han works in the *Huainanzi*. Of those, by far the largest number are from four sources: *Zhuangzi* (269 references in Charles Le Blanc's tabulation), *Lüshi chunqiu* (190 references), *Laozi* (99 references), and *Hanfeizi* (72 references). Chapter 1 of the *Huainanzi* is based heavily on the *Laozi*, and chapter 2, equally heavily on the *Zhuangzi*. While quotations from the *Lüshi chunqiu* can be found throughout the *Huainanzi* (in twenty of its twenty-one chapters), they are particularly prominent in chapters 3, 4, and 5. Indeed, much of chapter 5 is directly quoted from the first sections of each of the first twelve chapters of the *Lüshi chunqiu* (and thus also parallels the "Yueling" chapter of *Liji*, related to the same source). Chapter 10 develops concepts and terms that appear in a group of early texts typically associated with Confucius and his early followers, such as the *Lunyu*, *Mengzi*, *Xunzi*, and *Zisizi*. Chapter 12 draws extensively from the *Laozi*, effectively using it to ratify the analysis presented in the chapter itself of the meaning of various anecdotes.

Beyond these general remarks on sources, we refer readers to the discussion of the pertinent sources in the twenty-one separate chapter introductions.

The Debate over the Intellectual Affiliation of the *Huainanzi*

For many years, the intellectual affiliation of the *Huainanzi* has been the topic of much debate and dispute. But recently the affiliation debate has changed as a consensus has begun to emerge that perhaps all along trying to assign the text to one "school" or another was asking the wrong question. Nonetheless, a brief historical

42. This process has been brilliantly demonstrated by Le Blanc 1985, 86–98, in side-by-side readings of passages quoted from the *Lüshi chunqiu* and other sources and their *Huainanzi* adaptations. See also Sarah A. Queen, "The Creation and Domestication of the Techniques of Lao-Zhuang: Anecdotal Narrative and Philosophical Argumentation in *Huainanzi* Chapter 12," *Asia Major*, 3rd ser., 21, no. 1 (2008): 201–47.

survey of these debates is useful in trying to understand the state of the field of *Huainanzi* studies today and to assess where matters now stand.

The spectrum of opinion about "school" affiliation has produced many positions that differ in their subtle nuances, but generally, three broad approaches have dominated the field.

Over the long term, probably the most deeply entrenched approach has been to identify the *Huainanzi* as an "eclectic" or a "miscellaneous" (*za* 雜) text following Liu Xiang's classification of the *Huainanzi* in the "Monograph on Arts and Literature" chapter of Ban Gu's *Han shu*. The term *za* itself has been a source of confusion and often has been interpreted as pejorative. The traditional Chinese scholarly attitude toward the *Huainanzi* is exemplified by Feng Youlan: "This book, like the *Lü-shih Ch'un Ch'iu*, is a miscellaneous compilation of all schools of thought, and lacks unity."[43] The views of several influential French sinologists in the early twentieth century did much to bolster the tendency of Western scholarship before the 1960s to regard the *Huainanzi* as generally unworthy of notice.[44]

Recent scholarship on the *Huainanzi* and related texts has had the effect of refuting this older view, or at least of modifying it substantially. As John Knoblock and Jeffrey Riegel pointed out in their study of the *Lüshi chunqiu*, the classification *za* is in fact not pejorative in intent and does not denote a kind of miscellaneous intellectual chop suey (*zacai* 雜菜). In their words,

> The works of the "Mixed School" thus were not "miscellaneous," "eclectic," or "syncretic"; they were not ill-considered mish-mashes of extracts culled from other works and displaying little originality of thought. Rather, they belonged to a class of philosophical speculation that dealt especially with the relation of the human realm to the cosmos, governance to cosmology, the ruler to Heaven and Earth. We can see this directly in the two most important works of the "Mixed School," the *Lüshi chunqiu* and the *Huainanzi*.[45]

In another attempt to sort out the meaning of *za* with respect to the *Huainanzi* and the *Lushi chunqiu*, Mark Edward Lewis stated, "The syncretic nature of the two compendia was indicated by their classification as works that 'mixed' or 'combined' (*za* 雜) the schools."[46] In recent years, the eclectic position (variously understood) has been particularly popular among Chinese scholars. Chen Yiping and Hou Wailu, for example, support this position.[47] The eclectic position also has attracted some

43. Feng Yu-lan (Feng Youlan), *A History of Chinese Philosophy*, trans. Derk Bodde, 2 vols. (Princeton, N.J.: Princeton University Press, 1952, 1953), 1:395. Feng Youlan subsequently adopted a more favorable view of the *Huainanzi*. For a summary of the evolution of Feng's thinking, see Le Blanc 1985, 34n.45.

44. See the views of Leon Wieger, Henri Maspero, and Rolf Stein, as summarized by Le Blanc 1985, 32–33.

45. Knoblock and Riegel 2000, 46.

46. Lewis, *Writing and Authority*, 304.

47. See, for example, Chen Yiping 陳一平, *Huainanzi xiaozhuyi* 淮南子校註譯 (Guangdong:

Western scholars, notably Griet Vankeerberghen,[48] whose views will be discussed more fully later.

A second and very influential approach has been to identify the *Huainanzi* with the Daoist tradition, although with different understandings of what Daoism means and which understanding of Daoism the text represents. The case for *Huainanzi* as a Daoist work has been articulated by such scholars as Wing-tsit Chan, Kanaya Osamu, Benjamin Wallacker, Charles Le Blanc, Wolfgang Bauer, and Harold Roth. Some, like Chan and Kanaya, emphasize the text's conceptual links to ideas associated with the *Laozi* and the *Zhuangzi*.[49] Wallacker puts this argument in rather modest terms: "In referring to the general ideas of the eleventh chapter as 'Taoist' I mean that they can be derived from the classic Taoist texts, the *Lao-tzu Tao-te ching* and the *Chuang-tzu*."[50] Others, such as Hsiao Kung-ch'uan, Harold Roth, John Major, and Charles Le Blanc, have argued that the text is best understood as an exemplar of "Huang-Lao," a particular strain of Daoist syncretism popular among the elite during the early years of the Western Han.[51]

The view that the *Huainanzi* is a Huang-Lao text can be seen as perhaps a subset of the "Daoist" position; indeed some scholars who defend the Huang-Lao view regard the terms "Huang-Lao" and "early Han Daoism" as virtual synonyms.[52] The Huang-Lao view was strongly bolstered in the 1970s and 1980s by the gradual publication and analysis of works from the Mawangdui funerary library of silk manuscripts. The presence in that library of works ascribed to, or alleged to be based on the teachings of, the Yellow Emperor, in conjunction with the many obvious similarities between the four so-called Yellow Emperor silk manuscripts from Mawangdui[53] and the *Huainanzi* taken as a whole (for example, between the short text *Daoyuan* 道原 and *Huainanzi*'s chapter 1, "Yuan dao" 原道), led to a minor boom of scholarly interest in Huang-Lao as a new subject for investigation.[54] A number of scholars, including Major,[55] then argued strongly that the *Huainanzi* should be seen as a work, or perhaps as the exemplary work, in the Huang-Lao tradition. Robin Yates took the

---

Renmin Press, 1994), 5–7; and Hou Wailu 侯外盧, *Zhongguo sixiang tongshi* 中國思想通史 (Beijing: Renmin Press 1957), 2:78–83.

48. Vankeerberghen 2001.

49. See, example, Wing-tsit Chan, *A Sourcebook in Chinese Philosophy* (Princeton, N.J.: Princeton University Press, 1963), 305.

50. Wallacker 1962, 11.

51. Hsiao Kung-ch'uan, *A History of Chinese Political Thought*, trans. F. W. Mote (Princeton, N.J.: Princeton University Press, 1979), 570–82; Le Blanc 1985, 4–8; Major 1993, 8–14; Roth 1992, 13–19.

52. See, for example, Harold D. Roth, "Who Compiled the *Chuang Tzu*?" in *Chinese Texts and Philosophical Contexts: Essays Dedicated to Angus C. Graham*, ed. Henry Rosemont Jr. (La Salle, Ill.: Open Court Press, 1991), 79–128.

53. These four texts are "Jingfa," "Jing," "Cheng," and "Daoyuan." To these, Robin Yates adds a fifth, "Yiyin jiuzhu." See Robin D. S. Yates, *Five Lost Classics: Tao, Huang-Lao, and Yin-Yang in Han China* (New York: Ballantine Books, 1997). For a translation of "Daoyuan," see 172–77.

54. Among the pioneering works in this field were Tu Wei-ming, "The Thought of Huang-Lao: A Reflection on the *Lao Tzu* and *Huang Ti* Texts in the Silk Manuscripts of Ma-wang-tui," *Journal of Asian Studies* 39 (1979): 95–100; and Randall Peerenboom, *Law and Morality in Ancient China: The Silk Manuscripts of Huang-Lao* (Albany: State University of New York Press, 1993).

55. Major 1993, 8–14.

cautious position that "Huang-Lao was one of the three traditions of ancient Daoism . . . it was the philosophy or technique of greatest interest to the early Han emperors Wen and Jing, the powerful Empress Dowager Dou, [and] Liu An."[56]

Soon, however, a reaction set in. Angus Graham questioned how the *Huainanzi* could be a Huang-Lao work if in chapter 9 it privileges Shen Nong rather than the Yellow Emperor. Mark Csikszentmihalyi began to argue the case against *Huainanzi* as a Huang-Lao work and for caution in applying the label "Huang-Lao" to any work of the Warring States and Han periods without a clearer understanding of what Huang-Lao was and was not.[57] In the end, this debate was inconclusive; when everyone had had his or her say in the matter, it was, as Aihe Wang put it, "still open to question whether or not Huang-Lao was a single ideology and what its tenets were."[58] Pending further discoveries bearing on the nature and scope of Huang-Lao, the identification of the *Huainanzi* as a Huang-Lao text remains an intriguing possibility but not something that has been (or can be) established beyond dispute.

Most recently, Griet Vankeerberghen voiced support for the venerable view of the *Huananzi* as an "eclectic" work in her monograph *The Huainanzi and Liu An's Claim to Moral Authority*. Vankeerberghen took issue with two assumptions informing the dominant view that the *Huainanzi* is a Daoist work. First, she maintains that scholars who hold to this position claim that the *Huainanzi* was written with the intention of defending a Daoist or Huang-Lao school or tradition. (Many scholars who hold to the "Daoist" or "Huang-Lao" position would reject this characterization of their views, however.) Second, although they recognized that the text draws on a variety of sources, not all of which can be classified as Daoist, they wish to privilege the sources—and the chapters of the *Huainanzi* that draw most heavily and explicitly on them—that can be easily identified with the Daoist tradition, as exemplified by texts such as the *Zhuangzi* or the *Laozi*.[59] In contrast, Vankeerberghen argues, "the *Huainanzi* turns to texts or ideas of the past not to defend a single strand of thought against rival theories but to pick out of the large repertoire of statements, ideas, and stories available those that best represented its vision of the Way, and in the process establish the king of Huainan as one who possesses the authority needed for rulership."[60] Vankeerberghen concludes that if we are to apply a label to the text, Liu Xiang's "eclectic" rubric is most suitable because it underscores the text's "preference for drawing widely on disparate sources."[61]

Vankeerberghen's approach (in its arguments, if not in its conclusion) is not very different from that of a number of recent scholars who prefer to eschew altogether

56. Yates, *Five Lost Classics*, 42–43.

57. Angus C. Graham, quoted in Major 1993, 10; Yates, *Five Lost Classics*; Mark Csikszentmihalyi, "Emulating the Yellow Emperor: The Theory and Practice of Huang-Lao, 180–141 B.C." (Ph.D. diss., Stanford University, 1994).

58. Wang, *Cosmology and Political Culture in Early China*, 185.

59. Vankeerberghen 2001, 4.

60. Vankeerberghen 2001, 4.

61. Vankeerberghen 2001, 4.

the assignment of a particular intellectual label to the text. This is a position supported by Roger Ames, Mark Csikszentmihalyi, Paul Goldin, Mark Edward Lewis, Michael Loewe, Judson Murray, Michael Puett, and Sarah Queen.[62] Scholars in this group have rejected the "Daoist" or "eclectic" affiliation for a variety of reasons, based largely on internal features of the text itself. Thus this group of scholars tends to underscore the text's "syncretic," "synthetic," and "comprehensive" aspects, and they generally liken it to a "compendium," an "anthology," or an "encyclopedia." For example, based on a close reading of chapter 21 of the *Huainanzi*, "An Overview of the Essentials," Queen contended that associating the text with a single tradition contradicts the author's self-proclaimed vision of the text articulated in this chapter.[63] Adopting a rather dark view of the text, Goldin argued that the *Huainanzi* is marked by an "insidious syncretism" that aims to justify a political state that would subdue philosophical disputation altogether.[64] Ames used the word *syncretic* to describe the *Huainanzi* and also implied that he regards it as an encyclopedic work that defies classification: "The contents of the *Huai Nan Tzu's* twenty books and postface are broad and varied, probably following the *Lü-shih ch'un-ch'iu* in attempting to provide a compendium of existing knowledge. It is a syncretic text which borrows widely and heavily from pre-Ch'in sources and adapts earlier contributions to its own ends."[65] Csikszentmihalyi similarly argues: "The *Masters of Huainan* shows the influence of almost every philosophical or religious current, often filtered through a synthetic worldview that attempts to unify them under a broader conceptual scheme."[66] Lewis identifies the *Huainanzi* as one of several important works that "claimed to be [a] universal encyclopedia containing everything worth knowing." This is further borne out by the collective nature of the work, which involved a large number of scholars assembled at Liu An's court. Lewis further maintains, "This insistence on the large number of people who participated in the writing of the text is part of the program of comprehensiveness that defined the project of composing such an encyclopedia."[67] And again, "As comprehensive treatises produced by large numbers of scholars under the aegis of a leading political figure who aspired to guide a young ruler, both texts [*Lüshi chunqiu* and *Huainanzi*] aimed to bring together all the competing doctrines of the period."

---

62. Ames 1994; Paul R. Goldin, "Insidious Syncretism in the Political Philosophy of *Huai-nan-tzu*," *Asian Philosophy* 9, no. 3 (1999): 165–91; Michael Loewe, "Huang Lao Thought and the *Huainanzi*," *Journal of the Royal Asiatic Society*, 3rd ser., 4, no. 3 (1994): 377–95; Puett, *Ambivalence of Creation*, 260–61n.72; Michael Puett, *To Become a God: Cosmology, Sacrifice, and Self-Divinization in Early China*, Harvard-Yenching Institute Monograph Series 57 (Cambridge, Mass.: Harvard University Asia Center, 2002), 269; Lewis, *Writing and Authority*; Judson Murray, "The Consummate *Dao*: The 'Way' (*Dao*) and 'Human Affairs' (*shi*) in the *Huainanzi*" (Ph.D. diss., Brown University, 2007); Murray, "Study of 'Yao lüe.'"

63. Queen, "Inventories of the Past."

64. Goldin, "Insidious Syncretism."

65. Ames 1994, xxii.

66. Csikszentmihalyi, *Readings in Han Chinese Thought*, 63.

67. Lewis, *Writing and Authority*, 303.

After several years of close collaboration on this translation, our own views remain far from uniform. Roth continues to be a stout defender of the position that the *Huainanzi* is a Daoist work. He argues that despite the broad array of pre-Han sources from which it draws, in its cosmology and methods of self-cultivation, it remains squarely within a tradition of both philosophy and practice that borrows from earlier Daoist sources, including the four "Xinshu" texts of the *Guanzi*, the *Laozi*, and the *Zhuangzi*. In his view, these sources and the cosmology and techniques of apophatic inner cultivation that they profess are treated by the *Huainanzi* authors as the "root" or foundation of the entire work. This can be seen in the way the *Huainanzi* privileges Daoist cosmology in chapters 1 and 2 and the many and various ways in which it privileges a cosmology of the Way and the practice of inner cultivation as the root in many other chapters. While acknowledging with his colleagues that the *Huainanzi* regards itself as a work beyond comparison, Roth sees it as being in a tradition of Daoist syncretism that includes the three later *Guanzi* "Xinshu" chapters; the "Syncretist" chapters of the *Zhuangzi* (as identified by Graham and Liu Xiaogan); chapters 3, 5, 17, and 25 of the *Lüshi chunqiu* (as identified by Meyer); and the so-called Mawangdui Huang-Lao silk manuscripts, whether or not we call it—or this tradition—"Huang-Lao."

In contrast, Meyer and Queen emphasize the *Huainanzi*'s own claim to be above and beyond classification. Having proposed in 1993 that the *Huainanzi* could be regarded as a paradigmatic work of the Huang-Lao tradition,[68] Major now has adopted a more agnostic position toward the whole Huang-Lao question. With specific reference to the *Huainanzi*, he ultimately agrees with the internalist approach favored by Meyer and Queen.

After several decades of heated discussion, the debate over the "school" affiliation of the text by now may have played itself out. In any case, in this translation we have opted to adopt an emic view of the text; that is, we seek to understand the problem of the place of the *Huainanzi* in Han intellectual life in terms of what the authors of the *Huainanzi* themselves chose to say on this matter rather than to perpetuate further the "affiliation debate." We believe this approach to be the best way both of analyzing the text and presenting it to our readers.

A Brief Account of This Translation Project

This project had its genesis in the early 1990s when, amid an upsurge of interest in late Warring States and early Han intellectual history, the thought occurred to a number of scholars that the time was right to attempt a complete English translation of the *Huainanzi*. (At about the same time, another team began work on a full

68. Major 1993, 8–14. Major still stands by many of the points made in those pages, including the key statement that for the Huainan masters, "knowledge of the natural world translates into political power" (13). But the question of how to understand Huang-Lao doctrine is, for him, now less clear.

French translation, which was published in 2003.)[69] After a series of preliminary discussions, a collaborative project took shape, leading (with some changes of personnel) to the current team and this translation. Work on rough chapter drafts began in 1995. At that early stage, the team members agreed on principles that have guided the project throughout its course:

1. The translation would be complete and as accurate as it was possible to make it, with all Chinese words accounted for and nothing added or paraphrased.
2. The translation would use standard, highly readable English, with no jargon or esoteric vocabulary and no resort to contrived syntax.
3. The translation would preserve vital features of the Chinese original, such as parallel prose, verse, and aphoristic sayings.[70]

As our work progressed, two more principles were added to this list:

4. We would identify and pay special attention to the formal characteristics (precepts, sayings, persuasions, and so on) that distinguished some chapters and use them for guidance in assessing both the text's rhetorical strategies and its philosophical meaning.
5. We would try to understand the text as much as possible on its own terms, as laid out in the chapter summaries and other features of the book's postface (chapter 21, "An Overview of the Essentials").

When the translation work was well under way, we applied for a two-year fellowship for the academic years 1996 to 1998, which was granted by the Chiang Ching-Kuo Foundation. The *Huainanzi* Translation Project was then officially headquartered at Roth's home institution, Brown University. Thereafter the team met at Brown three to five times each year to read and discuss drafts, work toward a common understanding of numerous Chinese terms, resolve inconsistencies, and assign tasks to move the project forward.

By early 2007, revised drafts of all the chapters were complete, and the work of writing the chapter introductions and a general introduction and of preparing the manuscript for publication continued, with the completed manuscript being delivered to Columbia University Press at the end of that year.

The principal translator or translators of each chapter are indicated, showing who did the initial draft of a particular chapter, shepherded it through the revision process, and assumed final responsibility for the finished version. Similarly, appendix A was drafted by Meyer, appendix B by Major, and appendix C by Roth with the assistance of Matthew Duperon. Notwithstanding this assignment of responsibility (and credit), we have emphasized throughout the project the collaborative nature

69. Le Blanc and Mathieu 2003.

70. In this connection, we are deeply indebted to our colleague William Boltz, who kindly identified for us the Han rhymes that characterize the verse passages in the text.

of our work. Every draft, at the initial stage and at every round of revision, was read and critiqued by every member of the team. In that sense, each chapter, as well as this introduction, the chapter introductions, and the appendices, is the work of the entire team, and we have tried hard to ensure that the work overall reads as a uniform and seamless whole.

Conventions Used in This Work

Chapters and Chapter Sections

The earliest references to the *Huainanzi* indicate that the work, as submitted to Emperor Wu of the Han in 139 B.C.E., was divided into twenty-one chapters, the same arrangement as in the extant work. The original manuscript copy would have had either no punctuation or only minimal punctuation, with little or no indication of sentence and paragraph breaks, no differentiation of prose and verse, and no sections or other subdivisions within chapters. We have provided all these in our English translation.

In general, we have followed the suggested punctuation and, less often, the paragraph breaks suggested by D. C. Lau, editor of the standard edition on which we have based our translation.[71] We note our departures from Lau's punctuation and paragraph division only when they have a significant effect on how the meaning is construed.

We also have divided each chapter into sections. Although, as noted, these are not present in the original text, we believe they provide an important tool to enhance the reader's understanding of the text and also are useful in facilitating cross-references. As we have defined them, the chapter sections are by no means arbitrary; instead, we have tried with great care to follow natural breaks in the material itself. So, for example, the topic word *jin* 今 (now) might begin a section, and the conclusion-drawing word *gu* 故 (therefore) might end one. In some cases, several "now–therefore" passages that are similar in theme have been grouped to form a single section. In other cases (for example, chapter 12), section breaks appear naturally in the text because passages are "capped" by a quotation from an authoritative classic. Some chapters have many sections (especially chapters 16 and 17 and also chapters 12 and 14), while others have relatively few (for example, chapters 8 and 19).

Chapter sections are numbered in the translated text in the form "8.3," meaning "chapter 8, section 3." We use this numbering system in the notes for cross-references (for example, to important parallel passages) within or among chapters (for example, "see 8.3").

71. *Huainanzi zhuzi suoyin*; see section "Editions."

Format and Typography

Because parallel prose, especially, and verse are important components of the *Huainanzi*'s rhetorical structure, we have been careful to translate parallel prose lines and verse into parallel lines of English, indented and set line-for-line.

Words that do not appear in the Chinese text but are implied by the wording of the original or, in our judgment, are required to complete the sense of a phrase or sentence (taking care not to add anything that is not clearly implied by the text itself) are enclosed in square brackets.

Arrangement of Chapters and Appendices

Each of the twenty-one translated chapters is preceded by an introduction, except for chapters 16 and 17, which are very much alike in structure and content and so share an introduction.

Notes have been kept to a necessary minimum and generally cover such matters as *textual emendations*, such as when we disagree with D. C. Lau's proposed changes or propose emendations of our own; *explanations of terms*, such as obscure words or characters that are used in unusual ways; *people and places* mentioned in the text, whose importance can be better appreciated through a brief identification;[72] *cross-references* within the text and references to comparable passages in early texts; and *explanations of obscure passages* such as historical anecdotes that cannot readily be understood without information that supplements the original text. One way of keeping the number of notes under control was to use appendices, and the book has three. Appendix A, "Key Terms and Their Translations," comments on and explicates a number of words, compounds, and phrases that are of special importance to the text and, in many cases, present special challenges to translators. Appendix B, "Categorical Terms," lists and explicates terms that naturally group into categories

72. We identify persons and places only when, in our judgment, such identification would add significantly to the reader's understanding and enjoyment of the work. Figures are identified when they first are mentioned in the text. We do not identify famous historical figures like Confucius and Qin Shihuangdi who already will be familiar to most of the readers of this book. Nor do we always identify minor mythical or imaginary personages, especially when the context is sufficient to explain their presence in the text. For those wishing more information, we suggest the following: The recent French translation of the *Huainanzi* has a useful index of proper names, both personal and geographical (Le Blanc and Mathieu 2003, 1017–1140). Many but not all the people (both mythological and historical) mentioned in the *Huainanzi* can be found in the excellent "Glossary of Names" in David Hawkes's translation of the *Chuci* (Hawkes 1985, 322–45) and in the glossary in John Knoblock and Jeffrey Riegel's translation of the *Lüshi chunqiu* (Knoblock and Riegel 2000, 763–813). The standard Chinese reference work for biographical names is Huang Huixian 黃惠賢, ed., *Ershiwushi renming da cidian* 二十五史人名大辭典 (*Dictionary of Personal Names in the Twenty-five Histories*) (Zhengzhou: Zhongzhou guji chubanshe, 1997). The most convenient reference work for historical place-names is Wei Songshan 魏嵩山, ed., *Zhongguo lishi diming da cidian* 中國歷史地名大辭典 (*Dictionary of Chinese Historical Place-Names*) (Guangzhou: Guangdong jiaoyu chubanshe, 1995).

such as "Astronomical Terms" and "Weights and Measures." Appendix C, "A Textual History of the *Huainanzi,*" gives a brief account of the history and current status of *Huainanzi* studies in the form of a bibliographical essay.

Nonstandard Romanizations

In order to avoid the ambiguity caused by words that have different Chinese characters but are spelled identically in romanization, we used the following nonstandard romanizations:

The state of Wei 魏; the state of Wey 衛
The state of Han 漢; the state of Hann 韓
The Di 狄 "barbarians," the Dii 氐 "barbarians," and the Dee 翟 "barbarians"
The Zhou 周 dynasty, but Djou 紂, last king of the Shang dynasty

Terms Not Translated

While we have made every effort to avoid cluttering our pages with untranslated Chinese terms, we inevitably had to leave untranslated a number of words that simply have no good English equivalent. These include some words pertaining to measurement, such as

li, a linear distance equal to about one-third of a mile or about 500 meters
mu (or *mou*), a measure of area equal to about one-sixth of an acre or about 0.067 hectare
Other words of linear measure, such as *ren, zhang,* and *pi*
Words for units of weight, such as *jun* and *dan* (for all these, see "Weights and Measures" in appendix B)
The names of the five notes of the pentatonic scale, *gong, shang, jue, zhi,* and *yu*
The names of some musical instruments, such as the *se* and the *qin,* often but, in our view, inappropriately translated as "lute" or "zither"
The names of the ten heavenly stems and the twelve earthly branches and their sexagenary combinations
Some technical terms, notably *qi,* which we sometimes translate as "vital energy" when it is clearly used in a context of Daoist self-cultivation or related topics but which we more often leave untranslated

Citations

Editions

We take as our standard edition the work of D. C. Lau, *Huainanzi zhuzi suoyin* 淮南子逐字索引 (*A Concordance to the Huainanzi*), Chinese University of Hong Kong,

Institute of Chinese Studies Ancient Chinese Text Concordance Series (Hong Kong: Commercial Press, 1992), cited as HNZ. When we accept Lau's emendations, we do so without comment, but when we depart from his text, we explain why in the notes. Our standard form of reference to all the concordances in the ICS Ancient Chinese Text Concordance Series is to chapter/page/line in the form 10/83/19. Our standard reference text of the *Huainanzi* for collected commentaries is by Zhang Shuangdi 張雙棣, *Huainanzi jiaoshi* 淮南子校釋, 2 vols. (Beijing: Beijing University Press, 1997), cited as Zhang Shuangdi 1997.

References to Other Works

Classical works are usually referred to by standard divisions of chapter and verse, without reference to any particular edition—for example, *Odes* 96, stanza 2; *Laozi* 55; and *Zuozhuan*, Duke Cheng, year 18. Where an exact page and line reference is called for, unless otherwise indicated, we cite editions of pre-Han and Han works in the ICS Ancient Chinese Text Concordance Series (all edited by D. C. Lau and published in Hong Kong by the Commercial Press [Shangwu yinshuguan]) whenever they are available. Citations take the form of the abbreviated title plus chapter/page/line—for example, LieZ 2/6/20. Cited works (with publication dates) include

BSSZ	*Bing shu si zhong zhuzi suoyin* 兵術四種逐字索引 (1992)
CC	*Chuci zhuzi suoyin* 楚辭 逐字索引 (2000)
GZ	*Guanzi zhuzi suoyin* 管子逐字索引 (2001)
HFZ	*Hanfeizi zhuzi suoyin* 韓非子逐字索引 (2000)
HSWZ	*Hanshi waizhuan zhuzi suoyin* 韓詩外傳逐字索引 (1992)
LieZ	*Liezi zhuzi suoyin* 列子逐字索引 (1996)
LH	*Lunheng zhuzi suoyin* 論衡逐字索引 (2008)
LSCQ	*Lüshi chunqiu zhuzi suoyin* 呂氏春秋逐字索引 (1994)
LY	*Lunyu zhuzi suoyin* 論語逐字索引 (1995)
LZ	*Laozi zhuzi suoyin* 老子逐字索引 (1996)
MoZ	*Mozi zhuzi suoyin* 墨子逐字索引 (2001)
MZ	*Mengzi zhuzi suoyin* 孟子逐字索引 (1995)
SY	*Shuo yuan zhuzi suoyin* 說苑逐字索引 (1992)
WZ	*Wenzi zhuzi suoyin* 文字逐字索引 (1992)
XZ	*Xunzi zhuzi suoyin* 荀子逐字索引 (1996)
YZ	*Yanzi chunqiu zhuzi suoyin* 晏子春秋逐字索引 (1993)
ZGC	*Zhanguoce zhuzi suoyin* 戰國策逐字索引 (1992)
ZZ	*Zhuangzi zhuzi suoyin* 莊子 逐字索引 (2000)

Encyclopedia and Standard Histories

The *Huainanzi* is frequently quoted in the *Taiping yulan* 太平禦覽 (*Imperially Reviewed Encyclopedia of the Taiping Era*, 984 C.E.), cited as TPYL (in any standard edition; it is not included in the ICS Concordance Series).

For the standard histories of the Former Han period, we cite the following editions:

Han shu	*Han shu buzhu* 漢書補注 (Beijing: Zhonghua shuju, 1983)
Shiji	*Shiji* 史記 (Beijing: Zhonghua shuju, 1959)

Frequently Cited Works

The following works are cited frequently and therefore always in abbreviated form.

Ames 1994	Roger T. Ames, *The Art of Rulership: A Study in Ancient Chinese Political Thought* (Honolulu: University of Hawai'i Press, 1983; repr., Albany: State University of New York Press, 1994)
Csikszentmihalyi 2004	Mark Csikszentmihalyi, *Material Virtue: Ethics and the Body in Ancient China* (Leiden: Brill, 2004)
Graham 1982	A. C. Graham, *Chuang-tzu: The Seven Inner Chapters and Other Writings from the Book Chuang-tzu* (London: Allen & Unwin, 1982)
Hawkes 1985	David Hawkes, *The Songs of the South: An Ancient Chinese Anthology of Poems by Qu Yuan and Other Poets* (Oxford: Clarendon Press, 1959; repr., Harmondsworth: Penguin, 1985)
Knoblock 1988	John Knoblock, *Xunzi: A Translation and Study of the Complete Works,* 3 vols. (Stanford, Calif.: Stanford University Press, 1988)
Knoblock and Riegel 2000	John Knoblock and Jeffrey Riegel, *The Annals of Lü Buwei: A Complete Translation and Study* (Stanford, Calif.: Stanford University Press, 2000)
Le Blanc 1985	Charles Le Blanc, *Huai-nan Tzu: Philosophical Synthesis in Early Han Thought: The Idea of Resonance (Kan-ying) with a Translation and Analysis of Chapter Six* (Hong Kong: Hong Kong University Press, 1985)
Le Blanc and Mathieu 2003	Charles Le Blanc and Rémi Mathieu, eds., *Philosophes taoïstes,* vol. 2, *Huainan zi: Texte traduit, présenté et annoté,* Bibliothèque de la Pléiade (Paris: Éditions Gallimard, 2003)
Legge 1895	James Legge, trans., *The Chinese Classics,* 2nd rev. ed. (1895; repr., 5 vols. in 4, Hong Kong: Hong Kong University Press, 1960)
Mair 1997	Victor Mair, *Wandering on the Way: Early Taoist Tales and Parables of Chuang Tzu,* new ed. (Honolulu: University of Hawai'i Press, 1997)
Major 1993	John S. Major, *Heaven and Earth in Early Han Thought: Chapters Three, Four and Five of the*

	Huainanzi, SUNY Series in Chinese Philosophy and Culture (Albany: State University of New York Press, 1993)
Rickett 1985	W. Allyn Rickett, *Guanzi: Political, Economic, and Philosophical Essays from Early China*, vol. 1 (Princeton, N.J.: Princeton University Press, 1985)
Rickett 1998	W. Allyn Rickett, *Guanzi: Political, Economic, and Philosophical Essays from Early China*, vol. 2 (Princeton, N.J.: Princeton University Press, 1998)
Roth 1992	Harold D. Roth, *The Textual History of the Huai-Nan Tzu*, Monographs of the Association for Asian Studies, no. 46 (Ann Arbor, Mich.: Association for Asian Studies, 1992)
Roth 1999	Harold D. Roth, *Original Tao: Inward Training and the Foundations of Taoist Mysticism* (New York: Columbia University Press, 1999)
Vankeerberghen 2001	Griet Vankeerberghen, *The Huainanzi and Liu An's Claim to Moral Authority* (Albany: State University of New York Press, 2001)
Waley/Allen 1996	Arthur Waley, *The Book of Songs*, new ed., edited with additional translations by Joseph R. Allen (Boston: Houghton Mifflin, 1937; New York: Grove Press, 1996)
Wallacker 1962	Benjamin E. Wallacker, *The Huai-nan-tzu, Book Eleven: Behavior, Culture and the Cosmos*, American Oriental Series, vol. 48 (New Haven, Conn.: American Oriental Society, 1962)

We, the members of the *Huainanzi* translation project team, and our associates in this work, hope that we have been able to carry out this project in conformity with the preceding principles. Above all, we hope that this translation will have the effect of stimulating further new scholarship on the fascinating and rich book of Liu An, the Master of Huainan.

One

ORIGINATING IN THE WAY

"ORIGINATING IN the Way" (Yuan dao 原 道), the first of the eight foundational or "root" chapters of the text, is significant because it provides the cosmological basis for the entire *Huainanzi* collection. It opens with a beautiful poetic rhapsody on the cosmology of the Way (*dao* 道) and its Potency (*de* 德) in the tradition of the *Laozi* 老子, certainly one of the canonical sources for this particular essay and for the book as a whole. In it we see a detailed examination of how these cosmic foundations are manifested in the world and an in-depth description of how sages are able to use their unique penetrating vision of these foundations, attained through self-cultivation, to bring peace and harmony to the realm. Coming at the beginning of the entire twenty-one-chapter book and presented to the court at a time when its compiler, Liu An 劉安, was trying to dissuade his nephew, Emperor Wu 武 帝, against the arguments of his Confucian (*ru* 儒) advisers, this chapter serves a number of purposes.

First, even though the chapter never directly affirms a particular intellectual affiliation, its cosmological, psychological, and political philosophy shows its indebtedness to the *Laozi* and some other important early Daoist sources on the relationship of cosmology and self-cultivation to rulership.[1] Only such an ideal of rulership

---

1. For details on these texts and their relationships, see Harold D. Roth, "Psychology and Self-Cultivation in Early Taoistic Thought," *Harvard Journal of Asiatic Studies* 51, no. 2 (1991): 599–650; "Who Compiled the *Chuang Tzu?*" in *Chinese Texts and Philosophical Contexts: Essays Dedicated to Angus C. Graham*, ed. Henry Rosemont Jr. (LaSalle, Ill.: Open Court Press, 1991), 78–128; and "Redaction Criticism and the Early History of Taoism," *Early China* 19 (1994): 1–46.

comprehends the inner workings of the cosmos and applies that wisdom to governing in harmony with them. Second, as the opening chapter of the collection, "Originating in the Way" sets out general themes that will be pursued in more detail in much of the remainder of the work, such as cosmology, human psychology and self-cultivation, and political philosophy. Its importance to understanding the entire book and seeing it in a clearer light cannot be overemphasized.

The Chapter Title

We have translated the title of this chapter, "Yuan dao" 原道, as "Originating in the Way." The word *yuan* is a noun meaning "origin" or "source." The Han commentator Gao You takes it to mean "foundation." *Yuan* can also be used adjectivally and occasionally verbally, as in Roger T. Ames and D. C. Lau's translation of this chapter, "Tracing Dao to Its Source."[2] *Dao* means "the Way," the primary creative and destructive force in the cosmos that is simultaneously immanent in everything yet paradoxically transcendent of any one of them. It serves as a kind of invisible guide for the spontaneous self-generating activities of all phenomena. Because it is immanent, the Way can be directly apprehended or grasped by human beings through an apophatic meditative practice that I call "inner cultivation."[3] Our translation of the title, "Originating in the Way," reflects the verbal use of *yuan* and highlights its authors' demonstration that the cosmos, human consciousness, methods of inner cultivation, human history, and even the contents of the rest of the book "originate in the Way." While we might expect the preposition *yu* 於 (in) to appear between *yuan* and *dao* (原於道) in the title, it seems to have been left out in order to conform to the two-character title format for all the chapters, but it can be inferred. Furthermore, as a translation, "Originating in the Way" is meant to preserve the parallelism with the title of chapter 2, "Activating the Genuine." This parallelism, however, creates semantic problems in English, because constructing the title as a verb–object phrase is philosophically unsound from the perspective of the text (the *dao* cannot really be an object). If we were to cleave very closely to the grammar of the title, we

2. Roger T. Ames and D. C. Lau, *Yuan Dao: Tracing Dao to Its Source* (New York: Ballantine Books, 1998). Ames 1994, 14, earlier translated this title as "Tracing the Dao." Csikszentmihalyi 2004, 45, 102n.2, renders it variously as "Finding the Source of the Way" and "Origin of the Tao." For other versions of the chapter title, see the translations listed in app. C.

3. "Apophatic" refers to methods of self-transformative practice that involve the "forgetting" or negation of common dualistic categories of knowledge and experience. "Inner cultivation" is the term I use to refer to the apophatic practices of emptying the mind in order to realize the Way that are found in all early Daoist works. For details, see Harold D. Roth, "The Inner Cultivation Tradition of Early Daoism," in *The Religions of China in Practice*, ed. Donald Lopez and Stephen Teiser (Princeton, N.J.: Princeton University Press, 1995), 123–48; "Evidence for Stages of Meditation in Early Taoism," *Bulletin of the School of Oriental and African Studies* 60, no. 2 (1997): 295–314; and *Original Tao: Inward Training and the Foundations of Taoist Mysticism* (New York: Columbia University Press, 1999), 7–9 and passim.

could render it as "The Originating Way," but this does not make for good style or sense in English. "Originating in the Way," however, conveys the same sense and is stylistically better suited to English syntax and usage.

Summary and Key Themes

For the authors of the *Huainanzi*, because everything in Heaven and on Earth is both natural and supernatural, secular and sacred, the natures and patterns that constitute them attain a normative prominence often unfamiliar to us in the West. That is, these patterns, sequences, propensities, and natures are themselves divine. They are the basis through which all the multitudinous phenomena in the world adhere and function in harmony and, as such, serve as the models and standards for the communities of human beings who are an integral part of this order. Thus Nature is holy in and of itself—to be respected, adhered to, and even worshiped. According to the authors of this chapter, human beings can either ignore this normative natural order and fail in their endeavors, or they can follow it and succeed.

The sage-kings referred to in section 1.4, Feng Yi 馮夷 and Da Bing 大丙, are portrayed as having been the first to recognize this and to rule the cosmos by following the natural tendencies of phenomena and the patterns of their activities. Human beings cannot succeed by opposing these fundamental principles of the natural world. In order to govern effectively, the ruler must model himself on these sage-kings and develop the wisdom to discern these principles and then not interfere with how the myriad things follow them. Unfortunately, human beings tend to fall away from this normative natural order and lose their spontaneous functioning. The senses' desire for sense objects generates preferences and enticements, and people become so obsessed with them that they lose touch with their innate nature and natural spontaneity. Humans must learn to get back in touch with their natural and spontaneous side, for it is that part of them that is directly connected to the normative patterns through which the Way subtly guides the spontaneous self-generation of all things. Inner cultivation is the primary way in which human beings can realize the deepest aspects of their intrinsic nature, that part of their being that is directly in touch with the Way and, through it, with the inherent patterns and structures of the universe.

The universe is thus described as a "spiritlike vessel" (*shen qi* 神器), made up of the various innate natures (*xing* 性) of things that determine their course of development and their actions and of the great patterns (*li* 理) inherent in the cosmos that govern the characteristic ways in which things interact with one another. These natures and patterns are thoroughly infused with the empty Way, which mysteriously guides their spontaneous processes of development and their daily activities. This entire complex world functions completely spontaneously and harmoniously and needs nothing additional from human beings. All sages need to do is recognize these natures and patterns and adapt to them. It is because of this normative order that sages can accomplish everything without exerting their individual will to control things. In other words, they practice "non-action" (*wuwei* 無爲), which is effective because of the existence of this normative natural order. Sages cultivate themselves through the "Techniques of the Mind" (*xin shu* 心術) in order to fully realize the basis of this order within.[4] By realizing the Way at the basis of their innate nature, sages can simultaneously realize the intrinsic natures of all phenomena.

These interlocking ideas of order and structure in the universe as the foundation for non-action and sagely government are well summarized in section 1.9:

> Sages internally cultivate the root [of the Way within them]
> and do not externally adorn themselves with its branches.
> They protect their Quintessential Spirit
> and dispense with wisdom and precedent.
> In stillness they take no deliberate action, yet there is nothing left undone.
> In tranquillity they do not try to govern, but nothing is left ungoverned.
> What we call "no deliberate action" is to not anticipate the activity of things.
> What we call "nothing left undone" means to adapt to what things have [already] done.
> What we call "to not govern" means to not change how things are naturally so.
> What we call "nothing left ungoverned" means to adapt to how things are mutually so.

Thus, as section 1.5 states:

> The affairs of the world cannot be deliberately controlled.
> You must draw them out by following their natural direction.
> The alterations of the myriad things cannot be fathomed.
> You must grasp their essential tendencies and guide them to their homes.

The inner cultivation through which sages are able to realize the Way and practice non- action entails the systematic elimination of the emotions, distractions, desires, preferences, thoughts, deliberations, and attachments to the sense-objects that usually flood the conscious mind. Through this, one may break through to the level of "spiritlike illumination" (*shenming* 神明) and realize what lies deep within the innermost core of one's being, the one Way. Realizing this yields a profound and lasting contentment much greater than the fleeting pleasures of the senses. It also is conceived of as preserving the inherent balance among the functioning of the

4. The "Techniques of the Mind" is the title of two short texts in the seventy-six-text *Guanzi* compendium. Together with "Inward Training" and "The Purified Mind," they constitute a group that in modern scholarship is referred to as the four "Techniques of Mind" works. By the time of the *Huainanzi*, this phrase was probably used as a general term for what I have called "inner cultivation" practice. For details, see Roth, *Original Tao*, 15–30.

four basic aspects of human beings: physical body (*xing* 形), vital energy or breath (*qi* 氣), spirit (*shen* 神), and will or attention (*zhi* 志), which are part of the normative natural order that exists in human beings. Cluttering consciousness with lusts and desires disrupts this balance. The antidote for this is inner cultivation practice, which cleanses the mind and thus gradually restores the inherent balance among these activities. Thus by practicing inner cultivation that calms mind and body and yields a deep state of tranquillity, sages enable the four basic aspects of their beings to function spontaneously and harmoniously in accordance with their inherent natural patterns. This then allows them to align with the "heavenly dynamism" (*tianji* 天機), the normative natural order of which they are an integral part and thus act completely in accordance with the Way.

Another benefit of realizing the Way within is that those who do so can avoid the disasters associated with acting before the correct moment in time. When they detect that moment, they act spontaneously in response to it and are said to follow it and not anticipate it. This chapter contains an intricate matrix of interacting temporal sequences and natural patterns that guide the spontaneous responses arising from the natures of all phenomena. All these elements constitute the normative natural order, and failure to act in accordance with it will result in personal failure and, at times, natural disasters.

The authors of "Originating in the Way" also use the metaphor of water to express the most important aspects of this normative order. Water moves and acts as the Way does. It is both something from which we can learn about how the Way works in the world and a normative model for how the sages act. When they encounter difficulties, sages do not meet them with force but rather with a mental attitude based on the model of the persistent weakness of water. This is a quality of mind to be cultivated and is related to the notions of suppleness, pliancy, non-striving, and non-assertiveness. It is through this normative model of water that we can, as the *Laozi* says, understand the benefits of acting without asserting the human will over and against the patterns of nature (*tianli* 天理). The benefits of water are extolled in section 1.12:

> Therefore,
> without being partial or impartial, gushing and undulating, it totally merges with Heaven and Earth.
> Without favoring the left or the right, coiling and swirling, it ends and begins with the myriad things.
> This is what we call "Perfect Potency."

The reason that water is able to achieve its Perfect Potency within the entire world is that it is gentle and soaking, moist and slippery. Thus, in the words of Lao Dan:

> The most pliant things in the world
> ride roughshod over the most rigid.

[This is because] they emerge from the Nonexistent
and enter into the Seamless.
I thereby understand the benefits of taking no action.

Sources

The principal source for this chapter is the *Laozi*. It is the inspiration for the chapter's poetic rhapsodies on the Way and its vision of applying inner cultivation to governing. This chapter also shares its thought with the similarly entitled "Dao yuan" 道原 (The Source That Is the Way) essay that is part of the Mawangdui Huang-Lao silk manuscripts.[5] In its presentation of self-cultivation, "Originating in the Way" shares much of its language with the four works on "Techniques of the Mind" assembled in the *Guanzi*.[6] Its discussion of water as a metaphor for the Way comes from the *Laozi* and also perhaps from the *Taiyi sheng shui* (*The Grand One Generates Water*) text excavated at Guodian.[7]

The Chapter in the Context of the *Huainanzi* as a Whole

Coming at the beginning of the entire work, "Originating in the Way" establishes important elements of the philosophical framework in which the rest of the text functions. "An Overview of the Essentials," the concluding chapter of the *Huainanzi*, attributes to this chapter the ability to

> [begin with] the six coordinates contracted and compressed
> and the myriad things chaotic and confused.
> [It then] diagrams the features of the Grand One
> and fathoms the depths of the Dark Unseen,
> thereby soaring beyond the frame of Empty Nothingness.

5. For a translation, see Harold D. Roth and Sarah A. Queen, "Syncretic Visions of State, Society, and Cosmos," in *Sources of Chinese Tradition*, ed. Wm. Theodore de Bary and Irene Bloom, rev. ed. (New York: Columbia University Press, 1999), 252–56. For a translation and analysis of this text and the other silk manuscripts, see Robin D. S. Yates, *Five Lost Classics: Tao, Huang-lao, and Yin-yang in Han China* (New York: Ballantine Books, 1997), 171–77.

6. For details of these works and their ideas on self-cultivation, see Roth, "Redaction Criticism and the Early History of Taoism."

7. For the text and a preliminary discussion of this short but important work, see "Other Texts and the Question of Philosophical Schools," 162–71, and Edmund Ryden, "Edition of the Bamboo-Slip *Laozi* A, B, and C, and *Tai yi sheng shui* from Guodian Tomb Number One," 228–31, both in *The Guodian Laozi: Proceedings of the International Conference*, ed. Sarah Allan and Crispin Williams, Early China Special Monograph Series, no. 5 (Berkeley: University of California Press, 2000); and Sarah Allan, "The Great One, Water, and the *Laozi*: New Light from Guodian," *T'oung Pao* 89, nos. 4–5 (2003): 237–85.

> By relying on the small, it embraces the great;
> by guarding the contracted, it orders the expansive.
> It enables you to understand
> the bad or good fortune of taking the lead or following behind
> and the benefit or harm of taking action or remaining still
> If you sincerely comprehend its import, floodlike, you can achieve a grand vision. (21.2)

It thus ascribes to this first chapter an all-inclusive wisdom that provides the foundation for the rest of the book. In some important ways, "Originating in the Way" also is a parallel work to the second chapter, "Activating the Genuine," for which the *Zhuangzi* is the major influence.

The major themes in this chapter that occur in various combinations and contexts throughout the rest of the book are as follows: (1) the cosmology of the Way and its Potency; (2) the general framework for how the Way works in the world through the innate natures and propensities of things and through the natural patterns that form the structures through which things interact, thus forming a harmonious world order; (3) the basic theory that because of this order and structure, sages can act efficaciously in the world through non-action, a state of mind, and its derivative laissez-faire principle that leaving things alone allows them to spontaneously and harmoniously develop and interact; and (4) the theory that this state of mind can be developed through apophatic inner-cultivation practices.

Harold D. Roth

One

1.1

As for the Way:
It covers Heaven and upholds Earth.
It extends the four directions
and divides the eight end points.
So high, it cannot be reached.
So deep, it cannot be fathomed.
It embraces and enfolds Heaven and Earth
It endows and bestows the Formless.
Flowing along like a wellspring, bubbling up like a font,
it is empty but gradually becomes full.
Roiling and boiling,
it is murky but gradually becomes clear.
Therefore,
pile it up vertically: it fills all within Heaven and Earth.
Stretch it out horizontally: it encompasses all within the Four Seas.
Unwind it limitlessly: it is without distinction between dawn and dusk.
Roll it out: it expands to the six coordinates.[1]
Roll it up: it does not make a handful.

1. *Liu he* 六合; that is, the three dimensions: up-down, front-back, left-right. See 4.1.

It is constrained but able to extend.
It is dark but able to brighten.
It is supple but able to strengthen.
It is pliant but able to become firm.
It stretches out the four binding cords[2] and restrains yin and yang.
It suspends the cosmic rafters and displays the Three Luminaries.
Intensely saturating and soaking,
Intensely subtle and minute.
Mountains are high because of it.
Abysses are deep because of it.
Beasts can run because of it.
Birds can fly because of it.
The sun and moon are bright because of it.
The stars and timekeepers move because of it.
Qilins wander freely because of it.
Phoenixes soar because of it. [1/1/3–8]

1.2

The two August Lords of high antiquity[3]
grasped the handles of the Way
and so were established in the center.
Their spirits mysteriously roamed together with all transformations
and thereby pacified the four directions.
Hence, they could revolve like the heavens and stand still like the earth,
cycle round and round without stopping,
flowing unceasingly like water,
they ended and began together with all things.
As winds arose and clouds formed,
there was no event to which they did not respond.
As thunder rumbled and rain descended,
to all they responded without end.
Ghosts departed and spirits entered.
Dragons arose and phoenixes alighted.
Like the potter's wheel turning, like the wheel hub spinning,
they circled round and round.
Both carved and polished,

2. The four binding cords (*si wei* 四維) are the "corners" of the compass-circle: northeast, southeast, southwest, and northwest. See 3.10.

3. These two August Lords are the mythical organizer deities Fuxi and Nüwa. Fuxi is often depicted holding a carpenter's square and laying out the square earth; Nüwa is often depicted holding a compass and laying out the round heavens. See Major 1993, 267.

they returned to the Unhewn.[4]
They acted non-actively and were united with the Way.[5]
They spoke non-actively and were suffused by its Potency.[6]
They were peaceful and without cares and attained harmony.

Although there were a myriad of different things in the world, they accorded with their various natures. Their spirits could concentrate [on something as small as] the tip of an autumn hair[7] and something as vast as the totality of space and time.[8] Their Potency:

accorded with Heaven and the Earth and harmonized yin and yang;
delimited the four seasons and attuned the Five Phases.[9]

[Because] it affectionately supported and nurtured them,
the myriad things nourished their vitality.
It could seep into grasses and trees
and soak into metal and rock.[10]

Among the multitude of kinds of wild beasts
the hairs of their coats were sleek and moist.
Their feathers and wings fluttered;
their horns and antlers grew.
The embryos of beasts were not stillborn.
The eggs of birds were not infertile.
Fathers were spared the grief of mourning their sons.
Elder brothers were spared the sadness of mourning their younger brothers.
Children did not become orphans.
Wives did not become widows.
Double rainbows did not appear.
Baleful stars did not occur.[11]

This is all the result of the Potency with which they were imbued. [1/1/10–17]

---

4. The Unhewn (*pu* 樸) is a symbol for the desireless state found in both the Way and the sage-ruler who is united with the Way. Its *locus classicus* is *Laozi* 19 and 28.

5. To act non-actively (*wuwei* 無為) is to not exert intentional action from the perspective of a fixed and limited ego. This is the famous dictum found throughout the *Laozi*.

6. The Potency (*de* 德) of the Way is its manifestation, through which it serves as the subtle guiding force in all phenomena that enables them to spontaneously act in accord with their unique natures.

7. In early Chinese philosophical texts, autumn hair is a common metaphor for something minute. Animals of many species shed their undercoats at the beginning of summer and grow a new undercoat in the fall. The tip of a new hair as it emerges from the animal's skin at that time is extremely fine. See also chap. 16, n. 13.

8. In passages involving human cognition in the *Huainanzi*, the *shen* 神 (spirit, soul) is associated with consciousness and has the ability to concentrate on perceptions and thoughts.

9. The Five Phases (*wuxing* 五行)—Wood, Fire, Earth, Metal, and Water—are the basic categories of vital energy (*qi* 氣) of which all phenomena are manifestations.

10. Here Potency is thought of as a rarified kind of *qi* that infuses all phenomena and enables them to flourish. The *locus classicus* for this materialistic interpretation of *dao* and *de* is *Inward Training*. See Roth 1999, 46, 48, 96.

11. These last two are ominous portents indicating Heaven's displeasure. See Zhang Shuangdi 1997, 1:14n.37.

1.3

The most exalted Way
generates the myriad things but does not possess them,
completes the transforming images[12] but does not dominate them.
Creatures that walk on hooves and breathe through beaks, that fly through the air and wriggle on the ground,
depend on it for life, yet none understands its Potency;
depend on it for death, yet none is able to resent it.
Those who attain it and profit are unable to praise it;
those who use it and lose are unable to blame it.
It gathers and collects yet is not any richer for it.
It bestows and confers yet it not diminished by it.
It cycles endlessly yet cannot be fathomed.
It is delicate and minute yet cannot be exhausted.
Pile it up, but it will not get higher;
Collapse it, but it will not get lower.
Add to it, but it will not increase.
Take away from it, but it will not decrease.
Split it, but it will not get thinner.
Kill it, but it will not be destroyed.
Bore into it, but it will not deepen.
Fill it in, but it will not get shallower.
Hazy! Nebulous! You cannot imagine it.
Nebulous! Hazy! Your use will not exhaust it.
Dark! Obscure! It responds formlessly.
Deep! Penetrating! It does not act in vain.
It rolls and unrolls with the firm and the pliant.
It bends and straightens with the yin and the yang. [1/1/19–24]

1.4

In ancient times when Feng Yi and Da Bing rode chariots, they rose up in thunder carts and entered the cloudy rainbow. They roamed in the ethereal mists and galloped in the hazy and nebulous. Going farther and farther and higher and higher, they reached the pinnacle. They traversed the frost and snow but left no tracks. Illuminated by the light of the sun, they cast no shadows. Spiraling around, they ascended the whirlwind. Traversing mountains and rivers, they strode over Mount Kunlun. Pushing through the Chang He [gate] they surged through the gateway of Heaven.[13]

---

12. That is, the *bagua* 八卦, or "eight trigrams," of the *Yijing*.
13. For these mythical landscapes, see 4.3.

If we compare this with the charioteering in recent times, although there are lightweight carts and good horses, strong whips and sharp prods, they cannot compete with or overtake them.[14]

Therefore, the Great Man
calmly has no worries
and placidly has no anxieties
He takes
Heaven as his canopy;
Earth as his carriage;
the four seasons as his steeds,
and yin and yang as his charioteers.

He rides the clouds and soars through the sky to become a companion of the power that fashions and transforms us. Letting his imagination soar and relaxing his grip, he gallops through the vast vault [of the heavens].

When appropriate, he canters [his steeds].
When appropriate, he gallops them.
He orders the master of rain to moisten the byways
And directs the master of wind to sweep away the dust.
He takes lightning as his lash
and thunder as his chariot wheels.
Above, he roams freely in the misty and murky realms.
Below, he emerges from the gateway of the boundless.
Having observed all around and illuminated everything
He returns to guarding [the One] in order to remain whole.
He superintends the four corners [of Earth]
Yet always turns back to the central axis.

Thus,
with Heaven as your canopy, nothing will be uncovered.
With Earth as your carriage, nothing will be unsupported
With the four seasons as your steeds, nothing will be unemployed.
With yin and yang as your charioteers, nothing will be incomplete.

Therefore, why is it that
he hastens forth but does not wobble;
goes far but does not weary;
his four limbs do not weaken;
his perceptual acuity does not diminish;

and he comprehends the shapes and outlines of the eight outlying regions and the nine fields of the heavens? It is because he grasps the handles of the Way and roams in the land of the inexhaustible. [1/1/26–1/2/11]

---

14. This is a metaphor for the sorry state of present times in comparison with the era of the sage-kings of antiquity. The theme that government has declined from an earlier ideal state is pursued in several of the later chapters of the *Huainanzi*. For the metaphor of supernaturally talented charioteering, see also 6.6.

1.5

Therefore,

the affairs of the world cannot be deliberately controlled.
You must draw them out by following their natural direction.
The alterations of the myriad things cannot be fathomed.
You must grasp their essential tendencies and guide them to their homes.

When a water mirror comes in contact with shapes, it is not because of wisdom and precedent that it is able to flawlessly reflect the square, round, crooked, and straight.[15] Therefore, the echo does not respond at random, and the shadow does not independently arise. They mimic sounds and forms and tacitly grasp them.

That which is tranquil from our birth is our heavenly nature. Stirring only after being stimulated, our nature is harmed. When things arise and the spirit responds, this is the activity of perception. When perception comes into contact with things, preferences arise. When preferences take shape and perception is enticed by external things, our nature cannot return to the self, and the heavenly patterns are destroyed.[16]

Thus those who break through to the Way do not use the human to change the heavenly. Externally they transform together with things, but internally they do not lose their genuine responses.

They attain Nothing, but their needs are provided for.
They are always on the move but find a place to lodge for the night.

Small and great, tall or short, each has its proper role. The myriads spring forth and leap and prance in profusion, yet they do not lose track of their norms.[17]

So when they rest above, the people do not find them heavy.
When they are located in front, the multitudes do not injure them.

---

15. Wisdom and precedent are key ideas that the syncretic Daoist tradition criticizes in the Confucians. Casting these aside is one of their characteristic literary tropes. For details, see Harold D. Roth, "Who Compiled the *Chuang Tzu?*" in *Chinese Texts and Philosophical Contexts: Essays Dedicated to Angus C. Graham*, ed. Henry Rosemont Jr. (LaSalle, Ill.: Open Court Press, 1991), 95–128.

16. The authors are making a deliberate parallel between the dispassionate and accurate responses of the water mirror, the echo, and the shadow and the dispassionate and accurate responses of people's innate nature which, however, become perverted when preferences arise. Only those who break through to the Way are able to set aside selfish preferences and retain their "true condition," that is, the unbiased perception and knowing that is the inherent response of their intrinsic nature.

17. The "norms" (*shu* 數) appear to be the characteristic patterns of things. For example, in 12.1, the "norms" of the Way are detailed as follows:

Non-action responded, "The Way that I know
can be weak or strong;
it can be soft or hard;
it can be yin or yang;
it can be dark or bright;
it can embrace or contain Heaven and Earth;
it can respond to or await the Limitless.
These are the norms by which I know the Way.

All the world returns to them
The wicked and perverse fear them.
It is because they do not compete with the myriad things that none is able to compete with them. [1/2/11–19]

1.6

Now if someone spends an entire day pole-fishing along a riverbank he will not be able to fill up even a hand basket. Even though he may have hooked barbs and sharp spears, fine line and fragrant bait, and, in addition, the skills of Zhan He or Juan Xuan,[18] he would still be unable to compete with the catch hauled in by a trawling net. Or suppose a bowman were to stretch out the famous Wuhao bow and fit it with the fine arrows from Qi and add to this the craft of Yi or Feng Mengzi.[19] If he wanted to hunt birds in flight, he would still be unable to match the amount caught by a gauze net. Why is this? It is because what he is holding is small [by comparison].

If you stretch out the world and make it your basket
and follow the courses of rivers and oceans and make them your trawling net,
How could you lose any fish or miss any birds?

Thus the arrow cannot match the spear; the spear cannot match the trawling net; but the trawling net cannot match the Formless Image.[20] [1/2/21–25] Now if you let go of the great Way and rely on inferior methods,[21] this is no different from using a crab to catch a rat or a frog to catch a flea: it is insufficient to prevent wickedness and block depravity. It will only cause disorder to increase.

In ancient times, Gun[22] of Xia made a city wall twenty-four feet high,[23] but the Lords of the Land turned against him and those who dwelled beyond the seas had deceitful hearts. [His son] Yu[24] understood that the world had become rebellious and thereupon knocked down the wall, filled in the moat surrounding the city, gave away their resources, burned their armor and weapons, and treated everyone with beneficence. And so the lands beyond the Four Seas respectfully submitted, and the four Yi tribes brought tribute. When he assembled the Lords of the Land on Mount

18. Zhan He and Juan Xuan were legendary fishermen of superlative skill; both were said to be natives of Chu.

19. Yi 羿, or Archer Yi, is the legendary bowman who, when all ten of the world's suns came out at once, shot nine of them out of the sky. Feng was his student.

20. This is a metaphor for the Way, which is completely without form.

21. Reading *shu* 數 (numerical) for 術 (methods), a frequently substituted homophone.

22. Gun 鯀 was a mythical figure charged by sage-ruler Shun to tame the great flood; he attempted to do so by building dikes but failed to control the raging waters. For his failure, he was turned to stone.

23. We see no reason to accept Lau's emendation of "three *ren*" (each *ren* is eight feet) to "nine *ren*," which would be a ridiculous seventy-two feet high.

24. Yu 禹, or Yu the Great, succeeded in draining the flood by excavating new channels for the overflowing rivers. He became, at least in legend, the founder of the Xia, China's first dynastic state. For Gun and Yu, see Mark Edward Lewis, *The Flood Myths of Early China* (Albany: State University of New York Press, 2006); for an analysis of this passage, see 63.

Du, there were people from myriad principalities who brought in gifts of jade and silk. Thus when a deceitful heart is hidden in your chest, your inner purity will not glisten and your spiritlike Potency will not be whole. When what lies within your own person is not known to you, how can people from afar cherish you? Therefore when the armor is hard, the weapons are sharper; when city walls are built, battering rams are made. It is like using boiling water to reduce the boil: the disorder will simply increase. Therefore if you lash a snapping dog or whip a kicking horse in order to teach them, although you be as gifted as Yi Yin[25] or Zaofu,[26] you will not be able to transform them in this way. But if the heart that wishes to harm others disappears from within you, then you can pull the tail of a hungry tiger; how much more can you tame such things as dogs and horses?

Therefore those who embody the Way are relaxed and never exhausted.
Those who rely on [inferior] methods work hard but achieve little. [1/3/1–7]
Resorting to harsh laws and arbitrary punishments is not the practice of hegemons and kings.
Repeatedly using sharp whips is not the method of those who travel far.
Li Zhu's[27] vision was so acute that he could pick out the tip of a needle beyond a hundred paces, but he could not see the fish in the deep.
Music Master Kuang's[28] hearing was so accurate that he could harmonize the tones of the eight winds, yet he could not hear anything beyond ten *li*.

Thus relying on the talents of one person is insufficient to govern a holding of three *mou*. But if you comply with the norms of the Way[29] and follow the naturalness of Heaven and Earth, then none within the six coordinates will be able to be your equal.

Therefore, when Yu drained the flood,
he followed the water as his master.
When the Divine Farmer[30] sowed grain,
he followed the seedlings as his teacher. [1/3/9–13]

1.7

Plants like duckweed take root in water.
Plants like trees take root on land.
Birds beat their wings in the air in order to fly.

25. Yi Yin, legendary minister of King Tang, the founder of the Shang dynasty, was famous for his cooking (presumably of dogs, among other viands). For a passage similar to this one, see 16.34.

26. Zaofu appears frequently in the *Huainanzi* as the paragon of chariot drivers; he was said to have been the charioteer of King Mu of Zhou (tenth century B.C.E.) on his legendary journey to the West.

27. Li Zhu 離朱 was a famous (mythical) minister of Huangdi, the Yellow Emperor.

28. Kuang was a legendary music master. See also 6.1, 13.3, and 19.7; and *Zhuangzi*, chap. 2.

29. See n. 17.

30. The Divine Farmer is Shen Nong 神農, mythical inventor of agriculture and sage-emperor of high antiquity.

Wild beasts stomp on solid ground in order to run.
Serpents and dragons live in the water.
Tigers and leopards live in the mountains.
This is the nature of Heaven and Earth.[31]
When two pieces of wood are rubbed together, they make fire.
When metal and fire are pushed together, the metal becomes molten.
Round things always spin.
Hollow things excel at floating.
This is their natural propensity.

Therefore, when spring winds arrive, then sweet rains will fall; they vitalize and nurture the myriad things.

Those with wings sit on their nests and hatch eggs.
Those with hair gestate and give birth to their young.
Grasses and trees become lush and flowering.
Birds and wild beasts have eggs and embryos.
No one sees what effects these things, but these achievements are completed.
The autumn winds cause frost to descend,
and the living things [that are reached by the frost] are snapped and injured.
Eagles and falcons hawkishly seize [their prey];
swarming insects hibernate;
grasses and trees die back to their roots;
fish and tortoises plunge together into the deep.
No one sees what effects these things; they just disappear into the Formless.
Tree dwellers nest in the woods;
water dwellers live in caves.
Wild beasts have beds of straw;
human beings have houses.
Hilly places are suitable for oxen and horses.
For travel by boat, it is good to have a lot of water.
The Xiongnu produce rancid animal-skin garments,
The Gan and Yue [peoples] make thin clothes of *pueraria* fabric.[32]
Each produces what it urgently needs
in order to adapt to the aridity or dampness.
Each accords with where it lives
in order to protect against the cold and the heat.
All things attain what is suitable to them;
things accord with their niches.

From this viewpoint, the myriad things definitely accord with what is natural to them, so why should sages interfere with this? [1/3/15–22]

31. See 15.1.

32. The *ge* 葛, or "pueraria" (*Pueraria lobata*), is a plant with many creepers that can be used to make fine fabric for clothes.

1.8

To the south of the Nine Passes, tasks on dry land are few, while tasks on water are many. So the people cut their hair and tattoo their bodies in order to resemble scaly creatures. They wear short pants, not long trousers, in order to make swimming easier. And they have short sleeves in order to make poling their boats easier. In doing this, they are adapting [to their natural environment].

To the north of the Yanmen Pass, the Di tribes do not eat grain. They devalue the aged and value the strong, and it is a custom to esteem those with strength of vital energy. People there do not unstring their bows, nor do they remove the bridles from their horses. In doing this, they are adjusting [to their natural environment].

Thus when Yu went to the Country of the Naked, he removed his clothes when he entered and put them back on when he left. In doing this he was adapting [to his natural environment]. Nowadays, if those who transplant trees neglect the yin and the yang aspects of their natures, then none will not wither and die. Thus if you plant a mandarin orange tree north of the Yangzi, it will transform into an inedible orange. A mynah bird cannot live beyond [i.e., to the north of] the Qi River, and if a badger[33] crosses [to the south of] the Min River, it will die. Physical form and innate nature cannot be changed,[34] and propensity and locale cannot be shifted.

Therefore,

those who break through to the Way return to clarity and tranquillity.
Those who look deeply into things end up not acting on them.
If you use calmness to nourish your nature,
and use quietude to transfix your spirit,
then you will enter the heavenly gateway. [1/3/24–1/4/3]

What we call "Heaven"
is pure and untainted,
unadorned and plain,
and has never begun to be tainted with impurities.

What we call "human"
is biased because of wisdom and precedent.
Devious and deceptive,
it is what looks back to past generations and interacts with the vulgar.

Thus,

33. *He* 貈. The identity of this animal is uncertain. Commentators generally agree that it is the same as the *he* 狢, which Morohashi's *Dai kanwa jiten* (*Great Sino-Japanese Dictionary*) defines as a badger (*mujina*). However, the illustration accompanying that entry in Morohashi depicts a catlike animal, not at all resembling a badger. *Grand dictionnaire Ricci de la langue chinoise*, 7 vols. (Paris: Institut Ricci, 2001), 2:848, defines *he* as *Nyctereutes procyonoides*, sometimes called the raccoon dog in English but best known by its Japanese name, *tanuki*. (In 6.8 and 10.14, the raccoon dog, or *tanuki*, is referred to as a *li* 貍.) We provisionally accept the definition of *he* as a badger. The passage here reflects an accurate observation of wildlife. The mynah is a bird of the subtropics that cannot survive in northern latitudes; the badger is an animal of dry northern plains and steppes that does not thrive in the moist lands of the south.

34. Compare the discussion in 19.4.

that the ox treads on cloven hooves and grows horns
and that the horse has a mane and square hooves,
This is heavenly [i.e., natural].
Yet to put a bit in a horse's mouth
and to put a ring through an ox's nose,
This is human.
Those who comply with Heaven roam with the Way.
Those who follow the human interact with the mundane.
Now,
you cannot talk to a fish in a well about great things because it is confined by its narrow space.
You cannot talk to a summer bug about the cold because it is restricted to its season.
You cannot talk to petty scholars about the Utmost Way because they are confined by the mundane and bound up by their teaching.
Thus sages
do not allow the human to obscure the heavenly
and do not let desire corrupt their genuine responses.
They hit the mark without scheming;
they are sincere without speaking;
they attain without planning;
they complete without striving.
Their vital essence circulates into the Magical Storehouse, and they become human along with what fashions and transforms them. [1/4/5–10]

1.9

When an excellent swimmer sinks and an excellent rider falls, it is because, contrary to expectations, each has taken what he is fond of and used it to make misfortune for himself.
Therefore,
those who are fond of striving never miss falling into a trap,
and those who compete for gain are never not exhausted.

In ancient times, the strength of Gong Gong was such that he butted his head against Buzhou Mountain and caused the earth to tilt toward the southeast. He competed with Gao Xin[35] in order to become the thearch. Subsequently he disappeared into an abyss; his entire clan was destroyed; and the ancestral sacrifices of his clan line were cut off. The king of Yue fled to a cave in the mountains, but the people of Yue smoked him out,[36] and subsequently he had no choice [but to return with them].

---

35. That is, Zhuan Xu; for the battle between these mythical titans, see 3.1.
36. This story is told more fully in the *Zhuangzi* (ZZ 28/82/1–4).

When we look at things from this point of view,

attainment lies with the right moment and does not lie in competing with others.

Good order lies in the Way and does not lie in sages.

The soil lies beneath things and does not compete to be higher than them. Thus it is secure and in no danger.

Water flows downward and does not compete to take the lead. Thus it moves quickly without delay. [1/4/12–16]

In ancient times, Shun plowed on Mount Li. After a year the farmers competed to occupy the stony fields while they relinquished the fertile fields to one another. He fished on the riverbank. After a year the fishermen fought to occupy the rapids and shallows while they gave the remote coves and deep pools to one another. During this time his mouth did not speak, and his hands did not direct with banners. He held a mysterious potency in his mind, and he transformed things so rapidly it seemed spiritlike. If Shun had not had this awareness, although his mouth could argue so cogently that every household would be persuaded, he would not have been able to transform even a single person. Therefore the Way that cannot be spoken of is incredibly vast! Now he was able to regulate the San Miao and subjugate the Feathered People, to move to the Country of the Naked, and to receive tribute from the Sushan. It was not because he announced titles and proclaimed edicts that he was able to adjust their mores and change their customs; it was only because of his mental activity that he was able to do that. How could laws and measures, punishments and restrictions, enable him to achieve this?

Therefore,

sages internally cultivate the root [of the Way within them]

and do not externally adorn themselves with its branches.

They protect their Quintessential Spirit

and dispense with wisdom and precedent.

In stillness they take no deliberate action, yet there is nothing left undone.

In tranquillity they do not try to govern, but nothing is left ungoverned.

What we call "no deliberate action" is to not anticipate the activity of things.

What we call "nothing left undone" means to adapt to what things have [already] done.

What we call "to not govern" means to not change how things are naturally so.

What we call "nothing left ungoverned" means to adapt to how things are mutually so.

The myriad things all have a source from which they arise;

[the sages] alone understand how to guard this root.

The hundred endeavors all have a source from which they are produced;

[the sages] alone understand how to guard this gateway.

Thus exhausting the inexhaustible,

reaching the limit of the infinite,

illuminating things without bedazzling them,

and inexhaustibly responding to things like an echo [responds to sound]:
This is what we call "being released by Heaven." [1/4/18–26]

1.10

Thus those who attain the Way:

Their wills are supple, but their deeds are strong.
Their minds are empty, but their responses are dead on.

What we mean by a supple will is
being pliant and soft, calm, and tranquil;
hiding when others do not dare to;
acting when others are unable to;
being calm and without worry;
acting without missing the right moment;
and cycling and revolving with the myriad things.
Never anticipating or initiating
but just responding to things when stimulated.

Therefore,
the honored invariably take their titles from the base,
and those of high station invariably take what is below as their foundation.
They rely on the small to embrace the great;
they rest in the inner to regulate the outer;
they act pliantly to become firm;
they utilize weakness to become strong;
they cycle through transformations and push where things are shifting;
they attain the Way of the One and use the few to correct the many.

What we mean by strength of deeds is
responding with alacrity when encountering alterations;
pushing away disasters and warding off difficulties;
being so strong that there is nothing unvanquished;
facing enemies, there are none that are not humiliated;
responding to transformations by gauging the proper moment
and being harmed by nothing.

Therefore,
if you wish to be firm, you must guard it by being pliant.
If you wish to be strong, you must protect it by being supple.
When you accumulate pliability, you become firm.
When you accumulate suppleness, you become strong.
Keep a close watch on what you are accumulating
in order to know the tendencies toward fortune or misfortune.

Strength defeats what is not its equal. When it encounters its equal, it is neutralized.
Pliability defeats what exceeds itself. Its power cannot be measured.

Thus when an army is strong, it will be destroyed.

When a tree is strong, it will be broken.
When leather armor is hard, it will split open.
Because teeth are harder than the tongue, they wear out first.
Therefore, the pliant and weak are the supports of life,
and the hard and strong are the disciples of death.[37] [1/4/28–1/5/7]

1.11

To anticipate [the right moment] and initiate is the road to ruin;
to follow is the source of success.[38]

How do I know this is so? For most people, through a life span of about seventy years until they reach their death; they pursue things and then reject them; they divide them up and then reassemble them; and daily they regret what they are doing. Thus Qu Boyu[39] at age fifty had criticized himself for forty-nine of them. Why?

Because those who anticipate have a hard time acting with wisdom,
but those who follow have an easy time acting efficaciously.
When those who anticipate climb up high,
those who follow will pull them down.
When those who anticipate climb down,
those who follow will jump over them.
When those who anticipate fall into a pit,
those who follow will take counsel from this.
When those who anticipate accumulate defeats,
those who follow will avoid them.

Looking at it from this perspective, those who anticipate are the target that draws the bows and arrows away from those who follow. It is as the hilt is to the blade of the sword: the blade suffers the stress while the hilt remains unharmed. Why? Because it places itself in the position of following and has a protected spot.[40] This is something widely seen in the vulgar world and among ordinary people, and the worthy and wise cannot avoid it.

What we call "following" does not mean being stagnant and not developing or being congealed and not flowing. It is, rather, to value being able to revolve according to the norms and unite with the right moment.

Now those who grasp the Patterns of the Way and become companions of alterations, their anticipation governs what follows and their following after governs what

37. *Laozi* 76.

38. To anticipate (*xian* 先, to precede) or to act in advance of how situations will develop is a problem for the authors of the *Huainanzi*. It most certainly blocks the natural, spontaneous, and timely responses to situations as they arise and develop and causes much unnecessary thought, worry, and erroneous action. Acting spontaneously immediately after situations arise allows accurate responses.

39. Qu Boyu, an aristocrat (fl. sixth century B.C.E.) of the state of Wey, was known for his wisdom and humaneness.

40. Following the emendation suggested by Lau, HNZ 1/5/14. See also n. 7.

they anticipated. What is the reason for this? They do not lose what they use to govern others [i.e., the Patterns of the Way], and so others cannot govern them. [1/5/7–17]

Time turns over and over.
There is not a moment's rest.
To anticipate is to overshoot the mark;
to follow is to not fall short.
The days turn round and the months revolve:
Time does not play with mankind.

Thus sages do not value a foot of jade as much as they esteem an inch's movement of the sundial's shadow. Time is difficult to gain but easy to lose.

When Yu was chasing the right moment,
if he lost his sandal, he would not stop to pick it up.
If he snagged his cap on a branch, he would not even glance back at it.

It was not that he was striving to anticipate the right moment; he was striving to attain it.

Therefore, sages guard the Pure Way and embrace the limits of the feminine principle. They adapt to things and comply with them; they respond to alterations spontaneously; they constantly follow and do not anticipate.

They are pliant and supple and thereby become tranquil,
They are relaxed and calm, and therefore their minds are stable.

They defeat the great and grind down the hard, and none is able to compete with them. [1/5/19–22]

1.12

Of all things under Heaven, none is more pliant and supple than water.
Nonetheless, it is

so great that its limits cannot be reached;
so deep that it cannot be fathomed;
so high that it reaches the infinite;
so distant it merges into the boundless.
Increasing and decreasing, draining away and filling up,
it circulates without restraints into the immeasurable.
When it ascends into the heavens, it becomes the rain and the dew.
When it descends to the earth, it becomes moisture and dampness.
If the myriad things do not gain it, they will not be born.
If the various endeavors do not gain it, they will not succeed.
It completely embraces the various things without partiality or favoritism.
It seeps through to the tiniest of creatures without seeking their gratitude.
Its richness sustains the entire world without being depleted.
Its Potency extends to the hundred clans without being expended.
It circulates [everywhere], yet we cannot exhaust it.

It is so subtle that we cannot seize it in our hands.
Strike it, and it is not wounded.
Pierce it, and it is not injured.
Chop it, and it is not cut apart.
Try to set it alight, and it will not burn.
Seeping, draining, flowing, disappearing,
Mixing and blending, intertwining with [things], it cannot be differentiated.
It is so sharp it can pierce a hole in metal and stone.
It is so strong it can give sustenance to the entire world.
It dissolves into the realm of the Formless,
And soars beyond the region of the Nebulous.
It meanders its way through the rivers and valleys,
and surges out into the vast wildernesses.
Depending on whether it is abundant or deficient,
it takes from or gives to Heaven and Earth.
It gives to the myriad things equally without preferences.

Therefore,

without being partial or impartial, gushing and undulating, it totally merges with Heaven and Earth.
Without favoring the left or the right, coiling and swirling, it ends and begins with the myriad things.

This is what we call "Perfect Potency." [1/5/24–1/6/7]

The reason that water is able to achieve its Perfect Potency within the entire world is that it is gentle and soaking, moist and slippery. Thus, in the words of Lao Dan:

The most pliant things in the world
ride roughshod over the most rigid.
[This is because] they emerge from the Nonexistent
and enter into the Seamless.

I thereby understand the benefits of taking no action.[41] [1/6/9–10]

Now the Formless is the Great Ancestor of things,
and the Toneless is the Great Ancestor of sound.
Their son is light;
their grandson is water;

And both are generated by the Formless.

Light can be seen but cannot be held;
water can be held but cannot be destroyed.

Thus of all things that have shapes, none is more honored than water.

41. *Laozi* 43. According to William Boltz (private communication), it clearly reflects the *guben*, or "ancient text," version that survives in the Fu Yi recension rather than the more common Wang Bi or He Shanggong version.

1.13

Emerging into life, entering into death;
from Nothing treading into Something;
from Something treading into Nothing,
we thereby decline into lowliness. [1/6/10–13]

Therefore,

clarity and tranquillity are the perfections of Potency;
pliancy and suppleness are the essentials of the Way.

Empty Nonexistence and calm serenity are the ancestors of the myriad things.[42]

To quickly respond when stimulated,
to boldly[43] return to the Root,

is to be merged with the Formless.

What we call "the Formless" is a designation for the One. What we call "the One" is that which has no counterpart in the entire world.

Majestically independent,
immensely solitary;
above, it permeates the Nine Heavens;
below, it threads through the Nine Regions.
Though round, it does not fit within the compass;
though square, it does not fit within the carpenter's square.
Multifarious, yet constituting a unity;
proliferating, yet without a root.
It envelops Heaven and Earth like a sack;
it closes the gates to the Way.
Mysterious and vague, hidden and dark,
its whole Potency is preserved in its solitude.
Spread it out: it never ceases;
utilize it: it is never exhausted.

Therefore,

though you look for it, you will never see its form;
though you listen for it, you will never hear its sound;
though you hold it, you will never feel its contours.
It is a formlessness from which forms are generated;
It is a soundlessness from which the five tones call out.
It is a tastelessness from which the five flavors take shape.
It is a colorlessness from which the five colors develop.

Therefore,

the Existent arises from the Nonexistent;

---

42. Emending *yong* 用 (usefulness) to *zu* 祖 (ancestor), as in the *Wenzi* and following Liu Ji. See Zhang Shuangdi 1997, 1:88n.7.

43. Emending *yin* 殷 (abundant, flourishing) to *yi* 毅 (boldly), as in TPYL and following Zhuang Kuiji. See Lau, HNZ, 6n.6; and Zhang Shuangdi 1997, 1:88n.8.

the Real emerges from the Empty.
Because the entire world is encircled by it,
names and realities converge.
The number of the tones does not exceed five, yet their variations cannot be fully heard.
The harmony of the flavors does not exceed five, yet their transformations cannot be fully savored.
The number of the colors does not exceed five, yet their variations cannot be fully seen.

Thus,

as for tone: when the *gong* note is established, the five tones all take shape;
as for flavor: when sweetness is established, the five flavors all become fixed;
as for color: when white is established, the five colors all develop;
as for the Way: when the One is established, then the myriad things all are born. [1/6/15–23]

Therefore,

the guiding principle of the One
spreads throughout the Four Seas.
The diffusion of the One
extends throughout Heaven and Earth.
In its wholeness, it is pure like uncarved wood.
In its dispersal, it is jumbled like murky water.
Although it is murky, it gradually becomes clear;
although it is empty, it gradually becomes full.
Still! It resembles a deep pool.
Buoyant! It resembles floating clouds.[44]
It seems to be nonexistent yet it exists;
it seems to be absent yet it is present.
The myriad things in their totality
all pass through this one portal.
The roots of the hundred endeavors
all emerge from this one gateway.
Its movements are formless;
its alterations and transformations are spiritlike [i.e., unfathomable];
its actions are traceless;
it constantly anticipates by following after. [1/6/25–27]

Therefore, in the governing of the Perfected,

they conceal their mental acuity;
they extinguish their literary brilliance.

Relying on the Way, they set aside wisdom and, toward the people, act impartially.

44. These six lines of poetry have a similar syntax to the verses in the middle section of *Laozi* 15. Because they vary, it is possible that both are drawing on a common source, perhaps a collection of what I have called "early Daoist wisdom poetry" (Roth 1999, 190–92).

They limit their possessions
and reduce their needs.[45]
They cast off their ambitions,
discard lusts and desires,
and abandon worries and anxieties.
Limiting their possessions, they see things clearly;
reducing their needs, they attain them.

Now those who rely on their ears and eyes to hear and see, tire out their bodies, and are not clear. Those who use knowledge and deliberation to govern afflict their minds and achieve no success.

Therefore, sages make use of the one measure to comply with the tracks of things.

They do not alter its suitability;
they do not change its constancy.

Applying it as their level,[46] relying on it as their marking cord,[47] through the meanderings [of life], they follow it as their benchmark. [1/6/29–1/7/2]

1.14

Joy and anger are aberrations from the Way;
worry and grief are losses of Potency.
Likes and dislikes are excesses of the mind;
lusts and desires are hindrances to nature.

Violent anger ruins the yin;
extreme joy collapses the yang.
The suppression of vital energy brings on dumbness;
fear and terror bring on madness.

45. These two lines are from the Liu Ji redaction of 1501 and its descendants. Lau (HNZ, 6n.8) cites Wang Shumin as adding them as well.

46. Tools appear throughout the *Huainanzi*, often, as here, in metaphorical or symbolic senses. The *zhun* 準, "level" (unlike the much later spirit-level familiar in the West, which features an air bubble in a closed liquid-filled tube), relied on the self-leveling property of water. It consisted of a board into which a water reservoir and a narrow straight channel were carved. When the board was held exactly level, water from the reservoir would fill the channel to an even depth. Sometimes the *zhun* sometimes consisted of the board alone (for use on flat surfaces), and sometimes the board was fitted with a handle so that the level could be held up to a wall or other raised surface.

47. The *sheng* 繩, "marking cord," is a device consisting of a hollow box containing ink-soaked vegetable fiber, a string arranged to run through the ink box and be inked by it, and a reel or other device to control the string. It functions in the same way as a Western carpenter's chalk line, to mark a straight line (e.g., to indicate where to cut a plank or stone). It can also be hung from a high position to function as a plumb line. *Sheng* is sometimes translated as "marking line" or "line marker," which are appropriate renderings; it is also sometimes mistranslated as "measuring line" or "tape measure." But this is an error because the principal function of the device is to mark straight lines, not to measure linear distance.

When you are worried, aggrieved, or enraged,
sickness will increasingly develop.
When likes and dislikes abundantly pile up,
misfortunes will successively follow.

Thus,

when the mind is not worried or happy, it achieves the perfection of Potency.

When the mind is inalterably expansive, it achieves the perfection of tranquillity.

When lusts and desires do not burden the mind, it achieves the perfection of emptiness.

When the mind is without likes and dislikes, it achieves the perfection of equanimity.

When the mind is not tangled up in things, it achieves the perfection of purity.

If the mind is able to achieve these five qualities, then it will break through to spiritlike illumination. To break through to spiritlike illumination is to realize what is intrinsic.

Therefore,

if you use the internal to govern the external,
then your various endeavors will not fail.
If you are able to realize internally,
then the external can be attended to.
If you realize it internally
then your Five Orbs[48] will be in repose;
worries and anxieties will be at peace.
Your sinews will be powerful, and your muscles will be strong;
your ears and eyes will be acute and clear.
Though you are placid and calm, you do not waver.[49]
Though you are hard and strong, you do not break.
There is nothing you overshoot
and nothing you fall short of.
When you dwell in the small, you will not be cramped;
when you dwell in the great, you will be unrestrained.
Your soul will not be agitated;
your spirit will not be troubled.

---

48. The Five Orbs (*wu zang* 五臧) correspond to the five organs of the human physiology that were thought to be critical generative and coordinating junctures for the dynamic matrix of *qi* that composed the mind–body system: the lungs, liver, spleen, gall bladder, and kidneys. The term refers to organic systems, not just to the physical viscera; hence we speak of the pulmonary, renal, choleric, hepatic, and splenic orbs. See 7.2 and app. A.

49. We accept the interpretation of this line by Kusuyama Haruki, *Enanji*, in *Shinshaku kanbun taikei* (Tokyo: Meiji shōin, 1979–1988), 54:66.

Clear and limpid, still and calm,
you will become a hero[50] to the entire world. [1/7/4–11]

1.15

The Great Way is vast and serene.
It is never far away from your own person.
If you seek it in what is close at hand,
you will go forth with it and return to it.[51]
When stimulated, you will be able to respond;
when pressed you will be able to move.
Mysteriously subtle and inexhaustible,
you alter without form or image.
When you fully roam [with the Way] in complete abandonment,
you will be like an echo to it or a shadow of it.
Climbing up high and gazing down on what is below,
you will never lose what you are hanging onto.
When treading through dangers and traversing defiles,
you will never forget your mysterious support.

If you are able to preserve it here, then your Potency will not diminish. The myriad things commingle in profusion, and you can revolve and transform together with them and thereby listen to the entire world. It is like galloping with the wind at your back. This is called "Perfect Potency." If you attain Perfect Potency, then you will be truly content.

Among the people of olden times were those who lived in caves and grottoes but whose spirits did not depart from them [i.e., did not lose the centeredness derived from the spirit]. Among people of recent times are those who have the power of ten thousand chariots but who every day are worried and saddened.

If we look at things from this viewpoint,
sageliness is lost in governing people, yet it is found in attaining the Way.
Contentment is lost in wealth and station, but it is found in the harmony of Potency.

When you understand how to emphasize the self and deemphasize the [external] world, then you will be close to the Way. [1/7/13–18]

50. Literally, "an owl." The *xiao* 梟 (generally taken to be a kind of owl) is for the ancient Chinese a symbol of audacity and courage that in the *Huainanzi* is emblematic of perfected human beings. In Chinese mythology it is also known as the creature that devoured its own mother. See also 12.5.

51. In the Northern Song redaction, these four lines occur ten lines later in the text, after "You will never forget your mysterious support" (Lau, HNZ 1/7/14–15, 7n.3). They are totally missing in the *Daozang* redaction, but Lau adds them in the later position following the Northern Song redaction. We follow the Liu Ji redaction and its descendants in placing them here, at the beginning of a new section on the Way. This is also where Kusuyama places them (*Enanji*, 66). The textual evidence is equivocal, and we place these lines here because this location seems to better fit the flow of the argument.

What is called "contentment"? Why must it consist of residing in the Lofty Terrace or the Elegant Floral Terrace; or roaming in the Lake of Cloudy Dreams or Sandy Hillock?[52] The ear's listening to the "nine *shao* [songs]" or the "six *ying* [pieces]";[53] or the mouth's tasting finely prepared delicacies; or galloping on a level highway; or hunting the auspicious turquoise kingfisher—is this what is called contentment?[54] What I call "contentment" refers to a person realizing his [deepest] realization [i.e., the Way]. Now those who realize their [deepest] realization:

Do not find contentment in extravagance
or grief in frugality.
They close together with the yin
and surge together with the yang.

Thus when [Confucius's disciple] Zixia had conflict in his mind he grew thin, but when he attained the Way, he fattened up again. Sages do not allow their own persons to be enslaved by external things and do not allow desires to disrupt their [inner] harmony.

Therefore, when they are content, they do not delight in it;
when they are aggrieved, they are not distressed by it.

Through myriads of situations and hundreds of alterations, they flow freely and have nothing fixed:

"I alone remain detached;
I abandon external things,
and proceed together with the Way."[55]

Therefore if you have the resources to realize it [the Way] yourself, then

beneath [the canopy of] lofty forests
and in [the bowels of] the deepest caves,

you will have what it takes to respond appropriately to your situation. But if you do not have the wherewithal to realize it yourself, then although you take the entire world as your own family and the myriad people as your servants and concubines, you will not have what it takes to nurture life.

If you are able to perfect the condition of being totally devoid of contentment, then there is nothing that will not make you content. If there is nothing that does not content you, then you will attain perfect contentment.[56] [1/7/20–26]

52. According to the commentator Gao You, there was a Chu cult surrounding these mystic places. Le Blanc and Mathieu 2003, 36, identify them as two panoramic viewing locales in the Chu capital. They further identify the "Cloudy Dreams" as a vast marsh in the state of Chu and the "Sandy Hillock" as part of the pleasure garden of the tyrant Djou, last king of the Shang dynasty.

53. Zhang Shuangdi 1997, 1:104, cites the Gao You commentary to the LSCQ that attributes these pieces to these two mythical sage emperors. Mathieu further identifies them: the "nine songs" celebrated the accession of the mythical sage-emperor Shun, and the "six pieces" were favored music of the mythical sage-emperor Zhuan Xu, grandson of the Yellow Emperor and grandfather of Shun.

54. The kingfisher's iridescent feathers were used in items of women's jewelry, such as hair ornaments.

55. In their shift to the first person, these three lines appear to be a quotation from a source similar to *Laozi* 20: "I alone am inactive," and so on.

56. How to do this is the main theme of the *Zhuangzi*, chap. 20, "Zhile" (Perfect Contentment).

1.16

Now setting up bells and drums, lining up wind and string instruments, spreading out felt mats and cushions, hanging up banners and ivory carvings, the ears listening to the licentious court music from the last Shang capital region,[57] presenting beauties of an elegant complexion, setting up wine and passing around goblets all night into the next morning, powerful crossbows shooting at high-flying birds, running dogs chasing crafty hares: All these may bring you contentment, consume you with a blazing passion, and tempt you to lust after them. But when you unhitch the chariot, rest the horses, stop the wine, and halt the music,

your heart suddenly feels as if it is in mourning,
and you are as depressed as if you had a great loss.

What is the reason for this? [It is]

because you do not use what is intrinsic to bring contentment to what is extrinsic but, rather, use what is extrinsic to bring contentment to what is intrinsic. So when the music is playing, you are happy, but when the songs end, you are sad.

Sadness and happiness revolve and generate one another;
your Quintessential Spirit becomes chaotic and defensive

and cannot get a moment's rest.

If you examine the reasons for this, you cannot grasp their shapes, yet every day because of this, you injure your vitality and neglect your [deepest] realizations.

Therefore, if you do not realize the intrinsic [nature] that lies within you, then you will bestow your natural endowment [of Quintessential Spirit] on external things and use it to falsely adorn yourself.[58]

It will not seep into your flesh and skin;
it will not pass into your bones and marrow;
it will not stay in your mind and awareness;
it will not collect in your Five Orbs.

Thus,

unless you have an internal master, what enters you from the outside will not stop.
Unless it is responding to something external, what exits from within will not be activated.

Thus,

when they hear good words and sound advice, even fools know to accept it.

57. The text attributes this licentious music to the last Shang capital, Zhaoge 朝歌, and its northern suburbs, Beibi 北鄙. Le Blanc and Mathieu 2003, 37, locate it in the northeast of the state of Qi in Henan.

58. The authors seem to be differentiating between two words commonly used to refer to a person's interior experience, *nei* 內 and *zhong* 中. We understand their use of the former to refer to the intrinsic nature of human beings and the latter to refer to a person's interior life. Further, the authors imply that human nature also contains a supply of quintessential spirit, the essential vital energy of the spirit, which is the most important foundation of consciousness. Here they argue that we can waste this vital essence on extrinsic rather than intrinsic activities, to our detriment.

When they are told of Perfect Potency and lofty actions, even the unworthy know to yearn for it.

Yet while those who accept it are many, those who make use of it are few.

While those who yearn for it are many, those who practice it are few.

Why is this so? Because they do not know how to return to their natures.

When those whose intrinsic [nature] has not opened up within insist on studying [Potency and lofty actions], [the words] enter their ears but do not take hold within their minds. How is this different from the songs of deaf mutes? They simply imitate what others do, but they do not have the means to make music themselves. The sounds issue forth from their mouths, but they merely spill out and disperse. [1/7/28–1/8/9]

1.17

The mind is the master of the Five Orbs. It regulates and directs the Four Limbs and circulates the blood and vital energy, gallops through the realms of accepting and rejecting, and enters and exits through the gateways and doorways of the hundreds of endeavors. Therefore if you do not realize it [your intrinsic nature] in your own mind and still want to control the entire world, this is like having no ears yet wanting to tune bells and drums and like having no eyes and wanting to enjoy patterns and ornaments. You will, most certainly, not be up to the task.

Thus the world is a spiritlike vessel: you cannot act deliberately on it; you cannot control it.[59] Those who attempt to deliberately act on it will be defeated by it; those who try to control it will lose it. Now the reason that Xu You[60] devalued the world and would not trade places with Yao was because he had the intention of leaving the world behind. Why was this so? Because he thought that you should act on the world by adapting to it [and not trying to force your own will on it].

The essentials of the world:

do not lie in the Other
but instead lie in the self;
do not lie in other people
but instead lie in your own person.

When you fully realize it [the Way] in your own person, then all the myriad things will be arrayed before you. When you thoroughly penetrate the teachings of the Techniques of the Mind, then you will be able to put lusts and desires, likes and dislikes, outside yourself.[61]

Therefore [if you realize the Way],

59. Following Wang Shumin's emendation in Lau (HNZ 1/8/14n.3), and adding "you cannot control it" because of parallelism.

60. Xu You was a legendary hermit.

61. The "Techniques of the Mind" (*xinshu* 心術) refer at one and the same time to the methods of inner cultivation and the two texts in the *Guanzi* collection of the same name. These techniques are said to strip away desires and preferences from consciousness. For details, see Roth 1999.

there is nothing to rejoice in and nothing to be angry about,
nothing to be happy about and nothing to feel bitter about.
You will be mysteriously unified with the myriad things,
and there is nothing you reject and nothing you affirm.
You transform and nourish a mysterious resplendence
and, while alive, seem to be dead.[62] [1/8/9–18]

1.18

The world is my possession, but I am also the possession of the world. So how could there even be the slightest gap between me and the world?

Why must possessing the entire world consist of grasping power, holding onto authority, wielding the handles of life and death, and using them to put one's own titles and edicts into effect? What I call possessing the entire world is certainly not this. It is simply realizing it [the Way] yourself. Once I am able to realize it [the Way], the entire world will also be able to realize me. When the entire world and I realize each other, we will always possess each other. And so how could there be any gap between us to be filled in? What I call "to realize it yourself" means to fulfill your own person. To fulfill your own person is to become unified with the Way.

Thus roaming along riverbank or seashore, galloping with Yao Niao[63] or riding a chariot beneath a kingfisher-feathered canopy, the eyes seeing the "Plumes of the Pheasant" dance or the performance of the "Emblems of King Wu" music, the ears listening to lavishly clear, elegant, and rousing melodies or being stimulated by the licentious music of Zheng and Wey or getting wrapped up in the stirring traditional ballads of Chu or shooting at high-flying birds along the lakeshore or hunting wild beasts in hunting preserves: all these are things that average people find alluring and intoxicating.[64] Sages experience them but not so much as to dominate their Quintessential Spirit or to disrupt their vital energy and concentration or cause their minds to be enticed away from their true nature.

To reside in a remote village on the side of a deep gorge hidden amid dense vegetation in a poor hut with a thatched roof on which grass sprouts up, whose door is overgrown by vines and which has small round windows like the mouth of a jar and a mulberry staff for a hinge, a hut whose roof is leaky and whose floor is damp, whose sleeping quarters are drafty and blanketed by snow and frost so that the grass mats are soaked; to wander in a vast marsh and ramble on the side of mountain slopes:

62. You fully realize the Way as the unifying ground of your being and the myriad things in a conscious experience that is devoid of all opposites and in which you are in a deep trance and appear to others to be dead. This recalls the description in *Zhuangzi* 2 of the sage Nanguo Ziqi, whose "body is like withered wood and mind is like dead ashes" (ZZ 2/3/15).

63. Yao Niao was a legendary horse, renowned for speed and endurance.

64. The "Emblems of King Wu" were said to have been composed by the Duke of Zhou to celebrate the conquest of the Shang. Along with the "Plumes of the Pheasant," they are epitomes of artistic expression. See Zhang Shuangdi 1997, 1:115; and Le Blanc and Mathieu 2003, 337n.14.

these are things that would make average people develop dark moods and make them anxious and sad and unable to concentrate on anything. Sages live in places like this, but they do not make them worried or angry or make them lose what makes them content on their own. What are the reasons for this? Because they intrinsically have the means to penetrate to the Mechanism of Heaven, and they do not allow honor or debasement, poverty, or wealth to make them weary and lose their awareness of their Potency. Thus, the cawing of the crow, the squawking of the magpie: has cold or heat, dryness or dampness ever altered their sounds?[65] [1/8/18–1/9/4]

Therefore when the realization of the Way is secure, it does not depend on the comings and goings of the myriad things. It is not because of a momentary alteration or transformation that I have secured the means to realize it myself. What I am calling "realization" means realizing the innate tendencies of nature and destiny and resting securely in the calmness that it produces.[66] [1/9/6–7]

1.19

Now our nature and destiny emerge from the Ancestor together with our bodily shapes. Once these shapes are completed, our nature and destiny develop; once our nature and destiny develop, likes and dislikes arise.

Thus, scholars have the established format of essays; women have unchanging standards of conduct. The compass[67] cannot become square, and the carpenter's square[68] cannot become round, nor can the marking cord become crooked and the angle rule[69] become straight. The constancies of Heaven and Earth are such that climbing up a hill does not make you taller and sitting on the ground does not make you shorter.

---

65. Because sages totally penetrate the Mechanism of Heaven—which is a metaphor for the normative natural order—they are no more affected by living in exalted or demeaned circumstances than are the noises of crows and magpies affected by their climate.

66. Accepting Lau's (HNZ, 9n.3) emendation, which adds the character *de* 得 (to realize) directly in front of "the truth of our nature and destiny."

67. The *gui* 規, "compass," is a device for inscribing circles. Unlike the draftsman's dividers familiar in Western usage, the Han-era *gui* compass is often depicted as a device in the shape of a lowercase "h" having a long vertical member to mark the center point, an adjustable horizontal radial member, and a shorter vertical member supporting a scribing device to mark the circle itself.

68. The *ju* 矩, "square," is a carpenter's square. It is usually depicted as a right-angle (rather than T-shaped) device, sometimes braced diagonally.

69. The basic meaning of *gou* 鈎 is "hook" or "angle." As the name of a tool, we translate it as "angle rule." The *gou* seems to have been similar to a modern bevel-square, used to mark and duplicate variable angles. It also was used to make sets of objects, such as chariot axles, in a range of diameters. The *gou* probably resembled a *ju* "square," except that the arms of the device would have been free to assume any desired angle and it would have included some means of fixing the arms in place at that angle for as long as necessary.

A difficulty with this word is that it has multiple meanings. Depending on context, it can mean "hook" or "angle" (as in *si gou* 四鈎, the "Four Hooks" of the heavens [see 3.16] or of the *liubo* board or TLV mirror), or "hook" as in "fishhook" (as in 1.6); or as a kind of weapon, which we translate as "battle-hook." See 12.34. The appropriate meaning is not always clear.

Therefore, those who realize the Way:
when impoverished are not cowed,
when successful are not proud.
When they dwell on high, they are not stirred by it;
when they grasp a full vessel, they do not tip it over.
They are new but not shiny;
they are old but not faded.
They enter fire but are not scorched;
they enter water but are not drenched.

Therefore,
they do not depend on political position to be honored.
They do not depend on wealth to be rich.
They do not depend on physical force to be strong.
Even and empty, they flow downward,
and they soar upward along with transformations.

People like these
store their gold in the mountains,
hide their pearls in the deep,
do not profit by goods and wealth,
do not lust after political position and fame.

Therefore,
they do not take prosperity as contentment,
nor do they take privation as aggravation.
They do not take honor as security,
nor do they take debasement as danger.

Their bodies, spirits, vital energy, and awareness each dwell in their appropriate activities, and they thereby follow the workings of Heaven and Earth. [1/9/7–13]

The physical body is the abode of vitality;
the vital energy is the source of vitality;
and the spirit is what regulates vitality.

If one of these loses its position, then the other two will be harmed.

Therefore, sages ensure that each rests in its appropriate position, preserves its specific functions, and does not interfere with the others.

Thus, if the physical body resides where it is not safe, it will be destroyed;
if the use of vital energy does not match what replenishes it, it will drain away;
if the spirit acts in an inappropriate manner, it will become darkened.[70]

These three must be attentively guarded. [1/9/15–18]

70. Note the contrast between the darkened spirit here and the exalted spiritlike clarity spoken of in 1.16.

1.20

Now consider the myriad things of this world, even spiders and wasps that creep and crawl. All know what they like and dislike, what brings them benefit and harm. Why? Because they are constantly guided by their natures. If it were to suddenly leave them, their bones and flesh would have no constant guide. People today can see clearly and hear acutely; their bodies can support weight, and their hundred joints can bend and stretch; they can differentiate between white and black, discern ugliness and beauty; and they can understand sameness and difference and clarify right and wrong. Why? Because vital energy infuses these activities, and the spirit regulates them. How do we know this is so?

In general, when there is something that occupies peoples' awareness and their spirit is tied up in it, when they walk they stumble over tree roots or bump their heads on tree limbs without their realizing it. If you beckon to them, they cannot see you; if you call to them, they cannot hear you. Their eyes and ears have not left them, but they cannot respond. Why? Their spirit has lost what it is guarding [its concentration].

Thus,

when it focuses on the small, it forgets the great;
when it focuses on the inside, it forgets the outside;
when it focuses on the high, it forgets the low;
and when it focuses on the left, it forgets the right.

When there is nowhere it does not infuse, there is nowhere it does not focus. Therefore those who value emptiness [their concentration is so refined that] they take the tip of an autumn hair as their abode. [1/9/20–26]

1.21

Now there is a reason why madmen cannot avoid disasters of water and fire and why they cannot cross over obstacles like ditches and culverts. How could it be that they have no body, spirit, vital energy, and awareness? Despite this, they use them in a different fashion. They have lost the relative positions they are supposed to guard, and they have left their external or internal dwellings.[71]

Therefore,

if madmen make mistakes, they cannot compensate for them;
they cannot strike a balance between activity and rest.

Throughout their lives, they drag their withered bodies along the edge of mountain ridges and embankments, stumbling into filthy ditches and sewage pits. Although they were born the same as other people, they cannot escape their condemnation and ridicule. Why? Because their bodies and spirits have lost their relative positions.

71. A similar argument is made in chap. 7.

Thus, when the spirit rules, the body follows and benefits from this.
When the body governs, the spirit follows and is harmed by this.
People who are covetous and filled with desires
are blinded by political power and profit
and are enticed by their lust for fame and station.
If by surpassing the wisdom of others they hope to grow tall in the eyes of the world, then their Quintessential Spirit will daily be squandered and become increasingly distant from them.

If they indulge in this for long and do not reverse this pattern when their bodies close down during daily activities, then their spirit will have no way to reenter. [1/9/28–1/10/5]

Thus throughout the world, there are sometimes the misfortunes of people who lose themselves through blindness and stupidity. This is the same thing as the tallow of a candle: the more the fire burns it, the more it melts and eventually disappears.

Now the more that the vital essence, spirit, vital energy, and awareness are tranquil, the more they will be abundant and strong. The more they are agitated, the more they will be depleted and aged.

Therefore, sages nourish their spirits,
harmonize and soften their vital breath,
and pacify their bodies.
They sink and float, plunge and soar, through life along with the Way.
In calmness, they relax into it.
When pressed, they employ it.
Their relaxing into it is like their taking off clothes;
their use of it is like shooting a crossbow.
In this way, there are no transformations of the myriad things that they do not welcome,
and no alterations of the hundreds of affairs to which they do not respond. [1/10/7–10]

Translated by Harold D. Roth

Two

ACTIVATING THE GENUINE

"ACTIVATING THE Genuine" is the second of the eight "root" or foundational chapters of the text and serves as a companion to chapter 1, "Originating in the Way," in its overarching cosmology and self-cultivation themes. While "Originating in the Way" is very much indebted to the *Laozi*, "Activating the Genuine" is thoroughly steeped in the *Zhuangzi*, three of whose authorial voices recognized by A. C. Graham are powerfully represented in its pages.[1]

All the principal themes of chapter 2 are found in the *Zhuangzi*, although they are not, in all cases, intended to be understood in the same way as in the source text. These themes include cosmogony, the precariousness of life, the existence of archaic utopias governed by spiritually perfected sage-rulers, the devolution of history and the degradation of spiritual realization that have occurred over time, the nature of perfected human beings, the Way as the source of the entire universe, the spiritual perfection of sages who through apophatic inner cultivation return to the wellsprings of the spirit that lie deep within human nature, and the importance of the right

1. These three voices are the authentic writings of Zhuang Zhou, the "Primitivist," and the "Syncretist." The *Zhuangzi* is a layered text, written by several hands over a period of time, and some of its latest portions might be roughly contemporaneous with the *Huainanzi*. See Angus C. Graham, "How Much of *Chuang Tzu* Did Chuang Tzu Write?" in *A Companion to Angus C. Graham's Chuang Tzu: The Inner Chapters*, by Harold D. Roth, Monographs of the Society for Asian and Comparative Philosophy, no. 20 (Honolulu: University of Hawai'i Press, 2003), 58–102. Indeed, the text may have been edited into something like its received form at the court of Huainan; see Harold D. Roth, "Who Compiled the *Chuang Tzu*?" in *Chinese Texts and Philosophical Contexts: Essays Dedicated to Angus C. Graham*, ed. Henry Rosemont Jr. (La Salle, Ill.: Open Court Press, 1991), 79–128.

balance of nature and destiny in the human ability to attain sage-rulership and spiritual fulfillment.

The Chapter Title

The title of this chapter is "Chu zhen" 俶真, which we translate as "Activating the Genuine." The word *chu* is a verb meaning "to begin," "to undertake," "to move," and "to set in motion."[2] "To activate" also falls within this range of meanings and best fits the current context, because the chapter assumes that the reader will actively pursue a program of self-cultivation whose ultimate goal is realizing *zhen*. *Zhen* is a noun and an adjective meaning "real" or "genuine." The "genuine" of the title is one of a number of metaphors used in the chapter to refer to the *dao*, or Way, and its various aspects. (Others include the Unhewn, the Great Clod, and the Great Ancestor.) In this context, the Genuine is the deepest layer of our intrinsic nature, that which is grounded in the Way itself. To activate it is to attain Potency. The Way lies in all of us as the ground of our existence but usually remains outside our awareness because human beings have been led astray by their senses into desiring material things and power and fame. By following such apophatic inner-cultivation practices as outlined in the *Zhuangzi* and other early sources, like "Inward Training" (Nei ye) in the *Guanzi*, human beings are able to realize the Way in terms of their concrete daily experiences. To do this is to "Activate the Genuine." The term *zhen* also occurs in the compound *zhenren* "Genuine Persons." In earlier Daoist lore and in the text of the *Huainanzi* itself, three paragons of human perfection are described in terms that overlap and are to some extent interchangeable: the sage (*shengren*), the Perfected (*zhiren*), and the Genuine (*zhenren*). All are people who have discovered the Way that lies within them.

Summary and Key Themes

The principal themes of this chapter are various aspects of Potency and its attainment. As such, they complement the principal themes in chapter 1, which explore the nature of the Way and how it operates in the world. These themes in chapter 2 are the nature of human perfection, its different categories, the methods to attain it, its role in rulership, the tendency of human beings and human societies to fall away from it, and how attaining it relates to fate. Chapter 2, however, may be best known for its extended analysis of explicit stages of cosmogony that is essentially a detailed commentary on the famous infinite regress of stages of cosmogony from

2. *Grand dictionnaire Ricci de la langue chinoise*, 7 vols. (Paris: Institut Ricci, 2001), 2:109, lists the primary meanings of *chu* as "commencer, entreprendre; bouger, mettre en movement."

Zhuangzi's "Qiwulun."[3] The crucial difference is that while the author of chapter 2 of the *Zhuangzi* is satirizing the attempt to ascertain a cosmogony ("there is not yet having begun to have not yet beginning," and so on), the authors of chapter 2 of the *Huainanzi* see these mock stages as real stages of a cosmogonic process and attempt to specify the conditions of each stage. Rarely in the history of Chinese philosophy—or of any major world philosophy—has the first commentary on a set of ideas been so diametrically opposed to the original author's intended meaning. This passage is important, therefore, because it provides the oldest extant attempt by classical Chinese thinkers to detail a cosmogony in philosophical terms.[4]

The chapter moves on in section 2.2 to musings on the relativity and brevity of human existence that are variations on themes in the inner chapters of the *Zhuangzi*, especially chapters 2 and 6. This passage's debt to the *Zhuangzi* extends to using the image of the Great Clod as a metaphor for Earth and reflecting on the strange quasi reality of dreams, substituting a man's transforming into a tiger and eating his brother for the *Zhuangzi*'s butterfly dream. The point of the section is that life is precarious and perspectives constantly change. Hence our most profound attachment, self-identity, is far from fixed and secure in a world of constant change.

The rulership of spiritually perfected human beings in a hoary past is first broached in the next passage (2.3), one reminiscent of the ideal primitive society envisioned in chapters 8 through 11 of the *Zhuangzi*. The *Huainanzi*'s version contains a significant difference, however: the rulers are not reluctant minimalists, as in the *Zhuangzi*, but are mystically adept sages engaged in government. The authors of the *Huainanzi* wish to emphasize that despite its simple and impoverished appearance, the primitive state they envision is a society rich in a harmony that transcends material concerns. This theme reemerges at the end of the chapter.

Notions of human perfection loom large in "Activating the Genuine." This theme is pursued in considerable detail in sections 2.4 through 2.6, beginning with a description of a group of adepts simply referred to as "the Perfected" (*zhiren*). These are rare human beings who have directly experienced the Way and carry it with them throughout their daily activities. Whether in comfortable or in difficult straits, they never lose their awareness of the Way, which is a constant within them just as the pine and cypress trees retain their foliage through the cold winter months as well as the warm summers.[5] They remain indifferent to beauty of form and music, riches and high station, because the Way is present in them despite all these temptations

---

3. Charles LeBlanc, "From Cosmology to Ontology Through Resonance: A Chinese Interpretation of Reality," in *Beyond Textuality: Asceticism and Violence in Anthropological Interpretation*, ed. Gilles Bibeau and Ellen Corin (Paris: Mouton de Bruyter, 1995), 57–77; Michael Puett, "Violent Misreadings: The Hermeneutics of Cosmology in the *Huainanzi*," *Bulletin of the Museum of Far Eastern Antiquities* 72 (2000): 29–47.

4. A few texts of the Warring States period, including the Chu silk manuscript and the Guodian text *Taiyi sheng shui* (*The Grand One Generates Water*), contain what might be termed mythological cosmogonies.

5. See 2.4. This is evidently an allusion to *Analects* 9.27: "The Master said, 'When the year becomes cold, then we know how the pine and the cypress are the last to lose their leaves.'" The next line in the *Huainanzi* makes explicit the comparison with the sage.

and transformations. They are like the luster of the jade of Kunlun, which can withstand three days and nights in a charcoal-fired oven without being diminished one iota. They thus maintain a profound awareness of the Way and remain unhindered by physical or geographical limitations.

Because of the centrality of the Way in the phenomenal world, the sages (*shengren*) seek the Way that lies within them by entrusting their spirits to a deep inner realm called the "Numinous Storehouse" and by "peering into Dark Obscurity." Thus experiencing the Way, they use it without using it; they know of it without objectifying it. By doing this, they "activate the Genuine" within themselves. As explained in sections 2.7 and 2.8, when sages depart from the world, they retreat into an introvertive mystical experience that derives from turning consciousness completely inward and withdrawing to "wander outside the dust and dirt and freely roam in the activity of the effortless." As we read in 2.9:

> For this reason, sages inwardly cultivate the techniques of the Way and do not adorn themselves externally with Humaneness and Rightness. They are unaware of the demands of the ears and eyes and wander in the harmony of Quintessential Spirit.

This is to experience what is called "Potency."

People who fall away from the Way and those who have never realized it are said to "lack the Utmost Essence internally" (2.9). When they perceive and interact with the phenomenal world, they cannot avoid becoming enslaved to material things. The psychospiritual devolution of individual consciousness is paralleled in the historical devolution of human society. When the Way and Potency are abandoned, Humaneness and Rightness are established and human society is on the path of losing the unitary consciousness of the sage and thus headed for ruin. The authors of chapter 2 trace this decline from an "age of Utmost Potency" when sages governed in accord with the Way, when all people existed together in a harmonious union and all things flourished, through the times of Fuxi, the Divine Farmer, and the houses of Xia and Zhou, down to the decadent present age (2.10).

The remedy for this disorder is the "learning of the sages," which seeks to return human nature to its origins and the mind to its inherent emptiness in order to counteract "the vulgar learning of the age" that destroys Potency and intrinsic nature, vexes the Five Orbs, and belabors perception with external things (2.10). Particularly singled out as examples of this vulgar learning are Confucians, who seek nothing but fame for themselves and obsess over the picky minutiae of morally hollow values (2.12). In contrast to this inferior learning, the authors of "Activating the Genuine" assert that true contentment does not lie in these external things but in the internal satisfaction of wandering carefree at the boundaries of Something and Nothing, of life and death.

To the authors of chapter 2, all humans possess innate natures that contain the tendencies of the senses to clearly perceive their sense objects. Only sages use their nature to cultivate their innermost potential. How do they do this? They work with the spirit, the basis of consciousness which in turn is the storehouse of the mind. Its tendency to be still and calm is disrupted by desires caused by the senses' engagement with the many and various objects of the world. Sages discipline their senses and thoughts through an apophatic process of meditation in which they empty out the contents of consciousness until they can reconnect with the clear, bright, and tranquil spirit. With the spirit now present in their consciousness, they are able to mirror all external things with perfect clarity and not be enticed by sensory pleasures and self-aggrandizing goals. In so doing, they are united with the Way. Thus even if they were offered possession of the entire world and were widely praised, they would have no desire for such worldly things.

In section 2.12, the authors of "Activating the Genuine" criticize the disciples of Confucius and Mozi, who teach the techniques of Humaneness and Rightness yet cannot personally practice their own teachings. In contrast, when adepts break through to their own basic nature through the practice of apophatic inner cultivation, Humaneness and Rightness spontaneously result. This is the Way of the Genuine: they cannot be lured by profit, beauty, wisdom, and courage. Such rare cultivated human beings are conjoined with the Way even as they interact in the human realm. Only through inner cultivation are they truly able to govern the world.

Human nature is nourished by tranquillity; Potency is attained through emptiness; when external things do not disturb our internal realization of spirit, our nature attains suitable and harmonious expression in the world. Regrettably, many disturbances to our consciousness make this kind of realization very difficult to attain. Worries are generated daily by common occurrences so that our attention becomes absorbed in petty things and misses the significant ones. The spirit is easy to muddy and difficult to clarify. If even petty things disturb it, how much worse is it when the entire age disturbs the spirit? Under these circumstances, "How difficult it is to achieve even a moment of equanimity!"

In the chapter's concluding section (2.14), the authors admit that the ability to govern sagaciously depends not only on how the ruler cultivates his nature but also on the times in which he lives. In ancient times of great Potency, even hermits were able to attain their sagely Way. In the evil times of the Xia dynasty when royal cruelty was rampant and the natural world was in disarray, history recorded no sages, not because there were none but because the conditions did not allow them to achieve their Ways. So embodying the Way does not rest entirely with a person's effort, it also depends on the era in which he lives. Thus even though the great sages of the past were able to nourish and realize the deepest aspects of their natures, the very fact that they were able to govern was their destiny. Only when nature meets destiny can it be effective.

Sources

As mentioned earlier, the principal source for "Activating the Genuine" is the *Zhuangzi*, whose vision of spiritual perfection is taken directly from the inner chapters of that work attributable to Zhuang Zhou himself. The apophatic techniques it suggests to achieve that spiritual perfection derive ultimately from *Guanzi*'s "Inward Training." The ideal Daoist utopias of chapter 2 are closely reminiscent of those in the "Primitivist" chapters (8–11) of the *Zhuangzi*. The overall vision of sage-rulership in chapter 2 of the *Huainanzi* seems to owe much to the "Syncretist" final stratum of the *Zhuangzi* (12–15, 33), which advocates government led by rulers who have perfected themselves through Daoist inner-cultivation methods. Although phrases, paraphrases, and passages from the *Zhuangzi* abound in "Activating the Genuine," they are never attributed or often understood in precisely the same sense as they are in the *Zhuangzi* (for example, the cosmogonic regress that begins this chapter). This indicates that the text of the *Zhuangzi* was well known at Liu An's court but was not fixed into a final form or regarded as canonical by the authors who toiled there. It was influential but not canonical like the *Laozi*,[6] direct quotations from which are invariably attributed to their source.[7] When material that we now find in the extant *Zhuangzi* is used in the *Huainanzi*, it is virtually never attributed to the *Zhuangzi*.[8]

The Chapter in the Context of the *Huainanzi* as a Whole

Chapter 2 is based primarily on the *Zhuangzi*, whereas chapter 1 is based primarily on the *Laozi*. Chapter 2 also focuses on Potency, complementing the first chapter's focus on the Way. The visions of human perfection through the attainment of this Potency resonate throughout the text, especially in chapters 7, 8, 12, and 14. Chapter 7, "The Quintessential Spirit," seems so close to this chapter in its vocabulary and concern for attaining spiritual perfection and its indebtedness to the *Zhuangzi* that it might have been written by the same hand. The concept of rulership by sages who cultivated themselves according to the apophatic inner-cultivation practices

6. Roth, "Who Compiled the *Chuang Tzu*?"

7. As we point out in both the general introduction and the introduction to chap. 12, the *Laozi* is one of only four sources that are almost invariably attributed in the *Huainanzi*; the others are the *Odes*, the *Documents*, and the *Changes*.

8. If the *Zhuangzi* had been edited into something like its final form before or during the decade in which the *Huainanzi* was being composed (150–140 B.C.E.), it seems likely that it would have been considered a canonical source by the Huainan masters, given its influence in some of the *Huainanzi* chapters, particularly 2 and 7. Had that been the case, it then seems likely that passages quoted from the *Zhuangzi* would have been attributed to their source. The lack of such attribution is one reason that I concluded that the fifty-two-chapter *Zhuangzi* that represented the text in its most complete original form was compiled at Liu An's court after the *Huainanzi* was completed in 139 B.C.E. See n. 1.

discussed in chapter 2 also informs other chapters throughout the work. The theme that the sage, however cultivated, cannot arise within a society unless the time is right is a frequent refrain in the text—for example, in 6.9, 8.6, 10.82, and 19.5.

The juxtaposition of "Originating in the Way" and "Activating the Genuine" at the beginning of the *Huainanzi* appears to have been a deliberate attempt to privilege not only their arguments but also their primary sources, the *Laozi* and the *Zhuangzi*, as linked foundations for cosmology and self-cultivation in the entire work. We find another reflection of this linkage in chapter 12, "Responses of the Way," which contains more than fifty short illustrative narratives, almost every one of which is capped by a quotation from the *Laozi*. About 20 percent of the material in the illustrative narratives themselves is closely similar or parallel to passages in the *Zhuangzi*.[9] This heavy reliance on the *Laozi* and *Zhuangzi* materials seems deliberate, especially when combined with the following comment on chapter 12, "Responses of the Way," in the *Huainanzi*'s postface (chapter 21, "An Overview of the Essentials"): "'Responses of the Way' . . . investigates the reversals of ill and good fortune, benefit and harm, testing and verifying them according to the techniques of Lao and Zhuang."[10] [21/225/19–20]

Thus the *Zhuangzi* seems to be one of the main sources for this chapter's vision of the attainment of Potency and human perfection through apophatic inner-cultivation practices, a vision that the authors link to chapter 1's cosmology of the Way based on the *Laozi*. When seen in light of this juxtaposition of the first two chapters of the *Huainanzi*, the reference in "An Overview of the Essentials" to "the techniques of Lao and Zhuang" may provide evidence of the authors' attempt to build a new—or reflect an extant—intellectual tradition.

Harold D. Roth

9. See the introduction to chap. 12.
10. That is, *Laozi* and *Zhuangzi*.

Two

2.1

[1] There was a beginning.
[2] There was not yet beginning to have "There was a beginning."
[3] There was not yet beginning to have "There was not yet beginning to have 'There was a beginning.'"
[4] There was Something.
[5] There was Nothing.
[6] There was not yet beginning to have "There was Nothing."
[7] There was not yet beginning to have "There was not yet beginning to have 'There was Nothing.'"[1]

[1] What is called "There was a beginning":

> Pell-mell: not yet manifest;
> buds beginning, sprouts emerging;
> not yet having shape or outline.

Undifferentiated, wriggling, it is on the verge of desiring to be born and flourish but not yet forming things and categories.

1. Lau (HNZ 2/10/15) mistakenly omits this line, although it is present in all other editions. Thanks to our colleague Judson Murray for pointing this out. Also, we see no need to insert the character *you* 有 at the beginning of the chapter.

[2] [What is called] There was not yet beginning to have "There was a beginning":
The *qi* of Heaven beginning to descend;
the *qi* of Earth beginning to ascend;
yin and yang mixing and meeting;
mutually roaming freely and racing to fill the interstices of time and space,
enveloping Potency and engulfing harmony;
densely intermingling;
desiring to connect with things but not yet having formed boundaries and bodies.

[3] [What is called] There was not yet beginning to have "There was not yet beginning to have 'There was a beginning'":
Heaven engulfing harmony but not yet letting it fall;
Earth embracing the vital energy but not yet letting it rise;
empty and still,
inert and isolated,
Nothing and Something were a matched pair.
The vital energy pervaded and greatly penetrated Dark Obscurity. [2/10/14–19]

[4] [What is called] "There is Something":
Speaks of the flourishing of the myriad things. The roots, trunks, branches, and leaves were verdant and abundant, bountiful and brilliant. [Insects] wriggled and moved, crawled and walked, crept and gasped. [All these things] could be touched, grasped, and enumerated.

[5] [What is called] "There is Nothing":
Look at it; you do not see its form;
listen to it; you do not hear its sound.
Reach for it, and you cannot grasp it;
gaze at it, and you cannot fathom it.
Collected and fused,
floodlike and expansive,
It is something whose brilliance cannot be penetrated by any instrument.

[6] [What is called] There was not yet beginning to have "There was Nothing":
Encloses Heaven and Earth,
smelts the myriad things,
greatly penetrates the chaotic and obscure.
Deeply impenetrable, vast and great, it can have no exterior;
as fine as the tip of a hair, as sharp as a point, it can have no interior.
A space without containment, it generated the root of Something and Nothing.

[7] [What is called] "There was not yet beginning to have 'There was not yet beginning to have 'There was nothing.'"
Heaven and Earth had not yet split apart;

yin and yang had not yet been carved out;
the four seasons had not yet differentiated;
the myriad things had not yet been generated.
Enormously peaceful and tranquil,
silently clear and limpid,
none saw its form.

It was like Resplendent Light asking Not Something, who was withdrawn and had lost himself: "I can [conceive of] having Nothing, but I cannot [conceive of] not having Nothing. If I could reach [the state of] Not Nothing, how could even the most marvelous surpass this?"[2] [2/10/21–27]

2.2

The Great Clod
loads me with a body,
burdens me with a life,
eases me with old age,
rests me with death.

That I found it good to live is the very reason why I find it good to die.

[You can] hide a boat in a ravine,
hide a fishing net in a marsh:[3]
people call this "secure."

However, in the middle of the night, a strong man can put [the boat] on his back and run off with it, and the sleeper does not know about it. It is appropriate to hide small things within the large. But if you do so, your thing just might vanish from you. But if you hide the world in the world, then there is nothing that can conceal its form. [2/10/29–2/11/2]

How can it be said that things are not grandly indiscriminate? You once happen on the shape of a human being and are especially pleased. But humanity has a thousand alterations and ten thousand transformations, never reaching its limit, wearing out and then renewing; should not your joy be incalculable?[4] Compare it to a dream:

In a dream we become a bird and fly into the sky.
In a dream we become a fish and disappear into the deep.

When we are dreaming, we do not know it is a dream; only after we awaken do we realize it is a dream. Only when we have a great awakening do we realize that this

2. This is a shortened and somewhat altered version of a passage in *Zhuangzi* 22 "Knowledge wandered North" (ZZ 22/63/1–3). See Mair 1997, 220. Another version of this anecdote appears in 12.45.

3. Emending the word "mountain" 山 to "fishing net," following the interpretation of Yu Yue to the parallel passage in *Zhuangzi*. See Guo Qingfan 郭慶藩, *Zhuangzi jishi* 莊子集釋, ed. Wang Xiaoyu 王孝魚 (Beijing: Zhonghua shuju, 1961), 244. We do not accept Wang Shumin's proposal to emend "mountain" to "cart" 車. See Lau, HNZ, 11n.1.

4. This entire section to this point is found almost verbatim in ZZ 6/16/25. See Graham 1982, 86; and Mair 1997, 55.

present moment is the ultimate dream.[5] In the beginning before I was born, how could I have known the joy of being alive? Now in this moment when I have not yet died, how can I know that death is not also joyful?

In ancient times, Gongniu Ai suffered from a cyclical illness:[6] every seven days he would transform into a tiger. His older brother opened his door and entered to spy on him, and when he did, the tiger snatched and killed him. Thus,

his [outer] patterns and markings became those of a beast;
his fingernails and teeth shifted and changed;
his consciousness and mind altered;
his spirit and form transformed.

When he was a tiger, he did not know that he had ever been a human being. When he was a human being, he knew nothing about being a tiger. These two alternated in opposition, yet each found joy in the form it took. Cleverness and the confusion displace [each other] endlessly, and who knows from what they spring?[7] [2/11/4–10]

When water approaches winter, it congeals and becomes ice.
When ice welcomes spring, it melts and becomes water.

Ice and water shift and change in the former and latter positions as if they were running around in an eternal circle; which has the time to know bitterness or joy? Thus

The body is damaged by the privations of cold, heat, aridity, and dampness: the body weakens, yet the spirit remains strong.

The spirit is damaged by the distress of joy, anger, rumination, and worry: the spirit becomes exhausted, yet the body has reserves.

Therefore,

when you skin a worn-out horse after it dies, it is like desiccated wood;
when you skin a young dog after it dies, it still twitches.

Thus,

those who have been murdered, their ghosts haunt;
those who reach their [allotted] time, their spirits go silent.[8]

Neither of these has their spirit and form expire simultaneously.

In the use of their mind, sages lean on their natures and rely on their spirits. They [nature and spirit] sustain each other, and [so sages] attain their ends and beginnings.

---

5. These lines are found almost verbatim in ZZ 2/7/1. See Graham 1982, 59–60; and Mair 1997, 22–23.

6. Gongniu Ai 公牛哀 is what might colloquially be called a "weretiger." Gao You explains that this was a hereditary malady of the Gongniu clan. According to Gao, the ordinary transformation was evidently only psychological and temporary, but if the afflicted actually did eat human flesh, he would transform into a "real tiger." Those who refrained from eating human flesh would become human again. Gao You may be overinterpreting the HNZ text, however. See Zhang Shuangdi 1997, 1:151n.13, 152n.14.

7. This last phrase appears almost verbatim in ZZ 2/3/30. See Graham 1982, 50; and Mair 1997, 13. The point of the section is that life is precarious and perspectives constantly change. Hence our most profound attachment, self-identity, is far from fixed and secure.

8. This evidently refers to a state of dementia perceived in some who reach advanced age. In other words, they have lived on past their destined time, so their bodies live on but their spirits are inactive.

Thus when they sleep, they do not dream, and when they awaken, they are not sad. [2/11/12–16]

2.3

Among the people of antiquity were some who situated themselves in the chaotic and obscure. Their spirit and vital energy did not leak out to their exteriors. The myriad things were peaceful and dispassionate and so became contented and tranquil. The *qi* of [baleful comets such as] "magnolias," "lances," "colliders," and "handles"[9] was in every case blocked and dissipated so that they were unable to cause harm. At that time, the myriad peoples were wild and untamed, not knowing East from West;

> they roamed with their mouths full,
> drummed on their bellies in contentment.
> In copulation they followed the harmony of Heaven;
> in eating they accorded with the Potency of Earth.

They did not use minute precedent or "right and wrong" to surpass one another. Vast and boundless, this is what we call "Grand Order." And so those in high station

> directed [ministers] on their left and right and did not pervert their natures;
> possessed and pacified [the people] and did not compromise their Potency.

Thus,

> Humaneness and Rightness were not proclaimed, and the myriad things flourished.
> Rewards and punishments were not deployed, and all in the world were respected.

Their Way could give rise to great perfection, but it is difficult to find a quantitative measure for it. Thus,

> calculating by days there is not enough;
> calculating by years there is surplus.[10] [2/11/18–23]
> Fish forget themselves in rivers and lakes.
> Humans forget themselves in the techniques of the Way.[11]

The Genuine of antiquity stood in the foundation of Heaven and Earth, were centered in uninterrupted roaming, embraced Potency, and rested in harmony. The myriad things were to them like smoke piling higher.[12] Which of them would will-

9. These four sobriquets derive from the perceived shapes of ill-augured comets.

10. The utopia envisioned in this section is quite similar to that found in the "Primitivist" chapters of *Zhuangzi* (ZZ 8–11/12), but with a significant difference: it is governed by mystically adept sages who actively govern. This suits the overall syncretic vision of the text, which implicitly rejects the Primitivist call for a return to a simple agrarian society. The point of this passage is if you use a momentary materialist perspective to evaluate their society, it will seem impoverished, but if you observe it over a longer duration, you will understand that it embodies a harmony that transcends material concerns.

11. These two sentences appear also in ZZ 6/18/26. See Graham 1982, 88.

12. This line parallels ZZ 11/26/27, in which the author explains how an exemplary person would appear:

ingly create discord in human affairs or use things to trouble their nature and destiny? [2/11/25–26]

2.4

The Way has both a warp and a weft linked together. [The Perfected] attain the unity of the Way and join with its thousand branches and ten thousand leaves. Thus

because they have it in high position, they can promulgate their decrees;
because they have it in low position, they can forget their baseness;
because they have it in poverty, they can take pleasure in their work;
because they have it in distress, they can be settled amid danger.

When the great cold arrives, frost and snow descend: only then do we understand the vigor of pine and cypress;[13]

Withstanding difficulties, walking into danger, with profit and harm arrayed before them: only then do we understand how sages do not lose the Way.

Thus those who are able to

wear on their heads the Great Circle [of Heaven] will traverse the Great Square [of Earth];
mirror Vast Purity will contemplate Great Luminosity;
stand amid Vast Peace will be situated in the great hall;
roam amid Dark Obscurity will have the same brilliance as the sun and moon.

Thus,

they take the Way as their pole;
Potency as their line;
Rites and Music as their hook;
Humaneness and Rightness as their bait;
they throw them into the rivers;
they float them into the seas.

Though the myriad things are boundless in numbers, which of them will they not possess? [2/11/28–2/12/4]

---

sitting still as a corpse he will look majestic as a dragon, from the silence of the abyss he will speak with a voice like thunder, he will have the promptings which are daemonic and the veerings which are from Heaven, he will have an unforced air and *do nothing,* and *the myriad things will be like smoke piling higher and higher.* (Graham 1982, 212, italics added)

13. This is evidently an allusion to *Analects* 9.27: "The Master said, 'When the year becomes cold, then we know how the pine and the cypress are the last to lose their leaves.'"

2.5

Even those who narrowly rely on skewed techniques, who control the human realm, who seek profit above and below according to the customs of the age in order to grope for and link together the subtleties of things: even such people will achieve their ambitions and fulfill their desires. How much more will this be so of those who embrace the precious Way, forget the [emotions associated with the] hepatic and choleric orbs, abandon hearing and seeing, float solitarily beyond the boundless and do not become embroiled with worldly things, who within linger in the realm of the Formless and harmonize with Heaven and Earth? [2/12/4–6]

For such people, they stop perception and embrace Vast Simplicity.

They view benefit and harm as dust and dirt,
view life and death as day and night.

Thus,

when their eyes see the form of the imperial chariot adorned with jade and ivory;
when their ears hear the sounds of "White Snow"[14] and [the note] pure *jue*;[15]
these things are unable to disorder their spirit.
When they climb the thousand-*ren* gorge
or peer at a very steep cliff;
these are unable to disturb their harmony.

This is just like the jade of Bell Mountain:[16] if you roast it in a charcoal furnace for three days and three nights, its color and luster will not alter. They [sages] have attained the Quintessence of Heaven and Earth.[17]

For these reasons,

if life is not enough to motivate them, how could benefit be enough to move them?
If death is not enough to stop them, how could harm be enough to frighten them?
They are clear about the division between life and death
and penetrate the distinction between benefit and harm.

Though you offer them the greatness of the world in exchange for a single hair from their arm, none of this will catch their attention. [2/12/8–12]

14. According to Gao You, "White Snow" 白雪 was a song played by the ancient music master Shi Kuang 師曠 that made spirits descend. See Zhang Shuangdi 1997, 1:165n.15. See also 6.1.

15. *Jue* is the third note in the Chinese pentatonic scale. In traditional Chinese music theory, notes had "pure 清" and "muddy 濁" modulations, the latter being equivalent to the former flattened by one half-tone. For more on these terms, see app. B. The mention here of "pure *jue*" evidently alludes to an anecdote in which Shi Kuang declared that "pure *jue*" was the most melancholy of notes. See *Hanfeizi*, "Ten Faults" 十過 (HFZ 10/15/12).

16. Gao You claims that "Bell Mountain" is an alternative sobriquet for Mount Kunlun. Xu Shen says that it is "a terrain in the northern reaches, where there is no sun, which produces beautiful jade." Tao Fangqi deduces from this and other evidence that Bell Mountain must be north of Yanmen 雁門. See Zhang Shuangdi 1997, 1:166n.17.

17. Following the emendation of Yu Yue. See Lau, HNZ, 12n.3.

The significance of nobility and baseness to their persons is like the brief passing of a swift breeze.
The impact of blame and praise on their selves is like an encounter with mosquitoes and gnats. [2/12/14]

2.6

To grasp the intensely bright and not blacken it,
act with the perfectly pure and not sully it,
rest in profound obscurity and not darken it,
sit at the pivot of Heaven and not destroy it,
to be unobstructed by the Mengmen or Zhonglong mountains,[18]
unhindered by swift currents, deep chasms, or the depths of Lüliang,[19]
unimpeded by the obstructions of Taihang, Shijian, Feihu, or Gouwang.[20]
Only those who embody the Way are able to not be defeated [by these things].

For these reasons, their persons reside on rivers and seas, and their spirits roam under the palace gateway.[21] Had they not attained the One Source, how could they have reached this point? [2/12/14–18]

For these reasons, residing with the Perfected
makes families forget their poverty,
makes kings and dukes scorn honors and riches and delight in poverty and baseness,
makes the brave deflate their anger
and makes the greedy diminish their desires.
They sit and do not teach;
they stand and do not dispute.
When they are empty, they go;
when they are full, they return.

Thus they do not speak and can quench others with harmony.

18. The text here contains the line "only those who embody the Way are able to be undefeated." We accept its deletion by Wang Niansun (Lau, HNZ, 12n.9) as an intrusion from the commentary, where it must have explained the line "To rest at the pivot of Heaven and not be destroyed."

19. According to Gao You, Lüliang 呂梁 is the name of a river near Pengcheng (modern-day Xuzhou). See Zhang Shuangdi, 1:168n.26.

20. Taihang 太行 (Great Array) is a mountain range straddling the frontier between modern Shanxi and Hebei provinces. According to Gao You, Shijian 石澗 (Rocky Torrent) is the name of a deep gorge, though he gives no location. Also according to Gao You, Feihu 飛狐 (Flying Fox) and Gouwang 句望 (Angular View) are the names of narrow valleys, the former in Dai Prefecture and the latter at Yanmen. Wang Niansun argues that Gouwang is a mistake for Gouzhu 句注, the name of a pass mentioned in chap. 4, a judgment with which Lau agrees. See Zhang Shuangdi 1997, 1:168–69n.27.

21. The "palace gateway" (*weique* 魏闕) is the gate to a palace from which edicts are hung. The meaning here is dual: (a) although one's body is in the mundane world, one's consciousness inhabits a transcendent plane of awareness; and (b) although one's person may be on the periphery of the empire, one's character is suited to the halls of power.

For these reasons, [those who embody] the Utmost Way take no action.

Now a dragon, then a snake,
they expand and contract,
coil and uncoil,
and alter and transform with the seasons.
Outside, they follow prevailing customs;
inside, they guard their nature.
Their ears and eyes are not dazzled.
Their thoughts and reflections are not entangled.

Those who in this way lodge their spirit maintain the simple in order to roam in vast purity, draw into compliance the myriad things, and cause the many excellences to germinate.

For these reasons,

the spirit will depart those who belabor their spirit;
the spirit will lodge with those who rest their spirit.

The Way emerges from the One Source, penetrates the Nine Gateways,[22] is scattered through the Six Crossroads,[23] and is displayed in the domain of the boundless. It is still and silent and thereby empty and nonexistent. It is not that it acts on things; it is that things act on themselves. For these reasons, when affairs comply with the Way, it is not that the Way has accomplished them, but that the Way has impelled them.[24] [2/12/19–25]

2.7

That which Heaven overspreads,
that which Earth bears up,
that which is included in the six coordinates,
that which is animated by the yin and the yang;
that which is moistened by the rain and the dew;
that which is supported by the Way and its Potency:

These all are born from a single father and mother, and all partake of a single harmony.

For these reasons,

the locust and the elm, the orange and the grapefruit, together are brothers;
the You Miao [people] and the [people of] San Wei are joined as a single family.[25]

22. According to Gao You, these are the gates of Heaven. See Zhang Shuangdi 1997, 1:174n.1.

23. Gao You treats this as a figurative synonym for the six coordinates 六合. Zhang Shuangdi, 1997, 1:174n.1, takes issue with his reading, but if Gao is right that the "Nine Gateways" are celestial, this image must be a terrestrial counterpart.

24. Disregarding Lau's (HNZ 2/12/25) proposed addition of 非.

25. The You Miao 有苗 are identified as the San Miao 三苗 (Three Miao Tribes), a frontier people from the south who were banished by the legendary sage-emperor Shun for some unspecified fault. The people of San Wei 三危 are from a mountain (Three Dangers Mountain) in the area of Dunhuang

When your eyes see the flight of wild geese and swans,
when your ears hear the sounds of the *qin*[26] and the *se*,[27]
and your mind is in the midst of Yanmen,[28]

Within your single person, your spirit divides and splits up within the six coordinates so that in a moment you travel ten million miles.[29]

For these reasons,

when viewed from the perspective of their difference, [things as close as] the hepatic and choleric orbs can be as different as Hu [northern "barbarians"] and Yue [southern "barbarians"].

When viewed from the perspective of their similarities, the myriad things are a single set.[30]

The Hundred Traditions[31] have different theories, and each has its own origins. For example, the relationship of Mo[zi],[32] Yang [Zhu],[33] Shen [Buhai],[34] and [Lord] Shang[35] to the Way of Governing is like that of an individual [umbrella] rib to the

---

in Gansu Province. The idea is that the Way is able to make peoples as different as these two tribes into the same family.

26. The *qin* 琴, commonly but misleadingly translated as "lute," was a stringed instrument which in the Warring States and Han periods had a wooden sounding board attached to a thinner neck, with five to ten strings secured to the top of the neck and stretched over a wide bridge on the sounding board, beyond which they were attached to individual tuning pegs. As the *qin* later evolved in the post-Han period, the "neck" eventually disappeared, and the instrument consisted of the sounding board only, tapering from a wider end to a narrower one.

27. The *se* 瑟, sometimes translated as "zither," was a stringed instrument with a wide, hollow wooden sounding board and (usually) twenty-five strings that passed over fixed bridges at each end of the sounding board and were secured by pegs. The instrument was tuned by means of individual movable bridges. The *se* was popular in ancient China but fell into neglect after the Han period.

28. Yanmen 雁門 (Wild Goose Gate) is a mountain pass in the district of Yangguo, in the far north, to which geese fly.

29. Another of the psychological functions of the spirit is imagination. The text argues for a parallel between how the one Way embraces Heaven and Earth, the six coordinates, yin and yang, the rain and the dew; and how the spirit embraces different perceptions, thoughts, and imaginations.

30. Similar to ZZ 5/113/14.

31. For a discussion of the "schools" of early Chinese thought, see 27–28.

32. Mo Di 墨翟 (also known as Mozi 墨子 [fl. ca. 450 B.C.E.]) was an influential philosopher whose teachings stressed frugality and "Heaven's Will" and stood opposed to those of Confucius. A text bearing his name survives.

33. Yang Zhu 楊朱 (fl. ca. 400 B.C.E.) was a philosopher famous for declaring that he would not sacrifice one hair from his arm to save the empire. Little is known of his life, and no writings reliably attributable to him are extant. Graham and some others regard the first two chapters of the *Lüshi chunqiu* as products of Yang Zhu's followers but there is not universal agreement on this. See Angus C. Graham, "The Background of the Mencian Theory of Human Nature," in *Studies in Chinese Philosophy and Philosophical Literature* (Albany: State University of New York Press, 1986), 13.

34. Shen Buhai 申不害 (ca. 385–337 B.C.E.) was a native of Hann who served as prime minister under Marquis Zhao. He advocated basic reforms to increase the efficiency of government, such as the technique of "form and names" (*xingming*, see app. A) for the disciplined employment of civil officials. A text bearing his name survives in fragments.

35. Lord Shang 商君 (also known as Shang Yang 鞅, Wey 衛 Yang, and Gongsun 公孫 Yang [ca. 390–338 B.C.E.]) was a native of Wey who was employed as prime minister by Duke Xiao of Qin. He is credited with having increased the power of Qin through the institution of basic reforms, including a reliance on strict written laws and rewards and punishments. A text bearing his name survives but is generally regarded as a later attribution.

whole canopy and like that of an individual spoke to the whole chariot wheel. If you have any one of them, you can complete the number; if you are missing any one of them, it will not affect the utility [of the whole]. Each one thought that he alone had a monopoly [on true governing]; he did not understand the genuine disposition of Heaven and Earth. [2/12/27–2/13/6]

When a smith forges an implement and the metal flies out of the forge, it must be either an overflow or discard. When it hits the ground, it will harden and take the form of something. Although its shape may have some small use, it cannot be treasured as much as the Nine Tripods of the house of Zhou,[36] how much more the case when compared to the one who has molded them? And when compared to the Way, their distance is even greater. [2/13/8–10]

When the myriad things differentiate and branch off, when the hundred affairs proliferate and diverge, all have their foundation in a single root, despite their ten million branchings. Those that receive are not what gives [i.e., the Way]. What gives does not receive, and yet there is nothing it does not give. That of which there is nothing that it does not give is like thick rain clouds that accumulate, piling up and spreading they make rain, profoundly soaking the myriad things yet not getting wet themselves. [2/13/12–14]

A good archer has the standard of the sight and the target in the same way as the carpenter has the calibrations of the compass and the square. Each has ways of determining perfection. However, Xi Zhong[37] could not be Feng Meng,[38] and Zaofu[39] could not be Bo Le.[40] Each had articulated a single corner but did not comprehend the full domain of the myriad techniques.[41] [2/13/16–17]

> If you dye silk black in ferrous sulfate, it will become blacker than the ferrous sulfate;
> if you dye [fabric] blue in indigo, it will become bluer than the indigo.[42]
> Ferrous sulfate is not black; indigo is not blue.[43]

Although [the fabrics] have surpassed[44] their mother [i.e., the original dye], they are not able to transform back. What is the reason? This [would be] comparable to their

36. The Nine Tripods were a fabled set of sacrificial bronze tripods that served as talismans and regalia of the Zhou kings.

37. Xi Zhong 奚仲 was a cartwright of legendary skill.

38. Feng Meng 逢蒙 was an archer of legendary skill.

39. Zaofu 造父 was a charioteer of legendary skill.

40. Bo Le 伯樂 was a horse breeder of legendary skill and expertise.

41. This argument follows that found in *Zhuangzi* 33 in assessing the relative value of the Hundred Traditions.

42. A similar statement is found in the opening line of *Xunzi* 1 (XZ 1/3/3): "Though blue dye comes from the indigo plant, it is bluer than indigo" (Knoblock 1988, 1:135).

43. Accepting Yang Shuda's emendation of this line. See Lau, HNZ, 13n.12; and Zhang Shuangdi 1997, 1:180n.24. Ferrous sulfate crystals are greenish; the juice of the indigo plant is also greenish in its raw (unoxydized) state. These lines play on the meaning of *qing* 青, which embraces a wide range of colors from green through blue to gray.

44. Accepting Yu Chang's reading of *guo* 過, "surpass," for *yu* 遇, "encounter." See Zhang Shuangdi 1997, 1:180n.24.

[color's] becoming fainter with every turn [in the dye bath].[45] How much more is this so of those things that have not yet begun to be fashioned and transformed by ferrous sulfate and indigo?[46] Even if you were to etch their transformations onto metal and stone, inscribe them onto bamboo and silk, how could we ever enumerate them? [2/13/19–21]

From this perspective, no thing is not generated from something, and the small and great roam as companions.

> The tip of an autumn hair [may be minute], but slip it into space in which there is no gap and it becomes [in effect] enormous.
>
> If you take the thinness of a reed and insert it into something where there is no crack, it becomes [in effect] bulky.

[That which] lacks [even] the fineness of an autumn hair or the thinness of a reed, [extending] unboundedly to the four end points, pervading the Limitless: nothing can stop or impede it. It is exquisitely refined and doubly marvelous. It lifts and lowers the myriad things, harmonizes the nine alterations and transformations: how can anything in Heaven and Earth suffice to explain it?

A fast wind can snap trees, yet it cannot pull out feathers or hair. From the height of a cloud terrace, a person who falls will break his spine and shatter his skull, but for a mosquito or a gnat, it is high enough to take flight from it. Now we, alike with centipedes and worms, mount the Mechanism of Heaven,[47] and we receive our form as part of the same set [of living things], but it is the things that fly and are light and that are tiny and minute that find [their form] sufficient to escape with their lives. How much more is this so for that which has no category? Looked at from this perspective, it is even more apparent that what has no form generates what has form. [2/13/23–28]

2.8

For these reasons, sages entrust their spirits to the Numinous Storehouse and return to the beginning of the myriad things.

> They peer into Dark Obscurity
> and listen to the soundless.

---

45. The logic of the passage is this: through successive infusions of ferrous sulfate or indigo, the color of the dyed fabric surpasses (becomes darker than) its "mother" (i.e., the original dye), and this process cannot be reversed. If it could, it would be comparable to an impossible situation in which the color of a dyed fabric got fainter every time it was dipped in the dye bath (the opposite of what actually occurs). But for things that have not yet had the trajectory of their transformation determined (as the color of a fabric is determined by a dye), the possibilities are numberless. See also 16.58.

46. This metaphorically describes the manner in which the Way generates things: the further along the road to differentiation a thing is, the less likely it will be able to return to its source. This recalls the passage in *Laozi* 28 describing the breaking up of the Uncarved Block to make vessels.

47. *Tianji* 天機, a metaphorical term for the spontaneous nature and patterns of the cosmos, infused by the Way.

In the midst of Dark Obscurity, they alone see luminescence.
In the midst of the silent and still, they alone shine forth.

Their use of it is in not using it;
only by not using it are they able to use it.
Their knowing of it is in not knowing it;
only by not knowing it are they able to know it.

If Heaven were not stable, the sun and moon would have no support.
If Earth were not stable, the grasses and trees would have nowhere to be planted.

If what is established within your person is not tranquil, "that's it!" and "that's not!" cannot take form. For these reasons, only when there is a Genuine Person is there Genuine Knowledge. If what I grasp is not clear, how do I know that what I call knowledge is not ignorance? [2/14/1–5]

Now to accumulate wisdom and multiply generosity,
gather up love and concentrate kindness.

With a glorious reputation, love and protect the myriad people and hundred clans, causing them to be joyful and delight in their natures; this is Humaneness.

To achieve great merit,
establish an illustrious name,
support ruler and minister,
correct superiors and inferiors,
distinguish kin from stranger,
sort out the noble and the base,
preserve the endangered kingdoms,
continue the broken [ancestral] lines.

To break off the rebellious and control the disorderly, revive destroyed ancestral temples, and establish those with no descendants; this is Rightness.

To block off the nine orifices,
to store up the attention of the mind,
to discard hearing and vision,
to return to having no awareness,

to vastly wander outside the dust and dirt and freely roam in the activity of effortless, to inhale the yin and exhale the yang, and to completely harmonize with the myriad things; this is Potency.

For these reasons,

when the Way is scattered, there is Potency.
When Potency leaks away, there is Humaneness and Rightness.
When Humaneness and Rightness are established, the Way and its Potency are abandoned.[48] [2/14/7–11]

48. This section works out the implications of *Laozi* 19.

2.9

Take a tree of a hundred hand spans in diameter, cut it down, and make it into sacrificial goblets. You

engrave them with knives and awls,
sprinkle them with blue and yellow.
[They are] elaborately adorned and brilliantly inlaid,
[with] dragons, snakes, tigers, and leopards,
intricately finished with patterns and designs.

Yet as soon as one breaks, it [is discarded] in a ditch. Comparing a sacrificial goblet to what is discarded in the ditch, though as to ugliness and beauty they are different, yet in having lost the nature of wood, they are equal.

For this reason,

the words of one whose spirit pours away are elaborate;
the conduct of one whose Potency is blocked is artificial.

If you lack the Utmost Essence internally, yet perceive words and conduct externally, you will not be able to avoid becoming enslaved to material things. If in your choosing and rejecting your conduct is artificial, this is to seek Essence externally. If Essence leaks out completely but conduct is not curbed, this disturbs the mind and agitates the spirit, confusing and disordering the source.

What you preserve is not stable: outwardly you are steeped in the fashionable customs of the age.
Your mistakes are already made: inwardly your pure clarity is sullied.

Thus you are apprehensive to the last, never knowing a moment of contentment. [2/14/13–18] For this reason, sages inwardly cultivate the techniques of the Way and do not adorn themselves externally with Humaneness and Rightness. They are unaware of the demands[49] of the ears and eyes and wander in the harmony of the Quintessential Spirit.

Those who are so,

below survey the three springs,
above inspect the nine heavens,
broadly span the six coordinates,
bind and unite the myriad things,

Such are the wanderings of the sages.

The Genuine flow into utmost emptiness and wander in the wilds of extinction;

they ride the gryphon and follow the sphinx;[50]
they gallop beyond the bounds [of the world];
and rest beneath the roof [of the cosmos].[51]

They use ten suns as a lamp and command the wind and rain.

49. Rejecting Lau's (HNZ 2/14/20) proposed emendation of 宣 to 宜.

50. Gao You's commentary identifies the *feilian* 蜚廉 (gryphon) as a winged, hairy beast and the *dunyu* 敦圄 (sphinx) as a fabled cat, smaller than a tiger. See Zhang Shuangdi 1:193n.22.

51. Rejecting Lau's (HNZ 2/14/22–23) emendation of 方外 to 外方 and 宇內 to 內.

They subjugate the Duke of Thunder,[52]
employ Kuafu,[53]
take Mi Fei[54] as a concubine,
take the Weaver Girl as a wife.[55]

What between Heaven and Earth could be worthy of their ambition? Thus,

Emptiness and Nothingness are the lodging place of the Way;
equilibrium and simplicity are the basic fabric of the Way. [2/14/20–24]

When people belabor their spirits and disturb their essence, rationally searching for things externally, they all lose their spiritlike brilliance and expel it from its abode. Thus one who has frozen will use a double robe in spring, and one who has suffered heatstroke will hope for a cool breeze in autumn. When there is sickness within, it will always leave its complexion externally. The sweet osmanthus relieves cataracts;[56] the snail cures iritis; both these are medicines that can treat the eye. If people take these without cause, it will certainly obscure their vision. [2/14/26–2/15/1]

2.10

That by which the sages overawe the world has never been surpassed by the Genuine.
That by which the worthy condescend to the vulgar has never been noticed by the sages.

Now,

a puddle in an ox's footprint will not have [even] a one-foot carp;
a piled-earth hillock will not have [even] a tree one fathom in height.[57]

Why is this so? Because their limits are narrow and small and cannot accommodate what is grand and large. How much more is this true of what cannot envelope these very things? This is even further from the grandeur of mountains and abysses. When human beings grapple with the age, inevitably their form becomes entangled and their spirit depletes; thus they cannot avoid exhaustion. If I can be bound and harnessed, it is certainly because my destiny is grounded externally [to myself]. [2/15/1–4]

In an age of Utmost Potency, [people]

52. The Duke of Thunder was the mythical god of thunder. Many of these mythical figures appear in the *Chuci*. See CC 5/18/10.

53. Kuafu 夸父, "Bragging Father," was a strongman of legend who raced the sun. See also 4.16.

54. Mi Fei 宓妃 was the goddess of the Luo River. See CC 1/3/4 and 5/18/16.

55. The Weaver Girl 織女 was the divine daughter of the Heavenly Thearch, who took a humble cowherd as a husband.

56. 翳 literally means "a film over a diseased eye," thus possibly a disease of the cornea rather than (like cataracts) a disease of the lens. According to Gao You, the bark of the osmanthus 梣 is boiled to produce a green liquid with which the eye is washed. See Zhang Shuangdi, 1:195n.30.

57. Similar statements appear in 9.11 and 13.14. A *zhang* 丈, sometimes (as here) translated as "fathom," is a linear measure of ten Chinese feet (*chi* 尺), or approximately seven and a half feet in English measure.

contentedly slept in boundless realms
and moved [between] and lodged in indeterminate dwellings.

They clasped Heaven and Earth and discarded the myriad things. They took primal chaos as their gnomon and floated freely in a limitless domain. For this reason, the sages [merely] inhaled and exhaled the *qi* of yin and yang, and none of the myriad living things failed to flourish as they acknowledged [the sages'] Potency in harmonious compliance. At this time nothing was directed or arranged; separately and autonomously [things] completed themselves. Mixed and merged, simple and undispersed, they blended into a unity, and the myriad things were greatly abundant. For this reason, even if you had the knowledge of [Archer] Yi there was nothing for which to use it.[58]

When the age declined, in the reign of Fuxi, his Way was obscure and indistinct. He contained Potency and embraced harmony, broadcasting them subtly and comprehensively, yet even so knowledge first stirred and sprouted. [The people] all wanted to part from their childlike and ignorant mind and awareness appeared in the midst of Heaven and Earth; thus their Potency was vexed and could not be unified.

Coming to the age of the Divine Farmer and the Yellow Emperor,[59] they
split and sundered the Great Ancestor,
examining and directing Heaven and Earth,
enumerating the Nine Vacancies,
and demarcating the Nine Boundaries.[60]
They clasped yin and yang,
kneaded the hard and the soft,
split the branches, and sorted the leaves.

The myriad things and hundred clans were each given structure and rule. At this, the myriad people all were alert and awake, and there were none who did not straighten up to listen and look. Thus they were orderly but could not be harmonized.

Coming down to the age of Kun Wu[61] and the descendants of the Xia,
desires attached to things;
hearing and sight were lured outward,
[so that] nature and destiny lost their [proper] attainment.

Coming down to the house of Zhou, decadence dispersed simplicity; [people] deserted the Way for artifice; they were miserly of Potency in conduct; and cleverness and precedence sprouted. When the Zhou house declined, the kingly Way was abandoned. The Confucians and Mohists thus began enumerating their Ways

58. This description of the "age of Utmost Potency" is similar in sentiment to ZZ 9/23/28–9/24/4.

59. The Yellow Emperor, or Yellow Thearch (Huangdi 黃帝), was a legendary ruler of high antiquity, said variously to be the original ancestor of the Chinese people and the inventor of the state and of warfare.

60. The "Nine Vacancies" and "Nine Boundaries" are synecdoches for Heaven and Earth. See Zhang Shuangdi, 1:206n.23.

61. Kun Wu 昆吾 was the progenitor of the dynastic line of the Xia. See Zhang Shuangdi, 1:207n.28.

and debating, dividing up disciples, and reciting. From then on, broad learning cast doubt on the sages; elaborate deceit tyrannized the masses. They played and sang and drummed and danced, embroidering the *Odes* and *Documents* to purchase fame and praise in the world. They

proliferated rituals of ascending and descending,
adorned costumes of aprons and caps.

The assembled masses were insufficient for the extremes of their alterations; the collected wealth [of the world] was insufficient to meet their expenses. At this, the myriad people first forgot the trail and abandoned the path; all wanted to practice their own knowledge and artifice, seeking to force conditions[62] on the age and crookedly acquire fame and profit. For this reason, the common people were unleashed to profligacy and lost the root of the Great Ancestor. The [current] age being bereft of nature and destiny is the product of gradual decline; its origins are distant. [2/15/6–20]

For this reason,

the learning of the sage:
seeks to return nature to its origin
and to set the mind to roaming in emptiness.
The learning of the knowledgeable:
seeks to connect nature to the great expanse [of the world]
and to awaken to stillness and quiescence.
The vulgar learning of the age is not like this.
It tugs at Potency
and drags at nature.
Internally it vexes the five orbs;
externally it belabors the ears and eyes.

Then one begins to pick at the wriggling and curling minutiae of things; moving and swaying with Humaneness, Rightness, Ritual, and Music. You lord your conduct and project your cunning over the world, seeking title, fame, and reputation from the age. This I am too ashamed to do. [2/15/22–25]

For this reason, having the world does not compare with being content. Being content does not compare with wandering carefree through the ends and beginnings of things and penetrating the frontier between Something and Nothing. [Those who are] thus

are not more encouraged if the whole age praises them;
are not more melancholy if the whole age contradicts them.

They are firm in the boundary between life and death and comprehend the guiding pattern of honor and disgrace. Though raging fires and flooding waters wreak havoc throughout the world, their spirit remains undiminished in their breasts. Those who are like this view the realm of the world as flying feathers and floating twigs. How could they be willing to busily make things their affairs? [2/16/1–4]

62. 鑿枘, literally, "to bore a round socket for a square peg."

2.11

The nature of water is clear, yet soil sullies it.
The nature of humans is tranquil, yet desires disorder it.
What human beings receive from Heaven are [the tendencies]
for ears and eyes [to perceive] colors and sounds,
for mouth and nose [to perceive] fragrances and tastes,
for flesh and skin [to perceive] cold and heat.

The instinctive responses are the same in everyone, but some penetrate to spiritlike illumination, and some cannot avoid derangement and madness. Why is this? That by which they [these tendencies] are controlled is different.

Thus,

the spirit is the source of consciousness. If the spirit is clear, then consciousness is illumined.

Consciousness is the storehouse of the mind. If consciousness is impartial, then the mind is balanced.

No one can mirror himself in flowing water, but [he can] observe his reflection in standing water because it is still.

No one can view his form in raw iron, but [he can] view his form in a clear mirror because it is even.

Only what is even and still can thus give form to the nature and basic tendencies of things. Viewed from this perspective, usefulness depends on what is not used. Thus when the empty room is pristine and clear, good fortune will abide there.[63]

If the mirror is bright, dust and dirt cannot obscure it.
If the spirit is clear, lusts and desires cannot disorder it.

To work at reclaiming the Quintessential Spirit once it has already overflowed externally is to lose the root and seek it in the branches. If external and internal do not tally and you desire to interact with things; if you cover your mysterious light and seek to know [things] with the ears and eyes; this is to discard your brilliance and follow your blindness. This is called "losing the Way." When the mind goes somewhere, the spirit swiftly lodges there. By returning the spirit to emptiness, this lodging dissolves and is extinguished.[64] This is the wandering of the sage. [2/16/6–15]

Thus those in antiquity who ordered the world invariably penetrated the basic tendencies of nature and destiny. Their taking and giving were not necessarily the same, [but] they were as one in uniting with the Way.

You do not refrain from wearing fur in summer because you cherish it but because it is too hot for your person.

---

63. This line occurs in the famous "fasting of the mind" passage in ZZ 4/10/7.

64. When the mind focuses on an external object, energy in the form of Quintessential Spirit (*jingshen*) is projected onto it from the spirit within. Normatively, as the subject's attention moves on, this energy should return to the subject and dissolve into the larger internal fund of energy that composes the spirit (vacuity).

You do not refrain from using a fan in winter to conserve it but because it is too cold for comfort.

The sages

assess their bellies and eat;

measure their frames and dress.

They compose themselves, that is all; from whence can the mind of greed and dissipation arise?

Thus,

a person who can have the world is invariably someone who will not strive for it.

A person who can possess fame and praise is invariably someone who will not scurry in search of them.

The sage has broken through to it. Having broken through to it, the mind of lust and desire is external [to him]. [2/16/17–21]

2.12

The disciples of Confucius and Mozi all teach the techniques of Humaneness and Rightness to the age, yet they do not avoid destruction. If they personally cannot practice [their teachings], how much less may those they teach?[65] Why is this? Because their Way is external. To ask the branches to return to the roots: if even Xu You could not do it, how much less the common people? If you genuinely break through to the basic tendencies of nature and destiny, so that Humaneness and Rightness adhere [to your actions], how then can choosing and discarding suffice to confuse your mind? [2/16/23–25]

If

the spirit has no obstruction and the mind has no burden,

if they are pervasively comprehending and minutely penetrating,

calm and quiescent and free of tasks,

without any congealing or stagnancy,

attentive in empty stillness,

then

power and profit cannot lure them;

logicians cannot delight them;

sounds and colors cannot corrupt them;

beauty cannot debauch them;

wisdom cannot move them;

courage cannot frighten them;

This is the Way[66] of the Genuine. Those who are like this shape and forge the myriad things and in their being human are conjoined with what creates and transforms.

65. A similar criticism of Confucians and Mohists appears in 13.7.

66. Rejecting Lau's (HNZ 2/17/1) emendation of *you* 遊 for 道.

Amid Heaven and Earth,
in space and time,
nothing can destroy or impede them.
What generates life is not life;
what transforms things is not transformation.[67]
Their spirits:
cross Mount Li or the Taihang [Mountains] and have no difficulty;
enter the Four Seas or the Nine Rivers and cannot be trapped;
lodge in narrow defiles and cannot be obstructed;
spread across the realm of Heaven and Earth and are not stretched.
If you do not penetrate to this [point],
though your eyes enumerate a group of one thousand sheep,
though your ears distinguish the tones of the eight winds,
your feet perform the "Northern Bank"[68] dance;
your hands execute the "Green Waters"[69] rhythm;
your intelligence encompasses Heaven and Earth;
your brilliance illuminates the sun and moon;
your disputations unknot linked jewels;
your words add luster to jade and stone;
These will still be of no aid to governing the world. [2/16/27–2/17/6]

2.13

Tranquillity and calmness are that by which the nature is nourished.
Harmony and vacuity are that by which Potency is nurtured.
When what is external does not disturb what is internal, then our nature attains what is suitable to it.
When the harmony of nature is not disturbed, then Potency will rest securely in its position.
Nurturing life so as to order the age,
embracing Potency so as to complete our years,
This may be called being able to embody the Way.
Those who are like this:
Their blood and pulse have no sluggishness or stagnation;
their five orbs have no diseased *qi*;
calamity and good fortune cannot perturb them;
blame and praise cannot settle on them like dust;

67. This is a paraphrase of two lines from ZZ 6/17/15, which read 殺生者不死, 生生者不生: "What kills life is not death; what gives birth to life is not life." See Lau, HNZ, 17n.1.

68. "Northern Bank" 陽阿 was a song of ancient Chu. Apparently there was a dance that accompanied the music. See CC 9/23/13. "Northern Bank" appears as "Waving Lotuses" 揚荷.

69. "Green Waters" 綠水 was the name of a song, perhaps a lost *Ode*. See Zhang Shuangdi, 1:227–28n.6.

thus can they reach the ultimate. [However,] if you do not have the age, how can you succeed? If you have the right character but do not meet your time, you will not even be able to safeguard your person. How much less so one who is without the Way! [2/17/8–11]

Moreover, the instinctive responses of human beings are for

the ears and eyes to respond to stimulus and movement,

the mind and awareness to recognize worry and happiness.

The hands and feet to rub at pains and itches and to avoid cold and heat.

This is how we interact with things.

If a wasp or a scorpion stings your finger, your spirit cannot remain placid.

If a mosquito or a gadfly bites your flesh, your nature cannot remain settled.

The worries and calamities that come to disturb your mind are not limited to the poisonous bites of wasps or scorpions or the annoyance of mosquitoes and gadflies, yet you want to remain tranquil and vacuous. How can it be done?

The ears of one whose eyes are examining the tip of an autumn hair will not hear the sound of thunder and lightning.

The eyes of one whose ears are harmonizing the tones of jade and stone will not see the form of Mount Tai.

Why is this? They are attending to what is small and forgetting what is big. Now the arrival of the myriad things, pulling and plucking at my nature, grabbing and grasping at my feelings, is like a spring or fountain, even if one wanted to not be ruled [by them], could this be achieved? [2/17/13–18]

Now a person who plants a tree irrigates it with springwater and beds it in fertile soil. If one person nurtures it and ten people harvest it, there will certainly be no spare splinters;[70] how much less if the entire kingdom hacks at it together? Though one wanted it to live for a long time, how could this be accomplished?

If you leave a basin of water in the courtyard to settle for one full day, you will still not be able to see your eyebrows and lashes. If you muddy it with no more than one stir, you will not be able to distinguish square from circular. The human spirit is easy to muddy and difficult to clarify, much like the basin of water. How much more so when an entire age stirs and disturbs it; how can it attain a moment of equanimity? [2/17/20–23]

2.14

Antiquity was an age of Utmost Potency.

Merchants prospered in their markets;

farmers rejoiced in their work;

70. Disregarding Lau's (HNZ 2/17/20) proposed emendation. Wang Niansun argues that "one" and "ten" have been transposed and that this line should read, "If ten people nurture it and one person harvests it," but the original ordering seems to read well in context.

grandees rested secure in their posts;
and scholar-recluses practiced[71] their Way.

At this time,

winds and rains were not destructive;
grasses and trees did not die prematurely;
the Nine Tripods doubled the flavor [of offerings];[72]
pearls and jade were lustrous;
the Luo River gave forth the "Crimson Writings";
the Yellow River gave forth the "Green Chart."[73]

Thus Xu You, Fang Hui, Shan Juan, and Pi Yi[74] all attained their Way. Why was this? The rulers of the age had the mind that desires to benefit the world; thus the people could enjoy their ease. The talent of the four masters did not make them able to be wholly good, just like [people] of the current age. Yet no one [today] can match their brilliance, because they encountered the era of Tang and Yu.[75]

Coming to the age of [King] Jie of Xia and [King] Djou of Yin,[76] they

cooked people alive,
condemned remonstrators,
created the "roasting beam,"[77]
forged the "metal pillar,"[78]

---

71. Rejecting Lau's (HNZ 2/17/25) proposed emendation.

72. Lau (HNZ 2/17/26) proposes that this be amended to "The Nine Tripods were heavy," deleting the final character "flavor 味". Zhuang Kuiji 莊逵吉 notes that the *Taiping Yulan* contains an alternative reading without "flavor" and that the commentary remarks, "When the practice of the Moral Potency of the monarch was clear the tripods were heavy, when he was wicked the tripods were light" (Zhang Shuangdi 1997, 1:225n.3). The elimination of "flavor" here seems to break the parallelism, and the line as written works well thematically in context.

73. The "Crimson Writings" and the "Green Chart" are fabled texts variously understood as the revelations of powerful deities or of Heaven itself, which are said to have appeared at particularly auspicious moments in history to both guide and legitimate the efforts of great sages. These "texts" are alluded to occasionally in pre-Han literature (in *Analects* 9, Confucius laments, "The [Yellow] River does not give up its chart!"). The lore surrounding them became increasingly elaborate in the Han with the proliferation of *wei shu* 緯書 ("weft" texts or apocrypha).

74. Xu You 許由 was a legendary hermit, attested to in many early texts, who supposedly refused Yao's offer of abdication. According to Gao You, Fang Hui 方回, Shan Juan 善卷, and Pi Yi 披衣 all were hermits during the time of Yao. Pi Yi appears in ZZ 7/20/3, 12/30/13, and 22/60/31. Shan Juan appears in ZZ 28/81/15 and 29/90/16 and in LSCQ 15.3/83/6.

75. Tang 唐 and Yu 虞—that is, Yao and Shun—the last of the mythical predynastic sage kings. Yao found his sons unworthy and ceded the throne to the commoner Shun; Shun in turn ceded the throne to the flood-tamer Yu 禹.

76. Jie (ca. 1550 B.C.E.) and Djou (ca. 1050 B.C.E.) were the legendary or semilegendary last rulers of the Xia and Shang (Yin) dynasties, famous as exemplars of royal misrule.

77. A device with which King Djou tortured and killed people by making them walk across a red-hot metal beam, it is also mentioned in 10.89, 11.1, 12.35, 15.2, and 21.4. See chap. 11, n. 9.

78. Another torture device. The victim was placed on the metal pillar while fire was stoked below. When the pillar got too hot and the victim fell into the flames, the king would laugh. See Zhang Shuangdi, 1:237n.9.

opened the heart of a worthy man,[79]
cut off the feet of a talented knight,[80]
minced the daughter of the marquis of Gui,
pulverized the bones of the earl of Mei.[81]

During this time,

tall mountains collapsed;
three rivers dried up;
flying birds snapped their wings;
running beasts lost their hooves.

How could it be that at this time alone there were no sages? However, they could not fulfill their Way because they did not meet their age.

The heavenly bird flies above one thousand *ren*.
The beast runs into the dense forest.

[Yet] calamity still reaches them; how much more so for the common people of ordinary households? Seen from this [perspective], embodying the Way does not rest entirely with us; it is indeed also tied to the era [in which we live]. [2/17/25–2/18/4]

When the capital of Liyang became a lake in one night,[82] those of courageous strength and sage wisdom shared the same fate with the cowardly and unworthy.

When on top of Mount Wu, a chance wind let loose fire, the [great] *gaoxia* trees and the glossy ganoderma[83] died along with the oxtail-southernwood trees and moxa.

Thus,

the river fish does not have clear eyes;
young crops do not live an entire season.

This is the way they were born. Thus,

if the age is orderly, the foolish alone will not be able to disorder it.
If the age is chaotic, the wise alone will not be able to bring it to order.

To blame yourself for the Way's not being practiced while trapped in a corrupt age

---

79. King Djou supposedly ordered this done to Bi Gan, to see whether the heart of a worthy was any different from that of an ordinary man.

80. King Djou ordered this done to a knight who could ford cold streams, to see whether there was something unusual about his marrow. The story is recounted in LSCQ 23.4/152/13.

81. According to Gao You, the earl of Mei recommended the lord of Gui's daughter to Djou as a great beauty. On seeing her, Djou was displeased, whereupon he had both the daughter and the earl literally cooked into a meat sauce (the verbs translated here as "minced" and "pulverized"). Gao notes an alternative story in which the earl of Mei was punished for remonstrating. See Zhang Shuangdi, 1:237n.11.

82. Liyang 歷陽 was a district in Huainan (in present-day Anhui Province) whose administrative capital was evidently destroyed by some Atlantis-like natural disaster. Gao You recounts a story of an old widow who was warned of the impending disaster. See Zhang Shuangdi 1997, 1:239n.18.

83. *Gaoxia* 膏夏 is not identified, but it is evidently a plant with fatty or greasy properties. *Zizhi* 紫芝 is the Japanese glossy ganoderma, related to the fungus known as *lingzhi* 靈芝. See "Names of a Selection of Asian Fungi," at http://www.plantnames.unimelb.edu.au/Sorting/Fungi_Asian.html.

is like double-hobbling [the famous horse] Qiji[84] and asking him to travel a thousand *li*. If you put an ape in a cage, it will be just like a pig. It is not that it is no longer clever or agile but that it has nowhere to give free rein to its ability. When Shun was farming in Tao, he could not profit his village. When he faced south as king, his Potency spread through the Four Seas. It could not be that his Humaneness increased; his position was fortuitous and his strategic position advantageous.

For the ancient sages,

their harmony and tranquillity were their nature;
their achieving their ambition and practicing the Way were their destiny.

For this reason,

when nature meets destiny, only then can it be effective;
when destiny attains nature, only then can it be clarified.
Neither bows of cudrania tree [wood][85]
nor the crossbows of Xizi[86]
could be shot without a string.
Neither the boats of Yue
nor the skiffs of Shu
could float without water.

If now

the dart and line were shot above;
the net and snares were spread out below;

Even if [a bird] wanted to soar, how could it attain the force [to do so]? Thus the *Odes* says,

"I pick and pick the chickweed,
yet do not fill my shallow basket.
I sigh for the one I cherish,
posted to the ranks of Zhou."[87]

This speaks of longing for distant ages. [2/18/6–14]

Translated by Harold D. Roth and Andrew Meyer

84. Qiji 騏驥 was a legendary thoroughbred said to be capable of traveling a thousand *li* in a single day.

85. The *wuhao* 烏號, or *Cudrania tricuspidata*, is related to the mulberry. According to Gao You, its wood makes especially strong bows. See Zhang Shuangdi 1997, 1:241n.28. Its leaves can be fed to silkworms as a substitute for mulberry leaves. See 5.3. The *Cudrania* is the emblematic tree of the eighth month. See 5.8.

86. Gao You offers two explanations: (a) Xizi 谿子 was a southern land renowned for its excellent bows, and (b) Xi Ziyang was a great bowyer of Zheng. See Zhang Shuangdi, 1:241n.28.

87. *Odes* 3, "Juan'er 卷耳." Some commentators and translators understand the last line to mean that the narrator has laid down her basket by the side of the road.

Three

CELESTIAL PATTERNS

"Celestial patterns" introduces readers to astronomy and related subjects, including cosmology, positional astronomy, calendrics, mathematical harmonics, and astrology. Although some passages may strike modern readers as both obscure and highly technical, from the point of view of Han intellectual history this chapter treats its topics in rather general terms, omitting the sorts of technical detail that would be the province of specialists. Readers of this chapter would be able to understand a situation in which these topics arose (such as a discussion at court of astrologically based policy) but not themselves be practicing astrologers. The principal message of the chapter is that all things in the cosmos are interconnected, that human plans and intentions are subject to the influence of various cosmic cycles and correlations, and that such cycles and correlations can be understood and taken into account in the formulation of policy.

The Chapter Title

"Tianwen" 天文 can be understood as having two complementary meanings, depending on how one construes the grammar of the phrase: "Heaven Adorned," noun plus past-participle verb, and "Celestial Patterns," adjective plus noun. Both meanings are valid, and both would have been present to some extent in the mind of a Han-dynasty reader. In English, however, we must choose one or the other, and in our view the second sense is dominant. The modern Chinese word *tianwen* is translated in English as "astronomy," but generally with a wider range of meanings than the English term conveys; for example, it includes atmospheric phenomena such as meteorology and auroras.

Summary and Key Themes

The chapter begins with a lyrical account in parallel prose of how the cosmos originated in undifferentiation and evolved into the familiar world of phenomena through the action of yin and yang. This section ends with the battle between the Titan-like deities Gong Gong and Zhuan Xu, which, by knocking the axis of Heaven and Earth askew, brought an end to the primordial age and ushered in the era of human affairs. This section leads into a demonstration (3.2) that all phenomena conform to the cycles of yin and yang and (3.3) that human actions resonate with the cosmos.

These introductory sections are followed by a list of the principal heavenly bodies and the ninefold divisions of Heaven, correlated with the twenty-eight lunar lodges (constellations), and then by Five-Phase correlates of the five planets visible to the naked eye (Jupiter, Mars, Saturn, Venus, and Mercury, in the order in which they are given in chapter 3) and their motions. Sections 3.4 through 3.11 provide, in effect, instructions for drawing a diagram of significant correlations of heavenly bodies, directions, and seasonal time.[1] Such a diagram might form the base (the so-called Earth plate) of the cosmological model known as a *shi* 式, or "cosmograph," which consisted of a fixed Earth plate engraved with directions, names of months, lunar lodges, and other correlative categorical information, and a pivoted, movable "Heaven plate" depicting the Northern (Big) Dipper constellation. By rotating the Heaven plate in imitation of the stars' apparent daily and annual motion, astrological predictions could be made on the basis of where the "handle" of the Dipper pointed on any given day.[2] The cosmograph was the preeminent astrological instrument of the late Warring States and early Han periods (being replaced thereafter by the armillary sphere). Because it was a comprehensive microcosm, it allowed practitioners to calculate and interpret a wide range of correlations of astrological significance and is a concrete example of the normative natural order outlined so eloquently in chapter 1.

The remainder of the chapter consists largely of directions for reading and understanding the meaning of such correlations, including the sixty-day *ganzhi* cycle governed by the heavenly stems and earthly branches, the seasons, the twelve-year orbital cycle of Jupiter, a cycle of eight forty-five-day "wind seasons" correlated with

1. For an excellent study of Chinese schematic cosmography, see Mark Edward Lewis, *The Construction of Space in Early China* (Albany: State University of New York Press, 2006), esp. chap. 5, "World and Cosmos."

2. David Pankenier (private communication) suggests that these procedures, which involve rather mechanical readings of good and ill fortune on the basis of cyclical and directional phenomena, might better be known as "astromancy" rather than "astrology." See also the introduction to chap. 5, n. 4.

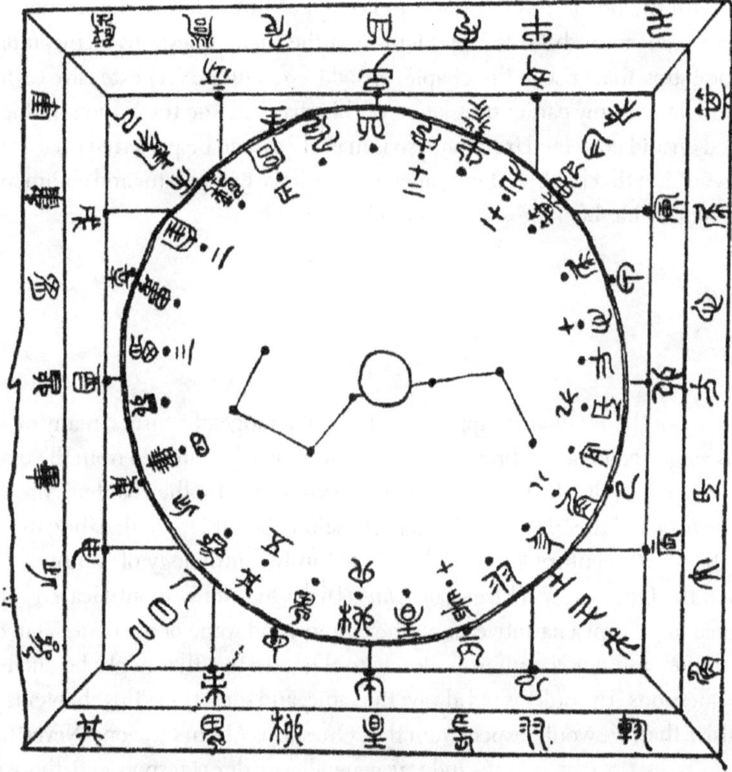

A *shi* 式 cosmograph from the early Han period, second century B.C.E. The Heaven plate, which can be rotated, is engraved with an image of the Northern Dipper (known in the West as the Big Dipper), allowing its annual movement around the horizon to be tracked so that predictions might be made in accordance with astrological correlative data encoded on the square Earth plate.

the eight cardinal directions, the twelve tones of the chromatic scale and the five of the pentatonic scale, and the lunar lodges. The chapter includes sections on deriving the twelve tones of the chromatic scale by the "ascending and descending thirds" method (3.29) and correlating the twelve tones with the pentatonic scale; a section on weights and measures correlated with the twelve-tone scale (3.31); the names and characteristics of the twelve years of the Jupiter cycle (3.32–3.34, 3.41); correlations of celestial phenomena with the states and territories of the Warring States period (3.35, 3.37, 3.40); and miscellaneous correlations, prognostications, and omens. The chapter ends with a section (3.43) on using gnomons to measure the size of the cosmos.

The astronomical and astrological correlations and calculations in this chapter are presented only in overview (enabling the ruler to understand what his astrologers were telling him, but not necessarily giving him enough technical information to perform the operations himself), and much of this material appears obscure to modern readers. Both textual problems and the many questions of meaning and interpretation that arise in this chapter are addressed in the very extensive commentary and notes to my earlier translation of this chapter.[3] The translation in this book is based on and corrected from (and so is in every case to be preferred to) that in my 1993 work, but that book contains much more scholarly apparatus and commentarial material than has been possible to include here.

Sources

Chapter 3 of the *Huainanzi* appears to draw on a range of sources, many of which are no longer extant and whose former existence must be inferred from the material in the chapter itself. The most important known source for the chapter is the poetic catechism called the "Tian wen" 天問 (Questions About Heaven), dating from perhaps the fourth century B.C.E. and included in the anthology of southern poetry entitled the *Chuci* 楚辭 (*Elegies of Chu*). The "Questions About Heaven" appear designed to prompt a narrative about the cosmos, and some of the material in chapter 3 of the *Huainanzi* conforms closely to the narrative that might be elicited by those questions. The order is not always the same, and sometimes this chapter is more expansive than we would expect from the "Questions About Heaven." Nevertheless, sections 3.1, 3.4, 3.13, 3.15, 3.16, and 3.25 generally are direct responses to those questions. Indeed, there can be no doubt of the connection between the "Questions About Heaven" and the *Huainanzi*.

One important source for this chapter was completely unknown before the 1970s: the Mawangdui text[4] *Wuxingzhan* 五星占 (*Prognostications of the Five Planets*). That text, lost for many centuries, gives Five-Phase correlates for the five visible planets, along with detailed information about their orbital periods, proper and retrograde motion, conjunctions, occultations, and other technical matters. The discovery of the *Wuxingzhan* not only supplies a hitherto-unknown source for the *Huainanzi* but also gives us an important insight into the working methods of Liu An and his court scholars. For this third chapter of the *Huainanzi*, they quoted verbatim the Five-Phase correlations that begin each of the five sections of the *Wuxingzhan*, grouping them together in a single section (3.6) that is followed by five sections (3.7–3.11) describing the apparent motions of the planets in terms similar to but much simpler than the text of the *Wuxingzhan*. In other words, the *Huainanzi* draws on the *Wuxingzhan* to give an "executive summary" of the astrology of the five planets but omits entirely the technical details that would have been of interest only to astrological specialists in the monarch's employ.

3. Major 1993.

4. Part of a funerary library of texts on silk found in the tomb of the younger marquis of Dai, at Mawangdui, Changsha, Hunan, dated 168 B.C.E.

We can only guess how many other lost texts are quoted or alluded to in chapter 3 of the *Huainanzi*. Some of the chapter's sections look very much like set pieces drawn verbatim from now-lost sources. These include 3.17, on the annual waxing and waning of yin and yang; 3.25, on the daily motion of the sun (related, as noted, to the "Questions About Heaven" but very likely quoted from a now-lost source); 3.27, in which puns are used to explain the correlations between the twelve earthly branches and the twelve chromatic notes; 3.31, on weights and measures; 3.33, on the twelve years of the Jupiter cycle; and 3.42, on the allocation of daily rations to the people on the basis of variations in the Jupiter cycle years. Section 3.44, on the use of gnomons, also was probably an independent text incorporated into this chapter. Many other sections of the chapter may have been derived from now-lost manuals on the use of the cosmograph. It is, in short, impossible to know how much of the *Huainanzi*'s chapter 3 is original writing by Liu An and his court scholars, but it appears likely that it is in large part an anthology of material quoted from now-unknown sources.

The Chapter in the Context of the *Huainanzi* as a Whole

Coming early in the *Huainanzi*, chapter 3 emphasizes the interconnectedness of all phenomena and the influence of cosmic cycles on human affairs. The overview of cosmology, astronomy, astrology, and related subjects presented here is intended to be sufficient for a ruler to understand, if not actively participate in, the techniques by which cosmic cycles and correlations are calculated (particularly by means of the cosmograph) and taken into account in the formulation of policy. The essential point is that acts of state must harmonize with celestial patterns and cycles in order to be successful.

Chapter 21 of the *Huainanzi*, "An Overview of the Essentials," says of this chapter that it enables a person to "possess the means to look upward to Heaven and uphold what to follow and thereby avoid disordering Heaven's regularities" (21.2). The "Overview" also regards this chapter as part of a subunit of text that includes chapters 4 and 5, and says of them, "Had we discussed ends and beginnings and not illuminated Heaven, Earth, and the four seasons, you would not know the taboos to avoid" (21.3). Thus even the seemingly esoteric subject matter of this chapter is presented by Liu An and his editors as an essential component of the art of rulership.

John S. Major

Three

3.1

When Heaven and Earth were yet unformed, all was
ascending and flying,
diving and delving.
Thus it was called the Grand Inception.
The Grand Inception produced the Nebulous Void.
The Nebulous Void produced space-time;[1]
space-time produced the original *qi*.
A boundary [divided] the original *qi*.
That which was pure and bright spread out to form Heaven;
that which was heavy and turbid congealed to form Earth.
It is easy for that which is pure and subtle to converge
but difficult for the heavy and turbid to congeal.
Therefore
Heaven was completed first;
Earth was fixed afterward.

---

1. Conventionally translated as "cosmos" or "universe," *yuzhou* 宇宙 more precisely means, as Angus C. Graham put it, "process enduring in time" and "matter extending in space" ("Reflections and Replies: Major," in *Chinese Texts and Philosophical Contexts: Essays Dedicated to Angus C. Graham*, ed. Henry Rosemont [La Salle, Ill.: Open Court Press, 1990], 279). "Space-time," a term borrowed from modern physics, captures the idea very well.

The conjoined essences of Heaven and Earth produced yin and yang.
The supersessive essences of yin and yang caused the four seasons.
The scattered essences of the four seasons created the myriad things.
The hot *qi* of accumulated yang produced fire; the essence of fiery *qi* became the sun.
The cold *qi* of accumulated yin produced water; the essence of watery *qi* became the moon.

The overflowing *qi* of the essences of the sun and the moon made the stars and planets.

To Heaven belong the sun, moon, stars, and planets;
to Earth belong waters and floods, dust and soil. [3/18/18–23]

In ancient times Gong Gong[2] and Zhuan Xu[3] fought, each seeking to become the thearch. Enraged, they crashed against Mount Buzhou;[4]

Heaven's pillars broke;
the cords of Earth snapped.
Heaven tilted in the northwest, and thus the sun and moon, stars and planets shifted in that direction.
Earth became unfull in the southeast, and thus the watery floods and mounding soils subsided in that direction. [3/18/25–26]

3.2

The Way of Heaven is called the Round;
the Way of Earth is called the Square.
The square governs the obscure;
the circular governs the bright.
The bright emits *qi*, and for this reason fire is the external brilliance of the sun.
The obscure sucks in *qi*, and for this reason water is the internal luminosity of the moon.
Emitted *qi* endows;
retained *qi* transforms.

Thus yang endows and yin transforms. [3/18/28–30]

The unbalanced *qi* of Heaven and Earth, becoming perturbed, causes wind;
the harmonious *qi* of Heaven and Earth, becoming calm, causes rain.

2. Gong Gong 共工 is a mythical figure of high antiquity, sometimes described as the "minister of works" to the ancient thearchs but also depicted as a rebel and fomenter of disorder.

3. Zhuan Xu 顓頊 is a divine thearch and god of the north, from whom many aristocratic lineages of the Bronze Age claimed descent. See also chap. 5, n. 46.

4. Mount Buzhou, conceptualized as the central peak of Mount Kunlun and therefore located to the northwest of China (see the introduction to chap. 4 and fig. 4.1), is the pivot of Heaven and Earth. *Zhou* 周 means "to circle" in the sense of "to circumambulate" or "to orbit"; it does not mean "to revolve on its own axis." Thus the common translation of "Unrotating Mountain" for Buzhou 不周 is not correct. The sense of the term is that the mountain rests unmoving at the very center of the universe, which rotates around it.

When yin and yang rub against each other,[5] their interaction produces thunder.

Aroused, they produce thunderclaps;
disordered, they produce mist.
When the yang *qi* prevails, it scatters to make rain and dew;
when the yin *qi* prevails, it freezes to make frost and snow. [3/19/1–2]
Hairy and feathered creatures make up the class of flying and walking things and are subject to yang.
Creatures with scales and shells make up the class of creeping and hiding things and are subject to yin.
The sun is the ruler of yang. Therefore, in spring and summer animals shed their fur; at the summer solstice, stags' antlers drop off.
The moon is the fundament of yin. Therefore when the moon wanes, the brains of fish shrink; when the moon dies, wasps and crabs shrivel up.
Fire flies upward;
water flows downward.

Thus,

the flight of birds is aloft;
the movement of fishes is downward.[6] [3/19/4–7]
Things within the same class mutually move one another;
root and twig mutually respond to each other.

Therefore,

when the burning mirror sees the sun, it ignites tinder and produces fire.
When the square receptacle[7] sees the moon, it moistens and produces water.
When the tiger roars, the valley winds rush;
when the dragon arises, the bright clouds accumulate.
When *qilins* wrangle, the sun or moon is eclipsed;
when the leviathan dies, comets appear.
When silkworms secrete fragmented silk,[8] the *shang* string [of a stringed instrument] snaps.
When meteors fall, the Bohai[9] surges upward. [3/19/9–11]

5. The same phrase, *yin yang xiang bo* 陰陽相薄, occurs five times in 4.19 and once in 17.174. The context of 17.174 requires a slightly different translation: "yin and yang erode each other."

6. See 10.27: "When an eagle hovers above the river, fish and turtles plunge and flying birds scatter. By necessity they distance themselves from harm."

7. A device intended to collect dew by condensation.

8. Reading *er* 珥 as *er* 餌. Essentially the same statement appears in 6.2. See chap. 6, n. 18.

9. That is, the Gulf of Bohai, a shallow body of water located off northeastern China and partly enclosed by the Liaodong and Shandong peninsulas.

3.3

The feelings of the rulers of men penetrate to Heaven on high.
Thus,

if there are punishments and cruelty, there will be whirlwinds.
If there are wrongful ordinances, there will be plagues of devouring insects.
If there are unjust executions, the land will redden with drought.
If there are unseasonable ordinances,[10] there will be great excess of rain. [3/19/13–14]
The four seasons are the officers of Heaven.
The sun and moon are the agents of Heaven.
The stars and planets mark the appointed times of Heaven.
Rainbows and comets are the portents of Heaven. [3/19/16–17]

3.4

Heaven has nine fields and 9,999 junctures. It is 150,000 *li* distant from the earth. There are five planets, eight winds, and twenty-eight lunar lodges. There are five offices and six departments. The [six departments] are called the Purple Palace, the Great Enclosure, the Chariot Frame,[11] the Pool of Xian,[12] the Four Guardians, and the Heavenly Slope. [3/19/19–20]

3.5

What are the nine fields?

The central one is called Balanced Heaven. Its asterisms are Horn, Neck, and Root.[13]
The eastern one is called Azure Heaven. Its asterisms are Room, Heart, and Tail.
The northeastern one is called Variable Heaven. Its asterisms are Winnowing Basket, Dipper, and Ox Leader.

10. Reading *ling bu shi* 令不時 as in the *Yiwen*, in place of the *ling bu shou* 令不收 of the *Huainanzi* text. My thanks to Michael Loewe (private communication) for suggesting this emendation. For the concept of "unseasonable ordinances," see chap. 5.

11. "Chariot Frame," Xuanyuan 軒轅, is the personal name of the Yellow Emperor, after the name of his supposed birthplace in Henan. The compound word means "axle and shafts"—that is, the basic frame of a chariot.

12. The Pool of Xian is a constellation. The word *xian* 咸 is open to various interpretations, but in this compound it seems to be the name of the legendary figure Shaman Xian, Wuxian 巫咸. For further discussion, see Major 1993, 199. See also chap. 11, n. 35.

13. The "asterisms" (*xing* 星) of this passage are the lunar lodges (*xiu* 宿). For the lunar lodges and the English translations of their names used in this work, see app. B.

The northern one is called Umbral Heaven. Its asterisms are Serving Maid, Emptiness, Rooftop, and Encampment.

The northwestern one is called Secluded Heaven. Its asterisms are Eastern Wall, Stride, and Bond.

The western one is called Luminous Heaven. Its asterisms are Stomach, Pleiades, and Net.

The southwestern one is called Vermilion Heaven. Its asterisms are Turtle Beak, Triad, and Eastern Well.

The southern one is called Fiery Heaven. Its asterisms are Ghost Bearer, Willow, and Seven Stars.

The southeastern one is called Yang Heaven. Its asterisms are Extension, Wings, and Chariot Platform. [3/19/22–26]

3.6

What are the five planets?

The East is Wood. Its god is Tai Hao.[14] His assistant is Gou Mang. He grasps the compass and governs spring. His spirit is Year Star [Jupiter]. His animal is the Blue-green Dragon. His musical note is *jue;* his days are *jia* and *yi.*[15]

The South is Fire. Its god is Yan Di.[16] His assistant is Zhu Ming. He grasps the balance beam and governs summer. His spirit is Sparkling Deluder [Mars]. His animal is the Vermilion Bird. His musical note is *zhi;* his days are *bing* and *ding.*

The Center is Earth. Its god is the Yellow Emperor. His assistant is Hou Tu. He grasps the marking cord and governs the four quarters. His spirit is Quelling Star [Saturn]. His animal is the Yellow Dragon. His musical note is *gong;* his days are *wu* and *ji.*

The West is Metal. Its god is Shao Hao. His assistant is Ru Shou. He grasps the T-square and governs autumn. His spirit is Great White [Venus]. His animal is the White Tiger. His musical note is *shang;* his days are *geng* and *xin.*

The North is Water. Its god is Zhuan Xu. His assistant is Xuan Ming. He grasps the

14. Tai Hao, Gou Mang, and the other planetary gods and "assistants" are mythical figures; many also appear in the poems of the *Chuci.* For further identifications, see the "Glossary of Names" in Hawkes 1985, 322–45.

15. This and the following four paragraphs are quoted verbatim from the Mawangdui manuscript text known as "Wuxingzhan." See Xi Zezong 席澤宗, "Zhongguo tianwenxue shi de yige zhongyao faxian—Mawangdui Hanmu boshu zhong de 'Wuxingzhan'" 中國天文學史的一個重要發現—馬王堆漢墓帛書中的五星占 (An important discovery for the history of Chinese astronomy—the Mawangdui silk manuscript "Prognostications of the Five Planets"), in *Zhongguo tianwenxue shi wenji* 中國天文學史文集 (Beijing: Science Press, 1978), 14–33. On the motions of the five planets, 3.7 through 3.11 are similar to but less detailed than the corresponding sections of the "Wuxingzhan."

16. Yan Di 炎帝, the "Flame Emperor," is a semidivine figure who figures variously in different myths. In some stories he is credited with having invented the use of fire for humankind, and in others he is depicted as a rebel against the legitimate authority of the Yellow Emperor, who is sometimes identified as his half brother.

weight and governs winter. His spirit is Chronograph Star [Mercury]. His animal is the Dark Warrior. His musical note is *yu*; his days are *ren* and *gui*. [3/20/1–6]

3.7

When *taiyin* 太陰 is in any of the four midpoints, the planet Jupiter passes through three of the lunar lodges.

When *taiyin* is in any of the four hooks, the planet Jupiter passes through two of the lunar lodges.

Two times eight is sixteen;[17] three times four is twelve. [16 + 12 = 28] Therefore, in twelve years [Jupiter] traverses [all] twenty-eight lunar lodges. The [average] daily motion [of Jupiter] is [approximately] one-twelfth of a [Chinese] degree. In one year, [Jupiter traverses] $30\frac{7}{16}^{d}$. In twelve years, [Jupiter] completes a circuit [of the heavens]. [3/20/8–10]

3.8

Mars normally enters the asterism Grand Enclosure in the tenth month. [The corresponding state thereupon] comes under its control. Then it emerges, passing through the lunar lodges in turn. [Mars] is in charge of states that lack the Way. It

causes disorder, causes violence;
causes sickness, causes death;
causes famine, and causes warfare.

Its leavings and enterings [of lunar lodges] are irregular. Its color perceptibly varies. [Its color] is sometimes visible and sometimes unnoticeable. [3/20/12–13]

3.9

On the day *jiayin* [no. 51], in the first year of the Epoch, Saturn is in [the lunar lodge] Dipper. Each year Saturn moves through one lunar lodge. If Saturn should be [in a particular lunar lodge] but is not there, the state [corresponding to that lodge] will lose its land. If Saturn ought not yet to be [in a particular lunar lodge] but [already] occupies it, the state corresponding to that lodge] will increase its land and [its] crops will ripen. The [average] daily motion [of Saturn] is one-twenty-eighth of a [Chinese] degree. Its annual motion is $13\frac{5}{112}^{d}$. In twenty-eight years it completes a circuit [of the heavens]. [3/20/13–15]

17. Each of the "four hooks" defines two points on the horizon, and Jupiter passes through two lunar lodges for each of those points. Thus four hooks equal eight points and therefore the "two times eight is sixteen" of the text. See Major 1993, 34, fig. 2.2.

3.10

In the first month, on the day *jiayin*, in the first year of the Epoch, Venus rises at dawn in the east in [the lunar lodge] Encampment. After 240 days, it disappears. It remains hidden for 120 days and then appears in the evening in the west. After 240 days, it disappears. After thirty-five days, it once again appears in the east. It appears in *chen* or *xu* and disappears in *chou* or *wei*. When [Venus] should appear but does not appear, or should not yet disappear but does disappear, throughout the world armies will be withdrawn. When [Venus] should disappear but does not disappear, or should not yet appear but does appear, throughout the world armies will set forth [on campaigns]. [3/20/15–18]

3.11

[The movements of] Mercury correspond exactly to the four seasons. Normally in the second month, at the spring equinox, it appears in [the lunar lodges] Stride and Bond. In the fifth month, at the summer solstice, it appears in [the lunar lodges] Eastern Well and Ghost Bearer. In the eighth month, at the autumn equinox, it appears in [the lunar lodges] Horn and Neck. In the eleventh month, at the winter solstice, it appears in [the lunar lodges] Dipper and Ox Leader. [Mercury] appears in [the chronograms] *chen* or *xu* and disappears in *chou* or *wei*. It appears for twenty days and then disappears.

At dawn it attends [the sun] in the east;
in the evening it attends [the sun] in the west.

If in any season it does not appear, that season will be unfortunate. If it does not appear for four seasons, throughout the world there will be famine. [3/20/20–23]

3.12

What are the eight winds?

Forty-five days after the winter solstice arrives, the Regular [northeast] Wind arrives.[18]

Forty-five days after the Regular Wind arrives, the Brightly Abundant [east] Wind arrives.

Forty-five days after the Brightly Abundant Wind arrives, the Clear Bright [southeast] Wind arrives.

Forty-five days after the Clear Bright Wind arrives, the Sunshine [south] Wind arrives.

18. These wind names are repeated in 4.18. A different list of wind names, perhaps representing an alternative tradition, is found in 4.1.

Forty-five days after the Sunshine Wind arrives, the Cooling [southwest] Wind arrives.

Forty-five days after the Cooling Wind arrives, the Changhe [west] Wind[19] arrives.

Forty-five days after the Changhe wind arrives, the Buzhou [northwest] Wind[20] arrives.

Forty-five days after the Buzhou wind arrives, the Broadly Expansive [north] wind arrives.

When the Regular Wind arrives, release those imprisoned for minor crimes and send away those [foreign intruders] who had been detained.

When the Brightly Abundant Wind arrives, rectify boundaries of fiefs and repair the fields.

When the Clear Bright Wind arrives, issue presents of silk cloth and send embassies to the Lords of the Land.

When the Sunshine Wind arrives, confer honors on men of position and reward the meritorious.

When the Cooling Wind arrives, report on the Potency of the earth and sacrifice at the four suburbs.

When the Changhe wind arrives, store away the suspended [bells] and hanging [chimestones]; *qin* and *se* [stringed instruments] [must be] unstrung.

When the Buzhou wind arrives, repair palaces and dwellings and improve dikes and walls.

When the Broadly Extensive Wind arrives, close up gates and bridges and execute punishments. [3/20/25–30]

3.13

What are the five offices?

That of the east is Agriculture.

That of the south is the Military Command.

That of the west is Public Order.

That of the north is Public Works.

That of the center is Metropolitan Affairs. [3/21/1]

What are the six departments? They are *ziwu, chouwei, yinshen, maoyu, chenxu,* and *sihai.*[21] [3/21/3]

The Grand Enclosure is the hall of the Grand One.[22]

19. Changhe 閶闔 is the name of the Gate of Heaven, the portal through which communication between Heaven and Earth is possible. See 4.3.

20. Mount Buzhou 不周 is the pivot of Heaven, around which the cosmos rotates. See 4.3 and chap. 4, n. 10.

21. Six imaginary diametral lines that span the celestial circle.

22. Yu Yan suggests that here *taiyi* 太一 should read *tianzi* 天子, "Son of Heaven." Wang Yinzhi suggests *wudi* 五帝, "five emperors" or "five thearchs." The suggested emendations are plausible but

> The Purple Palace is the dwelling place of the Grand One.
> Chariot Frame is the residence of the imperial concubine.
> The Pool of Xian is a park of water and fishes.
> The Heavenly Slope is the gate tower of the assembled spirits.
> The Four Guardians are those who bestow rewards and punishments.

The Grand Enclosure governs the Vermilion Bird. [3/21/5–7]

3.14

The Purple Palace controls the Dipper and turns to the left. The sun moves 1^d [in relation to the fixed stars] each time it makes a revolution across the heavens. At the winter solstice, the sun is in [the constellation] Lofty Wolf Mountain. The sun shifts 1^d per day. Therefore, after it has traveled $182\frac{5}{8}^d$, at the summer solstice the sun is in [the constellation] Ox Head Mountain. Then it turns back and, [after traveling through] $365\frac{1}{4}^d$, completes one year. [3/21/7–9]

3.15

At the beginning of a Heavenly Singularity Epoch, the first [civil] month being established in *yin,* the sun and moon together enter the fifth degree of [the lunar lodge] Encampment. Seventy-six years after the beginning of the Heavenly Singularity Epoch, the sun and moon again enter the fifth degree of Encampment, without any remainder fraction. This is called an Era. Twenty Eras make 1,520 years, called a Grand Conclusion. [After three Grand Conclusions], the sun, moon, and asterisms all recommence in *jiayin.* [3/21/9–11]

3.16

The daily motion of the sun is 1^d. Thus in a year there will be a surplus of $\frac{1}{4}^d$. Thus after four years, there will be an accumulation of 1,461 days, and [the fractional days] will come together again [to make a full day]. Thus after eighty years, [the days of the sixty-day cycle] will be repeated [on the same days of the year]. [3/21/11–13]

Thus it is said[23] that

> *ziwu* and *maoyu* are the two diametral chords;
> *chouyin, chensi, weishen,* and *xuhai* are the Four Hooks.

---

not compelling. *Taiyi,* the "Grand One," is a philosophical/cosmological concept, a star, and a god. All the places mentioned here (Grand Enclosure, etc.) are constellations; thus the location of Taiyi among them is reasonable within the framework of the cosmology presented here. See Zhang Shuangdi 1997, 1:290n.78.

23. Rejecting Lau's (HNZ 3/21/12–13) suggestion in the concordance text that *gu yue* 故曰 be emended to *gu ri* 故日 and attached to the end of the preceding paragraph.

Northeast is the binding cord[24] of Returning Accretion;
Southwest is the binding cord of Reverting Yang;
Southeast is the binding cord of Perpetual Ocean;
Northwest is the binding cord of Penetrating Cleft. [3/21/15–16]

When the sun is at the winter solstice, the Dipper [points] north, exactly on the [north–south] marking-cord line. The yin *qi* is at its maximum, and the yang *qi* begins to grow. Thus it is said that the winter solstice produces accretion.[25]

When the sun is at the summer solstice, the Dipper [points] south, exactly on the [north–south] marking-cord line. The yang *qi* is at its maximum, and the yin *qi* begins to grow. Thus it is said that the summer solstice produces recision.

When the yin *qi* is at its maximum, north is at its farthest extent [from the sun]. The Northern Limit penetrates down to the Yellow Springs. Hence one must not cut into the earth or bore wells. The myriad creatures are shut up in hibernation, and insects are head down in their burrows. Thus it is said that accretion is in the Room.

When the yang *qi* is at its maximum, south is at its farthest extent [from the sun]. The Southern Limit penetrates upward to the Vermilion Heaven. Hence one must not level hills or raise roof beams. The myriad creatures flourish and increase, and the five grains grow abundantly. Thus it is said that accretion is in the Field. [3/21/18–21]

When the sun is at the winter solstice, fire follows it.
When the sun is at the summer solstice, water follows it.

Thus,

in the fifth month, fire is at its maximum and water begins to seep out.
In the eleventh month, water is at its maximum and fire arises.[26]

Yang *qi* produces fire; yin *qi* produces water.

[Because] water [begins to be] dominant, the summer solstice is damp.
[Because] fire is [begins to be] dominant, the winter solstice is parched.
When [the weather] is parched, charcoal is light.
When [the weather] is damp, charcoal is heavy. [3/21/23–25]

When the sun is at the winter solstice, wells are full of water and basins overflow. Goats shed their hair, deer's antlers fall away, and magpies nest. An eight-foot gnomon[27] casts a shadow thirteen feet long [at noon].

---

24. The four "corner" directions (northeast, southeast, southwest, and northwest) are conceived of as cords (*wei* 維) binding the cosmos together and restraining the movements of yin and yang. See 1.1.

25. The terms "accretion" and "recision," *de* 德 and *xing* 刑, in this passage and after refer to the accumulation and paring away of the yang *qi* throughout the year. For an extended discussion of this idea, see John S. Major, "The Meaning of *Hsing-te*," in *Chinese Ideas About Nature and Society: Studies in Honour of Derk Bodde*, ed. Charles Le Blanc and Susan Blader (Hong Kong: Hong Kong University Press, 1987), 281–91.

26. Reading sheng 勝 as sheng 升, as suggested by Yu Yue. See Lau, HNZ, 21n.13.

27. A *biao* 表, "gnomon," is a straight stick or rod designed to cast a solar shadow. Gnomons used in sundials are aimed at the celestial north pole. Gnomons used to find direction (e.g., finding a true north–south line by bisecting the angle of shadows cast at sunrise and sunset) or to track the seasons (by measuring the length of the noon shadow) are usually exactly vertical.

When the sun is at the summer solstice, the yellow floods enrich the fields, and mineral essences emerge from the soil. Cicadas begin to sing, and the half-summer herb grows; flying insects do not bite foals and calves, and birds of prey do not seize nestlings. An eight-foot gnomon casts a shadow one foot and five inches [i.e., 1½ feet] long [at noon].

When the gnomon shadow is long, yin *qi* is dominant.
When the gnomon shadow is short, yang *qi* is dominant.
When the yin *qi* is dominant, there is water.
When the yang *qi* is dominant, there is drought. [3/22/1–4]

3.17

Yin and yang, recision and accretion, have seven habitations. What are these seven habitations? They are the Room, the Hall, the Court, the Gate, the Lane, the Road, and the Field. In the eleventh month, accretion dwells in the Room for thirty days, fifteen days before the winter solstice and fifteen days after. Thereafter it shifts its place every thirty days.

When accretion is in the Room, recision is in the Field.
When accretion is in the Hall, recision is in the Road.
When accretion is in the Court, recision is in the Lane.

When yin and yang are of equal power, then recision and accretion are together in the Gate. In the eighth month and the second month, the *qi* of yin and yang is equal, and day and night are of equal length. Thus it is said that recision and accretion are together in the Gate.

When accretion is in the south, there is birth;
When recision is in the south, there is death.

Thus,

at the meeting [in the Gate] at the second month, the myriad creatures come to life.
At the meeting [in the Gate] in the eighth month, the herbs and trees begin to die. [3/22/6–9]

3.18

Between the two binding cords is a span of 91⁵⁄₁₆^{d}. The sun's daily motion being 1^{d}, fifteen days makes one node [*jie* 節]. Thus are produced twenty-four seasonal alterations.

When the [handle of the] Dipper points to *zi* [at midnight], it is the Winter Solstice [node]. Its sound is like [the pitch pipe] Yellow Bell.[28]

28. Lau (HNZ 3/22/12–29) emends the text here and throughout the passage relating to the twenty-four solar nodes to shift the pitch-pipe notes by one unit in each case. For example, in this

After fifteen days, [the handle of the Dipper at midnight] points to *gui*. This is the Lesser Cold node. Its sound is like [the pitch pipe] Responsive Bell.

After fifteen more days, [the handle of the Dipper at midnight] points to *chou*. This is the Greater Cold node. Its sound is like [the pitch pipe] Tireless.

After fifteen more days, [the handle of the Dipper at midnight] points to the binding cord of Returning Accretion, and there is a surplus of yin in the land. Thus it is said that the forty-sixth day from the winter solstice marks the Beginning of Spring [node], when the yang *qi* dispels the cold. Its sound is like [the pitch pipe] Southern Regulator.

After fifteen more days, [the handle of the Dipper at midnight] points to *yin*. This is the Rain node. Its sound is like [the pitch pipe] Tranquil Pattern.

After fifteen more days, [the handle of the Dipper at midnight] points to *jia*. This is the Awakening of Insects node. Its sound is like [the pitch pipe] Forest Bell.

After fifteen more days, [the handle of the Dipper at midnight] points to *mao*. Thus it [is said that the forty-sixth day after the Beginning of Spring][29] is called the Spring Equinox [node]. Thunder is abroad. Its sound is like [the pitch pipe] Luxuriant.

After fifteen more days, [the handle of the Dipper at midnight] points to *yi*. This is the node of the Clear Bright wind-maximum. Its sound is like [the pitch pipe] Median Regulator.

After fifteen more days, [the handle of the Dipper at midnight] points to *chen*. This is the Grain Rain node. Its sound is like [the pitch pipe] Maiden Cleanliness.

After fifteen more days [the handle of the Dipper at midnight] points to the binding cord of Perpetual Ocean, and the portion [of the year allotted to] spring reaches its limit. Thus it is said that that the forty-sixth day [after the spring equinox] is the Beginning of Summer [node]. The great winds end. Its sound is like [the pitch pipe] Pinched Bell.

After fifteen more days, [the handle of the Dipper at midnight] points to *si*. This is the Lesser Fullness node. Its sound is like [the pitch pipe] Great Budding.

After fifteen more days, [the handle of the Dipper at midnight] points to *bing*. This is the Grain in Ear node. Its sound is like [the pitch pipe] Great Regulator.

After fifteen more days, [the handle of the Dipper at midnight] points to *wu*. Yang *qi* reaches its maximum. Thus it is said that the forty-sixth day [after the beginning of summer] marks the Summer Solstice [node]. Its sound is like [the pitch pipe] Yellow Bell.

---

line he emends Yellow Bell to read Responsive Bell and similarly throughout the passage. We believe that those emendations are not soundly based, and so we follow the original, unemended text in this translation.

29. Adding this line of text to maintain the pattern of the passage overall.

After fifteen more days, [the handle of the Dipper at midnight] points to *ding*. This is the Lesser Heat node. Its sound is like [the pitch pipe] Great Regulator.

After fifteen more days [the handle of the Dipper at midnight] points to *wei*. This is the Great Heat node. Its sound is like [the pitch pipe] Great Budding.

After fifteen more days [the handle of the Dipper at midnight] points to the binding cord of Reverting Yang. Thus it is said that forty-six days after [the summer solstice] is the Beginning of Autumn [node]. This is the node of the Cool Wind wind-maximum. Its sound is like [the pitch pipe] Pinched Bell.

After fifteen more days [the handle of the Dipper at midnight] points to *shen*. This is the End of Heat node. Its sound is like [the pitch pipe] Maiden Cleanliness.

After fifteen more days [the handle of the Dipper at midnight] points to *geng*. This is the Descent of White Dew node. Its sound is like [the pitch pipe] Median Regulator.

After fifteen more days, [the handle of the Dipper at midnight] points to *you*, on the central marking line. Thus it is called the Autumn Equinox [node]. Thunder ceases, and swarming insects turn toward the north. Its sound is like [the pitch pipe] Luxuriant.

After fifteen more days, [the handle of the Dipper at midnight] points to *xin*. This is the Cold Dew node. Its sound is like [the pitch pipe] Forest Bell.

After fifteen more days, [the handle of the Dipper at midnight] points to *xu*. This is the Descent of Hoarfrost node. Its sound is like [the pitch pipe] Tranquil Pattern.

After fifteen more days, [the handle of the Dipper at midnight] points to the binding cord of Perpetual Cleft. Thus the portion [of the year allotted to] autumn comes to its end. Thus it is said that the forty-sixth day [after the autumn equinox] is the Beginning of Winter [node]. Herbs, trees, and flowers die. Its sound is like [the pitch pipe] Southern Regulator.

After fifteen more days, [the handle of the Dipper at midnight] points to *hai*. This is the Lesser Snow node. Its sound is like [the pitch pipe] Tireless.

After fifteen more days, [the handle of the Dipper at midnight] points to *ren*. This is the Great Snow node. Its sound is like [the pitch pipe] Responsive Bell.

After fifteen more days, [the handle of the Dipper at midnight again] points to *zi*. Therefore it is said that

yang is born in *zi*;
yin is born in *wu*.

Yang is born in *zi*. Therefore in the eleventh month, the sun is at the winter solstice; magpies begin to nest; and human *qi* accumulates in the head.

Yin is born in *wu*. Therefore in the fifth month lesser punishments are carried out. Shepherd's purse and wheat stop growing and wither. The herbs and trees that sprouted in the winter must die. [3/22/11–29]

3.19

The handle of the Dipper makes the Lesser Year. In the first [civil] month [the Dipper] is established in *yin.* The months move from the left through the twelve chronograms.[30]

The Pool of Xian makes the Greater Year. The second month is established in *mao.* The moon moves from the right through the four quadrants. When it finishes, it begins again.

As for the Greater Year:

one who faces is it humiliated;
one who turns away from it is strong;
one who is on its left is in decline;
one who is on its right attains glory.
When the Lesser Year is in the southeast, there is birth;
when it is in the northwest, there is death.

This is what is meant by the saying

It must not be met, but it may be turned away from;
it must not be to the left, but it may be to the right.[31] [3/23/1–4]

The Great Season is [governed by] the Pool of Xian. The Lesser Season is that of the month establishments. The binding cords of Heaven establish the Epoch, which always begins with *yin.* Arising, [*taisui*] moves to the right for one year and then shifts. After twelve years, it [completes] a heavenly circuit and then begins again. [3/23/6–7]

In the winter of the first year of [the King of] Huainan, the Grand One[32] was in [the cyclical year] *bingzi.* The winter solstice was on [the cyclical day] *jiawu;* [the node] Beginning of Spring [began] on [the cyclical day] *bingzi.* [3/23/9]

3.20

One yin and one yang make two *qi.*
Two yang and one yin make three *qi.*
Combining these *qi* makes the [pentatonic] notes.
Combining the yin makes yang.
Combining [this number with] the yang makes the pitch pipes.

Thus there are five notes and six pitch pipes.

30. The "chronograms" (*chen* 辰) are the twelve earthly branches considered as markers of calendrical time: the twelve months distributed around the horizon circle (and around the Earth plate of the astronomical/astrological instrument known as the *shi* 式, "cosmograph"). See Major 1993, 34, fig. 2.2.

31. Although the details are obscure, this whole passage is an example of Han "military astrology" dealing in the vulnerability of states to attack, depending on their geographical location in relation to certain heavenly bodies and calendrical periods.

32. Rejecting Lau's (HNZ 3/23/9) emendation of *taiyi* 太一 to *tianyi* 天一.

The notes double to produce the number of the days.
The pitch pipes double to produce the earthly branches.
Thus there are ten days and twelve branches. [3/23/11–12]

3.21

The moon's daily motion is 13 26/76^{d}. A lunar month is twenty-nine and 499/940 days. Twelve months make a year. The [tropic] year is ten and 827/940 days longer [than the lunar year]. Hence in nineteen years there are seven intercalary months. [3/23/12–14]

3.22

The days of the winter solstice take the branches *zi* and *wu*.
The days of the summer solstice take the branches *mao* and *you*.
Adding three days to the [branches of] the winter solstice yields the days of the summer solstice. The whole year shifts by six days and begins again with *renwu*.

At the winter solstice, [the cyclical day] *jiazi* receives control. [The phase] wood is used in all affairs, and the smoke of fires is bluegreen.

After seventy-two days, *bingzi* receives control. [The phase] fire is used in all affairs, and the smoke of fires is vermilion.

After seventy-two days, *wuzi* receives control. [The phase] earth is used in all affairs, and the smoke of fires is yellow.

After seventy-two days, *gengzi* receives control. [The phase] metal is used in all affairs, and the smoke of fires is white.

After seventy-two days, *renzi* receives control. [The phase] water is used in all affairs, and the smoke of fires is black.

After seventy-two [more] days, the year comes to an end, and *gengwu* takes control. The year shifts by six days so that the number may extend [to the full count of 366]. After ten years, [the sequence] begins again with *jiazi*.

When *jiazi* is in control, act gently and graciously, and relax the many prohibitions. Open doors and covers, and penetrate barriers. It is prohibited to cut down trees.

When *bingzi* is in control, promote the worthy and the good, and reward the meritorious. Enfeoff nobles and distribute wealth.

When *wuzi* is in control, nourish the old and the widowed, distribute food alms, and bestow grace and favor.

When *gengzi* is in control, improve walls and enclosures, strengthen city walls and fortifications, scrutinize prohibitions [with a view toward strengthening them], refurbish the armor of the troops, admonish officials, and punish the lawless.

When *renzi* is in control, shut doors and gates, investigate strangers, execute punishments, kill the condemned, [command the people to] rest within their gates and under the beams of their roofs, and prohibit wandering outside [the city walls]. [3/23/16–23]

The *qi* of *jiazi* is dry and turbid.
The *qi* of *bingzi* is dry and bright.
The *qi* of *wuzi* is damp and turbid.
The *qi* of *gengzi* is dry and cold.
The *qi* of *renzi* is clear and cold. [3/23/25]

3.23

When [the day designated] *bingzi* opposes [the "season" governed by] *jiazi*, hibernating insects hatch forth prematurely, and there is [unseasonably] early thunder.

When *wuzi* opposes *jiazi*, the pregnant suffer calamities, eggs are infertile, and birds and insects suffer great injuries.

When *gengzi* opposes *jiazi*, there will be military operations.
When *renzi* opposes *jiazi*, there will be spring frosts.
When *wuzi* opposes *bingzi*, there will be claps of thunder.
When *gengzi* opposes *bingzi*, there will be bolts of lightning.
When *renzi* opposes *bingzi*, there will be hail.
When *jiazi* opposes *bingzi*, there will be earthquakes.
When *gengzi* opposes *wuzi*, the five grains will suffer calamities.
When *renzi* opposes *wuzi*, there will be cold spells in summer, with rain and frost.
When *jiazi* opposes *wuzi*, silkworms will not mature.
When *bingzi* opposes *wuzi*, there will be great drought; aquatic grasses will dry out entirely.
When *renzi* opposes *gengzi*, fish will not grow.
When *jiazi* opposes *gengzi*, herbaceous plants and trees die and then sprout again.
When *bingzi* opposes *gengzi*, herbaceous plants and trees bloom for a second time [out of season].
When *wuzi* opposes *gengzi*, some of the annual harvest will preserved and some lost.
When *jiazi* opposes *renzi*, [creatures] will not hibernate [as they should].
When *bingzi* opposes *renzi*, there will be meteors.
When *wuzi* opposes *renzi*, in winter insects depart from their places.
When *gengzi* opposes *renzi*, there will be thunder in winter. [3/23/25–3/24/5]

3.24

In the third [and final] month of spring, abundant thunder sounds forth, bringing in the rains.

In the third [and final] month of autumn, the *qi* of Earth has not yet become [completely] quiescent, and one gathers in the killed things.[33] All crawling things become torpid and hide away, and country dwellers shut their gates. Gray Woman[34] comes out and brings down frost and snow.

Thus the *qi* of the twelve times of the year progress until they reach an end [again] in the second month of spring, when what has been stored away is received forth [again] and the cold is shut away. Then Tranquil Woman drums and sings to regulate the harmony of Heaven and to make grow the hundred kinds of cereals, the beasts and birds, and the herbs and trees.

In the first month of summer the crops ripen; the cries of pheasants and pigeons become prolonged, causing the emperor to look forward to the annual harvest. Thus,

> if Heaven does not give forth yin, the myriad things cannot be born;
> if Earth does not give forth yang, the myriad things cannot grow to maturity.
> Heaven is round;
> Earth is square;

the Way is exactly in the middle.

> The sun [produces] accretion;
> the moon [produces] paring away.
> When the moon reverts [in its course], the myriad creatures die.
> When the sun attains its apogee, the myriad creatures are born.
> Separated from mountains, the *qi* of mountains is hidden away.
> Separated from water, aquatic insects become dormant.
> Separated from trees, leaves wither.

When the sun is not seen for five days, [the ruler] will lose his throne. Even a [ruler who is a] sage cannot withstand this. [3/24/7–12]

3.25

The sun rises up from the Bright Valley, bathes in the Pool of Xian, and rests in the Fusang Tree. This is called Dawn Light.

Ascending the Fusang Tree, it thereupon commences its journey. This is called Emergent Brightness.

> [When the sun] reaches the Bent Slope, this is called Dawn Brilliance.
> [When the sun] reaches the Steaming Spring, this is called the Morning Meal.

33. *Nai shou qi sha* 乃收其殺. It is not clear what is meant by this unusual phrase; perhaps it is a reference to bringing in game that has been killed in the hunt. Another possible interpretation would be "[the authorities] take charge of those who are to be executed."

34. Qing Nü 青女. The color word *qing* embraces a range of colors from blue to green; our usual translation is "bluegreen." But with respect to horses, dogs, and other mammals, it means "gray," a color that also would be appropriate for what is apparently a mythical winter goddess or fairy.

[When the sun] reaches the Mulberry Field, this is called the Late-Morning Meal.
[When the sun] reaches the Balance Beam of Yang, this is called Within the Angle.
[When the sun] reaches Kun Wu, this is called the Exact Center.
[When the sun] reaches the Bird Roost, this is called the Lesser Return.
[When the sun] reaches the Valley of Grief, this is called the Dinner Hour.
[When the sun] reaches Woman's Sequence, this is called the Great Return.
[When the sun] reaches the Angle of the Abyss, this is called the Raised Pestle.
[When the sun] reaches Carriage Stone, this is called the Descending Pestle.

[When the sun] reaches the Fountain of Grief, it halts; its female attendant rests her horses. This is called the Suspended Chariot.

[When the sun] reaches the Abyss of Anxiety, this is called Yellow Dusk.
[When the sun] reaches the Vale of Obscurity, this is called Definite Dusk.

The sun enters the floodwaters of the Abyss of Anxiety; sunrise emerges from the drainage stream of the Vale of Obscurity. [The sun] travels over the nine continents, [passing through] seven resting places, [covering a distance of] 507,309 *li*. The divisions [of its journey] make dawn, daylight, dusk, and night. [3/24/14–22]

3.26

At the summer solstice, yin [begins to be] ascendant over yang. For this reason, the myriad creatures come to an end and die.
At the winter solstice, yang [begins to be] ascendant over yin. For this reason, the myriad creatures lift up their heads and come to life.
Daylight is the portion of yang;
night is the portion of yin.
Thus when the yang *qi* dominates, days are long and nights are short.
When the yin *qi* dominates, days are short and nights are long.

Appearing in *mao* and *you* [at the equinoxes], yin and yang divide day and night equally. [3/24/24–3/25/2]

Thus it is said that

when the compass is born, the square dies;
when the balance beam[35] is [being] set up, the weight[36] is hidden away;

35. The *heng* 衡, "balance beam," is the horizontal member in a hand scale. The *heng* works in conjunction with a *quan* 權, "weight."

36. *Quan* 權 means a "weight." When using a hand scale, the object to be weighed is suspended from one arm of the balance, and a weight or combination of weights is suspended from the other arm. The weights are equal when the balance beam achieves a stable horizontal position. In the type of scale known as a steelyard, the object to be weighed is suspended from one arm of the beam, while a weight is moved along the other arm of the balance beam until the latter achieves a stable horizontal position.

when the marking cord occupies the center, it [marks out] the foundation of the four seasons.[37] ([3/25/14–15])

3.27

The Celestial Thearch stretches out the four binding cords of Heaven, and employs the Dipper to revolve [through] them. In a month it shifts by one chronogram, its location being successively displaced. In the first [civil] month, it points to *yin;* in the eleventh month it points to *zi.* It completes a circle in one year; finishing, it begins again.

[In the first civil month, the Dipper] points to *yin.* The myriad creatures stir like earthworms underground. The pitch pipes take the note Great Budding. Great Budding means that there are buds but they have not yet emerged.[38]

[In the second civil month, the Dipper] points to *mao. Mao* means "burgeoning," thus [living things] burgeon forth. The pitch pipes take the note Pinched Bell. Pinched Bell means that seeds first begin to swell.

[In the third civil month the Dipper] points to *chen. Chen* means "to stir up." The pitch pipes take the note Maiden Cleanliness. Maiden Cleanliness means that what is withered is done away with and the new comes forth.

[In the fourth civil month the Dipper] points to *si* [fetus]. There being a fetus, there is sure to be birth in consequence. The pitch pipes take the note Median Regulator. Median Regulator means that the center grows large.

[In the fifth civil month the Dipper] points to *wu. Wu* means "to oppose." The pitch pipes take the note Luxuriant. Luxuriant means that all is tranquil and fitting.

[In the sixth civil month the Dipper] points to *wei. Wei* means "flavor." The pitch pipes take the note Forest Bell. Forest Bell means to extend forth and then stop.

[In the seventh civil month the Dipper] points to *shen. Shen* means "chanting." The pitch pipes take the note Tranquil Pattern. Tranquil Pattern means that the pattern is changed. The [force of] accretion is expunged [from the annual cycle].

[In the eighth civil month the Dipper] points to *you. You* means "satiety." The pitch pipes take the note Southern Regulator. Southern Regulator means that it is recognized that the satiety is great.

The weight of the object being weighed then can be read on a scale inscribed onto the surface of the beam. Recent scholarship suggests that the steelyard became common in China only from the Latter Han dynasty onward. See Griet Vankeerberghen, "Choosing Balance: Weighing (*quan*) as a Metaphor for Action in Early Chinese Texts," *Early China* 30 (2005): 47–89, esp. 48–53.

Quan also sometimes refers to the plumb bob of a plumb line, rather than a weight for weighing things. The word also has a number of extended meanings, such as "heft" and "expediency," beyond its basic meaning of a "weight" as a physical object. See app. A.

37. This line has been transposed to here from 3/25/14–15, where it is clearly out of place. For textual notes relating to this and the following section, see also Major 1993, 299.

38. For the numerous puns, both phonetic and logographic, that give this section its meaning and make it very difficult to translate, see Major 1993, 299–300.

[In the ninth civil month the Dipper] points to *xu*. *Xu* means "destruction." The pitch pipes take the note Tireless. Tireless means that there is bringing in without satisfaction.

[In the tenth civil month the Dipper] points to *hai*. *Hai* means "hindrance." The pitch pipes take the note Responsive Bell. Responsive Bell means to respond to the bell.

[In the eleventh civil month the Dipper] points to *zi*. *Zi* means "black." The pitch pipes take the note Yellow Bell. Yellow Bell means that the bell is beginning to be yellow.

[In the twelfth civil month the Dipper] points to *chou*. *Chou* means "to tie." The pitch pipes take the note Great Regulator. Great Regulator means to go out one after the other. [3/25/4–13]

3.28

Thus it is said, "The Way begins with one." One [alone], however, does not give birth. Therefore it divided into yin and yang. From the harmonious union of yin and yang, the myriad things were produced. Thus it is said,

> "One produced two,
> two produced three,
> three produced the myriad things."[39]

[With regard to] Heaven and Earth, three months make one season. Thus a sacrifice of three [types or portions of] cooked grains are used in mourning rites. The year continues for three shifts [of seasons] to make the seasonal nodes [complete their cycle]. Armies emphasize three signal flags in order to maintain control.[40]

Using three to examine matters: $3 \times 3 = 9$. Thus the Yellow Bell pitch pipe is nine inches long and harmonizes with the note *gong*. Furthermore, $9 \times 9 = 81$. Thus the number of the Yellow Bell is established therein. Yellow is the color of the Potency of Earth; the bell is that by which the [seeds of] *qi* are sown. At the winter solstice the *qi* of accretion produces Earth; the color of Earth is yellow. Thus the [note of the winter solstice] is called Yellow Bell.

The number of pitch pipes is six, classified as female and male [for a total of twelve]. Thus it is said there are twelve bells to act as adjuncts to the twelve months. Each of the twelve is based on three. Thus if one sets up [the number] one and triples it eleven times [i.e., 3^{11}], the total is 177,147. The Great Number of the Yellow Bell is thereby revealed. [3/25/17–23]

---

39. *Laozi* 42.
40. Following the original wording of the text, rather than the emendation suggested by Lau.

3.29

There are twelve pitch pipes.

Yellow Bell makes the note *gong.*
Great Budding makes the note *shang.*
Maiden Cleanliness makes the note *jue.*
Forest Bell makes the note *zhi.*
Southern Regulator makes the note *yu.*
Matters are brought to completion by means of three;
Notes are established as [all together] five.

3 + 5 = 8. Creatures born from eggs have eight bodily orifices. This was the beginning of the pitch pipes. [The ancients] recorded the sounds of the phoenix; therefore the notes are born from eight. [3/25/23–25]

Yellow Bell makes the note *gong; gong* is the sovereign of the notes. Thus Yellow Bell is established in *zi;* its number is 81, and it governs the eleventh month.

Descending, [Yellow Bell] produces Forest Bell. The number of Forest Bell is 54 [81 × ⅔]; it governs the sixth month.

Ascending, Great Budding is produced. Its number is 72 [54 × 4/3]; it governs the first month.

Descending, Southern Regulator is produced. Its number is 48 [72 × ⅔]; it governs the eighth month.

Ascending, Maiden Cleanliness is produced. Its number is 64 [48 × 4/3]; it governs the third month.

Descending, Responsive Bell is produced. Its number is 42 [64 × ⅔]; it governs the tenth month.

Ascending, Luxuriant is produced. Its number is 57 [42 × 4/3 + 1]; it governs the fifth month.

Ascending, Great Regulator is produced. Its number is 76 [57 × 4/3]; it governs the twelfth month.

Descending, Tranquil Pattern is produced. Its number is 51 [76 × ⅔]; it governs the seventh month.

Ascending, Pinched Bell is produced. Its number is 68 [51 × 4/3]; it governs the second month.

Descending, Tireless is produced. Its number is 45 [68 × ⅔]; it governs the ninth month.

Ascending, Median Regulator is produced. Its number is 60 [45 × 4/3]; it governs the fourth month.

[Beyond this] limit, nothing [further] is produced. [3/26/1–7]

Those pipes that descend are [created by multiplying the previous pipe's number] by ⅔.

Those pipes that ascend are [created by multiplying the previous pipe's number] by 4/3.[41] [3/26/24]

41. This and the previous line have been moved here from 3/26/24, where they are out of place.

3.30

Gong produces *zhi*; *zhi* produces *shang*; *shang* produces *yu*; *yu* produces *jue*. *Jue* produces Maiden Cleanliness.

Maiden Cleanliness produces[42] Responsive Bell. Responsive Bell is comparable[43] to the fundamental note [i.e., Yellow Bell] and thus produces harmony.

Responsive Bell produces Luxuriant. Luxuriant is not comparable to the fundamental note and thus produces discord.

At the winter solstice, the note is like Forest Bell in a flattened tone;

At the summer solstice, the note is like Yellow Bell in a clear tone.[44]

The twelve pitch pipes respond to the alterations of the twenty-four seasonal nodes.

At *jiazi*, Median Regulator moves to *zhi*.

At *bingzi*, Pinched Bell moves to *yu*.

At *wuzi*, Yellow Bell moves to *gong*.

At *gengzi*, Tireless moves to *shang*.

At *renzi*, Tranquil Pattern moves to *jue*. [3/26/7–11]

3.31

In ancient times, weights and measures were created; lightness and heaviness were born from the Way of Heaven.

The length of the Yellow Bell pitch pipe is nine inches. All things are produced by [virtue of] three. [3 × 3 = 9.] 3 × 9 = 27. Thus the width of a standard bolt of cloth is two feet, seven inches.[45] This is the ancient standard.

There are shapes; thus there are [also musical] sounds. The musical notes are mutually produced by [means of] the number eight. Thus the span of a man's arms measures four feet.

A *xun* is double [this length]; thus eight feet make one *xun*. A *xun* is the height of an average man.[46]

The number of the notes is five. Using five to calculate in terms of eight, 5 × 8 = 40. Thus four *zhang* make one *pi*.[47] Therefore, one *pi* is used as [the standard unit in the cloth tax] administration.

---

42. Rejecting Lau's proposed emendation of *sheng* 生 to *zhu* 主.

43. Rejecting Lau's insertion of *bu* 不, "not," in this line.

44. In early Chinese musical terminology, notes could be designated as "turbid" or "muddy" (*zhuo* 濁) or "clear" (*qing* 清). The former were lower in pitch than the latter; so here we might speak of Forest Bell, flat. But the precise meaning of *ruo* and *qing* in ancient musical terminology is uncertain. See app. B.

45. That is, 2.7 *chi* 尺; one Chinese foot is equal to ten inches (*cun* 寸).

46. *Xun* 尋. The Han "foot" (*chi* 尺) was about nine modern inches long; thus eight Han feet equals approximately seventy-two inches, or six feet, probably in fact somewhat taller than the height of an "average man" in Han times. In 7.5, the height of a person is given as seven feet (*chi*)—that is, about five feet, three inches, in today's terms.

47. One *zhang* 仗 is ten feet; one *pi* 匹 is forty feet.

At the autumn equinox, the beards of grain husks are fully grown. When the beards of the husks are fully grown, the grain ripens. The number of the pitch pipes is twelve. Thus [the width of] twelve husk beards [laid side by side] equals one *fen.*[48]

The pitch pipes correspond to the chronograms. The [pentatonic] notes correspond to the sun. The number of the sun is ten. Thus ten *fen* make one inch; ten inches make one foot; and ten feet make one *zhang.*

For those units used to measure weight, twelve millet grains make one *fen.* Twelve *fen* make one *zhu.* Twelve *zhu* make one half-ounce [*ban liang*].[49] The balance beam has a left side and a right side. Therefore, doubling the weight, twenty-four *zhu* make one ounce.

Heaven has four seasons, completing one year. Therefore, reckoning by fours, $4 \times 4 = 16$. Therefore sixteen ounces make one catty. Three months make a season, and thirty days, a month. Therefore thirty catties make one *jun.* Four seasons make one year; therefore four *jun* make one *dan.*[50]

For [units of] musical measurement: One pitch pipe produces five tones; twelve pitch pipes produce sixty tones. Therefore, reckoning by sixes, $6 \times 6 = 36$. Therefore, 360 tones correspond to the days of one year. Thus the number of [notes of] the pitch pipes and [days of] the calendar are in accord with the Way of Heaven and Earth. [3/26/13–24]

3.32

The beginning of the Jovian cycle is established in *jiayin.*

After one completion, it [begins again,] established in *jiaxu.*
After two completions, it [begins again,] established in *jiawu.*
After three completions, it returns to its beginning in *jiayin.*

The year's annual shift is one chronogram. After the [seasonal node] Beginning of Spring, it attains its [proper annual] location by shifting its position [away from the previous one]. When it has moved forward three places and back five, then all matters may be taken in hand. [3/26/26–27]

Where *taiyin* is established, insects lie head down in their burrows and stay quietly [in them]; magpies nest in the countryside and make their homes.

[When] *taiyin* is in *yin,* the vermilion bird is in *mao;* the Hooked Array is in *zi;* the Dark Warrior is in *xu;* the White Tiger is in *you;* the Bluegreen Dragon is in *chen.*

48. Note that *fen* 分, a generic term meaning "portion," is used in 3.31 as both a unit of length (1/10 Han inch) and a unit of weight (1/12 *zhu* 銖, i.e., 1/144 of a half ounce, *ban liang* 半兩). It seems unlikely in fact that twelve husk beards side by side would add up to a breadth as small as 1/10 inch, and it also seems unlikely that the weight of 1/12 *zhu* (in modern terms, equal to about 0.05 gram) could have been measured accurately.

49. A half ounce, *ban liang,* was the weight of a standard Han coin.

50. A "catty" is a *jin* 斤; thirty catties make one *jun* 鈞; four *jun* make one *dan* 石. (The character for *dan* is normally pronounced *shi,* meaning "stone"; it has the unusual pronunciation *dan* when used as a unit of weight.)

If yin is the establishing chronogram, then *mao* is Removal; *chen* is Fullness; *si* is Evenness, governing birth; *wu* is Fixedness; *wei* is Holding Firm, governing pitfalls; *shen* is Breaking, governing the balance beam; *you* is Danger, governing the ladle; *xu* is Completion, governing minor Potency; *hai* is Receiving, governing great Potency; *zi* is Opening, governing *taisui*; *chou* is Closing, governing [. . .].[51] [3/27/1–4]

3.33

When *taiyin* 太陰 is in *yin*, the year is called Shetige.[52] The male [mate] of *taiyin* is Jupiter. It dwells in the [lunar lodges] Dipper and Ox Leader. In the eleventh[53] month, it rises with them in the east at dawn. [The lodges] Eastern Well and Ghost Bearer are opposite [i.e., setting in the west at dawn].

When *taiyin* is in *mao*, the year is called Ming'e.[54] Jupiter dwells in Serving Maid, Emptiness, and Rooftop. In the twelfth month, it rises with them in the east at dawn. Willow, Seven Stars, and Extension are opposite.

When *taiyin* is in *chen*, the year is called Zhixu. Jupiter dwells in Encampment and Eastern Wall. In the first month, it rises with them in the east at dawn. Wings and Chariot Platform are opposite.

When *taiyin* dwells in *si*, the year is called Dahuangluo. Jupiter dwells in Stride and Bond. In the second month, it rises with them in the east at dawn. Horn and Neck are opposite.

When *taiyin* is in *wu*, the year is called Dunzang. Jupiter dwells in Stomach, Pleiades, and Net. In the third month, it rises with them in the east at dawn. Root, Room, and Heart are opposite.

When *taiyin* is in *wei*, the year is called Xiexia. Jupiter dwells in Turtle Beak and Alignment. In the fourth month, it rises with them in the east at dawn. Tail and Winnowing Basket are opposite.

When *taiyin* is in *shen*, the year is called Tuntan. Jupiter dwells in Eastern Well and Ghost Bearer. In the fifth month, it rises with them in the east at dawn. Dipper and Ox Leader are opposite.

---

51. A character is evidently missing here.

52. *Yin* is the third of the earthly branches and thus the third astronomical month (after *zi*, the month in which the winter solstice occurs, and *chou*). In the so-called Xia calendar, the third astronomical month is, by convention, the first civil month; hence *yin* is associated with the first Jovian year, Shetige.

53. In the received text this passage reads "in the eleventh month," and subsequent passages read "twelfth month," "first month," and so on. Lau (HNZ 3/27/5–18) emends this to "first month," "second month," "third month," and so on, on the grounds that the civil year begins with *yin*. But part of the point of this passage is to correlate the civil months of the lunar year with the astronomical months of the solar year: the first astronomical month, *zi*, in which the winter solstice occurs, is the eleventh month of the civil year that begins with *yin*. It is important to remember that this passage, like much of the astronomical information in this chapter, refers primarily to manipulations of the *shi* 式 chronograph rather than to observations of the sky.

54. The character 單 is normally pronounced *dan*. For the name of the second Jovian year, it has the nonstandard pronunciation *ming*; hence, Ming'e.

When *taiyin* is in *you*, the year is called Zuo'e. Jupiter dwells in Willow, Seven Stars, and Extension. In the sixth month, it rises with them in the east at dawn. Serving Maid, Emptiness, and Rooftop are opposite.

When *taiyin* is in *xu*, the year is called Yanmao. Jupiter dwells in Wings and Chariot Platform. In the seventh month, it rises with them in the east at dawn. Encampment and Eastern Wall are opposite.

When *taiyin* is in *hai*, the year is called Dayuanxian. Jupiter dwells in Horn and Neck. In the eighth month, it rises with them in the east at dawn. Stride and Bond are opposite.

When *taiyin* is in *zi*, the year is called Kundun. Jupiter dwells in Root, Room, and Heart. In the ninth month, it rises with them in the east at dawn. Stomach, Pleiades, and Net are opposite.

When *taiyin* is in *chou*, the year is called Chifenruo. Jupiter dwells in Tail and Winnowing Basket. In the tenth month, it rises with them in the east at dawn. Turtle Beak and Alignment are opposite. [3/27/4–18]

3.34

When *taiyin* is in *jiazi*,[55] recision and accretion are harmoniously together in the Eastern [Celestial] Palace. In their normal movements, which cannot be overcome, they are together for four years and then part. They remain parted for sixteen years and then come together again. As for the reason why they part, recision cannot enter the Central Palace but moves into Wood.

In the place where *taiyin* dwells
    the day causes accretion.
    The chronograms cause recision.
With accretion, [the number of] unyielding days naturally doubles because pliant days cannot overcome them.

With recision,
    the chronograms [associated with] water move to wood.
    The chronograms [associated with] wood move to water.
Metal and fire stay in their [designated] places.

Generally, [*taiyin*] moves through the directional gods [as follows]:
    The Vermilion Bird is one place ahead of *taiyin*.
    The Hooked Array is three places behind.
    The Dark Warrior is five places ahead.
    The White Tiger is six places behind.
The Empty Star carries the Hooked Array, and Heaven and Earth are in accord with this. [3/27/18–22]

55. On this passage, see Donald Harper, "Warring States Natural Philosophy and Occult Thought," in *The Cambridge History of Ancient China: From the Origins of Civilization to 221 B.C.*, ed. Michael Loewe and Edward L. Shaughnessy (Cambridge: Cambridge University Press, 1999), 849–50.

Of the days [i.e., the heavenly stems], *jia* is unyielding, *yi* is pliant, *bing* is unyielding, *ding* is pliant, and so on to *gui*.

Wood is born in *hai*, matures in *mao*, and dies in *wei*. These three chronograms together are Wood.

Fire is born in *yin*, matures in *wu*, and dies in *xu*. These three chronograms together are Fire.

Earth is born in *wu*, matures in *xu*, and dies in *yin*. These three chronograms together are Earth.

Metal is born in *si*, matures in *yu*, and dies in *chou*. These three chronograms together are Metal.

Water is born in *shen*, matures in *zi*, and dies in *chen*. These three chronograms together are Water.

Thus [as for] the five overcomings, if birth [occurs in step] 1, then maturity [occurs in step] 5, and death [occurs in step] 9 [in any sequence of the earthly branches]: $5 \times 9 = 45$. Thus the [directional] gods shift one place every forty-five days. Taking three and responding with five, there are thus eight [such] shifts, and the year comes to an end.

In using *taiyin* [for prognostication], as a rule

whatever is to its left, that is, ahead of it, suffers cutting away;

whatever is to its right, that is, behind it, obtains increase.[56]

[As for] the chronogram that suspends the Hooked Array in the balance beam,

if there is war, [the state associated with that chronogram] certainly will be victorious;

if there is an assault, it must succeed. [3/27/24–29]

3.35

If one wishes to know the Way of Heaven, one takes the sun as the ruling factor. In the sixth month, it matches [the lunar lodge] Heart. Rotating leftward, it moves, dividing [the celestial circle] and making the twelve months. When they accord with [the movements of] the sun, Heaven and Earth are doubly in accord. Thereafter, there can be no calamitous asterisms. [3/27/29–30]

The first month is established in Encampment and Eastern Wall.[57]

The second month is established in Stride and Bond.

The third month is established in Stomach and Pleiades.

The fourth month is established in Net, Turtle Beak, and Alignment.

The fifth month is established in [Eastern] Well and Ghost Bearer.

The sixth month is established in Willow, Seven Stars, and Extension.

The seventh month is established in Wings and Chariot Platform.

56. Rejecting Lau's (HNZ 3/27/28–29) emendations of these two lines.

57. In almost all cases, the received text gives only one lunar lodge for each of the twelve months in this list. We follow Lau in giving the full allotment of lunar lodges to each month, but with some misgivings, as it is not clear to us that the abbreviated list in the received text was not what the author intended. For a translation of the list in its original form, see Major 1993, 127.

The eighth month is established in Horn, Neck, and Root.
The ninth month is established in Room and Heart.
The tenth month is established in Tail and Winnowing Basket.
The eleventh month is established in Dipper and Ox Leader.
The twelfth month is established in Emptiness and Rooftop. [3/28/1–4]

The angular extensions of [the stars in the lunar lodges are as follows]:

Horn: 12^{d}
Neck: 9^{d}
Root: 15^{d}
Room: 5^{d}
Heart: 5^{d}
Tail: 18^{d}
Winnowing Basket: 11.25^{d}
Dipper: 26^{d}
Ox Leader: 8^{d}

Serving Maid: 12^{d}
Emptiness: 10^{d}
Rooftop: 17^{d}
Encampment: 16^{d}
Eastern Wall: 9^{d}
Stride: 16^{d}
Bond: 12^{d}
Stomach: 14^{d}
Pleiades: 11^{d}
Net: 16^{d}

Turtle Beak: 2^{d}
Alignment: 9^{d}
[Eastern] Well: 30^{d}
Ghost Bearer: 4^{d}
Willow: 15^{d}
[Seven] Stars: 7^{d}
Extension: 18^{d}
Wings: 18^{d}
Chariot Platform: 17^{d}
[3/28/6–9]

The stars [= lunar lodges] are apportioned to territories, namely,
Horn and Neck to Zheng
Root, Room, and Heart to Song
Tail and Winnowing Basket to Yan
Dipper and Ox Leader to Yue
Serving Maid to Wu
Emptiness and Rooftop to Qi
Encampment and Eastern Wall to Wey
Stride and Root to Lu
Stomach, Pleiades, and Net to Wei
Turtle Beak and Alignment to Zhao
[Eastern] Well and Ghost Bearer to Qin
Willow, Seven Stars, and Extension to Zhou
Wings and Chariot Platform to Chu. [3/28/11–13]

When Jupiter dwells [in a lodge corresponding to a state, in that state,] the five grains will be bountiful. [The situation of the state corresponding to the lodge] opposite will be the reverse; the harvest will suffer calamity. If Jupiter should dwell [in a lodge] and does not dwell there, if it skips over and enters another place, the ruler of the country [governed by that lodge] will die and his state will be extinguished. [3/28/15–16]

3.36

When *taiyin* controls the ordinances of spring, [the ruler] should act [in a way that is] pliant, kind, mild, and good.
When *taiyin* controls the ordinances of summer, [the ruler] should publish, bestow, proclaim, and make clear.

When *taiyin* controls the ordinances of autumn, [the ruler] should repair, put in order, and make ready his troops.
When *taiyin* controls the ordinances of winter, [the ruler] should be fiercely brave and resolute and harden the frontier defenses.
In every three-year period, there is an alteration of what is usual.
In every six-year period, there are changes from what is normal.

Thus,
within three years, there is a year of famine;
within six years, there is a year of depression;
once in twelve years, there is abundance. [3/28/18–20]

3.37

[The territorial allotments of the celestial stems are as follows:]

jia with Qi	*ji* with Hann
yi with Eastern Yi	*keng* with Qin
bing with Chu	*xin* with Western Yi
ding with Southern Yi	*ren* with Wey
wu with Wei	*gui* with Yue

[The territorial allotments of the earthly branches are as follows:]

zi with Zhou	*wu* with Qin
chou with Di	*wei* with Song
yin with Chu	*shen* with Qi
mao with Zheng	*you* with Lu
chen with Jin	*xu* with Zhao
si with Wey	*hai* with Yan [3/28/22–24]

[The stem and branch correlations of the Five Phases are as follows:]

[stems]	[branches]	[phases]
jia and *yi*	*yin* and *mao*	Wood
bing and *ding*	*si* and *wu*	Fire
wu and *chi*	the four seasons	Earth
geng and *xin*	*shen* and *you*	Metal
ren and *gui*	*hai* and *zi*	Water [3/28/26–27]

3.38

Water produces Wood; Wood produces Fire; Fire produces Earth; Earth produces Metal; Metal produces Water.

If the child gives birth to the mother, this is called Rightness.
If the mother gives birth to the child, this is called fostering.

If the mother and child each give rise to the other, this is called concentration.
If the mother vanquishes the child, this is called control.
If the child vanquishes the mother, this is called obstruction.
If one employs victory to smite and kill, the victory will be without recompense.
If one employs concentration to pursue affairs, there will be achievement.
If one employs Rightness to carry out fixed principles, one's fame will be established and it will not diminish.
If one employs fostering to nurture the myriad creatures, there will be luxuriant growth and prosperity.
If one employs obstruction to pursue affairs, there will be destruction, extermination, death, and extinction [of the state]. [3/28/26–29]

3.39

The gods of the Northern Dipper are both female and male. In the eleventh month, at the beginning [of the year], they are established [together] in *zi*. Every month they shift by one chronogram. The male goes leftward, the female rightward. In the fifth month they coincide in *wu* and devise recision. In the eleventh month they coincide in *zi* and devise accretion. [3/29/1–2]

3.40

The chronogram in which *taiyin* is located[58] is called an "oppressive day." On oppressive days it is not possible to pursue the hundred [normal] affairs. Earth and Heaven[59] move with slow dignity; the male knows the female by the sound [of her singing]. Thus [the chronogram in which *taiyin* is located] is known as the "extraordinary chronogram." [3/29/2–3]

The numbers [of the sexagenary cycle] begin with *jiazi*. Offspring and mother seek each other out. The place where they come together is called a concurrence. Ten stems and twelve branches make a sexagenary cycle.

In all there are eight concurrences. If the concurrence is [at a point in the cycle] before [the stem–branch combination in which *taiyin* is located], there will be death and destruction; if the concurrence is later [in the cycle], there will be no calamity. [3/29/5–6]

[The territorial allocations of the "eight concurrences" are as follows:]

58. Rejecting Lau's (HNZ 3/29/2) suggestion that *taiyin* be replaced by *ci* 雌, "female [deity]." The context of this passage pertains to the celestial location of *taiyin*.

59. Not the usual phrase *tiandi* 天地 "Heaven and Earth" but *kanyu* 堪輿, literally "support and canopy," a poetic term for Earth and Heaven.

jiaxu is Yan	*gengchen* is Qin
yiyou is Qi	*xinmao* is the Rong tribes
bingwu is Yue	*renzi* is the Dai tribes
dingsi is Chu	*guihai* is the Hu tribes

[The territorial allocations of the "lesser conjunction" cyclical pairs are as follows:][60]

[*wuchen* is . . .]	*yiyou* is . . .
wuxu is . . .	*yimao* is Wei
[*yisi* is . . .]	*wuwu* is . . .
yihai is Hann	*wuzi* is . . .

The eight concurrences [together with the eight lesser conjunctions] [thus correspond to] the world. [3/29/8–10]

When *taiyin,* the Lesser Year, the asterisms [= lunar lodges], the branches, the stems, and the five [directional] gods all coincide on the same day, there will be clouds, vapors, and rain. The state and ruler match [the prognostication]. [3/29/12]

3.41

Of those prized by the heavenly spirits, none is more prized than the Bluegreen Dragon. The Bluegreen Dragon is otherwise called the Heavenly Unity, or otherwise *taiyin.* [The country corresponding to] the place where *taiyin* dwells cannot retreat but can advance. [The country corresponding to] the place beaten against by the Northern Dipper cannot withstand attack. [3/29/14–15]

When Heaven and Earth were founded, they divided to make yin and yang.

Yang is born from yin;
yin is born from yang;

they are in a state of mutual alternation. The four binding cords [of Heaven] communicate with them.

Sometimes there is death;
sometimes there is birth.

Thus are the myriad things brought to completion.

[Of all creatures that] move and breathe, none is more prized than humans. [The bodily] orifices, limbs, and trunk all communicate with Heaven.

Heaven has nine layers; man also has nine orifices.
Heaven has four seasons, to regulate the twelve months;
Man also has four limbs, to control the twelve joints.

60. The text here is obviously defective; most of the names of states to which these "lesser conjunctions" refer are missing; and it is not possible to reconstruct them with confidence. For what I have called the "lesser conjunctions," see Major 1993, 134.

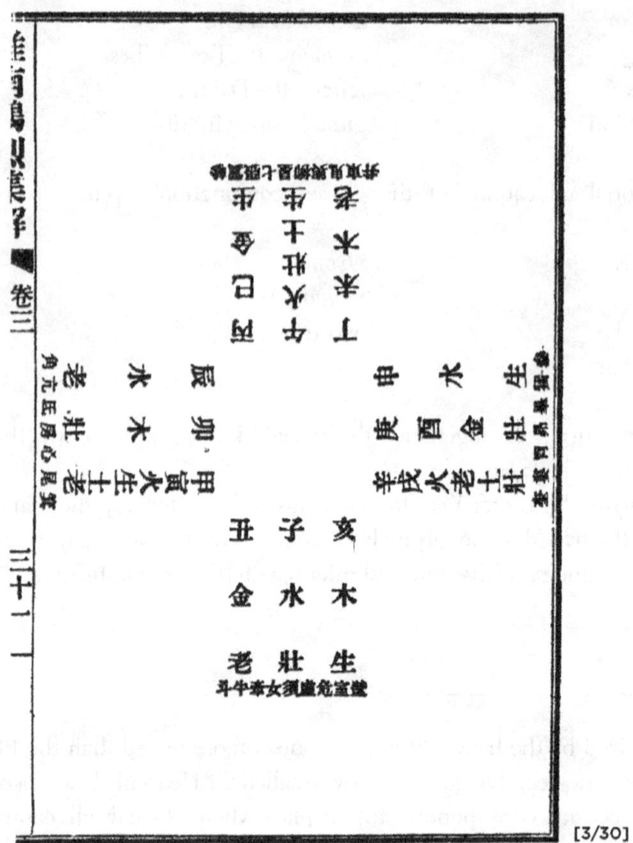

This diagram of the stems, branches, lunar lodges, and Five Phases is in the form of the Earth plate of a *shi* 式 cosmograph, showing significant alignments with the "pointer" of the Northern Dipper engraved on the rotating Heaven plate (not depicted here).

Heaven has twelve months, to regulate the 360 days;
Man also has twelve joints, to regulate the 360 nodes.[61]

A person who undertakes affairs while not obeying Heaven is someone who deviates from what gave birth to him. [3/29/17–20]

3.42

Take the arrival of the winter solstice and count to the first day of the first month of the coming year. [If] there are a full fifty days, the people's food supply will be sufficient. [If] there are fewer [than fifty days], [the people's rations] will be reduced

61. In this instance, "nodes" (*jie* 節) refers to any place in the body where two bones meet.

[SOUTH]

Chariot-Platform
Wings
Extension
Seven Stars
Willow
Bond
Horn
Neck
Root
Room
Heart
Tail
Alignment
Turtle-Beak
Net
Pleiades
Stomach
Bond
Earth Born
Metal Born
Fire Matures
Wood Old
ding si
wu
ding wei
chen
Water Old
mao
Wood Matures
jia yin
Fire Born
Earth Old
shen
Water Born
yu geng
Metal Matures
xin xu
Fire Old
Earth Matures
chou
Metal Old
zi
Water Matures
hai
Wood Born
Ox-Leader
Serving-Maid
Emptiness
Rooftop
Encampment
[Eastern] Wall

Translation of the diagram of the stems, branches, lunar lodges, and Five Phases.

by one pint per day. [If] there is a surplus [above fifty], [the people's rations] will be increased by one pint per day. This is what controls the harvest. [3/29/22–23]

The year Shetige: A year of early moisture and late drought. Rice plants are sickly and silkworms do not mature. Legumes and wheat flourish. The people's food ration is four pints [of grain per day]. *Yin* in *jia* is called "impeded seedlings."

The year Ming'e: The year is harmonious. Rice, legumes, wheat, and silkworms flourish. The people's food ration is five pints. *Mao* in *yi* is called "flag sprouts."

The year Zhixu: A year of early drought and late moisture. There is minor famine. Silkworms are obstructed, and wheat ripens. The people's food ration is three pints. *Chen* in *bing* is called "pliant omen."

The year Dahuangluo: A year of minor warfare. Silkworms mature in small numbers, wheat flourishes, and legumes are sickly. The people's food ration is two pints. *Si* in *ding* is called "strengthen the frontier."

The year Dunzang: A year of great drought. Silkworms mature, rice is sickly, and wheat flourishes, but the crops do not yield. The people's food ration is two pints. *Wu* in *wu* is called "manifestly harmonious."

The year Xiexia: A year of minor warfare. Silkworms mature, rice flourishes, and legumes and wheat do not yield. The people's food ration is three pints. *Wei* in *ji* is called "differentiate and separate."

The year Tuntan: The year is harmonious. The lesser rains fall in season. Silkworms mature; legumes and wheat flourish. The people's food ration is three pints. *Shen* in *geng* is called "elevate and make manifest."

The year Zuo'e: A year of great war. People suffer illness, silkworms do not mature, legumes and wheat do not yield, and crops suffer insect damage. The people's food ration is five pints. *You* in *xin* is called "redoubled brightness."

The year Yanmao: A year of minor famine and warfare. Silkworms do not mature, wheat does not yield, but legumes flourish. The people's food ration is seven pints. *Xu* in *ren* is called "umbral blackness."

The year Dayuanxian: A year of great warfare and great famine. Silkworms rupture their cocoons; legumes and wheat do not yield; crops suffer insect damage. The people's food ration is three pints. [*Hai* in *gui* is called . . .][62]

The year Kundun: A year of great fogs rising up and great waters issuing forth. Silkworms, rice, and wheat flourish. The people's food ration is three bushels. *Zi* in *jia* is called "dawning brilliance."

The year Chifenruo: A year of minor warfare and early moisture. Silkworms do not hatch. Rice plants are sickly, legumes do not yield, but wheat flourishes. The people's food ration is one pint. [*Chou* in *yi* is called. . . .][63] [3/29/25–3/31/8]

3.43

To establish the directions of sunrise and sunset, first set up a gnomon in the east. Take one [other] gnomon, and step back ten paces from the first gnomon. Use it to sight in alignment toward the sun when it first emerges at the northern edge [of its position on the eastern horizon?] When the sun is just setting, again plant one gnomon to the east [of the second gnomon], and use the gnomon to the west of it to sight in alignment toward the sun when it sets at the northern edge. Then establish the midpoint of the two eastern gnomons; this along with the western gnomon fixes a true east–west line. At the winter solstice, the sun rises at the southeastern binding cord and sets at the southwestern binding cord. At the spring and autumn equinoxes, it rises exactly in the east and sets exactly in the west. At the summer solstice, the sun rises at the northeastern binding cord and sets at the northwestern binding cord. At the zenith it is exactly in the south. [3/31/10–14]

62. This phrase, expected from parallelism with the other years of the Jovian cycle, is missing from the text.

63. This phrase, expected from parallelism with the other years of the Jovian cycle, is also missing from the text.

3.44

If you wish to know the numerical values for the east–west and north–south breadth and length [of the earth], set up four gnomons to form a square one *li* on each side. Ten or a few more days before the spring or autumn equinox, use the two gnomons on the northern edge of the square to sight in alignment on the rising sun when it first appears [above the horizon]. Wait until [the day when the gnomons] coincide [with the rising sun]. When they coincide, then this corresponds to the true [east] position of the sun. Then immediately also use the south[west]ern gnomon to sight on the sun in alignment. Take the amount by which [this sighting] is within the forward gnomons as the standard. Divide the width and length [between the gnomons [i.e., one *li*]] by this, and from this you will know the numerical value of [the width of the earth] from east to west. For example, observe the [alignment of the southwestern gnomon with] the rising sun to be one inch within the forward gnomons, and let one inch equate to one *li*. One *li* equals 18,000 inches, so the distance from [the point of observation] eastward to the sun is 18,000 *li*. Or [on the same day] observe the setting sun; [the alignment of the sun with the southeastern gnomon] lies one-half inch within the forward gnomons. For one-half inch, one obtains one *li*. Divide the number of inches in one *li* by one-half inch; one obtains the answer of 36,000 *li*. Thus one obtains the numerical value of the distance from [the point of observation] westward to the sun. Add [the two figures] together for the numerical value of the distance from east to west. This number represents the span between the extreme end points [of the earth].

If the alignment [of the gnomons on the northern edge of the square] occurs before the spring equinox or after the autumn equinox, you are to the south [of the midline of the earth]. If the alignment occurs before the autumn equinox or after the spring equinox, you are to the north. If the alignment occurs exactly on the equinox, then you are midway between north and south.

If you wish to know true south from a position in the exact center, [observe that] if the alignment [of the gnomons on the northern edge of the square] does not occur before the autumn equinox, the position is exactly between north and south. If you wish to know the distance to the extreme limits of south and north from a position in the center, use the southwestern gnomon to sight in alignment on the sun. When the sun at the summer solstice first rises, sight on the north[west]ern gnomon, and [you will see that] the sun is an equal distance to the east, [aligned with] the northeastern gnomon. The distance to the east is 18,000 *li*, so the distance from the center to the north is also 18,000 *li*. Double this to obtain the numerical value of the distance from south to north.

The amount by which [a position] departs from the center is larger or smaller, [proportional to the] amount by which [the sight line] is within or outside the forward gnomons. If [that line] is one inch inside the gnomons, the sun is closer by one *li*. If [the line] is one inch outside the gnomons, the sun is more distant by one *li*. [3/31/15–24]

3.45

If you wish to know the height of heaven, plant a gnomon one *zhang* [i.e., ten feet] tall in the south [and another] in the north, at a distance of a thousand *li*. Measure their shadows [at noon] on the same day. [Suppose that] the northern gnomon [casts a shadow of] two feet, and the southern gnomon [casts a shadow of] one foot, nine inches. Thus by going a thousand *li* to the south, the shadow is shortened by one inch.[64] Going twenty thousand *li* [to the south], there would be no shadow. That would be directly beneath the sun. A shadow two feet long results from a height of ten feet, so going south one [*li*] [increases] the height by five [*li*] Thus if one measures the *li* from [the northern gnomon] to a point directly beneath the sun and then multiplies that by five, it makes 100,000 *li*, and that is the height of heaven. Or if you suppose that the [length of] the shadow is equal to [the height of] the gnomon, then the height [of heaven] would be equal to the distance [southward to a point directly beneath the sun].[65] [3/32/1–4]

Translated by John S. Major

64. Note that in Chinese linear measure, one foot equals ten inches (not twelve, as in the English system); thus two feet minus one inch equals one foot, nine inches, as stated here.

65. For a highly detailed analysis of 3/31/10 to 3/32/4, see Christopher Cullen's annotated translation, "A Chinese Eratosthenes of the Flat Earth," in Major 1993, 269–90.

Four

TERRESTRIAL FORMS

"TERRESTRIAL FORMS" is an account of world geography from the point of view of the Western Han dynasty. It ignores political geography (such as the states of the Warring States period or the kingdoms, provinces, and counties of the Han Empire) in favor of the postdeluge geography of Yu the Great and the wider world beyond China's borders, with an emphasis on the mythical, the magical, the distant, and the strange. The chapter emphasizes that physical features of terrain interact in important ways with plants, animals, and people.

The Chapter Title

"Di xing" 墬形 can be understood correctly in either of two grammatical constructions: as a noun plus a past-participle verb (Earth Given Form) or as an adjective plus a noun (Terrestrial Forms). We have chosen the second as the English equivalent for this chapter title, but both meanings resonate with each other, and each informs our understanding of the other. The use in the chapter title of the unusual character *di* 墬 in place of the common character *di* 地 has no discernable significance, as the two seem to be exact synonyms or, rather, two precisely equivalent ways of writing the same word for "earth."

Summary and Key Themes

"Terrestrial Forms" gives its reader an account of the size, shape, and topography of the earth and of the dynamic interactions of the earth with its creatures. It does not, somewhat surprisingly, concern itself with political geography, of either the Warring States or the Qin–Han periods. (Astrological considerations concerning the states are treated in chapter 3, "Celestial Patterns.") There does not seem to be any continuous narrative or analytical thread that runs from section to section through the chapter as a whole, but it is possible to discern several important themes.

The chapter begins with a description of the main topographical features of the continent of which China is a part, including the nine provinces and their associated mountains, passes, marshes, and winds (4.1) and the dimensions of the world (4.2). In section 4.7, the chapter returns to the landscape of China, describing rare and valuable products of the nine provinces. Section 4.17 lists some forty rivers and their sources.

Having begun with the general size, shape, and layout of the world, in sections 4.3, 4.4, and 4.5 the chapter turns to the magical landscape of Mount Kunlun, the pivot of Heaven and Earth and the staircase of the gods for their ascents and descents to and from Heaven. Kunlun is taken as being located at the center of the entire terrestrial world. The authors of "Terrestrial Forms" envision that world as being divided into nine continents, in accordance with theories propounded by Zou Yan (ca. 305–240 B.C.E.). Those theories admit varying interpretations,[1] but in the version most pertinent to this chapter, each of the nine great continents is divided into nine subcontinents, and each of those into nine provinces. China comprises the southeastern subcontinent of the central continent. (The other eight continents are essentially ignored.) Kunlun is depicted as being in that continent's exact center and thus located to China's northwest.

Sections 4.6, 4.15, and 4.16 describe places far beyond the borders of China: a world of barbarians, monsters, and gods. These sections reflect a contemporary fascination with the distant and strange found also in such texts as the *Shanhaijing* (*Classic of Mountains and Seas*) and the *Mu tianzi zhuan* (*Travels of Son of Heaven Mu*). A few decades after the *Huainanzi* was compiled, much of the world to the west of China was shifted from the realm of mythic landscape to that of known geography, through the explorations of the celebrated Han intelligence agent Zhang Qian.

"Terrestrial Forms" is not just about geography, however; it also describes the interactions between the earth and its creatures. Section 4.8 shows that the *qi* of different terrains and waters has different effects on the creatures that live on or

1. For the complexities of Zou Yan's cosmology, see John S. Major, "The Five Phases, Magic Squares, and Schematic Cosmography," in *Explorations in Early Chinese Cosmology: Papers Presented at the Workshop on Classical Chinese Thought Held at Harvard University, August 1976*, ed. Henry Rosemont Jr., Journal of the American Academy of Religion Studies, vol. 50, no. 2 (1984; repr., Charleston, S.C.: Booksurge, 2006), 133–66; see esp. 134–37.

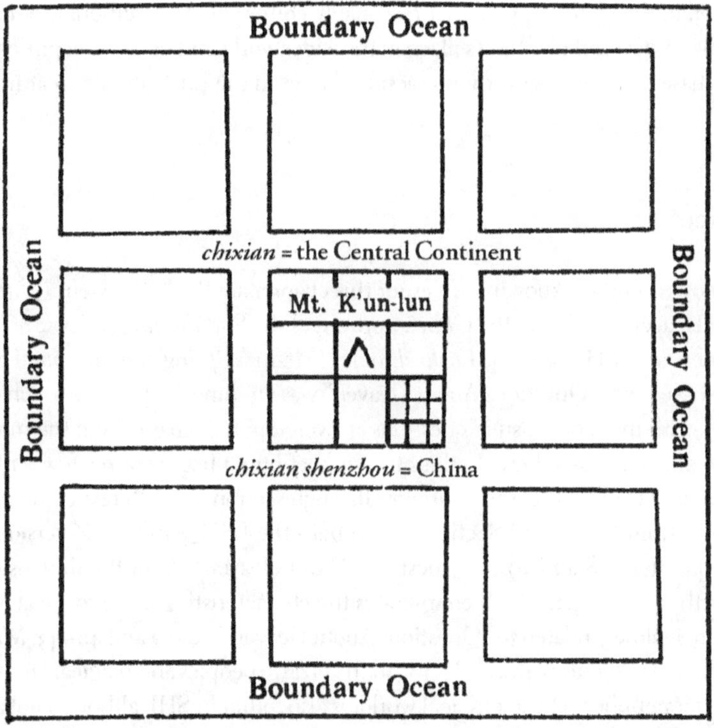

This diagram shows China's place in Zou Yan's nine-continent cosmological theory. China, divided into nine provinces, is located in the southeastern corner of the central continent, with Mount Kunlun to China's northwest.

near them; similarly, 4.9 gives correlations of soils, diet, and dispositions. Section 4.10 demonstrates that the gestation periods of various animals are numerologically linked to celestial and calendrical phenomena. Section 4.11 contains an interesting and unusual early Chinese example of what in the West would be called "natural history": it attempts a rudimentary taxonomic classification of animals on the basis of their physical characteristics. Also in this category of connections between topography and the "myriad things" are section 4.12, describing the relationship between types and colors of water, on the one hand, and minerals and crops, on the other; and 4.13, on the Five-Phase characteristics of people living in the four cardinal directions and in the center. Section 4.13 is complemented by section 5.13 in the following chapter of the *Huainanzi,* which defines the boundaries and characteristics of the territories of the four directions and the center. Section 4.14 focuses on the cycles of the Five Phases, which are shown to govern transformations of all kinds. The theme of transformation is central to sections 4.18, which recounts the "evolution" of various classes of animals and plants from mythical first ancestors, and 4.19, an alchemical demonstration that the growth of minerals in the earth is governed by the numerological principles of the Five Phases.

Overall, the chapter provides a reasonably comprehensive, although not always systematic, account of China's place in the wider world and of how the principles of Five-Phase cosmology govern interactions between the earth and its creatures.

Sources

The most important known sources for this chapter are the "Tian wen" (Questions About Heaven) section of the *Chuci*, portions of the *Shanhaijing* (*Classic of Mountains and Seas*, SHJ), and the *Lüshi chunqiu* (*Mr. Lü's Spring and Autumn*, LSCQ). As we have seen, "Questions About Heaven" was an important source for chapter 3 as well, with the more cosmic questions answered in that chapter and the more terrestrial ones addressed here. In this chapter, section 4.1 begins with a few sentences paraphrased from SHJ 6 and continues through section 4.2 with text copied nearly verbatim from LSCQ 13.[2] Section 4.2 (in both the LSCQ and HNZ versions) answers questions 38 and 39 in "Questions About Heaven" about the dimensions of the earth. Section 4.3, which enumerates the characteristics of the magical Mount Kunlun, is closely related to "Questions About Heaven," 29–34 and 40–43. Much of the material in sections 4.15 and 4.16, on the bizarre peoples and magical landscapes on the far periphery of the physical world, is also found in SHJ, although not always in quite the same form. Most of the rivers in section 4.17 (which returns from the realms of magic to the actual geography of China) are found also in SHJ 1–4. This section may derive from a now-lost text that anticipated the *Shuijing* 水經 (*Classic of Rivers*), a Han-period work that briefly describes more than one hundred Chinese waterways. Section 4.7, describing the valuable products of the nine provinces, is in the tradition of the "Yugong" (Tribute of Yu) chapter of the *Shujing* (*Documents*) but does not directly depend on it textually.

Sections 4.8 and 4.9, relating terrain, diet, and physical and psychological characteristics; 4.10, on the gestation periods of various animals; 4.13, on the characteristics of territories in the four directions (plus the center); and 4.14, on Five-Phase correlations, all seem to form self-contained units and were probably copied verbatim or nearly so from now-lost sources. So too with section 4.19, on the transmutation and maturation of mineral ores in the earth, which appears to be a set piece copied intact from some unknown source. This is considered to be China's oldest extant statement of the principles of alchemy.

Section 4.18, on the evolutionary genealogy of various classes of animals and plants, presents a less clear case because in its current form it seems to be rather garbled, in some places beyond recovery. It originally may have been copied from an earlier source, or it may represent an editor's not very successful attempt (perhaps subsequently mangled by later copyists) to distill or abridge an earlier source. The

2. Knoblock and Riegel 2000, 278–81. The *Lüshi chunqiu* was an important source for other *Huainanzi* chapters as well; for example, see the introductions to chaps. 5 and 12.

possibility that this section is derived in some way from an earlier source is bolstered by the presence in *Zhuangzi* 18 of a similar (and also now badly garbled) evolutionary passage.

Overall, this chapter (like chapter 3, "Celestial Patterns") reads largely as an anthology of passages quoted, paraphrased, or compiled from earlier sources, many of which are now unknown.

The Chapter in the Context of the *Huainanzi* as a Whole

Chapters 3, 4, and 5 form a distinctive subunit within the *Huainanzi*, a trilogy describing the cosmos, the earth, living creatures, and other concrete phenomena (the "myriad things"), and the correlative influences of seasonal and monthly time. The summary of chapter 4 in the *Huainanzi* itself (chapter 21, "An Outline of the Essentials") says, in part, that it "enables you to circulate comprehensively and prepare exhaustively, so that you cannot be roused by things or startled by oddities." By going beyond a description of the Chinese Empire to recount the strange territories and bizarre creatures beyond the periphery, the actual content of chapter 4 matches this objective very well, helping its royal reader achieve one of the goals of successful administration: no surprises.

John S. Major

Four

4.1

Everything that exists on earth lies

> within the six coordinates [and]
> within the outer limits of the four directions.
> To illuminate it, [it has] the sun and moon;
> for its warp threads, [it has] the stars and planets;
> to regulate it, [it has] the four seasons;
> to control it, [it has] the great Year Star. [4/32/8–9]

Between Heaven and Earth are nine continents and eight pillars. The dry land has nine mountains; the mountains have nine passes. There are nine marshes, eight winds, and six rivers.[1] [4/32/11–12]

What are the nine continents?

> In the southeast is Shen Province, called the land of agriculture.
> In the south is Zi Province, called the land of fertility.
> In the southwest is Rong Province, called the land of abundance.
> In the west is Yan Province, called the land of ripeness.
> In the center is Ji Province, called the central land.
> In the northwest is Tai Province, called the land of plenty.

1. We take *sai* (or *sou*) 塞, *deng* 等, and *pin* 品 as untranslated numerative adjuncts for *ze* 澤, *feng* 風, and *shui* 水, thus avoiding a more "literal" but very awkward translation as "Of marshes there are nine wetlands," and so on.

In the north is Qi Province, called the land of consummation.
In the northeast is Bo Province, called the land of seclusion.
In the east is Yang Province, called the land of beginning again. [4/32/14–16]

What are the nine mountains? They are Mount Guiji, Mount Tai, Mount Wangwu, Mount Shou, Mount Taihua, Mount Qi, Mount Taihang, Mount Yangchang, and Mount Mengmen. [4/32/18]

What are the nine passes? They are the Taifen Pass, the Min'ou Pass, the Jingruan Pass, the Fangcheng Pass, the Yaoban Pass, the Jingxing Pass, the Lingci Pass, the Gouzhu Pass, and the Juyong Pass. [4/32/20]

What are the nine marshes? They are The Juqu Marsh of Yue, the Yunmeng Marsh of Chu, the Yangyu Marsh of Qin, the Dalu Marsh of Jin, the Putian Marsh of Zheng, the Mengzhu Marsh of Song, the Haiyu Marsh of Qi, the Julu Marsh of Zhao, and the Zhaoyu Marsh of Yan. [4/32/22–23]

What are the eight winds?

The northeast wind is called the Blazing Wind.[2]
The east wind is called the Protracted Wind.
The southeast wind is called the Luminous Wind.
The south wind is called the Balmy Wind.
The southwest wind is called the Cooling Wind.
The west wind is called the Lofty Wind.
The northwest wind is called the Elegant Wind.
The north wind is called the Cold Wind. [4/32/25–26]

What are the six rivers? They are the [Yellow] River, the Vermilion River, the Liao River, the Black River, the [Yangzi] River, and the Huai River. [4/32/28]

4.2

The expanse within the four seas measures 28,000 *li* from east to west and 26,000 *li* from south to north. There are 8,000 *li* of watercourses passing through six valleys; there are six hundred named streams. There are 3,000 *li* of roads and paths.

Yu employed Tai Zhang to measure the earth from its eastern extremity to its western extremity. It measured 233,500 *li* and 75 double paces. He also employed Shu Hai to measure from its northern extremity to its southern extremity. It measured 233,500 *li* and 75 double paces.[3]

Concerning flood lands, deep pools, and swamps greater than three hundred fathoms[4] [in expanse?]: [Within the previously designated expanse of] 233,500 *li*, there are nine. [4/32/30–4/33/3]

2. This list of wind names differs from that in 3.12 and repeated in 4.18; perhaps it represents a different tradition.

3. Tai Zhang 太章 and Shu Hai 豎亥 are identified by Gao You as "good walkers" who served Yu as ministers. The *Shanhaijing* also reports that Yu ordered them to pace out the dimensions of the world. See Zhang Shuangdi 1997, 1:432–33n.4.

4. *Ren* 仞, a linear measure of eight feet, is thus equivalent to the *xun* 尋. See 3.31 and app. B. The

4.3

Yu also took expanding earth to fill in the great flood, making the great mountains. He excavated the wastelands of Kunlun to make level ground. In the center [of Kunlun] is a manifold wall of nine layers, with a height of 11,000 *li*, 114 double paces, two feet, and six inches. Atop the heights of Kunlun are treelike cereal plants thirty-five feet tall. [Growing] to the west of these are pearl trees, jade trees, carnelian trees, and no-death trees.[5] To the east are found sand-plum trees and malachite trees.[6] To the south are crimson trees. To the north are *bi* jade trees and *yao* jade trees.[7]

Nearby are 440 gates. There are four *li* between each gate, and each gate is fifteen *shun* wide. [One *shun* equals fifteen feet.][8]

Nearby are nine wells. The jade crossbar binds the northwestern corner.[9] The north[west]ern gate opens to admit the wind from Mount Buzhou.[10] Broad Palace, Revolving House, Hanging Garden, Cool Wind, and the Hedge Forest are within the Changhe Gate of the Kunlun Mountains.[11] This is [called] the Carved-Out Garden. The pools of the Carved-Out Garden flow with yellow water. The yellow water circulates three times and then returns to its source. It is called cinnabar water; anyone who drinks it will not die. [4/33/3–9]

4.4

The waters of the Yellow River issue from the northeast corner of the Kunlun Mountains and enter the ocean, flowing [eastward] along the route of Yu through the Piled-Stone Mountains.

The Vermilion River issues from the southeast corner and flows southwest to the

---

term *ren* also occurs in chaps. 2, 6, 12, 15, 17, 18, and 20; it seems to connote especially the height or depth of features in the natural landscape. This sentence as written appears to require that *ren* be understood as a measure of breadth. The sentence does not make good sense and appears to be textually corrupt. Lau (HNZ 4/33/3) omits "hundred" so that his text reads "three *ren*"; he also omits the word *li* 里. These changes do not improve the situation.

5. *Busi shu* 不死樹. This phrase has two interpretations: either the trees themselves are undying, or they are a kind of elixir of immortality or an ingredient thereof. For similar phrases, see Ying-shi Yü, "Life and Immortality in the Mind of Han China," *Harvard Journal of Asiatic Studies* 25 (1964–1965): 90–91.

6. *Lang'gan* 琅玕 is often taken to mean "coral." Edward H. Schafer argues that its usual meaning is "malachite," in "The Transcendent Vitamin: Efflorescence of Lang-kan," *Chinese Science* 3 (1978): 27–38.

7. *Bi* 碧 and *yao* 瑤 are two types of jade. The terms are untranslatable but signify roughly "jade suitable for disks" and "perfect jade" or "precious jade."

8. This sentence is apparently a line of commentary that has crept into the text.

9. Note that our punctuation of this sentence differs from that suggested by Lau. See Major 1993, 305, technical n. 4.III.10. For *wei* 維 as cords binding the "corners" of the cosmos, see 3.3.

10. Mount Buzhou is the unmoving pivot at the center of Heaven and Earth. See 3.1 and chap. 3, n. 20.

11. The Changhe 閶闔 Gate is the Gate of Heaven, allowing communication between Heaven and Earth.

Southern Sea, passing to the east of Cinnabar Marsh. The Weakwater [River] issues from the southwest corner; when it reaches Heli, its overflowing waves pass through the Flowing Sands and flow south to enter the Southern Sea.[12] The Yang River issues from the northwest corner and enters the Southern Sea south of [the country of] the Winged People.

The four streams [originate in] the divine springs of the [Yellow] Emperor, from which can be concocted all kinds of medicinal substances to bring physical well-being to the myriad creatures. [4/33/11–14]

4.5

If one climbs to a height double that of the Kunlun Mountains, [that peak] is called Cool Wind Mountain. If one climbs it, one will not die. If one climbs to a height that is doubled again, [that peak] is called Hanging Gardens. If one ascends it, one will gain supernatural power and be able to control the wind and the rain. If one climbs to a height that is doubled yet again, it reaches up to Heaven itself. If one mounts to there, one will become a spirit. It is called the abode of the Supreme Thearch. [4/33/16–17]

The Fu [= Fusang] Tree in Yang Province is baked by the sun's heat. The Jian Tree on Mount Duguang, by which the gods ascend and descend [to and from Heaven], casts no shadow at midday. If one calls [from that place], there is no echo. It forms a canopy over the center of the world. The Ruo Tree is to the west of the Jian Tree. On its branches are ten suns; its blossoms cast light upon the earth. [4/33/19–20]

4.6

The borders of each of the nine provinces encompass one thousand *li*.

Beyond the nine provinces are eight distant regions, each encompassing a thousand *li*.

The one to the northeast is called Impenetrable, [also] called Great Marsh.[13]

The one to the east is called Great Island, [also] called Sandy Sea.

12. Wang Yinzhi argues that the sentence "The Weakwater issues from the southwest corner" belongs much later in the chapter, in the section dealing with the rivers of China, and that much of the text of this passage is superfluous. See Zhang Shuangdi 1997, 1:439nn.22, 23. We translate the entire text here (not being persuaded that it is extraneous), with the exception of the phrase "east of the Vermilion River" (*chishui zhi dong* 赤水之東). We also duplicate the sentence about the Weakwater in the later sections on rivers.

13. Most of the "distant regions" are given alternative names as such-and-such marsh. Derk Bodde pointed out that the word *ze* 澤, conventionally translated as "marsh," does not imply a swamp or bog but a well-watered meadow, in "Marshes in *Mencius* and Elsewhere: A Lexicographical Note," in *Ancient China: Studies in Early Civilization*, ed. David T. Roy and Tsuen-hsuin Tsien (Hong Kong: Chinese University Press, 1978), 156–66.

The one to the southeast is called Juqu, [also] called Misty Marsh.[14]
The one to the south is called Great Dream, [also] called Vast Marsh.
The one to the southwest is called Island Wealth, [also] called Cinnabar Marsh.
The one to the west is called Nine Districts, [also] called Marsh of Springs.
The one to the northwest is called Daxia [Bactria], [also] called Ocean Marsh.
The one to the north is called Great Obscurity, [also] called Frigid Marsh.

All the clouds of the eight distant regions and eight marshes bring rain to the nine provinces. [4/33/22–25]

Beyond the eight distant regions are eight outlying regions, each also encompassing one thousand *li*.

The one to the northeast is called Harmonious Hill, [also] called Wasteland.
The one to the east is called Thorn Forest, [also] called Mulberry Wilderness.
The one to the southeast is called Great Destitution, [also] called Horde of Women.
The one to the south is called Duguang, [also] called Reversed [i.e., north-facing] Doors.[15]
The one to the southwest is called Scorched Pygmies, [also] called Fiery Earth.
The one to the west is called Metal Hill, [also] called Fertile Wilderness.
The one to the northwest is called One-Eye, [also] called Place of Sands.
The one to the north is called Amassing Ice, [also] called Abandoned Wings.

The *qi* of the eight outlying regions are those that emit cold and heat. In order to harmonize the eight proper [directional *qi*], there must be wind and rain. [4/34/1–4]

Beyond the eight outlying regions are eight ultimate regions.

The one to the northeast is called Square Soil Mountain, [also] called Azure Gate.
The one to the east is called Extreme East Mountain, [also] called Opening Brightness Gate.
The one to the southeast is called Mother-of-Waves Mountain, [also] called Yang Gate.
The one to the south is called Extreme South Mountain, [also] called Summer Heat Gate.
The one to the southwest is called String of Colts Mountain, [also] called White Gate.
The one to the west is called Extreme West Mountain, [also] called the Changhe Gate.
The one to the northwest is called Buzhou Mountain, [also] called the Gate of Darkness.

14. The name Juqu 具區 does not yield a satisfactory translation; perhaps this is a transcription of a non-Chinese name.

15. The doors in Chinese houses typically face south, to let in sunlight. The implication here is that the territory called Duguang lies south of the equator, and so the doors must face northward to let in the sun.

The one to the north is called Extreme North Mountain, [also] called Winter Cold Gate.

The clouds of the eight ultimate regions are those that bring rain to the whole world; the winds of the eight gates are those that regulate seasonal heat and cold.

The clouds of the eight outlying regions, the eight distant regions, and the eight marshes bring rain to the nine provinces and produce harmony in the central province. [4/34/6–10]

4.7

The beautiful things of the east are the *xun, yu,* and *qi* jades[16] of Yimulu Mountain.

The beautiful things of the southeast are the arrow bamboos of Mount Guiji.

The beautiful things of the south are the rhinoceros [horn] and elephant [ivory] of Mount Liang.

The beautiful things of the southwest are the precious metals and jade of Mount Hua.

The beautiful things of the west are the pearls and jade of Mount He.

The beautiful things of the northwest are the *qiu, lin,* and *lang'gan* jades[17] of the Kunlun Mountains.

The beautiful things of the north are the sinews and horn of Mount Youdu.

The beautiful things of the northeast are the patterned pelts of Mount Zhi.[18]

The beautiful things of the center are around Dai Peak, which produces the five grains, mulberry, and hemp. Fish and salt are produced there [also]. [4/34/12–16]

4.8

In the [fabric of] the earth's shape,
east and west are the weft;
north and south are the warp.
Mountains are the cumulative [result of] accretion;
valleys are the cumulative [result of] cutting away.
High places govern birth;
low places govern death.
Hills govern maleness;
valleys govern femaleness.

16. *Xun* 珣, *yu* 玗, and *qi* 琪 are names of types of jade, whose significance is now unclear.

17. *Qiu* 球, *lin* 琳, and *lang'gan* 琅玕 are, again, types of jade, mostly not identifiable with certainty. For *lang'gan* (possibly malachite), see n. 6.

18. For example, tiger and leopard skins.

Water [congealed] in a round shape forms pearls;
water [congealed] in a square shape forms jade.

Clear water yields gold; the dragon's lair in the depths yields the quintessential beauty of jade.

Various sorts of earth give birth [to living creatures], each according to its own kind.

For this reason,

The *qi* of mountains gives birth to a preponderance of men.
The *qi* of low wetlands gives birth to a preponderance of women.
The *qi* of dikes produces many cases of muteness.
The *qi* of wind produces many cases of deafness.
The *qi* of forests produces many cases of paralysis of the legs.
The *qi* of wood produces many cases of spinal deformity.
The *qi* of seashores produces many cases of ulcerations of the lower extremities.
The *qi* of stone produces much strength.
The *qi* of steep passes produces many cases of goiter.
The *qi* of heat produces many cases of early death.
The *qi* of cold produces much longevity.
The *qi* of valleys produces many cases of rheumatism.
The *qi* of hills produces many cases of rickets.
The *qi* of low-lying places produces much human fellow-feeling.
The *qi* of mounds produces much covetousness.
The *qi* of light soil produces much hastening after profit.[19]
The *qi* of heavy soil produces much sluggishness.
The sound of clear water is small;
the sound of muddy water is great.
People [who live near] rushing water are light;
people [who live near] placid water are heavy.

The central region produces many sages.

All things are the same as their *qi*; all things respond to their own class. [4/34/18–23] Thus,

In the south are herbs that do not die;[20]
In the north is ice that does not melt.
In the east are countries of superior people.
In the west is the corpse of Xing Can.[21] [4/34/25]

19. *Li* 利 normally means "profit, advantage"; here it is a paired opposite with *chi* 遲, "slow, sluggish," so it must mean something like "hastening after profit." Perhaps here it could be translated as "hustling."

20. *Busi zhi cao* 不死之草; another interpretation would be "herbs of no-death"—that is, a natural elixir of immortality. See n. 5.

21. Xing Can 形殘 was a mythological figure who contended with the Supreme Thearch for control of the world. After the thearch beheaded him, he used his nipples as eyes and his navel as a mouth, singing and dancing while brandishing a shield and an axe. Cosmologically, this gruesome account befits the correlation of West with metal and weapons.

4.9

Sleep sitting up and have straight dreams;[22]
a person dies and becomes a ghost.
Lodestone flies up;
mica draws water.
The earthen dragon brings rain;
swallows and wild geese fly in turn.
Clams, crabs, pearl [oysters], and tortoises
flourish and decline with the moon.[23]

Thus for the same reasons,

people who live in regions of hard soil are hard and unyielding;
people who live on easily worked soil are fat.
People who live on lumpy soil are large;
people who live on sandy soil are small.
People who live on fertile soil are beautiful;
people who live on barren soil are ugly.
People who live on level ground are clever.

People who live on flat land are sensitive and find the five [kinds of] grain suitable.[24]

Those [creatures] that feed on water excel at swimming and are able to withstand cold.
Those that feed on earth [i.e., earthworms] do not have minds but are sensitive.
Those that feed on wood[25] are very powerful and are fierce.
Those that feed on grass excel at running but are stupid.
Those that feed on [mulberry] leaves produce silk and turn into moths.
Those that feed on flesh are brave and daring but are cruel.
Those that feed on *qi* [attain] spirit illumination and are long-lived.
Those that feed on grain are knowledgeable and clever but short-lived.
Those that do not feed on anything do not die and are spirits. [4/34/25–4/35/3]

---

22. There is a pun here using the word *zhi* 直, which means both "straight" and "true"; thus *zhi meng* 直夢 means both "straight dreams" and "true dreams."

23. Such water creatures were thought to grow larger or smaller in synchrony with the phases of the moon. These eight lines are a sort of doggerel verse, perhaps putting conventional wisdom into easily remembered form.

24. This line is transposed from 4/35/24, where it is clearly out of place.

25. Supposedly this refers to bears, which rip apart dead trees in search of grubs and honey.

4.10

Concerning humans, birds, and beasts, the myriad creatures and tiny organisms,
each has that from which it is born.
Some are odd and some are even;
some fly and some go on foot,
but no one understands these instinctive responses.
Only one who knows how to trace the Way can get to the source and root of it. [4/35/5–6]

Heaven is one, Earth is two, man is three.

Three times three equals nine. Nine times nine equals eighty-one. One governs the sun. The number of the sun is ten. The sun governs man, so man is born in the tenth month [of pregnancy].

Eight times nine equals seventy-two. Two governs even numbers. Even numbers contain odd numbers. Odd numbers govern the chronograms.[26] The chronograms govern the moon. The moon governs the horse, so horses are born in the twelfth month [of pregnancy].

Seven times nine equals sixty-three. Three governs the Dipper. The Dipper governs the dog, so dogs are born in the third month [of pregnancy].

Six times nine equals fifty-four. Four governs the seasons. The seasons govern the pig, so pigs are born in the fourth month [of pregnancy].

Five times nine equals forty-five. Five governs the musical notes [of the pentatonic scale]. The musical notes govern the ape, so apes are born in the fifth month [of pregnancy].

Four times nine equals thirty-six. Six governs the notes [of the pitch pipes]. The pitch-pipe notes govern the deer, so deer are born in the sixth month [of pregnancy].

Three times nine equals twenty-seven. Seven governs the stars. The stars govern the tiger, so tigers are born in the seventh month [of pregnancy].

Two times nine equals eighteen. Eight governs the wind. The wind governs insects, so insects undergo metamorphosis in the eighth month. [4/35/8–13]

4.11

All birds and fish are born of yin but are of the class of yang creatures.[27] Thus birds and fish are oviparous. Fish swim through water; birds fly in the clouds. Thus at the beginning of winter, swallows and sparrows enter the sea and transform into clams.

The myriad [living] creatures all are born as different kinds.

---

26. The chronograms (*chen* 辰) are the twelve earthly branches in their role as markers of the twelve lunar months of the year. See 3.19 and 3.27.

27. Oviparous animals are considered yin, but swimming and flying are yang forms of locomotion.

Silkworms eat but do not drink.
Cicadas drink but do not eat.

Mayflies neither eat nor drink. Armored and scaly creatures eat during the summer but hibernate in the winter.

Animals that eat without mastication have eight bodily openings and are oviparous.
Animals that chew have nine bodily openings and are viviparous.

Quadrupeds do not have feathers or wings. Animals that have horns do not have upper [incisor] teeth.

[Some] animals do not have horns and are fat but do not have front teeth.
[Other animals] have horns and are fat but do not have back teeth.
Creatures born during the day resemble their fathers;
creatures born at night resemble their mothers.
Extreme yin produces females;
extreme yang produces males.

Bears hibernate, and birds migrate seasonally.[28] [4/35/13–20]

4.12

For the same reasons,

white water is appropriate for [white] jade;
black water is appropriate for black stone [slate?],
Bluegreen water is appropriate for azure jade;
red water is appropriate for cinnabar;
yellow water is appropriate for gold;
clear water is appropriate for turtles.
The waters of the Fen River are turbid and muddy and are suitable for hemp.
The waters of the Qi River flow harmoniously and are suitable for wheat.
The waters of the Yellow River are blended together and are suitable for legumes.
The waters of the Luo [雒] River are light and beneficial and are suitable for grains.
The waters of the Wei [渭] River are powerful and are suitable for pannicled millet.
The waters of the Han River are heavy and calm and are suitable for bamboo.
The waters of the Yangzi River are fertile and benevolent and are suitable for rice.[29] [4/35/22–24]

28. The word *yi* 移 here is ambiguous and could refer to different types of variation among birds—for example, the difference in spring and autumn plumage in many species. We chose to translate it as "migrate," as *yi* often refers particularly to spatial change.

29. The line that follows in the Chinese text, *pingtu zhi ren hui er yi wugu* 平土之人慧而宜五穀, is clearly out of place here and has been moved up to the middle of 4.9.

4.13

The east is where streams and valleys flow to and from whence the sun and moon arise. The people of the east are heavy bodied and have small heads, prominent noses, and large mouths. They have raised shoulders like hawks and walk on tiptoe. All their bodily openings are channeled to their eyes. The nerves and [bodily] *qi* belong to the east. The color green governs the liver. The people there are tall and large; they become knowledgeable early but are not long-lived. The land there is suitable for wheat; it is full of tigers and leopards. [4/35/26–27]

The south is where yang *qi* gathers. Heat and damp reside there. The people of the south have long bodies and are heavy above. They have large mouths and prominent eyelids. All their bodily openings are channeled to their ears. The blood and the blood vessels belong to the south. The color red governs the heart. The people there mature early but die young. The land there is suitable for rice; it is full of rhinoceroses and elephants. [4/36/1–2]

The west is a region of high ground. Rivers issue forth from there, and the sun and moon set there. The men of the west have ill-favored faces and misshapen necks but walk with dignity. All their bodily openings are channeled to their noses. The skin belongs to the west. The color white governs the lungs. The people there are daring but not humane. The land there is suitable for millet; it is full of yaks and rhinoceroses. [4/36/4–5]

The north is a dark and gloomy place where the sky is closed up. Cold and ice are gathered there. Insects in their larval and pupal stages lie concealed there. The bodies of the people of the north are tightly knit, with short necks, broad shoulders, and low-slung buttocks. All their bodily openings are channeled to their genitals. The bones belong to the north. The color black governs the kidneys. The people there are stupid as birds or beasts but are long-lived. The land there is suitable for legumes and is full of dogs and horses. [4/36/7–9]

The center is where the wind and *qi* come together from all directions and is the place of confluence of the rains and the dew. The people of the central region have large faces and short chins. They consider beards beautiful and dislike obesity. All their bodily openings are channeled to their mouths. Flesh and muscle belong to the center. The color yellow governs the stomach. The people of the center are clever and sagelike and are good at government. The land there is suitable for grain and is full of cattle and sheep and the various domestic animals. [4/36/11–12]

4.14

Wood overcomes Earth, Earth overcomes Water, Water overcomes Fire, Fire overcomes Metal, Metal overcomes Wood. Thus,

> grain is born in the spring and dies in the fall.
> Legumes are born in the summer and die in the winter.
> Wheat is born in the autumn and dies in the summer.

Green vegetables are born in the winter and die in midsummer. [4/36/14–15]
When Wood is in its prime, Water is old, Fire is about to be born, Metal is paralyzed [imprisoned], and Earth is dead.
When Fire is in its prime, Wood is old, Earth is about to be born, Water is paralyzed, and Metal is dead.
When Earth is in its prime, Fire is old, Metal is about to be born, Wood is paralyzed, and Water is dead.
When Metal is in its prime, Earth is old, Water is about to be born, Fire is paralyzed, and Wood is dead.
When Water is in its prime, Metal is old, Wood is about to be born, Earth is paralyzed, and Fire is dead. [4/36/17–18]
There are five [musical] notes, of which the chief is *gong*.
There are five colors, of which the chief is yellow.
There are five flavors, of which the chief is sweet.
For positioning there are five materials, of which the chief is Earth.

This is why
refining Earth produces Wood,
refining Wood produces Fire,
refining Fire produces clouds [of metallic *qi*],
refining clouds produces Water,
and refining Water reverts to Earth.
Refining sweet produces sour,
refining sour produces acrid,
refining acrid produces bitter,
refining bitter produces salty,
and refining salty reverts to sweet.
Altering *gong* [note 1] produces *zhi* [note 4];[30]
altering *zhi* produces *shang* [note 2];
altering *shang* produces *yu* [note 5];
altering *yu* produces *jue* [note 3];
altering *jue* produces *gong*.

Thus one uses
Water to harmonize Earth,
Earth to harmonize Fire,
Fire to transform Metal,
and Metal to rule Wood;
Wood reverts to Earth.

The Five Phases interact together, and so useful things are brought to completion. [4/36/20–24]

30. This refers to the "ascending and descending" method of deriving the twelve-tone scale from a fundamental note. See 3.29 and app. B.

4.15

Beyond the seas are thirty-six countries.

In the region stretching from the northwest to the southwest, there are the Long Thighs; the Sky People, the People of Sushen, the White People, the Fertile[-Land] People, the Female People, the Male People, the One-Legged People, the One-Armed People, and the Three-Bodied People.

In the region stretching from the southwest to the southeast, there are the Bound-Breast People, the Winged People, the People of Huantou, the Naked People, the Three Miao Tribes, the Cross-Legged People, the Undying People, the Pierced-Breast People, the Tongue-Tied People, the Hog-Snouted People, the Chisel-Toothed People, the Three-Headed People, and the Long-Armed People.

In the region stretching from the southeast to the northeast, there are the Land of Giants, the Land of Superior People, the Black-Toothed People, the Dark-Legged People, the Hairy People, and the Hardworking People.

In the region stretching from the northeast to the northwest, there are the Tiptoe-Walking People, the People of Juying, the Deep-Eyed People, the People Without Anuses, the People of Rouli, the One-Eyed People, and the People of Wuji. [4/36/26–4/37/3]

4.16

Luotang Mountain and Warrior Mountain are in the northwest corner. The Pang Fish is [found] to the south of them. Twenty-eight gods[31] link their arms and serve the thearch by watching over the night to the southwest of them. Three pearl trees are northeast of them. Jade trees are [found] along the banks of the Vermilion River.

The Kunlun Mountains and Artemesia Hill are to the southeast.[32] There are found precious jade and [the countries of] Grayhorse and Viewflesh; in that place carambola trees, sweet flowering quince trees, sweet flowers, and the hundred kinds of fruit are produced.

Harmonious Hill is in the northeast corner. The three mulberry trees without branches are to its west. Bragging Father[33] and Hanging Ears dwell northeast of it. Bragging Father cast aside his staff, which grew into the Forest of Deng.

31. These presumably are personifications of the twenty-eight lunar lodges (*xiu* 宿). See 3.35.

32. In the "nine continents" scheme associated with the third-century B.C.E. thinker Zou Yan, China was located in the southeastern corner of a great continent. Mount Kunlun was therefore thought to be northwest of China proper, at the center of the terrestrial world. See the introduction to chap. 4 and fig. 4.1; and, in greater detail, John S. Major, "The Five Phases, Magic Squares, and Schematic Cosmography," in *Explorations in Early Chinese Cosmology: Papers Presented at the Workshop on Classical Chinese Thought Held at Harvard University, August 1976*, ed. Henry Rosemont Jr., Journal of the American Academy of Religion Studies, vol. 50, no. 2 (1984; repr., Charleston, S.C.: Booksurge, 2006), 133–66, esp. 134–37.

33. Kuafu 誇父, "Bragging Father," was a mythical strongman who raced the sun. See also 2.9.

The Hill of Kun Wu is in the south. Chariot Frame Hill[34] is to its west. Shaman Xian[35] dwells to its north, standing on Dengbao Mountain. Sunrise Valley and the Fusang Tree are to the east.

The land of You Song [or You Rong] is north of Mount Buzhou. The older sister was Jian Di; the younger sister was Jian Ci.[36] The Queen Mother of the West[37] dwells at the edge of the Flowing Sands. The Happy People[38] and the Nalu People live on an island in the Weakwater in Kunlun. Three Dangers Mountain is to the west of the Happy People.

Lighting Darkness and Candle Gleam are on an island in the Yellow River; they illuminate an area of one thousand *li*. The Dragon Gate is in the depths of the Yellow River. The Torrential Pool is in Kunlun. Dark Smelting [is near] Mount Buzhou. Shen Pool is in the Haiyu Marsh. The Mengzhu Marsh is in Pei. The Lesser and Greater Mansions are in Ji Province.

The Torch Dragon[39] dwells north of Wild Goose Gate. He hides himself in Abandoned Wings Mountain and never sees the sun. This god has a human face and a dragon body, but no feet.

The grave mound of Lord Millet[40] is to the west of the Jian Tree. The people there come to life again after they die. There are demifish in their midst. Flowing Yellow and the Fertile-Land People are three hundred *li* to the north. Dogland is to the east. In Thunder Marsh are gods with dragon bodies and human heads. They drum on their bellies to amuse themselves. [4/37/5–14]

---

34. The supposed birthplace of Huangdi, the Yellow Emperor, who is also known by the cognomen Chariot Frame.

35. Shaman Xian 巫咸, a legendary figure who was supposedly an official at the court of Tai Wu, the seventh Shang king. His name is associated with the mythical place-name and constellation the Pool of Xian (Xian chi 咸池). See chap. 3, n. 12, and chap. 11, n. 35.

36. Jian Di 簡翟 was the legendary first ancestress of the Shang people. She gave birth after swallowing an egg dropped by a dark bird sent by Heaven. Jian Ci 建疵 was the younger sister of Jian Di. Both were consorts to the divinity Di Gu.

37. Queen Mother of the West 西王母, a goddess who ruled over a western paradise in the Kunlun Mountains and is said to have been visited by King Mu of the Zhou. She is conventionally depicted wearing a distinctive hair ornament called a *sheng* 勝. In later times, she became a popular Daoist deity. See Suzanne E. Cahill, *Transcendence and Divine Passion: The Queen Mother of the West in Medieval China* (Stanford, Calif.: Stanford University Press, 1993); and Elfriede R. Knauer, "The Queen Mother of the West: A Study of the Influence of Western Prototypes on the Iconography of the Taoist Deity," in *Contact and Exchange in the Ancient World*, ed. Victor H. Mair (Honolulu: University of Hawai'i Press, 2006), 62–115.

38. This could be read either as *le min* 樂民, "happy people," or (with the same characters) *yue min*, "music people." The pun on music/joy is integral to the Chinese phrase but impossible to convey in English. It appears elsewhere in the text as well. See, for example, 14.59.

39. Possibly a personification of the aurora borealis.

40. Lord Millet or Hou Ji 后稷, the legendary first ancestor of the Zhou people. He is said to have been born after his mother trod on the footprint of a god.

4.17

The Yangzi issues from Mount Min and flows eastward, passing through Han and entering the ocean. It [then] turns left and flows north to [a point] north of Kaimu Mountain. Then it turns right and flows eastward to the Eastern Pillar.

The Yellow River issues from the Piled-Stone Mountain.

The Qu River issues from Mount Jing.

The Huai River issues from Mount Tongbo.

The Sui River issues from Feather Mountain.

The Clear Zhang River issues from Mount Jieli.

The Turbid Zhang River issues from Mount Fabao.

The Qi River issues from Mount Wangwu.

The Shi River, the Si River, and the Yi River issue from Mount Tai [臺], Mount Tai [台], and Mount Shu.

The Luo [洛] River issues from Mount Lie.

The Wen River issues from Mount Fuqi and flows westward to join the Qi River.

The Han River issues from Mount Bozhong.

The Jing River issues from Mount Boluo.

The Wei [渭] River issues from Bird-and-Rat Cave.

The Yi River issues from Mount Shangwei.

The Luo [雒] River issues from Bear Ear Mountain.

The Jun River issues from Flower Hole.

The Wei [維] River issues from Overturned-Boat Mountain.

The Fen River issues from Mount Yanjing.

The Ren River issues from Mount Fenxiong.

The Zi River issues from Mount Muyi.

The Cinnabar River issues from Lofty Capital Mountain.

The Pan River issues from Mount Qiao.

The Hao River issues from . . .[41]

The Bo River issues from Mount Xianyu.

The Liang River issues from Mount Maolu and Mount Shiliang.

The Ru River issues from Mount Meng.

The Qi River issues from Mount Dahao.

The Jin river issues from Mount Jiezhu [also called Dragon Mountain].

The He River issues from Mount Fengyang.

The Liao River issues from Grindstone Mountain.

The Fu River issues from Mount Jing.

The Qi River issues from Stone Bridge Mountain.

The Hutuo River issues from Mount Luping.

The Nituyuan River issues from Mount Man.

The Wei [維] River and the Shi River flow north into Yan. [4/37/16–23]

41. The name of the source of the Hao River is missing from the text.

The Weakwater issues from Exhausted Stone Mountain and enters the Flowing Sands.[42]

4.18

Zhu Ji and She Ti[43] were born from the Regular [northeast] Wind.[44]
Tong Shi was born from the Brightly Abundant [east] Wind.
Chifenruo was born from the Clear Bright [southeast] Wind.
Gong Gong was born from the Sunshine [south] Wind.
Zhu Bi was born from the Cooling [southwest] Wind.
Gao Ji was born from the Changhe [west] Wind.
Yu Qiang was born from the Buzhou [northwest] Wind.
Qiong Qi was born from the Broadly Expansive [north] Wind. [4/37/25–27]

Downyhair gave birth to Oceanman. Oceanman gave birth to Ruojun. Ruojun gave birth to sages; sages gave birth to ordinary people. Thus creatures with scanty hair are born from ordinary people.

Winged Excellence gave birth to Flying Dragon. Flying Dragon gave birth to the phoenix. The phoenix gave birth to the symurgh.[45] The symurgh gave birth to ordinary birds. Feathered creatures in general are born from ordinary birds.

Hairy Heifer gave birth to Responsive Dragon. Responsive Dragon gave birth to Establish Horse. Establish Horse gave birth to the *qilin*.[46] The *qilin* gave birth to ordinary beasts. Hairy animals in general are born from ordinary beasts.

Scaly One gave birth to Wriggling Dragon. Wriggling Dragon gave birth to Leviathan. Leviathan gave birth to Establish Emanation. Establish Emanation gave birth to ordinary fishes. Scaly creatures in general are born from ordinary fishes.

Armored Abyss gave birth to First Dragon. First Dragon gave birth to Dark Sea-Turtle. Dark Sea-Turtle gave birth to Divine Tortoise. Divine Tortoise gave birth to ordinary turtles. Armored creatures in general are born from ordinary turtles.

Warm Damp gave birth to Countenance. Warm Damp was born from Hair Wind. Hair Wind was born from Damp Darkness. Damp Darkness was born from Feather Wind. Feather Wind gave birth to Mild Armored–Creature. Mild Armored–Creature gave birth to Scaly Meager. Scaly Meager gave birth to Warm Armored–Creature.[47]

---

42. This sentence has been duplicated here from 4/33/12. See n. 12.

43. The figures mentioned here are mythical divinities, in some cases (She Ti, Chifenruo) personifications of the Jupiter years, for which, see 3.42.

44. The wind names in this section are the same as those in 3.12 but quite different from the list in 4.1; perhaps the two lists represent two separate traditions.

45. The *luan* 鸞, a mythical bird supposedly of very large size and with beautiful plumage, is described here as the evolutionary descendant of the "phoenix" (*fenghuang* 鳳凰).

46. The *qilin* 麒麟 is a composite mythical beast whose appearance was regarded as an omen of sagely government.

47. The preceding paragraph is garbled in the original, without any satisfactory way to sort it out. As it stands, the passage does not make very much sense.

The five classes [of animals] in their various manifestations flourished in the outside world and multiplied after their own kind. [4/38/1–7]

Sun Climber gave birth to Brightness Blocker. Brightness Blocker gave birth to Lofty Ru. Lofty Ru gave birth to Trunktree. Trunktree gave birth to ordinary trees. All plants with quivering leaves are born from ordinary trees.

Rooted Stem gave birth to Chengruo. Chengruo gave birth to Dark Jade. Dark Jade gave birth to Pure Fountain. Pure Fountain gave birth to Sovereign's Crime. Sovereign's Crime gave birth to ordinary grasses. All rooted stems are born from ordinary grasses.

Ocean Gate gave birth to Swimming Dragon. Swimming Dragon gave birth to Lotus Flower. Lotus Flower gave birth to Duckweed. Duckweed gave birth to Aquatic Plant. Aquatic Plant gave birth to seaweed. All rootless plants are born from ordinary seaweed. [4/38/9–12]

4.19

The *qi* of balanced earth is received into the yellow heaven, which after five hundred years engenders a yellow jade [possibly realgar or amber]. After five hundred years this engenders a yellow quicksilver, which after five hundred years engenders gold ["yellow metal"]. After one thousand years, gold engenders the yellow dragon. The yellow dragon, going into hiding, engenders the yellow springs. When the dust[48] from the yellow springs rises to become a yellow cloud, the rubbing together of yin and yang[49] makes thunder; their rising and spreading out make lightning. What has ascended then descends as a flow of water that collects in the yellow sea.

The *qi* of unbalanced earth is received into the bluegreen heaven, which after eight hundred years engenders a bluegreen malachite. After eight hundred years this engenders a bluegreen quicksilver, which after eight hundred years engenders lead ["bluegreen metal"]. After one thousand years, lead engenders the bluegreen dragon. The bluegreen dragon, going into hiding, engenders the bluegreen springs. When the dust from the bluegreen springs rises to become a bluegreen cloud, the rubbing together of yin and yang makes thunder; their rising and spreading out make lightning. What has ascended then descends as a flow of water that collects in the bluegreen sea.

The *qi* of vigorous earth is received into the vermilion heaven, which after seven hundred years engenders a vermilion cinnabar. After seven hundred years, this engenders a vermilion quicksilver, which after seven hundred years engenders copper ["vermilion metal"]. After one thousand years, copper engenders the vermilion dragon. The vermilion dragon, going into hiding, engenders the vermilion springs. When the dust from the vermilion springs rises to become a vermilion cloud, the

48. *Ai* 埃 literally means "dust" but here implies something more like "smog," an impure miasma that rises from subterranean realms to become a purified cloud.

49. The phrase *yin yang xiang bo* 陰陽相薄 also occurs in 3.2 and 17.174. See chap. 3, n. 5.

rubbing together of yin and yang makes thunder; their rising and spreading out make lightning. What has ascended then descends as a flow of water that collects in the vermilion sea.

The *qi* of weak earth is received into the white heaven, which after nine hundred years engenders a white arsenolite. After nine hundred years, this engenders a white quicksilver, which after nine hundred years engenders silver ["white metal"]. After one thousand years, silver engenders the white dragon. The white dragon, going into hiding, engenders the white springs. When the dust from the white springs rises to become a white cloud, the rubbing together of yin and yang makes thunder; their rising and spreading out make lightning. What has ascended then descends as a flow of water which collects in the white sea.

The *qi* of passive earth is received into the black heaven, which after six hundred years engenders a black slate. After six hundred years, this engenders a black quicksilver, which after six hundred years engenders iron ["black metal"]. After one thousand years, iron engenders the black dragon. The black dragon, going into hiding, engenders the black springs. When the dust from the black springs rises to become a black cloud, the rubbing together of yin and yang makes thunder; their rising and spreading out make lightning. What has ascended then descends as a flow of water that collects in the black sea. [4/38/14–27]

Translated by John S. Major

Five

SEASONAL RULES

"SEASONAL RULES" is the third part of a trilogy with chapters 3 and 4. Having established, in those chapters, the patterns of Heaven (and their astrological significance) and the shape of Earth (and how creatures interact with topography), the *Huainanzi*'s authors turn here to the role of monthly and seasonal ritual time in the proper governing of the empire. Reflecting the annual waxing and waning of the powers of yin and yang and the successive seasonal potency of each of the Five Phases (Wood, Fire, Earth, Metal, and Water), the chapter prescribes ritual behavior, colors of vestments, and actions of government for each of the year's twelve months; proscribes certain other behaviors and actions; and warns of the bad consequences of applying the rules appropriate to any one season inappropriately to any of the others. The year is divided not into the four natural seasons of the solar year but into five seasons (with the third month of summer being treated as an artificial fifth season, "midsummer") so as to make all the ritual prescriptions of the seasons conform to the correlative cosmology of the Five Phases. The chapter thus integrates yin–yang and Five Phase theory in a detailed and holistic fashion for the guidance of government policy throughout the year.

The Chapter Title

The title of this chapter is "Shi ze" 時則. *Shi* means "season" and, by extension, "time." *Ze* is one of several words in classical Chinese sharing a spectrum of meanings such as "law," "pattern," "model," "rule," "ordinance," and "commandment." (Other words in this group include *fa* 法, *lü* 律, *du* 度, and *ling* 令.) We translate the chapter title as "Seasonal Rules." The grouping of the chapter's twelve monthly sections into five "seasons" (the four natural seasons plus an artificial "midsummer") emphasizes the importance of seasonal time. The connotations of the English word "rules" capture the cosmic and impersonal nature of the chapter's prescriptions, which allow no latitude for modification or abrogation.

Chapter 5 is one of three versions of a text otherwise known as *Yueling* 月令 (*Monthly Ordinances*). One version is found as the first section of each of the first twelve chapters of the *Lüshi chunqiu*, the so-called Almanac chapters of that work.[1] Another version, substantially identical to that in the *Lüshi chunqiu* but collected into a single chapter, is found as chapter 6 of the *Liji* (*Record of Rites*).[2]

Summary and Key Themes

"Seasonal Rules" prescribes appropriate ritual and administrative behavior for the ruler throughout the year, according to a scheme based on the annual cycles of yin and yang and the Five Phases. The chapter begins with twelve sections corresponding to the twelve months and concludes with three more sections that supplement and amplify the prescriptions contained in sections 5.1 through 5.12. The first month of spring—that is, the second lunar month following the month in which the winter solstice occurs—is designated by the third earthly branch, *yin*. (This is the first civil month according to the so-called Xia calendar, followed throughout the *Huainanzi*.) Each of the monthly sections follows a set pattern of correlations, with the correlates varying systematically from section to section:[3]

> In the nth month of season A, *zhaoyao*[4] points to [the direction indicated by] earthly branch B. Lunar lodge C culminates at dusk; lodge D culminates at dawn.

---

1. Knoblock and Riegel 2000, 60–64, 77–79, 95–98, 115–18, 133–35, 153–56, 172–75, 189–92, 206–9, 223–26, 241–44, 258–61.

2. James Legge, trans., *Li Chi: Book of Rites*, Sacred Books of the East, vols. 27 and 28 (1885; repr., New Hyde Park, N.Y.: University Books, 1967), 1:249–310.

3. Compare the schematic outline of the LSCQ/*Liji* version of the *Yueling* in Major 1993, 220–21.

4. *Zhaoyao* 招搖, "Far Flight" (in Schafer's translation; a more literal rendering would be "Resplendent"), is a bright star in Boötes that in Chinese astronomy was taken to be an extension of the "pointer" of the handle of the Northern Dipper. See Edward H. Schafer, *Pacing the Void: T'ang Approaches to the Stars* (Berkeley: University of California Press, 1977), 52. See the reference to the star Yaoguang (Gemlike Brilliance, the last star in the handle of the Dipper) in 8.5. The direction in which the Dipper's handle points could be observed directly in the sky, or indirectly by means of the cosmograph (*shi* 式). For the cosmograph, see Donald Harper, "The Han Cosmic Board (*Shih* 式)," *Early China* 4 (1978–1979): 2; and Christopher Cullen, "Some Further Points on the *Shih*," *Early China* 6 (1980–1981): 31–46, esp. 37, fig. 6.

Season A occupies direction E; the season's heavenly stems are XY. The fullness of power is in [seasonal] phase F. The [seasonal] class of creatures is G. The pentatonic note is H [seasonal], the pitch pipe is I [monthly]. The number is J, the taste is K, the smell is L [all seasonal]. Sacrifices are made to the M household god; organ O is offered first [seasonal].

Omens and portents from the world of living creatures; signs of the changing year [monthly].

The Son of Heaven wears [seasonal] P-colored clothing. He rides in a chariot drawn by dragon horses of [seasonal] color P, wears P-colored jade pendants, and flies a P-colored banner. He eats grain Q and meat R (for ritual meals). He drinks water gathered from the eight winds and cooks with a fire kindled from stalks of [seasonal] plant S. The ladies of the court wear P-colored clothing with P-colored trim. They play musical instruments T and U. The weapon of season A is V; its domestic animal is W.

The Son of Heaven holds court in the [monthly] chamber N of the Mingtang, from where he issues appropriate orders.

Inauguration of season A [first month of each season only]. The Son of Heaven personally leads the Three Sires, Nine Lords, and the great nobles to meet the A season at the altar in the (direction E) suburb.

The Son of Heaven issues regulations for sacrifices and promulgates prescriptions and prohibitions appropriate to the month and the season and makes pronouncements regarding the people's livelihoods. The Son of Heaven issues charges to appropriate officials.

The chapter warns of the disastrous consequence of applying, in any given season, the rules appropriate to each of the other seasons.

Month N governs office Z; its tree is AA.

There are minor but systematic differences between monthly sections that begin a season and those that do not. The signs and portents from the natural world, the orders given to officials, and the prohibitions and prescriptions naturally vary from month to month, but overall this outline is followed closely in the twelve chapter sections corresponding to the twelve months of the year.

The chapter concludes with three sections that build on the twelve monthly sections:

1. Section 5.13, the "five positions" (*wu wei* 五位), provides information, partly geographical and partly mythographical, about five regions: east, south, the center, west, and north, with the rules governing each. These rules are prescriptions for the conduct of government and are similar but not identical to those for the five "seasons" contained in the twelve monthly sections of the text.

2. Section 5.14, the "six coordinates" (*liu he* 六合),[5] are six pairs of months linked

5. Note that the meaning of *liu he* here is different from its usual meaning (as in the opening lines of chap. 4) of "up and down, left and right, back and front."

conceptually as if by diagonals drawn across the celestial circle, similar to the "six departments" found in *Huainanzi* section 3.13. The pairs thus are of opposites—for example, first month of spring–first month of autumn, middle month of spring–middle month of autumn, and so on. (Note that in this scheme the third month of summer is not singled out as a special "midsummer" season.) Each of the twelve months is characterized in a phrase or two, followed by formulas for the pairs: "If government fails in its duties in month N, in month N + 6, there will be bad consequence X." The section ends with a set of prognostications similar to those concluding each of the twelve monthly sections of the text: "If in season A the ordinances of season B (C, D) are carried out, there will be bad consequence X (Y, Z)."

3. Section 5.15, the "six regulators" (*liu du* 六度), is a *fu* (poetic exposition) celebrating six measuring instruments—the marking cord, the level, the compass, the balance beam, the square, and the weight—that are correlated with Heaven, Earth, spring, summer, autumn, and winter, respectively. Each instrument is the subject of a poetic paean to its virtues as a standard, and later lines tell how each should be applied "in the regulation of the Mingtang," or in other words, to the annual calendar of ritual observances. (The Mingtang, a term sometimes translated as "Hall of Light," was a special building in which monthly and seasonal rituals were conducted.)

Throughout the chapter, appropriate monthly and seasonal rules, rituals, and other human and natural phenomena are linked to the two complementary annual cycles of yin and yang (expressed through the correlation of the twelve months with the twelve earthly branches and their associated directions) and the Five Phases. The yin–yang cycle is seen as an annual round of months in which yang begins to grow in the first month of spring, becomes dominant in summer, is at its maximum in the midsummer month, and wanes in autumn and winter as the power of yin emerges and grows. The Five Phases are most apparent in the ritual colors associated with each of the five seasons, but these chapters embrace many other Five Phase correlations as well.[6]

The extent to which these prescriptions and prohibitions formed, or even could have formed, the basis for Han ritual and public policy is an important historical question worthy of consideration. Approached from a modern sensibility, they strike the reader as fanciful. Even with some knowledge of Han ritual and politics, two arguments point in the direction of considering "Seasonal Rules" no more than an unreachable ideal of imperial behavior. The first is the sheer complexity and rigidity of the rules themselves. It is difficult to imagine a busy and overburdened emperor taking the time and trouble to carry out these measures in person, as the text demands. The second is the artificiality of the prescriptions themselves. There was, of course, general agreement on key points: the branch correlations of the months, the annual cycle of yin and yang, and the color and directional correlations of the Five

6. For tables of chap. 5's earthly-branch correlations with the twelve months and associated phenomena, and the Five-Phase correlations with the seasons and associated phenomena, see Major 1993, 222–23.

Phases. These had been widely understood and accepted since at least the mid–Warring States period. But other correlations—seasonal weapons, monthly trees, and the like—were not as securely established, and the correlations given in the *Yueling* (in the *Huainanzi* or any other version) represented the prescriptions of only one text. Many other texts circulating at the time also contained ritual calendars, with lists of prescriptions, prohibitions, and correlates that differed to greater or lesser degree from those of the *Yueling*. The choice of which text to follow would not have been uncontested, and the decision would have inevitably been as much a political one—which advisers were backing which text, and why—as one based on ritual and cosmological principles alone.

Nevertheless, there is considerable evidence that the Han emperors did attempt to carry out a ritual program like that prescribed in "Seasonal Rules," at least in its broadest outlines. First, considerable attention was paid to selecting the ruling phase of the Han dynasty itself. This was a matter of state policy and was the subject of heated debate and (in 104 B.C.E.) an actual change in the ruling phase, from Water to Earth.[7] From the beginning of the dynasty, emperors had carried out suburban sacrifices to the Five Thearchs (*wudi* 五帝)—not the traditional sage-rulers of mythical antiquity, such as the Divine Farmer and Lord Millet, but personifications or deifications of the Five Phases, conceived of as the Bluegreen, Red, Yellow, White, and Black thearchs. (Later their altars were made subordinate to another deified principle, the Grand One.)[8] At these rites, the emperor and his attendants would have been dressed in vestments of the appropriate color, just as prescribed in the "Seasonal Rules." Moreover, several Mingtang buildings were constructed in the Han period, not only at the capital but also at the foot of the holy Mount Tai. In these simple structures, emperors could sit in the correct monthly room, face in the appropriate direction, and issue edicts and instructions, just as envisioned in the "Seasonal Rules." And at a more general level of government operation, the annual and seasonal cycles of yin and yang and the Five Phases were respected in practice. It was a matter of settled policy, for example, to avoid carrying out executions in the spring and summer and to schedule them for the fall and winter, thereby matching the supposed cycles of leniency and severity of the cosmos itself.

Overall, it appears that while "Seasonal Rules" may not have been the keystone of Han ritual and public policy (which involved many other kinds of observances and actions as well), the emperors and their advisers and ministers did make a serious effort to carry out their prescriptions and prohibitions, although perhaps not in every detail.

7. Michael Loewe, "The Concept of Sovereignty," in *The Ch'in and Han Empires, 221 B.C.–A.D. 220*, ed. Denis Twitchett and Michael Loewe, vol. 1 of *The Cambridge History of China* (Cambridge: Cambridge University Press, 1986), 730, 737–39. See also Gopal Sukhu, "Yao, Shun, and Prefiguration: The Origins and Ideology of the Han Imperial Genealogy," *Early China* 30 (2005): 91–153, esp. 118–21.

8. These matters are discussed in detail in *Shiji* 28, "The Treatise on the Feng and Shan Sacrifices."

Sources

"Seasonal Rules" belongs to a genre of early Chinese almanacs that give astronomical, stem–branch, yin–yang, and Five Phase correlations for each of the twelve months and prescribe appropriate ritual and administrative behavior for the ruler throughout the year. As noted earlier, the *Huainanzi*'s "Seasonal Rules" is one of three extant versions of a text usually known as the *Yueling* (*Monthly Ordinances*). This text may once have existed as an independent work, but if so, it was not transmitted independently in the received tradition. The earliest extant version of the *Yueling* (possibly quoted from this now-lost hypothetical independent source) is found in the first twelve chapters of the *Lüshi chunqiu*, a text whose earliest portions date to about 239 B.C.E.[9] The other version, substantially identical to that in the *Lüshi chunqiu* (and either derived from it or based on the same now-lost original source), is a chapter of the *Liji* (*Record of Rites*). These texts also are similar to other texts prescribing behavior for the ruler in accordance with the seasons and the months and based on the concept of *ganying* (resonance) between the cosmos as a whole and the actions of humans.[10] These texts include the "Zhou yue" (Months of Zhou) chapter of the *Yizhou shu* (*Remnant Writings of the Zhou Period*); the "You guan" (Dark Palace), "Sishi" (Four Seasons), "Wuxing" (Five Phases), and "Qingzhong ji" (Light and Heavy) chapters of the *Guanzi* (*Book of Master Guan*);[11] as well as the "Xia xiaozheng" (Lesser Annuary of Xia), which is usually published with the *Da Dai liji* (*The Elder Dai's Record of Rites*) as an appendix to that text;[12] and the Chu silk manuscript.[13] The previously unknown text *Sanshi shi* (*Thirty Periods*), excavated at Yinqueshan in 1972 and dated to about 134 B.C.E., is similar to the *Guanzi*'s "You guan" chapter. Several sections of the third chapter of the *Huainanzi*, "Celestial Patterns"—particularly 3.16, 3.17, 3.22–24, and 3.26—are also closely related to this cluster of texts dealing with calendrical astrology.[14]

9. Some scholars, notably E. Bruce Brooks of the Warring States Project, argue that portions of the *Lüshi chunqiu* postdate the 235 B.C.E. date of the suicide of Lü Buwei.

10. On *ganying* resonance, see John B. Henderson, *The Development and Decline of Chinese Cosmology* (New York: Columbia University Press, 1984), 22–28; and Charles Le Blanc, "The Idea of *Kan-Ying* in *Huai-nan Tzu*," in Le Blanc 1985, 191–206.

11. "You guan" is translated in Rickett 1985, 169–92. The other chapters mentioned are translated in Rickett 1998: "Sishi," 108–17; "Wuxing," 118–28; and "Qingzhong ji" (in several parts), 446–516.

12. Translated as an appendix to William Soothill, *The Hall of Light: A Study of Chinese Kingship* (London: Lutterworth Press, 1951).

13. Noel Barnard, ed., *Ch'u and the Silk Manuscript*, vol. 1 of *Early Chinese Art and Its Possible Influence in the Pacific Basin* (New York: Intercultural Arts Press, 1972), esp. Jao Tsung-yi, "Some Aspects of the Calendar, Astrology, and Religious Conceptions of the Ch'u People as Revealed in the Ch'u Silk Manuscript," 113–22, and Hayashi Minao, "The Twelve Gods of the Chan-Kuo Period Silk Manuscript Excavated at Ch'ang Sha," 123–86.

14. Discussions of the *Yueling* texts, with reviews of the appropriate scholarly literature, can be found in Major 1993, 217–21; Knoblock and Riegel 2000, 35–43; Henderson, *Development and Decline of Chinese Cosmology*, 20–24; and Rickett 1985, 148–69. See also Fung Yu-lan, *A History of Chinese Philosophy*, trans. Derk Bodde (Princeton, N.J.: Princeton University Press, 1952–53), 1:164–65; Joseph Needham, *Mathematics and the Sciences of the Heavens and the Earth*, vol. 3 of *Science and*

Chapter 5 of the *Huainanzi* therefore must be seen in the context of a substantial body of calendrical works (probably including some now-lost works that have not been transmitted from the past) that, while differing widely in details, all agreed that it was imperative for the ruler to match his personal, ritual, and political conduct to the annual rhythms of yin and yang and the Five Phases. But it seems very likely that in that context, "Seasonal Rules" is directly descended from the *Lüshi chunqiu*. The *Lüshi chunqiu*'s "Annals" and the *Huainanzi*'s "Seasonal Rules" are not identical, but their differences are significant and systematic rather than minor and random; that is, they are likely to reflect deliberate editorial choices rather than copyists' errors. It also is possible that both the *Lüshi chunqiu* and the *Huainanzi* versions of the text (and, as noted earlier, the *Liji* version as well) were derived separately from a now-lost original source. The possibility that the *Lüshi chunqiu* and the *Huainanzi* are related only by common descent fades, however, with the observation that other portions of the *Huainanzi* (for example, 4.1 and 4.2, as noted in the introduction to chapter 4) are also quoted verbatim from the *Lüshi chunqiu*. Liu An, the king of Huainan, was not only a famous scholar and patron of scholarship but a bibliophile as well. It would therefore be surprising if his famous library at the court of Huainan did not include a copy of the *Lüshi chunqiu*,[15] which would have been available to the king's court scholars to serve as the source for "Seasonal Rules." The reasons for the systematic differences between the current *Lüshi chunqiu* and *Huainanzi* versions may be (1) that Liu An's copy of the *Lüshi chunqiu* was different from the present received version, in ways reflected in the current *Huainanzi* "Seasonal Rules"; and (2) that as the *Lüshi chunqiu* material was incorporated into the *Huainanzi*, it was systematically edited and revised to suit the beliefs and preferences of Liu An and his circle.

Whichever of those possibilities is correct, the differences among the *Lüshi chunqiu*, *Liji*, and *Huainanzi* texts are consistent and not random. One of the most conspicuous variations between the *Lüshi chunqiu* and *Huainanzi* versions is the use of the formula "*Zhaoyao* points to branch X" instead of "the sun is in lunar lodge Y" to begin each of the twelve monthly sections of the text. This substitution probably represents a tendency in the second century B.C.E.—the time of Liu An and his circle—to use the *shi* (cosmograph) for determining the astronomical and astrological positions of the heavenly bodies, rather than the direct visual observation that would have been employed a century or so earlier in the time of Lü Buwei. Other differences include the additional correlations that were systematically added to the *Huainanzi* version, including seasonal correlations of weapons, domestic animals,

Civilisation in China (Cambridge: Cambridge University Press, 1959), 194–96; Derk Bodde, *Festivals in Classical China: New Year and Other Annual Observances During the Han Dynasty, 206 B.C. to A.D. 220* (Princeton, N.J.: Princeton University Press, 1975); Hsü Dau-lin, "Crime and Cosmic Order," *Harvard Journal of Asiatic Studies* 30 (1970): 111–25; and William G. Boltz, "Philological Footnotes to the Han New Year Rites," *Journal of the American Oriental Society* 99 (1979): 425–39.

15. Or parts thereof, specifically the first twelve chapters, which at that time might have circulated as an independent text. It is likely that the *Lüshi chunqiu*, like many other early Chinese texts, had not yet achieved its familiar final form by the time the *Huainanzi* was written.

fuel for the ruler's ritual cooking fire, and monthly correlations of offices and trees. The *Lüshi chunqiu* version includes a seasonal thearch (*di* 帝) and god (*shen* 神) in the text for each month. These are omitted in the *Huainanzi* version, perhaps because a similar (although not identical) roster of planetary gods and their "assistants" already appears in section 3.6 and again as deities of the five directions in 5.13, the "five positions."

Chapter 5 of the *Huainanzi* and the *Lüshi chunqiu/Liji Yueling* versions have two other conspicuous differences. The first is the treatment of the artificial fifth season of "midsummer." Early ritual calendars from the Warring States period, such as the *Guanzi*'s "Four Seasons," base their ritual prescriptions on the self-evident fact that the year contains four, and only four, seasons. These are correlated in the customary fashion with the phases Wood, Fire, Metal, and Water; phase Earth and its correlates play little or no role. In the *Lüshi chunqiu/Liji Yueling,* the section for the sixth month treats it as the third month of summer, and all correlations for that month are to phase Fire. This section also contains a short supplementary (or alternative) section that gives phase Earth correlations for a midsummer season of unspecified date and duration. In chapter 5 of the *Huainanzi,* however, Earth correlations are substituted for Fire ones throughout the sixth month; in other words, the sixth month is treated as a separate midsummer "season," in defiance of astronomical reality but incorporating the theoretical resonances of the Five Phase system.

The other significant difference is that the three additional sections of chapter 5 of the *Huainanzi* (5.13–15) are neither found in nor closely related to the *Lüshi chunqiu.* They do not seem to be derived from any extant Warring States or early Han text. Therefore, they either may be original to the *Huainanzi* or were copied or derived from now-lost ancient texts. The fact that each of these three sections has a "set piece" quality to it—that is, each could stand alone as an independent short treatise—argues (entirely speculatively) for the latter possibility.

Regardless of how the differences between various versions of the text came about, chapter 5 of the *Huainanzi* and the *Lüshi chunqiu* and *Liji* versions of the *Yueling* are all, in effect, the same text in the sense that their commonalities are far more substantial than their differences.

The Chapter in the Context of the *Huainanzi* as a Whole

"Seasonal Rules," "Celestial Patterns," and "Terrestrial Forms" comprise a distinct subunit of the *Huainanzi.* Their treatment of the key issues of Heaven, Earth, and Time demonstrates to readers that the entire cosmos is an integrated whole and that the phenomena of the universe are in constant resonant contact with one another through the workings of yin and yang and the Five Phases, and the subtleties of *qi* matter-energy. An understanding of these matters, sufficient for a ruler to understand and acquiesce in or modify ritual procedures as suggested by his technical advisers, was an integral part of the curriculum for a young ruler-in-training devised by the Huainan masters.

The summary of "Seasonal Rules" in chapter 21 of the *Huainanzi*, "An Overview of the Essentials," says that

> "Seasonal Rules" provides the means by which to
> follow Heaven's seasons above;
> utilize Earth's resources below;
> determine standards and implement correspondences,
> aligning them with human norms.
> It is formed into twelve sections to serve as models and guides.
> Ending and beginning anew,
> they repeat limitlessly,
> adapting, complying, imitating, and according
> in predicting bad and good fortune.
> Taking and giving, opening and closing,
> each has its prohibited days,
> issuing commands and administering orders,
> instructing and warning according to the season.
> [It] enables the ruler of humankind to know the means by which to manage affairs. (21.2)

The program of this chapter thus fits smoothly into that of the work overall, in training a ruler to govern the empire with sagelike wisdom and enabling him to harmonize with the rhythms and cycles of the cosmos itself.

John S. Major

Five

5.1

In the first month of spring, Zhaoyao[1] points to [the earthly branch] *yin* [ENE]. [The lunar lodge] Array culminates at dusk; Tail culminates at dawn. [Spring] occupies the east. Its days are [the heavenly stems] *jia* and *yi*. The fullness of Potency is in Wood. Its beasts are [those of the] scaly [class]. Its [pentatonic] note is *jue*. The pitch pipe [of the first month] is Great Budding. The number [of spring] is eight. Its flavor is sour. Its smell is rank. Its sacrifices are made to the door god. From the body of the sacrificial victim, the spleen is offered first.

The east wind dispels the cold. Hibernating creatures begin to stir and revive. Fish rise and [rub their] backs [against] the ice. Otters sacrifice fish.[2] Look for the

1. *Zhaoyao* 招摇, "Far Flight" in Schafer's translation, is a bright star in the constellation Boötes. It was envisioned by the Chinese as the last star in the "handle" of the constellation *beidou* 北斗, "Northern Dipper" (usually called the "Big Dipper" in English). See Edward H. Schafer, *Pacing the Void: T'ang Approaches to the Stars* (Berkeley: University of California Press, 1977), 239. The direction to which the Dipper's handle points shifts one Chinese degree (1^d) per day with respect to the horizon—that is, one full rotation per solar year. It thus marks out directions on the horizon, which in turn are correlated with the lunar months. In the context of the *Huainanzi*, the reference to *Zhaoyao* as a moving pointer is probably not to the constellation itself but to the depiction of the constellation on the round "heaven plate" of the "cosmograph" (*shi* 式), an astronomical/astrological instrument that mimicked the movements of the Dipper.

2. Otters, which sometimes arrange fish that they have caught in a neat line on the bank of a stream, were thus thought in ancient China to "sacrifice" fish in a ritualistic manner. See also 5.9 and 9.28.

geese [to return] north. The Son of Heaven wears bluegreen clothing. He mounts [a carriage drawn by] azure dragon [horses]. He wears azure jade [pendants] and flies a bluegreen banner. He eats wheat with mutton. He drinks water gathered from the eight winds[3] and cooks with fire [kindled from] fern stalks. The imperial ladies of the Eastern Palace wear bluegreen clothing with bluegreen trim. They play *qin* and *se* [musical instruments]. The weapon [of spring] is the spear. The domestic animal [of spring] is the sheep.[4] [The Son of Heaven] holds the dawn session of court in the corner [chamber of the Mingtang] to the left of [i.e., counterclockwise from] the Bluegreen Yang Chamber in order to promulgate the spring ordinances. He extends his Moral Potency, bestows favor, carries out [rites of] celebration and praise, and reduces corvée exactions and tax levies. [5/39/3–7]

On the first day of spring, the Son of Heaven personally leads the Three Sires, the Nine Lords, and the great nobles to welcome the year at [the altar of] the eastern suburbs. He repairs and cleans out the place of sacrifice and [employs] wealth offerings to pray to the ghosts and spirits. Only male animals are used as sacrificial victims. It is prohibited to cut down trees. Nests must not be overturned nor the unborn young killed, likewise neither young creatures nor eggs. People must not be assembled [for labor duty] or fortifications erected. Skeletons must be reburied, and corpses interred. [5/39/9–11]

If during the first month of spring the ordinances of summer were carried out, then there would be unseasonable winds and rain; plants and trees would wither early; and there would be fear in the state. If the ordinances of autumn were carried out, the people would suffer epidemics; violent winds and torrential rains would arrive at the same time; and thorns, weeds, briars, and overgrowth would spring up together. If the ordinances of winter were carried out, floods would create ruin, and there would be rain, frost, and great hailstones. The first-sown seeds would not sprout. [5/39/13–14]

The first month governs the Master of Works. Its tree is the willow.[5] [5/39/16]

5.2

In the middle month of spring, Zhaoyao points to *mao* [E]. [The lunar lodge] Bow culminates at dusk; Establishing Stars culminates at dawn. [Spring] occupies the

3. On "water gathered from the eight winds," see 4.6: "The clouds of the eight outlying regions, the eight distant regions, and the eight marshes bring rain to the nine provinces and produce harmony in the central province." The implication here would seem to be that rainwater was collected for ritual use.

4. The Chinese word *yang* 羊 means both "sheep" and "goat," without distinguishing between the two. A more exact but less graceful translation would be "ovicaprid." We choose the translation "sheep" rather than "goat" because in early China, sheep seem to have been preferred to goats as sacrificial animals.

5. *Yang* 楊 ordinarily means "poplar." We follow the *Er Ya* in taking it as a type of willow in this instance.

east. Its days are *jia* and *yi*. Its beasts are [those of the] scaly [class]. Its [pentatonic] note is *jue*. The pitch pipe [of the second month] is Pinched Bell. The number [of spring] is eight. Its flavor is sour. Its smell is rank. Its sacrifices are made to the door god. From the body of the sacrificial victim, the spleen is offered first.

The rains begin. Peaches and pears begin to blossom. The oriole sings. Hawks metamorphose into pigeons. The Son of Heaven wears bluegreen clothing. He mounts [a carriage drawn by] azure dragon [horses]. He wears azure jade [pendants] and flies a bluegreen banner. He eats wheat with mutton. He drinks water gathered from the eight winds and cooks with fire [kindled from] fern stalks. The imperial ladies of the Eastern Palace wear bluegreen clothing with bluegreen trim. They play the *qin* and the *se*. The weapon [of spring] is the spear. The domestic animal [of spring] is the sheep. [The Son of Heaven] holds the dawn session of court in the Bluegreen Yang [chamber of the Mingtang]. He orders those in authority to ameliorate penal servitude and to cause manacles and fetters to be struck off. [There is to be] no flogging, and criminal trials are halted. The young and the small are to be nourished [and] the orphaned and childless protected in order that [these policies] may communicate [their efficacy] to the growing sprouts.[6] He chooses an auspicious[7] day and orders the people [to sacrifice] at shrines. [5/39/18–23]

In this month, the days and nights are equally divided. The sound of thunder begins to be heard. Hibernating insects all stir and revive. Anticipating the thunder by three days, [he sends messengers to] strike bells with wooden clappers, proclaiming among the people, "The thunder is about to sound forth. Those who are not careful of their demeanor [and] who give birth without taking [appropriate] precautions will surely suffer catastrophes." He orders the Master of Markets to make uniform all weights and measures: the *jun*, the steelyard, the *dan*, the catty, the peck, and the pail. [In this month, one must] not drain rivers and marshes, draw off water from embanked ponds, set fire to the mountain forests, or undertake any large-scale works such as would impede the efficiency of farming. In sacrifices, animal victims are not used; [rather] one uses [jade] scepters and disks, fur pelts, and rolls of [silk] cloth. [5/39/25–5/40/2]

If during the second month of spring the autumn ordinances were carried out, the country [would suffer] great floods and cold winds at the same time. Bandits and Rong [barbarians] would attack. If the ordinances of winter were carried out, the yang *qi* would not prevail; wheat would not ripen; and the people thereby would suffer great ruin. If the ordinances of summer were carried out, the country [would suffer] great drought, [and] hot *qi* would arrive prematurely. Insect pests would wreak havoc. [5/40/4–5]

The second month governs the granary. Its tree is the almond. [5/40/7]

---

6. Reading *ju* 句 as *gou* 茍.

7. Following Gao You's gloss of *yuan* 元 as "auspicious."

5.3

In the final month of spring, Zhaoyao points to *chen* [ESE]. [The lunar lodge] Seven Stars culminates at dusk; Ox Leader culminates at dawn. [Spring] occupies the east. Its days are *jia* and *yi*. Its beasts are [those of the] scaly [class]. Its [pentatonic] note is *jue*. The pitch pipe [of the third month] is Maiden Purity. The number [of spring] is eight. Its flavor is sour. Its smell is rank. Its sacrifices are made to the door god. From the body of the sacrificial victim, the spleen is offered first.

The *tong* tree begins to bloom. Fieldmice transform into quail. Rainbows first appear. Duckweed begins to sprout. The Son of Heaven wears bluegreen clothing. He mounts [a carriage drawn by] azure dragon [horses]. He wears azure jade [pendants] and flies a bluegreen banner. He eats wheat with mutton. He drinks water gathered from the eight winds and cooks with fire [kindled from] fern stalks. The imperial ladies of the Eastern Palace wear bluegreen clothing with bluegreen trim. They play the *qin* and the *se*. The weapon [of spring] is the spear. The domestic animal [of spring] is the sheep. [The Son of Heaven] holds the dawn session of court in the corner [chamber of the Mingtang] to the right of the Bluegreen Yang Chamber. [He orders] the Master of Boats to turn over the boats [to inspect them] five times over and five times back and then to deliver a report [on their condition] to the Son of Heaven. The Son of Heaven thereupon[8] boards his boats for the first time [in the new year]. A sturgeon is offered in the inner chamber of the [ancestral] temple, and prayers are made that the wheat should bear grain. [5/40/9–13]

In this month, the production of *qi* reaches its fullest, [and] yang *qi* is released. Young plants grow no more, and the sprouting plants attain their maximum growth, but they cannot [yet] be gathered in. The Son of Heaven orders those in authority to open the granaries and storehouses to assist the impoverished and the bereft, to relieve the exhausted and [those who are] cut off [from their families], and to open the strong rooms and treasuries to distribute rolls of silk. He sends embassies to the nobles, inquires after eminent scholars, and performs courtesies to the worthy. He orders the Minister of Works, when the seasonal rains are about to descend, to mount his carriage as the water descends and, following all of the roads from the capital city, make an inspection of the plains and uncultivated fields, repairing the dikes and embankments, channeling the ditches and watercourses, following to its end every road and comprehending every byway,

> beginning at the metropolis,
> stopping [only] upon reaching the border.

Those who hunt, [whether with] nets or with arrows, with rabbit snares or bird nets, or by putting out poisoned bait, are prohibited from going out from the nine gates [of the city]. [The Son of Heaven] also [issues] a prohibition to the foresters in the wilderness, [saying that there must be] no cutting down of mulberry trees or cudrania

8. Reading *wu* 烏 as *yan* 焉.

trees.[9] The turtledove spreads its wings, [and] the crested hoepoe lands in the mulberry tree. Preparing plain cocoon frames,[10] round baskets and rectangular baskets, the royal consort and the royal concubines fast and perform austerities. Then they go[11] to the mulberry [groves] in the eastern suburbs where

the lady overseers initiate
and supervise [the work of] sericulture.[12]

[He] commands [those in charge of] the five storehouses to order the workmen to inspect the gold and iron, the pelts and hides, the sinew and horn, the arrowshaft bamboo and the bow-wood, the grease and glue, the cinnabar and lac, [seeing to it that] there is none that is not excellent. Selecting an auspicious day in the last ten-day period of the month, [he holds] a great musical performance, which brings jubilation. Moreover [he orders] bulls to be mated with cows and stallions with mares; afterward the female animals are driven out to their herdsmen. He orders on behalf of the kingdom an exorcism at the nine gates [of the capital city], [and] sacrificial [animal victims] are torn apart in order to bring an end to the *qi* of springtime.

If the ordinances for this month are observed, sweet rain will fall during the three ten-day periods of the month. [5/40/15–22] If during the last month of spring the ordinances of winter were carried out, then cold *qi* would from time to time issue forth; all the plants and trees would wither; and the state would [suffer] great fear. If the ordinances of summer were carried out, the people would [suffer] epidemics; the seasonal rains would not fall; and nothing would grow on the mountains and tumuli. If the ordinances of autumn were carried out, Heaven would produce a flood of yin. Rains would fall [unseasonably] early, [and] military rebellions would break out. [5/40/24–25]

The third month governs villages. Its tree is the pear. [5/40/27]

5.4

In the first month of summer, Zhaoyao points to *si* [SSE]. [The lunar lodge] Wings culminates at dusk; [the constellation] Widow culminates at dawn. [Summer] occupies the south. Its days are *bing* and *ding*. The fullness of Potency is in Fire. Its beasts are [those of the] feathered [class]. Its [pentatonic] note is *zhi*. The pitch pipe [of the fourth month] is Median Regulator. The number [of summer] is seven. Its flavor is bitter. Its smell is burnt. Its sacrifices are made to the stove god. From the body of the sacrificial victim, the lungs are offered first.

Crickets and tree frogs sing on the hillsides; earthworms emerge. The king melon [begins to] set fruit. Bitter herbs flourish. The Son of Heaven wears vermilion cloth-

9. The *Cudrania*, or false-mulberry tree, is an alternative source of food for silkworms when mulberry leaves are not available.

10. Reading *qu* 曲 as *qu* 笛.

11. Reading *qin* 親 as *jiu* 就, as in TPYL.

12. Reading *quan* 勸 as *guan* 觀, as in TPYL.

ing. He mounts [a carriage drawn by] black-maned vermilion horses. He wears vermilion jade [pendants] and flies a vermilion banner. He eats legumes with chicken. He drinks water gathered from the eight winds and cooks with fire [kindled from] cudrania branches. The imperial ladies of the Southern Palace wear vermilion clothing with vermilion trim. They play reed pipes and mouth organs. The weapon [of summer] is the glaive.[13] The domestic animal [of summer] is the chicken. [The Son of Heaven] holds the dawn session of court in the corner [chamber of the Mingtang] to the left of the Mingtang Chamber, in order to promulgate the summer ordinances. [5/41/1–5]

On the first day of summer, the Son of Heaven personally leads the Three Sires, the Nine Lords, and the great nobles to welcome the year at [the altar of] the southern suburbs. Returning [from this ceremony], he bestows favors, enfeoffs nobles, rectifies ceremonials and music, and gives a feast for [the officials of] the left and the right. He commands the Intendant-General to single out for praise the heroic and meritorious, to select the eminent and excellent, and to raise up the filial and fraternal. He carries out [ceremonies of] ennoblement and issues official emoluments; assisting [the work of] Heaven, he increases the nurture [of the people], lengthens what is long [and] piles up what is high. [There must be] no destructive or vicious [behavior]. It is prohibited to build up earthen [fortifications] or to cut down great trees. He orders the foresters to travel [through] the cultivated fields and the plains, to encourage the practices of agriculture, and to drive away [both] wild and domestic animals so as not to permit them to harm the [growing] grain. The Son of Heaven takes a pig [and] sacrificial wheat and presents them as the first offerings in the inner chamber of the [ancestral] temple. Domestic animals are rounded up, and the hundred medicinal herbs [are gathered]. The fragile grassy plants die, and wheat attains its autumn growth. Minor criminal cases are decided, and petty punishments are carried out. [5/41/7–10]

If during the first month of summer the autumn ordinances were carried out, then bitter rains would come on numerous occasions. The grain would not be nourished [by that rain]. Neighboring peoples on four sides would penetrate [the country's] defensive fortifications. If the ordinances of winter were carried out, the plants and trees would dry up early; thereafter there would be floods, destroying the city walls and outer fortifications. If the ordinances of spring were carried out, grasshoppers and locusts would cause devastation; scorching winds would come and attack [the fields, so that] the flourishing plants would not bear seed. [5/41/12–13]

The fourth month governs the tilled fields. Its tree is the peach. [5/41/15]

13. *Ji* 戟 is a weapon with a long, curved blade mounted to the end of a pole, similar to the medieval European glaive.

5.5

In the second month of summer, Zhaoyao points to *wu* [S]. [The lunar lodge] Neck culminates at dusk; [the lodge] Rooftop culminates at dawn. [Summer] occupies the south. Its days are *bing* and *ding*. Its beasts are [those of the] feathered [class]. Its [pentatonic] note is *zhi*. The pitch pipe [of the fifth month] is Luxuriant. The number [of summer] is seven. Its flavor is bitter. Its smell is burnt. Its sacrifices are made to the stove god. From the body of the sacrificial victim, the lungs are offered first.

The Lesser Heat arrives; mantises are born. The shrike begins to cry; the turn-tongue is not heard.[14] The Son of Heaven wears vermilion clothing. He mounts [a carriage drawn by] black-maned vermilion horses. He wears vermilion jade [pendants] and flies a vermilion banner. He eats legumes with chicken. He drinks water gathered from the eight winds and cooks with fire [kindled from] cudrania branches. The imperial ladies of the Southern Palace wear vermilion clothing with vermilion trim. They play reed pipes and mouth organs. The weapon [of summer] is the glaive. The domestic animal [of summer] is the chicken. [The Son of Heaven] holds the dawn session of court in the Mingtang Great Chamber. He commands the Music Master to repair the hand drums and kettle drums, the *qin* and the *se*, the flutes and panpipes; to polish the bells and chimestones; and to attend to the [ceremonial] shields, battle-axes, haldberds, and feather plumes [used in war dances].

[He] commands those in authority to pray and sacrifice to the mountains, rivers, and the hundred [= all] river sources. In the great prayer to the gods for rain, a full panoply of music is employed. The Son of Heaven takes a chicken [and] the sacrificial pannicled millet, along with a sacrificial offering of ripe peaches, and presents them [all] as first offerings in the inner temple of the [ancestral] temple. [He] issues prohibitions to the people, [saying that they must] not reap indigo for dyeing, bake charcoal, or dry bolts of cloth in the sun. City and village gates must not be closed, [and] taxes must not be levied on markets. Serious criminal cases are put off, and [the prisoners'] rations are increased. Widows and widowers are preserved [from want], and relief is distributed to [those incurring] funeral expenses. The [pregnant] female animals are separated out from the herds, [and] stallions and colts are tied up. [The ruler] promulgates regulations for [the raising of] horses. [5/41/17–24]

The longest day [of the year] arrives. Yin and yang contend. Life and death reach a dividing point. The nobles fast and perform austerities. They display no angry emotions, refrain from music and sex, and eat meagerly. Officials all rest in tranquillity from their duties and do not travel abroad; [all this] in order to make definite the establishment of the serene [forces of] yin. Deer shed their antlers, [and] cicadas begin to sing. The half-summer plant begins to grow, [and] the hibiscus tree blooms. A prohibition is issued to the people, [saying] they must not set fires. [But] it is per-

14. The turn-tongue, *fanshe* 反舌, is a kind of bird, possibly a blackbird, that can imitate the songs of other birds. The blackbird is more commonly known as the hundred-tongue (*bai she* 百舌). See 16.44.

mitted to dwell in high places [so as to] see clearly into the distance, to climb on hills and mounds, and to stay on estrades and towers. [5/41/26–28]

If during the middle month of summer the ordinances of winter were carried out, hail and sleet would damage the grain; the roads would be impassable; and fierce armies would invade. If the ordinances of spring were carried out, the five kinds of grain would not ripen; all kinds of destructive insects would spring up during the season; and the country would suffer famine. If the ordinances of autumn were carried out, the plants and trees would droop and fall; fruits and grains would ripen prematurely; and the people would suffer calamities of pestilence. [5/42/1–2]

The fifth month governs functionaries. Its tree is the elm. [5/42/4]

5.6

In the final month of summer, Zhaoyao points to *wei* [SSW]. [The lunar lodge] Heart culminates at dusk; [the lodge] Stride culminates at dawn. [Midsummer] occupies the center. Its days are *wu* and *jia*. The fullness of Potency is in Earth. Its beasts are [those of the] naked [class].[15] Its [pentatonic] note is *gong*. The pitch pipe [of the sixth month] is Hundred Bell.[16] The number [of midsummer] is five. Its flavor is sweet. Its smell is fragrant. Its sacrifices are made to the [god of the] drain hole. From the body of the sacrificial victim, the heart is offered first.

The cool winds begin to arrive, [and] crickets dwell in the snug corners [of the house]. [Young] geese begin to practice flying, [and] rotting vegetation transforms into millipedes.[17] The Son of Heaven wears yellow clothing. He mounts [a carriage drawn by] black-maned yellow horses. He wears yellow jade [pendants] and flies a yellow banner. He eats millet with beef. He drinks water gathered from the eight winds and cooks with fire [kindled from] cudrania branches. The imperial ladies of the Central Palace wear yellow clothing with yellow trim. They play reed pipes and mouth organs. The weapon [of midsummer] is the sword. The domestic animal [of midsummer] is the ox. [The Son of Heaven] holds the dawn session of court in the Central Palace [chamber of the Mingtang]. [He] commands the Master of Fisheries to spear scaly dragons, capture alligators, fetch up turtles [from the depths], and capture sea turtles. [He] commands the Marsh Masters to present timber and rushes. [He] commands the four supervisory lords to order all districts [to present] the customary [amount of] fodder to feed the sacrificial beasts. In service to the Supreme Thearch of August Heaven,[18] the illustrious mountains, the great rivers, and the gods

15. Reading *luo* 羸 as *luo* 裸, "naked"—that is, hairless. Five-Phase theory calls for creatures of the "naked class"—that is, humans—to be correlated with the center and midsummer.

16. Hundred Bell is another name for Forest Bell (*linzhong* 林鍾).

17. For the millipede, see also 13.22, 15.12, and 17.151.

18. Supreme Thearch (Shangdi 上帝) was the high god of the Shang culture. Here the term is being used in a more generic sense to indicate the deity who presides over the cosmos in like fashion to the rule of the Son of Heaven over the human realm.

of the four directions, he sacrifices millet in the great sanctuary of the [ancestral] temple, praying for the prosperity of the people.

[He] carries out benefactions, commanding that the dead should be mourned, the sick inquired after, and the elderly protected and cared for. He causes bran and gruel to be sent to them and sees to it that their sleeping mats are [comfortably] thick. [All this is] to speed the myriad things on their return [journey as the year begins to wane]. [He] commands the officials of the women's [quarters] to dye [fabrics] in various hues and multicolored designs, patterned and ornamented, bluegreen, yellow, white, and black. There may be none that are not beautiful and fine. [This is to] provide new vestments for the ancestral temple: There must be a display of [things] that are brightly new. [5/42/6–13]

In this month, the trees that were planted are fully flourishing, [and] one must not dare cut them. It is not permitted to call an assembly of the nobles, to raise earthworks, to recruit corvée labor, or to call up armies. [If these things were done], Heaven inevitably would call down calamities. The soil is richly wet from the humid heat, and the great rains fall in season, beneficially bringing to an end the life cycle of the grassy plants. It is permitted to[19] fertilize the fields and to enrich the boundary strips between the fields. [5/42/15–16]

If during the last month of summer the ordinances of spring were carried out, the kernels of grain would scatter and fall; [the people would suffer] many colds and coughs; and people would depart the country. If the ordinances of autumn were carried out, hills and lowlands alike would be flooded; the grain that had been sown would not ripen; and there would be many women's calamities [= miscarriages]. If the ordinances of winter were carried out, then winds and cold would arrive out of season; falcons and hawks would snatch their prey [unseasonably] early; and along the four borders of the country, people would withdraw to places of safety. [5/42/18–19]

The sixth month governs the Lesser Ingathering. Its tree is the catalpa. [5/42/21]

5.7

In the first month of autumn, Zhaoyao points to *shen* [WSW]. [The lunar lodge] Dipper culminates at dusk; [the lodge] Net culminates at dawn. [Autumn] occupies the west. Its days are *geng* and *xin*. The fullness of Potency is in Metal. Its beasts are [those of the] hairy [class]. Its [pentatonic] note is *shang*. The pitch pipe [of the seventh month] is Tranquil Pattern. The number [of autumn] is nine. Its flavor is pungent. Its smell is rancid. Its sacrifices are made to the door god. From the body of the sacrificial victim, the liver is offered first.

Cool winds arrive, [and] the hoarfrost descends. Cold-weather cicadas sing. Hawks sacrifice birds. [This is] used [as a signal to] begin executing criminals. The Son of Heaven wears white clothing. He mounts [a carriage drawn by] black-maned white

---

19. Reading *keyi* 可以, as in LSCQ.

horses. He wears white jade [pendants] and flies a white banner. He eats hemp seed with dog meat. He drinks water gathered from the eight winds and cooks with fire [kindled from] cudrania branches. The imperial ladies of the Western Palace wear white clothing with white trim. They play music on white[-metal] bells. The weapon [of autumn] is the halberd.[20] The domestic animal [of autumn] is the dog. [The Son of Heaven] holds the dawn session of court in the corner [chamber of the Mingtang] to the left of the Comprehensive Template [chamber], in order to promulgate the autumn ordinances. [He commands his officials to] search out the unfilial and unfraternal and those who are oppressive, cruel, tyrannical, and ruthless, in order to punish them, thus encouraging the waxing of baleful *qi*. [5/42/23–5/43/3]

On the first day of autumn, the Son of Heaven personally leads the Three Sires, the Nine Lords, and the great nobles to welcome the autumn at [the altar of] the western suburbs. Returning [from this ceremony], at court he bestows rewards on the leaders of his armies and on his soldiers. [He] orders the generals and commanders to select soldiers and sharpen weapons, seeking out and selecting men who are heroic and valiant, placing trust in those of proven accomplishments. [This is done] so that he might chastise the unrighteous and investigate and punish the overbearing and those who are derelict in their duties. [The execution of these orders] must extend to the farthest reaches of the realm.

[He] orders those in authority to set in order the laws and regulations and to repair the prisons, to prohibit licentiousness and bring an end to depravity, [and] to judge criminal cases and adjudicate disputes at law. Heaven and Earth now begin to be severe; it therefore is not permissible to act with mildness.

In this month the farmers begin to present their [newly harvested] grain to the throne. The Son of Heaven [ritually] tastes the new grain and then offers it as the first sacrificial offering in the inner shrine of the [ancestral] temple. [He] orders all the officials to begin to gather [the tax grain], to complete [the building of] barriers and embankments, to pay careful attention to embankments and dikes in order to prepare for floods, to repair city walls and boundary walls, and to refurbish palaces and mansions. There must be no enfeoffment of nobles or raising high officials to office; there must be no bestowals of costly gifts or any sending forth of important embassies. [5/43/5–9]

If the ordinances for this month are observed, the cool winds will arrive in thirty days. [5/43/9–10] If during the first month of autumn the ordinances of winter were observed, the yin *qi* would be excessive; land snails[21] would devour the grain; and Rong ["barbarian"] warriors would invade. If the ordinances of spring were observed, the country would suffer drought; the yang *qi* would return [out of season]; and the

20. The halberd or "dagger axe," *ge* 戈, had one or more short, broad daggerlike blades mounted transversely near one end of a pole several feet long. It was one of the principal weapons of ancient China, used by both foot soldiers and chariotmen from the Shang era through the Warring States period. Wang Niansun and Yu Dacheng argue strenuously that the weapon of autumn should be the battle axe, *yue* 戉. We have taken note of that opinion but have translated the text as written. See Zhang Shuangdi 1997, 1:575–76n.11.

21. *Jiechong* 介蟲, "shelled insects"; here the context calls for the meaning "land snails."

five kinds of grain would not yield any harvest. If the ordinances of summer were observed, there would be many disastrous fires; cold and heat would not conform to their seasonal order; and the people would suffer fevers. [5/43/12–13]

The seventh month governs the armory. Its tree is the Chinaberry. [5/43/15]

5.8

In the second month of autumn, Zhaoyao points to *you* [W]. [The lunar lodge] Ox Leader culminates at dusk; [the lodge] Turtle Beak culminates at dawn. [Autumn] occupies the west. Its days are *geng* and *xin*. Its beasts are [those of the] hairy [class]. Its [pentatonic] note is *shang*. The pitch pipe [of the eighth month] is Southern Regulator. The number [of autumn] is nine. Its flavor is pungent. Its smell is rancid. Its sacrifices are made to the door god. From the body of the sacrificial victim, the liver is offered first.

The cool winds arrive. Look for the wild geese to arrive. Swallows return [to their wintering grounds], [and] flocks of birds fly to and fro. The Son of Heaven wears white clothing. He mounts [a carriage drawn by] black-maned white horses. He wears white jade [pendants] and flies a white banner. He eats hemp seed with dog meat. He drinks water gathered from the eight winds and cooks with fire [kindled from] cudrania branches. The imperial ladies of the Western Palace wear white clothing with white trim. They play music on white[-metal] bells. The weapon [of autumn] is the halberd. The domestic animal [of autumn] is the dog. [The Son of Heaven] holds the dawn session of court in the Comprehensive Template [chamber of the Mingtang]. He orders those in authority to increase the strictness of all punishments. Beheadings and other capital punishments must be applied appropriately, with neither excess nor leniency.

> If the application of punishments is not appropriate,
> the penalty will revert to [those in authority].[22] [5/43/17–21]

In this month the elderly must be carefully attended to; they are given stools and walking sticks, congee and gruel, drink and food. [He] commands those in charge of sacrifices and prayer to go to the sacrificial beasts and see to their fodder and grain, examine their fatness or leanness, and see that they are of uniform color. [The officials] check the sacrificial beasts for suitability and color, examine their quality and type, measure whether they are small or large, and see whether they are immature or fully grown. When [they are sure that] none fail to meet the required standard, the Son of Heaven [sacrifices them] in an exorcism to lead in the autumn *qi*. [He] takes a dog and [ritually] tastes [its flesh, along with] hemp seed, and then offers them as the first sacrificial offerings in the inner chamber of the [ancestral] temple.

In this month, it is permitted to build city walls and outer fortifications, to establish metropolises and walled towns, to dig underground irrigation channels and storage

22. This is a rhymed couplet and could be translated loosely as "If a punishment's applied but does not fit, It reverts upon him who ordered it."

pits, and to repair granaries and storehouses. [He] also commands those in authority more urgently to collect the taxes [due from] the people, to store vegetables, and to accumulate large stores [of all sorts of things]. [The officials] exhort the people to plant the [winter] wheat,[23] without missing the time [for doing so]. If any should miss the time [for planting], they will be punished without fail.

In this month the thunder begins to recede. Hibernating creatures shut the doors [of their burrows]. The deadly [yin] *qi* gradually becomes abundant, [and] the yang *qi* daily declines. Water begins to dry up. Day and night are equally divided. [The Son of Heaven orders the Master of Markets to] calibrate correctly the weights and measures, equalize the balance beam and its weights; correct the weight of the *jun*, the *dan*, and the catty [and the volume] of the peck and the pail. [He orders his officials to] regulate barrier gates and markets and to bring in [to the capital] merchants and travelers [to] import goods and wealth so as to promote the affairs of the people. Coming from the four quarters and assembling from distant places, they arrive with wealth and goods. There is no deficiency in what is offered [in the markets], no exhaustion of what is [made available for] use; thus affairs of all sorts are facilitated. [5/43/23–5/44/6]

If during the second month of autumn the ordinances of spring were carried out, the autumn rains would not fall; plants and trees would blossom [out of season]; and the country would be in fear. If the ordinances of summer were carried out, the country would suffer drought; creatures that hibernate would not retire to their burrows; and the five kinds of grain would all [unseasonably] sprout again. If the ordinances of winter were carried out, calamities caused by wind would arise over and over again, the thunder that had abated would break out again prematurely, and plants and trees would die too soon. [5/44/8–9]

The eighth month governs military officers. Its tree is the cudrania. [5/44/11]

5.9

In the last month of autumn, Zhaoyao points to *xu* [WNW]. [The lunar lodge] Emptiness culminates at dusk; [the lodge] Willow culminates at dawn. [Autumn] occupies the west. Its days are *geng* and *xin*. Its beasts are [those of the] hairy [class]. Its [pentatonic] note is *shang*. The pitch pipe [of the ninth month] is Tireless. The number [of autumn] is nine. Its flavor is pungent. Its smell is rancid. Its sacrifices are made to the door god. From the body of the sacrificial victim, the liver is offered first.

Wild geese arrive as guests. Sparrows enter the ocean and turn into clams. Chrysanthemums bear yellow flowers. Dholes sacrifice small animals and kill birds.[24] The

23. Deleting the word *su* 宿; it is superfluous, and the rhetoric of this line calls for a three-character phrase.

24. The dhole (*chai* 豺) is a small wild dog of southern Asia. Like the otter, it sometimes leaves uneaten for a period of time small animals that it has killed and so was thought to "sacrifice" its prey. See 5.1 and 9.28.

Son of Heaven wears white clothing. He mounts [a carriage drawn by] black-maned white horses. He wears white jade [pendants] and flies a white banner. He eats hemp seed with dog meat. He drinks water gathered from the eight winds and cooks with fire [kindled from] cudrania branches. The imperial ladies of the Western Palace wear white clothing with white trim. They play music on white[-metal] bells. The weapon [of autumn] is the halberd. The domestic animal [of autumn] is the dog. [The Son of Heaven] holds the dawn session of court in the corner [chamber of the Mingtang] to the right of the Comprehensive Template [chamber]. [He] commands those in authority to further increase the severity of their proclamations. [He] orders all officials [to see to it that] among nobles and commoners [alike], there is none who does not fulfill his duty to bring in [the harvest] in accordance with the going-into-storage [= quiescence] of Heaven and Earth. Nothing must be taken out [of storehouses]. [He] also issues orders to the chief minister that when all agricultural affairs are settled and [the grain tax has been] received, [he should] present an accounting of receipts of the five kinds of grain. The grain harvested from the sacred fields is stored in the spirit granary. [5/44/13–18]

In this month the hoarfrost begins to descend, [and] the various artisans rest from their work. [He] therefore commands those in authority to make [a public announcement] saying, "The cold *qi* has definitely set in. The people's strength cannot withstand it. All should [now] stay inside their dwellings." On the first *ding* day of the month, [the musicians] enter the Hall of Study to practice playing wind instruments. A great sacrificial feast is held for the thearch.[25] The beasts offered in sacrifice are sampled. [The Son of Heaven] assembles the Lords of the Land and those who govern all of the districts so that they may receive [the almanac, which sets] the first days of the months of the coming year. [He] gives the Lords of the Land the light and heavy standard [weights] for the taxation of the people. The annual schedule for presenting tribute is set according to the distance [of the fief from the royal domain] and the quality of the land.

[He] also instructs them in hunting so that they may practice the use of the five weapons. [He] orders the grand charioteer and the seven [grades of] grooms to yoke up the chariots and set out banners. Chariots are assigned [to the nobles] on the basis of rank and [are] arrayed in correct order before the screen-of-state [of the ruler]. The minister-overseer, with his baton of office stuck into his sash, stands facing north and gives [the hunters] their instructions. Then the Son of Heaven, wearing martial garb and wide-spreading ornaments, grasps his bow and holds his arrows, and [goes forth] to hunt. [At the conclusion of the hunt,] he orders the Master of Sacrificial Rites to sacrifice [some of] the game to the [gods of] the four directions.

In this month [the leaves of] the plants and trees turn yellow and fall; then their branches are cut and made into charcoal. Hibernating creatures all go [farther] into concealment. Thereupon [those in authority] hasten [the process of] judgment and punishment and do not delay in executing the guilty. [The Son of Heaven] receives

25. That is, *di* 帝, presumably the same deity as the Supreme Thearch of August Heaven (*huangtian shangdi* 皇天上帝) mentioned in 5.6. See Lau, HNZ 5/42/11.

[the petitions of] those whose emoluments and rank do not correspond [to their due] and [of] those who [have] not [received] care and nurture according to right principles. [He orders the Master of Works] to go along the highways and open up the roads from the frontiers to the capital. In this month, the Son of Heaven takes a dog and [ritually] tastes [its flesh, along with] hemp seed, and then presents them as the first sacrificial offering in the inner chamber of the [ancestral] temple. [5/44/20–5/45/2]

If the ordinances of summer were observed in the final month of autumn,, then the country would suffer floods, and the winter stores would be destroyed. The people would suffer respiratory diseases. If the ordinances of winter were observed, there would be many robbers and bandits in the country; the frontiers would be unquiet, and the territory [of the state] would be divided and split up [by others]. If the ordinances of spring were observed, warm winds would arrive [out of season]; the people's energies [*qi*] would be dissipated accordingly; and battalions and companies [of troops] would thereupon rise up [in rebellion]. [5/45/4–5]

The ninth month governs the Lords of the Land.[26] Its tree is the sophora. [5/45/7]

5.10

In the first month of winter, Zhaoyao points to *hai* [NNW]. [The lunar lodge] Rooftop culminates at dusk; [the lodge] Seven Stars culminates at dawn. [Winter] occupies the north. Its days are *ren* and *gui*. The fullness of Potency is in Water. Its beasts are [those of the] armored [class]. Its [pentatonic] note is *yu*. The pitch pipe [of the tenth month] is Responsive Bell. The number [of winter] is six. Its flavor is salty. Its smell is putrid. Its sacrifices are made to the well god. From the body of the sacrificial victim, the kidneys are offered first.

Water begins to freeze. The earth begins to harden with cold. Pheasants enter the ocean and turn into large clams. The rainbow [dragon] remains hidden and is not seen. The Son of Heaven wears black clothing. He mounts [a carriage drawn by] black horses. He wears black jade [pendants] and flies a black banner. He eats millet with suckling pig. He drinks water gathered from the eight winds and cooks with fire [kindled from] pine branches. The imperial ladies of the Northern Palace wear black clothing with black trim. They play music on chimestones. The weapon [of winter] is the partisan.[27] The domestic animal [of winter] is the pig.[28] [The Son of Heaven] holds the dawn session of court in the corner [chamber of the Mingtang] to the left of the Dark Hall [chamber], in order to promulgate the winter ordinances. He

26. Taking *hou* 候, "marquises," here as equivalent here to *zhu hou* 諸候, "Lords of the Land"—that is, all high-ranking nobles.

27. *Sha* 鎩, a pole-mounted thrusting weapon with a swordlike blade fitted with quillons (crosspieces). The medieval European partisan is a rough equivalent.

28. *Zhi* 彘, literally, "suckling pig," but here clearly intended to mean swine in general.

commands those in authority to reinstitute the general prohibitions. It is prohibited to walk around [outside the city walls]. Gates of cities and outer fortifications are closed, [and] strangers are placed under detention. Punishments are speedily carried out, [and] those under sentence of death are killed. Those who have corruptly abused their positions to confound the law are punished. [5/45/9–14]

On the first day of winter the Son of Heaven personally leads the Three Sires, the Nine Lords, and the great nobles to welcome the year at [the altar of] the northern suburbs. Returning [from this ceremony], he bestows rewards on [the descendants of] those who were killed [while carrying on the ruler's] affairs, and he puts widows and orphans under his protection. In this month he commands the Master of Prayers to pray and sacrifice to the spirits that they might establish [as true and correct] the oracles of the tortoise and the milfoil stalks, inquiring by means of the trigrams and the bone crackings to foretell good fortune and ill fortune. [In this month] the Son of Heaven begins to wear fur garments. [He] commands all the officials to carefully cover up and store away [all articles for which they are responsible]. [He] commands the minister-overseer to carry out the collecting and gathering. City walls and outer fortifications are repaired, and their doors and gates [are] inspected. Door bolts and fastenings are repaired, [and] keys and locks [are] carefully attended to. Earthen mounds and boundary walls are strengthened, [and] frontier and border fortifications are repaired. [The defenses of] important passes are strengthened, and narrow defiles and byways are blocked up. Regulations are issued with regard to terms of mourning, and inquiries are made [regarding] the quality of inner and outer coffins, burial clothes, and shrouds. The designs of grave mounds and tumuli are regulated with regard to size and height, so that for nobles and commoners, the humble or the honorable, each has its proper gradation. In this month, the Master of Artisans verifies the results [of the year's] labors, displaying the ritual vessels and examining their conformity to the [prescribed] patterns; those that are of fine quality are offered to the throne. In the carrying out of the work of the artisans, if there is [anyone who,] through hateful and dilatory [conduct,] produces [things that are] meretricious or shoddy, the [appropriate] criminal sentence must be carried out. In this month there is a great feast.[29] The Son of Heaven prays [for blessings] for the coming year. A grand rite of prayer and sacrifice is conducted at the shrine of the founder of the lineage, and a general feast is given for the royal ancestors. [The Son of Heaven] rewards the farmers so that they may rest from their labors. [He] commands the generals and [other] military officers to give lectures on war craft [to the troops and to have them] practice archery and chariot driving [and to engage in] trials of strength. [He] also orders the Superintendent of Waters and the Master of Fisheries to collect the taxes [due on the products of] the rivers, springs, ponds, and marshes. There must be no embezzlement or overcollection [of these taxes]. [5/45/16–23]

If during the first month of winter the ordinances of spring were observed, then the freezing [of the earth] would not be complete. The *qi* of Earth would issue forth and spread about, [and] the people in large numbers would drift away and be lost [to

29. Literally, a "great drinking and steam-cooking."

the kingdom]. If the ordinances of summer were observed, there would be many hot windstorms. [Even in] the dead of winter, it would not be cold; hibernating creatures would reemerge. If the ordinances of autumn were observed, then snow and frost would not come in season. Minor warfare would break out from time to time, [and] territory would be usurped and seized [by invaders]. [5/45/25–26]

The tenth month governs the Master of Horses. Its tree is the sandalwood. [5/45/28]

5.11

In the middle month of winter, Zhaoyao points to *zi* [N]. [The lunar lodge] [Eastern] Wall culminates at dusk; [the lodge] Chariot Platform culminates at dawn. [Winter] occupies the north. Its days are *ren* and *gui*. Its beasts are [those of the] armored [class]. Its [pentatonic] note is *yu*. The pitch pipe [of the eleventh month] is Yellow Bell. The number [of winter] is six. Its flavor is salty. Its smell is putrid. Its sacrifices are made to the well god. From the body of the sacrificial victim, the kidneys are offered first.

The ice becomes stronger. The earth begins to crack. The *gandan* bird does not cry.[30] Tigers begin to mate. The Son of Heaven wears black clothing. He mounts [a carriage drawn by] black horses. He wears black jade [pendants] and flies a black banner. He eats millet with suckling pig. He drinks water gathered from the eight winds and cooks with fire [kindled from] pine branches. The imperial ladies of the Northern Palace wear black clothing with black trim. They play music on chimestones. The weapon [of winter] is the partisan. The domestic animal [of winter] is the pig. [The Son of Heaven] holds the dawn session of court in the Dark Hall [chamber of the Mingtang]. He commands those in authority, saying, "No works having to do with earth may be undertaken, nor may rooms and dwellings be opened." [He also commands them] to call together the masses and say to them, "If anyone opens up what has been shut away by Heaven and Earth, then hibernating creatures all will die; the people will surely suffer illness and pestilence; and in the wake of this will come destruction." It is obligatory to arrest thieves and robbers and to punish those who are debauched, licentious, deceitful, or fraudulent. [He issues a] pronouncement saying, "[This is] the month when nothing grows." [He] commands the superintendent of eunuchs to reissue the standing orders of the palace and to examine the doors and gates and attend to the rooms and apartments; all must be closed up tightly. [There must be] a general diminution of all affairs having to do with women. [He] also issues orders to the Master Brewer, [saying that] the glutinous millet and rice must be uniform [in quality]; the yeast cakes must be ready; the soaking and cooking must be done under conditions of cleanliness; and the water must be fragrant. The earthenware vessels must be of excellent quality, and the fire must be

30. The *gandan* 鳱鴠 is a night-flying bird of some kind, possibly a member of the nightjar family.

properly regulated. There must be no discrepancy or error [in these things]. The Son of Heaven also commands those in authority to pray to the Four Seas, the great rivers, and the illustrious marshes. [5/46/1–8]

In this month, if the farmers have any [crops] that they have not harvested and stored away in granaries, or any cattle, horses, or other domestic animals that they have allowed to stray and get lost, then anyone who takes such things will not be subject to prosecution. In the mountains, forests, marshes and moors, if there are any who are able to gather wild food to eat or to capture rats and other small game, the superintendent of uncultivated land should instruct and guide them [in these activities]. If there are any who encroach on or steal from [such folk], they will be punished without mercy.

In this month the day reaches its shortest extent. Yin and yang contend. The Superior Man fasts and practices austerities. His dwelling place must be closed, [and] his body must be tranquil. He abstains from music and sex and forbids himself to feel lust or desire. He rests his body and quiets his whole nature. In this month, lychee buds stand out [on their twigs], [and] the rue plant begins to grow. Earthworms wriggle. The palmate deer shed their antlers. Springs of water stir into movement.[31] Accordingly, [this is the time to] fell trees for wood and collect bamboo for arrow shafts. Unserviceable articles in offices and articles of equipment that are of no use, are discarded. Gate towers, pavilions, doors, and gates are [repaired with] mud plaster, and prison walls are repaired, thus assisting in the closing up of Heaven and Earth.

If during the middle month of winter the summer ordinances were observed, the country would suffer drought. Vapors and fog would spread gloom and obscurity, and the sound of thunder would break out. If the ordinances of autumn were observed, the season[32] would have [excessive] rain. Melons and gourds would not ripen. The country would experience major warfare. If the ordinances of spring were observed, insect pests and caterpillars would cause destruction. The rivers and springs all would run dry. The people would suffer greatly from ulcerating diseases. [5/46/10–16]

The eleventh month governs the metropolitan guards. Its tree is the jujube. [5/46/18]

5.12

In the last month of winter, Zhaoyao points to *chou* [NNE]. [The lunar lodge] Bond culminates at dusk; [the lodge] Root culminates at dawn. [Winter] occupies the north. Its days are *ren* and *gui*. Its beasts are [those of the] armored [class]. Its [pentatonic] note is *yu*. The pitch pipe [of the twelfth month] is Great Regulator. The number [of winter] is six. Its flavor is salty. Its smell is putrid. Its sacrifices are made to the well god. From the body of the sacrificial victim, the kidneys are offered first.

31. Rejecting Lao's suggested insertion here of the phrase *ri duan zhi* 日短至, "the day reaches its shortest extent," which already occurs earlier in this paragraph and seems out of place here.

32. Reading *qi* 其 in place of *tian* 天 here, contrary to Lao's suggestion.

Wild geese head north. Magpies add to their nests. The cock pheasant cries, [and] hens cluck and lay their eggs. The Son of Heaven wears black clothing. He mounts [a carriage drawn by] black horses. He wears black jade [pendants] and flies a black banner. He eats millet with suckling pig. He drinks water gathered from the eight winds and cooks with fire [kindled from] pine branches. The imperial ladies of the Northern Palace wear black clothing with black trim. They play music on chimestones. The weapon [of winter] is the partisan. The domestic animal [of winter] is the pig. [The Son of Heaven] holds the dawn session of court in the [chamber of the Mingtang] to the right of the Dark Hall [chamber]. He commands those in authority to conduct a grand exorcism, in which sacrificial victims are torn apart on all [four] sides [of the city walls]. An earthen ox is set out [to lead away the cold *qi*].

[He] orders the Master of Fisheries to commence fishing. The Son of Heaven personally goes [to take part in] the fish shooting. [The fish that are caught] are presented as first offerings in the inner temple of the [ancestral] temple. Orders are issued to the people to withdraw [from the storehouses] the five kinds of seed grain and to the farmers to calculate [the schedules? for] using the teams [of draft animals], to put in order their plowshares, and to equip themselves with the implements of cultivation. [He] commands the master of music to give a grand concert of wind instruments and then to stop [any further music making]. [He] also commands the superintendents of the four directions to collect and set in order firewood for use in the ceremonies of the inner temple of the [ancestral] temple, as well as firewood and kindling for sacrifices of every kind. [5/46/20–26]

In this month, the sun completes [its circuit] through the stages [of the twelve divisions of the celestial circle]. The moon completes its cycle. The stars have made a complete revolution around the heavens. The year is about to begin again. Orders are given that the farmers and commoners must rest, [that] they not be employed [in any public works]. The Son of Heaven calls together his sires, the lords, and the great officers to promulgate[33] the statutes of the realm and to discuss the seasonal ordinances, in order to plan what is suitable for the coming year. He commands the grand recorder to make a list of the nobles in order of rank, assigning to them their [appropriate] levies of sacrificial animals [for the coming year] for use in worship of the Sovereign of Heaven Supreme Thearch and at the shrines of the [gods of] the soil and the grain. [He] also commands the states [ruled by fief holders] having the same surname [as that of the ruler] to provide fodder and feed [for the sacrificial animals] used in worship in the inner temple of the [ancestral] temple. [He also commands all, from] the lords, knights, and great officials to the common people, to provide [articles for] use in worship at the sacrifices to the mountains, forests, and illustrious rivers. [5/47/1–4]

If during the last month of winter the ordinances of autumn were observed, then the white dew would descend too early, [and] shell-bearing creatures would suffer deformities;[34] on the four frontiers, people would enter places of refuge. If the

33. Reading *shi* 飾 as *chi* 飭.

34. Reading *yao* 祆 as *yao* 妖.

ordinances of spring were observed, pregnant females and the young would suffer injury; the country would suffer many intractable diseases. If one were to inquire about this fate, it would be called "adverse." If the ordinances of summer were observed, floods would cause ruin in the country; the seasonable snow would not fall; the ice would melt; and the cold would dissipate. [5/47/6–7]

The twelfth month governs the prisons. Its tree is the chestnut. [5/47/9]

5.13

There are five positions. [5/47/11]

The extreme limit of the eastern region begins from Stele-Stone Mountain, passing through the Land of Chaoxian[35] and the Land of Giants. In the east it reaches the place from whence the sun rises,[36] the land of the Fu [-Sang] tree, the wild fields of the Green-Land trees. The places ruled by Tai Hao and Gou Mang [encompass] 12,000 *li*.

The ordinances [of the East] say: Hold fast to all prohibitions. Open what is closed or covered. Penetrate to the utmost all blocked-up passes. Extend to the frontiers and passes. Wander afar. Reject resentment and hatred. Free slaves and those condemned to hard labor [for crimes]. Avoid mourning and grief. Refrain from imposing corporal punishments. Open gates and dams. Proclaim a [general] distribution of wealth [from the public treasury]. Harmoniously resolve [any] resentment [that may be] abroad. Pacify the four directions. Act with pliancy and kindness. Put a stop to hardness and [overbearing] strength. [5/47/13–16]

The extreme limit of the southern region begins from outside [= beyond] [the country of] the people of North-Facing Doors[37] and passes through the country of Zhuan Xu.[38] It extends to the wild lands of Stored Fire and Blazing Winds. The regions governed by the Vermilion Thearch and Zhu Rong encompass 12,000 *li*.

The ordinances [of the south] say: Ennoble the virtuous [and] reward the meritorious. Show kindness to the beneficent and excellent. Come to the aid of the hungry and thirsty. Raise up those who display prowess in agriculture. Relieve the poor and destitute. Show kindness to orphans and widows. Grieve with the infirm and ill. Dispense great emoluments [and] carry out great bestowals of rewards. Raise up ruined

35. Chaoxian 朝鮮 is an old name for a state occupying part of what is now Korea. The name was revived as the name of the dynastic kingdom that ruled Korea from 1398 to 1910. Chaoxian is often, but incorrectly, translated as "Land of Morning Freshness" or "Land of Morning Calm." It is probable that the Chinese term was an attempt to transliterate the sound of a now-lost toponym in a proto-Korean language.

36. Possibly a reference to Japan.

37. In China, doors normally faced south, thus facing the sun. The implication is that the land of "north-facing doors" must be below the equator, where doors would have to face north to capture the sunlight. See also 4.6.

38. Zhuan Xu was a legendary figure who fought with Gong Gong for rulership of the universe. See 3.1.

lineages. Support those who have no posterity. Enfeoff nobles. Establish [in office] worthy assistants. [5/47/18–20]

The extreme limits of the central region extend from Kunlun east through the region of [the two peaks? of] Constancy Mountain.[39] This is where the sun and the moon have their paths. It is the source of the Han and Jiang [= Yangzi] rivers. [Here are] the open fields of the multitudes of people, [the lands] suitable for the five [kinds of] grain. At Dragon Gate the He [= Yellow] and the Qi rivers merge. [Here, Yu the Great] took swelling earth to dam the floodwaters and traced out the [nine] provinces. [These territories] extend eastward to Stele-Stone Mountain. The territories governed by the Yellow Emperor and the Sovereign of the Soil encompass 12,000 *li*.

The ordinances [of the center] say: Be evenhanded without inconsistency. Be enlightened without petty fault finding. Embrace, enfold, cover over, [and] enrich as with dew, so that there is none who is not tenderly enwrapped in [the royal] bosom. Be vast and overflowing, without private considerations. Let government be tranquil, to bring about harmony. Succor, nurture, and feed the old and the weak. Send condolences to [the families of] the dead, inquire after the sick, [all] to escort the myriad creatures on their return.[40] [5/47/22–25]

The extreme limits of the regions of the west extend from Kunlun through the Flowing Sands and the Sinking Feathers, westward to the country of Three Dangers. [They extend to] the Walled City of Stone and the Metal Palace [and] the open fields of the people who drink *qi* and do not die. The territories governed by Shao Hao and Ru Shou encompass 12,000 *li*.

The ordinances [of the west] say: Scrupulously use the laws. Punishment of the guilty must be carried out. Take precautions against thieves and robbers. Prohibit sexual license and debauchery. Issue instructions regarding the general collection [of harvest taxes]. Make a careful record of all collections [of revenue]. Repair city walls and outer fortifications. Repair and clear out drainage pipes. Close off footpaths and lanes; block up sluices and ditches. Shut off flowing water, swamps, gorges, and valleys. Guard doors and gates. Set out [in readiness] weapons and armor. Select officials. Punish the lawless. [5/47/27–5/48/3]

The extreme limits of the regions of the north extend from the nine marshes and the farthest reaches of Exhaust-the-Summer Gloom, north to the Valley Where Ordinances Cease.[41] Here are the open fields of freezing cold, piled-up ice, snow, hail, frost, sleet, and of pooling, soaking, massed-up water. The regions governed by Zhuan Xu and Xuan Ming encompass 12,000 *li*.[42]

---

39. The word *liang* 兩 in *liangheng shan* 兩恒山, "Two(-Peaks?) Constancy Mountain," may be an intrusion into the text, as it does not appear in this passage as quoted in TPYL.

40. A similar phrase appears in the text for the sixth month. The sense is that the myriad creatures are being speeded on their journey in the waning half of the year. The year is "returning" to its yin phase, and the myriad creatures are returning to a state of quiescence.

41. Reading *ling zhi* 令止 instead of *ling zheng* 令正. The implication is that in the farthest reaches of the frozen north, the king's writ ceases to run.

42. The mythical ruler Zhuan Xu sometimes is associated with the south, as in the immediately

The ordinances [of the north] say: Extend all prohibitions. Firmly shut and store away. Repair [the fortifications of] the frontiers and passes. Fix gates and water barriers. Prohibit walking around [outside the city walls]. Speedily carry out corporal punishments. Kill those who are under sentence of death. Close up the city gates and the gates of the outer fortifications. On a large scale, conduct investigations of strangers. Put a stop to communications and travel. Prohibit the pleasures of the night. Close up [chambers] early and open them late, in order to restrain lewd folk. If lewd persons are already to be found, they must be seized and held under severe restraint. Heaven has already almost completed its cycle: Punishments and executions must [be carried out] without any being pardoned; even in the case of [royal] relatives of surpassing venerableness, the law must be carried out to the full degree.

There must be no travel by water.
There must be no opening up of that which is stored away.
There must be no relaxation of punishments. [5/48/5–9]

5.14

[There are] six coordinates. [5/48/11]

The first month of spring and the first month of autumn are a coordinate.
The middle month of spring and the middle month of autumn are a coordinate.
The last month of spring and the last month of autumn are a coordinate.
The first month of summer and the first month of winter are a coordinate.
The middle month of summer and the middle month of winter are a coordinate.
The last month of summer and the last month of winter are a coordinate.
In the first month of spring, [crops] begin to grow; in the first month of autumn, [crops] begin to wither.
In the middle month of spring, [crops] begin to emerge; in the middle month of autumn, [crops] begin to be brought in.
In the last month of spring, [crops] are fully grown; in the last month of autumn, [crops] are harvested on a large scale.
In the first month of summer, [things] begin to slow down; in the first month of winter. [things] begin to quicken.
In the middle month of summer, [the day] reaches its greatest length;
in the middle month of winter, [the day] reaches its shortest length.
In the last month of summer, accretion reaches its climax;
in the last month of winter, recision reaches its climax.

Thus,

preceding section on the southern regions. Here he is named as a ruler of the north. Some commentators speculate that this is a consequence of his having been exiled to the north after his battle with Gong Gong. See chap. 3, n. 3.

if the government fails in its duties in the first month, the cool winds will not arrive in the seventh month.

If the government fails in its duties in the second month, the thunder will not go into hiding in the eighth month.

If the government fails in its duties in the third month, the frost will not descend in the ninth month.

If the government fails in its duties in the fourth month, it will not be cold in the tenth month.

If the government fails in its duties in the fifth month, hibernating creatures will emerge in the winter in the eleventh month.

If the government fails in its duties in the sixth month, grasses and trees will not be bare of leaves in the twelfth month.

If the government fails in its duties in the seventh month, the great cold will not disperse in the first month.

If the government fails in its duties in the eighth month, the thunder will not be heard in the second month.

If the government fails in its duties in the ninth month, the spring winds will not cease in the third month.

If the government fails in its duties in the tenth month, the grasses and trees will not bear seed in the fourth month.

If the government fails in its duties in the eleventh month, there will be hail and frost in the fifth month.

If the government fails in its duties in the twelfth month, the five [kinds of] grain will sicken and become weedy in the sixth month. [5/48/13–19]

In spring,

if the ordinances of summer are carried out, there will be inundations.

If the ordinances of autumn are carried out, there will be [too much] water.

If the ordinances of winter are carried out, there will be severity.

In summer,

if the ordinances of spring are carried out, there will be [excessive] winds.

If the ordinances of autumn are carried out, there will be wild growth of vegetation.

If the ordinances of winter are carried out, there will be interruption [of natural processes].

In autumn,

if the ordinances of summer are carried out, there will be [untimely] blooming of flowers.

If the ordinances of spring are carried out, there will be [untimely] breaking out of new buds.

If the ordinances of winter are carried out, there will be spoilage of the harvest.

In winter,

if the ordinances of spring are carried out, there will be excessive flows [of water].

If the ordinances of summer are carried out, there will be drought.
If the ordinances of autumn are carried out, there will be fog. [5/48/21–22]

5.15

Regulating the standards:
For the great regulation of yin and yang, there are six standards.

Heaven is the marking cord.
Earth is the level.
Spring is the compass.[43]
Summer is the balance beam.
Autumn is the square.
Winter is the weight.[44]
The marking cord is that by which the myriad things are marked out.
The level is that by which the myriad things are leveled.
The compass is that by which the myriad things are made round.
The balance beam is that by which the myriad things are equalized.
The square is that by which the myriad things are made square.
The weight is that by which the myriad things are weighed. [5/48/24–28]

The marking cord as a standard:

It is straight without swerving.
It is long and inexhaustible.
It is long enduring and does not wear out.
It reaches to far distances without deviation.
It matches Heaven in Potency.
It matches the spirits in illumination.
[By its means,] what one desires may be obtained,
and what one loathes may be caused to perish.

From ancient times to the present, there can be no deviation from its trueness. Its innate Potency is vast and subtle; it is broad and capacious. For this reason, the Supreme Thearch takes it as the ancestor of things. [5/48/30–5/49/2]

The level as a standard:

It is flat and not bumpy,
balanced and not inconsistent,
broad and capacious,
spacious and abundant,
so as to be harmonious.

43. *Gui* 規—that is, the drafting instrument, not the (much later) navigational magnetic compass.

44. For the various meanings and metaphorical usages of the word "weight" (*quan* 權), see chap. 3, n. 36; and Griet Vankeerberghen, "Choosing Balance: Weighing (*quan*) as a Metaphor for Action in Early Chinese Texts," *Early China* 30 (2005): 47–89.

It is pliant and not hard,
acute but not injurious,
flowing and not stopped up,
simple [to use] and unsullied,
expansively penetrating and [proceeding in] an orderly course.
It is comprehensive and subtle but not sluggish.
The level makes things perfectly flat without error,
thereby the myriad things are leveled.

The people are without malice or scheming; resentment and hatred do not arise. Therefore the Supreme Thearch uses it to make all things level. [5/49/4–6]

The compass as a standard:

It revolves without repeating itself.
It is round without turning [from its course].
Great but without excess,
broad and spacious,
feelings and actions are ordered [thereby].
It is expansively penetrating and [proceeds] on an orderly course.
Abundant! Simple!
The hundred forms of resentment do not arise.
The standard of the compass does not err;
it gives birth to both *qi* and pattern. [5/49/8–9]

The balance beam as a standard:

It is deliberate but does not lag behind.
It is impartial and not resented.
It bestows but is not benevolent.
It condoles but does not rebuke.
It adjusts to an appropriate level the people's emoluments.
It continues but does not heap up.
Majestic! Brilliant!
Only those [possessing] Potency act thus.
Nurturing, bringing to full growth, transforming, rearing;
the myriad creatures abundantly flourish.
It makes the five [kinds of] grain bear seed,
and the bounded fields be fruitful.

Government [by this standard] does not err; Heaven and Earth are illuminated thereby. [5/49/11–13]

The square as a standard:

It is majestic and not contrary.
It is hard and unbroken.[45]
It seizes but does not provoke resentment,
[Penetrates] within but does no injury.

45. Reading *kui* 憒 as *gui* 轒, as suggested by Yu Dacheng.

It is stern and severe but not coercive.
Its ordinances are carried out but without wasteful destruction.
In killing and smiting, its ends are attained;
the enemy is brought to submission.

The square's trueness is without error; all punishments are [thereby] suitably fulfilled. [5/49/15–16]

The weight as a standard:

It is hasty but not excessive.
It kills but does not slaughter.
It is filled to completion.
It is comprehensive and subtle but without sluggishness.
It inflicts destruction on things but does not single things out.
It punishes and kills without pardon.
Sincerity and trustworthiness are essential to it,
Strength and sincerity make it firm.
Cleanse away filth! Chastise the evil!
Wickedness may not be tolerated.

Therefore, if correct [policies] for winter are to be carried out, [the ruler] must appear

weak in order to be strong,
pliant in order to be firm.

The weight's trueness is without error; through it the myriad things are shut away. [5/49/18–20]

In the regulation of the Mingtang,

be tranquil, taking the level as a pattern.
Be active, taking the marking cord as a pattern.
For the government of spring, adopt the compass.
For the government of autumn, adopt the square.
For the government of winter, adopt the weight.
For the government of summer, adopt the balance beam.
Thus dryness and dampness, cold and heat, will arrive in their proper seasonal nodes.
Sweet rain and fertile dew will descend in their proper times. [5/49/22–23]

Translated by John S. Major

Six

SURVEYING OBSCURITIES

THE FIRST five chapters of this book established the characteristics of the Way and its primacy in cosmogony and in the cosmological realms of Heaven, Earth, and Time. In chapter 6, "Surveying Obscurities," the Huainan masters turn to a phenomenon the existence of which they are certain but cannot fully explain. This is "resonance" (*ganying* 感應), thought of as a kind of sympathetic vibration in the force field of *qi* that pervades the cosmos.[1] Resonance acts not only on physical objects but on emotions and intentions as well; thus the actions of humans have clear and predictable effects in the natural world. Impiety, injustice, and bad government lead to human catastrophes and natural disasters, whereas following the Way and instituting good government lead to human happiness and celestial harmony. Thus it is imperative, the chapter maintains, for the ruler to look into the roots of bad and good government, identify himself with the One, and make his actions conform to the Way, so as to lay the foundation for the whole world to be harmonious and tranquil. In the end, however, the means by which resonance operates remain cloaked in obscurity, so the phenomenon can be observed but not fully explained. That perhaps accounts in part for why "Surveying Obscurities" is one of the shortest chapters in the entire *Huainanzi*, although it is arguably also one of the most important.

1. For an alternative translation and detailed study of chap. 6, including a particular inquiry into the theory of resonance, see Le Blanc 1985; and Le Blanc's revised translation and chapter introduction (in French) in Le Blanc and Mathieu 2003, 251–87.

The Chapter Title

The title of chapter 6 is "Lanming" 覽冥, which we translate as "Surveying Obscurities."[2] *Lan* means "to look at, inspect, or perceive something"; it has connotations of seeing something from afar, making a survey, or obtaining an overview rather than getting a minutely detailed look from up close. *Ming* means "dark, obscure, distant, hard to see"; it has connotations of something obscured from vision by darkness or a miasma. The title well suits the chapter's content, about which the authors admit, "Even if one has enlightened understanding, it is not possible to [explain why] these things are so" (6.3).

Summary and Key Themes

The chapter begins with two striking images that set the theme for the chapter as a whole.[3] A music master is ordered to play sacred music out of its proper context, and his lord is stricken with calamities; a virtuous widow is falsely accused of a crime, and the ruler who authorized her prosecution suffers disasters. When Heaven sends punishments, the authors affirm, there is nowhere one can go to escape from them.

But how does this come about? Admitting that the process is "dark, mysterious, deep, and subtle" (6.2), the authors do not attempt to explain it directly but approach the problem in a roundabout manner. First, they give examples of resonance in the physical world: the burning mirror takes fire from the sun; the "square receptacle" takes water from the moon. These effects occur because they follow the natural propensity of things, but that does not completely explain resonance. It can be understood only by the sage who fully embraces the Way, who himself is like a mirror. Deeply unmoving, he is able to apprehend the transformations of the myriad things. He is as far above the common herd of humankind as dragons are above snakes and eels, or as phoenixes are above sparrows and swallows (6.5).

Are we astonished by the charioteering skills of Wang Liang and Zaofu, whose control of bits and reins was such that their horses galloped with uncanny speed and smoothness? Consider, then, Qian Qie and Da Bing, who had no need of harness and whips and who controlled their horses through the strength of their will alone (6.6). This was not brought about by "reason or thought, or through the exercise of manual skill." Rather, it was a manifestation of identifying with the One. So, too, were the regimes of the sage-rulers of high antiquity, such as the Yellow Emperor and, even before him and with still greater perfection, Fuxi and Nüwa. Under those

2. Ames 1994, 16, translates this title as "Perceiving the Imperceptible"; Le Blanc and Mathieu 2003 render it as "De l'examen des choses obscures."

3. For a somewhat different view of the organization and arguments of the chapter, see Le Blanc 1985, 191–94.

worthies, the world spontaneously brought itself to order, responding resonantly to the Potency of the rulers themselves. Nonhuman beings likewise responded to this Potency, so that such auspicious beasts as dragons, phoenixes, and *qilins* were seen abroad in the land, and normally dangerous animals posed no threat to people. All this was so because the sage-rulers themselves relied on the Way and its Potency rather than on such qualities as wisdom and precedent (6.7).

Conversely, at the time of the tyrant Jie, last king of the Xia dynasty, not only was misrule prevalent throughout the land, but the myriad things also responded resonantly to that misrule: the seasons were out of joint, mountains became deforested, marshes dried up, and animals behaved strangely. People rejected their own kin and officials conspired in cabals; rulers and ministers were estranged. Endless divinations revealed no answers to these problems, which persisted from the Xia down to modern times, and the breakdown of state order led to incessant warfare and corpses piled on roads and in ditches (6.8).

Which model, then, will the rulers of today emulate? The emperors of the Han dynasty sit on the throne in the manner of the Five Thearchs themselves. Will they continue to follow that Way, practicing Humaneness and Rightness? Or will they rely on the counsel of Lord Shang, Shen Buhai, and Han Feizi, employing the expedients of laws and punishments, warfare, and self-aggrandizement? Those methods, the authors assert, are as ephemeral as shoots from the rootstock of a tree or vine, springing up quickly, only to wither and die. Far better to rely on the fundamentals in the manner of Fuxi and Nüwa, who "achieved Empty Nothingness and Pure Unity, and they did not dabble in petty matters." Just so, the chapter concludes, "begging for fire is not as good as getting a fire starter, and asking for a drink is not as good as boring a well" (6.9).[4]

At the end of the chapter, it is evident that the authors have not given an adequate account of how resonance produces its effects. Even though they have surveyed the topic, it remains obscure. But the chapter does offer arguments concerning resonance that many contemporary readers would have found persuasive.

First, the phenomenon of resonance is real. This can be demonstrated by a well-known and widely accepted (and true) test: "When a person who tunes a *se* plays [the note] *gong*, [another] *gong* string responds" (6.4). Second, extraordinary individuals transcend the boundaries of human knowledge and skill, and their feelings provoke responses that seem to have no physical basis; the charioteering of Qian Qie and Da Bing illustrates this. Thus the phenomenon goes beyond commonplace physical effects. Third, because the sage-rulers of high antiquity (alluded to again and again in the *Huainanzi*) were such individuals, it is not surprising that their reigns were times of joyful simplicity and extraordinary cosmic harmony. Fourth, in reigns of surpassingly bad rulers, such as the tyrant Jie, the cosmos responded with portents and anomalies such as unseasonable weather and the strange behavior of animals.

4. This chapter's striking description of the world's devolution from an archaic age of unity, harmony and simplicity (6.7–6.9) is echoed in chap. 8, which uses the theme of decline from primordial unity as the starting point of an analysis of how sage-rulership might be reinstituted in the present age.

Finally, one who has the Way of Heaven, who practices non-action (*wuwei* 無爲) and is thus-of-himself (*ziran* 自然)is in a resonant relationship with the entire cosmos, just as a string that has not yet begun to be tuned is not limited to resonating with a single note but (potentially) resonates with every other string on the instrument.

Thus the authors demonstrate that the phenomenon of resonance operates most completely in the person of one of the Genuine (*zhenren* 真人), and this leads to the essential message for the young monarch-in-training who is the intended reader of the *Huainanzi:* it is possible for a transcendent ruler to arise in our own time, to bring about (through the resonant response of the cosmos to his own perfected Potency) a new era of sagely government. Charles Le Blanc puts it well: the power of resonance "is based on the persistent affinity and attraction of things that were originally one, but that became scattered when the world began. Through the True Man, it [that is, *ganying*] recreates the original unity."[5]

Although the concept of resonance forms the entire focus of this chapter, the term *ganying* itself does not appear in "Surveying Obscurities" or indeed anywhere in the *Huainanzi. Gan* means "an influence" or "to influence," "a stimulus" or "to stimulate," "to evoke a response." It appears twice in chapter 6. *Ying* appears seven times in the chapter, with its usual meaning of "to respond" or "a response"—for example, in 6.3: "The sage is like a mirror, . . . responding but not storing up." Overall throughout the *Huainanzi, ying* appears much more frequently (151 times) than *gan* does (39 times), and the two terms are closely coupled in only a few instances. But these instances conform exactly to the meaning of resonance that one expects from the concept of *ganying:* "responding to things when stimulated" (*gan er ying zhi* 感而應之, 1.10); "when stimulated they respond" (*gan er ying* 感而應, 7.7); "the stimulus impels a response externally" (*gan dong ying yu wai* 感動應於外, 10.27); "[non-action] does not mean that a stimulus will not produce a response" ([*wuwei*] *fei wei qi gan er bu ying* [無爲] 非謂其感而不應, 19.2).

While "Surveying Obscurities" must be counted as a key text arguing for the importance of resonance as an operative principle of yin–yang and Five Phases cosmology and attempting to explain how it worked, it would appear that at the time the chapter was written (mid-second century B.C.E.), the term *ganying* itself had not yet stabilized as a technical term for the phenomenon.

Sources

Because this chapter relies mainly on anecdote and analogy to make its argument for the pervasive reality of resonance, it draws extensively on a fund of mythological, legendary, historical, and other lore that was broadly familiar to all educated people in the early Han. Such figures as Fuxi and Nüwa, the Yellow Emperor and the Queen

5. Le Blanc 1985, 209.

Mother of the West, the tyrants Jie and Djou, the expert charioteer Zaofu, and the lugubrious musician Yong Menzi all were part of Han China's common cultural heritage. General references to them are difficult or impossible to trace to specific sources. Much of the content of this chapter shows a broad familiarity with such material but little evidence of direct quotations or borrowing from known sources.

Some passages do have strong parallels to other texts, however, including the *Zhuangzi*, *Lüshi chunqiu*, *Hanfeizi*, and *Guanzi*. Of these, by far the most important is the *Zhuangzi*. That is hardly surprising; in the *Huainanzi* overall, the *Zhuangzi* is quoted or alluded to far more than any other source, although the quotations are not at all evenly distributed across the book's twenty-one chapters.[6] Chapter 6, for instance, has more than twenty allusions to the *Zhuangzi*.[7] Some are brief and relatively trivial, but others are of central importance to the chapter's argument and shed light on how the *Huainanzi*'s authors went about their work.

The key passage in this chapter is also the most dramatic instance of borrowing from an earlier source. The observation that a string tuned to a particular note causes vibrations in an identically tuned string on a nearby instrument is central to the chapter's argument for the concept of resonance. In chapter 13 of the *Lüshi chunqiu*, this appears as a simple statement of fact: a *gong* string resonates with a *gong* string, a *jue* string with a *jue* string. Chapter 24 of the *Zhuangzi*, like section 6.4 of the *Huainanzi*, makes the additional—physically impossible but philosophically intriguing—claim that an untuned string resonates with all twenty-five of the musical instrument's strings (presumably because it represents an underlying unity that still contains all possible tunings). Chapter 24 of the *Zhuangzi* represents a late stratum of that text, very likely not much (if at all) older than the *Huainanzi*. The idea of resonating tuned strings thus would seem to date back to the pre-Qin period, whereas the notion of the superior resonance of an untuned string represents the milieu of the early Han.

Other passages in "Surveying Obscurities" show considerable ingenuity in the use of sources. For example, the passage in 6.2 beginning with "mountain clouds are like grassy hummocks" quotes five lines from chapter 13 of the *Lüshi chunqiu*. A few lines later, the text refers to Fu Yue bestriding the lunar lodges, alluding to chapter 6

---

6. More than half the total appear in just four chapters: 1, 2, 6, and 7. See the chart in Le Blanc 1985, 83.

7. In ascribing passages to "the *Zhuangzi*," we do not mean to suggest that the entire *Zhuangzi* was written by its putative author, Zhuang Zhou, sometime in the late fourth century B.C.E. The *Zhuangzi* is a layered text, written by several hands over a period of time, so some of its latest portions might be roughly contemporaneous with the *Huainanzi*. Parallel passages linking the *Zhuangzi* and the *Huainanzi* therefore do not in themselves argue for a well-developed theory of *ganying* resonance in the mid- to late Warring States period. For more on the *Zhuangzi* as a source for the *Huainanzi*, see the introduction to chap. 2, esp. n. 1.

Similarly, some material in the *Lüshi chunqiu* might well date from after the death of Lü Buwei (see the discussion of the LSCQ in the introduction to chap. 5), and the complex textual history of the *Hanfeizi* has not been sorted out satisfactorily (see our further discussion of the *Hanfeizi* in the introduction to chap. 12).

of the *Zhuangzi*; immediately thereafter, it quotes from chapter 21 of the *Zhuangzi* on maximum yin and maximum yang, capping that quotation with another from chapter 7 of the *Zhuangzi* about the consequences of having too many males and not enough females. Section 6.2 concludes with a quotation from chapter 2 of the *Guanzi* and an allusion to chapter 46 of the *Laozi*. The authors of chapter 6 of the *Huainanzi* evidently knew these texts and had deft editorial hands in stringing them together to create a novel argument that went beyond the original sources.

One can see a similar process at work in section 6.7, where the passage beginning with "[people] rested in tranquillity" is cobbled together with lines from, successively, chapters 7, 9, and 11 of the *Zhuangzi*, with the whole passage as strung together from the *Zhuangzi* seeming to allude to chapter 80 of the *Laozi*.

A final point about creative allusion pertains to section 6.5, the allegories of the dragons and the mud eels and the phoenixes and the swallows, which strongly echo the allegories of the Kun fish and the Peng bird in the opening paragraphs of chapter 1 of the *Zhuangzi*. As Le Blanc observed, "The actors (animals) and style are different . . . , but the point of the allegories is, in both works, the same: namely, that petty men are hemmed in by the trivia of their own existence, and cannot understand the grand designs and ambitions of superior men, who have attained the Tao."[8]

The Chapter in the Context of the *Huainanzi* as a Whole

Chapter 21's summary of "Surveying Obscurities" says in part,

> It begins by
> grasping things and deducing their categories,
> observing them, taking hold of them,
> lifting them up, and arranging them,
> and pervasively positing them as categories of similarity,
> by which things can be understood as ideas and visualized as forms. . . .
> [It] then thereby illuminates
> the stimuli of the various categories of things,
> the responses of identical *qi*,
> the unions of yin and yang,
> and the intricacies of forms and shapes.
> It is what leads you to observe and discern in a far-reaching and expansive way. (21.2)

Chapter 21's rationale for including "Surveying Obscurities" in the *Huainanzi* states:

8. Le Blanc 1985, 144.

> Had we discussed Heaven, Earth, and the four seasons and not introduced examples and elucidated categories,
> you would not recognize the subtleties of the Quintessential *qi*. (21.3)

The phrase "introduced examples and elucidated categories" seems to be the key to the importance of the chapter itself, by arguing through examples and elucidation for the reality and pervasiveness of *ganying* resonance within categories of yin and yang and the Five Phases and then contending also that resonance operates on a deeper and more mysterious level so as to permit the sage (who conforms to the Way and identifies with the One) to resonate with the entire cosmos. This contention provides the operative principle for the *Huainanzi*'s political philosophy of sagely rule. Thus the principle propounded in this chapter pervades the entire work.

John S. Major

Six

6.1

In ancient times Music Master Kuang played the tune "White Snow,"[1] and because of that, spiritlike creatures descended [from heaven]; wind and rain arrived violently; Duke Ping[2] became impotent and ill; and the lands of the state of Jin reddened [with drought].

The Commoner Woman[3] cried out to Heaven. Thunder and lightning beat down; Duke Jing's[4] lookout tower collapsed; his limbs and body were broken and slashed; and floodwaters gushed from the sea.

Now the blind music master and the Commoner Woman
were of a [social] rank as lowly as swaying weeds;[5]
their [political] weight was as light as windblown feathers;
yet

1. "White Snow" evidently was a work of sacred music. When the Jin ruler Duke Ping ordered his music master to play it outside its proper liturgical context, the misfortunes named here resulted. A much more detailed version of the story appears in *Hanfeizi*, chap. 10.

2. Duke Ping 平公 of Jin (r. 557–532 B.C.E.).

3. As the Gao You commentary explains, the Commoner Woman (*shu nü* 庶女) was a virtuous widow, falsely accused by her sister-in-law of murdering her mother-in-law. She cried out to Heaven about the injustice of this, and calamities ensued.

4. Duke Jing 景公 of Qi (r. 547–490 B.C.E.).

5. Reading *shang* 尚 as *chang* 徜, to preserve the parallelism of *shangxi* 尚 (徜) 葈 and *feiyü* 飛羽, and rejecting the rather contrived argument of commentators that *shangxi* should be understood to mean "Master of Hemp," supposedly a lowly office in the Zhou royal administration.

by concentrating their essences and disciplining their intentions,
abandoning their [mundane] responsibilities and storing up spirit [energy],
upward, they penetrated to ninefold Heaven, rousing and putting into action[6] the utmost essence.

Looking at things from this perspective in regard to the punishments [sent by] Heaven on high: Though one dwells
in a broad wasteland or a dark valley,
at a remote distance or a secluded hideaway,
in a multilayered stone refuge,
or at a frontier barrier or narrow defile,
there is no place where one may escape them. This is clear. [6/49/27–31]

King Wu[7] carried out a punitive campaign against [the tyrant] Djou. As he crossed [the Yellow River] at Meng Ford, the waves of the marquis of Yang[8] flowed against the current and smashed into [his army]. In the sudden wind and obscure gloom, men and horses were unable to see one another. Thereupon King Wu grasped a yellow battle-ax in his left hand and raised a white battle flag with his right hand and, with flashing eyes, brandished them, saying, "I am here! Who under Heaven dares to violate my will?" Immediately the winds quieted and the waves ceased.

Duke Luyang[9] was engaged in a difficult [battle] with Hann. As the battle grew fiercer, the sun began to set. He raised his halberd and waved it, and the sun reversed [its course] for him by three lunar lodges.

Now if you keep intact your nature and guard your authenticity
and do not do damage to your person,[10]
[when you] meet with emergencies or are oppressed by difficulties,
your essence will penetrate [upward] to Heaven;
You will be like one who has not yet begun to emerge from his Ancestor[11]—how can you not succeed?

One for whom death and life are the same territory, who cannot be threatened, such a single brave warrior is the hero of the Three Armies.[12] Such a one simply seeks fame yet is able for the sake of his own desire to ignore death in this manner. How much more so for one who
holds sway over Heaven and Earth,

6. Reading *li* 厲 as *li* 勵.

7. King Wu was the second king of the Zhou dynasty, after his father, King Wen. King Wu (the "martial king") completed the conquest of Shang, defeating the Shang army at the battle of Muye (in present-day Qi County, Henan Province), ca. 1046 B.C.E.

8. Marquis Yang, ruler of the state of Lingyang 陵陽, was supposed to have drowned in the Yellow River; his ghost sometimes caused deadly waves to arise. See also 16.139.

9. Duke Luyang 魯陽公 was a vassal of the state of Chu, the grandson of King Ping of Chu (r. 528–516 B.C.E.) and son of Master of Horse Ziqi.

10. These two lines are repeated in 13.9, where they are said to describe the philosophy of Yang Zhu.

11. The Ancestor (*zong* 宗)—that is, the Way. This phrase recurs in 6.4.

12. The Three Armies, a conventional phrase for the entire armed forces of a kingdom. A version of this anecdote is also found in ZZ 5/13/19–21.

embraces the myriad things,
befriends creation and transformation,
and cherishes utmost harmony,

who simply finds himself fitted up in human form, who scrutinizes the Nine and penetrates to the One,[13] thereby knowing the unknown so that his mind has no notion of death! [6/50/1–7]

In ancient times, Yong Menzi[14] used weeping to gain an audience with Lord Mengchang.[15] Having [been received,] he marshaled his phrases and communicated his ideas, laying his hands on his heart and breaking into song. [As he did so,] Lord Mengchang increasingly sobbed and wailed until he choked, and his tears ran down copiously without stopping. [Thus] when Quintessential Sincerity takes form within, outwardly it communicates grief to the hearts of others. [But] the Way of [doing] this cannot be transmitted [to others]. If a commoner who, lacking his ruler's form, were to imitate [the ruler's] demeanor, surely he would be laughed at by others. That Bo Juzi[16] could draw a bead on a bird a hundred *ren*[17] up [in the air], and Zhan He could scare up fish in the midst of a great abyss, was all because they had obtained the Way of Clarity and Purity and the Harmony of Supreme Vastness. [6/50/9–12]

6.2

That things in their [various] categories are mutually responsive is [something] dark, mysterious, deep, and subtle.

Knowledge is not capable of assessing it;
argument is not capable of explaining it.

Thus,

when the east wind arrives, wine turns clear and overflows [its vessels];
when silkworms secrete fragmented silk,[18] the *shang* string [of a stringed instrument] snaps.

Something has stimulated them.

---

13. Both Heaven and Earth have nine divisions, but each also has an underlying unity.

14. According to Gao You, Yong Menzi 雍門子 lived near the Yong Men gate of the Qi capital of Linze and thus derived his sobriquet. See Zhang Shuangdi 1997, 1:640n.18. See also 10.94.

15. Lord Mengchang 孟嘗君 (also known as Tian Wen 田文 [ca. 330–ca. 280 B.C.E.]) was a powerful scion of the royal house of Qi. He was renowned as a great patron and statesman; his biography is recounted in detail in *Shiji* 75.

16. According to Gao You, Bo Juzi 蒲且子 was a native of Chu famed for his skill with a dart and line. See Zhang Shuandgi 1997, 1:642n.22.

17. A *ren* 刃 equals eight feet and is thus equivalent to a *xun* 尋. Eight Han feet would equal about six feet in English measure, hence the translation "fathom" in 6.5. See also 3.31 and 4.1.

18. Reading *er* 咡 as *er* 餌. Essentially the same statement appears in 3.2. In an earlier translation of chap. 3, I followed commentators who read 珥 as "ear ornament" (Major 1993, 65–66). I now believe that the interpretation of "brittle" or "crumbly" (*er* 餌) is more convincing. See also the discussion in Le Blanc 1985, 117. It is possible that neither explanation is correct; in any case, the basic notion involved clearly is derived from the concept of resonance in the Five-Phase categories.

When a picture is traced out with the ashes of reeds, the moon's halo has a [corresponding] gap.[19]

When the leviathan dies, comets appear.[20]

Something has moved them.

Thus, when a sage occupies the throne, he embraces the Way and does not speak, and his nurturance reaches to the myriad people. But when ruler and ministers [harbor] distrust in their hearts, back-to-back arcs[21] appear in the sky. The mutual responses of spirit *qi* are subtle indeed!

Thus,

mountain clouds are like grassy hummocks;
river clouds are like fish scales;
dryland clouds are like smoky fire;
cataract clouds are like billowing water.

All resemble their forms and evoke responses according to their class.[22]

The burning mirror takes fire from the sun;
the square receptacle takes dew from the moon.[23]

Of [all the things] between Heaven and Earth, even a skilled astrologer cannot master all their techniques. [Even] a hand [that can hold] minutely tiny and indistinct things cannot grasp[24] a beam of light. However, from what is within the palm of one's hand, one can trace [correlative] categories to beyond the extreme end point [of the cosmos]. [Thus] that one can set up [these implements] and produce water and fire is [a function of] the mutually [responsive] movement of yin and yang of the same *qi*. That is how Fu Yue bestrode [the lunar lodges] Winnowing Basket and Tail.[25] [6/50/14–20]

Thus,

maximum yin is freezing cold;
maximum yang is blazing hot.

The two of them come together and interconnect to bring about harmony, and the myriad things thereby are born.[26] If there were lots of males and no females, how indeed would transformation be able to create [anything]?[27] This is what is known as

---

19. Commentators' efforts to elucidate this enigmatic statement are generally unconvincing. Some sort of military divination or prognostication, using ashes to make a drawing on the ground, is evidently involved. For further discussion, see Le Blanc 1985, 117nn.41, 42.

20. The same statement appears in 3.2.

21. *Beijue* 背譎 is regarded by commentators as a technical term referring to convex halos appearing on either side of the sun. For a discussion, see Le Blanc 1985, 118.

22. These five lines also appear in LSCQ 13.2. See Knoblock and Riegel 2000, 283–84.

23. For these two quasi-magical implements, see also 3.2.

24. Reading *lan* 覽 as *lan* 攬, following Wang Niansun. See Lau, HNZ, 50n.8.

25. Reading *ji* 箕 in place of *chen* 辰, as in ZZ 6/17/7. For the lunar lodges, see app. A. Tail (*wei* 尾) and Winnowing Basket (*ji* 箕) are the sixth and seventh in the usual sequence of lodges, beginning with Horn (*jue* 角). The legendary Shang-dynasty minister and sage Fu Yue is said to have ascended to Heaven by riding on these constellations.

26. There is a parallel passage in ZZ 21/57/23–24.

27. There is a similar passage in ZZ 7/20/27–28.

the argument that is not spoken
and the Way that is not [called] "the Way."

Thus

to attract those who are far-off [i.e., emissaries], one employs non-action;
to cherish those who are close by, one employs non-interference.[28]

But only one who "walks by night"[29] is able to have this [technique]. Thus [he] retires [his] fast horses so they [only] make dung,[30] and [his] chariot tracks do not need to extend beyond far-off lands. This is what is called

racing while sitting, bathing on dry land,
darkness at noon, bright light at night,
melting pitch in winter,
making ice in summer. [6/50/22–25]

6.3

One who has the Way of Heaven has

no private motives in what he accepts,
no private motives in what he rejects.
One who is capable has more than enough;
one who is inept has an insufficiency.
One who accords with it prospers;
one who opposes it suffers setbacks.

It is like

the pearl of Marquis Sui[31]
or the jade disk of Mr. He:[32]
Those who achieved it became rich;
those who lost it became poor.

The standard of [what constitutes] getting or losing is deep, minute, elusive, and obscure. It is hard to use knowledge to discuss it or to explain it by means of debate. How can we know that this is so? Now [the medicinal herb] Earthyellow is sovereign

---

28. Rejecting Lau's (HNZ 6/50/23) proposed emendation of shi 使 to yan 言. If the emendation were accepted, the lines would have a very different interpretation: "to attract those who are far-off emissaries is of no use; to cherish those who are close by words is of no avail." These two lines (with *yan*, not *shi*) appear in a parallel passage in *Guanzi* 2.4. See Rickett 1985, 131–32. For an extensive discussion of these two lines, see Le Blanc 1985, 122.

29. *Ye xing zhe* 夜行者—that is, one who acts in a concealed and mysterious manner.

30. *Laozi* 46.

31. Marquis Sui 隋侯 was a vassal of Chu of unknown date. He was given a fabulous pearl by a snake that he had saved from being killed, and the pearl became a renowned heirloom of his lineage.

32. Mr. He 和氏, or Bian He 卞和, was the discoverer of a marvelous piece of raw jade that went unrecognized by successive Chu monarchs until it was finally acknowledged as a priceless jewel, though not before Bian He himself was brutally punished for attempted fraud. See chap. 14, n. 57; and 16.19 and 16.90. His story is also recounted in *Hanfeizi* 13.

for mending bones, and Sweetgrass is sovereign for healing [injured] flesh. But to take what is good for mending bones and expect it to heal flesh or to take what is good for healing flesh and promote it for mending bones would be like Wangsun Zhuo, who wanted to use a double dose of a medicinal plant used for [curing] partial paralysis in order to revive a man who had been killed in battle—really, one could say that he had lost his senses![33] Now if one were to accept [that] fire can burn wood and use it to melt metal, that would [follow] the movement of the Way. But if one were to accept [that] lodestone can attract iron and use it to attract tile, that would certainly be difficult. Things certainly cannot be assessed according to their weight [alone]. [6/51/1–6]

Now,

> the burning mirror can draw fire [from the sun];
> lodestone can draw iron;
> crabs spoil lacquer;[34]
> and sunflowers incline to the sun—

[but] even if one has enlightened understanding, it is not possible to [explain why] these things are so. Thus investigations by ear and eye are not adequate to discern the principles of things; discussions employing the mind and its conceptions are not adequate to distinguish true and false. Thus he who uses knowledge as the basis for government will have a hard time holding on to his state. Only he who penetrates to Supreme Harmony and who grasps the responses of the natural will be able to possess it [i.e., his state].

Thus when Mount Yao collapsed, the Boluo River dried up. When Ou the Smelter was born, the sword Chunjun was completed.[35] When [the tyrant] Djou acted without the Way, Zuo Qiang was at his side.[36] The Grand Duke[37] served through two generations; thus King Wu succeeded in establishing [his rule]. Seen from this perspective, the paths of benefit or harm, the gateways of calamity or good fortune, cannot be obtained [just] by seeking them out. [6/51/8–12]

Now,

> how the Way compares with Potency
> is like how leather compares with rawhide.

---

33. A version of this story appears in LSCQ 25.2. See Knoblock and Riegel 2000, 628.

34. Reading *jie* 解 as *xie* 蟹. Compare 16.124: "If exposed to the sight of crabs, lacquer will not dry." According to later Chinese pharmacopeias, a compress of crushed shellfish was used to treat the rash caused by exposure to raw lac sap (the lac tree is related to poison sumac). The enzymes in the shellfish medicine also are capable of preventing lacquer from drying properly, and so it must be kept away from lacquer that is still in the process of being manufactured. We are grateful to Anthony Barbieri-Low (private communication) for this insight.

35. Ou the Smelter 區冶, also written 歐冶, was a renowned swordsmith of Yue who fashioned legendary swords for King Goujian of Yue (r. 496–465 B.C.E.) and King Zhao of Chu (r. 515–489 B.C.E.). Chunjun was one of five precious swords he crafted for the former monarch.

36. The sycophant Zuo Qiang served as minister to Djou, "bad last ruler" of the Shang dynasty.

37. The Grand Duke 太公 (also known as Lü Wang 呂望) was a wise commoner who became counselor to King Wen and assisted in the Zhou conquest of Shang. He was made the first Duke of Qi, and his descendants ruled that state until they were usurped by the Tian clan in 379 B.C.E.

From a distance they [seem] close;
close together they [seem] far apart.[38]
[One who] does not get the Way is like [someone] watching minnows.[39]
Therefore,
the sage is like a mirror,
neither holding onto nor welcoming [anything],
responding but not storing up.
Thus he can undergo ten thousand transformations without injury.
To [claim to] get it is indeed to lose it;
so is not losing it really to get it? [6/51/14–16]

6.4

Now when a person who tunes a *se*
plays [the note] *gong*, [another] *gong* [string] responds;
when he plucks a *jue* [string], [another] *jue* responds.[40]
This is the harmony of notes that are the same. But if [he] tunes one string eccentrically, so that it does not accord with [any] of the five notes and then strikes it, and all twenty-five strings [of the *se*] respond, this is [a case of] the sounds not yet having begun to differentiate but the ruler of [all] notes having already achieved its form.[41] Thus one who penetrates to Supreme Harmony is as confused as [a person who] is stupified by drink, who wanders about in a sweet daze without knowing where he has come from or where he is going.
Simple and mild, he [descends] the vortex;
simple and stupified, he [reaches] his end.
He is like
one who has not yet begun to emerge from the Ancestor.
This is called the Great Penetration. [6/51/18–21]

38. This simile of leather and rawhide has prompted several commentarial attempts at explication, most of them improbable. We think the most likely interpretation is the one implied by the translation given here, involving a play on words (close/similar and distant/dissimilar).

39. That is, their attention is distracted in all directions.

40. This statement, apparently well known in third and second centuries B.C.E. China, also appears, inter alia, in *Zhuangzi* 24 (ZZ 24/69/21–22), *Lüshi chunqiu* 13.2 (Knoblock and Riegel 2000, 283), and *Chunqiu fanlü* 57.

41. Compare 3.29, where the "ruler of all notes" (*yin zhi jun* 音之君) is equated with the fundamental note *gong*. Here, in contrast, the "ruler of all notes" seems to refer to some quality that lies behind and before music itself—perhaps to be understood as profound silence. Compare also the "ruler of form" (*jun xing* 君形), in 16.91 and 17.61.

6.5

Now a red *chi* dragon and a green *qiu* dragon[42] were roaming around in Ji [Province].[43]

The sky was blue,
the earth tranquil.
Venomous animals did not make an appearance;
flying birds did not startle them.
Entering a thorny thicket,
they fed on plums and fodder.

Enjoying the taste and savoring the sweetness, they did not stray outside a space of a hundred *mou.*[44] So the snakes and swamp eels[45] took them lightly and thought that they would not be able to tussle with them and win, [whether] in the river or the ocean. But when [the dragons ascended] to the dark clouds in the pale dawn, yin and yang engaged and struggled. [The dragons] descended on the wind, tangled in squalls of rain, rode the billows, and ascended again, awesomely moving Heaven and Earth. The sound of thunder penetrated to the midst of the ocean. [Then] the salamanders[46] and swamp eels burrowed a hundred *ren* [fathoms] into the mud; black bears and brown bears crawled away to the crags of hills and mountains; tigers and leopards sheltered in caves and did not dare to roar; gibbons and monkeys tumbled down headfirst and lost their grip on the trees and branches—how much more [affected] were mere snakes and swamp eels?

The soaring aloft of a female and a male phoenix reached [such a state of] Utmost Potency that thunder and lightning did not occur; wind and rain did not arise, the rivers and valleys did not flood; and grasses and trees did not tremble. So the swallows and sparrows mocked them, saying that they were incapable of matching them in squabbling among the roof beams and rafters.[47] Turning about, [the phoenixes] departed to a height of ten thousand *ren,* wheeled and soared beyond the four seas, [flew] past the Carved-Out Garden of Kunlun,[48] drank from the rushing rapids of the Polished Pillar,[49] flew to and fro over the banks of the Dark Oxbow,[50] curved around

42. Commentators explain that the *chi* 螭 dragon is hornless and that the *qiu* 虯 dragon has horns.

43. Ji 冀 is described in 4.1 as the central province of the known world.

44. *Qing mou* 頃畝; the expression does not make much sense because a *qing* normally means "one hundred *mou.*"

45. The *shan* 鱓 is generally assumed to be the swamp eel (*Monopterus albus*), a very aggressive freshwater eel.

46. Emending *she* 蛇 to *yuan* 蚖, as proposed by Lau, HNZ 6/51/26. See also Zhang Shuangdi 1997, 1:664n.17.

47. The text here makes a play on words: *yuzhou* 宇宙 is used literally in its sense of "roof beams and rafters" (e.g., of a barn, the natural habitat of swallows and sparrows), but it also calls to mind its more usual meaning of "universe" (i.e., the habitat of phoenixes).

48. For the Carved-Out Garden and other magical places in Kunlun, see 4.3.

49. The Polished Pillar was a boulder in the midst of the Yellow River, in Henan Province.

50. *Mengsi* 蒙汜, probably the same as *menggu* 蒙谷, the Vale of Obscurity, into which the sun sets and from which the sun rises again. See 3.25.

the borders of Ji [Province], lightly cleared [the peak of] Duguang [Mountain], entered with the [setting] sun into Yijie [Valley], washed their wings in the Weakwater [River], and, at dusk, [roosted] in Wind Cave. During this whole time, geese, swans and cranes were, without exception, awestruck and slunk away to hide, sticking their beaks into the riverbank. How much more [affected] were mere swallows and sparrows? This [is a case of] being clear about the traces of small matters but being unable to know the origins of great events. [6/51/23–6/52/5]

6.6

In ancient times, when Wang Liang[51] and Zaofu went driving, [as soon as] they mounted their chariots and took hold of the reins, the horses set themselves in order and wanted to work together.

They obediently paced in step with one another;
[whether] pulling hard or easing off, they were as one.
Their hearts were in tune and their *qi* harmonious;
their bodies [became] more and more light and coordinated.
They were content to work hard and happy to go forward;
they galloped away as if they would vanish.
They went right and left like [the waving of] a whip;
they circled around like a jade bracelet.

All people of that era considered [Wang Liang and Zaofu] to be superlative [charioteers], but that was because they had not yet seen any [truly] worthy ones.
Now consider the charioteering of Qian Qie and Da Bing.[52] They
considered reins and bits superfluous,
got rid of whips and cast aside goads.
Before the chariot began to move, it was starting on its own.
Before the horses were given the signal, they were walking on their own.
They paced [like the] sun and moved [like the] moon.
They flashed [like the] stars and advanced [like the] dark.
They raced [like] lightning and leaped [like] ghosts.[53]
Advancing or withdrawing, gathering strength or stretching out,
they did not see the slightest barrier.

Thus,
with no gesturing or pointing,
with no cursing or scolding,
they overtook the wild geese flying to Piled Stone Mountain,

51. Wang Liang 王良, a grandee of Jin during the Spring and Autumn period, was renowned for his skill as a charioteer.

52. According to Gao You, Qian Qie 鉗且 and Da Bing 大丙 were the charioteers of the Grand One (*Taiyi* 太一) in his guise as a god of the royal cult. Another account says that they were adepts of the Way who mounted the yin and yang using their spirit *qi*. See Zhang Shuangdi 1997, 1:673n.8.

53. Emending *teng* 騰 to *hai* 駭, following Wang Niansun. See Lau, HNZ, 52n.6.

passed the jungle fowl [flying to] Guyu Mountain.
Their galloping was like flying;
their bursts of speed like thread snapping.
[It was] like riding an arrow or mounting the wind,
like following a cyclone and returning in an instant.
At dawn they started from Fusang
and set with the sun at Luotang.

This was taking something unused and obtaining its usefulness: it was not done by examining things through reason or thought or through the exercise of manual skill. Whenever urgent desires took form in the breasts [of Qian Qie and Da Bing], their quintessential spirits were [already] communicated to the six horses.[54] This was a case of using non-driving to go driving. [6/52/7–14]

6.7

In ancient times, the Yellow Emperor ruled the world. Li Mu and Taishan Ji assisted him in

regulating the movements of the sun and the moon,
setting in order the *qi* of yin and yang,
delimiting the measure of the four seasons,
correcting the calculations of the pitch pipes and the calendar.

They

separated men from women,
differentiated female and male [animals],
clarified the high and the low,
ranked the worthy and the mean;

they took steps [to ensure that]

the strong would not oppress the weak;
the many would not oppress the few.
People lived out their allotted life spans and did not suffer early death;
crops ripened in season and were not subject to calamities.
All the officials were upright and not given to partiality.
High and low were in concord and did not find fault.
Laws and commandments were clear and there was no confusion.
Officials assisted the ruler and did not engage in flattery.
Hunters[55] did not encroach on field boundaries.
Fishers did not struggle over coves.

On the roads, people did not pick up [and keep] things that were dropped [by others]; in the markets, [goods] did not have predetermined prices.

54. According to tradition, the imperial carriage was drawn by six horses (or six dragons).

55. *Tianzhe* 田者, could mean "those who work in fields"; *tian,* however can also mean "to hunt," and here *tianzhe* as "hunters" makes a better parallel with "fishers" in the following line.

City and town [gates] were not closed.
Towns were without bandits and thieves.
Humble travelers shared their supplies with one another.
[Even] dogs and pigs spat out beans and millet [that they found] on the road.

And no one cherished thoughts of conflict in their hearts. Because of that,

the essence of the sun and moon was bright.
The stars and celestial chronograms[56] did not deviate from their orbits.
Winds and rain were timely and moderate.
The five grains grew and ripened [as they should].
Tigers and leopards[57] did not roar wildly.
Raptors did not snatch prey wildly.
Phoenixes soared above the [royal] courtyards.
The *qilin* wandered in the suburbs.
Green dragons drew the [royal] carriage,
and Flying Yellows[58] were put away in their stables.

Of the various northern states and the country of Hanging Ears, there were none that did not offer their tribute and skills. And yet this [age of the Yellow Emperor] did not come up to the Way of Lord Fuxi. [6/52/16–22]

Going back to more ancient times,

the four pillars were broken;
the nine provinces were in tatters.

Heaven did not completely cover [the earth];
Earth did not hold up [Heaven] all the way around [its circumference].[59]
Fires blazed out of control and could not be extinguished;
water flooded in great expanses and would not recede.
Ferocious animals ate blameless people;[60]
predatory birds snatched the elderly and the weak.

Thereupon, Nüwa

Smelted together five-colored stones[61] in order to patch up the azure sky,
cut off the legs of the great turtle to set them up as the four pillars,
killed the black dragon[62] to provide relief for Ji Province,[63]

---

56. *Chen* 辰—that is, time-keeping heavenly bodies such as planets and lunar lodges.

57. Reading *bao* 豹 instead of *lang* 狼 (wolf), following Wang Niansun. See Lau HNZ, 52n.12.

58. Flying Yellows (*feihuang* 飛黃) were special horses, dragonlike or actual dragons, supposedly used to pull the imperial chariot.

59. *Di buzhou dai* 墬不周載. It is interesting that the mountain in the northwest, where a gap is said to have existed between Heaven and Earth, is called Mount Buzhou. For the myth of the fight between Gong Gong and Zhuan Xu that supposedly caused the disruption of Heaven and Earth described here, see 3.1.

60. *Zhuan min* 顓民 conveys the sense of people who are unsophisticated and blameless. Yu Dacheng advocates emending *zhuan* to *jing* 精, understood to mean "pure in spirit." This seems unnecessary.

61. That is, stones embodying the essence of each of the Five Phases. Compare the five minerals described in the alchemical passage that ends chap. 4.

62. The essence of water, thus responsible for floods.

63. That is, the central regions, the Sinitic world. See 4.1.

and piled up reeds and cinders to stop the surging waters.
The azure sky was patched;
the four pillars were set up;
the surging waters were drained;
the province of Ji was tranquil;
crafty vermin died off;
blameless people [preserved their] lives.
Bearing the square [nine] provinces on [her] back
and embracing Heaven,
[Fuxi and Nüwa[64] established]
the harmony of spring and the yang of summer,
the slaughtering of autumn and the restraint of winter.[65]

[People] kept their heads squarely on their pillows and slept straight as a marking cord. Whatever obstructed yin and yang, [causing them to be] deeply blocked up and unable to connect,[66] [Fuxi and Nüwa] thoroughly set in order.

[Whoever] ran counter to *qi* and [thereby] perverted things;
[whoever] through hoarding provisions harmed the people;
[they] interrupted and stopped them.

At that time, [people]
rested in tranquillity,
woke up with alacrity.
One considered himself a horse;
another considered himself an ox.[67]
Their motions were calm and unhurried;
their gaze was tranquil and uncurious.[68]
In their ignorance, they all got what they needed to know,
but they did not know where it came from.
Aimlessly drifting, they did not know what they were looking for;
zombielike,[69] they did not know where they were going.[70]

At that time, birds and beasts, noxious vermin and snakes, without exception, sheathed claws and fangs.[71] They stored away their venom and poison, and none of them were disposed to attack or bite.

---

64. The subject here is unstated; given the reference in 6/52/22 immediately preceding, it would seem that the rule of Fuxi in addition to Nüwa, or even subsequent to her labors in repairing Heaven and Earth, is implied.

65. For these attributes of the four seasons, see chap. 5, passim.

66. This sentence does not read very smoothly in the original Chinese and may be defective. Various commentarial suggestions have been made for emendations, none of them very satisfactory.

67. These four lines appear (in slightly different form) in ZZ 7/20/5; the first two are also in ZZ 29/87/24.

68. These two lines also appear in *Zhuangzi* 9 (ZZ 9/23/27). The state of bovine tranquillity described here is also reminiscent of the peasants depicted in *Laozi* 80 (LZ 80/27/10–11).

69. A *wangliang* 魍魎 is a kind of corpse monster, said to feed on the brains of the buried dead.

70. These two lines, with some differences in wording, appear in ZZ 11/28/12.

71. Closely similar lines appear in *Hanfeizi* 49 and *Wenzi* 2.

Examining into these glorious achievements, [we find that]
they reach up to the ninefold Heaven;
they extend down to the Yellow Clods.[72]
Their fame resounded down through later generations;
their brilliance dazzled successively the myriad things.
[They] mounted their thunder chariot,
with flying *long* dragons[73] as the inner pair
and green *qiu* dragons as the outer pair.
They grasped their incomparable jade emblems;
their sitting mat was a floriate diagram;
they spread out[74] clouds like silken threads.
Preceded by white *chi* dragons,
followed by hurrying snakes,
aimlessly drifting, rambling at random,
leading [a retinue of] ghosts and spirits,
they climbed to ninefold Heaven,
paid court to the [Supreme] Thearch at the Numinous Gate,
silent and reverent they ended [their journey] in the presence of the Great Ancestor.
Even then, they
did not make a great show of their accomplishments,
did not heap praise on their own reputations.
They concealed [within themselves] the Way of the Genuine
and followed the imperatives of Heaven and Earth.
How was this so? [In them] the Way and its Potency achieved the highest penetration, and wisdom and precedent were extinguished. [6/52/24–6/53/8]

6.8

Coming down to the time of [the tyrant] Jie of the Xia [dynasty],
rulers had become benighted and unenlightened.
Their Way was excessive and lacked restraint;
they rejected the pardons and punishments of the Five Thearchs[75]
and rescinded the laws and ordinances of the Three Kings.[76]

72. Not merely surface soil, but the earth at the floor of the subterranean Yellow Springs, land of the dead.

73. *Ying long* 應龍, conventionally understood to mean a dragon that is able to fly.

74. The first character of this three-character sentence should be a verb, in parallel with the two that come before it and the two that follow. We read *huang* 黃, "yellow," as *guang* 廣, "broad; to spread out," even though there is no commentarial tradition to suggest this. Yu Yue proposed changing the order of the sentence to *lo huang yun* 咯黃雲, "they made tendrils of yellow clouds."

75. Lists of the "Five Thearchs" (*wu di* 五帝) vary; here, presumably, the list would include both Fuxi and the Yellow Emperor, mentioned favorably earlier, possibly also the Divine Farmer, and would probably end with Yao and Shun.

76. Conventionally, Yu the Great, Cheng Tang, and King Wen, supposed founders of the Xia,

As a result,

Utmost Moral Potency was obliterated [rather than] publicly promoted;
the Thearch's Way was suffocated [rather than being] made to flourish.
Their conduct of affairs offended Azure Heaven;
their issuing of proclamations contravened [the rhythms of] the four seasons.
Spring and autumn recoiled from their [accustomed] harmonies;
Heaven and Earth discarded their Potency.
The rulers of humankind occupied their positions but were uneasy;
great lords concealed their Way and did not speak out.

The multitude of officials took as their standard[77] the wishes of their superiors and embraced what matched [those wishes]. Flesh and bone drifted apart[78] and [followed] their own interests. Depraved persons strolled about by threes and twos and hatched secret plots. They interposed themselves between rulers and ministers and fathers and sons, and competed for rewards.

They flattered their rulers and aped their ideas
and caused chaos for the people while carrying out their own affairs.

For this reason,

rulers and ministers became estranged and were not on intimate terms;
bone and flesh drifted apart and were not close.
Well-established [earthen] altars dried out and cracked apart;
[state] banquet pavilions shuddered and collapsed.
Packs of dogs howled and entered deep waters;
pigs gobbled mouthfuls of rushes and bedded down in river coves.[79]
Beauties messed up their hair and blackened their faces, spoiling their appearance.
Those with fine voices filled their mouths with charcoal, kept their [talent] shut away, and did not sing.
Mourners did not [express] the fullness of grief;
hunters did not obtain any joy [from it].[80]
The Western Elder snapped her hair ornament;[81]
the Yellow God sighed and moaned.[82]

Shang, and Zhou dynasties. Note, however, that this passage refers specifically to Jie, last king of Xia, so strictly speaking, Cheng Tang and Wen Wang do not fit chronologically.

77. *Zhun* 準—that is, a water level.

78. That is, people disregarded kinship ties.

79. The sense of this enigmatic pair of sentences would seem to be that dogs and pigs fled from their usual associations with humans in response to the breakdown of government and morality and to the earthquakes that occurred as a consequence of that breakdown.

80. *Ting qi le* (or *yue*) 聽其樂 is a complicated phrase. Usually one would take it to mean "hear its (or the) music," but here it is parallel to the phrase "express the fullness of grief" (*jin qi ai* 盡其哀) in the previous line and so must mean "obtain joy (from it)." As usual, the double meaning of *le/yue* cannot be conveyed in English.

81. That is, Xiwangmu 西王母, the "Queen Mother of the West." See chap. 4, n. 37. She is conventionally depicted wearing a distinctive headdress called a *sheng* 勝.

82. That is, Huangdi, the Yellow Emperor. His sighing and moaning, like Xiwangmu's snapping her hair ornament, is presumably a sign of frustration at the parlous state of humanity.

Flying birds folded their wings;
running animals lost their footing.
Mountains were without towering trees;
marshes were without pooling waters.
Foxes and raccoon dogs[83] headed for their burrows;
horses and cattle scattered and were lost.
Fields were without standing grain;
roadsides were without cattails or sedge.[84]

Gold ingots were cracked and missing their corners; jade disks were piled up but had their surface engraving worn off.[85]

[They] used up[86] turtles [for divination] until they had no plastrons left; they set out milfoil stalks and cast them daily. [6/53/10–18]

Coming down to a later era, the seven states set up unrelated clans [of rulers].[87] The various lords took control of the laws, each practicing their own customs in different ways. Vertical and horizontal [alliances][88] came between them; raising troops, they locked horns with one another, besieging cities and wantonly slaughtering [their inhabitants]. They overthrew those in high [positions] and endangered the peaceful.

They exhumed burial mounds
and scattered human bones,
enlarged the frames of [war] chariots
and raised high the thick ramparts.
They dispensed with the Way of Warfare,
and easing onto the Road of Death,
they engaged dreaded enemies
and plundered beyond reason.

For every hundred soldiers that advanced, one returned [alive]. [These rulers'] fame and renown flourished in a meretricious way.

All that being so, those who were sound in body and light on their feet were made into armored soldiers and sent a thousand *li* or more away [to fight], while the household elders and those who were sickly or weak remained, anxious and sad, at home.

Servant battalions and horse wranglers
pushed carts and handed out rations.

83. For *hu* 狐 and *li* 狸, see 10.14 and (for *li*) chap. 1, n. 32.

84. Leaves of both cattails and sedge were used for making raincoats.

85. The implication is that the disks were being used so excessively in divinatory and other rituals that their surface decorations were worn away. This pair of four-character phrases is enigmatic: in particular, *bi xi wu luo* 璧襲無蠃 depends on nonstandard interpretations of *xi* and *luo*. The translation given here relies on the commentary of Wang Yinzhi and should be regarded as tentative.

86. Taking *qing* 磬 as *qing* 罄.

87. According to the Gao You commentary, the seven states referred to here are Qi 齊, Chu 楚, Yan 燕, Zhao 趙, Hann 韓, Wei 魏, and Qin 秦.

88. That is, alliances of northern and southern states versus eastern and western states.

The ways and roads were endlessly far;
frost and snow interminably piled up;
their rough woolen tunics were not sufficient.
People were exhausted and chariots fell apart.
Mud and muck reaching to their knees,
they helped drag one another along the way.
Dauntlessly raising their heads on the roads,
their bodies [nevertheless] fell and died.

What is called "annexing states and having [their] land" [really] means fallen corpses by the tens of ten thousands and smashed chariots counted up by the thousands and hundreds, with those wounded by bows or crossbows, spears or glaives, arrows or stones, supporting one another along the roads.

Thus the world reached the point that people used human skulls for pillows, fed on human flesh, made mincemeat of human livers, drank human blood, and [found] these things sweeter than [the flesh of] fattened cattle. [6/53/20–26]

Thus from the Three Dynasties onward, the world was never able to obtain
[a sense of] security in their instinctive responses and their natures
or joy in their habits and customs
or preserve their natural life spans

or avoid dying young in consequence of the tyranny of others. Why was that so? [It was because] the various rulers [used their] strength to attack [one another], and so the world was unable to come together and be as one family. [6/54/1–2]

6.9

Coming down to the present time, the Son of Heaven occupies his position on high,
sustaining [his rule] with the Way and its Potency,
supporting [his rule] with Humaneness and Rightness.
Those nearby augment his knowledge;
those far away embrace his Moral Potency.

He folds his hands and bows, gestures with his finger, and [all within] the Four Seas respectfully submit to him. Spring and autumn, winter and summer, all offer up their goods in tribute to him. The whole world blends together and becomes one; sons and grandsons succeed one another. This was the way the Five Thearchs welcomed the Potency of Heaven. [6/54/4–6]

Now a sage cannot create [an opportune moment of] time. [But] when the [opportune] time comes, he does not miss it. He
promotes those who have ability,
dismisses the initiators of slander or flattery,
puts a stop to clever or argumentative talk,
does away with the laws [requiring punishments of] cutting or amputating,
banishes matters that are vexatious or petty,

avoids any traces of gossip,
shuts the door on cabals and parties.

He

extirpates [conventional] knowledge and ability,
complies with the Supreme Constant,[89]
sloughs off his limbs and body,
minimizes perception and intelligence,[90]
greatly penetrates into formless obscurity,
liberates his awareness and releases his spirit.

Completely indifferent, as if lacking ethereal and material souls,[91] he causes the myriad things all to return to their own roots, thus in these ways following in the footsteps of Lord Fuxi and reverting to the Way of the Five Thearchs.

Now, how is it that Qian Qie and Da Bing were able to achieve a reputation for charioteering throughout the world while not using reins or bits and that Fuxi and Nüwa were able to transmit Utmost Potency to later generations while not setting up laws and standards? They achieved Empty Nothingness and Pure Unity, and they did not dabble in petty matters. The *Book of Zhou*[92] says, "If you try to catch cock pheasants and do not get any, adjust [your hunting techniques] to suit their habits." [6/54/8–14]

Now take, for example, the methods of government [proposed by] Shen [Buhai], Han [Feizi],[93] and Shang Yang. They [proposed to]

pluck out the stems [of disorder]
and weed out the roots [of disobedience],

without fully investigating where [those undesirable qualities] came from. How did things get to that point? They

forcibly imposed the five punishments,
employed slicing and amputations,

and turned their backs on the fundamentals of the Way and its Potency while fighting over the point of an awl.[94] They mowed the common people[95] like hay and extermi-

89. Le Blanc 1985, 181, and Le Blanc and Mathieu 2003, 285, translate *tai chang* 太常 as "minister of rites," one of the chief ministers in the Han government. We think that is too literal and that a philosophical principle rather than a government office is intended here. We suspect that this is an allusion to the "constant Way" (*chang dao* 常道) of *Laozi* 1.

90. This and the previous line appear, with variations, in ZZ 6/19/21, where (through the mouthpiece of Confucius's disciple Yan Hui) they are part of a passage about achieving "sitting in forgetfulness" (*zuo wang* 坐忘). A longer version appears in ZZ 11/28/16–18, where the speaker is Hung Meng.

91. For the *hun* 魂 and *po* 魄 souls, see also 7.6, 7.7, and 16.1.

92. Presumably the *Yi Zhou shu* 逸周書, but this quotation does not appear in the surviving fragments of that work.

93. Han Feizi 韓非子 (also known as Han Fei [d. 233 B.C.E.]) was a scion of the royal house of Hann and a prolific writer on politics and political theory. The text that bears his name, the *Hanfeizi*, is one of the richest works of early statecraft thinking and a source from which much material in the *Huainanzi* may have been drawn.

94. That is, disputing over fine points of no importance.

95. *Baixing* 百姓, the "hundred surnames."

nated more than half of them. Thus filled with self-admiration, they constantly took themselves as [the model of] government; but this was just like adding fuel to put out a fire or boring holes to stop water [from leaking].

Now shoots may grow from the wooden casing of a well, not leaving room for the bucket; and branches may grow from the wooden casing of a canal, not leaving room for the boats. But not more than three months later, [these growths] will be dead. How is it that this is so? They all are wild growths with no roots of their own. That the Yellow River makes nine bends before it flows into the sea, but its flow is not interrupted by them, is because [the water] is carried [by the flow from] Mount Kunlun. But that floodwaters do not find an outlet but spread out widely to the limits of [one's] vision, [so that] after ten days or a month of no rain they dry up and turn into a stagnant wetland is because they receive [only] an overflow but have no source [of replenishment].

This may be compared with [the situation of] Yi [the Archer], who requested the elixir of immortality from the Queen Mother of the West. Heng E[96] stole it [from him] and fled [with it] to the moon. [Yi] was downcast and grief stricken because he had no way to get more of it. Why? Because he did not know where the elixir of immortality came from.

Thus begging for fire is not as good as getting a fire starter, and asking for a drink is not as good as boring a well. [6/54/14–21]

Translated by John S. Major

96. Heng E 恒娥 (also known as Chang 長 E) was the wife of Archer Yi. To this day, many Chinese people still speak of her living on the moon.

Seven

QUINTESSENTIAL SPIRIT

"QUINTESSENTIAL SPIRIT" is the first chapter of the *Huainanzi* to introduce human beings systematically into the grand scheme of things. The text continues its methodical explication of the underlying powers, patterns, and forces of the cosmos and its creatures before turning, in the later chapters of the work, to illustrations and amplifications of the workings of the Way in the world of affairs. Chapters 1 and 2 introduced cosmology and ontology; chapters 3 through 5 explored the various dimensions of Heaven, Earth, and Time; and chapter 6 explained the mysterious operations of *ganying* resonance by which things in the world interact through stimuli and responses. In chapter 7, the authors now turn their attention to human beings, the third leg of the early Chinese conceptual tripod of Heaven, Earth, and Man.

The chapter begins with a brief reprise of the cosmology relevant to understanding the origins of the vital energy that constitutes the cosmos and the creatures that inhabit it before going on to consider humans in their guise as physical/spiritual bodies and microcosms of the universe. The chapter then introduces the concept of the Quintessential Spirit as the force that animates the physical body and consciousness itself. It also discusses the paragons of human perfection, Genuine Persons (*zhenren*), sages, and Perfected Persons (*zhiren*), who are characterized by, among other qualities, their ability to ignore external stimuli and to draw Potency from their source in the Way and by their indifference to the exigencies of life and death. The qualities of human perfection are not cultivated through self-mortification but through an apophatic inner-cultivation practice in which the adept empties the mind and body of passions, prejudices, and thoughts until realizing the unification of innate nature and the Way. The resultant indifference to ordinary desires and the ability to respond spontaneously and harmoniously to whatever situation arises takes on political coloration in a discussion of the attitude of the sage toward government: able to serve unerringly as ruler when the time is right but not covetous of power, not greedy for wealth, and not concerned with self-aggrandizement. The chapter ends with a striking image of the goal of this inward training and the self-discipline it requires: it is not the arrow that misses the bull's-eye but the archer who fails to guide it accurately.

The Chapter Title

The title of the chapter is "Jing shen" 精神, which we translate as "Quintessential Spirit."[1] *Jing* means "essence" or "quintessence" or, in adjectival form, "quintessential." It refers to the most highly refined and true to its own nature form of any quality. It is often used nominally as a shortened form of *jingqi* (quintessential vital energy). *Shen* is "spirit," covering a wide range of meanings within the spectrum of that term, from "deity" and "divine" to "animating spirit" or "vital force." In the *Huainanzi*, it is associated with properties of consciousness and having the ability to oversee or coordinate the various mental activities of perception and cognition (see 1.20). As section 7.1 explains, everything in the world is made of *qi*, "vital energy," whether the pure, rarified *qi* of Heaven or the turbid, gross *qi* of Earth. *Shen* can be thought of as composed of the most highly rarified and purified kind of *qi*, and *jingshen* as the quintessence of *shen*. To the extent that *shen* itself has a basis as a form of *qi*, it is this *jingshen*, the quintessential vital energy of the spirit. The Quintessential Spirit occupies and animates the physical form but must be guarded lest it leak away or become sullied. A good way to prevent this leakage is to minimize perception and the passions and prejudices that result from it.

Although we prefer to see the primary meaning of the chapter title as an adjective–noun phrase, it can also be understood as a double noun phrase, "quintessence (= quintessential *qi*) and spirit." In some passages of the *Huainanzi* this meaning is confirmed by parallelism with another double noun phrase; for example in 7.6:

> Their ethereal and corporeal souls are settled in their dwelling;
> their Quintessence and spirit are preserved in their root.

It would not be incorrect to render the chapter title as "Quintessence and Spirit," but "Quintessential Spirit" more nearly captures the subject matter of the chapter itself. Moreover, contextual research indicates that when *jing* and *qi* are unqualified,

1. For more extensive discussions of the terms *jing* and *shen* and the compound *jingshen*, see app. A.

they are most often followed by predicates of fluid motion (for example, "flows," "swirls," "seeps"). When *shen* is unqualified, it is often followed by a predicate of instrumentality (for example, "directs," "makes," "orders"). However, the compound *jingshen* is most frequently followed by predicates of fluid motion, as are *jing* and *qi*. Thus *jingshen* has the properties of a type of *qi*. It is, basically, the quintessential vital energy of the spirit, its most quintessential form. Hence in most passages, it is translated as "Quintessential Spirit."[2]

Summary and Key Themes

"Quintessential Spirit" begins with a recapitulation of chapter 1's *Laozi*-based cosmogony, but in this instance with the specific purpose of explaining the origins of the Quintessential Spirit. Two "spiritlike powers" differentiated into yin and yang and became manifested as *qi*, and various sorts of *qi* congealed to form different sorts of creatures. Humans are distinguished from beasts by being made of purer and more refined vital energy. They contain Quintessential Spirit—that is, their heavenly dimension that is preserved by sages who can maintain tranquillity and emptiness. Section 7.2 differentiates between Quintessential Spirit, received from Heaven, and physical form, received from Earth. Humans recapitulate the cosmos in microcosm. Their heads are round, like Heaven; their feet (side by side) form a square, like Earth; and their 366 joints match the year's 366 days. The fetus develops in stages over a ten-month period, and the five visceral orbs connect to the organs of sense and correlate with various natural forces.

The Quintessential Spirit is exalted above all these aspects of human beings: it alone, as section 7.6 states, is more precious than "the jade half-disk of the Xiahou clan." It is important both to preserve one's innate store of Quintessential Spirit and to generate new stores. The way to do this is consistent with the recommendations of the Daoist inner-cultivation tradition to avoid excessive sense stimulation, perception, and concomitant desires (as we find in sections 7.4 and 7.5). Sections 7.3, 7.4, and 7.12 offer advice on how to accomplish this: concentrate your breathing and attention and relinquish thoughts, feelings, and desires, "cast aside wisdom and precedent." Eventually, you will reach a condition of complete equanimity and pure emptiness, a state in which your "inborn nature is merged with the Way" (7.7). Then when returning to the world of dualities, you will have many valuable qualities. Your sense perceptions are always clear and accurate; your emotions are always calmed; and you rest in harmony amid the turmoil of the world. People like this are sages and are able to avoid the pitfalls of the physical body: the eyes and ears that can drain off vital energy and the lusts that excite the senses. This is very much in

2. Harold D. Roth, "The Early Taoist Concept of *Shen*: A Ghost in the Machine?" in *Sagehood and Systematizing Thought in the Warring States and Early Han*, ed. Kidder Smith (Brunswick, Maine: Bowdoin College Press, 1989), 11–32.

the tradition of thinkers like the author, for example, of *Laozi* 12: "The five colors blind human eyes; the five notes deafen human ears," and so on. Sections 7.5, 7.6, and 7.7 explain that sages exhibit a cultivated indifference to life and death, to sorrow and joy, and to success and failure; they do not allow emotional states to cause their Quintessential Spirit to leak out externally. When they become perfected, they are profoundly spiritlike; "they contain nothing, and things cannot disturb them."

This chapter also discusses some of the paragons of inner cultivation. In addition to sages are the Perfected (*zhiren*) and the Genuine (*zhenren*). Both are described in sections 7.7 and 7.10 as being able to concentrate on their inner lives and take their outer lives lightly. They can maintain the Origin (that is, the Way) amid the chaos of the dusty world by practicing non-action (*wuwei*) and maintaining a body like "withered wood" and a "mind . . . like dead ashes." They are metaphorically said to "study with the Undying Teacher" and to be so indifferent to self-preservation that "they take life and death to be a single transformation."

Perhaps this treasured indifference is why the authors of this chapter take pains to differentiate their practices from common techniques of physical self-cultivation to attain health and longevity, known in the late Warring States and early Han periods as *daoyin* 導引 (guiding and pulling [of *qi*]), that now survive principally among the early Chinese medical corpus, especially the texts discovered at Mawangdui and Zhangjiashan.[3] These exercises, which often involved stretching and bending and mimicking the positions of animals, are criticized in section 7.8, which opens with a surprisingly dismissive reference:

> If you huff and puff, exhale and inhale,
> blow out the old and pull in the new,
> practice the Bear Hang, the Bird Stretch,
> the Duck Splash, the Ape Leap,
> the Owl Gaze, and the Tiger Stare:
>
> This is what is practiced by those who nurture the body. They are not the practices of those who polish the mind.

This criticism, also found in *Zhuangzi* 15, gives a fascinating glimpse into the similarities, perceived even then, between the *qi* cultivation practiced for physical benefits and the *qi* cultivation practiced for more transformative and deeply satisfying spiritual benefits, which seems to have involved more still sitting than active movement.[4] The reference here is to a process of "nourishing the spirit" (*yangshen*), the aspect of human beings that is "born together with Heaven and Earth" and that is not transformed at death.

---

3. For a brilliant translation and analysis of this literature, see Donald Harper, *Early Chinese Medical Literature* (London: Kegan Paul International, 1998).

4. Compare ZZ 15/5–6. Some of these positions are depicted in the chart of the *qi* cultivation exercises known as "guiding and pulling" (*daoyin* 導引) found at Mawangdui Tomb 3.

Having established the definitions of spiritual paragons and their qualities and methods of attainment and after having given some examples of such people in the narratives of section 7.9, the authors of "Quintessential Spirit" then address the reasons why a government led by such perfected human beings is superior to any other kind. They emphasize the assertion that these sages do not have any ambitions to rule; power, wealth, and the elaborate trappings of state are of no interest to them. As section 7.12 states: "Possessing and not possessing the empire are the same reality to them." True sages are utterly indifferent to such things, simple in their tastes and tranquil in their demeanor; possessing the empire is nothing to them. They eat enough to survive and wear enough clothing to be protected from the elements, that is all. Various examples of sage rulers—familiar figures such as Yao and Shun—are used to illustrate these points and to contrast with the shallow scholars and narrow-minded literati of the present age.

Sections 7.11 and 7.15 single out the Confucians for such criticism. While the authors do express a grudging admiration for exemplars of the ethically superior Confucian paragon of the *junzi* (Superior Man), they see them as inferior to their own Daoist paragons: "People like them act only according to what is right and are not drawn to material things. How much more is this so for those who act through non-action?" (7.11). Section 7.11 then compares scholars who study the *Odes* and the *Documents* with impoverished villagers who are satisfied with the music they make by drumming on pots and pans. By contrast, those who "know the meaning of the Great Discourse" are like those who make the music of the great ceremonial bells and drums. Section 7.14 states,

> Shallow scholars in this declining age do not understand how to get to the origins of their minds and return to their root. They merely sculpt and polish their natures and adorn and stifle their genuine responses in order to interact with their age.

They are contrasted with "those who penetrate through to the Way" who cultivate the "Techniques of the Mind," find repose in Potency, and desire nothing yet attain what they desire. Section 7.15 explicitly critiques Confucians who "do not get to the foundations of why they have desires but instead prohibit what they desire." They are contrasted with perfected adepts who "rest in the vast universe, roam in the country of the Limitless, ascend Tai Huang, [and] ride Tai Yi . . . [and] play with Heaven and Earth in the palms of their hands."

The chapter's final section (7.16) lists those rulers who allowed themselves to be distracted by desires and so came to bad ends.

The message of the latter parts of the chapter especially is that incompetent and greedy rulers and advisers abound in the present age and that sage-rulers are in short supply. Because of this, it is important that we create them through the inner-cultivation practices outlined in this chapter.

Sources

"Quintessential Spirit" appears to draw its cosmogony and cosmology from the *Laozi* and, perhaps more directly, from the early chapters of the *Huainanzi* (which themselves are based on the *Laozi*) and to borrow its image of the Perfected Person—tranquil, empty, self-contained—from the *Zhuangzi*. In particular, chapter 15 of the *Zhuangzi*, "Ingrained Ideas" (Keyi 刻意), shares much of this chapter's perspective on the attainment of spiritual perfection. Specific turns of phrase, technical terminology, and critiques of practitioners of *daoyin* (Grandfather Peng's Ripe Old Agers) and of embittered or self-promoting moralists (Confucians) are so close that one could make a fair case for common authorship.[5] The other major influence of this chapter is the inner-cultivation tradition preserved in such texts as *Guanzi*'s "Neiye" (Inward Training) and "Xinshu" (Techniques of the Mind). The interest in the cultivation of *jing, qi, shen,* and *jingshen* in chapter 7 of the *Huainanzi* seems to be directly drawn from this tradition. Indeed, as explained earlier, although the actual phrase "Techniques of the Mind" is used and advocated, it is not clear in this instance if it is the specific text or the psychospiritual cultivation practices that is intended.

It is important to note that "Quintessential Spirit" and these earlier sources discuss and refer to the same methods of psychospiritual cultivation that we find in the later organized Daoist religion. While specific historical evidence linking this text with those later practices is lacking, there is little doubt that chapter 7 of the *Huainanzi* was transmitted through the Han at local courts and centers of power in what Mark Csíkszentmihalyi calls an "unofficial transmission."[6] Local academies and learning salons preserved methods and techniques associated with the rise of the late Han Daoist millennial rebellions and the religious traditions they formed. He suggests that many of the texts from Liu An's court were part of this kind of unofficial transmission.

The Chapter in the Context of the *Huainanzi* as a Whole

"Quintessential Spirit" builds on and complements the six chapters that precede it. The *Huainanzi*'s basic cosmological orientation is extended to the world of humans, who are made like all things of *qi*, partaking of both Heaven and Earth, each person a microcosm of the universe. But people are also portrayed as frail, mortal, and subject

5. For parallel passages from the *Zhuangzi*, see the notes to chap. 7.

6. Mark Csikszentmihalyi, "Traditional Taxonomies and Revealed Texts in the Han," in *Daoist Identity: History, Lineage, Ritual*, ed. Livia Kohn and Harold D. Roth (Honolulu: University of Hawai'i Press, 2002), 94–97; Harold D. Roth, "Han Cosmology and Mantic Practices," in *Daoism Handbook*, ed. Livia Kohn (Leiden: Brill, 2000), 52–73.

to all sorts of distractions and ills occasioned by stimulation of the sensory organs. The chapter then develops the notion of *jingshen*, introduced in chapter 1, as the force animating the physical body whose retention is the focus of sagely self-cultivation.

"Quintessential Spirit" paves the way for the many chapters of the *Huainanzi*, especially those in the second part of the book, that deal extensively with the idea of the sage-ruler, by defining more clearly what a sage is (especially the highly self-cultivated manifestation of sagehood, the Perfected) and what a sage's attitude is toward holding the reins of power. When we read those later chapters in light of chapter 7, we realize why sages are so rarely encountered in the world. In addition, easy as it may be to talk about the concept of "sagely rule" (*sheng zhi* 聖治), finding it practiced in the world as we know it is a rare event indeed. This message from the latter sections of chapter 7 is picked up again later in the text and becomes one of the principal themes of chapter 14, "Sayings Explained." There, too, we find the idea that true sages are tranquil and self-contained and that they do not lust after political power.

That message, in both this chapter and chapter 14, may have had immediate relevance to the life and fortunes of its author/editor Liu An. An example is the fraught political climate in which the *Huainanzi* was compiled and written and Liu An's own ambiguous roles as an ambitious intellectual, a possible heir to Emperor Jing's throne, a would-be adviser to Emperor Wu, and a potentially seditious imperial kinsman. The later sections of chapter 7 maintain that sages are indifferent to power, have no interest in ascending a throne, desire tranquillity and self-cultivation, and are unaffected by the lusts and desires to which ordinary men are subject. These all add up to a subtle plea by Liu An to his imperial cousin (Jing) and nephew (Wu) that the writing of the *Huainanzi*—despite its implicit (and dangerous) advocacy of a partly decentralized imperial realm in which the imperial central government coexisted with neofeudal kingdoms—really did not pose a threat to the imperial throne. Sages, according to this subtle message, are above that sort of thing. As chapter 21, "An Overview of the Essentials," puts it,[7] the sage is not "foolishly immersed in the advantages of political power, [nor] seductively confused by the exigencies of affairs." The *Huainanzi* is, among other things, a political document written during a very dangerous time in the history of the former Han dynasty. The image of the sage presented in this chapter is thus intimately bound up with the political concerns of Liu An's time.

Harold D. Roth and John S. Major

7. In 21.2, as part of the summary of chap. 13, "Boundless Discourses," addressing a related point.

Seven

7.1

Of old, in the time before there was Heaven and Earth:

> There were only images and no forms.
> All was obscure and dark,
> vague and unclear,
> shapeless and formless,
> and no one knows its gateway.

There were two spirits, born in murkiness, one that established Heaven and the other that constructed Earth.

> So vast! No one knows where they ultimately end.
> So broad! No one knows where they finally stop.

Thereupon

> they differentiated into the yin and the yang
> and separated into the eight cardinal directions.
> The firm and the yielding formed each other;
> the myriad things thereupon took shape.
> The turbid vital energy became creatures;
> the refined vital energy became humans.

Therefore,

> the Quintessential Spirit is of Heaven;
> the skeletal system is of Earth.
> When the Quintessential Spirit enters its gateway

and the skeletal system returns to its root,
how can I still survive?
For this reason, the sages
model themselves on Heaven,
accord with their genuine responses,
are not confined by custom,
or seduced by other men.
They take
Heaven as father,
Earth as mother,
yin and yang as warp,
the four seasons as weft.
Through the tranquillity of Heaven, they become pure.
Through the stability of Earth, they become calm.
Among the myriad things,
those who lose this perish;
those who follow this live. [7/54/25–7/55/2]
Tranquillity and stillness are the dwellings of spiritlike illumination;
emptiness and nothingness are where the Way resides.
For this reason,
those who seek for it externally lose it internally;
those who preserve it internally attain it externally as well.
It is like the roots and branches of trees: none of the thousands of limbs and tens of thousands of leaves does not derive from the roots. [7/55/4–5]

7.2

The Quintessential Spirit is what we receive from Heaven;
the physical body is what we are given by Earth.
Therefore it is said:
"The one generates the two;
the two generate the three;
the three generate the myriad things.
The myriad things carry the yin and embrace the yang and, through the blending of vital energy, become harmonious."[1]
Therefore it is said:
"In the first month, fertilization occurs.
In the second month, a corporeal mass develops.
In the third month, an embryo forms.
In the fourth month, the flesh is produced.
In the fifth month, the muscles form.

1. *Laozi* 42.

In the sixth month, the bones develop.
In the seventh month, the fetus forms.
In the eighth month, the fetus starts to move.
In the ninth month, its movements become more pronounced.
In the tenth month, the birth occurs."

In this way,
the physical body is completed
and the five orbs are formed.

Therefore,
the pulmonary orb[2] regulates the eyes;
the renal orb regulates the nose;
the choleric orb regulates the mouth;
the hepatic orb regulates the ears;
and the splenic orb regulates the tongue.
The external ones are on the outer side;
the internal ones are on the inner side.
They open and close, expand and contract,
and each has its conduits and connections.

Therefore,
the roundness of the head is in the image of Heaven;
the squareness of human feet is in the image of Earth.[3]
Heaven has four seasons, five phases, nine regions, and 366 days.
Humans have four limbs, five orbs, nine apertures, and 366 joints.
Heaven has wind, rain, cold, and heat;
humans have taking, giving, joy, and anger.

Therefore,
the choleric orb parallels[4] the clouds;
the pulmonary orb parallels the air;
the hepatic orb parallels the wind;
the renal orb parallels the rain;
and the splenic orb parallels the thunder.

In this way human beings form a triad with Heaven and Earth, and the mind is the ruler of this.

Therefore,
the ears and eyes are the sun and moon;
the blood and vital energy are the wind and rain.
In the sun there is a three-legged crow;
in the moon there is a speckled toad.[5]

---

2. The five "orbs" (*zang* 藏) are the spheres of vital energy in the human body.

3. The paired footprints of a person standing in a comfortable stance form approximately a square.

4. *Wei* 為 generally means "make," but here it has the more technical meaning of "is the same as, in parallel systems."

5. The sun bird is called a *cun wu* 踆烏, "hopping crow," conventionally depicted as having three

When sun and moon err in their periodic motions, fireflies have no light, wind and rain are not appropriate to the season, and destruction occurs and disasters arise.

When the five asterisms err in their periodic movements, provinces and states meet with calamity. [7/55/7–16]

7.3

The Way of Heaven and Earth is immense and grand, yet it still must
restrict its brilliance
and conserve its spiritlike illumination.
The ears and eyes of human beings, how can one expect them to toil for long periods without rest?
The Quintessential Spirit, how can one expect it to course [through the body] for long periods without respite?
Therefore,
the blood and vital energy are the flowerings of humankind,
and the Five Orbs are the essence of humankind.
If the blood and vital energy are concentrated within the Five Orbs and [the Quintessential Spirit] does not flow out, then the chest and belly are replete and lusts and desires are eliminated.
When the chest and belly are replete and lusts and desires are eliminated, then the ears and eyes are clear, and hearing and vision are acute.
When the ears and eyes are clear and hearing and vision are acute, we call this "clarity."
When the Five Orbs can be subordinated to the mind and their functioning is without error, then fluctuating attention will be done away with, and the circulation [of the vital energy] will not be awry.
When fluctuating attention is done away with and the circulation is not awry, then the Quintessential Spirit is abundant, and the vital energy is not dispersed.
When the Quintessential Spirit is abundant and the vital energy is not dispersed, then you are functioning according to Underlying Patterns.
When you function according to Underlying Patterns, you attain equanimity.
When you attain equanimity, you develop penetrating awareness.
When you develop penetrating awareness, you become spiritlike.
When you are spiritlike,
with vision, there is nothing unseen;
with hearing, there is nothing unheard;
with actions, there is nothing incomplete.
For this reason,

legs. There are illustrations of these two mythical animals on the funerary banners found at Mawangdui Tombs 1 and 3.

anxiety and worry cannot enter,
and aberrant vital energy cannot seep in. [7/55/18–24]

Thus there are certain things that you seek outside the Four Seas yet never meet and others that you guard within the physical frame yet never see.

Therefore,

the more you seek, the less you attain;
the more you see, the less you understand. [7/55/26–27]

7.4

The apertures of perception [eyes and ears] are the portals of the Quintessential Spirit.

The vital energy and attention are the emissaries and servants of the Five Orbs.

When the eyes and ears are enticed by the joys of sound and color, then the Five Orbs oscillate and are not stable.

When the Five Orbs oscillate and are not stable, then the blood and vital energy are agitated and not at rest.

When the blood and vital energy are agitated and not at rest, then the Quintessential Spirit courses out [through the eyes and ears] and is not preserved.

When the Quintessential Spirit courses out and is not preserved,

then when either good fortune or misfortune arrives, although it be the size of hills and mountains, one has no way to recognize it.

But

if you make your ears and eyes totally clear and profoundly penetrating and not enticed by external things;

if your vital energy and attention are empty, tranquil, still, and serene and you eliminate lusts and desires;

if the Five Orbs are stable, reposed, replete, and full and not leaking [the vital energies];

if your Quintessential Spirit is preserved within your physical frame and does not flow out;

then even gazing back beyond bygone ages and looking further than things that are to come; even these things would not be worth doing, much less discriminating between bad and good fortune.

Therefore it is said, "The farther you go, the less you know."[6] This says that the Quintessential Spirit cannot be allowed to be enticed by external things.

Therefore,

the five colors disrupt the eyes and cause them to be unclear;
the five sounds confuse the ears and cause them to not be acute;
the five tastes disrupt the mouth and cause it to lose the ability to taste;

6. *Laozi* 47. This line also is quoted in 12.46.

preferences confuse the nature and cause it to fly about [from one thing to the next].[7]

These four things are how the people of this world commonly nourish their natures. However, they all are human attachments.

Therefore it is said:

"Lusts and desires cause humans' vital energy to dissipate;
likes and dislikes cause human' minds to tire."

If you do not quickly eliminate them, your attention and vital energy will diminish daily. [7/55/27–7/56/8]

7.5

Why is it that common people are not able to complete the full course of their lives and, along the way, die young by execution? "It is because they set too much store in living. Now only those who are able to not make living their concern are able to attain long life."[8]

Heaven and Earth revolve and interpenetrate;
the myriad things bustle about yet form a unity.
If one is able to know this unity, then there is nothing that cannot be known;
if one cannot know this unity, then there is not even one thing that can truly be known.

For example, I live within the world, yet I am also a thing in it. I do not know whether the things of the world are complete because of me or whether only without me are things not incomplete. However, I am also a thing and things relate to things.[9] A thing is related to other things [by this underlying unity], so why must we be things to [i.e., objectify] one another? Even though this may be so,

what gain is there in its giving me life;
what loss is there in its taking my life away?

Because what fashions and transforms us treats me as an unfired brick, I have no way to defy it.[10] How do I know that to practice acupuncture and moxibustion and to desire life is not a delusion and to seek death by strangulation is not a blessing? Perhaps life is just servitude, and death is a respite from this toil.[11]

The world is vast: who understands it?

It gives me life, but not because I intentionally seek it.
It takes my life away, but not because I intentionally seek an end.
Desire life, but do not strive for it.
Detest death, but do not refuse it.

7. We follow the interpretation of Kusuyama Haruki, *Enanji*, in *Shinshaku kanbun taikei* (Tokyo: Meiji shōin, 1979–1988), 54:328. This is a paraphrase of *Laozi* 12.

8. This is a paraphrase of *Laozi* 47.

9. This paragraph is a musing on ZZ 4/9/8ff.

10. This is similar to but more succinct than ZZ 6/17/27–6/18/8.

11. This is similar to ZZ 2/6/28.

Demean it, but do not detest it.
Honor it, but do not rejoice in it.

Follow your heavenly endowment and be at peace until you develop it to the fullest.

In life I have a form that is seven feet tall;[12]
in death I have [the space of] a coffin's worth of soil.
My life classes me with the things that have form;
my death sinks me into the oblivion of the formless.

Thus,

because of my life, a thing is not added to the multitude;
because of my death, the soil does not get any thicker.

So how can I know what is pleasant or hateful, beneficial or harmful in all of this? [7/56/10–20]

The way in which what fashions and transforms us takes hold of things can be compared with the way in which the potter molds his clay. The earth that he has taken hold of and made into bowls and pots is no different from the earth before it had been taken from the ground. The earth that remains after he has made the vessels and then smashed them to pieces and thoroughly soaked them with water so that they return to their cause is no different from the earth that had been in the bowls and pots that had existed earlier.

Now the people who live along the banks of a river draw water from it to irrigate their gardens, but the water in the river does not resent it. The families who live near filthy ponds break through their banks and drain them into the river, but the water from these ponds does not rejoice in this. Thus there is no difference between the water in the river and the water irrigating gardens, and there also is no difference between the water in the ponds and the water in the river. Thus

sages adapt to the times and are at peace with their station in life;
they conform to their age and so find happiness in their calling. [7/56/22–26]

7.6

Sadness and joy are aberrations of Potency,
pleasure and anger are excesses of the Way;
fondness and resentment are the fetters of the mind.[13]

Therefore it is said [that sages]:

"In their life, act in accord with Heaven;
in their death, transform with other things.
In tranquillity, share the Potency of the yin;
in activity, share the surge of the yang."[14]

---

12. A Han "foot" (*chi* 尺) was approximately nine English inches long, so "seven feet" here means about five feet, three inches. In 3.31, the "height of an average man" is defined as eight feet (*chi*).

13. This parallels ZZ 15/42/3.

14. This poem is also found in ZZ 13/34/27–28 and 15/41/26–27.

Being calm and limitless, their Quintessential Spirit is not dissipated amid external things, and the world naturally submits to them.

Thus,

the mind is the ruler of the physical form;
the spirit is the treasure of the mind.
When the physical form toils without rest, it becomes exhausted;
when the Quintessence is used unceasingly, it runs out.[15]

Thus sages honor and esteem it and do not dare to allow it to seep out. [7/56/28–7/57/3]

The owner of the jade half-disk of the Xiahou clan stores it in a strong box because it is supremely precious.[16] The preciousness of the Quintessential Spirit is not merely that of the jade half-disk of the Xiahou clan.

For this reason, sages

based in Nothing respond to Something
and invariably fathom the Underlying Patterns;
based in the empty accept the full;
and invariably fathom the temporal nodes.[17]
Calm and still, empty and tranquil,
by this they reach the end of their life spans.

Thus,

there is nothing from which they are too aloof;
nothing with which they are too intimate.
Embracing the Potency and blending with the harmonious,
they accord with Heaven.

They make

the Way their boundary
and Potency their neighbor.
They do not make [attaining] good fortune a priority;
they do not make [avoiding] misfortune an antecedent.[18]

Their ethereal and corporeal souls are settled in their dwelling;[19]
their Quintessence and spirit are preserved in their root.

Death and life do not alter them. Therefore we say they are supremely spiritlike. [7/57/5–9]

---

15. This is similar to ZZ 15/42/5.

16. The jade half-disk (*huang* 璜) of the Xiahou 夏后 clan was a fabulous jewel that supposedly formed part of the regalia of the ducal house of Lu. See *Zuozhuan*, Ding 4; and 13.15, 16.90, and 17.2. There is a similar passage in ZZ 15/42/7–8.

17. The temporal nodes (*jie* 節) are twenty-four divisions of the solar year, each consisting of fifteen days. See 3.18 and app. B. The implication is that sages intuitively understand the right moment to act and the right moment to be still and thus they adapt to the seasons (*yinshi* 因時).

18. These two lines are found in a similar context in ZZ 15/41/27.

19. That is, the *hun* 魂 and *po* 魄 souls. In Han belief, living humans had two souls: (a) the *po*, a substantive, earthy, corporeal soul associated with yin that was buried with the body after death and consumed funerary offerings, and (b) the *hun*, an ethereal soul associated with yang that left the body at the time of death.

7.7

Those whom we call the Perfected are people whose inborn nature is merged with the Way.

Therefore,

they possess it but appear to have nothing.
They are full but appear to be empty.
They are settled in this unity and do not know of any duality
They cultivate what is inside and pay no attention to what is outside.
They illuminate and clarify Grand Simplicity;
taking no action, they revert to the Unhewn.[20]

They embody the foundation and embrace the spirit in order to roam freely within the confines of Heaven and Earth.[21] Untrammeled, they ramble outside this dusty world and wander aimlessly in their taskless calling.[22] Unfettered and unhindered, they harbor no clever devices or cunning knowledge in their minds.

Thus death and life are great indeed, but they do not alter them. Although Heaven and Earth support and nourish, they are not protected by them. They discern the flawless and do not get mixed up with things. While seeing the chaos of affairs, they are able to preserve their origin.[23]

Beings like these

negate obsession and fear
and cast aside sensory perceptions.[24]
Their mental activity is concentrated internally
and penetrates through to comport with the One.
At rest, they have no objectives;
in motion, they set no goals.
Artlessly they go forth;
peacefully they come back.
Their bodies are like withered wood;
their minds are like dead ashes.[25]
They forget the Five Orbs;
lose their physical frames;
know without studying;

20. The *locus classicus* of these two terms is *Laozi* 19 and 28, in which they signify conditions of undifferentiated selflessness and desirelessness.

21. This line and the previous six are found almost verbatim in ZZ 12/32/21–22.

22. This parallels ZZ 6/18/21–22 and 19/52/20–21.

23. This parallels ZZ 5/13/12–13.

24. For "obsession and fear," the text reads literally "negates liver and gall," but this actually refers to the negative mental states associated with the hepatic and choleric orbs. In the Chinese medical literature, these states are said to be obsession, for the hepatic, and fear, for the choleric. See *Grand dictionnaire Ricci de la langue chinoise*, 7 vols. (Paris: Institut Ricci, 2001), 6:621. The corresponding phrase in the parallel line, "sensory perceptions," literally reads "ears and eyes."

25. The *locus classicus* for this vivid description of a profound state of tranquillity attained through meditation is ZZ 2/3/14.

see without looking;
complete without acting;
and differentiate without judging.
When stimulated, they respond;
when pressed, they move;
when it is unavoidable, they go forth,[26]
like the brilliant glow of a flame,
like the mimicry of a shadow.

Taking the Way as their guiding thread, they are necessarily so. Embracing the foundation of Grand Purity, they contain nothing,[27] and things cannot disturb them. Vast and empty, they are tranquil and without worry.

Great marshes may catch fire, but it cannot burn them.
Great rivers may freeze over, but it cannot chill them.
Great thunder may shake the mountains, but it cannot startle them.[28]
Great storms may darken the sun, but it cannot harm them.

For this reason,

they view precious pearls and jade as being the same as gravel.
They view the supremely exalted and maximally favored [at court] as being the same as wandering guest [scholars].
They view [the beauties] Mao Qiang and Xi Shi[29] as being the same as funerary figurines.
They take life and death to be a single transformation
and the myriad things to be a single whole.
They merge their vital essence with the Root of Great Purity
and roam freely beyond the boundless.

They have vital essence but do not [recklessly] expend it;
and have spirit but do not [thoughtlessly] use it.
They identify with the artlessness of the Great Unhewn
and take their stand amid the supremely pure.

Thus,

their sleep is dreamless;[30]
their wisdom is traceless.
Their corporeal soul does not sink;
their ethereal soul does not soar.[31]

---

26. These three lines parallel ZZ 15/41/26–27.

27. As Lau (HNZ, 57n.10) noted, the text is corrupt here, missing several characters, so this translation is conjectural.

28. These lines parallel ZZ 2/6/17–18.

29. Mao Qiang 毛嬙 and Xi Shi 西施 were famed beauties of Yue, credited with having helped bring about the destruction of the state of Wu by distracting King Fuchai (r. 495–477 B.C.E.) with their charms. Their names became emblematic of perfect feminine beauty.

30. The idea that the Perfected sleep without dreaming is found in ZZ 6/16/2 and 15/41/29.

31. According to ancient beliefs, at death the *po* eventually sank into the ground, and the *hun* eventually rose into the sky. This text maintains that it is not the case for perfected human beings.

They repeatedly cycle from end to beginning, and we cannot know their starting and stopping points.

They behold the dwelling place of Total Darkness
and contemplate the lodging place of Total Brightness.
They rest in the realms of the Unfettered
and roam in the fields of the Nebulous.
At rest, they have no appearance.
In place, they have no location.
In movement, they have no form.
In stillness, they have no body.
They are present yet seem to be absent.
They are alive yet seem to be dead.
They emerge from, and enter into, the Dimensionless[32]
and employ ghostly spirits as their servants.

They plunge into the Fathomless
and enter the Nonexistent.[33]

In order that their different forms evolve into one another,

Ending and beginning like a circle,
of which no one can trace an outline.

This is how their Quintessential Spirit is able to verge upon the Way; this is the roaming of the Perfected.[34] [7/57/10–7/58/3]

7.8

If you huff and puff, exhale and inhale,
blow out the old and pull in the new,
practice the Bear Hang, the Bird Stretch,
the Duck Splash, the Ape Leap,
the Owl Gaze, and the Tiger Stare:

This is what is practiced by those who nurture the body.[35] They are not the practices of those who polish the mind [e.g., the Perfected]. They make their spirit overflow, without losing its fullness. When, day and night, without injury, they bring the spring to external things,[36] they unite with, and give birth to, the seasons in their own minds.

---

32. This alludes to *Laozi* 43: "The most flexible in the world can gallop through the most rigid: that which has no substance enters that which has no space."

33. Following the emendation of Wang Shu-min of *wu-jian* 無間, "the Dimensionless," to *wu-yu* 無有, "the Nonexistent." See Lau, HNZ, 58n.1.

34. Following the emendation of Yu Yue to drop "therefore" (*gu* 故) as an erroneous insertion. See Zhang Shuangdi 1997, 1:758.

35. ZZ 15/41/19–20. Some of these positions may be depicted in the chart of the *qi* cultivation exercises known as "guiding and pulling" (*daoyin* 導引) found at Mawangdui Tomb 3.

36. "When, day and night, without injury, they bring the spring to external things" is quoted almost verbatim from ZZ 5/15/3. The idea seems to be that the Perfected become such powerful generators of vital energies that they can infuse the external world with the vitality of springtime.

Moreover, there are those who mortify their bodies without harming their minds,
and those who cede their dwelling [i.e., the mind] without diminishing their Quintessence.
The thinking of the leper is not altered;[37]
the body of the madman not impaired.

But when their spirits eventually make their far-off journey, who will have time to think about what they did [in their lives]? Thus even though the body disappears, the spirit is never transformed. If you use what does not transform in response to transformations, [even through] a thousand alterations and ten thousand evolutions, you will not have begun to reach a limit.

What transforms returns to the Formless;
what does not transform is born together with Heaven and Earth.

A tree dies because its greenness has departed. But can that which gives life to a tree be a tree itself? Analogously, what fills the body is not the body. Thus,

What gives birth to the living never dies,[38] yet that to which it gives birth does die.
What transforms things never transforms, yet that which it transforms does transform.
If you take the world lightly, then your spirit will have no attachments.
If you minimize the myriad things, then your mind will not be led astray.
If you equalize death and life, then your mentality will not be fearful.
If you take all alterations and transformations as [being] the same, then your clarity will not be darkened.

The masses take these as empty words, but I take them as my ideal and prove them true. [7/58/3–10]

7.9

The reason people find pleasure in ruling is that they can fulfill the desires of their senses and facilitate the ease of their bodies.

Nowadays,

people find tall towers and lofty pavilions beautiful, but Yao did not trim the bark off the rough timber beams [of his house] and did not adorn the columns with capitals.
People find strange rarities and unusual tastes attractive, but Yao ate coarse millet and a simple vegetable soup.
People find elaborate embroidery and white fox fur pleasing, but Yao clothed himself in plain garments and deer pelts to ward off the cold.

His practice of nourishing his nature was to not overlay it by adding great responsibilities and burdening it with grief. Thus his transmitting the world to Shun was like

37. Reading 趨 as 趣, following the suggestion of Yang Shuda. See Zhang Shuangdi 1997, 1:761.
38. There is an identical line in ZZ 6/17/15.

the releasing of a burden from his back. This was not merely a polite offer: he really had no interest in ruling. This was the result of his taking the world lightly.

Yu traveled south to inspect the region and was crossing a river when a yellow dragon picked up his boat on its back. Five other people in the boat were so frightened that their faces kept altering color, but Yu laughed heartily and announced, "I received the Mandate from Heaven. I have exerted all my effort and toiled on behalf of the myriad people. Life is a sojourn; death is a return. How could this disturb my harmony?" He looked upon the dragon as if it were a lizard, [so he was unafraid] and his color did not change. The dragon thereupon hung his ears, picked up his tail, and fled. Yu's way of regarding [serious] things was to take them lightly, indeed.

A spiritlike shaman from Zheng checked the physiognomy of Huzi Lin, saw the signs [of a short life span], and informed Liezi.[39] Liezi ran crying to report this to his teacher. Huzi, balancing Heaven and Earth, remained indifferent to the idea and the reality of it and allowed the dynamism [of the breath] to rise up from his heels.[40] From Huzi's viewpoint, life and death were indeed equal.

Ziqiu had lived for fifty-four years when an injury made him hunchbacked.[41] The arch of his spine was higher than his forehead; his chin pressed down on his chest; his two buttocks were on top; his rectum pointed to the sky. He crawled over to peer at himself in a well: "Amazing! That which fashions and transforms us! How has it turned me into this crumpled thing?" This shows that from his viewpoint, alterations and transformation are the same.

Thus,

> If we examine the Way of Yao, we thereupon know how light the world is.
> If we observe the mentality of Yu, we thereupon know how insubstantial the world is.
> If we get to the source of Huzi's teaching, we thereupon know how equivalent death and life are.
> If we see the actions of Ziqiu, we thereupon know how identical alterations and transformations are. [7/58/12–23]

7.10

The Perfected

> lean on the unbudgeable pillar,
> walk on the unblocked road,

39. Liezi 列子 (also known as Lie Yukou 御寇 [fourth century B.C.E.]) was a Daoist thinker frequently mentioned in the *Zhuangzi* and other early texts. An extant text bears his name but is widely considered a later forgery. A longer version of this story is found starting at ZZ 7/20/25. In that version, the shaman is made to be the fool, but not here.

40. This passage seems to be alluding to the rising and falling of the breath that is discussed in the earliest source of breath cultivation in China, the "twelve-sided jade cylinder," dated to the fourth century B.C.E. For details, see Roth 1999, 161–64. *Zhuangzi* 6 (ZZ 6/16/2–3) also contains the idea that the Perfected breathe from their heels and that in them, the "heavenly dynamism" is deep.

41. This is a shortened and paraphrased version of the story in ZZ 6/17/25–31.

draw from the inexhaustible storehouse,
and study with the undying Teacher.
There is nowhere they go that they do not go all the way.
There is nowhere they get to that they do not push on through.
Living is not sufficient to preoccupy their thinking.
Dying is not sufficient to occlude their spirit.

Crouching and stretching, looking up and down, they embrace their life span and delight in its revolutions.

Bad and good fortune, profit and loss,
a thousand alterations and myriad turns:

Which of these is sufficient to disturb their minds?

People like them
embrace simplicity, guard Essence;
like locusts molting and snakes shedding their skin [they leave this world and],
they wander in Vast Clarity.
They lightly rise up and wander alone
and suddenly enter the Obscure.

Even the phoenix cannot be their match, how much less the barn swallow! Power and station, rank and reward, how could these be sufficient to perturb their mentality? [7/58/25–29]

7.11

When Yanzi was offered a covenant by Cui Shu, even though he was facing death, he would not change his sense of rightness.[42] Zhi and Hua[43] were going to fight to the death, and the lord of Ju offered them a large sum of money to stop, but they would not change their conduct. Thus,

Yanzi could be moved by Humaneness but could not be threatened by force of arms.
Zhi and Hua could be halted by Rightness but could not be bound up by profit.

The Superior Man
will die for what is right but cannot be made to pay attention to wealth and honor;
will do what is right but cannot be made to fear threats of death.

42. Yanzi 晏子 (also known as Yan Ying 嬰 [d. 500 B.C.E.]) was a celebrated minister who served three successive dukes of Qi with great loyalty and dedication. His exploits are chronicled in a text known as the *Yanzi chunqiu*. Cui Shu murdered Duke Zhuang of Qi and tried to force the Qi feudal lords to make a covenant with him. Yanzi resisted.

43. These are Ji Zhi 杞植 and Hua Huan 華還, two grandees of Qi. They fought a suicidal rearguard action to cover the retreat of Duke Zhuang of Qi from his failed attack on Ju 莒. The lord of Ju offered them money to surrender, but they refused. This incident occurred in 550 B.C.E. See *Zuozhuan*, Xiang 23.

People like them act only according to what is right and are not drawn to material things. How much more is this so for those who act through non-action?

Yao did not regard possessing the world as valuable, and thus he was able to hand it down to Shun.
Gongzi Zha[44] did not regard possessing a state as honorable, and thus he ceded his position.
Zihan[45] did not regard jade as wealth, and thus he would not receive precious objects.
Wu Guang[46] did not regard life as worth retaining through forsaking Rightness, and thus he threw himself into the deep.

From this perspective,

supreme honor does not depend on a title;
supreme wealth does not depend on goods.
The world is supremely great, yet it can be given to others.
Your self is very dear, but it can be thrown away in the deep.

Other than these things, there is nothing else worthy of considering beneficial. It is people like them whom we call "without attachments." People without attachments do not value the world. Above, when they contemplate the discourses of the Perfected, they profoundly trace to the origin the meaning of the Way and its Potency; below, when they examine the customary practices of the age, they find them shameful. Thus if we comprehend the significance of Xu You, the "Metal-Bound Coffer" and the "Leopardskin Quiver" will be set aside.[47] Jizi of Yanling would not accept [the rulership of] the state of Wu, and as a result, people who pursued land-boundary lawsuits dropped them.[48] Zihan was not interested in a precious jade, and as a result, people who disputed contracts were ashamed. Wu Guang was not corrupted by the attractions of his age, and those who lusted for profit more than life itself were filled with unease.

Thus,

those who do not contemplate the Great Meaning do not understand that life is not worth coveting.
Those who have not listened to the Great Words do not understand that the empire is not worth valuing.

Nowadays in impoverished rural villages, people bang on pots, drum on jars, and sing together, and they take this to be their music. But when they first hear the rhythmic striking of great ceremonial drums and the ringing of the great ceremonial

---

44. Gongzi Zha 公子札 was a prince of Wu, the youngest son of King Shoumeng (r. 585–561 B.C.E.). He is celebrated for having refused to displace his elder brother as heir.

45. Zihan 子罕 was an official of the state of Song during the sixth century B.C.E. renowned for his incorruptibility.

46. Wu Guang 務光 was a righteous hermit who, according to legend, when King Tang (founder of the Shang dynasty) offered to abdicate to him, drowned himself rather than bear the insult.

47. The "Metal-Bound Coffer" (Jin deng) is a chapter in the *Documents*. The "Leopardskin Quiver" (Bao dao) is a chapter in the *Liu Tao*.

48. Jizi of Yanling 延陵季子 is another name of Gongzi Zha. The suing peasants were affected by the example of his detachment from wealth and power.

bells, they suddenly feel disappointed and think their pots and jars are shameful. To collect the *Odes* and the *Documents*, to cultivate literary studies and yet not know the meaning of the Utmost Discourse [like the Confucians] is like those who bang on pots and drum on jars. To not strive to obtain the empire is the great drum of study.

Honor, position, riches, and profit are what people covet. But tell someone to hold in his left hand a writ for the empire and with his right hand to cut his own throat, and not even a fool would take the latter. From this perspective, life is more valuable than empire. [7/59/1–16]

7.12

Sages
eat enough to maintain their vital energy
and wear clothes sufficient to cover their bodies.
They satisfy their genuine responses and do not look for more.
To not possess the empire does not diminish their natures;
to possess the empire does not add to their inner harmony.
Possessing and not possessing the empire are the same reality to them.
If you offer someone the entire granary on Mount Ao
or give them all the water in a river,
were they to eat enough to sate their hunger
and drink enough to quench their thirst,
what would enter their bellies would not exceed a plate of food or a ladle of drink.
So
their bodies would be satisfied, and yet the granary on Mount Ao would not be diminished;
their stomachs would be full, and yet their waters in the river would not be lessened.
To own [these great supplies] would not make their satiation any greater,
and to not own them would not make their hunger any worse.
When we compare this with someone who has his bamboo jars of grain and his own small well, it is the same reality.
When someone is extremely angry, it shatters his yin energy,
and when someone is extremely happy, it collapses his yang energy.
Great sorrow destroys his interior,
and great fear drives him mad.
Yet if you eschew the dust [of daily living] and relinquish attachments, you will be as calm as if you had never left your Ancestor and thereupon will become grandly pervasive.[49]

49. This alludes to the *Zhuangzi*'s famous "sitting and forgetting" passage in chap. 6 (ZZ 6/19/21), in which Yan Hui asserts that he "merges with the Great Pervader" (*tong yu datong* 同於大通).

Purify your eyes and do not look with them;
still your ears and do not listen with them;
close your mouth and do not speak with it;
relax your mind and do not think with it.
Cast aside clever brilliance and return to Vast Simplicity;
Rest your Quintessential Spirit and cast aside wisdom and precedent.[50]

Then,

you will be awakened but seem to be obscured;
you will be alive but seem to be dead.

In the end, you will return to the foundation of the time before your birth and form one body with transformations. Then, to you, death and life will be one body. [7/59/16–23]

7.13

Now take the example of corvée laborers: they work with shovels and hoes and carry dirt in baskets on their backs until the sweat pours off them and their breathing becomes halting and their throats dry. If they are able to rest for a while beneath a shady tree, they will become relaxed and happy. Yet the profound shade deep within a mountain cave is incomparably better than that found beneath this shady tree.

Take the example of people afflicted with intestinal tumors: they pound their chests, scrunch up their stomachs, hit their heads on their knees, curl up into a ball, and moan all night long without being able to sleep. During this time, if they can get even a moment's rest, then their parents and brothers will be pleased and happy. Yet the repose of a long night ['s sleep] is incomparably better than this momentary joy.

Thus, if you know the immensity of the cosmos, you will not be concerned about life and death.
If you know the harmony of nourishing vitality, you will not be attached to the world.
If you know the happiness of not yet being born, you will not be afraid of dying.
If you know that to be Xu You is more valuable than Shun, you will not covet things.
A standing wall is better once it topples; how much better if it had never been built.

50. To "cast aside wisdom and precedent" (*qi zhigu* 棄知故) is a phrase frequently found in syncretic Daoist works. It means that one does not rely on the past wisdom of sages or on the precedents they set (as recorded in such works as the *Documents* and *Spring and Autumn Annals*), but on direct experience. This is intended as a contrast with the Confucians. For a discussion of this phrase in early Daoist syncretism, see Harold D. Roth, "Who Compiled the *Chuang Tzu*?" in *Chinese Texts and Philosophical Contexts: Essays Dedicated to Angus C. Graham*, ed. Henry Rosemont Jr. (La Salle, Ill.: Open Court Press, 1991), 93–98.

Ice is better once it melts; how much better if it had never been frozen.[51]

From Nothing treading into Something; from Something treading into Nothing; from beginning to end there are no traces; and no one knows from whence it springs. Without penetrating the exteriority and the interiority [of the Way], who is able to be without likes and dislikes?

The exterior that has no exterior:
that is supremely grand.
The interior that has no interior:
that is supremely precious.[52]
If you are able to know the grand and the precious,
where will you go and not reach the end?[53] [7/59/25–7/60/4]

7.14

Shallow scholars in this declining age do not understand how to get to the origins of their minds and return to their root. They merely sculpt and polish their natures and adorn and stifle their genuine responses in order to interact with their age. Thus,

when their eyes desire something, they forbid it with measures;
when their minds delight in something, they restrict it with rites.

They hasten forth in circles and formally scrape and bow

while the meat goes bad and becomes inedible
and the wine goes sour and becomes undrinkable.
Externally they restrict their bodies;
internally they belabor their minds.
They damage the harmony of yin and yang
and constrain the genuine responses of their nature to fate.

Thus throughout their lives, they are sorrowful people.

Those who penetrate through to the Way are not like this.

They regulate the genuine responses of their natures,
cultivate the techniques of the mind,
nourish these with harmony,
take hold of these through suitability.
They delight in the Way and forget what is lowly;
They find repose in Potency and forget what is base.
Since their natures desire nothing, they attain whatever they desire.
Since their minds delight in nothing, there are no delights in which they do not partake.

---

51. This pair of parallel lines emphasizes the value of the pure potential of the Way.

52. When you are merged with the Dao, nothing is outside you: the apparently external is part of your own subjectivity. In addition, your own subjectivity is no longer "inside" you: both subject and object are part of one whole.

53. After having once merged with the Way, when you return to the phenomenal world, you are aware of its "presence" wherever you go.

Those who do not exceed their genuine responses do not allow them to tie down their Potency.
Those who find ease in their natures do not allow them to injure their inner harmony.

Thus with

their relaxed bodies and untrammeled awareness,
their standards and regulations,

they can become models for the empire. [7/60/6–11]

7.15

Nowadays the Confucian literati

do not get to the foundations of why they have desires but instead prohibit what they desire;
do not get to the source of why they delight in things but instead restrict what they enjoy.

This is like breaking open the source of rivers and streams and then damming them up with your hands.

Shepherding the people is like taking care of wild beasts. If you do not lock them up in enclosed pens, they will have savage hearts, but if you bind up their feet in order to prohibit their movement and still wish to raise them through a long life, how is this possible? Now Yan Hui, Ji Lu, Zixia, and Ran Boniu were Confucius's most brilliant students.[54] Still,

Yan Yuan died young;
Ji Lu was pickled in Wey;
Zixia lost his eyesight;
and Ran Boniu became a leper.

These disciples all constrained their natures and stifled their genuine responses and did not attain harmony in their lives. Thus when Zixia met Zengzi,[55] sometimes he was thin and sometimes he was fat. Zengzi asked him the reason for this. Zixia replied: "When I went out and saw the delights of wealth and honor, I desired them. But when I returned and saw the Way of the former kings and took pleasure in that, the two feelings fought each other in my mind, and I became thin. But when the Way of the former kings won out, I got fat."

---

54. Yan Hui 顏回 (also known as Yan Yuan 淵) was Confucius's most gifted disciple, and his early death deeply saddened the Master.

Ji Lu 季路 (also known as Zilu 子路 and Zhong You 仲由 [542–480 B.C.E.]) was a disciple of Confucius. Militarily inclined, he served as steward to the powerful Ji clan.

Zixia 子夏 (also known as Bu Shang 卜商 [b. 507 B.C.E.]) was a disciple of Confucius and traditionally is ascribed a major role in the transmission of the Classics.

Ran Boniu 冉伯牛 was another disciple of Confucius.

55. Zengzi 曾子 (also known as Zeng Can 曾參 [505–435 B.C.E.]) was a prominent disciple of Confucius mentioned in many early texts. A text attributed to him once circulated but exists now only in fragments.

Based on this, it is not that his will was able to not covet positions of wealth and honor and not appreciate the delights of excess; it was merely that by constraining his nature and restricting his desires [that] he used Rightness to guard against them.

Although their emotions and minds were depressed and gloomy and their bodies and natures were constricted and exhausted, they [i.e., the individuals just named] had no choice but to force themselves [to follow the Confucian Way]. Thus none was able to live out his allotted years.

Contrast these with the Perfected:

They eat exactly what suits their bellies
They wear precisely what fits their forms.
They roam by relaxing their bodies.
They act by matching their genuine responses [to the situation].
If left the empire, they do not covet it,
If entrusted with the myriad things, they do not profit from it.

They rest in the vast universe, roam in the country of the Limitless, ascend Tai Huang, [and] ride Tai Yi.[56] They play with Heaven and Earth in the palms of their hands: how is it possible that people like them would grow fat or thin by coveting wealth?

Thus, because the Confucians

are unable to prevent people from desiring, they can only try to stop them from being fulfilled;
because they are unable to prevent people from delighting in things, they can only try to forbid those delights.

They cause the world to fear punishments and not dare to steal, but how can they cause people not to have the intention to steal? [7/60/13–23]

7.16

When the people of Yue catch a python, they take it to be quite a [valuable] rarity, but when [the people of] the Middle Kingdom get hold of one, they discard it as useless. Thus,

if he knew something was useless, even a greedy person would be able to give it away.
If he did not know something was useless, even an incorruptible person would not be able to relinquish it to someone else.

Now, the reason that rulers of people

ruin and destroy their states and families,
abandon and renounce their altars to the soil and grain,
lose their lives at the hands of others,

and become the laughingstocks of the world is that they have never *not* acted selfishly and not desired [for themselves].

---

56. Tai Huang 太皇 (Great Sovereign) and Tai Yi 太一 (Grand One or Primal Unity) are constellations.

The Qiu You tribe coveted the gift of a great bell and lost their state.[57]
The prince of Yu was obsessed with the jade disk of Chuiji and was captured.[58]
Duke Xian was bewitched by the beauty of Lady Li and created chaos for four generations.[59]
Duke Huan was besotted by the harmonious flavors of chef Yi Ya and was not buried in a timely fashion.[60]
The king of the Hu tribe was debauched by the pleasures of female musicians and so lost his best territories.[61]

If these five princes[62] had matched their genuine responses to the situation and relinquished what they did not really need, if they had taken their inner selves as their standard and not run after external things, how could they have possibly arrived at such disasters?

Thus,

in archery, it is not the arrow that fails to hit the center of the target; it is the one who studies archery who does not guide the arrow.
In charioteering, it is not the reins that fail to make the chariot go; it is the one who studies charioteering who does not use the reins well.[63]

If you know that a fan in winter and fur clothes in summer have no use to you, then the alterations of the myriad things will be like dust in the wind to you. Thus, if you use hot water to stop something from boiling, the boiling will never stop. But if you really know its root, then all you need to do is put out the fire. [7/60/25–7/61/2]

Translated by Harold D. Roth

---

57. The Qiu You were a tribe of northern "barbarians" who were given the gift of a great bell by Earl Zhi. But in order to bring it home, they had to build a road, which provided a convenient path for Earl Zhi to invade and conquer them. A passage similar to this line and the following three lines appears in 9.25.

58. The prince of Yu sold the right of passage across his territory for a rare jade disk of Chuiji, and this route was later used by the state of Jin to conquer him. See *Zhu zhuan*, Xi 2. See also 10.47, 11.7, 17.57, and 18.5.

59. Duke Xian of Jin (r. 676–651 B.C.E.) had his own heir killed in order to replace him with the son he had fathered with the "barbarian" Lady Li Ji, and the struggle for title to the throne lasted for four generations.

60. Duke Huan of Qi 齊桓公 (r. 685–643 B.C.E.) was one of the most powerful rulers of the Spring and Autumn period. He was the first to hold the post of hegemon and employed the famous statesman Guan Zhong as his prime minister. He is said to have been so taken with Yi Ya's cuisine that he gave him many favors. Thus when the duke died, Yi Ya was powerful enough to fight for several months for the throne against the duke's heirs. Because of this, no one had time to bury the duke.

61. The king of the Hu, a Western tribe, was so taken by the allures of dancers and singers that he totally neglected his defenses and lost a great deal of territory to Duke Mu of Qin. See Claude Larre, "Les Esprits légers et subtils," in *Les Grands Traités du Huainanzi*, vol. 75, *Variétés sinologiques*, ed. Claude Larre, Isabelle Robinet, and Elisabeth Rochat de la Vallée (Paris: Institut Ricci, 1993), 102n.30.

62. Three of these anecdotes are recounted again in 9.25.

63. A somewhat similar statement appears in 9.10.

Eight

THE BASIC WARP

"THE BASIC Warp" uses several different but generally complementary descriptions of an imagined historical past to raise questions about the nature of sage-rulership and to criticize government in the present era. In all these scenarios, an archaic era of agrarian primitivism is idealized as a time when sages, embodying the Way and its Potency, could govern almost invisibly by means of non-action. Both the human and the natural worlds responded resonantly to the sages' superior qualities. Qualities like Humaneness and Music were intrinsic to the sage and were not (as they later became) mere expedients to control the populace in times that departed ever more profoundly from the Way. But inevitably the world began to devolve from the archaic ideal. People perceived deficiencies in their lives and increasingly took steps to satisfy their desires. The more they did so, the more the situation degenerated from primordial simplicity and unity. Thus we find ourselves in an era of discord and turmoil. What is to be done?

The answer is perhaps surprising: although latter-day calamities have led to suffering and turmoil, they also create an opportunity for a contemporary ruler—one wise enough to avoid the pitfalls of extravagance, excess, cruelty, and greed—to establish a new era of sagely rule. In tranquil times, there is no need for remarkable men or extraordinary measures. But in times of danger and trouble, a ruler who knows how to embody the unmediated unity of the Grand One, align himself with the Way and its Potency, match his actions to the rhythms of the cosmos, and become imbued with spirit illumination, has a golden opportunity to govern as a sage.

The Chapter Title

The title of the chapter is "Ben jing" 本經, which we have translated as "The Basic Warp." *Ben* means "root," as opposed to branch; therefore "basis, basic; foundation, fundamental." *Jing* is often encountered in extended or metaphorical meanings, such as "constant, standard, norm," and especially as "classic, canonical work of literature," and it would be possible to understand *ben jing* in that way, translating it as "The Fundamental Classic." But we do not think that that is the intended meaning in this case. The literal meaning of *jing* is "warp"—that is, the tensioned threads strung on a loom as a substrate into which weft threads (*wei* 緯) are woven to create a fabric. We are confident that the word is used here in that literal sense, hence our translation as "The Basic Warp."[1]

Weaving metaphors appear a number of times in the *Huainanzi.* For example, in 8.7 we read that the Grand One "knots the net of the eight directional end points and weaves the web of the six coordinates." A closely similar expression appears in the opening lines of chapter 21, where the authors announce that they have written this book "to knot the net of the Way and its Potency, and weave the web of humankind and its affairs." The image is of a cloth that is integral, tightly woven, strong, and seamless. Chapter 2 likens the Way to a fabric: "The Way has both a warp and a weft that are linked together."[2] Chapter 13 also uses a weaving metaphor, in this case applied to two of the conventional virtues: "Humaneness is the warp, Rightness is the skein of [weft] threads."[3]

A warp cannot consist of one thread but must be made up of many, strung in parallel and evenly tensioned; only then can the weft be woven in to create a fabric. As this chapter argues, the warp of the *Huainanzi*'s philosophy consists of several strands that together make up the character of the sage.

Summary and Key Themes

The chapter begins with a paean to an archaic (and mythical) era of Grand Purity, a time of primitive agrarian communitarianism when people were ignorant and industrious; rulers had little to do; and everything conformed to the Way. Accordingly, crops ripened in timely fashion, and auspicious beasts such as *qilins* and phoenixes appeared. This vision of archaic bliss is reiterated in several other sections (8.3, 8.5, 8.6, 8.11, 8.12), with differing emphases. Section 8.3, for example, stresses a lack of

1. Csikszentmihalyi 2004, 134n.71, and Le Blanc and Mathieu 2003 reach the same understanding: "The Basic Warp" and "De la chaîne originelle," respectively. Ames 1994, 22, translates the title as "The Fundamental Constancy."

2. See 2/11/28, *dao you jing ji tiao guan* 道有經紀條貫; *ji* (a skein of threads) is often used as a synonym for *wei* 緯, "weft."

3. See 13/121/25, *ren yi wei jing, yi yi wei ji* 仁以爲經, 義以爲紀.

social controls and conventions, while 8.5 emphasizes that a Perfected Person must resemble the primitive era in being free of artifice and contrivances. Sections 8.11 and 8.12 stress the harmony and perfection of government in antiquity and the unity of will that bound the ruler and his people. Thus the chapter as a whole is consistent in positing an ideal archaic age of unity and harmony but describes that era in several different ways.

Whatever its specific characteristics, the era of primitive unity and harmony was followed by an age of decline, when people became acquisitive and competitive, and the natural world responded by falling out of joint, with yin and yang confused, the four seasons disordered, and various natural disasters ensuing. The age degenerated further; the extravagance of the rich and the exploitation of the poor knew no bounds; and warfare and suffering permeated the world. The conventional villains Jie (last ruler of the Xia dynasty) and Djou (last ruler of the Shang dynasty) are cited in 8.6 as exemplars of degenerate rule at its worst.

All this conforms with the model established in chapter 6, "Surveying Obscurities": *ganying* resonance operates everywhere and always, so it is entirely to be expected that a degenerate age in the human realm will provoke both social and natural disasters. Section 8.2 provides a mechanism by which we can understand the decline of the world into degeneracy: "when the hearts of high and low become estranged from each other," "noxious *qi*" (*zei qi* 賊氣) is generated, which in turn communicates the disorder of the human world to the natural realm.

Echoing *Laozi,* sections 8.3 through 8.5 emphasize the importance of holding to the fundamental and disregarding the peripheral and of identifying with the Way and its Potency and eschewing artifice. Yet here, as so often in the *Huainanzi,* the Huainan masters put their own spin on the canonical work that they use as their point of departure. They are not willing to advocate a return to primitivism or to dispense altogether with expedient means to govern during an era in decline.

We become aware of this as the chapter's argument takes an unexpected turn in section 8.6, initiating a line of persuasion that continues to the end of the chapter. We live in a degenerate age, the writer concedes, but the very turbulence of chaotic times offers an opportunity for a true sage to emerge. The Five Thearchs and the Three Kings adapted their actions to suit the exigencies of their times. To be an embodiment of the Grand One is the best thing of all, but not every ruler can achieve that, so kings, hegemons, and princes must use methods appropriate to their own stations. Meanwhile, to be successful, any ruler must follow (as does Yaoguang, the bright star at the end of the handle of the Northern Dipper, whose annual circuit of the heavens points out the seasons) the natural rhythms of the cosmos, avoid being distracted by sensory stimuli, avoid being seduced by extravagance, understand the wellsprings of emotion and their appropriate expressions, and make use of the lessons of history. He must also (as 8.6 reminds us) be fortunate enough to live in an era in which the qualities of a sage can be recognized and employed. The true ruler embraces the Moral Potency of Humaneness and Rightness and uses his power to maintain a proper hierarchy in the realm of human affairs. Thus, the chapter concludes, "If the foundation is established, the Way can be implemented."

While this chapter takes an idealized vision of an era of agrarian primitivism under the rule of a sage as its point of departure, it neither advocates nor concedes the possibility of returning to such a state. The picture painted here is a more accommodating view of sage-government, in which the sage-ruler employs such expedient means as circumstances and the historical era may require. In the *Huainanzi*'s view, a sage must be of and for his time.

Sources

Much of "The Basic Warp" reads like an anthology of passages on the subject of the ideal primitivism of high antiquity, but in most cases it is no longer possible to identify the sources of those passages. We think it is highly likely that many, if not all, of these passages are quoted from works now lost. An exception is section 8.3, which approaches the theme of agrarian primitivism by taking as its point of reference the famous chapter 38 of the *Laozi*, which describes society's gradual decline from conformity with the Way. The *Huainanzi* paraphrases the key lines from *Laozi* 38:

> When the Way is lost, then there is Potency.
> When Potency is lost, then there is Humaneness.
> When Humaneness is lost, then there is Rightness.[4]
> When Rightness is lost, then there is Ritual.

Thus as primordial unity disappears, there is a concomitant rise of the human virtues: Rightness and Humaneness, Ritual and Music. The closing lines of section 8.3 identify *shenming*, "spirit illumination," as more important than even the Way and its Potency for the implementation of sage-government.[5] Sections 8.4 and 8.5 show little regard for virtues such as Humaneness and Rightness and for rulership that depends on inventions and contrivances rather than the qualities of a sage.

The grounding of section 8.3 in *Laozi* 38 is unmistakable. But while it seems likely that the other descriptions of harmonious archaic eras found in "The Basic Warp" were assembled into an anthology from other sources available to the Huainan masters, the actual language of those descriptions can no longer be traced to works that have come down as part of the received literature of early China. Nonetheless, the many mythical and historical figures mentioned in the chapter are known today

4. This passage in turn echoes *Laozi* 18: "[Where] the Great Way is dispensed with, there is Humaneness and Rightness."

5. *Shenming* as a characteristic of the sage is introduced in 1.14 and extensively explored in some of the later chapters of the *Huainanzi*. See also 2.9, 2.11, 4.9, 7.1, 7.3, 8.3, 8.4, 11.12, 12.44, 13.21, 15.3, 15.25, 19.5, 20.1, 20.6, 20.10, 21.2, and 21.3. The passage in 12.44 is especially noteworthy. The term *shenming* carries a double charge of significance, as it means both "spiritlike illumination" (i.e., the sort of illumination characteristic of a spirit) and "spirit illumination" (the means by which one attains that state; i.e., illumination by means of or through one's inner spirit).

from a wide range of received literary works. Although such figures are part of the broad cultural heritage of early China, their appearances here again cannot generally be traced to a specific extant source.

Based on their literary style, two other sections of the chapter probably borrowed from now-lost works. Section 8.9, a poetic essay about "Profligate Indolence," is written in a highly ornate and richly metrical style, adhering to the literary form of *fu* (poetic exposition) that was fashionable at the time. Its language is quite different from that of the rest of the chapter, and it has the quality of a set piece, composed for oral recitation, that can stand on its own. It seems likely, therefore, that this was originally a separate composition, now lost as an independent work, that was copied in its entirety into (or composed especially for) "The Basic Warp." For analogous reasons, we might surmise that section 8.10, a short and rather self-contained essay on the emotions of joy, sorrow, and anger, may have been copied into chapter 8 from some other source.

Nevertheless, while much of the chapter seems to comprise a congeries of earlier material, it cannot be said to be lacking in originality. Instead, its originality lies primarily in its interpretation of the concept of sage-government. The chapter's line of argument coheres through an artful arrangement of borrowed passages.

The Chapter in the Context of the *Huainanzi* as a Whole

As usual, chapter 21 of the *Huainanzi* gives us a useful and pertinent summary:

"The Basic Warp" provides the means by which to
 illuminate the Potency of the great sages,
 and penetrate the Way of the Unique Inception.[6]
 Delineating and summarizing the devolution of decadent eras from past to present,
 it thereby praises the flourishing prosperity of earlier ages
 and criticizes the corrupt governments of later ages.
It is what enables you to
 dispense with the acuity and keenness of hearing and sight,
 still the responses and movements of the essence and spirit,
 restrain effusive and ephemeral viewpoints,
 temper the harmony of nourishing your nature,
 distinguish the conduct of [the Five] Thearchs and [Three] Kings,
 and set out the differences between small and great. (21.2)

6. *Wei chu* 維初; this puzzling phrase is not mentioned by the commentators. We take it to refer to the uniqueness of the inception of the cosmos, but it could also be understood to be equivalent to *tai chu* 太初, "Grand Beginning." The French translation takes that approach and renders the phrase as "commencement suprême" (Le Blanc and Mathieu 2003, 1014).

As we noted, "The Basic Warp" begins with an idealized picture of an archaic era of unity and harmony, and humankind's gradual decline from that idyllic time. The theme of decline appears also in chapters 2 and 11, which complement the vision of history presented here. The other side of the coin is found in chapters 7 and 19, the first of which argues that sagely self-cultivation is possible in the present era, just as it was in the past, whereas the second vigorously challenges the notion that the remote past was a time when sages had nothing to do.

"The Basic Warp" is linked in interesting ways with other chapters of the *Huainanzi*. It echoes the theme of devolution from an early age of unity, simplicity, and harmony that had already been explicated in detail in sections 6.7 through 6.9. Looking ahead in the text, we could consider this chapter as forming a pair with chapter 9, "The Ruler's Techniques," because the discussion of sage-rulership in history in chapter 8 provides the basis for chapter 9's more specific discussion of the means by which government can succeed. At the same time, chapter 8 is the last of the "theoretical" (or "root") chapters of the *Huainanzi*. With chapter 9, the book shifts to more practical ("branch") considerations. These later chapters offer numerous illustrations and suggested applications of the arts of rhetoric and persuasion, as well as an overview of the military, advice on how to evaluate and employ subordinates, how to apply the principles of non-action, and other matters of pragmatic concern to the ruler.

As its own title implies, chapter 8 delineates the warp threads on which the fabric of sage-government is to be woven. What are those threads of the "basic warp"? This chapter privileges the Laoist qualities of identification with a personified primordial unity (variously called, in the *Huainanzi*, by such names as "Grand Inception," "Grand Purity," "Grand Beginning," and "Grand One");[7] spirit illumination; and identification with *dao* and *de*, the Way and its Potency. The conventional virtues (Humaneness, Rightness, Ritual, Music) are generally treated here as derived and secondary qualities, weft threads rather than part of the warp, although nonetheless necessary for the completion of the fabric. We could say that the viewpoint of chapter 8 is broadly consistent with that of the *Huainanzi* overall: enlightenment and the ability to respond appropriately to the circumstances of his time are the essential characteristics of the sage, whereas the conventional virtues are functional but not fundamental.

John S. Major

7. "Grand Inception" (*taishi* 太始) appears in 3.1; "Grand Purity" (*taiqing* 太清), in 2.5, 7.7, 8.1, and 12.1; "Grand Beginning" (*taichu* 太初), in 14.1; and "Grand One" (*taiyi* 太一), in 8.7 and numerous other passages throughout the text.

Eight

8.1

The reign of Grand Purity[1]
was harmonious and compliant and thus silent and indifferent;
substantial and true and thus plain and simple;
contained and tranquil, it was not intemperate;
exerting and shifting, it [followed] no precedents.
Inwardly it accorded with the Way;
outwardly it conformed to Rightness.
When stirred into motion, it formed [normative] patterns;
when moving at full speed, it was well matched to things.
Its words were concise and in step with reason;
its actions were simple and in compliance with feelings.
Its heart was harmonious and not feigned;
its [conduct of] affairs was simple and not ostentatious.
That being so,
there was no selecting of [auspicious] times and days,
no divining by trigrams or shell cracking,
no scheming about where to begin,
no discussion of where to end.

1. *Tai qing* 太清. Another possible translation would be "Supreme Clarity," as the Chinese term means both "clarity" and "purity."

When tranquil, it stopped;
when roused, it moved.
It was of one body with Heaven and Earth,[2]
and one essence with yin and yang.
In its oneness it accorded with the four seasons;
in its brightness it shone as the sun and the moon.

As one with what fashions and transforms us, it was [both] female and male.

That being so,

Heaven overspread it with Potency;
Earth upheld it with Music.
The four seasons did not lose their order;
wind and rain did not descend with violence.
The sun and moon, with purity and clarity, spread their radiance;
the five planets held to their paths and did not fail in their movements.

At that time, the Mysterious Origin came to brightness and shed its brilliance all around.

The phoenix and the *qilin* arrived;
the milfoil and the tortoise gave omens.
Sweet dew descended.
Bamboo produced abundant shoots;
"flowing yellow"[3] emerged [from the ground];
vermilion grass grew.

Contrivances and falsehoods were not harbored in people's minds.

Coming down to the age of decline,

people delved in mountains for [precious] stones.
They engraved metal and [carved] jade,
pried open oysters and clams [to get pearls],
smelted bronze and iron,

and the myriad things were not nurtured [thereby].

People ripped open pregnant animals and killed young ones, [so] the *qilin* no longer wandered abroad.
They overturned nests and broke eggs, [so] the phoenix no longer soared.
They bored wood to get fire,
cut timber to build terraces,
burned forests to make fields,
drained marshes to catch fish,

so tortoises and dragons no longer frequented the earth.

[Nevertheless,] the implements of the common people were insufficient,
[while] the hoarded treasures [of the rich] were excessive.

Thus among the myriad things, more often than not,

2. Compare this and the following three lines with the opening lines of 20.1.

3. "Flowing yellow" (*liu huang* 流黃) usually means "sulfur"; here it evidently signifies an auspicious plant of some sort, not otherwise identifiable.

calamities damaged sprouts and shoots,
and eggs and pregnancies failed to reach fruition.
People piled up earth so as to live on hills,
manured their fields to plant grain,
dug into the earth to make wells for drinking,
channeled streams to improve [their usefulness],
pounded earth into walls to make fortifications,
captured wild animals to domesticate them.
[Thus] yin and yang became twisted and tangled;
The four seasons lost their [proper] order;
thunderclaps caused things to overturn and break;
hailstones fell violently;
noxious vapors [descended and] did not disperse;
and the myriad things suffered premature deaths.

People cleared fields that were overgrown and weedy to consolidate and enclose acreage;
they mowed open lands and thickets so as to grow seedlings and sprouting grain;
and there were innumerable instances of misshapen shoots, unblossoming flowers, and pendant fruit that died [in an untimely way].

So things reached the stage when [people]
built great mansions, houses, and palaces,
with linked rooms and ranks of pillars,
with jointed eaves and rafter ends,
all patterned, polished, carved, and graven,
with twisting and trailing caltrop branches,
with hibiscus and lotus,
the five colors vying with one another,
flowing together or standing apart.
All was smoothly contrived with great craft,
bent and contorted and doubled into knots,
minutely fussed over with great pains,
all in accordance with instructions,
so that [even legendary artisans like] Gongshu[4] and Wang Er would have found no fault with the chiseling and graving, the carving and scrollwork. Yet [even] this did not suffice to fill the desires of the rulers of men. Thus the pine, the cypress, and the flowering bamboo[5] drooped and rotted in the summertime; the Yangzi, the Yellow River, and the Three Streams became exhausted and ceased flowing.

Foreigners' sheep [flocked] in the meadows;
flying locusts filled the open lands;

4. Gongshu was a legendary artisan, also known as Gongsun Ban or Lu Ban; under the last name, he appears in 11.17.

5. *Junlu* 箘露, evidently a bamboo of some type, but not reliably identifiable.

Heaven dried up and Earth cracked open;
the phoenix did not descend.

Hook-clawed, bare-toothed, horn-bearing, marauding wild animals became [even] fiercer. The common people had only small reed huts for houses, with nowhere [for travelers] to find lodging; those who died of cold and hunger lay as close together as pillows to mats.

Then it came to pass
that they divided mountains and streams, gorges and valleys, to make territories and boundaries.
They counted the population to divide the masses of people by numbers.
They pounded earth to make walls and dug moats.
They set up military contrivances in defiles and passes to prepare [against attack].
They created insignia for those who managed affairs,
made regulations of clothing and rank,
differentiated between noble and base,
distinguished the worthy from those who were not,
codified [terms of] disapprobation and praise,
instituted rewards and punishments.

That weapons and armor flourished, and contention and conflicts broke out; that the common people suffered extermination, repression, and disasters; that they were oppressively executed though guiltless, and suffered mutilating punishments though not guilty of crimes, was all due to this. [8/61/6–27]

8.2

The concord and harmony of Heaven and Earth,
the transformations of yin and yang and the myriad things

depend on one *qi*.[6] For this reason, when the hearts of high and low become estranged from each other, *qi* rises up like a vapor; when ruler and minister are not in harmony, the five grains do not yield [a harvest].

For forty-six days after the winter solstice,[7]
Heaven withholds its responses and does not yet descend;
Earth harbors its *qi* and does not yet scatter it abroad.
Yin and yang are stored up together,
exhaling and inhaling as if in deep water.
They embrace and enfold [all] customs,

6. *Yi qi* 一氣. This is a rich term with several layers of meaning. Here it denotes "a single (unitary, undivided) *qi*," "unifying the *qi*," and even "the *qi* of the Grand One" (*taiyi* 太一). The term should be understood in all these senses simultaneously.

7. This is a reference to the calendar of twenty-four solar periods (*jieqi*). See 3.18.

deliberate on the myriad differences [among things],
set aside what is unsuitable and amass the seemly,

thus together soaking and steeping, brewing and fermenting, they bring to completion the multitude of living things. For this reason,

when things are stunted in spring and flourish in autumn,
when there is thunder in winter and frost in summer,

it all is generated by noxious *qi*. From this one can see that

Heaven and Earth, space and time, are as the body of a single person,
and everything within the six coordinates are as the shape of a single person.[8]

For this reason,

one who discerns the natures of things cannot be alarmed by anything in Heaven or Earth;
one who investigates auspicious omens cannot be affected by strange phenomena.

Thus the sage knows the far by means of the near, so that the myriad differentiations become unified. [8/62/1–6]

8.3

The people of antiquity made their *qi* the same as that of Heaven and Earth; they wandered in an era of unity.[9] At that time,

there was no garnering advantage by praise and rewards,
no intimidation by mutilations and punishments.
Ritual and Rightness, purity and modesty, had not yet been established;
slander and flattery, Humaneness and contempt, had not yet been set up;

and the myriad peoples had not yet [begun to] treat one another with fraud and oppression, cruelty and exploitation—it was as if they were still immersed in turbid obscurity.[10]

Coming down to the era of decline, [it transpired that]

people were abundant, but wealth was scarce;
people labored to the utmost, but their nourishment was insufficient.

Thus competition and strife were born, and Humaneness was valued. The Humane and the petty minded were [, however,] not treated equitably.

Neighbors formed groups,

8. This microcosm–macrocosm is developed further in 7.1.

9. This section reads as an expansion of, or a commentary on, *Laozi* 38, which was the first chapter of the *Laozi* in some Han versions of that work (e.g., the Mawangdui A and B *Laozi* texts). See Robert G. Henricks, *Lao Tzu Te Tao Ching* (New York: Ballantine Books, 1989). To a Han audience, this would have been an authoritative and immediately recognizable text.

10. The primitive society of high antiquity is thus compared with the state of undifferentiated matter-energy (*hun ming* 混冥) that preceded the coming-into-being of the phenomenal world. See the opening section of chap. 3.

and friends formed cabals.
They promoted falsehood and deceit,
cherished a spirit of contrivance and artifice,
and lost [their] natural tendencies.

Thus Rightness was valued.

None of [the people's] feelings associated with yin and yang [i.e., sexual feelings] were free from the stimulation of blood and *qi.* Men and women [therefore] gathered in places and promiscuously dwelt together without distinction. Thus Ritual was valued.

Instinctive feelings overflowed and were mutually conflicting. They could not stop themselves and therefore were discordant. Thus Music was valued.

Thus, Humaneness, Rightness, Ritual, and Music, though able to save [the world] from ruin, are still not the perfection of comprehensive governance.

Humaneness is able to save people from strife;
Rightness is able to save people from errors;
Ritual is able to save people from lewdness;
Music is able to save people from melancholy.
When spirit illumination is established in the world, then minds revert to their original state.
When minds revert to their original state, then people's natures become good.
When people's natures become good, they are followed by Heaven and Earth and by yin and yang.

Wealth then becomes sufficient. When wealth becomes sufficient, the people are respectful; covetousness, petty mindedness, anger, and competition have no occasion to arise. From this one can see that [under these circumstances,] there is no need for Humaneness and Rightness.

When the Way and its Potency are established in the world, then the people become pure and simple. Thus

their eyes are not fixed on beauty;
their ears are not drawn to sounds.

If there were [entertainers] sitting in rows and singing songs or prancing about with their hair hanging loose—

even if they were as alluring as Mao Qiang or Xi Shi, [the audience] would take no pleasure in them;
even if the tunes were "Falling Wings" or "Martial," they would not find any joy in them.[11]

Even if the lewdness had no limit, it would come to nothing.

From this one can see that [under these circumstances,] there is no need for Ritual and Music. Thus,

11. The Chinese character 樂 is used to write both the word *yue* (music) and the word *le* (joy); thus this sentence contains a double-entendre impossible to convey gracefully in English: "They would not find any music/joy in them."

when Potency declines, Humaneness is born;[12]
when conduct fails, Rightness is established.
When harmony is lost, there are sounds and ditties;
when rituals are decayed, comportment is gaudy.

Thus,

if one understands spirit illumination, then one can understand the inadequacy of the Way and its Potency for effecting things;
if one understands the Way and its Potency, then one can understand the inadequacy of Humaneness and Rightness in putting things into practice;
if one understands Humaneness and Rightness, then one can understand the inadequacy of Ritual and Music in regulating conduct. [8/62/6–19]

8.4

Now,

people who turn their backs on the fundamental but seek it in the peripheral
or who wish to explain the essential but inquire into details,

are not yet able to take part in discourses that reach the utmost. [8/62/19–20]

The size of Heaven and Earth may be known by means of the [carpenter's] square and the gnomon;
the motions of the stars and the moon can be obtained from the calendar and from investigations;
the sound of thunder can be approximated by means of drums and bells;
the alterations of rain and wind can be known by means of the notes and the pitch pipes.

Thus,

if the size of a thing can be seen, it is possible to gauge its weight;
if the brightness of a thing can be observed, it is possible to know its obscurities;
if the sound of a thing can be heard, it is possible to know its melodies;
if the colors of a thing can be examined, it is possible to distinguish among them.
But as for the limit of vastness, Heaven and Earth cannot contain it;
as for the limit of minuteness, spirit illumination cannot comprehend its fineness.

When the time came that

the pitch pipes and calendar were established,
the five colors were distinguished,
the tonic and flattened [scales] were differentiated,
and sweet and bitter were distinguished as tastes,

12. This line is a close paraphrase of several lines in *Laozi* 38 and echoes *Laozi* 18.1: *dadao fei, you renyi* 大道廢 有仁義, "[Where] the great Way is dispensed with, there is Humaneness and Rightness."

then it was that the Unhewn Block was shattered and made into implements.

When Humaneness and Rightness were established
and Ritual and Music were reformed,
then Potency was done away with,
and the meretricious was brought into being.
When the meretricious was born,
fake wisdom was used to startle the ignorant,
and clever deceptions were used to inveigle those in high positions.

Thus in the world there were those who were able to manage things, but there was none who was capable of [true] rule. [8/62/22–27]

8.5

In ancient times,

when Cang Jue invented writing, Heaven rained corn, and demons wept all night.
When Bo Yi[13] invented wells, dragons ascended to the dark clouds, and the spirits [fled to] their abode on Kunlun.

As wisdom and ability grew ever more abundant, Potency grew ever more scarce. Thus on the Zhou tripods was cast a depiction of Chui[14] biting his fingers, signifying that great ingenuity is [ultimately] unable to accomplish anything.

Therefore the rule of the Perfected Person is like this:

His mind is coextensive with his spirit;
his physical form is in tune with his nature.
When he is still he embodies Potency;
when he acts, he patterns himself on penetration.

He follows his spontaneous nature and aligns himself with inevitable transformations.

He is profoundly non-active, and the world naturally becomes harmonious;
He is tranquilly devoid of desires, and the people naturally become simple.
He does not augur for good omens, so the people do not suffer calamities.
He is not angry or contentious, so food supplies are sufficient.

He unites and binds together all within the [Four] Seas, and the benefits reach to future generations, but none knows who it is who has done this.

While he is alive, he has no cognomen.
When he is dead, he has no posthumous title.
He accumulates no wealth, so his fame is not established.

When bestowing, he does not accumulate Potency, and when receiving, he does not

13. Bo Yi 伯益 was the legendary leader of the Eastern Yi tribe who served Shun as a gamekeeper.

14. Chui was a mythical craftsman and master woodworker to the divine emperor Di Ku, for whom he made musical instruments, bows, plows, boats, marking cords, and other contrivances. See Anne Birrell, *Chinese Mythology: An Introduction* (Baltimore: Johns Hopkins University Press, 1993), 53, 63.

cede it.[15] Potency circulates and returns again to its source, and there is none who is not replete with it. So

where Potency is pervasive, the Way cannot be harmed;
what knowledge cannot understand, discrimination cannot explicate.
Wordless discrimination,
the Way of No-Way:

How can penetration get there? It is called Heaven's Storehouse. One can

take from it without diminishing it,
pour from it without exhausting it.

No one knows from whence it comes. It is called Yaoguang.[16] Yaoguang is the wealth and provender of the myriad things. [8/62/27–8/63/6]

8.6

When [the ruler] relieves hardships and supplements insufficiencies, then his fame is born. [When he] upholds the beneficial and eliminates the harmful, [when he] chastises the disorderly and prohibits cruelty, then his merit is established.

When an age is without calamity or harm, even a spirit would find no occasion to display his Potency.
When high and low are [united in] harmonious amity, even a worthy would have no occasion to show forth his merits.

In antiquity, in the time of Rong Cheng,[17] people walked along on the roads like geese [in single file] and arranged themselves in rows. They [trustingly] cradled their infants and children in birds' nests, [and] they put their surplus grain in mounds in the fields [without it being stolen]. They could grasp the tails of tigers and leopards and tread upon cobras and pythons [and come to no harm].[18] But they did not understand how it came to be so.

Coming down to the time of Yao, the ten suns [once] came out together. They scorched the standing grain and the sheaves and killed herbs and trees, so that the people had nothing to eat. [Moreover,] Chayu, Nine Gullet, Typhoon, Mound Pig,

15. Giving something to another causes the giver to accumulate Potency (*de* 德) by creating an obligation on the part of the person who receives. The Perfected Ruler described here can bestow or receive without reference to calculations of obligation and reciprocity.

16. Yaoguang 瑤光 (Gemlike Brilliance) is the name of the third (and final) star in the "handle" of the Northern Dipper constellation. As the indicator of where the "dial" of the Dipper is pointing in its annual circuit around the sky, it plays a significant role in some forms of Chinese astrology. Another star, Zhaoyao 招搖, which forms an extension of the Dipper's handle, is used similarly to designate the successive months in chap. 5. See the introduction to chap. 5, n. 4.

Adopting the stance of *wuwei* 無爲 (taking no purposive action) and bringing about results without striving for them, the ruler is a microcosmic analogue of the macrocosmic Yaoguang, which impersonally dispenses good and ill fortune to the states as it revolves through its annual round.

17. Rong Cheng 容成 was a (mythical) official of the Yellow Emperor credited with inventing the calendar.

18. For a quite different view of archaic society, see 19.1.

Chisel Tusk, and Long Snake all were causing the people harm.[19] Yao therefore commanded Yi [the Archer] to slaughter Chisel Tusk in the water meadows of Chouhua, to kill Nine Gullet on the banks of the Xiong River, to shoot down Typhoon in the wilds of Greenhill, upward to shoot the ten suns and downward to kill Chayu, to chop Long Snake in two at Dongting Lake, and to capture Mound Pig in Mulberry Forest. The multitudes of people all were happy and established Yao as Son of Heaven. And thus for the first time under Heaven, there were roads and mileposts in the plains and canyons, in [difficult] passes and easy [terrain], far and near.

In the time of Shun, Gong Gong stirred up the torrents and [unleashed] floods of water, extending as far as Hollow Mulberry. The Dragon Gate Pass was not yet opened, [and] the Lu Berm had not yet been breached. The Yangzi and the Huai flowed as one; the four seas [became] a boundless expanse of water. The people all climbed hills and mounds and leaped into trees. Shun [thereupon] employed Yu to drain the three rivers and the five lakes [and] to tunnel through Yujue Mountain and make channels for the Chan and Jian rivers. He leveled the land and conducted the waters, leading them to flow into the eastern sea. The flooding waters flowed away, and the nine provinces became dry again. The multitudes were at peace with their natures, and thus they considered Yao and Shun to be sages.

Coming to the time of later generations, there were the emperors Jie and Djou. Jie built the Revolving Palace and the Jade Terrace, [with] porches of ivory and bedsteads of jade. Djou made a forest of meat and a lake of wine; he gathered [for his own use] all the wealth of the world and exhausted in bitterness the labor of the multitudes. He cut open [and extracted the heart of a minister] who remonstrated and ripped open a pregnant woman [to expose her fetus]. [In these ways, Jie and Djou] plundered the world and ill treated the people.

Accordingly, then, Tang employed three hundred war chariots to attack Jie south of Chao and imprisoned him at Xia Terrace. King Wu used three thousand armored warriors to destroy Djou at Muye, [later] executing him at Proclamation Hall. The world became peaceful and orderly, and the people came together harmoniously. Thus Tang and Wu were considered men of surpassing goodness.

From this, one can see that if one is to acquire the reputation of a worthy or a sage, it is necessary to encounter the calamities of a disorderly age. [8/63/8–21]

Nowadays a Perfected Person [who is] born in the midst of a chaotic age, who internalizes Potency, embraces the Way, and is filled with inexhaustible wisdom, [nevertheless must] gag his mouth and stifle his speech. Consequently, there are many [such] who die without ever having spoken, and under Heaven, no one [even] knows to honor this not-speaking. Thus

> the Way that can be called the Way is not the enduring Way;
> names that can be named are not enduring names.[20]

---

19. These mythical monsters are mentioned in various Warring States and Han works; they seem to be paradigms of harmful natural forces. Chayu is a dragon-headed monster armed with a shield and spear; Nine Gullet is a Hydra-like monster; Typhoon (lit., "big wind") is conceived of as a gigantic, malevolent bird.

20. *Laozi* 1.

[Words] written on bamboo or silk or engraved in metal or stone, so as to be passed down to [later] people, are only the rough equivalents.

The Five Thearchs[21] and Three Kings[22] had
different affairs
but the same intentions;
different roads
but the same destinations.[23]

But the scholars of later times know nothing about how to form one body with the Way or how to comprehensively epitomize its Potency. They merely take up the track of things that have already been done. They sit facing one another with a dignified air and talk about it;[24] they drum, chant, and express themselves in dance. But [despite] their broad studies and extensive instruction, they still do not avoid being deluded. It is as the *Odes* says:

"One does not dare to attack a tiger bare-handed;
one does not dare to cross the [Yellow] River without a boat."

Everyone knows this, but no one knows anything else.[25] [8/62/23–8/64/3]

8.7

The thearch embodies the Grand One;
the king emulates yin and yang;
the hegemon follows the four seasons;
the prince uses the six pitch pipes.[26]

Now the Grand One
encloses and contains Heaven and Earth,
weighs on and crushes the mountains and streams,
retains or emits yin and yang,
stretches out and drags along the four seasons,
knots the net of the eight directional end points,
and weaves the web of the six coordinates.

It renews the dew and universally overflows without partiality; it [causes the] waterflies to fly and wriggling things to move; there is nothing that does not rely on it and its Potency in order to live.

Yin and yang

---

21. Five semidivine mythical rulers of high antiquity; the usual list includes the Yellow Emperor, Zhuan Xu, Di Ku, Yao, and Shun.

22. That is, the three royal dynasties of antiquity: Xia, Shang, and Zhou.

23. This formulaic phrase is repeated in 19.3.

24. The same image is found in 19.7.

25. *Odes* 195, "Xiaomin." The poem as a whole is a warning to behave with caution in an age of bad counsel.

26. *Liu lü* (六律) means both "six pitch pipes" and "six standards."

uphold the harmony of Heaven and Earth and shape the physical forms of the myriad diversities.
[They] retain *qi* and transform things in order to bring to completion the kinds of the myriad categories.
They stretch out and draw back,
roll up and uncoil.[27]
They sink into the unfathomable,
end and begin [again] in emptiness and fullness,
revolving in the without-origin.

The four seasons:
spring birth,
summer growth,
autumn harvest,
winter storage.
For obtaining and bestowing, there are times;
for going out and entering, there are measures.
Opening and closing, expanding and contracting, they do not deviate from their [proper] order;
happiness and anger, hardness and pliancy, do not depart from their principles.

The six pitch pipes are
life and death,
reward and punishment,
granting and taking away.

Anything that is otherwise lacks the Way. Therefore
pay heed to the balance beam and weight, the level and the marking cord;[28]
examine into the light and the heavy.

This is sufficient to govern within the boundaries [of a state]. [8/64/5–11]

Therefore one who embodies the Grand One
discerns the true responses of Heaven and Earth[29]
and penetrates the regularities of the Way and its Potency.
His comprehensive brilliance bedazzles like the sun and moon;
his essence and spirit penetrate the myriad things.
His motion and rest are in tune with yin and yang;
his happiness and anger harmonize with the four seasons;
his Moral Potency and magnanimity extend to beyond the borderlands;
and his fame and reputation pass down to later generations.

One who emulates yin and yang
has Potency comparable to Heaven and Earth
and brilliance like that of the sun and moon;

27. Compare 1.1.
28. See 5.15.
29. Compare this and the following five lines with 20.1.

his essence is as comprehensive as that of ghosts and spirits.
He wears roundness as a hat
and squareness as shoes;[30]
he embraces the gnomon
and holds fast to the marking cord.
Within, he is able to govern his person;
without, he is able to win people's minds.

When he promulgates edicts and issues commands, there is no one in the world who does not comply with them.

One who follows the four seasons
is pliant but not fragile,
hard but not brittle,
lenient but not reckless,
demanding but not overbearing.

He is liberal, pliant, responsible, and indulgent in his nourishing the multitudes of creatures; in his Moral Potency he is magnanimous to the simpleminded and forgiving of the deviant; he is devoid of partiality.

One who uses the six pitch pipes
quells disorder and prohibits violence;
advances the meritorious and demotes the unworthy.
He supports the reliable so as to create order;
he drives away the treacherous in order to create peace;
he straightens out the bent in order to create uprightness.

He discerns the Way of prohibitions and pardons, openings and closings. He relies on timeliness and utilizes the power of circumstance in order to win over the hearts of the people.

If a thearch [merely] embodies yin and yang, [his throne] will be usurped.
If a king [merely] models himself on the four seasons, [his territory] will be seized.
If a hegemon [merely] regulates himself by the six standards, he will be disgraced.
If a prince neglects the level and the marking cord, he will be eradicated.
If [a person of] small [standing] carries out great [affairs], the results will be turbulent, insubstantial, and uncongenial.
If a great [person] carries out petty [matters], the results will be narrow, cramped, and unpleasing.

If honorable and mean do not lose their [proper] embodiments, then the world will be [properly] governed. [8/64/11–21]

30. That is, his head resembles the roundness of Heaven, and the outline of his two feet side by side resembles the squareness of Earth. This image is also found in 7.2.

8.8

Heaven loves its [own] essence;
Earth loves its [own] properties;
people love their [own] instinctive responses.
Heaven's essential qualities are the sun, moon, stars, planets, thunder, lightning, wind, and rain.
Earth's properties are water, fire, metal, wood, and earth.
People's instinctive responses are thought, forethought, comprehensiveness [of hearing], clarity [of sight], happiness, and anger.

Thus if one
closes the Four Gates [of perception][31]
and puts an end to the Five Extravagances,
then one will be immersed in the Way. Therefore
when spirit illumination is stored up in the Formless,
and the Quintessential *qi* reverts to ultimate genuineness,
then the eyes are clear, but they are not used for seeing;
and the ears are comprehensive, but they are not used for hearing;
the mouth is apt, but it is not used for speaking;
and the heart is orderly and penetrating, but is not used for thinking and planning.
[Under such circumstances,]
there are responsibilities but no intentional action,
harmonious actions but no boastfulness.

There is a true expression of the instinctive responses invoked by [the ruler's] nature and life circumstances, so that wisdom and precedent are unable to confuse [him].

When the vital essence flows to the eye, vision is clear;
when it is present in the ear, hearing is comprehensive;
when it resides in the mouth, speech is apt;
when it collects in the heart, its feelings are appropriate.
So when one shuts the Four Gates, in the end,
the body suffers no adversity;
the hundred joints have no diseases.
There is neither death nor birth;
neither vacuity nor repletion.
This is what is called the Genuine Person. [8/64/23–28]

8.9

Generally speaking, disorder arises from profligate indolence. The sources of profligate indolence are fivefold:

31. These are the eyes, ears, mouth, and heart (mind), as elucidated several lines below this one.

[erecting] great roof beams and framing timbers;
building palaces and halls;
courtyard buildings, storied towers, and covered walkways;
aviaries and well houses;
with pillars and planks of fruitwood;
all joined together in mutual support;
masterpieces of skillful carpentry;
carved into twists and coils;
overflowingly engraved and carved and polished;
adorned with peculiar patterns and spiraling waves;
[with ornamentation] dripping, floating, billowing, subsiding;
water chestnut and dwarf oak twining and enfolding;
extensive, profuse, disordered, fecund;
cleverly artificial, joined together in apparent confusion;
each [effect] exceeding the last:

Such is profligate indolence based on wood.

The depths of excavated ponds and lakes;
the distance of aligned dikes and embankments;
the flow of diverted [streams] through gorges and valleys;
the straitness of ornamental zigzag channels;
the piling up of stone slabs and the strewing about of stones
in order to make borders and set out stepping-stones;
the placing of barriers and dampers in the furious rapids
so as to stir up the surging waves;
the making of angles and riffles, bends and meanders
to imitate the rivers of [Fan]yu and [Cang]wu;
the augmenting of lotus and water-chestnut plantings
so as to feed turtles and fish,
swans, geese, kingfishers,
fed with leftover rice and sorghum;
dragon boats with prows carved like water birds,
wafted along by the breeze for pure pleasure:

Such is profligate indolence based on water.

High pounded-earth city walls and fortifications,
plantings of trees [as barriers] in passes and defiles;
the impressiveness of lofty belvederes and observation posts;
the immensity of extravagant gardens and walled parks,
the sight of which satisfies every desire and wonder,
the height of lofty gate towers that ascend to the clouds and blue [sky];
great mansions rising tier upon tier,
rivaling the height of Kunlun;
the construction of barrier walls and enclosures,
the making of networks of roads,

the leveling of highlands and filling in of depressions,
the piling up of earth to make mountains,
for the sake of easy passage to great distances;
the straightening of roads through flatlands and hills,
so that [drivers] may ceaselessly gallop and race
without [fear] of stumbles or falls:

Such is profligate indolence based on earth.

Great bells and tripods,
beautiful and heavy implements,
engraved all over with floral and reptilian designs,
all twisting and intertwined,
with recumbent rhinos and crouching tigers,
coiling dragons interlacing together;
blazingly bright and confusingly contrived,
shiningly dazzling, brilliantly glittering,
topsy-turvy, convoluted, luxuriant, tangled,
[with] overall fretwork and written inscriptions,
[with] engraved and polished ornamentation;
cast tin-alloy decorated mirrors,
now dark, now bright,
rubbed minutely, every flaw removed;
frost patterns and deep-cut inlay work,
resembling bamboo matwork, basketry, or netting,
or brocade wrappings, regular or irregular,
the lines numerous but each one distinct:

Such is profligate indolence based on metal.

Frying, boiling, roasting, grilling,
the quest to blend, equalize, and harmonize [flavors],
trying to capture every permutation of sweet and sour in the manner of Jing and Wu;
burning down forests in order to hunt,
stoking kilns with entire logs,
blowing through *tuyères* and puffing with bellows
in order to melt bronze and iron
that extravagantly flow to harden in the mold,
not considering an entire day sufficient to the task.
The mountains are denuded of towering trees;
the forests are stripped of cudrania and catalpa trees;
tree trunks are baked to make charcoal;
grass is burned to make ash,
[so that] open fields and grasslands are white and bare
and do not yield [vegetation] in season.
Above, the heavens are obscured [by smoke];
below, the fruits of the earth are extinguished:

Such is profligate indolence based on fire.

Of these five, [even] one is sufficient for [a ruler] to lose control of the world. For this reason, in ancient times the making of the Mingtang was such that

below, mud and dampness should not rise up [in the walls];
above, drizzle and fog should not enter into [the building];
and on all four sides, the wind should not come in.
The earthen [walls] were not patterned;
the woodwork was not carved;
the metal fittings were not ornamented.
Clothing [was made] with untrimmed corners and seams;
hats were designed without fancy corners and folds.
The [Ming]tang was sufficiently large for the movement of [those who] arranged the liturgies;
it was sufficiently quiet and clean for sacrifices to the high gods and for ceremonies [directed at] the spirits and deities.

This was to show forth to the people knowledge, simplicity, and economy. [8/65/1–19]

8.10

Now, sounds, colors, and the five flavors, precious and strange things from distant countries, things that are extraordinary, different, and surprising are enough to cause alterations and changes in the heart and will, to agitate and unsettle one's essence and spirit, and to stir up the blood and the *qi* so that it becomes impossible to keep control of them. Now, the ways in which Heaven and Earth bring forth their products do not basically exceed five. The sage adheres to the five modes of conduct,[32] and thus his government does not become disordered.

As a general rule, human nature [is such that] when the heart is harmonious and desires are obtained, there is joy.

Joy gives rise to movement;
movement gives rise to stepping about;
stepping about gives rise to agitation;
agitation gives rise to singing;
singing gives rise to dancing.

If there is dancing, [even] animals and birds will jump about.[33]

Human nature [is such that] when the heart harbors sorrow or mourning, there is grief.

32. *Wuxing* 五行 here appears to be used in its Mencian sense of five modes of conduct—Humaneness, Wisdom, Rightness, Ritual Correctness, and Sagehood—rather than (as is usually the case in the *Huainanzi*) as the Five Phases: Wood, Fire, Earth, Metal, and Water.

33. We drop the words *ge* 歌 and *jie* 節 from this sentence, following Yu Yue's commentary. See Zhang Shuangdi 1997, 1:879–80n.2.

Grief gives rise to lamentation;
lamentation gives rise to aroused feelings;
aroused feelings give rise to anger;
anger gives rise to movement;[34]

Movement causes the hands and feet to be restless.

Human nature [is such that] when [the heart] harbors [feelings of] being encroached upon or insulted, there is anger.

With anger, the blood becomes replete;
when the blood becomes replete, *qi* is aroused;
when *qi* is aroused, anger is manifested externally;
when anger is manifested externally, there is some release of feelings.

Thus,

bells and drums, flutes and panpipes, shields and war hatchets, feather plumes and oxtail banners, all are means to express joy.

Unfinished hempen garments, unbleached headcloths, and mourners' staffs, and weeping, thrashing about, and restraints [on conduct] all are means to express sorrow.

Weapons and leather [armor], feather plumes and oxtail banners, metal drums, battle-axes and pole-axes, all are means to express anger.

First there must be the inner substance [of the emotion]; then one can make an outward expression of it. [8/65/21–8/66/4]

8.11

In ancient times when the sage-kings occupied the throne, governance and instruction were equitable; humaneness and love were harmoniously blended.[35]

High and low were of one mind;
ruler and minister were friendly and in accord [with each other].
Clothing and food were in surplus;
families supplied people with the necessities.
Fathers were compassionate and sons were filial;
older brothers were nurturing and younger brothers compliant;
in life there was no resentment;
in death there was no regret.

---

34. The text here may be corrupt; the reference to "movement" (*dong* 動) appears to belong with the previous paragraph, while the reference to "anger" (*nu* 怒) appears to belong with the following paragraph. But commentators make no suggestions for emendations, and we have translated the text as given.

35. This passage contrasts in an interesting way with the idealized picture of archaic agrarian primitivism in *Laozi* 80, the famous passage that begins "Let the state be small and the populace sparse." While the *Laozi* envisions small village communities willfully oblivious of one another's affairs, the vision of the archaic era in 8.11 is of a substantial empire marked by unity and concord between ruler and subjects.

The world was harmonious and in concord,
and the people obtained what they desired.

People were happy with one another but without the means to give expression to [this happiness] and bestow it [on one another]. Therefore the sages devised ritual and music for them so as to harmonize and regulate them.

In the government of later ages,
hunting and fishing were heavily taxed;
gate tolls and market fees were sharply increased;
the use of wetlands and bridges was prevented and prohibited.
There was no place to deploy nets and snares;
no advantage to using mattock and plow.
The people's strength was exhausted by corvée labor;
their wealth and necessities were depleted in order to pay taxes.
Residents had nothing to eat;
travelers had no provisions;
the old were not nurtured;
the dead were not buried.
Wives were prostituted and children sold,
in order to meet the demands of the higher-ups,
but even so they were unable to satisfy them.

Clueless common men and simple women all were left with their hearts in turmoil and flux and with their wills sick and sorrowful. Under such circumstances, to strike the great bells, to pound the resounding drums, to blow on pipes and mouth organs, to pluck *qin* and *se*, would be to cast away the basis of music [itself]. [8/66/6–12]

In ancient times, the demands of those on high were light, and the people's needs were met.

Princes bestowed their Moral Potency;
ministers amply fulfilled [their duty of] loyalty.
Fathers behaved compassionately;
sons outdid themselves in filiality.

Each attained the [proper degree of] love, and there were no feelings of resentment among them. The three years' mourning was not imposed by force, but it was accomplished [nevertheless, so that]

people heard music but were not joyous,
ate delicacies but did not find them sweet;

They were mindful of thoughts of the deceased and were unable to leave off [thinking about them].

In later ages, habits were dissipated and customs grew depraved.
Lusts and appetites proliferated;
Ritual and Rightness were eradicated.
Rulers and ministers deceived one another;
fathers and sons distrusted one another.
Anger and rancor filled every breast;
thoughtful minds were entirely extinct.

Those who wore mourning clothes and tied on unbleached headcloths
fooled around and laughed in the midst [of their mourning].

Although they attained the full three years, they cast away the fundamental principle of mourning. [8/66/14–17]

8.12

In ancient times, the Son of Heaven had his royal domain, and the Lords of the Land each had the same [domains as called for by their rank]; each took care of his own portion, and none was permitted to usurp another. If there was one who did not follow the kingly Way,

who was cruel and oppressive to the masses,
who fought over land and tried to usurp territory,
who disrupted the government and violated prohibitions,
who when summoned [to the king's court] would not come,
who when given commands would not carry them out,
who when forbidden [things] would not desist,
who when admonished would not alter,

then [the Son of Heaven] raised an army and went forth to punish him,

executing the prince,
getting rid of his supporters,
shutting his ancestral tombs,
sacrificing at their altars of the soil,

[and] then selecting by divination one of his sons or grandsons to replace him.

But in later ages, [rulers]

endeavored to enlarge their lands and encroach on the territory of others, forming alliances ceaselessly,
raised armies for unrighteous causes and mounted punitive expeditions against the guiltless;
killed innocent people and cut off the lineages of the former sages.
Large countries set off to attack [others];
small countries built fortifications to defend themselves.
[Such rulers] confiscated people's oxen and horses,
took captive their sons and daughters,
destroyed their ancestral temples,
carried off their weighty treasures,
[so that] streams of blood flowed for a thousand *li*,
and sun-bleached skeletons choked the wild lands.

To satisfy the desires of greedy lords—this is not how armies should be managed. [8/66/19–24]

Now the purpose of armies is to punish cruelty, not to commit cruelties.
The purpose of music is to bring forth concord [in human relations], not to create licentiousness.

The purpose of mourning is to bring about a consummation of grief, not to create what is meretricious.

Thus,

there is a Way of serving close relations, and love is the principal means of serving them.

There is substance in the [rituals of] attendance at court, and respect is its highest expression.

There are rituals for the implementation of mourning, and grief is their principal quality.

There are techniques for the use of arms, and Rightness is their foundation.

If the foundation is established, then the Way can be implemented;

if the foundation is harmed, then the Way will be abandoned. [8/66/26–29]

Translated by John S. Major

Nine

THE RULER'S TECHNIQUES

"THE RULER'S Techniques" begins by stating: "The ruler's techniques [consist of] establishing non-active management and carrying out wordless instructions." This serves notice that the chapter is not a handbook of tips and tricks for an energetic bureaucrat but a comprehensive plan for achieving the kind of effective self-cultivation, charismatic appeal, and radiant moral force required for a person to be a true universal monarch, a "Son of Heaven." The ruler's non-active orientation is made possible by time-tested techniques that have proved efficacious in creating a harmonious and just society in which the common people flourish and officials support their ruler as spokes to the hub. His ability to instruct and yet remain silent as he does so lies in the wondrous power of vital energy (*qi*), which, through self-cultivation, he possesses in quintessential form. By means of this Quintessential *qi*, which in its most refined state is referred to in this chapter interchangeably as the Utmost Essence (*zhijing*) or spirit (*shen*), the ruler can avail himself of the Way of Heaven above and transform the people below.[1] In this manner, the ruler achieves a kind of profound and pervasive resonance with his subjects. Stirring their hearts as a fine melody would, such "wordless instructions" are infinitely more persuasive, far-reaching, and influential than any verbal command or purposeful act could be.

---

1. For an extensive discussion of the subject of resonance as it relates to Utmost Essence (*zhijing*)—that is, the most refined quintessential *qi*—see chap. 6. The concept of Quintessential Sincerity (*jingcheng*) is developed in chap. 10. For both terms, see also app. A.

The Chapter Title

We have translated the title of this chapter, "Zhu shu" 主術, as "The Ruler's Techniques." *Zhu* is the most general of several possible Chinese words that could be translated as "ruler." A Zhou-dynasty word known from bronze inscriptions and early literature (but not from Shang oracle bones), its earliest meaning seems to be "one who presides" (for example, over a ceremony) or "host" (of a banquet). Two close cognates are *zhu* 拄, "to prop up," and *zhu* 柱, "pillar" (specifically, a load-bearing pillar of a building). The *Huainanzi* authors had other choices: this chapter could have been entitled "Jun shu" 君術, "The Prince's Techniques"; or "Wang shu" 王術, "The King's Techniques"; or even "Huangdi shu" 皇帝術, "The Emperor's Techniques." The choice of a word with broad implications of "presiding, axial, upholding" therefore was surely deliberate.

Shu straightforwardly means "techniques," the ways in which an expert exercises his profession or carries out some task. The word implies skill, practice, and specialized knowledge but also a kind of fluency of action beyond verbal description. To exercise *shu* is to act with an ease possible only as a result of long and diligent practice. *Shu* was a word much on the minds of late Warring States and Han thinkers because it fit the prevailing ideal of a person whose actions went beyond mere skill or expertise and were derived from being attuned to the Way.

The well-known translation of this chapter by Roger Ames is entitled "The Art of Rulership."[2] We hope that our translation, "The Ruler's Techniques," conveys more precisely that this chapter outlines the specific "Techniques of the Way" (*dao shu*) that enable an individual to succeed as a ruler.

Summary and Key Themes

"The Ruler's Techniques" describes the methods that a ruler should use to create a beneficent and orderly government and stay on top of it. As the authors assert: "Thus, with techniques, one rules others; without techniques, one is ruled by them" (9.24). As the chapter makes clear, the list of techniques required for successful rule is long and daunting.

Practicing Non-Action

The first and perhaps most important technique to be identified is "non-active management." With a quiet and tranquil demeanor, impartial and detached, the ruler delegates to his underlings the day-to-day responsibilities of running the govern-

2. Ames 1994.

ment. As the authors expressly point out, this does not mean that the ruler should become inert and do nothing. Even though he acts, nothing emanates from him personally (9.23), so his policies are not biased by his private preferences (9.25), nor are they restricted by the limits of his individual intelligence (9.9–9.11). Rather, the techniques he implements conform to the patterns of the Way implicit in the natural propensities of things. For example, because the ruler adjusts his policies to the yin–yang rhythm of the four seasons, the people find those policies suitable because they seem natural. With non-action as his foundational orientation, the ruler can implement laws and dispense rewards and punishments without being swayed by personal bias. Freed from the quotidian concerns of ruling, his role as "model or gnomon for the world" is given due prominence, and the weighty responsibility of transforming the people moves to the foreground.

Transforming the People by Means of Quintessential *qi*

If you refine your heavenly and earthly *qi*, the authors argue, you can merge with the Grand One and, through the Grand One, avail yourself of the unlimited and mysterious Way of Heaven (9.2). Readers of the *Huainanzi* have already encountered (in chapter 7) a detailed description of the meditative regimens that foster refinement of the bodily energies, and an argument for why the ruler will obtain benefits from adhering to them. "The Ruler's Techniques" returns to that theme and considers the public and political implications of the ruler's self-cultivation. The ruler uses his Quintessential *qi* because, as with the technique of non-action, he needs it to conduct the grand symphony of transformation on the universal scale envisioned by the *Huainanzi* authors.

The ruler transforms the people most effectively by approaching them not with words but through the demonstrational power of his moral conduct, through a projection of his Quintessential *qi* in a way that naturally evokes a response from everyone within range: "A great shout can be heard at most only within a hundred paces, but the human will can project over a thousand *li*" (9.4). The transformation of the people is made easier when the ruler is virtuous and holds on to the handles of authority and positional advantage (9.26). Thus the ruler's power and his ability to motivate his officials and to persuade the people to do his will depend on charisma rather than coercion: "By proclaiming laws and establishing rewards, [however], one cannot alter habits and change customs because sincerity of heart would not be stirred" (9.7).

Using Positional Advantage and Following Natural Propensities

Positional advantage[3] is a key element in the ruler's capacity to transform the people because it allows him to project his Moral Potency along with the innate force of

3. For a discussion of *shi* 勢 "positional advantage," see app. A and the introduction to chap. 15.

his Quintessential *qi*. When the ruler is morally potent and maintains his positional advantage, this transformative process is made easier. Moral Potency without positional advantage is ineffective, but positional advantage without Moral Potency leads to coercion and tyranny (9.19). The goal of the self-cultivated ruler is thus to use his positional advantage to transform the people in a positive way. The ruler possesses positional advantage in part because he is able to appropriate to himself the collective talent and strength of the people and officials: thus the ruler "is carried by the capabilities of others as if they were his feathers and wings" (9.25). He does this by following their natural propensities. The people wish to be good, as naturally as "boats floating on water and carts going on land" (9.10), and the ruler's task is to allow those natural propensities to emerge and flourish.

Laws, Taxes, Officials, and Administration

Chapter 9's advice to the ruler is not confined to political theory. On the contrary, "The Ruler's Techniques" contains a great deal of practical information on how to run a successful administration.

The chapter makes clear that successful rule is grounded in fair and impartial laws, and it makes an extraordinary claim about the origin of law: "Law comes from Rightness. Rightness comes from what is appropriate for the people. What is appropriate for the people accords with the human heart. This is the *sine qua non* of government" (9.23). At the same time, this is not what in the West would be called "natural law." Instead, law is defined as a purely human invention: "Law is not a gift of Heaven, not a product of the Earth. It was devised by humankind but conversely is used [by humans] to rectify themselves" (9.23). At the same time, once instituted, "Law is the standard of measurement for the world, the level and marking cord of the ruler" (9.23). According to this theory, good law is a reflection of peoples' capacity for goodness; bad, coercive, biased, tyrannical laws will fail because they violate the people's inborn sense of what is right.

The ruler must implement his laws (and other aspects of his administration) through his officials. But the ruler also must constantly be on guard against bad officials, those who engage in flattery, deceit, corrupt practices, and oppression of the people: "The ruler of men values uprightness and esteems loyalty. When the loyal and the upright are in high positions and affairs are dealt with by cleaving to rectitude, flattering deceivers and wicked villains will have no place to advance" (9.18). When those whom he employs are appropriate, the administration will be orderly, and the populace will be harmonious. The officials will feel close to the ruler, and the masses of the people will submit (9.18).

Taxation is an essential function of government, and excessive taxation is recognized as one of the chief complaints that people might have about their rulers. The authors of the chapter thus name the ruler's unrestrained desire for luxury as a key source of excessive taxation: If "the ruler is eager to carry out projects that are of no use, and the people look haggard and worn" (9.21), then the ruler's government is on the verge of ruin. In contrast, the sagely ruler demonstrates concern for the people by ensuring that their material needs are satisfied; by amassing adequate reserves so the people can withstand natural disasters; and by instructing them in the rudiments of agriculture and animal husbandry so they have the means to feed and clothe themselves.

The point of the ruler's techniques is to benefit the people, not to exploit or repress them; and if the people benefit from the government, they will support it: the ruler and his people reciprocally support each other.

Moral Potency and Sage-Rulership

Finally, the authors of "The Ruler's Techniques" insist that exemplary rulers embody Potency (9.4, 9.10, 9.14, 9.20, 9.21, 9.22).[4] Commensurate with the syncretic and comprehensive goals of the Huainan masters and illustrative of their efforts to devise a theory of governance that harmonizes the various wisdom traditions of China's great past, the salient features of non-action—silence and tranquillity—are refashioned here to allow the ruler's Potency to shine through. Potency (both in its broadest sense and with the specific connotations of "virtue" that we term Moral Potency) is associated with such rich and varied attributes as Humaneness, Wisdom, Rightness, Sincerity, Rectitude, Kindness, Grace, Filial Piety, Uprightness, Moderation, Restraint, and Frugality (9.18, 9.27, 9.30, 9.31). Potency is exemplified by the great sage-kings of the past, who frame the chapter like two bookends, opening with the Divine Farmer (9.3) and concluding with the paradigmatic Confucian sages Yao, Shun, Yu, Tang, Wen, and Wu, and Confucius as the "uncrowned king" (9.29).

Sources

As is the case with so many other chapters in the *Huainanzi*, the variety of sources from which the authors of "The Ruler's Techniques" draw is astounding for its breadth. Moreover, as we have seen elsewhere, the *Huainanzi* draws on its diverse sources through direct and indirect quotations, paraphrases, and allusions. Chapter 12 of the *Huainanzi*, with its more than fifty references to the *Laozi*, represents one end of the spectrum of how sources are used, and chapter 9, with only a few citations of named sources, represents the other. The authors usually hide the warp and weft threads of the conceptual tapestry that constitutes chapter 9 of the *Huiananzi*. Nevertheless, it is clear that the chapter shares ideas and historical references (but less often specific quotations) with the *Laozi*, *Zhuangzi*, *Lüshi chunqiu*, *Guanzi*, *Zuozhuan*, *Liji*, *Hanfeizi*, and other texts. Many passages in this chapter also have clear parallels with the *Wenzi*. Readers interested in pursuing further the chapter's

4. For the full range of meanings and connotations of the difficult term *de*, see app. A.

sources should consult Roger Ames's rigorous and insightful study of this chapter, which identifies and discusses them in more detail.[5]

The Chapter in the Context of the *Huainanzi* as a Whole

According to the opening lines of the chapter summary in chapter 21 of the *Huainanzi*, "'The Ruler's Techniques' [addresses] the affairs [*shi* 事] of the ruler of humankind." With this seemingly modest claim, however, the *Huainanzi* turns an important conceptual corner, making a transition from the text's first eight "root" chapters, which are primarily concerned with elucidating the Way (*dao*), and beginning the second half of the book with the first of twelve "branch" chapters, which focus on affairs (*shi*). In keeping with this transition from theoretical underpinnings to the more practical and detailed affairs of government, the first topic addressed in this chapter is the spectrum of specific techniques (*shu*) that will enable the ruler to establish an efficacious and judicious regime.[6] The chapter describes methods for appointing, overseeing, and evaluating officials so that they exert their abilities to the utmost to regulate the multitudes below, thus enabling the ruler to "straighten the bent and correct the crooked, set aside self-interest [*si* 私] and establish the public good [*gong* 公]" (21.2) so that a mutually beneficial and harmonious relationship between ruler and ruled is established throughout the empire. Such, claim the authors, "is the brilliance of the ruler's techniques" (21/225/8–11).

Sarah A. Queen and John S. Major

5. Ames 1994; sources and parallels are discussed in detail in the endnotes to his translation, 239–55.

6. The *Huainanzi* returns to the important theme of "techniques" in chap. 12.

Nine

9.1

The ruler's techniques [consist of]
establishing non-active management
and carrying out wordless instructions.
Quiet and tranquil, he does not move;
by [even] one degree he does not waver;
adaptive and compliant, he relies on his underlings;
dutiful and accomplished, he does not labor.
Therefore,
though his mind knows the norms, his savants transmit the discourses of the Way;
though his mouth can speak, his entourage proclaims his words;
though his feet can advance, his master of ceremonies leads;
though his ears can hear, his officials offer their admonitions.[1]
Therefore,
his considerations are without mistaken schemes;
his undertakings are without erroneous content.
His words [are taken as] scripture and verse;
his conduct is [taken as] a model and gnomon for the world.

1. This sentence breaks the parallelism of the whole passage, so we suspect that the text might have originally read, "his officials receive the admonitions [of others]."

His advancing and withdrawing respond to the seasons;
his movement and rest comply with [proper] patterns.
His likes and dislikes are not based on ugliness or beauty;
his rewards and punishments are not based on happiness or anger.
Each name names itself;
each category categorizes itself.
Affairs emerge from what is natural;
nothing issues from [the ruler] himself.

Thus kings in antiquity wore caps
with strings of pearls in front so as to mask their vision
and silk plugs in their ears so as to obstruct their hearing.
The Son of Heaven surrounded himself with screens so as to isolate himself.
Thus,
what the ruler patterns himself on is far away, but what he grounds himself in is nearby;
what he governs himself with is great, but what he preserves is small.
Now,
if his eyes looked recklessly, there would be profligacy;
if his ear listened recklessly, there would be delusion;
if his mouth spoke recklessly, there would be disorder.
One cannot fail to guard carefully these three gateways.
If you wish to regulate them, that is in fact to distance yourself from them;
if you wish to embellish them, that is in fact to injure them. [9/67/3–11]

9.2

Heavenly *qi* becomes your ethereal soul;
earthly *qi* becomes your substantive soul.[2]
Return them to their mysterious dwelling place, so that each resides in its proper place.
Preserve and do not lose them, so that above you communicate with the Grand One,
for the essence of the Grand One communicates with Heaven,
and the Way of Heaven is mysterious and silent, shapeless and without pattern.
Heaven's limit cannot be reached;
its depths cannot be plumbed.

2. For heavenly and earthly *qi*, see 3.1: "[The *qi* that] was pure and bright spread out to form Heaven; [the *qi* that] was heavy and turbid congealed to form Earth." In Han belief, the body of a living person was inhabited by two souls: (a) the *hun* 魂, an ethereal yang soul that departed from the body at death, and (b) the *po* 魄, an earthy, substantive, corporeal yin soul that remained with the corpse after death and was entombed with it. Funerary offerings placed in the tomb were for the benefit of the *po* soul. See also 7.7 and 16.1. The link made here between heavenly and earthly *qi* and the *hun* and *po* souls of the ruler suggests a direct macrocosm–microcosm relationship between the cosmos and the sage.

Still it transforms together with humans, [though] knowledge cannot grasp it. [9/67/13–15]

9.3

In ancient times, when the Divine Farmer ruled the world,
his spirit did not lunge forth from his chest;
his wisdom did not go beyond the four sides [of his body].
He cherished his humane and sincere heart.
Sweet rains fell in their season;
the five grains multiplied and prospered.
In the spring there was birth, in summer growth;
in the fall, harvest; in the winter, storage.
He inquired monthly and investigated seasonally;
when the harvest ended, he reported the achievements [to the ancestors].
Each season he tasted the grain offerings
and sacrificed [to the ancestors] in the Mingtang.
The construction of the Mingtang was [such that] it had a roof but no sides.
Wind and rain could not assail it;
cold and heat could not harm it.
Slowly and haltingly [the ruler] entered the hall. He nurtured the people with public spiritedness; the people [in turn] were simple and steady, straight and sincere.
They did not engage in angry struggle, but goods were sufficient.
They did not strain their bodies, but they completed their accomplishments.
They availed themselves of the gifts of Heaven and Earth and lived in harmony and unity with them.
Therefore,
his awesome demeanor was stern but not exercised;
his punishments existed but were not used;
his laws were sparing and uncomplicated.
Thus [the Divine Farmer's] transformation [of the people] was spiritlike. His territory
to the south went as far as Jiaozhi
and in the north to the Youdu Mountains.[3]
To the east it stretched to Sunrise Valley,
and to the west it reached to Three Dangers Mountain.
There was none who failed to follow him. At that time
the law was generous and punishments were lenient;
prisons and jails were vacant and empty.
Throughout the world, customs were one, and none harbored wickedness in their hearts. [9/67/17–23]

3. Jiaozhi is identified with a kingdom in part of what is now northern Vietnam, in the floodplain of the Red River, and the Youdu Mountains are near the Gulf of Zhili. See 20.28.

Government in the era of decline was not like that.

Those above loved to seize and knew no limit;
those below were as rapacious as wolves and would not yield.
The people, impoverished and suffering, struggled angrily;
affairs exhausted their energy without achieving anything.
Cleverness and deceit sprouted forth;
theft and plunder flourished openly.

Those above and those below resented each other; laws and commands had no currency.

Officials had authority but did not take responsibility for returning to the Way; instead, they went against the root and embellished the branches.

They diminished and decreased rewards
and strengthened and increased punishments,

hoping in this way to govern well. This is no different from

grasping a crossbow and calling a bird
or wielding a club and approaching a dog[4]

—the disorder will only increase. [9/68/1–4]

9.4

When waters are muddy, fish gasp for air [near the surface];[5]
when the government is harsh, the people become disorderly.

Thus those who raise tigers, leopards, rhinoceroses, and elephants

give them pens and cages,
provide for their desires,
feed them appropriately,

yet the animals still harbor great anger and cannot live out their normal life spans because they live under compulsion. Thus it is that

when those above have many clever schemes, those below have much deceitfulness.
When those above have many matters to deal with, those below have many fabrications.
When those above are troubled and vexed, those below are unsettled.
When those above have many wants, those below struggle harder against one another.
Failing to correct the root
but attending to the branches

is like

spreading dirt to stop a dust storm
or bringing firewood to put out a fire. [9/68/4–8]

---

4. See 16.157.
5. This proverb recurs in 10.97, 16.59, and 20.2.

Thus with sages,

their undertakings are sparing and thus easily managed;
their desires are few and thus easily satisfied.
They do not give but are humane;
they do not speak but are trustworthy.
They do not seek but they attain;
they do not act but they succeed.

Clodlike,[6] they preserve Genuineness, embrace Potency, and project Sincerity. The world follows them as an echo responds to a sound or a shadow imitates the form [that casts it], for what they cultivate is the root.

Punishments and chastisements are not enough to modify habits;
executions and mutilations are not enough to proscribe wickedness.

Only spirit transformation is [to be] prized. Essence at its utmost is spirit. [9/68/10–12]

A great shout can be heard at most only within a hundred paces, but the human will can project over a thousand *li*.

Winter's sunshine,
summer's shade—

everyone seeks them, but no one makes them so.

Thus the semblance of Utmost Essence
is not called forth but comes of itself;
is not waved off but departs of itself.

It is obscure and dark; we do not know who made it. Its achievements accomplish themselves.

The wise cannot discourse about it;
the analytical cannot describe it. [9/68/14–16]

9.5

Long ago, Sunshu Ao[7] slept peacefully, and the men of Ying had no occasion to use their weapons. Yiliao of Shi'nan juggled crossbow pellets, and [although] the two houses [i.e., those of Duke Bo and Zixi] had difficulties, none could take issue with [Yiliao's] refusal.[8]

Armor of leather and metal,
belligerent stares and clenched fists—

6. *Kuairan* 塊然 (lit., "clodlike") probably is a reference to the "Great Clod" (*dakuai* 大塊) in *Zhuangzi* 2. The concept of a self-contained and inviolable state is similar to that of the "Unhewn" (*pu* 樸), for which see, for example, 1.2.

7. Sunshu Ao (fl. ca. 598 B.C.E.) was the prime minister of Chu.

8. Yiliao 宜遼 of Shi'nan was a mighty knight of Chu, surnamed Xiong 熊, whose aid was sought by Duke Bo in a vendetta against Prime Minister Zixi but who refused despite bribery and threats. See *Zuozhuan*, Ai 16. Stories about him appear in *Zhuangzi* 20, 23, and 25. The remark here about "juggling crossbow pellets" parallels a speech attributed to Confucius in *Zhuangzi* 24. According to Gao You, when Duke Bo's emissary Shi Qi came to appeal to Yiliao, he was juggling crossbow pellets and did not stop even when Shi Qi threatened him with a sword. See Zhang Shuangdi 1997, 1:903n.18.

how inadequate these are as a defense against weapons and swords;
scrolls of treaties, rolls of silk,
mutilating punishments and [executioners'] axes—
how meager these are as ways to get out of difficulties!
To rely on the eyes [alone] to see
or to depend on words [alone] to command—
it is hard to rule that way. [9/68/16–19]

When Qu Boyu was prime minister, Zigong[9] went to see him and asked, "How do you govern a country?" He answered, "I govern it by not governing."

Viscount Jian [of Zhao],[10] wanting to attack Wey, sent Scribe An[11] to look things over. He came back and reported, saying, "Qu Boyu is prime minister. We cannot send in troops yet."

How could strong fortifications and precipitous defiles be as effective as [men like] these]?

Thus,

Gao Yao,[12] who was mute, served as minister of justice, and there were no cruel punishments in the world. He had [qualities] of greater value than speech.

Music Master Kuang, who was blind, served as grand tutor, and Jin had no disorder in government. He had [qualities] more valuable than sight.

Thus,
the commands that do not [rely on] words,
and the vision that does not [rely on] seeing,
are what make Fuxi and the Divine Farmer our teachers. [9/68/21–25]

9.6

The transformation of the people comes not from what [the ruler] says but from he does.

Thus,

Duke Zhuang of Qi[13] was fond of bravado and would not allow [anyone] to argue with him about fighting. So his state had many difficulties, and its decline led to the rebellion of Cui Zhu.

---

9. Zigong 子貢 (also known as Duanmu Si 端木賜) was a disciple of Confucius who, after the death of the Master, went on to a career as a merchant and diplomat.

10. Viscount Jian of Zhao 趙簡子 (also known as Zhao Yang 鞅 [d. 475 B.C.E.]), a ministerial vassal of Jin, was the successful leader of the Zhao clan in factional struggles against rival vassal clans. He was a proponent of government reform known for casting the penal laws of Jin onto bronze tripods for public display.

11. Scribe An 史黯 (also known as Scribe Mo 墨) was a knight of Jin, surnamed Cai 蔡, who served as grand scribe of the ducal court.

12. Gao Yao 皋陶 was a legendary sage official in the time of Yao and Shun.

13. Duke Zhuang of Qi (r. 553–548 B.C.E.) consorted with the wife of, and was consequently murdered by, his minister Cui Zhu.

King Qingxiang of Chu[14] liked sex and did not allow [anyone] to discuss his habits [with him]. So many of the people fell into disorder, culminating in the affair of Zhao Qi.[15]

Thus the movements of the Utmost Essence are like
the generative [power] of springtime *qi*
and the slaying [power] of autumn *qi*.

Not even a relay carriage or a galloping horse could go that far. Thus a ruler of men is like an archer. When he [releases an arrow] if his aim is slightly off, it will always miss [the target] by a wide margin. Thus the ruler is very careful in how he evokes a response. [9/68/25–9/69/2]

9.7

Rong Qiji[16] plucked his *qin* just once, and Confucius was joyful for three days in response to its harmony.

Zou Ji[17] played one note on his *qin*, and King Wei of Qi[18] was mournful all evening in response to its sadness.

By playing on the *qin* and the *se*
and giving form to the notes,

one can make others sad or joyful. By proclaiming laws and establishing rewards, [however], one cannot modify habits and change customs, because sincerity of heart would not be stirred.[19]

When Ning Qi[20] sang a song in the *shang* mode from under the cart,[21] Duke Huan of Qi sighed and suddenly understood [and appointed him a high official]. How deeply the Utmost Essence enters into humans!

Thus it is said,

"If you hear the sound of music,
you know the customs of the place from which it arises;
if you see the customs, you know their transformations."

14. King Qingxiang of Chu 楚頃襄王 was the ruler of Chu from 299 to 263 B.C.E.

15. Zhao Qi 昭奇, according to Gao You, was a grandee of Chu. See Zhang Shuangdi 1997, 1:907n.4. He is otherwise unknown.

16. Rong Qiji 榮啟期 was a hermit of the Spring and Autumn period. The story of his encounter with Confucius is recounted in *Liezi* 1.

17. Zou Ji 鄒忌 (d. ca. 341 B.C.E.), a minister of Qin under two sovereigns, rose to the post of prime minister under King Wei, and oversaw sweeping government reforms.

18. King Wei 齊威王 of Qi (r. 356–320 B.C.E.) was the second Tian-clan sovereign to hold the throne of Qi and the first to assume the title of king. He was famous for his patronage of scholars at Jixia in the Qi capital of Linze.

19. See the discussion of sincerity of heart in 20.7.

20. Ning Qi 甯戚, a native of Wei during the Spring and Autumn period, began life in poverty and ultimately rose to succeed Guan Zhong as prime minister of Qi. See 10.94, 11.6, 12.14, and 13.16.

21. This incident is described most fully in 12.14 and is alluded to several times in the text. See 10.94, 11.6, and 13.16.

Confucius studied music under Master Xiang[22] and [thereby] understood the will of King Wen of Zhou. This was because upon seeing subtleties, he could know the obvious.

Jizi of Yanling, hearing the music of Lu, knew the customs of the Shang and Xia dynasties. From assessing the close at hand, he recognized the distant.

What was created in highest antiquity and disseminated a thousand years ago has not been extinguished. This is emphatically so in the case of what transforms the people in the present era. [9/69/4–9]

9.8

During the reign of King Tang [of the Shang dynasty], there was a seven-year drought.[23] The king offered himself as sacrifice at Mulberry Forest. Thereupon

clouds from the Four Seas gathered,
and rain fell for a thousand *li*.

Embracing his basic substance and imparting his sincerity, he evoked a response from Heaven and Earth, his spirit making itself known beyond the [four] quarters. How could promulgating orders and prohibitions suffice to accomplish something like this?

In ancient times, the Utmost Essence of the sage-kings took form within themselves, and their personal likes and dislikes were forgotten outside themselves. They

spoke simply to express their emotions,
issued orders to make clear their intentions,
displayed [their essential qualities] in rites and music,
and exemplified them in songs and ballads.

Their achievements

have spread to a myriad generations without being impeded
and have pervaded the four directions without being depleted.

Even birds, beasts, and insects were refined and transformed[24] by them. How much more so were they effective in maintaining laws and carrying out commands. [9/69/11–15]

Thus,

the loftiest [of rulers] transforms by means of his spirit.
The next lower [ruler] convinces the people to act without transgressions.
The next lower one rewards the worthy and punishes the unruly. [9/69/17]

22. Master Xiang 師襄 is identified by Gao You as the grand musician of Lu, but several later commentators take issue with this, noting that that the *Analects* gives a different name to that figure. See Zhang Shuangdi 1997, 1:909n.11.

23. According to other sources, a five-year drought.

24. *Taohua* 陶化—that is, transformed as clay is transformed into ceramic by being fired in a kiln.

9.9

The balance beam, in regard to left and right, is unbiased in its weighing, and thus it can be level.
The marking cord, in regard to inside and outside, is unbiased about the crooked and the straight, and thus it can be true.
The ruler, in regard to law, is unbiased in his likes and dislikes, and thus he can promulgate commands.
The steelyard, in weighing the light and the heavy, is not off by [even the weight of] the head of a mosquito.
The stretched string, in straightening the crooked, makes no mistake [even as small as] the tip of a needle.

The ruler, in rectifying the deviant, is without personal bias.
Wickedness cannot distort him;
slander cannot disorder him.
When
Potency has no place to stand,
and hatred is not stored away,
this is to employ the techniques of rulership and dispense with the human mind. Therefore the wisdom of the one who rules does not enter into it. [9/69/17–20]

9.10

Now,
for boats to float on water
and carts to go on land
is their natural propensity. If
a carriage hits a tree and breaks an axle,
or if a boat runs aground and shatters the hull,
there is no reason for people to bear resentment against the tree or the rock; they will blame the lack of skill [of the carriage driver or the boatman]. They know that [trees and stones] possess no [conscious qualities]. Thus
when the Way includes wisdom, there is confusion;
when Potency includes the mind, there is danger;
when the mind includes the eyes, there is bedazzlement.
No weapon is more powerful than awareness and the will. Even the great sword Moye is inferior to them.[25]
No brigand is as strong as yin and yang. The drumsticks and drums [signaling attack] are inferior to them.

25. The precious sword Moye, mentioned several times in the *Huainanzi*, took its name from Mo Ye 莫耶, wife of the legendary swordsmith Gan Jiang 干將 and herself a superlatively skilled smith. See 19.4. See also Olivia Milburn, "The Weapons of Kings: A New Perspective on Southern Sword Legends in Early China," *Journal of the American Oriental Society* 128 (2009): 427.

Now the weight and the balance beam, the compass and the square, once fixed do not change.

Their calibrations are not altered for the sake of Qin or Chu;
their form does not change for the Hu or the Yue [tribes].

Constant and unswerving, going straight and not meandering, taking form in a single day and passed down for ten thousand generations, they act through non-action. Thus,

states have rulers who perish, but no era can see the destruction of the Way.
People have distress and poverty, but principles never fail to be passed on.

From this standpoint, non-action is the Ancestor of the Way. Attaining the Ancestor of the Way, one responds to things without limit. When one relies [merely] on human talents, the highest kind of statecraft is difficult. [9/69/22–27]

9.11

[King] Tang [of Shang] and [King] Wu [of Zhou] were sage-rulers but could not equal the people of Yue in managing small craft and staying afloat on rivers and lakes.[26]

Yi Yin was a worthy prime minister, but he could not equal the Hu people in mounting fine steeds or taming wild northern horses.

Confucius and Mozi were erudite but could not equal the mountain-dwelling people in navigating dense undergrowth or traversing dangerous passes.

From this perspective, human knowledge, in relation to things, is shallow. Desiring to illuminate all within the seas and preserve the ten thousand places, if the ruler does not accord with the norms of the Patterns of the Way but relies on his own ability instead, then he will not reach his goal. Thus wisdom is not sufficient to rule the world. [The tyrant] Jie's strength could

break an ox's horn, straighten an iron hook,
twist [strands of] iron together, and fuse metals.

[His men] Qin Yi and Da Xi[27]

in the water could kill the giant *yüan*-turtle and the crocodile
and, on land, could catch the [common] bear and the brown bear.[28]

Nevertheless, Tang, with only three hundred armored chariots, surrounded [Jie's forces] at Mingtiao and captured them at the [Nan]Jiao Gate. From this perspective,

strength[29] is not sufficient to control the world;
wisdom is not sufficient to rule;
bravery is not sufficient to be strong.

26. A similar point is made in 19.5.

27. Qin Yi is the same as 推 哆 in the *Mozi*; Da Xi is not mentioned in extant literature.

28. The brown bear, *pi* 羆 (*Ursus arcticus*), is a large northern Eurasian bear similar to the North American grizzly bear.

29. The text reads *yong li* 勇力. Wang Niansun argues strongly for deleting *li* and retaining *yong*. We feel that, on the contrary, *yong* should be dropped here, as it duplicates the *yong* two lines later.

Thus, that human talents are not enough to do the job is obvious. A ruler of men need not descend from his palace halls to know about matters beyond the Four Seas because

he avails himself of things to know about things;
he avails himself of people to know about people.
Where collective strength is employed, it is always victorious;
where collective wisdom is employed, it is always successful.
A tube well does not house giant turtles or crocodiles; it is too narrow.
An ordinary courtyard does not contain giant trees; it is too small.[30]

Now when it comes to lifting a heavy *ding* vessel, [a person] with meager strength will not be able to do it. As to picking it up and transporting it, one need not wait for someone who is stronger.[31] Thus a village of a thousand people has no broken rafters, and a population of ten thousand has no project they cannot carry out. [9/70/1–11]

9.12

Now [the horses] Hualiu and Lü'er[32] could go a thousand *li* in a day, but if we made them chase a rabbit, they would not be comparable to a wolf or a dog. [This is because] their skills and abilities have limits.

An owl at night can grab a flea or a mosquito and can distinguish the tip of an autumn hair, but in daylight the focus of its eyes cannot discern hills and mountains. Its form and nature are at odds with each other.

Now,

the *teng* snake floats in the fog and soars;
the *ying* dragon rides on the clouds and ascends.
When an ape gets in a tree, it jumps with agility;
when a fish gets in water, it swims quickly.

Thus in ancient times when they made a carriage,

the one who painted its surface did not draw designs on it,
and the one who drilled holes did not carve designs.
Workers did not have two different skills;
scholars did not hold two positions;
each stuck to his profession
and did not interfere with others.
Each person obtained what was suitable to him;
each thing obtained what gave it security.

Hence,

tools and utensils were not cumbersome;
duties and tasks were not despised.

---

30. A similar statement appears in 2.10.

31. That is, several people can join together in accomplishing that task. See also 9.16.

32. Hualiu 華騮 and Lü'er 綠耳 were two of the legendary "eight thoroughbreds" that formed the chariot team of King Mu of Zhou, described in the *Mu tianzi zhuan*.

When debts are small, they are easy to repay;
when duties are few, they are easy to sustain;
when responsibilities are light, they are easy to fulfill.
When those above reduce the workload,
those below find it easy to do it successfully.

In this way, the ruler and his ministers work closely together for a long time without imposing on each other. [9/70/13–18]

9.13

The Way of [one who] governs people is like [that of] the corpse impersonator in [the sacrificial rite of] the *ling* star.[33] Austere, mysterious, and silent, he auspiciously and happily receives the blessing. He who has attained the Way does not try to embellish what is ugly or make good what is false. He is like a cloak that if worn by one person is not too large and if by ten thousand is not too small.

If the ruler
gravely implements generosity
and gravely implements severity,
then the Way of ruling will come through.

"Generosity" means to emphasize the awarding of largesse. When those without merit are richly rewarded and those who do not work hard receive high rank, those attending to their duties will grow lax, and those who roam about [seeking official position] will press to advance their situations.

"Severity" means to punish recklessly. When those who are innocent are put to death and those who act honestly are punished, then those who cultivate their persons will not encourage goodness, and the wicked will look lightly on defying their superiors. Thus acting generously gives birth to licentiousness, and acting severely gives birth to disorder.

Customs of licentiousness and disorder
are habits of a perishing state. [9/70/20–25]

Thus in the governance of an enlightened ruler,
when the state implements punishments, there is no place for the ruler's anger.
When the court bestows rewards, there is no place for the ruler's involvement.
One who is punished does not resent the ruler, for the punishment suits the offense.
One who is rewarded does not feel gratitude toward the ruler, for the reward has been earned by merit.

In such a state the people understand that rewards and punishments all come from themselves. Thus they perform their duties and serve their callings, not feeling that they should receive special tribute from their ruler. Thus

33. *Ling* 零 here is probably used as an alternative form of *ling* 靈, "numinous." The corpse impersonator (*shi* 尸) represented the soul of a dead person in certain sacrificial rituals.

the court is full of weeds and devoid of footprints;
farmers' fields are well tilled and devoid of weeds.
"Of a great ruler,
those below know only that he exists."[34] [9/70/27–9/71/1]

9.14

The axle tree of a swape is planted upright and does not move, [but] in tipping up and down, [the balance arm] is constrained by it.
The ruler is tranquil and calm and does not become agitated, [but] the hundred officials obtain their compliance from him.

It is like the soldier who carries the battle flag: if he points it the wrong way, there will be disorder.

Cleverness does not suffice to bring great peace;
wisdom does not suffice to dispel danger.

Praising Yao and disparaging Jie is not as good as casting aside intelligence and cultivating the Way.

If [the ruler is] pure, tranquil, and non-active,[35] Heaven will provide the seasons for him.
If [the ruler is] honest, frugal, and keeps to moderation, Earth will yield its wealth for him.

If [he] empties out his intelligence yet accords with Potency, the sage will make a course of action for himself.

Thus,

to the [one who is] low, the myriad things revert;
to the [one who is] empty, the world gives what it has. [9/71/1–5]

In this way,[36] the ruler begins by displaying his propriety, establishing it as the foundation. Thus using the natural propensity of the people as his carriage and the wisdom of the people as his horse, though [traversing] dark wastelands and perilous defiles, still no confusion can arise.

Because the ruler dwells in a deeply secluded place, avoiding scorching heat and damp cold [and because] he makes layers of doors to separate the gate from his inner rooms, he is prepared against evil men and deceivers.

Inside [his state], he knows nothing of the situation in village houses or gates;
outside it, he knows nothing of the forms of mountains and marshes.

Even outside the curtains,

34. *Laozi* 17.

35. The phrase *qing jing wuwei*, describing the attributes of the ideal ruler, occurs often in the Mawangdui Huang-Lao silk manuscripts.

36. The thirty-six characters preceding this sentence in the text are repeated almost verbatim at the beginning of 9.16. They were mistakenly duplicated here at some unknown time in the past, and we have deleted them in this translation as an inappropriate interpolation.

the eye cannot see beyond ten *li*,
and the ear cannot hear more than a hundred paces away.

Nevertheless, there is nothing in the world that [the ruler] does not perceive, [because] his sources of information are rich and those who draw from him are many. Thus,

without going out his door, he knows the world,
and without glancing out his window, he knows the Way of Heaven.[37]
If he relies on the wisdom of the people, the whole world will not suffice to contain it;
if he relies on his own mind alone, he will not be able to protect even himself. [9/71/7–13]

Thus the ruler covers [the world] with his Potency. He does not act on [the basis of] his own wisdom but follows what will bring benefit to the myriad [common] people. Just raising his heel is enough to bring benefit to the people. Hence,

though he places himself on top of the people, they do not find him heavy;[38]
though he situates himself in front of the people, they do not find him injurious.
Though they elevate him, they do not feel he is too lofty;
though they support him, they do not tire of him. [9/71/15–17]

9.15

The Way of the ruler is round, revolving and turning endlessly, transforming and sustaining, like a spirit, vacant, gliding without apparent purpose, always at the rear and never taking the lead.

The way of the official is square, discussing practicalities and being in the right place. In accomplishing tasks, he is the first to take the lead. Guarding his store of knowledge and parceling out his insight, he thereby establishes his success.

Therefore,

when the ruler and [his] officials follow different Ways, there is order.
[When they follow] identical Ways, there is disorder.

When each obtains what is appropriate to him and situates himself in his proper place, above and below can work with each other.[39] [9/71/17–20]

9.16

In listening to affairs of government the ruler is

empty of mind and soft of will;
clear, bright, and unclouded.

37. *Laozi* 47.
38. *Laozi* 61.
39. This section closely parallels LSCQ 3, section 5. See Knoblock and Riegel 2000, 109–13.

Thus the many officials work with him like the spokes of a wheel and advance in unison. Whether foolish or wise, worthy or unsatisfactory, none fails to use his abilities to the fullest extent. In this way, the ruler obtains the means to control his ministers, and they obtain the means to serve their ruler, so the Way of ruling the state is clear.

King Wen [of Zhou] was wise. He [also] was fond of soliciting opinions. Thus he was a sage.
King Wu was brave. He [also] was fond of soliciting opinions. Thus he was victorious.
If one uses the knowledge of many people, there is nothing that cannot be undertaken.
If one employs the strength of many people, there is nothing that cannot be overcome.

Even Wu Huo[40] could not lift the weight of a thousand *jun*,[41] but if many people work together as one, then a hundred men would have more than enough strength [to lift it]. Thus,

if [the ruler] relies on the strength of just one man, then even that of Wu Huo would not be enough;
if he relies on the knowledge of many people, then the world will not suffice to contain it.[42] [9/71/22–26]

9.17

Yu diverted the Yangzi and cleared the Yellow River in order to bring great benefit to the world, but he could not get the water to flow westward.
Lord Millet extended arable land and reclaimed grasslands so the people could devote their strength to agriculture, but he could not get grain to grow in winter.

Is it that the efforts of these men were inadequate? [No,] the natural propensity [of water and grain] made it impossible. Now to advance a project that the natural propensity [of things] makes impossible, rather than to comply with the norms of the Patterns of the Way— this is something that [even] a sage, however spiritlike, could not accomplish. How much more so would this be the case with any contemporary ruler!

Now,

if the load in the cart is heavy and the horses are weak, even Zaofu could not get them to go very far.
If the cart is light and the horses fine, even a middling workman could get it to go fast.

40. Wu Huo 烏獲 was a strongman of Qin who served King Wu (r. 310–307 B.C.E.).
41. A *jun* 鈞 equals thirty catties (*jin* 觔 or 斤), thus roughly sixteen pounds.
42. Compare 9.15.

Thus how can even sages, in carrying out affairs, oppose the norms of the Patterns of the Way or go against the constraints of nature, making

the crooked straight
and the bumpy smooth?

[The sage] never fails to use things according to their natural qualities.

Therefore,

if you combine the strength [of many] to lift something, there is nothing in which you cannot succeed.

If you collect the wisdom of many, there is nothing you cannot accomplish.

You can make a deaf person chew sinews [to soften them], but you cannot make him hear.

You can make a mute tend the stables, but you cannot make him talk.

Physical forms [may] have what is incomplete;
abilities may have aspects that are limited.

Thus a particular form belongs in a particular place, and a particular ability addresses a particular task.

If one's strength surpasses his burden, lifting it will not be heavy;
if one's ability is appropriate to the task, accomplishing it will not be difficult.

When each matter—small or large, long or short—obtains what is appropriate to it, the world will be as one, and no one will have the means to surpass another. The sage makes use of people's various capacities; thus no talent is wasted. [9/72/1–10]

9.18

The ruler of men values uprightness and esteems loyalty. When the loyal and the upright are in high positions and affairs are dealt with by cleaving to rectitude, flattering deceivers and wicked villains will have no place to advance. It can be compared to the way [that]

the square and the circular cannot cover each other,
and the crooked and the straight cannot fit inside each other.

That birds and beasts do not gather in the same place is because they belong to different species.

That tigers and deer do not travel together is because their strength is unequal.

Thus when a sage accomplishes his will and ascends the throne, the flattering deceivers and depraved villains who wish to oppose him become like

a sparrow catching sight of a hawk
or a rat encountering a fox.

There certainly will not be much more life for them!

Therefore, the ruler of men in every matter cannot fail to be careful. When those whom he employs are appropriate, then

above, the country will be orderly;
below, it will be harmonious.

The officials will feel close to the ruler;
the masses of the people will submit.
When those employed are not appropriate, then
the country will be in danger;
superior and inferior will disagree;
officials will be resentful;
and the people will be disorderly.

Thus if a matter is dealt with wrongly, to the end of his life the ruler will suffer. In gaining or losing the Way, the power must lie with the ruler. Thus,

if the [line of the] marking cord is straight above,
the board will be straight below.

There is no great affair involved. It is just a matter of following what has been laid out, and it will be so. [9/72/12–18]

Thus,

when the ruler is sincere and upright, honest officials will carry out their duties, and wicked men will go into hiding.
When the ruler is not upright, evil men will achieve their goal, and loyal ones will hide themselves.

Why is it that people do not break open jade and stones but do break open melons and gourds? It is because there is nothing to be gained [by cutting open] jade and stones, so we do not assault them. If the ruler holds fast to rectitude and exercises fairness, it will be [as easy as] using the marking cord and the level [to mark a line] from high to low. [Even] if officials bring in wicked practices, they will [have as little effect as]

eggs thrown against stones
or fire tossed into water.

Thus,

King Ling of Chu[43] admired narrow waists, and the people cut down on their food and starved themselves.
King Goujian [of Yue][44] loved bravery, and people all put themselves in danger and vied at risking death.

From this perspective, [he who wields] the handles of power and positional advantage finds it easy to modify habits and change customs.

When Yao was [only] a commoner, he could not transform people through Humaneness even for an area of [only] a *li*.
When Jie ascended the throne, his commands were carried out, and what he forbade stopped.

---

43. King Ling of Chu 楚靈王 (r. 540–529 B.C.E.) was a powerful ruler who expanded Chu's territory through conquest. His throne was usurped by his younger brother, and he died ignominiously in exile.

44. King Goujian of Yue 越王句踐 (r. 496–465 B.C.E.) was a powerful ruler and colorful character of the late Spring and Autumn period whose story figures in many texts. He was initially humbled in defeat and forced to serve as the personal servant of King Fuchai of Wu. Later he rose to destroy Wu and become hegemon of the Zhou realm.

From this perspective, it is clear that worthiness is not sufficient to create order, but positional advantage can change customs. The *Documents* says, "When the One Man [i.e., the ruler] encounters good fortune, the myriad people depend on it."[45] This is what is meant here. [9/72/20–25]

9.19

In the world, many are confused by name and fame, and few investigate the real situation. Therefore

hermits are venerated for their reputations;
roving debaters are noted because of their persuasiveness.

If we look into the reasons why they are venerated and noted, we will find it is due to nothing other than the fact that the ruler does not distinguish clearly between the grounds of benefit and harm and esteems the disputations of great masses of people. A well-governed country is not like this.

Those who discuss policy must be looked into [in accordance with] the law;
those who carry out official matters must be regulated by bureaucrats.
Superiors uphold [official] titles and use them to evaluate actual performance;
officials take care of their duties and carry out their work efficiently.
Words are not permitted to exceed reality;
actions are not permitted to overstep the law.

The numerous officials come together like the spokes of a wheel, with no one daring to usurp the prerogatives of the ruler. If a matter does not lie within the scope of the law but can benefit the state or support its administration, then one must carry out [procedures of] threes and fives to make a covert investigation, in order to discern its outcome [for the ruler].[46] [He] must also use [the technique of] listening on all sides to investigate its transformations, not leaning toward one viewpoint or favoring one side. Thus he stands at the center yet is omnipresent, spreading his light to all within the Four Seas, while the numerous officials are impartial and upright, none daring to do anything wicked. The hundred officeholders transmit [the details of] their duties and strive to leave behind a meritorious legacy. When

the ruler is the essence of enlightenment above,
the officials exhort [one another] to work hard below.
The traces of wickedness are [thus] extinguished,
and many successes follow day after day.

This is why brave men will give their utmost to the armed forces.

In a disordered country, it is not thus.

---

45. *Shang Shu* 47/0476. See Qu Wanli, *Shang Shu jinchu jinyi* (Taipei: Commercial Press, 1970), 180. This line is also quoted in 10.60.

46. We follow Lau (HNZ, 73n.1) in emending this line to read *bi xing canwu yi yin kao zhi* 必行參五以陰考之. *Canwu* refers to a procedure for analyzing problems; "threes," to the triad of Heaven, Earth, and Man; and "fives," to the Five Phases. See also 20.11 and 21.2; and Ames 1994, 247–48n.129.

Those who are praised by the multitudes are richly rewarded though devoid of accomplishments.
Those who stick to their duties are punished though free of guilt.
The ruler above is in the dark and does not understand.
Officials form factions and are disloyal.
Persuasive talkers roam about engaging in debates.
People who embellish their actions compete for offices.

When the ruler above issues a law, [such officials] denounce it according to [their respective factions]. What the law prohibits, they transgress in their wickedness.

Those who are taken to be wise devote themselves to artifice and deceit;
those who are taken to be brave devote themselves to contention and struggle.
High officials usurp authority;
low functionaries seize positional advantage.

Cliques and factions become widespread and toy with their superiors. Although the state seems to [still] exist, people of antiquity would have said, "It has [already] fallen."

Moreover,

not to regulate official functions,
not to take up shield and armor,
not to cultivate the southern fields,

yet still to enjoy fame as a worthy or a sage—that is not the way to promulgate one's teachings in a state.

Qiji and Lü'er were the fastest horses in the world, but if [charioteers] had goaded them and they did not go, reined them in and they did not stop, then not even fools would have driven them. Now at the crux of chaos and order,[47] there are signs that can be observed, yet none of the rulers of our age can discern them. Their way of governing is obstructed. [9/72/27–9/73/10]

Expediency and positional advantage are the ruler's carriage.[48]
Rank and emolument are the officials' harness and bit.

Thus the ruler

institutes central control of expediency and positional advantage,
wields the handles of rank and emoluments,
surveys carefully the regulation of slowness and speed,
and apportions what is given and taken.

Thus all the world works hard but is not tired. Now the relationship between official and ruler

47. *Zhi luan zhi ji* 治亂之機. This phrase recurs in 9.22 (9/74/27–28), as well as in 13.12. It seems to refer to the concept of a "tipping point" at which order and chaos hang in the balance.

48. *Quan* 權 in the sense of "expediency" refers to a policy or course of action that, *on balance*, is preferable to other available choices. Compare *Mozi* 44 (MoZ 11.1/192/17): "[Selecting] from among concrete [choices] by weighing them is called expediency." The term *quan* in this sense occurs frequently in the later chapters of the *Huainanzi*, notably in chap. 13. See chap. 13 also for *quan* as "balance" or "moral equilibrium," and chap. 15 for *quan* as "heft."

is not as close as [that] between father and son
or as intimate as that between bones and flesh [i.e., blood relations].
Nevertheless [the official] will use all his strength and even risk his life and will not reject his ruler's control. Why? It is [the ruler's] use of positional advantage that makes [the official] behave like this. [9/73/12–14]

9.20

Formerly Yu Rang[49] was an official of Viscount Wen of Zhonghang[50] when Earl Zhi[51] attacked the Zhonghang clan and annexed its territory. Yu Rang turned against his ruler and served as an official for Earl Zhi. Earl Zhi and Viscount Xiang of Zhao[52] fought near Jinyang. Earl Zhi was killed, and his country was divided into three. Yu Rang, hoping to get revenge against Viscount Xiang of Zhao, lacquered his body to raise leprous [sores], swallowed ashes to disguise his voice, and pulled out his teeth to change his looks. Can it be that with the heart of one man, he served two masters? In one case he turned against his master and left him, while in another case he sacrificed his life to follow him. Can it be that the positional advantage of following one master and abandoning the other was different? [No,] the kindness and grace with which he was treated was what made it so.

When [the tyrant] Djou ruled the world, he assembled the Lords of the Land. [Everywhere]
people used their feet to arrive
and plied their oars to come through.
No one failed to submit to him. Nevertheless, King Wu, with only three thousand armored warriors, captured him at Muye. Can it be [simply] that the Zhou people were willing to die and the Yin [Shang] were rebellious? [No,] because [King Wu]'s Moral Potency and Rightness were abundant, his commands were carried out.

Now,
when the wind is strong, the waves rise;
when trees flourish, birds gather.
Each engenders *qi* in the other.

---

49. Yu Rang 豫讓 was a famous knight of Jin whose legend is recounted in many texts as an ideal of devoted service and indomitable resolve. His biography is recorded in *Shiji* 86.

50. Viscount Wen of Zhonghang 中行文子 (also known as Xun Yin 荀寅) was the leader of the Zhonghang clan, one of the six great ministerial clans of Jin. He was driven into exile, at which point his clan's holdings were divided among the other vassals of Jin.

51. Earl Zhi 知伯 (also known as Earl Yao 瑤 of Zhi [d. 453 B.C.E.]) was a colorful figure whose tale is recounted in many texts as an example of overreaching ambition. As leader of the Zhi clan, he seemed poised to bring all the vassal clans of Jin under his sway, until his overbearing belligerence drove the Hann, Wei, and Zhao clans to unite to destroy him.

52. Viscount Xiang of Zhao 趙襄子 (d. 425 B.C.E.) was the leader of the Zhao clan who orchestrated the alliance that brought down Earl Zhi and led ultimately to the partition of the state of Jin into the three independent kingdoms of Hann, Wei, and Zhao.

Thus,

if the official does not get what he wants from the ruler,

the ruler also cannot get what he wants from the official.

What transpires between rulers and officials is due to the positional advantage of reciprocal obligations. Thus if the official gives all his efforts and is willing to risk his life for his ruler, the ruler will measure the official's accomplishments and issue ranks on that basis. Thus,

the ruler cannot reward an official who has no accomplishments;

an official also will not die for a ruler who lacks Moral Potency.

If the ruler's Moral Potency does not flow down to the people but he still desires to make use of them, it is like beating a wild horse or like not waiting for the rain yet seeking the ripe grain: methods that are surely impossible. [9/73/16–24]

9.21

The Way of the ruler is

to abide in tranquillity and thereby to cultivate the self;

to practice economy and thereby lead those below.

If he is tranquil, those below will not be disturbed.

If he is frugal, the people will not be resentful.

When those below are disturbed, government is disordered.

When the people are resentful, [the ruler's] Moral Potency is wanting.

When government is disordered, worthies will not offer proposals.

When [the ruler's] Moral Potency is wanting, brave men will not die for him.

Thus if the ruler

is fond of fierce birds and wild animals,

precious curiosities and exotic things,

is violent and excitable,

does not cherish the people's strength,

goes riding and hunting at inappropriate times,

then

the responsibilities of the hundred officials will be disordered;

their affairs will be labored, and their resources will be exhausted.

The populace will grow miserable and sorrowful;

their means of livelihood will be neglected.

If the ruler is fond of

high terraces and deep pools,

carved, polished, engraved, and figured [gemstones],

finely embroidered and artfully ornamented [designs],

fine and thick silks and linens,

precious baubles of pearl and jade,

then taxes will be unrestrained, and the people's strength will be exhausted.

When Yao governed the world, he did not covet the wealth of the people, nor did he rest secure in the position of ruler. Perceiving that the people expended their strength in struggle, [so that]

the strong mistreated the weak, and
the many oppressed the few,

therefore Yao practiced personal economy in his actions and made clear the humaneness of mutual love so as to harmonize and pacify [the people]. Therefore

the thatching [on his house] was not trimmed;
the beams and pillars were not carved.
His state carriage was not decorated;
his floor mats were not hemmed.
His sacrificial broth was not seasoned;
his grain was not hulled.
He made tours of inspection and taught by example;
he labored hard for [the sake of] the world;

[his influence] spread throughout the Five Peaks.

Could it be that the support he received was not sufficient for his enjoyment? He treated the whole world as his altar of grain [i.e., as his state] but did not seek personal gain from it. When he became old and his will grew weary, he abdicated in favor of Shun, as if stepping back to kick off his sandals.[53]

It follows that an age in decline is not like this. Upon gaining the wealth of the world and the positional advantage of rulership, [the ruler] exhausts the strength of the people just to satisfy the desires of his eyes and ears. His will is preoccupied with

palaces, pavilions, ponds and gardens,
wild animals, [common] bears and brown bears,
amusing himself with fine objects and judging the merits of rarities.

Thus,

the impoverished people do not have even the dregs of grain from the brewery to eat,
yet tigers, wolves, [common] bears and brown bears gorge themselves on fodder and meat.
The people wear short garments of the coarsest cloth that do not even completely cover them,
while those in the palaces wear brocade and embroidered gowns.
The ruler is eager to carry out projects that are of no use,
while the people look haggard and worn.

All this makes [the people of] the world disquieted in their natures. [9/73/26–9/74/10]

---

53. That is, his giving up the throne was no more difficult for him than discarding a pair of worn-out sandals.

9.22

The ruler of men, [by virtue of] his position, is like the sun and moon in their brightness. The people of the world, as one,

strain their eyes to look at him,
strain their ears to hear him,

crane their necks, and stand on tiptoe to gaze at him. For this reason,

unless he is calm and indifferent, he will not be able to shine forth his Moral Potency.
Unless he is still and tranquil, he will not be able to extend [his rule] to distant places.
Unless he is lenient and great [hearted], he will not be able to bind together and cover [the realm].
Unless he is kind and generous, he will not be able to embrace the people.
Unless he is fair and upright, he will not be able to render judgments. [9/74/12–14]

Thus the worthy ruler's employment of others is like a skillful artisan's management of wood.

Large pieces are used for boats and barges or pillars and rafters;
small ones are used for tholes and pegs.
Long pieces are used for eaves and rafters;
short pieces for red [-lacquered] brackets and capitals.

Whether small or large, long or short, each has something for which it is appropriate. The compass and the square [shape them] square or round; each has something for which it is suitable. They have different shapes and varying qualities, but there is nothing that does not find its [proper] use. Of all things in the world, none is more poisonous than the *xitu* plant,[54] but an accomplished doctor puts it in his bag and keeps a supply of it, for it is useful in some treatments. Thus, if among the products of the forests and the thickets, there are none that may be ignored, how much more so is this the case with people?

Now [it may be] that someone is not promoted at court and his fame is not celebrated in country songs, not because the person is unsatisfactory, but because the office he holds is not appropriate to his true abilities. When a deer ascends a mountain, a roebuck cannot follow. Yet when [the deer] descends again, [even] a shepherd boy can chase it. Natural talents have long suits and shortcomings. For this reason,

someone with a talent for grand schemes cannot be entrusted with [a task requiring] nimbleness and cunning.
Someone with petty wisdom cannot be given responsibility for a great project.
People have abilities;
material things have shapes.

54. *Xitu* 奚毒, also identified as *wutou* 烏頭, or *Aconitum*, is a genus of plants that includes wolfsbane.

For some, taking responsibility for one thing is too burdensome;
for others, taking responsibility for a hundred things seems light.

Thus,

one who can calculate things in minute detail would be lost [dealing with] large numbers on the scale of Heaven and Earth;
someone who never misses in small calculations would become confused when dealing with grand affairs.

Likewise,

a fox cannot be used to attack an ox;
tigers cannot be used to catch rats.

People's talents are such that some wish to

pacify the nine provinces,
unite the lands beyond,
preserve an endangered state,
or revive an extinguished [royal] line.

Their will is set on

straightening the Way and rectifying evil,
resolving difficulties and ordering the disorderly.

Yet they are charged with the minutiae of court ceremonies.

Others are

adept and clever, petty and backbiting.
[They] advance through flattery, rely on persuasion,
follow the vulgar customs of country lanes,
and defile themselves before the ears and eyes of the masses.

Yet they are entrusted with authority over the world, at the crux of order and disorder. This is like

using an ax to split a hair
or a knife to cut down a tree.[55]

In each case it is inappropriate. [9/74/16–28]

The ruler of men uses

the eyes of the world to see,
the ears of the world to hear,
the wisdom of the world to make plans,
and the strength of the world to contend.

Thus his orders and commands are able to penetrate to those below, and the true feelings of the ministers are known by [the ruler] above.

The hundred offices are regulated and efficient;
the numerous officials work together like spokes [at the hub of a wheel].
The personal pleasure [of the ruler] does not determine the granting of rewards;
[his] personal anger does not determine the meting out of punishments.

Thus,

his awesome dignity will be established and not be destroyed;

55. The same image is used in 16.126.

his comprehensive illumination will shine and not be obscured;
his laws and commands will be clear and precise and will not be [considered] harsh;
his ears and eyes will penetrate everywhere and will not be blocked.

The dispositions of good and bad will be laid out before him daily, and there will be nothing to which he is opposed.

Thus worthies will use their wisdom to the utmost, and the untalented will use all their strength [to serve him]. His Moral Potency and grace will cover the world impartially; the many officials will work hard to fulfill their duties and will not be indolent.

The near at hand will find security in [the ruler's] nature;
the far-off will respond to his Moral Potency.

Why is this so? [It is because the ruler] has attained the Way of making use of people and does not rely merely on his own qualities. Thus,

those who travel with chariots and horses do not wear out their legs but can go more than a thousand *li*.
Those who rely on boats and oars need not [know how to] swim but can cross the rivers and seas. [9/75/1–6]

Now, [of those who have] the feelings of a ruler of men, there is none who does not want to gather unto himself all the wisdom in the world and use to the fullest extent the strength of the masses. Yet making known their intentions to act with exemplary loyalty, the numerous officials rarely escape putting themselves in danger. If someone offers a proposal and it is correct, even if it is from a brushwood gatherer in coarse clothing, it should not be rejected. If someone offers a proposal and it is incorrect, even if it comes from the chief minister or the ruler himself and is extolled in writing in the ancestral hall, it should not necessarily be implemented. When deciding where truth or falsity lies, wealth and poverty, honors or meanness, may not be discussed. When an enlightened ruler listens to his ministers,

if their proposals are such as can be used, he will not feel ashamed of the [low] rank [of the proposer].
If their words are such as can be put into action, he will not criticize their rhetorical style.

A benighted ruler is not like this.

Even if his favorites and intimates are wicked and dishonest, he will not be capable of seeing it.
Even if those far away from him and in low positions exert all their strength and show the utmost loyalty, he will not be capable of knowing it.
Those who speak forthrightly are beaten down by [the ruler's] own words.
Those who [loyally] admonish are punished as if guilty of crimes.

[A ruler who] acts in this way yet still wants to shine his light throughout the world and preserve the myriad districts [of the realm] is like someone who

blocks his ears and tries to distinguish high from low [tones]
or who covers his eyes and tries to distinguish between blue and yellow.

That is a long way from enjoying sharp hearing and keen eyesight! [9/75/8–14]

9.23

Law is the standard of measurement for the world, the level and the marking cord of the ruler.

[He who] proclaims the laws does so to [impose] law on the lawless;
[he who] sets up rewards does so to reward those who deserve rewards.

After the laws are set,

those who obey the laws are rewarded,
and those who fall short of the marking cord['s line] are punished.
For the honorable and noble, the punishments are not decreased,
and for the lowly and base, the punishments are not increased.
If someone disobeys the law, even if he is [otherwise] worthy, he must be punished.
If someone meets the standard, even if he is [otherwise] unworthy, he must be found innocent.

Thus the Way of the public good will be opened up, and that of private interest will be blocked.

In ancient times,

a system of responsible officials was established so as to restrain the people and thus prevent them from doing just as they pleased.
The position of ruler was set up to control the officials so that they could not carry out [policy] on their own.

Laws, records, propriety, and Rightness were used to restrain the ruler so that he could not exercise absolute authority.

When none of the people could blindly follow their own desires, the Way was triumphant.
When the Way was triumphant, Patterns were apparent.

Thus government returned to non-action. Non-action does not mean [that the ruler] froze and was inert but that nothing any longer emanated from the ruler personally. [9/75/16–21]

Now the inch comes from the millet grain; the millet grain comes from physical forms. Physical forms come from shadows; shadows come from the sun. This is the root of standards of measurement.[56]

Music comes from the [pentatonic] notes; the notes come from the pitch-pipe tones; and the pitch-pipe tones come from the wind. This is the ancestry of sound.[57]

Law comes from Rightness. Rightness comes from what is appropriate for the people. What is appropriate for the people accords with the human heart. This is the *sine qua non* of government.

56. Compare 3.31.

57. Compare LSCQ 6.2/29/8: "In the age of the great sages, when great wisdom ruled the world, the *qi* of Heaven and Earth joined together and produced the wind. When the sun had reached its utmost point the moon gave the wind a sound and this gave birth to the twelve tones of the pitch pipe" (Knoblock and Riegel 2000, 157).

Thus,

those who penetrate to the root are not confused about the branches.

Those who see the fundamental are not confused about the details.

Law is

not a gift of Heaven,

not a product of Earth.

It was devised by humankind but conversely is used [by humans] to rectify themselves. Thus,

what you have in yourself you must not criticize in others;

what you lack in yourself you must not seek in others;

what is established for inferiors must not be disregarded by superiors;

what is prohibited to the people must not be practiced by [the ruler] himself.

A country that can be said to be lost is not one without a ruler but one without laws.

To twist[58] the law does not mean to have no laws [at all] but, rather, that the laws are not employed. That is equivalent to not having laws. Thus when the ruler first establishes laws, he begins by making himself an example and a standard; thus the laws are implemented in the world. Confucius said,

"If the ruler himself is upright, even though he does not issue orders, they are carried out;

if he is not upright, though he issue orders, they are not followed."[59]

Thus when the prohibitions apply to [even the ruler] himself, then his orders will be carried out among the people. [9/75/23–30]

9.24

The sage-ruler's [conduct of] government is like Zaofu's charioteering.[60] He smoothes the ride by controlling the reins and bit and regulates the speed by harmonizing with [the horse's] lips and breathing. Having the correct standard within his own breast, he exercises control with the whip in his hands.

Inwardly he draws on what is within his heart;

externally he accords with the horse's will.

Thus he is able

to advance and retreat in a line as straight as if laid out with a marking cord

and to turn circles as round as if drawn with a compass.

He selects a route that will take him far away and still has energy (*qi*) and strength left over. [He can do this] because he has sincerely mastered the [necessary] technique. Thus,

---

58. *Bian* 變 usually means "to vary" in a positive sense but here clearly is a pejorative term meaning "to twist" or "to pervert."

59. *Analects* 13.6.

60. A closely similar passage is in *Liezi*, chap. 5 (LieZ 5/32/13–16). See A. C. Graham, trans., *The Book of Lieh-tzŭ: A Classic of Tao* (New York: Columbia University Press, 1990), 114.

[the exercise of] authority and positional advantage is the ruler's chariot chassis,
and the high-ranking ministers are the ruler's team of horses.

For the body to leave the safety of the chariot chassis and the hands to lose their responsiveness to the team of horses' intentions and yet still be able to avoid danger is something that has never been accomplished from ancient times to the present.

Thus if the chariot and the horses are not coordinated, [even the master charioteer] Wang Liang would not be able to choose a route.
If the ruler and his ministers are not in harmony, even Tang and Yu [i.e., Yao and Shun] would not have the ability to govern.
If [the ruler] uses the [proper] technique to drive them, even the wisdom of Guan [Zhong][61] and Yan [Ying] would be employed to the fullest.
If [the ruler] illuminates distinctions to control them, even the wickedness of [men like] [Robber] Zhi[62] and [Zhuang] Qiao[63] could be stopped. [9/76/1–6]

If you lean over the railing and peer into the bottom of a well, even if you have superior eyesight, you could not see the reflection of your own eye's pupil. But if you look at your reflection in a mirror, you can see it in only a one-inch portion of the mirror. Thus an enlightened ruler's

eyes and ears are not worn out;
his essence and spirit are not exhausted.
When things come into view, he looks at their appearance;
When events transpire, he responds to their transformations.
When what is near at hand is not in disorder,
then what is far away will be ordered.

Thus,

he does not use haphazard methods
but carries out the unalterable Way.

Thus of his myriad undertakings, none fails to go according to plan. [9/76/8–11]

Now if the horses are matched to the chassis and the driver's heart is in harmony with the horses, a charioteer can travel perilous roads and go for long distances, advancing and retreating and turning circles, with nothing failing to accord with his will. [But if] even steeds as fine as Qiji and Lü'er were given to female bondservants to drive, they would revert to their own intractable ways, and the servants could not control them. Thus the ruler does not prize [people] being the way he wants them

61. Guan Zhong 管仲 (also known as Guanzi 管子, Guan Yiwu 夷吾, and Zhongfu 仲父 [d. 645 B.C.E.]) was perhaps the most famous statesman of early China. He served as prime minister under Duke Huan of Qi, increased the power of his ruler through basic reforms and policies, and invented the office of hegemon. Scholars agree that the well-known text bearing his name (*Guanzi*) was written and compiled long after his death.

62. Robber Zhi 盜跖 was a legendary bandit of great daring, cunning, and ferocity. His name is preserved in the title of chap. 29 of the *Zhuangzi* and is invoked in many early texts as an exemplar of rapine.

63. Zhuang Qiao 莊蹻 was a man of Chu who led a revolt during the reign of King Huai (r. 328–299 B.C.E.).

of their own accord but prizes there being no chance for them to go wrong. Thus it is said,

"Do not make it possible for people to have desires; then you need not tell them not to seek things.

Do not make it possible for people to grab things; then you need not tell them not to struggle."

In this way, [individual] talents are set aside and the Way of public service will be carried out. Those who have ample [talent] will be restrained by appropriate measures, while those whose [abilities] fall short will be used [for something]. Thus all within the seas can be made as one. [9/76/13–17]

Now if a ruler ignores [the relationship between] position and duties and listens to undeserved reputations, rejects those who work for the public good, and employs people according to friendship and factions, then those of bizarre talents and frivolous ability will be promoted out of turn, while conscientious officials will be hindered and will not advance. In this way, the customs of the people will fall into disorder throughout the state, and accomplished officials will [have to] struggle at court.

Thus laws, regulations, standards, and measures are the means by which the ruler controls his subordinates. If he ignores them and does not use them, it is like trying to drive a horse without reins and bit. The numerous officials and the common people [alike] manipulate the ruler instead. Thus,

with technique, one rules others;
without technique, one is ruled by them. [9/76/19–21]

9.25

If a fish [large enough to] swallow a boat leaps out of the water, it will be overcome by crickets and ants because it has left its dwelling place.

If an ape or a monkey leaves its tree, it will be caught by a fox or raccoon dog because it is out of [its proper] place.

If the ruler of men ignores what he should preserve and struggles with his ministers and subordinates about [the conduct of] affairs, then those with official posts will be preoccupied with holding on to their positions, and those charged with official duties will avoid dismissal by following the whims of the ruler. This will cause capable ministers to conceal their wisdom and not put it to use, and so their responsibilities will instead shift back to the ruler. [9/76/22–24]

Now what makes the wealthy and noble work hard, the adept at management examine things judiciously, and the proud and unruly be respectful is the fact that their positional advantage does not equal that of the ruler. If the ruler does not rely on capable people

but wants to do everything himself, then his wisdom will be taxed daily, and he will be burdened with responsibilities.

If the ruler is frequently exhausted by attending to lesser duties, he will not be able to make broadly known [the proper] patterns.
Proper conduct will deteriorate throughout the state, and he will no longer be able to exert exclusive control.
His knowledge by itself will be insufficient to govern,
and his majesty will be insufficient to impose punishments.

Thus he will lack what it takes to deal with the world.

If joy and anger form in [the ruler's] heart
and desires manifest themselves in his outward appearance,

those charged with official duties will abandon what is proper and pander to the ruler,
while those who hold office will distort the law and follow the prevailing wind.

Rewards will no longer match accomplishments;
punishments will no longer correspond to crimes.
The hearts of superiors and subordinates will part ways;
ruler and ministers will resent each other.

Thus, when those who hold the reins [of government] pander to their superiors and commit errors, there will be no way to hold them accountable. When those who commit crimes are not punished, the numerous officials will lapse into turmoil and disorder, and wisdom will not be able to resolve the situation. Baseless slander and unwarranted praise will sprout forth, and enlightenment will not be able to clarify the situation. If he does not rectify the root by returning to the natural, then the ruler will be taxed even more, and his ministers will become even less restrained. It would be like skinning an animal yourself instead of letting a master cook do it or [trying to] carve wood for a master carpenter. If a man were to race a horse on foot, even though he tore his tendons [in the effort], he would not catch up, but if he mounted a chariot and took the reins, the horse would be responsive to its bit. Thus if Bo Le selects the steeds and Wang Liang drives them, an enlightened ruler can ride without the trouble of selecting horses or driving and can undertake a journey of a thousand *li*. He is carried by the capabilities of others as if they were his feathers and wings. [9/76/26–9/77/5]

Thus the ruler of men practices non-action; he has a basis [for what he does] but is devoid of personal preferences. If he practiced action, slander would arise. If he had personal preferences, flattery would come forth.

In ancient times,

Duke Huan of Qi was fond of exotic flavors, so Yi Ya[64] boiled his eldest son to entice him.
The ruler of Yu was fond of treasures, so Jin used jade disks and fine horses to lure him.

64. Yi Ya 易牙 (also known as Yong Wu 雍巫) was a servitor of Duke Huan of Qi who gained great favor through his surpassing skill as a chef. When Guan Zhong was dying, he advised Duke Huan to banish Yi Ya, but the duke was too fond of his cooking to do so. Ultimately, Yi Ya joined in a rebellion against Duke Huan and starved him to death in his own palace.

The king of the Hu [tribes] loved music, so Duke Mu of Qin[65] used female musicians to seduce him.

In all these cases,[66] because some benefit was presented to them, they fell under the control of others. Thus,

"what is planted well cannot be uprooted";[67]
what is established by [mere] words has no physical form.

Now,

Fire is hot but water extinguishes it.
Metal is hard but fire melts it.
Wood is strong but axes cut it;
water flows but earth blocks it.

Only what fashions and transforms us cannot be overcome by things.

Thus,

not [letting inner] desires emerge is called "barring the door";
not letting external depravity enter is called "blocking the gate."
If what is inside is locked in
and what is outside is blocked out,

what matter would not be properly regulated?

If what is outside is blocked out
and what is inside is locked in,

what matter would not be successful?

Only if you do not use something [now] can you use it later;
only if you do not act [now] can you act later.
If the essence and spirit are overworked, they become dispersed;
if the ears and eyes are [employed] excessively, they become exhausted.

Thus a ruler who has the Way extinguishes planning and discards intent. Quiet and empty, he waits.

He does not speak for the officials;
he does not do their jobs.
According to their job titles, they are assigned responsibilities;
as their offices are employed, they discharge their duties.
[They have] responsibilities without [written] instructions,
duties without [formal] teaching;
he takes "I don't know" as the Way,
and "How is it done? as a treasure.

In this way, someone is responsible for each of the affairs [handled by] the numerous officials. [9/77/7–15]

65. Duke Mu of Qin (r. ca. 650–621 B.C.E.). See chap. 7, n. 61.
66. A similar passage appears in 7.16.
67. *Laozi* 54.

9.26

Holding on to the handles of authority and positional advantage makes it easy to transform the people.

That the ruler[68] of Wey took into service [Confucius's disciple] Zilu was because [the ruler's] authority was heavy.

That Dukes Jing[69] and Huan of Qi made ministers of Guan Zhong and Yan Ying was because [the rulers'] positions were exalted.

That [sometimes]

the timid can subdue the brave

and the unintelligent can control the wise

is because they can use positional advantage successfully. Now,

the limbs of a tree cannot be larger than its trunk,

the stem cannot be stronger than the root.

So it is said that light and heavy, large and small, have that by which they mutually control each other. It is like the way the five fingers are attached to the arm. They can grasp, extend, snatch, or grab, and none [happens] other than as we wish it. This is to say, the small are appendages of the large. Thus to have the benefit of positional advantage means that what you hold is very small but what you manage is very large; what you guard is very compact, but what you control is vast. Thus a tree trunk ten [hand]spans [in circumference] can support a roof weighing a thousand *jun*, and a key five inches long can control the opening and closing [of a door]. How can this small amount of material be sufficient for the task? The position they occupy is the important thing.

Confucius and Mo Di cultivated the techniques of the former sages and had a penetrating understanding of the theories of the six arts. Their utterances adhered to their doctrines, and their personal actions embodied their will. [Yet] those who, admiring their Rightness and following their influence, submitted to them and served them did not amount to more than a few tens of individuals. But if they had occupied the position of Son of Heaven, everyone in the world would have become Confucians or Mohists.

King Zhuang of Chu[70] was distressed because Wen Wuwei was killed in [the state of] Song.[71] He pushed up his sleeves in anger and arose [to invade Song]. [Officials] in robes and caps fell in with him at every stage along the road so that at last they

68. Duke Chu 出公 (r. 492–481 B.C.E.).

69. Duke Jing of Qi 齊景公 (r. 547–490 B.C.E.) was placed on the throne by the rebel Cui Zhu. He is reputed to have been a harsh and licentious ruler but to have improved somewhat under the edifying influence of Yan Ying.

70. King Zhuang of Chu 楚莊王 (r. 613–591 B.C.E.) initially had little interest in government, but through the remonstrance of loyal ministers, he became a competent and forceful leader and rose to be hegemon of the Zhou realm.

71. Wen Wuwei 文無畏 (also known as Shen Zhou 申舟), a Chu vassal, was sent on a diplomatic mission to Qi without asking the ruler of Song for free passage through his territory and was killed. See *Zuo zhuan*, Xuan 14.

formed a whole army beneath the walls of Song. [His grasp of] the handles of authority was weighty.

King Wen of Chu[72] liked to wear a cap of *xie* fur,[73] and the people of Chu imitated him. King Wuling of Zhao[74] attended court wearing a belt [decorated with] shells and a cap [plumed] with pheasant feathers, and the [entire] state of Zhao transformed [their dress] along with him. Yet if an ordinary person were to go to court wearing a *xie*-fur hat, a belt of shells, and a cap [plumed] with pheasant feathers, he could not avoid being laughed at by others. [9/77/17–26]

There is not one in ten thousand among the common people who loves goodness, rejoices in uprightness, and, without waiting to hear what is forbidden or punishable, naturally stays within the scope of the laws and standards. But if [the ruler] hands down commands that must be followed, so that those who obey them benefit and those who disobey them suffer, then before the sun [dial's] shadow has moved, no one within the Four Seas will fail to toe the line.

Thus, grasping a sword or a glaive by the blade and [advancing to fight]—not even Beigongzi[75] or Sima Kuaikui[76] could be used to respond to an enemy attack [in that manner]. But if he were to grasp the hilt and raise the tip of the blade, then even an ordinary person might prevail. If [even] Wu Huo [or Jie Fan][77] were to pull on an ox's tail from behind, even though the tail might break off, still the ox would not go where they wanted it to [because] that would be working against [its natural propensities]. But if you put a mulberry stick through [the ox's] nose, even a five-foot-tall child could lead it anywhere within the Four Seas, [because] that would be complying with [its natural propensities].

With a seven-foot oar you can steer a boat to the right or to the left because it uses the water [itself] to assist it. The Son of Heaven issues commands. His orders are implemented and his prohibitions observed because he uses the people [themselves] as his positional advantage. [9/77/28–9/78/4]

If the ruler defends the people against what does them harm and opens [a way] for the people to have what brings them benefit, then his awesomeness will spread

72. King Wen of Chu 楚文王 (r. 689–677 B.C.E.) was the ruler who first established Chu's capital at Ying. He is credited for contributing to Chu's status as a major power through territorial expansion.

73. The *xie* 獬 is identified as a single-horned bovine animal said to be able to distinguish between people who told the truth and those who did not. A cap supposedly made from the animal's fur was popular for a time in Chu and was adapted for use at the court of Qin.

74. King Wuling of Zhao 趙武靈王 (r. 325–295 B.C.E.) was a dynamic ruler who initiated political and military reforms, most famously the adoption of "Hu tribe dress" (i.e., trousers) for a new corps of mounted archers. He expanded Zhao's territory but fell victim to factional fighting among his sons and was starved to death in his own palace.

75. Beigongzi 北公子 (also known as Beigong You 幼) was a famous swordsman of Qi mentioned in *Mencius* 2A.2 as a paragon of courage.

76. Sima Kuaikui 司馬蒯蕢 was a knight of Zhao during the Warring States period, famed for his skill with a sword.

77. The phrase *jie fan* 藉蕃 is troublesome. Some commentators read it as a personal name, presumably a legendary strong man like Wu Huo. Others see it as a meaningful phrase, indicating that the strong men pulled the ox's tail "so hard that . . . " We have tentatively come down on the side of the former possibility but put the binome in brackets to indicate the uncertainty surrounding it.

like the bursting of a dike or the breaking of a dam. Thus if you follow the current and head downstream, it is easy to reach your goal; if you gallop with your back to the wind, it is easy to go far.

When Duke Huan of Qi set up his government, he got rid of meat-eating animals, [got rid of] grain-eating birds, and took down snares and nets. With these three undertakings, he pleased the common people.

When [Tyrant] Djou murdered his uncle, Prince Bi Gan,[78] his blood relatives[79] grew resentful. When he cut off the legs of people who were crossing the river in the early morning, tens of thousands of people rebelled. With these two undertakings, he lost the world.

Now,

> [a ruler's] Rightness cannot be relied on to benefit everyone in the world, but if it benefits one person, the world will follow his example.
>
> [A ruler's] cruelty might not be enough to harm everyone in the world, but if it harms one person, the whole world might rise in rebellion.

Thus,

> Duke Huan made three undertakings and [subsequently presided over] nine gatherings of the Lords of the Land.
>
> Djou performed two undertakings, and [subsequently] he could not live even as a commoner. Thus one cannot but be careful of one's actions. [9/78/6–10]

9.27

When the ruler levies taxes on the people, he must first calculate what the harvest will bring in, weigh what the people have in storage, and find out, [in anticipation of] abundance or dearth, the numbers of people who have a surplus or a shortage. Only after this should he use [tax revenues to pay for] chariots, carriages, clothing, and food to satisfy his desires.

High terraces and multistoried pavilions, serried rooms, and linked chambers—it is not that they are not elegant, but when the people do not even have hollowed-out caves or wattle huts in which to shelter themselves, an enlightened ruler does not enjoy them.

Rich [food], strong wines, and sweet pastries—it is not that they are not good, but when not even husks of the grain or beans and peas make it to the mouths of the people, then the enlightened ruler does not find [such delicacies] sweet.

A well-made bed and finely woven mats—it is not that these are not restful, but when the people live in frontier walled towns, braving danger and hardship, dying in

78. Prince Bi Gan 王子比干, a minister to the tyrant King Djou of the Shang, was renowned for his sagacity. Because he remonstrated with the king, Djou ordered his heart cut out, reportedly to see whether the heart of a sage was different from that of an ordinary human being.

79. Literally, his "bones and flesh" (*gurou* 骨肉).

the meadowlands [leaving] sun-bleached bones, an enlightened ruler does not [lie] peacefully [in his fine bed].

Thus those who ruled over humanity in antiquity felt such sorrowful despondency[80] for [the troubles of] the people that

if some went hungry in the state, his food would not be heavily seasoned;
if some people were cold, in winter he would not wear furs.

When the harvest was abundant and the people prosperous, only then would the ruler set up the bells and drums and display the shields and axes [used in ceremonial dances]. Ruler and ministers, superiors and subordinates, then with one mind took pleasure in them, so that there was not a single sorrowful person in the state. [9/78/10–17]

Thus people in ancient times created

[instruments of] metal, stone, bamboo, and strings to express their joy;[81]
weapons, armor, axes, and halberds to display their anger;
wine cups and libations, [sacrificial] meat stands and platters, pledges and toasts, to verify their happiness;
unbleached mourning garments and straw sandals, breast-beating and gyrating, crying and weeping, to communicate sorrow.

These all are cases of things that swell up internally and then become manifest externally. But] coming down to [the times of] disorderly rulers,

in taking from the people, they did not calculate their strength;
in seeking [taxes] from those below, they did not measure their savings.

Men and women were not able to pursue their callings of farming and weaving because they had to supply the demands of their superiors. Their strength was exhausted and their resources were depleted. Rulers and ministers despised one another. Thus [if just when] the people reached the point that, with parched lips and agitated livers, they had only enough for the moment with nothing put aside, the rulers began to have the great bells struck, the drums beaten, the reed pipes played, and the *qin* and *se* plucked, it would have been just like descendants donning armor to enter the ancestral temple or wearing silk gauze to go on a military campaign. [One could say that] they had lost sight of that from whence joy in music arises. [9/78/19–24]

Now as people pursue their livelihoods, if a single man follows the plow, he can till no more than ten *mu* of land. The yearly harvest from fields of middling quality would not exceed four *dan* per *mu*. His wife and children and the elderly and infirm must also rely on this. Sometimes there are diverse calamities such as floods, droughts, and natural disasters. He also has to pay the taxes to the ruler for the expenses of chariots and horses, and soldiers and armor. From this point of view, the

80. *Canda* 慘怛; this phrase also occurs in 10.28 (10/85/3) as a feeling that is "conveyed [from the ruler] to the hearts of others."

81. "Joy" here includes the concept of "music," the single character 樂 meaning both "joy" (pronounced *le*) and "music" (pronounced *yue*).

life of commoners is pitiful indeed! Now over the great [expanse] of Heaven and Earth, [on average] a three-year period of farming should produce a surplus of one year's grain. Thus roughly

over nine years, there should be three years' savings,
six years' accumulation in eighteen years,
and nine years' reserve in twenty-seven years.

Even if there were floods, droughts, or natural disasters, none of the people would become distressed and impoverished and be left to wander about in utter destitution.

Thus if the state does not have

a reserve of nine years' production, it is called "insufficient."
Without six years' accumulation, it is called "pitiful."
Without three years' surplus, it is called "impoverished."

Thus humane princes and enlightened rulers are restrained in what they take from those below; they are measured in supporting themselves. As a result, the people can receive the bounty of Heaven and Earth and not encounter the difficulties of hunger and cold. But if there are greedy rulers and violent princes, they vex those below, plundering and confiscating [goods] from the people to gratify their insatiable desires. Consequently, the people have no means to avail themselves of Heaven's Harmony or tread the path of Earth's Bounty. [9/78/26–9/79/6]

9.28

Food is the root of the people;
the people are the root of the state;
the state is the root of the ruler.

For this reason, the ruler of men

above, follows the seasons of Heaven;
below, relies on the resources of Earth;
and in their midst, uses the strength of the people.

Thus

living things grow to maturity;
the five grains flourish abundantly.

The ruler [is responsible for] teaching the people how to

nourish and care for the six [kinds of] domestic animals,
plant trees in the [proper] season,
work at laying out paddy fields and open fields,
start [seedlings of] and plant mulberry trees and hemp.

According to whether the soil is fertile or infertile, high or low, they sow each place with what suits it. In hilly and precipitous places where the five grains will not sprout, they plant trees and bamboo.

In spring they prune the dry branches.
In summer they take fruits and melons.

In autumn they gather vegetables and grains.
In winter they cut firewood.

All these are resources for the people. Thus while alive, they have no lack of things to use, and when dead, their corpses are not abandoned.

Thus by the laws of the former kings,
when hunting they did not wipe out herds;
they did not catch fawns or baby animals;
they did not drain marshes to get fish;
they did not burn forests to capture [animals].

[In the ninth month],[82] before dholes had offered their sacrifices, the nets [for catching animals] were not spread out in the wild.

[In early spring] before otters had sacrificed fish,[83] the fishnets were not put in the water [because the fish were too small].

[At the beginning of autumn,] when the eagles and falcons had not yet been used to seize [other] birds, nets [for catching birds] were not placed in valleys and gorges.

[In the ninth month,] before the leaves had fallen, axes were not brought into the mountains and forests.

[In the tenth month,] before the insects had gone into hibernation, the fields were not burned off.

Pregnant animals were not killed;
fledgling birds and eggs were not taken.
Fish that were not [at least] a foot long were not caught;
pigs that were not [at least] a year old were not eaten.

Thus grasses and trees grew like steam rising into the air, and birds and beasts returned [to their habitats] like the flowing of a spring. Flying birds ascended to the sky like smoke or clouds. This was [all] because the conditions were ripe for them. [9/79/8–16]

Thus, according to the administrative policies of the former kings,

When the clouds from the Four Seas gathered [at the beginning of spring], the field boundaries were repaired.

When frogs and toads called and the swallows descended and arrived [in the third month], the roads were opened and byways cleared.

When yin [*qi*] descended to the hundred springs [in the tenth month], the bridges were repaired.

When the [lunar lodge] Extension culminated [at dusk in the third month], various grains were industriously planted.

When the star Great Fire [Antares] culminated [at dusk in the fourth month], millet and beans were sown.

82. In this passage, the designations of seasons and months are not in the text but have been supplied by commentators.

83. For the supposed habit of dholes and otters of "sacrificing" small animals and fish, see 5.1 and 5.9.

When the [lunar lodge] Emptiness culminated [at dusk in the eighth month], winter wheat was planted.
When the [lunar lodge] Pleiades culminated [at dusk in the twelfth month], reserves of grain were stored, and firewood was cut.[84]

The ruler reported upward to Heaven, and he made pronouncements downward to the people. The reason that the former kings in those ways

responded to the seasons and put all in order,
strengthened the state and benefited the people,
and populated the wilds and attracted [settlers] from distant lands,

was because their Way was complete. It was not that they were able too see with their own eyes and personally went on foot [to investigate]. They wanted to benefit the people. Their wanting to benefit the people was never neglected in their [own] hearts, so the officials naturally were conscientious. The heart is incapable of accomplishing even one of the tasks of the nine apertures and the four limbs [of the body], but in moving, resting, hearing, and seeing, all take the heart as their master because it never forgets to benefit them. [9/79/18–22]

Thus Yao did good, and much additional goodness came about [because of it].
[The tyrant] Jie did wrong, and much additional evil came about [because of it].
When goodness accumulates, success is reached;
When wrong accumulates, failures proliferate. [9/79/24–25]

9.29

Generally people say that you want

your heart to be small [cautious] and your will to be large [expansive];
your wisdom to be round [full] and your conduct square [proper];
your abilities to be many and your affairs few.

"The heart should be cautious" means that you should consider difficulties before they arise, prepare for calamities before they occur, guard against transgressions and be careful about small matters, and not dare to give rein to your desires.

"The will should be expansive" means that you should bring together and embrace the myriad states, unify and standardize diverse customs, ally and shelter the commoners as if uniting them as a single people, and act as the hub when [opinions about] right and wrong converge like the spokes of a wheel.

"Wisdom should be round" means that you turn like a circle with no distinction between beginning and end, and flow to the four directions like a deep and inexhaustible spring. When the myriad things arise together, there is nothing to which you fail to turn your attention and respond.

"Conduct should be square" means that you should be straight and unswerving,

84. For the twenty-eight lunar lodges (*xiu* 宿), see chap. 3 and app. B. The association of calendrical months with the culminations of particular lunar lodges is a feature of chap. 5's ritual calendar.

pure and uncorrupted. Even if you are destitute, you never change your patterns, and when successful, you never force your will [on others].

"Abilities should be many" means that you must be competent in both civil and military matters, and adhere to proper deportment both in movement and at rest. In your actions, in promoting and demoting, you always do what is appropriate. You meet with no opposition, and so nothing is incomplete or inappropriate.

"Affairs should be few" means that you grasp the handles and wield the techniques [of governance], get what is important so as to respond to the multitudes, grasp the essence so as to govern widely, dwell in quietude and stay centered, revolve at the pivot, and use the one to bring together the myriads, like bringing together [the two halves of] a tally.

Thus,

if your heart is cautious, you can put a stop [to problems] in their incipient stages.
If your will is great, there will be nothing you do not embrace.
If your knowledge is round, there will be nothing you do not know.
If your conduct is square, you will not act in certain instances.
If your abilities are many, there will be nothing you cannot put in order.
If your affairs are few, the essence will be what you grasp. [9/79/27–9/80/7]

In ancient times when the Son of Heaven held court, he arranged for
lords and ministers to present forthright admonitions,
scholars of wide learning to chant the *Odes*,[85]
music masters to sing critiques of government,
and the populace to offer their opinions.
Secretaries recorded the ruler's misconduct;
chefs cut down on his delicacies.

But still this was not considered sufficient, so
Yao put in place a drum [at the palace gate] for anyone wishing to admonish [him];
Shun set up a board on which to post criticisms;
Tang had a superintendent of rectitude;
King Wu set up a small drum to remind him to be careful.

[Thus], when mistakes were still trivial, there already were precautions taken against them.

According to the sage's concept of goodness, no act [of goodness] is so small that it should not be carried out.
According to his concept of misconduct, no act [of misconduct] is so trivial that it should not be corrected.

Yao, Shun, Yu, Tang, King Wen and King Wu confidently faced south and ruled the world. In those times,

85. This appears to be a reference to the *Odes*, although *shi* 詩 could also refer to poetry in general.

when a gong was struck, they ate;
when the [musical composition] "Concord"[86] was played, the table was cleared.

After finishing their rice, they offered a sacrifice to the stove god. In their conduct, they did not make use of shamans' invocations.

Ghosts and spirits did not dare to work black magic on them;
mountains and rivers did not dare to harm them.

They could be said to be [truly] noble. Yet they were
preoccupied and fearful,
daily more and more careful.

From this point of view, then, the sage's heart is cautious. The *Odes* says,

"Indeed this King Wen
was cautious and reverent;
illustriously he served the High God,
thus securing good fortune."[87]

Is this not what is referred to here?

When King Wu of Zhou attacked the Shang dynasty, he
disbursed the grain from the Zhuqiao granaries,
distributed the money from the Lutai treasury,
built a mound over Bi Gan's tomb,
designated as exemplary the [ancestral] village of Shang Rong,[88]
brought under royal control the ancestral temple of Cheng Tang,
and freed Ji Zi from prison.[89]

He let people of all sorts remain in their own homes and till their own fields.

He did not distinguish between old and new [friends]
but drew near only to those who were worthy.
He made use of those who had not previously served him
and employed those who were not [previously] his own men,

comfortably treating the newcomers as if they had long been in his employ. From this point of view, then, the sage's will is expansive.

King Wen of Zhou
comprehensively surveyed successes and failures
and everywhere investigated right and wrong.
[He considered] what made Yao and Shun glorious
and [why] Jie and Djou perished,

86. *Yong* 雍 is described in books of ritual as a musical composition to accompany the end of a meal.

87. *Odes* 236, verse 3.

88. Shang Rong was a (possibly legendary) Shang-dynasty worthy who was punished by the tyrant Djou for honest admonitions against the king's abuses. King Wu's actions are also mentioned in XZ 98/27/53. Interestingly, the *Huainanzi* itself serves as the *locus classicus* for the identification of Shang Rong as Laozi's teacher. See also 12.47 and 20.28.

89. Ji Zi had been imprisoned by the tyrant Djou for his admonitions against the king. He was to have been executed but feigned madness and was imprisoned instead. See *Shiji* 3 /12b–13a.

then recorded all [his findings] in the Mingtang. Thereby he increased his wisdom and expanded his erudition so he could respond to anything that departed from the foursquare. From this point of view, then, the sage's wisdom is round.

King Cheng and King Kang
carried on the task of Kings Wen and Wu,
preserved the institution of the Mingtang,
looked into the traces of [ancient states] that endured or perished,
and observed the alterations of success and failure.

If something
contravened the Way, they would not say it;
contravened Rightness, they would not do it.
Their words were not spoken heedlessly;
their actions were not carried out heedlessly.

They selected what was good, and only then would they pursue a course of action. From this point of view, then, the conduct of the Superior Man is square.

Confucius's penetrating qualities [were such that]
in wisdom he surpassed Chang Hong;[90]
in bravery he was superior to Meng Ben.[91]
His feet were quicker than an agile rabbit;
his strength could lift a city gate.

His abilities certainly were many. Nevertheless,
his bravery and strength were not heard about;
his skills and mastery were not known.

It was only through carrying out filial piety and the Way that he became an "uncrowned king." His affairs certainly were few.

In the 242 years of the Spring and Autumn period, fifty-two states perished and thirty-six rulers were assassinated. Confucius
upheld goodness and condemned wickedness, [thereby]
perfecting the Way of [the True] King.

His discussions certainly were broad. Nevertheless,
when he was besieged in Kuang,
his expression and complexion did not alter.
He plucked [his *qin*] and sang without pausing.
When it came to the point that his life was in danger,
when he encountered calamities and dangerous difficulties,

he clung to Rightness and practiced his principles, and his will was fearless. His sense of discrimination [between life and death] certainly was clear.

Thus, [in serving] as minister of justice in Lu, when he heard cases, he invariably

---

90. For Chang Hong, see 13.12 and 16.52. He is mentioned as a worthy in *Zuozhuan*, Ai 3/1; ZZ 73/26/2; and elsewhere.

91. Meng Ben (also known as Meng Yüe) was a fearless hero known for his acute vision. See, for example, *Mencius* 10/2a/2.

came to a decision. In compiling the *Spring and Autumn Annals*, he did not give accounts of ghosts and spirits, nor did he dare to [inject] his personal opinions.

Now the wisdom of sages certainly embraces many things; what they preserve gets to the essence. Thus when they take some action, the outcome is invariably glorious. The wisdom of a foolish person certainly is very little, yet the things he tries to do are numerous. Thus when he acts on something it is certain to fail. In wisdom, Wu Qi[92] and Zhang Yi[93] did not compare with Confucius and Mo Di, yet they contended with rulers of ten-thousand-chariot states. This is why they eventually had their bodies torn apart by chariots and their lineage wiped out.[94] Now

> if [the ruler] uses uprightness to transform [the people] by teaching, that is easy and he will certainly succeed.
>
> If he uses depravity to manipulate society, that is difficult and he will certainly fail.

Now, if you are going to establish a pattern of conduct and make it general throughout the world, to abandon the easy route that is sure to succeed and to follow the difficult way that is bound to fail would be the height of stupidity and confusion.

The six opposites must, without fail, be scrutinized carefully. [9/80/9–9/81/4]

9.30

> To be thoroughly knowledgeable about the ten thousand things yet not to know about the Way of humankind—this cannot be called Wisdom.
>
> To be thoroughly loving toward all sorts of [living] things yet not love humankind—this cannot be called Humaneness.
>
> Humaneness is the love of one's own kind.
>
> Wisdom means one cannot be confused.
>
> A humane person may be in the midst of [witnessing] a mutilating punishment or an execution, but it is evident from his countenance that he cannot bear to do so.
>
> A wise person may be in the midst of dealing with a vexing and challenging matter, but it is evident from his efficacy that he is not in the dark.

His inner sense of reciprocity is reflected in his [outward] feelings. What he does not wish for himself he does not do to others.[95]

92. Wu Qi 吳起 (d. 381 B.C.E.) was a famous statesman and soldier of the Warring States period. He led armies for Lu and Wei and eventually was employed as prime minister by King Dao of Chu. He led Chu effectively until the king's death, when the aristocratic clans of Chu murdered him out of resentment. A text on military strategy attributed to him, the *Wuzi*, is extant.

93. Zhang Yi 張儀 (d. 310 B.C.E.) was a statesman, strategist, and diplomat of the Warring States period. A native of Wei, he traveled as a "roaming persuader" seeking employment at various courts until he was made prime minister of Qin by King Hui. In this post, he was able to forge a league of states subordinate to Qin and to greatly expand the state's power.

94. Zhang Yi was not torn apart by chariots. Commentators suggest that this may be an error for Su Qin or Shang Yang, who were indeed dismembered. See Zhang Shuangdi 1997, 1:1022n.52.

95. Compare LY 22/12/2 and 32/15/24.

From [knowing] the near, he knows the distant;
from [knowing] himself, he knows others.
That is how [the sage] acts on the concord of Humaneness[96] and Wisdom.

If in small matters there is teaching, then in great matters there is preservation [of the state].
If in small matters there are punishments, then in great matters there is peace.

How compassion is to be expressed in action is a matter for the man of wisdom alone to decide. Thus Humaneness and Wisdom sometimes disagree and sometimes agree. When they agree, [the ruler employs] uprightness, when they disagree, [he employs] expediency. The [standard of] Rightness is the same. [9/81/6–11]

Functionaries and secretaries adhere to the law, but the ruler controls them through Rightness. [A ruler] who is lawful but lacks Rightness is no different from the functionaries and secretaries; this is not sufficient for [true] government.

Farming as an occupation is laborious;
weaving as an occupation is burdensome.

Though they are laborious and burdensome, the people do not abandon them because they know that it is through those means that they can clothe and feed themselves. It is an essential quality of human beings that they cannot do without clothing and food. The Way of clothing and feeding oneself must begin with farming and weaving. This is something that the people in their tens of thousands all recognize. Things like farming and weaving begin with hard work, but in the end they are inevitably beneficial.

Things for which preparations can be made in advance are innumerable, but the number of preparations [actually] undertaken by the foolish are few.
Matters in which expedient measures may be applied are many, but those in which expedient measures are [actually] undertaken by the foolish are few.

This is why foolish people have so many troubles.

Things for which one can prepare, the wise prepare for as completely as possible.
Things to which expedient measures can be applied, they apply them as completely as possible.

This is why the wise have so few troubles. Thus,

the wise first meet with resistance but later [bring about] concord;
the foolish begin in joy and end in grief. [9/81/13–18]

Today, what should we do to win honors?
Tomorrow, what should we do to accord with Rightness?

All this is easy to say.

Today, what should we do to accord with Rightness?
Tomorrow, what should we do to win honors?

This is hard to know.

If you ask a blind musician, "What is plain white like?"
he will say, "It is like unbleached silk."

---

96. Reading *ren* 人 as *ren* 仁.

If you ask him, "What is black like?"
he will say, "It is like deepest black."[97]

If you take something white and something black and show them to him, however, he will not be able to distinguish between them. People use their eyes to perceive white and black and their mouths to speak of white and black. The blind music master has the means to speak of white and black but not the means to know white and black. Thus in speaking of white and black, he is the same as other people, but in not being able to distinguish them, he is different from other people.

Everyone, whether foolish or wise, worthy or deficient, knows that internalizing filial piety toward his parents and outwardly displaying loyalty to his ruler is Rightness. But few can set an example of loyal and filial conduct or know whence [those qualities] arise. Now as to people's thoughts, there is no one who does not first consider his [opinion] correct and then act on it. What distinguishes whether their [conduct] is correct or incorrect is the difference between foolishness and wisdom.[98] [9/81/20–25]

In human nature
nothing is more valuable than Humaneness;
nothing is more urgently needed than Wisdom.
Humaneness is used as the basic stuff;
Wisdom[99] is used to carry things out.

These two are the root. Add to them
bravery, strength, eloquence, mental acuity,
cleverness, quickness, diligence, discrimination,
ingenuity, mental agility, sharpness, keenness,
thoroughgoing brilliance, and penetrating insight,

and they all would serve to increase [a person's] advantages. But if someone who is personally lacking in self-cultivation is trained in skills and arts but has no Humaneness or Wisdom that he can manifest as his fundamental character, then the more he augments his strong points, the more it will add to the damage he can do. Thus,

someone who lacks Humaneness but is brave and daring is like a madman brandishing a sharp sword.

Someone who lacks Wisdom but is eloquent and quick tongued is like driving a fine horse but not knowing which way to go.[100]

Even though you may have talent and ability, if you apply it where it is not suitable, it will suffice only to promote deception and cover up wrongdoing. [In that case,] having many skills would be not as good as having few. Thus those who are consumed with ambition cannot be given access to positional advantage, and those who are basically foolish cannot be given a "sharp tool."[101] [9/81/27–9/82/2]

---

97. *Dan* or *tan* 黮, a deep black presumably with some special tactile quality, now unknown.

98. Reading *zhi* 知 as *zhi* 智, to maintain the consistency of the argument in this passage.

99. Again reading *zhi* 知 as *zhi* 智, to maintain the consistency of the argument in this passage.

100. The text is corrupt at this point and seems to be missing two or three words, but the general sense of this sentence is clear from the context.

101. The "sharp tool" is a reference to political power. Compare *Laozi* 36.

9.31

When fish have water, they swim in it and enjoy themselves; but if [the dikes] break and the water dries up, then they will be eaten by insects. If you strengthen and repair the dikes and embankments and replace the water that leaked out, the fish will be restored and benefit from it.

A country has something by means of which it is preserved;
people have something by means of which they stay alive.
What preserves a state is Humaneness and Rightness;
what keeps people alive is good conduct.
If a state lacks Rightness, even if it is large, it will certainly perish.
If people lack goodness of will, even if they are brave, they will be injured.

The government of a state is by the fiat of the ruler and no one else. Being filial to parents, brotherly to siblings, and honest with friends all can be accomplished without commands from above. To put aside what you can accomplish and seek to do what you cannot control is absurd. [9/82/4–7]

9.32

If a scholar living in low and obscure circumstances wants to gain access to the ruler, he must first revert to himself.

There is a Way to gain access to the ruler. But if you lack fame and reputation, you cannot gain access.
There is a Way to gain a reputation. But if you do not gain the trust of your friends, you cannot gain a reputation.
There is a Way to gain the trust of your friends. But if in your dealings with relatives you do not make them happy, your friends will not trust you.
There is a Way to make your relatives happy. But if your self-cultivation does not [lead to] sincerity, you cannot manage your family.
There is a Way to make yourself sincere. But if your mind is not focused on the One, you cannot be sincere.
The Way lies in what is easy, but [people] seek it in what is hard.
The proof lies in what is near, but [people] seek it in the far away.

That is why no one gets it. [9/82/7–11]

Translated by Sarah A. Queen and John S. Major

Ten

PROFOUND PRECEPTS

"PROFOUND PRECEPTS" poses a question: How is the ideal ruler to bring order and harmony to society? The chapter's answer is that the ruler must follow the promptings of his inner heart and honor his innermost feelings as the basis of his rule, rather than relying on laws, rituals, institutions, or the advice of worthies. "Profound Precepts" thus evinces a deep commitment to concepts of moral autonomy and moral agency that echo the radical optimism of Mencius, who centuries earlier argued passionately for the potential and power of human emotions to uplift the world. Thus the ideal ruler seeks goodness within himself[1] and thereby brings goodness to the world. He is able to do so because the moral inclinations of his human heart, expressed in such intrinsic feelings as Humaneness and Rightness, are shared by all humanity. Thus guided by his own inherent feelings, he is able to connect in a profound way with his people, leading them by means of a kind of empathetic resonance that is more powerful than any commands he might utter. Through vigilant introspection, the ruler establishes a close communion with the stirrings of his inner heart, relying on his personal Humaneness and Rightness to establish a government under which the people are loved and benefited as a father loves his son. There is a perfect resonance between ruler and ruled; thus by cultivating his inherent feelings, the ruler sets the world in order.

1. "Profound Precepts" argues frequently that the Superior Man is one who seeks (the Way) within himself (e.g., 10.17).

The Chapter Title

The title of this chapter is "Mou cheng" 繆稱. Both elements of that phrase present challenges to the translator.

Mou (skein, bundle) is generally understood to be a loanword for either of two closely similar graphs: *miu* 謬 (erroneous, fallacious) or *mu* 穆 (ponderous, weighty). The implications of the two possibilities for understanding the chapter title overall point in opposite directions.

The root meaning of *cheng* is "to weigh in a scale"; thence "weigh, assess, evaluate," "assessment, evaluation," and from there a host of extended and metaphorical meanings, including "to declare" and "to praise."

Most commonly, the chapter title has been read as *miu cheng* and accordingly has been rendered as "Erroneous Appraisals" or equivalent phrases such as "Des évaluations fallacieuses."[2] Presumably the implication is that the reader will learn from this chapter how to identify and guard against erroneous opinions. That reading finds some support in the chapter 21 summary of this chapter, which says it will enable a person "to find fault with persuasions and attack arguments, responding to provocations without error." Nevertheless, that interpretation seems strained, and the phrase understood as *miu cheng* seems unsatisfactory as a chapter title.

Read alternatively as *mu cheng*, the title could mean "Profound Evaluations" or "Profound Appraisals." In this case, advocated by some commentators, the title would allude to the content of the chapter and its intellectual profundity, the very kind of wisdom one might hope to consult when confronted with the "false explanations and combative arguments" that one sought to challenge and correct.

Both these approaches are acceptable, but we believe that there is a third and better alternative that would interpret the title to mean "Profound Precepts." Such a rendering would point specifically to the literary form of the chapter and allude to its potential utility in the formal debates and other kinds of oral exchanges characteristic of the period. In this reading, the *cheng* of the title is understood to refer to a type of gnomic wisdom encapsulated in brief precepts. These could be cited in various oral contexts to argue against false opinions, precisely as the chapter 21 summary suggests.

In fact, several texts from the late Warring States through the Han, such as the *Yanzi chunqiu*, *Guanzi*, *Shuo yuan*, and *Lun heng*, support such a reading, as these texts use the word *cheng* to denote the utterance of a precept or indicate when a precept is about to be cited in the course of a conversation. This usage takes the form "someone presented a precept saying" (*jin cheng yue* 進稱曰, sometimes abbreviated to simply *cheng yue* 稱曰). A typical example from *Yanzi chunqiu* depicts Yan Ying (d. 500 B.C.E.) offering a precept to Duke Jing of Qi (held title, 547–489 B.C.E.): "With clothing, nothing compares with what is new; with people, nothing

2. Respectively, Donald Harper, "*Huai Nan Tzu* Chapter 10: Translation and Prolegomena" (master's thesis, University of California, 1978); Le Blanc and Mathieu 2003.

compares with what is old."[3] Chapter 32 of the *Guanzi*, "Minor Appraisals" (Xiao cheng 小稱), includes a handful of brief precepts attributed to Guanzi like the following: "It is good to criticize oneself. Then the people will have nothing to criticize. If you are incapable of criticizing yourself, you will be criticized by the people."[4] The *Shuo yuan* cites many precepts, including the following from the *Changes*: "The eastern neighbor slaughtering an ox does not compare with the western neighbor's Yue sacrifice."[5] Similarly, the *Lun heng* contains a passage in which Confucius cites the following precept: "Life and death are a matter of fate; wealth and honor rest with Heaven."[6] Thus the meaning of *cheng* as "precept" seems to have been well established in the Han era.

The translation of this chapter title is indeed a complicated matter, and a good case can be made for each of the versions discussed here. We believe that the translation "Profound Precepts" both best conforms to how the words of the chapter title would have been understood at the time the *Huainanzi* was written and best describes the content of the chapter, which does in fact contain many brief precepts.

Summary and Key Themes

"Profound Precepts," like so many chapters before it, opens with a poetic and moving exaltation of the inclusiveness, perfection, and limitlessness of the Way. Accordingly, those who "embody the Way" (10.1) or "follow Heaven's Way," identifying their *qi* with that of the origins of all things (10.3), do so through direct experience (10.113). With this identity established, they transcend the vast majority of human beings. Leaving behind the more typical human emotions that arise in response to the phenomenal world—such as sorrow, joy, happiness, and anger—for a deeper level of inner experience that enables one to generate a range of different feelings from deep within the interior of the self, they respond to others with a profound sense

3. YZ 5.5/41/28: 晏子稱曰: "衣莫若新, 人莫若故."

4. GZ 32/85/11: 善罪身者,民不得罪也;不能罪身者,民罪之. See also 32/84/31. Unfortunately, it appears that this chapter has survived through the ages only in partial form, as the second half of the chapter currently consists of two anecdotes unrelated to the materials that constitute the first half of the chapter. The following chapter of the *Guanzi*, entitled "Four Evaluations" (Si cheng 四稱) and consisting of four exchanges between Duke Huan of Qi and Guan Zhong, uses the term *cheng* in the alternative sense of "appraisal" or "evaluation."

5. SY 20/173/17–18: 易稱: 東鄰殺牛不如西鄰之禴祭 (The western neighbor, being on the right side [all doors face south], is more highly esteemed than the eastern neighbor). For another example from the *Shuo yuan*, see the anecdote in which the humble attendant Zhao Cangtang seeks to persuade his lord, the heir Ji of Zhongshan, to send an emissary to visit his father, Marquis Wen of Wei. Zhao Cangtang initiates his persuasion by presenting a precept saying: "When a son for three years does not listen to his father's inquiries, he cannot be called filial; when a father for three years does not inquire after his son, he cannot be called kind" (為人子三年不聞父問,不可謂孝;為人父三年不問子,不可謂慈) (SY 12.6/95/20). Additional precepts are recited as the story unfolds. See SY 12.6/96/18 and 12.6/96/20.

6. LH 28/127/6: 孔子稱曰: 死生有命,富貴在天.

of inner equanimity and move them with these feelings of a wholly different order (10.1). Such is the basis of Moral Potency in the world embodied in the ideal of the Superior Man and the sage.[7]

The Superior Man is associated with many virtues, chief among them being Humaneness, Rightness, and Goodness (10.32, 10.77, 10.101). Undoubtedly, the pair Humaneness and Rightness are most important. As section 10.6 explains, "If not for Humaneness and Rightness, the Superior Man would have nothing to live for." He acts out of Humaneness and Rightness at every turn (10.82, 10.106). More "intimate than a father" (10.29), Humaneness is understood as the "visible proof of accumulated kindness" (10.5). The kindness of a humane heart is particularly valued for its ability to move others in profound ways (10.34).[8]

The Superior Man's ability to embody Rightness is attributed to the inner state of his heart and mind: he persistently "ponders Rightness" (10.67), "fears losing Rightness" (10.6), wishes to practice Rightness (10.33), and either "advances and obtains" or "withdraws and yields by means of Rightness" (10.82). "More exalted than a ruler" (10.29), the Rightness of the Superior Man includes "a sense of appropriateness" (10.87). More specifically, it is "what comports with the human heart and conforms to what is appropriate for the majority of humankind" (10.5).[9]

The Superior Man also is synonymous with Goodness, which he reflects on constantly, assessing the measure of his personal virtue (10.32) and attending to acts of goodness, no matter how trivial. Through persistence and dogged determination, his seemingly banal acts of goodness slowly accrue to become something truly outstanding (10.9, 10.101, 10.102): "Radiantly it rivals the brilliance of the sun and moon. No one in the world can restrain or repress it" (10.71). Ever mindful of doing good in the world, the Superior Man understands that such goodness is rooted in his Heaven-ordained nature, and whether or not he encounters good or bad fortune is a matter of destiny (10.77).[10] Accordingly, it is always better to seek for goodness not in others but in the deepest recesses of oneself (10.42).

The Superior Man stands out from the crowd because he possesses a number of additional qualities. When he acts, he is mindful of the consequences of his actions (10.23). He is a perfect blend of cultural refinement and natural substance (10.23). And he is able to foretell the course of an affair by the characteristics it exhibits at its inception (10.21). He also is marked by a willingness to speak the truth and disregard the consequences of doing so, making him a reliable critic of the ruler (10.10) and giving him a sense of circumspection when his person is concerned (10.46) and a sense of vigilance when pondering the stirrings of his innermost heart (10.31).

7. For other references to the Way, see 10.1, 10.3, 10.5, 10.62, 10.65, 10.74, 10.77, 10.79, 10.85, 10.86, 10.88, 10.100, 10.107, and 10.114.

8. For other discussions of Humaneness, see 10.5, 10.6, 10.28, 10.34, and 10.106.

9. For other references to Rightness, see 10.5, 10.6, 10.29, 10.33, 10.46, 10.48, 10.67, 10.70, 10.82, 10.87, 10.88, 10.91, and 10.104.

10. For other references to the randomness of good and bad fortune, see 10.7, 10.60, 10.76, 10.77, 10.83, 10.99, 10.111, and 10.112.

Indeed, the Superior Man is decidedly preoccupied with his interior landscape, for this is where his moral compass lies. As the autonomous author of his moral destiny, he cannot do otherwise. The text clearly explains: "Thus, goodness or evil is our own doing; bad or good fortune is not our own doing. Thus the Superior Man complies with what lies within him; that is all he can do" (10.76). Accordingly, the Superior Man's Way, the ultimate ethical model of emulation for the remainder of humankind, must be sought within the self:

> The Way of the Superior Man is
> close but cannot be attained,
> low but cannot be ascended,
> contains nothing inside it, but cannot be filled. It is
> enduring yet brilliant,
> far-reaching yet illustrious.
>
> To understand this and so follow the Way is something that cannot be sought in others but only attained from the self. If you abandon the search within yourself and seek it in others, you will have strayed far from it. (10.65)[11]

The sage, like the Superior Man, does not follow the crowd. He is marked by an equal dose of moral autonomy; listening to his own heart and disregarding the opinions of others, he "reverts to himself and does not take [the lead from others]" (10.113; see also 10.58). Indeed, for both the Superior Man and the sage, "obtaining oneself" and "seeking within the self" are the most important qualities of the morally perfected person.[12] Thus the sage, like the Superior Man, is also fiercely independent and self-reliant. One passage explains that this independence is the very quality that enables the sage to connect to others. There the sage is likened to a drum: "There is no instrument that is in tune with it, and no instrument that cannot be accompanied by it" (10.51). And like the Superior Man, he is unconcerned with the evaluations of others; he follows his own inner compass (10.113).

Yet the sage differs from the Superior Man in possessing certain qualities unique to this ideal. Although the sage shares with the Superior Man the ability to know the future of an event before it unfolds, based on the qualities it exhibits at its inception (10.7, 10.83, 10.96), the sage's perspicacity endows him with additional qualities not associated with the Superior Man. It enables him to do such things as recognize and understand the subtleties of things that would confuse the average person (10.115), act in a timely fashion (10.89), and find something of use in everything, preparing "even the shavings from the timber" (10.16). His intellectual prowess is

11. For other references to the Superior Man, see 10.6, 10.10, 10.21, 10.23, 10.27, 10.28, 10.31, 10.32, 10.46, 10.65, 10.66, 10.67, 10.77, 10.82, 10.101, and 10.106.

12. For the importance of the self as the ultimate arbiter of the virtuous life, see 10.17, 10.22, 10.24, 10.31, 10.32, 10.42, 10.49, 10.58, 10.65, 10.86, 10.106, and 10.113.

matched by certain emotive qualities that contribute to his unique qualities as an ideal personality: chief among them are a sense of foreboding (10.111) and anxious concern (10.20, 10.48, 10.72, 10.79), which appear as persistent emotions of his inner landscape.

When he occupies a position of political leadership, the sage nurtures the people (10.21), moving and transforming them with his intrinsic feelings (10.25) in a spiritlike fashion (10.31) that is commensurate with their inherent qualities (10.56).[13] So vital and powerful are these two aspects of sagely governance that one passage claims: "If you cherish feelings and embrace inherent qualities, Heaven cannot kill you; Earth cannot bury you. Your voice will resound throughout the space between Heaven and Earth; your brightness will match the sun and moon" (10.41). The spiritlike transformation of the people is accomplished by means of nonverbal communication through the Quintessential *qi* of the human heart, providing the physiological basis for unspoken forms of communication between the ruler and his people and among people in general (10.24).[14] Accordingly, the sage's government is marked by Perfect or Utmost Potency (*zhi de* 至德).[15] When the ruler embodies the sage's Perfect Potency, "His words are identical with his plans; his actions are identical with his intentions. Above and below are of one mind" (10.3). His government is a balanced admixture of the guiding patterns of culture and the intrinsic feelings of humanity (10.54). He thereby gains the hearts of the people by promoting what they love (10.20).[16] Thus although the text readily concedes that verbal communication is essential to governance, it is what is communicated nonverbally that is most clearly prized. As one passage explains:

> A three-month-old infant does not yet understand the distinction between benefit and harm, but the love of a kind mother is conveyed to the infant because of her feelings.
>
> Thus the usefulness of what is spoken—how manifestly tiny it is!
> The usefulness of what is not spoken—how vastly great it is! (10.26)

The central claim of the chapter is that the best rulers conduct themselves in accordance with their innermost feelings (10.11) and thereby move the hearts of those whom they rule. Accordingly, much of the chapter outlines the details of how human resonance works, demonstrating the centrality of the human heart and the feelings that correspond to this deeper psychic world and how these feelings evoke various

13. For additional references to the sage, see 10.7, 10.8, 10.15, 10.25, 10.30, 10.36, 10.37, 10.40, 10.48, 10.51, 10.58, 10.83, 10.89, 10.90, 10.91, 10.96, 10.111, 10.113, and 10.118.

14. For other references to the essence or Quintessential *qi*, see 10.18, 10.24, 10.94, and 10.103.

15. For additional references to Moral Potency, see 10.73, 10.85, 10.91, 10.102, 10.104, 10.105, and 10.106.

16. For further discussions of the ideal ruler and government described in this chapter, see 10.2, 10.3, 10.4, 10.9, 10.13, 10.29, 10.44, 10.52, 10.55, 10.56, 10.64 (Mandate of Heaven), 10.74, 10.78, 10.84, 10.85, 10.86, 10.89, 10.98, 10.100, and 10.104.

kinds of sympathetic and resonant responses from other human beings.[17] Of particular relevance here is the concept of inner sincerity, apparently an emotion or attitude that appears to be identified with one's deepest psychic landscape that should ideally precede one's speech and actions and accompany the expression of other feelings. Of the many kinds of intrinsic feelings prized in the chapter and distinguished from the more pedestrian emotional responses to external stimuli, feelings that arise purely as responses to the external world, there is no doubt that sincerity enjoys pride of place.[18] Sincerity is said to make people responsive to the commands of their leaders: The ruler wills it, and the people fulfill it. This is because of inner sincerity (10.56, 10.17, 10.25). Sincerity has the power to move things that are quite distant from oneself (10.22) and gives rise to an internal joy and calm (10.57).[19]

Sources

"Profound Precepts" confirms and develops concepts and terms that appear in a group of early texts typically associated with Confucius and his early followers: the *Lunyu, Liji, Mengzi, Xunzi, Zisizi,* and *Wuxingpian* (Mawangdui and Guodian versions). The Superior Man, the morally perfected ideal of these early texts, figures prominently in the chapter and is frequently contrasted, as in the *Lunyu*, with its counterpart, the petty man.[20] Moreover, the Superior Man is associated with a number of characteristics consonant with these texts: he embodies the twin virtues of Humaneness and Rightness. He also is associated with Rightness, Goodness, Trustworthiness, and Loyalty. As in the *Lunyu*, he is a perfect blend of cultural ornamentation (*wen*) and natural substance (*zhi*) (10.23). He also is mindful, cautious, or circumspect of his solitude (*shen qi du* 慎其獨), a quality commensurate with the Superior Man of the *Zhongyong, Wuxingpian,* and *Liji.* Most important, as in these early texts, the Superior Man follows the moral inclinations of his own heart and is guided primarily by this internal compass rather than the opinions of others. Other concepts as well bear the stamp of these early texts. The chapter's discussion of the related concepts of Heaven and destiny draws on or alludes to the *Mengzi* and *Xunzi.* The chapter's emphasis on human feelings as the primary source of ethical action is clearly indebted to the *Mengzi,* as are the arguments for accumulating small acts of goodness so as to establish truly outstanding virtue. "Profound Precepts" follows the *Lunyu* and *Mengzi* in contrasting the Superior Man's concern for Rightness with

17. For various references to the heart, see 10.2, 10.4, 10.5, 10.11, 10.17, 10.20, 10.21, 10.41, 10.47, 10.53, and 10.94.

18. For references to feelings, see 10.11, 10.25, 10.26, 10.34, 10.35, 10.36, 10.41, 10.45, 10.50, 10.53, 10.54, 10.58, 10.62, 10.67, 10.68, 10.69, 10.81, and 10.99.

19. For more on sincerity, see 10.17, 10.22, 10.25, 10.56, 10.57, 10.72, 10.103, and 10.116. Is sincerity an emotion or a quality of emotions? See 10.72. Note that Mencius regarded sincerity as one of the hallmarks of the morally perfected person.

20. See 10.6, 10.33, 10.39, 10.60, 10.66, 10.67, 10.71, 10.87, and 10.106.

the petty man's concern with profit. The concept of sincerity, which is mentioned often, is reminiscent of that in the *Zhongyong*.[21] "Profound Precepts" develops these foundational ideas by linking them to the more recent vocabulary of inner cultivation centering on the "Quintessential *qi*" as the physiological basis for human resonance evident in such texts as chapter 49, "Inner Cultivation" (Nei ye 內業), of the *Guanzi* and chapter 9.5, "Breaking Through (via the Quintessential *qi*)" (Jing tong 精通), and chapter 18.3, "Communicating (via the Quintessential *qi*)" (Jing yu 精諭), of the *Lüshi chunqiu*.

The Chapter in the Context of the *Huainanzi* as a Whole

As the chapter summary in chapter 21, "An Overview of the Essentials," suggests, "Profound Precepts" analyzes and differentiates various assessments of four essential concepts—the Way, Moral Potency, Humaneness, Rightness—and a number of additional notions intimately related to these four. As the summary explains: "It proposes similes and selects appositions to match them with analogies. It divides into segments and forms sections, to respond with brief aphorisms." Such a collection of profound precepts (*mou cheng*) is meant to provide the reader with the first of several weapons in a growing conceptual arsenal meant to be deployed to defend certain kinds of intellectual territory: "It is what makes it possible to respond without error when provoked by devious explanations and combative assessments" (21/225/13–14).

Sarah A. Queen and John S. Major

---

21. In addition, in "*Huai Nan Tzu* Chapter 10," Harper has pointed out that the style of argumentation prominent in the first half of the chapter, which draws heavily on the *Odes* and *Changes*, is reminiscent of a style of argumentation associated most typically with the *Xunzi* and the evaluation of historical figures is consistent with various positions articulated in the *Analects* and *Mengzi*. He also argues for strong affinities between this chapter and the *Zisizi*.

Ten

10.1

The Way at its highest has nothing above it;
at its lowest it has nothing below it.
It is more even than a [carpenter's] level,
straighter than a marking cord,
rounder than a compass,
and more square than a [carpenter's] square.

It embraces the cosmos and is without outside or inside. Cavernous and undifferentiated, it covers and supports with nothing to hinder it.

Therefore, those who embody the Way
are not sorrowful or joyful;
are not happy or angry.
They sit without disturbing thoughts,
and sleep without dreams.[1]
Things come, and they name them.
Affairs arise, and they respond to them.[2] [10/82/15–17]

1. This claim is paralleled in 2.2, where it argues similarly: "In the use of their mind, sages lean on their natures and rely on their spirits. They [nature and spirit] sustain each other, and [so sages] attain their ends and beginnings. Thus when they sleep, they do not dream, and when they awaken, they are not sad."

2. Similarly, "When affairs arise, the sage regulates them; when things appear, the sage responds to them" (14.43).

10.2

The ruler is the heart of the state.
When the heart is well ordered, the hundred joints are all secure;
when the heart is unsettled, the hundred joints are all confused.

Thus
if your heart is well ordered, your limbs and body [can] ignore each other.
If your state is well ordered, ruler and minister [can] forget each other.[3] [10/82/19–20]

10.3

The Yellow Emperor said,
"Broad and infinite,
[I] follow Heaven's Way,
and my *qi* is identical with the Origin."[4]

Thus when [the ruler] has perfected Potency,
his words are identical with his plans;
his actions are identical with his intentions.
Above and below are of one mind. [10/82/20–21]

10.4

Those who have no divergent paths or distorted views
erect barriers to falling into depravity;
open the path to following goodness.
Thus the people will turn toward the foursquare.

Thus the *Changes* says,
"Unite the people in the fields.
It is advantageous to cross the Great River."[5] [10/82/21–22]

---

3. For a similar body/state analogy, see GZ 13.2/98/16.

4. This statement attributed to the Yellow Emperor also appears in 20.17 and LSCQ 13/2.2, for which see Knoblock and Riegel 2000, 284.

5. *Changes*, hexagram 13, *Tong ren* 同人, "The Same as Others."

10.5

The Way is what guides things;
Potency is what supports nature.

Humaneness is visible proof of accumulated kindness.[6] Rightness is what comports with the human heart and conforms to what is appropriate for the majority of humankind.[7]

Thus

when the Way was extinguished, Potency was employed.
When Potency declined, Humaneness and Rightness were born.[8]

Thus

the earliest era embodied the Way but did not have Potency.
The middle period had Potency but did not cherish it.[9]

The latter-day era was anxious and fearful lest even Humaneness and Rightness be lost. [10/82/24–26]

10.6

If not for Humaneness and Rightness, the Superior Man would have nothing to live for.
If he loses Humaneness and Rightness, he will lose the reason for his existence.
If not for cravings and desires, the petty man would have nothing to live for.
If he loses his cravings and desires, he will lose his reason for living.

Thus

the Superior Man fears losing Rightness.
The petty man fears losing what is valuable to him.[10]

When we look at what people fear, we understand how different they are. [10/82/24–28]

The *Changes* says,

"Chasing a deer without a guide.
It goes into the forest.
For the Superior Man to follow it would not be so good as to abandon it.
Should he follow it, he would encounter difficulty."[11] [10/82/30]

---

6. Similarly, "Humaneness is the application of kindness" (11.8).

7. Similarly, "Rightness comes from what is appropriate for the people. What is appropriate for the people accords with the human heart. This is the *sine qua non* of government" (9.23).

8. *Laozi* 18 and 38. This point also informs 8.3 and introduces chap. 11 (11.1).

9. Reading *huai* 壞 as *huai* 懷, as in the *Wenzi*. See Lau, HNZ, 82n.2B.

10. For other instances of this contrast, see 10.33 and 10.67.

11. *Changes*, hexagram 3, *Tun* 屯, "Gathering Support."

10.7

If your generosity is ample, your reward will be great;
if your hatred is great, your misfortune will be profound.
To give meagerly yet hope extravagantly, to nurture hatred yet be free of suffering—such has never been the case from ancient times until the present.

This is why the sage
looks into things that have gone before
and so understands what is to come. [10/82/30–10/83/2]

10.8

Might not one say that the sagely Way is like a wine jar set up in the middle of an intersection? People passing by will pour some out. [Some will take] more, some less, in unequal amounts; but all will get what they think is appropriate.[12]

For this reason, the way to obtain [the allegiance of] one person is the same as the way to obtain [the allegiance of] a hundred. [10/83/2–3]

10.9

If people take as the standard what they desire from their superiors and apply it to the way they treat their subordinates, who would not support them?
If they take what they desire from their subordinates as a standard for treating their superiors, who would not like them?

The *Odes* says,
"Beloved is the One Man [the king].
In his responses to the Lords of the Land, he follows Potency.[13]
The careful exercise of Potency is great.
The One Man is small.

---

12. Compare *Laozi* 77: "Heaven's Way . . . subtracts from the have-mores, and supplies those in want" (Moss Roberts, trans., *Dao De Jing: The Book of the Way* [Berkeley: University of California Press, 2001], 181).

13. The reference is to *Odes* 243 (no. 9 of the "Da ya" section), but only the first two lines of the stanza are quoted here. The four lines that follow here, "The careful exercise of Potency is great," and so on, continue the sense of the *Shijing* ode but are not part of it, at least in the received version. Also note that in the second line, the *Shijing* verse has *shun de* 順德, rather than *shen de* 慎德, as it is here. We follow the unanimous view of commentators in taking *shen* as a loanword for *shun* and retaining the meaning of "follow." See Zhang Shuangdi 1997, 1:1037.

If you do good in the small,
you can do good in the great." [10/83/3–5]

10.10

When the Superior Man sees [the ruler's] transgressions, he forgets about punishment [for pointing it out]. Thus he is able to remonstrate.
When he sees a worthy, he forgets about [the worthy's low] rank. Thus he is able to yield modestly.
When he sees others who do not have enough, he forgets [his own] poverty. Thus he is able to give charitably.[14] [10/83/7]

10.11

Feelings are attached to one's center [i.e., the heart];
conduct is manifested on one's outside.

Whenever conduct stems from feelings, though [it is] excessive, [it will cause] no resentment.
Whenever it does not stem from feelings, though one's conduct is loyal, it will bring bad consequences. [10/83/7–8]

10.12

Lord Millet brought wide-ranging benefits to the world, but still he did not brag about it. Yu neither wasted his efforts nor wasted his resources, but he still regarded himself as deficient.

Those to whom
fullness is like a sinkhole,
and substance is like emptiness
get the most out of them. [10/83/10–11]

14. This echoes themes in *Mozi* 49 (yield to the worthy and give to the poor) and 39 (remonstrance).

10.13

All people
find worthy what pleases them
and are pleased by what makes them happy.

There is no age that does not promote "worthies." [But] some [rulers] thereby bring order, some bring chaos. It is not that [rulers] deceive themselves; it is just that they seek out "worthies" who are the same as themselves. But if the ruler is not necessarily a worthy himself and he looks for someone just like himself hoping in that way to obtain a worthy, it certainly is not going to work. To let Yao evaluate Shun is permissible, but to let Jie evaluate Yao is like using a *sheng* to measure a *dan* [i.e., they are incommensurable].[15] [10/83/13–15]

10.14

Now if you call a fox a raccoon dog,[16] it is certain that you do not know what a fox is, nor do you know what a raccoon dog is. If it is not that you have never seen a fox, then surely you have never seen a raccoon dog. [In one sense,] a fox and a raccoon dog do not differ, as they belong to the same class of animals. But if you call a fox a raccoon dog, you do not know either the fox or the raccoon dog.[17]

For this reason,
if you call a worthless person a worthy, it is certain you do not know what a worthy is.
If you call a worthy a worthless person, it is certain you do not know what a worthless person is. [10/83/15–17]

10.15

When a sage is above [i.e., in power],
then the people rejoice in his governance;
when he is below [out of power],
then the people admire his steadfastness.

15. A *sheng* is a small measure of dry volume (pint), while a *dan* is a large measure of weight (120 catties [*jin* 觔]).

16. *Grand dictionnaire Ricci de la langue chinoise*, 7 vols. (Paris: Institut Ricci, 2001), 3:1212, defines *li* 貍 as *Nyctereutes procyonoides*, commonly known as the raccoon dog and also widely known by its Japanese name, *tanuki*. It has "the appearance of a small fox-like canid with fur markings similar to those of a raccoon." For further discussion, see chap. 1, n. 33.

17. For the parallel passage in the reconstructed *Zisizi*, see Donald Harper, "*Huai Nan Tzu* Chapter 10: Translation and Prolegomena" (master's thesis, University of California, 1978), app. 1, A; and Csikszentmihalyi 2004, app. 1, no. 31.

When a petty man is in high position, it is like bedding down on a gate or keeping cocoons in the sunshine.[18] One would not get a moment's peace.

Thus the *Changes* says,

"Mounting the horse, it turns about;
weeping blood, it flows torrentially."[19]

This means that when a petty man is in a position beyond his station, he will not last long in it. [10/83/19–21]

10.16

There is nothing that does not have some use.

Tianxiong and *wuhui*[20] are the [most] virulently poisonous of herbs, but a good physician uses them to save people's lives.

Dwarves and blind musicians are the troubled invalids of humankind, but the ruler of men uses them to perform music.

For this reason, the sage prepares even the shavings from the timber.[21] There is nothing that he does not use. [10/83/23–24]

10.17

With one shout, a brave warrior can cause the Three Armies to retreat. What disperses them is his complete sincerity.[22]

Thus

if you command, but [the troops] do not [comply] harmoniously;
if you have intentions, but [the troops] do not support you,

it surely is the case that something is not in accord with your inner heart.[23]

---

18. If cocoons are kept in the sunshine, the overheated pupae thrash around inside them until they eventually die.

19. *Changes*, hexagram 3, *Tun* 屯, "Gathering Support," line 6.

20. Both *tianxiong* 天雄, "heavenly male bird," and *wuhui* 烏喙, "crow's beak," are kinds of *Aconitum*, also known as *xitu*, *jitu*, or *wutou*. See chap. 9, n. 54.

21. Following the emendations suggested by Lau, HNZ, 83n.10.

22. For other references to sincerity, see 10.22, 10.25, 10.56, 10.57, 10.72, 10.103, and 10.116. Section 20.7 similarly maintains: "Thus when the sage nurtures his heart, nothing is better than sincerity. With utmost sincerity, he can move and transform [others]." See also *Zhongyong* (*Liji* 32.20/145/27, 32.21/145/32, 32.22/146/1–2, 32.23/146/6, 32.30/147/14). For the physiological basis of sincerity, see the discussions of quintessential sincerity (*jingcheng* 精誠) in 6.1, 20.3, 20.9, and 20.17.

23. For the notion of the inner heart (*zhong xin*), see GZ 16.1/116/21. There the *Guanzi* explains: "Within the heart there is yet another heart." For the inner versus the outer heart, see also Guodian and Mawangdui *Wuxingpian*.

Thus the reason that Shun, without descending from his mat, [was able to] preserve the world was because he sought it within himself.[24] Thus if the ruler makes more and more excuses, the people will practice more and more deceit. To have a body that is crooked and a shadow that is straight—such a thing has never been heard of. [10/83/26–10/84/2]

10.18

What persuasive speech cannot get at, appearance and demeanor can get at.
What appearance and demeanor cannot get at, a flash of emotion can express.

What is stimulated in the mind then becomes clear in the intelligence; finally it issues forth and takes form. The essence,[25] at its utmost, can shape the dynamics of an encounter, but it cannot give clear warning. [10/84/4–5]

10.19

The horses of the Rong and Dee people all can run and gallop. Some go short distances, some go far, but only Zaofu could get the most out of the horses' strength.
The peoples of the Three Miao tribes all can be made loyal and trustworthy. Some are worthy, some are worthless, but only Tang[26] and Yu[27] could integrate their good points.
They must have possessed something that cannot be transmitted.

Earl Mu of Zhonghang seized a tiger with his bare hands, but he could not capture it alive. No doubt his physical strength was outstanding, but his ability did not extend that far.[28] [10/84/7–9]

24. For further reiterations of this notion of self-reflective moral autonomy (seeking in oneself), see 10.31, 10.40, 10.42, 10.49, 10.58, 10.66, and 10.113.

25. For additional references to the workings of the essence or Quintessential *qi* (*jing* 精), see 10.18, 10.24, 10.94, and 10.103. Other chapters of the *Huainanzi*—for example, chaps. 6–8—discuss in great detail the working of the essence. For an important earlier discussion, see GZ 16.1/115/17–16.1/117/25.

26. 唐, not 湯—that is, not Tang, the supposed founder of the Shang dynasty, but a cognomen of the sage-emperor Yao.

27. 虞, not 禹—that is, not Yu the flood tamer and founder of the Xia dynasty, but a cognomen for the sage-emperor Shun.

28. Earl Mu of Zhonghang (also known as Xun Wu) was a minister in the state of Jin. See *Zuozhuan*, Duke Zhao, year 15; and 18.12. For the parallel passage in the reconstructed *Zisizi*, see Harper, "*Huai Nan Tzu* Chapter 10," app. 1, B; and Csikszentmihalyi 2004, app. 1, no. 33.

10.20

If you use what a hundred people can do, you will obtain the strength of a hundred people.
If you promote what a thousand people love, you will gain the hearts of a thousand people.

By analogy, it is like chopping down a tree and pulling out its roots. Of the thousand branches and the ten thousand leaves, none can fail to follow. [10/84/9–10]

10.21

The kindly father's love for his son is not in order to be repaid[29] but because [the love] cannot be removed from his heart.
The sage-king's nurturance of his people is not because he seeks to use them but because his nature cannot do otherwise.

It is like
fire, which is naturally hot,
and ice, which is naturally cold,
what cultivation is necessary for that?

When it comes to relying on the strengths of others or trusting to the merits of others, it is like a fire on a boat.[30] Thus the Superior Man sees the beginning and knows the end. [10/84/12–14]

10.22

Matchmakers praise people, but not because they esteem them.
[People] hire laborers and force-feed them, but not because they love them.

One's own loving father and kind mother could do no more than this. But when something is done for a purpose, kindness does not enter into it.

Thus you do not see off guests in the same way you greet them.[31]
What you give to the dead is not what you set aside for the living.
Sincerity comes from the self, but what is moved by it is far-off. [10/84/14–16]

29. By being cared for in old age.
30. Which people naturally act to put out without thought of rewards.
31. That is, one greets them joyfully and sees them off sadly.

10.23

To dress in brocades and embroidery and ascend the ancestral temple is to value [outer] refinement.
To hold *gui* and *zhang* tablets[32] in front of yourself is to esteem [inner] substance.

If your [outer] refinement does not overwhelm your [inner] substance, you may be called a Superior Man.[33]

Therefore,

it takes a year to build a chariot, but if it lacks a three-inch long linchpin, you cannot gallop off in it.[34]
It takes a carpenter to frame up a door, but without a foot-long door latch, you cannot close it securely.

Therefore when the Superior Man acts, he thinks about the results. [10/84/18–20]

10.24

The essence of the heart can transform [others] like a spirit, but it cannot point out things to them.
The essence of the eye can cut through obscurities, but it cannot give clear warning.

What lies within the dark and obscure cannot be verbalized to others.

Thus,

Shun did not descend from his mat, and the world was ordered.
[The tyrant] Jie did not leave his throne, and the world was disordered.[35]

Certainly, feelings are deeper than spoken commands. To seek from others what one lacks in oneself—such has never been heard of from ancient times to the present. [10/84/22–24]

---

32. *Gui* 圭 and *zhang* 璋 tablets: jade tablets that conferred the right to speak or perform certain duties at court.

33. See *Analects* 6.18.

34. For the parallel passage in the reconstructed *Zisizi*, see Harper, "*Huai Nan Tzu* Chapter 10," app. 1, C; and Csikszentmihalyi 2004, app. 1, no. 12.

35. For the parallel passage in the reconstructed *Zisizi*, see Harper, "*Huai Nan Tzu* Chapter 10," app. 1, D; and Csikszentmihalyi 2004, app. 1, no. 29.

10.25

If the speech is identical but the people trust it [in some cases], it is because trust preceded the speech.
If the command is identical but the people are transformed by it [in some cases], it is because sincerity lay beyond the command.[36]

When sages rule above and the people are moved and transformed, it is because their feelings have paved the way for them. When there is movement above and no response below, it is because feelings and orders are at variance with one another.

Thus the *Changes* says,

"The overbearing dragon will have [reason to] regret."[37] [10/84/24–26]

10.26

A three-month-old infant does not yet understand the distinction between benefit and harm, but the love of a kind mother is conveyed to the infant because of her feelings.

Thus the usefulness of what is spoken—how manifestly tiny it is!
The usefulness of what is not spoken—how vastly great it is! [10/84/26–27]

10.27

To personify the words of a Superior Man is trustworthiness.
To internalize the resolve of a Superior Man is loyalty.[38]
When loyalty and trust form internally,
the stimulus impels a response externally.

Thus

[when] Yu grasped a shield and a battle-axe and danced on the double staircase, the Three Miao tribes submitted [to his rule].[39]

36. For the parallel passage in the reconstructed *Zisizi*, see Harper, "*Huai Nan Tzu* Chapter 10," app. 1, E; and Csikszentmihalyi 2004, app. 1, no. 4.

37. *Changes*, hexagram 1, *Qian* 乾, line 6.

38. These two lines contain graphic puns: between *yan* 言, "words," and *xin* 信, "trustworthiness," and between *zhong* 中, "internalize," and *zhong* 忠, "loyalty."

39. Section 11.11 attributes these actions to Shun: "Thus in the time of Shun, the Youmiao did not pay tribute. At this, Shun cultivated [good] governance and ceased military [operations]. Thus he grasped the shield and battle-ax and danced with them." See also HFZ 49/146/11–12.

When an eagle hovers above the river, fish and turtles plunge and flying birds scatter.
By necessity they distance themselves from harm. [10/84/27–10/85/1]

10.28

A son dying for his father or a minister dying for his ruler is something that has happened throughout the ages. It is not that they died for the sake of fame but that they harbored within themselves a kindly heart, and so they could not walk away from the troubles [of the father or ruler].

Thus people's delight in what they find agreeable does not exactly create a path for them; the path is [simply] there and they follow it.
The Superior Man's sorrowful despondency does not exactly take definite form, but it is conveyed to the hearts of others.
It is not something that comes in from outside but something that emerges from within [one's own] center [i.e., the human heart]. [10/85/1–3]

10.29

Rightness is more exalted than a ruler.
Humaneness is more intimate than a father.
Thus
the ruler in relation to his ministers [has the power to] kill them or let them live, but he cannot force them to do their jobs with negligent unconcern.
A father in relation to his children [has the power to] reject them or raise them, but he cannot force them to be without anxious concern.[40]

Thus
when Rightness transcends the ruler himself,
and Humaneness transcends the father himself,
the ruler is exalted and his ministers are loyal;
the father is compassionate and his children are filial. [10/85/5–6]

10.30

When sages rule, they transform and nurture [the people] in a spiritlike way.
[If the ruler was of] the highest type, [the people] said, "I [do this because] it is my nature!"

40. For this notion of "anxious concern" (*youxun* 憂尋), see also 10.72 and 10.79.

[If the ruler was of] the next rank, [the people] said, "How subtle he is to be that way!"

Thus the *Odes* says,

"He manages the reins [of government]
as if they were the silk ribbons [of a dancer]."[41]

The *Changes* says,

"Concealing his elegance, he is able to persevere."[42] [10/85/8–9]

10.31

Actions undertaken near at hand cause a civilizing influence to spread far away. Now when he examined his evening gait, the Duke of Zhou was embarrassed by his shadow.

Thus the Superior Man scrutinizes [himself] in solitude.[43] To abandon what is close at hand in expectation of what is far-off is to obstruct [one's path]. [10/85/9–10]

10.32

To hear of goodness is easy. To use it to correct oneself is difficult.

Now when the Master saw the three alterations of grain [i.e., seed, sprout, and ripened form], he sighed deeply and said, "The fox turns its head toward its burrow and dies. But my head [droops like] grain."[44] Thus when the Superior Man sees goodness, he takes pains with respect to himself. If your own self is rectified, then transforming the far-off [by example] will be easy.

Thus the *Odes* says,

"You do not [act] personally; you do not [show] affection;
and the common people do not trust you."[45] [10/85/12–14]

---

41. *Odes* 38. This seems to refer to an aristocratic warrior performing a war dance; the reference to "reins" is probably a reference to actual chariot reins, only much later taken by commentators to refer to the "reins of government." The overt reference is to physical prowess and personal poise.

42. *Changes*, hexagram 2, *Kun* 坤, line 3.

43. This quality of being mindful, cautious, or circumspect of oneself when alone (*shen qi du* 慎其獨) is found in a number of early texts, such as *Zhongyong*, Mawangdui *Wuxingpian*, Guodian *Wuxingpian*, *Xunzi*, and *Liji*.

44. This quotation does not appear in the received Confucian canon.

45. *Odes* 191, stanza 4.

10.33

In his pursuit of affairs,
the petty man says, "If only I could get what I want."
The Superior Man says, "If only I could [practice] Rightness."
In seeking something they are the same;
what they are expecting is different.

If you strike [the planks of] a boat in the middle of the water,
fish plunge and birds scatter.
They hear the same thing; they behave differently.
Their feelings are one.[46] [10/85/16–17]

10.34

For setting out a pot of food, Xi Fuji[47] received a commendatory inscription at his village gate.
For giving a packet of dried meat [to Ling Zhe],[48] Zhao Xuanmeng[49] saved his own life.
As acts of propriety, these were not outstanding, but they overflowed with Moral Potency.

Thus when a humane heart's responsive kindness connects [with another], sympathetic sorrow is born. Thus it enters deeply [into the hearts of] others. [10/85/17–18]

10.35

With a piercing cry,
the family elder arouses kindness and generosity,
whereas the creditor elicits competition and strife.

Therefore it is said,

46. A parallel saying is reiterated in 11.19, where it is attributed to Zengzi.

47. Xi Fuji 僖負羈 was a minister of Cao during the Spring and Autumn period. He sent a plate of food containing a jade disk to the ducal scion Chong'er during his wanderings in exile. Chong'er later went on to become Duke Wen of Jin and hegemon. See *Zuozhuan*, Xi 23.

48. Ling Zhe 靈輒 was a knight of Jin who served in the palace guard of Duke Ling. He had been saved from starvation by Zhao Xuanmeng and later aided Zhao's escape from an ambush that the duke had laid for him. See *Zuozhuan*, Xuan 2.

49. Zhao Xuanmeng 趙宣孟 (also known as Zhao Dun 盾 and Viscount Xuan 宣子 of Zhao) was a minister of Jin during the late seventh century B.C.E. He consolidated control over the Jin court and presided over a period of peace and stability. In 607 B.C.E., he fell out of favor with Duke Ling (r. 620–607 B.C.E.) and was forced into exile.

"There are no weapons more fearsome than the human will. The Moye sword is inferior to it.
There are no assailants greater than Yin and Yang. The drum and drumstick are smaller than them." [10/85/18–20]

10.36

When sages practice goodness, it is not to seek fame, yet fame follows. They do not expect fame to be accompanied by profit, yet profit comes to them.

Thus people's anxiety and happiness are not the result of following a deliberate path. The path takes them there, and the feelings emerge. Thus the very highest [sages] do not [concern themselves with] outward appearances. Thus they are as if

rubbing their eyes when smarting,
grabbing a support when stumbling. [10/85/22–23]

10.37

The sage's conduct of government is silent and does not make a display of worthiness. Only after [his reign] has come to an end do you know that it can be [considered] great.

It is like the movement of the sun: [even the great horse] Qiji cannot compete with how far it goes. [10/85/23–24]

10.38

When we seek something at night, we are as blind as a music master. But when the eastern sky opens, how bright it is!

When you act with a view toward gain, loss follows.

Thus the *Changes* says,

"Stripping them away, they are not successively exhausted,
Thus they are received again in returning."[50] [10/85/24–26]

---

50. This paraphrases a line from the *Xu gua* 序卦 (*The Order of the Hexagrams*), ninth of the "Ten Wings" (appended commentaries) of the *Changes*. The line refers to hexagrams 23, *Bo* 剝, "Stripping Away," and 24, *Fu* 復, "Returning." The logic of the statement is as follows: Bo is one yang line above five yin lines; Fu is five yin lines above one yang line. Ascending the lines of the Bo hexagram, there is still one yang line left in the end, and a yang line is the first one encountered in the next hexagram, Fu.

10.39

Amassing the thin makes the thick.
Amassing the low makes the high.

Thus
every day the Superior Man works diligently and thereby attains glory.
Every day the petty man works shoddily and thereby reaps ignominy.
But [the increments of] diminution and increase [are such that] even Li Zhu could not clearly discern them. [10/86/1–2]

10.40

King Wen
listened for what was good as if he could not attain it
and dwelt on what was not good as if it were an unlucky portent.
It was not that the days were insufficient. His anxious concern [within himself] compelled him to do so.

Thus the *Odes* says,
"Though Zhou is an old country,
its mandate is new."[51] [10/86/2–3]

10.41

If you cherish feelings and embrace inherent qualities,
Heaven cannot kill you;
Earth cannot bury you.
Your voice will resound throughout the space between Heaven and Earth, [and] your brightness will match the sun and moon. This is because you take joy in it. [10/86/3–4]

10.42

If you turn to goodness, even if you err, you will not be censured.
If you do not turn to goodness, even if you are loyal, you will invite calamity.

Thus

51. *Odes* 235. The reference is to Zhou King Wen, who attained the "new mandate" (*ming* 命) that brought the Zhou dynasty to power.

being censorious toward others is not so good as being censorious toward yourself.
Seeking it [i.e., goodness] in others is not so good as seeking it in yourself.[52] [10/86/4–5]

10.43

Sounds sound themselves.
Appearances display themselves.
Names announce themselves.
People[53] find their appropriate functions themselves.
There is nothing that is not intrinsic.[54]

The spear is wielded to pierce.
The sword is wielded to stab.
That things announce themselves is apparent. What cause do they have to resent others?

Thus,
Guanzi's patterned brocade was ugly, but he ascended the ancestral temple.
Zichan's[55] dyed silk was beautiful, but he gained no respect.[56] [10/86/7–8]

10.44

Empty yet able to be filled,
insipid yet acquiring flavor,
wearing coarse garments but embracing a jade [scepter].[57]

Thus,
when of two minds, you cannot obtain [the allegiance of even] one person;
when of one mind, you can obtain [the allegiance of] a hundred.[58] [10/86/9–10]

52. For the parallel passage in the reconstructed *Zisizi*, see Harper, "*Huai Nan Tzu* Chapter 10," app. 1, F.

53. Reading *ren* 人 in place of *wen* 文, as in the *Wenzi*. See Lau, HNZ, 86n.4.

54. For the parallel passage in the reconstructed *Zisizi*, see Csikszentmihalyi 2004, app. 1, no. 24.

55. Zichan 子產 (d. 522 B.C.E.), a scion of the ducal house of Zheng, served as that state's prime minister from 554 B.C.E. He reformed the agricultural, judicial, and fiscal systems of his state and helped preserve it from the encroachments of powerful neighbors.

56. For the parallel passage in the reconstructed *Zisizi*, see Harper, "*Huai Nan Tzu* Chapter 10," app. 1, G; and Csikszentmihalyi 2004, app. 1, no. 32.

57. Compare *Laozi* 70.

58. For the parallel passage in the reconstructed *Zisizi*, see Harper, "*Huai Nan Tzu* Chapter 10," app. 1, H; and Csikszentmihalyi 2004, app. 1, no. 32, with reference to app. 1, no. 13.

10.45

If a boy plants an orchid, it will be beautiful but will not be fragrant.
If a stepson is fed, he will grow fat but will not flourish.

[This is because] feelings are not mutually shared in the intercourse between them.[59] [10/86/12]

10.46

Life is [a dwelling] that you borrow;
death is [a home] to which you return.

Thus,

Hong Yan,[60] upright and humane, stood up and died.
Prince Lü[61] bared his chest to receive the knife.

They would not let what was [temporarily] entrusted to them harm that to which they would return.

Thus,

When the age is well governed, you use Rightness to protect yourself.
When times are disordered, you use yourself to protect Rightness.[62]

The day that you die [marks] the end of your actions. Therefore, the Superior Man is careful every single time he uses his person. [10/86/12–14]

10.47

Those who lack bravery are not initially fainthearted, but when difficulties arise, they lose their self-control.

Those who are greedy and covetous are not initially lustful, but when they see profit they forget the harm involved.

---

59. That is, between the boy and the (feminine) orchid, and between the stepparent and the stepchild.

60. Hong Yan 弘演 was a knight in the service of Duke Yi of Wey (r. 668–660 B.C.E.). The duke was killed and eaten by the Di people, leaving only his liver. Hong Yan killed himself, cutting himself open and putting the duke's liver inside himself so that his own body would serve as his lord's corpse. On hearing of this sacrifice, Duke Huan of Qi reestablished the state of Wey. See *Lüshi chunqiu* 11.4.

61. Prince Lü 王子閭 (d. 479 B.C.E.) was a scion of the royal house of Chu. When Duke Bo rebelled, he attempted to force Prince Lü to take the throne. The prince refused and was killed. See *Zuozhuan*, Ai 16.

62. For the parallel passage in the reconstructed *Zisizi*, see Harper, "*Huai Nan Tzu* Chapter 10," app. 1, I.

When the Duke of Yu saw the jade *bi* of Chuiji, he did not know that the calamity of Guo would befall him.[63] Thus [only] the most advanced human beings cannot be repressed or diverted. [10/86/16–17]

10.48

People's desire for glory is for their own sake. What good is that to others? [But] when sages act to implement Rightness, their anxious concern emanates from within. What benefit is it to them personally?

Thus

> emperors and kings have been numerous, but the Three Kings alone are praised.
> The poor and lowly have been numerous, but Bo Yi[64] alone is esteemed.
> Does being wealthy make you a sage? Then sages would be numerous.
> Does being poor make you humane? Then the humane would be numerous.

Why, then, are sages and humane people so rare? Oh, what a joy is an independent and focused resolve! [10/86/19–21]

10.49

As each day rolls by hastily and the days renew themselves, you forget that old age will come upon you.

> From your young and tender years,
> to your becoming gray and old,

[the years] inevitably pile up in this way. If you do not deceive yourself, you will not deceive others.

It is like crossing a bridge [made from] a single [log]. Just because there is no one else present does not mean you do not struggle [to maintain] your countenance. Thus it is easy to get people to trust you, but difficult to trust yourself should you cloak yourself in [deceptive] clothing. [10/86/21–24]

---

63. *Zuo zhuan*, Xi 2. The story of the jade disk of Chuiji, the Duke of Jin, and the rulers of Yu and Guo is also found in 7.16 (see chap. 7, n. 58), 11.7, 17.57, and 18.5.

64. Bo Yi 伯夷 was the legendary son of the lord of Guzhu who was so offended by the overthrow of the Shang by the Zhou that he and his brother Shu Qi 叔齊 starved themselves to death rather than suffer the shame of eating the grain of a usurper. Their joint biography is found in *Shiji* 61.

10.50

When feelings precede actions, no action is unsuccessful. When nothing is unsuccessful, there is no vexation. Released from vexation, you become content.

Thus,

the comportment of Tang [Yao] and Yu [Shun] was such that it did not violate their feelings. They pleased themselves, and the world was well ordered.

[The tyrants] Jie and Djou were not intentionally thuggish. They pleased themselves, and the many concerns [of government] were laid waste.

When their likes and dislikes are critiqued, order and disorder are distinguished. [10/86/24–10/87/2]

10.51

The actions of the sage

are not joined with anything

and are not separated from anything.

By analogy, it is like a drum.

There is no instrument that is in tune with it,

and no instrument that cannot be accompanied by it. [10/87/4]

10.52

With instruments of silk (strings) and bamboo or metal and stone, their size and length have gradations.[65] They make different sounds, but they harmonize.

With ruler and official or superior and subordinate, their offices and functions have grades. They perform different tasks but act in unison.

Now

the weaver daily advances

while the tiller daily retreats.

Their tasks move in opposite directions, but in accomplishment they are one. [10/87/4–6]

---

65. Stringed instruments have long and short strings, and metal bells, chimestones, and the keys of bamboo xylophones come in sets, from very large to very small.

10.53

Shen Xi heard a beggar's song and was saddened. When he went out to see who it was, it was his mother.[66] At the battle of Ailing, [King] Fuchai of Wu[67] said, "The Yi raise their voices. Such is the multitude of Wu!"[68] What was the same was that there were voices, but the beliefs derived from them were different; they were inherent in the [respective] feelings [of the singers].[69]

Thus,

if the heart is sad, the song is not joyful.

If the heart is joyful, the wailing is not sorrowful.

After the three years of mourning were over, Minzi Jian picked up his *qin* and played. The Master said, "His playing was correct, but it sounded wrong."[70] [10/87/6–8]

10.54

Culture is the means by which we connect to things.

Feelings bind inwardly,

but desires manifest themselves externally.

If you use culture to obliterate feelings, feelings will be lost.

If you use feelings to obliterate culture, culture will be lost.

When the guiding patterns of culture and feelings interpenetrate, the phoenix and the *qilin* will roam extensively. That is to say, the embrace of your Utmost Potency will be far-reaching. [10/87/8–11]

10.55

Shu Ziyang[71] said to his son, "A good workman immerses himself in his square and his chisel." Between the square and the chisel, there certainly is nothing than cannot be brought to completion.

What sage-kings used to control the people,

66. See 16.4.

67. King Fuchai of Wu 吳王夫差 (r. 495–473 B.C.E.) initially led Wu to great triumph over King Goujian of Yue, but his later negligence led to his state's destruction by Yue and his own suicide. See 12.23.

68. The "Yi music" refers to the Yi "tribe," an important ethnic group in the state of Wu.

69. Compare 19.3: "An ardent feeling internally is manifested as a response externally. The cause [of the response] lies in the feeling itself."

70. For the parallel passage in the reconstructed *Zisizi*, see Harper, "*Huai Nan Tzu* Chapter 10," app. 1, J; and Csikszentmihalyi 2004, app. 1, no. 30.

71. Shu Ziyang 輸子陽, otherwise unknown.

what Zaofu used to control horses,
what Physician Luo[72] used to control illnesses:
they all took what they needed from the same basic material. [10/87/11–13]

10.56

The ruler wills it.
The people fulfill it.
This is because of his inner sincerity.
Before saying a word, he is trusted;
without being summoned, they come.
Something precedes it. [10/87/15]

10.57

Those who are worried about others not knowing them do not know themselves.
Arrogance and pride are born from inadequacy.
Flamboyance and deceit are born from arrogance.
People who have inner sincerity are joyful and unworried.

It is like
the owl loving to hoot
or the bear loving to pace—
Where is there anyone who should be arrogant? [10/87/15–17]

10.58

In spring the maid grieves.
In autumn the warrior mourns.
They know that things will transform.[73]

With howling or weeping, sighing and grieving, we recognize sounds that are [genuinely] actuated.
With bearing and visage, rouge and tint, and with bending and stretching, standing and crouching, we recognize feelings that are feigned.

72. According to Xu Shen, Physician Luo 醫駱 was a physician of Yue. See Zhang Shuangdi 1997, 1:1069n.29.

73. The implication is that in spring the power of yin is waning. It is the season for girls to marry and move to their husbands' households, so they grieve for having to leave their own families. In autumn the power of yang is waning. It is the season for warfare, when many warriors will be killed on the battlefield.

Thus the sage trembles at [what he keeps] within himself and so attains the highest ultimate. [10/87/19–21]

10.59

When a meritorious reputation follows success, that is Heaven's doing;
when compliant principles meet with acceptance, that is humankind's doing.

Grand Duke Wang and Duke Dan of Zhou were not created by Heaven for [the benefit of] King Wu.
Marquis Chong and Wulai[74] were not engendered by Heaven for [the benefit of the tyrant] Djou.
As with the era, so with the men. [10/87/23–24]

10.60

Education is rooted in the Superior Man, [but] the petty man is enriched by it.
Profit is rooted in the petty man, [but] the Superior Man fattens on its results.

Formerly, in the time of Donghu Jizi,[75] people did not take goods that were left on the road. Hoes and plows and leftover grain were stored at the head [of the fields], enabling the Superior Man and the petty man each to obtain his appropriate [share].[76]

Thus, "when the One Man[77] encounters good fortune, the many people depend on it."[78] [10/87/26–27]

10.61

Those in the highest position esteem their left side. Thus subordinates say to superiors, "I am on your left." Such is the artful speech of a minister.

---

74. Marquis Chong 崇侯 and Wulai 惡來 were ministers of King Djou, the tyrannical last ruler of the Shang, who encouraged the king's bad tendencies.

75. According to Xu Shen, Donghu Jizi 東戶季子 was a ruler of antiquity. See Zhang Shuangdi 1997, 1:1072n.42.

76. For a more detailed description of Donghu Jizi in the reconstructed *Zisizi*, see Harper, "*Huai Nan Tzu* Chapter 10," app. 1, K; and Csikszentmihalyi 2004, app. 1, no. 34.

77. That is, the ruler.

78. This line from the *Documents* is also quoted (with a slight variation in wording) in 9.18.

Those who are below esteem their right side. Thus superiors say to subordinates, "I am on your right." Such is the condescension of the ruler.[79]

Thus,

if the superior moves to the left, he loses what makes him respected.
If the minister shifts to the right, he loses what makes him esteemed. [10/87/29–30]

10.62

Small instances of haste harm the Way;
false pretenses disrupt the proper order.

When Zichan drafted his writings, lawsuits proliferated, [even though] there was no depraved [intent].[80] If you lose touch with your feelings, your words will be obstructed. [10/88/1–2]

10.63

The way of perfecting a country is that
tradesmen should have no false dealings;
farmers should have no wasted labor;
scholars should take no clandestine actions;
officials should make no evasion of the laws.

It is analogous to someone setting out nets. When he pulls on the guide rope, the myriad eyes open. [10/88/4–5]

10.64

Shun and Yu did not accept the Mandate of Heaven the second time [it was offered].[81] What Yao and Shun transmitted[82] was great, but it first took shape in something small.

79. This passage is a pun between two sets of words that are homophones and synonyms. *Zuo* 左, "left," puns on *zuo* 佐, "to assist"; and *you* 右, "right," puns on *you* 佑, "to help." Thus "I am on your left" is a pun for "I will assist you," and "I am on your right" is a pun for "I will help you."

80. That is, no depravity on Zichan's part. His drafting of a law code was not undertaken with bad intentions.

81. They accepted only after the third offer.

82. That is, the principle that the mandate should be bestowed on a meritorious successor.

"He tested [Shun] with the royal wives,
extended it to the brothers as well.
When he abdicated clan and state,"[83]
the whole world followed his example.

Thus,

with weapons, one uses what is great to understand what is small;
with humankind, one uses what is small to understand what is great. [10/88/5–7]

10.65

The Way of the Superior Man is
close but cannot be attained,
low but cannot be ascended,
contains nothing inside it, but cannot be filled. It is
enduring yet brilliant,
far-reaching yet illustrious.

To understand this and so follow the Way is something that cannot be sought in others but only attained from the self. If you abandon the search within yourself and seek it in others, you will have strayed far from it. [10/88/9–10]

10.66

The Superior Man has ample joy but insufficient reputation.
The petty man has insufficient joy but ample reputation.

When one looks at the difference between being ample and being insufficient, they are clearly very far apart. To hold something [noxious] in your mouth and not spit it out, or to have something in your feelings and not let it blossom forth—these are things that have never been heard of. [10/88/12–13]

10.67

The Superior Man ponders Rightness and does not anticipate profit.
The petty man craves profit and does not regard Rightness.

83. *Odes* 240, stanza 2. The reference to King Wu, second founder of the Zhou dynasty, seems to have been emended in this passage to refer instead to Yao and Shun. For the story of how Yao tested Shun, first by marrying him to two of his daughters and then by giving him nine of his sons to care for, see 20.11 and *Shiji* 1, "The Basic Annals of the Five Thearchs."

The Master said, "Both weeping said, 'Oh! What to do? You took advantage of me!' Their sorrow was the same, but the reasons for it were different."

Thus sorrow and joy penetrate deeply into people's feelings.[84] [10/88/13–15]

10.68

If digging ditches and damming ponds is not done properly, it will overwork and distress the people. If each [project planner] follows his own desire, disorder will result. The feelings [behind their actions] are the same, but the way [each] applies [those feelings] to people is different.[85]

Thus

Tang [Yao] and Yu [Shun] strove daily, thereby leading to their kingships.
Jie and Djou erred daily, thereby leading to their deaths,

without knowing that later ages would condemn them. [10/88/17–19]

10.69

Human feelings are such that

people are joyful when they avoid what brings them suffering
and sorrowful when they lose what brings them joy.

Thus,

knowing the joy of life,
you will necessarily know the sorrow of death. [10/88/21]

10.70

If you have Rightness, you cannot be deceived by profit.
If you have courage, you cannot be intimidated by fear.

Similarly those who are starving and thirsty cannot be deceived with an empty bowl.

When people multiply desires, they decrease Rightness.
[When people] multiply anxieties, they injure knowledge,
[When people] multiply fears, they injure courage. [10/88/23–24]

84. The point here is that two people said the same thing to each other, but for different reasons.

85. The point would seem to be that both ditching and damming are valid ways of managing water resources, but you must choose one or the other, lest one person's ditch interfere with another person's dam.

10.71

Rudeness is born of the petty man.
[Even] the ["barbarian"] Man and Yi can [behave like] that.
Goodness is born of the Superior Man.
Radiantly it rivals the brilliance of the sun and moon. No one in the world can restrain or repress it.

Thus,
a well-governed state rejoices in the means by which it is preserved;
a perishing state rejoices in the means by which it is lost. [10/88/26–27]

10.72

If metal[86] and tin are not melted, they cannot be poured into the mold.
If the ruler's anxious concern is not sincere, he cannot serve as a model for the people.
If his anxious concern is not grounded in the people, the ruler will cut his ties to them.
If the ruler returns to the root, his ties to the people will be firm. [10/88/29–30]

10.73

The Utmost Potency [is attained when]
small matters are completed
and great matters are initiated.

Duke Huan of Qi initiated [great matters] but was not attentive to details.
Duke Wen of Jin[87] was attentive to details but did not initiate [great matters].
Duke Wen obtained what he wanted within his private quarters but failed beyond the borders.
Duke Huan failed within his private quarters but obtained what he wanted at court. [10/89/1–2]

86. That is, copper; the reference is to the casting of bronze.

87. Duke Wen of Jin 晉文公 (also known as Chong'er 重耳 [r. 636–628 B.C.E.]) was a storied ruler who, despite a crippling physical deformity and despite being forced to live in exile in early life, rose to become one of the most powerful leaders of the state of Jin and the second Zhou vassal lord to assume the title of hegemon. He figures in many early texts.

10.74

Water flows downward, becoming wide and great.
The ruler puts himself below his minister, becoming comprehensive and brilliant.

If the ruler does not contend with his ministers for achievement, the Way of governing will prevail.

Guan Yiwu and Baili Xi[88] were the ones who properly aligned and brought to completion their various achievements; Duke Huan of Qi and Duke Mu of Qin[89] [merely] accepted them and assented to them. [10/89/4–5]

10.75

On a bright day you might confuse east for west, but if you are confused, you have only to see the sun to realize your mistake.

Marquis Wu of Wey[90] said to his officials, "You young fellows should not call me old and treat me like a dotard. If I make mistakes, you must point them out to me." Actually, if Marquis Wu had not shown in this way that he was not a dotard, he would in fact have been in his dotage. Thus he grew old but was not ignored. He comprehended the principles by which [states] are preserved or lost. [10/89/7–10]

10.76

People do not possess the ability to create, but they possess the ability to act.
They possess the ability to act, but they do not possess the ability to perfect.

What people do is perfected by Heaven.

Even if people do good deeds all their lives, if not for Heaven, they would not succeed.
Even if people do evil deeds all their lives, if not for Heaven, they would not fail.

Thus,

goodness or evil is our own doing;
bad or good fortune is not our own doing.

---

88. Baili Xi 百里奚 was a worthy of Yu who was ransomed out of captivity by Duke Mu of Qin and raised to be his prime minister.

89. Duke Mu of Qin 秦穆公 (r. 659–621 B.C.E.) was a powerful ruler who purportedly became one of the "five hegemons" of the Zhou era.

90. Marquis Wu of Wey 衛武侯 (r. 812–758 B.C.E.) was a vassal who led forces in defense of the Zhou when they were forced from their capital in 771 B.C.E.

Thus the Superior Man complies with what lies within him; that is all he can do. [10/89/12–14]

10.77

Nature is what is received from Heaven;[91]
destiny is what depends on the times.[92]

If you possess talent but do not encounter the right era for it, that is Heaven's doing.

What made Grand Duke [Wang] strong?
What made [Prince] Bi Gan a criminal?

They both complied with their natures and acted on their intentions. One was harmed, one was benefited.

For seeking something there is a Way,
but attaining it is a matter of destiny.[93]

Thus, the Superior Man
can do good but cannot make certain that he will encounter good fortune;
cannot bear to do evil but cannot make certain that he will avoid misfortune.[94]
[10/89/14–16]

10.78

The ruler is the trunk and roots;
his officials are the branches and leaves.
A [tree's] trunk and roots that are not beautiful
but whose branches and leaves are luxuriant—such a thing has never been heard of.[95] [10/89/18]

10.79

In an age that has the Way, a man is given to the state.
In an age that does not have the Way, the state is given to a man.

---

91. Compare *Xunzi* 22 (XZ 22/111/14); a similar phrase also appears in *Zhongyong* (*Liji* 32/242/21).

92. A similar phrase is found in *Xunzi* 28 (XZ 28/141/6).

93. See MZ 13.3/67/221–22.

94. These two lines are also a reference to Mencius. See MZ 13.3/67/21–22.

95. For the parallel passage in the reconstructed *Zisizi*, see Harper, "*Huai Nan Tzu* Chapter 10," app. 1, L; and Csikszentmihalyi 2004, app. 1, no. 13.

When Yao ruled the world as king, his anxiety did not abate. When he conferred [his rulership] on Shun, his anxiety disappeared. Anxiously he watched over it; joyfully he gave it to a worthy. To the end he did not consider the benefit [of rulership] to be his private possession. [10/89/20–21]

10.80

The myriad things all have some use. Nothing is so small that it is useless.

If you view things from the perspective of their uselessness, precious jades are [no different from] manure. [10/89/23]

10.81

Human feelings [are such that]

when encountering harm, people struggle to obtain [only] the smallest portion;
when encountering benefit, they struggle to obtain the largest portion.

Thus,

when the flavor is the same and one craves a bigger piece of meat, it is certainly because one savors it.
when the teacher is the same and one [student] surpasses the group, it is certainly because he finds joy in the teacher.

Who has ever heard of someone setting an outstanding example in something that he neither savored nor enjoyed? [10/89/25–26]

10.82

When the time is right, the Superior Man advances and obtains [it] by means of Rightness. What good luck does he possess?
When the time is not right, he withdraws and yields [it] by means of Rightness. What bad luck does he possess?

Thus when Bo Yi starved [himself] to death at the foot of Mount Shou[yang], it was without personal regrets;

he abandoned what he considered worthless
and gained what he considered valuable. [10/89/28–29]

10.83

The sprouts of good fortune are flossy and fine,
and the birth of bad fortune is tiny and trifling.

Since the beginnings of good and bad fortune are tiny as a sprout, people overlook them. Only sages see their beginnings and know their ends.

Thus a chronicle says,

"The wine of Lu was weak and Handan was surrounded;
the lamb broth was not poured, and the state of Song was endangered."[96] [10/90/1–2]

10.84

An enlightened ruler's rewards and punishments
are not employed on his own behalf;
they are employed for the state.
If someone suited the ruler personally but was of no benefit to the state, the ruler would not confer a reward on him.
If someone defied the ruler personally but was helpful to the state, he would not impose a punishment on him.[97]

Thus King Zhuang of Chu said to Gong Yong,[98] "Those who have Potency receive rank and emoluments from me. Those who have achievements receive fields and residences from me. Of these two, you do not have even one. I have nothing to give you." It can be said that he did not go beyond his principles. He rejected Gong Yong and [also] avoided encouraging him. [10/90/4–7]

10.85

The governing of Zhou was supreme.
The governing of Shang was good.
The governing of Xia was effective.
Effective governing is not necessarily good.
Good governing is not necessarily supreme.

96. Both of these are incidents of the minor failure of diplomatic etiquette leading to important military confrontation. The second line is an allusion to the Song general Hua Yuan's failure to distribute lamb meat to his charioteer before an important battle. The incident is recorded in *Zuozhuan*, Duke Xuan 2.

97. He would not allow personal pique to interfere with the larger interests of his state.

98. According to Xu Shen, Gong Yong 共雍 was an official of Chu. See Zhang Shuangdi 1997, 1:1085n.16.

People who have attained the utmost do not envy [participating in governing] that is effective nor are they ashamed to [take part in governing] that is good. They hold steadfastly to their Moral Potency as they tread the Way, and superior and subordinate rejoice in each other without knowing the reason why. [10/90/9–10]

10.86

Those who possessed states were numerous, but Duke Huan of Qi and Duke Wen of Jin are uniquely renowned. On Mount Tai there are seventy royal altars, but the Three Kings are uniquely [known for having followed] the Way.

> The ruler does not seek things from his ministers,
> and the ministers do not borrow things from their ruler.

The ruler cultivates what is near and extends [his influence] to what is far, so that later ages proclaim his greatness. Without encroaching on his neighbors, he achieves a glorious reputation, so that no one compares with him.

Thus someone might behave with Xiao Ji's[99] perfect propriety but still not be able to challenge his reputation, for certainly no one can attain what he embraced in himself. [10/90/12–14]

10.87

> One whose Rightness includes a sense of appropriateness is called a Superior Man.
> One whose appropriateness abandons a sense of Rightness is called a petty man.

> Penetrating wisdom achieves [its goals] without exertion;
> the next best kind exerts itself without becoming worn out;
> the lowest kind becomes worn out without exerting itself.
> Men of antiquity tasted [the food offered in sacrifice] but did not covet it.
> Men of today covet [the sacrificial food] but do not care about its taste. [10/90/16–17]

99. Xiao Ji 孝已 (Ji the Filial), the son of King Wuding of the Shang dynasty, was renowned for his filial piety. He fell victim to his stepmother's slander and died in exile.

10.88

When singing improves on the score, it is because the score itself is not sufficiently beautiful. [Instruments of] metal, stone, string, and bamboo bolster and accompany the music, but that still does not suffice to reach the utmost [excellence].

When people are able to revere the Way and practice Rightness, happiness and anger [are things they can] take or leave; their desires are like grass following the wind. [10/90/17–19]

10.89

In the season for picking mulberry leaves, raising silkworms' cocoons, and plowing and planting, the Duke of Shao[100] opened the jails and released the prisoners. Thus the common people all were able to resume their occupations and return to their work.

King Wen declined [a grant of] a thousand *li* of land, but requested instead that [Tyrant Djou] should eliminate the punishment of the roasting beam.[101]

Thus in carrying out their duties, sages do not lose the moment in advancing and withdrawing. This is like the saying, "In the summer you wear hemp; when you mount a chariot you hold the strap." [10/90/21–23]

10.90

> Laozi studied under Shang Rong. He got a look at Shang Rong's tongue and understood preserving the soft.[102]
> Liezi studied under Huzi. He saw the shadow of his walking stick and understood the principle of following behind.

Thus sages do not go ahead of things, and so they constantly control them. Things of this sort are analogous to a stack of firewood. The last [logs] are laid on top.[103] [10/90/25–26]

100. The Duke of Shao 召公, a loyal official who served as grand protector to King Wu of Zhou, was enfeoffed at Shao.

101. A cruel punishment attributed to the tyrant Djou, last ruler of the Shang dynasty. A person was forced to walk to his death across a red-hot metal beam. It is also mentioned in 2.14, 11.1, 12.35, 15.2, and 21.4.

102. The point is that the soft (the tongue) outlasts the hard (the teeth); this is presented as the inspiration for Laozi's emphasis on water and other "soft" metaphors.

103. For the notion that the sage follows behind, see 1.11 and 14.56; and *Laozi* 66.

10.91

People
love by means of Rightness,
gather together by means of cliques,
and grow strong by gathering together.

For this reason,
when Moral Potency is applied broadly, then might is effective distantly.
When Rightness is applied parsimoniously, then what is controlled militarily will be small. [10/90/28–29]

10.92

The Wu bell destroyed itself with its sound.
The wax lamp melted itself with its brightness.

The markings of tigers and leopards attract archers.
The agility of monkeys and apes invites pursuit.[104]

Thus,
Zilu died because of his bravery.
Chang Hong[105] was captured because of his cleverness.
He could use his cleverness to be clever, but he could not use his cleverness to not be clever.

Thus,
If you traverse a pass, you cannot tread [as straight as] a marking cord.
If you come out of a forest, you cannot follow a straight path.[106]
When traveling at night, your vision becomes obscured, and you lead with your hands.[107]

Sometimes situations arise in which clarity [of vision] is not of much use.[108] If a person can connect to Dark Obscurity to enter into Brilliant Brightness, that is someone with whom you can discuss the ultimate. [10/90/32–10/91/3]

---

104. This saying paraphrases *Zhuangzi*, chap. 7 (ZZ 7/20/20), where it is attributed to Laozi. It does not, however, appear in the received version of the *Daodejing*. This saying also appears in 14.4 and 17.84.

105. Chang Hong 萇弘 (d. 492 B.C.E.) was an officer of the state of Liu famed for his skill in astronomy, calendrics, and divination. There was once a text in his name, now lost.

106. This saying also appears in 17.70.

107. A variant of this saying occurs in 17.133.

108. The implication is that when it is dark, there may still be an inner clarity that is not impaired by the darkness because it goes beyond mere visual acuity.

10.93

To build its nest, a magpie [must] know from which way the wind arises.
To build its burrow, an otter [must] know the height of the water.
The "Bright Day" knows when it will be clear;
The "Shady Accord" knows when it will be rainy.[109]

But if because of this you were to say that human knowledge is inferior to that of birds and beasts, it would not be true. Thus a person who has

mastered one skill
or investigated one text

can explain one corner [of a subject] but cannot give a comprehensive response. [10/91/5–6]

10.94

Ning Qi beat time on a cow's horn and sang, and Duke Huan raised him up with a great grant of land. Yong Menzi used crying to gain an audience with Lord Meng Chang.[110] His tears flowed down so that they soaked his hat strings. Singing and crying are things that anyone can do.

You make a sound;
it enters someone's ears;
it moves his heart—

it is something that reaches the essence.

Thus you might emulate the models of Tang [Yao] and Yu [Shun], but you will not achieve their communion with the hearts of others. [10/91/8–10]

10.95

Duke Jian of Qi[111] was murdered because of his weakness;
Ziyang[112] was put to death because of his fearlessness.

Both were unable to attain their Way.

Thus if you sing without following the notes, the high and low notes will all be the same.

---

109. Commentators gloss the names "Bright Day" (*hui ri* 暉日) and "Shady Accord" (*yin xie* 陰諧) as poetic names for the male and female of a species of falcon.

110. See 6.1.

111. Duke Jian of Qi 齊簡公 (r. 484–481 B.C.E.) was overthrown by his prime minister, Tian Chang, marking the ascendancy of the Tian clan over the Qi court.

112. Ziyang 子陽 (d. 398 B.C.E.) was a prime minister of Zheng who led that state in resisting the aggression of Chu. The ruler of Zheng killed him in an attempt to appease the king of Chu.

Outside the marking cord [line]
or inside the marking cord [line],
in either case it is not straight. [10/91/12–13]

10.96

[The tyrant] Djou made ivory chopsticks, and Jizi lamented.
Lu used figurines in their burials, and Confucius sighed.[113]
They saw the beginning and knew the end.[114]

Thus
water comes out of the mountains and flows into the sea.
Grain grows in the fields and is stored in storehouses.
Sages see where things begin and know where they will end up.[115] [10/91/15–16]

10.97

When waters are muddy, fish gasp for air [near the surface].[116]
When laws are harsh, the people rebel.[117]
When city walls are precipitous, they invariably crumble.
When riverbanks are steep, they invariably collapse.

Thus
Shang Yang established laws and was dismembered.
Wu Qi instituted mutilating punishments and was torn apart by chariots. [10/91/18–19]

10.98

Governing a country is like tuning a *se*.
If the thick strings are tightened too much,
the thin ones will break.

Thus if you yank the reins and whip [your horses] many times, you are not a thousand-*li* driver. [10/91/21–22]

113. See also MZ 1.4/2/22–23.

114. This saying is repeated in 16.102, with slightly different wording. This anecdote also appears in *Hanfeizi*, chaps. 21 and 22. See HFZ 21/44/5 and 22/49/21.

115. For this quality of the sage, see also 9.7, 9.30, 13.13, 14.65, and 20.35.

116. This proverbial phrase also appears in 9.4, 16.59, and 20.2. See also HSWZ 1.23/5/13 and SY 7.4/47/23.

117. See also 9.26.

10.99

The sound that has sound
cannot go farther than a hundred *li*.
The sound that has no sound
extends throughout the Four Seas.

For this reason,
when emoluments exceed merit, there is harm;
when reputation exceeds reality, there is deception.
If feelings and actions are in accord and reputation is secondary to them, the arrival of ill or good fortune will not be without reason. [10/91/22–23]

10.100

If you personally have bad dreams, you have not yet mastered proper conduct.
If a state witnesses unlucky omens, it has not yet mastered good government.

For this reason,
if at first you are rewarded with the carriage and cap [of office], you will not get anything out of it if you have no merit.
If later you are punished with the executioner's ax, you will not suffer from it if you have no guilt.
If you are in the habit of cultivating what is proper, you will not depart from the Way. [10/91/23–25]

10.101

The Superior Man does not say,
"Small [acts of] goodness are not important enough to do" and therefore sets them aside. Small [acts of] goodness accumulate to become great goodness.
[He also does not say],
"Small [acts of] misconduct do not do any harm" and therefore does them. Small [acts of] misconduct accumulate to become great misconduct.

For the same reason,
a pile of feathers can sink a boat;
lots of light things can break an axle.
Thus the Superior Man observes prohibitions [even] regarding minutiae. [10/92/1–2]

10.102

A single pleasing act is not sufficient to constitute goodness. Accumulate pleasing acts and they become Moral Potency.

A single hateful act is not sufficient to constitute wrong. Accumulate hateful acts and they will become evil.

Thus

the [reputation for] goodness of the Three Dynasties [Xia, Shang, and Zhou] [reflects] the accumulated praise of a thousand years;

the [reputation for] evil of Jie and Djou [reflects] the accumulated condemnation of a thousand years. [10/92/2–4]

10.103

Heaven has four seasons;
people have four functions.

What is meant by the four functions?

For seeing and giving shape to things, nothing is clearer than the eyes.
For hearing and refining things, nothing is keener than the ears.
For holding and shutting up something, nothing is firmer than the mouth.
For containing and concealing something, nothing is deeper than the heart.

When

the eyes see the form,
the ears hear the sound,
the mouth expresses the sincerity,
and the heart communicates the essence,

the transformation of the ten thousand things will reach their limit. [10/92/6–8]

10.104

When a territory is enlarged by means of Moral Potency, the ruler will be respected for his Moral Potency. This is best.

When a territory is enlarged by means of Rightness, the ruler will be respected for his Rightness. This is next best.

When a territory is enlarged by means of might, the ruler will be respected for his might. This is inferior.

Thus

a pure ruler is a [true] king;
a ruler of mixed qualities is a hegemon.

A state that has neither will perish.[118] [10/92/10–11]

10.105

[In the time of] the "two ancients,"[119] a phoenix came to the palace.
During the Three Dynasties, it came to the gate.
In the Zhou,[120] it came to the meadow.

As Potency became coarser, the phoenix kept itself more distant;
As Potency becomes more refined, the phoenix will approach more closely.[121] [10/92/13–14]

10.106

The Superior Man is sincere in Humaneness.
When he acts, it is out of Humaneness;
when he does not act, it is also out of Humaneness.
The petty man is sincere in his own inhumaneness.
When he acts, it is out of inhumaneness;
when he does not act, it is [also] out of inhumaneness.
[Someone whose] goodness comes from the self, rather than coming from others, is [a person] in whom Humaneness and Moral Potency flourish.

Thus,
if your feelings overcome your desires, you will flourish.
If your desires overcome your feelings, you will perish.[122] [10/92/16–17]

10.107

If you want to know the Way of Heaven, examine its cycles.
If you want to know the Way of Earth, differentiate[123] its plants.
If you want to know the Way of Humankind, follow its desires. [10/92/19]

118. This saying appears in *Xunzi*, chaps. 11, 16, and 26.

119. That is, the two mythical sage-kings Fuxi and the Divine Farmer.

120. The "Three Dynasties" are Xia, Shang, and [Western] Zhou; "Zhou" in this line apparently refers to the (decadent) Eastern Zhou.

121. This is possibly a reference to (though not a direct quotation from) *Odes* 252, verses 7–9.

122. The interplay of feelings and desires is an important theme in *Mencius*.

123. Wu 物; lacking an English verb "to thing," one might translate this *in extenso* as "differentiate and gain concrete knowledge of."

10.108

Do not startle [them], do not frighten [them],
and the myriad things will set themselves in order.
Do not disturb [them], do not stir [them] up,
and the myriad things will purify themselves. [10/92/19–20]

10.109

If someone has examined just one corner of something, you cannot discuss transformations with him;
if someone has investigated only one age, it is not possible to discuss anything of significance with him.

The sun does not know the night.
The moon does not know the sunshine.

The sun and moon make light, but they cannot combine [their light] with each other. Only Heaven and Earth can embrace them [both]. When it comes to being able to encompass Heaven and Earth, it is said that only the Formless can do so. [10/92/20–22]

10.110

An arrogant and extravagant ruler has no loyal ministers.
A person with a clever mouth [says] nothing that compels belief.
A tree you can span with both hands does not have branches that will hold [your weight].
A ditch eight feet wide does not contain fish that can swallow a boat.
If the trunk is shallow[ly rooted], the branches will become stunted.
If the root is damaged, the branches will wither away. [10/92/24–25]

10.111

Good fortune is born of non-action;
bad fortune is born of many desires.
Harm stems from not preparing;
weeds stem from not hoeing.

Sages do good as if afraid they will not attain it; they prepare against disaster as if afraid they cannot avoid it. [10/92/25–26]

10.112

To cover yourself with dust and want it not to get in your eyes;
to wade in water and want it not to get you wet—
these things cannot be done.

Thus,
those who know themselves do not resent others;
those who know their destiny do not resent Heaven.[124]
Good fortune springs from oneself;
bad fortune is born from oneself. [10/92/28–29]

10.113

The sage does not seek praise, nor does he avoid condemnation. He corrects his person and acts with rectitude, and the various evils dissipate of their own accord.

Now were he to
abandon rectitude and follow the crooked,
turn his back on truth and follow the crowd,
this would be to consort with the vulgar and to internalize acting without standards. Thus the sage reverts to himself and does not take [the lead from others]. [10/93/1–2]

10.114

The Way that [is written down in] chapters and sections, with shape and boundaries, is not the utmost [Way].
You can taste it, but it has no flavor;
you can observe it, but it has no form.
It cannot be transmitted to others. [10/93/4]

10.115

The *daji* bush expels water,
while the *tingli* plant heals boils,[125]
but if you use them without measuring [the dose], they will make you ill instead.

124. See also MZ 4.13/24/21–26 and 13.1–13.2/67/15–19; the phrase also appears in XZ 4/13/19–20.

125. *Daji* 大戟 and *tingli* 亭歷, not securely identifiable but evidently medicinal plants.

Many things seem to be of the same sort but are not; only sages know their subtleties. [10/93/6–7]

10.116

A good charioteer does not neglect his horses.
A good archer does not neglect his bow.
A good superior does not neglect his subordinates.

If he can love genuinely and benefit the people, the world will follow him. If a father can neither love nor benefit [his children], then even his own sons will rebel against him. [10/93/9–10]

10.117

In the world,

something is most highly honored, and it is not power and position;
something is most highly valued, and it is not gold and jade;
something has the most longevity, and it is not a [lifetime of] a thousand years.
To return your heart to its original nature is most highly honored;
to discipline your feelings to know what is sufficient is most highly valued;
to understand the apportionment of life and death is the greatest longevity. [10/93/12–13]

10.118

Someone whose words are not always true and whose actions are not always appropriate is a petty person.
Someone who has examined into one matter and has mastered one skill is a middle type of person.

Gaining or losing [the realm] but always having it, skilled and capable but using those [attributes] in a measured way, that is a sage. [10/93/15–16]

Translated by Sarah A. Queen and John S. Major

Eleven

INTEGRATING CUSTOMS

"INTEGRATING CUSTOMS" is an extensive treatise on the subject of ritual. "Ritual," in the context of both ancient Chinese thought and the text of the *Huainanzi,* encompassed all forms of symbolic action from the most austere to the most mundane, ranging from the grand sacrifices of the imperial cult to the small courtesies (such as bowing) that transpired between people at a chance meeting. "Integrating Customs" explores the origins of ritual in cosmic and human history and discourses on how the current sage-ruler should establish the rituals appropriate to his age.

The Chapter Title

Like many of the chapter titles of the *Huainanzi,* that of chapter 11 is a verb–object phrase: "Qi su" 齊俗. The verb, *qi,* is a richly multivalent word, among whose meanings are "to equalize," "to put on a par," "to bring together," and "to bring into agreement." The object, *su,* means "customs," with a general connotation of "folkways." As an adjective, *su* can be used to express the meaning of "common," "unrefined," or "vulgar."

The title "Qi su" is a clear allusion to that of chapter 2 of the *Zhuangzi,* the "Qi wu lun" 齊物論,[1] variously translated as "The Discussion of Making All Things Equal"

1. The relationship between the titles "Qi su" and "Qi wu lun" may be more than an allusion, as the authors of the *Huainanzi* may have appended the latter title to the second chapter of the *Zhuangzi.* See

or "The Sorting That Evens Things Out."[2] Previous American and European scholars have thus translated *qi su* as "Equalizing Customs / Placing Customs on a Par,"[3] and this is undoubtedly one meaning that the title would have evoked for a Han readership. In this context, the title refers to the perspective that views all "customs," whether the crude folkways of non-Sinic people living at the periphery of the empire or the elegant ceremonials of the imperial court, as being normatively indistinguishable from one another.

This is only one dimension of the concept of *qi su*, however; the term is not merely passive or perspectival. Chapter 11 calls on the ruler to harmonize the prevailing and divergent cultural practices in the empire so that customary variation will not obstruct the integral functioning of the universal imperium envisioned by the text. As the summary provided in chapter 21 declares, the teachings of chapter 11 enable one to

> unify the weaknesses and strengths of the various living things,
> equate the customs and habits of the nine Yi [tribes],
> comprehend past and present discourses,
> and thread together the patterns of the myriad things. (21.2)

From this summary, we can see that even though a translation like "Placing Customs on a Par" is valid, "Integrating Customs" better preserves the self-conscious parallel between the chapter titles in the *Huainanzi* and the *Zhuangzi*. A common double entendre is implied in both texts: the *dao* of the *Qi wu lun* integrates all things in the universe in much the same way that the sage of the *Huainanzi* integrates all the customs of the world. Thus we render the title of the chapter as "Integrating Customs."

Summary and Key Themes

Whereas "ritual" was a matter of supreme importance for Confucians (*ru*),[4] "Integrating Customs" immediately makes clear that ritual is the "creation of a declining age" (11.1) and does not rank among the forces to which the *Huainanzi* grants primacy and maximum potency. Thus the title of the chapter speaks more generically

---

Harold D. Roth, "Who Compiled the *Chuang Tzu*?" in *Chinese Texts and Philosophical Contexts: Essays Dedicated to Angus C. Graham*, ed. Henry Rosemont Jr. (La Salle, Ill.: Open Court Press, 1991), 118.

2. Respectively, Burton Watson, *The Complete Works of Chuang Tzu* (New York: Columbia University Press, 1968); and Graham 1982.

3. Wallacker 1962. Csikszentmihalyi 2004, 18, also translates this title as "Equalizing Customs"; Le Blanc and Mathieu 2003 translate it as "De l'équivalence des mœurs."

4. For a discussion of the term *ru* and its translation as "Confucians," see the introduction to this book.

of "customs," implicitly asserting (in opposition to Confucius and others) that no set of "rituals," no matter how sophisticated or wisely conceived, can be ultimately normative. The validity of any "ritual" is contingent on its appropriateness to the time and place in which it is practiced, and the distinction between the tribal customs of the "barbarians" living outside the Han domain and the rituals of the Han court is ultimately arbitrary. The willingness to grant normative validity to non-Han customs was unusual in the milieu of early Han China and may reflect the physical location of the kingdom of Huainan near the ethnically diverse southern frontier of the Han Empire.

Although the text may deem ritual to be a latter-day phenomenon of secondary potency, it openly admits that ritual is indispensable to effective rulership in the current age. This admission is tactically astute, as in pragmatic terms it is unlikely that any imperial government during the Han dynasty could have succeeded without ritual. The cycle of sacrifices and feasts held in honor of various ancestral spirits and divinities at the imperial court was a vast enterprise that drew heavily on the state treasury and kept hundreds (if not thousands) of functionaries employed.[5] Moreover, these ceremonial functions of the court could not be separated from the "practical" organs of government. Protocols and rituals joined court ceremonial offices with the functional bureaus engaged in the day-to-day exercise of imperial power. Attempting to reorganize the Han government in the absence of ritual would be the equivalent of burning a house down and rebuilding it from the ground up.

In the Han, the topic of ritual also was seen as a matter of some urgency because of the new scope of imperial rule. Even though ritual had been a prime topic of statecraft thinking during the entire Warring States period, the consolidation of imperial rule and the spread of imperial authority outward under the Qin and Han had created a new critical awareness of cultural diversity throughout the imperial domain. Not only were there striking differences in ritual and custom among the Sinic people united under the empire, but, with the expansion of the territorial boundaries into the non-Sinic world, imperial officials now had to face the challenge of governing people who had no knowledge of or sense of participation in the culture of the central court.[6] Under these conditions, anyone who lacked advice on how one might "integrate customs" had little of value to offer the rulers of the Han domain.

These tactical concerns naturally lead us to question whether the *Huainanzi*'s admission of the utility of ritual is hypocritical or self-contradictory. The text's theory of "deep history" does offer some rationalization in this regard. In earlier ages of human history (closer to the cosmic origins of the universe), it was possible to rule only on the basis of the Way and its Potency. But as human society matured and human civilization became more complex, the natural process of devolution made

5. For a review of the Han state structure, see Hans Bielenstein, *The Bureaucracy of Han Times* (Cambridge: Cambridge University Press, 1980).

6. For a study of the expanding geoethnographic scope of Han rule, see Yü Ying-shih, "Han Foreign Relations," in *The Cambridge History of China*, vol. 1, *The Ch'in and Han Empires, 221 B.C.–A.D. 220*, ed. Denis Twitchett and Michael Loewe (Cambridge: Cambridge University Press, 1986), 377–462.

it impossible to establish order without artifices like ritual. The Han came to power in a latter age and thus were compelled to use those implements that current social and historical conditions demanded.

"Integrating Customs" invests ritual with intrinsic value and power as an indispensable tool of the current age. In this respect, the text's perspective is like that of the Han Confucians. Ritual is an effective implement of rule because when the channels of power are ritualized, the exercise of state authority does not require the dehumanizing application of threats or bribery. Beyond this, unlike rewards and punishments, which act only on people's bestial impulses of greed and fear, ritual provides a medium through which human beings may be saved from their self-destructive impulses and gradually transformed so that their spontaneous responses to conditions and events become more harmonious and constructive.[7]

The *Huainanzi* diverges from the Confucian theory of ritual in its view of how rituals originate and are maintained. The Confucians would insist that the only effective path to human perfection involves the acceptance and practice of normatively correct rituals. Accordingly, the ritual order must be reproduced and maintained through painstaking study and reconstruction of the ritual institutions of the ancient sages. Unlike Confucians, the *Huainanzi* holds that human perfection does not require ritual. There was thus a time when there were sages but not rituals. Sages could create rituals, but ritual itself was never (nor is it now) an indispensable path to sagehood itself. Past sages are therefore not the only or even the best source of effective rituals for the present. The key to creating effective ritual (if and when it is needed) is in the mystical self-cultivation of the sage-ruler in the current age. Only a sage who has come to personally embody the Way and its Potency can produce and maintain rituals that are perfectly suited to creating order and harmony in the current age and to integrating the culturally diverse peoples under his rule.

Sources

The rather deflated view of ritual implied by the title "Integrating Customs" naturally raises the question of why the *Huainanzi* would devote an entire chapter to this topic. This may be answered in part by reference to the text's claim of comprehensiveness. When the *Huainanzi* was composed, there already existed a voluminous literature on ritual and its relationship to government. Three texts devoted to ritual—the *Liji* (*Record of Rites*), the *Yili* (*Ceremonial and Rites*), and the *Zhouli* (*Rites of Zhou*)—were ultimately included in the classical canon propounded by the Confucians at the Han court. These Confucian ritual texts, especially the *Liji*, provide the clear intellectual context in and against which "Integrating Customs" was created.

7. For Confucian ritual theory, see Herbert Fingarette, *Confucius: The Secular as Sacred* (New York: HarperCollins, 1972), 1–17; and Paul Goldin, *Rituals of the Way: The Philosophy of Xunzi* (La Salle, Ill.: Open Court Press, 1999), 55–82.

Numerous parallels and influences may be found in the *Liji* and chapter 11 of the *Huainanzi*, although when these texts echo each other, the context and rhetoric of the shared passages are often quite divergent. For example, in chapter 31 of the *Liji* ("Fang ji" 坊紀, one of the four chapters of the *Rites* reputed to have been written by, or otherwise associated with, Confucius's grandson Zisi),[8] we read that "the rites accord with human feeling and make for them an ordered pattern,"[9] a line that appears verbatim in "Integrating Customs." In the *Liji*, however, this principle is adduced by demonstrating how ritual serves to curb people's worst impulses, "Thus in his control of wealth and nobility, the sage makes it so that the people will not be arrogant when wealthy, or miserly when poor, or insolent to their seniors when noble."[10] In the *Huainanzi*, by contrast, this line states that ritual is most effective when it corresponds most closely to what is spontaneous to human nature:

> The three-year mourning period forces a person to what he cannot reach; thus he supplements his feelings with pretense.
> The three-month observance breaks off grief, coercing and hacking at nature.
>
> The Confucians and the Mohists do not [find the] origin [of their doctrines] in the beginnings and ends of human feelings and are committed to practicing mutually opposed systems. (11.8)

Another example of parallelism between the *Rites* and the *Huainanzi* is the famous second phrase of the "Zhong yong":[11] "following nature is called the Way."[12] An only slightly altered version of this axiom forms the opening line of "Integrating Customs": "Following nature and putting it into practice is called 'the Way.'" The conclusions the *Huainanzi* derives from this principle are quite different from those of the "Zhong yong," however:

> For this reason,
> when Humaneness and Rightness were established, the Way and Potency receded;
> when Ritual and Music were embellished, purity and simplicity dissipated.

This argument, coming at the very beginning of the chapter (11.1), is based on *Laozi* 38: "When the Way is lost, then there is Potency; when Potency is lost, then there is Humaneness; when Humaneness is lost, then there is Rightness; when Rightness

---

8. For an extensive study of these texts, see Jeffrey K. Riegel, "The Four 'Tzu Ssu' Chapters of the *Li Chi*: An Analysis of the *Fang Chi*, *Chung Yung*, *Piao Chi*, and *Tzu I*" (Ph.D. diss., Stanford University, 1978).

9. *Liji* 31.2/139/14.

10. *Liji* 31.2/139/15.

11. That is, the "Doctrine of the Mean," another of the supposed "Zisi" chapters of the *Liji*, often also printed as an independent text as one of the Confucian "Four Books."

12. *Liji* 32.1/142/21.

is lost, then there is Ritual."[13] By contrast, the authors of the "Zhong yong" attribute ultimate normative authority to the rites of Zhou antiquity: "If one comprehends the rites of the suburban altar and the altar of the soil, and the significance of the *di* and *chang* [sacrifices], one may order the kingdom as if holding it in one's palm."[14]

The date of the *Liji*'s composition is a matter of some complexity and controversy. Thus when comparing "Integrating Customs" with those chapters in the *Rites* containing parallel passages, the question of which text was the "source" for the other is an open one. The *Rites* was composed through a much more fluid and decentralized process than the *Huainanzi* was;[15] thus the mechanism by which parallel passages appeared in both texts may have been very complicated. The *Rites* may be citing the *Huainanzi*; the inverse may be true; or both texts might be sourcing other material circulating in written or oral forms of various kinds. What can be inferred with some certainty, however, is that a debate over the nature and origins of ritual took place in the Former Han, and the patron and authors of the *Huainanzi* were resolved to engage it.

The Chapter in the Context of the *Huainanzi* as a Whole

The position of "Integrating Customs" in the structure of the *Huainanzi* reflects the philosophical priorities underpinning the text as a whole. In the same way that the *Huainanzi* describes the cosmos moving farther and farther through time from the undifferentiated and potent state of its cosmogonic origins, the text itself moves from a discussion of the Way, the concept in which it invests ultimate value, through successively less fundamental concerns. In this context, the place of "Integrating Customs," after chapters on cosmology and personal cultivation but before those on rhetoric and military affairs, represents the medial role to which the *Huainanzi* authors consign ritual in their system of prescriptions for the Han era. The opening section of this chapter recapitulates the argument in chapter 8 that Humaneness, Rightness, and Ritual are symptoms of, and arise only in successive stages of, an age of decline. Chapter 11 then builds on that fundamental assertion. Although ritual is thus shown to be a secondary concern, an imperfect substitute for primordial rule by means of the Way and its Potency, it is counted as more essential to efficacious governance in the current age than are modes of instrumental cunning or naked state power.

Andrew Meyer

13. *Laozi* 38/13/17. A devolutionary argument based on *Laozi* 38 is also found in 8.3. See the introduction to chap. 8.

14. *Liji* 32.13/144/21–22.

15. For a recent discussion of the exemplary case of one of the four "Zisi" chapters, see Edward L. Shaughnessy, "Rewriting the *Zi Yi*: How One Chinese Classic Came to Read as It Does," in *Rewriting Early Chinese Texts* (Albany: State University of New York Press, 2006), 63–130.

Eleven

11.1

Following nature and putting it into practice is called "the Way";[1]
attaining one's Heaven[-born] nature is called "Potency."
Only after nature was lost was Humaneness honored;
only after the Way was lost was Rightness honored.

For this reason,

when Humaneness and Rightness were established, the Way and Potency receded;
when Ritual and Music were embellished, purity and simplicity dissipated.[2]
Right and wrong took form, and the common people were dazzled;
pearls and jade were revered, and the world set to fighting [over them].

These four were the creations of a declining age and are the implements of a latter age. [11/93/20–22]

Now Ritual

distinguishes the revered and the lowly,
differentiates the noble and the base.

Rightness is what unites sovereign and minister, father and son, elder brother and younger brother, husband and wife, friend and friend.

1. This line echoes the famous opening lines of the *Zhongyong* (*Doctrine of the Mean*).
2. Like 8.3, which this passage closely resembles, these lines paraphrase *Laozi* 38.

What the current age considers Ritual [demands] reverence and respect yet [causes] jealousy.
What it considers Rightness is boastful and condescending yet [is deemed] potent.

[Because of them,]

ruler and minister oppose each other;
blood kin become resentful of one another.

This is to lose the basis of Ritual and Rightness. Thus [government] is confused and complicated.

When water accumulates, it generates fish that eat one another;
when earth accumulates, it generates beasts that [devour] one another's flesh;
when Ritual and Rightness are embellished, they generate false and hypocritical scholars.
To blow on ashes yet not to want to get a mote in one's eye,
to wade through water yet not to want to get soaked:

these [things] are impossible.

In antiquity, the people were naïve and ignorant, [and] they did not know west from east. The [expressions on] their faces did not exceed their feelings [within], [and] their words did not outstrip their deeds.

Their clothes were warm and without pattern;
their weapons were blunt and had no edge.
Their songs were joyful yet without warbling;
their sobbing was mournful yet without shouting.
They dug wells and drank,
plowed fields and ate.

They had nothing with which to adorn their beauty, nor did they grasp for acquisitions.

Kinsmen did not praise or deprecate one another;
friends did not resent or revere one another.

Upon the creation of Ritual and Rightness and the valuation of goods and wealth, deception and falsehood sprouted, [and] blame and praise proliferated together; resentment and reverence arose in concert. Because of this,

there was the perfection of Zeng Can and Xiao Ji,
the perversity of Robber Zhi and Zhuang Qiao.

Thus where there is the Great Chariot[3] and the Dragon Banner,[4] the feathered canopy and hanging straps, teams of horses and columns of riders, there must be the wickedness of drilling [peep]holes and removing crossbars, digging up graves and climbing over walls. Where there are cunning patterns and complex embroidery, fine cloth and gossamer silk, there must be clomping along in straw sandals and those whose short coats have unfinished hems. Thus it is clear that high and low depend on each other, the short and the long give form to each other. [11/93/24–11/94/4]

---

3. Taking *dalu* 大路 as equivalent to *dalu* 大輅; commentators describe this as a royal chariot.
4. A banner with two intertwining dragons, a symbol of the Son of Heaven. See *Zhou li* 6.3/80/5.

Now the frog becomes the quail, [and] the water scorpion becomes the dragonfly.[5] These all give rise to what is not of their own kind. Only the sage understands their transformations.

When the Hu [northern "barbarians"] see hemp, they do not understand that it can be used to make cloth.

When the Yue [southern "barbarians"] see fleece, they do not know that it can be used to make a [felt] rug.

Thus with one who does not comprehend things, it is difficult to discuss transformation. [11/94/6–8]

In ancient times, Grand Duke Wang[6] and Duke Dan of Zhou met with each other after receiving fiefs.

Grand Duke Wang asked the Duke of Zhou, "How will you govern Lu?"

The Duke of Zhou said, "I will exalt the noble and draw close to my kindred."

The Grand Duke said, "Henceforward Lu will grow weaker!"

The Duke of Zhou asked the Grand Duke, "How will you govern Qi?"

The Grand Duke said, "I will raise up the worthy and promote those of merit."

The Duke of Zhou said, "In later generations, there will certainly be a ruler who rises through assassination."

Afterward, Qi grew daily larger, to the point of becoming hegemon. After twenty-four generations, [the ducal house] was replaced by the Tian clan.[7] Lu grew daily smaller, being destroyed in the thirty-second generation. Thus the *Changes* says,

"Treading on frost, hard ice descends."

The sages' perception of outcomes at their origin is [truly] subtle![8] Thus the "mountain of dregs" originated with the use of ivory chopsticks; the "roasting beam" originated with a hot ladle.[9] [11/94/10–15]

11.2

Zilu saved someone from drowning and accepted an ox by way of thanks. Confucius said, "[People in] the state of Lu will certainly favor saving [others] from calamity."

---

5. Wallacker 1962, 30nn.30, 31. For similar metamorphoses, see 4.11 and 5.3.

6. Grand Duke Wang (Taigong Wang 太公望) is said to have been the military commander of the Zhou army at the battle that resulted in the overthrow of the Shang dynasty. His Jiang clan ruled Qi until overthrown by the Tian.

7. The Tian was a clan of Qi vassals who overthrew the ruling Jiang house and established themselves as "dukes" (subsequently "kings") of Qi.

8. Following Sun Yirang's reading of *yan* 言 as *yi* 矣 (11/94/14). The quotation is from *Changes*, hexagram 2, *Kun* 坤.

9. These two phrases allude to traditional stories about the tyrant Djou, the evil last ruler of the Shang dynasty. Djou was supposed to have had a drinking party so excessive that at the end a mountain was made from the dregs of the wine consumed. He is also said to have invented the *pao luo*, a metal beam kept white hot by coals across which one condemned to torture was forced to walk. According to the *Huainanzi*, each of these monstrosities had incipient beginnings, the former in the frivolous use of ivory chopsticks at Djou's court (the first sign of his predilection for luxury), and the latter in the accidental burning of someone by a hot ladle (the initial inspiration for the *pao luo* torture). The "roasting beam" is also mentioned in 2.14, 10.89, 12.35, 15.2, and 21.4.

Zigong ransomed someone and did not accept gold from the [state] treasury.[10] Confucius said, "No one in Lu will pay ransom for anyone again."

By accepting, Zilu encouraged virtue;
by refusing, Zigong put a stop to goodness.

Confucius's clarity was such that

he used the small to know the great, [and]
he used the near to know the distant.

He was one who penetrated reasoning.

Viewed on this basis, although incorruptibility has its place, it cannot be universally practiced. Thus

when one's actions accord with customs, they may be followed;
when one's affairs correspond to one's abilities, they are easily accomplished.

Arrogant falsehood that deludes the age and haughty conduct that separates one from the masses—these the sage does not take as customs for the people.

Wide mansions and broad houses, series of doors and spacious rooms, these are what [make] people secure, but if birds enter them, they are afraid.

Tall mountains and difficult passes, deep forests and thick grass, these are what delight tigers and leopards, but if people enter them, they are terrified.

River valleys and broad ponds, deep water and profound springs, these are what serve the [water] turtle and the monitor lizard, but if people enter them, they die.

The "Xian Pool" and the "Riding on Clouds," the "Nine Shao" and the "Six Ying,"[11] these are what people delight[12] in, but if birds and beasts hear them, they are alarmed.

Deep valleys and sheer cliffs, tall trees and spreading branches, these are what please monkeys and apes, but if people climb them, they tremble.

Their forms are different and their natures divergent, thus

what delights one upsets the other;
what makes one secure endangers the other.

Now, with regard to all that is covered by Heaven and supported by Earth—all that is illuminated by the sun and overseen by the moon—make each facilitate its nature, rest secure in its position, occupy what is appropriate to it, and accomplish what it is able. Thus even

the stupid have their strong points;
the wise have that for which they are not equipped.
A pillar cannot be used as a toothpick;
a hairpin cannot support a house.
A horse cannot carry heavy loads;
an ox cannot chase in fast [pursuit].

---

10. This story is told in 12.12.

11. These all are types of ancient music. Xian chi 咸池, "Pool of [Shaman] Xian," is also the name of a constellation. See 3.4, 3.19, 3.25, and 4.16; and Major 1993, 199.

12. The character 樂 here implies both *le* (joy) and *yue* (music).

Lead cannot be used to make a sword,
and bronze cannot be used to make a crossbow;
iron cannot be used to make a boat,
and wood cannot be used to make an ax.

Each is
used where it is best suited
and applied to what is appropriate to it,

thus all the myriad things are placed on a par, and none transgresses the others.

A bright mirror is convenient for reflecting a form, but for steaming food, it does not measure up to a bamboo basket.

A sacrificial ox with red hair[13] is fit to be offered up in the [ancestral] temple, but for bringing rain, it does not match a black snake.[14]

Viewed on this [basis], there is no [distinction] of noble or base among things.

If one values things in accordance with what ennobles them, there is nothing that is not noble.

If one degrades things in accordance with what debases them, there is nothing that is not base. [11/94/15–30]

11.3

Uncut jade can never be thick enough;
jade inlay can never be thin enough;
lacquer can never be black enough;
rice powder can never be white enough.

These four are opposites, yet when urgently [needed], they are equal, their usefulness is the same. Now of furs and straw garments, which is more urgently [needed]? If one encounters rain, then furs are useless, when one ascends the [regal] hall, straw is not worn. These things alternate in being "emperor."[15] They are comparable to boats and chariots, mud sledges and sand chariots, [palaces and] tents—each definitely has its appropriate [use]. Thus *Laozi* says,

"Do not elevate the worthy."

This means that one [should] not put fish in trees or plunge birds into the depths. [11/95/1–4]

When Yao ruled the world,
Shun was his minister of education;
Xie[16] was his minister of war;
Yu was his minister of works;

13. Lau, HNZ, 94n.12; Wallacker 1962, 55n.54.

14. See 11/94/29. The *li* 蜧 is said to be a snake with supernatural qualities. See Wallacker 1962, 55n.55. Some editions read "spirit snake" instead of "black snake." See Zhang Shuangdi 1997, 2:1125n.10.

15. Reading *chang* 常 as *di* 帝. The quotation is from *Laozi* 3.

16. Xie 契, according to tradition, was the ancestor of the Shang royal house. He is mentioned in the "Canon of Shun" of the *Documents*.

Lord Millet was his minister of agriculture;
Xi Zhong was his palace craftsman.
In his guiding of the myriad people,
those who lived near the water were fishers;
those who lived in the mountains were foresters;
those who lived in valleys were herdsmen;
those who lived on the plains were farmers.
Their location was appropriate to their occupation;
their occupation was appropriate to their tools;
their tools were appropriate to their functions;
and their functions were appropriate to the people [who used them].
On marshes and coastlines, nets were woven;
on hillsides and slopes, fields were plowed.
They obtained [things]
by using what they had to exchange for what they lacked,
using what they were skilled [in making] to exchange for what they were incapable [of producing].
For this reason,
those who rebelled were few;
those who obeyed were many.

It was comparable to rolling chess pieces on the ground. The round ones will roll into depressions; the square ones will rest on high [ground]. Each follows what is natural to it. How can there be superior and inferior? It is like the wind encountering pitch pipes, spontaneously activating them; each responds with a high or a low [note]. [11/95/6–11]

11.4

Monkeys and apes, on obtaining a luxuriant tree, do not quit it for a cave;
porcupines and badgers, on finding an embankment, do not quit it for a hedge.
Nothing
abandons what is of benefit to it
and seeks out what is of harm to it.
For this reason,
neighboring states can see one another,
and each can hear the sound of the other's chickens and dogs,[17]
yet
footprints never reach the rulers' boundary;
cart ruts never run beyond a thousand *li*—
everyone rests in what makes him secure.
Thus a chaotic state seems full;

17. *Laozi* 80.

an ordered state seems empty;
a collapsing state seems lacking;
a surviving state seems to have surplus.
The emptiness is not a lack of people; it [arises from] each maintaining his position.
The fullness is not a plethora of people; it [arises from] each chasing after nonessential [tasks].
The surplus is not an abundance of goods; it [arises from] desires being restricted and affairs being few.
The lack is not a dearth of wealth; it [arises from] the people being agitated and expenses being excessive.

Thus

the methods and statutes of the former kings were not inventions; they were compliance.
Their prohibitions and executions were not initiatives; they were preservation. [11/95/13–18]

What controls all objects is not objects, it is harmony.
What controls harmony is not harmony, it is people.
What controls people is not people, it is the ruler.
What controls the ruler is not the ruler, it is desire.
What controls desire is not desire, it is nature.
What controls nature is not nature, it is Potency.
What controls Potency is not Potency, it is the Way. [11/95/20–22]

11.5

If the original nature of human beings is obstructed and sullied, one cannot get at its purity and clarity—it is because things have befouled it. The children of the Qiang, Dii, Bo, and Dee [barbarians] all produce the same sounds at birth. Once they have grown, even with both the *xiang* and *diti* interpreters,[18] they cannot understand one another's speech; this is because their education and customs are different. Now a three-month-old child that moves to a [new] state after it is born will not recognize its old customs. Viewed on this basis, clothing and ritual customs are not [rooted in] people's nature; they are received from without.

It is the nature of bamboo to float, [but] break it into strips and tie them in a bundle and they will sink when thrown into the water—it [i.e., the bamboo] has lost its [basic] structure.

18. The *xiang* 象 and *diti* 狄鞮 were interpreters employed to facilitate interactions between the Chinese Central States and their "barbarian" neighbors. See the similar phrasing that appears in the *Lüshi chunqiu*: "[All states] that do not use the *xiang* and *di* interpreters" (LSCQ 17.6/105/16). Their exact functions are unknown. See Chen Qiyou 陳奇猷, *Lüshi chunqiu jiaoshi* 呂氏春秋校釋, 2 vols. (Shanghai: Xuelin chubanshe, 1984), 2:1108, 1112n.7; Zhang Shuangdi 1997, 2:1134n.8; and 20.8.

It is the nature of metal to sink, [but] place it on a boat and it will float—its positioning lends it support.

The substance of raw silk is white, [but] dye it in potash and it turns black.

The nature of fine silk is yellow, [but] dye it in cinnabar and it turns red.

The nature of human beings has no depravity; having been long immersed in customs, it changes. If it changes and one forgets the root, it is as if [the customs one has acquired] have merged with [one's] nature.

Thus

the sun and the moon are inclined to brilliance, but floating clouds cover them;

the water of the river is inclined to purity, but sand and rocks sully it.

The nature of human beings is inclined to equilibrium, but wants and desires harm it.

Only the sage can leave things aside and return to himself.

Someone who boards a boat and becomes confused, not knowing west from east, will see the Dipper and the Pole Star and become oriented. Nature is likewise a Dipper and a Pole Star for human beings.

If one possesses that by which one can see oneself, then one will not miss the genuine dispositions of things.

If one lacks that by which one can see oneself, then one will be agitated and ensnared.

It is like swimming in Longxi:[19] the more you thrash, the deeper you will sink.

Confucius said to Yan Hui, "I serve you by forgetting [you], and you also serve me by forgetting [me]. Although it is so, even though you forget me, there is still something that has not been forgotten that persists."[20] Confucius understood the root of it.

The actions of one who gives free rein to desires and loses his nature have never been correct.

Controlling one's person [in this way leads to] danger;

controlling a state [in this way leads to] chaos;

leading an army [in this way leads to] destruction.

For this reason, those who have not heard the Way have no means to return to nature.

---

19. Longxi was a commandery in the northwestern territory of the Han Empire (in what is today Gansu Province). "Swimming in Longxi" evidently was or became a recognizable trope for a dangerous or foolhardy activity, but if there was an antecedent text that helps explain why, it has been lost. Ying Ju (d. 252) evokes it in his "Letter to Cousins Junmiao and Junwei" (*Wen xuan* 42:1918–22). Li Shan's (d. 689) commentary to the *Wen xuan* cites this *Huainanzi* passage by way of explanation, thus by the Tang period, whatever source text (if any) to which the *Huainanzi* is alluding must have been lost.

20. This reproduces part of a dialogue found in *Zhuangzi* 21 (21/57/16–18). See the translation of the *Zhuangzi* parallel in Burton Watson, *The Complete Works of Chuang Tzu* (New York: Columbia University Press, 1968), 224. As Watson notes, the meaning here is not completely transparent in either the *Zhuangzi* parallel or the *Huainanzi* context. The sense seems to be that true personal advancement depends on "forgetting" the constituents of individual identity. Thus Confucius teaches best when he forgets Yan Hui, and Hui studies best when he forgets Confucius. What "persists" in the wake of such forgetting is pristine nature, which is merged with the Way.

Thus the sage-kings of antiquity were able to attain it in themselves, and their orders were enacted and their prohibitions were binding. Their names were carried down to later ages, [and] their Potency spread throughout the Four Seas. [11/95/24–11/96/7]

11.6

For this reason, whenever one is about to take up an affair, one must first stabilize one's intentions and purify one's spirit.

When the spirit is pure and intentions are stable,
only then can things be aligned.

It is like pressing a seal into clay:

if it is held straight, [the impression] will be straight;
if it is held crookedly, [the impression] will be crooked.

Thus

when Yao chose Shun, he decided simply with his eyes;
when Duke Huan chose Ning Qi, he judged him simply with his ears.

If on this basis one were to give up technique and measurements and rely on one's ears and eyes, the [resulting] chaos would certainly be great. That the ears and eyes can judge is because one returns to feelings and nature.

If one's hearing is lost in slander and flattery
and one's eyes are corrupted by pattern and color,

if one then wants to rectify affairs, it will be difficult.

One who is suffused with grief will cry upon hearing a song;
one suffused with joy will see someone weeping and laugh.
That grief can bring joy
and laughter can bring grief—

being suffused makes it so. For this reason, value emptiness. [11/96/6–12]

When water is agitated, waves rise,
when the *qi* is disordered, the intellect is confused.
A confused intellect cannot attend to government;
agitated water cannot be used to establish a level.

Thus the sage-king holds to the One without losing it, and the genuine dispositions of the myriad things are discovered, the four barbarians and the nine regions all submit. The One is the supremely noble; it has no match in the world. The sage relies on the matchless; thus the mandate of the people attaches itself [to him]. [11/96/14–16]

One who practices Humaneness must discuss it [in terms of] grief and joy;
one who practices Rightness must explain it [in terms of] grasping and yielding.
If the human eye does not see beyond ten *li* and one wants to comprehensively reach all people within the [four] seas, grief and joy will not suffice.
If one does not have the amassed wealth of the world and wants to comprehensively supply the myriad people, [material] benefit cannot be enough.

Moreover, pleasure, anger, grief, and joy arise spontaneously from a stimulus. Thus,

a cry issues from the mouth,
tears flow from the eyes—
all burst forth within
and take form externally.

It is like

water flowing downward
or smoke rising upward:

What compels them? Thus,

though one who forces oneself to cry feels pain, he does not grieve;
though one who forces intimacy will laugh, there is no harmony.

Feelings come forth within, and sounds respond externally. Thus,

the jug of food of Xi Fuji was better than the Chuiji jade of Duke Xian of Jin,[21]
the bound meat-strips of Zhao Xuanmeng were more worthy that the great bell of Earl Zhi.[22]

Thus [though] ritual may be elaborate, it does not suffice for effecting love, yet a sincere heart can embrace [those at] a great distance. [11/96/18–23]

11.7

Thus,

in caring for his family, Gongxi Hua[23] resembled one living among friends.
In caring for his family, Zeng Can resembled one serving an austere lord or a fierce ruler.

[Yet] in terms of caring, they were as one.

The Hu people strike bones together [to seal an oath];
the Yue people make cuts in their arms;
[the people of] the Middle Kingdom smear their mouths with blood.

The origins of all [these customs] are different, but in terms of [establishing] trust, they are as one.

The Three Miao [tribes] bind their heads with hemp;
the Qiang people bind their necks;
the [people of] the Middle Kingdom use hat and hairpin;
the Yue people shear their hair.

In regard to getting dressed, they are as one.

---

21. Xi Fuji gave Duke Wen of Jin some food when the latter wandered through Cao in exile, thus establishing himself in the duke's good graces after he assumed the title of hegemon. See *Zuozhuan*, Xi 23. See also 12.22 and 18.18. Duke Xian of Jin used the offer of the Chuiji jade as a ruse to destroy the states of Yu and Guo. See 7.16, 10.47, 17.87, and 18.5; and *Zuozhuan*, Xi 2.

22. Zhao Dun (Xuanmeng) gave some dried meat to a starving man who later spared Zhao's life. See *Zuozhuan*, Xuan 2; and LSCQ 15.4/84/8–18. Earl Zhi used the gift of a great bell as a ruse to destroy the Qiuyou people. See ZGC 24/8/22–29 and LSCQ 15/2/82/8–14.

23. Gongxi Hua 公西華 was a disciple of Confucius. See *Analects* 7.34 and 11.22, 26.

According to the institutes of Thearch Zhuan Xu, if wives did not avoid men on the roads, they would be beaten at a four-way crossroads. Now in the capital, men and women touch shins and rub shoulders in the street. In regard to being customs, they are as one.

Thus the rites of the four Yi ["barbarians"] are not the same, [yet] they all
revere their ruler,
love their kin,
and respect their elder brothers.
The customs of the Xian and Yun are opposite, [yet] they both
are kind to their children
and venerate their elders.
Birds in flight form a line;
beasts in the field form groups,
who was there to teach them? [11/97/1–6]

Thus the state of Lu observed the rites of the Confucians and practiced the arts of Confucius. Its territory was stripped away and its name brought low; it was unable to befriend those nearby or attract those far away.

King Goujian[24] of Yue shaved his head and tattooed his body; he did not have leather caps or jade belt ornaments; [he lacked] the postures of bowing and bending. Even so he defeated Fuchai at Five Lakes; facing south he was hegemon of the world. All twelve feudal rulers from north of the Si River led the nine Yi [tribes] in paying court [to him].

In the countries of the Hu, Mo, and Xiongnu, [people] leave their limbs unwrapped and their hair unbound; they sit cross-legged and talk back [to their superiors]. Yet their states have not collapsed, and they do not necessarily lack Ritual.

King Zhuang of Chu wore thin lapels on a broad robe,[25] [yet] his commands were effective throughout the world, and as a consequence he became hegemon of the Lords of the Land.

Lord Wen of Jin wore clothes of coarse cloth and sheepskin, and he belted his sword with leather, [yet] his might was established within the seas. How can it be that only the rites of Zou and Lu [may be] called Rites? For this reason,
when entering a state, one follows their customs,
when entering a household, one respects their taboos.
If one does not violate a prohibition in entering,
if one does not go forward contrary [to custom],
then even on traveling to the (countries of) the Yi or Di or to the Country of the Naked, or going beyond the farthest limits of chariot tracks, one will have no trouble. [11/97/8–13]

24. Goujian 句踐 ruled Yue from 491 to 465 B.C.E. See *Shiji* 41.

25. Following the gloss in Zhang Shuangdi 1997, 2:1145n.34.

11.8

Ritual is the patterning of substance.
Humaneness is the application of kindness.

Thus Rites accord with human feeling and make for them an ordered pattern, and Humaneness bursts forth as a blush that appears in one's countenance.

When Ritual does not surpass substance
and Humaneness does not surpass [the proper degree of] kindness,

this is the Way of ordering the world.

The three-year mourning period[26] forces a person to what he cannot reach; thus he supplements his feelings with pretense.

The three-month observance[27] breaks off grief, coercing and hacking at nature.

The Confucians and the Mohists do not [find the] origin [of their doctrines] in the beginnings and ends of human feelings and are committed to practicing mutually opposed systems [for] the five grades of observance.[28] Sorrow and grief are contained in feelings; burial and interment correspond to nurturing.[29]

Do not force people to do what they are incapable of;
do not interrupt what people are able to complete.

When standards and measurements do not deviate from what is proper, there is no source from which slander and flattery can arise.

In antiquity, it was not that they did not know the elaborate rites of ascending and descending, turning and circling, the postures of the "dignified" and "hastening" steps.[30] They felt that these wasted the day, burdened the people, and were useless; thus they instituted only those rites that aided substance and expressed one's intentions.

It was not that they were unable to display bells and drums, array pipes and flutes, brandish shields and axes, hoist plumes and banners. They felt that these wasted wealth and disordered government; [thus] they instituted only music that sufficed to harmonize joy and expound one's intentions; the tune did not exceed the pleasure [it expressed].

It was not that they were unable to exhaust the state and mislead the people, empty the treasury and waste wealth, sending off the dead with pearls in their mouth, wrapped in scales [of jade], girdled in cotton and bamboo. They felt it impoverished the people, interrupted their work, and was of no aid to dry bones and rotting flesh. Thus burials were sufficient to gather the remains and cover the grave, that is all.

---

26. That is, the lengthy mourning period advocated by Confucius and his followers.

27. The brief mourning period advocated by Mozi and his followers.

28. Following Xu Shen. See Zhuang Shuangdi 1997, 2:1148n.3.

29. The authors of the *Huainanzi* are distinguishing between feelings (such as sorrow and grief), which are internal, and actions (such as specific rites of burial and interment), which reflect learned behavior (nurture) and thus are external.

30. The *Caiqi* 采齊 and *Sixia* 肆夏 were music purportedly played at state occasions at the Zhou court. When the occasion called for walking, the *Sixia* would be played, and when protocol demanded hurrying, the *Caiqi* would be played. See *Zhou li* (*Rites of Zhou*), Spring Offices, the Master of Music (*yue shi*).

Of old when Shun was buried at Cangwu, stalls were not altered in the marketplace [and] when Yu was buried at Mount Kuaiji, farmers did not move their fields. They were clear about the division between death and life, the mean between expenditure and frugality. Chaotic kingdoms are not this way.

Their words and conduct are at odds;
their feelings and facial expressions are opposed.
Their rituals are binding to the point of oppression;
their music is stirring to the point of license.
They revere death to the point of harming life;
they extend mourning to the point of obstructing work.

For this reason, their customs are corrupting to the age; flattery and slander sprout at court; thus the sage abandons and does not use them. [11/97/15–26]

11.9

Rightness is following the patterns and doing what is appropriate;
Ritual is embodying feelings and establishing a design.
Rightness is appropriateness;
Ritual is embodiment.[31]

Of old,

the Youhu[32] clan acted with Rightness and perished; they understood Rightness but did not understand appropriateness.

Lu instituted Rites and was pared down; they understood Rites but not embodiment.

In the rites of Youyu,[33] the altar was made of earth; sacrifices were to the central eaves; the tombs were one *mu* square; his music[34] was the "Pool of Xian," the "Bearing Clouds," and the "Nine Harmonies."[35] His clothing gave prominence to yellow.[36]

---

31. Wang Yinzhi feels that this sentence should be omitted. See Lau, HNZ, 98n.1.

32. The Youhu 有扈 were a clan that rebelled against the Xia upon the investiture of their second king, Qi.

33. Youyu 有虞—that is, the sage-king Shun.

34. The musicological history outlined in this section roughly parallels that laid out in *Lüshi chunqiu* 5.5. The two texts share most of the same basic elements and sequence them in the same chronological order. LSCQ, however, begins the sequence earlier, before the reign of the Yellow Emperor, so the two texts do not closely accord until the latter eras of the Shang and Zhou.

35. For the referent of "Pool of Xian," see 3.4 and 4.16. "Pool of Xian" is listed as accompanying a Zhou-dynasty ritual dance in *Zhou li* 3.21/41/16. "Bearing Clouds" 承雲 is invoked in CC 5/18/17; Wang Yi's commentary equates it with the "Cloud Gates" 雲門, an ancient musical form mentioned throughout the early literature. The "nine harmonies" 九韶 are also mentioned in the *Zhou li* as part of the ritual repertory of the Zhou, where they are rendered as 九磬.

36. This and the following three paragraphs describe the historical succession from the era of sage-kings through Xia, Shang, and Zhou, according to the "mutual overcoming" order of the Five Phases as indicated by the attributes and colors described for each reign. Earth (yellow) is overcome by Wood (green), which is overcome by Metal (white), which is overcome by Fire (red). The next stage in the

The altar of the lords of Xia was made of pine; they sacrificed to the door [god]; their tombs were walled; and their coffins were shrouded.[37] Their music was the nine movements[38] of the "Pipes of Xia," the "Six Dance Troops," the "Six Lines," and the "Six Blossoms."[39] Their clothes gave prominence to green.

In the rites of the Yin, their altar was made of stone; they sacrificed to the gate; [and] their tombs were planted with pines. Their music was the "Great Melody" and "Morning Dew."[40] Their clothing gave prominence to white.

In the rites of the Zhou, their altar was made of chestnut; they sacrificed to the stove; their tombs were planted with cypress; their music was the "Grand Martiality," the "Three Elephants," and the "Beneath the Mulberry." Their clothing gave prominence to red.[41]

Their Ritual and Music were contradictory; their clothes and regulations were opposed; yet none lost the affection [appropriate to] kinship and remoteness, the discipline of superior and inferior. Now to seize on one ruler's methods and statutes while rejecting the customs transmitted from ages [past] is like tuning a *se* and [then] gluing the bridges in place.[42] [11/98/1–9]

Therefore the enlightened ruler clothes himself with rites and propriety [and] girdles himself with discipline and conduct. His clothes suffice

to cover his frame,
to follow the ancient canons,
to accommodate bowing and bending,
to convenience his body and frame,
to ease his movement and steps.

He does not strive for an extraordinary or beautiful appearance or a cornered, diagonal cut.

---

sequence would be Water (black). An implicit argument is being made here for Water and black to be the appropriate emblems of the current dynasty.

37. The *sha* was a fan-shaped shroud draped over the coffin of the entombed.

38. Lau takes the phrase 夏籥九成 to refer to two proper nouns: the "Pipes of Xia" and the "Nine Perfections." There is little corroboration for the reading of "Nine Perfections," however, so we followed Knoblock and Riegel's 2000, 150, translation of the parallel passage in LSCQ 5.5, rendering 九成 as "nine movements."

39. The "Pipes of Xia" are mentioned in *Liji* 29.4/137/15. The "Six Dance Troops" 六佾, "Six Lines" 六列, and "Six Blossoms" 六英 are unique to the *Huainanzi* and its parallel *Lüshi chunqiu* text.

40. The "Great Melody" is translated on the acceptance of Lau's proposed emendation from 大護 to 大濩. The latter is a form of ancient music mentioned in *Zhou li* 3.21/41/12. "Morning Dew" 晨露 is first mentioned as a form of ancient music in the *Lüshi chunqiu*.

41. "Grand Martiality" is given as the name of a Zhou musical form in the *Zhou li*. "Three Elephants" 三象 and "Beneath the Mulberry" 棗下 are first mentioned in the parallel *Lüshi chunqiu* text.

42. The syntax of the original text is convoluted, but this seems to be the sense of the metaphor. Chinese zitherlike instruments, such as the twenty-five-string *se*, had wooden bridges that could be moved back and forth along the strings to adjust their pitch. A Three Kingdoms (220–265 C.E.) text contains this anecdote: "A man of Qi went to a man of Zhao to study the *se*. He relied on [the teacher] to first tune it, then glued the bridges in place and went home. For three years he could not play a single melody" (Handan Chun 邯鄲淳 [fl. ca. 221 C.E.], *Xiao lin* 笑林). Something akin to this anecdote seems to be the context of the *Huainanzi*'s imagery.

His belt suffices
to tie a knot and gather the flaps,
to bind tightly and cinch fast.
He feels no urgency that [it be made of] round and square patterned [embroidery].[43]

Thus he institutes Rites and Rightness; he acts with utmost Moral Potency, but he is not fixated on the Confucians and the Mohists. [11/98/11–13]

11.10

What is called "clarity" does not refer to seeing another, it is seeing oneself, that is all.
What is called "acuity" does not refer to hearing another, it is hearing oneself, that is all.
What is called "attainment" does not refer to understanding another, it is understanding oneself, that is all.

Thus the person is where the Way is lodged; when the person is achieved, the Way is achieved. As for achievement of the Way,
in seeing, it is clarity,
in listening, it is acuity,
in speech, it is impartiality,
in conduct, it is compliance.

Thus the sage shapes and fashions things
the way the carpenter chops, pares, drills, and fastens;
the way the cook slices, cuts, divides, and separates.

Each detail achieves what is appropriate to it, and nothing is broken or harmed. A clumsy artisan is not this way.
Big things become so blocked up that nothing can penetrate them;
small things become so tenuous that nothing can get around them.

He is
agitated in his mind,
shaky in his hands,
and makes things worse.

As for the sage's chopping and paring things,
he splits them, he halves them,
he separates them, he scatters them.
[Those that are] already dissolute, already lost, he unites again.
Having emerged from their root, they return again to their gateway.

43. We follow Sun Yirang's comments in translating *wenju shuduan* 文句疏短 as "round and square patterns." We also follow Sun in dropping the final character, *xie* 鞵, from the end of the sentence. *Xie* literally means "shoes," and Sun notes that it would be incongruent for the text to begin discussing shoes at this point. See Zhang Shuangdi 1997, 2:1156n.27.

Already carved, already polished, they return again to simplicity.
Merged, they are the Way and its Potency,
separated, they are standards and decorum.
He concentrates[44] and penetrates the Mysterious Obscurity;
he disperses and responds without form.

How can even Ritual, Rightness, discipline, and conduct exhaust the source of perfect order? [11/98/15–22]

11.11

Many of those who oversee affairs in the world depart from the source of the Way and its Potency, saying that Ritual and Rightness suffice to order the empire. One cannot discuss techniques with people like them. What is called "Ritual and Rightness" is the methods, statutes, ways, and customs of the Five Thearchs and the Three Kings. They are the remnants of a [former] age. Compare them to straw dogs and earthen dragons when they are first fashioned.[45]

They are patterned with green and yellow,
wrapped with silk and embroidery,
bound with vermilion silk,
clothed in white and black garb.

Grandees wear the peaked cap to send them off and welcome them. Once they have been used, they are buried in the soil and grown over by grass and brambles, that is all. What is there to be valued in them?

Thus in the time of Shun, the Youmiao did not pay tribute. At this, Shun cultivated [good] governance and ceased military [operations]; thus he grasped the shield and battle-ax and danced with them.[46]

In the time of Yu, there was a great flood in the world. Yu ordered the people to gather earth and wood, forming hills and mounds to lodge [the dead].

When King Wu attacked [the tyrant] Djou, he carried the corpse [of his father] on the march. All within the seas was not yet pacified; thus [the custom] of three years' mourning began.

Yu encountered the calamity of the flood, the tasks of ditches and embankments; thus those who died in the morning were buried in the evening.

These all are examples of how the sage follows alterations and responds to the times, views the form and effects what is appropriate. Now to cultivate the staff and battle-ax and laugh at the hoe and the spade, or to know of the three-year [mourning period before burial] and reject [burial after only] one day, is [as absurd as] to follow

44. The character in the original text, *zhuan* 轉, literally means "to turn." It comprises the semantic element *zhuan* 專 (to concentrate) plus the "cart" radical on the left. The latter *zhuan* (concentrate) seems to fit the context of the passage better.

45. This refers to two forms of ancient ritual practice. Straw dogs were made to carry the transgressions of the community, and earthen dragons were fashioned to pray for rain.

46. This refers to a particular martial ritual dance performed in the ancestral temple.

the ox and reject the horse, or to take up the *zhi* tone but laugh at the *yu* tone.[47] Responding to transformation like this is no different from playing "Beneath the Mulberry" by plucking only one string. [11/98/24–11/99/5]

Now to desire to follow transformation and respond to the times on the basis of the alterations of a single era can be compared to wearing straw in winter and fur in summer.

A single aim cannot be used for a hundred shots;
a single garment cannot last the entire year.
The aim must respond to high and low;
the garment must be appropriate to cold or heat.

For this reason,

in different ages, affairs alter,
when times shift, customs change.

Thus the sage

assesses the age in establishing methods;
follows the times in initiating affairs.

The kings of high antiquity performed the *feng* [sacrifice] on Mount Tai and the *shan* [sacrifice] on Mount Liangfu.[48] The seventy or more sages [all] had methods and standards that were different. They were not deliberately opposed to one another; it was that times and the age were different.

For this reason,

they did not follow already established methods;
they followed those for which there was a basis.

Methods that had a basis were those that extended and shifted with transformations. He who can extend and shift with transformations is the noblest among men, that is all. [11/99/7–11]

11.12

Thus,

the songs of Hu Liang[49] can be followed, but how he created his songs cannot be [re]created.
The methods of the sages can be observed, but how they established their methods cannot be plumbed.

47. *Yu* and *zhi* were two of the tones on the Chinese pentatonic scale; thus this phrase means something like "they laugh at F sharp on the basis of A flat."

48. The *feng* 封 and *shan* 禪 sacrifices were considered the most august prerogative of the imperial government from Qin times onward. Their preimperial origins (if any) are obscure. The earliest information on them is recorded in *Shiji* 28.

49. Although the current text of the *Huainanzi* gives this figure's name as 狐梁, several commentators suggest emending this to 瓠梁 on the basis of Tang citations. No extant early texts mention Hu Liang, but the commentaries to two Tang-era encyclopedias gloss the name as that of "an excellent singer of antiquity" (Zhang Shuangdi 1997, 2:1163n.20).

The words of disputing scholars can be heard, but how they formulate their words cannot be given form.

The Chunjun sword[50] can be cherished, but Ou Ye's[51] skill cannot be evaluated.[52]

Now Wang Qiao and Chi Songzi[53]

exhaled and inhaled,
spitting out the old and internalizing the new.
They cast off form and abandoned wisdom;
they embraced simplicity and returned to genuineness;
in roaming with the mysterious and subtle
above, they penetrated to the clouds and Heaven.

Now if one wants to study their Way and does not attain their nurturing of the *qi* and their lodging of the spirit but only imitates their every exhale and inhale, their contracting and expanding, it is clear that one will not be able to mount the clouds and ascend on the vapors.

The Five Thearchs and the Three Kings

viewed the world as a light [affair],
minimized the myriad things,
put death and life on a par,
matched alteration and transformation.

They embraced the great heart of a sage by mirroring the dispositions of the myriad things.

Above, they took spirit illumination as their friend;
below, they took creation and transformation as their companions.

Now if one wants to study their Way and does not attain their pure clarity and mysterious sagacity, yet maintains their methods, statutes, rules, and ordinances, it is clear that one cannot achieve order.

Thus it is said:

"Obtaining ten sharp swords is not as good as attaining the skill of Ou Ye;
obtaining one hundred fleet horses is not as good as attaining the arts of Bo Le." [11/99/11–18]

---

50. A fabled sword, comparable to Excalibur in Arthurian legend.

51. Ou Ye 歐冶 (Smelter Ou) was a fabled sword maker of Yue during the reign of King Goujian (r. 496–465 B.C.E.). He is mentioned in texts such as the *Yue jue shu* and *Wu Yue chunqiu*.

52. Emending the text to preserve the parallelism with the context that precedes it. The original reads: "A pure steel sword can not be cherished, but Ou Ye's skill can be valued [*gui*]."

53. Wang Qiao 王喬 and Chi Songzi 赤誦子 (usually rendered 赤松子) were fabled adepts whose personal cultivation had elevated them to the level of "immortals" 仙 and imbued them with uncanny powers. *Hanfeizi* 20 mentions Chi Songzi; both figures are prominent in lore about immortals from the Han onward.

11.13

The ultimate greatness of the Uncarved Block is its being without form or shape;
the ultimate subtlety of the Way is its being without model or measure.
The roundness of Heaven cannot be tested by the compass;
the squareness of Earth cannot be tested by the [carpenter's] square.
From furthest antiquity to the present days is called "extension-in-time";
the four directions [plus] up and down are called "extension-in-space."[54]

The Way is within their midst, and none can know its location. Thus,
with those who cannot see far, one cannot speak of greatness;
with those whose intelligence is not capacious, one cannot discuss ultimacy.

Of old,
Feng Yi attained the Way and thus became immersed in the Great River,
Qin Fu[55] attained the Way and thus lodged on Kunlun.

Through it [i.e., the Way],
Bian Que[56] cured illness,
Zaofu drove horses,
Yi shot [arrows],
Chui worked as a carpenter.

What each did was different, yet what they took as the Way was one.

Now those who penetrate things by embodying the Way have no basis on which to reject one another. It is like those who band together to irrigate a field—each receives an equal share of water.

Now if one slaughters an ox and cooks its meat, some will be tart, some will be sweet. Frying, stewing, singeing and roasting, there are myriad ways to adjust the flavor, but it is at base the body of a single ox.

Chopping down a cedar or camphor [tree] and carving and splitting it, some [of it] will become coffins or linings, [and] some [of it] will become pillars and beams. Cutting with or against the grain, its uses are myriad, but it all is the material from a single tree.

Thus, the designations and prescriptions of the words of the Hundred Traditions are mutually opposed, but they cleave to the Way as a single body.

Compare it [i.e., the Way] to silk, bamboo, metal, and stone.[57] In concert, they all [make] music. The sound and tradition of each is different, but none is lost from the structure.

54. For the terms *yu* 宇 (extension in space) and *zhou* 宙 (extension in time), see chap. 3, n. 1.

55. Qin Fu 欽負 is evidently the same legendary figure who appears in a roughly parallel passage in *Zhuangzi* 6. There his name is given as Kan Pi 堪坏. See Zhang Shuangdi 1997, 2:1167n.3.

56. Bian Que 扁鵲 was physician of legendary skill who lived in the late sixth century B.C.E.

57. That is, stringed instruments, wind instruments, bells, and chimestones.

The assessment methods of Bo Le, Han Feng, Qin Ya, and Guan Qing[58] were all different, but their understanding of horses was as one.

Thus the methods and statutes of the Three Augusts and the Five Thearchs vary, but their attainment of the people's hearts was equivalent.

Tang entered Xia and used their methods;
King Wu entered Yin and used their rituals.
[The tyrants] Jie and Djou were destroyed using [these methods and rituals],
yet Tang and Wu used them to create order. [11/99/20–11/100/2]

11.14

Thus,

[even] when the knife and saw are laid out, if one is not a good craftsman, one cannot shape the wood.

[Even] when the furnace and the earthen molds are prepared, if one is not a skillful smith, one cannot shape the metal.

Butcher Dan cut up nine cows in one morning,[59] and his knife was sharp enough to split a hair.

Cook Ding used his knife for nineteen years, and his knife was as if just cast and sharpened.[60]

Why is this? It roamed among the many spaces.

The compass, the square, the angle rule, and the marking cord are the tools of the skillful but do not make one skilled. Thus if the *se* has no strings, even a music master[61] could not make a tune. [Yet] strings alone cannot produce sorrow. Thus strings are the tools of sorrow; they do not cause one to be sorrowful. The master artisan's construction of the repeating crossbow, the revolving aperture, the hidden lock, and *trompe l'oeil* inlays[62] enters into the darkest of subtleties, the ultimate of spiritlike harmony. What wanders in the spaces between the heart and the hand, and is not in the realm of things, is something [even] fathers cannot teach to their sons. A blind musician's abandoning thought on encountering things, releasing the spirit and rising to dance, [thus] giving it form with strings, is something [even] an elder brother cannot describe to his younger brother.

---

58. Han Feng 韓風, Qin Ya 秦牙, and Guan Qing 筦青 were fabled horse assessors of olden times and are mentioned in tandem as adhering to mutually distinctive methods in LSCQ 20.8/138/5–9, although the names of Han Feng and Guan Qing are rendered slightly differently. For Bo Le, see 11.10 and 12.25.

59. *Guanzi* 29 records this incident but gives no further information about Butcher Dan.

60. Cook Ding is a sagely chef famously portrayed in *Zhuangzi* 3.

61. Following Xu Shen's gloss of 師文 as 樂師. See Zhang Shuangdi 1997, 2:1172n.23.

62. The term *lianji* 連 機 is reasonably securely identifiable as a "repeating crossbow." Translations of the other terms in this sentence are tentative. The sliding shutter mechanism of the famous Han gilded lamp in the shape of a servant, from the tomb of Dou Wan, may be an example of a *yun kai* 運開, "revolving aperture." See *Historical Relics Unearthed in New China* (Beijing: Foreign Language Press, 1972), pl. 99. For *xuanzuo* 眩錯, which seems to mean "fool-the-eye inlay," see the cunningly contrived and deceptive objects named as "extravagances of wood" in 8.9. See Lau, HNZ 8/65/1–3.

Now,

one who makes [something] true uses the level;

one who makes something straight uses the marking cord.

Making true or straight without being in the line or on the level is an art that cannot be shared. When one strikes the [note] *gong*, *gong* responds; pluck the *jue* [string], and [another] *jue* [string] moves. This is the mutual response of identical tones.[63] What does not correspond to any of the five tones, but to which all twenty-five strings respond, is the Way, which cannot be transmitted.[64] Thus,

solitude is the lord of form;

silence is the ruler of tone. [11/100/4–13]

11.15

In the world, "right" and "wrong" have no immutable basis. Each age affirms what it [deems] right and rejects what it [deems] wrong.[65] What each calls right and wrong is different, [yet] each [deems] itself right and others wrong. Seen from this [basis],

there are facts that accord with one's self, yet they are not originally "right."

There are those that are repellent to one's heart, yet are not originally "wrong."

Thus,

those who seek what is "right" do not seek the pattern of the Way; they seek what accords with their selves.

Those who reject what is "wrong" do not criticize what is crooked, they discard what is repellent to their hearts.

What is repellent to me is not necessarily not in accord with others.

What accords with me is not necessarily not rejected by custom.

The "right" of the utmost right has no wrong;

the "wrong" of the utmost wrong has no right.

This is genuine "right" and "wrong."

As for its being "right" here and "wrong" there, "wrong" here and "right" there, this is called "one right, one wrong." This one "right" and "wrong" is one corner [of the universe]. The unity [of all] "rights" and "wrongs" is the whole cosmos.[66] Now if I want to chose a "right" and lodge there, chose a "wrong" and abandon it, I still

63. This is an example of musical resonance often cited as a demonstration of greater "cosmic" resonance. *Gong* and *jue* are tones in the pentatonic scale. If two stringed instruments in the same room are tuned to each other, when the *gong* string on one is struck, the corresponding string on its counterpart will vibrate.

64. This paragraph echoes a passage in 6.4.

65. Some of the sense of the Chinese has been sacrificed to smooth English usage here. The original text literally reads "Each age rights [*shi* 是] what it rights and wrongs [*fei* 非] what it wrongs."

66. The text is somewhat unclear at this point. We translated it to agree with the overall sense of the passage. Tao Hongqing suggests that the text may be corrupt at this point and that it might have read originally as something like "This is the right and wrong of one corner, not the right and wrong of the cosmos" (Zhang Shuangdi 1997, 2:1175n.4).

cannot know, among what the age calls "right" and "wrong," which is "right," and which is "wrong."[67] [11/100/15–21]

The *Laozi* says:

"Ruling a great state is like cooking a small fish."[68]

Those who favor leniency say [it means] "Do not disturb it too much";
those who favor strictness say, "Give it salt and vinegar, that's it."

Duke Ping of Jin let slip words that were not correct. Music Master Kuang raised his *qin* and bumped into him, so that he tripped on his robe and [struck] the wall. The courtiers wanted to plaster [the damaged spot]. Duke Ping said, "Leave it. This will [remind] me of my fault."[69]

Confucius heard this and said, "It is not that Duke Ping did not cherish his body, but that he wanted to attract those who would admonish him."

Han [Fei]zi heard this and said, "The assembled officials abandoned Ritual and were not punished. This is to condone transgression. This is why Duke Ping did not become hegemon!"[70]

There was a guest[71] who presented someone to Mizi.[72] When the visitor[73] left, Mizi said, "Your visitor has only three faults.

He looked at me and laughed, this is arrogance.
In conversation he did not mention his teacher, this is effrontery.
His manner was light and his words were deep, this is rebelliousness."

The guest said,

"He looked at you and laughed, this is impartiality.
In conversation he did not mention his teacher, this is comprehensiveness.
His manner was light and his words were deep, this is loyalty."

Thus the demeanor [of the visitor][74] was the same,
but one thought him a gentleman, [and]
the other thought him a petty man.

This is the difference of one's own perspective. [11/100/23–11/101/4]

Thus,

if what they choose and discard correspond, then the words [of a minister to a ruler] will be [deemed] loyal, and they will become increasingly intimate. If their persons are distant, then [although their] plans are appropriate, suspicion will arise.

---

67. Following an emendation of the text suggested by Chen Guanlou, eliminating the characters *bu zhi* before "which is right and which is wrong" (Zhang Shuangdi 1997, 2:1176n.5).

68. *Laozi* 60.

69. A more detailed version of this anecdote appears in HFZ 36/115/22–25.

70. The current text of the *Hanfeizi* does not give this judgment verbatim, but it does record a very negative assessment of Music Master Kuang's actions.

71. This anecdote appears in ZGC 257/136/22–25.

72. Mi Zijian 密子賤 (b. 511 B.C.E.) was a disciple of Confucius. He is mentioned in *Analects* 5.3.

73. The character translated as "visitor" here (*bin* 賓) is the same as that translated as "guest" in the previous sentence, but the context makes clear that the referent is different in both cases. The text seems to have been corrupted in transmission. See Lau, HNZ, 100n.8; and Zhang Shuangdi 1997, 2:1177n.13.

74. The text refers here to "the demeanor of the guest," but again the reference is to the person who was introduced to Mizi, not to the "guest" who introduced him.

If his own mother were to treat her son's scalp boils and blood flowed past his ears, those who saw would consider it the utmost of love. If it were his stepmother, then those passing would think it was jealousy.

The dispositions of these affairs are the same; the point of view is different. From the top of the city wall

oxen look like sheep,
sheep look like pigs,

because where one stands is high.

Peer at your face in a pan of water and it is round;
peer at it in a cup of water and it is oval.

The shape of one's face has not altered from what it was. It is now round, now oval because where one looks at it is different.

Now although I want to rectify my person in facing things, how can I, without deliberation, know the viewpoint from which the age peers at me? If I turn and transform and race along with the age, this is like trying to flee the rain. There is nowhere to go where I will not get wet.

If I constantly want to reside in emptiness, then I cannot become empty. If I do not make myself empty and become empty spontaneously, none of my goals will not be met.[75]

Thus one who comprehends the Way is like the axle of a cart. He himself does not move, yet with the wheel he reaches one thousand *li*. He turns at the limitless origin. One who does not comprehend the Way is as if lost and confused. If you tell him east, west, south, north, his position is clear. As soon as there is a turn, he strays and suddenly does not grasp it; again he is lost and confused. Thus to the end of his days, he is a servant to others, like a weather vane[76] in the wind. He is not stable for an instant. Thus the sage embodies the Way and returns to nature; he does not transform in facing transformation, thus he comes close to withdrawal. [11/101/4–14]

11.16

In an ordered age,

the structure is easy to maintain;
its affairs are easy to do;
its rites are easy to practice;
its duties are easy to fulfill.

For this reason,

no person occupies two offices;
no officer manages two affairs.

Scholars, farmers, artisans, and merchants [keep] separate communities and [live in] different regions.

75. Emending the text as suggested by Wang Niansun. See Zhang Shuangdi 1997, 2:1179n.26.

76. The type of weather vane used in ancient China would have been a plume or a pennant on a staff set to blow in the wind. Thus the next line, "he is not stable for an instant."

Farmers discuss strength with one another;
scholars discuss conduct with one another;
artisans discuss skill with one another;
merchants discuss numbers with one another.

Thus,

scholars have no negligent conduct;
farmers have no wasted effort;
artisans have no odious tasks;
merchants have no debased goods.

Each rests secure in his nature; they are not able to interfere with one another.

Thus when Yi Yin started earthworks,

those with long legs were set to treading on shovels,[77]
those with strong backs were set to carrying earth,
those who were blind in one eye were set to [reading the] level,
hunchbacks were set to applying stucco.

Each had (a task) that was appropriate to him, and people's natures were put on a par.

The people of Hu are accustomed to horses;
the people of Yue are accustomed to boats.

They have different forms and separate categories.

If they exchange tasks, they will be upset;
if they lose their positions, they will be denigrated;
if they achieve their [potential] force, they will be honored.

The sage takes up [both] and uses them; their worth is as one [to him]. [11/101/16–21]

11.17

Foreknowledge and farsightedness,
vision reaching to a thousand *li* away,
are the zenith of human talent,

yet in an ordered age this is not expected of the people.

Broad learning and strength of will,
eloquent speech and fluent words,
are the perfection of human intelligence,

yet the enlightened ruler does not demand this of his subordinates.

Disdaining the age and scorning [material] things,
being uncorrupted by vulgarity,
are the upright conduct of a scholar,

yet in an ordered age these are not used to transform the people.

77. Emending the text in accordance with Wang Niansun and others. See Zhang Shuangdi 1997, 2:1183n.2.

The repeating crossbow and the hidden lock,
the curved knife leaving no trace,[78]
are the most marvelous [products] of human skill,
yet an ordered age does not make these the task of the people.

Thus Chang Hong and Music Master Kuang had foreknowledge of calamity and good fortune; their words contained no failed plans; yet they could not serve in office among the many.

Gongsun Long[79] broke arguments and repelled words, distinguishing like and unlike, discriminating between the hard and the white, [yet] he could not share his Way with the multitude.

Beiren Wuze[80] rejected Shun and threw himself into the Qingling Pool, [yet] he could not serve as a model for the age.

Lu Ban and Mozi made kite hawks out of wood and they flew, not landing for three days,[81] yet no one could employ them as carpenters.

Thus
what is so lofty as to be unreachable cannot be the measure of humans;
conduct that cannot be matched cannot be made the custom of the kingdom.
[11/101/23–11/102/3]

[One who] can judge heavy and light by holding [things] without being off by a *zhu* or a *liang*[82] the sage does not use; [instead,] he hangs things on the scales.

[One who] can judge high and low [deviations from the horizontal] by sight without being off by a foot or an inch the enlightened ruler does not employ; [instead,] he seeks it with the water level.

Why is this? Human talent cannot be employed reliably, but standards and measures can be passed down from generation [to generation].

Thus
the order of the kingdom may be maintained with the foolish,
and the control of the army can be used with the powerful.

If you wait to harness [only] Yaoniao or Feitu,[83] then you will not mount a chariot in this age.

If you wait to be matched only with Xi Shi or Mao Qiang, then you will not be married to the end of your life.

---

78. This translation breaks the parallelism of the two clauses *shenji yinbi* 神機陰閉, *jijue wuji* 剞劂無跡. It is possible that *wuji* should also be translated nominally, referring to some artifact of the Western Han known as a "traceless," the record of which has been lost. Alternatively, *yinbi* might be meant to modify *shenji;* thus the first clause would read "the repeating crossbow with its hidden lock," and the second phrase would then mean something like "the engraving tool that leaves no traces."

79. Gongsun Long 公孫龍 (b. 498 B.C.E.) was a renowned logician of the Warring States period, famous for his assertion that "a white horse is not a horse."

80. The legendary figure Beiren Wuze 北人无擇 appears in LSCQ 19.1 and ZZ 28.

81. *Mozi* 49 records that Lu Ban 魯般 (also known as Gongshu 公輸 Ban [fl. ca. 450 B.C.E.]) constructed an ingenious bird, which Mozi himself derided as impractical.

82. A *liang* was an ancient unit of weight roughly comparable to an ounce. One *liang* was equal to twenty-four *zhu*.

83. Yaoniao 騕褭 and Feitu 飛兔 were famous horses of legend, sire and foal.

This being so, if people have made do without awaiting the heroes of antiquity, it is because they went along with what they had and used it. Qiji could traverse one thousand *li* in a single day. An inferior horse requires ten rest stops, but in ten days it will still get there. Looking at it from this [perspective], human talent cannot be exclusively relied on, yet the techniques of the Way can be universally practiced. In the methods of a chaotic age,

the lofty is made the measure, and those who do not reach it are incriminated;
duties are weighty, and those who cannot overcome them are punished;
tests are perilous, and those who do not dare are executed.

The people are trapped by these three demands, thus

they ornament their intelligence and cheat their superiors;
they commit depravity and shirk [their duties].

Thus although there are harsh laws and severe punishments, one cannot contain their wickedness. Why is this? Force is insufficient. Thus a maxim says:

"When a bird is desperate, it grasps for food with its beak;
when a beast is desperate, it roots for food with its horns;
when a person is desperate, he deceives."

This says it. [11/102/5–13]

11.18

The standard of the Way and Potency is comparable to the sun and moon.

[Moving] south of the Yangzi or north of the Yellow River cannot change its position.
Speeding across one thousand *li* cannot alter its location.

Choosing and rejecting, rites and customs are comparable to a home.

The house to the east calls it "the west house";
the house to the west calls it "the east house."

Even if Gao Yao ordered it for them, he could not fix its location.[84]

Thus,

choosing and rejecting are equal;
blame and praise are rooted in custom.
Intentions and conduct are matched;
failure and success reside in the [circumstances of] the time.

Tang and Wu's accrual of conduct and accumulation of goodness can be matched. Their meeting Jie and Djou was a bequest of Heaven. Now if you have the intention of Tang or Wu yet lack the timely [circumstances] of [encountering] Jie and Djou and want to complete the task of a hegemon or king, you will not get close to it.

In the past, King Wu raised the spear and grasped the battle-axe in conquering Yin.

84. That is, even a sage could not make it consistently "the east house" or "the west house"; the terminology always depends on the frame of reference.

He held the jade tablet and leaned on the wooden cane in attending court. When King Wu died, the people of Yin revolted. The Duke of Zhou moved into the Eastern Palace and mounted the royal chariot. Assuming the position of the Son of Heaven [and] with his back to the screen, he convened the Lords of the Land. He exiled Cai Shu, executed Guan Shu,[85] conquered Yin, and punished the Shang. Sacrificing to King Wen, after seven years he gave over the government to King Cheng. Now that King Wu was first martial and then civil is not that his intentions had altered; it was that he responded to the times. That the Duke of Zhou exiled his older brother and executed his second brother was not that he was not humane; it was that he was rectifying chaos. Thus when one's affairs comprehend the age, one's merit will be complete; when one's tasks accord with the times, one's name will be established. [11/102/15–22]

In the past, Duke Huan of Qi convened the Lords of the Land with ceremonial chariots; withdrawing, he punished his state with the battle-axe.
Duke Wen of Jin convened the Lords of the Land with war chariots; withdrawing, he managed his kingdom with Ritual and Rightness.
Duke Huan was soft at first and hard later.
Duke Wen was hard at first and soft later;

yet in their orders being carried out throughout the world, their authority controlling the Lords of the Land, they were the same. They had investigated the alterations of the strategic situation.

The ruler of Lu wanted to make Yan He[86] his prime minister, yet [Yan He] was unwilling. [The duke] sent someone with silk as an advance [gift], but [Yan He] cut a hole in his wall and absconded, [later] becoming a renowned warrior in the world. If he had met with Shang Yang or Shen Buhai, the death penalty would have extended to the third [degree of relatedness] of his family, not to mention his own person![87] The age often singles out people of antiquity and looks up to their conduct. All ages have those who are the same, yet their nobility is not known. It is not because their talent was inferior; it is because the times were not right.

For crossing the Yangzi or the Yellow River, six [horses like] Qiji or four Northern Di stallions do not match the convenience of a hollow log. The dynamic of the location makes it so. For this reason, a person who establishes his merit is relaxed about his conduct yet meticulous about the time. The common people of the current age

take completed merit as worthiness,
triumph over adversity as intelligence,

---

85. Cai Shu 蔡叔 and Guan Shu 管叔 were, like the Duke of Zhou, younger brothers of King Wu. They defied the Duke of Zhou's assumption of the regency on behalf of the underage King Cheng. Their punishment by the Duke of Zhou is described in the *Documents*. See *Shang shu* 37/32/21–37/34/6. See also 20.14 and 20.25; and chap. 21, n. 31.

86. Yan He 顏闔 was reportedly a hermit-knight of Lu during the reign of Duke Ai (r. 494–467 B.C.E.). A slightly altered version of this tale appears in ZZ 28 and LSCQ 2.2.

87. That is, the Duke of Lu was willing to overlook Yan He's desire to decline office; but if a Legalist had been in control of the state, Yan He would have been liable to drastic punishment for the same act.

encountering difficulty as foolishness,
and dying for duty as stubbornness.

I regard each as having reached one's limit, that is all. [11/102/24–11/103/2]

Prince Bi Gan was not unaware of [the strategy of] disheveling his hair and feigning madness to avoid [injury to] his person.[88] However, he took joy in [maintaining] upright conduct and utmost loyalty in dying for his duty; thus he would not do it.

Bo Yi and Shu Qi[89] were not unable to accept a salary and hold office to extend their merit. However, they took joy in departing from the age and acting loftily in transcending the multitude; thus they would not serve.

Xu You and Shan Juan were not incapable of grasping the world, pacifying the realm in making the people virtuous. However, they were ashamed to allow things to pollute their harmony; thus they would not accept it.

Yu Rang and Yao Li[90] were not unaware of enjoying one's home, resting content with one's wife and children in living easily. However, they took joy in extending their sincerity and fulfilling obligation in dying for their ruler; thus they would not refrain.

Now,

if we follow Jizi in viewing Bi Gan, he was foolish.
If we follow Bi Gan in viewing Jizi, he was base.
If we follow Guan [Zhong] and Yan [Ying] in viewing Bo Yi and Shu Qi, they were stubborn.
If we follow Bo Yi and Shu Qi in viewing Guan and Yan, they were greedy.

Their choosing and rejecting negated each other; their wants and desires were mutually opposed; yet each took joy in his affairs. Who can be employed [to judge] which was correct?

Zengzi said: "When you strike [the side of] a boat in the water,
the birds hear it and fly high;
the fish hear it and plunge deep."[91]

Where each tends is different, yet each attains what is suitable to it.

Huizi[92] crossed the Mengzhu [Marsh] with a retinue of one hundred chariots. Zhuangzi saw him and threw away his leftover fish.[93]

---

88. Prince Bi Gan 比干 was the uncle of King Djou, the wicked last ruler of the Shang dynasty. He admonished the rulèr for his excesses and was put to death. Here he is implicitly contrasted with Jizi 箕子, another uncle and retainer of King Djou, who was able to escape Bi Gan's fate by feigning madness.

89. Shu Qi 叔齊 was the younger brother of Bo Yi. Both died of starvation together on Mount Shouyang. See *Shiji* 61.

90. Yao Li 要離 was a retainer of King Helü of Wu who consented to being falsely incriminated and to his wife's being executed so that he might get close to one of his king's enemies. His story is recounted in LSCQ 11.3.

91. A parallel saying is found in 10.33.

92. Huizi 惠子 (Hui Shi 施) was a sophist who served as chief minister of King Hui of Liang (r. 370–319 B.C.E.).

93. Zhuangzi's gesture was one of disgust at the display of excess he had just witnessed.

The pelican drinks several *dou* of water, yet it is not enough.
If the cicada gets so much as a mouthful of mist, it is full.[94]
Earl Zhi had all three Jin [states], and his desires were not sated;
Lin Lei's[95] and Rong Qiji's clothes were ragged and tattered, but their thoughts were unperturbed.

Viewing it from this [perspective], each of their predilections and conduct was different, how could they refute one another?

One who highly values life will not harm himself for profit;
one who establishes discipline will not negligently avoid difficulty when faced with it;
one who lusts for emolument will not consider his person in the face of profit;
and one who loves reputation will not [accept] gain in neglect of Rightness.

These standards set against one another are like ice and charcoal, angle rule and marking cord;[96] when will they ever accord? If you take the sage as a standard, then he comprehensively covers and completely contains them, so there never can be a "right" and a "wrong."

The flying bird favors the nest;
the fox favors the burrow.
Nesters attain a perch when the nest is complete;
burrowers attain a rest when the burrow is made.

Choosing and rejecting, conduct and Rightness are also the perch and rest of human beings. [When] each takes joy in what makes him secure [and] arrives at his destination, [then] he is called a "complete person." Thus the standard of the Way combines them and puts them on a par. [11/103/4–17]

11.19

In the Way of the ordered state,

superiors do not give harsh orders;
officials do not confuse the government;
scholars do not falsify their conduct;
artisans do not make licentious use of their skill.
Its affairs are regular and untroubled;
its implements are complete and unornamented.

A chaotic age is not like this.

Those who partake in conduct vie to outdo one another in loftiness;
those who partake in Ritual take pride in [surpassing] one another in artifice.

---

94. Following Sun Yirang's proposed emendation. See Zhang Shuangdi 1997, 2:1194n.26.

95. Lin Lei 林類 was, according to Xu Shen, a "worthy recluse." See Zhang Shuangdi 1997, 2:1195n.28.

96. These two pairs are meant to exemplify cold and hot, curved and straight. For ice and charcoal, see also 16.14.

Chariots are excessively carved;
implements are exhaustively engraved.
Those who seek goods vie for those that are hard to obtain as treasures.
Those who value writing fix complexity and distortions as [signs of] intelligence.

They compete to create false disputations. Accumulating for a long while without cease, these are of no aid to order. Craftsmen make exotic implements. Complete only after a year has passed, these do not increase utility.

Thus the laws of the Divine Farmer said:

"If a man is able-bodied[97] and does not farm, someone in the world will be hungry as a result.
If a woman does not weave over the course of a year, someone in the world will be cold as a result."
Thus each man farming for himself
and each wife personally spinning

was made the priority of the world. In guiding the people,

he did not value goods that were hard to obtain;
he did not take useless objects as implements.

For this reason,

those who did not exert strength in farming did not have the means to nourish life;
those who did not exert effort in weaving did not have the means to cover their bodies.

Surplus or dearth came back to each person individually.

Clothing and food were plentiful;
wickedness and deviance did not appear.

[People were] secure, happy, and without incident, and the world was at peace.

Thus Confucius and Zeng Can had nowhere to practice their goodness,
Meng Ben and Cheng Jing[98] had nowhere to effect their might. [11/103/19–26]

11.20

In the customs of a declining age, people employ their understanding and skill to [create] the fake and the false; they ornament every kind of useless [thing].

They value goods from distant places,
treasure materials that are hard to obtain,

and do not accumulate the instruments for nurturing life.

They dilute what is concentrated in the world;
they fragment what is uncarved in the world;

97. *Zhangfu* 丈夫, "a full-grown man."

98. Cheng Jing 成荊 was a knight of Qi renowned for his courage during the Spring and Autumn period. He is mentioned in LSCQ 8.2.

they corral and subjugate horses and oxen as sacrificial beasts. They fool the myriad people, turning the pure into the sullied. Nature and destiny fly away; all is chaotic and confused. Sincerity and trust are thrown into turmoil; people lose their genuine dispositions and nature.

With this there appears

kingfisher feathers, rhino [horn] and ivory, embroidery and elegant patterns to confuse their eyes;

grass-fed and grain-fed [animals]; the aromas of Jing and Wu to tempt their mouths;

[the sound of] bells, drums, pipes and flutes, strings, bamboo, metal, and stone to seduce their ears;

choosing and rejecting, conduct and Rightness, Ritual and discipline, criticism and argumentation to bind their minds.

At this point, the common people are turbulent and confused; all day they chase after profit. They are vexed and shallow. The laws and Rightness negate each other; conduct and profit oppose each other. Even ten Guan Zhongs could not bring [this situation] to order. [11/103/28–11/104/4]

Moreover, the rich have

carriages draped with red silk and embroidery;
and horses ornamented with plumes and ivory.
Their tents and seat cushions,
silken clothes and belts,
have interweaving [patterns of] green and yellow;

they cannot be pictured.

In the summer the poor wear hemp clothes belted with rope; they gulp beans and drink water to fill their bellies and to repel the heat. In the winter their wools and furs are torn and tattered; their short hemp coats do not cover their frames; and they blow into the stove's mouth. Thus, while in being registered as commoners in the household registers, they are no different, the [actual] difference between the rich and the poor cannot even compare with that between the ruler and a slave or a captive.

Those who employ strange arts and practice deviant ways have enough to last a generation.

Those who maintain rectitude, follow order, and do not acquire negligently cannot avoid the calamity of hunger and cold.

Yet we want the people to discard the branches and return to the root. This is like opening up a spring and stopping its flow. Moreover,

carving, polishing, cutting and engraving are what harm the tasks of farmers.
Embroidering cloth and patterning belts are what impair the work of women.
When the task of farmers is abandoned
and women's work is injured,

this is the root of hunger and the source of cold. One who can avoid committing crime and facing punishment when both hunger and cold arrive has never been known. [11/104/6–13]

11.21

Humaneness and depravity reside in timeliness, not in conduct;
profit and harm reside in fate, not in intelligence.
Among the soldiers of a defeated army brave warriors will flee; the commander cannot stop them.
Within the ranks of a victorious army, cowards will march to their deaths; the fearful cannot run away.

Thus when the Yangzi and the Yellow River overflow, the fathers and sons, elder and younger brothers, of a single village will abandon one another and flee. They will fight to mount high mounds or to climb high hills. Those who are fleet of foot will get there first; they cannot look after one another. When the age is happy and wills are set on peace, if they see the people of a neighboring kingdom drown, they still will grieve for them, how much more so for their own family and kin!

Thus,

when one's person is secure [and] kindness reaches to the neighboring kingdom, one will exert oneself to the utmost.
When one's person is endangered, then one forgets one's family and kin, [and] Humaneness offers no solution.
One who is swimming cannot save [another] from drowning; his hand and feet are occupied.
One who is burning cannot save [another] from the flames; his body is in pain.
If the people have surplus, they will yield;
if they lack enough, they will fight.
When they yield, then Ritual and Rightness are generated;
if they fight, then tyranny and chaos will result.

If you knock on someone's door and ask for water or fire, none will fail to give it, because they have enough to lend.

In forests no one sells firewood;
on lakes no one sells fish;

Because there is a surplus. Thus,

when things are plentiful, desires are reduced,
when demands are fulfilled, fighting ceases.
During the time of the king of Qin [i.e., Qin Shihuangdi], some people cooked their own children because material benefits were insufficient.
When the Liu clan took control of the government, widows took in orphans because there was surplus wealth.

Thus,

when the age is ordered, petty people will maintain rectitude; they cannot be enticed by profit.
When the age is in chaos, gentlemen will commit wickedness; the law cannot restrain them. [11/104/15–24]

Translated by Andrew Meyer

Twelve

RESPONSES OF THE WAY

"RESPONSES OF the Way" is summarized in chapter 21 of the *Huainanzi* as follows:

> [It] picks out and draws together the relics of past affairs,
> pursues and surveys the traces of bygone antiquity,
> and investigates the reversals of bad and good fortune, benefit and harm.
> It tests and verifies them according to the techniques of Lao and Zhuang,
> thus matching them to the trajectories of gain and loss. (21.2)

Thus the qualities of the ideal ruler unfold through negative and positive examples from the past. This comprehensive vision of rulership is expressed through fifty-six anecdotes, each capped with a citation from the *Laozi* that supports the anecdote's didactic claims.[1] These anecdotes and many others of the same kind appear to have circulated in various forms (written, oral, or both) during the Warring States and Han periods and may be considered a distinctive genre. Those collected in "Responses of the Way" contain everything from profound and recondite accounts of mystical wandering to moralizing speeches, ethical prescriptions, and practical political counsel. They illustrate the manner in which the Way may be known to the ruler and be used to ensure the success and prosperity of his reign.

1. The *Laozi* is quoted fifty-three times. These citations correspond to sections from the following forty chapters in the received *Wang Bi* edition: 1, 2, 3, 4, 7, 9, 10, 13, 14, 15, 18, 19, 20, 21, 22, 23, 25, 27, 28, 36, 38, 39, 43, 44, 45, 47, 52, 54, 55, 56, 57, 58, 62, 70, 71, 72, 73, 74, 75, and 78.

Rhetorically, these anecdotes and their "capping" passages from the *Laozi* also demonstrate the versatility of that text as an authoritative source of sagely rule. Read as "the relics of past affairs," they were the ideal literary medium to illustrate the relationship between the Way and human affairs as unfolding in the context of change.[2] In addition, the citations from the *Laozi* demonstrate that text's wide scope and its ability to address nearly every occasion that might arise. The combination of illustrative anecdote and apposite citation created a mix of didactic principles (in chapter 21, called "the techniques of Lao-Zhuang") that the compilers of chapter 12 saw as instrumental to a ruler's success. Moreover, the *Laozi* here is given a canonical authority[3] that enhanced the credibility of the vision of empire and sage-rulership promoted in the *Huainanzi* more generally.

The Chapter Title

The title of this chapter is "Dao ying" 道應, which we translate as "Responses of the Way." Here *dao* denotes an all-embracing, singular, and abstract concept that lies beyond the multiplicity of things as well as the particular, varied, and concrete ways that come into play in different situations. *Ying*, meaning "response," has strong resonances with the Han *ganying* stimulus–response cosmology (see chapter 6). In "Responses of the Way," *ying* suggests that the ruler must choose the appropriate response (*ying*) grounded in the Way that is evoked (*gan*) by the circumstances of the moment. When rulers of bygone days did so, they succeeded; when they did not, they failed. Separately and cumulatively, these illustrative anecdotes address issues of royal responsiveness and virtuous rule, such as how a ruler should orient himself toward his people and his bureaucracy.

Other translators have rendered the title "The Response of Matter to the Move-

---

2. The opening lines of chap. 21 of the *Huainanzi* state:

> We have created and composed these writings and discourses as a means to
> knot the net of the Way and its Potency
> and weave the web of humankind and its affairs.

The idea is repeated later in the same paragraph where the author explains:

> Thus,
> if we speak of the Way but do not speak of affairs,
> there would be no means to shift with the times.
> [Conversely,]
> if we speak of affairs but do not speak of the Way,
> there would be no means to move with [the processes of] transformation.

3. As we discuss in the introduction to this book, the *Laozi* is one of four texts that the *Huainanzi* authors treat as canonical by (usually) citing them by name (rather than, as with many other texts, quoting or paraphrasing them without attribution); the others are the *Odes*, the *Changes*, and the *Documents*.

ment of the Cosmic Spirit"[4] or "Des résonances du 'dao.'"[5] We have chosen "Responses of the Way" to emphasize the chapter's central concern with demonstrating the relevance and applicability of the Way and its methods of resolving the often complex and multifarious challenges of rulership. Accordingly, this chapter portrays the ruler as the conduit enabling Moral Potency and the virtues of the Way to work through him to respond to whatever may arise.

Summary and Key Themes

The subject and the literary form of "Responses of the Way" are closely linked.[6] The chapter is written in a distinctive anecdotal form that we regard as unique to early Chinese prose literature. Each anecdote has a beginning, a middle, and an end, with its setting and characters loosely conforming to conventional patterns. The time frame and *dramatis personae* are limited, and locales generally are common stereotypes that provide a frame for the action (a royal court, a battlefield, a riverbank, a gateway, a bridge). A skillfully crafted anecdote memorably illustrates an abstract principle ("what many consider right is often wrong") or some quality of a significant cultural icon ("Confucius knew how to judge the subtle tendencies of things"). Furthermore, some anecdotes have a "snapshot" quality that conveys a historical moment captured in writing.

Although these anecdotes might now be identified as a subgenre of prose composition in the Warring States and Han periods, there was no word when they were written that unambiguously meant "anecdote." The genre most closely associated with the anecdote as a written form was the *shui* 說, or "persuasion." As chapters 16 and 17 demonstrate, a "persuasion" could be reduced to a "talking point" on which a speaker could frame an argument designed to sway the opinion of his listeners. Although an anecdote was often worked into the body of a persuasion using various techniques of contextualization and rhetorical framing, it was not itself a *shui* but was part of the raw material out of which a persuasion could be built. Moreover, unlike the *shui* collected in the "Shui lin" (A Forest of Persuasions) chapter of the *Hanfeizi,* in which anecdotes predominate as the material from which most persuasions are built, the two collections of *shui* in the *Huainanzi* do not consist mainly of anecdotes. Instead, they favor a shorter generic form of persuasive utterance, also found in the *Hanfeizi*'s "A Forest of Persuasions," albeit less developed there.[7]

Anecdotes were the building blocks of much of the prose writing of the late War-

4. Evan Morgan, *Tao, the Great Luminant: Essays from Huai Nan Tzu* (Shanghai: Kelly and Walsh, 1933).

5. Le Blanc and Mathieu 2003.

6. The same may be said of chap. 18, which uses the anecdotal form to great effect. See the introduction to that chapter.

7. For a more detailed discussion of the persuasions in the *Hanfeizi* compared with chaps. 16 and 17 of the *Huainanzi,* see the introduction to those chapters.

ring States and Former Han periods, on which authors constructed larger prose pieces. Besides the *Lüshi chunqiu*, one of the longest earlier works assembled from anecdotal prose, all or part of many other texts also use this form. Indeed, these anecdotal units became so common that eventually entire texts of deracinated anecdotes, such as the *Zhanguoce* and *Shuo yuan*, were compiled to meet the demand for them.

As is true of several other chapters of the *Huainanzi* consisting of many short sections (for example, chapters 10, 14, 16, 17, and 18), "Responses of the Way" begins with an establishing anecdote that sets the theme for the chapter as a whole. Here, section 12.1 features short dialogues between Grand Purity and Inexhaustible, Non-action and Non-beginning, concerning the nature of the Way. These dialogues affirm the unity of the Way (a unity that is beyond the power of words to describe) and are reinforced by two quotations from the *Laozi*, the first stating that "when all the world recognizes good as good, there is ill" and the second, the famous affirmation that "those who know do not speak; those who speak do not know." The reader thus is prepared to read the anecdotes that follow as a discourse on the nature of the Way, with interpretations backed by the authority of the *Laozi*.

These anecdotes depict crucial moments and dilemmas in a wide range of political contexts, discussing the principles to be implemented and attributes to be embodied by the ideal ruler under varying circumstances to ensure that he will succeed and not fail. The text also recommends to the ruler highly syncretic techniques, thereby reconciling disparate received traditions into an idea of rulership within the larger context of change. In "Responses to the Way," these anecdotes can be grouped in three categories: (1) epistemology, (2) ethics, and (3) pragmatics.

Epistemology: Knowing, Articulating, and Transmitting the Way

The seventeen anecdotes in the category of epistemology address such fundamental questions as: Can knowledge of the Way be acquired? How does one know the Way? How does one communicate knowledge of the Way to others?[8] These stories share many parallels with anecdotes found in the later chapters of the received *Zhuangzi*.[9] They suggest that the dual aspects of the Way as changing/unchanging, differentiated/undifferentiated, and eternal/ephemeral may be known by following two distinct but complementary epistemological routes: "knowing" and "not knowing." In turn, these correspond to learning through others and learning through the self.

8. These anecdotes correspond to the following sections: 12.1, 12.2, 12.3, 12.4, 12.7, 12.11, 12.18, 12.20, 12.25, 12.34, 12.37, 12.39, 12.42, 12.44, 12.45, 12.46, and 12.48.

9. By noting such parallels, we do not intend to argue that the *Huainanzi* compilers necessarily drew on the *Zhuangzi* and that if they did, it had already achieved a static form or its final form as we know it today. Moreover, Roth has argued that the received *Zhuangzi* may have been compiled at the court of Huainan. For his arguments, see Harold D. Roth, "Who Compiled the *Chuang Tzu*?" in *Chinese Texts and Philosophical Contexts: Essays Dedicated to Angus C. Graham*, ed. Henry Rosemont Jr. (La Salle, Ill.: Open Court Press, 1991), 79–128, and the introduction to chap. 2.

Learning the Way through others refers to articulating and transmitting the Way through conventionally accepted understandings of wisdom, mediated through human culture and involving reading, writing, and speaking. Learning the Way through direct experience necessitates practicing "apophatic" regimens of inner cultivation.[10] The knowledge thus gained cannot be transmitted through reading, writing, and speaking but must rely on nonverbal forms of communication.

"Responses of the Way" depicts knowledge that elucidates the eternal, unchanging, and undifferentiated Way as profound, refined, and internal and describes knowledge of the ephemeral, changing, and differentiated Way as shallow, coarse, and external. Although the eternal Way is prized more highly, the ephemeral Way also is recognized as valuable. Each complements the other. This hierarchical reading of wisdom is used to resolve and harmonize conflicting positions on the fundamental question of epistemology represented in the various intellectual positions found in preunification China. In this way, the most extreme claims of the *Zhuangzi* that eschew politics altogether are tamed, and the most potentially subversive readings of the *Laozi*, supportive of a minimalist government and an undetectable ruler, are domesticated as a vision of ideal rule conducive to the intellectual unity and harmony embodied in the *Huainanzi* as a whole.

Ethics: Bringing the Moral Potency of the Way to the Realm

The second group, ethics, consisting of twenty-three anecdotes,[11] portrays a more public wisdom grounded in details of the political realm and notions of ethical leadership, judgment, and a responsibility to the collective future. These anecdotes provide moral inspiration to do the greatest good for the greatest number of people. Accordingly, they deal with the ethical conduct and moral character of rulers in relation to the people and members of the bureaucracy, illustrating the ways in which they affect current political circumstances. Through these illustrations, the ruler is advised to embody certain kinds of virtue and exhibit certain kinds of ethical conduct so as to bring Moral Potency to ruler and ruled alike.

This group of anecdotes also shows a deep commitment to a vision of governance in which the ruler nurtures and transforms the people through his moral example and feels himself to be bound up with them in a mutually beneficial and harmonious

10. Harold D. Roth, "Bimodal Mystical Experience in the 'Qiwulun' Chapter of the *Zhuangzi*" (paper presented at the annual meeting of the Association for Asian Studies, Chicago, March 1997); "Evidence for Stages of Meditation in Early Taoism," *Bulletin of the School of Oriental and African Studies* 60, no. 2 (1997): 295–314; and "The Yellow Emperor's Guru: A Narrative Analysis from *Chuang Tzu* 11," *Taoist Resources* 7, no. 1 (1997): 43–60. See also Lee Yearley, "The Perfected Person in the Radical Chuang Tzu," in *Experimental Essays on Chuang-tzu*, ed. Victor Mair (Honolulu: University of Hawai'i Press, 1983), 125–39, and "*Zhuangzi*'s Understanding of Skillfulness and the Ultimate Spiritual State," in *Essays on Skepticism, Relativism, and Ethics in the Zhuangzi*, ed. Paul Kjellberg and Philip J. Ivanhoe (Albany: State University of New York Press, 1996), 152–82.

11. See 12.8, 12.9, 12.10, 12.12, 12.15, 12.16, 12.17, 12.21, 12.22, 12.24, 12.26, 12.27, 12.28, 12.30, 12.31, 12.36, 12.43, 12.47, 12.49, 12.50, 12.51, 12.53, and 12.54.

relationship. He exhibits concern for the welfare of people, even those from a foreign state, through his commitment to cultivating the moral aspects of his person[12] and seeking the advice, heeding the counsel, and using the ability of his worthy ministers.[13] These anecdotes demonstrate that when rulers govern through such virtues as humaneness, rightness, sincerity, trustworthiness, and moderation, they will not only receive support from their officials and their people but also generate the requisite conditions for humans to flourish. These anecdotes speak of enduring ideals of ethical rule and the common good, which contrast with the last group of stories, which deal with the exigencies of political power and purchase.

Pragmatics: Surviving Potential Harm and Destruction

The last group of anecdotes counsels the ruler to implement practical measures to ensure that his positional advantage (*shi* 勢) will not be compromised, his political power will not be challenged, and his state or person will not be destroyed. These anecdotes emphasize techniques of bureaucratic recruitment and control, recommending those that enable the ruler to secure men of worth and talent and arguing that the most efficacious rulers do not overlook talented men. That is, such rulers employ men with a wide range of talents, since a ruler cannot predict when a seemingly insignificant talent may become indispensable to his ability to avoid harm or to resolve a challenging problem. Good examples are the humorous and entertaining vignettes in which Gongsun Long hires a rustic man who is good at yelling and the Chu general Zifa hires an infamous thief.[14] Ideal rulers, moreover, concentrate on the strong points of others and overlook their minor flaws. According to the *Huainanzi* compiler(s), this is the lesson to be gleaned from the well-known story of neglect and discovery in which Duke Huan of Qi employs Ning Qi.[15] We also read about those who lost their states and suffered defeat as well as those who managed to hang on to them and enjoy long-term prosperity. This collection of sixteen anecdotes contains the greatest number of parallels and near parallels with the *Lüshi chunqiu*.[16]

12. See, for example, 12.17.

13. See, for example, 12.10, which attributes the perfect merit achieved by Yao, Shun, and King Wu to their able ministers whose capabilities surpassed those of their respective rulers.

14. See 12.29 and 12.38. Note that the story of Zifa concludes: "Thus, there are no petty skills and there are no insignificant abilities; it all depends on how the ruler uses them" (12.38).

15. See 12.14.

16. For these anecdotes, see 12.5, 12.6, 12.13, 12.14, 12.19, 12.23, 12.29, 12.32, 12.33, 12.35, 12.38, 12.40, 12.41, 12.52, 12.55, and 12.56.

Sources

Each of the fifty-six sections of "Responses of the Way" begins with an anecdote and is usually capped by a citation from the *Laozi*.[17] In that way, chapter 12 of the *Huainanzi* is reminiscent of chapter 21 of the *Hanfeizi*, "Illustrating the *Laozi*" (Yu Lao 喻老). *Hanfeizi* 21 is the earliest extant example of a commentary attached to the *Laozi* that uses well-known and widely circulated stories to illustrate the relevance of the *Laozi* to statecraft concerns.[18] "Illustrating the *Laozi*" sees the *Laozi* primarily as a resource for exercising political power rather than as a guide for cultivating the body or achieving one's place in the natural and cosmic realms.[19] "Responses of the Way" also personifies and contextualizes passages of the *Laozi* but uses the anecdotes and quotations to demonstrate their relevance to contemporary political concerns. This chapter is thus an important descendant of a literary prototype represented by the *Hanfeizi* in the Warring States period.

Nonetheless, "Responses of the Way" departs from *Hanfeizi* 21 in noteworthy ways. Perhaps one of the most striking deviations from the earlier model is its linking of several narratives in the received *Zhuangzi*[20] with *Laozi* citations to promote "the techniques of Lao-Zhuang" in a single commentary. These anecdotes thus help

17. The three exceptions to this general rule close respectively with a citation from the *Zhuangzi*, *Shenzi*, and *Guanzi*. See 12.42, 12.50, and 12.51.

18. *Hanfeizi* 21 comments on lines that appear in the following chapters of the extant *Wang Bi* edition of the *Laozi*: 26, 27, 33, 36, 41, 46, 47, 52, 54, 63, 64, and 71. It uses anecdotes mainly to explicate the *Laozi* but not exclusively so, as in chap. 12 of the *Huainanzi*. Sometimes lines from the *Laozi* are introduced with brief philosophical explanations as in the chapter's discussion of political purchase (*shi* 勢). See HFZ 21/42/31–21/43/4. *Hanfeizi*, chap. 20, "Explaining the *Laozi*" (Jie lao 解老), comments on the following chapters from the *Laozi*: 1, 14, 38, 46, 50, 53, 54, 58, 59, 60, and 67. It is structured very differently from *Hanfeizi* 21 by not using stories to gloss lines from the *Laozi*, preferring philosophical prose. See HFZ 20/34/8–20/41/31. These two early commentaries have not received the scholarly attention they deserve, given their ability to illuminate two important and influential readings of the *Laozi*. Bertil Lundhal and Zheng Liangshu 鄭良樹 have reviewed the most important features of these two commentaries and the debates concerning their authorship and dating, but the field is in great need of a more detailed study of these two works. See Bertil Lundhal, *Han Fei Zi: The Man and the Work*, Stockholm East Asian Monographs, no. 4 (Stockholm: Stockholm Institute of Oriental Languages, Stockholm University, 1992); and Zheng Liangshu, "Hanfeizi Jie Lao pian ji Yu Lao pian chutan" 韓非子解老篇及喻老篇初探, *Hanxueyanjiu* 漢學研究 6, no. 2 (1988): 299–332.

19. *Huainanzi* 12 and *Hanfeizi* 21 also share two parallels. See HNZ 12/110/17–19 and HFZ 21/44/18–21; and HNZ 12/117/12–15 and HFZ 21/45/9–13. HNZ 12/111/4–7 recounts the tale of Goujian's servitude to and ultimate defeat of King Wu, and HFZ 21/44/10–13 refers briefly to this same story. Other chapters in the *Huainanzi* contain additional anecdotes that also appear in the *Hanfeizi* but vary in their details and are used for different didactic purposes. Compare, for example, the narrative of the ivory chopsticks in HFZ 21/44/5–8 with the version in HNZ 20.4.

20. Chap. 12 shares nine parallels or near parallels with the received *Zhuangzi*, two of which also appear in the *Lüshi chunqiu*. Compare the following anecdotes: HNZ 12/105/3–18 and ZZ 22/62/18–22; HNZ 12/106/28–12/107/4 and ZZ 22/60/31–22/61/2; HNZ 12/109/12–19 and ZZ 28/81/23–28; HNZ 12/109/21–25 and ZZ 28/84/7–11; HNZ 12/110/1–8 and ZZ 13/37/10–13; HNZ 12/114/26–29 and ZZ 10/24/27–10/25/3; HNZ 12/115/12–17 and ZZ 6/19/17–20; HNZ 12/116/18–19 and ZZ 1/1/19; HNZ 12/117/1–4 and ZZ 2/7/17–19; and HNZ 12/117/6–10 and ZZ 22/63/1–3.

readers interpret key *Laozi* passages as specific references to the meditative techniques and mystical gnosis of the *Zhuangzi*.[21] Conversely, using citations from the *Laozi* to gloss these *Zhuangzi* narratives gives these stories new nuances of meaning as well as canonical authority.

"Responses of the Way" also resembles the *Lüshi chunqiu*, which uses "historical" anecdotes to illustrate both broad ethical themes and practical political advice. In addition, twenty-three of the anecdotes in "Responses of the Way" also appear in the *Lüshi chunqiu*.[22] Although such an extensive overlapping of material is common in Western Han literature, its implications are not entirely clear. The compilers of chapter 12 of the *Huainanzi* may have used the *Lüshi chunqiu* as a source of anecdotal literature; the chapter may have used another written source or sources not known to us; or both the *Huiananzi* and the *Lüshi chunqiu* may have drawn from a common pool of anecdotal literature that circulated as modular units of "text" in written or oral form.[23] Whatever the case, the *Huainanzi* compiler(s) clearly used these stories to promote practical knowledge and techniques that rulers needed to successfully navigate the political challenges of administering a complex bureaucracy and heading a vast empire. These anecdotes were consistent with the syncretic aims of the *Huainanzi* project as a whole and summarized, illustrated, and reiterated concepts and themes developed elsewhere in the text.

"Responses of the Way" does not simply reiterate anecdotes that also appear in the *Lüshi chunqiu* to advance similar arguments but also uses them to highlight different didactic principles.[24] In the *Lüshi chunqiu*, many chapters begin with a general

21. Other tropes from the *Zhuangzi* developed in chap. 12 are "the usefulness of the useless" (12.34) and "valuing life" (12.15 and 12.16).

22. For the parallel and near parallel anecdotes, compare HNZ 12/105/20–26 and LSCQ 18.3/111/16–21; HNZ 12/106/1–6 and LSCQ 18.5/114/21–24; HNZ 12/106/8–13 and LSCQ 17.8/107/23–26; HNZ 12/106/15–20 and LSCQ 25.4/163/24–28; HNZ 12/107/6–14 and LSCQ 15.1/80/19–1/81/6; HNZ 12/107/16–12/108/3 and LSCQ 15.5/85/13–26; HNZ 12/108/5–9 and LSCQ 15.6/86/20–21; HNZ 12/108/11–15 and LSCQ 26.2/167/20–23; HNZ 12/108/17–21 and LSCQ 16.6/95/29–16.6/96/2; HNZ 12/108/23–27 and LSCQ 19.5/124/16–20; HNZ 12/109/1–10 and LSCQ 19.8/128/10–17; HNZ 12/109/12–19 and LSCQ 21.4/141/11–17; HNZ 12/109/21–25 and LSCQ 21.4/141/27–29; HNZ 12/109/27–30 and LSCQ 17.8/107/18–21; HNZ 12/111/9–13 and LSCQ 19.8/128/10–17; HNZ 12/112/19–12/113/3 and LSCQ 6.4/31/20–6.4/32/4; HNZ 12/113/16–20 and LSCQ 19.6/126/3–8; HNZ 12/114/26–29 and LSCQ 11.4/55/25–11.4/56/1; HNZ 12/115/19–28 and LSCQ 16.4/93/20–16.4/94/11; HNZ 12/116/21–28 and LSCQ 18.8/118/7–13; HNZ 12/117/22–26 and LSCQ 24.5/158/24–29; HNZ 12/117/28–12/118/8 and LSCQ 20.3/131/1–5; and HNZ 12/118/17–21 and LSCQ 14.3/72/25–14.3/73/4. As we saw earlier, chap. 4 also draws heavily on the LSCQ.

23. For the circulation and interchange of anecdotes as modular units of meaning, see David Schaberg, *A Patterned Past* (Cambridge, Mass.: Harvard University Press, 2001), 163–90. For one proposed strategy to sort out textual parallels through isocolometrical analysis, see William G. Boltz, "Notes on the Textual Relation Between the 'Kuo yü' and the 'Tso Chuan,'" *Bulletin of the School of Oriental and African Studies* 53, no. 3 (1990): 491–502. See also William G. Boltz, "The Composite Nature of Early Chinese Texts," in *Text and Ritual in Early China*, ed. Martin Kern (Seattle: University of Washington Press, 2005), 50–78.

24. See, for example, 12.3, an anecdote about Hui Shi drafting a set of laws for King Hui of Wei. Another version of this story appears in LSCQ 18.5/114/21–24. See Knoblock and Riegel 2000, 459–60. For a comparative analysis of the *Huainanzi* and *Lüshi chunqiu* versions, see Le Blanc 1985, 86–90.

claim or statement that frames the anecdotes that follow. In contrast, "Responses of the Way" presents the anecdote first and ends it with a quotation from the *Laozi*. Thus an anecdote that might be read in different ways uses the quotation to narrow it down to one interpretation. In anchoring well-known stories to particular lines in the *Laozi*, "Responses of the Way" not only explains the *Laozi* in novel ways but also refashions ancient stories to suit its own aims and goals.

Finally, "Responses of the Way" shares important similarities of structure and content with Han Ying's *Hanshi waizhuan* (*Master Han's Supplementary Disquisitions on the Book of Odes*). Han Ying's text also is a collection of anecdotes containing moral disquisitions, ethical prescriptions, and practical advice, with most entries concluding with a quotation from the *Shijing* to reinforce the point of the story or argument.[25] Likewise, Han Ying's text borrows from a wide range of disparate sources—in this case, the *Xunzi*, *Zhuangzi*, *Lüshi chunqiu*, *Yanzi chunqiu*, *Laozi*, and *Mengzi*[26]—and some of the same anecdotes appear in both texts.[27] The two also serve a similar function as texts meant primarily to instruct through the use of anecdotes linked to suitable quotations. For the *Hanshi waizhuan*, the *Odes* has the same function as the *Laozi* does for chapter 12 of the *Huainanzi*.

The Chapter in the Context of the *Huainanzi* as a Whole

"Responses of the Way" describes the eternal, unchanging, and undifferentiated aspects of the Way that the ideal ruler learns through firsthand experience. The sagely ruler understands that once discovered, such "knowledge" cannot be transmitted to others through verbal communication. Instead, he must rely on nonverbal forms of communication. Other anecdotes in this chapter offer a public wisdom based on daily political matters and encompassing leadership, judgment, and responsibility, which in turn provides a kind of moral inspiration to do the greatest good for the greatest number of people. Still other anecdotes address more pragmatic political issues to illustrate how the ruler can keep his person safe, his state intact, and his

---

As Le Blanc points out, the *Lüshi chunqiu* concludes the anecdote by emphasizing the importance of laws, whereas the *Huainanzi* ends by quoting Laozi's famous dictum, "The more detailed the laws and edicts; the more thieves and robbers there are."

25. Michael Loewe, ed., *Early Chinese Texts*, Early China Special Monograph, no. 2 (Berkeley: Society for the Study of Early China and the Institute of East Asian Studies, University of California, 1993), 125. The *Hanshi waizhuan* cites the *Laozi* twice. See Lau, HNZ, 7.10 and 9.16.

26. Loewe, *Early Chinese Texts*, 125.

27. For parallel and near parallel anecdotes with chap. 12, compare HSWZ 3.21/20/27–3.21/21/2 and HNZ 12/113/22–26; HSWZ 3.30/23/14–20 and HNZ 12/119/14–20; HSWZ 5.6/35/26–5.6/36/3 and HNZ 12/110/1–8; HSWZ 6.15/48/5–9 and HNZ 12/111/9–13; HSWZ 7.10/51/30–10/52/5 and HNZ 12/110/10–15; HSWZ 7.12/52/16–21 and HNZ 12/113/28–12/114/3; and HSWZ 10.23/78/1–4 and HNZ 12/108/23–27. The *Hanshi waizhuan* also shares other anecdotes and traditional sayings found in chaps. 10, 11, 13, 14, 18, and 20 of the *Huainanzi*.

ministers in line. In short, the ideal ruler envisioned in chapter 12 of the *Huainanzi* should be a mystic, a moralist, and a realist. Through paired narrative and citation, "Responses of the Way" describes a program of intellectual, moral, and strategic behavior. Filtered through the lens of the *Laozi*, these anecdotes illustrate the applicability of the Way to a variety of human affairs.

Sarah A. Queen

Twelve

12.1

Grand Purity asked Inexhaustible, "Do you know the Way?"
Inexhaustible responded, "I don't know it."
[Grand Purity] then asked Non-action, "Do *you* know the Way?'
Non-action replied, "I know it."
[Grand Purity said,] "Does this Way that you know have norms?"[1]
Non-action responded, "Yes, the Way that I know has norms."
[Grand Purity] inquired, "What are the norms, then?"
Non-action responded, "The Way that I know

can be weak or strong;
it can be soft or hard;
it can be yin or yang;
it can be dark or bright;
it can embrace or contain Heaven and Earth;
it can respond to or await the Limitless.

These are the norms by which I know the Way." [12/105/3–7]

Grand Purity then asked Non-beginning, "Earlier, I asked Inexhaustible about the Way and Inexhaustible replied, 'I don't know it.' I then asked Non-action and Non-action responded, 'I know it.' So I asked him, 'Does this Way that you know

1. *Shu* 數, more commonly "numbers," but here clearly used in one of its secondary meanings, "norms."

have norms?' Non-action then responded, 'Yes, the Way that I know has norms.' When I asked him whether he could [name] the norms, he responded, 'I know that the Way

can be weak or strong;
it can be soft or hard;
it can be yin or yang;
it can be dark or bright;
it can embrace or contain Heaven and Earth;
it can respond to or await the Limitless.

These are the norms by which I know the Way.' This being so, between Inexhaustible's not knowing and Non-action's knowing, which is right and which is wrong?"

Non-beginning answered,

"Not knowing it is deep while knowing it is shallow;
not knowing it is internal while knowing it is external;
not knowing it is refined while knowing it is coarse."

Grand Purity then gazed up at the heavens and said with a long sigh,

"Then is not knowing, in fact, knowing?
And is knowing, in fact, not knowing?
Who knows that knowing it is not knowing
and that not knowing it is knowing?"

Non-beginning responded,

"The Way cannot be heard, for what is heard is not the Way;
the Way cannot be seen, for what is seen is not the Way;
the Way cannot be spoken, for what is spoken is not the Way.
Who knows the formlessness of what gives form to form?[2]

Therefore the *Laozi* says:

"When all the world recognizes good as good,
there is ill."[3]

Therefore

those who know do not speak;
those who speak do not know.[4] [12/105/9–18]

12.2

The Duke of Bo asked Confucius: "Is it possible for people to share subtle words?"[5] Confucius did not respond. The Duke of Bo asked again: "Isn't it like throwing stones into the water?"

Confucius replied: "Skilled divers from Wu and Yue could retrieve them."

2. A version of this anecdote appears in ZZ 22/62/18–22.
3. *Laozi* 2.
4. *Laozi* 56.
5. *Wei yan* 微言.

"Then perhaps it is like throwing water into water?" the Duke of Bo asked.

Confucius replied: "When the waters of the Zi and Sheng rivers were blended together, Yi Ya tasted [the water] and recognized [which was which]."

The Duke of Bo responded: "Then is it not the case that people certainly cannot transmit subtle words?"

"Why consider it impossible?" asked Confucius. "[But it is possible] only for those who really know to what words refer. Now those who know to what words refer do not rely on words to speak. Fishermen get wet and hunters chase after their prey, but not because they like to do so. Therefore, the best words reject words [altogether], and the best acts are devoid of action. What [those of] shallow knowledge squabble over is inconsequential." The Duke of Bo did not grasp Confucius's meaning and consequently died in a bathhouse.[6]

Therefore the *Laozi* says:

> "Words have an ancestor and affairs have a sovereign.
> It is only because people lack this knowledge that they fail to understand me."[7]

These words describe the Duke of Bo. [12/105/20–26]

12.3

Huizi drafted the state laws on behalf of King Hui [of Wei].[8] When he had completed them, he showed them to the elders,[9] all of whom praised them. He then submitted them to King Hui. King Hui was elated by them and showed them to Zhai Jian.[10] Zhai Jian exclaimed, "Excellent."

King Hui inquired, "Since they are excellent, can we implement them?"

Zhai Jian responded, "We cannot."

King Hui then asked, "If they are excellent, why can we not implement them?"

Zhai Jian answered, "Now take those who haul heavy logs: those in front call,

---

6. For parallels of this story, see LSCQ 18.3/111/16–21, as well as *Liezi* 8, "Shuofu," and the "Weiyan" chapters of *Wenzi*. Compare the translation by Knoblock and Riegel 2000, 450, for LSCQ 18/3.4 and that by A. C. Graham, *The Book of Lieh-tzŭ: A Classic of Tao* (New York: Columbia University Press, 1990), 166–67. See Graham's note: "The Duke of Pai was the grandson of King Ping of Ch'u (528–516 B.C.E.). After the execution of his father in Cheng, he urged the Prime Minister of Ch'u to make war on Cheng. Instead a Ch'u army was sent to help Cheng against an invasion by Chin. The Duke rebelled, killed the Prime Minister, but was himself killed in a bath-house" (167).

7. *Laozi* 70.

8. King Hui of Wei 魏惠王 (also known as King Hui of Liang 梁 [r. 369–319 B.C.E.]) was the first ruler of Wei to assume the title of king. He moved the capital of Wei to Da Liang and oversaw the building of several large-scale public works. At the end of his long reign, after suffering successive defeats by powerful neighbors, he initiated a campaign to attract scholars and drew figures like Mencius to his court. See Zhang Shuangdi 1997, 2:1211n.1. This anecdote also appears in LSCQ 18, where King Hui is explicitly identified as the king of Wei. See Knoblock and Riegel 2000, 460.

9. Following the original text and rejecting Lau's emendation, which changes *xiansheng* 先生 to *minren* 民人, based on parallels with the *Lüshi chunqiu*.

10. Zhai Jian 翟煎 was a hereditary minister at the court of Wei during the Warring States period. His ancestor Zhai Huang had recruited many talented knights for Marquis Wen of Wei.

'Heave!'[11] while those behind respond, 'Ho!' This is a chant to encourage the strength of those who haul heavy loads. Could it really be that they do not know either the melodies of Zheng and Wey or the [tune called] 'Whirling Chu'? Although they know such melodies, they do not use them because they do not suit the circumstance as well as this chant does. Governing a state is a matter of ritual and not a matter of literary eloquence."[12] Therefore the *Laozi* says:

"The more detailed the laws and edicts,
the more thieves and robbers there are."[13]

This is what is meant here. [12/106/1–6]

12.4

Tian Pian[14] offered a persuasion on the techniques of the Way to the king of Qi, whereupon the king of Qi responded to Tian Pian: "What I possess is the state of Qi. The techniques of the Way are difficult to rely on to eradicate [its] troubles. I would much rather hear about governing the state of Qi."

Tian Pian replied: "My words said nothing [about] governing, but they may be used to create governing. [My words] may be compared to trees in a forest. They are not lumber, but they may be used to create lumber. I implore Your Majesty to investigate what has been said and then extrapolate from that the means to govern Qi. Although my [persuasion] might not eradicate the troubles of Qi, it can alter and transform what lies between Heaven and Earth and what is within the six coordinates. How can it suffice [for Your Majesty] to ask only about the governance of Qi?"[15]

This is what Lao Dan referred to as

a shape without a shape [of its own],
a form without an object [of its own].[16]

What the king asked about was Qi, and Tian Pian made an analogy to lumber.

Now,

the lumber is not so important as the forest;
the forest is not so important as the rain;
the rain is not so important as yin and yang;
yin and yang are not so important as harmony;
and harmony is not so important as the Way. [12/106/8–13]

11. Literally, *ye xu* 邪許.

12. For another version of this story, see LSCQ 18.5/114/21–24; and Knoblock and Riegel 2000, 459–60. For a comparative analysis of the HNZ and LSCQ versions, see Le Blanc 1985, 86–90.

13. *Laozi* 57.

14. Tian Pian 田駢 (also known as Tianzi 田子 and Chen 陳 Pian) was a philosopher and Qi native known for teaching the "arts of the Way." He was ranked among the venerable masters of Jixia in the Qi capital of Linze during the Warring States period. A text bearing his name once circulated but exists now only as fragments.

15. A version of this story appears in LSCQ 17.8/107/23–26. See Knoblock and Riegel 2000, 435.

16. *Laozi* 14.

12.5

When the Duke of Bo won possession of the state of Jing [i.e., Chu], he could not [bring himself to] distribute among the people the grain [kept in] the storehouses. On the seventh day [after the conquest], Shi Qi[17] entered [the capital] and said [to the Duke of Bo]: "You obtained this wealth through unrighteous means. Moreover, you could not [bring yourself to] share it. Calamity is sure to arrive. If you are incapable of giving [this wealth] to the people, it would be best to burn it so as not to give them cause to harm us." The Duke of Bo did not heed his advice.

On the ninth day [after the conquest], the Duke of She[18] entered [the capital]. He brought out the goods from the Supreme Storehouse in order to distribute them to the multitudes. He then removed the weapons from the Lofty Repository in order to distribute them to the common people. Thereafter he attacked the Duke of Bo, and on the nineteenth day [after the conquest] he captured him.

To desire the state when one does not yet possess it may be called the utmost avarice. To be incapable of acting on behalf of others, not to mention being incapable of acting on behalf of oneself, may be called utmost foolishness. How is the Duke of Bo's stinginess any different from the cannibal owl's love for its offspring?[19]

Therefore the *Laozi* says:

> "Rather than holding it upright and filling it to the brim,
> better to have stopped in time.[20]
> Hammer it to a point,
> and the sharpness cannot be preserved forever."[21] [12/106/15–20]

12.6

When Viscount Jian of Zhao selected Viscount Xiang as his successor, Dong Anyu[22] asked: "Wu Xie is of humble origins; why did you select him as your successor?"

17. Shi Qi 石乞 (d. 479 B.C.E.) was a knight of Qi who assisted the Duke of Bo in his rebellion against the throne. When the rebellion was put down, he was boiled alive as punishment.

18. The Duke of She 葉公 (also known as Shen Zhuliang 沈諸梁) was a grandee and vassal of Chu who led the forces that put down the rebellion of the Duke of Bo.

19. It is said that the *xiao* 梟 bird (generally taken to be a type of owl) loves her offspring, but because the mother bird teaches them to be fierce, the nestlings devour her when they mature. See also 1.14. In other words, the Duke of Bo loved wealth, but this love ultimately destroyed him. See Zhang Shuangdi 1997, 2:1215n.5. This story also occurs in LSCQ 25.4/163/24–28. See Knoblock and Riegel 2000, 635.

20. D. C. Lau explains: "This refers to a vessel which is said to have been in the temple of Zhou (or Lu). It stands in position when empty but overturns when full. The moral is that humility is a necessary virtue, especially for those in high position" (*Tao Te Ching* [Harmondsworth: Penguin, 1964], 65). For a story that revolves around the same type of vessel, see 12.55.

21. *Laozi* 9.

22. We follow Yu Dacheng in emending this name from Dong Jianyu (as given in the text but otherwise unknown) to Dong Anyu. See Lau, HNZ, 106n.4. Dong Anyu 董安于 (d. 496) was a knight who served in the household of Viscount Jian. His prescient counsel drew the suspicion of Earl Zhi, who forced him to commit suicide. Dong Anyu figures in several anecdotes about Viscount Jian in the *Lüshi chunqiu* and other texts.

Viscount Jian replied: "It was on account of [the type of] person he is. He is someone capable of enduring humiliation for the sake of the altars of soil and grain."

On another day Earl Zhi and Viscount Xiang were drinking wine together when Earl Zhi knocked Viscount Xiang on the head. The great ministers suggested that Earl Zhi should be executed for this, but Viscount Xiang replied: "When the former ruler appointed me, he said that I was a man who was capable of enduring humiliation for the sake of the altars of soil and grain. Did he say that I was a man capable of murdering another man?"

[Viscount Xiang] had been in office for ten months when Earl Zhi besieged him at Jinyang. Viscount Xiang dispatched a small force that attacked Earl Zhi and soundly defeated him. He split Earl Zhi's skull[23] and made a drinking vessel from it.

Therefore the *Laozi* says:

"Know the male
but keep to the role of the female
and be a ravine for the world."[24] [12/106/22–26]

12.7

Gaptooth asked Ragbag about the Way.

Ragbag replied:

"Straighten your body,
focus your gaze,
and Heaven's Harmony will arrive.
Concentrate your perception,
straighten your posture,
and the spirit will come to take up its abode.[25]
Potency will beautify you,
and the Way will reside in you.
You will be naïve as a newborn calf who does not seek out the reason for it."

Before Ragbag had finished speaking, Gaptooth fell into a deep sleep, having become a companion to the infinite. Ragbag broke out in song and went away singing:

23. A version of this story appears in *Shuo yuan*, chap. 3, "Jian ben" (Establishing the Root); there the text reads "lacquered his skull" rather than "split his skull." See Lu Yuanjun, *Shuoyuan jinzhu jinyi* (Taibei: Shangwu, 1967), 100–101. The story of Earl Zhi's (知伯 or 智伯) rise and fall is very famous, especially as a tale of strategic insight on the part of Viscount Xiang of Zhao. At a certain moment, Earl Zhi could easily have triumphed over Zhao, Hann, and Wei, but his own arrogance and presumption ultimately defeated him. Earl Zhi is a stock figure, and his story is retold many times down through the Han in such texts as the *Zhanguoce*, *Hanfeizi*, and *Lüshi chunqiu*, but the earliest known version appears in the final pages of the *Zuozhuan*. The greatest fund of "Earl Zhi stories" is likely the *Zhanguoce*, where he (listed in the index under Chih Po-yao or Earl Yao of Zhi) figures in chaps. 5, 75, 90, 97, 107, 158, 229, 292, 363, 461, 482, and 483 of James I. Crump, trans., *Chan-kuo Ts'e*, rev. ed., Michigan Monographs in Chinese Studies, vol. 77 (Ann Arbor: Center for Chinese Studies, University of Michigan, 1996).

24. *Laozi* 28.

25. This line could also be rendered, "And spirits will come to take up their abode."

"His form is like a withered carcass;
his mind is like dead ashes.
He authenticates his true knowledge
but does not rely on precedent to grasp it by himself.
Obscure and dim,
he has no mind with which to scheme.
What a man he is!"[26]

Therefore the *Laozi* says:

"When your discernment illuminates the four quarters,
can you do so without relying on knowledge?"[27] [12/106/28–12/107/4]

12.8

Viscount Xiang of Zhao dispatched an attacking force against [the "barbarian" state of] Dee and defeated it. When the inhabitants of [the two cities of] Zuo and Zhong had been captured, a messenger arrived to report the victory to Viscount Xiang, who was just about to eat his meal. When Viscount Xiang heard the news, an anxious expression appeared on his face. His attendants asked: "Capturing two cities in one morning is a cause for celebration. Why, then, do you appear so anxious?"

Viscount Xiang replied: "The swelling of the Yangzi and Yellow rivers does not last more than three days; wild winds and violent rains do not last a morning;[28] the sun at high noon lasts for less than a moment. Now the virtuous conduct of the Zhao clan has not yet amounted to anything, and yet in one morning two cities have been captured. Our demise is imminent!"

When Confucius heard about this, he said: "The Zhao clan will surely prosper!"

Anxiety leads to prosperity;
happiness leads to ruin.

Winning is not difficult, but preserving victory presents real challenges. The worthy ruler relies on his sense of anxiety to preserve victory, and so his good fortune extends to his descendants. The states of Qi, Chu, Wu and Yue all were victorious for a time, yet eventually their rulers were captured and ruined because they did not understand how to preserve victory. Only the ruler who possesses the Way can preserve victory. Confucius had enough strength to draw back the bolted gate of the capital, but he did not want to become known for his strength. Mozi engaged in defensive warfare that forced Gongshu Ban to submit to him, yet Mozi did not want to be known as a warrior. Those who are skilled at preserving victory consider their strength as weakness.[29]

---

26. This anecdote also appears in ZZ 22/60/31–22/61/2.

27. *Laozi* 10.

28. Supplying *bu zhongchao* 不終朝, based on Zhang Shuangdi 1997, 2:1221n.5.

29. A near parallel of this story appears in LSCQ 15.1/80/19–15.1/81/6. See Knoblock and Riegel 2000, 341–42.

Therefore the *Laozi* says:

"The Way is empty,
yet when you use it, you need not refill it."[30] [12/107/6–14]

12.9

Hui Ang[31] had an audience with King Kang of Song.[32] Stamping his feet and clearing his throat impatiently, King Kang replied hastily: "I am persuaded by courage and strength. I am not persuaded by Humaneness and Rightness. What could you possibly have to teach me?"

Hui Ang replied: "I possess a Way that goes to this point. It can cause people, however courageous, never to penetrate when they stab and, however strong, never to hit the mark when they strike. Could Your Majesty really not be interested in this?"

King Kang of Song replied: "Excellent! These are indeed matters that I want to hear about."

Hui Ang continued: "Stabbing but not penetrating and striking but not hitting the mark is nevertheless still an insult. I possess a Way that goes to this [further point]. It can cause courageous men not to dare to stab you and strong men not to dare to strike you.

"Still, not daring to stab you and not daring to attack you is not the same as lacking the intention to do so. I possess a Way that goes to this [further point]. It can cause men to lack such intentions altogether.

"Still, lacking such intentions is not the same as wanting to love and benefit you. I possess a Way that goes to this [further point]. It can cause every grown man and woman in the world without fail to have it in their hearts to love you ardently and wish to benefit you. This is worthier than courage and strength and is the top of the pile of the four ways [I have just mentioned]. Could Your Majesty really not be interested in this?"

King Kang of Song replied: "These are indeed matters that I want to understand."

Hui Ang responded: "Kong [i.e., Kong Qiu, Confucius] and Mo [i.e., Mo Di, Mozi] exemplify this way. Kong Qiu and Mo Di

possessed no territory yet were treated as rulers;
had no officials [in their service] yet were treated as chief ministers.

Without fail, every grown man and woman in the world craned their necks and stood on tiptoe,[33] wanting to secure their safety and benefit. Now Your Majesty is a ruler of [a state possessing] ten thousand chariots. If you were to sincerely manifest

30. *Laozi* 4.

31. Hui Ang 惠盎 was a native of Song and a knight in the service of King Kang.

32. King Kang of Song 宋康王 (r. 328–286 B.C.E.), the last ruler of the state of Song, was comparable to the tyrant Jie for his avarice and profligacy.

33. That is, they looked for every opportunity to be helpful.

the will [of such men], then everyone within the borders of your state would enjoy the benefits. In that case, [Your Majesty's] worthiness would far exceed that of Kong or Mo."

The king of Song had nothing to say in response. When Hui Ang departed, the king of Song commented to his attendants: "What eloquence! This guest has won me over with his persuasion!"[34]

Therefore the *Laozi* says:

> "One who is fearless in being bold will die;
> one who is fearless in being timid will live."[35]

Looking at the matter from this perspective, great courage paradoxically consists of nothing other than timidity. [12/107/16–12/108/3]

12.10

In ancient times, Yao's assistants numbered nine; those of Shun numbered seven; and those of King Wu numbered five. Yao, Shun, and Wu were not as capable as those nine, seven, and five assistants in any single task, and yet with hanging robes and folded hands, they achieved perfect merit because they excelled at availing themselves of the natural abilities of others.[36] Thus, if a man tries to outrun a thoroughbred, he will not beat the thoroughbred. But if he relies on the use of a chariot, the thoroughbred will not be able to beat him.

In the northern regions there is an animal called the "stumbler." It has forelegs that resemble those of a rat and hind legs that resemble those of a hare. When it runs it tumbles forward, and when it walks it falls backward, but it always picks out the sweet grasses to give to the [creature called the] "fabulous-big-and-small." Whenever the "stumbler" encounters danger or harm, the "fabulous-big-and-small" invariably carries it on its back to safety. This exemplifies the principle of relying on one's capabilities to supplement what is beyond one's capabilities.[37]

Therefore the *Laozi* says:

> "Those who carve wood in place of the master carpenter
> rarely fail to hurt their hands."[38] [12/108/5–9]

---

34. This story also appears in LSCQ 15.5/85/13–26. See Knoblock and Riegel 2000, 357–58.

35. *Laozi* 73.

36. A similar argument is made in 19.5.

37. This anecdote also appears in LSCQ 15.6/86/20–21; we follow Knoblock and Riegel's 2000, 360, translations of the term *qiong qiong ju xu* 蛩蛩駏驉 as "fabulous-big-and-small" and *jue* 蹶 as "stumbler." Apparently, the *jue* has short forelegs and long hind legs, while the *qiong qiong ju xu* has long forelegs and short hind legs. The fabulous-big-and-small is said to have trouble with his sense of smell; thus the *jue*, although a stumbler, is able to use his capacities to help the *qiong qiong ju xu* and thereby augment those capacities he lacks. See Chen Yiping, *Huiji ge jia xueshuo de juzhu: Huainanzi* (Beijing: Zhongguo wenlian chuban gongsi, 1997), 559n.5.

38. *Laozi* 74.

12.11

Bo Yi[39] offered a persuasion on the techniques of kingship to Lord Si of Wey.[40] Lord Si replied: "I possess a state of [only] one thousand chariots. I wish to receive [the appropriate] instruction."[41] Bo Yi answered: "Wu Huo [could] lift a thousand *jun*, so he certainly could lift a single *jin*."[42]

Du He[43] offered a persuasion to Lord Zhaowen of Zhou[44] on the means to pacify the world. Lord Zhaowen replied to Du He: "I would like to learn how to pacify [the state of] Zhou."

Du He responded: "If what I say is unacceptable [i.e., incorrect], then you will not be able to pacify Zhou. If what I say is acceptable [i.e., correct], then Zhou will pacify itself. This is what is meant by the expression 'Pacify it by not pacifying it.'"[45]

Therefore the *Laozi* says:

> "Great handiwork does not involve cutting.[46]
> Therefore, if you fully count [the pieces of] a carriage, there is no longer a carriage."[47] [12/108/11–15]

12.12

According to the laws of the state of Lu, if a native of Lu is captured by another Lord of the Land as a servant or a concubine, and if there is someone who is able to ransom [the captive], that person will be reimbursed from the state treasury. Zigong ransomed a native of Lu from a Lord of the Land but when [the ransomed party] returned to Lu, [Zigong] declined and did not accept reimbursement.

Confucius heard of the matter and said: "Si[48] has committed an error! When sages initiate undertakings, they are able to shift with prevailing habits to change local cus-

39. Bo Yi 薄疑, an official of Wey.

40. During the reign of Lord Si of Wey 衛嗣君 (r. 324–283 B.C.E.), Wey became an effective vassalage of Qin with little territory; thus his rank was reduced from "marquis" to "lord."

41. That is, in techniques appropriate to the prince of a medium-size state, not to a great king.

42. A *jun* (鈞) is an ancient measure of weight equal to thirty *jin* (斤), approximately sixteen pounds.

43. Du He 杜赫 was a native of Zhou who embarked on a career as a wandering persuader and strategist during the Warring States period. He figures in several anecdotes in the *Zhanguoce*.

44. Lord Zhaowen of Zhou 周昭文君 was, according to Gao You, a ruler of East Zhou during the period of decline in which the Zhou royal domain broke into two competing courts, East and West. See Zhang Shuangdi 1997, 2:1230n.4.

45. See also LSCQ 26.2/167/20–23; and Knoblock and Riegel 2000, 649.

46. *Laozi* 28.

47. *Laozi* 39. Lau's translation reads: "Hence the highest renown is without renown" (*Tao Te Ching*, 100). Based on the Mawangdui manuscript, Lau's emendations seem to be erroneous, a conclusion that is further supported by the detailed discussion in Robert Henricks, trans., *Lao-tzu: Te-Tao Ching: A New Translation Based on the Recently Discovered Ma-wang-tui Texts* (New York: Ballantine Books, 1989), 100. We follow Henricks in our rendering of this line.

48. Another name for Zigong. See chap. 9, n. 9.

toms. Their teachings and instructions can be applied by future generations. It is not the case that they suit their personal conduct alone.[49] Now the wealthy of Lu are few, but the poor are numerous. Ransoming others and receiving recompense is not the most honorable practice, but if no reimbursement is received, no one will ever again ransom others, and henceforth the people of Lu might never again redeem others from the Lords of the Land." It may indeed be said that Confucius understood how to transform others.[50]

Therefore the *Laozi* says:

> "To notice the details is called discernment."[51] [12/108/17–21]

12.13

Marquis Wu of Wei asked Li Ke:[52] "Why did the state of Wu perish?"

Li Ke responded: "Countless battles and countless victories."

Marquis Wu retorted: "But countless battles and countless victories are the good fortune of the state and its ruling family. How could such things be the sole cause of Wu's downfall?"

Li Ke replied:

> "With countless battles, the populace grows exhausted;
> with countless victories, the ruler grows arrogant.

Rare indeed is the state that does not perish when an arrogant ruler governs an exhausted populace!

> Arrogance leads to recklessness, and recklessness depletes material resources.
> Exhaustion leads to resentment, and resentment drives the people to their wits' end.

Given that both superior and subordinate were depleted, the demise of Wu appears

49. The main point in this passage, ascribed to Confucius, is that the Superior Man must not arbitrarily follow his own standards of morality but must take into account the customary practices of the populace at hand. Confucius does not approve of the practice of being given a cash reward for ransoming people, but that custom can be reformed only by first using it as the local populace does, not by disregarding it. Confucius expressly states: "When sages initiate undertakings, they are able to shift with prevailing habits to change local customs." It is precisely their sensitivity to the particular circumstances on the ground or the local nuances of customary practice that enables sages to transform the common people through their virtuous conduct.

50. A version of this story appears in LSCQ 16.6/95/29–16.6/96/2. See Knoblock and Riegel 2000, 394. This story is also alluded to in 11.2.

51. *Laozi* 52. *Hanfeizi* 21 links a different anecdote to this citation exemplifying the interchangeability of these stories as compact and portable ciphers of intellectual exchange. There the ability to "notice the details" enables the viscount of Ji to foretell impending catastrophe. See HFZ 21/44/5–8.

52. Marquis Wu of Wei 魏武侯 (r. 396–371 B.C.E.), the second ruler of the independent state of Wei, expanded his state's territories through a series of aggressive campaigns. Li Ke 李克 (also known as Li Kui 悝 [ca. 455–395 B.C.E.]) was a statesman and government reformer who served as prime minister of Wei under Marquis Wen. He is credited with inventing certain techniques of rule, such as using the sale and purchase of state grain reserves to stabilize prices. A text attributed to him once circulated but now exists only as fragments.

to have occurred rather late. This is why King Fuchai [of Wu] took his life at [the battle of] Gansui."[53]

Therefore the *Laozi* says:

> "To withdraw when merit is achieved and reputation established
> is the Way of Heaven."[54] [12/108/23–27]

12.14

Ning Qi hoped to seek office from Duke Huan of Qi, but being poverty-stricken he had no means to have himself recommended. Consequently he made his way to Qi by driving a cart [laden with goods] for a traveling merchant. When night descended, he took up lodging outside the city gate. [Just at that time] Duke Huan of Qi was traveling to the suburbs to welcome guests so that when night fell, he [ordered] the gate to be opened and the cart drivers removed from the road. His lighted torches filled the night sky, while those who followed him collected in a great throng.

[Meanwhile] Ning Qi sat under his cart, feeding his ox and gazing despondently at Duke Huan. Tapping on his ox's horn he wailed out a tune composed in the *shang* key. When Duke Huan heard it, he clutched his charioteer's hand and said: "How extraordinary! Surely the singer is no ordinary man!" [Duke Huan then] ordered a rear carriage to bring him along [with his entourage].

When Duke Huan returned to his court, his followers asked him what he wished to do. Duke Huan honored Ning Qi with a robe and cap and granted him an audience. During the audience, Ning Qi offered a persuasion for governing the world. Duke Huan was elated by the persuasion and was about to appoint Ning Qi to an official post when his ministers objected, saying: "Our guest is a person from Wey. Wey is not far from Qi. It would be best if you sent someone to inquire about him. If you find that Ning Qi is truly worthy, then it will not be too late to appoint him."

"Not so," replied Duke Huan. "If we inquire about him, I fear that we will discover some minor flaw. To dismiss a man's great strengths on account of his minor flaws is precisely the reason why rulers lose the scholar-knights of the world."

As a general rule, what is heard will always be verified. Once something is heard, there is no need to inquire further, for you have already connected with what caused it to be so. Moreover, it is certainly difficult for men to be perfect. You should simply evaluate and use their strengths. In accordance with this principle, appoint them to office. Duke Huan understood this.[55]

---

53. See 12.23. King Fuchai of the southeastern, non-Sinitic state of Wu was renowned for both his military prowess and his arrogance. In the battle of Gansui (473 B.C.E.), he was surrounded by an army of the neighboring state of Yue and committed suicide. He is mentioned several times in the *Huainanzi*, most fully in 15.25; see also 11.7 and 18.27. The exchange between Marquis Wu of Wei and Li Ke also appears in LSCQ 19.5./124/16–20. See Knoblock and Riegel 2000, 494. See also HSWZ 10.23/78/1–4.

54. *Laozi* 9.

55. LSCQ 19.8/128/10–17. See Knoblock and Riegel 2000, 507–8. For Ning Qi, see also 9.7, 10.94, 11.6, and 13.16.

Therefore the *Laozi* says:

> "The Way is great;
> Heaven is great;
> Earth is great;
> and the king is also great."

Within the realm, there are four things that are great and the king counts as one.[56] These words mean that Duke Huan was able to embrace this principle. [12/109/1–10]

12.15

When the Great King Danfu[57] resided in Bin, the Dee people attacked him. He offered them hides, silks, pearls, and jades, but they would not accept them and said: "What we, the Dee people, want is [your] land. We will not accept these material goods as a substitute."

The Great King Danfu said [to his subjects]: "I cannot bear to reside with your elder brothers while leading your younger brothers to death, or to dwell with your fathers while causing your sons to die. You all [must] do your utmost to remain here. Does being my subject really differ from being the subject of the Dee people? Moreover, I have heard it said that you should not rely on the means by which you are nourished [i.e., the land] to harm those you nourish [i.e., a ruler's subjects]." He left with his staff and whip, but his people led one another along and followed him. Subsequently, he reestablished his state at the foot of Mount Qi.[58]

It may be said of the Great King Danfu that he was able to preserve life.

> When wealthy and eminent, he did not allow what nourished him to injure his person;
> when impoverished and humble, he did not allow what brought him material benefit to burden his physical form.

Today, those who have received the rank and emoluments of their predecessor invariably consider losing them to be a serious matter. Life comes to us over a long period of time, yet we consider losing it a trivial matter. Is this not sheer folly?

Therefore the *Laozi* says:

> "Those who value their person as if it were the world can be entrusted with the world.
> Those who cherish their person as if it were the world can be given custody of the world."[59] [12/109/12–19]

56. *Laozi* 25.

57. Great King Danfu 大王亶父 was an ancient ancestor of the Zhou royal house. He was awarded the title Great King posthumously after the Zhou ascended to the throne of the Son of Heaven.

58. The version of the Danfu story presented here is almost identical to that in ZZ 28/81/23–28. See Mair 1997, 285–86. Abbreviated versions appear in 14.14 and 20.9, and see also LSCQ 21.4/141/11–17; and Knoblock and Riegel 2000, 557–58.

59. *Laozi* 13.

12.16

Prince Mou of Zhongshan[60] said to Zhanzi: "Although I dwell here secluded among the rivers and seas, my heart remains at the court of Wei. What can I do?"

"Emphasize life," replied Zhanzi, "If you emphasize life, you will take material benefits lightly."

"Although I understand this principle, I still cannot achieve self-mastery," responded Prince Mou of Zhongshan.

Zhanzi continued: "If you cannot achieve self-mastery, you must simply follow [your inclinations]. If you follow [your inclinations], your spirit will be free from resentment. If you cannot achieve self-mastery and yet compel yourself not to follow [your inclinations], it may be said that you injure yourself on two accounts. Those who injure themselves on two accounts cannot be included among those who are long-lived."[61]

Therefore the *Laozi* says:

> "Knowing harmony is called constancy;
> knowing constancy is called clarity.
> Augmenting life is called auspiciousness.
> The mind directing the *qi* is called compulsion."[62]

For this reason,

> "use its brilliance
> and repeatedly return to its clarity."[63] [12/109/21–25]

12.17

King Zhuang of Chu inquired about Zhan He [i.e., Zhanzi]: "How should I bring order to my state?"

Zhan He replied: "I, [Zhan] He, know how to order my person but know nothing of ordering the state."

The king of Chu responded: "I, the orphaned one, have inherited the shrines and temples of my ancestors and the altars to the soil and grain. I would like to learn how to preserve them."

Zhan He replied:

> "I have never heard of a ruler who brought order to his person yet found his state to be in disorder.

60. Prince Mou of Zhongshan 中山公子牟 was a prince of Wei who was enfeoffed at Zhongshan after Wei destroyed that state. A text in four chapters attributed to him is recorded in the "Daoist" section of the *Hanshu yiwenzhi*.

61. See also ZZ 28/84/7–11; LSCQ 21.4./141/27–29; and Knoblock and Riegel 2000, 558–59.

62. *Laozi* 55. Presumably the text argues here that one should neither try to extend one's natural life span nor use the mind to direct the vital energy. One values the preservation of life but not longevity; one relies on emptiness and nothingness, rather than the mind, to direct the vital energy.

63. *Laozi* 52.

I have never heard of a ruler whose person was disordered yet found his state to be ordered.

Thus when the root of the matter rests with bringing order to your person, I would not presume to answer your query by speaking of the branches."

The king of Chu exclaimed: "Excellent!"[64]

Therefore the *Laozi* says:

"Cultivate it in your person,
and your Potency will be genuine."[65] [12/109/27–30]

12.18

Duke Huan [of Qi] was reading in the upper part of his hall while Wheelwright Flat[66] was hewing a wheel in the lower part. Setting aside his hammer and chisel, the wheelwright asked Duke Huan, "I venture to ask what books you are reading?"

"The books of the sages," said the duke.

"Are the sages still alive?"

"They already are dead," said the duke.

"Then what you are reading are merely the lees and dregs of the sages."

Flushing in anger, Duke Huan replied, "How dare you, a wheelwright, presume to criticize the books I am reading? If you can explain yourself, all right. If you cannot explain yourself, you shall die."

"Yes, I can explain. I will put it in terms of my occupation as a wheelwright," said Wheelwright Flat. "If [the blows of the mallet] are too hard, [the chisel] will bite and not budge; if they are too gentle, [the chisel] will slide and not take hold. To make the chisel neither slide nor stick is something you can sense with your hand and feel with your heart.[67] Then you can get it down to the utmost subtlety. But I have not been able to teach it to my son, and my son has not been able to learn it from me. That's why I am an old man still hewing wheels after sixty years. Now what the sages have said contains some truth, but since they are dead and long gone, all that remains is the lees and dregs [of their teachings]."[68] Therefore the *Laozi* says:

"The Way that can be spoken
is not the constant Way;
the Name that can be named
is not the constant Name."[69] [12/110/1–8]

64. For a variant of this story, see LSCQ 17.8/107/18–21; and Knoblock and Riegel 2000, 435.

65. *Laozi* 54.

66. *Bian* 扁.

67. Our translation of these challenging lines follows Burton Watson, *The Complete Works of Chuang Tzu* (New York: Columbia University Press, 1968), 152–53.

68. For the *Zhuangzi* variant of this parable, see ZZ 13/37/10–13. For the *Hanshi waizhuan* version of this story, see HSWZ 5.6/35/26–5.6/36/3.

69. *Laozi* 1.

12.19

Previously, when Sicheng Zihan acted as minister to the state of Song, he said to the lord of Song, "The danger or safety of this state and the orderliness or disorderliness of its people depend on how you execute rewards and punishments. Now the gifts of rank and reward are what the people love—these you should carry out personally. The punishments of execution and mutilation are what the people hate—may I ask that I administer them?"

The lord of Song responded: "Excellent! I will enjoy the peoples' praises while you will suffer their resentments. This way I'll be sure to know how to avoid being the laughingstock of the Lords of the Land."

The lord of Song then carried out the rewards while Zihan [implemented] the punishments. When the people of the state came to understand that the regulations concerning executions and amputations rested solely with Zihan, the grand ministers of state treated him with affection, and the hundred surnames [i.e., the common people] feared him. Before a year had passed, Zihan had murdered the lord of Song and usurped his government.[70] Therefore the *Laozi* says:

> "The fish must not be allowed to leave the deep;
> the efficacious instruments of state must not be revealed to anyone."[71]
> [12/110/10–15]

12.20

Royal Longevity was traveling with a bundle of books on his back when he bumped into Dignified Ascent in Zhou. Dignified Ascent remarked:

> Affairs arise in response to alterations, and alterations are born of the times. Therefore those who understand timeliness are not constant in their actions.
> Books are the product of speech, and speech is the product of the knowledgeable. [Therefore] those who understand speech do not hoard books.[72]

---

70. This story also appears in HSWZ 7, 10/51/30–10/52/5.

71. *Laozi* 36. *Hanfeizi* 21 explains these lines:

> When political purchase is weighty, it constitutes the "deep abyss" of the ruler. To shepherd the people, your political purchase must be weightier than that which rests with the ministers. If it is lost, it cannot be regained. When Duke Jian lost it to Tian Cheng and the Duke of Jin lost it to the six ministers, their states were destroyed and their lives lost. Thus "fish must not be allowed to leave the deep." Rewards and punishments are the efficacious instruments of state. If they rest with the ruler, he controls the ministers; if they rest with the ministers, they defeat the ruler. If the ruler reveals his rewards [to his ministers], the ministers will disparage them as acts of virtue; if the ruler reveals his punishments [to his ministers], the ministers will exaggerate them as acts of authority. If the ruler exhibits his rewards, the ministers will make use of his political purchase; if the ruler reveals his punishments, the ministers will avail themselves of his authority. (HFZ 21/42/31–21/43/4)

The "Inner Collection of Discourses, Lower Section" (Nei zhu shuo xia 內諸說下) also comments on these lines in a somewhat similar fashion. See HFZ 31/72/1–4.

72. This line has generated some debate over the years. Lau proposes emending it by supplying the

Upon hearing this, Royal Longevity made a bonfire of his books and danced about with joy.[73] Therefore the *Laozi* says:

> "An excess of words leads to countless impoverishments;
> it cannot compare to preserving the center [i.e., the heart]."[74]
> [12/110/17–19]

12.21

Chief Minister Zipei[75] invited King Zhuang [of Chu] to a drinking party, and King Zhuang accepted his invitation. Zipei made the necessary preparations for the drinking party at Qiang[76] Terrace, but King Zhuang never arrived. The next morning Zipei arrived at the palace barefooted and bowed to King Zhuang. Facing north and standing at the front of his palace, Zipei addressed King Zhuang: "Earlier you agreed to come to my drinking party, but you never came. Was the reason that I committed some offense?"

King Zhuang replied: "I heard that you were preparing to fete me at Qiang Terrace. [Now,] Qiang Terrace

---

negative *bu* before *cang shu*, yielding the reading 書者言之所出也.言出於知者, 知者不藏書. He follows the near parallel from the "Yu Lao" chapter of *Hanfeizi*:

> Royal Longevity was traveling with a bundle of books on his back when he bumped into Dignified Ascent in Zhou. Dignified Ascent remarked: "Affairs are [what one] does, and [what one does] is born of the times. [Thus] the times have no constant affairs. Books are [what one] says. [What one] says is born of knowledge. Thus one who knows does not hoard books. Why then do you make an exception by carrying books on your back?" Upon hearing this, Royal Longevity made a bonfire of his books and danced with joy. Thus, those who are knowledgeable do not rely upon spoken communication to teach; those who are intelligent do not rely upon hoarded books to learn. Such a principle, our present age has passed by but Royal Longevity returned to it. This is to learn not to learn. Thus it is said: "Learn not to learn and return to what the multitudes pass by." (HFZ 21/44/18–21)

In his emendation and reading of this passage, Rudolph Wagner argues that Lau is mistaken in following the *Hanfeizi* text and supplying the negative. He follows the *Wenzi*, in which no negative appears, and proposes leaving the line as is: 書者言之所出也.言出於知者, 知者藏書: "Books are the product of speech and since speech is the product of the knowledgeable, those who are knowledgeable hoard books" (*Language, Ontology, and Political Philosophy in China* [Albany: State University of New York Press, 2007], 35–36).

Finally, Zhang Shuangdi bases his emendations on citations of the *Hanfeizi* preserved in various encyclopedias. He appears to have dug the deepest into this problem, and accordingly we follow Zhang Shuangdi, who proposes 書者言之所出也.言出於知者, 知言者不藏書: "Books are the product of speech and speech is the product of the knowledgeable. Those who understand speech do not hoard books" (1997, 2:1249n.2).

73. Books at the time were written on wooden or bamboo strips and so burned readily.

74. *Laozi* 5.

75. Chief Minister Zipei 子佩. According to Yu Dacheng, this figure is Chief Minister Zixia 子瑕 or Yang Gai 陽匄, who is recorded in the *Zuozhuan*, Zhao 19, as having served as chief minister to King Zhuang of Chu. See Lau, HNZ, 110n.8.

76. Lau (HNZ 12/110/21) supplied the graphs *jingtai* 京臺 here, but it should read Qiangtai 強臺 based on the several references to this terrace in the following passage.

to the south overlooks Ke Mountain,
to the north approaches Fang Huang;
to the east lies the Yangzi River,
and to the west flows the Huai River.[77]

The joy they bring causes men to forget their mortality.[78] A man of meager Potency like me cannot deal with such joy. I feared that if I tarried there, I would be unable to return."

Therefore the *Laozi* says:

"If you do not look at what you desire,
you will make your heart free from turmoil."[79] [12/110/21–25]

12.22

Prince Chong'er of Jin was fleeing. When he passed through the state of Cao, the ruler of Cao failed to treat him according to the proper etiquette.[80] Xi Fuji's wife then said to Xi Fuji:[81] "Our prince has failed to treat the prince of Jin with the proper etiquette. I have observed his followers. They all are worthy men. If they help him return to the state of Jin, he will certainly attack Cao. How could you fail to take the lead in augmenting his Potency?" Xi Fuji then provided Chong'er with a calabash of food to which he added a jade disk. Chong'er accepted the food but returned the jade disk. When he finally returned to his state, Chong'er raised troops to attack the state of Cao. He vanquished Cao but forbade his three armies from entering the territory of Xi Fuji.[82]

Therefore the *Laozi* says:

"Contorted, you will become whole;
bent, you will become upright."[83] [12/110/27–12/111/2]

12.23

The king of Yue, Goujian, battled with Wu but was not victorious. His capital city was demolished, and he was driven into exile. He was surrounded at Mount Kuaiji.

[Though] with indignant heart and rising gall,
with *qi* like a gushing spring,

77. *Zuo* 左 (left) corresponds to the east and *you* 友 (right) to the west because the monarch faces south.

78. *Wang si* 忘死; an alternative reading has *wang gui* 忘歸, "forget to return home."

79. *Laozi* 3.

80. The ruler wanted Chong'er to go fishing naked so that he could see his joined ribs, a deformity for which he was well known. The story is recounted in 18.18 and mentioned again in 20.37.

81. Xi Fuji was a minister and fief holder in the state of Cao in the seventh century B.C.E. See *Zuozhuan*, Xi 23; and 11.6 and 18.18.

82. A rather different version of this story appears in HFZ 21.

83. *Laozi* 22.

his handpicked, well-trained armored troops
rushed into the conflagration as if [determined to] perish,

[defeated], Goujian requested that he serve as King [Fuchai] of Wu's attendant and his wife serve as the king's concubine. Armed with a halberd, Goujian became the king's forward guard.[84] In the end, Goujian took [the king of Wu] captive at Gansui.[85]

Therefore the *Laozi* says:

"The soft overcomes the hard;
the weak overcomes the strong.
Everyone in the world knows this,
but no one can practice it."[86]

The king of Yue personally practiced such principles. Consequently he became a hegemon over the Central States. [12/111/4–7]

12.24

Viscount Jian of Zhao died and had not yet been buried when the people of Zhongmou shifted their allegiance to the state of Qi. When Viscount Jian of Zhao had been buried for five days, Viscount Xiang [his son] raised troops to attack and encircle them. The encirclement was not yet complete, when a one-hundred-foot[87] section of the city wall suddenly crumbled. Viscount Xiang then beat the gong and withdrew his troops. An official of his army remonstrated with him, saying, "When you were punishing the crimes of Zhongmou, its city walls crumbled. This is a sign that Heaven supports us. Why, then, should we abandon the attack?"

Viscount Xiang replied, "I heard that Shuxiang[88] once said: 'A Superior Man does not impose on others when they profit, nor does he attack others in distress.' Let the people of Zhongmou repair their walls. Only when the walls have been repaired, will we attack them." When the people of Zhongmou heard of the viscount's [sense of] justice, they asked to surrender.[89]

Therefore the *Laozi* says:

"Now,
it is because he alone does not contend
that no one can contend with him."[90] [12/111/9–13]

84. Literally, "one who marches ahead of the horse and chariot of the king."

85. *Hanfeizi* 21 also refers to this story, but in a much abbreviated manner. See HFZ 21/44/10–13.

86. *Laozi* 78.

87. Ten *zhang* 丈.

88. Shuxiang 叔嚮 was the nickname of Yangshe Xi 羊舌肸, a grand officer of the state of Jin during the Spring and Autumn period who was known for his worthiness and ability. For references to additional anecdotes in which he appears, see Knoblock and Riegel 2000, 798.

89. A variant of this anecdote appears in LSCQ 19.8/128/10–17. See Knoblock and Riegel 2000, 507–8. See also HSWZ 6.15/48/5–9.

90. *Laozi* 22.

12.25

Duke Mu of Qin addressed Bo Le saying: "You are getting on in years. Is there anyone in your family who can take over for you and find me a good steed?"

Bo Le replied: "A good horse may be judged by his physique, countenance, sinews, and bones. But in judging the best horse in the world, it seems

as if it is not there at all, as if it has disappeared,
as if it had lost its singular identity.

A horse like that raises no dust and leaves no tracks. All my sons are lesser talents. They can judge a good horse, but they lack the talent to judge the best horse in the world. However, there is a man who is my porter and firewood gatherer who is called Nine-Cornered Hillock. In judging horses, he is not inferior to my abilities. I respectfully request that you grant him an audience."

Duke Mu granted him an audience and commanded him to search out a fine steed. After three months Nine-Cornered Hillock returned and reported: "The horse has been located. It is in Shaqiu."

Duke Mu replied: "What kind of horse is it?"

"It is a yellow mare," answered Nine Cornered Hillock.

Thereupon Duke Mu sent men to Shaqiu to obtain the horse. The horse, however, turned out to be a black stallion. Duke Mu was quite displeased. Summoning Bo Le, he inquired of him saying: "What a loss! The man you sent to find me a good steed cannot distinguish the color of one coat from another nor a female from a male, what could he possibly know about horses?"

Bo Le let out a long sigh and replied: "It always comes to this! This is precisely why he surpasses me by a thousand or ten thousand fold and is infinite in his capabilities. What Hillock observes is the dynamism of Heaven.[91]

He recognizes the refined essence and discards the dross.
He focuses on the internal and disregards the external.
He looks at what is to be seen and does not look at what is not to be seen.
He scrutinizes what is to be scrutinized and disregards what is not to be scrutinized.

It appears that what he has judged is [a quality] more precious than just a horse."

The horse arrived and ultimately proved to be an excellent horse.[92]

Therefore the *Laozi* says:

"Great straightness is as if bent;
great skill is as if clumsy."[93] [12/111/15–25]

---

91. *Tianji* 天機.

92. Literally, "a ten thousand-*li* horse." A version of this story appears in *Liezi*. See LieZ 8/49/1–11. Bo Le is mentioned twice in *Zhuangzi* 9 in different contexts. See ZZ 9/23/23 and 9/24/7.

93. *Laozi* 45.

12.26

When Wu Qi was acting as chief minister of the state of Chu, he traveled to the state of Wei and asked Qu Yijiu:[94] "The king does not know how unworthy I am and has appointed me to be chief minister. Will you, sir, please test and evaluate my [plan of] action?"

Master Qu replied: "What do you plan to do?"

Wu Qi answered: "I plan to diminish the nobility of the state of Chu and equalize the system of official salaries, decreasing the salaries of those who receive too much and increasing the salaries of those who receive too little. I plan to train and drill the armored and foot soldiers so that when the opportune time arises, they will contend for advantage with [everyone in] the world."

Master Qu responded: "I, Yijiu, have heard that in ancient times those who excelled at governing their states did not alter precedents nor change norms. Now you plan to diminish the nobility of the state of Chu and equalize the system of official salaries, decreasing the salaries of those who receive too much and increasing the salaries of those who receive too little. This is to alter precedents and change norms. If you do this, it will not bring benefit.

"I, Yijiu, have also heard it said: 'Anger is contrary to Potency; weapons are ill-augured instruments; and fighting is something that human beings will always avoid.' Now you secretly conspire to oppose Potency, are fond of using ill-augured instruments, and practice what others would avoid. This is the height of perversity! Moreover,

> it is not proper for you to employ the troops of Lu to realize your ambitions in Qi, and yet you do so.
> It is not proper for you to employ the troops of Wei to realize your ambitions in Qin, and yet you do so.

I have further heard that if you do not harm others, then you will not bring harm on yourself. I have certainly suspected that my king has repeatedly opposed the Way of Heaven and perverted the principles of humankind. Yet, until today he has avoided harm. Oh, he must have been waiting for you!"

Wu Qi responded in alarm: "Is it still possible to change?"

Master Qu replied: "When one has already committed the crime, it is impossible to change the outcome. It would be best if you loved with sincerity and acted with genuineness."

Therefore the *Laozi* says:

> "Blunt the sharpness;
> untangle the knots;
> soften the glare;
> be as dust."[95] [12/112/1–11]

---

94. Qu Yijiu 屈宜咎 was a grandee of Chu who had been exiled to Wei.

95. *Laozi* 4.

12.27

When the state of Jin attacked the state of Chu, [the Jin forces] advanced three stages without stopping.[96] The grand ministers [of Chu] asked the king's permission to counterattack. King Zhuang responded: "When the former lords ruled Chu, Jin did not attack Chu. It is only during my reign that Jin has attacked Chu. I am to blame for this. How could I [attach] this disgrace to my grand ministers?"

The grand ministers answered: "When the former ministers took up their posts, Jin did not attack Chu. It is only since we have served as ministers that Jin has attacked Chu. Your ministers are to blame for this. We implore Your Majesty to counterattack." King Zhuang bowed his head and burst into tears, soaking his collar. When he raised his head, he saluted his grand ministers.

When the people of Jin heard of this incident, they said: "The ruler and his ministers vied to take responsibility for their mistakes. Moreover, the ruler of Chu humbled himself before his ministers. We could not possibly attack such a state." That evening the Jin troops retreated and returned home.

Therefore the *Laozi* says:

> "One who can accept the humiliation of his state
> may be called the lord of the altars of soil and grain."[97] [12/112/13–17]

12.28

During the reign of Duke Jing of Song,[98] when Mars was in [the lunar lodge] Heart,[99] the duke became fearful and summoned Zi Wei[100] to question him, saying: "Mars is in Heart. What does it mean?"

Zi Wei responded: "Mars corresponds to the Heavenly Executioner; [the lunar lodge] Heart corresponds to the territory of Song. Disaster awaits you. Nonetheless it is possible to shift the blame to the prime minister."

The duke replied: "The prime minister is entrusted with governing the state. If the blame is shifted to him and he is put to death, it would be unlucky. I request to take the onus on myself."

"You can shift the blame to the people," Zi Wei stated.

The duke responded: "If the people die, for whom would I act as lord? It would be better if I were the only one to die."

96. A "stage," *she* 舍, is a day's march, equal to thirty or thirty-five *li*.

97. *Laozi* 78. A state could be said to exist only as long as its altars of soil and grain remained intact and functioning; thus it was the ruler's responsibility to protect them at all costs.

98. Duke Jing of Song 宋景公 ruled from 517 to 452 B.C.E.

99. For the lunar lodges (*xiu* 宿; here called "stages," *she*), see chap. 3 and app. B.

100. Zi Wei 子韋, court astronomer of Song, was renowned for his skill at divination. He was granted the surname Zi (that of the ducal house) in reward for his services.

Zi Wei responded: "Then you can shift the blame to the harvest."[101]

The duke retorted: "The harvest is the people's life. If there were a famine due to the harvest, then the people would surely die. I am the people's lord. If I wanted to kill my people in order to survive, who would consider me a true lord? My life has certainly reached its end. Zi Wei, speak no more."

Zi Wei turned to go. Facing north[102] he bowed twice and said: "I dare to congratulate you. Even though Heaven dwells on high, [Heaven] hears what lies below. You have spoken as a true lord on three occasions, so Heaven will certainly reward you three times. This evening Mars will surely travel through three lunar lodges,[103] [signaling] that you will extend your life by twenty-one years."

The duke responded: "How is it that you know this to be the case?"

Zi Wei replied: "You have spoken as a true lord on three occasions. Therefore, you will be rewarded three times. Mars will surely travel through three lunar lodges. Each lodge traverses seven stars. Each movement of Mars corresponds to one year. Three [lunar lodges through which Mars will move] times seven [stars for each lodge] equals twenty-one. Thus, I stated that you would extend your life by twenty-one years. I beg to be allowed to kneel at your throne and wait. If Mars does not shift its location, I request the death penalty."

The duke responded, "It is allowed."

That very night Mars did, in fact, pass through three lunar lodges.[104]

Therefore the *Laozi* says:

> "One who can accept the misfortunes of his state
> may be called a king of the world."[105] [12/112/19–12/113/3]

12.29

In former times, when Gongsun Long resided in Zhao, he said to one of his disciples, "If a person has no ability, I have no interest in keeping company with him."

A guest, clad in coarse cloth with only a rope for a belt, received an audience with Gongsun Long and said: "I can shout."

101. *Sui* 歲. The meaning of Zi Wei's suggestion and Duke Jing's response depends on a pun. In the context of this astrological conversation, Zi Wei might be suggesting that the duke shift the blame to the planet Jupiter, called *sui xing* (year star); Jupiter was regarded as having a powerful influence on the fate of states. But *sui* means "harvest" as well as "year," and Duke Jing elects to understand *sui* here as meaning not *sui xing*, Jupiter, but "harvest," which allows him to reply to Zi Wei's suggestion in suitably moralistic terms.

102. That is, turning toward the ruler, whose throne faces south.

103. A shift of a planet through three lunar lodges in one night is not physically possible; however, it would be possible to emulate such a shift on the cosmograph (*shi* 式), allowing the astrological consequences of the shift to be demonstrated.

104. This story also appears in LSCQ 6.4/31/20–6.4/32/4. See Knoblock and Riegel 2000, 165–66.

105. *Laozi* 78.

Gongsun Long turned to his disciples and asked: "Among my disciples is there already one who can shout?"

The disciples all replied, "There is not."

Gongsun Long responded: "Register him as a disciple."

Several days had passed when Gongsun Long was on his way to present a persuasion to the king of Yan. When they arrived at the bank of the [Yellow] River, a ferry rested on the opposite shore. He then directed the disciple who was good at shouting to call the ferry. When he did, the ferry promptly arrived.

Thus when sages dwell in the world, they do not disregard knights who possess specific talents.

Therefore the *Laozi* says:

> "Among men to abandon no one,
> among things to abandon no thing,
> this is called embracing clarity."[106] [12/113/5–9]

12.30

[The Chu general] Zifa attacked and defeated the state of Cai. King Xuan of Chu[107] [traveled] to the suburbs to welcome [Zifa when he returned]. He presented him with one hundred *qing* of land[108] and enfeoffed him as "Holder of the Jade Baton."[109] Zifa, however, declined to accept [these honors], saying:

> "Governing a state and setting it in order so that the Lords of the Land will come as guests [to offer their submission] is due to the Potency of the ruler.
> Issuing commands and handing down orders so that, even before your troops assemble, the enemy is routed, is due to the awesomeness of the general.
> Arraying your troops in battle order and achieving victory over the enemy is due to the strength of the common people.

Taking advantage of the people's achievements and efforts to secure rank and emoluments for oneself is not the way of Humaneness and Rightness. Thus I declined to accept [the rewards offered me]."[110]

---

106. This citation of *Laozi* 27 differs from the *Wang Bi* and *Heshanggong* recensions. It is shorter than the other versions but carries the same general message. Lau's translation of Wang Bi's recension of this passage reads: "Therefore the sage always excels in saving people, and so abandons no one; always excels in saving things, and so abandons nothing. This is called following one's discernment" (*Tao Te Ching*, 84).

107. King Xuan of Chu 楚宣王 (r. 369–340 B.C.E.) presided over a period of declining power for his state.

108. One *qing* 頃 equals a hundred *mu* 畝. See app. B.

109. We follow Knoblock and Riegel's translation of the title *zhi gui* in LSCQ 20/3.2. Charles O. Hucker renders the title as "Baton Holder," in *A Dictionary of Official Titles in Imperial China* (Stanford, Calif.: Stanford University Press, 1985), 1017.

110. The story of Zifa 子發 is reminiscent of the story of Jiezhi Tui 介之推 (*Zuozhuan*, Xi 24.2), who refused all rewards on the grounds that the achievement was really Heaven's doing.

Therefore the *Laozi* says:

> "Succeed but do not dwell in it—
> it is only by not dwelling in it
> that [success] is not erased."[111] [12/113/11–14]

12.31

When Duke Wen of Jin attacked the city of Yuan, he agreed with his grand ministers on [a period of] three days [to capture the city]. When three days passed and Yuan did not surrender, Duke Wen ordered a retreat. A military officer said: "Yuan is sure to surrender in another day or two."

The ruler responded: "I did not realize that it would not be possible to defeat Yuan in three days and so agreed with the grand ministers on [a period of] three days to capture the city of Yuan. Now if we do not end this campaign, even though the designated time has elapsed, it would mean forfeiting my trustworthiness to obtain Yuan. I will not do it."

When the people of Yuan heard about this, they said: "With a ruler like this, how could we refuse to surrender?" They promptly surrendered. When the people of Wen heard about this, they also asked to surrender.[112]

Therefore the *Laozi* says:

> "How dim! How obscure!
> Yet within it is the Quintessence.
> This essence is profoundly genuine,
> for what lies within is trustworthy.[113]
> Therefore beautiful words can buy honor,
> [but] beautiful deeds can raise a man above others.[114] [12/113/16–20]

12.32

Gongyi Xiu,[115] the prime minister of Lu, had an insatiable craving for fish. Although everyone in the state presented him with fish, Gongyi Xiu did not accept them. His disciple asked him about it, saying: "Master, you always crave fish. Why, then, do you never accept these gifts of fish?"

He responded: "It is because I always crave fish that I do not accept the fish. If I accept the fish and am thereby dismissed from my post as minister, although I always

111. *Laozi* 2.

112. See also LSCQ 19.6/126/3–8; and Knoblock and Riegel 2000, 499–500.

113. *Laozi* 21.

114. *Laozi* 62. Note the linking of the two *Laozi* passages here with the graph *gu* 故 (therefore).

115. Gongyi Xiu 公儀休, prime minister under Duke Mu of Lu (r. 407–376 B.C.E.), enjoyed a reputation for frugality and incorruptibility.

crave fish, I will not be able to provide myself with fish. If I do not accept the fish and avoid being dismissed from office, then I will be able to supply myself with fish for a long time to come."

This is a case of discerning the difference between acting for others and acting for oneself.[116]

Therefore the *Laozi* says:

"[Sages] put themselves last and so come first,
treat themselves as extraneous and so are preserved.
Is it not because they are selfless
that they are able to accomplish their private ends?"[117]

Another [passage] states:

"Know contentment
and you will not be humiliated."[118] [12/113/22–26]

12.33

An elderly man named Hu Qiu said to Sunshu Ao: "There are three things people resent. Do you know what they are?"

Sunshu Ao responded: "What do you mean?"

Hu Qiu replied:

"If your rank is high, those of low rank will envy you;
if your post is great, the ruler will detest you;
if your salary is substantial, resentment will crop up everywhere."

Sunshu Ao commented:

"The higher my rank, the humbler my ambitions;
the greater my post, the smaller my desires;
the more substantial my salary, the more widespread my charity.

If I rely on these things to avoid the three resentments, will that do?"[119]

Therefore the *Laozi* says:

"The superior must have the inferior as its root;
the high must have the low as its base."[120] [12/113/28–12/114/3]

116. For another account of this story, see HSWZ 3.21/20/27–3.21/21/2.
117. *Laozi* 7.
118. *Laozi* 44.
119. See also HSWZ 7.12/52/16–21.
120. *Laozi* 39.

12.34

The forger of battle hooks[121] for the minister of war was already eighty years old but had not lost the sharp edge of his battle hooks. The minister of war asked him, "Is it just a matter of skill? Or do you possess the Way?"

He replied, "It is that I have something to which I hold exclusively. By the time I was twenty, I [already] liked to forge hooks. I did not look at anything else. If it was not a hook, I did not pay any attention to it."

Thus using something must depend on not using something, and in this way its usefulness is maintained. This is even truer if there is nothing that one does not use. Which things, then, would not be equal [to all other things]?

Therefore the *Laozi* says:

"Those who manage their affairs according to the Way
identify with the Way."[122] [12/114/5–8]

12.35

King Wen tempered his Moral Potency and consolidated his government so that within three years, two-thirds of the world submitted to his rule. [The tyrant] Djou learned of this and grew fearful, saying: "Rising early and retiring late, I strive to compete with him and so exhaust my mind and weary my body. Yet if I relax my vigilance, I fear that he will attack me."

Marquis Hu of Chong[123] replied:

"Earl Chang of Zhou [i.e., King Wen] is humane and just and is good at strategizing;
his Heir Apparent, [Ji] Fa, is courageous and resolute and knows nothing of indecision;
and his younger son [Ji] Dan is reverent and frugal and understands timeliness.

If you allow them to go on as they have, then you will not be able to sustain the calamities they will bring, and if you relax your vigilance and pardon them, you will also surely suffer misfortune. Even though a hat may be worn out, the only place you can put it is on your head.[124] I implore you to devise a plan before King Wen has consolidated his power." Subsequently Qu Shang[125] held King Wen at Youli.

---

121. The word *gou* 鉤 in this context refers to a kind of double-edged, slightly curved, sicklelike weapon. For an illustration, see Meng Jianmin and Zhang Lin, *Awakened: Qin's Terra-Cotta Army* (Xi'an: Shaanxi Travel & Tourism Press, 2001), 113.

122. *Laozi* 23.

123. Marquis Hu of Chong was an adviser to King Djou, the tyrannical last ruler of Shang. He appears in 10.59 as "Marquis Chong."

124. This recalls a proverb of the era: "Although a hat is old, it is certainly placed on the head [i.e., in a position of honor]; although a pair of shoes is new, it is certainly worn on the feet [i.e., in an inferior position]" (quoted from a court debate recounted in *Shiji* 121/3122–23, in Sarah A. Queen, *From Chronicle to Canon* [Cambridge: Cambridge University Press, 1996], 18).

125. Qu Shang 屈商 was another minister of the tyrant Djou.

After King Wen was captured, San Yisheng[126] expended thousands of catties of gold to seek out and obtain the most precious items and rare forms of animals in the world [as ransom]: the fabulous *zongyu* tiger and *jisi* chicken, one hundred pieces of black jade, one hundred large cowry shells, a black panther, a yellow bear, a black moose, and one thousand mottled white tiger skins. He presented these gifts to Djou, relying on Fei Zhong[127] to act as an intermediary. When Djou cast his eyes on them, he was elated and released King Wen, killing and sacrificing an ox and presenting it to him.

When King Wen returned to his state, [he made a show of changing his ways by] constructing gates carved in jade, building Ling Terrace, consorting with his concubines, and amusing himself with the music of the bronze drums, all the while waiting for Djou to slip up.

When Djou learned of King Wen's behavior, he declared: "Earl Chang of Zhou has modified his ways and changed his behavior. My worries are over!" Subsequently Djou engaged in [such nefarious conduct as] creating the "roasting beam,"[128] cutting out Bi Gan's heart, slicing open the wombs of pregnant women, and executing those who dared to disagree with him. It was then that King Wen implemented his plan [and defeated Djou].

Therefore the *Laozi* says:

"Know honor
but accept humiliation
and be a valley to the world."[129] [12/114/10–18]

12.36

King Cheng[130] questioned Yin Yi[131] about governing. "What kind of virtuous conduct will inspire the people to feel affection for their ruler?" he asked.

Yin Yi replied: "Employ them according to the proper seasons. Treat them with respect and compliance."

King Cheng inquired: "To what extent should one practice such things?"

Yin Yi responded: "Practice them as if you were facing a deep abyss or treading on thin ice."[132]

King Cheng said: "How frightening to be a king!"

126. San Yishing 散宜生 was a worthy who entered the service of King Wen on hearing the report of his virtue.

127. Fei Zhong 費仲 was a sycophantic minister of Djou credited with exacerbating his ruler's flaws.

128. This is a famously cruel punishment, also mentioned in 2.13, 11.1, 15.2, and 21.4.

129. *Laozi* 28.

130. King Cheng 成王, the third ruler of the Zhou dynasty, was the son of King Wu and ward of the Duke of Zhou.

131. Yin Yi 尹佚 (also known as Scribe 史 Yi), the grand historian of the Zhou court, was an astronomer and a diviner of renowned skill. A text bearing his name was listed in the "Mohist" section of the *Hanshu yiwenzhi* but now exists only as fragments.

132. *Odes* 195.

Yin Yi replied: "Those between Heaven and Earth and within the Four Seas who are good are loved by the people; those who are not good are despised by the people. In ancient times, the subjects of the Shang and Xia reversed their allegiances; they came to despise [the tyrants] Jie and Djou and submitted to the rulership of Kings Tang and Wu. The people of Susha all took it upon themselves to attack their lord and shift their allegiance to the Divine Farmer. Such things are well understood in our age. How could you not be frightened!"

Therefore the *Laozi* says:

> "What others fear
> you also must fear."[133] [12/114/20–24]

12.37

One of Robber Zhi's followers asked him: "Do even thieves possess the Way?"

Robber Zhi replied: "Would it be fitting for a thief not to possess the Way? To surmise where the goods are hidden is sagacity, to enter first is courage, to leave last is Rightness, to share the spoils equitably is Humaneness, and to know what actions are [well] advised or ill advised is wisdom. There is no one in the world capable of becoming a great thief without completely mastering these five things. From this perspective, it is evident that even those who possess a heart bent on thievery must rely on the Way of the sage before realizing their intentions."[134]

Therefore the *Laozi* says:

> "Exterminate sagacity, abandon wisdom,
> and the people will benefit a hundredfold."[135] [12/114/26–29]

12.38

Zifa, the general of the Chu army, was fond of seeking out knights skilled in the Way. A person from Chu who was an outstanding thief went to see Zifa and said: "I have heard that you are seeking out knights skilled in the Way. I am a petty thief of the Chu markets. I want to offer my talents and become one of your soldiers."

Upon hearing these words, clothes unfastened and hat askew,[136] Zifa rushed out to meet the man and pay him his respects. Zifa's assistants remonstrated with him saying: "This thief is known to everyone. How can you pay him such respect?"

133. *Laozi* 20.

134. This story also appears in LSCQ 11.4/55/25–11.4/56/1 and ZZ 10/24/27–10/25/3. For other translations, see Riegel and Knoblock 2000, 251; and Mair 1997, 85.

135. *Laozi* 19.

136. That is, ignoring all the norms of propriety. Zifa is so overwhelmed by his guest's significance that he "forgets his manners." Compare Mencius (4B.29), who taught that a gentleman should never leave his house, no matter what the provocation or emergency, unless his hair was properly arranged and his hat strings tied.

He responded: "This is not something that you can understand."

Shortly thereafter, the state of Qi raised troops and attacked the state of Chu. Zifa led his troops to repulse Qi but three times retreated in defeat. The worthy and incorruptible ministers of Chu all made full use of their best plans and most sincere efforts to repulse Qi, and yet the Qi forces daily grew more powerful. The petty thief of the markets then presented himself and implored Zifa saying: "I request to serve you by practicing my meager skills."

Zifa replied: "You may." Without asking the thief to explain himself, Zifa sent him off.

The thief departed, and in the dark of the night stole the curtain belonging to the Qi general and presented it to Zifa. Zifa subsequently ordered it returned to the Qi general, saying: "When my troops were out gathering brush for their fire, they came upon your curtain, so I have directed them to return it to their owner." The next evening, the thief once again made his way toward the Qi general, this time absconding with his pillow. Zifa again ordered someone to return it. The following evening, once again, the thief made his way to the Qi general, this time taking his hairpin. Once again Zifa had the item returned to him.

When the Qi troops learned of this, they were greatly alarmed. The general and his officers then took counsel together, saying: "If we do not depart today, I fear the Chu troops will take our heads!" The general commanded his army to turn around, and the army promptly departed. Thus, there are no petty skills and there are no insignificant abilities; it all depends on how the ruler uses them.

Therefore the *Laozi* says:

> "Do not praise the person;
> praise the substance of the person."[137] [12/115/1–10]

12.39

"I am making progress," said Yan Hui.

"What do you mean?" asked Confucius.

"I have forgotten Rites and Music."

"Not bad, but you still haven't got it."

Yan Hui saw Confucius again on another day and said: "I am making progress."

"What do you mean?"

"I have forgotten Humaneness and Rightness."

"Not bad, but you still haven't got it."

Yan Hui saw Confucius again on another day and said,

"I sit and forget."

"What do you mean 'sit and forget'?" Confucius asked with surprise.

"I slough off my limbs and trunk," said Yan Hui, "dim my intelligence, depart

137. *Laozi* 27.

from my form, leave knowledge behind, and immerse myself in the conduits of transformation. This is what I mean by 'sit and forget.'"

"If you are immersed," said Confucius, "then you have no preferences. If you are transformed, then you have no more constants. It is you who is really the worthy one! Please permit me to follow after you."[138]

Therefore the *Laozi* says:

> "When nourishing your ethereal soul and embracing the One—
> can you not let them go?
> In concentrating your *qi* and attaining softness,
> can you be like an infant?"[139] [12/115/12–17]

12.40

Duke Mu of Qin raised an army and was about to launch a surprise attack on the state of Zheng when Jian Shu[140] said to him: "You cannot do that! I have heard that when one launches a surprise attack on a state,

> chariots should go no farther than one hundred *li*
> and foot soldiers no farther than thirty *li*,

for confined to these distances,

> plans will not yet be leaked;
> armored soldiers will not yet lose their acuity;
> provisions will not yet be depleted;
> and people will not yet give up in exhaustion.

This is because they reach the peak of their vigor and the pinnacle of their strength. This is the way to repulse the enemy and fill them with awe. Now if you send troops several thousand *li* and cross the territory of the Lords of the Land several times to launch a surprise attack on the state of Zheng, I doubt you will succeed. You should rethink your plans!"

Duke Mu did not heed Jian Shu's advice. Jian Shu bid the army farewell, rending his garments and weeping [as if in mourning]. The army departed, passed Zhou, and proceeded eastward. A merchant of Zheng named Xian Gao, feigning that he was acting on the orders of the earl of Zheng, prepared twelve head of oxen to provide sustenance for the Qin army and played host to them [at a banquet]. The three generals of the Qin army were frightened and, speaking among themselves, said: "Even though we have traveled several thousand *li* to launch this surprise attack, the people of Zheng knew about us before we even arrived at our destination. They must already be fully prepared for us. We cannot possibly proceed with the attack." The generals commanded their armies to turn around and left promptly.[141]

138. This anecdote also appears in ZZ 6/19/17–20.

139. *Laozi* 10. For the *hun* "ethereal soul," see 7.7.

140. Jian Shu 蹇叔 was a grandee of the Qin court.

141. A briefer version of this story appears in 13.11 and another version in 18.12; Xian Gao is mentioned again in 20.34. See also LSCQ 16.4/93/20–16.4/94/11.

During this same time, Duke Wen of Jin died en route and had not yet been buried when Xian Zhen advised Duke Xiang,[142] "In the past, when our former ruler communicated with Duke Mu, everyone in the world heeded it and all the Lords of the Land took note of it. Now our ruler has died and has not yet been buried. Duke Mu neither condoled us in mourning nor asked permission to have free passage [across our territory], considering that our ruler was dead and that our orphan [i.e., the newly enthroned heir] was weak. I ask that we attack him!" Duke Xiang assented. Xian Zhen[143] led his troops to Mount Xian where he attacked the Qin army and defeated it soundly. He captured their three commanders and brought them back to Jin. When Duke Mu of Qin learned of the defeat, he clothed himself in mourning garb and paid a visit to the ancestral temple to announce the defeat to the multitudes of his ancestors.[144]

Therefore the *Laozi* says:

> "To know that you do not know is best;
> to not know but think you know is a disease."[145] [12/115/19–28]

12.41

The queen consort of the king of Qi died. The king wanted to appoint a new queen consort but had not yet decided who it would be, so he directed his ministers to deliberate the issue. The Duke of Xue,[146] hoping to discover the king's choice, presented him with ten pairs of earrings, one of which was especially beautiful. The next morning he asked about the whereabouts of the most beautiful pair of earrings and urged that the woman who now had them should be appointed queen consort. The king of Qi was delighted by this and thereafter respected and valued the Duke of Xue even more. Thus, if the intentions and desires of the lord are visible on the outside, he will fall subject to the control of his subjects.

Therefore the *Laozi* says:

> "Block the openings,
> shut the doors,
> and all your life you will not labor."[147] [12/116/1–3]

---

142. Duke Xiang of Jin 晉襄公 (r. 627–621) was the successor of Duke Wen.

143. Xian Zhen 先軫 (d. 627) was a high minister of the Jin court, commander of the Army of the Center.

144. This anecdote first appears in the *Zuozhuan*, Xi 33. A longer version appears in LSCQ 16.4/93/20–16.4/94/11. See Knoblock and Riegel 2000, 385–89.

145. *Laozi* 71.

146. The Duke of Xue 薛公 (also known as Tian Ying 田嬰 and Lord Jingguo 靖郭君) was a scion of the Qi royal house during the Warring States period and the father of Lord Mengchang. He served as prime minister under King Xuan (r. 319–301 B.C.E.).

147. *Laozi* 52.

12.42

When Lu Ao[148] roamed around the Northern Sea, having passed through Great Yin,[149] he entered Dark Gate and arrived at the top of Hidden Valley.[150] There he saw a gentleman with deep-set eyes and abundant dark hair, an ample neck and hawk-like shoulders, corpulent above and cadaverous below, who was spinning round and round as if welcoming the winds in dance. When [the man] turned around and saw Lu Ao, he slowly lowered his arms and ran away to hide himself in the shadow of a large rock. Lu Ao pursued him, and when his eyes once again fell on the gentleman, he found him perched on a tortoise shell eating a clam.

Lu Ao then addressed him, saying: "I have turned my back on my companions and left my associates to see all that lies beyond the realm of the six coordinates. There has never been a wanderer like me, don't you think? When I was young I loved to wander, and when I grew to adulthood I never lost my love of wandering. I wandered to the farthest extremes of the four directions[151] but had never seen northern Yin. Now, unexpectedly, I find a Son of Heaven in this place. Could we strike up a friendship?"

It appeared that the gentleman grinned and laughed, saying, "Oh, my! You are one of those folk from the central continent. It is not true that you have come all that far to get here. Here, too, we are illuminated by the sun and moon and blanketed by the arrayed stars. It is where the yin and yang circulate and where the four seasons emerge. Compared with the places that are nameless [and vast], where we are here is just like the front corners of a house. One such as I—

to the south, I wander to the wilderness of Wangliang [Penumbra];[152]
to the north, I rest in the countryside of Chenmu [Sunken Tomb];
to the west, I go as far as the hamlet of Yaoming [Deep Obscurity];
to the east, I close myself up within Hongmeng [Profound Mist].

"In such places,

no Earth lies below;
no Heaven spreads above.
You listen but do not hear;
you look but do not see.

Beyond that place is something rather like a cleansing, encircling stream. Beyond that, there are perhaps another thousand or ten thousand *li*, but I have not been able to go there.

---

148. Lu Ao was a famous (but possibly legendary) erudite of the time of Qin Shihuangdi, late third century B.C.E.

149. A reference to the darkness, damp, and cold (all yin qualities) of the northern regions. At its most extreme, north could be regarded as entirely yin, beyond the influence of yang.

150. Although Lau does not emend the text here, he does suggest two possible emendations in his notes to this passage. We follow emendation A. See Lau, HNZ, 116n.1. Menggu, the "Hidden Valley" or "Vale of Obscurity," also is found in 3.25, as part of a passage describing the sun's path across the sky.

151. For the "extremes of the four directions," see 4.1 and 4.2.

152. The "Wangliang" of this passage appears to be a nonstandard graphic loanword for "Wangliang" (Penumbra [see 12.44]), and we translate it accordingly.

"Now you, sir, have traveled here and announced that you have seen everything there is to see. Have you really come all that far? Nonetheless, stay if you would like; but I have already arranged to meet Vast Waters beyond the Nine Limits, so I cannot remain here for long." Then it appeared that the gentleman lifted his arms, raised his body, and flew off into the clouds.

Lu Ao looked upward to gaze after him but did not see him. He then stopped his horse, his mind unsettled. Perplexed and at a loss, he said: "If I compare myself to this man, it will be like comparing a worm to a swan. All day long the worm crawls just to go no farther than a few inches, but it seems like a long way to him. How lamentable is that!"

Therefore the *Zhuangzi* says:

> "A few years are not as good as many years;
> small knowledge is not as good as great knowledge.
> The morning mushroom knows nothing of dusk and dawn;
> the cicada knows nothing of spring and fall."[153]

That is, even clarity cannot discern everything. [12/116/5–19]

12.43

Mizi[154] had governed Shanfu for three years when Wuma Qi[155] changed his appearance by wearing tattered clothes and a short hemp jacket so that he could [secretly] observe what transformations had taken place there. He saw a night fisherman catch a fish and let it go. Wuma Qi asked him: "You sir, being a fisherman, want to catch fish. Why then do you catch them and let them go?"

The fisherman replied: "Mizi does not want us to catch small fish. Since all the fish I caught were small ones, I let them go."

Wuma Qi returned home and reported his findings to Confucius: "Mizi is the most Morally Potent of all! He is able to inspire people to conduct themselves in the dark of the night as if they were facing a strict punishment for their actions. How is Master Mi able to achieve such things?"

Confucius replied: "I, Qiu, once asked him about governing. He replied, 'Sincerity in this takes shape in that.' Mizi must be practicing this technique."[156]

Therefore the *Laozi* says:

> "He discards that and takes this."[157] [12/116/21–28]

---

153. ZZ 1/1/19.

154. Mizi 宓子 (also known as Mi Buqi 不齊 and Zijian 子賤 [b. 521 B.C.E.]) was a disciple of Confucius.

155. Wuma Qi 巫馬旗 (also known as Wuma Shi 施) was a native of Lu and a disciple of Confucius.

156. This parable appears as part of a longer story in LSCQ 18/8.2. See Knoblock and Riegel 2000, 471.

157. *Laozi* 72.

12.44

Penumbra asked Shadow:[158] "Is the brilliance of the sunlight spirit illumination?"

"No, it is not," replied Shadow.

"How do you know that?" queried Penumbra.

Shadow replied: "When the Fusang Tree falls into darkness,[159] the sun illuminates the universe, the radiance of its light illuminating [all within] the Four Seas. But if you shut your doors and close your windows, it has no means to enter your home. If it were spirit illumination,

it would flow to the four [directions] as far as they reach,
and there would be nowhere to which it did not extend;
above, delimiting Heaven,
below, encircling Earth.

It would transform and nourish the myriad things, and yet it could not be construed as having any particular appearance. In the twinkling of an eye, it would embrace all that lies beyond the Four Seas. How could 'the brilliance of the sunlight' be sufficient to denote spirit illumination?"

Therefore the *Laozi* says:

"The softest thing in the world
rides roughshod over the hardest thing in the world."[160] [12/117/1–4]

12.45

Resplendent Light asked Nothing There, "Master, is there really something there, or is there really nothing there?" Nothing There did not respond. Not getting an answer to his question, Resplendent Light looked intently at the other's sunken, hollow, appearance.

He looked for him but did not see his form,
listened for him but did not hear his voice,
groped for him but could not grasp him,
gazed after him but could not reach him.

"How superb!" said Resplendent Light. "Who could achieve this state? I am able to be without Something, but I am not yet able to be without Nothing. When it comes to being without Nothing, what then would one follow to arrive at this state?"[161]

Therefore the *Laozi* says:

158. Penumbra and Shadow appear as characters in *Zhuangzi* 2, but in the context of quite a different anecdote.

159. The Fusang Tree falls into darkness when the sun crow takes off from its branches to begin its daily journey across the sky.

160. *Laozi* 43.

161. This anecdote also appears in *Zhuangzi*, chap. 22. See ZZ 22/63/1–3; and Mair 1997, 210. It is also quoted in an abbreviated version in 2.1.

"Nothing There enters where there is no space;
this is how I know that non-action brings benefit."[162] [12/117/6–10]

12.46

Preoccupied with thoughts of rebellion,[163] Duke Sheng of Bo left the court and was standing alone when he picked up a riding crop upside down and pierced his chin. Even though his blood flowed all over the ground, he was not conscious of it. When a person from Zheng learned of this, he said: "If you forget your chin, what won't you forget!"

That is, if your Quintessential Spirit overflows outside, your knowledge and forethought will waste away inside, and you will not be able to regulate your body in a measured fashion. For this reason, the more distant the location in which the spirit is employed, the closer will be the things that are lost.[164]

Therefore the *Laozi* says:

"Do not go out your door,
thereby know the whole world;
do not peer out your window,
thereby know the Way of Heaven.
The farther you go,
the less you know."[165]

This is what is meant here. [12/117/12–15]

12.47

When the First Emperor of Qin[166] conquered the world, he feared that he would not be able to defend it. Thus, he attacked the Rong [border tribes], repaired the Great Wall, constructed passes and bridges, erected barricades and barriers, equipped himself with post stations and charioteers, and dispatched troops to guard the borders of his empire. When, however, the house of Liu took possession of the world, it was as easy as turning a weight in the palm of your hand.

In ancient times, King Wu attacked and vanquished [tyrant] Djou at Muye. He then

162. *Laozi* 43.

163. Duke Sheng was said to be consumed by a desire to avenge the murder of his father by the state of Zheng. Hence the comment of the "person from Zheng" is an expression of apprehension.

164. This anecdote also appears in *Hanfeizi* 21. See HFZ 21/44/18–21.

165. *Laozi* 47. This line is also quoted in 7.4.

166. The First Emperor of Qin 秦始皇帝 (also known as Zhao Zheng 趙政 and King Zheng of Qin [259–210 B.C.E., r. 221–210 B.C.E.]) conquered the Warring States and founded the Qin dynasty (221–206 B.C.E.). He created the title of emperor and thus is known as the first ruler of China's imperial period. His reign is chronicled in *Shiji* 6.

erected a tumulus at the grave of Bi Gan,
hung [his] banner over the [palace] gate of Shang Rong,
erected a fence to protect the home of Jizi,
paid his respects at the ancestral temple of Cheng Tang,
distributed the grain in the Juqiao granary,
and disbursed the wealth in the Deer Pavilion.[167]
He destroyed the war drums and drumsticks.
He unbent his bows and cut their strings.
He moved out of his palace and lived exposed to the wilds to demonstrate that life would be peaceful and simple.
He lay down his waist sword and took up the breast tablet to demonstrate that he was free of enmity.

As a consequence of King Wu's actions, the entire world sang his praises and rejoiced in his rule while the Lords of the Land came bearing gifts of silk and seeking audiences with him. [His dynasty endured] for thirty-four generations without interruption.

Therefore the *Laozi* says:

"Those good at shutting use no bolts,
yet what they shut cannot be opened;
those good at tying use no cords,
yet what they tie cannot be unfastened."[168] [12/117/17–21]

12.48

Yin Ru[169] was studying charioteering, but three years passed and he had not yet mastered it. He was so troubled and grieved by this that when he slept, his thoughts often drifted to charioteering. Once in the middle of the night he dreamed that he received instruction in "Autumn Driving"[170] from his teacher.

The next morning he visited his teacher, who looked at him and said: "It is not that I have been withholding my Way from you; it is just that I feared you were not capable of receiving my instruction. Today I will instruct you in 'Autumn Driving.'"

Yin Ru turned around to take his leave; facing north he bowed twice and replied: "I have enjoyed Heaven's good fortune. This past evening I already received such instruction in my dreams!"[171]

167. All the actions of King Wu illustrate the ways in which he reversed the course of rulership adopted by Djou Xin, the last ruler of the Shang. According to Chinese tradition, the tyrant-king Djou Xin cut out the heart of Bi Gan. Shang Rong was supposedly prime minister under King Djou. Jizi was the uncle of King Djou and feigned madness to avoid being associated with his nephew's actions. Cheng Tang was the virtuous founder of the Shang dynasty. The Juqiao Granary and Deer Pavilion were places where King Djou stored his grain and money.

168. *Laozi* 27.

169. Yin Ru 尹儒 was a famous charioteer of the Spring and Autumn period.

170. This was the name of a special technique of charioteering.

171. A version of this story appears in LSCQ 24.5/158/24–29. See Knoblock and Riegel 2000, 619.

Therefore the *Laozi* says:

> "I do my utmost to attain emptiness;
> I hold firmly to stillness.
> The ten thousand things act in succession,
> and I observe their reversions."[172] [12/117/22–26]

12.49

In the days of old, Sunshu Ao thrice rose to the position of prime minister but felt no joy because of it, and thrice he left the office but felt no anxiety over it. The people of Wu wanted Jizi of Yanling to be their king, but he would not accept. Xu You was given the empire, but he would not accept it. Master Yan Ying made a covenant with Cui Shu, and even though he faced death, he did not seek to alter his obligations. In every case, these men possessed far-reaching understanding. Their Quintessential Spirit plumbed the distinction between death and life; how then could worldly things delude them?[173]

There was a person from Jing [i.e., Chu] named Ci Fei who obtained a precious sword at Gansui.[174] On his way home, he crossed the Yangzi River. When he was in midstream, a massive wave arose, and two scaly dragons pressed in on his boat and coiled around it. Ci Fei asked the boatman: "When you encountered these dragons before, how did you survive?" The boatman responded: "I have never seen them before." Thereupon Ci Fei laid bare his arms and drew his sword declaring: "A courageous knight can be persuaded by Humaneness and Rightness, but he cannot be intimidated by force.[175] On behalf of this rotten flesh and putrid bones floating in the river, if I were to give up my sword to preserve myself whole, what more would I have to cherish?" Ci Fei then jumped into the river and beheaded the dragons. The passengers survived, and the waves subsided. The king of Jing rewarded Ci Fei by making him "Holder of the Jade Baton."

When Confucius learned about Ci Fei's exploits, he commented: "Excellent, indeed! 'To not discard a sword on behalf of rotten flesh and putrid bones'—does not this say [it all] about Ci Fei?"

Therefore the *Laozi* says:

> "Only those who do not act for the sake of life
> are worthier than those who value life."[176] [12/117/28–12/118/8]

172. *Laozi* 75.

173. For parallels with this section, see LSCQ 20.3/131/1–5; and Knoblock and Riegel 2000, 518.

174. Presumably as a reward or as plunder from that famous battlefield; see 12.13. The story of Ci Fei 佽非 is mentioned in 13.21 and 18.25, and a version appears in LSCQ 20.3/131/1–5.

175. Emending 此 to 以. The implication is that the two dragons were trying to steal Ci Fei's rare and valuable sword; he refused to give it up without a fight.

176. *Laozi* 75.

12.50

Chunyu Kun,[177] a person from Qi, offered a persuasion to the king of Wei on [the merits of joining] the Vertical Alliance. The king of Wei found it convincing, so he gave him ten chariots and ordered him to proceed to Jing [Chu]. When Chunyu Kun was about to take his leave, he had second thoughts about the merits of joining the Vertical Alliance and so again offered a persuasion, this time regarding [the merits of joining] the Horizontal Alliance. Chunyu Kun then took his leave as before, but the king of Wei halted his expedition and distanced himself from Chunyu Kun. In [both] his failing to realize his ambitions concerning the Vertical Alliance and his being unable to complete the task [of persuading the king to join] the Horizontal Alliance, the reason was constant.

Now words have an ancestor, and affairs have a root. If you lose sight of them, even if you possess much skill and capability, it would be better if you possessed less. For this reason, when Chui is depicted on the Zhou tripods, he is shown chewing his fingers because the former kings hoped to illustrate that excessive skill should not be practiced.[178]

Therefore the *Shenzi* says: "A craftsman who knows how to make a door that can [only] stay open does not truly know about [making] doors. He must be able to make them close. Only then does he know how to [make] doors."[179] [12/118/10–15]

12.51

A Mohist named Tian Jiu[180] wished to have an audience with King Hui of Qin. He readied his chariot and aligned his wheels, but after remaining in Qin for three years, he still had not seen the king. A certain retainer spoke to the king of Chu on Tian Jiu's behalf, and consequently Tian Jiu [traveled to Chu and] had an audience with the king. The king of Chu was delighted with Tian Jiu, so he bestowed on him the tally [of the general of the army] and sent him off to Qin. When he arrived in Qin with his tally, he obtained an audience with King Hui of Qin and offered him a persuasion. When he left the king and was on his way to his lodging, Tian Jiu let out a long sigh and remarked to one of his followers: "I remained in Qin for three years and did not obtain an audience. I did not realize that the path to Qin would be through the state of Chu."

---

177. Chunyu Kun 淳于髡, a native of Qi, was a scholar who served at the Qi court during the Warring States period and was ranked among the venerable masters of Jixia. He wrote a text, the *Wang du ji* 王度記, which has not survived.

178. The story of Chunyu Kun also appears in LSCQ 18/4.6. See Knoblock and Riegel 2000, 455–56. The image of Chui portrayed as biting his fingers also appears in 8.5.

179. This incomplete citation is from a lost passage of the *Shenzi*. Although Lau does not emend the main text here, we follow his suggested possible emendations at HNZ 12/118/14nn.2, 3. See also Zhang Shuangdi 1997, 2:1315n.8.

180. Tian Jiu 田鳩 (also known as Tian Qiu 俅) was a native of Qi and a latter-day disciple of Mozi. A text bearing his name, the *Tian Qiuzi*, once circulated, but now exists only as fragments.

There definitely are some things that are near but are put far away, and some things that are far away but are brought near.[181] Thus, the movements of a great man cannot be marked out with [the straightness of] a marking cord; he arrives at his objective, that is all. This is what the *Guanzi* means when it says:

The flight of birds is like the level and marking cord.[182] [12/118/17–21]

12.52

The waters of Feng River are a thousand *ren*[183] deep, yet it takes in no dirt or dust. Toss a metal needle into the deep waters, and the needle will remain visible. It is not that the water is not deep; it is that the water is clear, so that fish, turtles, dragons, and snakes are not willing to make their home there. Similarly, the five grains will not grow on top of stones and boulders, and deer will not roam on bare mountains, for they have no place in which they can hide and find shelter.[184]

In ancient times Viscount Wen of Zhao[185] asked Shuxiang,[186] "[Among] the six [hereditary] generals of [the armies of] Jin,[187] who will be the first to perish?"

Shuxiang replied: "[The generals of] the Zhonghang and Zhi [clans]."

Viscount Wen asked: "Why?"

Shuxiang answered: "In administering the affairs of government, they consider
cruelty to be scrutiny;
severity to be discernment;
treating their subordinates harshly to be loyalty [to their lord];
and devising numerous stratagems to be meritorious.

They may be compared to stretching hide. If you stretch it, the hide will grow larger but enlarging the hide is also the way to rupture it."

Therefore the *Laozi* says:

181. For parallels, see LSCQ 14.3/72/25–14.3/73/4; and Knoblock and Riegel 2000, 313.

182. The translation of this passage follows Rickett 1985, 203.

183. Some commentators emend "thousand" to "ten," which yields a more plausible picture of the river's depth as eighty feet rather than eight thousand feet.

184. Although Lau (HNZ 12/118/21–24) attaches this paragraph to the end of 12.51, we follow the majority of Chinese and Japanese commentators, who include it at the beginning of the current passage. The paragraph, however, does not seem to fit either of the two passages very well.

185. Viscount Wen of Zhao 趙文子 (also known as Zhao Wu 武), head of the Zhao clan and minister of Jin during the reigns of Dukes Dao (r. 572–558 B.C.E.) and Ping (r. 557–532 B.C.E.), was credited with helping revive the prosperity and power of Jin.

186. Shuxiang 叔向 (also known as Yangshe Xi 羊舌肸) was an influential grandee and minister of Jin who served in several capacities at the Jin court and whose ideas helped shape its policies.

187. Jin was unique among Spring and Autumn states in organizing its military forces into Six Armies instead of the customary three. As in many other states, in Jin the command of each of the armies was the hereditary privilege of a particular ministerial clan. In effect, the "Six Generals" is an alternative designation for the "Six Counselors" (or "Six Excellencies," *liu qing* 六卿) of the Zhonghang, Fan, Zhi, Zhao, Hann, and Wei clans. The term "general" here thus denotes a hereditary privilege or title held by an aristocratic clan rather than its Warring States period meaning of the professional rank of an individual.

"When the government is muddled,
the people are simple.
When the government is alert,
the people are cunning.[188] [12/118/21–29]

12.53

Duke Jing [of Qi] said to the chief prognosticator: "What can you accomplish with your Way?"

He replied: "I can move the earth."

When Yanzi went to have an audience with Duke Jing, the duke said to him: "I asked the chief prognosticator what he could accomplish with his Way. He replied that he could move the earth. Is it really possible to move the earth?"

Yanzi was silent and did not respond. After he left Duke Jing, he went to see the chief prognosticator and said to him: "Earlier I observed a comet between [the lunar lodges] Room and Heart. Is there about to be an earthquake?"

"There will be," said the chief prognosticator.

After Yanzi left, the chief prognosticator had an audience with Duke Jing in which he said: "I cannot move the earth, but the earth will definitely move."

When Tian Ziyang[189] heard this, he commented: "When Yanzi chose to remain silent and not speak, it was because he did not want to see the chief prognosticator die. When Yanzi sought an interview with the chief prognosticator, it was because he feared that the duke would be deceived. It may be said of Yanzi that he was loyal toward his superiors and generous toward his subordinates."[190]

Therefore the *Laozi* says:

"[The sage] is square edged but does not scrape,
has corners but does not jab."[191] [12/119/1–6]

12.54

Marquis Wen of Wei[192] feasted his grand ministers at Quyang. When they had drunk enough wine to become inebriated, Marquis Wen sighed deeply and exclaimed: "I, alone, lack a minister like Yu Rang."

Jian Zhong[193] raised a cup and approached him saying: "Please, drink a cup as a forfeit."

188. *Laozi* 58.

189. Tian Ziyang 田子陽 was a minister of Qi.

190. This story also appears in *Yanzi chunqiu* (*Master Yan's Spring and Autumn*).

191. *Laozi* 58.

192. Marquis Wen of Wei 魏文侯 (r. 446–396 B.C.E.), the first ruler of the independent state of Wei, was renowned for undertaking vigorous reforms and attracting able knights to his court.

193. Jian Zhong 蹇重 was a minister of Wei.

The lord responded: "Why?"

Jian Zhong answered: "I have learned that those who follow their true destinies as mothers and fathers know nothing of the filial son, while the ruler possessed of the Way knows nothing of the loyal minister. Besides, what became of Yu Rang's ruler?"

Marquis Wen accepted the cup and drank it. When he had drained the goblet, he replied: "If one lacks ministers like Guan Zhong and Bao Shu,[194] then one gets the meritorious service of a Yu Rang."[195]

Therefore the *Laozi* says:

> "When the state is confused and chaotic,
> there are loyal ministers."[196] [12/119/8–12]

12.55

Master Kong[197] was paying a visit to the temple of Duke Huan[198] when he happened to catch sight of a vessel called a Warning Vessel.

"How wonderful to have caught sight of such a vessel!" Master Kong exclaimed in delight. He turned his head around toward his disciples and called out: "Disciples, fetch some water!"

When they brought the water, Master Kong poured it into the vessel. When the vessel was half full, it remained upright, but when Master Kong filled it completely, it toppled over on its side.

Suddenly Master Kong's expression changed, and he exclaimed: "How splendid to grasp the significance of fullness."

Standing at the master's side, Zigong said: "Please, what does it mean 'to grasp the significance of fullness'?"

"What increases will decrease," replied Master Kong.

"What does that mean?" asked Zigong.

Master Kong replied:

> "Things prosper then decline.
> Joy reaches its utmost then becomes sorrow.
> The sun reaches its apogee then shifts.
> The moon reaches its fullness then begins to wane.

This is why

194. Bao Shu 鮑叔 (also known as Bao Shuya 叔牙) was an adviser to Duke Huan of Qi who convinced him to employ Guan Zhong, even though the latter had served the duke's brother in the struggle over his succession.

195. Yu Rang 豫讓 appears in *Shiji* 86:2519–2522. His story is told in the "Book of Zhao" of the *Zhanguoce*, chap. 232 in Crump, *Chan-kuo Ts'e*, 279–81.

196. *Laozi* 18.

197. That is, Confucius.

198. Duke Huan 桓公 was the ruler of Lu from 711 to 694 B.C.E.

the perceptive and wise preserve themselves with stupidity;
the learned and eloquent preserve themselves with restraint;
the martial and courageous preserve themselves with timidity;
the wealthy and powerful preserve themselves with frugality;
and those whose Potency operates throughout the world preserve themselves with docility.

These five things are the means by which the former kings defended their empires without losing them. If you oppose these five things, you will always be endangered."[199]

Therefore the *Laozi* says:

"If you submit to the Way,
you will not want to be full.
It is because he is not full
that he can be worn and yet newly made."[200] [12/119/14–20]

12.56

King Wu asked the Grand Duke: "If I attack [the tyrant] Djou, the world will consider that a subject has murdered his lord and a subordinate has attacked his superior. I fear that later generations will employ their troops incessantly and will struggle with one another unceasingly. What can I do about this?"

The Grand Duke replied: "The king's question is excellent indeed! Those who have not yet caught their prey fear the wound will be too small. But once they have caught it, they fear the wound is so large as to spoil much of the meat. If the king persistently wants to hold onto the empire, then block up the peoples' senses. Guide them all into useless occupations and pointless teachings. When they all rejoice in their respective callings and are at ease with their emotions, those who are bright and shining will lead those who are [still] dark and obscure.

Then, and only then, discard their helmets and adorn their heads with caps of duck feather; unfasten their waist swords; and direct them to carry breast tablets. Establish three years of mourning, directing the mourning clothes to be simple. Elevate and praise those who are modest and retiring so that the people will not compete with one another. Use wine and meat to communicate with them, the [music of] the mouth organ and the *qin* to amuse them, and ghosts and spirits to intimidate them.

[Next] employ sumptuous ornamentation and opaque ritual to obscure their inner substance. Enhance funerals and extend mourning periods to make their households sincere. With pearls for the mouths of the deceased, fish scales [of jade] for their clothing, and silken thread and cords to bind their bodies, you will deplete

199. For a different version of this story, see HSWZ 3.30/23/14–20.

200. *Laozi* 15; Lau, *Tao Te Ching*, 71. Lau notes that the negative *bu* must have crept into the text by mistake.

their resources. With tombs that have been chiseled deep with ornamentation and tumuli that have been mounded high above the earth, you will use up their strength. When the families are impoverished and the clans have decreased, your worries and anxieties will be few. If you employ these methods to modify customary practices, then you will be able to maintain the empire without losing it."

Therefore the *Laozi* says:

> "After they are transformed, should they want to act,
> I shall suppress them with the Nameless Uncarved Block."[201]
> [12/119/22–29]

Translated by Sarah A. Queen

---

201. *Laozi* 38.

Thirteen

BOUNDLESS DISCOURSES

USING NUMEROUS examples, "Boundless Discourses" shows that change has always been a part of human history, from remote antiquity to the present day. It argues that successful rulers do not resist change in a futile attempt to uphold the policies and standards of the past but instead modify their actions to suit changing customs and circumstances. Sages, on whom rulers are urged to model themselves, are portrayed as having a unique insight that allows them to see the enduring reality behind superficial qualities. That in turn enables them to adapt to change and innovate while following diverse strategies to realize the Way under varying circumstances.

The Chapter Title

The title of the chapter is "Fan lun" 氾論, which we translate as "Boundless Discourses," although "Far-reaching Assessments" would also be a suitable rendering. *Fan* is closely related to the word *fan* 凡, "general" or "common," but with the "water" radical, it has connotations of "floodlike," "inundating," "boundless," and "spreading in all directions." *Lun* was used in many senses during the Han, from the verbal senses of "to consider, examine, appraise, argue, elucidate," and, most prominently, "to discuss, argue, or dispute," to the nominal sense of "discussion" and "discourse."

As is often the case in the *Huainanzi*, the authors exploit the multivalence of ancient Chinese words so that the chapter title exhibits several important resonances germane to understanding the aims and import of the chapter, nuances that are nearly impossible to capture in a single English translation. On the one hand, rendering the title as "Boundless Discourses" underscores two important aspects of the chapter. It highlights the human phenomenon addressed in this chapter and the object of the sage's acuity: the "boundless" quality of human society to develop over time toward ever-increasing differentiation, complexity, and multidimensionality. It also relates the chapter title to a genre of writing known as the *discourse*. Here, however, we would argue that the term is employed rather loosely, as the chapter is not one long discursive essay but is constituted from smaller segments of discourse that together yield a coherent and cogent argument.

On the other hand, translating the title as "Far-Reaching Assessments" would capture a central theme of the chapter, the sage's far-reaching ability to assess change and diversity in the world. Such a rendering proposes a narrower and more focused reading of *lun*. In the Qin legal system, which, largely intact, continued to be used in Han times, the judgment rendered by the presiding official in a legal case was a *lun*—an "opinion" or a "judgment" legally binding on all parties to the case. Here the term "assessment" indicates that this chapter provides numerous illustrations of how the sage assesses a wide range of situations and historical examples and renders judgments about them to guide the ruler. These are wide-ranging and can be generalized to inform the conduct of the ruler in many kinds of situations; hence the alternative translation "Far-Reaching Assessments."[1]

Summary and Key Themes

The *Huainanzi*'s own summary of "Boundless Discourses" in chapter 21, "An Overview of the Essentials," says that the chapter will enable a reader to "stitch up the spaces in ragged seams and hems, and plug up the gaps in crooked and chattering teeth." This vivid metaphor for the shortcomings of the present age, depicted as a ragged and disreputable vagrant, uses the image of how things grow old and unserviceable over time to suggest that sage-rulers cannot rest content to follow the ways of ancient times but instead must remain attuned to changes wrought by time and circumstance. The sage must be deeply acquainted with the historical past but not in servitude to bygone ways; he must be prepared to abandon old policies when they become obsolete, innovate when faced with new challenges, and adopt diverse approaches as the circumstances warrant. Nowhere in the text do we find a more com-

1. Both Ames and Csikszentmihaly regard *fan* as adjectival: "Perennial Discussions" (Ames 1994, 20) and "All-Encompassing Discussions" (Csikszentmihalyi 2004, 174). Le Blanc and Mathieu 2003 render the title as "De l'inconstance des choses" (On the Uncertainty of Things).

prehensive discussion of change, replete with an elaborate vocabulary that brings out subtle distinctions within the concept, including such terms as "to change" (*yi* 易), "to transform" (*hua* 化), "to alter" (*bian* 變), and "to adjust" (*yi* 移). Numerous historical anecdotes illustrate how sages through the ages have assessed, responded to, and adapted to changing circumstances, and, indeed, one subtheme of the chapter is the ruler's need for a historically grounded understanding of human affairs.

The authors of "Boundless Discourses" accept the view, common at the time, that in the most ancient eras of human history, life was idyllic, sages ruled through the inherent Potency of the Way, and governance was uncomplicated. But time, the chapter insists, has marched on and brought with it changes and new challenges that sages met by constantly innovating in diverse ways, including the invention of such virtues as Humaneness and Rightness. Even the sages of remote antiquity are not portrayed as static figures but are celebrated for inventing devices and techniques—rudimentary forms of shelter, clothing, agriculture, transportation, and weaponry—that eased the peoples' daily struggle to survive and improved their material well-being. The Duke of Zhou provides an example of a sage who often altered his course of action to adapt to changing circumstances. Change is both normal and necessary. Early rulers and dynasties that were able to transform themselves and adapt to times and customs thrived; those that did not, perished. Most recently, the founding emperor of the Han is lauded as a model ruler because he adjusted his policies to suit the demands of his day, all the while cultivating moderation as he did so. (This no doubt reflects not only Liu An's pride in the imperial Liu clan, of which he was a member, but also his strong political interest in the dynastic founder's policy of establishing and maintaining large, semiautonomous kingdoms such as Huainan.)

Because sages embrace change, they are anything but uniform in their actions. Rather, they follow historical precedents for both creativity and diversity. Do not blindly revere or follow antiquity, the authors argue, or your state will perish. Laws and rites suitable for any given age will become obsolete with the passage of time. Rulers of the present day must emulate the ancient sages (as they are portrayed here), not in their specific actions and policies, but in their willingness to adjust rites and laws to changing circumstances. In some instances, this adjustment demands promulgating new laws or reforming rites; in others, it recognizes that it is sometimes necessary for a ruler to depart from the usual legal regulations and ritual standards of his time.

Sages think and act in the context of change, guided by their cultivated and internalized understanding of the Way. Thus they are able to discard obsolete policies that no longer suit the times and use timeliness and expediency to respond to changing circumstances. As in other chapters, timeliness (*shi* 時) involves seizing the opportune moment to implement a particular course of action. Expediency (*quan* 權) sanctions the suspension of normal standards of conduct, as the context demands, to achieve a greater good. Expediency involves the weighing, sorting, and prioritizing of competing moral imperatives. Choosing properly leads to moral equilibrium (another meaning of *quan*); the choice depends on the sage's innate sense of moral values, guided by the Way. Only a sage understands expediency and the power of circumstance from which it derives.[2]

Although "Boundless Discourses" emphasizes that the ability to change is an essential component of successful rulership, it also insists that a ruler has to possess the qualities of a sage to understand when and how to change. This begs the question: What, then, is a sage? This chapter points to a number of qualities that add up to sageliness. Attuned to the Way, sages enjoy a unique capacity to assess (*lun*) the world around them. They can understand and evaluate, in the context of the times in which they live, the circumstances of the moment, the actions of other men, and their own strengths and weaknesses. Sages understand that self-preservation is the foundation of all future policies. They weigh and assess circumstances and preserve themselves, even at the cost of temporary setbacks or humiliation, so as to make their policies effective in the long run.

Sages seek out worthy individuals wherever they may be found, and they can assess their worth before it is apparent to others, sometimes on the basis of a single word or deed. Ordinary people equate lowly position with lack of merit, but sages overlook superficial negatives to discover underlying worth. Similarly, sages are not confused by strange phenomena and aberrations but use the ordinary and the usual as the basis for assessing situations. Nor are sages distracted by tales of ghosts and spirits, but understand that the common people are guided by superstition and fear, which can be used to control them. But sages do not rely on terrifying and cruel punishments to deter misconduct or on extravagant rewards to encourage good conduct. They understand that the love and loyalty of the people cannot be commanded through fear or bought with bribes, but it can be won through Moral Potency. Sages look for the best in their subordinates and for ways to bring out their best, and they overlook minor shortcomings in favor of significant strengths. Thus good judgment is an essential quality for a ruler: many things are superficially alike but really different, or superficially different but really alike. Sages know how to tell them apart.

Despite the chapter's emphasis on the sages' ability to assess and adapt, they also must consistently conform to certain fixed principles embodied in the Way. "Boundless Discourses" identifies these principles as Humaneness and Rightness. As both sections 8.3 and 11.1 have demonstrated (drawing on *Laozi* 38 in both cases), such qualities of Moral Potency as Humaneness and Rightness (along with Ritual and Music) themselves came into being only in the course of changing times and circumstances, after the primordial Way and its Potency had been lost. But having been established through this process of change, Humaneness and Rightness are treated here as enduring qualities that transcend time and circumstance, whereas legal regulations and ritual standards will continue to vary and be adapted to their times.

2. For the various meanings of the word *quan*, including the weighing of courses of action that we term "expediency," see Griet Vankeerberghen, "Choosing Balance: Weighing (*quan*) as a Metaphor for Action in Early Chinese Texts," *Early China* 30 (2005): 47–89. See also chap. 9, n. 48.

Harmony also is an enduring principle embodied by the sages. Mirroring the vital energy of Heaven and Earth, which perfectly blends yin and yang to generate cosmic harmony, sages are said to "reside between hardness and softness and thereby obtain the root of the Way." They are the perfect balance of leniency and firmness, strictness and kindness, pliancy and rigidity, forcefulness and humaneness. In contrast, unsuccessful rulers often vacillate between leniency and strictness, with disastrous results in either case. Accordingly, it is necessary to adapt to circumstances and choose a path of moderation. Thus, the chapter concludes, if the ruler embraces the Way and conducts himself in accordance with its Harmony, good government will naturally result.

Sources

This chapter, like others in the *Huainanzi*, synthesizes materials from disparate sources, many of which were pitted against one another in the late Warring States context of doctrinal competition but which are made to fit comfortably together in this text. As the authors of "Boundless Discourse" explain,

> The hundred rivers have different sources, yet all return to the ocean.
> The hundred lineages [of learning] have different specializations, yet all strive for [good] governance. (13.3)

Here we find passages inspired by the *Mozi*, *Xunzi*, *Hanfeizi*, *Gongyang Commentary* (to the *Spring and Autumn Annals*), *Odes*, *Changes*, and *Laozi* placed side by side, with appropriate lessons drawn from each. The idea that the sages of antiquity cannot serve as unchanging models of royal conduct may be seen as a criticism of one strand of Confucian doctrine, but Confucius himself is portrayed sympathetically in the chapter, and the normative qualities of Humaneness and Rightness, seen here as essential elements of sage rulership, are fundamental to Confucian doctrine. But if the chapter is open to Confucian ideas, it also is heavily indebted to sources that are normally seen as anti-Confucian. Especially the opening sections of the chapter show the strong influence of the "Ciguo" 辭過 (Refusing Extravagances) chapter of the *Mozi* and the "Wudu" 五蠹 (Five Vermin) chapter of the *Hanfeizi* in arguing that the sages of antiquity were not merely passive and quiescent but also "active creators of the material culture of humanity." Drawing from those sources, the conclusion of "Boundless Discourses" is that "it is necessary for sages to create anew with the changing times."[3]

Chapter 13 draws on these diverse sources not to set them in opposition to one another but to enlist them in various ways in support of the central arguments

3. Michael Puett, *The Ambivalence of Creation* (Stanford, Calif.: Stanford University Press, 2001), 160.

that change is normative and that sages perfectly attune their conduct to the ever-changing contexts they confront. Thus, through illustrations of past sages, the authors urge the ruler to establish a comprehensive view of things that entails not siding a priori with the perspective of any one particular viewpoint but availing himself of the diverse contributions of all of them, thereby enabling him to contend with whatever challenges that change might bring.

The Chapter in the Context of the *Huainanzi* as a Whole

"Boundless Discourses" is one of the most overtly political chapters in a text that overall can be read as a prescription for sage-rulership or a curriculum for a sage-ruler in training. Here Liu An is arguing for the necessity of the ruler making creative responses to change, a plea for the emperor and his regime being open to new ideas (such as those contained in the *Huainanzi*). The chapter criticizes those who seek the answers to the political questions of the age in canonical texts (13.4) and argues against the extravagance and militarism of Qin-style centralized rule (13.9). The statement in 13.10 that "survival lies in obtaining the Way; it does not lie in being large. Destruction lies in losing the Way; it does not lie in being small" is overtly about the importance of conforming to the Way, but in terms of contemporary early Han politics, it can also be read as daring attempt to persuade the imperial regime not to increase the territory under central control by wiping out and absorbing neofeudal kingdoms like Huainan.

The summary of chapter 13 in the work's final chapter, "An Overview of the Essentials," reinforces the chapter's political claims. The statement in chapter 21 that "Boundless Discourses" "welcomes the straightforward and straightens out the devious, in order to extend the Original Unhewn," could be read as a reference to the many historical personages referred to in the chapter's anecdotal sections, but it also could be a plea for Liu An to be made welcome at court in his hoped-for role as uncle and adviser to the young emperor Wu. The summary's claim that the chapter will enable the reader to

> not be foolishly immersed in the advantages of political power,
> not be seductively confused by the exigencies of affairs,
> and so tally with constancy and change
> to link up and discern timely and generational alterations,
> and extend and adjust [your policies] in accordance with transformations (21.2)

is surely a plea to the emperor not to pursue unsound policies (such as abolishing the neofeudal kingdoms) in pursuit of short-term gains.

In the *Huainanzi* as a whole, this chapter has links in many directions, including the value of self-cultivation (chapter 7), a devolutionary view of history (chapter 8), and the importance of flexibility on the part of the ruler (chapter 11). Perhaps most striking is the consonance between the emphasis in chapter 13 on the importance of the ruler's creative responses to change and the insistent message of chapter 19 that sage-rulership demands constant effort and rigorous training. A sage-ruler does far more than "sit on his throne and face south."

Sarah A. Queen and John S. Major

Thirteen

13.1

In ancient times, those who wore [plain] caps and [simple] rolled collars ruled the world.[1] Their Potency was of life, not death, of giving, not usurping. None in the world rejected their service; all embraced their Potency. In those times,

> yin and yang were harmonious and tranquil;
> the winds and rains were timely and moderate.
> The myriad things prospered and flourished;
> nests of birds and owls could be inspected on bended knee;[2]
> wild animals could be ensnared and kept compliant.

What need was there for official costumes, wide sashes, buckled collars, grand insignia? [13/120/3–5]

1. There is a good deal of commentarial disagreement about the exact nature of these garments, but the point of the sentence is clear: ancient rulers wore simple clothing rather than elaborate royal regalia. See Zhang Shuangdi 1997, 2:1332n.2.

2. That is, the nests were made low to the ground because birds had no fear of humans. These lines appear to have been inspired by *Xunzi*, chap. 31.3, Duke Ai. See Xiong Gongzhe 熊公哲, ed., *Xunzi jinzhu jinyi* 荀子今註今譯 (Taibei: Shangwu yinshuguan, 1975), 626; compare the translation by Knoblock 1988, 3:261.

13.2

In ancient times, the people lived in humid lands, hollowing out caves again and again.

In the winters, they could not bear the frost, the snow, the fog, the dew;
in the summers, they could not bear the oppressive heat, the sultry days, the mosquitoes, the flies.

The sages therefore created for them the pounding of earth and the cutting of trees to make houses. Above they placed ridgepoles, and below they placed rafters

to protect against the winds and rain
and to keep out the cold and heat.

The common people[3] were put at ease.

Bo Yu[4] was the first to make clothing. He spun the hemp, working the warp with his hand, suspending it through his fingers, and forming it like netting. Later generations [of sages] made looms for doubled weaves to increase their usefulness. The people were thus able to protect their bodies and drive off the cold.

In ancient times, [the people]

sharpened sticks to plow,
polished clam shells to weed,
cut firewood to make fuel,
and hauled jars to draw water.

The people labored, but their gains were few. Later generations [of sages] made them plows, plowshares, and hoes; axes for cutting firewood; and well sweeps for drawing water. The people were at ease, [and] their gains multiplied.

In ancient times, the great rivers and famed waterways cut across the roads and impeded the comings and goings of the people. Consequently, [the sages] hollowed logs and squared timbers to make rafts and boats. Therefore, according to a place's circumstances of plenty or dearth, things could be exchanged and transported.

They made shoes from hides and traversed a thousand *li*;
they endured the labor of carrying loads on their backs.

[The sages] thus created for them

the bending [of wood] into wheels and the constructing of carts,
the hitching of horses and the yoking of oxen.

The people could thus go great distances without tiring.

Since ferocious beasts would injure people and there was nothing with which to stop them, [the sages] created for them the casting of metal and the forging of iron to make weapons and arms. The animals could harm them no more.

Thus,

pressed by difficulties, [the sages] searched for what was advantageous;
bound by adversity, they created what was necessary.

---

3. *Bai xing* 百姓 (lit., "hundred surnames"), a standard term for the people as a whole.

4. Bo Yu 伯余, according to Gao You, was a minister of the Yellow Emperor. See Zhang Shuangdi 1997, 2:1336n.17.

In each case, the people used what they had come to know [from the sages]
to eliminate what harmed them
and to seek what benefited them.
If the unchanging past cannot be followed, if the martial implements [of the past] cannot be relied on, then there will be [occasions when] the laws and standards of the former kings must be adjusted to changing [circumstances]. [13/120/7–17]

13.3

According to the ancient regulations,

in the marriage ritual, no reference is made to the host [i.e., the bridegroom]. [But in the *Spring and Autumn Annals* there is an instance in which the bridegroom is named.][5] Shun married without announcing it [to his father]. These [actions] were not in accord with the rites.[6]

One establishes one's eldest son as the heir. [But] King Wen set aside Bo Yikao[7] and used King Wu. This was not in accord with the regulations.

According to the rites, one marries at age thirty. [But] King Wen was fifteen and had King Wu. This was not in accord with the law.

In the time of the Xia, the tablet for the deceased was placed above the eastern steps; the Yin placed it between two pillars; the Zhou placed it above the western steps. These rites were not the same.

Shun used earthen coffins; the Xia encircled them with stonework; the Yin used double coffins; the Zhou built a partition and arranged feathers on it. These burial practices were not the same.

The Xia sacrificed at night; the Yin sacrificed during the day; the Zhou sacrificed when the sun rose at dawn. These sacrifices were not the same.

For Yao, the [music was] the "Great Measure";[8] for Shun, the "Nine Harmonies"; for Yu, the "Great Xia"; for Tang, the "Great Melody"; for Zhou, the "[Grand] Martiality" and the "[Three] Elephants."[9] These tunes were not the same.

---

5. The regulation is quoted from the *Gongyang Commentary*, Duke Yin, year 2, month 9. See *Chunqiu*, Duke Yin, II.5.

6. *Mencius* 4A:26 and 5A:2. The first passage cited notes, "There are three ways of being a bad son. The most grave is failing to produce an heir. Shun married without telling his father because he feared not having an heir. To the gentleman, this was as good as having told his father" (Legge 1895, vol. 2, *Mencius*, 313). The suggestion seems to be that Shun's actions were ultimately approved by Confucius because when weighing the different expressions of filial piety—announcing one's bride to one's father or taking a wife to some day produce an heir—Shun weighed the moral choices at hand and made the correct choice.

7. Bo Yikao 伯邑考, King Wen's eldest son, was boiled alive by King Djou.

8. The "Great Measure" 大章 is recorded as the music of Yao in LSCQ 5.5.

9. Zhang Shuangdi generally reconciles this historical musicology with that presented in 11.9. He identifies the "Great Xia" 大夏 with the "Pipes of Xia" (1997, 2:1346n.18). He moreover claims that the two characters *wu xiang* 武象 are not a single musical form but a contraction of the two forms attributed to King Wu in 11.9 (1997, 2:1346n.20). We follow his reading here. For more background on all these musical forms, see the notes to 11.9.

Therefore,

the Five Thearchs had different ways, but their Potency covered the world.

The Three Kings had distinct activities, but their fame has been handed down to later generations.

They all instituted rites and music in accord with alterations in the times. It was like [the blind] Music Master Kuang's setting the bridges on a *se:* he moved and adjusted them up and down [the sounding board] without measuring by inches or feet, yet none failed to [be tuned to] the proper note. Thus, those who comprehend the essential qualities of rites and music are able to create [accurate] notes. The basis and ruling principle lies within them; therefore they understand how standards and measures should be applied comprehensively. [13/120/19–27]

Duke Zhao of Lu[10] had a nurse whom he loved. When she died, he had a cap of silk made on her behalf. Thus there came to be mourning clothes for nurses.[11]

The lord of Yang killed the lord of Liao and took his wife. Thus there came to be the protocol of excusing women from great feasts.[12]

When the regulations of the former kings were not appropriate, they were discarded; in the actions of the later ages, if they were good, they were promoted. This is why the rites and music have never [even] begun to have constancy. Therefore, the sages regulate rites and music; they are not regulated by them.

Ordering the state has a constant, and benefiting the people is its basis.

Correcting education has its norms, and carrying out orders is the apogee.

If one investigates benefiting the people, one does not necessarily imitate the ancients.

If one investigates activities, one does not necessarily accord with the old.

Now,

as for the decline of the Xia and Shang: they did not alter their laws, and they were destroyed.

As for the ascendancy of the Three Dynasties: they ruled without imitating their predecessors and so suited [their circumstances].

Thus, sages'

laws alter with the times;

[their] rites transform along with customs.

Their clothes and utensils were each determined according to their use; the laws, measures, regulations, and commands accorded with what was appropriate. Therefore,

altering what is ancient is not something that can be rejected,

---

10. Duke Zhao of Lu 魯昭公 reigned from 541 to 510 B.C.E.

11. This story is recorded in *Liji* 7.

12. Dates are not known for the lord of Yang 陽侯 and the lord of Liao 蓼侯, if in fact they ever lived. Gao You explains that in antiquity it was the custom of both husband and wife to serve their guests at a feast but that on seeing the beauty of Liao's wife, Yang was moved to murder. The story is cited in *Liji* 31. Zheng Xuan's commentary to that passage notes that these figures' states are unknown, in which case Yang and Liao would be posthumous titles (thus they would be Marquis Yang and Marquis Liao). See Zhang Shuangdi 1997, 2:1347–48n.24.

and following what is customary is not enough [to warrant being called] "excessive."
The hundred rivers have different sources, yet all return to the ocean.
The hundred lineages [of learning] have different specializations, yet all strive for [good] governance. [13/121/1–8]

13.4

When the way of the kings grew deficient, the *Odes* was created. When the house of Zhou fell into ruin and their ritual standards were destroyed, the *Spring and Autumn Annals* was created. Those who study the *Odes* and the *Spring and Autumn Annals* view them as beautiful; both are products of ages of decline. The Confucians follow them in order to teach and guide the generations. But how can they compare to the flourishing of the Three Dynasties? Taking the *Odes* and the *Spring and Autumn Annals* as the way of the ancients, they honor them. But there is also the time before the *Odes* and the *Spring and Autumn Annals* were created.
Now,
the deficiency of the Way is not as good as the entirety of the Way;
reciting the poems and texts of the former kings is not as good as hearing and attaining their words;
hearing and attaining their words is not as good as attaining that about which they spoke.
As for attaining that about which they spoke, speaking cannot speak it. Therefore: "The Way that can be spoken is not the enduring Way."[13] [13/121/8–13]

13.5

When the Duke of Zhou served King Wen,
he never encroached on the regulations.
He never acted on his own behalf.
It was as if his person was not equal to his regalia;
it was as if his speech did not emanate from his mouth.
When receiving instructions from King Wen, he was submissive and weak, as if incapable, as if afraid he might stray from them. It can be said that he was able to be a true son.

King Wu died; King Cheng was young. The Duke of Zhou continued the work of Kings Wen and Wu:
he took the position of the Son of Heaven;
he oversaw the governance of the world.

13. *Laozi* 1.

He pacified the rebellions of the Yi and Di [tribal peoples];
he punished the crimes of Guan and Cai;[14]

he turned his back to the north; he brought the Lords of the Land to court; he meted out punishments; he gave out rewards—all without taking counsel. His authority moved Heaven and Earth, and his voice extended to all within the seas. It can be said that he was able to be martial.

When King Cheng attained maturity, the Duke of Zhou gathered together the population registers and resigned from the government. He faced north, offered gifts, and served as a minister. He

acted only after being asked
and put [policies] into practice only after [the request] was repeated

—without the will to arrogate authority to himself and without a proud countenance. It can be said that he was able to be a minister.

Thus the same person altered three times in order to accord with the times. How much more so

for rulers who frequently change generations[15]
and states that frequently change rulers?

People use their positions to attain their wishes and use their authority to obtain their desires. It is clear that if one wants to use

rituals that are uniformly implemented
and laws that are uniformly established

to respond to the times and accord with alteration, he will be incapable of attaining equilibrium.[16] [13/121/15–22]

Therefore, what the sage follows is called the "Way"; what he does is "activities." The Way is like metal and stone [musical] instruments: once tuned, they do not change. Activities are like the *qin* and *se*; they need to be retuned continuously. Therefore, law, regulations, Ritual, and Rightness are instruments for governance, but not the means by which to govern. Thus,

Humaneness is the warp;
Rightness is the skein of [weft] threads;[17]

this does not change in ten thousand generations. It is like the fact that one can test the abilities of the people and study the ways they can be used, even though daily there are alterations. Does the world have unchanging laws? If you

---

14. Guan 管 and Cai 蔡 (more often cited as Guan Shu 管叔 and Cai Shu 蔡叔) were brothers of King Wu who rebelled against the authority of their nephew, the young King Cheng, and were executed by the Duke of Zhou, who was acting as regent. See also 11.18, 20.14, and 20.25; and chap. 21, n. 31.

15. It is difficult to convey the sense of *yishi* 易世 in a short English phrase. It refers to a type of political instability in which rule devolves rapidly from grandfather to son to grandson.

16. *Quan* 權 in this phrase refers to the ruler's moral, as well as political, equilibrium—literally, a weight that will balance the scale. The term is an important concept in the philosophy of Mencius. See his example of a drowning woman who needs to be rescued. Ritual forbids her brother-in-law from touching her, but he nevertheless grabs her by the hand to save her life. He is said to have adopted a balanced position between a ritual requirement and a moral imperative. See *Mencius* 4A.17.

17. *Ren yi wei jing, yi yi wei ji* 仁以爲經, 義以爲紀; *ji* 紀, a "skein of threads," is often used as a synonym for "weft."

fit with affairs of the age,
obtain the patterns of man,
accord with Heaven and Earth,
and bring happiness to the ghosts and spirits,
then you can rectify and govern. [13/121/24–27]

13.6

In antiquity,
the people were pure, the artisans skillful,
the merchants straightforward, the women simple.
This is why
governance and education were easily transformed [in response to circumstances],
and habits and customs were easily adjusted [to suit changing times].
In the present age, Moral Potency is declining more and more, and the customs of the people are becoming more and more stingy. Wanting to use straightforward and simple laws to put in order a people already corrupted is like wanting to control a horse without a bit and a whip.

In ancient times, the Divine Farmer used no regulations or commands, yet the people followed. Tang [i.e., Yao] and Yu [i.e., Shun] had regulations and commands but no punishments.
The Xia used no false words;
the Shang made oaths;
the Zhou made covenants.
When one comes down to the present time, people accept shame and think lightly of being disgraced, value taking, and belittle giving. Wanting to use the way of the Divine Farmer to put things in order would only make chaos inevitable. When Bocheng Zigao[18] resigned from being a Lord of the Land and simply tilled the fields, the world exalted him. Now, those who resign from office and become hermits occupy the bottom [rung] of their locales. How can this be considered the same?

The armies of antiquity had bows and swords; their lances had no sharp points; their halberds, no tips.

The armies of the later ages have siege weapons and battering rams with which to attack, spiked balls with which to defend, arrays of crossbows with which to shoot, and iron chariots with which to fight.

When states fought in ancient times, they did not kill the young, [and] they did not capture the old.

What in antiquity was proper is today laughable; what was taken to be honorable

18. Bocheng Zigao 伯成子高, a Lord of the Land, was appointed by Yao but resigned his rank on the appointment of Shun to be Son of Heaven, complaining that government had become too burdensome and complex. His story is recorded in *Lüshi chunqiu* 20.2.

in antiquity is taken to be disgraceful today; what was taken to be order in antiquity is taken to be chaos today. [13/122/1–9]

Now,

the Divine Farmer and Fuxi did not give out rewards and punishments, yet the people did no wrong; but those who govern [today] are unable to dispense with laws and rule the people.

Shun grasped a shield and axe and brought the Miao rulers to submission, yet those who lead campaigns [today] are unable to use arms to reduce the violence.

Looking at the issue from this perspective, it is clear that laws and standards are the means to assess the customs of the people and regulate relaxation and work; instruments and implements accord with the alterations of the times and are regulated to fit what is suitable. Now,

the sages created laws and the myriad people were regulated by them;
the worthies established rituals and the ignorant were restrained by them.

[But] people who are regulated by laws cannot propose far-reaching initiatives;
those who are restrained by rituals cannot effect responsive alterations.

An ear that does not know the difference between high and low [tones] cannot order tunes and notes;
a mind that does not understand the source of order and disorder cannot impose regulations and laws.

It is necessary to have

an ear that uniquely hears,
discernment that uniquely sees;

for only then can you take personal responsibility for implementing the Way. [13/122/11–18]

Now,

the Yin replaced the Xia;
the Zhou replaced the Yin;
the Spring and Autumn period replaced the Zhou.

The rites of the Three Dynasties were not the same. Why should antiquity be followed? [13/122/20]

13.7

Great men create and [their] disciples follow. If you understand from whence law and governance arise, then you can respond to the times and alter. If you do not understand the origin of law and governance, even if you accord with antiquity, you will end up in disorder. The legal edicts of the current age should alter with the times; ritual standards should change with customs. Scholars accord with those who came before, inherit their practices, rely on their records, and hold fast to their teachings—thinking that if they oppose them there will be no order. This is like trying to use a square tool to chisel out a round hole: you hope to obtain a proper fit and a fixed starting point, but it is very difficult.

Now the Confucians and Mohists revere the Three Dynasties and Wen and Wu, but they do not put this into practice. This is to affirm in words what they do not practice. They oppose the current age, but they do not reform it; this is to affirm in practice what they oppose. They praise what they affirm but put into practice what they oppose. They thereby expend their days with utmost anxiety yet without contributing anything to governance. They weary their bodies and strain their understanding without giving any aid to the ruler.

Nowadays artisans like to paint demons and detest representing dogs and horses. Why? Because demons do not appear in the world, while dogs and horses can be seen daily.

Now, to maintain oneself [in times of] danger and to govern [in times of] disorder cannot be done without intelligence, but even a fool can praise what came before and revere antiquity. Thus,

a sage-king does not implement useless laws;
a sage-king does not heed unverifiable words. [13/122/20–27]

13.8

As for the *qi* of Heaven and Earth, nothing is as grand as Harmony. Harmony means

the blending of yin and yang,
the dividing of day and night,
and the birth of the myriad things.
In the period of spring there is birth;
in the period of autumn there is maturation;

with birth and maturation, [things] invariably obtain the quintessence of harmony. Therefore, the way of the sages is

lenient yet firm,
strict yet kind,
pliant yet upright,
forceful yet humane.
Too much hardness leads to inflexibility;
too much softness leads to laxity.

Sages properly reside between hardness and softness and thereby obtain the root of the Way.

If they accumulate [only] yin, they will sink;
if they accumulate [only] yang, they will fly away.

With yin and yang conjoined, they thereby perfect harmony. [13/122/29–13/123/2]

Considering the marking cord as a standard,

it can be rolled up and tucked away;
it can be drawn out and stretched;
it can be straightened and followed [with the eye].

Therefore, sages use their bodies to incarnate it. Now,

when lengthened, it is not crooked;
when shortened, it is not deficient;
when straightened, it is not rigid.
Long lasting and not ephemeral:

this is a marking cord! Therefore,

kindness pushed too far is feebleness; being feeble, one has no authority.
Strictness pushed too far is fierceness; being fierce, one is not harmonious.
Loving pushed too far is laxity; being lax, one cannot command.
Punishing pushed too far is cruelty; being cruel, one cannot win affection. [13/123/4–7]

In earlier times, Duke Jian of Qi let go the reins of his country and transferred responsibility to his ministers. They took up the authority; they arrogated power to themselves; they acted selfishly; they formed factions; and the public way was not put into practice. As a result, Chen Chengchang[19] and Chiyi Zipi[20] fell into difficulties; the house of Lü broke off their sacrifices; and the house of Chen took the country. This is what arises from too much softness and feebleness.

Ziyang of Cheng was firm and harsh and fond of punishments. In his use of punishments, he carried them out without pardons. One of his officers broke a bow; fearing retribution and terrified of being put to death, he took advantage of the panic caused by a mad dog and killed Ziyang.[21] This is what firmness and fierceness bring about.

Nowadays, those who do not understand the Way,

seeing the soft and feeble being usurped, turn to acting firmly and harshly;
seeing firmness and harshness being destroyed, turn to acting softly and feebly.

This is due to the lack of a basis within and to one's hearing and seeing being dragged along from the outside. Therefore, to the end of one's days, one will have no stable way of acting. This is like singing without knowing the melody: the low notes will be flat and will not be in tune with the other notes; the high notes will be too sharp and will not harmonize. When it came to the melodies of Han E, Qin Qing, and Xue Tan and the songs of Hou Tong and Wan Sheng:[22] [the music]

aroused their inclinations
and accumulated inside them,

---

19. Chen Chengchang 陳成常 (also known as Tian Chang and Tian Heng), leader of the Tian clan in Qi, served as prime minister under Duke Jian. In 481 B.C.E., he killed the duke and established his brother as Duke Ping. From that point forward, the Tian clan was ever more firmly in control of Qi, until it finally replaced the Lü clan altogether as rulers of Qi in 379 B.C.E.

20. Chiyi Zipi 鴟夷子皮, a follower of Tian Chang identified by some commentators with Fan Li 范蠡, was a fugitive aristocrat from Chu who ultimately settled in Qi after the fall of Yue. See Zhang Shuangdi 1997, 2:1372–74n.15.

21. See 10.95. There the implied reason for Ziyang's death is somewhat different from that presented here.

22. Of these figures, Gao You notes that they were "skilled at singing." See Zhang Shuangdi 1997, 2:1377n.24. Little other lore concerning them survives in extant texts.

welling up and emerging as notes, so that
none failed to be in tune with the pitch pipes,
and all harmonized with the hearts of others [who heard them].

How so? Within themselves they had a basis and a ruling principle that let them hit exactly the low and high notes. They received nothing externally; they themselves were the standard.[23]

Now, if a blind man is walking down a road,
when people say to go left, he goes left;
when people say to go right, he goes right.
If he meets a gentleman, then he will follow an easy path;
if he meets a petty man, he will fall into a ditch.

How so? His eyes have nothing with which to connect.

Therefore,
Wei used both Lou [Bi] and Zhai [Qiang][24] and lost its lands west of the Yellow River;
King Min [of Qi][25] used only Nao Chi[26] and died at Dongmiao:
They did not possess the technique for "driving the chariot" [of state].
King Wen used both Lü Wang and Duke Shi of Zhao and became king;
King Zhuang of Chu used only Sunshu Ao and became hegemon:
They possessed the technique for "driving the chariot" [of state]. [13/123/7–18]

13.9

Singing to stringed instruments and dancing to drums so as make music;
turning, bestowing, diminishing, yielding so as to practice the rites;
having lavish burials and lengthy mourning so as to send off the dead:

23. *Yi biao* 儀表, literally, "sundial and gnomon," but metaphorically the instruments that set a standard of accuracy.

24. Lou Bi 樓鼻 and Zhai Qiang 翟強 were simultaneously employed as high officials of the Wei court under King Ai (r. 318–296 B.C.E.). They felt intense mutual animosity and worked at cross-purposes to each other in planning foreign policy, thereby bringing disaster on Wei. See *Zhanguoce* 317B (James I. Crump, trans., *Chan-kuo Ts'e*, rev. ed., Michigan Monographs in Chinese Studies, vol. 77 [Ann Arbor: Center for Chinese Studies, University of Michigan, 1996], 385–87). The extant text of the *Huainanzi* contains the name of Wu Qi here directly after the contracted names of Lou Bi and Zhai Qiang, but Gu Guangqi 顧廣圻 argues persuasively on the basis of a parallel passage from HFZ 36/117/14–15 that Wu Qi's name must be an extraneous interpolation at this point in the text. See Zhang Shuangdi 1997, 2:1378n.6.

25. King Min of Qi 齊湣王 (r. 300–284 B.C.E.) was exceedingly powerful for a time, expanding his territories through aggressive conquests. He agreed with King Zhao of Qin on their mutual recognition as "thearchs" 帝 of the West and East, respectively. Ultimately, his belligerence brought the enmity of the other states on him, and he was driven from his capital and to death by a combined army under the command of the Yan general Yue Yi.

26. Nao Chi 淖齒 (d. 284 B.C.E.) was a general of Chu employed by King Min as prime minister. According to one account, when King Min was driven from his capital, Nao Chi, in an attempt to curry favor with the victors, seized King Min, pulled out his tendons, and suspended him by them from a bridge at a place called Miao (here Dongmiao).

These were established by Confucius, but Mozi opposed them.
Universal love, honoring the worthy,
esteeming ghosts, opposing fatalism:
These were established by Mozi, but Yangzi[27] opposed them.
Keeping your nature intact, protecting your authenticity,
not allowing things to entangle your form:[28]
These were established by Yangzi, but Mencius[29] opposed them.
In accepting or rejecting [something], people differ, for each has a particular understanding in mind. Thus, right and wrong are based on a particular perspective.
Gain [a particular] perspective, and something is not "wrong";
lose [that particular] perspective, and [the same] thing is not "right."
As for the people of Danxue, Taimeng, Fanzhong, Kongtong, Daxia, Beihu, Qihong, Xiugu:[30] Each have their different rights and wrongs, [and] their customs are mutually opposed.
Ruler and minister, superior and inferior,
husband and wife, father and son:
each has its related service.
What is right for the one is not right for the other;
what is wrong for the one is not wrong for the other.
It is like an axe, hatchet, hammer, and chisel, each having its own function. [13/123/20–25]

In the time of Yu, he listened to proper order by means of the five tones. Suspended [by silk cords] were bells, drums, chimestones, and bells with clappers; and set up [on frames] were small drums, all to greet officers from the four quarters. It was proclaimed:
"If it is someone to teach me the Way, strike the drum.
If it is someone to discuss with me Rightness, strike the bell.
If it is someone to announce to me affairs of state, shake the bells with clappers.
If it is someone to talk to me of troubles, strike the chimestones.
If it is someone with a legal dispute, play the small drums."
At this time,
he would get up ten times during a single meal,
and he would be interrupted three times when washing his hair—

27. Yangzi 楊子 (also known as Yang Zhu 朱 [fourth century B.C.E.]) was a philosopher famously said to have declared that he would not sacrifice a hair off his arm to save the world. Little is known of his origins or history, and he is not reported to have left any writings, but according to the testimony of many early texts, he and his followers were quite influential at the height of the Warring States period.

28. These two lines also appear in 6.1, where they are used in connection with Duke Lu Yang's miraculous victory in a battle with Hann.

29. Mencius 孟子 (also known as Meng Ke 軻 [ca. 390–305 B.C.E.]) was a latter-day disciple of Confucius and a follower of the tradition of Confucius's grandson Zisi. He traveled to many states in search of a sovereign who could become a true king. The text attributed to him, the *Mencius*, ultimately became one of the most influential works of the Confucian tradition.

30. All these are peoples or countries beyond the area of Sinitic culture and political control.

all to labor for the people in the world. If one failed to attain this level of goodness and loyalty, then even talent was insufficient.

In the time of Qin, they

built to great height towers and pavilions,
made extensive gardens and enclosures,
and built far-reaching imperial roads.
They cast bronze figures,
sent out troops,
and brought in grasses and grains.

Taxes, levies, and duties were transported to the treasuries. Young men and grown men were sent

west to Linchao and Didao,
east to Huiji and Fushi,
south to Yuzhang and Guilin,
north to Feihu and Yangyuan.

On the roads, the dead filled the ditches. At this time, those who loyally remonstrated were called inauspicious, and those who took Humaneness and Rightness as their Way were called mad.

When we come down to the time of Emperor Gao,[31] [the founder of the Han],

he survived in the face of destruction;
he continued what had been cut off.

He upheld the great Rightness of the world; he personally worked and grasped a sword so as to beseech August Heaven on behalf of his people. At this time, those in the world who were courageous, brave, valiant, and talented endured sun and rain in the fields and marshes; the vanguard were exposed to arrows and stones; the rearguard fell into ravines and ditches. For every hundred sent out, one would survive in the struggle for the balance of the world. With a determined martiality and a rigorous sincerity, they cut short their allotted life span to a single day. At this time, those who wore sumptuous clothing and wide sashes and who took [the teachings of] the Confucians and Mohists as their Way were taken as unworthy. This continued until the tyranny and disorder was ended and overcome. He

settled [the affairs of] all within the seas;
continued the undertakings of civility
and established the merits of martiality.[32]
He compiled the land registers of the Son of Heaven;
created a [ceremonial] cap for the house of Liu;
unified the Confucians and Mohists of Zou and Lu,
and penetrated the transmitted teachings of the former sages.

31. Emperor Gao 高帝 (also known as Han Gaozu and Liu Bang [265–195 B.C.E., r. 206–195 B.C.E.]) was the founder of the Han dynasty and grandfather of Liu An, eponymous patron of the *Huainanzi*. He rose from humble origins to unite the realm in the wake of the collapse of the Qin dynasty.

32. It also is possible to read these two lines as "He continued the undertakings of [King] Wen and established the merits of [King] Wu"; that is, in establishing the Han dynasty, he balanced the virtues of the two founders of the Zhou.

He displayed the banners of the Son of Heaven,
traveled the great roads,
established the nine pennants,
rang the great bell,
struck the drum,
played "The Pool of Xian,"[33]
[and] raised the shield and battle-ax.

At that time, those who established martiality were viewed with suspicion. In the span of a single era, civility and martiality alternated as female and male; at the right time each was used.

In the present time,
those who practice martiality reject civility.
Those who practice civility reject martiality.

[Supporters of] civility and martiality oppose each other, but they do not understand timely utilization. Each sees only a finger pointing at one corner or angle and does not understand the length and greatness of all the eight points [of the horizon circle]. Therefore,
when one looks to the east, one does not see the western wall;
when one looks to the south, one does not see the north.

Only if one does not incline toward any side will one comprehend everything. [13/123/27–13/124/13]

13.10

The means by which a state survives is the Potency of the Way; the means by which its [ruling] family perishes is the obstruction of its principles.
Yao did not possess even a suburb of one hundred families;
Shun did not possess even enough territory in which to stick an awl;
yet they took possession of the world.
Yu did not possess even a group of ten men;
Tang did not possess even a distribution of seven *li*
yet they ruled as true kings over the Lords of the Land.

King Wen resided in the environs of Qi Zhou, and his territory did not exceed one hundred *li*; yet he was established as the Son of Heaven, for he possessed the Way of a True King.

During the height of Xia Jie and Yin Djou's rule,
where human footsteps trod,
where boats and chariots penetrated,
no [lands] failed to become their prefectures and commandaries. Yet they personally died at the hands of other men and became the laughingstock of the world. These are

33. The "Pool of Xian" (Xianchi 咸池) is the name of a constellation and of a classical musical composition. See 11.2 and 11.9.

cases of their losing sight of the shape of things. Thus, sages observe transformations and look for their [future] verification.

Potency has [times of] waxing and waning;
winds precede the budding of plants.
Thus those who attained the Way of the True King, though [initially] small, invariably became great.
While those who lost sight of the shape of things, though [initially] successful, invariably suffered defeat.
Now when Xia was about to perish, Grand Astrologer Zhong Gu first fled to Shang. In three years, Jie was already lost.
When Yin was about to collapse, Grand Astrologer Xiang Yi first returned home to King Wen. Within a year, [the tyrant] Djou was already lost.[34]

Thus when sages view
the traces of survival and destruction
and the borderline between success and defeat,
they do not [resort to]
reading animals' cries in the wilderness
or [divining] the [auspiciousness of] *jia* and *zi* days.

Today,
those who are called strong prevail, measuring their territories and calculating their population.
Those who are called wealthy benefit, measuring their grain and weighing their gold.

This being the case,
among rulers of ten thousand chariots, there were none who did not become hegemon or king.
Among states of one thousand chariots there were none who were not destroyed or imperiled.

Since the traces of survival and destruction are like this, they are easy to recognize; even a foolish husband or daft wife could assess them.

Viscount Xiang of Zhao became preeminent because of the walls of Jinyang;
Earl Zhi was captured for the territory of the three Jin;
King Min was destroyed for the great state of Qi;
Tian Dan[35] had merit because of Jimo.
Thus, when it comes to the destruction of a state, even if the state is large, it does not suffice to depend on its size.
When it comes to putting the Way into effect, even if the state is small, it does not suffice to take it lightly.

34. The flight of the grand astrologers from these failing dynasties was the first sign of their imminent collapse. The stories of Zhong Gu 終古 and Xiang Yi 向藝 (called Xiang Zhi in that text) are related in *Lüshi chunqiu* 16.1.

35. Tian Dan 田單 was a general of Qi during the reign of King Min. When Qi was overrun by the army of Yue Yi in 284 B.C.E., Tian Dan successfully defended the city of Jimo, the last piece of Qi territory to resist the invaders' onslaught.

Looking at it from this perspective,

survival lies in obtaining the Way; it does not lie in being large.

Destruction lies in losing the Way; it does not lie in being small.

The *Odes* states:

"So he turned his gaze west,
and here made his dwelling place."[36]

This says that [the High God] left Yin and moved to Zhou.

Thus the ruler of a chaotic state

strives to enlarge his territory but does not strive for Humaneness and Rightness;

strives to elevate his position but does not strive for the Way and its Potency.

This is to lose that by which one survives

and to create that by which one perishes.

Thus,

when Jie was taken captive at Jiaomen, he was not able to negate what he had put into effect; he [only] regretted that he had been unable to slay Tang at Xia Tai.

When Djou was fettered at Xuanshi, he did not reverse his errors; he [only] regretted that he had been unable to chastise King Wen at Qiaoli.

These two rulers enjoyed the positional advantage of strength and size, but cultivating the Way of Humaneness and Rightness, Tang and Wu sought out their faults and did not give up. What plans did they dare think up?

If above you disorder the brightness of the three luminaries

and below you lose the hearts of the myriad people,

even if you are a Tang or Wu, who would not be capable of usurping you?

Now,

if you do not look for [flaws] within yourself

but, on the contrary, search for them in others,

the world will be without a single Tang or Wu. If you kill a single person, that is something that will have repercussions for generations.

Moreover,

the reason why Tang and Wu, though occupying a small and weak position, could become king was because they possessed the Way.

The reason why Jie and Djou, though occupying a strong and great position, in the end witnessed their usurpation, was because they lacked the Way.

Now,

if you do not practice the means by which one becomes a king

and, on the contrary, increase the means by which one is usurped,

this is the path of speedy destruction. [13/124/15–13/125/6]

When King Wu vanquished Yin, he wanted to construct a palace on the Wuhang Mountains. The Duke of Zhou exclaimed: "It is not permissible! The Wuhang Mountains are a rugged, blocked, precipitous, and sheer place. If we conduct ourselves so

36. *Odes* 241, verse 1.

that our Moral Potency can cover over them, those in the world who offer up tribute and knowledge will turn themselves toward us. If we engage in violent and disorderly conduct, the world will attack us when we are in difficulty." For this reason, in thirty-six generations there was not [a single] usurpation. It can be said of the Duke of Zhou that he was able to "grasp when enough was enough." [13/125/8–10]

13.11

In days of old, the *Documents of Zhou*[37] had a saying that read:

"[Sometimes] one elevates words and denigrates practicalities;
[sometimes] one denigrates words and elevates practicalities.
Elevating words is the norm;
denigrating words is expedient."

This is the technique for surviving in the face of destruction. [But] only a sage is capable of understanding expediency.

To speak and invariably elicit trust [and] to anticipate and invariably elicit a match are examples of lofty conduct in the world. When his father stole a sheep, "Straight Body" testified against him.[38] When Wei Sheng and his wife were to meet, he died on account of it.[39] Being upright and testifying against one's father or being trustworthy and dying for one's woman—although this may be upright and trustworthy, who would think it honorable?

Now when the Three Armies feign orders,[40] the trespass is great indeed! [But] when Duke Mu of Qin raised an army to attack Zheng, he passed through Zhou and headed east. A merchant from Zheng named Xian Gao was heading west to sell his oxen. On the road he encountered the Qin forces between Zhou and Zheng, whereupon he feigned orders from the viscount of Zheng, feted them with twelve oxen, hosted them, and withdrew, thereby saving the state of Zheng.[41] Thus events have their causes, so that

trustworthiness, contrary to expectation, might go too far,
and prevarication, contrary to expectation, may be meritorious.

---

37. According to tradition, there were many more texts from previous dynasties than those anthologized into the extant *Documents*. The cited passage is presumably from one of the excised and subsequently lost *Documents of Zhou*.

38. This figure appears in *Analects* 13.18, in which the Duke of She boasts of him to Confucius. Confucius replies that where he comes from, those deemed "straight" cover up for their kin rather than informing on them.

39. Wei Sheng 尾生 refused to leave the spot of their appointed rendezvous, even though the water in the river was rising, and eventually drowned. See also 16.100 and 17.242.

40. *Jiao ming* 矯命; that is, when they act as if orders have been issued when in fact none have been. "Three Armies" is a conventional term for the armed forces of a state.

41. A longer version of this story appears in 12.40 and another in 18.12. See also LSCQ 16.4/93/20–16.4/94/11; and *Zuozhuan*, Xi 33. The merchant pretended to be an official ambassador from the court of Zheng, sent to greet the Qin troops. The Qin army, believing that the element of surprise had been lost, then abandoned its campaign.

What does it mean to abandon ritual yet be greatly meritorious? In the days of old, when King Gong of Chu[42] [and Duke Li of Jin[43]] battled at Yinling,[44] [Lü Qi[45] shot an arrow at King Gong, hit him in the eye, and took him captive.][46] Shen Wang, Yang Youji, Huang Shuaiwei, and Gong Sunbing were in the midst of recapturing their sovereign when, in his fright, King Gong physically lost consciousness. Only when Huang Shuaiwei raised his foot to kick him in the gut did King Gong return to consciousness. Angry that Huang Shuaiwei had strayed from ritual protocol, King Gong aroused himself and stood up, and the four ministers [were able to] carry him off and leave.[47]

In the days of old, Cang Wurao[48] married a wife who was beautiful and thus gave her to his elder brother. This is what is called being loyal and loving yet behaving incorrectly.

For this reason, when sages assess whether an affair be crooked or straight, they bend or stretch themselves and curl or straighten alongside it. They do not adhere to a constant standard, so sometimes they bend and other times they stretch. When they are weak and yielding like a thin sheaf of grass, they do not take or snatch. When they are resolute, strong, fierce, and bold and their wills are oppressive like gray clouds, they do not brag or boast. They thereby avail themselves of timeliness and respond to alterations. [3/125/12–22]

In the intercourse between ruler and minister, there is the bending of the knee and the humble salutation [of the subordinate], employing the rites of mutual respect. But when it comes to being pressed by a calamity, so that one raises a foot to kick one's superior in the gut, no one in the world can repudiate such an action. For this reason, where loyalty is [securely] present, ritual norms are not sufficient to challenge it.

When the filial son serves his father, with pleasing expression and submissive posture he offers him his sash and lays out his shoes. But if the father is drowning, he grabs him by the hair and pulls him [out of the water]; this is not because he is presuming to be arrogant or haughty but because he means to rescue his father from death. Thus, when a father is drowning, to grab him by the hair and, when a ruler is celebrating, to call him by name—these things derive from the power of circumstance and so cannot be otherwise. This is what establishes the basis for expediency.

---

42. King Gong of Chu 楚恭王 reigned from 590 to 560 B.C.E.

43. Duke Li of Jin 晉厲公 reigned from 580 to 573 B.C.E.

44. The actual name of the historic battle site was Yanling 鄢陵. It is rendered as "Yin" 陰 in the *Huainanzi* because the two characters were homophones in the Han. See Zhang Shuangdi 1997, 2:1407n.13.

45. Lü Qi 呂騎 was a knight of Jin.

46. This line is currently not in the extant text but is contained in the Gao You commentary. Most modern scholars agree it has been mistakenly moved from the text into the commentary and should be replaced here. See Lau, HNZ, 125n.5; and Zhang Shuangdi 1997, 2:1404n.14.

47. The battle of Yanling took place in 575 B.C.E. It is recounted in *Zuozhuan*, Cheng 16. The *Zuo*'s account does not contain the episode of King Gong's capture, though it does report that he was shot in the eye by Lü Qi. Shen Wang, Yang Youji, and the others all were grandees of Chu.

48. Cang Wurao 蒼吾繞, according to Gao You, was a man who lived at the time of Confucius. See Zhang Shuangdi 1997, 2:1404n.17.

Thus Confucius said:

"A person might be suitable as someone with whom to study and yet not suitable as someone with whom to pursue the Way;

a person might be suitable as someone with whom to pursue the Way and yet not suitable as someone with whom to take a stand;

a man might be suitable as someone with whom to take a stand and yet not suitable as someone with whom to exercise expediency."[49]

Expediency is something the sages alone perceive. Thus,

those who [first] disobey [ritual norms] but ultimately accord with them are said to understand expediency.

Those who first accord [with ritual norms] but later oppose them are said to lack an understanding of expediency.

For those who do not understand expediency, goodness conversely [appears to be] ugliness. Thus, ritual is the efflorescence of reality, but [people] mistakenly take it to be [mere] ornamentation. [So] when they are in the midst of being unexpectedly pressed by difficulties, exhausted and agitated, they have nothing to use [to cope with them]. For this reason, sages use

[external] ornamentation to communicate with the world

but [inner] reality to pursue affairs in a suitable way.

They are not bound by the path of [a single line of] footprints, becoming fixed and rigid so as to fail to transform. For this reason,

their unsuccessful affairs are few,

but their successful affairs are numerous;

their commands and directives fill the world, and no one can deny them. [13/125/24–13/126/3]

13.12

The orangutan knows the past but does not know the future;

the male goose knows the future but does not know the past.

Such is the distinction between long and short.

In the days of old, Chang Hong served as a calendrical specialist to the house of Zhou. With regard to the *qi* of Heaven and Earth, the movements of the sun and moon, the alterations of the winds and rain, and the calculations of the calendar, there was nothing he failed to comprehend. Yet he was incapable of self-knowledge and died by dismemberment when torn apart by the chariot.

Su Qin[50] was a common mendicant, with no more than leather sandals and the

49. *Analects* 9.30.

50. Su Qin 蘇秦 (d. 284 B.C.E.) was a statesman, wandering persuader, and diplomat who figures in many colorful stories from the Warring States period. A native of Zhou, he reportedly rose to hold the prime minister's seal of six states simultaneously, which he wielded in a failed attempt to forge an

open sky for his umbrella, yet be manipulated the rulers of ten thousand chariots and won the admiration of the Lords of the Land. But he did not avoid the calamity of being split by a chariot.

King Yan of Xu,[51] with compassion and kindness as his bedding and clothes, personally practiced Humaneness and Rightness, and [those who resided in] no fewer than thirty-two states [traveled] overland to hold an audience with him. Yet he perished and his state was destroyed, with his sons and grandsons devoid of offspring.[52]

Grand Minister Zhong[53] assisted and aided King Goujian of Yue, avenging his grievances and cleansing his shame, capturing Fuchai, and opening up for cultivation several thousand *li* of land. Yet he fell on the "Shu Lou" sword[54] and died.

These all are examples of comprehending the linchpin of order and disorder yet not understanding the basis of keeping one's nature intact.

Thus,

Chang Hong understood the Way of Heaven, but he did not understand human affairs;

Su Qin understood expedient strategies, but he did not understand bad and good fortune;

King Yan of Xu understood Humaneness and Rightness, but he did not understand timeliness;

and Grand Minister Zhong understood loyalty, but he did not understand strategy. [13/126/5–12]

Sages are not like this.

They assess the age and determine their actions accordingly;

they weigh affairs and devise their strategies accordingly.

For this reason,

they propagate them throughout the [vastness of] the world, but they are not isolated;

they contain them within the [smallness of] a *xun* and *chang*, but they are not obstructed. [13/126/14–15]

---

anti-Qin alliance. He was ultimately caught spying on behalf of Yan in the state of Qi and met his grisly end. His biography is recorded in *Shiji* 69.

51. King Yan of Xu 徐偃王 was a semilegendary figure variously identified in early sources. The *Shiji* has him as the leader of a non-Chinese people in south-central China who rose in rebellion against King Mu of Zhou. The *Hanfeizi* has him as the leader of a Chinese vassal state during the Spring and Autumn period.

52. According to *Hanfeizi* 49, King Wen of Chu (r. 689–676 B.C.E.) destroyed Xu out of fear of King Yan's growing power.

53. Grand Minister Zhong 大夫種 (also known as Wen 文 Zhong) was a native of Chu who devised a plan on behalf of King Goujian of Yue (then held captive in Wu), explaining how he might avert the destruction of his state by bribing the prime minister of Wu. After Goujian was restored to his own throne, he was persuaded by slander to order Zhong to commit suicide.

54. Shu Lou 屬鏤 is the name of a treasured sword. The *Huainanzi* presumably means that Goujian presented Zhong with this sword, with which to commit suicide. Both the *Shiji* and the *Hanfeizi* report that this sword was presented by King Fuchai of Yue to his minister Zixu for the purpose of committing suicide. See Zhang Shuangdi 1997, 2:1416n.8.

13.13

When [a ruler] causes the world to be desolate and chaotic,
Rites and Rightness are cut off;
bonds and ties are dispensed with.
The strong take advantage of the weak;
attackers force the submission of the vanquished;
minister and ruler lack hierarchical distinction;
the noble and the humble lack deferential order;
armor and helmets become infested with lice and fleas;
swallows and sparrows roost in the tents and canopies;

so that the soldiers never get any rest. At that point, he may begin to adopt a cautious demeanor and [conduct] reverent rites, but [it will be too late and] he will invariably be destroyed with no possibility of being restored.

When [a ruler causes] the world to be secure and peaceful,
administration and instruction are harmonious and equitable;
the one hundred names [i.e., the common people] are reverent and affable;
superiors and subordinates are mutually affectionate.

At that point, [the ruler] might begin to establish an atmosphere of leniency. [If so,] he will embolden the courageous and strong and so will be unable to avoid falling subject to the laws of those who have authority.

For this reason,
sages can be yin, and they can be yang;
they can be weak, and they can be strong;
in tempo with the times, they are active or still;
in accordance with the inner substance of things, they establish merit.
When things become active, they know their reversions;
when affairs sprout forth, they anticipate their alterations;
when things transform, they act in their image;
when things move, they respond to them;

this is why to the end of their days, they are effective and free of troubles. [13/126/15–20]

13.14

Precedents and affairs [have]
some that can be practiced but cannot be discussed,
some that can be discussed but cannot be practiced,
some that are easy to do but difficult to perfect,
some that are difficult to perfect but easy to ruin.

What is meant by "can be practiced but cannot be discussed" is pursuing and abandoning.

What is meant by "can be discussed but cannot be practiced" is lying and cheating.
What is "easy to do but difficult to perfect" is management.
What is "difficult to perfect but easy to ruin" is a reputation.

These four tendencies are things that the sages uniquely see and where they focus their minds.

Curling up to the shortness of an inch or extending to the length of a foot are things the sages do.
Minimizing wrongs and maximizing rights are things the Superior Man practices.
The Duke of Zhou was saddled with the burden of killing a brother,
and Duke Huan of Qi had a reputation for competing with other states.
Yet the Duke of Zhou relied on Rightness to compensate for his shortcomings,
and Duke Huan relied on his merit to eradicate evil,

so that both became worthies.

Now if on account of others' insignificant errors, you conceal their significant goodness, the world will be bereft of sage-kings and worthy ministers.

Thus,

if at the center of the eye there is a blemish, it does not harm one's vision, [though] it cannot be cauterized by burning.
If at the center of the throat there is a defect, it does not harm one's breathing, [though] it cannot be cut away.
The mounds and hillocks along the riverbank are too numerous to be counted, but [the riverbank] is still considered level.
When water surges to give rise to waves, the high and the low approach each other and can differ [in height] by a *xun* or a *chang*, yet we consider the [water] to be level.

In days of old, Caozi[55] commanded an army on behalf of Lu. Three times in battle he was not victorious and lost thousands of *li* in territory. If Caozi had persisted in his plans and had not reversed course, had [planted his] feet without budging, he [might have] had his throat cut at Chenzhong or ended his days as the captive commander of a defeated army. But Caozi was not embarrassed by his defeat and did not die in shame and without merit. [Instead], during the interstate meeting at Ke, he took a sword three feet long and pointed it at the midriff of Duke Huan [of Qi]. Thus the effects of three defeats in battle were reversed in the course of a morning. His courage was heralded throughout the world, and his accomplishments were established in the state of Lu.[56]

---

55. Caozi 曹子 (also known as Cao Mo 曹沫) was a general of Lu during the reign of Duke Zhuang (r. 693–622 B.C.E.). His biography is included among those of the "assassin retainers" in *Shiji* 86, and a text bearing his name was recently discovered among a group of bamboo manuscripts looted from a tomb of ancient Chu.

56. The meeting at Ke occurred in 681 B.C.E. It is recorded in the *Zuozhuan*, Zhuang 13, although

Guan Zhong assisted Prince Jiu,[57] but with no good outcome. It cannot be said that he was wise. He escaped and hastily fled, failing to die during [his lord's] troubles. It cannot be said that he was brave.[58]

When you are bound and tied in fetters and manacles and cannot avoid being shamed, it cannot be said that you are lucky.

If you correspond to these three [kinds of] conduct, the commonly clad [i.e., the people] will not offer their friendship, and the ruler of men will be bereft of true ministers. Yet Guan Zhong avoided the inside of prisons, established the government of the state of Qi, nine times united the Lords of the Land, and unified and rectified the world. If Guang Zhong had sought death by sacrificing his life and had not [been willing to] reverse his plans, what hegemonic merit would there have been in this? [13/126/22–13/127/6]

Now when the ruler of men assesses his ministers, if he
does not calculate their significant achievements
or evaluate their overall conduct
but [instead] seeks out their petty merits,
he will lose [the services of] worthies in untold numbers.

Thus,

when someone possesses generous amounts of Moral Potency, none notes their trifling matters,

and when someone possesses a great reputation, none faults their small excuses.

A puddle in a cow's hoofprint[59] cannot [suffice to] give birth to a sturgeon.
A bee's honeycomb cannot hold a goose egg.[60]
A small form is not sufficient to embrace a large body. [13/127/8–10]

13.15

Now, it is the essential quality of humankind to possess shortcomings.

Truly,

if in general they are correct, even if they commit minor transgressions, it will not be sufficient to be considered burdensome.

---

no mention is made in that text of the dramatic events involving Cao Mo. Many other early texts inscribe this story, however. See, for example, *Lüshi chunqiu* 19.7; and *Guanzi* 18.

57. Prince Jiu 公子糾 (d. 685) was the older brother of Duke Huan of Qi and a potential heir to the ducal throne of that state. When their older brother Duke Xiang died, Prince Jiu and Duke Huan fought over who would succeed him. Prince Jiu ultimately lost, dying as a prisoner in Lu.

58. Guan Zhong originally served Prince Jiu. Upon the prince's death, Guan accepted service as prime minister of Qi under Duke Huan. See *Guanzi* 18, 19; and *Zuozhuan*, Zhuang 8.

59. The same vivid image occurs in Sanskrit in the word *gospada*. See Zhu Qingshi, *Some Linguistic Evidence for Early Cultural Exchange Between China and India*, Sino-Platonic Papers, no. 66 (Philadelphia: Department of East Asian Languages and Civilizations, University of Pennsylvania, 1995), 3–5.

60. Variants of this proverb appear in 2.10 and 9.11.

If in general they are incorrect, even if they have some rustic accomplishments, it would not be enough to [qualify them for] a great promotion.
Yan Zhuoju[61] was a great bandit of [Mount] Liangfu, but he became a loyal minister to the state of Qi.
Duangan Mu[62] was a swindler in the state of Jin, but he became a teacher to the Duke of Wen.
Meng Mao[63] married his sister-in-law and had five sons by her. Yet when he became minister in Wei, he quelled its danger and relieved its suffering.
Jing Yang[64] was licentious and drunken, unloosing hairpins and forcing himself on his wives, yet he awed the Lords of the Land into submission.

These four men all possessed weaknesses, yet their meritorious reputation was not eradicated, for their general conduct was efficacious.[65]

Ji'ai[66] and Chen Zhongzi[67] established their purity with their unyielding conduct. They would not enter the court of a corrupt ruler; they would not eat food [produced during] an unrighteous age. Subsequently they starved to death and died. Were they not able to survive in the face of danger or continue [their lineages] in the face of being cut off? As their trivial acts of purity expanded, the significance of their general conduct contracted.

Those who are small-minded and cautious do not enjoy great accomplishments.
Those who calculate their actions do not find acceptance by the masses.
A large-bodied person is long in the joints.
A person with a long stride can go high and far.

From antiquity to the present, [even among] the Five Emperors and Three Kings, there were none who perfected their conduct. Thus the *Changes* says: "Should minor transgressions prosper, beneficial and lucky."[68] This means that there is

---

61. Yan Zhuoju 顏啄聚 was an intriguing figure mentioned in many early texts about whom little concretely is known. He is said to have studied with Confucius and to have assisted Tian Chang in his rise to power in the state of Qi.

62. Duangan Mu 段干木 was a celebrated recluse. See 19.3.

63. Meng Mao 孟卯 (also known as Mang 芒 Mao) served as minister of education under King Zhao of Wei (r. 295–277 B.C.E.). *Zhanguoce* 309 records his meritorious service to Wei. See Crump, *Chan-kuo Ts'e*, 390–91.

64. Jing Yang 景陽 was a general of Chu. In 275 B.C.E., he led an expedition to lift the siege of Handan by the armies of Qin. *Zhanguoce* 212 records a clever stratagem with which he caused the armies of Yan and Qi to withdraw without giving battle. See Crump, *Chan-kuo Ts'e*, 261–62. This may be what the *Huainanzi* means by "awed the Lords of the Land."

65. This passage, which continues chap. 13's emphasis on *quan* 權, "balance" or "equilibrium," recalls *Gongyang zhuan*, Duke Huan 11.4, where it states, "one eventually achieves goodness, although at an initial stage one has acted contrary to constant standards."

66. This is Gongxi Ai 公晳哀 (courtesy title Ji'ai 季哀 or Jici 季次), a disciple of Confucius. *Shiji* 67:2209 records Confucius's praise of Gongxi Ai as the only one of his disciples who refused on principle to serve in government.

67. Chen Zhongzi 陳仲子 was a recluse knight of Qi during the fourth century B.C.E., famous for absolutely refusing to sully himself with the vulgar concerns of politics or commerce. He is the subject of a long anecdote in *Mencius* 3B.10.

68. *Changes*, hexagram 62, *Xiaoguo* 小過.

not a single person who does not err, but one hopes [the errors] will not be great. [13/127/10–21]

Yao, Shun, Tang, and Wu were eminent rulers of their age.
Duke Huan of Qi and Duke Wen of Jin were the martial and brave of the Five Hegemons.[69]

Yet

Yao had a reputation for being unloving;
Shun slandered his humble father;
Tang and Wu were implicated in liberating murderers,
and the Five Hegemons[70] produced schemes [that led to] tyranny and disorder.[71]

For this reason, the Superior Man does not place the entire blame [for something] on a single person.

If he is square and correct, [the Superior Man] does not make mincemeat of him;
If he is incorruptible and upright, [the Superior Man] does not slice him to death;
If he is expansive and penetrating, [the Superior Man] does not slander him;
If he is civil or martial, [the Superior Man] does not upbraid him.
When he makes demands on others, he does so in accordance with their strength.
When he reforms himself, he does so in accordance with the Way's Potency.
If you make demands on others in accordance with their strength, it is easy to get what you want;
if you cultivate yourself by relying on the Way's Potency, it is difficult to do.
If it is difficult to do, then carrying it out will be lofty;
if it is easy to get what you want, then seeking it will suffice.

Now,

[even] the jade half disk of the Xiahou clan[72] cannot be without [some flaw] on examination;
the Moonglow Pearl cannot be without [some imperfection] on classification.

Yet they are [among] the great treasures of the world. Why? Their slight imperfections do not suffice to obstruct their great beauty.

---

69. Various lists of the "Five Hegemons" are recorded in early texts. Gao You identifies them as Duke Huan of Qi, Duke Wen of Jin, Duke Xiang of Song (r. 650–637 B.C.E.), King Zhuang of Chu, and Duke Mu of Qin (Zhang Shuangdi 1997, 2:1429n.18). Other lists include King Helu of Wu (r. 514–496 B.C.E.) and King Goujian of Yue rather than the former rulers of Song and Qin.

70. Lau renders this phrase 伍伯, but Zhang Shuangdi 1997, 2:1424, reads 五伯, an alternative label for the "Five Hegemons" indicated earlier in the text by the phrase 五霸. As the Gao You commentary to this line indicates, the Five Hegemons are clearly the subject.

71. This reflects the ambivalent normative position of the Five Hegemons in early literature. Although they were praised as dynamic leaders, they also were denigrated as expedient operators who usurped the legitimate authority of the Zhou kings. See app. A.

72. A famous jade ritual object that was part of the ducal regalia of the state of Lu. See 7.6, 16.90, and 17.2.

Now if you set your mind on others' shortcomings and forget others' strengths yet seek to obtain worthies throughout the empire, it will be difficult indeed! [13/127/22–27]

13.16

Now [regarding]

Baili Xi's cooking the calf,
Yi Yin's shouldering the tripod,
The Grand Duke's drumming on his sword,
and Ning Qi's singing a song in the *shang* mode:

The beauty of these things was inherent [in the acts themselves]. [But] the masses saw [only] their humble and lowly position and treated them with rudeness; they did not recognize the larger meaning of their actions and considered them to be worthless. But when [these men] rose to the rank of Son of Heaven or [one of] the Three Dukes or became a Lord of the Land or worthy minister, only then did [the masses] begin to believe that such people differed from the average person.

Now take

[a cook] who emerges from amid the tripods and stands,
[a glutton] who comes out of the butcher's or wine seller's shop,
[a cowherd] who rises from below a cow's horn,
[a felon] liberated from bonds and fetters:
Clean him up with a hot bath,
warm him by a fire,
and set him up at the pinnacle of the present dynasty
or rely on him to take the position of one of the Three Dukes;
at home he will not feel shame before the great families of state,
while abroad he will not be abashed before the Lords of the Land;

his tally of office and his positional power will be inwardly in conformity.

Thus as for knowing that someone is worthy before his achievements have been manifested, only Yao knew Shun. But to know someone is worthy after his achievements have been accomplished and his tasks brought to success, all the people in the marketplace [then] knew Shun. Now if on account of this [i.e., Yao's extraordinary ability to recognize merit], you abandon measures and methods and seek out good men in the morning market or among weeds and thickets, you would surely miss many [competent] people. Why is this so? You may imitate them in searching but you will not know the means by which they chose people. [13/128/1–7]

13.17

Now what confuse and bewilder people of the present age are the comparative categories of things.

What bedazzle and baffle the masses are things that are deceptively alike in a doubtful and suspicious way.

Thus,

fierceness is [sometimes] categorized as "knowledge," but it is [fundamentally] not knowledge.

Foolishness is [sometimes] categorized as "humaneness," but it is [fundamentally] not humaneness.

Stupidity is [sometimes] categorized as "courage," but it is [fundamentally] not courage.

If we could make the comparative differences among people [as evident as]

the comparison between jade and stone

or the comparison between beauty and ugliness,

then assessing people would be easy. Now what confuses people is like

makino being taken for *Ligusticum*,

or *Cnidi fructus* being taken for deer parsley,[73]

they all look like one another.

Thus,

a swordsmith might wonder whether a sword resembles [the famous sword] Moye, but only [a master like] Ou the Smelter can name its type.

A jade worker might be in the dark about whether a jade resembles Bilu [azure jade], but only [a master like] Qi Dun[74] will not lose sight of its essential qualities.

A benighted lord might be confused by seductive ministers who say that a petty man resembles a Superior Man, but only a sage can see what is obscured, thereby knowing what is evident.

Thus,

if a snake raises its head a foot, its length can be known;

if an elephant reveals its tusk, its size can be assessed.

If Zhuyongzi of Xue[75] saw [a piece of] a sword the size of a fingernail,[76] he could judge the sharpness of the sword.

---

73. All these are medicinal herbs indigenous to East Asia. According to Gao You, the members of each pair look alike but have different scents. See Zhang Shuangdi 1997, 2:1436–37n.7.

74. Qi Dun 猗頓, a poor knight of Lu during the Spring and Autumn period, became wealthy raising cattle and sheep. He was renowned as the world's greatest connoisseur of jade.

75. The identity of this figure is unclear. A displaced scion of the ducal house of Wu bore the name Zhuyong 燭庸, but he defected to Chu and was enfeoffed at Shu. See *Shiji* 31. A knight of Qi named Zhuyong Zhiyue 之越 is mentioned in *Zuozhuan*, Ai 23. Xue ultimately became a vassalage of Qi, but at that time it was still an independent state. Thus the Zhuyongzi of the *Huainanzi* may be a different person entirely.

76. Accepting Yu Yue's proposed emendation. See Lau, HNZ, 128n.5.

If the water of the Zai and Sheng rivers were combined, Yu Er[77] and Yi Ya would taste one mouthful, and their respective flavors [lit., "bitter and sweet"] would be recognized.

Thus when sages assess worthiness, they observe a single action and [from it] distinguish worthiness or worthlessness.

Confucius refused the fief of Granary Hill, [and] in the end he would not steal emolument;[78]

Xu You yielded the empire, [and] in the end he did not value land or title.

Thus,

those who have never been burned [even so] do not dare to grasp fire because they recognize that it burns;

those who have never been injured [even so] do not dare grasp a blade because they recognize that it injures.

Looking at the issue from this perspective, the observer can assess what has yet to unfold; and by watching trifling things, it will suffice to know significant entities.

Thus [this is] the Way of assessing others:

If they are noble, observe what they acclaim;
if they are wealthy, observe what they bestow;
if they are exhausted, observe what they refuse to accept;
if they are lowly, observe what they refuse to do;
if they are impoverished, observe what they refuse to take.
Watch them when pressed by hardship to know their courage;
arouse them with happiness and joy to observe their steadfastness;
entice them with goods and property to assess their Humaneness;
startle them with fear and loathing to know their self-restraint.

Then the feelings of others will be fully [apparent to you]. [13/128/9–21]

13.18

In antiquity,

those who excelled at rewarding rewarded the few, and the many were encouraged;

those who excelled at punishing punished sparingly, and licentiousness was stopped;

those who excelled at giving used restraint and put Potency into practice;

those who excelled at taking brought in the many and prevented resentment.

77. Yu Er 臾兒 was a renowned gourmet of ancient times. *Zhuangzi* 8 calls him Yu 俞 Er. Xu Shen identifies him as having lived during the time of the Yellow Emperor. See Zhang Shuangdi 1997, 2:1439n.14.

78. *Lüshi chunqiu* 19.2 reports that Duke Jing of Qi offered this fief to Confucius during an audience, but Confucius declined because the duke had rewarded him before putting any of his advice into practice.

When Viscount Xiang of Wei was surrounded in Jinyang, he broke the siege and rewarded the five men who were meritorious, and Gao He[79] was the first to be rewarded. Those who flanked him to the right and left exclaimed: "As for the hardships at Jinyang, [Gao] did not possess any great merit, yet today he is the first to be rewarded. Why?"

Viscount Xiang of Wei responded, "During the siege of Jinyang, our altars to the soil and grain were endangered, and our state and families were imperiled. Among our numerous officials, there was not one who did not harbor a proud and arrogant heart, [but] only He did not stray from the ritual pertaining to ruler and minister." Thus through the rewarding of this one man, those who served as ministers in the world, without exception to the end of their lives, showed loyalty to their ruler. This is an example of rewarding the few to encourage the many.[80]

When King Wei of Qi set up the grand *ding* vessel at the center of his court, he upbraided the commander of Wuyan, saying: "Your acclaim daily reaches my ears. [Yet] having examined your actions, I find that your cultivated fields are overgrown with weeds, your granaries are empty, and your prisons are full. You rely on treachery to serve me." Then [the king] had him boiled alive. In the state of Qi for thirty-two years thereafter, none who traveled the roads and byways picked up any items left on the road. This is an example of punishing sparingly so that treachery is stopped.

Duke Mu of Qin was traveling abroad when his chariot broke down, and his right-hand assistant lost control of the horses. Some local rustics caught them. Duke Mu of Qin followed them in pursuit to the southern slope of Mount Ji. There he observed that the local rustics had just cooked the horses and were eating them. Duke Mu of Qin exclaimed: "If you eat the meat of a fine steed but do not follow it with a drink of wine, you will harm yourselves. I fear this harm will befall you." Then he passed out drinks and went away.

That same year, Duke Mu of Qin waged a war with Duke Hui of Jin at Hann[yuan]. The Jin forces surrounded Duke Mu's chariot. Just as Liang Youma grabbed the reins of the two outside horses of the four-abreast team and was about to take Duke Mu captive, the three hundred or so men who had dined on the meat of Duke Mu's horse, disregarding death, fought to the bitter end below Duke Mu's chariot. Subsequently they defeated Jin and, contrary to expectation, captured Duke Hui and returned home. This is an example of using moderation to put Potency into practice.[81]

---

79. Gao He 高赫 was a knight in the retinue of Viscount Xiang, identified in the *Lüshi chunqiu* as Gao She 赦.

80. This anecdote also appears in 18.10, *Lüshi chunqiu* 14.4, and *Hanfeizi*, chap. 36, "Refutations, Part 1" (*nan yi* 難一). See HFZ 36/115/9–20. *Hanfeizi* takes this as an example of not rewarding officials correctly. See the introduction to chap. 19, where we translate the *Hanfeizi* version.

81. An abbreviated version of this story appears in 20.9 with a somewhat different moral. See also the version in *Lüshi chunqiu* 5, in which Duke Mu explains to the rustics that if they eat the meat of a piebald horse without taking a drink of liquor afterward, it will be dangerous to their health. See Knoblock and Riegel 2000, 202–3.

Duke Huan of Qi was hoping to launch a punitive expedition. His armor and weapons being insufficient, he directed those who had committed serious crimes to contribute armor of rhinoceros hide and a glaive. Those who had committed light offenses were fined gold in accordance with [the severity of their crime]. Those who brought suit [against someone] and did not win had to contribute one quiver of arrows.[82] The common people all were pleased by this. So they straightened plant stems to make arrows and smelted metal to make knives, in order to attack the unjust and punish those who had lacked the Way. Thereupon [Duke Huan] became hegemon of the world.[83] This is an example of bringing in the many and so preventing resentment.

Thus sages
 accord with what the people like and thereby encourage them to do good;
 accord with what the people hate and therefore put a stop to wantonness.
 When they reward a single person, the whole world praises them;
 when they punish a single person, the whole world fears them.
Thus,
 the best rewards are not wasteful;
 the best punishments are not excessive.
 When Confucius punished Vice-Director Mao,[84] evil in the state of Lu was obstructed;[85] when Zi Chan punished Deng Xi,[86] wantonness in the state of Zheng was stopped.[87]
 They used what was near to assess what was distant;
 they used what was small to know what was great.
Thus sages preserve frugality and govern broadly. This is what is meant. [13/128/23–13/129/11]

13.19

In the world,
 nothing is easier than doing good,
 and nothing is harder than doing evil.
 What is meant by "doing good" is to be quiescent and non-active;

82. Yang Shuda and Yu Dacheng propose emendations to this section of text based on *Guo yu* and *Guanzi* parallels. See Lau, HNZ, 129n.2; and Zhang Shuangdi 1997, 2:1445n.15.

83. Parallels to this anecdote appear in *Guanzi* 19 and 20 and in *Guo yu* 6.

84. Vice-Director Mao 少正卯 (d. 496 B.C.E.) was a grandee of Lu who, according to *Shiji* 47:1917, had "disordered" the government of Lu. Confucius executed Vice-Director Mao, even though he was quite popular, because he combined all five types of wicked character singled out by the ancient sage-kings for extirpation.

85. This anecdote is recorded in *Xunzi* 28, *Shuo yuan* 15, and *Yantie lun* 58.

86. Deng Xi 鄧析 (ca. 545–501 B.C.E.) was a legal reformer and logician of Zheng. A text bearing his name is extant but is generally thought to be a later forgery.

87. Zichan's execution of Deng Xi is recounted in *Lüshi chunqiu* 18.4.

what is meant by "doing evil" is to be impulsive and harbor many desires.
If you accord with your feelings and eschew excess, there will be nothing to entice and mislead you;
if you follow your nature and preserve your authenticity, there will be no alteration to yourself.

Thus I say: To do good is easy.
To clamber over city walls;
to sneak around precipices and barriers,
to feign tallies of authority,
to rob offices of their gold,

or to commit regicide and usurpation and [presume to] carry out punishments in the ruler's name; such actions are not in the nature of human beings. Thus I say: To do evil is difficult.

Now the reason why people commit crimes that bring imprisonment or sink into the calamities of mutilating punishments is that [their] lusts and desires are not satiated and they do not comply with limits and measures. How do I know that this is so? The laws of the district magistrates across the world state: "Those who open graves will be executed; those who steal will be punished." These [are the measures] employed to uphold order. Now,

laws and ordinances entrap wickedness and depravity,
and restraints and fetters follow in the footsteps [of crime].

Neither a foolish husband nor a daft wife fails to know that if they commit evil there is no escape and if they defy the prohibitions they will not obtain a pardon. Yet no-account children fail to restrain their desires and so commit crimes that warrant the death penalty or suffer the disgrace of undergoing judicial mutilation. Moreover, after the beginning of autumn,[88] the troops of the commandant of justice ceaselessly bring [criminals] to the town gates, so that the blood of those put to death in the market flows copiously into the streets. Why so? They are led astray by the pursuit of wealth and advantage so that they become blind to the calamity of the death sentence.

Now [suppose that] foot soldiers are lined up in military formation, with opposing armies facing each other, and the commanders gives the order, saying: "Those who behead [the enemy] will be rewarded with noble rank, while those who duck or flinch will be beheaded." The front line of soldiers will not be able [i.e., will be afraid] to advance and pursue the merit of beheading the enemy, while the rear ranks [unable to engage the enemy] will suffer the punishment of being beheaded. This is to avoid the fear of death and pursue the inevitability of death. Thus the reversions of benefit and harm, the meeting of good and bad fortune, must be investigated. [13/129/13–23]

88. According to the "Seasonal Rules," autumn is the season for carrying out punishments. See chap. 5.

13.20

With regard to actions,

there are some that you want to carry out, but circumstances warrant that you abandon them;

there are some that you want to avoid, but circumstances warrant that you pursue them.

There was a man of Chu who boarded a boat and encountered a typhoon. The waves were upon him, and in his fright he threw himself into the water. It is not that he did not covet life and fear death but that sometimes in fearing death, you commit the contradiction of being forgetful of your life. Thus human lusts and desires are also like this.

Among the people of Qi was someone who stole gold. Just when the market was most crowded, he arrived, grabbed it, and fled. When held by force and asked: "Why did you steal gold from the market?" He responded: "I did not see anyone, I only saw gold." When the mind is preoccupied with desires, it forgets what it does. For this reason, sages

scrutinize the alterations of movement and rest,
accord with the due measures of receiving and giving,
order the feelings of liking and loathing,
and harmonize with the occasions of happiness and anger.

When [the distinctions of] movement and rest are attained, calamities will not be encountered;

when receiving and giving are in accord, crimes will not accumulate;
when liking and loathing are ordered, anxiety will not come near;
when happiness and anger are in [proper] occasion, resentment will not encroach.

Thus, those who have achieved the Way are not indifferent to obtaining [things] but are not ravenous for wealth;

what they have, they do not abandon,
but what they do not have, they do not seek.
They are constantly full but not overflowing;
they persevere in emptiness but are easily satisfied. [13/129/25–13/130/4]

Now the rain that drips from the eaves is sufficient to fill to overflowing a *hu* vessel, but the waters of the Yangzi and Yellow Rivers cannot fill a leaking *zhi* cup.[89] Thus the human heart is like this. If you make yourself conform to the Techniques of the Way in measurement and limitation, food will fill the emptiness; clothes will block the cold; and it will suffice to care for the body of one seven feet tall.[90] But if you lack the Techniques of the Way in measurement and limitation and try to practice

89. A *hu* is a large storage vessel; a *zhi* is a small drinking cup.

90. A Han "foot" (*chi* 尺) was about nine inches long, so a person "seven feet tall" in Han measure would have been about five feet, three inches, in modern terms.

restraint and moderation on your own, the positional advantage of ten thousand chariots will not suffice to make you honored, and all the wealth in the world will not suffice to make you happy. [13/130/6–8]

13.21

Sunshu Ao thrice declined the post of prime minister but was free of a worried expression, for rank and emolument could not entangle him.

Ci Fei of Jing [encountered] two scaly dragons that wrapped around his boat, but his mind was not moved, for strange creatures could not startle him.[91]

When the minds of sages are regulated and their wills are at ease, their essence and spirit are preserved within,[92] so that things are not sufficient to mislead them. [13/130/8–10]

If a drunkard endeavors to enter the city gates, he will consider it to be like the seven-foot [door to] the women's quarters.

If he is crossing the Yangzi or the Huai River, he will consider it to be a ditch no [wider than] a *xun* or a *chang*.

The wine has muddled his spirit.

When a nervous person sees a standing gnomon at night, he will take it to be a ghost;

when he sees an oddly shaped rock, he will take it to be a tiger.

Fear has seized his *qi*. How much truer is this for the strange creatures of the world!

When male and female join in intercourse and yin and yang cleave to each other, then feathered creatures produce chicks and fledglings, [and] furry creatures produce foals and calves. The soft parts become skin and flesh; the hard parts become teeth and bones. People do not find this strange. [Likewise,] when water gives birth to waterbugs and clams, or mountains give birth to gold and jade, people do not find it strange. [Likewise,] when an old locust tree bursts into flame or dried blood becomes phosphorescent, people do not find it strange. But when mountains give off Xiaoyang, water gives birth to Wangxiang, wood gives birth to Bifang, and wells give birth to Fenyang, people find it strange.[93] Since they hear and observe them infrequently, their knowledge of these things is superficial. The strange things of the world are matters about which sages have a unique vision; the reversions of benefit and harm are matters about which the knowledgeable have a unique understanding

91. This anecdote is recounted in 12.49 and 18.25.

92. The grammar here suggests a translation of *jingshen* as "essence and spirit," in parallel with "mind and will," rather than as the usual "Quintessential Spirit."

93. All these are fabulous creatures of uncertain description. The Xiaoyang 梟陽 is a bird, sometimes said to be emblematic of a perfected human being; the Wangxiang 罔象 is a water monster of some kind; the Bifang 畢方 is another magical bird, with gorgeous plumage, said to be responsible for forest fires; and the Fenyang 墳羊 is an earth deity in the shape of a sheep that has neither male nor female characteristics.

and comprehension.[94] [13/130/12–17] [But] identifying and differentiating the suspicious and the doubtful are what confuse and befuddle the common people of our age.

Because [sages]

see things that cannot be generally made known within the [Four] Seas,

and hear things that cannot be made clear to the masses of people,

they therefore make use of [vulgar beliefs in] ghosts and spirits and inauspicious and auspicious omens to establish prohibitions for them, and they generalize shapes and expand categories to alter appearances[95] for them. How do we know this is so? The proverbs of the common people of our age say:

"In the great sacrifice to the Most High Ones, a pig may serve as the supreme sacrificial animal";

or, "when interring a dead person, it is not necessary to place his fur garments in the tomb";

or, "when two people are engaging in swordplay, the Grand Ancestor will bump them on the elbow";

or, "whoever lies down with his head pillowed on a door frame, the ghosts and spirits will step on his head."

But none of these are written in the laws and ordinances or handed down among the oral teachings of the sages.

Now that in the great sacrifice to the Most High Ones, the pig is considered the supreme sacrificial animal is not because it is superior to wild animals such as deer or that [those having] spirit illumination uniquely savor it. So what about it? It is simply because householders generally raise pigs and so they are easily obtained; therefore they are [really] honored because of their convenience.

That when burying a dead person his fur garments are not entombed with him is not because [the fur garments] are better than silk or cotton cloth at warming the body. Rather, it is because the world considers fur to be something that is difficult to obtain and high priced, and it can be passed on to the next generation. Whereas it is of no advantage to the deceased, it can [be used to] care for the living. Thus in accordance with its value, its use [as grave goods] is avoided.

[The reason it is said that] when two people are engaging in swordplay, the Grand Ancestor will bump them on the elbow is that when engaging in swordplay, [the participants inevitably] must have accidents, and if they accidentally injure each other, the rancor necessarily will be great. The enmity from a bloodless match becomes angry combat, and what is a small matter in itself [escalates into] something

94. Compare this usage of *du* 獨, "unique," with the sage's "ear that uniquely hears, discernment that uniquely sees" near the end of 13.5, and "things that the sage uniquely sees" near the beginning of 13.13.

95. This line apparently refers to the making of actual physical statues, sculptures, and funerary goods, such as the *taotie* 饕餮, "glutton mask," and the *bixie* 避邪, "tomb-guardian monster," metamorphic images that embody common people's beliefs in monsters and prodigies. They draw on "expanded forms" (there are real four-footed animals, so why not *bixie*?) and "extended categories" (there are ravenous beasts, so why not *taotie*?).

involving mutilating punishment. This is because the foolish do not know to restrain themselves,, so [the sages] rely on the Grand Ancestor to constrain their minds.[96]

Now [it is said that] if anyone lies down with his head pillowed on a door frame, the ghosts and spirits will leave footprints on his head. If ghosts and spirits can mysteriously be transformed, they will not rely on doorways and windows to come and go. If in accordance with their ethereal quality they come and go, then likewise they cannot tread on things. Now the doorway and windows are things that windy *qi* passes through, and windy *qi* is the coarse and bulky stuff of yin and yang. Those who encounter it necessarily fall ill. Therefore we rely on the ghosts and spirits to warn and caution them.

Now all things of this kind are not of the sort that can successfully be written down in annals and documents of bamboo or silk and kept in official archives; therefore we use blessings and portents to make them clear. When simpletons do not know enough [to realize] their own transgressions, we rely on the terrors of ghosts and spirits to teach them a lesson. This is something that arose in the far-distant [past]. If the gullible [really] think that there are blessings and portents, and the fearless think that there are not, only one who has the Way can figure out what they are thinking. [13/130/19–13/131/4]

That the present age sacrifices
to the well and the stove, the gate and the door,
the basket and the broom and the mortar and pestle,
is not because these spirits are able to enjoy these sacrifices but because [people] presume on and rely on their Potency, so that hardship and suffering will not visit them personally. For this reason, when people in season observe the Potency [of these spirits], they do not [afterward] forget their efficacy.

[The clouds] touch its stones and disperse,
spread over every inch [of the land] and gather,
and in the space of one morning bring rain to the whole world.
[This happens] only on Mount Tai.[97]
They flow ceaselessly, though the world reddens with drought for three years,
and moisten [an area] extending one hundred *li*, soaking the grass and trees with water.
Only the Yangzi and the Huai rivers:
This is why the Son of Heaven sacrifices to them in accordance with their rank.
Thus,
if there is a horse that has saved someone from danger, when it dies people bury it with its carapace for a shroud.

---

96. The point here is that the foolish need some reason to believe that an accidental injury incurred during a fencing match was not inflicted intentionally, so this "folk saying" (in fact a clever piece of propaganda by the sages) provides a convenient pretext to explain why such mishaps occur: the Grand Ancestor "bumped the elbow" of the fencer who inflicted the accidental injury.

97. The description of Mount Tai's clouds is quoted from the *Gongyang zhuan*, Duke Xi 31.

If there is an ox that has been virtuous toward a person, when it dies people bury it with the passenger box of a large carriage for its burial mat.

If when an ox or horse is meritorious, it cannot be forgotten, how much more so is this the case with people? This is the reason why sages emphasize humaneness and embrace kindness.

Thus Yan Di[98] invented fire. When he died, he became the [god of the] kitchen.

Yu used his strength to the fullest extent on behalf of the world. When he died, he became the [god of the] soil.

Lord Millet invented sowing and reaping. When he died, he became the [god of the] grain.

Yi [the Archer] eradicated harm from the world. When he died, he became the [god of the] ancestral shrine.

This is why ghosts and spirits were set up [to receive sacrifices]. [13/131/6–13]

13.22

There was a man in northern Chu who became a vigilante. His sons implored him to give it up, but he would not listen. Some bandits in the district undertook a massive search to determine his whereabouts. Eventually he was discovered; surprised, at night he fled. Pursuing him, [the bandits] caught up to him on the road. Those on whose behalf he had striven[99] all fought for him. He got out of it unscathed and returned home. He said to his sons: "You repeatedly [tried to] stop me from acting as a vigilante. Now there was trouble, and in the end I relied on everyone[100] and got away. Your remonstrances were of no use." He knew how to save himself when there was trouble, but he did not know how to avoid trouble altogether. If you assess affairs in this way, will not the outcome be in doubt?

A man from Song was about to marry off his daughter. He said to his child, "This marriage may not turn out successfully. If it looks like you will be sent away, you had better have some savings of your own. If you have something saved up and are rich, it will be easy to marry again later." The child listened to her father's scheme and stole [some money] and hid it away. When her lord and master realized she was a thief, he expelled her from the house. Her father did not repudiate her but, on the contrary, reaped the benefits of his scheme. He knew that [if a bride were] expelled [she should have] saved up money, but he did not know about saving up money and therefore being expelled. If you assess matters in this way, will not the outcome be a surprise!? [13/131/15–22]

98. Yan Di was a fire god who warred with the Yellow Emperor. See 15.1. In 3.6, he is depicted as the god of the south and the planet Mars.

99. 所施德者 (lit., "those for whom he had exercised his Potency"). In other words, all those who had benefited from his efforts as a vigilante rallied to defend him from the bandits.

100. Accepting Yu Dacheng's proposed emendation. See Lau, HNZ, 131n.2.

Now suppose someone were looking for something to haul freight and sought out a single cart to do the job. [He reasoned that] if a single ox exerted all its strength, the axle might break, so he added another cart shaft to make it more secure. He did not know that it is the pressure of the cart shaft itself that makes the axle break!

The king of Chu wore a jade circlet at his waist. He went hunting rabbits, and as a result of his movement, the jade circlet broke. So [next time] he wore two jade circlets at his waist, in order to be prepared. But the two jade circlets banged together, and so their destruction was hastened.

The government of a chaotic state much resembles these examples. [13/131/24–28]

Now,

> the eyes of the owl are large, but its vision does not compare with that of the rat;
> the feet of the millipede are numerous, but its speed does not compare with that of a snake.

With things, it is certainly true that there are instances in which

> being large does not compare with being small,
> or being numerous does not compare with being few.

When it comes to

> the strength within weakness and the weakness within strength,
> the danger within safety and the survival within destruction,

if not for a sage, who could see it! Greatness or smallness, honor or disgrace, [alone] do not suffice for an assessment to be made. Only the Way that resides in each is to be valued. How can I clarify this point?

When the Son of Heaven takes up residence in his suburban pavilion, the Nine Ministers hasten to him, and the grandees follow along; those who are seated prostrate themselves, and those who are leaning [against the walls] set themselves in order. Meanwhile [to prepare for] a great audience in the Mingtang, [the Son of Heaven]

> hangs up his hat, takes off his sword,
> undoes his sash, and retires.

It is not that the suburban pavilion is large or that the audience hall is narrow and cramped but that the most highly honored reside there.

Now the nobility of the Way of Heaven does not depend on whatever the Son of Heaven holds in esteem. Wherever it resides, the masses welcome it. When hibernating insects [emerge] and jays nest, they all turn toward the Supreme One. Perfect Harmony lies precisely in this and nothing else. When the emperor sincerely embraces the Way and cleaves to Perfect Harmony, then [even] the birds and beasts, grasses and trees, do not fail to come under his beneficent influence. Is this not even more true for the people themselves? [13/131/30–13/132/6]

Translated by Sarah A. Queen, John S. Major, and Michael Puett

Fourteen

SAYINGS EXPLAINED

"Sayings Explained" is a collection of gnomic sayings (*yan* 言), most of which are further expanded or explicated to clarify their significance. Although at first glance, the sayings and explications seem to be merely a congeries of received wisdom, on more careful perusal they can be seen to recapitulate and reinforce important concepts and themes addressed elsewhere in the *Huainanzi:* What are the essential attributes of the sage? How does the sage bring order to his intrinsic self and, by extension, to the world? The sayings collected in this chapter address these central concerns, and the truths they are intended to express are explained through various analogies and illustrations that usually follow each saying. The sayings and explications also depict several ideal types that illustrate what a sage-ruler can and should be. The Genuine Person (*zhen ren* 真人) embodies a pristine, primeval time before time, when there was perfect unity; he identifies completely with the Grand One, the primal nondifferentiation. The sage is fundamentally, although not exclusively, associated with the empty, nameless, formless, non-active, non-striving, non-intervening attributes of the Way. His ability to embody these aspects of the Way empowers him to sustain an inner equanimity in his person and a harmonious unity in his governance. Thus in ordering his person, the sage avoids the various external distractions that can entangle the mind and disturb the nature. In ruling, the sage's qualities enable him to have to suffer neither the malice of his underlings nor the resentment of the common people. The Superior Man (*junzi* 君子) is more deeply engaged with the differentiated world of affairs but nevertheless rises above petty concerns. The Genuine Person, the sage, and the Superior Man all have lessons to teach about the nature and practice of sage rulership.

The Chapter Title

The title of this chapter is "Quan yan" 詮言, which we translate as "Sayings Explained." We take the phrase *quan yan* to be essentially a verb–object construction (explaining sayings), but we have reversed the order of the words to make a more graceful construction in English. The primary meanings of *quan* are "to explain" or "to comment on," giving the word an association with elucidation and explication. The second term, *yan*, means "a saying" or "an utterance"; all the word's connotations revolve around spoken language. "Sayings Explained" expresses its authors' aim of gathering together and explaining sayings that express basic truths about the ideal ruler and his governance.

Some other scholars have translated the chapter title as "Explanations and Theories" (taking *quan yan* as a double noun) or as "Des paroles probantes" (that is, "convincing sayings," a somewhat unconventional understanding of *quan*).[1] In our view, these renderings overlook the important literary form of the chapter. That is, it consists of not "explanations and sayings" but rather discrete sayings that are explained to bring out their sometimes subtle or recondite significance. The chapter summary in chapter 21 of the *Huainanzi* supports this interpretation. The summary comments only briefly and generally on the chapter's content, focusing instead on the literary techniques employed throughout the chapter:

> "Sayings Explained" provides the means by which to
> compare through analogy the tenets of human affairs
> and elucidate through illustration the substance of order and disorder.
> It ranks the hidden meanings of subtle sayings,
> explaining them with literary expressions that reflect ultimate principles.
> Thus it patches up and mends deficiencies due to errors and oversights.
> (21.2)

This summary makes clear that the goal of this chapter is to remedy potential conceptual deficiencies by collecting a number of "subtle sayings" and "literary expressions" whose hidden meanings and recondite principles are clarified through literary techniques like "comparing through analogy" and "elucidating through illustration." Such literary techniques enabled the *Huainanzi*'s compilers to shape this inherited oral wisdom and make it their own.

The *Huainanzi*'s authors have organized this chapter as a series of sayings (言) with their attendant explanations (詮). The opening section (14.1) serves as a preamble to the chapter as a whole and does not follow the chapter's standard format. Thereafter, most sections begin with a saying that is explained through an illustration, an analogy, or a definition. In several instances, the sayings are layered or inter-

1. Csikszentmihalyi 2004, 150n.117; Le Blanc and Mathieu 2003, 658.

leaved with explanations within a single section. In a few cases, the section concludes with a flourish, quoting a passage from the *Odes* or *Changes.* Generally, however, this chapter, like chapters 16 and 17, does not rely very much on canonical authority. Rather, it collects and conserves a genre of oral literature that seems to have been a ubiquitous part of intellectual life in the late Warring States and early Han periods: well-known sayings.

In order to make this apparent to the reader, we italicized the sayings that open each section of the chapter. Distinguishing the sayings from their corresponding explanations proved to be challenging because the sayings are not introduced with the conventions—"a tradition says" (傳曰) or "there is a saying that states" (有言曰)—typically used in Warring States and Han texts to introduce oral maxims. We thus relied on several criteria to parse the materials, including grammatical structure, parallelism, rhyme, and an analysis of the ways in which various grammatical particles are used here. Parallel passages in other texts (such as the *Zhuangzi, Wenzi,* and *Hanshi waizhuan*) also were helpful. In many cases, the repetition of a theme or concept from a previous line indicates the beginning of the explication. In other cases, the explication is introduced with the standard marker "therefore" (是故) or "thus" (故). In still other cases, standard phrases such as "this is what is meant by X" or "this is what is called X" (此之謂) identify the explanation. This list of criteria is by no means exhaustive.

Despite our best efforts, in some cases our demarcations remain tentative simply because the materials in some sections are more ambiguous and challenging, containing few or no markers of which we can be confident. In some cases, other scholars might have made different decisions about sectioning. Nonetheless, we believe that our understanding of chapter 14 of the *Huainanzi* as a series of sayings (言) with corresponding explanations (詮) is correct and that such an approach will enable the reader to appreciate the chapter's rhetorical coherence, which in turn will offer new interpretive possibilities for others to explore in the future. For these reasons, we have chosen to translate the chapter title as "Sayings Explained," to underscore and clarify the chapter's special rhetorical aims and characteristics.

Summary and Key Themes

This chapter opens with a description of the "Grand One" (*taiyi* 太一), portrayed as a personification of the primordial state of the Way before things as discrete entities came into existence. This first section of the chapter thus establishes a conceptual framework for the many (and otherwise seemingly random and disconnected) sayings and explications. This structural strategy is similar to that of other chapters consisting of a fairly large number of short sections that collect various types of oral literature, such as precepts (chapter 10), anecdotes (chapter 12), and persuasions (chapters 16 and 17). The opening passage of those chapters also serves as a frame, a kind of preamble, showing how the content of the chapter is to be understood. The placement of the opening anecdote concerning the "Grand One" and the closely related "Grand Inception" thus strikes us as not only the consequence of a deliberate editorial choice by the Huainan masters but also a key to the chapter as a whole.

The Grand One: Human Ontogeny Reflects Cosmogony

The Grand One personifies the state of things at the primeval time before time began, when there was only Oneness, a state of utter nondifferentiation. The Grand One represents unmediated unity characterized by emptiness and nondifferentiation, thus containing the full potentiality of all that will come to be in the world but that has not yet been formed and fashioned. The Grand One is both anterior to the creative (that is, differentiating) process of the Way and implicit in it as the source from which the differentiation of things proceeds: "It is not that there was nothing that made things into things; rather, what made things into things is not among the myriad things" (14.1).

Both individual human ontogeny and human history echo this grand cosmogonic movement from a state of formlessness to the acquisition of physical form, a transition from Nonbeing to Being. This process, the "Grand Inception," is understood to be both inevitable and regrettable, a devolution from the primeval and ideal state of the Grand One. (This theme of cosmic and historical devolution is important throughout the *Huainanzi* and is emphasized especially in chapters 6 and 8.) Once human beings acquire physical form, they willingly fall under the sway of the phenomenal world and thus lose their original unity. This need not happen, however. As the opening passage of this chapter points out, some can "return to that from which they were born as if they had not yet acquired a physical form." These are the "Genuine," idealized beings that represent the highest level of identification with the cosmos.

The Grand One, the Sage, and the Superior Man

With this conceptual mooring in place, the chapter uses gnomic verse to describe the sage, the Superior Man, and the manner in which they represent various aspects of sagely governance. What specific qualities does the sage possess? Just as the nondifferentiated and timeless Grand One is a manifestation of the Pole Star, the sage is identified with the stillness and constancy of the unmoving center (14.22, 14.67). This stability engenders inner harmony (*he* 和) or equanimity (*ping* 平), which enables the sage to remain unburdened and unperturbed by the world (14.5, 14.29). A number of sayings explicitly identify the sage with qualities associated with the Way, as described in the *Laozi*. The sage is nameless, formless, and empty. He is unassuming, keeping to the soft and weak. He is identified with non-action, nonstriving, naturalness, nonassertiveness, non-knowledge, and nonintervention.[2] He is selfless and devoid of mind, desires, and preferences. He follows the natural tendencies of things and does not initiate or innovate. He prizes (apparent) weakness and despises (apparent) strength, recognizing, as the *Laozi* states, that "the power of tigers and leopards attracts archers. The agility of monkeys and apes invites pursuit." But the description of the sage in this chapter draws on other sources besides the *Laozi.* The sage is the traceless sage of the *Hanfeizi,* who through his non-action and invisibility stands beyond the criticisms and judgments of his underlings. He is the timely sage of the *Lüshi chunqiu,* who, indifferent to worldly success and failure, simply waits for the opportune moment to arise (and understands the limitations imposed on his actions should that time not come). By following the natural course of things, the sage is able to keep his life secure and his innate nature intact while avoiding for both himself and his governance such negative outcomes as bad fortune, harm, danger, criticism, and chaos.

The Superior Man, although not achieving the perfection of the sage, cultivates his virtuous conduct in the world and extends his kindness to the world but goes to great pains to ensure that his goodness does not bring him fame or that his humaneness does not bring him notice. Like the sage, he remains in the background, barely discernible to those around him yet contributing to the harmony and unity of the world. By inwardly following his nature and the principles of the Way, the Superior Man outwardly accords with Rightness and is not burdened by the external world. The virtuous conduct of the Superior Man interacts (by means of the natural force of resonance) with the world of phenomena to generate "upright *qi*" (as opposed to the "noxious *qi*" generated by such historical monsters of bad rulership as Jie and Djou [see 14.31]). Like the sage, the Superior Man embodies unity or oneness, but his oneness is associated with the mental focus identified as an essential quality of the sage as described by Xunzi. In short, the Superior Man is synonymous with Moral Potency in the world; he simply does good and refuses to do evil, all the while recognizing that such conduct will not ensure that good fortune comes to his person and bad fortune does not. Like the sage, he is indifferent to the conventions of worldly success and failure. Thus, echoing the *Laozi,* one passage concludes: "Therefore, within himself his mind is constantly tranquil and still, and his Moral Potency is unencumbered. Even the barking of a dog cannot startle him because he naturally trusts his genuine responses" (14.71).

The Grand One and the Ordering of the Intrinsic Self

Echoing a theme that pervades the *Huainanzi,* "Sayings Explained" insists that an essential step on the path to sagehood is returning to primordial unity by identifying the intrinsic self with the Grand One. The sage must constantly cultivate his intrinsic Potency so as to become as unitary and self-sufficient as the Grand One, finding

2. See 14.3, 14.4, 14.18, 14.19, 14.22, 14.35, 14.46, 14.67, and 14.68.

self-realization within rather than looking to what lies outside the self. He does so by relying on the Way and its Techniques (*dao shu* 道術) to cultivate such essential aspects of the self as mind, natural tendencies, and the spirit.[3] Of equal importance is the necessity of restraining or eradicating responses to the external world that are expressed as human desires or preferences. By cultivating his identification with the Grand One and purging himself of desires for particular things and outcomes in the differentiated world, the sage achieves Grand Vacuity (*taichong* 太沖), a psychic state that enables him to respond to the external world from a unified and still center.

The Grand One and the Ordering of the Extrinsic World

Having cultivated the qualities of the Grand One in his intrinsic person, the sage is empowered to bring order to the world. With this conceptual frame in place, the chapter turns to a number of themes found throughout the *Huainanzi*. A clear homology is established between ordering the self and ordering the world; one must begin by ordering what lies within.[4] Because the Grand One represents a state of cosmic unity temporally and epistemologically prior to the differentiation of the ten thousand things, the ruler is urged to emulate the Grand One in his governance: "When the ruler grasps the One [*zhi yi* 執一], there is order; when he lacks constancy [*chang* 常], there is disorder."[5] The Huainan masters are quick to identify this immersion in unity with non-action : "The Way of rulership is not the means by which one acts; it is the means by which one does not act."[6] This saying is elucidated further:

> What does "non-action" mean? [It means that]
> the wise do not avail themselves of their position to intervene;
> the courageous do not avail themselves of their position to engage in violence;
> and the humane do not avail themselves of their position to confer kindness.

---

3. These themes are found in many sections of the chapter: for example, 14.8, 14.11, 14.12, 14.23, 14.37, 14.38, 14.39, 14.46, 14.49, 14.51, 14.52, 14.53, 14.67, and 14.68.

4. See, for example, 14.7, 14.8, and 14.12.

5. *Lüshi chunqiu* 17/7.1, "No Duality" (Bu er) similarly states: "Where there is unity, order results; where there are differences, chaos ensues; where there is unity, security results; and where there are differences, danger arises" (Knoblock and Riegel 2000, 434). *Lüshi chunqiu* 17/8.1, "Upholding Unity" (Zhi yi), also states:

> The true king by holding fast to the One makes the myriad things correct. An army must have a general, for he is what unifies it; a state must have a ruler, for he is what unifies it; and the world must have a Son of Heaven, for he is what unifies it. The Son of Heaven must hold fast to the One, for that is what makes him unique. Where there is unity, there is order; where there is duality, there is chaos. (Knoblock and Riegel 2000, 434)

6. See also WZ 5/26/12–13.

This may be called "non-action." Through non-action, you can grasp the One. The One is the root of the myriad things. It is the Way that is unopposed. (14.35)

We see here that non-action is the chief characteristic of the sagely ruler, but it is not the only one. All the qualities of a sage—being nameless, selfless, formless, empty, and unassuming; without mind, desires, or preferences; natural, nonstriving, nonassertive, unknowing and noninterventionist—come into play in sage-governance. Repeatedly, the authors warn that only those who do not seek to rule the world, who rise above the worldly conventions of success and failure, who are indifferent to bringing fame and reputation to their person or ensuring that they enjoy good fortune, and who avoid misfortune are truly fit to rule. The ruler must rely on the Way and not his personal preferences (14.48). In short, the sage rules by extinguishing his personal preferences and biases so that he follows the natural tendencies of things and is as impartial as Heaven and Earth (14.44, 14.45). Thus he rules as a sage but (fortunately) is not recognized as such; fame and reputation are contradictions of the Way and only bring disaster.

Sources

In this chapter, as throughout the *Huainanzi*, we see the Huainan masters weaving together various strands of gnomic verse and philosophical concepts derived from diverse wisdom traditions of the pre-Han era. Here, the authors demonstrate how gnomic sayings—most, if not all, of which would have been familiar to educated people of the time—exemplify themes seen elsewhere in the *Huainanzi* concerning the sage and his governance of the world. As we saw earlier, the sayings are explained through the literary techniques of "comparing through analogy" and "elucidating through illustration." Apothegms that at first glance seem unrelated to the sage are read analogically as descriptions of this ideal personality.[7] For example,

Yang qi *arises in the northeast and culminates in the southwest.*
Yin qi *arises in the southwest and culminates in the northeast.*

This description of the yearly waxing and waning of yin and yang, which the authors flesh out in the following lines, is read as a metaphor for the sage who "is cautious and circumspect concerning what he accumulates" (14.64). We also find the following apothegm describing the trajectory of two commonplace items from their origins to their destinations:

7. See, for example, 14.3, 14.23, 14.32, 14.40, 14.43, 14.64, 14.65, and 14.66.

> *Water comes out of the mountains and flows to the sea;*
> *grain grows in the fields and is stored in granaries.*

This saying similarly is read analogically as descriptive of the sage who "observes the beginning of things and knows their end" (14.65).

An example of the second literary technique, "elucidating through illustration," is

> *Those who excel at swimming do not study how to move a boat with a pole yet find [boats] easy to use.*
> *Those who possess strong muscles do not study how to ride a horse yet find [horses] easy to mount.*
>
> *Those who look lightly upon [taking possession of] the world do not allow their person to become entangled by external things; thus they can occupy such a position.* (14.14)

Here the compilers illustrate the deep meaning of this expression by linking it to the following anecdote concerning the Great King Danfu:

> When the Great King Danfu resided in Bin, the Dee people attacked him. He offered them skins, silks, pearls, and jades, but they did not heed him. Danfu then bid farewell to his elders and moved his residence to the foot of Mount Qi. Carrying their young and supporting their old, the common people followed Danfu, and subsequently he established a state there. By this principle, is it not fitting that the house of Zhou attained the world in four generations? Those who do nothing deliberately to take possession of the world assuredly are those who can rule the world.[8] (14.14)

By explaining the implications of these sayings through analogy and illustration, the authors shape this gnomic literature by identifying how these sayings should be interpreted.

This chapter reiterates arguments concerning the ideal ruler and his governance found elsewhere in the *Huainanzi* and echoes sayings that appear in early texts such as the *Mozi, Laozi, Zhuangzi, Hanfeizi, Guanzi, Lüshi chunqiu, Wenzi,* and *Hanshi waizhuan.* As part of the common intellectual property of educated people of the time, the origins of the gnomic sayings quoted in this chapter usually cannot be traced to particular literary sources so might best be described as part of early China's cultural inheritance. The contribution of the Huainan masters has been to use those sayings as the basis for their arguments about the nature of ideal rulership.

---

8. Great King Danfu also appears in 12.15 and 20.9.

The Chapter in the Context of the *Huainanzi* as a Whole

The summary of chapter 14 in chapter 21 of the *Huainanzi* describes the literary methods employed in this chapter, and the concluding line of the chapter summary refers to its broader conceptual goals: chapter 14 "patches up and mends deficiencies due to errors and oversights." Therefore, any arguments or themes presented earlier in the work that were misunderstood or overlooked are meant to be redressed in this chapter. A striking example of how this chapter harks back to earlier material is the way in which it recapitulates and expands on a theme from chapter 7—the tranquil, self-cultivated nature of the sage and the sage's complete lack of interest in pursuing political power and its worldly trappings. This is why the chapter might at first glance seem redundant, although as argued earlier, the chapter is not simply a repetition of themes that appear elsewhere in the work. Rather, it presents such themes within an overarching conceptual framework that foregrounds the notion of the Grand One, a concept to which the book returns repeatedly, exploiting this symbol with its associations ranging from cosmogony, cosmology, and human ontogony to self-cultivation and human governance in order to underscore the concept of self-identification with primordial unity as characteristic of a sage and foundational to one who would rule the world as a sage.[9]

Sarah A. Queen

9. For a particularly illuminating discussion of the Grand One and its associations with the *Laozi*, see Sarah Allan, "The Great One, Water, and the *Laozi*: New Light from *Guodian*," *T'oung Pao* 89 (2003): 237–85.

Fourteen

14.1

Cavernous and undifferentiated Heaven and Earth, chaotic and inchoate Uncarved Block, not yet created and fashioned into things: this we call the "Grand One."[1] Together emerging from this unity, so that each acquired its distinctive qualities, there were birds, there were fish, there were animals: this we call the "differentiation of things."

Regions became distinguished according to their categories;
things became differentiated according to their groupings.

Their natures and destinies were dissimilar; all acquired their physical forms in the realm of "Being."

Separate and not interconnected, differentiated as the myriad things, none could return to their Ancestor.[2] Thus,

1. For the "Grand One" (*tai yi* 太一), see also 3.13, 7.15, 8.7, 9.2, and 21.2.
2. For the notion of "returning to your Ancestor," see 16.1 and 16.15. The latter explains:

> The crumbling of a wall is better than its building;
> the melting of ice is better than its freezing
> because they [thus] return to the Ancestor.

For "returning to the Ancestor of Nature and Destiny," see the summary of chap. 7 in 21.2. For the "Great Ancestor," see *Zhuangzi*, chap. 6. For a different point of view, see 17.27.

when animated, things are said to be alive;
when dead, things are said to be expired.

In both cases, they are things. It is not that there was nothing that made things into things; rather, what made things into things is not among the myriad things. [14/132/10–13]

In antiquity, at the Grand Beginning,[3] human beings came to life in "Non-being" and acquired a physical form in "Being." Having a physical form, [human beings] came under the control of things. But those who can return to that from which they were born, as if they had not yet acquired a physical form, are called the "Genuine."[4] The Genuine are those who have not yet begun to differentiate from the Grand One. [14/132/15–16]

14.2

The sage
does not for the sake of a name become a corpse;
does not for the sake of stratagems store things up;
does not for the sake of affairs take on responsibility;
does not for the sake of wisdom become a ruler.[5]

[The sage]
dwells in the Formless,
moves in the Traceless,
and wanders in the Beginningless.
He does not initiate things for the sake of good fortune,
nor does he begin things to deal with misfortune.
He remains in Emptiness and Non-being
and moves when he cannot do otherwise.
For those who desire good fortune, sometimes suffer misfortune,
and those who desire benefit, sometimes suffer harm.[6]

Thus,
those who are secure through non-action become endangered when they lose that by which they are secure [i.e., non-action].
Those who are well ordered through nonintervention become disordered when they lose that by which they are well ordered. [14/132/18–20]

3. *Tai chu* 太初. Compare the "Grand Beginning" (*tai shi* 太始) in 3.1.

4. The concept of the "Genuine" (*zhen ren* 真人) is developed most extensively in chap. 2 but also appears in chaps. 6–8. See also extensive references in the *Zhuangzi*, especially in chaps. 6 and 24.

5. This saying also appears in *Zhuangzi* 7 (ZZ 7/21/19–20).

6. The *Wenzi* parallels this passage to the end of this line, and then the two texts diverge. See WZ 4/18/22–4/19/1.

14.3

Stars arrayed in the heavens are bright. Therefore people point at them.
Rightness arrayed in one's Moral Potency is obvious. Therefore people observe it.

What people point at has a manifestation because it moves;
what people observe leaves a trace because it acts.
When movements have manifestations, they will be criticized;
when actions have traces, they will be appraised.

Thus, the sage conceals his brilliance in the Formless and hides his traces in non-action. [14/132/20–22]

14.4

Prince Qingji[7] perished by the sword;
Yi died by a cudgel made of peach wood;
Zilu was dismembered in Wey;
and Su Qin died because of his eloquence.

There are no people
who do not cherish their strengths
and despise their weaknesses.
Yet,
while they indulge their strengths,
their weaknesses become pronounced.
So that
while what they cherish assumes definite form;
what they despise [seems to] leave not a trace.
Thus,
the power of tigers and leopards attracts archers.
The agility of monkeys and apes invites pursuit.[8]
Those who can
cherish their weaknesses
and despise their strengths
can join in discussions of the highest principles. [14/132/24–28]

7. Prince Qingji 王子慶忌 was the son of King Liao of Wu (r. 526–515 B.C.E.). He fled into exile when his brother, King Helü, usurped the throne. He was renowned as a fierce warrior and an expert swordsman.

8. This saying paraphrases *Zhuangzi* 7 (ZZ 7/20/20), where it is attributed to Laozi. It does not, however, appear in the received version of the *Daodejing*. This saying also appears in 17.84 and 10.92.

14.5

Those who trust themselves cannot be swayed by slander or flattery.
Those whose knowledge is sufficient cannot be enticed by power or profit.

Thus,

those who fully comprehend the genuine qualities of their nature do not strive to accomplish what their nature cannot accomplish.
Those who fully comprehend the genuine qualities of their destiny do not concern themselves with what their destiny cannot control.

For those who fully comprehend the Way, things are not enough to disorder their inner harmony.[9] [14/133/1–3]

14.6

Zhan He said:

"I have never heard of a ruler who was ordered in his person yet found his state disordered.
Nor have I heard of a ruler who was disordered in his person yet found his state to be well ordered." [14/133/5]

14.7

If the carpenter's square is not true, it cannot create a square.
If the compass is not true, it cannot create a circle.

Your person is the carpenter's square and compass of all your undertakings. I have not heard that it was possible to correct others by perverting yourself. [14/133/5–6]

14.8

Trace to the source Heaven's decree,
cultivate the techniques of the mind,
regulate likes and dislikes,
follow your disposition and nature,
and the Way of governing [oneself] will come through.

9. Following Lau, who follows Wang Niansun and emends *wu mo bu zu gu qi diao* (無莫不足滑其調) to *wu mo zu gu qi he* (無莫足滑其和), based on other occurrences of the expression in, for example, *Huainanzi*, chaps. 1, 2, and 7. See Lau, HNZ, 133n.2. See also Zhang Shuangdi 1997, 2:1475n.2. For the similar expression *bu zu yi gu he*, see ZZ 5/15/2.

If you trace to the source Heaven's decree, you will not be deluded by bad or good fortune.
If you cultivate the techniques of the mind, you will not be unrestrained in your happiness and anger.
If you regulate your likes and dislikes, you will not covet what is useless.
If you follow your disposition and nature, your desires will not exceed the appropriate limits.
If you are not deluded by bad or good fortune, your movement and stillness will comply with the inherent principles of things.
If you are not unrestrained in your happiness and anger, your rewards and punishments will not be partial.
If you do not covet what is useless, you will not allow your desires to harm your nature.
If your desires do not exceed the appropriate limits, you will nurture your nature and know contentment.

As a general rule, these four things cannot be sought after in what is outside the self nor can you bestow them on others. You can obtain them only by returning to the self.[10] [14/133/7–11]

14.9

The world
cannot be acted on by knowledge;
cannot be discerned through perceptiveness;
cannot be governed by intervening;
cannot be subjugated through humaneness;
and cannot be vanquished through strength.

These five are all aspects of human talent. If your Potency does not flourish, you will not be able to perfect even one of them. Where Potency is established, these five will not be endangered. But where these five appear, Potency will not be established. Thus,

if you grasp the Way, stupidity will be more than sufficient;
if you lose the Way, knowledge will be insufficient to the task. [14/133/13–15]

10. For the sage's ability to "return to the self" (*fan ji* 反己) or the closely related expression "return to [one's] nature" (*fan xing* 反性), see 10.113, 10.117, 11.5, 11.6, and 11.15. For "returning to [one's] nature" as the root of governance, see 20.28. For a parallel passage in the *Wenzi*, see WZ 4/19/23–26.

14.10

When crossing a river,

if you lack the technique[11] *of swimming, you will assuredly drown despite your strength.*

If you possess the technique of swimming, you will assuredly cross to the other side despite your weakness.

Then again, how much better to rely on taking a boat! [14/133/17]

14.11

The root of governance lies in bringing security to the people.
The root of bringing security to the people lies in using them sufficiently.
The root of using them sufficiently lies in not taking them from their seasonal tasks.
The root of not taking them from their seasonal tasks lies in decreasing what they need to attend to.
The root of decreasing what they need to attend to lies in moderating their desire.
The root of moderating their desire lies in returning to their nature.
The root of returning to their nature lies in eradicating [what] burdens [their mind].

If you eradicate [what] burdens [their mind], they will become empty. Being empty, they will become balanced.

Balance is the beginning of the Way.
Emptiness is the abode of the Way. [14/133/19–21]

14.12

Those who can take possession of the world assuredly do not forfeit their states.
Those who can take possession of a state assuredly do not forfeit their families.
Those who can govern their family assuredly do not neglect their persons.
Those who can cultivate their persons assuredly do not forget their minds.
Those who can trace their minds to the source assuredly do not injure their natures.
Those who can keep their natures intact assuredly are not confused about the Way.

11. For the justification of reading *shu* 數 as *shu* 術, see the numerous examples from the *Huainanzi* and other texts listed in Zhuang Shuangdi 1997, 2:1475n.7.

Thus the "Master of Broad Perfection"[12] said:

> "Reverently preserve what lies inside;
> comprehensively shut out what lies outside.
> Too much knowledge gives rise to defeat.
> Do not look.
> Do not listen.
> Embrace the spirit by means of stillness,
> and your physical form will correct itself."[13]

To be unable to grasp it within yourself and yet to be able to know it in others—this has never been possible.

Thus the *Changes* says:

> "Tie it up in a sack.
> No blame, no praise."[14] [14/134/1–4]

14.13

Those who can succeed as hegemons and kings assuredly achieve victory.
Those who can vanquish their enemies assuredly are powerful.
Those who can be powerful assuredly use the strength of others.
Those who can use the strength of others assuredly win the people's hearts.
Those who can win the people's hearts assuredly understand their own hearts.
Those who can understand their own hearts assuredly are soft and weak.

Strength triumphs when others' strength does not compare to your own. Should you encounter those whose strength is equal to your own, you will be resisted. But softness triumphs over those who exceed you [in strength], because its power is immeasurable. Thus, only the sage can accomplish great victories where most people would suffer defeat.[15] [14/134/6–9]

14.14

Those who excel at swimming do not study how to move a boat with a pole yet find [boats] easy to use.[16]
Those who possess strong muscles do not study how to ride a horse yet find [horses] easy to mount.

12. Guang Chengzi 廣成子.

13. For a longer and differently ordered version of this passage in which the Master of Broad Perfection imparts his teachings to the Yellow Emperor, see *Zhuangzi* 11 (ZZ 11/27/15–28).

14. For this line, see *Changes*, hexagram 2, *Kun*.

15. See also *Wenzi* 4 (WZ 4/24/4–7).

16. See the exchange in *Zhuangzi* 19 (ZZ 19/50/18–23) between Yen Hui and Confucius on what enables a good swimmer to handle a boat deftly.

Those who look lightly upon [taking possession of] the world do not allow their person to become entangled by external things; thus they can occupy such a position.

When the Great King Danfu resided in Bin, the Dee people attacked him. He offered them skins, silks, pearls, and jades, but they did not heed him. Danfu then bid farewell to his elders and moved his residence to the foot of Mount Qi. Carrying their young and supporting their old, the common people followed Danfu, and subsequently he established a state there. By this principle, is it not fitting that the house of Zhou attained the world in four generations? Those who do nothing deliberately to take possession of the world assuredly are those who can rule the world.[17] [14/134/11–15]

14.15

Frost, snow, rain, and dew bring life and death to the myriad things.
Heaven does not act deliberately in such matters,
yet Heaven is revered for accomplishing them.
Slaving over civil documents and worrying about legal decrees;
managing offices and keeping the people in order:
[such things are the tasks] of the officials.
The ruler does not intervene in such matters,
yet he is honored for accomplishing them.

The one who cultivated the fields and reclaimed the wastelands was Lord Millet;
the one who opened up the Yellow River and dredged the Yangzi was Yu;
the one who heard court cases and settled them appropriately was Gao Yao;
yet the one who enjoyed a sagely reputation for accomplishing them was Yao.

Thus if you rely on the Way in directing the world, even though you may be devoid of ability, you will invariably use those who are capable. But if you do not rely on the Way, though you may possess much skill and artistry, they will not bring you any benefit.[18] [14/134/15–18]

17. Danfu was the (legendary) grandfather of King Wen, founder of the Zhou dynasty. The story of Great King Danfu is also found in 12.15 and 20.9. The version in chap. 12 is in turn nearly identical to the story as it appears in *Zhuangzi* 28 (28/81/23–28). See Mair 1997, 285–86. See also LSCQ 21.4/141/11–17; and Knoblock and Riegel 2000, 557–58.

18. For a near parallel to this passage, see HSWZ 2/10.

14.16

Suppose you are crossing the river in a twin-hulled boat[19] *and an empty boat comes from another direction and crashes into your boat and overturns it. Even if you have a violent temper, you certainly will not exhibit an angry expression. [But] if there had been someone in the [other] boat, you might first have shouted, "Trim the sail," and next, "Stay to one side." And if you had called two or three times with no response, certainly a stream of insulting words would have followed in the wake of the boat.*

[Thus], although in the former case you would not be angry, in the latter case you would be angry; although in the former case you would be empty [of emotion], in the latter case you would be full. But as for those who are able to empty themselves [of emotions] and drift through the world, who could criticize them?[20] [14/134/20–22]

14.17

If you disregard the Way and rely on knowledge, invariably you will be endangered.
If you abandon technique and employ talent, invariably you will encounter difficulties.
There have been those who perished because their desires were numerous;
there have never been those who were endangered because they were free from desires.
There have been those who desired order but suffered disorder;
there have never been those who preserved what is constant and yet lost their state.

Thus,
while knowledge [alone] will not suffice for you to avoid trouble,
stupidity [alone] will not suffice to jeopardize your peace.
If you preserve these distinctions
and act in accordance with these principles,
when you lose, you will not feel vexed,
and when you succeed, you will not feel happy.
For when you accomplish something, it is not because you have acted deliberately,
and when you acquire something, it is not because you have sought after something.
What you receive, you take without [consciously] accepting;
what you give, you confer without [consciously] distributing.

---

19. *Fang chuan* 方船, which we understand to be a vessel comprising two boats lashed together side by side.

20. For a near parallel to this passage in *Zhuangzi* 20, see ZZ 20/54/4–6.

If you [nourish] life in accordance with spring,
and you kill in accordance with autumn,
those to whom you grant life will not view you as exerting Moral Potency,
and those whom you subject to death will not view you as expressing anger.
[Thus] you will have come close to the Way. [14/134/24–28]

14.18

The sage does not do things that are wrong
yet does not hate those who do wrong to him.
He cultivates Moral Potency worthy of praise
yet does not seek the praise of others.
He cannot prevent ill fortune from arising
yet trusts that he personally will not summon it.
He cannot assure that good fortune will invariably befall him
yet trusts that he personally will not yield to it.

[Thus,]
if misfortune befalls him, because it is not something he sought to bring about, should he fail, he feels no anxiety.
If good fortune befalls him, because it is not something he sought to bring about, should he succeed, he feels no pride.
He knows that what determines bad and good fortune is beyond his control.
Thus, he is joyful abiding at his leisure and governs through non-action.[21] [14/134/30–14/135/3]

14.19

The sage preserves what he already has
and does not seek after what he has not yet attained.
If he seeks after what he has not yet attained,
he will lose what he already has.
If he cultivates what he has within himself,
what he desires will be obtained.[22]

Thus,
those who employ an army
first make sure they cannot be defeated,
then await the enemy that can be defeated.

21. See also WZ 4/20/1–5.
22. See also WZ 4/20/6–7.

Those who rule a state,
first make sure that it cannot be captured,
then await the enemy that can be captured. [14/135/3–5]

14.20

Shun cultivated himself on Mount Li, and all within the Four Seas were transformed by his influence.
King Wen cultivated himself on Mount Qi, and the world was moved by his example.

Had Shun hastened after the benefit [of ruling] the world,
had he abandoned the Way of Self-Cultivation,
he would not have been able to preserve himself. How then would he have been able to take possession of [even] an inch of territory?
Thus,
if your governance is not yet secure enough to avoid disorder, and yet you intervene to create order, you will certainly encounter danger.
If your conduct is not yet secure enough to avoid censure, and yet you anxiously seek to establish a reputation, you will certainly fail in your attempt to do so.
There is no good fortune greater than being free of calamity.
There is no benefit better than avoiding death.[23] [14/135/5–8]

14.21

The thing about movement is
if you do not gain, you will lose;
if you do not succeed, you will fail;
if you do not benefit, you will suffer harm.
These things are dangerous; those who follow such a course are in peril.

Thus,
Qin won victory over the Rong [tribe] but was defeated at Mount Yao.
Chu won victory over the Central States but was defeated at Boju.
Thus,
the Way does not allow for seeking benefit through force
but does allow for avoiding harm through tranquillity.
Thus,

23. For these two couplets of parallel prose (beginning with "Thus"), see also WZ 4/20/8–9.

constantly avoid ill fortune,
but do not constantly seek good fortune.
Constantly avoid blame,
but do not constantly seek achievements.[24] [14/135/8–10]

14.22

The sage has no conscious deliberations;
he has no fixed ideas.
He neither welcomes what arrives
nor sends off what departs.
Though others occupy positions north, south, east, and west,
he alone is established at the center.

Thus, he encounters various crooked ways, but he does not lose his rectitude; the world flows to and fro, but he alone does not leave his [ancestral] shrine and walled city.

Thus,

he does not encourage what he likes,
nor does he avoid what he dislikes;
he simply follows Heaven's Way.
He does not initiate,
nor does he personally assume authority;
he simply complies with Heaven's Principles.
He does not make plans in advance,
nor does he miss the opportune moment;
he simply complies with Heaven's Times.
He does not seek to obtain things,
nor does he shun good fortune;
he simply goes along with Heaven's Patterns.
He does not seek after what he does not possess,
nor does he lose what he has obtained.
Inwardly he experiences no unexpected misfortune;
outwardly he experiences no unexpected good fortune.
Since neither ill fortune nor good fortune arises,
how can others harm him?[25] [14/135/10–14]

24. The six lines following "Thus" have near parallels in WZ 4/20/8–10.
25. See also WZ 4/20/10–13.

14.23

If you do good, you will be admired.
If you do ill, you will be criticized.
Admiration generates honor.
Criticism generates resentment.

Thus the Techniques of the Way
cannot be used to advance and seek a reputation
but can be used to retreat and cultivate one's person.
They cannot be used to obtain benefit
but can be used to distance oneself from harm.
Thus the sage
does not rely on his conduct to seek a reputation,
does not rely on his knowledge to demonstrate his praiseworthiness.
He imitates and complies with the natural so that nothing interferes with him.[26] [14/135/16–18]

14.24

Forethought is not superior to techniques;
acting is not superior to Potency;
intervening is not superior to the Way.

If you act deliberately, there will be things you do not achieve.
If you seek after things, there will be things you do not obtain.
Though human beings possess their limits,
there is nothing the Way does not penetrate.[27]
If you compete with the Way, you will suffer misfortune.
Thus the *Odes* says:
"Without recognizing them, without knowing them,
comply with the thearch's regulations."[28] [14/135/20–21]

14.25

To have knowledge but not act purposively is at one with the Way of no-knowledge;
to have ability but not intervene is at one with the Potency of no-ability.

26. See also WZ 4/20/17–18.
27. For these four lines, see also WZ 4/20/18–19.
28. *Odes* 241.

This knowledge is such that only when someone comes to report to him do we become aware that he has [already] acted.
This ability is such that only after someone comes to employ him do we become aware that he has already done it.
When having knowledge resembles no-knowledge,
when having ability resembles no-ability,
the Patterns of the Way are rectified.
Thus,
when your merit spreads over the world but does not evoke praise,
and when your beneficence extends to future ages but does not earn fame,
the Patterns of the Way will pervade [the world], and human artifice will be destroyed.[29] [14/135/21–24]

14.26

Reputation and the Way cannot simultaneously be brilliant.
When humans cherish a reputation, the Way is of no use.
When the Way prevails over humans, reputation vanishes.

The Way and humans compete for priority. What embellishes the human diminishes the Way. When the human is embellished and the Way vanishes, danger is not far off. Thus, when an age enjoys a reputation for sageliness, the day of the Way's decline has already arrived.[30] [14/135/26–28]

14.27

One who desires to have a posthumous reputation invariably performs good deeds;
one who desires to perform good deeds invariably initiates various undertakings.

If undertakings are initiated, then
you will abandon the public good and pursue self-interest
and will spurn techniques and rely on yourself.
Desiring to solicit praise for good deeds
and establish a reputation for worthiness,
your governance will not comply with precedent,
and your undertakings will not be in accord with the seasons.
When governance does not comply with precedent,
it will elicit numerous criticisms.

29. See also WZ 4/20/19–20.
30. See also WZ 4/20/20–21.

When undertakings do not accord with the seasons,
they will not be meritorious.

When criticisms are numerous and merit rare, and you do not possess the means to stop such tendencies, then

you will incite recklessness, even though you strive for what is appropriate,
and you will act recklessly, [even] though you seek to hit the mark.
Should your undertakings eventually succeed, it will not suffice to stop the criticisms;
should your undertakings eventually fail, it will suffice to cause you distress.[31]

Thus, if

you value doing what is approved
equally with doing what is disapproved,

you will have come close to the Way. [14/136/1–5]

14.28

It is not the case that the world lacks trustworthy men.

It is just that in the management of goods and the distribution of wealth, when you invariably seek to make calculations and determine distributions accordingly, you should consider that intending to be fair does not compare with being without intentions altogether.

It is not the case that the world is devoid of honest men.

It is just that in preserving valuable and precious things, as you invariably secure the doors and seal in the valuable and precious goods, you should consider that the desire to be honest does not compare with being without desires altogether. [14/136/7–9]

14.29

If a person points out your flaws, you will despise that person.
But should a mirror reveal your imperfections, you will praise the mirror.

Those who can interact with things and not take them personally can thus avoid encumbrances. 14/136/11]

31. See also WZ 4/18/18–20.

14.30

Gongsun Long was gifted with words but bought his way to fame;
Deng Xi was a clever disputer but confounded the laws;
Su Qin excelled at offering persuasions but lost his life.

If you follow the Way, you will excel at not being conspicuous;
if you comply with its principles, you will be skillful at not gaining fame.

Thus,

those who rely on cleverness to compete for supremacy start out in yang but always end up in yin.[32]
Those who rely on intelligence to govern a state start out in order but always end up in disorder.

If you allow water to flow downward, who cannot regulate it? But should you force it to flow upward, without [exceptional] skill, you will not be able to do so.

Thus,

when outer ornamentation prevails, inner substance is concealed.
When artful depravity succeeds, uprightness is blocked. [14/136/13–16]

14.31

Moral Potency can be used to cultivate oneself, but it cannot be used to make others tyrannical.
The Way can be used to order oneself, but it cannot be used to make others disorderly.

Although you possess the inner qualities of a worthy or sage, if you do not encounter a tyrannical or disorderly age, you can perfect your person, but you cannot become a hegemon or king. Kings Tang and Wu encountered the tyranny of Jie and Djou. Jie and Djou were not tyrannical on account of Tang's and Wu's worthiness, but Tang and Wu encountered the tyranny of Jie and Djou and so became kings. Thus, however worthy, whether a person becomes king invariably depends on encountering an

32. This claim appears in *Zhuangzi* 4 (ZZ 4/10/25–26). Graham translates:

> Another point: competitors in a game of skill begin in a bright Yang mood, but it is apt to end up by darkening to Yin; when they have gone too far they play more and more unfair tricks. Drinkers at a formal banquet are mannerly at first, but generally end up too boisterous; when thy have gone too far the fun gets more and more reckless. This happens in all sorts of affairs. (1982, 71)

Mair's version reads,

> Moreover, those who contest for supremacy with cleverness begin openly but invariably end up in deception. In their excesses, they are full of chicanery. Those who drink according to etiquette begin politely but invariably end up disorderly. In their excesses, they are full of debauchery. It's the same with all affairs. (1997, 35)

opportune moment. Encountering an opportune moment means obtaining something by happening upon the right moment. It is not something you can seek and perfect with your knowledge and ability.[33] [14/136/18–21]

14.32

The Superior Man cultivates his conduct yet makes certain that his goodness does not bring him fame.
He extends his kindness yet makes certain that his humaneness does not bring him notice.

Thus,
the scholars practice goodness but do not know the source of their goodness.
The people enjoy the benefits [they receive] but do not know the origins of their benefits.
Thus,
if you do not act, things will become regulated by themselves.
If your goodness becomes manifest, functionaries will compete [to establish] reputations.
If your benefits [are seen to] have a basis, the people will vie with one another to obtain them.
When these two types of competition arise, [even] though you are a worthy ruler, you will not be able to govern. Thus, the sage
hides his tracks when doing good
and conceals his reputation when acting humanely. [14/136/23–25]

14.33

Associating with foreign states to seek assistance
and serving large states to seek security
do not compare with
establishing order within your borders
and waiting for the opportune moment.

As a general rule, when serving others,
if you do not rely on jade and silk,
you will surely use humble speech.
If you serve others by means of jade and silk, once the goods have been given away, [their] desires may not be satiated.

33. A similar point is made in LSCQ 14.5/74/23. See Knoblock and Riegel 2000, 319.

If you humble yourself and use servile speech, once the phrases have been spoken, the relationship may not be clinched.
If you conclude a treaty and swear an oath, once the treaty has been established, it may be abrogated that very day.

Even though you diminish your state by a *zi* or a *chui*[34] to serve others and do not follow the Way of self-reliance, it will not suffice to keep your state intact. If you stop pursuing foreign policy schemes and truly attend to cultivating the affairs within your state, fully developing the resources of your land to increase the state reserves, exhorting your people to avoid death by repairing their city walls, [so that]

superior and subordinates are of one mind,
and ruler and ministers are of one will,

so that together with your ministers you preserve the altars of the soil and grain and the people are inspired to remain within the state even when facing death, then

those who aspire to establish a reputation will not punish the innocent,
and those who endeavor to bring benefit will not attack those who are difficult to defeat.

Surely this is the Way of keeping [one's state] intact. [14/136/27–14/137/3]

14.34

The people have a Way that they will uniformly follow;
the people have laws that they will uniformly uphold.
Rightness cannot make the people secure with one another;
coercion cannot make the people be bound to one another.

Thus a ruler is established to unify the people.

When the ruler grasps the One, there is order;
when he lacks constancy, there is disorder.[35] [14/137/5–6]

34. *Zi* 錙 and *chui* 錘 are trifling amounts.

35. LSCQ 17.7/107/6–7, "No Duality" (Bu er), similarly states: "Where there is unity, order results; where there are differences, chaos ensues; where there is unity, security results; and where there are differences, danger arises" (Knoblock and Riegel 2000, 434). LSCQ 17.8/107/13–15, "Upholding Unity" (Chi yi), also states:

> The true king by holding fast to the One makes the myriad things correct. An army must have a general, for he is what unifies it; a state must have a ruler, for he is what unifies it and the world must have a Son of Heaven, for he is what unifies it. The Son of Heaven must hold fast to the One, for that is what makes him unique. Where there is unity, there is order; where there is duality, there is chaos. (Knoblock and Riegel 2000, 434)

14.35

The Way of Rulership is not the means by which one acts;
it is the means by which one does not act.[36]

What does "non-action" mean? [It means that]
the wise do not avail themselves of their position to intervene;
the courageous do not avail themselves of their position to engage in violence;
and the humane do not avail themselves of their position to confer kindness.
This may be called "non-action." Through non-action, you can grasp the One. The One is the root of the myriad things. It is the Way that is unopposed. [14/137/6–8]

14.36

As a general rule, human nature
is glittering and unruly when young,
is violent and vigorous when mature,
and loves what brings it benefit when elderly.

In the course of one's life, a person undergoes these several alterations. How much more is it the case that rulers change the laws countless times and that states change their rulers! If people rely on their position in life to satisfy their likes and dislikes, they will not be able to bring order to [those who take] the "low road." Thus, when the ruler loses the One and there is chaos, it is worse than when there is no ruler at all.[37]

Thus, the *Odes* states:
"Do not err. Do not forget.
Follow the ancient regulations."[38]
That expresses it. [14/137/8–11]

14.37

When the ruler favors knowledge,
he will turn his back on timeliness and rely on himself;
he will abandon technique and rely on forethought.

36. See also WZ 5/26/12–13.
37. This sentence also appears in WZ 5/26/15–16.
38. *Odes* 249.

Since the things of the world are extensive while knowledge is limited, it is not possible to rely on what is limited to tend to what is extensive. When the ruler relies solely on knowledge, his mistakes will invariably multiply. Thus, favoring knowledge is an inferior policy.

When the ruler favors courage,
he will underestimate the enemy and be lax with his defensive preparations;
he will rely on himself and dismiss the assistance of others.

When he confronts a powerful enemy with the strength of [only] his one person and does not avail himself of the multitudes but instead relies solely on his own capabilities, invariably he will not survive. Thus, favoring courage is a dangerous policy.

When the ruler favors charity,
he will lack a fixed standard for making distributions.
When there is no fixed standard of distribution above,
resentments will not cease below.[39]

If he increases taxes and fills the storehouses with surplus, the people he is helping will despise him. If he appropriates little and gives much, the quantity of his surplus will not be sufficient. Thus, favoring charity is a Way that only gives rise to resentment.

Humaneness, knowledge, courage, and strength[40] constitute the outstanding capacities of human beings, yet none suffices to rule the world. Considering the matter from this perspective,
it will not suffice to rely on the worthy and capable.
Yet it is possible to follow the Techniques of the Way.
This is clear.[41] [14/137/13–18]

---

39. LSCQ 17.6/106/11–14, "Heeding the Circumstances" (Shen shi), quotes Shen Dao:

> When a rabbit runs by, a hundred people chase it. The reason is not that a hundred people could divide one rabbit but that its distribution has not yet been settled. Since its distribution has not yet been settled, even a Yao might exhaust his strength chasing it. How much more would this be the case with an ordinary man! But when the market is filled with rabbits, passersby pay them no heed. The reason is not that they do not desire rabbits but that their distribution is settled. When distribution is settled, no one, no matter how backward, contests with another over it. Therefore, governing the world, as well as a single state, rests on nothing more than settling distribution. (Modified from Knoblock and Riegel 2000, 431–32)

For a variation on this passage in the reconstructed *Zisizi*, see Csikszentmihalyi 2004, app. 1, no. 27. The *Zisizi* version does not attribute the passage to Shen Dao.

40. Note that the qualities described here in the explanation do not precisely match those in the sayings.

41. See also WZ 5/26/1–4.

14.38

The sage makes his mind victorious;
the ordinary person makes his desires victorious.
The Superior Man disseminates upright qi;
the small man disseminates noxious qi.

That which
inwardly suits nature
outwardly accords with Rightness,
complies with Patterns when acting,
and is not burdened by external things
is upright *qi*.

That which is
attracted by succulent aromas and tastes,
excited by sounds and colors,
moved by happiness and anger,
and unmindful of the dangers that lie ahead
is noxious *qi*.

Noxious *qi* and upright *qi* injure each other;
desires and nature harm each other.
They cannot both stand.
Uphold one and the other falls.

Thus the sage rejects desires and follows his nature.

The eyes being fond of color,
the ears being fond of sounds,
the mouth being fond of taste,

coming into contact with them [i.e., color, sound, and taste], they delight in them without understanding the benefit or harm that lies therein. [These are] the desires.

When eating is not good for the body,
when hearing does not accord with the Way,
when seeing does not suit nature,

and when the three sense organs [of taste, hearing, and sight] are in conflict with one another, what relies on Rightness to bring them under control is the mind.

When you cut out a boil it cannot but be painful.
When you drink toxic medicine, it cannot but be bitter.

Yet you do these things because they are good for the body.

If you are thirsty and drink [too much] water, it cannot but be pleasing,
and if you are hungry and eat a huge meal, it cannot but be satisfying.

Yet you do not do such things because they are harmful to the nature.

In these four cases, the ears, eyes, nose, and mouth do not understand what to take and what to reject. When the mind controls them, each achieves what is appropriate.

Considering the matter from this perspective, desires cannot be made victorious. This is clear.[42] [14/137/20–27]

14.39

To regulate your body and nourish your nature,
moderate your sleep and rest,
be appropriate in your food and drink,
harmonize your happiness and anger,
and make suitable your movement and stillness.

When you achieve the [ability to] carry out these things within the self, noxious *qi* will have no means to be produced.[43] Is not this similar to one who, fearing an asthmatic attack might occur or a skin ulcer burst forth, takes the proper precautions in advance? [14/137/27–29]

14.40

Now ox meat in a ding *tripod is boiling, so flies and gnats do not dare approach it.*
The jade of the Kunlun Mountains is dense, so dirt and dust will not defile it.

The sage
does not have a rejecting mind, yet his mind is free of imperfections
and does not have an acquisitive beauty, yet his beauty is never lost.
Thus,
when offering sacrifices, he thinks of his parents but does not seek their blessings;
when feasting guests, he cultivates reverence but does not think about how he will be repaid.
Only those who do not strive after things are able to take possession of them. [14/137/29–14/138/2]

14.41

When those who occupy an honored position follow the way of public mindedness and abandon personal preferences, they are recognized as honorable but not recognized as worthy.

42. See also WZ 4/21/6–11.
43. See also WZ 4/21/13–14.

When those who possess large territories rely on enduring techniques and avoid secret stratagems, they are recognized as fair but not recognized as knowledgeable.

Inside [their states], they avoid violent acts that would arouse the resentment of their people.
Outside [their states], they avoid worthy conduct that would incite the jealousy of the Lords of the Land.
The propriety between superior and inferior
is compliant and does not deviate [from what is proper].

Those who would judge them are silenced, for what they look at is not visible. This is what is meant by the phrase "hiding in the Formless." If not those who hide in the Formless, who then can give shape to what has form?[44] [14/138/4–6]

14.42

The Way of the Three Dynasties was "to follow the natural course of things."

Thus,

when Yu dredged the Yangzi and Yellow rivers, he followed the natural properties of the water.
When Lord Millet scattered seed and planted grain, he followed the natural properties of the land.
When Tang and Wu quelled violence and rebellion, they accorded with timeliness.
Thus the empire can be attained, but it cannot be appropriated.
The title of hegemon or king can be conferred, but it cannot be sought.
If you rely on knowledge, others will dispute with you.
If you rely on strength, others will contend with you.
Though you cannot ensure that others will lack knowledge, you can ensure that others will not be able to use their knowledge against you.
Though you cannot ensure that others will lack strength, you can ensure that others will not be able to use their strength against you.

These two techniques have existed for a long time and have long been observed.

Thus,

if the ruler does not reveal his worthiness, the Lords of the Land will not be on guard.
If he does not reveal his stupidity, the common people will not feel resentment.
If the common people do not feel resentment, it is possible to obtain the usefulness of the populace.

44. Emending *shu neng xing* 孰能形 to *shu neng xing xing* 孰能形形, based on Zhang Shuangdi 1997, 2:1504n.3.

If the Lords of the Land are not on guard, it is possible to avail oneself of the world's opportune moments as they arise.

When undertakings are commensurate with those of the multitudes,
when achievements depend on the opportune moment to succeed,
the sage will have nothing to do.

Thus the *Laozi* says:

"Tigers have no place to thrust their claws;
rhinos have no place to butt their horns."[45]

The passage likely refers to such things as this. [14/138/8–14]

14.43

A drum does not absorb sounds; consequently it can produce [various] sounds.
A mirror does not retain forms; consequently it can reflect [various] forms.
Metal [bells] and stone [chimes] possess the ability to make sounds, but if you do not strike them, they will not sound.
The flute and panpipes possess the ability to emit tones, but if you do not blow them, they will not sound.

The sage internalizes what [should be] hidden and is not drawn out by things.
When affairs arise, the sage regulates them;
when things appear, the sage responds to them.[46]
Those who adorn their exterior harm their interior.
Those who cling to their emotions injure their spirit.
Those who manifest their outer refinement obscure their inner substance.
Those who do not for a moment forget their worthiness will invariably obstruct their nature.
Those who within a hundred paces do not forget their appearance will invariably encumber their bodies.

Thus,

when feathers and wings are beautiful, they injure the skeleton and marrow.
When leaves and branches are beautiful, they injure the roots and stems.

Of both being able to be beautiful, there is no instance in all the world.[47] [14/138/16–20]

---

45. *Laozi* 50.
46. See also WZ 6/33/1–2.
47. The lines beginning "Those who adorn their exterior" to "all the world" also appear in WZ 4/21/14–16.

14.44

Though Heaven possesses light, it does not worry about the people's darkness.
The people bore out doors and chisel out windows and, of their own accord, appropriate the light of Heaven.
Though Earth possesses resources, it does not worry about the people's poverty.
The people fell trees and cut grasses and, of their own accord, appropriate the resources of Earth.

[Thus,]

those who perfect Potency and the Way are like hills and mountains. Solitary and unmoving, travelers take them as their guides. They rectify themselves and find sufficiency in things. They do not offer charity to others, and those who use them likewise do not receive their kindness. Thus they are peaceful and able to endure.[48] [14/138/22–24]

14.45

Since Heaven and Earth do not confer things, there is nothing to take.
Since the sun and the moon do not exhibit kindness, there is nothing to resent.
Those who enjoy exhibiting kindness invariably increase resentments;
those who enjoy giving invariably praise taking.

Only those who hide their tracks in non-action and follow the naturalness of Heaven and Earth can make [their] patterns victorious and abandon a love of reputation.

Where reputation flourishes, the Way does not operate.
Where the Way operates, people have no status.[49]

Thus,

where praise arises, insult follows.
Where good appears, evil follows.[50] [14/138/24–27]

14.46

Benefit is the starting point of harm.
Good fortune is the harbinger of bad fortune.
Only those who do not strive after advantage are free from disadvantage.
Only those who do not strive after benefit are free from harm.[51]

48. See also WZ 4/21/18–19.
49. See also HSWZ 1.13/3/18–19: "Only those who hide their tracks . . . status." The preceding couplet, identified as "tradition says," is closely similar but not identical.
50. See also WZ 4/21/18–21.
51. See also HSWZ 1.13/3/19–20 and WZ 4/21/21–22.

A marquis who strives to become a hegemon invariably will lose his standing as a marquis.
A hegemon who strives to become a king invariably will forfeit his standing as a hegemon.

Thus,
a state considers remaining intact as the norm, becoming hegemon or king as the extraordinary exception.
A person considers life as the norm, becoming wealthy or noble as the extraordinary exception.
Only those who will not injure their kingdom for the sake of the world or harm themselves for the sake of a kingdom can be entrusted with the world. [14/138/29–31]

14.47

Those who do not understand the Way
abandon what they already possess
and strive after what they do not yet possess.

With a distressed mind and anxious thoughts, they try to realize misguided precedents.
When good fortune arises, they feel happy.
When bad fortune arises, they feel frightened.
Their spirit is exhausted by various stratagems;
their intelligence is wearied by various affairs.
Bad fortune and good fortune sprout forth,
yet to the ends of their lives they are undeterred,
for what they themselves have caused,
they turn around and blame others.
Unhappy and anxious,
their center is never balanced.
They hold to what is unexamined.
This is called "a reckless life." [14/139/1–3]

14.48

When the people's ruler favors Humaneness,
those who lack merit will be rewarded,
and those who are guilty will be pardoned.
When he favors punishments,
those who possess merit will be disregarded,
and those who are innocent will be punished.

Only the ruler who has no preferences
punishes without [causing] resentment,
exhibits kindness without [eliciting] gratitude,
accords with the level and complies with the marking cord,
and does not personally intervene.
Like Heaven and Earth,
there is nothing that he does not cover or support.

Thus,
what unifies and harmonizes is the lord;
what controls and punishes is the law.
When the people receive their punishments
yet feel no resentment or hatred,[52]
this is called "The Way." Where the Way is victorious, people have nothing to do. [14/139/5–9]

14.49

The clothing of the sage is neither long nor short.
His conduct is neither extraordinary nor unusual.

His clothing does not arouse notice.
His conduct does not elicit observation,
and his speech does not incite criticism.
When successful, he is not ostentatious.
When impoverished, he is not afraid.
When honored, he is not showy.
When ignored, he is not bereft.
He is extraordinary yet does not appear unusual.
He is always appropriate yet identifies with the multitudes.
There are no means to name him. This is what is called "Great Merging."[53] [14/139/10–11]

14.50

Whether ascending or descending,
bowing with clasped hands or yielding to another,
moving quickly or slowly,
circulating forward or back,
do so spontaneously.

52. See also WZ 5/28/15–18.
53. See also WZ 4/21/24–25.

If they are not inherent to your person by nature, none among your spontaneous feelings will tally with them. Do those things that come spontaneously, and do not abandon the prescribed framework. That's it. What need is there to apply a precedent? Thus,

those who sing spontaneously do not work at being sorrowful.
Those who dance spontaneously do not strive at being graceful.

Those who sing and dance but do not work at being sorrowful or graceful [can do so] because in all cases there is nothing rooted in their minds. [14/139/13–15]

14.51

The adept gambler neither desires a win nor fears a loss.

With a tranquil mind and settled will,
he casts the dice in a uniform fashion,
and his movements follow definite patterns.
Though he does not always win,
he invariably accumulates many tallies.

Why is this so? It is because

winning is determined by technique
and not by desires. [14/139/17–18]

14.52

The chariot driver

does not covet being the very first,
does not fear being dead last.

He regulates the pace of the horse with his hands
and harmonizes his mind with the horse.
Though he does not always win first place,
he invariably causes his horse to do its utmost.

Why is this so? It is because

winning is determined by technique
and not by desire.

For this reason,

when you eradicate desire, technique will prevail.
When you banish knowledge, the Way will become established. [14/139/18–20]

14.53

Too many deals impoverish the merchant.
Too much artistry exhausts the craftsman.

It is because their minds are not [focused on] one thing.

Thus,

when the span of a tree is great, its height is compromised.
When the flow of a river is wide, its depth is compromised.

If you possess knowledge but lack technique, though you bore with an awl you will never get through anything.

If you possess a hundred different kinds of skills but lack a single Way, though you achieve things you will not be able to sustain [your achievements].

Thus the *Odes* states:

"The good man, the Superior Man,
his propriety is one.
His propriety is one.
His heart is as if bound."[54]

How bound by oneness is the Superior Man! [14/139/22–24]

14.54

Shun plucked the five-stringed qin *and chanted the poems of the "Southern Airs" [section of the* Odes*] and thereby governed the world.*

The Duke of Zhou, before the fine meats could be removed from in front of him and before the bells and drums could be taken down from their suspension cords, had already assisted King Cheng in pacifying the world.[55]

If a person maintains one hundred *mu* of land, he will have no time for leisure, but neither is there anything that would induce him to move [away].

[But] if you rely on the One Man to listen to petitions from the whole world,
every day there will be an excess [of work]
[and so] governance will be deficient.

[Thus] he employs others to manage things [for him].[56] [14/139/26–28]

54. *Odes* 152.
55. The same image appears in 20.16.
56. For another version of this passage, see HSWZ 4.7/27/9–11.

14.55

One who occupies a revered position is like the impersonator of the dead at a sacrifice;
one who has an official post is like the invoker.

Though the impersonator of the dead is capable of skinning a dog or roasting a pig, he does not do so. [Thus], if he is not able to do such things, nothing is lost.

Though he understands the proper arrangement of the dishes and platters used to offer sacrifices and the proper sequence in which the various types of millet are offered, he does not instruct others [in these matters]. [Thus] if he is incapable of instructing others, nothing is lost.

One who is incapable of offering prayers and invocations cannot be compelled to assume the responsibilities of the invoker, yet there is no harm in such a person acting as the impersonator of the dead.

One who is incapable of driving a chariot cannot be compelled to assume the responsibilities of a charioteer, yet there is no harm in such a person acting as the rider on the left.

Therefore, the more revered the position, the more idle the occupant. The more significant the post, the fewer duties it entails. It is similar to stringing a *qin:* The short strings are made tight, but the long strings must be looser. [14/140/1–4]

14.56

Non-action is the substance of the Way.
Following behind is the outward form of the Way.

Those who do not act control those who act; this is [called] technique.
Those who follow behind control those who take the lead; this is [called] the proper sequence of things.
If you rely on technique, you will be strong.
If you understand the proper sequence of things, you will be calm.

Now when it came to giving away Mr. Bian's jade disk,[57] when he had not yet obtained it, [Mr. Bian] was ahead. When he pleaded to present it and would not give up despite his indignation, he was behind.

If three men live together and two begin to quarrel, each will think he is right,

57. Mr. Bian's jade disk 卞氏之璧, also known as Mr. He's 和 jade disk, was a fabulous jewel that was discovered by Bian He 卞和, a man of Chu, in the mountains of that state. When the jade was presented to King Li of Chu as an uncut matrix, the king suspected Bian He of fraud and had his left foot cut off as punishment. When King Li died and Bian He tried to present the jade to his son, King Wu, the king ordered that his right foot be cut off. When King Wu finally had the stone cut and polished, its precious nature was revealed. See also 6.3, 16.19, and 16.90.

and neither will listen to the other. Though the third man is a fool, he will invariably resolve the dispute from the sidelines. This is not due to his intelligence but is because he was not fighting.

If two men begin to fight and a weakling stands at their side, if he helps one man, that man will win. If he aids the other man, that man will avoid defeat. Though the two fighters are strong, invariably [the outcome is] controlled by the single weakling. This is not due to his courage, but due to the fact that he does not fight.

Looking at it from this perspective,

that those who follow behind control those who take the lead
and that those who are still defeat those who are excitable

is due to following the proper sequence of things.

To defy the Way and abandon the proper sequence of things, hoping thereby to encounter good luck;
to alter constant norms and change precedents, relying on your intelligence in your desire to cover up for yourself;
to pass over your own errors and to take credit when you hit the mark;
to conduct yourself from a position of darkness and recklessly change things;
to remain throughout your life unaware;

such actions are called "reckless."

To be dissatisfied with misfortune and satisfied with good fortune,
to regret committing errors and feel satisfied when you achieve merit,
to push ahead and not know to return,

this [too] is called "reckless." [14/140/6–14]

14.57

When your circles coincide with the compass,
when your squares coincide with the [carpenter's] square,
when your going constitutes ferocity,
when your stopping constitutes civility,
you will be able to lead a small number of people,
but you will not be able to lead the multitudes.

When you raise knotweed in rows,
when your [ceremonial] cups are [furnished with] pedestals,
when you measure out millet and pound it [to remove the husk],
when you count out rice to prepare for steaming it,
you will be able to govern a household,
but you will not be able to govern a state.

When you wash the cup before eating from it,
when you clean the goblet before drinking from it,
when you bathe before offering up food,

you will be able to nourish the elderly of your household,
but you will not be able to offer a feast to the Three Armies. [14/140/16–18]

14.58

If you are not unassuming, you cannot govern what is great.
If you are not simple, you cannot unite the multitudes.

The greatest music is invariably unassuming.
The greatest rites are invariably simple.
Unassuming, you thus may be like Heaven.
Simple, you thus may be like Earth.
The greatest music [provokes] no resentment.
The greatest rites do not [evoke] censure.

All within the Four Seas will attach themselves to your rule, and thus you will be able to become emperor. [14/140/20–21]

14.59

When the mind is agitated,
though provided with a well-made bed and soft mats, you will not feel comfortable.
Though provided with a meal of wild rice and succulent beef, you will not find the taste good.
Though provided with the [music of] the qin *and* se, *and the piping of the flute, you will not feel joy.*

Only when vexations dissipate and agitations disappear will food taste good, a bed feel peaceful, a dwelling feel secure, and wanderings be joyful.

Looking at it from this perspective,
Nature has the means to be joyful,
and the means to be sorrowful.
Now if you try to promote what cannot bring joy to your nature
and you harm what brings joy to your nature,

though enriched by possessing the world and revered as the Son of Heaven, you will not be able to avoid becoming a sorrowful person.

In all cases, human nature
enjoys peace and quiet and dislikes discord and noise;
it enjoys rest and relaxation and dislikes toil and hard work.
When the mind is consistently free of desires, it is said to be "peaceful."
When the body is consistently free of tasks, it is said to be "resting."
If you allow the mind to wander in peace and quiet

and abandon the body to leisure,
thereby awaiting Heaven's decree,
within you will find joy,
and without you will be free from worries.
Even something as grand as the world will not be sufficient to change your unitary vision.
Should the sun or moon be eclipsed, it will not be sufficient to compel you to change your intentions.
Thus,
though lowly, it is as if you were honored;
though impoverished, it is as if you were wealthy. [14/140/23–28]

14.60

The greatest Way is devoid of form.
The greatest Humaneness is devoid of affection.
The greatest disputation is devoid of sound.
The greatest honesty is devoid of modesty.
The greatest courage is devoid of haughtiness.

When you do not abandon these five, you are heading in the right direction. [14/141/1]

14.61

When armies contend with too many orders, they will grow chaotic.
When wine [drinking] is under too many constraints, there will be disputes.
When armies grow chaotic, they will be routed.
When there are disputes, there will be mutual harm.

Therefore,
what begins as beautiful and elegant always ends up vulgar and vile.
What begins joyfully always ends up sorrowfully.
Yet things that begin in simplicity
invariably end up in perfect harmony.

Now suppose you prepare good wine and savory food to fete your guests and greet them with a modest bearing and humble words, hoping in this way to join with them in happy concord. Yet while contending to fill your guest's cup, contrary [to expectations], a quarrel ensues. In the course of the quarrel, both parties are injured, arousing the enmity of each other's clans for three generations. Thus contrary to expectations, you have elicited the very thing you despise. Such are the dangers of wine! [14/141/3–6]

14.62

The shortcoming of the Odes *lies in its partiality;*
the shortcoming of the Music *lies in its critiques;*
the shortcoming of the Rites *lies in its criticisms.*[58] [14/141/8]

14.63

It is not the case that the zhi *tone lacks a* yu *sound or that the* yu *tone lacks the* zhi *sound.*

Of the five tones, none is without overtones, but it is the dominant tone that determines the name of a specific note.

Thus, Humaneness and Rightness, wisdom and courage are equally possessed by the sage,

Yet they all contribute to the single designation of the sage; all speak of his greatness. [14/141/10–11]

14.64

Yang qi *arises in the northeast and culminates in the southwest.*
Yin qi *arises in the southwest and culminates in the northeast.*

From their inception the evolutions of yin and yang are synchronized.
Daily [the one that is waxing] strengthens [within its own] category.
[Moving] slowly and keeping equidistant from each other,
One becomes hot enough to melt sand;
The other becomes cold enough to freeze water.
Thus, the sage is cautious and circumspect concerning what he accumulates. [14/141/13–14]

14.65

Water comes out of the mountains and flows to the sea;
grain grows in the fields and is stored in granaries.

The sage observes the beginning of things and knows their end. [14/141/16–17]

58. A fuller version of this statement is found in 20.13.

14.66

We offer up astringent mushrooms from a sitting mat;
we offer up dark wine in a zun *goblet;*
we offer up raw fish on a zu *stand;*
we offer up unsalted soup in a dou *vessel.*

Such foods neither please the ears or eyes nor suit the palate or belly, yet the former kings valued them, because they attended first to the root and only afterward to the branches. [14/141/19–21]

14.67

When the sage encounters things in the world amid their thousand alterations and myriad evolutions, he invariably relies on what never transforms to respond to what is always transforming.

Cold and heat stand in opposition to each other.
During the season of intense cold, the ground cracks and water freezes, yet fire's capacity to burn is not diminished as a consequence.
During the season of intense heat, stones melt and metal fuses, yet fire's capacity to burn is not enhanced as a consequence.
The alterations of cold and heat neither harm nor benefit his person, for his inner substance is unchanging. [14/141/23–25]

14.68

The sage constantly follows behind and does not take the lead;
he constantly responds and does not initiate;
he does not advance to seek after things;
nor does he retreat to decline things.

"I follow the times for three years;
when the time's departed, there I would go.
I fled the times for three years,
so the time was at my back.
I have no discarding or seeking,
in the center I find my place."

The Way of Heaven is without affection; it gives only to those who have Potency.[59] Those who possess the Way do not lose the opportune moment to accommodate

59. See also WZ 4/21/27–4/22/1.

others, and those who do not possess the Way lose the opportune moment to accommodate others. If you rectify yourself and await your fate, once a propitious moment arrives, you can neither welcome nor oppose it. Whether you impede it or seek convergence with it, once the opportune moment passes, you cannot pursue it or change its course.

Thus, you will not say: "I have done nothing and yet the empire remains distant."

Nor will you say: "I desire nothing yet the empire does not come to me." [14/141/27–14/142/3]

14.69

In ancient times, those who preserved themselves
rejoiced in their Moral Potency and forgot their lowly status; therefore fame could not alter their wills.
They rejoiced in the Way and forgot their poverty; therefore profit could not disturb their minds.[60]

Though concerns for fame and profit filled the world, it did not suffice to alter their wills.

Thus,
they were pure and able to be joyous;
they were tranquil and able to live peacefully.
Thus, those who govern themselves are those with whom you may speak of the Way. [14/142/5–6]

14.70

Now the difference between your own life and the time dating back to the Great Vastness is distant indeed.
The difference between your own death and the eternity of Heaven and Earth is immense indeed.

To expend the life span of a single person worrying about the chaos of the world is like worrying that there is insufficient water in a river and trying to augment it with one's tears. The turtle lives for three thousand years, whereas the mayfly does not live more than three days. Now if you rely on the mayfly to augment the turtle's life, people will surely laugh at you. Thus, those who stop worrying about the chaos of

60. For the notion of the undisturbed or unmoved mind (*budongxin* 不動心), see *Mencius* 2A.2.

the world and simply delight in governing themselves are those with whom you may speak of the Way.[61] [14/142/6–9]

14.71

When the Superior Man does good, he cannot ensure that it will bring good fortune;
when he refuses to do evil, he cannot ensure that it will not bring bad fortune.

If good fortune arrives, since it is not something he sought, he does not proclaim his achievements;
if bad fortune arrives, since it is not something he elicited, he does not regret his actions.

If he should cultivate himself inwardly to the utmost and still adversity and bad fortune arrive, it is due to Heaven and not the person. Therefore, within himself his mind is constantly tranquil and still, and his Moral Potency is unencumbered. Even the barking of a dog cannot startle him because he naturally trusts his genuine responses.

Thus,
those who understand the Way are not confused;
those who understand fate are free from anxiety.[62] [14/142/11–14]

14.72

When the ruler of a state possessing ten thousand chariots passes away, we bury his bones in the wild lands and worship his spirit in the Mingtang.

[This is because] the spirit is more highly honored than the physical form.

Thus,
when the spirit regulates, the physical form complies,
but when the physical form prevails, the spirit dissipates.

Acuity and keenness may be employed, but you must revert to the spirit. This is called "Grand Vacuity."[63] [14/142/16–17]

Translated by Sarah A. Queen

61. See also WZ 4/22/6–8.
62. See also WZ 4/22/1–3.
63. See also WZ 4/22/3–4.

Fifteen

AN OVERVIEW OF THE MILITARY

As THE title makes clear, "An Overview of the Military" is devoted to military affairs in a very broad sense. Its purpose is to instruct the ruler in all aspects of this subject, from tactics and strategy to the role of the military in state and society at large. Although it is highly derivative of earlier military literature of the Warring States, it is a unique synthesis of these materials that is in keeping with the broader perspective of the *Huainanzi* as a whole. In its treatment of the normatively correct principles guiding the monarch's use of the military, the perspective of chapter 15 dovetails closely, and unsurprisingly, with the political interests of Liu An and his court of Huainan.

The Chapter Title

"Bing lüe" 兵略, translated here as "An Overview of the Military," parallels the title of chapter 21, "Yao lüe" 要略, "An Overview of the Essentials." The basic meaning of *bing* is an "edged weapon." Through a process of metonymy over the course of the Spring and Autumn and Warring States periods, this character came to signify first the common foot soldier who carried a weapon into battle and then, when large infantry armies became the norm, the military and its affairs in the abstract.

Lüe can mean "to plan," and so this chapter title is sometimes rendered "Military

Strategies" or "Military Plans."[1] It can also, as in the case of this chapter and chapter 21, have the sense of "overview" or "general summation." As we demonstrate, this chapter draws on and gives an overview of the large body of military writing that already existed in the early Han period. The same impulse to "survey the field" likely informed the similarly titled "Bing shu lüe" (An Overview of Military Writings), which Liu Xiang (ca. 77–ca. 6 B.C.E.) eventually included in his *Qi lüe* (*Seven General Categories*),[2] the first known attempt to systematically classify the written legacy of the empire.

As the chapter summary in chapter 21 makes clear, "An Overview of the Military" not only discusses "the techniques of battle, victory, assault, and capture," but also

> is what [enables you] to
> know that when you form for battle or deploy to fight contrary to the Way, it will not work;
> know that when you assault and capture or fortify and defend contrary to Moral Potency, it will not be formidable. (21.2)

In other words, the chapter is not concerned exclusively with tactics and strategy but encompasses the larger cosmic patterns and ethical norms that constrain the use of military force. Moreover, when chapter 21 enumerates the chapter themes by demonstrating their organic integrity, it explains the segue from chapter 15 to chapter 16 as follows:

> To know grand overviews but not know analogies and illustrations,
> you would lack the means to clarify affairs by elaboration. (21.3)

This shows that the *Huainanzi* authors viewed chapter 15 as not simply a treatise on military affairs but also a well-crafted literary work exemplary of an "overview" as a generic form. Thus we render the title of chapter 15 as "An Overview of the Military."

Summary and Key Themes

A number of words are used in chapter 15 (and elsewhere in the *Huainanzi*) in a technical sense derived from the military literature of the Warring States. One example of this is the distinction between the "extraordinary" and the "usual."[3] Earlier texts

1. See, for example, Ames 1994, 70, "Summary of Military Strategies"; and Csikszentmihalyi 2004, 89, "Military Strategies."

2. *Han shu* 30, 1701.

3. For a discussion of these terms in the history of the military literature, see Ralph D. Sawyer, *Sun Tzu: The Art of War* (Boulder, Colo.: Westview Press, 1993), 147–50.

like the *Wuzi*, *Weiliaozi*, and *Sunzi*[4] worked these terms into a theory of the tactical dialectic ruling the field of battle: the skilled commander must know the "usual" tactics to be applied in each situation, but he must always be ready to achieve surprise by producing an "extraordinary" tactical innovation (and correspondingly be prepared for the same from his opponent). Thus when the *Huainanzi* declares that "the mutual response of the extraordinary and the usual are like [the way that] water, fire, metal, and wood take turns being servant and master" (15.23), it is asserting a fundamental correlation between the dynamics of the battlefield and those of the basic energies of the cosmos. Most of these uses of technical vocabulary from the earlier literature are glossed in the notes or included in appendix A, but two terms merit special discussion here.

The first is *quan* 權. One of its original meanings is, as a verb, "to weigh" and, as a noun, the weight used in conjunction with a scale for measuring weight. From this root, other meanings, such as "authority," were derived during the Warring States period. The image of the scales informs most usages of *quan* in Warring States military texts and generally refers to a capacity that enables a unit or its commander to achieve certain outcomes ("tip the scales") on the field of battle. Chapter 15 identifies two types of *quan* that are operative in warfare: the superior knowledge of the commander and the superior training of the troops. We translate this concept as "heft."

A term closely related to *quan* is *shi* 勢.[5] In both pre-Han military texts and the *Huainanzi*, *shi* denotes the total combat effectiveness (actual or potential) of a unit, deployment, or invested position. This measure is determined by both the intrinsic and extrinsic factors affecting the military formation in question at any given time. Thus, all things being equal, ten highly trained archers have more *shi* than do ten poorly trained ones, but if the former are placed in a valley and the latter are deployed on a hilltop, the differential in *shi* might be reversed. Because the calculation of *shi* combines intrinsic and extrinsic factors in this way, we distinguish it from *quan* by translating it as "force" in chapter 15.[6] In keeping with its roots in the military literature of the Warring States, "force" is the cornerstone of the tactical and strategic philosophy of chapter 15. It is adduced as the single indispensable factor on which the final outcome of conflict depends, vastly more determinative than the relative moral qualities of matched combatants or the intercession of supernatural powers. (Note that *shi* appears in other chapters of the *Huainanzi* with other meanings and connotations and that a common translation of the term in other contexts is "positional advantage.")

---

4. The *Sunzi bingfa* discusses the "extraordinary" and the "usual" in 5/4/11–16, and the *Weiliaozi* in 18/30/7–8. The *Wuzi* advises "executing the extraordinary" to achieve victory in 5/43/13.

5. Both *quan* and *shi* are discussed at length in Victor Mair, *The Art of War: Sun Zi's Military Methods* (New York: Columbia University Press, 2007), and *Soldierly Methods: Vade Mecum for an Iconoclastic Translation of Sun Zi bingfa*, Sino-Platonic Papers, no. 178 (Philadelphia: Department of Asian Languages and Civilizations, University of Pennsylvania, 2008).

6. *Shi* is a concept that ultimately migrated into the political literature of the Warring States, where it denoted the forms of power or advantage that accrued to civil officials by virtue of their position or circumstances. The *Huainanzi* also uses this term with this meaning in other chapters, and in those places we have opted for translations better suited to the particular context.

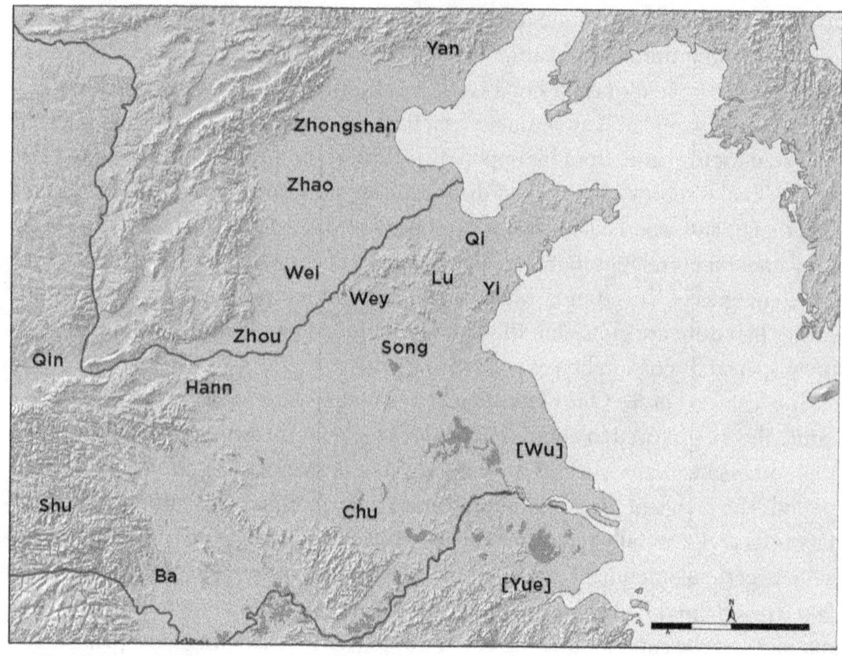

Many of the historical anecdotes recounted in the *Huainanzi* involved rivalries and conflicts among the major states of the Warring States period, whose approximate locations around 400 B.C.E. are shown. The state of Wu had been conquered by Yue in 473 B.C.E., and the once-powerful state of Jin had fragmented into the states of Hann, Wei, and Zhao in 403 B.C.E. The territory of the Yi peoples in southern Shandong was not recognized as a state by the Sinitic polities of the central plains. (Map by Sara Hodges, with data from the China Historical Geographic Information Service [CHGIS], version 4, Harvard Yenching Institute, Cambridge, Mass., January 2007)

As indicated earlier, the perspective of chapter 15 differs in several respects from that of the earlier military literature. First, "An Overview of the Military" treats military affairs in a manner that expresses the intrinsic interests and concerns of the *Huainanzi*'s eponymous patron, Liu An. The chapter addresses how the military may be used efficiently and when and under what circumstances the military may be used legitimately. Borrowing a formula from Warring States and early Han political literature, "An Overview of the Military" establishes that military force may be legitimately applied only "to sustain those who [were] perishing, [and] revive those [lineages] that had been cut off."[7]

7. The phrase "sustain those that are perishing, [and] revive those [lineages] that had been cut off" 存亡繼絕 appears in many Warring States texts, including the *Guanzi*, *Xunzi*, and *Lüshi chunqiu*. It originally denoted the definitive virtuous merit of a hegemon, a leader who used military power to moral rather than coercive ends. By the Han period, this phrase had become associated with the Confucian exegetical tradition of the *Spring and Autumn Annals* and is used in the *Chunqiu Guliang zhuan*, Duke Xi, year 17, to describe the merit of Duke Huan of Qi.

These lines were used to evoke their original context. The "perishing" and "cut off" to which they refer are not people in general but the hereditary noble houses chartered by the Zhou kings to carry on ancestral cults and exercise local authority. This Zhou model was precisely the institutional structure on which Liu An's position as "king of Huainan" was predicated. The larger import of "An Overview of the Military" is thus clear: that military power cannot be used to centralize routine power over the entire empire, that it can be applied only in a proper spirit of deference to the hereditary privileges of the noble houses that honeycombed the Han domain (such as that of Huainan).

This assertion is not a mere moral injunction. As "An Overview of the Military" asserts at several points, the normatively correct and practically efficacious uses of the military are ultimately one and the same. Any assault directed at other than a "kingdom without the Way" will result in either defeat or, through the cosmic processes described in chapter 6, calamity rebounding on the state and person of the victorious aggressor. In this respect, the *Huainanzi* agrees with the *Jing fa* (*Constant Standard*), the first of five texts appended to the *Laozi* B manuscript discovered at Mawangdui. That text declares that "if your achievement [that is, your conquest] is complete and you do not stop, your person will be endangered and suffer calamity."[8] The *Huainanzi* extends this principle to a further extreme. Chapter 15 closes with a detailed description of purifying rituals that must be performed by both the ruler and the commander of a victorious army in order to avoid calamity, even if they took care not to transgress cosmic limits.

Another theme of chapter 15 that distinguishes it from earlier military texts like the *Sunzi* centers on its discussion of the commander. Like the latter text, "An Overview of the Military" celebrates knowledge and skill as definitive capacities of the victorious commander. These qualities are not enough, however. Consistent with the perspective of the rest of the *Huainanzi*, chapter 15 asserts that knowledge and skill must be wedded to a potency that is rooted more deeply than rational thought. Only a commander who has come to embody the Way and its Potency through mystical self-cultivation will be completely unfathomable to his enemies and perfectly effective in responding to the constantly changing conditions of the battlefield:

> [H]e sets his mind in the Field of Profound Mystery
> and lodges his will in the Spring of the Nine Returns. (15.17)

Sources

"An Overview of the Military" is one of the most derivative chapters of a highly synthetic text, its structure drawing heavily from the classical military writings,

8. Mawangdui Hanmu boshu zhengli xiaozu, *Mawangdui Hanmu boshu* (Beijing: Wenwu, 1980), 45.

especially the *Sunzi bingfa*,[9] inherited by Han literati from the Warring States.[10] For example, the lines

Thus,
a complete soldier is first victorious and only then seeks battle;
a defeated soldier gives battle first and only then seeks victory. (15.9)

are quoted almost verbatim from the *Sunzi*.[11] And whereas chapter 15 declares,

[T]he force of one who is skilled at using arms is
like releasing amassed water from a thousand-*ren*[-high] dike,
like rolling round stones into a ten-thousand-*zhang*[-deep] gorge (15.18)

the *Sunzi* asserts, "One who is victorious [leads] the people into battle like releasing amassed water into a thousand-*ren*[-deep] gorge"[12] and elsewhere states, "The force of one who is skilled at battle is like rolling round stones down a thousand *ren*[-high] mountain."[13]

Warring States texts like the *Sunzi* developed a novel view of military affairs that contrasted with the aristocratic warrior ethos of the Bronze Age. Whereas the latter stressed personal courage, chivalric honor, and public displays of martial prowess, the new literature represented the military as a pragmatic implement of state power unrelated to qualities of valor, the use of which necessitated the application of skill, cunning, and deception. The aristocratic commander had been expected to be a martial hero, but the new Warring States commander was expected to be a sagacious and coldly calculating strategist.[14] By the time of the Han Empire, this novel Warring States perspective on military affairs had become the hegemonic view and the basic template informing the state's ongoing practices of military recruitment and organization. In echoing texts like the *Sunzi*, the *Huainanzi* is thus acknowledging the received and broadly accepted wisdom.

The *Huainanzi*'s discussion of military affairs is not, however, entirely constrained by the new "professionalism" of the *Sunzi* and its ilk. Chapter 15 presents a unique synthesis of ideas. Those regarding tactics, strategy, and the art of command cor-

---

9. For a complete translation of all the extant military texts of the early period, see Ralph D. Sawyer, *The Seven Military Classics of Ancient China, Including The Art of War* (Boulder, Colo.: Westview Press, 1993).

10. Many English translations of the *Sunzi bingfa* are available for review and comparison with chap. 15 of the *Huainanzi*. Among the best are Sawyer, *Sun Tzu*; Roger Ames, *Sun-tzu: The Art of Warfare* (New York: Ballantine Books, 1993); Samuel B. Griffith, *Sun Tzu: Art of War* (Oxford: Oxford University Press, 1963); and Mair, *Art of War*.

11. BSSZ A4/3/24. The only difference in the text of the *Sunzi bingfa* is that it refers to the "victorious soldier" rather than the "complete soldier."

12. BSSZ A4/4/6.

13. BSSZ A5/4/28.

14. Mark Edward Lewis, *Sanctioned Violence in Early China* (Albany: State University of New York Press, 1990), 15–136.

respond most closely to that of the Warring States military texts. But as suggested earlier, these ideas are framed in a larger discussion of the purposes and ethics of military power based on Confucian canonical texts, especially the *Spring and Autumn Annals* and its commentaries, and Daoist texts such as the silk manuscript texts appended to the *Laozi* B text discovered in Mawangdui Tomb 3.

The Chapter in the Context of the *Huainanzi* as a Whole

"An Overview of the Military" serves several purposes in the overall structure of the text. Inasmuch as the text claims to be a comprehensive compendium of all knowledge necessary to rule, it could not fail to include some discussion of military affairs. Chapter 15's synthesis of Warring States military literature is thus partly an exercise in "due diligence" by the *Huainanzi*'s authors. In accordance with the text's overarching syncretic scheme, this perusal of military affairs logically comes in the late sections of the text. Elsewhere in its discussion of cosmogony and human history, the *Huainanzi* makes clear that warfare and weaponry were late, "devolutionary" developments in the evolution of both the cosmos and human society. They thus represent instruments of state power that are of lower efficacy and priority and are placed toward the back of the text, after more fundamental realms of concern like cosmology, personal cultivation, and even ritual. This late positioning of "An Overview of the Military" is somewhat misleading, however. Because military force and military organization are the organs of state power most closely associated with the routinization and centralization of political authority that threatened the very survival of the court of Huainan, chapter 15 provides a platform on which the authors and patron of the *Huainanzi* defended their own political priorities and interests.

Andrew Meyer

Fifteen

15.1

In antiquity, those who used the military did not value expanding territory or covet the possession of gold and jade. They sought to sustain those who [were] perishing, revive those [lineages] that had been cut off,[1] pacify the chaos of the world, and eliminate harm to the myriad people.

All beasts that have blood and *qi*,
are equipped with teeth and horns.[2]
They have claws in front and paws behind.
Those with horns gore;
those with teeth bite;
those with poison sting;
those with hooves kick.
When they are happy, they play with one another;
when they are angry they injure one another;
this is their Heaven[-born] nature.

Humans have instincts for clothing and food, yet [material] things are lacking. Thus they settle together in various locations. If the division is not equal, if demands

1. The phrase "sustain those that are perishing, [and] revive those [lineages] that had been cut off" (*cun wang ji jue* 存亡繼絶) is used in the *Chunqiu Guliang zhuan*, Duke Xi, year 17, to describe the merit of Duke Huan of Qi.

2. A similar description of animals is found in 19.5. See also 1.7.

are not fulfilled, they fight. When they fight, the strong threaten the weak and the brave attack the cowardly.

People do not have strong muscles and bones or sharp claws and teeth, thus

they cut leather to make armor;
they forge iron to make blades.

Greedy and cruel people brutalize and rob the world. The myriad people are shaken; they cannot rest in tranquillity with what they possess. The sage rises up vehemently, punishing the strong and the violent [and] pacifying the chaotic age. He suppresses danger and eliminates disorder.

He makes the sullied pure;
he makes the imperiled calm.

Thus people are not cut off in mid[life].
The origins of the military are distant!

The Yellow Emperor once warred with Yan Di;[3]
Zhuan Xu once fought with Gong Gong.[4]
The Yellow Emperor warred in the wilds of Zhuolu;[5]
Yao warred on the banks of the River Dan;[6]
Shun attacked the Youmiao;[7]
Qi attacked the Youhu.[8]

Since the time of the Five Thearchs, [no one] has been able to ban [the military], much less in a declining age! [15/142/21–29]

15.2

The military sees to it that the violent are curtailed and the disorderly [are] punished.

Yan Di created a conflagration, thus the Yellow Emperor captured him;
Gong Gong created a flood, thus Zhuan Xu executed him.

If one teaches them the Way, guides them with Potency but they do not listen, then one displays martial might to them. If one displays martial might to them but they do not obey, one controls them with weapons and armor. Thus the sage's use of the military is like combing hair or weeding seedlings; those he eliminates are few, [and] those he benefits are many.

There is no harm greater than killing innocent people to support an unrighteous king;

---

3. The primeval conflict between the Yellow Emperor and Yan Di is mentioned in *Lüshi chuhqiu* 7.2. For Yan Di, the god of the south, fire, and the planet Mars, see 3.6.

4. For the battle between Zhuan Xu and Gong Gong, see 3.1.

5. This refers to the ancient battle between the Yellow Emperor and Chi You. See *Zhuangzi* 29.

6. *Lüshi chunqiu* 20.4 records a campaign by Yao against the Southern Man on the River Dan.

7. Shun's campaign against the Youmiao (Miao) is recorded in the "Shun dian" chapter of the *Documents*.

8. Qi's campaign against the Youhu is recorded in the "Gan shi" chapter of the *Documents*.

there is no calamity more profound than to exhaust the wealth of the world to satisfy one person's desires.

If [King] Jie of Xia and [King] Djou of Yin had met with calamity as soon as they harmed the people, they would not have reached [the point of] creating the "roasting beam."[9]

If [Duke] Li of Jin and [King] Kang of Song had [met with] the death of their persons and the destruction of their states as soon as they committed one act of unrighteousness, they would not have reached the point of invading and conquering or unleashing tyranny.

These four rulers all committed small transgressions and were not punished, thus they arrived at unsettling the world, harming the common people [and] extending the calamity of the realm by giving free rein to a single man's deviance. This is what the standard of Heaven will not accept. A ruler is established in order to curtail the violent and punish the disorderly. Now if one commands the strength of the myriad people yet conversely commits cruelty and robbery, this is like a tiger sprouting wings. How can it not be eliminated? [15/143/1–8]

One who raises fish in a pond must fend off otters;
one who raises birds and animals must likewise fend off wolves.

How much more so the one who governs people!
Thus the military of a hegemon or king

is given forethought according to standards,
is planned for according to strategy,
is applied according to Rightness.
It is not used to destroy those that survive
[but] to sustain [those that] are perishing.

When he hears that the ruler of an enemy state is being cruel to his people, he raises the military and descends on [the enemy's] borders.

He blames the enemy for his lack of Rightness;
he criticizes him for his excessive actions.

When the military reaches the suburbs [of the enemy capital], he commands the army, saying:

"Do not cut down trees;
do not disturb graves;
do not scorch the five grains;
do not burn property;
do not take the people as slaves;
do not steal the six domestic animals."

Then he issues a pronouncement and effects an edict, saying, "The ruler of X kingdom has scorned Heaven and insulted the ghosts.

He has imprisoned the innocent;
he has wrongfully executed the blameless.

9. A cruel punishment famously associated with King Djou, it is also mentioned in 2.14, 10.89, 11.1, 12.35, and 21.4.

This is what is punished by Heaven,
what is hated by the people.

The coming of the military is to cast aside the unrighteous and to restore the virtuous. Anyone who opposes the Way of Heaven and leads those who rob the people will be killed and his clan exterminated.

Anyone who leads his family to obey will be given an income for his household;
anyone who leads his village to obey will be rewarded with [control of] his village;
anyone who leads his town to obey will be given his town as a fief.
Anyone who leads his district to obey will be made marquis of his district."

His conquest of the kingdom does not touch the people; he [only] discards their ruler and changes their government.

He reveres their excellent scholars and gives prominence to the worthy and the good;
he uplifts their orphans and widows and shows compassion to their poor and desperate.
He releases those [unjustly] imprisoned;
he rewards those who have merit.

The common people open their doors and await him; they cook rice and supply him; only fearing that he will not come.

This was how Tang and Wu became kings
and how [Duke] Huan of Qi and [Duke] Wen of Jin became hegemons.

Thus when the ruler is without the Way, the people yearn for the military [just] as they hope for rain during a drought or plead for water when they are thirsty. Who among them will lift a weapon to meet the military? Thus to conclude without battle is the ultimate of the righteous military. [15/143/10–21]

15.3

In regard to the military of later ages, although rulers may be without the Way, none do not dig moats, build battlements, and defend [them]. Those who attack do not do so to curtail violence or eliminate harm; they want to invade the land and expand their territory. For this reason, the bodies pile up and the blood flows; they face one another all day, yet the achievement of a hegemon does not appear in the age. It is because they act selfishly.

One who wars for territory cannot become a king;
one who wars for himself cannot establish his merit.
One who takes up a task on behalf of others will be aided by the multitude;
one who takes up a task on his own behalf will be discarded by the multitude.
One who is aided by the multitude must [become] strong even if he is weak;
one who is discarded by the multitude must perish even if he is great. [15/143/23–26]

The military is
weak if it loses the Way;
strong if it obtains the Way.
The commander is
inept if he loses the Way;
skillful if he obtains the Way.
What is called the Way
embodies the circle and is modeled on the square,
shoulders the yin and embraces the yang,
is soft on the left and hard on the right,
treads in the obscure and carries illumination.

It alters and transforms without constancy; it obtains the source of the One and thereby responds limitlessly. This is called spirit illumination.

The circle is Heaven;
the square is earth.
Heaven is circular and without terminus, thus one cannot view its form;
the earth is square and without boundaries, thus one cannot see its gateway.
Heaven transforms and nurtures yet is without form;
Earth generates and rears and yet is without measure.
Vague, hazy, who knows their capacity?

All things have that which defeats them;[10] only the Way is invincible.[11] It is invincible because it has no constant shape or force. It cycles ceaselessly, like the motion of the sun and moon.

Just as summer and autumn alternate,
just as the sun and the moon have day and night,
it reaches an end and begins again;
it illuminates and becomes dark again.
None can attain its pattern. [15/144/1–7]
It controls form yet is formless;
thus its merit can be complete.
It objectifies things yet is no object;
thus it triumphs and does not submit. [15/144/9]

15.4

Form/punishment[12] is the ultimate of the military. Arriving at being without form/punishment may be called the ultimate of the ultimate. For this reason, the great

10. Following Wang Shumin's proposed emendation. See Lau, HNZ, 144n.3.

11. Following Wang Shumin's proposed emendation. See Lau, HNZ, 144n.4.

12. This is a deliberate pun. The character translated (*xing* 刑) means both "form" (形) and "punishment," and both meanings are being invoked here. The latter sense is that punishing wrongdoing is the ultimate end of the military, but the ultimate fulfillment of this end is achieved when punishments are no longer necessary. The former sense is that "form" (the formation of the army in battle, the form

military does no injury; it communicates with the ghosts and spirits. It does not brandish the five weapons, [yet] none in the world dares oppose it. It sets up its drums [but] does not open its arsenal, and none of the Lords of the Land do not freeze in terror. Thus

one who wars from the temple becomes emperor;[13]
one who [effects] spirit transformation becomes king.

What is called "warring from the temple" is modeling [oneself] on the Way of Heaven.

Spirit transformation is modeling [oneself] on the four seasons.

He cultivates governance within his borders and those afar long for his Potency;
he achieves victory without battle, and the Lords of the Land submit to his might.

It is because internally his government is ordered. [15/144/9–12]

In antiquity those who obtained the Way

in stillness modeled [themselves] on Heaven and Earth,
in motion complied with the sun and moon.
In delight and anger they corresponded to the four seasons;
in calling and answering they were comparable to the thunder and lightning.
Their voice and breath did not oppose the eight winds;
their contracting and extending did not exceed the five standards.[14]
Below to those [creatures] that have armor and scales;
above to those that have fur and feathers;

all were ordered from first to last. Among the myriad creatures and the hundred clans, from beginning to end, none was without its proper place.

For this reason, [the Way]

enters what is small without being pressed,
lodges in what is vast without being exposed.
It seeps into metal and stone;
it washes over grasses and trees.

[From] something that expands to fill the limits of the six coordinates to the end of a single hair, nothing does not cleave to it. The penetration of the Way suffuses what is [most] subtle. There is nowhere it does not reside; this is why it triumphs over the powerful and the many. [15/144/14–18]

---

of plans and operations) is the ultimate arbiter of success for the military, but achieving a state of "formlessness" (or accessing the power of the Formless) is the ultimate embodiment of martial skill.

13. "Warring from the temple" 廟戰 alludes to the first chapter of the *Sunzi bingfa*, which discusses the calculations made in the ancestral temple before battle has been joined. The basic notion here is that victory is achieved in the careful preparation before the battle, not in heroics on the field of battle itself. See 15.9.

14. Compare the "five positions" (*wu wei* 五位) in 5.13.

15.5

In archery, if the calibration of the sights is not correct, the target will not be hit.
With the thoroughbred, if [even] one tally goes unused, a thousand *li* will not be reached.[15]

Being defeated in battle does not happen on the day the drums give the order [to advance]; one's daily conduct has been without discipline for a long time. Thus in the military that has obtained the Way,

the chocks are not removed from the chariot [wheels];
the mounts are not saddled;
the drums raise no dust;
the banners are not unfurled;
the armor is not removed from its casings;[16]
the blades do not taste blood;
the court does not change its location;
the merchants do not leave the market;
the farmers do not leave the fields.

When [the ruler] issues a righteous summons and charges them,

large kingdoms pay court;
small cities submit.

He follows people's desires and marshals the people's strength by eliminating cruelty and dispelling thievery.

Thus,

those who value the same [thing] will die for one another;
those who share the same feelings complete one another;
those who have the same desires will find one another;
those who hate the same thing will assist one another.
If one moves in compliance with the Way, the world will [respond as] an echo.
If one plans in compliance with the people, the world will be one's weapon.

When hunters are pursuing game, the chariots race and the men run, each exhausting his strength. There is no threat of punishment, yet they scold one another for stumbling and urge one another on because they [all] will share in the benefit.

When those in the same boat are crossing a river and meet suddenly with wind and waves, the sons of the hundred clans all quickly grab the oars and row the vessel,[17] as if they were the right and left hands [of a single person]. They do not contend with one another because they share the same distress.

15. "Thoroughbred" (*ji* 驥) is literally a horse capable of traversing a thousand *li* in a single day. The point here is that despite its remarkable talents, the thoroughbred cannot complete the journey unless its rider is equipped beforehand with all the official tallies that will afford passage through government gate stations along the way.

16. Following Zhang Shuangdi 1997, 2:1558n.22.

17. Following Yang Shuda's reading. See Zhang Shuangdi 1997, 2:1559n.26.

Thus the enlightened king's use of the military is to eliminate injury to the world, and he shares its benefits with the people. The people work as sons do for their fathers, as younger brothers for their elder brothers. The impact of [the king's] might is like a mountain collapsing or a dike bursting, what enemy would dare to oppose him? Thus, he who excels at using the military uses [the people] for their own sakes.

If you use [people] for their own sakes, then none in the world may not be used.

If you use [people] for your own sake, what you achieve will be scanty. [15/144/20–29]

15.6

The military has three foundations:

In ordering the kingdom, regulate within the borders.

In effecting Humaneness and Rightness, spread Moral Potency and Benevolence.

In establishing correct laws, block deviant paths.[18]

[When]

the collected ministers are intimately close,
the common people are harmonious,
superiors and inferiors are of a single mind,
ruler and minister unite their efforts.
The Lords of the Land submit to your might and the four directions cherish your Moral Potency;
you cultivate governance in the temple hall and extend control beyond one thousand *li*;
you fold your hands, issue commands, and the world responds as an echo.

This is the highest use of the military.

[When]

the territory is broad and the people numerous;
the ruler is worthy and the commanders loyal;
the kingdom is rich and the military strong;
covenants and prohibitions are trustworthy;
pronouncements and orders are clear.
The two armies oppose each other;
the bells and drums face each other;

yet the enemy flees before the soldiers meet or blades clash. This is the middling use of the military.

[When]

18. In accordance with William Boltz's (private communication) identification of the rhyme scheme, preserving *sui* 隧, instead of Lau's (HNZ 15/145/1) suggested emendation to *dao* 道.

you understand what suits the terrain,
practice the beneficial [use of] narrow and obstructed [positions],
discern the alterations of the extraordinary and the usual,[19]
investigate the rules for marching and formation, dispersion and concentration;
bind the drumsticks [to your forearms] and roll the drums.
White blades meet;
flying arrows are exchanged;
you wade through blood and tread through guts;
you cart the dead away and support the wounded;
the blood flows for a thousand *li;*
exposed corpses fill the field;

thus victory is decided. This is the lowest use of the military.

Now everyone in the world

knows to work at studying its branches,
and none knows to resolve to cultivate its root.

This is to discard the root and plant the limbs. [15/145/1–8]

Those things that assist the military in victory are many; those that ensure victory are few.

If armor is sturdy and weapons sharp,
chariots are solid and horses excellent,
rations and equipment sufficient,
officers and men numerous,

these are the great foundations of the army, yet victory is not [found] here. If one is clear about

the movements of the stars, planets, sun, and moon;
the rules of recision and accretion[20] and the occult arts;[21]
the advantages of the rear, front, left, and right;

these are aids to warfare, yet completeness is not [found] here.

That by which the excellent commander is ensured victory is his constant possession of a knowledge without origin, a Way that is not a Way. It is difficult to share with the multitude. [15/145/10–13]

---

19. *Qi* 奇 and *zheng* 正 are used here in a special technical sense established by military texts like the *Sunzi bingfa.* "Extraordinary" and "usual" refer to the commander's selective and timely use of surprise tactics that break with conventional military doctrine. Both terms are discussed at length in Victor Mair, *The Art of War: Sun Zi's Military Methods* (New York: Columbia University Press, 2007), and *Soldierly Methods: Vade Mecum for an Iconoclastic Translation of Sun Zi bingfa,* Sino-Platonic Papers, no. 178 (Philadelphia: Department of Asian Languages and Civilizations, University of Pennsylvania, 2008).

20. Here *xingde* 刑德 is not used in the conventional sense of "punishment and beneficence" but refers to the recision and accretion of yin and yang as seen in various cosmic cycles, especially the cycle of lengthening and shortening days throughout the solar year. See 3.16 and 3.17. Accretion and recision are mentioned in the context of military astrology in 3.33 and 3.39, where the directional movements of counter-Jupiter (*taiyin*) are linked to victory or defeat. See Major 1993, 122–26, 132–33.

21. The phrase *qi gai zhi shu* 奇賌之數 is somewhat obscure. We follow the commentaries compiled in Zhang Shuangdi 1997, 2:1564n.12, in rendering it as "occult arts." Xu Shen glosses it as "the strange and secret essentials of yin and yang, extraordinary arts."

15.7

Meticulously recruiting [personnel],
being timely in movement and rest,
distinguishing officers and enlisted men,
maintaining weapons and armor,
ordering marching squadrons,
organizing platoons and companies,
clarifying drum and banner [signals],
these are the office of the adjutant.[22]
Distinguishing army camps,
scouring the terrain thoroughly,
choosing the location of the army,
these are the office of the master of horse.
Knowing [which terrain] is obstructed or passable to the front or the rear;
on encountering the enemy knowing what is difficult or easy;
issuing reprimands so that there is no negligence or idleness;
this is the office of the commandant.
[Ensuring that] movement along the route is swift,
that transport of the baggage is orderly,
that the size [of the camp] is standard,
that the positioning of the army is concentrated,
that the wells and stoves are dug [properly],
these are the office of the master of works.
Collecting and storing [materials] in the rear,
leaving nothing behind when camp is moved,
that there are no poorly packed carts,
that there is no missing baggage,
these are the office of the quartermaster.

These five officers are to the commander as the arms, legs, hands, and feet are to the body. He must choose men, assess their talents, [and] make sure that [each] officer can shoulder his responsibilities [and each] man is capable of his task.

He instructs them with regulations;
he applies them with orders;
using them the way that
tigers and leopards use their claws and teeth;
flying birds use their wings.

None is not employed. However, they all are implements that assist victory; they are not that by which victory is ensured. [15/145/13–19]

22. This reading rejects Lau's (HNZ 15/145/13) proposed interpolation of *da* to read the title as *dawei* (大尉, = 太尉), or "defender-in-chief" (a court office). All five offices listed here are army ranks, not court offices.

15.8

The victory or defeat of the military has its basis in governance.

If governance overcomes the people, subordinates will follow their superiors, and the military will be strong.

If the people overcome [their] government, subordinates will rebel against their superiors, and the military will be weak.

Thus,

if Moral Potency and Rightness are sufficient to encompass the people of the world,

if tasks and works are sufficient to meet the urgency of the world,

if selection and promotion are sufficient to win the minds of the worthies and scholars,

if plans and designs suffice to comprehend the heft of strength and weakness,

this is the root of certain victory. [15/145/19–21]

Vast territory and numerous people do not suffice to make one strong;
sturdy armor and sharp weapons do not suffice to make one victorious;
high walls and deep moats do not suffice to make one secure;
strict orders and complex punishments do not suffice to make one mighty.

One who practices the governance of survival, though [his kingdom] is small, will certainly survive.

One who practices the governance of extinction, though [his kingdom] is large, will certainly perish.

In antiquity, the territory of the Kingdom of Chu[23]

on the south was ringed by the Yuan and Xiang [rivers],
on the north was circled by the Ying and Si [rivers],
on the west was contained by [the states of] Ba and Shu,
on the east, was wrapped by [the states of] Tan and Pi.
[It had] the Ying and Ru [rivers] as ditches;
the Yangzi and Han [rivers] as moats.
Fenced in by the Deng Forest,
screened by a defensive wall.
The mountains [were] so high they scraped the clouds;
the valleys so deep there were no shadows.
The terrain [was] advantageous, the conditions favorable;
the soldiers and people courageous and daring.
They had shark's leather and rhinoceros [hide] to make armor and helmets;
they had long halberds and short spears together to make up the vanguard.
They had repeating crossbows to bring up the rear,
massed chariots to guard the flanks.

23. Ancient Chu spanned western Hubei and southwestern Henan Province. The geographical frontiers listed in this passage fall within or border on that general region.

At the quick they were like bolts and arrows,[24]
concentrated they were like thunder and lightning,
dispersed they were like the wind and rain.

However,

their soldiers fell at Chuisha;[25]
their multitudes were broken at Boju.[26]

The might of Chu spanned the earth and encompassed the masses; their portion was half the world. Yet King Huai[27] feared Lord Mengchang to the north, [so] he abandoned the defense of his ancestral altars and became a hostage of mighty Qin. His soldiers defeated and his territory pared away, he died without returning home.

The Second Emperor [of Qin][28] had the force of the Son of Heaven and the wealth of the world.

Nowhere that human footprints reached
or that was traversed by boat and oar

was not his prefecture or district.

Yet,

he was ensnared in the desires of the ears and eyes;
he practiced every possible variety of license and wickedness.

He paid no heed to the people's hunger, cold, poverty, and distress. He raised a chariot force of ten thousand chariots and built the A-fang palace; he

dispatched conscripted villagers for garrison duty
and collected taxes of more than half [of income].

Those among the common people who were conscripted or executed, who died gripping the crossbar of a wagon or at the head of the road, numbered countless myriads every day.

The world

was feverish as if scorching hot,
bent as if bitterly belabored.
Superior and inferior were not at peace with each other;
officials and commoners were not in harmony.

Chen Sheng,[29] a conscript soldier, arose in Daze. He bared his right arm and raised it, proclaiming himself "Great Chu," and the empire responded like an echo. At that time, he did not have

---

24. There seems to be one part of the parallelism missing here. "Concentrated" and "dispersed" (in the following two lines) are in parallel, so immediately after this line there should be a phrase parallel with "at the quick."

25. Chu was defeated by the combined armies of Qin, Han, Wei, and Qi at Chuisha in 301 B.C.E. The event is recorded in *Xunzi* 15 and *Zhanguoce* 179.

26. Chu was defeated by the combined armies of Cai and Wu at Boju in 506 B.C.E. See *Zuozhuan*, Duke Ding, year 4.

27. King Huai of Chu 楚懷王 reigned from 328 to 299 B.C.E.

28. The Second Emperor 二世皇帝, or Hu Hai 胡亥, was the son and heir of the First Emperor of Qin. He reigned from 210 B.C.E. until his death by suicide in 207 B.C.E.

29. Chen Sheng (d. 208 B.C.E.) was a minor Qin official who initiated the uprising that brought down the Qin dynasty. He is commemorated with his own "Hereditary House" in *Shiji* 48.

strong armor or sharp weapons,
powerful bows or hard spears.
They cut date trees to make spears;
they ground awls and chisels to make swords.
They sharpened bamboo
and shouldered hoes

to meet keen halberds and strong crossbows, [yet] no city they attacked or land they invaded did not surrender to them. They roiled and shook, overran and rolled up an area of several thousand square *li* throughout the world. [Chen Sheng's] force and station were supremely lowly, and his weapons and equipment were of no advantage, yet one man sang out and the empire harmonized with him. This was because resentment had accumulated among the people. [15/145/23–15/146/12]

When King Wu attacked Djou, he faced east and welcomed the year.[30]

When he reached the Si River, there was a flood;
when he reached Gongtou, [a mountain] collapsed.[31]

A comet appeared and presented its tail to the men of Yin. During the battle;

ten suns rioted above;
wind and rain struck below.[32]

Yet,

in front there were no rewards for braving danger;
at the rear there were no punishments for flight.

Clean blades were never fully drawn and the empire submitted. For this reason,

he who is good at defending cannot be overcome,
and he who is good at battle cannot be attacked.

He understands the Way of restricting entries and opening blockages. He takes advantage of the force of the moment, accords with the desires of the people, and seizes the world. [15/146/14–17]

15.9

Thus,

one who is good at governing accumulates Moral Potency;
one who is good at using the military stores anger.
When Moral Potency accumulates, the people may be employed;
when anger is stored, our awesomeness may be established.

Thus,

when our culture has been applied shallowly, what is brought to submission by heft will be meager.

30. A ritual performed to mark the beginning of spring. It is presumably noted here to demonstrate that the following events occurred out of season. What follows are a sequence of bad auguries for the endeavor of King Wu, despite which he prevails because of his superior Moral Potency.

31. Following Wang Shumin's emendation. See Lau, HNZ, 146n.13.

32. Following Wang Shumin's emendation. See Lau, HNZ, 146n.14.

If our Potency functions broadly, what is controlled by our awesomeness will be expansive.

When what is controlled by our awesomeness is broad, we are strong and the enemy is weak.

Therefore, one who is good at using the military first weakens the enemy and only after does battle. In this way the expense is not even half, and the effect is naturally doubled.

The territory of Tang was seventy *li* square, and he became king. This was because he cultivated his Moral Potency.

Earl Zhi had a thousand *li* of land and perished. This was because he was exclusively martial.

Thus, [the ruler of]

a thousand-chariot state that practices civility and Potency will become king;

a ten-thousand chariot state that is fond of using the military will perish.

Thus,

a complete soldier is first victorious and only then seeks battle;

a defeated soldier gives battle first and only then seeks victory.

If Potency is equal, the many will defeat the few.

If strength is matched, the intelligent will defeat the stupid.

If intelligence is the same, then the one with numbers will capture the one without. In all use of the military, one must first fight from the temple.

Whose ruler is more worthy?

Whose commander is more able?

Whose people are more obedient?

Whose state is better ordered?

Who has prepared more stores?

Whose troops are better trained?

Whose armor and weapons are better?

Whose equipment is more efficient?

In this way, one moves counters in the upper hall of the temple and decides victory more than a thousand *li* away. [15/146/19–26]

15.10

What has form and outline will be seen and praised by the world;

what has chapter and verse will be transmitted and studied by the ages.

These all are [examples] of forms overcoming one another. The one who is skilled at form does not use them as a model. What ennobles the Way is its formlessness. Having no form, it thus

cannot be controlled or coerced;

cannot be measured or ruled;

cannot be tricked or deceived;

cannot be schemed against or planned for.

People will make plans for one whose wisdom is apparent;
they will attack one whose form is apparent;
they will ambush one whose numbers are apparent;
they will defend against one whose weapons are apparent.

Those who
move and initiate, circulate and turn,
straighten and bend, contract and extend
may be tricked and deceived; none is skilled. The movement of the skilled
is as apparent as that of a spirit and yet proceeds like that of a ghost,
is as brilliant as the stars and yet operates in obscurity.

Advancing and retreating, contracting and extending, none sees its form or outline.
It alights like the halcyon and rises like the *qilin*,
flies like the phoenix and leaps like the dragon.
It emerges like a gale;
it speeds like lightning.
it beats death with life;
it overcomes decline with virility;
it defeats torpor with speed;
it controls hunger with fullness. [It is]
like water eradicating fire,
like heat melting snow.
Where can one go where it does not follow?
Where can one move where it does not reach?
Within, empty and spiritlike;
without, barren of will;
it moves in the formless;
it emerges where it is not expected;
it leaves tumultuously;
it returns unexpectedly.

None knows its destination.
Sudden as thunder and lightning,
swift as wind and rain,
as if bursting from the earth,
as if falling from the sky,
none can respond to or defend against it.
Fast as bolts and arrows, how can it be matched?
Now dark, now bright, who can know its beginning and end?
Before one has seen its launching, it invariably has already arrived. [15/147/1–11]

15.11

Thus the one skilled in arms, on seeing the deficiency of the enemy,
takes advantage of it and does not rest,
pursues it and does not let it go,
presses it and does not [let it] get away.
He
strikes while [the enemy] is in doubt,
overruns him while he hesitates.
[He is like]
swift thunder that does not give [the enemy] time to cover his ears,
fast lightning that leaves [the enemy] no leisure to cover his eyes.
The one skilled in arms
is like the sound to the echo,
is like the gong to the drum.
If a mote gets into [the enemy's] eye, he does not allow him to wipe it away;
if [the enemy] exhales, he does not allow him to inhale.
At this time,
he does not look up to see Heaven;
he does not look down to view Earth;
his hand does not lift his spear;
his weapon is not fully drawn.
He strikes [the enemy] like thunder;
he hits him like the wind;
he scorches him like fire;
he overcomes him like a wave.
The enemy
does not know where to stay while at rest,
does not know what to do while in motion.

Thus when the drums sound and the flags wave, none facing him do not give up or collapse. Who in the world dares to display might or maintain discipline when facing him? Therefore, one who anticipates others is victorious; one who awaits others is defeated; one who is led by others dies. [15/147/11–16]

15.12

[One]
whose soldiers are still stands firm,
who is concentrated and united is mighty,
whose duties are apportioned is brave,
whose mind is in doubt flees,
whose strength is divided is weak.

Thus, if you can divide his soldiers and cause his mind to doubt, [having] a small fraction [of his strength] will be more than enough. If you cannot divide his soldiers and cause his mind to doubt, [having] many times [his strength] will not suffice.

Djou's soldiers numbered one million and had one million minds;
King Wu's soldiers numbered three thousand and all were concentrated and united.

Thus,

one thousand men of the same mind yield the strength of a thousand men;
ten thousand men with different minds do not have the usefulness of one man.

When commander and soldiers, officials and people, all move and rest as if one body, you may respond to the enemy and join battle. Thus,

[when] you set off after plans are firm,
move after duties are apportioned,
the commander has no doubtful designs;
the soldiers have no separate mind;
in motion there is no lax demeanor;
in speech there are no empty words;
in tasks there is no tentativeness;
[then you] will surely respond to the enemy quickly;
[you] will surely initiate actions swiftly.

Thus,

the commander takes the people as his body,
and the people take the commander as their mind.
When the mind is sincere, the limbs and body will be close and cleave [to it];
when the mind is doubtful, the limbs and body will rebel and flee.
If the mind is not concentrated and unified, the body will not be disciplined in action;
if the commander is not sincere and sure, the soldiers will not be brave and daring.

Thus the soldiers of a good commander

are like the fangs of the tiger,
like the horn of the rhinoceros,
like the wings of a bird,
like the feet of a millipede.
They can advance;
they can withdraw;
they can bite;
they can butt.
They are strong without defeating one another;
they are numerous without harming one another;

one mind moves them.

Thus,

when the people earnestly follow orders, though they are few, there is nothing to fear;
when the people do not follow orders, though they are many, they act as few.

Thus,

when inferiors are not close to superiors. [the commander's] mind is of no use;
when the soldiers do not fear the commander, his formations will not do battle.
Among defenses there are those that are sure to hold;
among attacks there are those that are sure to triumph

before weapons cross or edges meet the crux of survival and destruction has invariably formed. [15/147/18–28]

15.13

The military has three [types of] force and two [forms of] heft.[33]

There is the force of *qi*;
there is the force of terrain;
there is the force of circumstance.
When the commander is full of courage and scorns the enemy;
when soldiers are daring and take joy in battle;

when amid the three armies and within the myriad hosts,

their will leaps to the sky;
their *qi* is like the whirlwind;
their sound is like thunder.

Their sincerity amasses and their [essence][34] overflows, so that their might falls on the enemy. These are called "the force of *qi*."

Mountain trails and marshy passes,
great mountains and famous obstructions,
"dragon coils," "umbrella peaks,"
"sheep intestine paths," "fish trap gates":[35]

when one person holds the defile, one thousand men do not dare pass. These are called "the force of terrain."

Relying on their being

belabored and fatigued, negligent and disordered,
hungry and thirsty, frozen or scorched,

---

33. The word translated here as "heft," *quan*, is a very richly multivalent term used in a technical military sense. *Quan* literally refers to the weight of a scale, and in different philosophical contexts it can mean "authority" or "expediency." In military texts and here in *Huainanzi* 15, it means the forms of advance training or preparation that can "tip the scales" on the field of battle, ergo "heft." See app. A.

34. Following Wang Niansun's emendation. See Lau, HNZ, 148n.2.

35. All four of these phrases seem to be set literary terms for types of terrain.

pushing them where they are unsteady,
squeezing them where they are spread thin,
these are called "the force of circumstance."
Skillfully using spies,
carefully laying plans,
establishing ambushes,
concealing their form,
emerging where he does not expect, [thus] giving the enemy's soldiers no suitable defense: these are called "the heft of knowledge."
[When]
the formations of soldiers are correct,
the front rank is elite,
they advance and retreat together;
the units and squads [maintain] tight [formation];
the front and the rear do not restrain each other;
the left and the right do not interfere with each other.
[When] the blows received are few,
the enemy wounded are many:
these are called "the heft of training."
[When]
advantage and force are surely formed,
officers and soldiers are concentrated and excellent,
the able are chosen and the talented employed;
each office finds its [right] person.
[When]
plans are set and strategies decided,
death and life are clear.
[When] taking and releasing attain their [proper] time [and] none are not aroused and alert, then
before the assault [employs] the battering ram or siege ladder, the city is taken;
before in battle weapons cross or edges meet, the enemy is broken.
This is to be enlightened about the arts of certain victory.
Thus,
if arms are not sure to be victorious, one does not rashly cross blades;
if the assault is not sure to take [its object], one does not rashly launch [it].
Only after victory is certain does one give battle;
only after the scales[36] have weighed does one move.
Thus,
the masses form up and do not vainly scatter;
the soldiers set out and do not fruitlessly return. [15/148/1–11]

36. Following commentators' reading of *ling* as *quan*. See Lau, HNZ, 148nn.1, 10.

15.14

On moving, only one who is devoid of a single movement scrapes the sky and shakes the earth.

Lifting Mount Tai,
blocking the Four Seas,
moving and shifting ghosts and spirits,
alarming and startling birds and beasts,

[when] one is like this,

in the countryside there are none who study arms;
throughout the kingdom there are no defended cities.
Meet agitation with stillness,
match chaos with order,
be without form and control what has form,
be without purpose and respond to alterations,

though this will not yet make you able to gain victory over the enemy, it will allow the enemy no path to victory.

When the enemy moves before me, then from this I see his form.
When he is agitated and I am still, then with this I can obstruct his strength.
When his form is seen, then victory may be fashioned.
When his strength is obstructed, [my] might may be established.
View his purposes and transform in accord with them,
observe his deviancy and straightness and thereby control his fate,
feed him what he desires and thereby stop up his contentment.

If he has a fissure,

quickly rush into the crack.
Compass his alterations and bind him,
plumb his rhythms and unbalance[37] him.
If the enemy returns to stillness, produce something unexpected for him;
if he does not respond, unilaterally extinguish his [sense of] security.
If I move and he responds, I can see his purposes;
if he holds back, push him to move him;
if he has accumulated something, there must be something that he lacks.
If his best troops turn left, trap his right flank;
if the enemy breaks and runs, his rear may definitely be moved.

[When] the enemy is pressed and does not move, this is called "lingering."

Strike him like thunder;
cut him like grass or trees;
burn him like fire or lightning.

You must hurry fast

[so that] his men have no time to run,
his carts have no time to roll,

37. Accepting Lau's (HNZ, 148n.11) proposed emendation.

his weapons are like wooden plants,
his crossbows are like sheep horns.
Though his men are numerous, [your] force is such that he dare not strike. [15/148/11–21]

15.15

Of all things that have an image, there is not [one] that cannot be defeated;
of all things that have form, there is none for which there is no response.
This is why the sage lodges in Nothingness and lets his mind roam in Emptiness.
Wind and rain can be blocked and screened,
but cold and heat cannot be shut out;
it is because they have no form. What can suffuse the essentially subtle,
pierce metal and stone,
reach the farthest distance,
rise above the Nine Heavens,
[and] coil below the Yellow Springs
is only the Formless.
One who is skilled at using arms
should attack [the enemy's] disorder
[but] should not assault his order.
Do not attack well-dressed ranks;
do not assault upright flags.
If his demeanor cannot yet be seen, match him with equal numbers. If he has the form of death, follow and control him. If the enemy holds [superior] numbers, stay hidden while moving. If you meet fullness with deficiency, you surely will be captured by him.
If tigers and leopards did not move, they would not enter the pit.
If deer and elk did not move, they would not be taken by nets.
If flying birds did not move, they would not be caught in snares.
If fish and turtles did not move, they would not be grabbed by lips and beaks.
Among things there is none that is not controlled by its motion. For this reason, the sage values stillness.
He is still and thus can respond to agitation;
he follows and thus can respond to one who leads;
he is artful and can thus defeat one who is coarse;
he is broad-reaching and can thus capture one who is deficient. [15/148/21–15/149/5]

15.16

Thus, for the good commander's use of soldiers,
he merges their minds;
he unites their strength;
the brave cannot advance alone;
the cowardly cannot retreat alone.
At rest like hills and mountains,
unleashed like the wind and rain,
what they hit surely breaks; nothing is not destroyed or drenched. They move as a single body; none can respond to or defend against [them].

The five fingers tapping in turn are not as good as the whole hand rolled into a fist;
ten thousand men advancing in turn are not as good as one hundred men arriving together.
Tigers and leopards have better speed;
bears and grizzlies have more strength;
yet people eat their meat and make mats of their hides because they are not able to communicate their knowledge and unite their strength.[38]

The force of water overcomes fire, [but] if the Zhanghua Tower[39] caught fire, if one sought to save it by dousing it with ladles and spoons, though one emptied a well and drained a pond, it would be no use. [But] if one picked up pots, urns, bowls, and basins and drenched it, [the fire's] being extinguished would only be a matter of time.

Now humans with respect to [other] humans do not have the advantage of water over fire, and if they wish to match the many with the few, they will clearly not achieve their aim. One of the military traditions has a saying: "The few can match the many." This refers to what one commands, not with which one gives battle. Some command many but use only a few, thus their force is not on a par [with their numbers]. One who commands a few but uses many [of them] increases his functional strength. If people employ their talents to the fullest and completely use their strength, it has never been heard of from antiquity to the current day that the few have defeated the many. [15/149/7–15]

15.17

There is no spirit nobler than Heaven;
there is no force more versatile than Earth;
there is no motion more swift than time;
there is no resource more advantageous than people.

38. A similar point about the advantage that humans have over animals is made in 19.5.
39. A fabled tower erected by King Ling of Chu (r. 540–529 B.C.E.).

These four are the pillars and trunks of the military, yet they must rely on the Way to operate because [the Way] can unite their functions.

The advantage of terrain overcomes Heaven and time;
clever tactics overcome the advantage of terrain;
force overcomes people.

Thus,

one who relies on Heaven can be led astray;
one who relies on Earth can be trapped;
one who relies on time can be pressured;
one who relies on people can be fooled.

Humaneness, courage, trustworthiness, and incorruptibility are the most excellent qualities among people. However,

the brave can be lured;
the humane can be robbed;
the trustworthy are easily cheated;
the incorruptible are easily schemed against.

If the commander of a host has even one of these [flaws], he will be taken captive. Seen from this perspective, it also is clear that victory in arms is produced by the Pattern of the Way, not by the worthiness of human character.

Thus, deer and elk can be seized by snares;
fish and turtle can be taken by nets;
geese and swans can be collected with the dart and line.

Only to the Formless may nothing be done. For this reason, the sage

lodges in the Sourceless, so his feelings cannot be grasped and observed;
moves in the Formless, so his formations cannot be attained and traced.
He has no model and no protocol;
he does what is appropriate [for what] arrives;
he has no name and no shape;
he fashions [a new] image for [each] alteration.
How deep!
How distant!
Through winter and summer,
through spring and fall,
above reaching the highest branch,
below fathoming the deepest depth,
altering and transforming,
never hesitating or halting,
he sets his mind in the Field of Profound Mystery
and lodges his will in the Spring of the Nine Returns.[40]

Though one has acute eyes, who can detect his feelings? [15/149/15–24]

---

40. The provenance of this metaphor is obscure. Gao You notes that "nine returns" denotes a spring that is "supremely deep." Apparently, both this sobriquet and that of the preceding line signify the Way.

15.18

What soldiers discuss secretly is the Way of Heaven;
what they chart and draw is the terrain;
what they speak of openly is human affairs;
what decides victory for them is heft and force.

Thus the superior commander's use of soldiers:

Above reaches the Way of Heaven,
below reaches the benefit of the terrain;

between [these], he reaches the minds of the people. He then moves them at the fulcral moment and launches them [replete] with force. This is why he never has broken armies or defeated soldiers.

Coming to the mediocre commander:

Above he does not understand the Way of Heaven;
below he does not understand the benefit of the terrain;

he exclusively uses people and force. Though he will not be perfectly [successful], his balance will mostly be victories.

About the inferior commander's use of soldiers:

He is broadly informed yet is himself disordered;
he has much knowledge yet doubts himself;
at rest he is afraid;
setting forth he hesitates.

For this reason, when he moves he becomes another's captive. [15/149/26–30]

Now let two people cross blades. If their skill or clumsiness is no different, the braver warrior will certainly win. Why is this? It is because of the sincerity of his actions. If you use a great ax on logs and firewood, you need not wait for a beneficial time or a good day to chop it. If you put the ax on top of the logs and firewood without the aid of human effort, though you accord with the "far-flight" asterism[41] and have hold of recision and accretion,[42] you will not chop it because there is no force. Thus,

when water is agitated, it dries up;
when an arrow is agitated, it flies far.

The end of an arrow made of Qiwei bamboo[43] and capped with silver and tin could not on its own pierce even a vest of thin silk or a shield of rotten leaves. If you lend it the strength of sinew and bone, the force of bow or crossbow, then it will pierce rhino[-hide] armor and pass through a leather shield!

---

41. For the "far-flight" asterism, see Major 1993, 218. Far-flight, at the tip of the "handle" of the Northern Dipper constellation, acts as a moving pointer that indicates the directions associated with the twelve months. See 5.1–12.

42. For this usage of *xingde*, see n. 20.

43. The phrase *qiwei junlu* 淇衛箘簬 is obscure. *Junlu* clearly refers to a type of thin but durable bamboo that is well suited to making arrows. Xu Shen glosses *qiwei* as the name of a region from which (presumably very excellent) bamboo is harvested, but other commentators offer divergent readings. See Zhang Shuangdi 1997, 2:1602nn.14, 37.

The speed of the wind can reach the point of blowing away roofs or breaking trees, [but] if an empty carriage reaches a great thoroughfare from atop a high hill, a person has pushed it.[44] For this reason, the force of one who is skilled at using arms is

> like releasing amassed water from a thousand-*ren*[-high] dike,
> like rolling round stones into a ten-thousand-*zhang*[-deep] gorge.[45]

When the world sees that my soldiers will certainly be effective, then who will dare offer me battle? Thus one hundred men who are sure to die are worth more than ten thousand men who are sure to flee; how much more is the multitude of the three armies who will enter fire and water without turning tail! Even if I challenged the entire world to cross blades, who would dare step up first? [15/150/1–9]

15.19

[These are] what are called the "divisions of Heaven":

> The Bluegreen Dragon to the left, the White Tiger to the right,
> the Vermilion Bird in front, the Dark Warrior behind.[46]

What is called the "advantages of Earth"?

> Life behind and death in front,
> valleys on the left and hills on the right.

What is called "human affairs"?

> Rewards being trustworthy and punishments sure,
> movement and stillness being timely,
> withdrawal and emplacement being swift.

These are what the ages have passed down as models and signs, [and] they are venerable.[47] But they are not that by which one survives. [True] models and signs are those that alter and transform in accordance with the times. Thus,

> One stands in the shade of the upper hall and knows the progress of the sun and moon;
> one sees the ice at the bottom of the jar and knows the cold and hot [seasons] of the world.

That by which things give form to one another is subtle; only the sage fathoms its utmost. Thus,

> though the drum is not among the five tones, it is the master of the five tones;
> though water is not among the five flavors, it blends the five flavors;
> though the commander is not among the five officers, he controls the five officers.

---

44. Accepting Sun Yirang's proposed emendation. See Lau, HNZ, 150n.5. The carriage in question is a two-wheel rig, which is why the force of the wind would not make it simply roll down the hill.

45. One *ren* is eight Chinese feet, and one *zhang* is ten Chinese feet.

46. These are constellations marking the four cardinal directions; the orientation implied here is a ruler's-eye view, facing south.

47. Accepting Lau's (HNZ, 150n.6) emendation.

[The drum] can harmonize the five tones because it is not among the five tones;
[water] can blend the five flavors because it is not among the five flavors;
[the commander] can order the affairs of the five officers because he [himself] cannot be surveyed or measured.

For this reason, the mind of the commander is
warm like the spring, hot like the summer,
cool like the fall, cold like the winter.

He
accords with conditions and transforms with them,
follows the seasons and shifts with them. [15/150/11–19]

15.20

A shadow cannot be crooked if the thing [itself] is straight;
an echo cannot be a high note if the sound [itself] is a low note.

Observe what he sends and respond to each with what defeats it. For this reason,
hold up Rightness and move, promote order and set forth;
conceal your nodal points, and discard your injuries;
rely on your strengths, and complete your objective.

Make him
know your coming out but not know your going in;
know your withdrawing but not know your amassing.
Be at first like a fox or a raccoon dog,
then he will advance at ease.
On meeting, be like a rhino or a tiger,
then the enemy will take flight.
When a soaring bird strikes, it pulls in its head;
when a ferocious beast attacks, it conceals its claws.
The tiger and leopard do not let their fangs show;
biting dogs do not show their teeth.

Thus the Way of using arms is to
show them softness and meet them with hardness,
show them weakness and ride them with strength,
make [as if] contracting and respond to them by expanding.
When the commander wants to go west, he shows them east.
At first he stands aloof, yet after he engages,
in front he is dark yet behind he is bright.
Like ghosts, leaving no tracks;
like water, bearing no scars.

Thus
where he tends toward is not where he arrives;
what he reveals is not what he plans.

Taking, giving, moving, resting, none can recognize him. Like the stroke of thunder, one cannot prepare for him. He does not repeat [any tactic] he uses, so he can always be victorious. He communicates with the Mysterious Brilliance; none knows his portals. This is known as the Supremely Spiritlike. [15/150/21–28]

15.21

What makes the military strong is being set on death.
What makes the people set on death is Rightness.
What makes Rightness able to be practiced is awesomeness.

For this reason,

gather them with civility;
order them with martiality.

This is called "sure attainment." When awesomeness and Rightness are practiced together, this is known as "supreme strength."

What people take joy in is life,
and what they hate is death.

Even so,

at high walls and deep moats,
when arrows and stones fall like rain;
on flat plains and broad marshes,
where naked blades cross and meet,

soldiers will compete to advance and engage [the enemy]. It is not that they scorn death and take joy in injury; it is because rewards are trustworthy and punishments are clear. [15/151/1–4]

For this reason,

if superiors view inferiors as sons,
inferiors will view superiors as fathers.
If superiors view inferiors as younger brothers.
inferiors will view superiors as older brothers.
If superiors view inferiors as sons, they will surely be king over the Four Seas;
if inferiors view superiors as fathers, they will surely rectify the world.
If superiors are intimate with inferiors as with younger brothers, then [the inferiors] will not [find it] difficult to die for [their superiors].
If inferiors see their superiors as older brothers, then [the superiors] will not [find it] difficult to perish [for their inferiors].

For this reason, one cannot fight with opponents who are [as close as] fathers, sons, older brothers, and younger brothers because of the goodwill accumulated over previous generations.

Thus,

if the four horses were not in harmony, [even] Zaofu would not be able to travel far;

if bow and arrow were not in harmony, [even] Yi would not be able to always hit the mark;
if ruler and minister were of separate minds, [even] Sunzi[48] would not be able to face the enemy.

Thus,
within, [the ruler] cultivates his governance in accumulating Potency;
without, he stops up resentment [by causing people to] submit to his awesomeness. [15/151/6–10]

15.22

Investigate the [soldiers'] labor and ease so as to be aware of their fullness and hunger, so when the day of battle arrives, they will view death as a homecoming. The commander must share the troops' sweetness and bitterness, matching their hunger and cold. Thus he can win their [loyalty unto] death, even to the last man.

Thus in antiquity, skillful commanders were sure to personally take the lead.
In the heat, they did not spread a canopy;
in the cold, they did not don furs,
so as to equal [the soldiers'] heat and cold.
In narrow defiles they would not ride;
going uphill they would always dismount,[49]
so as to match [the soldiers'] fatigue and ease.
When the army's food was cooked, only then did they dare eat;
when the army's well had been bored, only then did they dare drink,
so as to share [the soldiers'] hunger and thirst.

When battle was joined, they would stand where the arrows and stones were arriving, so as to partake of [the soldiers'] safety and danger.

Thus the good commander's use of soldiers constantly
struck accumulated resentment with accumulated Potency,
struck accumulated hatred with accumulated love.
Why would he not triumph? [15/151/10–15]

What the ruler asks of the people is twofold:
He asks the people to labor for him;
he wants the people to die for him.
What the people hope of the ruler is threefold:
That if they are hungry, he will feed them;
that if they are fatigued, he will rest them;
that if they have merit, he will be able to reward them.

---

48. Sunzi 孫子 (also known as Sun Wu 武) was a native of Qi and general of the state of Wu during the Spring and Autumn period. He is the putative author of the *Sunzi bingfa*.

49. Accepting Wang Shumin's emendation. See Lau, HNZ, 15n.9A. The reference is probably to dismounting from a chariot, not from riding astride.

If the people fulfill their two duties and the ruler disappoints their three hopes, though the kingdom is large and the people numerous, the military will be weak.

The embittered must attain what they take joy in;
the belabored must attain what they find profit in.
The merit of "cutting heads" must be fully [remunerated];
service unto death must be posthumously rewarded.

If in these four, one keeps faith with the people, even if the ruler

shoots at birds in the clouds, angles for fish in the deep abyss,
plucks the *qin* and *se*, listens to bells and pipes,
plays *liubo* or tosses "high pots,"[50]
the military will still be strong;
orders will still be carried out.

For this reason, if superiors are worthy of reverence, inferiors may be used; if one's Potency is worthy of admiration, one's awesomeness may be established. [15/151/17–22]

15.23

The commander must have three guides, four ethics, five conducts, and ten disciplines.

What are called the three guides

above understand the Way of Heaven,
below study the shape of the terrain,
among them investigate the feelings of the people.

What are called the four ethics? [They are]

to benefit the kingdom without favoring the military,
to serve the ruler without thought for yourself,
to face difficulty without fearing death, and
to decide doubts without avoiding punishment.

What are called the five conducts? [They are]

to be soft but unable to be rolled up;
to be hard but unable to be snapped;
to be humane but unable to be insulted;
to be faithful but unable to be cheated; and
to be brave but unable to be overcome.

What are called the ten disciplines?

Your spirit is pure and cannot be sullied;
your plans are far-reaching and cannot be anticipated;
your training is firm and cannot be moved;
your awareness is lucid and cannot be blocked;

50. *Liubo* was a board game, played for gambling stakes and used as a form of divination. For an anecdote involving a chesslike game, possibly *liubo*, see 18.27. "Tossing pots" was also a popular game.

you are not greedy[51] for wealth;
you are not corrupted by things;
you are not taken in by disputation;
you are not moved by [occult] arts;
you cannot be pleased;
you cannot be angered.

This is called the perfect model. Obscure! Mysterious! Who understands his feelings? [The ideal commander's]

initiatives surely accord with the heft;[52]
his words surely correspond to the measure;
his actions surely comply with the seasons;
his resolutions surely hit the [correct] pattern.
he comprehends the activation of motion and stillness;
he is enlightened to the rhythm of opening and closing;

he has investigated the benefit and harm of removing and deploying, so that [they are] as if merging two halves of a tally.

He is swift like a cocked crossbow;
his force is like that of a released arrow,
Now a dragon, now a snake;
his movements have no constant shape.
None sees his middle;
none know his end.
When he attacks, there is no defense;
when he defends, he cannot be attacked. [15/151/24–15/152/2]

It has been said that one who is skilled at the use of arms must first cultivate it in himself [and] only afterward seek it in other people. He must first make himself invincible and only then seek out victory.

To [look for] self-cultivation from others and beg victory from the enemy, not yet being able to order oneself and yet attacking another's disorder; these are like

extinguishing fire with [more] fire,
responding to a flood with [more] water.

What can it accomplish?

Now if a potter were to be transformed into clay, he could not fashion plates and pots.
If a weaver girl were to be transformed into silk, she could not weave patterned cloth.

Like [things] do not suffice to control one another, thus only [something] different can be extraordinary. If two sparrows are fighting with each other, the arrival of a falcon or a hawk will break them apart because they are of a different sort.

Thus stillness is extraordinary to agitation, [and] order is extraordinary to chaos;
fullness is extraordinary to hunger, [and] ease is extraordinary to labor.

---

51. Following the reading in Zhang Shuangdi 1997, 2:1613, of *tan* 貪 in place of *shi* 食.
52. Accepting Lau's (HNZ, 151n.12) emendation of the character *quan*: 權, not 詮.

The mutual response of the extraordinary and the usual are like [the way that] water, fire, metal, and wood take turns being servant and master.

The one who is skilled at the use of arms maintains the five lethal [conducts] in responding, so he can complete his victory. The one who is clumsy abides in the five fatal [failings] and overreaches, so when he moves he becomes another's captive.[53] [15/152/4–9]

15.24

The military values plans being unfathomable and formations being concealed. Emerge where one is not expected, so [the enemy] cannot prepare a defense.

> If plans are seen, they will fail;
> if formations are seen, they will be controlled.

Thus one who is skilled at using arms,

> above hides them in Heaven,
> below hides them in Earth,
> between hides them among people.

One who hides them in Heaven can control anything. What is called "hiding them in Heaven"? It is to alter in accordance with

> great cold, profound heat,
> swift wind, violent rain,
> heavy fog, or dark night.

What is called "hiding it in Earth"? It is being able to conceal one's formations amid

> mountains, hills,
> forests, and valleys.

What is called "hiding it among people"?

> Blocking their view in front,
> facing them in the rear.

While producing an unexpected [maneuver] or moving a formation,

> breaking forth like thunder,
> rushing like the wind and rain.

Furling the great banners, silencing the loud drums so that one's coming and going has no traces; none knows their beginning or end. [15/152/11–15]

> When front and rear are correctly aligned, the four corners are as if bound together;
> when coming and going, disengaging and continuing do not interfere with one another;
> when light [troops] are at the wings and crack [soldiers] are at the flanks, some forward and some at the rear;

53. This appears to refer to the "five conducts" (and the implicitly corresponding "five failings") listed earlier in this section as aspects of the ideal commander.

when in parting and merging, dispersing and concentrating, companies and squads are not broken up;
this is to be skilled at deploying moving formations.

When one is clear as to freak occurrences and anomalies, yin and yang, recision and accretion, the Five Phases, the observance of *qi*, astrology,[54] and spirit supplication,[55] this is to be skillful at the Way of Heaven.

When one establishes plans, places ambushes,
uses fire and water,[56] produces anomalies.
When one has the army shout and drum so as to confuse [the enemy's] ears and drags bundled sticks to kick up dust and confuse [the enemy's] eyes; all these are being skilled at deception and dissimulation.

When the *chun*[57] sounds resolutely,
when one's will is firm[58] and not easily frightened,
when one cannot be lured by force or advantage,
when one cannot be shaken by death or defeat,
these are to be skilled at bolstering strength.

When one is agile and quick to strike,
when one is brave and scorns the enemy,
when one is swift as [a horse at] the gallop,
these are to be skilled at using speed and creating surprise.

When one assesses the shape of the terrain,
when one lodges at rest camps,
when one fixes walls and fortifications,
when one is careful of depressions[59] and salt marshes,
when one occupies the high ground,
when one avoids exposed positions,
these are to be skilled at using the shape of the terrain.

When one relies on [the enemy's] hunger, thirst, cold and heat,
when one belabors his fatigue and aggravates his disorder,
when one deepens his fear and hampers his steps,
when one hits him with elite troops,
when one strikes him at night,
these are to be skilled at according with the seasons and responding to alterations.

---

54. These all are cosmological categories and forms of divination used to forecast battlefield conditions. Observing *qi* is a form of military prognostication by means of which one ascertains victory or defeat by surveying the *qi* emanating from the enemy army. It is described in *Mozi* 68.

55. That is, rituals, and prayers, used to solicit the aid of the spirit world.

56. The character *jian* 見 is a superfluous intrusion into the text. See Lau, HNZ, 152n.2.

57. A *chun* 錞 is a kind of bell with a bulbous top, played by being struck with a stick or mallet. The word *yue* 鉞 in this sentence is used as an onomatopoetic representation of the sound of a bell; thus we translate *yue* freely as a verb, "sounds."

58. Reading *zhi* 植 as "will." See Zhang Shuangdi 1997, 2:1620n.8.

59. Reading *yan* 煙 as having a water radical on the left: 湮. See Sun Yirang's proposed emendation in Lau, HNZ, 152n.4.

When one uses chariots on easy [terrain],
when one uses mounted horsemen on obstructed [terrain],
when one uses more bowmen while crossing water,
when one uses more crossbowmen in a narrow pass,
when one uses more flags by day,
when one uses more fires by night,
when one uses more drums at dusk,
these are to be skilled in logistics.

One cannot lack even one of these eight, even though they are not what is most valuable to the military. [15/152/17–26]

15.25

The commander must see singularly and know singularly.
Seeing singularly is to see what is not seen.
Knowing singularly is to know what is not known.
To see what others do not is called "enlightenment."
To know what others do not is called "spiritlike."
The spiritlike and enlightened is one who triumphs in advance. He who triumphs in advance
cannot be attacked when he defends,
cannot be defeated in battle,
cannot be defended against when he attacks.
This is because of emptiness and fullness.

When there is a gap between superiors and inferiors, when the commander and officials do not cooperate, when what one upholds is not straight, when the minds of the soldiers accumulate insubordination, this is called "emptiness."

When the ruler is enlightened and the commander competent, when superiors and inferiors are of the same mind, when [the soldiers'] *qi* and intentions both are aroused, this is called "fullness."

It is like throwing water at fire:
What it lands on squarely will collapse;
what it hits sparsely will be moved.
Hard and soft do not interpenetrate,
victory and defeat[60] are alien to each other.
This speaks of emptiness and fullness.
Being skilled at battle does not reside in the few;
being skilled at defense does not reside in the small;
victory resides in attaining awesomeness;

60. Following Yang Shuda's proposed emendation. See Lau, HNZ, 153n.3.

defeat resides in losing *qi*. [15/152/27–15/153/4]
The full should fight, the empty should run;
the thriving should be strong, the declining should flee.

The territory of King Fuchai of Wu was two thousand *li* square, and he had seventy thousand armored warriors.

To the south he fought with Yue and routed them at Kuaiji.
To the north he fought with Qi and broke them at Ailing.
To the west he met the Duke of Jin and captured him at Huangchi.[61]

This is to use the people's *qi* when it is full. Afterward

he became arrogant and gave free rein to his desires;
he scorned admonition and took delight in slander;
he was violent and followed erroneous [advice];

he could not be spoken to honestly.

The great officials were resentful;
the people were insubordinate.

The king of Yue and three thousand elite troops captured [Fuchai] at Gansui.[62] This was taking advantage of his emptiness.

That *qi* has empty and full [phases] is like the darkness following the light. Thus,

a victorious military is not always full;
a defeated military is not always empty.
He who is skilled can fill his people's *qi* while awaiting others' emptiness.
He who is incapable empties his people's *qi* while awaiting others' fullness.

Thus the *qi* of emptiness and fullness are what is most valued by the military. [15/153/6–11]

15.26

Whenever the kingdom has difficulty, from the palace the ruler summons the commander, charging him: "The fate of the altars of the soil and grain are on your person. The kingdom faces a crisis, I wish you to take command and respond to it."

When the commander has accepted his mandate, [the ruler] orders the Supplicator and Great Diviner to fast, sequestered for three days. Going to the Great Temple, they consult the Magic Tortoise to divine a lucky day for receiving the drums and flags.

The ruler enters the temple portal, faces west, and stands. The commander enters the temple portal, rushes to the foot of the platform, faces north, and stands.

The sovereign personally grasps the *yue* ax. Holding it by the head, he offers the commander its handle, saying, "From here up to Heaven is controlled by [you,] the commander." [The ruler] again grasps the *fu* ax. Holding it by the head, he offers

61. The battle at Kuaiji occurred in 494 B.C.E., that at Ailing in 489 B.C.E., and that at Huangchi in 482 B.C.E.

62. Fuchai's final defeat at the hands of Yue occurred in 473 B.C.E.

the commander its handle, saying, "From here down to the Abyss is controlled by [you,] the commander."[63]

When the commander has accepted the *fu* and *yue* axes, he replies,

"[Just as] the kingdom cannot be governed from without,
the army cannot be ruled from within.[64]
[Just as] one cannot serve the ruler with two minds,
one cannot respond to the enemy with a doubtful will.

Since [I,] your minister, have received control from you, I exclusively [wield] the authority of the drums, flags, and *fu* and *yue* axes. I ask nothing in return. I [only] hope that Your Highness likewise will not hand down one word of command to me.

If Your Highness does not agree, I dare not take command.
If Your Highness agrees, I will take my leave and set out."

[The commander] then trims his fingernails,[65] dons funeral garb, and exits through the "ill-augured" portal.[66] He mounts the commander's chariot and arrays the banners and axes, tied as if not [yet] victorious. On meeting the enemy and committing to battle,

he pays no heed to certain death;
he does not have two minds.

For this reason,

he has no Heaven above;
he has no Earth below;
he has no enemy in front;
he has no ruler behind;
he does not seek fame in advancing;
he does not avoid punishment in retreating;
he [seeks] only to protect the people;
his benefit is united with that of the ruler.

This is the treasure of the kingdom, the Way of the superior commander.

If he is like this,

the clever will plan for him;
the brave will fight for him;
their *qi* will scrape the azure clouds;
they will be swift as galloping [steeds].

Thus before weapons have clashed, the enemy is terrified.

If the battle is victorious and the enemy flees, [the commander] thoroughly dispenses rewards for merit. He reassigns his officers, increasing their rank and emolu-

63. The *yue* 鉞 and *fu* 斧 axes are military regalia of the ruler. The conferring of these symbols on the commander represents the transfer of sovereign authority to him for the duration of the campaign.

64. Here "within" is used with the meaning of "within the king's court."

65. Following Yang Shuda (although retaining the original order of the text). See Lau, HNZ, 153n.5.

66. These all are rituals demonstrating the commander's resolve to die. The "ill-augured" portal is the north portal.

ment. He sets aside land and apportions it, making sure it is outside the feudal mound.[67] Last, he judges punishments within the army.

Turning back, he returns to the kingdom, lowering his banners and storing the *fu* and *yue* axes. He makes his final report to the ruler, saying, "I have no further control over the army." He then dons coarse silk and enters seclusion.

[The commander goes] to ask pardon of the ruler. The ruler says, "Spare him." [The commander] withdraws and dons fasting garb. For a great victory, he remains secluded for three years; for a middling victory, two years; for a lesser victory, one year.

That against which the military was used was surely a kingdom without the Way. Thus

> one can triumph in battle without retribution,
> take territory without returning it;
> the people will not suffer illness;
> the commander will not die early;
> the five grains will flourish;
> the winds and rains will be seasonable;
> the battle is won without;
> good fortune is born within.

Thus one's reputation will be made, and afterward there will be no further harm. [15/153/13–29]

Translated by Andrew Meyer

67. In other words, the commander makes sure that all lands dispensed as rewards fall outside the sacred ground used for the ancestral cult of the defeated sovereign, so that sacrifices to the ancestors of the defeated line may be continued.

Sixteen and Seventeen

A MOUNTAIN OF PERSUASIONS AND A FOREST OF PERSUASIONS

As their similar titles suggest, chapter 16, "A Mountain of Persuasions," and chapter 17, "A Forest of Persuasions," are collections of brief, persuasive utterances that share the same literary form and didactic function in the text. Given these similarities, we have chosen to treat these chapters together as a pair and to follow chapter 21 of the *Huainanzi*, "An Overview of the Essentials," which similarly summarizes these chapters together. Their purpose seems to be to provide a kind of repository of aphorisms that could be used in a variety of settings where the performative aspects of language were crucial, such as in oral deliberation, instruction, and debate. According to the summary in chapter 21, the brief utterances collected in these two chapters would enable the reader "to skillfully and elegantly penetrate and bore open the blockages and obstructions of the many affairs and thoroughly and comprehensively penetrate and pierce the barriers and hindrances of the myriad things." These "talking points" then would give a person engaged in oral argument or instruction a kind of arsenal of well-turned phrases with which to capture the essence of difficult concepts and thereby avoid potential snags and obstructions.

The Chapter Titles

The character 說 can be read, as we explain at greater length later, as either *shuo* or *shui*. We read the titles of chapters 16 and 17 as "Shui shan" 說山 and "Shui lin" 說林

and have translated them as "A Mountain of Persuasions" and "A Forest of Persuasions." Even though an alternative reading of "Shuo shan" and "Shuo lin" (with the rendering "A Mountain of Talk" and "A Forest of Talk") also would be legitimate, we have chosen "Persuasions" to highlight the particular genre of persuasive oratory collected in these chapters and to underscore its possible function in oral argument and debate. In other words, the short sayings collected in these chapters were meant both to illustrate and to persuade the listener to accept some fundamental point about the nature of a wide array of topics from the "many affairs" to the "myriad things."

We believe the various readings and usages of this character, *shuo/shui* 說, are important keys to understanding the manner in which oral literature—by which we mean any composition (either transmitted orally or recorded in writing) that was meant to be performed orally rather than simply read—was collected, collated, anthologized, and interpreted to serve the broader philosophical purposes of various Warring States and Han collections.

The character 說 is found in a number of chapter and book titles from the late Warring States period through the Han dynasty, with several distinct readings and related connotations as *shuo* and *shui*. When read as *shuo*, the term in its most general sense of "talk" indicates the originally oral character of materials collected in a chapter or book or materials in the literary form of a spoken story. In this broadest sense, *shuo* could be either short expressions or narratives or more extended conversations between two or more people. Thus Liu Xiang's famous collection *Shuo yuan* 說苑 might be rendered *A Garden of Talk*. It was likely given that title to indicate the author's intention of creating an anthology of various types of oral lore and performative literature. Its chapter titles give a sense of the collection's range, from well-known brief maxims, ditties, or sayings (Tan cong 談叢 [A Thicket of Remarks]) to exemplary exchanges between famous statesmen and philosophers trying to persuade those who held power to accept their particular point of view (Shan shui 善說 [Admirable Persuasions]) to outright remonstrations meant specifically to critique and redirect the actions or policies of a ruler (Zheng jian 正諫 [Upright Remonstrances]). When read as *shuo*, the character could also denote more specifically an "explanation" or "illustration," as in the "Nei chu shuo" 內儲說 (Inner Collection of Illustrations), "Wai chu shuo" 外 (Outer Collection of Illustrations), and "Shuo yi" 說疑 (Illustrations of Questionable [Conduct]) chapters of the *Hanfeizi*.

Read as *shui*, the character indicates a particular form of oral exchange or discourse for which we use the English term "persuasion" somewhat unconventionally as a countable noun. Accordingly, *shui* could be understood as a particular type of *shuo*—that is, as a recorded conversation or exchange in which the chief speaker tries to persuade the listener of a clearly articulated point of view or policy position. As Xunzi explained, a successful persuasion adheres to a carefully modulated series of techniques of oration:

> Approach the topic with dignity and gravity; dwell on it with seriousness and sincerity; hold to it with firmness and strength; clarify it by providing examples and

precepts; illustrate it by making distinctions and differences; and present it with exuberance and ardor. If you make it something precious, rare, noble, and sublime, your persuasion will always and invariably be well received. Even if you do not persuade others [of your point], none will fail to esteem you. This may indeed be described as "being able to bring esteem to what one esteems." A tradition says: "It is only the gentleman who is capable of bringing esteem to what he esteems." This expresses it.[1]

A well-known early example of such a usage of the term denoting a collection of persuasions is the similarly titled "Shui lin" (A Forest of Persuasions) chapter of the *Hanfeizi*. The "Shui nan" 說難 (The Difficulties of Persuasion) chapter of the *Hanfeizi* discusses the principal challenges that might impede a successful persuasion. (According to the *Hanfeizi*, the greatest difficulty is "to know the mind of the one to be persuaded, so as to match your persuasion to it.") A Han example of a similar usage of *shui* is the "Shan shui" (Admirable Persuasions) chapter of the *Shuo yuan*, in which a number of outstanding persuasions are collected.

Summary and Key Themes

Both chapters 16 and 17 open with introductory paragraphs meant to frame the chapters as a whole and elucidate their main purpose. Chapter 16 begins with an anecdote in which the Way is related to the subject of "form and names"—that is, speech. This playful anecdote, reminiscent of the *Zhuangzi*, recounts a conversation between a person's *po* 魄 (substantive spirit) and *hun* 魂 (ethereal spirit). These are fitting characters to embody within a single figure, and to frame a discussion of, the dual aspects of the Way: what has form and what is formless. This critical distinction between what has form and what is formless is used throughout the *Huainanzi* to harmonize and demonstrate the unity of two apparently separate approaches to the Way. Here this distinction reminds the reader that speech may assume various forms as particular expressions of the Way in a given moment and in a given context but that words do not possess universal or eternal validity. They are useful as transitory and instrumental expressions of the formless and inexpressible "Dark Mystery" or "Ancestor" that is the ultimate sense of the Way. So we also are given to understand that the forms of the myriad things are contingent and transitory, not fixed and immutable, that only the Way is unchanging.

Chapter 17 begins with three short analogies cautioning the reader that "just because something is suitable for a particular time is not enough to make it valuable [always]." This brief preamble reiterates an argument appearing elsewhere in the text: that the standards of ancient times—things that were suitable to a particular era,

1. *Xunzi*, chap. 5, "Fei xiang." Translation modified from Knoblock 1988, 1:209.

time, or circumstance—do not enjoy eternal relevance or universal validity. Even though an earthen dragon is made in times of drought and a straw dog in times of epidemic, such things are "sovereign" only at those particular times. When the time passes, these things lose their efficacy. So, too, with words: certain words fit certain occasions; the same expression is not suitable to all occasions. One thus must choose one's words judiciously, employing the right expressions for the context. One must employ the "sovereign" expression.

To do so, chapters 16 and 17 have collected an astounding array of "persuasions," exceeding in number and variety of topic all surviving collections that had been compiled before the *Huainanzi* was completed and surpassed only by the later Western Han collection, Liu Xiang's *Shuo yuan*. Chapter 16 of the *Huainanzi* collects 162 sayings, and chapter 17 brings together 246. Some are accompanied by brief editorial comments that clarify their meaning in some way. These collections of persuasive oratory, with their titles suggesting the height of a mountain and the number and density of trees in a forest, indicate that together they represent a particular genre of persuasion. In fact, the various subjects addressed in these persuasions are just the point: they enable the reader to "wander in accord with Heaven and Earth" rather than be limited to "follow[ing] a path made by a solitary footprint or adher[ing] to instructions from a single perspective," as chapter 21, "An Overview of the Essentials," explains. We might speculate that armed with such a comprehensive collection, the reader would be equipped with a wide variety of "talking points" commensurate with every conceivable aspect of the Way and suitable for any oral debate or discussion.

Sources

The collections of persuasions most relevant to chapters 16 and 17 of the *Huainanzi* are the earlier *Hanfeizi* and later *Shuo yuan*. These texts help us understand how this particular genre of performative literature was collected and preserved through the ages. Chapters 22 and 23 of the *Hanfeizi*, "Shui lin shang" and "Shui lin xia" (A Forest of Persuasions, Parts 1 and 2), with the same title as chapter 16 of the *Huainanzi*, are the most pertinent here. The duplication of the title by the *Huainanzi* authors suggests that these chapters belong to the same genre of persuasive oratory and that *Hanfeizi* 22 and 23 are examples of such literature of which the *Huainanzi* authors were well aware.

This chapter, and others in the *Hanfeizi* that preserve this genre of persuasive oratory, collects "persuasions" in various guises. The first genre, a more typical and longer form of persuasion characteristic of the *Hanfeizi* and other Warring States texts, generally is in the form of an anecdote with an oral element following a more or less set literary form. It usually consists of a narrative frame setting the scene, historical or mythical figures (often a holder of political power and a "persuader" trying to convince him of something), the pronouncement meant to persuade, and a response. As a kind of denouement, the response may take the form of verbal approval or disapproval or action indicating that the recipient of the persuasion has either embraced or rejected what has been proposed. The editorial comment that sometimes follows the persuasion proper shapes the persuasion along the philosophical lines intended by the author of the specific collection.[2] The following excerpt from *Hanfeizi* 22, which revolves around the colorful and insatiable Earl Zhi, exemplifies this type of persuasion:

> Earl Zhi demanded territory from Viscount Huan of Wei. Viscount Huan of Wei did not yield it. Ren Zhang said: "Why do you not yield it to him?" Viscount Huan responded: "He is demanding territory from us for no reason. This is why I refused to yield it to him." Ren Zhang responded: "If he demands territory without reason, neighboring states surely will grow fearful of him. If the earl's desires increase without cease, the world surely will grow apprehensive of him. [But] if you give him territory [now], Earl Zhi will surely grow arrogant and slight his enemies so that neighboring states surely will grow fearful of him and form mutual alliances. If you rely on the troops of states forming mutual alliances to address a state that slights its enemies, Earl Zhi's life will not be long. The *Book of Zhou* states: 'When you desire to conquer, you must first assist; when you desire to take, you must first give.' It would be best to give Earl Zhi territory and thereby feed his arrogance. Moreover, why would you hesitate to join with the rest of the world to conspire against the Zhi clan so that our state alone would become a target for Earl Zhi?" The Viscount responded: "Superb." He then gave Earl Zhi a fief of ten thousand households. Earl Zhi was greatly pleased. Earl Zhi then demanded territory from [Viscount Xiang of] Zhao. [Viscount Xiang of] Zhao refused to grant it. Consequently Earl Zhi besieged Jinyang. The states of Hann and Wei plotted against Earl Zhi from beyond [Jinyang] while the state of Zhao responded to him from within [Jinyang], and Earl Zhi was ultimately destroyed.[3]

The second common literary treatment of a persuasion is typically briefer and decontextualized. It is a short oral pronouncement, usually without a narrative frame or an identified speaker or listener.[4] The point of these persuasive utterances seems to be their very commonplace character and unremarkable lineage. They appear to be a kind of public wisdom handed down through the ages, highly prized not because they derive from the mouth of the sages but because they capture enduring truths. What is recorded is a brief statement, often characterized by parallelism or rhyme that exhibits varying degrees of transparency to the modern reader. Some stand out for their pithiness or wittiness, while others appear to relate to quite banal aspects of the phenomenal world. Whatever the particular meaning might be, the didactic

---

2. The vast majority of persuasions collected in *Hanfeizi*, chaps. 22 and 23, "A Forest of Persuasions, Parts 1 and 2," follow this format, as do those collected in *Shuo yuan*, chap. 11, "Admirable Persuasions."

3. HFZ 22/47/1–7. For the *Huainanzi* account of this story, see 18.5.

4. There are, of course, exceptions to this general rule. For example, in the "Tan cong" chapter of the *Shuo yuan*, three utterances are attributed to Zengzi.

point to be extracted from the pronouncement is sometimes identified by an editorial comment that directly follows a given pronouncement. Examples of this shorter form of persuasive utterance may be found in such texts as the *Hanfeizi*'s chapter 23, "A Forest of Persuasions, Part 2" (Shui lin xia) and the *Shuoyuan*'s chapter 16, "A Thicket of Remarks" (Tan cong). The following are three such examples:

Example 1

Saying: "Among birds there is one called the cuckoo. It has a heavy head and a curved tail. When it is about to take water from the river, it inevitably falls on its head. Only when it flattens its wings with its mouth can it drink from the river."

Comment: "When people do not have enough to drink, they too must find their wings."[5]

Example 2

Saying: "There is a type of worm called a 'tapeworm.' It has a single body and two mouths. When it struggles to get food, the two mouths bite one another so that each mouth kills the other and eventually the tapeworm kills itself."

Comment: "When ministers struggle over their affairs and forget the state, they all belong to the likes of a tapeworm."[6]

Example 3

Saying: "When buildings are whitewashed and furniture is cleaned with water, then they are immaculate."

Comment: "Human conduct and character is just the same. When there is no place left to be whitewashed or cleaned, then faults are few."[7]

The sayings collected in chapters 16 and 17 of the *Huainanzi* resemble most closely this second (shorter) form of persuasive utterance and therefore comprise an important collection of such materials from the time between when the *Hanfeizi* and *Shuoyuan* collections were compiled. In fact, as the next example demonstrates, we find the same persuasive utterance used for different interpretive aims in these three collections:

5. HFZ 23/51/17–18.
6. HFZ 23/52/1–2.
7. HFZ 23/52/4.

Hanfeizi 23

Saying: "Eels resemble snakes; silkworms resemble caterpillars. When people see snakes, they become alarmed and frightened; when they see caterpillars, their hair stands on end. But fishermen hold eels and women pick up silkworms."

Comment: "Thus, where benefit resides, everyone resembles a Meng Ben or Zhuan Zhu [in their courage]."[8]

Huainanzi 17.56

The eel and the snake,
the silkworm and the caterpillar—
In appearance they belong to the same category. But how they are liked or disliked makes them different.

Shuoyuan 16

The eel is akin to the snake; the silkworm is akin to the caterpillar. When people see a caterpillar or snake, none fails to be personally alarmed. [Yet] women cultivate silkworms and fishermen handle eels. Why do they not loathe such things? Desiring to make a living, those who hunt fish must get wet, and those who hunt prey must hasten their pace, but not because they like to do so. It is due to the circumstances of the situation.[9]

The Chapters in the Context of the *Huainanzi* as a Whole

The existence of collections of *shui* from the Warring States period and the Western Han dynasty suggests that there was a clear demand for them from bureaucrats, advisers, teachers, and others who regularly offered lessons or advice to others and tried to influence their actions. We can think of such collections as handbooks for people who knew that they would be asked to speak on a regular basis. A modern analogy might be the many collections of jokes, anecdotes, and apt turns of phrase for masters of ceremony, toastmasters, and after-dinner speakers.

But if we are correct in believing that the primary audience for the *Huainanzi* was the actual or aspiring ruler of a kingdom or an empire, it is necessary to ask about the

8. HFZ 23/51/20–21. Meng Ben was a fearless warrior from the state of Wei. Zhuan Zhu was a courageous inhabitant of Wu who assassinated King Liao of Wu, thereby permitting Prince Guang to become King Helü of Wu.

9. *Shuo yuan*, "Tan cong." Interestingly, Liu Xiang conflates two *Huainanzi* passages here: the persuasion about "eels and snakes" comes from 17.56, and "those who hunt fish" comes from 12.3.

value of a collection of persuasions for such a figure. A ruler might have been more likely to be moderating and listening to court debates than marshaling persuasions to make points of his own. For this highly selective audience, a ruler might want these collected *shui* on hand to shape his own participation in court debates, but he might also want to have them in mind as persuasions that he was likely to hear from debaters in his presence. That is, they should prepare him for stereotyped arguments that his advisers and other participants might use in court sessions, so he could distinguish genuinely new ideas from hackneyed talking points. In this context, the comment in "An Overview of the Essentials" that these persuasions

> skillfully and elegantly penetrate and bore open the blockages and obstructions of the many affairs
> and thoroughly and comprehensively penetrate and pierce the barriers and hindrances of the myriad things (21.2)

takes on a subtle double meaning. The "blockages and obstructions" concerned might be the rhetorical obfuscations that debaters in the ruler's own presence offered and that he could detect through his own familiarity with such stereotyped talking points.

Of course, this effect is not limited to an imperial "audience of one." Anyone who engages in oratory might benefit by adding to his rhetorical arsenal the persuasions collected in these two chapters, and he would also recognize when another speaker was using these same prepackaged arguments. Thus the use of such material was always a two-edged sword: Did these persuasions help a speaker be seen as a brilliant orator, or did they leave him open to a charge of using stale and stereotypical arguments? It would seem impossible to have one effect but not the other.

A Note on the Format of Chapters 16 and 17

The paragraph numbers used in chapters 16 and 17 follow those of D. C. Lau's *Concordance to the Huainanzi* and replace the references by chapter, page, and line that we have used in all but these two chapters. In a few cases, where we believe that Lau has conflated two or more sayings, we have divided the paragraph and renumbered the subsequent parts of it with the letters "a," "b," and so on, such as 4, 4a, and 4b.

Sarah A. Queen and John S. Major

Sixteen

16.1

The *po* [substantive soul] asked the *hun* [ethereal soul],[1] "How does the Way take physical form?" The *hun* replied, "It takes Nothing There as its physical form." The *po* asked, "Does Nothing There have a physical form, then?" The *hun* replied, "It does not." The *po* asked, "If there is Nothing There, how can one apprehend it and be informed about it?" The *hun* replied, "I only have ways to encounter it, that is all. When we look at it, it has no form; when we listen to it, it has no sound. We call it 'the Dark Mystery.' The Dark Mystery can be used to refer to the Way, but it is not the Way." The *po* said, "Now I get it." Thereupon he turned his gaze inward and reverted to himself. The *hun* said, "Those who have attained the Way have forms that cannot be seen and names that cannot be expressed. *You* still have 'form' and 'name.' How can you attain the Way?" The *po* said, "What use is speech, then? I shall return to my Ancestor." The *po* turned to look, and suddenly the *hun* could not be seen. The *po* then turned and got a grip on himself and also entered the formless.

1. In Han belief, living humans had two souls: the *po* 魄, a substantive, earthy, corporeal soul associated with yin, which was buried with the body after death and consumed funerary offerings; and the *hun* 魂, an ethereal soul associated with yang, which left the body at the time of death. See also 7.6 and 9.2; and chap. 9, n. 2.

16.2

If not for small learning, a person would not be greatly misled;
if not for small intelligence, a person would not be greatly deluded.

16.3

No one uses running water for a mirror. Rather, you look at yourself in clear water because it is still and unmoving.

16.4

Mr. Zhan's[2] fishing [skill] could catch a thousand-year-old carp.
So hard did Zengzi tug at the planked cart [carrying his father's coffin] that the catafalque puller was forced to stop.
When his elderly mother walked by singing, Shen Xi was moved right on the spot.[3]

These are clear examples of the highest attainment of the Essence.

16.4a

Hu Ba[4] played the *se*, and the sturgeons[5] came up to listen.
Bo Ya[6] played the *qin*, and the quadriga horses raised their heads while grazing.
Jie Zi[tui][7] sang about the dragon and the snake, and Lord Wen of Jin broke down in tears.

---

2. See 1.6 and 6.1. Here Zhan He is called Zhan Gong; *gong* 公 must be understood here not as "duke" but as an honorific term for a respected older man.

3. Shen Xi 申喜 was a man variously said to have been from Zhou or Chu. Having lost his mother when he was young, he was once strangely moved by the song of an old beggar woman. On closer inspection, she turned out to be his long-lost mother. His story is recorded in *Lüshi chunqiu* 9.5.

4. Hu Ba 瓠巴 appears in *Xunzi* 1. According to Gao You, he was a man of Chu. See Zhang Shuangdi 1997, 2:1632n.7.

5. Following Lau's (HNZ, 154n.1) identification of *yin-yu* 淫 魚 as *xun* 鱘.

6. Bo Ya 百牙 (also known as 伯牙) was a master musician who famously broke his instrument when Zhongzi Qi, the person who most appreciated his music, died. See *Lüshi chunqiu* 14.2. The story of his effect on horses is recorded in *Xunzi* 1.

7. Jie Zitui 介子推 (also known as Jie Zhitui 之推) was a knight of Jin who accompanied Duke Wen of Jin during his long years in exile but who alone among the duke's retinue was not rewarded on the latter's accession to the ducal throne. Many versions of Jiezi Tui's legend appear in various texts. He is said to have gone as far as cutting off some of his own flesh to feed Duke Wen when provisions had run low and the group was starving. Gao You relates a version of Jie Zitui's legend (alluded to here in the *Huainanzi*) in which Jie sang a song comparing himself to a snake that had nurtured and been

Thus,

if there is jade in the mountains, the plants and trees are enriched;
if a pool produces pearls, its banks do not dry up.

16.4b

The earthworm lacks strength of muscles and bones and sharpness of claws and teeth, but

above it eats dry earth
and below it drinks of the Yellow Springs,

for it uses its mind in a unitary way.

16.5

With the clarity of what is pure, a cup of water reveals [the reflection of] an eyeball.
With the darkness of what is murky, the water of the [Yellow] River does not reveal [even the reflection of] Mount Tai.

16.6

If you stare at the sun, you will go blind.
If you listen to thunder, you will become deaf.
If you act without purpose, you will be well ordered.
If you act with purpose, you will be harmed.

Being well ordered through purposelessness is dependent on Nothingness. If you act with purpose, you will be unable to have anything. If you are unable to act without purpose, you will be unable to have anything purposeful.

16.6a

One who is without words is spiritlike.
One who has words is harmed.

One who is spiritlike through wordlessness is dependent on Nothingness. Having words harms the spirit.[8]

---

abandoned by a dragon (i.e., Duke Wen), moving the duke to tears of regret. See Zhang Shuangdi 1997, 2:1634n.9. *Shiji* 39 records an alternative version of this story in which Jie writes a snake/dragon poem on the gates of the ducal palace.

8. We omit the next three characters (*zhi shen zhe* 之神者—) as being a stray fragment that does not belong here.

16.6b

That by which the nose breathes,
and that by which the ears hear—
In the end it is their Nothingness that makes them function.

Among things, none do not rely on what they have and use what they do not have. If you do not believe this, look at the flute and reed pipes.[9]

16.7

Those who ponder and worry cannot sleep. If pondering and worrying are ended, then there [must be] a means by which they are ended. When both [pondering and worrying] are completely extirpated, one may attain [a state of] Potency and Purity.

16.8

Sages spend their lives talking about governing. What is of use is not their words [as such] but what they have to say. Singers use lyrics, but what people really enjoy hearing is not the lyrics themselves. A parrot can speak, but it cannot engage in meaningful discourse. Why is this? It has the power of speech but does not have anything to say.

Thus if someone follows you and walks in your tracks, he cannot produce fresh footprints of his own.

16.9

A divine snake can be cut in two and grow back [the severed part], but it cannot prevent someone from cutting it in two.
A divine tortoise could appear in a dream to King Yuan [of Song],[10] but it could not free itself from the fisherman's trap.

9. That is, the nose and the ears (like wind instruments) rely on both their physical structure and their empty passages to function.

10. King Yuan of Song 宋元王 poses a historiographic puzzle. This name appears in many Warring States and Han texts, but reconstructed chronologies of the period do not seem to accommodate his historicity. Only one Song ruler for whom a clear record exists took the title of king: King Kang of Song (r. 329–286 B.C.E.), the last ruler of Song before its destruction. There was a Duke 公 Yuan of Song (r. 531–517 B.C.E.), but he lived too early to fit plausibly into many of the contexts in which "King Yuan" is evoked in later texts. Qian Mu 錢穆 believes that "King Yuan" may have been a crown prince of Song, son of King Kang, who briefly held the throne during the crisis surrounding the state's collapse (*Xian Qin zhuzi xinian* 先秦諸子繫年, 2nd ed. [Hong Kong: Hong Kong University Press, 1956; repr., Taipei: Dongda, 1990], 402–4). *Zhuangzi* 26 reports that Lord Yuan 元君 (in this case, most likely

16.10

The four directions are the gates and doors, windows and back gates of the Way; which one you go through [determines] how you view things. Thus

fishing can be used to teach someone horseback riding;
horseback riding can be used to instruct a person in charioteering;
and charioteering can be used to teach someone how to pole a boat.

16.11

When the people of Yue studied the [unfamiliar] art of long-distance archery, they looked up at the sky and shot, but their arrows landed only five paces away because they did not change their aim.[11] To stick to old ways of doing things after the times have altered is like the people of Yue practicing archery.

16.12

When the moon is seen [in the daytime], the sun steals the moon's light. The yin cannot take precedence over the yang. When the sun comes out, the stars cannot be seen. The stars cannot compete in brightness with the sun. Thus

branches cannot be stronger than the roots;
fingers cannot be larger than the arms.

If

the bottom is light
and the top is heavy,

[an object] surely will be easy to overturn.

16.12a

One pool cannot [house] two sharks;
one perch cannot [house] two male birds.
If there is one, there is stability;
if there are two, there is strife.

Duke Yuan) encountered a dream tortoise claiming to be an emissary of the god of the Yangzi on his way to the god of the Yellow River that had been caught in a fisherman's basket. The ruler summoned the fisherman, retrieved the turtle, and killed it so as to use its shell for prognostication.

11. Commentators explain that the people of Yue were familiar with shooting overhead (e.g., at birds in trees) but not at shooting at things far away. They were unable to adapt their familiar technique to a new goal.

16.12b

When water is still, it is clear and even; when it moves, it loses its evenness. Thus it is only by not moving that nothing is unmoved.

16.13

The reason why the Yangzi and the Yellow rivers can extend through a hundred valleys is because they are able to descend through them. As a general rule, only by being able to occupy a lower position will you be able to rise to the top.

16.14

In the world,

> there are no two things so mutually repellent as glue and pitch,
> and none more attracted to each other than ice and charcoal.
> Glue and pitch detract from each another.
> Charcoal and ice enhance each other.[12]

16.15

> The crumbling of a wall is better than its building;
> the melting of ice is better than its freezing

because they [thus] return to the Ancestor.

16.16

The appearance of Mount Tai is majestically high, but if you go a thousand *li* away from it, it looks smaller than an earthen embankment. This is because of the distance.

12. Glue will not stick to pitch; each "steals" the other's stickiness. Charcoal was used to insulate ice in ice houses during the summertime. See also 11.18; and chap. 11, n. 96.

16.17

The tip of an autumn hair[13] can get lost in the unfathomable. This means that what is so small that nothing can be placed inside it is [the same as] something so large that nothing can be placed outside it.

16.18

Orchids grow in dark valleys. They are no less fragrant just because no one [happens to] wear them.[14]
Boats ply rivers and oceans. They are no less buoyant just because no one [happens to] ride in them.
The Superior Man practices Rightness. He does not stop doing so just because no one [happens to] know about it.

16.19

When a piece of jade is moistened, it looks bright. [When struck], its sound is slow and harmonious. How expansive are its aspects! With no interior or exterior, it does not conceal its flaws or imperfections. Close up, it looks glossy; from a distance, it shines brightly. It reflects like a mirror revealing the pupil of your eye. Subtly it picks up the tip of an autumn hair. It brightly illuminates the dark and obscure. Thus the jade disk of Mr. He and the pearl of the marquis of Sui emerged from the essence of a mountain and a spring. When the Superior Man wears them, he complies with their purity and secures his repose. When lords and kings treasure them, they rectify the world.

16.20

Chen Chengheng's[15] threatening of Ziyuan Jie;[16] Zi Han's refusal of what he did not desire [a valuable jade] and achieving what he most desired [a reputation for covetlessness]; Confucius's seeing a man catching cicadas;[17] Duke Sheng of Bo holding his

13. The tip of a downy hair just beginning to emerge through an animal's skin in autumn is a standard ancient Chinese metaphor for the smallest possible thing.

14. Many species of orchids have little or no scent; nevertheless, orchids (*lan* 蘭) are strongly associated with fragrance in Chinese literary imagery.

15. Chen Chengheng is the same as Chen Chengchang. See 13.8.

16. Ziyuan Jie 子淵捷 (also known as Ziju 子車) was a grandee of Qi who served at the court of Duke Jian. Chen Chengheng threatened Ziyuan Jie because the latter would not join in his plot to assassinate Duke Jian of Qi.

17. This refers to a story in *Zhuangzi* 48 (ZZ 48/19/18) about a man who could capture the insects on the end of a pole by being able to concentrate his whole spirit on the task.

lance and whip upside down;[18] the daughter of the king of Wey asking Duke Huan of Qi to punish her [instead of invading her state]; Zengzi looking at Zi Xia and asking, "Why are you so fat?";[19] Duke Wen of Wei seeing a man with the leather side and the fur side of his garment reversed and carrying straw [and making fun of him]; Ni Yue[20] untying the closed knot for the king of Song:
These are all cases in which from a tiny instance one can see the whole situation.

16.21

A man was marrying off his daughter. He counseled her, "Go, but be careful not to do anything good." She replied, "If I don't do anything good, should I do something bad?" [Her father] responded, "If you shouldn't even do anything good, how much less should you do anything bad!" This was [how she could] keep her natural qualities intact.[21]

16.22

Those who are in prison consider a day a long time.
Those who are about to be executed in the marketplace consider a day to be very short.
The length of a day has a set standard, but
from where one person stands it is short
and from where another stands it is long.
This is because their center is not balanced. Thus when one uses what is not balanced to consider what is balanced, then what one takes to be balanced will not be balanced.

16.23

If you marry off a daughter to a man with a disease that makes him impotent, then when the husband dies, [people will] say, "The woman put him off." Later she will find it difficult to remarry.
Thus,

18. Duke Bo of Sheng was so preoccupied with a rebellion that he injured his chin with a whip held upside down and was not even aware of it. See 12.46.

19. See 7.15; and *Hanfeizi*, chap. 7.

20. Ni Yue 兒說 was a logician of Song who is said to have defeated all the debaters at Jixia by arguing the proposition that "a white horse is not a horse." He "untied" (i.e., "solved") the duke's knot by showing that it could not be untied. See 17.193; and chap. 18, nn. 131, 132.

21. The father's advice seems useful; a good strategy for a young bride entering her husband's household was to avoid being conspicuous in any way.

you cannot sit near a house that is ready to collapse;
you cannot stand next to a wall that is about to fall over.

16.24

A man who is held in jail has no illnesses.
A man who faces execution is fat and healthy.
A man who has been castrated lives a long time.

Their minds are free of entanglements.

16.24a

A doctor constantly treats illnesses that are not [yet] illnesses; thus he prevents illnesses.

A sage constantly deals with calamities that are not [yet] calamities; thus he prevents calamities.

16.25

One who has mastered carpentry does not use an angle rule or marking cord;
one who excels at shutting himself away does not use a door and latch.

Chunyu Kun's warning of a fire hazard is [an example of] the same kind of thing.[22]

16.26

When what is clear mixes with what is muddy, [muddiness] is diminished and diluted.

When what is muddy mixes with what is clear, [clarity] is overturned and subverted.

16.26a

When the Superior Man resides in the Good, he resembles the wood gatherer who,

upon seeing a twig, picks it up
and, upon seeing a green onion, plucks it too.

22. Chunyu Kun warned a neighbor that his chimney was defective and might cause a fire. See Zhang Shuangdi 1997, 2:1651n.25.

16.27

When the two *qi* [contend] in Heaven, they cause rainbows;
when the two *qi* [contend] on Earth, they cause emissions;
when the two *qi* [contend] in a human body, they cause disease.[23]
Yin and yang cannot make it be both winter and summer [simultaneously].
The moon does not know daylight;
the sun does not know night.

16.28

A good archer shoots and does not miss the target. That is good for the archer, but not good for the target.
A good fisherman never loses a fish. That is good for the fisherman, but not good for the fish.
Thus where there is that which is good, there also is that which is not good.

16.29

If you compare [the sounds of] bells and chimestones,
close by the sound of bells is richer,
but far away the sound of the chimestones is clearer.
There are certainly things that
are better near than far away,
[and others that are] better far away than near.

16.30

Now it is said that
rice grows in water, but it cannot grow in a turbulent flow [of water].
The *zhi* fungus grows on mountains, but it cannot grow on barren boulders.
A lodestone can attract iron, but if you put it near bronze it will not move.

16.31

When the waters are vast, the fish are huge;
when the mountains are high, the trees are tall.

23. Yin and yang (the two *qi*) are always simultaneously present in everything, but usually in unequal amounts; thus one or the other is naturally dominant. When they are present with equal force and contend for dominance, the effects described result.

But if you extend its area too much, its Potency will be diminished. It is like a potter making a vessel. If he makes it large but not thick enough, it will be all the more likely to break.

16.32

A sage does not blow before the wind [does it for him];
he does not destroy in advance of the thunder.
He acts only when he cannot avoid it, and so he has no entanglements.

16.33

As the moon waxes and wanes above,
snails and clams respond below.[24]
Those of the same *qi*[25] bestir each other;
they cannot get very far apart.

16.34

If you
grasp a crossbow and call a bird
or brandish a club and beckon a dog,
then what you want to come will surely go away instead.[26] Thus,
a fish cannot be hooked without bait;
an animal cannot be lured with an empty trap.

16.35

If you tear off an ox's hide and stretch it to make a drum, you can use it to direct the multitudes of the Three Armies.[27] But from the ox's point of view, it would be better to wear a yoke and continue working.

A robe of white fox fur is worn by the Son of Heaven as he sits at court. But from the fox's point of view, it would be better to be running around in the meadow.

---

24. A similar statement appears in 4.9.

25. Some editions use the character *qi* 氣, which in this usage means something like "nature" (almost equivalent to *xing* 性), while others use *qi* 器, as in 16.21. There is a clear point of congruence of the terms, but *qi* 氣 appears to be correct here. See 4/34/23: *jie xiang qi qi, jie ying qi lei* 皆相其氣,皆應其類. This expresses the same idea as *tong qi xiang dong* 同氣相動 here.

26. A passage in 1.6 makes a similar point.

27. See 16.111.

16.36

If you lose a sheep but gain an ox, no one would fail to [consider it] a beneficial loss.
If you cut off a finger to avoid being beheaded, no one would fail to [consider it] a beneficial act.

Thus human emotion,
when surrounded by benefits, struggles to gain as much as possible
and, when surrounded by harm, struggles to get as little as possible.

16.37

A general dares not ride a [conspicuous] white horse.
An escaped prisoner dares not carry a torch at night.
A wine shop proprietor[28] dares not keep a dog that bites people.

16.38

The rooster knows the approaching dawn;
the crane knows the middle of night;
but neither can avoid the pot and the platter.

16.39

If there is a fierce beast in the mountains, because of that the forest's trees are not cut down.
If there are poisonous insects in the garden, because of that the greens are not picked.

Thus if a state has worthy ministers, it can defend itself [against attacks at a distance of] a thousand *li*.[29]

---

28. *Baozhe* 抱者, shopkeeper, explained by the commentators as the proprietor of a wine shop. He dares not keep a biting dog because it would frighten away his customers.

29. This sentence is transposed from 16.59, following the suggestion of Wang Niansun. See Lau, HNZ, 157, 159.

16.40

To be a Confucian and yet squat in the village lanes,[30]
or to be a Mohist and yet play the pitch pipes at court,[31]
is like someone who wants to conceal his tracks but walks in the snow
or who tries to rescue a drowning man without getting his clothes wet.

He repudiates what he practices and practices what he repudiates.

16.41

If someone drinks in the dark, he invariably will spill his drink.
If you enable him to hold the cup level, he will not spill any, even if he is a fool.

For this reason, he who does not identify with harmony and yet is able to succeed in his affairs—in the world there has never been such a thing.

16.42

If you look for beauty, you will not get it.
If you do not look for beauty, you will acquire beauty.
If you look for ugliness, you will not get it.
If you do not look for ugliness, you will acquire ugliness.

If you do not look for beauty and [also] do not look for ugliness, then you will be without beauty or ugliness. This is called "Mysteriously the Same."[32]

16.43

Shen Tudi[33] [tied] a stone on his back and jumped into deep water. But drowning yourself cannot be considered a protest.
Xian Gao used deception to preserve Cheng[34] But deception should not be taken as a standard.

Some actions [are effective as] a single response but may not be repeatedly practiced.

---

30. A major violation of etiquette. Compare 16.79.
31. Mozi opposed music as wasteful.
32. Some commentators interpret the "beauty" and "ugliness" of this passage as referring to one's reputation. See also *Laozi* 56; and *Zhuangzi* 24 (ZZ 24/10/27).
33. Shentu Di 申徒狄 was a minister of King Djou of Shang who committed suicide out of shame that he could not reform his ruler.
34. *Zuozhuan*, Xi 33; *Gongyang zhuan*, Xi 33.

16.44

An effusive person is like the sound of the hundred-tongue [bird].[35]
A reticent person is like a door whose hinges have not been greased.[36]

16.45

If one of the six domestic animals is born with an additional ear or eye, it is unlucky, [but] it is recorded in the books of omens.[37]

16.46

A hundred men trying to lift a gourd is not as good as one person grabbing it and running off. Thus there certainly are situations in which a crowd is not as good as a few people.

Two people pull a cart, and six more push behind. Thus there certainly are affairs in which mutual cooperation is necessary for success.

If two people are drowning, they cannot rescue each other, but if one is on shore, he can [save the other]. Thus identical things cannot set each other in order. It is necessary to depend on difference; only then there will be a good outcome.

16.47

Where below [ground] there is "hidden moss,"[38] above it there will be rabbit floss.[39]
Where above [ground] there is a patch of milfoil, beneath it there will be hidden a turtle.

A sage knows from external appearances what lies within. He uses the visible to know the hidden.

35. That is, the blackbird, which can imitate the songs of many other birds. Also called the turn-tongue (*fan she* 反舌). See 5.5.

36. That is, his voice has become rusty from disuse.

37. The lives of most animals pass unnoticed; these anomalies, though bad omens, receive a kind of immortality by being recorded in writing.

38. That is, *fuling*, written 伏苓 or 茯苓, which is said to grow on the roots of pine trees and to embody the "hidden spirit" of the tree. See *Shiji* 128/3b–4a.

39. A parasitic plant that has no roots.

16.48

Taking pleasure in military matters does not make one a soldier;
taking pleasure in literature does not make one a Confucian.
Liking formulas does not make one a doctor;
liking horses does not make one a charioteer.
Knowing music does not make one a court drummer;
knowing flavors does not make one a chef.

This is to have an approximation [of the skill] but not yet to have earned a reputation as a master [of that skill].

16.49

Armor does not [protect against arrows] at a distance of less than ten paces. Beyond a hundred paces, [arrows] contend [with the armor so as to pierce] deeply or shallowly. If deep, they will penetrate the five vital organs; if shallow, they will graze the flesh and stop. The distance between life and death cannot be attributed to the principles of the Way.

16.50

The king of Chu lost his [pet] ape,[40] and [to recapture it] he destroyed every tree in the forest.
The prince of Song lost his pearl, and [to recover it] he wiped out all the fish [in the lake he drained].

Thus when a meadow blazes with fire, the forest worries.

16.51

When the ruler wants a plank, his officials cut down a tree.
When the ruler wants a fish, his officials dry up a valley.
When the ruler wants an oar, his underlings give him a whole boat.
When the ruler's words are like threads, his underlings' words are like rope.
When the ruler likes one thing, his underlings praise it twice.
When the ruler faults three [people], his underlings kill nine.

40. See 16.89.

16.52

Great Officer Zhong knew how to strengthen Yue, but he did not know how to preserve his own life.[41]
Chang Hong knew the reason why Zhou would endure, but he could not discern why he would perish.
[They] knew what was distant but did not perceive what was close at hand.

16.53

To fear a horse will throw you and thus not daring to mount one;
to be anxious that a cart might overturn and thus not daring to ride in one:
these are cases of an "empty calamity" causing you to avoid real benefits.

16.54

Those who are unfilial or unbrotherly might sometimes scold their fathers and mothers. When you have children, you cannot rely on their necessarily being filial, but even so you nourish and raise them.

16.55

When the Fan clan[42] was defeated, someone stole their bell, slung it on his back, and ran away. It made a clanging noise. Fearing that someone might hear it, the thief covered his ears. That he would fear others might hear it was reasonable, but for him to cover his own ears was perverse.

16.56

A *sheng* cannot be bigger than a *dan* because a *sheng* is contained within a *dan*.[43]
A night cannot be longer than a year, because a night is contained within a year.

---

41. That is, Wen Zhong. He was forced to commit suicide by a suspicious king. See *Shiji* 28/7a–b; and *Zuozhuan*, Ai 3.

42. The Fan clan 范氏 was one of the "six ministerial clans" of the Jin. The clan was destroyed and its territory divided among the Hann, Zhi, Zhao, and Wei clans in 458 B.C.E.

43. For these and other weights and measures, see app. B.

Humaneness and Rightness cannot be greater than the Way and its Potency because Humaneness and Rightness are contained within the Way and its Potency.

16.57

If the needle goes first and the thread follows, you can make a tent.
If the thread [were to] go first and the needle to follow, you could not make [even] a garment.
The needle makes [possible] the curtain;
the basket makes [possible] the wall.

Whether an enterprise succeeds or fails necessarily starts from what is small. This is to say that it is a gradual process.

16.58

In dyeing things,
if something is at first blue and you dye it black, that is possible;
if something is first black and you [wish to] dye it blue, that is not possible.[44]
If an artisan
applies the lacquer first and then applies the cinnabar over it, that is possible;
if he applies the cinnabar first and then the lacquer over it, that is not possible.

Everything is like this: you cannot fail to attend to what is first and what is last, what is on top and what is underneath.

16.59

When the water is muddy, fish gasp for air [near the surface].
When your body is overworked, your spirit is disordered.

16.60

You rely on a matchmaker to bring about a marriage, but you cannot rely on the matchmaker to make the marriage successful.
You rely on people to relate to one another, but you cannot rely on people to be close.

44. For a similar argument, see 2.7.

16.61

If people's actions correspond and their inclinations[45] are the same, even if they are separated by a thousand *li*, they can follow one another.
If people's inclinations are not the same and their actions differ, even though their gates face one another, they will not communicate [with one another].

16.62

Though the waters of the sea are vast, it does not accept carrion and weeds.[46]
The sun and moon do not respond to things not of the same *qi* [as themselves];
the Superior Man does not associate with those not of his own type.

16.63

People do not love the hand of [the legendary master artisan] Chui, but they do love their own fingers.
People do not love the pearls of the Yangzi and the Han rivers, but they do love their own belt hooks.

16.64

You might mistake a bundle of firewood for a ghost
or fire and smoke for an emanation [of *qi*].
If you mistake the firewood for a ghost, you [might] turn and run away;
if you mistake smoke for an emanation you [might] kill a pig and boil a dog [as sacrifices].
To prejudge things like this is not as good as reflecting about them later.

16.65

A skillful workman is good at measuring things carefully.
A knowledgeable person is good at preparing [for future possibilities].

45. *Qu* 趨 here is equivalent to *qu* 趣 in the following line; in this context, we take both as having the sense of "inclinations."

46. A similar statement is found in 17.141.

16.66

When [the great archer] Yi was killed [in an ambush] by [men wielding] peach-wood clubs, he had no chance to shoot [his arrows].
When [the mighty wrestler] Qingji was killed by swords and spears, he had no chance to grapple [with his attackers].[47]

16.67

Someone who wanted to put a stop to slander went from door to door saying, "I really did not have an affair with my elder sister-in law!" The slander increased more and more.

Trying to stop words with more words
or affairs with more affairs
is like making piles of dirt to ward off dust
or using armloads of firewood to douse a fire.

Spouting words to expunge slander is like using black dye to clean something white.

16.68

An arrow at ten paces will pierce rhino-hide armor. At three hundred paces, it cannot even pierce the plain white silk of Lu.[48]

The great horse Qiji can travel a thousand *li* in a day, but when he has used [his strength] to the utmost and the harness is taken off, he collapses.

16.69

If a great family attacks a small family, that is taken to be oppression;
if a great state annexes a small state, that is taken to be worthiness.

16.70

Little horses are in the same category as big horses,
[but] petty knowledge is not in the same category as great knowledge.

47. These stories of Yi the Archer and the wrestler Qingji are alluded to in 14.4.
48. An almost identical statement appears in 17.222.

16.71

To wear sheepskin and labor for wages is quite ordinary;
to wear leopardskin and carry a bamboo basket [like a laborer] would be very strange.

16.72

To use what is pure and white to do something filthy and disgusting is like bathing and then mucking out a pigsty, or perfuming oneself with artemisia and then carrying a pig to market.

16.73

If you treat an abscess and do not distinguish between the good [flesh] and the bad and repulsive flesh but merely cut it all off,
or if you till the fields and do not distinguish between sprouts and weeds and simply hoe indiscriminately,
would this not be fruitless?

16.74

To spoil a pond to seek a turtle,
to wreck a house to look for a fox,
to dig up [the floor of] a room to search for a mouse,
to cut off the lips to cure a toothache:
These are the ways of [the tyrant] Jie and [Robber] Zhi. A Superior Man does not do this.

16.74a

To kill a warhorse but catch a fox,
to acquire two ordinary turtles and lose a divine tortoise,
to chop off the right arm but struggle for a single hair,
to break the [legendary sword] Moye to struggle for an [ordinary] carving knife:
How can using knowledge in this way suffice to be called lofty?

16.75

It is preferable to be pricked with a needle a hundred times than to be slashed by a knife just once.
It is preferable to pull something heavy just once than carry something light for a long time.
It is preferable to eat sparingly for a month than to starve for ten days.
For ten thousand to stumble is better than for one to fall into a pit.

16.76

There was a person who praised someone for working well beyond capacity, hulling grain until sunrise. But still the quota was not filled, and so it was as if the person deserved censure. When the case was investigated, it was discovered that the person [who did the work and was fraudulently praised] was his mother. Thus when petty people praise others, it can be harmful instead.[49]

16.77

In a family to the east, the mother died. Her son cried but was not sorrowful. A son from a family to the west saw this and returned home to his mother, saying, "Mother, why don't you die right away? I would certainly cry very sorrowfully for you!"

Now if someone really wants his mother to die, if she did die, he certainly would not be able to cry sorrowfully for her.

[Likewise,] if someone says, "I have no free time to study," even if he had free time, he would still not be able to study.

16.78

You might see a hollow log floating and understand how to make a boat
or see flying leaves spinning in the air and understand how to make a cart [wheel]
or see a bird scratching and understand how to write characters:
This is to acquire things by means of correlative categories.

---

49. That is, the praise itself drew attention to the case, and thus it was discovered that the mother of the convict laborer was in fact doing the work for him.

16.79

Taking what is not right to do right;
taking what is not proper to do [what is] proper:

This is like

running naked to chase a madman,
robbing things to give them to beggars,
stealing bamboo strips to write laws on them,
squatting to recite the *Odes* and the *Documents*.

16.80

If broken and cast aside, [the great sword] Moye could not [even] cut meat.
Grasped tightly and not released, a [hair from a] horse's tail cuts jade.

The sage has no [unvarying] stopping point or starting point. [He regards] this year as worthier than the past and today as better than yesterday.

16.81

A horse that looks like a deer could be worth a thousand pieces of gold, but there is no deer in the world worth a thousand pieces of gold.
Jade must be worked on with grit to become an object of art.[50]
There are jade disks worth a thousand pieces of gold, but no grit is worth even a trifling amount.

16.82

If you get light through a crack [in the wall], it can illuminate a corner;
if you get light from a window, it can illuminate the north wall;
if you get light from a doorway, it can illuminate everything in the room, omitting nothing.

How much more [would be illuminated] if the light received were from the whole universe! There would be nothing in the world it did not illuminate.

Looking at things in this way,

if what you get [light from] is small, what you see is shallow;
if what you get [light from] is large, what is illuminated is vast!

50. A similar point is made in 17.28 and 19.5.

16.83

The Yangzi River issues from the Min Mountains;
the Yellow River issues from Kunlun;
the Ji River issues from Wangwu;
the Ying River issues from Shaoshi;
the Han River issues from Bozhong.

Flowing separately, eddying or rushing, they eventually empty into the Eastern Sea.

[The places] from where they flow are different;
[the place] to which they return is one.

16.84

Those who are penetrating in their studies are like the axle of a cart. Within the turning wheel hubs, it does not itself move, but with it one travels a thousand *li*. Ending [its rotation, the wheel] begins again, turning like an inexhaustible stream.

Those who are not penetrating in their studies are like [one who is] confused and muddled. If you tell him [the location of] east, west, south and north, when he is standing there he is clear about them, but when he turns his back he does not get it. He does not understand the crux of the matter.

16.85

Cold cannot produce cold;
heat cannot produce heat.

What is not cold or not hot can produce cold and heat. Thus what has form comes from the formless, and the not-yet-Heaven-and-Earth gave birth to Heaven and Earth—how profoundly subtle and expansively vast it is!

16.86

The falling of the rain cannot soak anything. Only when it stops [by hitting something] can it soak anything.

The shooting of an arrow cannot pierce anything. Only when it stops [by hitting something] can it pierce anything.

Only stopping can stop all stoppings.

16.86a

In accord with the high ground, you build a terrace.
Following low ground, you dig a pond.
In each case one follows its natural tendency; one does not dare do more.

16.87

The way in which sages uses things is like
using red ribbon to tie up straw dogs,
making earthen dragons to seek rain.
Straw dogs: he uses them to seek prosperity.
Clay dragons: he uses them to obtain food.

16.88

A man from Lu was good at making hats; his wife was good at making cloth shoes. When they went [south] to Yue, they became greatly distressed and impoverished. To take skill to a place where it cannot be used is like
planting lotuses on a mountaintop,
or cultivating a fire within a well;
grasping fishing tackle and climbing a mountain,
or shouldering an ax and entering an abyss.
It is hard to get what one wants like this.
To take a chariot to [the marshy land of] Yue
Or ride a raft to [the dry land of] the Hu:
Though you may have an inexhaustible desire [to do these things], you will not be able to accomplish them.

16.89

The king of Chu had a white ape. When the king himself shot at it, the ape grabbed his arrows to show off. He ordered Yang Youji[51] to shoot it. When [Yang] began to draw the bow and aim the arrow, [even] before he shot, the ape hugged a tree and shrieked.

This is hitting the target before hitting the target.

---

51. Yang Youji appears in 13.11 in an anecdote about King Gong of Chu. That is presumably the "king of Chu" in this anecdote as well.

16.90

As for [ritual emblems like] the jade disk of Mr. He and the jade half-disk of the Xiahou clan,[52] if [courtiers] bow courteously and advance with them, they create harmony and amity. [But] at night because of thieves, they create resentment. Such is the difference between the right time and the wrong time.

16.91

When one paints [a picture] of the face of Xi Shi, it is beautiful but cannot please;
when one draws with a compass the eyes of Meng Ben, they are large but cannot inspire awe;
What rules form[53] is missing from them.

16.92

There are people such as elder and younger brothers who divide things between themselves without measuring. The multitudes praise the Rightness of that. This can only [be called] "measureless"; therefore it cannot be obtained through measurement.

16.93

Ascending a high place makes people want to look out;
approaching a deep place makes people want to peer down.
The location makes this so.
Archery makes people precise.
Fishing makes people circumspect.
The activity makes this so.

16.94

If someone said that by killing a worn-out ox we could avert the death of a good horse, nobody would do it. If an ox is killed, the one who kills it will be executed. To face

52. For Mr. He's jade disk, see 6.3 and 16.19; and chap. 14, n. 57; for the jade half-disk of the Xiahou clan, see 7.6, 13.15, and 17.2.

53. For the term *junxing* 君形, see also 17.61; compare the "ruler of [all] notes" (*yin zhi jun* 音之君) in 3.29 and 6.4.

certain execution in order to redeem a death that might not occur—there has never been anyone able to act in this way.[54]

16.95

The Jisun clan[55] took control of the ducal house. Confucius was pleased. He first went along with what the Jisun did and later entered the government under them. He said: "To use the bent to make something straight—what's wrong with that? To use the straight to make something bent—that's a policy that cannot be followed."

This is called following different paths to the same wickedness.

16.96

When the majority are crooked, they cannot tolerate the straight;
when the majority are bent, they cannot tolerate the upright.
Thus,
when people are in the majority, they eat wolves;
when wolves are in the majority, they eat people.

16.97

Those who want to be evil must seem to shine forth their uprightness;
those who want to be crooked must seem to establish their straightness.

From ancient times to the present, for the Public Way to not be established and for private desires to achieve currency has never been heard of [except through] taking the good and entrusting it to the wicked.

16.98

Popular rumor is like a forest:
it flies without wings.
If three people say there is a tiger in the market,
the whole village will turn out to chase it.

54. That is, the horse might not die after all, but the one who kills the ox will be executed. The commentators explain that an ox is crucial to agriculture and that to kill one is a capital offense.

55. The Jisun clan 季孫氏 was one of the three branch lineages descended from Duke Huan of Lu (r. 712–694 B.C.E.) that became the most powerful factions in that state during the late Spring and Autumn period. Gao You tentatively identifies the head of the Jisun clan during this period as either Ji Kangzi 康子 (d. 468 B.C.E.) or Ji Huanzi 桓子 (d. 492 B.C.E.). See Zhang Shuangdi 1997, 2:1688n.1.

16.99

[Animals] that float and sink do not try to wash or bathe; it is already enough for them to be in the middle of the water.

Thus,

animals that eat grass do not rush to change their pastures;
insects that live in water do not rush to change their rivers.

They may carry out small alterations, but they do not stray from their constant habits.

16.100

There are false beliefs;
there are breaches of propriety.
Wei Sheng died under the pillars of a bridge.[56] This was a case of a belief being false.
Mr. Kong [Kong Bo] did not mourn the death of his repudiated mother. This was a case of propriety being breached.[57]

16.101

Zengzi took his stand on filial piety. He would not walk past a village called Defeated Mother.
Mozi opposed music. He would not enter the city of Courtsong.[58]
Confucius[59] took his stand on incorruptibility. He would not drink from Robbers' Well.

This is what is called "nourishing the will."

16.102

[Tyrant] Djou used ivory chopsticks and Jizi sighed;
the people of Lu used figurines in burials and Confucius sighed.

Thus sages see frost and anticipate ice.

---

56. He drowned in a rising river while waiting for a woman who never arrived despite her promise. See also 13.11 and 17.242.

57. Kong Bo 孔白 was a great-grandson of Confucius. His mother had been repudiated by his father, but he nevertheless should have mourned her.

58. Zhaoge 朝歌 (Courtsong) was the name of a pre-Anyang capital of the Shang dynasty. Supposedly the court music of Shang was composed there, so Mozi, who opposed music, considered it a place to avoid. See Le Blanc and Mathieu 2003, 773n.40.

59. Correcting "Zengzi" to "Confucius," as suggested by Liu Wendian. See Lau, HNZ, 163n.5.

16.103

When birds are about to arrive, people spread out nets to await them. What catches the bird is a single eye of the net, but a single-eyed net will never catch a bird.[60]

Now a person who dons armor prepares for an arrow to strike him. If he knew for sure where the arrow would hit, he could wear just one tiny scale of armor.

Matters sometimes cannot be measured beforehand;
things sometimes cannot be foreseen.

Thus sages cultivate the Way and await the right time.

16.104

A homely piebald cow, hornless and tailless, still had her nose pierced and was put in a halter. She gave birth to a calf, and it was sacrificed. When the impersonator of the dead and the invoker carried out the sacrificial ceremony and drowned it in the river, would the Earl of the Yellow River[61] be ashamed of its origin and refuse the sacrifice?

16.105

Acquiring an army of ten thousand men does not compare to hearing one word that is apposite;

acquiring the pearl of the marquis of Sui does not compare to understanding from whence events arise.

Acquiring the jade disk of Mr. Gua[62] does not compare to understanding where events will lead.

16.106

One who selects a fine steed does not use it to chase a fox or a raccoon dog if he is preparing to shoot a deer or a stag.

One who sharpens a sword with a whetstone does not use it to cut plain silk robes if he is preparing to slash rhino-hide armor.

Thus,

---

60. A similar statement appears in 17.176.

61. He Bo 河伯, not (as the name might suggest) a human ruler, but a god. See also 17.210.

62. Regarded as the same as the jade disk of Mr. Bian 卞 or Mr. He 和. See chap. 14, n. 57; and 6.3, 16.19, and 16.90.

"With high mountains he looks to the summit,
with scenic byways he travels to the end."[63]

What this [ode] refers to is such a person.

16.106a

To see a crossbow pellet and expect a roast owl;
to see an egg and expect dawn to end the night;
to see a hemp seed and expect finished cloth:

although there is a principle here, still one cannot hasten the sunset.

16.107

If an elephant loses its tusks, it does not begrudge the person who profits from them;[64]
if a person dies and leaves behind his bed mat, he does not resent the person who takes it.

If a person is able to use what is of no benefit [to others] to benefit himself, that is permissible.

16.108

A madman runs to the east. The person pursuing him also runs to the east. They are the same in running to the east, but the reasons why they are running to the east are different.
A drowning person enters the water. The person rescuing him also enters the water. They are the same in entering the water, but the reasons why they are entering the water are different.

Thus,

sages equate life and death;
fools also equate life and death.
Sages equate life and death because they fully comprehend the rationale of making distinctions;
fools equate life and death because they do not know where benefit and harm lie.

63. *Odes* 218.
64. Compare 17.113.

16.109

On account of Humaneness and Rightness, King Yan of Xu lost his state. [But] losing a state is not necessarily due to Humaneness and Rightness.

On account of loyalty, Bi Gan lost his life. [But] being executed is not necessarily due to loyalty.

Thus,

one who is cold shivers;
one who is afraid also shivers.

They are the same in name but differ in substance.

16.110

The Moonglow Pearl came from a cricket oyster.
The great jade tablet of Zhou came from a dirty stone.
The divine tortoise of Dazai came from a city moat.

16.111

The ruler of [a state of] ten thousand chariots wears a hat not worth more than a pennyweight to ride a chariot worth a hundred pieces of gold.

The skin of an ox made into a drum directs the multitudes of the Three Armies.

16.112

Someone who wants to learn songs and ballads must begin with the *zhi* and *yu* [tunings] and the *yue* and *feng* [classical airs].

Someone who desires beauty and harmony must first start with the [classical compositions] "Yang'a" and "Cailing."[65]

In both cases he must study what he does not wish to study in order to get to what he does wish to study.

16.113

To attract cicadas, you try to make your fire bright;
to catch fish, you try to make your bait fragrant.

65. "Yang'a" 陽阿 (Sunny Slope) and "Cailing" 采菱 (Brightly Colored Water Chestnuts) were famous melodies of the state of Chu.

By making your fire bright, you thereby attract and catch them;
by making your bait fragrant, you thereby lure and profit from them.
If you want to get fish, you must [first] channel water;
if you want to get birds, you must [first] plant trees.
Where water collects, fish abound;
where trees flourish, birds flock.
If you enjoy bow hunting, you start by equipping yourself with bowstrings and arrow shafts;
if you enjoy fishing, you start by equipping yourself with fine-mesh and large-mesh nets.

It is not possible to secure any advantage without having the right equipment.

16.114

When you give someone a horse but [first] take off the harness,
when you give someone a chariot but [first] detach the yoke rings,
what you have kept is [worth] little,
and what you have given away is [worth] a lot.

Thus the peasants have a saying: "If you boil beef without salt, you defeat the purpose."

16.115

[Tyrant] Jie had some accomplishments.
[The sage] Yao had some departures from the Way.
[The ugly] Mo Mu[66] had some beautiful points.
[The great beauty] Xi Shi had some ugly points.

Thus
among the laws of a perished state, there are some that may be followed;
among the customs of a well-governed state, there are some that may be rejected.

16.116

The round and sharp-pointed [ritual] jades,[67] placed amid filth and mud, would not be rejected even by a fastidious person.

66. Mo Mu 嫫母 was the wife of the Yellow Emperor. Alhough ugly, she was virtuous. See *Lüshi chunqiu* 14.7.

67. *Wan* 琬 and *yan* 琰, ritual jade implements, said to represent mercy and severity, respectively.

A worn-out fish trap or rice steamer, placed on felt cushions, would not be taken even by a greedy person.
That in which beauty is present, even if soiled, cannot be disparaged by the ages;
that in which ugliness is present, even if elevated, cannot be valued by the ages.

16.117

If with spring you lend and with fall you tax, the people will be pleased.
If with spring you tax and with fall you lend, the people will be resentful.
The gains and losses are the same, but the happiness and anger are distinct; the seasons make the difference.

16.118

If you "indulge" a fish, you do not catch him but let him dive in the deep;
if you "reward" a monkey, you do not carry him away but let him swing from the trees.
You let them pursue what brings them benefit, that is all.

16.119

Sable fur that is mottled
cannot compare with
fox fur that is uniform.
Thus, people detest nothing more than someone whose conduct is not consistent.

16.120

One who judges horses may miss a [fine] horse, but the fineness of the horse is still there during the judging.

16.121

Now someone sets a fire;
some add fuel to make it burn;
others pour on water to extinguish it.

Before either has had any effect,
the resentment [that follows the one]
and the gratitude [that follows the other]
are already far apart.

16.122

A man from Ying [in Chu] was buying a beam for a house and sought a timber three hand spans in diameter. Someone gave him the axle of a cart. Kneeling down to measure it, he discovered that although it was thick enough, it was not long enough.

16.123

Qu Boyu used Potency to transform;
Gongsun Yang used slicing to punish.
Their goal was the same.
When a sick person is lying on his mat,
what a physician uses are needles and stones;
what a shaman uses are [sacrificial] grain and rushes;
their objectives are compatible.

16.124

The fox-head [plant] cures a rat bite;
the rooster-head [plant] cures a tumor;[68]
powdered mosquitoes clot blood;
pecked wood cures a toothache.
These are example of things that are extended within like categories.
To use grease to kill a tortoise,
feathered darts to shoot a hedgehog,
ash from rotted wood to breed flies,
[and the fact] that if exposed to the sight of crabs, lacquer will not dry[69]—
These [are examples of] things that cannot be extended within like categories.

68. Both "fox-head" and "rooster-head" are medicinal herbs, the first a kind of bean and the second a type of water lily.

69. A similar statement appears in 6.3. According to later Chinese pharmacopeias, a poultice of crushed shellfish was used to treat the rash caused by exposure to raw lac sap (the lac tree is related to poison sumac). But the enzymes in the shellfish medicine also are capable of preventing lacquer from drying properly, so it must be kept away from lacquer that is still being manufactured. We are grateful to Anthony Barbieri-Low (private communication) for this insight.

What can be extended or not extended [within categories] resembles what "is not" but [really] is; or what "is" but [really] is not. Who can comprehend their subtleties?

16.125

There are no pure white foxes in the world, and yet there is pure white fox fur; it is put together from many pieces of white fur. A person who loves to study resembles the king of Qi when he ate chicken. He had to eat several tens of chicken feet before he was satisfied.

16.126

A knife is handy for cutting hair, but when it comes to felling a large tree, without an ax you won't [be able to] cut it down. Thus among cutting implements, there certainly are ones that are appropriate and others that are not.

16.127

If you look at only a square inch of an ox, you will not know that it is bigger than a sheep. But take an overall look at both their bodies, and you will know that the difference between the two is very great.

16.128

If a pregnant woman sees a rabbit, the child will be born with a cleft palate.
If she sees a deer, the baby will have four eyes.

16.129

If a little horse has big eyes, it cannot be called a big horse.
If a big horse has a blind eye, it can be called a blind horse.[70]

There are things that seem to be so and things that seem not to be so.
Thus,

cut off your finger and you might die;
cut off your arm and you might live.

Categories of like things cannot necessarily be extended.

70. There is a play on words here. The character *miao* 眇, "blind in one eye," has the eye radical on the left, and the character for "few" (i.e., "small" with an additional stroke) on the right.

16.130

If you [want to] sharpen a sword, you must have a soft whetstone.
If you [want to] strike bells and chimestones, you must have a damp wooden mallet.

For the hub of a wheel to be strong, the spokes must be weak.

Two hard things cannot harmonize with each other,
two strong things cannot submit to each other.

Thus [soft] *wutong* wood can cut horn, and horsehair can cut jade.

16.131

A matchmaker doesn't [make a point of] studying deception, but when she does her work, it gives rise to untrustworthiness.
A man of upstanding bravery doesn't [make a point of] studying battle, but he bravely takes his stand and gives rise to indomitableness.

Thus,

the Superior Man does not enter a jail because it might harm his kindness;
he does not enter a market because it might harm his purity.

The accumulated [effect of things] cannot be overlooked.

16.132

When [people] walk, they do not use their hands, but if [a person's] hands are tied, he cannot walk swiftly.
When [birds] fly, they do not use their tails, but if [a bird's] tail is bent, it cannot fly very far.

In what is used we use what is not used.

Thus,

what is used for seeing does not itself see;
what is used to beat a drum does not itself make a sound.

16.133

By tasting one piece of meat, you can know the flavor of a potful.
By suspending feathers and charcoal [in a balance beam],[71] you can know the humidity of the air.

71. If you place feathers in one end of a scale and charcoal in the other and it balances evenly in dry weather, then the charcoal end will drop down when it is humid (because charcoal absorbs moisture better than feathers). Such a device could act as a sort of weather-forecasting tool.

One uses the small to illuminate the large.

By seeing one leaf fall, you can know that the year will soon end;

By noticing ice in a jug, you can know the temperature throughout the world.

One uses the near to assess the far.

16.134

If three people [walk] shoulder to shoulder, they cannot go out the door;
if two people follow each other, they can go anywhere in the world.

16.135

Treading the ground makes footprints [which remain behind];
walking in bright sunlight makes shadows [which do not].

These are easy [to observe] but difficult [to explain].

16.136

When King Zhuang [of Chu] executed [his minister] Li Shi,[72] Sunshu Ao mended his [official] cap and laundered his robe.[73]

Duke Wen [of Jin] discarded his [worn-out] rush mats and [relegated] to the rear those [soldiers] whose faces were blackened [with hardship and age]. Maternal Uncle Fan [therefore] declined to return with him.[74]

When the mulberry leaves fall, the elderly lament.

16.137

Ordinary cooking pots are used daily but are not of substantial value.

The Zhou royal *ding* are not used for cooking but cannot be considered valueless.

There certainly are things whose usefulness consists of not being used.

72. According to Gao You, Li Shi 里史 was a "devious official." See Zhang Shuangdi 1997, 2:1716n.10. Yu Dacheng proposes that the characters in his name be transposed to produce "Scribe Li" 史里. See Lau, HNZ, 166n.6.

73. He anticipated that he would be promoted to serve in Li Shi's place.

74. Maternal Uncle Fan (also known as Hu Yan [d. 622 B.C.E.]) was the uncle of Duke Wen of Jin and one of his most influential advisers. The story of his refusing to return home is recorded in *Hanfeizi* 32. Duke Wen was returning from a ten-year exile; Maternal Uncle Fan was outraged by his treatment of his faithful veterans.

If land is flat, water will not flow;
if the weights are equal, the balance beam will not tilt.

Excessiveness in anything will necessarily provoke a response. Thus there certainly are things that find great use in not being used.

16.138

To undress and then to wash is possible.
To wash and then to undress is not possible.
To sacrifice and then to feast is possible.
To feast and then to sacrifice is not possible.

In the sequence of things, in each case there is [a way] that is proper.

16.139

On the day of a sacrifice, to call someone a son of a bitch;
on one's wedding night, to mention funeral clothing;
on the day of a wine party, to talk of raising a funeral altar

[is] to cross the Yangzi or the Yellow River and speak of the waves of the marquis of Yang.[75]

16.140

Someone said, "If one knew that on a certain day there would be a great amnesty, many people would be killed [beforehand]."

Someone else said, "If one knew that on a certain day there would be a great amnesty, many people would stay alive [as a result of it]."

In looking at the amnesty, they were alike, but in considering it beneficial or harmful, they differed.

Thus,

sometimes you blow on a fire and it burns more brightly;
sometimes you blow on a fire and it goes out.

The reason you blow on it differs.

75. All these are examples of inappropriate behavior. The "waves of the marquis of Yang" are sudden waves in the river, caused by the drowned marquis's ghost, that can overturn boats and cause people to drown. See 6.1.

16.141

If someone cooked a cow and feasted his village but then cursed his landlord's mother,[76] not only would his kindness not be repaid, but he would put his life in danger.

16.142

King Wen [of Chu] had a sunken chest.
Bao Shen[77] was a hunchback.
Together they brought good government to Chu.

Pi Chen[78] became wise when he left the capital; he thereby brought about the success of Zichan's affairs.[79]

16.143

A dwarf asked a tall man about heaven. The tall man said, "I don't know." The dwarf replied, "Even if you don't know, you're still closer than I am."
Thus whenever you ask about affairs, you must ask someone close to them.

16.144

"Robbers make it hard to get there," said the lame man to the blind man. The blind man carried [the lame one] and went on his way; they both arrived alive. [This was because] each used his own ability.

To force a mute person to speak or a lame person to walk [would be] to lose [the use of] their actual abilities.

---

76. Literally, "the mother of his neighbor to the east." "Eastern neighbor" is a conventional term meaning "landlord."

77. Bao Shen 鮑申 served as prime minister of Chu during the reign of King Wen.

78. Pi Chen 裨諶 was an influential minister of Zheng. According to Gao You, he was unable to devise plans in the capital, only in the countryside, so Zichan would take him out into the countryside to discuss policy. See Zhang Shuangdi 1997, 2:1722n.2.

79. The message of all these examples is that contrary to expectations, unpromising people sometimes prove useful.

16.145

A man from Ying was going to sell his mother. He said to a [prospective] buyer, "This mother is old. Please feed her well and don't let [her life] be bitter." This is to carry out a large offense against Rightness while hoping to perform a small act of Rightness.

16.146

The movement of armored bugs [e.g., mollusks, turtles] facilitates rigidity;
the movement of asexual bugs [e.g., bees and wasps] facilitates poisonous stinging.
The movement of black and brown bears facilitates seizing and grasping;
the movement of rhinos and oxen facilitates butting and goring.
No animals abandon their strong points to use their shortcomings.

16.147

Governing a country is like hoeing a field. One gets rid of harmful plants, that is all.

When one washes, some hairs fall out, but we don't stop [washing] merely for that reason. What one loses is little and what one gains is much.

16.148

A whetstone is not sharp, but it can sharpen metal.
A bow maker's frame is not straight, but it can straighten a bow.
Thus there definitely are things
that [although] not straight can make things straight;
that [although] not sharp can make things sharp.

16.149

With strength we value agility;
with knowledge we value acumen.

16.150

When the results are the same, speed is considered superior;
when the triumph is equal, sluggishness is considered inferior.

The reason we value [the great sword] Moye is because it responds to things by cutting sharply and cleanly.

But a doorsill may break suddenly from the constant vibrations of ox carts.

16.151

Although Confucius encountered difficulties in [the borderlands of] Chen and Cai, [for that reason] to abandon the six arts[80] would be foolhardy.

Although doctors sometimes are unable to cure their own illnesses, [for that reason] not to use medicine when one falls ill would be rash.

Translated by Sarah A. Queen and John S. Major

80. The "six arts" of Confucianism were rites, music, archery, charioteering, writing, and mathematics.

Seventeen

17.1

To apply the standards of a bygone era in governing the world [today] is like a passenger in a boat who lost his sword in midstream. Right away he made a mark on the boat, intending to come back at night to look for the sword. His lack of knowledge of how to sort things out was certainly profound! Now to follow the footprints in one small corner [of the world] and not to know how to wander in accord with Heaven and Earth—no confusion can be greater than that. Just because something is suitable for a particular time is not enough to make it valuable [always]. It can be compared with making earthen dragons in time of drought or making [sacrificial] straw dogs during an epidemic. They are sovereign only at a particular time.

17.2

The torn remnants of a baby's swaddling cloth[1] are of value for treating bites of the *qiu* insect,[2] but it is not the jade half-disk of the Xiahou clan.[3]

---

1. Commentators generally agree that the text is corrupted here. It currently reads *cao shi zhi lie bu* 曹氏之裂布, "the Cao clan's tattered cloth," but the Gao You commentary evinces that the character 氏 (clan) is an interpolation. Moreover, the word 曹 is a lexical variant for 褿, which means "baby's swaddling cloth." According to Gao You, a folk cure for insect bites was to burn a soiled swaddling cloth and apply the ashes to the affected area. See Zhang Shuangdi 1997, 2:1728–29n.6.

2. The *qiu* 蛷 was a type of noxious insect, not clearly identifiable.

3. A *huang* 璜 was a type of ritual jade implement in the shape of a half disk. For the half disk of the Xiahou clan, part of the ducal regalia of the state of Lu, see 7.6, 13.15, and 16.90.

17.3

It has no antiquity and no present,
no beginning and no end.

Before there were yet Heaven and Earth, it generated Heaven and Earth. It is the profoundly subtle and expansively grand.

17.4

Where feet tread is shallow, but we [must] rely on where we do not tread before we [can] walk.

What a knowledgeable person knows is narrow, but we [must] rely on what we do not know before we [can] understand.

17.5

A swimmer uses his feet to kick and his hands to sweep [through the water]. But if you have not mastered the technique of swimming, the more you kick, the more you will get into trouble. When you do learn to swim, it is not [just] a matter of hands and feet.

17.6

Birds fly back to their home;
rabbits return to their burrow;
dying foxes head for their lair;
gnats hover over the water.

All things rely on what bring them into being.

17.7

One does not give a mirror to a person who has lost his sight;
one does not give a pair of shoes to a person who has lost a foot;
one does not give a ceremonial cap to a person from Yue;

they are of no use to them.

17.8

Although a hammer has a handle, it cannot pound itself;
although eyes can see a hundred paces away, they cannot see their own eyelids.

17.9

Dogs and pigs do not eat from plates and cups. Carelessly they fatten their bodies; [consequently] self-regard hastens their own deaths.

Phoenixes fly more than a thousand *ren*[4] high; consequently, no one can reach them.

17.10

The moon illuminates the sky, but it is swallowed by the toad;[5]
the *deng*[6] reptile wanders in the fog, but it is endangered by the cricket;
the crow's strength vanquishes the sun, but it submits to the *zhuizha* bird.[7]

[Things] can possess [both] strengths and weaknesses.

17.11

No one lives longer than a child who dies in infancy;
Ancestor Peng was short lived.[8]

17.12

If the rope is short, it cannot be used to draw water from the depths;
if the implement is small, it cannot be used [on things that are] abundantly large.

It is not within its capacity.

17.13

Anger arises from non-anger,
action arises from non-action.

4. One *ren* is eight Chinese feet.

5. During an eclipse, according to legend.

6. Lau, HNZ 17/169/1. According to legend, a kind of flying snake.

7. According to legend, the sun is personified as a three-legged crow that flies across the sky each day. The *zhuizha* 鵻札 is a legendary bird, perhaps resembling a dove, that announces the dawn even before the cock does, thus rousing the sun crow from its sleeping perch on the Fusang Tree in the east.

8. Ancestor Peng 彭祖 was a descendant of Zhuan Xu who was enfeoffed by the sovereign Shun at Peng. According to legend, he lived to be more than eight hundred years old. This paradox is quoted from *Zhuangzi* 2 (ZZ 2/5/21). The point is that there is no fixed standard of comparison; a baby who dies young is long-lived compared with a mayfly, whereas Ancestor Peng was short-lived compared with a mountain.

17.14

Look for the formless and you will see what you look for.
Listen for the soundless and you will hear what you listen for.

17.15

The best flavor does not satiate;
the highest language does not embellish.
The highest joy does not [elicit] laughter;
the loftiest sound does not call out.
The greatest artist does not chop;
the greatest cook does not carve;
the greatest hero does not fight.[9]

When you attain the Way, its Potency follows. This is like the correspondence of the [pitch-pipe] note Yellow Bell and the [pentatonic] note *gong*, or the correspondence of the [pitch-pipe] note Great Budding and the [pentatonic] note *shang*—their consonance cannot be altered.

17.16

If someone is gambling for [a piece of tile], his pace will be measured.
If he is gambling for gold, he will be excited.
If he is gambling for jade, he will be very ill at ease.

For this reason, if what you value is external, then what is internal will be dulled.[10]

17.17

When you pursue a wild animal, your eyes will not notice Mount Tai.
When you crave and desire something external, your perception will be impaired.

9. We follow Lau (who himself is following Yu Yue) in emending these three lines in accordance with *Lüshi chunqiu*, chap. 4. See Knoblock and Riegel 2000, 72. See also Zhang Shuangdi 1997, 2:1736n.5. The line "the greatest cook does not carve" is apparently a reference to the famous "Cook Ding" passage in *Zhuangzi*, chap. 3. Note, however, that the unemended form of this line can be understood to mean "the greatest *dou* [ritual vessel] does not display [sacrificial] offerings," which resonates with 16.137: "The Zhou royal *ding* [ritual vessels] are not used for cooking but cannot be considered valueless."

10. This persuasion is quoted from *Zhuangzi* 19 (ZZ 19/50/22–23). See also Mair 1997, 177.

17.18

Those who hear the sound of a sound are deaf.
Those who hear the sound of no sound are discerning.
Those who are neither deaf nor discerning have penetrated through to spirit illumination.

17.19

The diviner grasps the tortoise shell;
the shaman arranges the [milfoil] slips.
When inquiring about their calculations, how can it be numbers that we ask about?

17.20

Those who are dancing set the beat while those sitting unconsciously clap their hands in unison. What brings them to that point is the same.

17.21

The sun rises in the Bright Valley
and sets in the Abyss of Anxiety.[11]
No one is aware of its movements,
but in a moment's time
it turns your head around.

17.22

No one wants to learn to ride a dragon, but everyone wants to learn to ride a horse.
No one wants to learn to rule ghosts, but everyone wants to learn to rule men.
[People] hasten after what is of use.

11. For the mythical path of the sun across the sky, see 3.25; and Major 1993, 102–5.

17.23

To dismantle a gate to make firewood;
to plug a well to make a mortar:
When people do things, sometimes they are that stupid.[12]

17.24

Water and fire repel each other, but when a small cauldron lies between them, the five flavors are harmonized.
Bone and flesh[13] attract each other, but when slander intervenes, the father–son relationship is threatened.

17.25

Now when the means by which you nurture something harms what you nurture, it is like shaving the foot to fit the shoe or trimming the head to fit the hat.

17.26

Calamus repels fleas and lice but attracts centipedes.[14] It alleviates a minor irritation but invites a great harm. Thus small pleasures [can] undermine significant benefits.

17.27

A collapsing wall does not compare with one that does not [collapse].[15] But it is better than a falling-down house.

12. Following the interpretation of Gao You. See Zhang Shuangdi 1997, 2:1741n.5.

13. That is, the actual constituents of a physical body, but the term also is a metaphor for blood relatives.

14. Centipedes were said to bore into the ear. See 20.38.

15. Interestingly, 16.15 seems to make the opposite point: "When a wall has crumbled, it is superior to when it was standing" (because it has returned to its origin).

17.28

That the *bi* and *yuan* [jade ritual objects] become implements is due to the merits of the grit;[16]
that the Moye [sword] cuts so cleanly is due to the strength of the whetstone.

17.29

When the cunning rabbit is caught, the hunting dog is cooked.
When the high-flying bird is shot down, the strong crossbow is put into storage.

17.30

The gadflies that accompany a thoroughbred go a thousand *li* but do not fly. They do not have stores of grain, yet they do not starve.

17.31

Suppose you have an accidental fire and it happens to rain. Having the accidental fire is unfortunate but its happening to rain is fortunate. Thus within ill fortune there is good fortune.

17.32

The purveyor of coffins desires human illness and plague;
the hoarder of grain desires yearly drought and famine.

17.33

When water is still, it is level.
When it is level, it is clear.
When it is clear, it reveals the shapes of things.
Nothing can hide; thus it can be used to make things correct.

---

16. *Jian* 礛 is an abrasive stone or grit used to shape jade. Similar comments about grit appear in 16.81 and 19.5. *Bi* and *yuan* were types of disk-shaped jade ritual implements, known in China from predynastic antiquity. See 17.2.

17.34

Where streams dry up, valleys become empty.
Where hills level off, gorges fail to flow.
Where lips dry out, teeth grow cold.

17.35

[Although] river water runs deep, its silt lies in the mountains.

17.36

From the same plain white silk,
one piece might be used for a [mourning] cap
and one piece for socks.
The cap is worn on the head,
but the socks are worn on the feet.

17.37

If you know yourself, you cannot be enticed by things.
If you understand life and death, you cannot be put off by danger.
Thus a good swimmer cannot be frightened by wading.

17.38

No blood relationship is closer than one's own bones and flesh; they unite joints and connective tissue. But when the mind loses control over them, they can turn around and cause harm to oneself. How much more so is that true with more distant [relations].

17.39

The sage's relation to the Way is like that of the sunflower to the sun. Although he does not begin and end with it, he faces it with utter sincerity.

17.40

The imperial reservoir overflows in times of flooding and dries up in times of drought, [but] the sources of the Yangzi waters are deep springs that cannot dry up.

17.41

An awning that is not framed cannot screen out the sun.
A wheel that is not spoked cannot turn fast.
Nonetheless, frames and spokes are not in themselves sufficient to be relied on.

17.42

Metal overcomes wood, but it is not possible to destroy a forest with a single knife.
Earth overcomes water, but it is not possible to plug the Yangzi with one clod of earth.

17.43

When a cripple sees a tiger and he does not run away, it is not due to his bravery but because his situation is not conducive to it.[17]

17.44

What is tilted readily overturns.
What is slanted readily topples.
A person who is close is readily helped.
A place that is damp readily [gets] rain.

17.45

When the rat is caught, the trap moves;
when the fish is hooked, the float jerks;
when the load is moved, the cart squeaks.

17. The phrase *shi bu bian* 勢不便, which we translate as "his situation is not conducive to it," implies *both* that the crippled person's ability is impaired relative to an ordinary person's and that his strength is inferior to the tiger's. Compare 17.80.

17.46

Straw dogs can stand, but they cannot walk.
The "snake-bed" plant resembles the *miwu* plant,[18] but it cannot [give off] a scent.

17.47

No one who says
Xu You had no Potency
or Wu Huo had no strength
could fail to show disgrace in his face. No one fails to avoid revealing his own inadequacies.

17.48

Suppose the stride of a rabbit were made as big as that of a horse. It could keep up with the sun and pursue the wind. If [a rabbit] actually became [as big as] a horse, though, it would not be able to run at all.

17.49

In winter there might be thunder and lightning,
and in summer there might be frost and snow.
Nevertheless, the inherent tendencies of heat and cold do not change. Small differences are not enough to hinder constant principles.

17.50

The Yellow Emperor produced yin and yang.
Shang Pian produced ears and eyes;
Sang Lin produced shoulders and arms.[19]
Nüwa used these to carry out the seventy transformations.[20]

18. *Miwu* 蘪蕪 (*Ligusticum wallichii*, known as Sichuan lovage) is used medicinally to treat headache, menstrual cramps, and other painful symptoms.
19. Both Shang Pian 上駢 and Sang Lin 桑林 are mythical divine beings.
20. By means of which she created everything in the world.

17.51

To talk all day, one would need the traits of a sage;
to hit a bull's-eye a hundred times [in a row], one would need the skill of an [Archer] Yi or a Peng Meng.[21]
But the present era does not praise them; such adherence to standards is reviled.

17.52

Both the ox's hoof and the pig's skull are bone, but the world does not heat-crack them [for divination]. The reason why we must ask the tortoise if an outcome will be good or bad is because people have been doing so for years.

17.53

If you live near the Ao granary, you do not eat more because of it;
if you live close to the Yangzi or the Yellow River, you do not drink more because of it.[22]
You hope to fill your stomach; that is enough.

17.54

The orchid and the iris give forth their fragrance[23] but never [live to] see the frost.
The owl[24] evades the weapons [of his attackers], but his life ends in the fifth month.[25]

17.55

The tongue or the teeth—which decays first?
The spear handle or the blade—which dulls first?
The bowstring or the arrow—which snaps first?

21. Peng Meng 逢蒙 was a legendary archer of high antiquity. Having learned all that Yi could teach of the art of archery, he killed his teacher so as to be the greatest archer in the world. See *Mencius* 4B.24. He appears in 1.6 as Feng Mengzi.

22. A similar statement appears in 7.12.

23. See chap. 16, n. 9.

24. Literally *gu zao* 鼓造, "drum herald," understood by commentators as referring to an owl.

25. Supposedly, thick owl soup was traditionally served in the fifth month. This whole sentence is rather obscure, and its interpretation is heavily dependent on the glosses of commentators. See Zhang Shuangdi 1997, 2:1752n.14.

17.56

The eel and the snake,
the silkworm and the caterpillar—
In appearance they belong to the same category. But how they are liked or disliked makes them different.

17.57

Jin used the Chuiji jade disk to acquire [the states of] Yu and Guo;[26]
the Rong chieftain Li used a beautiful woman to destroy the state of Jin.[27]

17.58

Deaf people cannot sing, for they have no means to imagine music.
Blind people cannot observe, for they have no means to discern things.

17.59

If you watch the archer, you will lose sight of his skill.
If you watch the calligrapher, you will lose sight of his passion.
If you focus on what is there [on the outside], you will lose sight of what is preserved [on the inside].

17.60

If nothing from ancient times could ever be improved, then solid wagon wheels would never [have evolved into] wheels with separate hubs.[28]

17.61

If you get a female musician to blow through the reed pipes
and [another] musician to put his fingers on the holes,

26. *Zuozhuan*, Xi 2. See also 7.16, 10.47, 11.7, and 18.5.

27. Compare 7.16 and 17.145.

28. The terms *chuiche* 椎車 and *chanyue* 蟬匷 are extremely obscure. *Chuiche* means something like "pounding cart," which some commentators take as a reference to carts with solid (i.e., spokeless) wheels made from single logs. Commentators differ on the meaning of *chanyue* (or *jue*), but the most plausible explanation appears to be that it refers to a type of cart whose wheel, hub, and axle are made as separate pieces, as is the standard Chinese chariot.

even though they might keep the beat, no one could stand to listen to it. [The music] would lack its ruling form.[29]

17.62

If you have the same illness as one who is dying, it will be difficult to be a good doctor [for him];
If you share the same Way as a state that is perishing, it will be difficult to make plans for it.

17.63

When you make rice for your guest but eat greens yourself, you [show that you] prize reputation more highly than reality.

17.64

A nursing bitch will bite a tiger;
a brooding hen will peck a fox.
When their [maternal] concern has been aroused, they do not take account of [relative] strengths.

17.65

What makes the shadow crooked is the [original] form;
what makes the echo distorted is the [original] sound.
When emotions are divulged, the inner [sentiment] is easy to infer;
when flowers are untimely, [their fruit] is inedible.

17.66

If you go to Yue,
you can go by boat
or go by carriage.
The routes are different, but the destination is the same.

29. For the term *junxing* 君形, "ruler of form," see 16.91. See also the "ruler of [all] notes" (*yin zhi jun* 音之君) in 3.29 and 6.4.

17.67

Good-looking men do not [all] have the same body.
Beautiful women do not [all] have the same face.
But they all are pleasing to the eye.
Pears, oranges, dates, and chestnuts do not have the same flavor,
but they all are satisfying to the palate.

17.68

There are people who rob and get rich, but not all rich people are necessarily robbers.
There are people who are pure and poor, but not all poor people are necessarily pure.

17.69

Reed floss is like [silk] floss but cannot be used as floss (to pad winter clothing);
hemp [fiber] is not in the category of cloth, but it can be made into cloth.

17.70

If you come out of a forest, you cannot follow a straight path.
If you traverse a pass, you cannot tread [as straight as] a marking cord.

17.71

The means by which Yi shot far and pierced the center of small things was not the bow and arrow.
The means by which Zaofu drove fast and far was not the reins and bit.

17.72

The sea retains what it has expelled;[30] thus it is expansive.
The wheel returns where it has gone; thus it is far-reaching.

30. Presumably, a reference to the flow and ebb of waves on a beach.

17.73

Mutton does not long for ants, but ants are drawn to mutton because it smells rank.
Pickling brine does not long for gnats, but gnats are drawn to pickling brine because it is sour.

17.74

By tasting a small piece of meat, you know the flavor of the whole cauldron.
By suspending a feather over hot coals, you know the dryness and humidity of the *qi*.[31]

By the small, you judge the large; by the near, you extrapolate the far.

17.75

A ten-*qing* reservoir can irrigate forty *qing* of land,[32]
[but] a one-*qing* reservoir cannot irrigate four *qing* of land.

The decrease in scale from large to small is like this.

17.76

Under the light of a bright moon you can see far, but you cannot write in minuscule.
On a very foggy morning you can write in minuscule, but you cannot see beyond a few feet.

17.77

An artist concerned about a single hair will lose sight of the face.
An archer who aims at a small [point] will miss the big [target].

17.78

To dig out a rat hole and ruin the village gate,
to burst a small pimple and erupt a great boil

31. See 16.133.
32. One *qing* equals a hundred *mu;* one *mu* 畝 equals about one-sixth acre.

resembles

a pearl with a defect,
a jade with a flaw:
Leave it alone and it will remain whole;
remove it and you will spoil it all.

17.79

A bird that builds a nest makes its home in the dense forest because it is safe.
An animal that digs a hole relies on a raised embankment because it is convenient.

17.80

Prince Qingji could run as fast as tailed deer and [ordinary] deer, and he caught rhinoceroses and tigers with his bare hands. Placed in a dark room, though, he could not even catch a tortoise or a turtle because conditions were not conducive to it.[33]

17.81

Tang banished his ruler and enjoyed a glorious reputation.
Cui Shu assassinated his prince and was greatly despised.
What they did was comparable; why they did it was different.

17.82

Lü Wang encouraged the old to be vigorous.
Xiang Tuo[34] caused the young to be proud.
[People] admire those of [their own] kind.

17.83

What causes the leaves to fall is the wind that shakes them.
What causes the water to cloud are the fish that stir it.

33. Compare the use of *shi bu bian* 勢不便 here and in 17.43. In both cases, the combination of external conditions and inherent capabilities makes the task difficult.

34. Xiang Tuo 項託 was a precocious youngster who at the age of seven supposedly instructed Confucius. The story is subjected to an extended critique by Wang Chong in *Lun heng* 78.

17.84

The markings of tigers and leopards attract archers;
the agility of monkeys and apes brings hunters.[35]

17.85

Moving one chess piece is not sufficient to display your wisdom.
Plucking one string [of an instrument] is not sufficient to show your sorrow.

17.86

If a three-inch pipe has no stopper [in its lower end], the whole world cannot fill it.
If a ten-*dan* vessel has a stopper [in its drain hole], a hundred pecks will suffice.

17.87

Using a bamboo pole to measure the depth of the Yangzi River and, when the bamboo pole has reached its limit, considering that the water's [depth] has been measured, is [truly] deluded.

17.88

Those who fish hasten to the deeps;
those who fell trees hasten to the mountains,
for [they know] what they hurry after will be there.
In the morning, people hasten to the market;
in the evening they stroll leisurely home,
for what they sought is gone.

35. This paraphrases *Zhuangzi* 7 (ZZ 7/20/20), where it is attributed to Laozi; it does not, however, appear in the received version of the *Daodejing*. This saying, with minor variations in wording, also appears in 10.92 and 14.4. Here we take *zha* 乍 as a phonetic loan for *cuo* (or *ce*) 措, "pursuit," as in those earlier occurrences of the passage.

17.89

Sable fur that is mottled cannot compare with fox fur that is uniform.[36]
A white jade disk with spots is not highly treasured.

This describes the difficulty in achieving purity.

17.90

The ghosts of those who died in battles hate spirit shamans;
robbers and thieves hate barking dogs.

17.91

It is easy to make sacrifices of millet and meat at an altar of the soil without a village;
it is easy to pray for prosperity at an altar of grain without a state.[37]

17.91a

A tortoise lacks hearing, but his sight cannot be fooled; its quintessence lies in its clear sight.
A blind musician lacks sight, but his hearing cannot be obstructed; his quintessence lies in his acute hearing.

17.92

The posthumous son does not yearn for his father, for there is no impression in his mind. He does not see his image as he dreams because he has never laid eyes on his form.

17.93

A cobra cannot grow legs;
tigers and leopards cannot be made to climb trees.[38]

36. The same statement appears in 16.119.

37. The deities of such neglected temples are impoverished and willing to accept whatever sacrifices they can get.

38. This statement betrays unfamiliarity with leopards, which often climb trees.

17.94

A horse does not feast on lard;
a hawfinch does not peck up millet;
[but] not because they are abstemious.

17.94a

When Qin penetrated the Yao Pass, Wei built up its ramparts.

17.95

Starving horses in the stables are still and silent, but throw down some hay by their side and the covetous heart is born.

17.96

When you draw a bow and shoot, without the [whole] bowstring the arrow would not fly. But [the portion of] the bowstring that makes the shot is just one part in a hundred.

17.97

The Way and its Potency can be taken as a constant [model];
expediency cannot be taken as a constant [model].
Thus,
[someone who] slips through the pass [and flees the country] cannot be [allowed to] return;
an escaped prisoner cannot be rehabilitated.

17.98

A ring can be used to illustrate a circle, but it cannot necessarily be used as a wheel.
A silk cord can be used to make edging for a sandal, but it cannot necessarily be used as a ribbon.

17.99

The sun and the moon do not rise together.
Foxes do not form male twosomes.
The spirit dragon has no mate.
Fierce beasts do not form herds.
Birds of prey do not pair off.

17.100

If you follow a marking cord to cut [things], you will not make a mistake.
If you suspend a scale to weigh [things], you will not go wrong.
If you set up a gnomon to look into the distance, you will not be confused.[39]

17.101

If you subtract years [from your age], you will incur jealousy from your younger brother.
If you add years [to your age], you will incur suspicions from your elder brother.

Better just to follow principles and act according to what is suitable.

17.102

People do not see the dragon in flight. It can rise so high because the wind and rain serve it.

17.103

Where grubs proliferate, trees snap.
Where fissures widen, walls crumble.

17.104

Things that are hung up will eventually fall down.
Limbs that stick out will eventually break off.

---

39. Gnomons (*biao* 表) can be used to determine both direction and distance. See 3.43–3.45.

17.105

If you endure freezing cold and do not die, you will not impair your sturdiness.
If you face scorching heat and do not suffer sunstroke, you will not lose your sturdiness.
But if you have never been unsturdy, you will lose your sturdiness.[40]

17.106

When a bath is prepared, the lice console one another;
When a large building is finished, swallows congratulate one another.
Sorrow and joy are far apart.

17.107

When Liuxia Hui[41] saw the sweetmeats, he said, "[These] can nourish the elderly."
When Robber Zhi saw the sweetmeats, he said, "[These] can grease the door bolt."
What they saw was the same, but how they would use it was different.

17.108

The silkworm eats but does not drink. In thirty-two days it transforms.[42]
The cicada drinks but does not eat. In thirty days it sheds its skin.
The ant neither eats nor drinks. In three days she dies.

17.109

When people eat riverstones,[43] they die; when silkworms eat them, they avert starvation.
When fish eat *ba* beans, they die; when rats eat them, they grow corpulent.
Correlative categories cannot necessarily be inferred.

---

40. In other words, someone whose sturdiness has never been tested cannot be considered sturdy.

41. Liuxia Hui 柳下惠 was a grandee of Lu during the Spring and Autumn period. He is much praised in the *Mencius* as a moral paragon.

42. In other words, it undergoes metamorphosis and becomes a pupa.

43. *Youshi* 礜石, said to be a kind of mineral.

17.110

Tile is made with fire, but you cannot get fire from it;
Bamboo grows in the water, but you cannot get water from it.

17.111

To scatter dust around and want to keep from getting dirty;
to wrap yourself in furs and fan yourself too;
—wouldn't it be better just to wear appropriate clothes?

17.112

Dry bamboo has fire [within it], but without a fire drill it will not ignite;
within the earth there is water, but without a spring it will not emerge.

17.113

The maladies of oysters and elephants[44] are the treasures of humankind. But human maladies—who would treasure them?

17.114

If you are so worried about the wine seller's profits that you do not buy his wine, you will just go thirsty.
If you are so worried about the chariot driver's profits that you do not hire his chariot, you will not reach your destination.
If you seize fire to throw it at someone else, you will be burned first instead.

17.115

If your neighbor's mother died, you [would] go over to shed tears with him. But if your own wife died, you would not weep [publicly] because [people would] consider it a violation [of propriety].

---

44. This refers to oysters growing pearls and to elephants losing their tusks. The statement thus appears to reflect a mistaken belief that elephants shed their tusks as deer shed their antlers. See also 16.107 and 17.195.

17.116

In the Country of Naked People, in the western regions, birds and beasts [and people] do not avoid one another; together they all are as one.

17.117

If you grab a single piece of roasting meat, you will burn your fingers.
If you stand ten paces away from ten thousand *dan* of roasting meat, you will not burn to death.

Though the same with respect to their *qi*, they differ with respect to how much is amassed. [The difference between] great and small courage is like this.

17.118

With a mat six feet long,
if you lay it flat to be stepped over, even an inept person could do it;
if you stand it on end to be jumped over, even a highly talented person would not find it easy.

This is because the conditions have been changed.

17.119

A hundred plums is sufficient to make vinegar for a hundred people,
[but] one plum is not sufficient to make vinegar[45] for one person.

17.120

Forbidding the world to eat because [one person] was killed by food,
forbidding the world to ride because [one person] was injured by a carriage,
would be perverse.

17.121

If you use a hook, you are quiet;
if you use brushwood,[46] you tap the boat;

45. Reading *he* 和 as *suan* 酸, as suggested by Lau, HNZ, 176n.2.
46. To make a weir to trap fish.

if you use a trap, you press it down;
if you use a net, you lift it up.
The means differ, but in getting fish they are the same.

17.122

When you see an elephant's tusk, you know he was bigger than an ox.
When you see a tiger's tail, you know it was bigger than a fox.
One portion appears, and the remaining one hundred portions are known.

17.123

Small states do not fight in the space between large states;
two deer do not fight when there is a rhinoceros close by.

17.124

If you assist the sacrificer, you get to taste the offering.
If you aid a brawler, you get injured.
If you take shelter under an unlucky tree, you will be struck by lightning.

17.125

Some call it a *zhong*, some call it a *long*.[47]
Some call it a *li*, some call it a *deng*.[48]
The name is different, but the reality is the same.
Se meaning "head lice"
and *se* meaning "a musical instrument made from a hollow piece of wood":
The name is the same, but the reality is different.

17.126

The sun and the moon want to shine, but drifting clouds can cover them.
Orchids and irises want to endure, but autumn winds will vanquish them.

47. Both *zhong* 冢 and *long* 隴 mean "burial mound."
48. Both *li* 笠 and *deng* 簦 are kinds of bamboo rain-covers.

17.127

If a tiger has a cub that cannot grasp and tear [prey with its claws], it will kill the cub right away because it is not fierce enough.

17.128

A jade seal carved in the shape of a tortoise is something the worthy turns into an ornament;
topsoil dispersed in the fields is something the capable turns into wealth.
To give a drowning person gold and jade is not as good as a few feet of rope.

17.129

In looking at writings,
if there is the character "wine" above, the character "meat" will certainly be below.[49]
If "year" is above, "month" will certainly be below.
We can pick them out according to their categories.

17.130

If you're covered with dust and you squint, that is a good reason; but if you cover [your eyes] before you have [even] gone out your door, that is contrary to the Way.[50]

17.131

The butcher dines on coarse vegetables.
The carriage maker travels on foot.
The potter uses broken bowls.
The carpenter lives in cramped quarters.
The one who makes it does not [necessarily] use it;
the one who uses it is not willing to make it.

49. Ancient Chinese texts were typically written in vertical columns, so "below" here has the meaning of "next."

50. This is apparently a criticism of eremitism: if you retire from office after spending some time in the "dust" of the world of affairs, that is permissible, but to refuse to engage in public affairs at all is not in accordance with the Way.

17.132

With the wheel hub [properly] set up, each of its thirty spokes makes full use of its strength but does not detract from the others. If you take one spoke alone and set it into the hub, discarding all the others, how would it be possible to go ten thousand *li*?

17.133

If you walk at night, you close your eyes and stretch your hand in front of you.[51]
If you cross [a body of] water, you untie your horses and take a boat.

In doing things, there are appropriate [actions], and there are things that should not be done.

17.134

Tangerines and pomelos have their native places.
Phragmites reeds and metataxis vines have places where they cluster.
Wild animals with identical feet follow one another in migration.
Birds with identical wings follow one another in flight.

17.135

Rainwater from the fields empties into the sea;
words whispered in someone's ear can be heard for a thousand *li*.

17.136

When Su Qin walked slowly, people said, "Why is he walking?"
When he hurried along, they said, "Why does he hurry?"
When he galloped his horse, they said, "Why does he gallop?"

Whatever he did, people discussed it. Many activities bring much criticism.

51. A variant of this saying occurs in 10.91.

17.137

If the skin is nowhere to be seen,
where will you look for the hair?[52]
If you fear the head and fear the tail,
what about all that is hidden in the body?

17.138

To want to see the nine continents [of the world][53] when your feet have not gone [even] a thousand *li*;
to be ignorant of the sources of government and education but to wish to reign over myriads of people—
these things are difficult!

17.139

If [the prey is] too obvious, it will be taken;
if [the bird is] too leisurely, it will be shot down.
Thus,
Great Purity is as if sullied;
Great Potency is as if deficient.[54]

17.140

If you have never planted nor harvested, yet grain fills your warehouses;
if you have never raised mulberry trees or silkworms, yet silk fills your sacks,
then you obtained them [through conduct] not in accord with the Way, and their use must be contradictory [to the Way].

52. Compare *Zuozhuan*, Duke Xi, year 14: "When the skin has been lost, where can you place the hair?" See Legge 1895, vol. 5, *The Ch'un Ts'ew* [*Chunqiu*] *with the Tso chuen* [*Zuozhuan*], 162.

53. For Zou Yan's theory that the world comprises nine continents (*jiu zhou* 九洲), see John S. Major, "The Five Phases, Magic Squares, and Schematic Cosmography," in *Explorations in Early Chinese Cosmology: Papers Presented at the Workshop on Classical Chinese Thought Held at Harvard University, August 1976*, ed. Henry Rosemont Jr., Journal of the American Academy of Religion Studies, vol. 50, no. 2 (1984; repr., Charleston, S.C.: Booksurge, 2006), 133–66; see esp. 134–37.

54. Compare *Laozi* 41.

17.141

The sea does not accept floating carrion;
Mount Tai does not elevate the petty person.[55]
The bladder is not offered up on an offering stand;[56]
the piebald horse does not qualify for sacrifice.

17.142

Using a fan to cool yourself in midsummer but not knowing enough to put it away when winter comes;
raising the hem of your clothing when crossing a stream but not knowing enough to lower it when you reach the [other] bank—
[some people] are unable to respond to alterations.

17.143

There are mountains that have no forests.
There are valleys that have no wind.
There are rocks that have no metal.

17.144

The people sitting in a hall all have different belt hooks, but they all hold their sashes closed in the same way.

17.145

Duke Xian [of Jin]'s worthiness [did not save him from being] deceived by Lady Li.[57]
Shusun [Bao]'s[58] knowledge [did not save him from being] tricked by Shu Niu.[59]

55. Meaning, apparently, that the sacred Mount Tai will not allow itself to be climbed by an unworthy person.

56. A *zu* was a kind of raised platter used to hold meat placed on the sacrificial altar.

57. The chieftain of the Rong tribe sent the beautiful Lady Li 驪姬 to seduce Duke Xian 獻公 (r. 676–651 B.C.E.). See 7.16 and 17.57.

58. Shusun Bao 叔孫鮑 (d. 538 B.C.E.), a grandee of Lu, was head of the Shusun clan; he served for a time as prime minister.

59. Shu Niu 豎牛 was a knight who served as Shusun Bao's steward and enjoyed his total trust. He

Thus when Zheng Zhan[60] entered Lu, the *Spring and Autumn Annals* said, "A deceitful person is coming, a deceitful person is coming!"

17.146

When the gentleman has wine,
the rustic beats his ceramic jar.[61]
Though [the gentleman] does not show approval,
he also does not show scorn.

17.147

By nature, people find silk suitable, but when being shot at, they suit up in armor. Thus they find that what doesn't suit them serves very suitably.

17.148

When the spokes are set into the hub of a wheel, each meeting its respective hole, they do not pierce one another. It resembles officials, each of whom tends to his respective duties and does not interfere with the others.

17.149

Because he had avoided being shot by wearing armor, he wore it to enter water;
because he had crossed a river by holding on to a gourd, he used it to smother a fire.
We can say he did not understand how to categorize things.

17.150

When the Superior Man presides over the people, it is like
using a rotted rope to drive a racehorse,

---

tricked Shusun Bao into killing his own two sons and eventually starved him to death when he became ill and was bedridden. The story is recorded in *Zuozhuan*, Zhao 4; and *Hanfeizi* 30.

60. Zheng Zhan 鄭詹 was a grandee of Zheng during the Spring and Autumn period. When Qi was ascendant, Zhan counseled that Zheng should switch its allegiance to Chu. The judgment of him as a "deceitful person" is recorded in the *Chunqiu Gongyang zhuan*, Zhuang 17.

61. The object of doing so is to beg some wine from the gentleman.

treading on thin ice with a *jiao* dragon beneath it,
or entering a forest and encountering a nursing tiger.

17.151

Skillfully using others is like the feet of a millipede; though numerous they do not harm one another.

Or like the lips and the teeth, the hard and the soft rub up against each other but do not overcome each other.

17.152

The beauty of clear wine begins with the plow and the spade;
the beauty of fine brocade begins with the shuttle and the loom.

17.153

Rough linen when new is not as good as burlap;
burlap when old is not as good as rough linen.
Some things are best when new;
others are best when old.

17.154

A dimple is attractive on a cheek, but on the forehead it is ugly;
embroidery is appropriate on a robe, but on a cap it is reprehensible.

17.155

Horse teeth are not ox hoofs.
Sandalwood roots are not catalpa branches.

Thus if you see the root of their singularity, the myriad things can be known.

17.156

When it is formed, a stone is hard;
when it emerges, an orchid is fragrant.

When they are young, they [already] possess these qualities;
when they mature, they [become] obvious.

17.157

Propping it up or knocking it over,
thanking him or scolding him,
gaining it or losing it,
permitting it or forbidding it—
they are a thousand *li* apart.

17.158

To dirty your nose but to powder your forehead,
to have [dead] rats rotting in the courtyard but to burn incense in the palace,
to go in the water but to hate to get wet,
to embrace the odorous but to seek out the fragrant,
—even someone who is good at things cannot manage these.

17.159

Second sprouts are not harvested; flowering plants that grow large too early miss their [proper] season and wilt.

17.160

Do not say that things are unlucky. After all, a rice pot will not fall into a well by itself.
If you pull out a hairpin and get a spark, why should you be surprised?

17.161

To prevent someone from crossing a river is possible, but if a person has already reached the middle of the river, it is not possible to prevent him from crossing.

17.162

Seeing a single stripe of a tiger, you do not know how fierce he is.
Seeing a single hair of a steed, you do not know how well he runs.

17.163

Larva produce dragonflies;
tiny eggs produce mosquitoes;
rabbit-tooth [insects] produce dragon ants.
What things have for their making
emerges from what cannot be reasoned.
Those who do not know this are amazed;
those who know this do not think it strange.

17.164

Bronze sparkles with green;
gold sparkles with yellow;
jade sparkles with white.
An oilseed lamp shines dimly;
a tallow lamp shines richly.
You can use
the obscure to know the obvious
and the external to know the internal.

17.165

Simulated meat[62] cannot be tasted by the mouth;
the appearance of ghosts and spirits cannot be perceived by the eyes;
the pleasure of seizing a shadow cannot assume reality in the heart.

62. *Xiang rou* 象肉 can be taken literally to mean "elephant meat," but that leads to the demonstrably false statement that "elephant meat cannot be tasted by the mouth." The extended meaning of *xiang* (representational, simulated) is correct here, as the statement refers to simulated goods made of wood, ceramic, or other materials for burial with the dead—a practice that was gaining currency at the time the *Huainanzi* was written.

17.166

Winter ice can crack;
summer trees can bear fruit.
The right moment is hard to get and easy to lose.

17.167

When the trees are thick and luxuriant on all sides, you can chop them down all day long, and no one would know [the difference]. But when the autumn winds bring down the frost, in just one night, they [all] die of cold.

17.168

To force-feed someone with a fever,
to give cold drinks to someone with sunstroke,
to pull on the rope to rescue a hanged person,
to throw a stone to save a drowning person:
[Although] one wants to help, [these things] do harm instead.

17.169

Although you may wish to prevent runaway horses, you need not rush out the door for [every] rumbling cart;
although you want to be careful when taking wine, you need not cling to your sleeping mat.

17.170

Once Meng Ben[63] reaches into a rat hole, the rats will die in no time; [nevertheless] they assuredly will bite his fingers because he has lost his positional advantage.

63. See chap. 9, n. 91. Meng Ben was known for his acute vision. See 16.91. The rats "would die in no time," even though he could not see them, because of his skill at finding, catching, and killing them, but this would come at a cost to Meng Ben himself.

17.171

When clouds rise in the mountains, the bases of pillars grow damp.
When the *fuling* fungus is dug up, the [parasitic] convolvula vine dies.

17.172

When one house is lost to fire, one hundred houses burn.
When liars plot in secret, the "hundred names" become sun-bleached bones.[64]

17.173

When grain gets wet, it becomes warm;
when clay pots are fired, they emit water.
In water there is fire;
in fire there is water.

17.174

Swift lightning breaks stone.
Yin and yang erode each other.[65]
These are natural forces.

17.175

When hot [bath] water is poured into a river, it does not increase [its volume] by much. When floodwaters drain into the sea, although they cannot increase its expanse, they still add to what was already there.

64. That is, they will be killed in battle. Note the pun here: "hundred names" normally means "the common people," but here it also has the more literal meaning of "one hundred commoners," in parallel with the "one hundred houses" of the previous line.

65. The phrase *yin yang xiang bo* 陰陽相薄 also occurs in 3.2 as an explanation of thunder, and in 4.19 five times as part of an explanation of how mineral ores grow and mature within the earth. See chap. 3, n. 5.

17.176

A one-eyed net cannot catch a bird.[66]
A baitless hook cannot catch a fish.
If you meet up with a scholar and lack propriety, you will not catch his respect.

17.177

The convolvula vine has no roots, but it can grow.
The snake has no feet but it can go.
A fish has no ears, but it can hear.
A cicada has no mouth, but it can sing.
They all have what makes them so.

17.178

The crane lives for a thousand years, so it may fulfill its wanderings; the mayfly is born in the morning and dies in the evening but gets its fill of enjoyment.

17.179

When [the tyrant] Djou minced Earl Mei, King Wen plotted with the Lords of the Land against him.
When [the tyrant] Jie showed no gratitude toward one who remonstrated, Tang had the people weep for him.
A wild horse does not butt into a tree;
a mad dog does not throw himself into a river;
and even a deaf insect does not immolate itself.
How much more so should people [avoid self-destruction].

17.180

If you like bears but feed them salt;
if you like otters but give them wine to drink;
though you may wish to raise them well, this contradicts their Way.

66. A similar statement appears in 16.103.

17.181

If it made you happy, you might destroy a boat to get its rudder;
if it were your heart's desire, you might destroy a bell to get its clapper.

17.182

For every small disgrace Master Guan accomplished something glorious.
For every hundred deceptions Su Qin performed one honest act.

17.183

Where a target is displayed, bow and arrows gather.
Where a forest's trees flourish, hatchets and axes enter.
It is not that someone summoned them. The force of circumstance attracts them.

17.184

The expectation of a reward might lead you to rescue a drowning man; still, it also certainly benefits the drowning man.

17.185/186

If a boat is as likely to sink as to float, even a fool would not set foot on it.
Even [the famous horse] Qiji,
if he did not go when spurred on,
or if he failed to stop when reined in,
would not be selected by the ruler of men to travel [a single] *li*.

17.187

Those who criticize my conduct wish to be my friends;
those who demean my goods wish to barter with me.

17.188

Water blended with water is not worth drinking.
A one-stringed *se* is not worth listening to.

17.189

A fine horse will die from being tied up;
an honest scholar will grow poor from being upright.
A worthy is spurned at the court;
a beautiful woman is spurned at the palace.

17.190

When the traveler thinks [of his loved one] on the road,
the one at home dreams in her bed.
When the kindly mother sighs in Yan [in the north],
her son misses her in Jing [in the south].

These are [cases of] Essence going back and forth.

17.191

Where red meat hangs, crows and magpies gather.
Where hawks and buzzards soar, throngs of birds disperse.

Whether creatures disperse or gather depends on how they respond to one another.

17.192

If you eat [someone's] food, don't destroy his utensils;
If you eat fruit [from a tree], don't break its branches.

17.192a

If you block up a spring, you'll go dry;
If you turn your back on your roots, you'll grow rotten.

17.193

Interlacing brushstrokes cannot extend far.
Linked rings cannot be separated.

The way to "solve" them is by not separating them.[67]

---

67. The implication seems to be that linked circles—for example, interlinked rings of jade—can be separated only by breaking them. Compare the story of Ni Yue (16.20), who "solved/untied" the knot of Song by recognizing that it could not be untied. See also 18.21 and chap. 18, n. 132.

17.194

Going down to the river and hoping for a fish is not so good as going home and knotting a net.

17.195

A moon-bright pearl is
an oyster's ailment
but my profit.
Tigers' claws and elephants' tusks are
good for the animals
but harmful to me.[68]

17.196

An easy road and a fine horse make people want to gallop.
Drinking wine and feeling happy make people want to sing.

17.197

To do what you know is right can certainly be called decisiveness.
To do what you know is wrong can surely be called delusion.

17.198

An arrow's speed cannot carry it more than two *li*. But if you go a hundred stages without resting,[69] you can go a thousand *li*.

17.199

Sages live in the yin;
the masses live in the yang.[70]
Sages walk in the water

68. See 17.113.
69. *Bai she bu xiu* 百舍不休; *she* means a "stage"—that is, a day's journey.
70. Sages conceal their virtues and stay in the background, whereas ordinary people live more visible lives.

where they leave no traces;
the masses walk on frost
where their tracks remain.

17.200

Different notes cannot be heard from the same pitch pipe;
Different shapes cannot be accommodated within the same body.

17.201

The peasants work hard, and the nobleman is nourished thereby;
The foolish speak, and the man of knowledge selects therefrom.

17.202

If you abandon a flourishing forest to gather amid dead trees,
If you don't shoot a swan but do shoot a crow,
It will be difficult to make plans with you.

17.203

If a broad hill has no gullies, the spring and streams cannot be very extensive. But even a narrow creek can fill a wetland of a thousand *qing*.[71]

17.204

If we see things in bright light, we can distinguish them [as clearly] as jade and stone.
If we see things in dim light, we must remain in doubt.

17.205

To take the immensity of the world and entrust it to the talent of a single person is like hanging a weight of a thousand *jun* on a single branch of a tree.

71. One *qing* equals a hundred *mu*. See n. 32.

17.206

To carry one's son while climbing a wall is considered unlucky. Should one person fall, two will be injured.

17.207

Someone who excels at initiating things is like a person who rides in a boat and sings a sad song. One person sings and a thousand others join in.

17.208

> You cannot plow but you want grain;
> you cannot weave but you want fine clothes.

Not to do the work but to look for the benefit—that is hard.

17.209

> If there are some who flourish, there must be others who decline;
> if there are some who wear fine silks, there must be others who wear coarse hemp.

17.210

There is a bird that stirs up the waves.[72] On account of this, [even] the Earl of the [Yellow] River avoids the tides, for he fears the bird's sincerity [of purpose].[73] If even a single warrior comes forth [ready to] die, [an army of] a thousand chariots will not take it lightly.

17.211

If a cobra bites you, if you treat it with the *hejin* plant[74] you will recover. There certainly are things that are very harmful[75] yet can instead be beneficial.

---

72. Commentators describe it as a great eagle that flies close to the water's surface and flaps its wings to roil the waters, thereby exposing fish that it then grabs and eats.

73. *Cheng* 誠 here implies something like an irresistible perfection of will.

74. The *hejin* 和菫 plant is not securely identifiable; presumably, from context, it is a poisonous plant that is also an antidote to poison.

75. Following Lau's (HNZ 17/183/11) reading of the passage and rejecting the interpolation of *qing*

17.212

A sage living in times of disorder is like being under a broiling sun in summer and waiting for dusk. Between the mulberry and the elm, the passage gets easier to bear.[76]

17.213

Though the water is level, it will certainly have waves.
Though the scale is correct, it will certainly have errors.
Though the markings on a measuring rule are consistent, there are sure to be discrepancies.

17.214

What is not a compass or a square cannot fix squares and circles;
What is not a level or a marking cord cannot establish the crooked and the straight.

Thus, those who use compasses, squares, levels, and marking cords also have compasses, squares, levels, and marking cords within them.

17.215

Only when the boat overturns do we see who are the skilled swimmers.
Only when the horses bolt do we see who are the good charioteers.

17.216

If you chew something and it has no flavor, you will not be able to get it down your throat.
If you look at something but it has no form, you will not be able to get a concept of it in your mind.

---

er fan 輕而反 before *zhong* 重, as suggested by Tao Hongqing and other commentators. See Zhang Shuangdi 1997, 2:1817n.9.

76. This is a reference to the [Fu]Sang mulberry tree of the east, from the branches of which the sun crow rises at dawn, and the Jian elm tree of the west, on whose branches the sun crow perches at sunset.

17.217

With a rhinoceros and a tiger behind you and the pearl of the marquis of Sui in front of you, do not try to grab [the pearl]. First avoid the calamity, and then go for the profit.

17.218

If you are pursuing a deer, you do not pay attention to rabbits; if you are making a deal for goods worth a thousand [pieces of] gold, you do not haggle over a penny or an ounce of silver.

17.219

Bows must first be adjusted; later you can seek out the strong ones.
Horses must first be trained; later you can seek out the fine ones.
People must first prove trustworthy; later you can seek out the able ones.

17.220

The potter discards a rope, but the chariot maker grabs it.
The butcher throws away a piece of scrap metal, but the blacksmith takes it.

Priorities differ.

17.221

The brilliance of a hundred stars does not compare to the radiance of the single moon.
The light from ten open windows is incomparably [brighter] than that from a single doorway.

17.222

An arrow from ten paces can penetrate rhinoceros hide [armor]. At its limit, though, it cannot pierce the thin white silk of Lu.[77]

77. An almost identical statement appears in 16.68.

17.223

Even something higher than Mount Tai cannot be seen if you turn your back; the tip of an autumn hair can be examined if you look at it.

17.224

Mountains produce metals but are cut by them.
Trees engender grubs but are eaten by them.
People generate affairs but are harmed by them.

17.225

Even a skillful foundryman cannot cast wood;
even a master carpenter cannot carve metal.
The form and nature [of the materials] make that so.

17.226

You do not carve a pure white jade;
you do not inscribe a beautiful pearl.
The basic material is more than enough [already].
Thus,
if it strides forth without resting, even a lame turtle can go a thousand *li*;
if you pile things up without stopping, you can amass a great heap.

17.226a

If a wall is made from earth, trees will grow from beneath it. They have no particular purpose [in doing so]; they just have an affinity for it.

17.227

The Way of employing people is like drawing fire from a mirror:
If you're too far away [from the tinder], you won't get anything;
if you're too close, it won't work.
The right [distance] lies between far away and close.

17.228

Observing the dawn, he [calculates] the shift [of the sun] at dusk;
measuring the crooked, he tells [how far] something departs from the straight and level.

When a sage matches things up, it is as if he holds up a mirror to their form; from the crooked [reflection], he can get to the nature [of things].

17.229

Yang Zhu came to a fork in the road and shed tears because he could go either south or north.
Mo Di saw raw silk and wept because it could be dyed either black or yellow.[78]

17.230

The accord between [one who] leaves and [one who] stays behind is like a bell and a chimestone tuned in the same way. After a thousand years of separation, they would still [make] the same note together.

17.231

Birds that are not harmful are not shot, even if they are nearby;
birds that are a nuisance are not allowed to escape, even if they are far away.

17.232

If you buy wine that has turned sour,
if you buy meat that is spoiled,

and you still go back to the wineshop or the butcher that is not far from your home, you must really be someone who likes to seek things close by.

78. Once the choice was made, the potentiality would be lost.

17.233

If you respond to
cheating with cheating
and deceit with deceit, it is like
wearing a straw cape to douse a fire
or digging a ditch to stop the water. Your problems will just proliferate.

17.234

Xi Shi and Mao Qiang were not alike in their appearance but in judging their good points, the world considered them equally beautiful.
Yao, Shun, Yu, and Tang made laws that were different, but in winning the hearts of the people they were alike.

17.235

Sages
raise matters at the proper time and
accomplish things by following natural [tendencies].
When it rains hard, they prepare rain barrels;
When it is dry, they construct an earthen dragon [to pray for rain].

17.236

While weaving, a woman from Linzi thought of her absent [lover]; thus the cloth she made was coarse. If there is a beautiful woman [left] at home, her cloth will be like unraveled threads.

17.237

[Music] in the *zhi* and *yu* modes[79] is something the ears of the vulgar cannot comprehend. But if it is [something with] a catchy consonance and quick tempo, they will sit down and enjoy it.

79. *Zhi* and *yu* are two of the five pentatonic notes; the reference is to stately music that takes those notes as dominant.

17.238

If you walk past a storehouse with hands clasped behind your back, it would be strange if you did not have robbery in mind.
Likewise, someone who has been disrespectful to a person's ghost walks past their ancestral shrine and sets its branches aquiver.

17.239

Yang Chufu of Jin attacked Chu and saved Jiang.[80]

Thus releasing a captive does not rely on removing the yoke;[81] it relies on attacking [the one] wielding the stick.

17.240

If the tree is large, its roots grip strongly;
if a mountain is high, its foundation is firm.
The longer your stride, the farther you will go;
the bigger your body, the more spread out your bones and joints will be.

17.241

If a madman hurts someone, no one will resent him personally.
If a small child scolds an elderly person, no one will hate [the child].
The intent to do evil is absent.

17.242

Wei Sheng's trustworthiness[82] was not as good as Sui Niu's deceit [which saved his country].[83] Yet how much less [admirable] is one who is never trustworthy?

---

80. *Zuozhuan*, Duke Wen, year 3 (624 B.C.E.). The *Zuo* account states that Chu was besieging Jiang. Du You's commentary to the passage records that the Chu commander, Zizhu, lifted the siege on hearing that the Jin army was on the march for Chu and that the Jin army also withdrew on hearing that the siege was lifted.

81. Possibly a reference to the *cangue*, a heavy wooden yoke that criminals were made to wear as a punishment. But that interpretation is speculative; the text may be simply making an analogy between an (enslaved) captive and an ox.

82. See 13.11 and 16.100; and ZZ 29/88/10. Wei Sheng waited for a woman under a bridge. When she did not come, he continued to wait for her until he was drowned by the rising waters.

83. Sui Niu 隨牛. The identity of this figure is unclear. Gao You associates him with Xian Gao, the merchant of Zheng who was able to stave off a surprise attack by Qin through subterfuge. See 12.40. Yu

17.243

The one who worries over the father's illness is the son, but the one who cures him is the physician.
The one who presents sacrifices is the celebrant, but the one who prepares them is the cook.

Translated by Sarah A. Queen and John S. Major

Yue suggests that 牛 is a mistake for 生, making this figure "Mr. Sui," or Sui He 何, a rhetorician who served the early Han court. Yu Shengwu rejects that reading and proposes that 隨 is a mistake for 犒. Thus the two characters are not a proper name at all but mean "to present cattle," making the entire phrase read "the deceit of presenting cattle." This would explain the association with Xian Gao, as part of his ruse was to present the Qin army with some cattle, claiming that they were a gift of the ruler of Zheng. See Zhang Shuangdi 1997, 2:1828n.15.

Eighteen

AMONG OTHERS

"AMONG OTHERS" explores the vagaries of human affairs and the paradoxical impulses that constantly change the patterns of human society. This chapter is essentially an extended exercise in persuasive prose, using symmetrically arranged anecdotes to demonstrate that radically divergent principles and forces direct events from situation to situation and from moment to moment. The overarching theme of the chapter is that only a sage can hope to navigate the turbid waters of human politics and social intercourse.

The Chapter Title

Chapter 18 of the *Huainanzi* shares its title—"Ren jian" 人間—with chapter 4 of the *Zhuangzi*, and although stylistically they differ, the two texts are thematically quite close. The title of chapter 18 shows the elasticity of classical Chinese syntax; that is, the part of speech of each of the characters in the title can have multiple variant readings. For example, *ren* means "person" or "human being" but also "humanity" in general or "human" as a quality. *Jian* usually is a preposition meaning "between" or "among/amid," but it can also be used as a noun meaning "realm" or "domain." The chapter title thus could also be translated as "Among Human Beings" or "The Human Realm."[1]

1. Le Blanc and Mathieu 2003 translate the title as "Du monde des hommes."

Also of significance to chapter 18 is its place in the overall structure of the *Huainanzi.* Whereas earlier chapters of the text move sequentially through the cosmogonic processes and energies at the root of all existence and the interior spaces of the human psyche, "Among Others" and the other later chapters articulate the gross dimensions of the phenomenal world. Thus one of the common nominal meanings of *ren* is germane to the thematic valence of the chapter's title. In classical literature, *ren* could be the antonym of *ji* 己, "self," thus generating the meaning of "other people." As the introductory section of chapter 18 explains, here we have left the internal domain of the mind and nature and entered the multidimensional world of time and space populated by *ren,* "other people" or, simply, "others." For this reason, we translate the title of chapter 18 as "Among Others."

Summary and Key Themes

Even though most of "Among Others" is composed of the same discrete prose units that constitute both earlier texts like the *Lüshi chunqiu* and later anthologies like the *Shuo yuan,* in structure it resembles the former text much more than the latter. The anecdotes compiled in chapter 18 are not grouped into topics, as they are in the *Shuo yuan.* Rather, as in the *Lüshi chunqiu* (albeit in an even more deliberate and stylized manner than that text evinces),[2] the anecdotes in chapter 18 are set in a formal matrix framed by linking segments of parallel prose and verse. Viewed as a whole, the chapter is designed to follow (or establish) the conventions of a particular prose genre.

The sections into which this translation is divided correspond to the formal, generic segments into which the chapter as a whole naturally breaks (with the exception of the first segment, which serves as a thematic introduction). Each of the twenty-six segments following the first exhibits the same basic structural properties, with some slight degree of deviation overall. The structure of each segment has the following outline (the examples here are from 18.2):

Proem: A short introductory passage, often in verse or parallel prose, which establishes the topic of the segment.

The world has three perils:
To have little Potency but [enjoy] much favor is the first peril.
To have lower talent and high position is the second peril.
For one's person to be without great merit and yet to receive rich emolument is the third peril.

2. In the *Lüshi chunqiu,* anecdotes are generally grouped together and linked so that all anecdotes in an essay support its central thesis.

Motif: A symmetrically counterpoised pair of aphorisms, usually outlining a contradiction or paradox and delivered as the linked "legs" of a parallel prose dyad.[3]

> Thus, as for things,
> some are increased by being decreased;
> some are decreased by being increased.

First example: A modular prose anecdote that illustrates the first leg of the motif. This often opens with the formulaic segue "How do we know that this is so?" and is concluded by the formula "This is what is called X." Section 18.2 relates an anecdote about Sunshu Ao safeguarding his descendants by requesting a poor fief from his king.

Second example: A modular prose anecdote that illustrates the second leg of the motif. This often opens with the formulaic segue "What is called X?" and concludes with the formula "This is what is called X." Section 18.2 here has an anecdote about how Duke Li of Jin was destroyed because he overextended his power through conquest.

Envoy: A closing statement, sometimes delivering a "moral" to be derived from the motif, usually in verse or parallel prose.

> When Confucius read the *Changes*, on arriving at [the hexagrams] "Loss" [損] and "Gain" [益],[4] he never failed to sigh loudly, saying, "Gain and loss, are these not the affairs of a king?"[5]

Whether this structural arrangement invokes a prose genre that would have been recognizable to a literarily educated Han audience is an open question. Existing testimony of generic prose forms during the Han is sparse, and examples of many of the attested genre forms are lacking. One attested genre that could be compared with the prose composition of "Among Others" is that of *lianzhu*, or "Linked Pearls." Shen Yue (441–512) attributes the origins of this genre to Yang Xiong (53–18 B.C.E.);[6] thus it is of somewhat later provenance than the *Huainanzi.* No Han examples of the genre survive, but one piece by the Western Jin author Lu Ji (261–303), "Linked Pearls Elaborated to Fifty Stanzas," is anthologized into the imperially sponsored *Literary Selections* of the Liang-dynasty court. Each stanza in that composition is constructed from a pair of symmetrically counterpoised aphorisms parallel to the typical motif of each section of "Among Others." One stanza reads:

---

3. A significant structural variant is 18.27, whose motif has four rather than two legs, thus altering the section's subsequent structure.

4. *Changes*, hexagrams 41, *Sun*, and 42, *Yi*, respectively.

5. The conclusion of 18.2 contains more material that I have omitted, as this short section is more typical of a common envoy.

6. Ouyang Xun, *Yiwen leiju* (Beijing: Zhonghua shuju, 1965), 57.1039.

I have heard,
though accumulated substance may be subtle,
it will certainly move objects.
Though exalted vacuity may be expansive,
it will not shift hearts.
Thus,
a capital denizen of charming mien
will take no delight in the shadow of Xi Shi.
A carriage horse that is running in circles
will not be stopped by the shade of Mount Tai. (*Wen xuan* 55)[7]

Although much more laconic, the parallels between this generic form and the compositional structure of "Among Others" are clear.[8] Whether "Among Others" is a generic antecedent of the "Linked Pearls" form cannot be determined, but both texts illustrate common aesthetic preferences of literary artisanship. In this sense, whether the formal structure of chapter 18 was a conventional or recognizable genre of the Former Han or a novel invention of Liu An and his collaborators is moot. In either case, there is good evidence to suggest that the *Huainanzi*'s authors would have expected "Among Others" to be perceived as a virtuosic performance of literary composition. Any cursory survey of the surviving works of the Han and later eras demonstrates the building enthusiasm for symmetrical construction and parallelism in all fields of literary production.[9] Accordingly, at the very least the authors of "Among Others" would have congratulated themselves for showing how the modular anecdotes that had become so important to the philosophical and rhetorical prose of the Warring States and Han could be worked into a structure with the elegance and aesthetic refinement increasingly attributed to symmetrical and parallel literary forms.

Moreover, whether the formal structure of "Among Others" was received or invented, it was perfectly suited to the thematic valence of the chapter. As the introductory section of chapter 18 declares:

The arrival of calamity is generated by human beings [人];
the arrival of good fortune is effected by human beings.

---

7. Xiao Tong, *Wen xuan* (Shanghai: Shanghai guji, 1994), 2387.

8. The paradoxical juxtaposition of "accumulated substance" and "exalted vacuity" mirrors the common construction of a typical motif in chap. 18, although the subsequent lines provide examples only of "exalted vacuity."

9. "Parallel prose" is generally considered a hallmark of the Six Dynasties period, but its origins date to the Former Han. Already the *fu* of celebrated authors like Sima Xiangru (ca. 145–86 B.C.E.) relied heavily on parallelism for aesthetic effect, and the text of the *Huainanzi* itself is replete with parallel and symmetrical constructions. See Christopher Leigh Connelly, "Sao, Fu, Parallel Prose, and Related Genres," in *The Columbia History of Chinese Literature*, ed. Victor H. Mair (New York: Columbia University Press, 2001), 223–47; and Andrew H. Plaks, "Where the Lines Meet: Parallelism in Chinese and Western Literatures," *Chinese Literature: Essays, Articles, Reviews (CLEAR)* 10, nos. 1–2 (1988): 43–60.

> Calamity and good fortune share a gateway;
> benefit and harm are neighbors.
> No one who is not a spirit or sage can distinguish them.

This passage plays self-consciously with the multiple significances of *ren*. The first line reads simultaneously as "the arrival of calamity is generated by human beings" and "the arrival of calamity is generated by *others*." When an individual ventures into the realm of time and space inhabited by other people, he will encounter among them both benefit and harm, and both are engendered in identical contexts and by identical means. Demonstrating this is the object of juxtaposing anecdotes throughout the chapter that operate at cross-purposes to each other.

The conclusion to chapter 18 is thus encapsulated in the final line just quoted, that one must be a *spirit* or a *sage* to distinguish whether others are bringing harm or benefit from instance to instance and moment to moment. Here, again, the ambiguity of *ren* as human beings or other people is significant. The resource that empowers us to discriminate between benefit and harm—the *spirit* that when actualized through personal cultivation transforms the individual into a *sage*—does not lie with *others* but within ourselves. Simultaneously, actualizing the spirit raises the practitioner to a plateau that transcends the *human* realm. As Michael Puett notes in *To Become a God*,[10] by using the character *shen* (spirit) to describe the realized adept, texts like the *Huainanzi* claim for such individuals, literally and audaciously, the acquisition of superhuman qualities like those of the deities of the ancestral cult. This is the rhetorical stance underpinning all the literary gymnastics of chapter 18: conditions, "among others," are such that only a person who has transcended them through the forms of personal cultivation advocated earlier in the *Huainanzi* can even hope to survive them, much less exercise any significant leadership over them.

Sources

"Among Others" is closely related to another chapter of the *Huainanzi* that likewise is a composite of short, modular units of anecdotal prose: chapter 12, "Responses of the Way." The bulk of chapter 18 is composed of the same type of short prose anecdotes[11] that also make up chapter 12, although these two chapters use the anecdotes for quite different ends. Included among these modular units are many that seem to have been taken verbatim from the *Lüshi chunqiu*, the *Hanfeizi*, the *Zhuangzi*, the *Zhanguoce*, and the *Liezi*, to name only a few; some appear again a century later in

10. Michael J. Puett, *To Become a God: Cosmology, Sacrifice, and Self-Divinization in Early China* (Cambridge, Mass.: Harvard University Asia Center, 2002), 3–4.

11. For a discussion of the anecdote and its historical usage in Warring States and Han prose composition, see the introduction to chap. 12.

Liu Xiang's *Shuo yuan*. The transfer of these prose units from text to text leads to the question of which texts constitute the definitive "sources" of "Among Others." Many anecdotes appear in more than one other text besides the *Huainanzi*, and even for those that do not (or for which the *Huainanzi* stands as the current *locus classicus*), we cannot be certain of their original source. An anecdote that appears only in the *Hanfeizi* and the *Huainanzi* may have entered the latter text from the former, but it just as easily may have been circulating in another now-lost text or as a unit of "loose prose" in either written or oral form.[12] As our fund of archaeologically recovered manuscripts has increased, we have learned more about the material media in which various forms of writing were produced and circulated. Nevertheless, we still do not know enough about the pathways of textual transmission during the Han era to describe confidently the process by which the textual components of "Among Others" were collected and compiled.

The Chapter in the Context of the *Huainanzi* as a Whole

"Among Others" is a late chapter in the *Huainanzi*, and as such it is structurally relegated to a position in the text that is emblematic of "branch" concerns. Chapter 18 forcefully and elegantly describes the paradoxical nature of human affairs and reinforces the importance of personal cultivation and transcendence to political leadership. Neither of these accomplishments is enough, however, to account for its inclusion in the text as a whole. To understand the role of chapter 18, therefore, we must appreciate both the efforts by Liu An and his collaborators to establish their credentials as literary stylists and connoisseurs and their motives for doing so. The *Huainanzi* was written for an audience of intellectuals[13] who increasingly defined themselves as producers and consumers of texts, in a milieu in which literary skill was highly prized. If the *Huainanzi*'s novel vision of universal empire failed to identify a place for literary artistry and refinement, its authors could not have hoped for an enthusiastic reception. The *Huainanzi*'s veneration of ideas like those of the *Daodejing* ("those who know do not speak; those who speak do not know") left its authors open to the charge of endorsing literary primitivism or Philistinism. In other words, the authors of the *Huainanzi* would have been sensitive to the possibility that their political opponents might charge that they had taken a stand against literary elegance and refinement as a criterion for state employment and promotion. In "Among Others" (and in many other of the later chapters), the authors of the *Huainanzi* reassure their

---

12. For a discussion of some of these issues, see David Schaberg, *A Patterned Past: Form and Thought in Early Chinese Historiography* (Cambridge, Mass.: Harvard University East Asia Center, 2002); and William G. Boltz, "The Composite Nature of Early Chinese Texts," in *Text and Ritual in Early China*, ed. Martin Kern (Seattle: University of Washington Press, 2005), 50–78.

13. The text was certainly intended to reach a wide intellectual audience even if, as suggested elsewhere, its "ideal reader" was a young monarch or emperor-in-training.

readers that the intrinsic values of their vision do not denigrate or preclude literary artisanship and aesthetic engagement.

There is one other context in which the place of chapter 18 must be understood. "Among Others" is one of a sequence of chapters beginning with "A Mountain of Persuasions" (chapter 16) and continuing through "Cultivating Effort" (chapter 19) that deal with aspects of oral argumentation as a court activity. The symmetrical structure of chapter 18 makes it a compendium of exemplars of the art of debate itself and an illustration of how anecdotes may be deployed in oral argumentation. Beyond this, by demonstrating that anecdotes can be found to support, with apparently equal validity, both the "pro" and "con" sides of any argument, "Among Others" implicitly declares that although debate may be a versatile instrument of court policy, it can never serve as the ultimate arbiter of truth. Skilled debate may effectively lay out the merits of contrasting policy positions, but a ruler not fully realized in the Way will not be able to discern the future trajectories of good or ill fortune prefigured by either side of such a contest.[14]

Andrew Meyer

---

14. David Schaberg noted the relationship between "Among Others" and the issue of oral argumentation in "Oratorical Training in the *Huainanzi*" (paper presented at the conference "Liu An's Vision of Empire: New Perspectives on the *Huainanzi*," Harvard University, Cambridge, Mass., May 31, 2008).

Eighteen

18.1

The nature of humans is pure, clear, peaceful, and content.
The regulators of affairs are models, gnomons, the compass, and the square.
If you understand the nature of humans, you will not err in nurturing yourself.
If you understand the regulators of affairs, you will not be confused in your taking and giving.[1] [18/185/20–21]

When one end emerges,
it comprehends limitlessly.
Roaming the eight limits,
it gathers it all into a single straw.

It is called "the mind."

Looking at the root and knowing the branches, observing the finger and seeing the return [path], holding to the One and responding to the many, grasping the essentials and ordering the details. These are called "techniques." [18/185/23–24]

What the wise are at rest, where the wise go in motion, what the wise wield in affairs, that from which the wise act: this is known as "the Way."

The Way:

Place it in front, and [the cart] will not lean forward;
place it behind, and [the cart] will not lean backward.

1. Accepting the alternative *Daozang* reading of 惑 for 或. See Lau, HNZ, 185n.4.

Put in inside a cramped space, and it will not fill it,
Spread it over the world, and it will not be stretched.

For this reason,

what cause others to exalt and praise you are the strengths of the mind. [18/185/26–28]
What cause others to denigrate and slander you are the faults of the mind.
Words that issue from the mouth cannot be halted among others;
actions that are manifest nearby cannot be kept from afar.
Affairs are difficult to complete and easily defeated;
reputation is difficult to establish and easily abandoned.
A thousand-*li* dike will breach because of a cricket or ant burrow;
a hundred-*xun* roof will burn because of a spark from a crack in the chimney.[2]

The *Admonitions of Yao* says, "Trembling and shaking, take heed day by day. People do not stumble over a mountain; they stumble over an anthill."[3] This is why those who look lightly on small harms and scorn minor affairs will have many regrets. Worrying about a calamity once it has arrived is like a sick person's searching for a good doctor once he has already become critically ill. Even if [the doctor] has the skill of a Bian Que[4] or a Yu Fu,[5] [the patient] will still not live. [18/185/30–18/186/4]

The arrival of calamity is generated by human beings;
the arrival of good fortune is effected by human beings.
Calamity and good fortune share a gateway;
benefit and harm are neighbors.

No one who is not a spirit or sage can distinguish them. [18/186/6–7]

In all people's undertaking of affairs, none dares set his plans before using his intelligence to reflect and assess. Some lead to benefit, others to harm; this is the difference between the stupid and the wise. Those who thought that they clearly knew the fulcrum of survival and extinction, the portal of calamity and good fortune, and who, having used it, become trapped in difficulty, cannot be counted. If whenever one knew what was right, one's affair would succeed, there would be no unfinished ventures in the world. For this reason,

intelligence and reflection are the portals of calamity and good fortune;
motion and stillness are the fulcrums of benefit and harm.

The alterations and transformations of the hundred affairs, the order and chaos of the state and the household, wait [for them] to be effected. [For this reason, one who does not fall into difficulty succeeds.][6] Thus one cannot but take heed of them. [18/186/9–13]

2. Reading 煙 as a mistake for 熛. See Lau, HNZ, 186n.1.

3. The *Admonitions of Yao* 堯戒 seems to be a lost text; it is not mentioned in any of the early histories or bibliographical treatises. HFZ 46/138/27 quotes the second sentence of this passage, citing it as "a saying of a former sage."

4. Bian Que 扁鵲 was a famous physician who lived in the fifth century B.C.E. See *Shiji* 105:2785–94.

5. According to Xu Shen, Yu Fu 俞跗 was a physician at the time of the Yellow Emperor. See Zhang Shuangdi 1997, 2:1835n.12.

6. Yang Shuda asserts that this line is a superfluous interpolation, as the context would seem to suggest. See Lau, HNZ, 186n.7.

18.2

The world has three perils:

To have little Potency but [enjoy] much favor is the first peril.
To have lower talent and high position is the second peril.
For one's person to be without great merit and yet to receive rich emolument is the third peril.

Thus, as for things,

some are increased by being decreased;
some are decreased by being increased. [18/186/15–16]

How do we know this is so? In olden times, King Zhuang of Chu had just defeated Jin between the [Yellow] River and Yong.[7] Returning, he offered Sunshu Ao a fief, but Sunshu Ao declined it. When [Sunshu Ao] was sick and about to die, he told his son, "When I have died, the king will certainly enfeoff you. You must decline the rich and fertile land and accept sandy and rocky land. Between Chu and Yue are the hills of Qin.[8] Its land is lacking and its reputation is bad. The people of Wu[9] and Yue both think it haunted.[10] No one considers it of any benefit." Sunshu Ao died, and the king indeed did offer his son rich and fertile land as a fief. His son declined it, requesting the hills of Qin. According to the customs of Chu, officials of merit received title and emolument in the second generation, [yet] Sunshu Ao alone survived.[11] This is what is called "increasing it by reducing."

What is called "reducing it by increasing?" In antiquity, Duke Li of Jin attacked Chu to the south, Qi to the east, Qin to the west, and Yan to the north. His soldiers marched the breadth of the world without being defeated; he awed the four directions into submission without [himself] surrendering. Thereupon he assembled the Lords of the Land at Jialing.[12] His *qi* was replete, his will arrogant, [and] he tyrannized the myriad people. Within, he had no supporting ministers; without, he had no aid from the Lords of the Land. He slaughtered his great ministers; he drew close to manipulators and slanderers. The next year he went traveling to [the fief of] the Jiangli clan. Luan Shu and Zhonghang Yan seized and imprisoned him.[13] None of the Lords of the Land would save him; none of the common people grieved for him. After three months he died. Now, victory in battle and conquest in assault [and making] one's territory expansive and one's name revered; these are what [everyone

7. This battle took place in 597 B.C.E. See *Zuozhuan*, Xuan 12. Yong 雍 was a town in present-day Shaanxi Province.

8. Qin 寢 was a frontier region of Chu located in present-day Anhui Province.

9. Accepting Yu Dacheng's proposed emendation. See Lau, HNZ, 186n.8.

10. Reading 機 as the character *qi* (second tone; 幾 on top, 鬼 on the bottom). See Zhang Shuangdi 1997, 2:1841n.8.

11. This anecdote also appears in LSCQ 10.4/50/24–28 and HFZ 21/42/21–23.

12. The gathering took place in 574 B.C.E. The *Zuozhuan* gives the name of the meeting site as Keling 柯陵 (Cheng 17; Yang 895).

13. *Zuozhuan*, Cheng 17. The Jiangli 匠麗 clan, Luan Shu 欒書, and Zhonghang Yan 中行偃 all were vassals of Jin.

in] the world desires, yet [for Duke Li] they ended with his person dead and his state lost.[14] This is what is called "reducing it by increasing."

Sunshu Ao's requesting the hills of Qin, a sandy and rocky territory, was why it was not vied for by successive generations. Duke Li of Jin's assembling of the Lords of the Land at Jialing was why he died in [the fief of] the Jiangli clan. [18/186/18–18/187/3]

The mass of people all know to view benefit as benefit and illness as illness; only the sage understands that illness is benefit, benefit is illness. The trunk of a tree that is doubly solid will certainly be harmed; the family that digs up graves [to rob them] will certainly suffer disaster. These speak of great benefits that conversely become harm. Zhang Wu instructed Earl Zhi to wrest away the territory of Hann and Wei, and [Earl Zhi] was taken at Jinyang. Shenshu Shi instructed King Zhuang [of Chu] to enfeoff the descendants of the Chen clan, and [King Zhuang] became hegemon.[15]

When Confucius read the *Changes*, on arriving at [the hexagrams] "Loss" and "Gain,"[16] he never failed to sigh loudly, saying, "Gain and loss, are these not the affairs of a king?" [18/187/5–8]

18.3

Actions:

Some are taken in order to benefit a person and ultimately only injure him;
some are taken in order to injure a person and conversely [only] benefit him.
The reversals of benefit and injury
are the portal of calamity and good fortune.

They cannot but be investigated. [18/187/8–9]

Yang Hu rebelled in Lu.[17] The ruler of Lu ordered the people to bar the city gate and seize him. Anyone who apprehended him would be rewarded greatly; anyone who lost him would be heavily incriminated. Being encircled three times, Yang Hu was about to take up his sword and cut his own throat. One of the gatekeepers stopped him, saying, "I will let you out." Yang Hu thus went to the encirclement and drove them back; raising his sword and lifting his spear, he ran. The gatekeeper let him out. Turning around, [Yang Hu] went back to the one who let him out, stabbing him with his spear, grabbing his sleeve, and hitting him in the armpit. The one who let him out [said] resentfully, "I had no reason to befriend you. For you, I have risked

14. This anecdote occurs in LSCQ 20.7/136/7–11.

15. The two anecdotes alluded to here, concerning Zhang Wu and Shenshu Shi, form the body of 18.13. Because their summary mention at this point is rather odd and breaks the flow of the envoy, these lines may be an interpolated note from a later commentator. For the provenance and background of these stories, see 18.13 and its attendant notes.

16. *Changes*, hexagrams 41, *Sun*, and 42, *Yi*, respectively.

17. This incident occurred in 502 B.C.E. See *Shiji* 14:667. Yang Hu 陽虎 was a knight of Lu who was briefly able to consolidate control over the ducal court.

death and incurred incrimination, yet you turn and injure me. It is fitting that you should have this trouble!"

When the ruler of Lu heard that Yang Hu had escaped, he was greatly angry. He asked which gate [Yang Hu] had left through and ordered his officers to seize [its gatekeeper]. Thinking that if he were injured, it was because he fought and that if he were uninjured, it was because he had let [Yang Hu] go, [he ordered that] if he were injured, he would receive a great reward [and that] if he were not injured, he would be severely punished. This is what is called "injuring him and yet benefiting him." [18/187/11–17]

What is called "wanting to benefit [a person] and yet injuring him?" King Gong of Chu and the people of Jin did battle at Yanling.[18] When the fighting was fierce, King Gong was injured and withdrew. Commander Zifan[19] was thirsty and asked for a drink; his page Yang Gu brought wine and gave it to him. Zifan was fond of wine, and when he tasted it, he could not stop drinking; thus he became drunk and lay down. King Gong wanted to resume battle and sent someone to summon Commander Zifan. Zifan excused himself on account of a heart malady. The king drove to see him; entering his tent, he smelled wine. King Gong, greatly angry, said, "In today's battle I was personally wounded. The one I depended on was you, and yet you are like this. You abandon the altars of the soil and grain of Chu and have no concern for my people; I will not go into battle with you again!" Thereupon he halted the army and withdrew, beheading Zifan as punishment. Thus the page Yang Gu's giving Zifan wine was not out of a desire to cause him calamity. He truly loved and wanted to please him, and ultimately it only killed him.[20] This is called "wanting to benefit him and conversely injuring him." [18/187/19–25]

"If they are sick with a fever, force them to eat,
If they are sick with chills, give them a cold drink."

This is what the mass of people consider therapeutic, but a good physician considers them unhealthy.

What delights the eye,
what delights the mind,

these are what the foolish consider benefit but what those possessed of reason avoid.

Thus,

the sage first scrutinizes [something] and only later adopts [it];
the mass of people adopt [something] and only later scrutinize [it]. [18/187/27–18/188/2]

18. This battle took place in 575 B.C.E. See *Zuozhuan*, Cheng 16. Yanling 鄢陵 is in present-day Henan Province. King Gong 共 reigned from 590 to 575 B.C.E.

19. Zifan 子反 was an aristocrat of the Chu royal clan. According to the *Zuozhuan*, he committed suicide after the battle.

20. This anecdote occurs in LSCQ 15.2/81/13–21 and HFZ 10/14/1–7.

18.4

To possess merit is the duty of all ministers;
to be incriminated is what all ministers avoid.
[Yet] some who possess merit have fallen under suspicion;
some who commit crimes are trusted even more.

Why is this? It is because those who have merit were alienated from the Rightness of mercy; those who committed crimes did not dare lose their humane heart. [18/188/4–5]

The Wei general Yue Yang attacked Zhongshan.[21] His son was held in the city, and those in the city hung up his son to show Yue Yang. Yue Yang said, "The Rightness of ruler and minister does not allow me to have selfish concern for my son." He assaulted [the city] even more vigorously. Zhongshan then cooked his son, sending him a cauldron of soup containing his head. Yue Yang touched it and cried over it, saying, "This is my son." He knelt before the emissary and drank three cups [of the soup]. The emissary returned and reported. [The ruler of] Zhongshan said, "This is one who is bound to the spot and will persist unto death; we cannot endure." Thus he surrendered to him. [Yue Yang] had greatly expanded Marquis Wen of Wei's territory; he possessed merit. [Yet] from this point on, he was daily less trusted.[22] This is what is called "having merit and falling under suspicion." [18/188/7–11]

What is called committing a crime yet being trusted even more? Meng Sun[23] was hunting and caught a fawn. He ordered Qinxi Ba to take it back and cook it. The fawn's mother followed him, crying. Qinxi Ba could not endure it, [so] he freed [the fawn] and gave it [to its mother]. Meng Sun returned and asked where the fawn was. Qinxi Ba replied: "Its mother followed and was crying. I truly could not endure it, so I let [the fawn] go and gave it [to its mother]." Meng Sun was angry and exiled Qinxi Ba. After one year, he took [Qinxi Ba] as his son's teacher. Those around him said, "Qinxi Ba has transgressed against you, [yet] now you make him your son's teacher, why?" Meng Sun said: "If he could not endure [the suffering] of a single fawn, how much less [will he endure] that of a human being?"[24] This is what is called "committing a crime and yet being trusted even more." [18/188/13–17]

Thus one cannot but be careful in one's taking and relinquishing. This is why when Gongsun Yang[25] incurred recrimination in Qin, he could not enter Wei. It was not

21. This occurred in 400 B.C.E. See *Shiji* 44:1840. Yue Yang 樂羊 was a general of Wei. Zhongshan 中山 was a state established by the White Di people in present-day Hebei Province.

22. This anecdote appears in HFZ 22/49/7–9.

23. Meng Sun 孟孫 was a grandee of Lu during the Spring and Autumn period.

24. This anecdote appears in HFZ 22/49/11–14.

25. Gongsun Yang 公孫陽 (also known as Lord Shang 商 [ca. 390–338 B.C.E.]) was the prime minister of Qin. After falling out of favor in Qin, he fled to Wei but was refused refuge because of an old injury he had done to a Wei prince. See *Shiji* 68:2236–37.

that his merit was not great, yet his feet were bound and he had nothing upon which to tread.[26] It was because he was unrighteous. [18/188/19–20]

18.5

Actions:

Some are [undertaken] to take something and conversely give it away;
some are [undertaken] to give something away and conversely accept it.

Earl Zhi demanded territory from Viscount Huan of Wei.[27] Viscount Huan did not want to yield it. Ren Deng[28] said, "Earl Zhi's strength is such that he spreads awe throughout the world. If he demands territory and you do not grant it, this will be accepting calamity before the Lords of the Land. It would be better to grant it." Viscount Huan said, "If he demands territory without end, what shall I do?" Ren Deng said, "Give it to him; make him pleased. He will certainly go on to demand territory from the Lords of the Land, and they will surely fall in line. When we join minds to make plans with the entire world, what we gain[29] will not merely be what we have lost." Viscount Huan of Wei detached territory and gave it to him. [Earl Zhi] then demanded territory from Viscount Kang of Hann. Viscount Kang of Hann did not dare fail to grant it. The Lords of the Land were all afraid. [Earl Zhi] further demanded territory from Viscount Xiang of Zhao;[30] Viscount Xiang refused to grant it. At this Earl Zhi allied with Hann and Wei and besieged Viscount Xiang at Jinyang. The three states[31] plotted together, seizing Earl Zhi and dividing his state into three.[32] This is what is called "taking it and conversely giving it away." [18/188/22–27]

What is called "giving it away and conversely taking it?" Duke Xian of Jin wanted to obtain free passage from [the state of] Yu in order to attack [the state of] Guo.[33] He sent Yu a steed of Qu and the jade disk of Chuiji. The Duke of Yu was beguiled by the disk and the horse and wanted to grant free passage. Gong Zhiqi admonished him, saying, "You cannot. Yu and Guo are like the cart and its wheels.[34] The wheels depend on the cart; the cart also depends on the wheels. Yu and Guo naturally depend on each other. If we give free passage, then Guo will perish in the morning and

26. This appears to allude to Gongsun Yang's ultimate fate of being torn apart by chariots.

27. Accepting Yu Dacheng's emendation. See Lau, HNZ, 188n.7.

28. The *Zhanguoce* gives this figure's name as Ren Zhang 任章.

29. Deleting the characters *yixin* 一心, as recommended by Yang Shuda. See Lau, HNZ, 188n.10.

30. Viscount Huan of Wei 魏桓子 (d. 446 B.C.E.), Viscount Kang of Hann 韓康子, and Viscount Xiang of Zhao 趙襄子 (d. 425 B.C.E.) were the leaders of great ministerial lineages of Jin. Each lineage ultimately founded an independent kingdom.

31. That is, Hann, Wei, and Zhao.

32. This anecdote appears in ZGC 264A/140/7–12 and HFZ 22/47/1–7.

33. This occurred in 658 B.C.E. See *Zuozhuan*, Xi 2; and Yang Bojun 楊伯峻, *Chunqiu Zuozhuan zhu* 春秋左轉注 (Beijing: Zhonghua shuju, 1990), 281–83. Duke Xian 獻 ruled Jin from 676 to 651 B.C.E. Yu 虞 and Guo 虢 were small states in what is present-day Shaanxi Province. See also 7.16, 10.47, 11.7, 17.57, and 20.21.

34. Reading the original 輪 instead of Lau's proposed emendation of 輔 (side rail).

Yu will follow that night." The Duke of Yu did not listen, thus giving [Jin] free passage. Xun Xi[35] attacked Guo and defeated it. On his return he attacked Yu and took it too.[36] This is what is known as "giving it and conversely taking it." [18/189/1–6]

> The sage king spreads his Potency and applies his compassion, never demanding recompense from the common people.
> The various sacrifices[37] are all performed, never requesting good fortune from the ghosts and spirits. [18/189/8]

18.6

> Mountains reach their heights and clouds and rain arise there;
> water reaches its depths and sea serpents and dragons are born there;
> the gentleman achieves his Way, and good and fortune and emolument come to him.

Thus,

> the Potency of yin will certainly meet the response of yang;
> he who conducts himself [nobly] in obscurity will certainly have a resplendent name.

In antiquity there were no canals and dikes; floods harmed the people. Yu dug out Longmen and walled in Yinque. Leveling and ordering the water and soil, he gave the people dry land to inhabit.

> The common people did not hold [one another] close;
> the five grades [of relatedness][38] were not respected.

Qi taught them the Rightness of ruler and minister, the closeness of father and son, the distinction between husband and wife, the order of elder and younger.

> The fields were left wild and not cultivated;
> the people did not have enough to eat.

Lord Millet thus taught them how to break the earth and clear the plants, fertilize the soil, and plant the grain, [thereby] giving each household among the common people sufficiency.

After the Three Dynasties there was no [ruler] who was not "king"; theirs was the Potency of yin. The Zhou house declined; Ritual and Rightness were abandoned. Confucius instructed and guided the age with the Way of the Three Eras. His descendants have continued his line down to the present day without break; he conducted

---

35. Xun Xi 荀息, a grandee of Jin, was commander of the assault against Guo.

36. This anecdote occurs in LSCQ 15.2/81/23–82/6 and HFZ 10/14/10–19.

37. Four sacrifices are listed: *jiao, wang, di*, and *chang* (郊, 望, 褅, 嘗). According to Xu Shen, the first is to Heaven; the second is to the spirits of the sun, moon, stars, planets, mountains, and rivers; and the third and fourth are ancestral sacrifices. See Zhang Shuangdi 1997, 2:1856n.2.

38. This presumably refers to the so-called five cardinal relationships of ruler to minister, father to son, husband to wife, older to younger brother, and friend to friend. Only four of these are subsequently mentioned, however. See Lau, HNZ, 189n.2.

himself nobly in obscurity. The king of Qin, Zhao Zheng,[39] annexed the world and perished. Earl Zhi conquered territory and was exterminated. Shang Yang was dismembered; Li Si[40] was torn apart by chariots.[41]

The Three Eras cultivated their Potency and became kings;
Duke Huan revived broken [lineages] and became hegemon.

Thus,

the one who plants glutinous millet will not harvest pannicled millet;
the one who plants resentment will not be repaid with Moral Potency. [18/189/10–18]

18.7

In olden times, among the people of Song there was [a family] whose [members] were very close. The three generations[42] did not separate. Without warning, the household's black cow gave birth to a white calf. They asked the grandfather[43] and he said, "This is a good omen. Offer it up to the ghosts and spirits." After one year, the father suddenly went blind, and the cow again gave birth to a white calf. The father again sent his son to consult the grandfather. His son said, "Before we listened to grandfather and you lost your sight. If we consult him again now, what will happen?" His father said, "According to the words of the sages, one must first scrutinize and then adopt. The affair is not yet clear; we must still try asking him once more." The son again went to consult the grandfather. The grandfather said, "This is a good omen. I again instruct you to offer it to the ghosts and spirits." [The son] returned to convey these orders to his father. The father said, "Carry out grandfather's instructions." In one year, the son also suddenly went blind. Afterward Chu attacked Song, besieging the city. At this time, people traded their children for food; they cut up corpses and cooked them. The able and strong were dead; the old, sick, and children all had to mount the city walls. They defended them without failing. The king of Chu was furious. When the walls were breached, all those defending them were slaughtered. It was only because the father and son were blind that they did not mount the walls. When the army retired and the siege was lifted, both the father and son [regained] their vision. [18/189/20–27]

As for the revolutions and the mutual generation of calamity and good fortune, their alterations are difficult to perceive.[44] At the near frontier, there was a [family

39. Zhao Zheng 趙政—that is, Qin Shihuangdi.

40. Li Si 李斯 (d. 208 B.C.E.) was the prime minister of Qin during the unification of the empire.

41. The symmetrical structure here is less clear than in other sections but nonetheless accords with the chapter as a whole. The example of Yu, Qi, and Lord Millet of high antiquity, whose activism produced meritorious results, is contrasted with that of Confucius, whose quietism during a later era of "yin Potency" was the correct path to a "resplendent name."

42. That is, grandfather, father, son.

43. Literally, "the first born," *xian sheng* 先生—that is, the oldest of the "three generations."

44. This line seems displaced from the beginning of the section, as it introduces the topic of both linked anecdotes.

of] skilled diviners whose horse suddenly became lost out among the Hu[45] [people]. Everyone consoled them. The father said, "This will quickly turn to good fortune!" After several months, the horse returned with a fine Hu steed. Everyone congratulated them. The father said, "This will quickly turn to calamity!" The household was [now] replete with good horses; the son loved to ride, [but] he fell and broke his leg. Everyone consoled them. The father said, "This will quickly turn to good fortune!" After one year, the Hu people entered the frontier in force; the able and strong all stretched their bowstrings and fought. Among the people of the near frontier, nine out of ten died. It was only because of lameness that father and son protected each other. Thus,

good fortune becoming calamity,
calamity becoming good fortune;
their transformations are limitless,
so profound they cannot be fathomed. [18/189/27–18/190/6]

18.8

Some are correct in word yet not comprehensive in action; some are faulty of ear and stubborn of mind yet accord with substance.

Gaoyang Tui was about to build a house, [so] he consulted a carpenter. The carpenter replied, "It cannot be done yet. The wood is still living. If plaster is applied to it, it will definitely warp. When green material is covered with heavy plaster it may [seem] completed now, [but] it will definitely collapse later." Gaoyang Tui said, "Not so. As the wood dries, it gets harder; as the plaster dries, it gets lighter. When hard material is covered with light plaster, even though it is bad now, it will certainly be better later." The carpenter was out of words, he had no reply. He accepted his orders and built the house. When it was completed, it was apparently fine, but afterward it indeed collapsed.[46] This is what is known as "correct in word yet not comprehensive in action."

What is called faulty of ear [and] stubborn of mind yet according with substance? Lord Jingguo was about to fortify Xue.[47] Most of his guest clients tried to stop him; he did not listen to them. He told his heralds, "Send no word from my guest clients." A man of Qi requested an audience, saying, "I will speak only three words. If I surpass three words, please cook me [alive]." Lord Jingguo heard this and granted him an audience. The guest rushed forward, bowed twice, and rising, said, "Great sea fish," then retreated. Lord Jingguo stopped him, staying, "I want to hear your persuasion." The guest said, "I do not dare die for sport." Lord Jingguo said, "You, honored sir,

45. Mounted nomads of the northern steppes.

46. This anecdote appears in LSCQ 25.2/161/22–26 and HFZ 32/83/7–9. According to Xu Shen, Gaoyang Tui was a grandee of Song. See Zhang Shuangdi 1997, 2:1863n.3.

47. Lord Jingguo 靖郭君 (also known as Tian Ying 田嬰) was a scion of the Tian clan who became prime minister of Qi in 311 B.C.E. His son attained fame as Lord Mengchang. His fief of Xue 薛 is located in present-day Shandong Province.

have paid no heed to distance in coming here, I want you to explain it to me." The guest said, "The great sea fish: nets cannot stop it, hooks cannot catch it. [But] if it beaches and is out of the water, then crickets and ants will have their way with it. Now Qi is your sea. If you lose Qi, do you think that Xue can survive alone?" Lord Jingguo said, "Excellent" and thereby halted the fortification of Xue.[48] This is what is called "being faulty of ear and stubborn of mind, yet attaining the substance in action." [18/190/8–19]

Now using "do not fortify Xue" as a persuasion to halt the fortification of Xue was not as good as "great sea fish."

Thus things
  sometimes are distant yet near to it,
  sometimes are near yet far off the mark. [18/190/21–22]

18.9

Some [persons'] persuasions are heeded and assessments are correct, yet they become estranged [from the ruler].

Some [persons'] words are not used and assessments are not effected, yet they draw closer. How do we illustrate this?

Three states attacked Qi,[49] besieging Pinglu. Kuozi reported to Niuzi, saying, "The territory of the three states does not abut ours; they crossed neighboring states to besiege Pinglu. The profit in this is not worth coveting; thus they must have come to make a reputation from us. I request that we give them the marquis of Qi." Niuzi thought this was correct. Kuozi left, and Wuhaizi entered.[50] Niuzi related Kuozi's words to Wuhaizi. Wuhaizi said, "This is different from what I heard." Niuzi said, "The state is imperiled and cannot be secured; calamity ensnares us and cannot be escaped. What wisdom do you have to offer?" Wuhaizi said, "I have heard of ceding land to secure the altars of the soil and grain; I have heard of killing one's person and destroying one's household to preserve the state; I have never heard of giving away one's ruler for the sake of one's fief." Niuzi did not listen to Wuhaizi's words and carried out Kuozi's plan. The armies of the three states retired, and the territory of Pinglu was preserved. From this time on, Kuozi was daily more estranged [from his lord], [but] Wuhaizi daily advanced [in rank]. Thus in strategizing for and resolving calamity, in planning for and preserving the state, Kuozi's wisdom was effective. Wuhaizi's thoughts did not lead to [the proper] plan; his strategies were of no benefit to the state, yet his mind harmonized with that of the ruler; he had the right conduct. [18/190/22–18/191/4]

48. This anecdote also appears in HFZ 23/55/4–9 and ZGC 99/49/10–15.

49. It is unclear to which historical event the text is alluding, if any. See Zhang Shuangdi 1997, 2:1865n.1.

50. According to Xu Shen, Niuzi 牛子, Kuozi 括子, and Wuhaizi 無害子 all were ministers of Qi.

Now people
 await a hat to adorn their head.
 await shoes to tread the ground.
Caps and shoes
 do not keep people warm when it is cold,
 do not shelter [them] from the wind,
 do not shade [them] from the heat.
Nonetheless [people] wear caps and shoes because they have come to expect them. [18/191/6–7]

18.10

Jiu Fan conquered Chengpu, and [in the battle] Yong Ji did not earn an ounce of merit.[51] Yet Yong Ji was the first to be rewarded, and Jiu Fan was considered afterward. This was because [Yong Ji]'s words were more noble. Thus Rightness is what the world considers noble.[52] To speak correctly one hundred times in one hundred utterances is not as good as choosing one's direction and being careful of one's conduct.

Some are without merit and are promoted first;
some have merit and are rewarded last.

How do we illustrate this? In antiquity when Duke Wen of Jin was about to do battle with Chu at Chengpu, he consulted Jiu Fan, saying, "What should we do?" Jiu Fan said, "In matters of Humaneness and Rightness, one can never be loyal and trustworthy enough. In matters of the battle array, one can never be deceiving or artful enough. You should deceive them, that is all." Duke Wen excused Jiu Fan and asked Yong Ji. Yong Ji replied, "If in hunting, you burned the woods, you would get more animals [that way], but afterward there would surely be no more animals [left]. If you engage others with deception and artifice, although you will increase your profit, afterward there will be no further [profit]. You should rectify them, that is all." But [Duke Wen] did not listen to Yong Ji's plan, and using Jiu Fan's strategy he did battle with Chu, soundly defeating them. Upon returning home, when rewarding those who earned merit, Yong Ji was placed before Jiu Fan. Everyone said, "The battle at Chengpu [was conducted according to] Jiu Fan's strategy; why did Your Majesty reward Yong Ji ahead [of others]?" Duke Wen said, "Jiu Fan's words were the expediency of a single moment; Yong Ji's words were the benefit of myriad generations. How could I place the expediency of the moment before the benefit of myriad generations!"[53] [18/191/9–18]

---

51. This battle took place in 632 B.C.E. See *Zuozhuan*, Xi 28. Jiu Fan 咎犯 (d. 622 B.C.E.) was a minister and Yong Ji 雍季 was a ducal scion of Jin, respectively. Chengpu 城濮 was a city located in present-day Shandong Province.

52. This passage seems to be out of place, as the preamble to this section seems to begin in the following line. These lines should be at the conclusion of the section. See Zhang Shuangdi 1997, 2:1867–68n.9.

53. This anecdote appears in LSCQ 14.4/73/26–14.4/74/2 and HFZ 36/113/9–16.

Earl Zhi led the two states of Hann and Wei to attack Zhao. They besieged Jinyang, releasing the Jin River to flood it. Inside the city, people climbed trees to survive, suspended pots to cook. Viscount Xiang said to Zhang Mengtan,[54] "The strength of [those] within the city is already exhausted, provisions are low, and most of the military officers are sick. What should we do?" Zhang Mengtan said, "What is lost cannot be preserved; what is imperiled cannot be secured. I have no valuable wisdom [to offer]. I request to attempt to go [out] in secret to treat with the lords of Hann and Wei." He then saw the lords of Hann and Wei and persuaded them, saying, "I have heard, 'If the lips are lost, the teeth become cold.' Now Earl Zhi leads you two lords in attacking Zhao, and Zhao will be lost. Once Zhao is lost, you two lords will be next. If you do not plan for it now, calamity will overtake you two lords." The two lords said, "Earl Zhi is a man who suspects those close to him and has few intimates. If our plan leaks out, the action will certainly fail. What is there to do?" Zhang Mengtan said, "The words have left your two lordships' mouths and entered my ears, who will know of them? Moreover, those of common feeling succeed together; those with the same interests die together. Think about it!" The two lords then plotted with Zhang Mengtan and set a time with him. Zhang Mengtan reported back to Viscount Xiang, and on the evening of the appointed day the soldiers of the Zhao clan killed the officers guarding the dike, releasing the river to flood the army of Earl Zhi. While Earl Zhi's army was thrown into chaos fighting the flood; Hann and Wei attacked them on the flanks, Viscount Xiang led his troops in a frontal assault. Earl Zhi's army was greatly defeated; he was killed and his state was divided into three parts.[55]

When Viscount Xiang was rewarding those who had earned merit in lifting the siege, Gao He[56] was the first to be given a reward. The assembled ministers all asked, "The survival of Jinyang was thanks to Zhang Mengtan's merit; why has [Gao] He been rewarded first?" Viscount Xiang said, "During the siege of Jinyang, my state and household were imperiled, [and] my altars of soil and grain were threatened. None among the various ministers was without an arrogant and offensive mind-set. Only He did not abandon the propriety appropriate between ruler and minister. This is why I placed him first."[57] Viewed from this [perspective], Rightness is people's great foundation. Although one might have the merit of victory in battle or preserving [the state] from extinction, this does not equal the splendor of practicing Rightness.

Thus the *Laozi* says:

> "Beautiful words can buy one prestige;
> beautiful deeds can advance one above others."[58] [18/191/20–18/192/6]

---

54. Zhang Mengtan 張孟談 was a vassal of Viscount Xiang of Zhao.

55. This anecdote appears, in a much extended version, in HFZ 10/15/10–10/17/2 and ZGC 203/103/24–203/105/6.

56. Gao He 高赫 was another vassal of Viscount Xiang of Zhao.

57. This anecdote appears in HFZ 36/115/9–12 and LSCQ 14.4/74/9–13. It also occurs in 13.18. The *Hanfeizi* 36 version is translated in the introduction to chap. 19.

58. *Laozi* 62. The transmitted text of the *Laozi* and the two versions discovered at Mawangdui all are missing the second *mei* 美 (beautiful).

18.11

Some are incriminated yet may be rewarded;
some have merit yet may be incriminated.
[When] Ximen Bao administered Ye,[59]
no millet was gathered in the granaries;
no money was collected in the storehouses;
no armor or weapons were [stored] in the armory;
there were no planning meetings among the officials.

People spoke several times to Marquis Wen [of Wei] about [Ximen Bao]'s oversights. Marquis Wen went personally to the district, and indeed it was as people said. Marquis Wen said, "Di Huang[60] appointed you to bring order to Ye, and it is greatly disordered. If you can lead, then do so. If you cannot, I will punish you." Ximen Bao said, "I have heard that

'a kingly ruler enriches the people;
a hegemonic ruler enriches the military;
a lost state enriches the storehouses.'

Now because you want to be hegemon or king, I have accumulated materials among the people. If you do not believe it is so, please let me mount the wall and beat the drum. Armor, weapons, millet, and grain can be immediately produced." At this he mounted the wall and beat the drum. At the first drum roll, the people donned armor, grabbed arrows, and came out carrying weapons and bows. At the second drum roll, [the people] came pushing handcarts loaded with millet. Marquis Wen said, "Stand them down." Ximen Bao said, "Entering this bond of trust with the people has not been the work of a single day. If [now] you muster them falsely [even] once, you will not be able to use them again. Yan has occupied eight of Wei's cities.[61] I ask permission to strike north and reclaim our occupied territory." Thus he raised troops and attacked Yan, returning after reclaiming the territory. This is [an example of] "being incriminated yet worthy of reward."

Xie Bian[62] was administering the eastern fief and turned in three times what his superiors had assessed [as his revenue]. The court officers asked that he be rewarded. Marquis Wen said, "My territory has gotten no bigger; my people have not grown more numerous. How has he tripled revenue?" They replied, "In winter he cuts wood and collects it; in spring he floats it downriver to be sold." Marquis Wen said, "The people use their effort in the spring to plow; they use their strength in the summer to plant; in the autumn they harvest. To make them also cut and store wood [and] carry and ship logs during the winter [when] they have no tasks is to refuse the people

59. Ximen Bao 西門豹 was a knight in the service of Marquis Wen of Wei. Ye 鄴 is in present-day Hebei Province.

60. Di Huang 翟璜 was one of Marquis Wen of Wei's court ministers.

61. Following Lau, HNZ, 192n.4.

62. Xie Bian 解扁 was a magistrate of Wei.

rest. If the people are exhausted, what use will even triple revenue be to me?" This is "to have merit and yet be [worthy] of incrimination." [18/192/8–20]

18.12

A worthy ruler does not attain [anything] ignobly;
a loyal minister does not profit ignobly.

How do we illustrate this?

Earl Mu of Zhonghang assaulted Gu but could not capture it.[63] Kui Wenlun[64] said, "I know the sheriff of Gu. I ask that you not withdraw the military officers; if so, Gu can be taken." Earl Mu did not agree. His subordinates said, "If Gu can be taken without breaking a single halberd or having a single soldier wounded, why will you not send him?" Earl Mu said, "Wenlun is a devious and inhumane sort of person. If I send Wenlun to capture [Gu], can I fail to reward him? If I reward him, this would be rewarding a devious person. If a devious person achieves his ambition, this would cause the warriors of the state of Jin to abandon Humaneness and take up deviousness. Even if I took Gu, what use would it be!" [Earl Mu] assaulted the city out of a desire to expand his territory. He did not take the territory when [he could] acquire it because he looked at the roots and knew the branches. [18/192/22–27]

Duke Mu of Qin sent Meng Meng[65] to raise troops and launch a surprise attack on Zheng.[66] As he passed Zhou while moving east, two merchants of Zheng, Xian Gao and Jian Tuo,[67] plotted together, saying, "The army has traveled several thousand *li*, avoiding the territory of several Lords of the Land. It must be heading to attack Zheng. Whoever launches a surprise attack against a state assumes that [the target] is unprepared. If now we create the appearance that [Zheng] knows their dispositions, they will not dare advance." Then, falsifying orders from the earl of Zheng, they made a gift [to the Qin army] of twelve head of cattle. The three commanders [of the Qin army] conferred together, saying, "When one launches a surprise attack, [the target] must not be aware. Now that they already know about it, their defenses will certainly be strengthened. If we carry on, we definitely will not succeed." Thus they turned the army and headed back. Xian Zhen of Jin raised troops and attacked them, defeating them badly at Yao.[68]

The earl of Zheng thus offered a reward to Xian Gao for meritorious service in having preserved the state. Xian Gao declined it, saying, "If I were to receive a reward after having lied, this would destroy the credibility of the state of Zheng. To rule a

---

63. Earl Mu of Zhonghang 中行穆伯 led the forces of Jin against Gu 鼓 in 527 B.C.E. See *Zuozhuan*, Zhao 15. Gu was a small state in present-day Hebei Province.

64. Kui Wenlun 餽聞倫 was a grandee of Jin.

65. Meng Meng 孟盟, a grandee of Qin, according to Xu Shen, was the son of the prime minister Baili Xi.

66. This attack occurred in 627 B.C.E. See *Zuozhuan*, Xi 33.

67. Xian Gao 弦高 and Jian Tuo 蹇他 were merchants of Zheng.

68. Xian Zhen 先軫 (d. 627 B.C.E.) was a noble of Jin. Yao 殽 is a mountain in present-day Henan Province.

state without credibility would ruin its customs. To ruin the customs of the state by rewarding one person is not something a humane person would do. To attain rich rewards from being untrustworthy is not something a righteous person would do." Then he took his dependents and moved out among the Eastern Yi, never returning to the end of his life.[69]

Thus,

a humane person does not harm life for the sake of desire;
a wise person does not harm Rightness for the sake of profit.
The sage thinks of the long term;
the fool thinks of the short term. [18/192/29–18/193/8]

18.13

A loyal minister works at exalting his ruler's Potency;
a sycophantic minister works at expanding his ruler's territory.

How do we illustrate this?

Xia Zhengshu[70] of Chen murdered his ruler.[71] King Zhuang of Chu attacked him; the people of Chen complied with [Chu's] orders. When King Zhuang had already punished the criminal, he sent troops to garrison Chen. All the nobles congratulated him. At the time Shenshu Shi[72] was on an embassy to Qi; when he returned, he did not congratulate [the king]. King Zhuang said, "Chen was without the Way. I raised the Nine Armies to punish them. I marched against a cruel rebel and punished a criminal; all the nobles congratulated me. You alone have not, why?" Shenshu Shi said, "[Suppose] a man leads an ox into someone else's field. The owner of the field kills the man and takes the ox. A crime had indeed been committed, but the punishment was even worse. Now you feel that Chen is without the Way; you take up arms and rectify them. You punish the criminal and send troops to garrison Chen. When the Lords of the Land hear about it, they will not think that you did it to punish a criminal; [they will assume] that you coveted the state of Chen. I have heard that 'the gentleman does not abandon Rightness to obtain profit.'" The king said, "Excellent!" He thus withdrew the garrison from Chen and established descendants of [the ruling house of] Chen [to rule once more]. When the Lords of the Land heard of it, they all paid court to Chu. This is [an example of] one who exalts his ruler's Potency.

Zhang Wu[73] plotted for Earl Zhi, saying, "Of Jin's six commanders, Viscount Wen

69. An alternative version of this anecdote appears in LSCQ 16.4/93/20–16.4/94/11. Another version appears in 12.40 and a brief version in 13.11.

70. Xia Zhengshu 夏徵舒 was a grandee of Chen.

71. This event occurred in 598 B.C.E. See *Zuozhuan*, Xuan 11.

72. Shenshu Shi 申叔時 was a minister of King Zhuang of Chu. This anecdote is mentioned in 18.2.

73. Zhang Wu 張武 was a vassal of Earl Zhi. He is mentioned in LSCQ 2.4/10/2 and 22.6/148/25 as having encouraged the earl in his belligerent course. This anecdote is mentioned in 18.2.

of Zhonghang[74] is the weakest. He is estranged from his subordinates, [so] we may attack him to expand our territory." At this they attacked Fan and Zhonghang. When these had been exterminated, [Zhang Wu] also instructed Earl Zhi to demand territory from Hann, Wei, and Zhao. Hann and Wei detached territory and ceded it, [but] the Zhao clan would not do so. Then [Earl Zhi] led Hann and Wei in attacking Zhao. They besieged Jinyang for three years. The three states plotted together and agreed on a plan to attack the Zhi clan, thus exterminating it.[75] This is [an example of] one who expands his ruler's territory.

He who exalted his ruler's Potency [made him] hegemon;
he who expanded his ruler's territory [caused him to be] exterminated.

Thus,

the states of one thousand chariots that became king through the exercise of civil Potency were those of Tang and Wu;
The state of ten thousand chariots lost through expanding its territory was that of Earl Zhi. [18/193/10–21]

18.14

Do not undertake affairs that are not your own;
do not assume a reputation that is not yours.
Do not abide in riches and honor if you are without merit.
One who assumes another's reputation will be cast aside;
one who undertakes another's affair will fail.

One who enjoys great profit without merit will ultimately come to harm.

Compare it to climbing a tall tree and gazing at the four directions. Although one may feel delighted and happy, if a strong wind were to come up, no one would fail to be afraid. If you worry about calamity only after it has reached your person, a team of six fast horses cannot [help you] catch up to it. For this reason, in serving his ruler a loyal minister

accepts reward only after calculating his merit; he obtains nothing profligately;
accepts office only after measuring his strength; he does not covet rank and emolument.
What he is able to do, he accepts without demur.
What he is incapable of, he declines without pleasure.
To decline what one is capable of is to dissemble;
to desire what one is incapable of is to deceive.

If he declines what he cannot do and accepts what he can, he will acquire an unflagging force and have no tasks at which he is unsuccessful. [18/193/23–28]

In ancient times, Earl Zhi was arrogant; having attacked and conquered Fan and

74. Viscount Wen of Zhonghang 中行文子 was the leader of one of the "six ministerial clans" that for a time controlled the state of Jin.

75. Earl Zhi died in 453 B.C.E. See ZGC 203/105/8–14.

Zhonghang, he further extorted territory from Hann and Wei. Still, he felt he did not have enough, so he took up arms to attack Zhao. Hann and Wei turned on him; his army was defeated before Jinyang. He was killed east of Gaoliang; his head was made into a drinking vessel. His state was divided into three parts; he was laughed at by the world. This is the calamity of not knowing contentment.

The *Laozi* says:

"Know contentment and you will [suffer] no disgrace;
know when to stop and you will not expire,
[thus] may you endure a long time."[76]

This says it. [18/194/1–3]

18.15

Some praise others yet ultimately bring them to defeat;
some slander others yet conversely bring them success.

How do we know this is so?

Fei Wuji told King Ping of Jing,[77] "Jin became hegemon by becoming close to all the Xia[78] [states]. Jing cannot compete with them because we are so remote. If you want to gather the Lords of the Land into an alliance, nothing would serve as well as greatly fortifying Chengfu and ordering Crown Prince Jian to garrison it, so as to receive [the tribute] of the north. You would personally collect [the tribute] of the south." The king of Chu liked this [idea]. He then ordered the crown prince to garrison Chengfu and commissioned Wu Zishe to assist him.[79] After one year Wu Zishe traveled to the royal residence. He said that the crown prince was extremely humane and courageous; he had been able to win the hearts of the people. The king told this to Fei Wuji. Wuji said, "I have consistently heard that the crown prince is cultivating the common people internally and treating with the Lords of the Land externally. Qi and Jin are also assisting him; they are about to injure Chu. The action is already prepared." The king said, "He is already my crown prince; what more does he demand?" [Fei Wuji] said, "He resents you for the affair of the Qin woman."[80] The king thus killed Crown Prince Jian and executed Wu Zishe.[81] This is what is called "being praised yet experiencing calamity." [18/194/5–11]

What is called "slandering someone, yet conversely benefiting him?"

---

76. *Laozi* 44.

77. These events took place in 523 and 522 B.C.E. See *Zuozhuan*, Zhao 19, 20. Fei Wuji 費無忌 (d. 515 B.C.E.) was the junior mentor of Crown Prince Jian 建 of Jing (Chu), with whom he had a falling out. King Ping 平 ruled from 529 to 516 B.C.E.

78. That is, all the civilized or culturally "Chinese" states.

79. Wu Zishe 伍子奢 was the grand mentor of Crown Prince Jian. Chengfu 城父 was a city in present-day Anhui Province.

80. The king had taken away one of his son's wives, a particularly beautiful woman from Qin. See LSCQ 22.1/144/1–2.

81. This anecdote occurs in altered form in LSCQ 22.1/144/1–5.

Tangzi denigrated Chen Pianzi to King Wei of Qi.[82] King Wei wanted to kill him; Chen Pianzi fled to Xue with his dependents. Lord Mengchang heard of this and sent men with a carriage to receive him. After he arrived [in Xue], five-flavored meals of grass- and grain- [fed meats], millet, and sorghum were sent to him three times daily. In winter he was clothed in fur and down; in summer he donned ramie and linen. When he traveled, he rode in a heavy carriage drawn by fine horses. Lord Mengchang asked him, "You, master, were born in Qi and grew up in Qi, is there anything about Qi that you think of?" He replied, "I think about Tangzi." Lord Mengchang said, "Is not Tangzi the one who slandered you?" [Chen Pianzi] said, "He is." Lord Mengchang said, "Why do you think about him?" He replied, "When I lived in Qi, I ate coarse grain for my staple; pigweed and bean sprouts for my main course. On winter days I froze; on summer days I sweltered. Since Tangzi slandered me, and I came to you, I dine on grass- and grain- [fed animals]; I eat millet and sorghum for my staple; I wear light and warm clothes; I ride in a heavy carriage. This is why I think of him." This is called "slandering someone yet conversely benefiting them." For this reason, one cannot be too careful of slander and praise. [18/194/13–20]

18.16

Some covet life yet conversely die;
some scorn death yet manage to live;
some go slowly yet conversely hurry.

How do we know this is so?

Among the people of Lu, there was a man who avenged his father in Qi. Having split open his [enemy's] abdomen and exposed his heart, he sat and straightened his cap, rose, and readjusted his robe. Walking slowly out the door, he mounted his carriage and walked the horses; his countenance did not alter. His driver wanted to gallop; he grabbed [his driver] and stopped him, saying, "Today I set out to avenge my father intent on death. Now the deed is already done, what reason is there to leave?" Those pursuing him said, "This is a man of discipline; we cannot kill him." They opened their cordon and let him go. If he had not taken the time to belt his robe or adjust his cap; if he had crawled out, mounted his carriage, and sped off; he would not have survived to go ten paces.

Now,

sitting and straightening his cap,
rising and readjusting his robe,
walking slowly out the door,
mounting his carriage, and walking the horses,

---

82. Xu Shen identifies Tangzi 唐子 as a grandee of Qi. Chen Pianzi 陳駢子 may be the Jixia scholar identified in other texts as Tian 田 Pian. See Zhang Shuangdi 1997, 2:1887n.7. King Wei 威 of Qi reigned from 356 to 320 B.C.E.

his countenance never altering is what the mass of people would think leads to death. Yet, in fact, it conversely gained him life. This is what is known as "running[83] at the gallop is slower than walking."

Running is what people deem fast;
walking is what people deem slow.

In this case, [he] conversely used what people deem slow to go fast; [he] was clear as to the distinction. One who understands the speed of slowness and the slowness of speed is near the Way.

When the Yellow Emperor lost his Dark Pearl, he sent Grieving for Pearl and Grabbing-Grasping to search for it. Yet they could not get it; so he sent Forget Sorrow and only then got it back.[84] [18/194/22–18/195/3]

18.17

The sage respects the small and is cautious of the subtle; in action he does not lose a moment. He [makes] one hundred preparations and [takes] double precautions, thus calamity never arises. When planning for good fortune, he underestimates; when contemplating calamity, he overestimates.

If frost descends [on both] in the same day,
those who take shelter will suffer no harm.
If the fool has prepared,
his merit will be the same as that of the wise.

When the flame is still sputtering, one finger can extinguish it. When the leak in the dike is the size of a mouse hole, it can be plugged by a clump of earth.

Once the fire has ignited Mengzhu and set Yunmeng ablaze;
once the water has breached the Nine Rivers and flooded Jingzhou;[85]

even if one raised the multitudes of the Three Armies, one could not save [the situation]. [18/195/5–10]

Accumulated love creates good fortune;
accumulated resentment creates calamity.

Once the carbuncle bursts, the pus will be copious.

Zhuyu Yang[86] told Duke Jian [of Qi],[87] "Chen Chengchang and Zai Yu[88] hate

83. Following Lau, HNZ, 194n.7.

84. This anecdote appears in a different form in ZZ 12/30/9–11. Li Zhu 離朱 or 離珠 (here, "Grieving for Pearl") appears in 1.6, and Jue Duo 攫掇 (here, "Grabbing-Grasping") in 19.5.

85. Both Mengzhu 孟諸 and Yunmeng 雲夢 are marshes in present-day Henan and Hubei provinces, respectively; the Nine Rivers are tributaries of the Yangtze; and Jingzhou 荊州 is a region encompassing central and southern Hubei, northern and central Hunan, and parts of Sichuan.

86. Yang Bojun suspects that this figure's surname is Chen 陳 and that *zhuyu* is an official title meaning something like "ordinary charioteer" (*Chunqiu Zuozhuan zhu*, 1683).

87. These events occurred in 481 B.C.E. See *Zuozhuan*, Ai 14. Duke Jian 簡 reigned from 484 to 481 B.C.E.

88. The names of these two figures are somewhat garbled. Chen Chengchang 陳成常 is more

each other intensely. I fear this will develop into a problem that will endanger the state. You had best dismiss one of them." Duke Jian did not listen. Not long afterward, Chen Chengchang indeed attacked Zai Yu in the palace hall and murdered Duke Jian at court.[89] This is [an example of] not knowing to respect the small origins [of affairs].

The Ji clan and Hou clan had a cockfight.[90] The Hou clan armored its cock, [and] the Ji clan gave its cock metal spurs. The Ji clan cock did not win. Ji Pingzi[91] was angry, so he invaded the palace of the Hou clan and attacked them. Earl Zhao of Hou was angered, and he denounced him to Duke Zhao of Lu,[92] saying, "When the *di* sacrifice is performed to Duke Xiang in the ancestral temple, there are only two [rows of] dancers; all the rest of them dance for the Ji clan. The Ji clan's being without the Way and [recognizing] no authority has gone on for a long time. If you do not punish them, they will endanger the altars of the soil and grain." The duke was enraged and spoke of this to Zijia Ju.[93] Zijia Ju said, "The Ji clan has gained the masses; they are the first of the Three Families.[94] Their Potency is great, their might is strong, what can Your Majesty do?" Duke Zhao did not listen to him and sent Earl Zhao of Hou to lead soldiers in an assault on [the Ji clan]. The Zhongsun clan and the Shusun clan plotted together, saying, "Without the Ji clan, our death will not be long off." Then they raised troops to save [the Ji clan]. Earl Zhao of Hou died defeated; Duke Zhao of Lu fled to Qi.[95] Thus the birth of a calamity can begin with a rooster's foot and, at its greatest extent, end with the loss of the altars of the soil and grain. [18/195/12–24]

When the woman of Cai rocked the boat,
the army of Qi invaded Chu.[96]
Two men formed a grudge,
and Zai Yu was killed in the palace hall.
Duke Jian met with death,
perishing without issue.
When the Chen clan replaced them,

frequently recorded as Tian Chang 田常. He was a grandee of Qi and the leader of the powerful Tian clan. He initially shared the prime ministership of Qi with Jian Zhi 監止, whom he killed in the incident described in this anecdote. Zai Yu 宰予 (522–458 B.C.E.) was a disciple of Confucius. It is possible that Jian Zhi and Zai Yu were the same figure. See Zhang Shuangdi 1997, 2:1893–94n.7.

89. This anecdote occurs in LSCQ 17.6/106/19–23.

90. These events took place in 517 B.C.E. See *Zuozhuan*, Zhao 25. The Ji 季 and Hou 郈 clans were grandee families of the state of Lu.

91. Ji Pingzi 季平子 (d. 505 B.C.E.) was head of the Ji, or Jisun 季孫, clan.

92. Earl Zhao of Hou 郈昭伯 was head of the Hou clan. Duke Zhao of Lu 魯昭公 reigned from 541 to 510 B.C.E.

93. Zijia Ju 子家駒 was a grandee of Lu and kinsman of the ducal house.

94. That is, the Jisun, Mengsun 孟孫, and Shusun 叔孫 clans, three branch lineages of the ducal house of Lu that had consolidated great power in the sixth century B.C.E.

95. This anecdote appears in LSCQ 16.6/96/18–26.

96. The "woman of Cai" 蔡女 married Duke Huan of Qi. One day while boating with her husband, she rocked the boat and frightened him, for which he divorced her. This began a chain of events that ultimately led to a war between Qi and Chu. See HFZ 32/84/14–19.

Qi was without the Lü [house].[97]
Two houses fought cocks;
the Ji clan [used] metal spurs.
The Hou clan created trouble;
[Duke] Zhao of Lu fled.

Thus, "where the army camps; thorns and brambles will grow."[98] Once it is born, calamity is not soon eradicated; it is like fire reaching an [arid] place [or] flood reaching a wetland. Soak it and it grows greater. A carbuncle breaks out on a finger, but its pain spreads to the entire body. Thus,

moths and ants can fell pillars and bridges;[99]
mosquitoes and gadflies can stampede cattle and sheep.

This says it all. [18/195/26–29]

18.18

All people diligently make preparations in case of disaster, yet none is able to understand how to prevent a disaster from occurring. Preventing a disaster is easier than preparing for a disaster, yet none apply themselves to this task, so there is not yet anyone with whom to discuss this art.

The ducal scion of Jin, Chong'er,[100] was crossing Cao. The ruler of Cao wanted to see his joined ribs,[101] and so he ordered him to fish naked. Xi Fuji[102] stopped him, saying, "The ducal scion is not an ordinary person. The three men who are following him all [could] be aides of a hegemon or king. If you treat him without propriety, it will certainly bring distress to the state." The ruler did not listen. When Chong'er returned to his state, he raised an army and assaulted Cao, thus exterminating it. [The ruler of Cao's] death at another's hand, the ruination of his altars of the soil and grain: all these calamities originated in [forcing Chong'er] to fish naked. Qi and Chu wanted to save Cao; they could not preserve it.[103] If Xi Fuji's words had been listened to, the disaster of extinction would not have occurred. [18/196/1–6]

Now if you do not apply yourself to preventing disasters from occurring [but] attempt to deal with them once they have occurred, even if you had the wisdom of a sage, you could not plan for it. Moreover, the sources of disaster and calamity have a myriad starting points and no [sure] direction. This is why the sage abides remotely and avoids disgrace, [remaining] quiescent and tranquil and awaiting the moment.

Petty people do not understand the portals of calamity and good fortune. They

97. The Lü 呂 clan was the original ducal house chartered at Qi by the Zhou kings. They were usurped by their vassals, the Chen (or Tian) clan, in 386 B.C.E.

98. *Laozi* 30.

99. Following Liu Taigong's 劉台拱 alternative reading. See Lau, HNZ, 195n.3.

100. Chong'er 重耳, later Duke Wen of Jin. See 12.22 and 20.37.

101. A physical anomaly for which Chong'er was known.

102. Xi Fuji was a minister and fief holder of Cao. See 11.6 and 12.22.

103. A somewhat different version of this anecdote occurs in *Zuozhuan*, Xi 23.

move erratically, impeded by nets and snares. Although they make detailed precautions, how will this suffice to preserve their persons? It is comparable to digging a pond after [one's house] is lost to fire [or] using a fan after one has donned a coat. Moreover,

if the walls of [the pond] have ten thousand holes,
and you plug one, will the fish not quickly find an escape?
If the house has one hundred doors,
and you lock one, will the thief not quickly find an entrance?
The collapse of the wall [begins] with a crack;
if the sword breaks, there was definitely a nick.

The sage sees them early, thus none of the myriad things can do him harm.

Great Steward Zizhu served food to Prime Minister Ziguo.[104] Prime Minister Ziguo tried the stew and it was hot, so he grabbed a goblet of grain water[105] and poured it into [the stew]. The next day, Great Steward Zizhu resigned his post and went home. His driver said, "The grand stewardship of Chu is not easily attained, [so] why did you resign your post and give it up?" Zizhu said, "The prime minister is careless in conduct and neglects propriety; it will not be difficult for him to disgrace others." The next year [the prime minister] threw down the director of court gentlemen and flogged him three hundred [strokes]. A superior official first avoids calamity and only afterward pursues benefit, first distances himself from disgrace and only afterward seeks reputation. Great Steward Zizhu's perception of ends and beginnings was subtle! [18/196/6–16]

Before the goose or the swan has hatched from the egg, if you poke[106] it with one finger, it will disintegrate and become shapeless. Once its sinews and bones are already formed and its feathers and wings have matured, then

it flaps its wings and flies up,
leaping to the floating clouds.
Its back carries the blue sky;
its breast scrapes the red mists.
It soars above the atmosphere;
it roams among the rainbows.

Even if one had a strong bow, sharp arrows, a fine tether cord, and the skill of Bo Juzi,[107] one still could not reach it. Where the waters of the Yangzi first emerge from Mount Min, one can hitch up one's robe and jump across it. Coming to where it passes Dongting, rushes through Shicheng, and crosses Dantu,[108] it throws up waves

104. According to Xu Shen, both Zizhu 子朱 and Ziguo 子國 were grandees of Chu. They are unrecorded elsewhere. See Zhang Shuangdi 1997, 2:1902n.12.

105. This character seems to indicate drinking water thickened with millet or barley.

106. Following Lau's (HNZ, 196n.2) proposed emendation.

107. Bo Juzi 蒲且子 appears in 6.1, where he is said to have been able to bag a bird at a height of a hundred *ren*. Gao You's commentary identifies him as a skilled bird hunter of Chu. See Zhang Shuangdi 1997, 1:642n.22. The "tether cord" mentioned in this passage refers to a thin line connecting the arrow to the bow so that a bird shot on the wing cannot get away.

108. Mount Min 岷 is in present-day Sichuan Province; Dongting 洞庭 is a lake in present-day

and billows. In a boat, one can not cross it in a single day. For this reason, the sages often pursue affairs beyond the Formless and do not rest their thoughts or exhaust their reflections on actual events. Thus disaster and calamity cannot harm them. [18/196/18–23]

18.19

Someone asked of Confucius, "What type of person is Yan Hui?"

[He] replied, "A humane person. I do not equal him."

"What type of person is Zigong?"

[He] said, "An eloquent person. I do not equal him."

"What type of person is Zilu?"

[He] said, "A brave person. I do not equal him."

The guest said, "These three people are all more worthy than you, yet you lead them, why?" Confucius said, "I can be humane or stern, eloquent or inarticulate, brave or timorous. If I could trade my three students' abilities for my one Way, I would not do it." Confucius knew how to apply [these qualities]. [18/196/25–28]

Niu Que of Qin[109] was passing through the mountains and encountered bandits. They stole his carriage and horses, took his sacks and boxes, and stripped him of his robe and coat. When the bandits looked back at him, he did not have a frightened countenance or a distressed disposition; he was cheerful as if content. The bandits thus asked him, "We having taken your possessions and your goods, robbed you at knifepoint, yet you are not upset, why?" Niu Que of Qin said, "Carriages and horses are what carry my person; robes and coats are what cover my physical frame. The sage does not harm what he nurtures for the sake of that with which he nurtures it." The bandits looked at one another and laughed, saying, "If he will not harm his life on account of desire or encumber his physical frame for the sake of profit, he is a sage of this generation. If someone like this was ever to meet the king, he would certainly make us his business." [Thus] they went back and killed him.[110]

This [shows] that one can be wise to the wise, but one cannot be wise to the unwise. One can be brave to the courageous, but one cannot be brave to the cowardly. All those who have the Way respond to all [situations] yet are never lacking. They encounter difficulty and are able to avoid it; thus the world honors them. In this case [Niu Que] understood how to act for himself, but he did not understand how to act for others. His reasoning was not yet penetrating. When people can move from brilliance to obscurity, they are near the Way.

The *Odes* say,

Hunan Province; Shicheng 石城 was a city in present-day Henan Province; Dantu 丹徒 is a district in present-day Hubei Province.

109. According to LSCQ 14.8/78/25, Niu Que 牛缺 was a "great Confucian" who lived in the mountains. Gao You notes that he was a native of Qin. See Zhang Shuangdi 1997, 2:1905n.4.

110. This anecdote appears, somewhat altered, in LSCQ 14.8/78/26–14.8/79/4.

"People have a saying,
'There is no wise [man] who is not a fool.'"[111]
This says it all. [18/197/1–8]

18.20

Actions:
Some are done in order to cause something and ultimately ruin it;
some are done to ward off something and ultimately bring it about.
How do we know this is so?

The [First] Emperor of Qin spread out the "records and charts." Their text read, "Hu will destroy Qin."[112] Thus he sent out five hundred thousand troops and dispatched Duke Meng[113] and Yang Wengzi[114] to command. They built the Great Wall extending from Liusha to the west, striking north as far as the Liao River,[115] and terminating to the east in Korea. The [people of] the internal commanderies of the Middle Kingdom pulled carts to supply them.

[The First Emperor of Qin] also valued the rhinoceros horn, ivory, jade, and pearls of Yue. Thus he sent Commandant Tu Sui[116] with five hundred thousand troops. These were made into five armies.
One army fortified the mountain peak at Xincheng;[117]
one army defended the pass at Jiuyi;[118]
one army was positioned at the capital of Fanyu;[119]
one army guarded the frontier at Nanye;[120]
one army encamped at the Yugan River.[121]
For three years, they did not take off their armor or unstring their bows. Supervisor Lu[122] was sent to transport their provisions; he also used soldiers to dig canals and

111. *Odes* 256, "Grave" (抑).

112. According to the *Shiji*, these "records and charts" were presented to the First Emperor of Qin by Lu Sheng 盧生 in 215 B.C.E. after an expedition to "the island of the immortals." See *Shiji* 6:252.

113. This is the famous Qin general Meng Tian 蒙恬 (d. 210 B.C.E.).

114. According to Xu Shen, Yang Wengzi 楊翁子 was a Qin general. See Zhang Shuangdi 1997, 2:1908n.2.

115. Liusha 流沙, or "Flowing Sands," was a desert region of the northwestern imperial domain (in the area of present-day Gansu Province). The Liao 遼 River flows through Manchuria in northeastern China.

116. Tu Sui 屠睢 was dispatched to campaign against the Yue in 214 B.C.E. See *Shiji* 112:2958.

117. According to Xu Shen, Xincheng 鐔城 is in present-day Hubei Province.

118. Jiuyi 九嶷 is a mountain in present-day Hunan Province.

119. Fanyu 番禺 was a district in present-day Guangdong Province.

120. Nanye 南野, or "Southern Wilderness," was the name of a region in present-day Hubei Province.

121. The Yugan 餘干 River is in present-day Hubei Province.

122. 監祿. The *Shiji jijie* notes that the first character of this binome (*jian*) is an attenuated office title and that the second (*lu*) is the individual's name, his surname not having been transmitted. See *Shiji* 112:2959n.5.

thus open the route for supplies. They fought with the people of Yue and killed Yi Xusong, the ruler of Xi'ou.[123]

But all the Yue people went into the forests and lived with the birds and beasts; none was willing to be captured by the Qin. They conferred with one another in establishing a brave and outstanding [man] as commander and attacked the Qin by night, greatly crushing them. They killed Commandant Tu Sui, [and] there were tens of thousands of bloody corpses. [Qin] thus sent more guards to defend against [the Yue].

At this time men could not farm their fields, [and] women could not gather hemp or make thread. The emaciated and weak pushed carriages on the roads; noblemen met one another at the crossroads carrying baskets. The sick were not cared for; the dead were not buried. At that point Chen Sheng rose in Daze.[124] He raised his arm, gave a great shout, and rolled the world up like a rug all the way to Xi.[125] Liu [Bang] and Xiang [Yu][126] raised righteous soldiers following after [Chen Sheng] and secured [his victory].

Like snapping a withered tree or shaking loose [hanging fruit], [the Qin] thus lost the empire. The calamity resided in defending against the Hu and seeking profit in Yue. They wanted to know that building the Great Wall would defend against collapse; they did not know that building the Great Wall would be the cause of their collapse. They sent more guards to defend against the Yue and did not know that their troubles would arise from within.

When the magpie first notices that the [season of] the year is becoming very windy, it leaves the high trees and makes its nest in the lower branches. Adult [humans] who pass by thus take their chicks; children who come by steal their eggs. It knows to prepare against distant troubles yet forgets the closer disaster. Thus,

the preparations of Qin
equal the wisdom of the magpie. [18/197/10–22]

18.21

Some contend for profit yet conversely strengthen [their opponent];
some listen and obey yet conversely impede [their leader].

How do we know this is so?

Duke Ai of Lu[127] wanted to expand his residence westward. The court scribe fought this, saying that to expand the residence westward would be inauspicious.

123. According to Xu Shen, Xi'ou 西嘔 was a tribe of the Yue people, and Yi Xusong 譯吁宋 was their leader. See Zhang Shuangdi 1997, 2:1910n.15.

124. Daze 大澤 was a village in present-day Anhui Province.

125. Xi 戲 was a pavilion in present-day Shaanxi Province.

126. Liu Bang 劉邦 (247–195 B.C.E.) was a rebel leader against the Qin who became the founding emperor of the Han dynasty. Xiang Yu 項羽 (232–202 B.C.E.) was a rival rebel leader who briefly held the title of "hegemon king" before being defeated by Liu Bang.

127. Duke Ai 哀 of Lu reigned from 494 to 468 B.C.E.

Duke Ai flushed and became angry. Many of his attendants admonished him, but he would not listen. Thereupon [the duke] asked his tutor, Zai Zhesui,[128] "I want to expand my residence, and the court scribe thinks it is inauspicious. What do you think?" Zai Zhesui said, "In the world there are three bad auguries and expanding one's residence to the west is not among them." Duke Ai was greatly pleased.[129] After a moment, he asked, "What are called the 'three bad auguries?'" [Zai] replied, "Not practicing Ritual and Rightness is one bad augury. Unchecked greed is the second bad augury. Not listening to forceful admonition is the third bad augury." Duke Ai became silent and deep in thought. Sighing,[130] he reversed himself and thus did not expand the residence westward.

The court scribe thought that contending with [the duke] could halt him, but he did not understand how he could be enticed by not contending with him. The wise leave the path and attain the Way; fools stick to the Way and lose the path. The skill of Ni Yue[131] was such that there was no knot he could not "untie."[132] It was not that he could untie all knots; he did not untie what could not be untied. One who has reached the point of "untying it by not untying it" is one with whom one can reach the utmost[133] reasoning. [18/197/24–18/198/6]

18.22

Some make manifest Ritual and Rightness and promote the essence of the Way, but do not succeed.

Some abandon structure and speak rashly, but conversely hit the mark.

How do we illustrate this?

Confucius was traveling in the eastern countryside when his horse escaped and ate some farmers' crops. The country people were angry, [so] they took the horse and tethered it. [Confucius] sent Zigong to persuade them. He used polite phrases,[134] but they did not understand. Confucius said, "If [what] you use to persuade them [is] what people are unable to listen to, it is like using the great *lao* sacrificial feast to feed a wild animal or the 'Nine Harmonies'[135] to serenade the flying birds. This is my mistake; it is not your oversight." Thereupon he sent the groom to persuade them.

128. 宰折睢.

129. Following Yu Dacheng's proposed emendation. See Lau, HNZ, 198n.1.

130. Following Wang Shumin's proposed emendation. See Lau, HNZ, 198n.2.

131. Ni Yue 兒說 was a noble and famed debater of Song. See chap. 16, n. 20. He is mentioned in HFZ 32/82/6–7.

132. The text here is working off a pun: the same character, *jie* 解, means both to "untie" a knot and to "solve" a puzzle or a riddle. This alludes to an anecdote in LSCQ 17.2/100/26–17.2/101/2. There the story is told about "a disciple of Ni Yue" who reportedly solved a knot puzzle by recognizing that it was impossible to untie. A similar point is made in 17.193, and the story is alluded to in 16.20.

133. Accepting Lau's (HNZ, 198n.3) proposed emendation.

134. Conforming to the original text rather than following Lau's emendation of 卑 to 畢 ("When his words were finished").

135. The music of the sage-king Shun 舜.

Tian Zifang sheltered an old horse, and the kingdom of Wei exalted him;
Duke Zhuang of Qi avoided one mantis, and brave warriors turned to him.

Tang taught how to bless the nets, and forty states paid court.[157] King Wen buried the bones of the dead, and the Nine Yi submitted.[158] King Wu shaded the sun-stroked man beneath a tree, cradling him with his left [arm] and fanning him with his right, and the world cherished his Potency.[159] King Goujian of Yue released one innocent man from jail. He grabbed [his sword] Dragon Abyss and cut his thigh, so that the blood ran down to his feet, to punish himself, and [his] warriors resolved to die. They were moved by his mercy. Thus the sages act on the small [scale] so that they may encompass the large [scale]; they are thorough with respect to the near so that they may embrace the far.

When Sunshu Ao released the river at Qisi and irrigated the countryside of Yulou,[160] King Zhuang knew he could be prime minister. When Zifa divided tasks up so that work and leisure were equal, the state of Qi knew that he could be commander of the military. These both are [cases of] taking shape in the small and the subtle yet penetrating to the Grand Pattern. [18/199/24–18/200/10]

18.26

When the sage undertakes an affair, he does not pay extra attention to it. He investigates its basis; that is all. If ten thousand people were to tune a bell, they could not get it near the [proper] pitch. If you find someone who really understands [music], one person will suffice. The arguments of persuaders are also like this. If they truly achieve their aim, there is no need for more. The essence of what makes a cart able to travel one thousand miles is in three inches of axle. If you exhort people and cannot move them, if you warn people and cannot halt them, it is because the basis [of your words] is not reasonable.

In the olden days, the lord of Wey paid court to Wu and the king of Wu[161] imprisoned him, intending to cast him out to the sea. The persuaders and officials opposed [the king] yet could not stop him. When the lord of Lu heard of this, he unhooked his bells and drums and attended court in white [mourning] clothes. When Confucius saw him, he said, "Why do you look distressed?" The lord of Lu said, "The Lords of the Land have no kin; only [the other] Lords of the Land are our kin. The nobles

157. Tang prevented a hunter from using a prayer that would summon all birds into his net and instead taught him a prayer that would limit his catch to the birds he needed. See LSCQ 10.5/51/25–10.5/52/2.

158. According to LSCQ 10.5/52/4–7, King Wen's workers discovered bones while digging a pond, and he ordered them ceremonially reinterred. Xu Shen gives an alternative version of the story. See Zhang Shuangdi 1997, 2:1924n.20.

159. Discounting Lau's proposed deletion of "his Potency."

160. Qisi 期思 was the native place of Sunshu Ao, located in present-day Henan Province. Yulou 雩婁 was a neighboring town.

161. Xu Shen identifies the lord of Wey 衛 as Zhe 輒, Duke Chu 出 (r. 493–481 B.C.E.), and the king of Wu as Fuchai. See Zhang Shuangdi 1997, 2:1927nn.1, 2.

have no companions; only [other] nobles are their companions. Now the lord of Wey has paid court to Wu, and the king of Wu has imprisoned him and wants to cast him out to sea. Who would think that someone as Humane and Righteous as the lord of Wey would encounter this difficulty! I would like to save him but am unable. What can I do about it?" Confucius said, "If you would like to save him, then please [let] Zigong go." The lord of Lu summoned Zigong and granted him a general's seal. Zigong declined it, saying, "Rank is of no aid in resolving calamity; it resides in the Way that one takes as one's basis." Traveling incognito, he arrived in Wu and saw Great Steward Pi.[162] Great Steward Pi was very pleased with him and wanted to recommend him to the king. Zigong said, "You are not able to make a persuasion for the king; why don't I [make one] for you?" Great Steward Pi said, "How do you know that I am not able?"

Zigong said, "When the lord of Wey came, half of Wey said that it would be better to pay court to Jin; the other half said that it would be better to pay court to Wu. However, the lord of Wey felt that he could consign his flesh and bones to Wu, so he bound himself [by oath] and awaited orders. Now you receive the lord of Wey and imprison him and also want to cast him out to sea. This is rewarding those who spoke for paying court to Jin and punishing those who spoke for paying court to Wu. Moreover, the Lords of the Land all consider the arrival of the lord of Wey as an augury. If now he pays court to Wu and does not benefit, they all will shift their hearts to Jin. If you hope to complete the work of becoming hegemon, will it not be difficult?" Great Steward Pi went in [to court] and repeated this to the king. The king responded by issuing orders to the hundred officials that said, "For the next ten days, anyone who does not treat the lord of Wey with perfect propriety will die!" Zigong may be said to have understood how to persuade.[163] [18/200/12–27]

Duke Ai of Lu was building living quarters, and they were [very] large. Gongxuanzi[164] admonished him, saying, "If rooms are big,

> when one occupies them with a great many people, they are cacophonous;
> when one occupies them with few people, they are gloomy.

I would urge you to amend them." The duke said, "I hear and obey." [Yet] the building of the living quarters continued uninterrupted. Gongxuanzi had an audience again and said,

> "When the state is small and the living quarters are large;
> when the common people hear of it, they will certainly resent my ruler.
> When the Lords of the Land hear of it, they will certainly scorn my state."

The lord of Lu said, "[I] hear and obey." [Yet] the building of the living quarters continued uninterrupted. Gongxuanzi had an audience again and said, "To the left is [the ancestral temple of Duke] Zhao, and to the right [is the ancestral temple of

---

162. Great Steward Pi 太宰嚭 (also known as Bo Pi 伯嚭 [d. 473]), a great minister of Wu under King Fuchai, is often cited as a negative exemplar.

163. A much briefer and altered version of this anecdote appears in *Zuozhuan*, Ai 7.

164. Wang Shumin asserts that this figure's name should be Gongyizi 公儀子. See Lau, HNZ, 201n.1.

Duke] Mu. To build such grand rooms next to the temples of the two former lords, can it not be harmful to the son?"[165] The duke thereupon ordered that work be stopped and that the frame be disassembled and discarded.

The lord of Lu was determined in his desire to build the living quarters; Gongxuanzi was persistent in curbing him. Yet of three persuasions, only one was listened to; the other two were not [the duke's] Way. If you cast a hook at the riverside, and after it has been in all day, you are unable to catch a single white fish, it is not that the river fish do not eat, it is that what you are using as bait is not what they desire. When a skilled hand grasps the pole, casts [the hook,] and pierces biting lips, he is able to do so because he has lured [the fish] with what they desire. There is no thing about which nothing can be done, [only] people who have nothing they can do. Lead and cinnabar are of different categories and have separate colors. Yet if one can use [both of] them to produce scarlet, it is because one has grasped the technique. Thus intricate formulas and elegant phrases are of no aid to persuasion. Investigate what they take as the basis; that is all. [18/201/1–9]

18.27

The juxtapositions of the categories of things so that they are close [to one another] but of a different family are numerous and difficult to recognize. Thus

some are placed in categories to which they do not belong;
some are excluded from categories to which they do belong.
Some seem so and are not;
some are not and seem so.

A proverb says, "When a hawk dropped a rotten mouse, the Yu clan was lost." What does this mean? It is said that the Yu clan were tycoons of Liang. Their household was replete with riches; they had limitless gold and coins, immeasurable wealth and goods. They raised a lofty tower on the edge of the highway on which they staged musical [performances], served wine, and played games of chess.[166] As some wandering swordsmen passed under the tower together, one of the chess players above[167] moved against his friend's position and laughed as he turned over two pieces.[168] [Just at that moment] a flying hawk dropped a rotten mouse as it passed and hit the wandering swordsmen.

The wandering swordsmen said to one another, "The Yu clan's days of wealth and

165. Discounting Lau's (HNZ, 201n.2) proposed emendation, "to being a son."

166. Accepting Wang Shumin's proposed emendation. See Lau, HNZ, 201n.5.

167. Accepting Wang Shumin's proposed emendation. See Lau, HNZ, 201n.6.

168. We translate the received text as it reads, assuming that the players are playing a game akin to *wei qi* 圍棋 ("encirclement chess," known also by its Japanese name, *go*). Many commentators, however, would emend it according to the version of this anecdote that appears in LieZ 8/50/12–16, in which the players are playing a game that uses dice, such as *liubo* (for which, see chap. 15, n. 50). See Zhang Shuangdi 1997, 2:1932n.5; and A. C. Graham, trans., *The Book of Lieh-tzü: A Classic of Tao* (New York: Columbia University Press, 1990), 172–73.

happiness have been long, and they often are scornful of other people's will. We did not dare to disturb them, yet they insult us with a dead mouse. If this is not avenged, we will not be able to stand and proclaim ourselves to the world. Let us unite our strength to a single purpose, lead all our followers, and resolve to exterminate their house." That night they attacked the Yu clan and exterminated the house. This is what is called "placing it in a category in which it does not belong." [18/201/11–18]

What is called "excluding [it] from a category to which [it] does [belong]"? Qu Jian[169] told Shi Qi, "Duke Sheng of Bo[170] is about to rebel." Shi Qi said, "Not so. Duke Sheng of Bo humbles his person and exalts knights; he would not dare treat the worthy arrogantly. His house lacks the safeguards of keys and locks or the security of crossbars and bolts. He uses oversized *dou* and *hu* [measures] in distributing [grain] and undersized *jin* and *liang* [weights] when collecting [it]. Your assessment of him is inaccurate." Qu Jian replied, "These [conditions] are precisely why he will rebel." After three years, Duke Sheng of Bo indeed did rebel,[171] killing Prime Minister Zijiao[172] and Minister of War Ziqi.[173] This is what is called "being excluded from a category yet belonging to it." [18/201/20–23]

What is called "seeming so and yet not"? Zifa was the magistrate of Shangcai.[174] A common person committed a crime and faced punishment. The case was disputed and the arguments made. When it was decided before the magistrate, Zifa sighed with a pitiful heart. When the criminal had been punished, he did not forget Zifa's kindness. After this, Zifa committed a crime against King Wei[175] and fled. The man who had been punished thus disguised the one who had been kind to him, and the man who had been kind fled with him to a hut below the city walls. When pursuers arrived, [the man] stamped his foot and said angrily, "Zifa oversaw and decided my crime and had me punished; my hatred for him makes my bones and marrow ache. If I could get his flesh and eat it, I could never have enough!" The pursuers all felt he was truthful and did not search the interior, so Zifa survived. This is what is called "seeming so and yet not."[176] [18/201/25–29]

What is called "not yet seeming so"? In antiquity, King Goujian of Yue humbled himself to King Fuchai of Wu.[177] He asked to serve [Fuchai] personally as his minister and to give [Fuchai] his wife as concubine. He supplied the four seasonal sacrifices and remanded tribute every spring and autumn. He took down the altars of the soil and grain, exerted his energies [like a] commoner, lived in seclusion, and fought in the front ranks. He was extremely humble in all courtesies and extremely

169. According to Xu Shen, Qu Jian 屈建 was a grandee of Chu.
170. See 12.5.
171. This occurred in 479 B.C.E. See *Zuozhuan*, Ai 16.
172. 子椒. *Zuozhuan* gives this figure's name as Zixi.
173. 子期. According to Xu Shen, both Zijiao and Ziqi were paternal uncles of Duke Sheng.
174. Shangcai 上蔡 was a district of ancient Chu in present-day Henan Province.
175. King Wei 威 of Chu reigned from 339 to 329 B.C.E.
176. Lau's (HNZ 18/201/29) text contains a seemingly superfluous *ruo* (若) that is not in other editions and should be excised. See Zhang Shuangdi 1997, 2:1935n.18.
177. These events occurred in 493 B.C.E. See 12.23; and *Shiji* 31:1468–76.

submissive in all speech. He distanced himself far from the mind of a rebel, yet with three thousand men he captured Fuchai at Guxu.[178]

One cannot fail to examine these four cases. What makes it difficult to understand affairs is that [people] hide their origins and conceal their tracks; they establish the selfish in the place of the impartial; they incline toward the deviant over the correct and confuse other people's minds with victory. If one could make what people harbor internally tally perfectly with what they express externally, then the world would have no lost states or broken households. When the fox catches the pheasant, it must first prostrate its body and lower its ears[179] and wait for [the pheasant] to come. The pheasant sees this and believes it, thus it can be enticed and captured. If the fox were to widen its eyes and stare directly [at the pheasant], manifesting its lethal inclination, the pheasant would know to be alarmed and fly far off, thus escaping [the fox's] wrath.

> The mutual deception of human artifice
> is not merely the cunning of birds and beasts.

The resemblances between things and categories that cannot be externally assessed are numerous and difficult to recognize. For this reason, they cannot but be investigated. [18/202/1–8]

Translated by Andrew Meyer

---

178. Guxu 姑胥 is likely an alternative rendering of Gusu 蘇, a town in present-day Jiangsu Province. See He Ning, *Huainanzi jishi* (Beijing: Zhonghua shuju, 1998), 1308.

179. Discounting Lau's (HNZ 18/202/6) emendation of 耳 to 毛. Lau seems to be emending on the basis of a parallel text found in Gao You's commentary to LSCQ 8.4/41/11. See Chen Qiyou, *Lüshi chunqiu jiaoshi* (Shanghai: Xuelin, 1995), 458n.36. But the original text of the *Huainanzi* is more logical. Lowering the ears is a recognizable sign of submission among canines, whereas it is not clear how "smoothing its fur" would be at all observable.

Nineteen

CULTIVATING EFFORT

ACCORDING TO the summary in chapter 21, "Cultivating Effort" was written for those "whose entry into the Way is not yet profound, and whose appetite for debate is not yet deep." Substantively, chapter 19 provides arguments that can be used to challenge a number of political and philosophical views that seem to have been in vogue at the time the *Huainanzi* was created. Together, these arguments support the general theme of the chapter, that cultivating effort is necessary in a wide variety of contexts and among a wide variety of people, from the sage who tries to bring benefit to the world to the common man who tries to lift himself morally through education and training. Rhetorically, the chapter instructs the reader in techniques of assertion and refutation that can be used in oral debate. Each of the chapter's seven sections lays out a sustained argument that begins by asserting or refuting a particular proposition. In every case, personal effort is seen to be indispensable even when it pertains to the key concept of "non-action" (*wuwei* 無為), advocated throughout the *Huainanzi* as a technique of sagely government. Here, "non-action" is redefined to highlight the importance of human agency and human exertion.

The Chapter Title

We have translated the title of chapter 19, "Xiu wu" 脩務, as "Cultivating Effort."[1] Even though "Cultivation and Effort" also would be an acceptable translation of this chapter title, we prefer the verb–object reading because we believe that it best expresses the chapter's main theme as developed in all seven of its sections. *Xiu* is associated with a constellation of concepts such as to regulate, to cultivate, and to improve, with connotations of beginning with the natural tendency of a person or thing and developing it to perfection. *Wu* is associated with working hard, making an effort, trying to do something, and exerting oneself to the utmost. Both words point to the importance of human agency and its indispensable role in perfecting oneself and the world. The message of the title, as of the chapter itself, is that no ruler can hope to succeed unless he devotes himself to the task of ruling.

Summary and Key Themes

Each of this chapter's seven sections addresses a philosophical issue to be affirmed or refuted. The first two sections take up the concept of non-action but differ in the arguments they employ.

Section 19.1 is a refutation of what may have been a particularly popular early Han reading of the concept of non-action—that the non-active sage is "solitarily soundless and indifferently unmoving." It challenges this depiction through a detailed description of the Divine Farmer, Yao, Shun, Yu, and Tang and their contributions to human society. As "rulers who made the world flourish," these five sages are said to have "labored their bodies and used their minds to the utmost on behalf of the people to bring benefit and eradicate harm, yet they never tired of doing so."

Section 19.2 also addresses the concept of non-action but does so differently. Instead of refuting one particular understanding of the concept, it redefines non-action, linking the concept to the natural propensity of things (*shi* 勢), on the one hand, and to human effort, on the other:

> The propensity of terrain [is such that] water flows east, but people must work on it so that the floodwaters flow through the valleys.
> Grain and crops grow in the spring, but people must apply their efforts to them so that the five grains can reach maturity.
> If they had let the water flow naturally or waited for the plants to grow by them-

1. This chapter title has many shades of meaning and so can have many possible translations. Ames 1994, 19, uses "Striving with Effort." Csikszentmihalyi, 2004, 24, translates it as "Discipline and Facility." Le Blanc and Mathieu's 2003 understanding of the title is similar to our own: "Du devoir de se cultiver."

selves, the accomplishments of Gun and Yu would not have been established, and the wisdom of Lord Millet would not have been employed.

Having set out this fundamental position for understanding the concept of non-action, the section then refines its definition. Non-action means

> not allowing private ambitions to interfere with the public Way,
> not allowing lustful desires to distort upright techniques.
> [It means]
> complying with the inherent patterns of things when initiating undertakings,
> according with the natural endowments of things when establishing accomplishments,
> and advancing the natural propensities of things so that misguided precedents are not able to dominate.

Thus the section distinguishes between those who take deliberate action (*youwei* 有為) in a vain effort to contradict the natural propensities of things and those who engage in non-action by understanding and harnessing the natural course of things—for example, by using a boat on water or choosing a low-lying area as a place to dig a pond.

Section 19.3 argues that sages act differently to achieve the same ends: "As sages carry out their affairs, they differ in specific [details] but agree on matters of principle; they start out along different paths but return to the same place."[2] The section illustrates this point through a pair of anecdotes. In one, Mozi acts urgently to save the state of Song from potential destruction; in the other, the hermit Duangan Mu uses his prestige as a virtuous recluse to save Wei from a similar fate. The message is that the sage-ruler must choose appropriate means but never lose sight of the end: "In preserving [their states] against danger and stabilizing them against collapse, they are as one, and their wills never deviated from the desire to bring benefit to others."

Judging from the acerbic tone of the section's opening lines, section 19.4 challenges a particular understanding of human nature that may also have been popular when this chapter was composed. The claim is made, we are told, that human nature cannot be altered: "People's natures in each case possess strengths and weaknesses, just as fish are swift and cranes are particolored. This is something natural that cannot be diminished or enhanced." The section's rebuttal of that claim begins by denying its validity, using the same formula employed in section 19.1: "I believe that this is not so." The writer concedes that some traits are inherent; for example, people and horses alike receive their muscles, bones, frame, and body from Heaven, and these Heaven-endowed aspects of their physical form cannot be changed. Yet when a horse is a young colt, it exhibits many different kinds of natural tendencies: it jumps and kicks and raises its tail and runs, making it difficult for people to control it. Moreover,

2. This statement is nearly the same as in 8.6.

> its bite is strong enough to pierce flesh and break bones,
> and its kick is hard enough to break a skull or crush a chest.

But when tamed by a groom or trained by a charioteer, the wild and unrestrained colt can be controlled with bridle and harness and led with rein and bit so that it will traverse even the most precarious terrain. The argument concludes: "A horse is a dumb brute and yet it is possible to penetrate through to its vital energy and will by relying on training to perfect the horse. How much more is this true of people!" Admitting that one might cite examples of goodness or depravity so extreme as to defy the bad effects of corruption or the good effects of education, the writer points out that when formulating policies or making general assessments, one must be careful of reasoning from extreme examples. The vast majority of people who "in loftiness do not reach Yao and Shun and in baseness do not compare with Shang Yun" can be perfected through education and instruction.

Section 19.5 builds its argument around the following opening claim:

> The weakness of a wise person [in some field] makes him not as good [in that field] as a foolish person who is strong [in it].
> The deficits of a worthy [in some field] make him not as good [in that field] as an ordinary person who surpasses [in it].

Even the sages of antiquity, the section continues, were not good at everything. Rong Cheng invented the calendar, Lord Millet invented agriculture, and so on. People have their particular talents: some are smiths, some weavers, some musicians. None achieves his or her skill without effort. This section then concludes: "Looking at it from this perspective, a wise person who makes no effort does not compare with a foolish person who loves to learn. From the rulers, dukes, and ministers on down to the common people, there has never been a case of someone succeeding without exerting himself to the utmost."

Section 19.6 again takes up the theme of human agency, arguing that effort and perseverance are the crucial ingredients enabling a person to establish reputation and merit. The Superior Man then

> musters his will and commits himself to uprightness, hastening toward brilliant teachers;
> encourages moderation and exalts loftiness, separating himself from the conventions of the age.

These claims are supported by two illustrative and moving anecdotes in which the actors undergo all kinds of physical travails to achieve the goals just outlined.

Section 19.7, which concludes the chapter, turns to the benefits that come to those who have made the effort to educate themselves:

Those who fully comprehend things cannot be startled by the unusual;
those who are versed in the Way cannot be moved by the strange;
those who examine into words cannot be bedazzled by their designations;
those who investigate into forms cannot be misled by their appearances.

Sources

The literary form of "Cultivating Effort" belongs to a tradition extending back into the Warring States period, of using examples to teach people the techniques of oral debate by showing both how to assert and how to refute a philosophical claim. Sections 19.1 and 19.4 follow the literary form of a refutation or rebuttal (*nan* 難, "a proposition with which one has difficulty"). Each begins by stating a philosophical proposition attributed to an anonymous source, "someone says" (*huo yue* 或曰). The validity of the claim is immediately denied with the author's declarative statement "I believe this is not so" (*wo yi wei bu ran* 我以爲不然). The bulk of the section is then devoted to the refutation itself, so that the reader learns through examples and argumentation precisely why the particular proposition has been rejected. The oral and performative nature of the arguments in this chapter is underscored by the literary form of 19.1, which begins the chapter with an intricately metrical passage in the *fu* (poetic exposition) style. *Fu*, which generally were recited orally from a written script, were very popular and much admired during the Han period, and it was generally felt that their literary elegance lent heft to the arguments they contained. Section 19.1 thus gives us a very good sense of how a formal argument might have been presented at a ruler's court.

Sections 19.2, 19.3, 19.5, 19.6, and 19.7 are affirmations. Each begins by stating a philosophical principle that in most cases is followed by the interrogative "How might I illustrate this point?" (*He yi ming zhi* 何以明之) or "How do I know this to be so?" (*He yi zhi qi ran* 何以知其然). The explanation then follows, sometimes closing with a flourish by quoting from the *Odes*, as in sections 19.5, 19.6, and 19.7.

These model arguments in *Huainanzi* 19 likely belong to a long tradition of refutation and argumentation of which examples survive in various Warring States and Han collections—such as the *Xunzi*, *Hanfeizi*, *Chunqiu fanlu*, and *Lun heng*—and records of two Han court debates, the *Yantie lun* (*Debates on Salt and Iron*) and the *Bohu tong* (*Comprehensive Discussions in the White Tiger Hall*). Each of these collections contains various kinds of assertions, refutations, critiques, and rebuttals. Chapter 5 of the *Xunzi*, "Fei xiang" (Opposing Physiognomy), and chapter 6, "Fei shi er zi" (Opposing the Twelve Masters), are perhaps the best-known earlier examples. In "Opposing Physiognomy," Xunzi refutes the notion popular in his day that the destiny of a person could be predicted by assessing his physical attributes. He does so using numerous examples to demonstrate that physical attributes are essentially serendipitous. Rather than referring to physiognomers and their clients in his own time,

Xunzi cites mainly famous figures from the past, such as Confucius, the Duke of Zhou, and King Djou, whose accomplishments and faults were beyond question to an audience in the Warring States period.[3] In "Opposing the Twelve Masters,"[4] Xunzi rails against twelve philosophers whose teachings and influences he found to be especially pernicious and injurious to social harmony. Since Xunzi's preferred style of rhetorical combat is to support his arguments with specific historical examples, we might characterize his particular style of refutation as "peremptory refutation."

Less well known are the four "Nan" chapters of the *Hanfeizi*. "Refutations, Parts 1 to 4" (Nan yi, er, san, si) follow a similar format, which we might call the "anecdotal refutation." These chapters include a number of anecdotes that illustrate a didactic moral or state a particular philosophical position that is then followed by the refutation in the words of an anonymous critic, beginning with the set phrase *huo yue* 或曰 (someone says).[5] These "anecdotal refutations" were likely well known to Han audiences from the examples collected in the *Hanfeizi* or other sources that have since been lost. On one occasion, the *Huainanzi* explicitly attributes such an "anecdotal refutation" to Hanfeizi.[6] This form of refutation seems to have been frequently employed by Master Han Fei, judging from the numerous examples preserved in the work that carries his name. The following example typifies this literary form:

> Anecdote: Viscount Xiang was surrounded in Jinyang. When he broke the siege, he rewarded five men who served meritoriously, and Gao She was the first to be rewarded. Thereupon Zhang Mengtan said: "During the siege at Jinyang, She rendered no great meritorious service. Why now do you reward him first?" Viscount Xiang replied: "During the crisis at Jinyang, our state and families were imperiled and our altars of soil and grain were endangered. Among our officials, there was not one who did not harbor a proud and arrogant heart. She alone did not stray from the propriety owed by the minister to the ruler. This is why I rewarded him first." When Zhongni [Confucius] heard about this, he said: "Viscount Xiang [truly]

3. See Knoblock 1988, 1:196–205; and the comment on 198.

4. Knoblock 1988, 1:212–29.

5. "Refutations, Part 1," contains nine anecdotes and refutations; "Refutations, Part 2," contains eight anecdotes and refutations; and "Refutations, Part 3," contains nine anecdotes, three of which have lost their rebuttals, as well as two statements attributed to Guanzi, each of which is followed by a rebuttal. "Refutations, Part 4," preserves four anecdotes, each followed by two rebuttals.

For a different style of refutation, see *Hanfeizi*, chap. 40, "A Refutation of Political Purchase" (Nan shi 難勢), in which Shen Dao's ideas about political purchase are quoted and critiqued. See HFZ 40/127/31–40/129/22.

6. Compare HFZ 36/115/22–25 with *Huainanzi* 11.15 (11/100/24–26), which refers explicitly to Han Feizi:

> Duke Ping of Jin let slip words that were not correct. Music Master Kuang raised his *qin* and bumped into him, so that he tripped on his robe and [struck] the wall. The courtiers wanted to plaster [the damaged spot]. Duke Ping said, "Leave it. This will [remind] me of my fault."
>
> Confucius heard this and said, "It is not that Duke Ping did not cherish his body, but that he wanted to attract those who would admonish him."
>
> Han[Fei]zi heard this and said, "The assembled officials abandoned Ritual and were not punished. This is to condone transgression. This is why Duke Ping did not become hegemon!"

excelled at bestowing rewards! He rewarded one man, and all those who served as ministers in the world, without exception, did not dare stray from propriety."[7]

Rebuttal: Someone said: Zhongni did not understand excellence in rewarding. When the ruler excels at conferring rewards and punishments, the numerous officials will not dare overstep their commissions, and the innumerable ministers will not dare stray from propriety. If the ruler promulgates the laws [clearly], then subordinates will not harbor treacherous and deceitful hearts. When the ruler acts in this manner, it may be said that he excels at conferring rewards and punishments. If when Viscount Xiang was in Jinyang, his orders were not implemented and his prohibitions stopped nothing, this would amount to Viscount Xiang's having no state and Jinyang's having no ruler. Then with whom could he defend the city? Now, when Viscount Xiang was surrounded in Jinyang, even though the Zhi clan inundated the city until frogs made their nests inside the mortars and ovens, the people still did not harbor rebellious hearts. Thus, too, should ruler and minister have cleaved to each other with affection. Now if Viscount Xiang had been bathed in the affection owed by his ministers to their ruler, and if Viscount Xiang wielded the laws in such a way that his orders were effective and his prohibitions were enforceable, yet there still remained ministers who harbored proud and arrogant hearts, it must have been the case that Viscount Xiang strayed from the [appropriate] punishments [in dealing with his ministers]. When ministers serve meritoriously when situations arise, they should be rewarded. Now She alone was neither proud nor arrogant, and so Viscount Xiang rewarded him. This is a case of straying from the [appropriate] reward. The enlightened ruler neither rewards those who are not meritorious nor punishes those who are not guilty. Now Viscount Xiang did not punish those ministers who harbored a proud and arrogant heart, yet he rewarded the unmeritorious She. Where, then, does his excellence in bestowing reward reside? Thus the claim: "Zhongni did not understand excellence in rewarding."[8]

The tradition of affirmation and rebuttal continues in several works that were composed after the *Huainanzi* but that apparently preserve earlier materials. The

---

7. *Hanfeizi* 36. Note that *Huainanzi* 13.18 (13/128/23–27) uses the same anecdote to make a quite different didactic point:

> When Viscount Xiang of Wei was surrounded in Jinyang, he broke the siege and rewarded the five men who were meritorious, and Gao He was the first to be rewarded. Those who flanked him to the right and left exclaimed: "As for the hardships at Jinyang, [Gao] did not possess any great merit, yet today he is the first to be rewarded. Why?"
>
> Viscount Xiang of Wei responded, "During the siege of Jinyang, our altars to the soil and grain were endangered, and our state and families were imperiled. Among our numerous officials, there was not one who did not harbor a proud and arrogant heart, [but] only He did not stray from the ritual pertaining to ruler and minister." Thus through the rewarding of this one man, those who served as ministers in the world, without exception to the end of their lives, showed loyalty to their ruler. This is an example of rewarding the few to encourage the many.

8. HFZ 36/115/9–20.

Chunqiu fanlu (*Luxuriant Gems of the Spring and Autumn*), attributed to Dong Zhongshu of the Western Han dynasty (late second century B.C.E.), contains fragments of various debates and discussions in this tradition. Chapter 25, "Yao and Shun Did Not Presumptuously Transfer the Throne; Tang and Wu Did Not Unauthorizedly Murder the Ruler" (Yao Shun bu shan yi; Tang Wu bu zhuan sha 堯舜不擅移; 湯武不專殺), preserves a brief record of the historically documented court debate between Master Huang and Yuan Gu[9] held before Emperor Jing (r. 156–140 B.C.E.), as well as other exchanges of opinion ranging from propositions concerning the *Spring and Autumn Annals* to certain aspects of yin–yang cosmology. Here the critical voice is introduced by the set phrase *nan zhe yue* 難者曰, which may be variously understood as "one raising an objection stated" or "someone who found this difficult to accept said." This form of rebuttal differs from the "anecdotal rebuttal" typical of the *Hanfeizi*. In the *Chunqiu fanlu*, the rebuttals are part of dialogues, so we might call them "diaological rebuttals." There is a kind of back-and-forth or give-and-take between the person who sets out a particular proposition and the person who expresses an objection or difficulty with the given assertion.[10]

A number of chapters in Wang Chong's *Lun heng* (*Discourses Weighed in the Balance* [first century C.E.]) preserve various refutations and critiques. Chapter 28, "Questioning Confucius" (Wen Kong 問孔), chapter 29, "Opposing Han [Feizi]" (Fei Han 非韓), and chapter 30, "Negating Mencius" (Ci Meng 刺孟) contain refutations of philosophical propositions attributed to Confucius, Han Feizi, and Mencius. These differ yet again from those preserved in the *Hanfeizi* and the *Chunqiu fanlu*. Not "peremptory," "anecdotal," or "diaological," each of these refutations begins with a citation from the *Analects* or *Mencius* (or, in the case of "Opposing Han," a paraphrase of the views of the *Hanfeizi*) that is then critiqued by means of a detailed prose analysis. Accordingly, we might identify this form of critique as the "extended refutation."

The importance of techniques of oral debate in the Han period can be gauged from the two records of imperially mandated court debates mentioned: the *Debates on Salt and Iron*[11] and the *Comprehensive Discussions in the White Tiger Hall*.[12] *Salt and Iron* records a debate on state economic policy held in 81 B.C.E. in the presence of Emperor Zhao (r. 87–73 B.C.E.) and purports to transcribe verbatim the arguments made by Grand Secretary Sang Hongyang in favor of an authoritarian policy, and the equally vehement rebuttals made by Huan Kuan and other representatives of the literati. *Comprehensive Discussions* summarizes a debate about how the clas-

9. For a discussion of this debate, see Sarah A. Queen, *From Chronicle to Canon: The Hermeneutics of the Spring and Autumn According to Tung Chung-shu* (Cambridge: Cambridge University Press, 1996), 17–19, 82.

10. For examples of the "dialogical rebuttal," see *Chunqiu fanlu zhuzi suoyin* 1.2/3/15, 2.1/6/17, 2.1/7/4, 3.1/10/16, 3.1/11/4, 3.1/11/16, 3.1/12/4, 3.2/12/18, 3.2/12/27, and 11.6/53/20.

11. Esson M. Gale, *Discourses on Salt and Iron: A Debate on State Control of Commerce and Industry in Ancient China* (Leiden: Brill, 1931).

12. Tjan Tjoe Som, *Po Hu T'ung: The Comprehensive Discussions in the White Tiger Hall*, 2 vols. (Leiden: Brill, 1949, 1952).

sics should be understood and their role in the formulation of policy, convened in 79 C.E. by Emperor Zhang (r. 76–89 C.E.) of the Later Han dynasty. The record is in the form of topical questions followed by answers and explanations. Behind these rather bland summaries are some of the high-stakes arguments among scholars and court officials over which editions and commentarial traditions of the classics should be considered authoritative.

From these examples, it is clear that the kinds of debating skills featured in "Cultivating Effort" were an essential part of the education of anyone who hoped to play a role in politics and government in the Han era.

The Chapter in the Context of the *Huainanzi* as a Whole

As noted in the general introduction to this book, one way of looking at the *Huainanzi* and understanding the principles of its organization is to regard it as a curriculum for the education of an aspiring monarch. Seen in this light, chapter 19 plays a dual role. It instructs, using examples, how to frame affirmations and refutations in oral debate, and as chapters 16 and 17 do as well, it equips its reader to evaluate the arguments of others. But as important as this training in rhetorical techniques was, the content of the chapter is given equal weight. In earlier chapters of the *Huainanzi* (for example, chapter 8), the reader encountered numerous instances in which the moral authority of a sage apparently was sufficient to bring about good government. Here, however, the author warns the reader that there is no easy path to the cultivation of sagehood and that it is a mistake to think that "non-action" is a license to do nothing. On the contrary, the chapter states in no uncertain terms that effort is, and has always been, an essential quality of a ruler. The chapter summary in chapter 21 reinforces this point, saying bluntly that idleness and laziness will surely obstruct one from the Great Way. A later passage from chapter 21 then reiterates the same point when it insists that he who fails to familiarize himself with chapter 19 will surely "lack the means to inspire scholars to exert their utmost strength" (21.3). No ruler can hope to have energetic officials if he does not cultivate effort himself. Chapter 19 thus sets the stage for the next chapter, "The Exalted Lineage," which recapitulates many of the themes of the book as a whole. When the book's young royal reader has learned to cultivate effort, his education will be nearly complete.

Sarah A. Queen and John S. Major

Nineteen

19.1

Some people say: "Those who are non-active
are solitarily soundless
and indifferently unmoving.[1]
Pull them, and they do not come;
push them, and they do not go.
Only those who are like this give the appearance of having attained the Way."

I believe this is not so. I might ask them: "Is it possible to refer to such men as the Divine Farmer, Yao, Shun, Yu, and Tang as sages?' [Even] those who hold to this view [of non-action] certainly could not contend otherwise. [But] if you examine these five sages, it is clear that none of them achieved non-action.

In ancient times,
the people fed on herbaceous plants and drank [only] water,
picked fruit from shrubs and trees
and ate the meat of oysters and clams.
They frequently suffered tribulations from feverish maladies and injurious poisons. Consequently, the Divine Farmer first taught the people to plant and cultivate the five grains.

1. This echoes the opening line of chap. 8: "The reign of Grand Purity was harmonious and compliant and thus solitary and indifferent." The key term *jimo* 寂漠 also appears several times in chap. 2.

He evaluated the suitability of the land,
[noting] whether it was dry or wet, fertile or barren, high or low.
He tried the taste and flavor of the one hundred plants
and the sweetness or bitterness of the streams and springs,

issuing directives so the people would know what to avoid and what to accept. At the time [he was doing this], he suffered poisoning [as many as] seventy times a day.

Yao established filial piety, compassion, humaneness, and love, inspiring the people to become like sons and brothers.

To the west, he taught the People of the Fertile Lands;
to the east, he reached the Blackteeth People;
to the north, he soothed the Yudu People;
and to the south he made inroads to Jiaozhi.[2]
He exiled Huan Dou[3] to Mount Chong,
pursued the Three Miao [tribes] to Three Dangers [Mountain],
banished Gong Gong to Yuzhou,
and executed Gun at Feather Mountain.[4]

Shun created homes.

Constructing walls and thatching roofs,
opening lands and planting grains,

he directed all the people

to abandon their caves and
each to establish a family dwelling.
These are the practices he initiated.
To the south he chastised the Three Miao [tribes],
dying along the way at Zangwu.

Yu,

bathed by torrential rains
and combed by violent winds,
cleared the waterways and dredged the rivers,
bored through Dragon Gate,
opened up Yin Pass,

repaired the embankments of Peng Li [i.e., Boyang Lake],

mounted the four vehicles,[5]
followed the mountains,

2. For these mythical people and countries, see chap. 4; and Major 1993. They also are mentioned in the *Shanhaijing*.

3. Huan Dou 讙兜, a minister of Yao, was exiled for opposing the accession of Shun to the throne.

4. See chap. 4; and Major 1993. These four figures—Huan Dou, the Three Miao, Gong Gong, and Gun—are collectively known as the "four fierce ones" (*xiong* 兇), traditionally identified as enemies of sagely government.

5. Most of the several explanations include boats for water and carts for land, but the remaining vehicles could be *chun* 輴, a mud sledge; *lei* 蔂, a vehicle or shoes especially useful in climbing mountains; *qiao* 橇, another mud sledge; and *qiao* 橋, sometimes associated with *jiao* 轎, a sedan chair.

and marked their trees,
leveling and ordering the water and land
so as to determine [the boundaries of] the eighteen hundred states.

Tang
rose early and retired late
to take full advantage of his perspicacious intelligence;
reduced taxes and lightened demands
to enhance the people's livelihood;
displayed virtue and bestowed favor
to rescue the impoverished and bereft.
He mourned the dead and inquired about the afflicted
to take care of orphans and widows.
[Consequently,]
the common people grew close to and cleaved to him.
His policies and directives flowed forth and circulated [everywhere].
Thus he subsequently
marshaled his troops at Mingtiao,
surrounded [Jie] of the Xia at Nan Guo,
punished him for his transgressions,
and banished him to Mount Li.

These five sages were rulers who made the world flourish. They labored their bodies and used their minds to the utmost on behalf of the people to bring benefit and eradicate harm, yet they never tired of doing so.

Now if you raise a beaker of wine,
no one would notice [the strain] from your face,
but if you lift a vat [weighing] a *dan*, sweat will flow profusely.
How much more so will this be the case if you take on the worries of the world
and assume responsibility for all the affairs within the [Four] Seas!
This is far heavier than a vat weighing a *dan*.

Moreover, these sages
were not embarrassed by their humble status
but regretted that the Way did not prevail;
were not anxious about their brief life spans
but worried that the people were impoverished.
For this reason,
when Yu acted on the waterways,
he used his own body to break through the banks of the Yangxu [River];
and Tang, at the time of the great drought,
offered himself as a sacrifice at the edge of Mulberry Forest.
If the sages' solicitousness for the people was as clear as this, is it not deluded to accuse them [of being] "non-active"? [19/202/12–30]

Furthermore, in ancient times

when emperors and kings were established, it was not to serve and nourish their [own] desires;
when sages took office, it was not to indulge and delight their own persons.
It was because in the world,
the strong oppressed the weak,
the many violated the few,
the clever deceived the ignorant,
and the brave dispossessed the timid.
Those who possessed knowledge did not impart it;
those who accumulated wealth did not distribute it.[6]
Thus the Son of Heaven was established in order to equalize them.

Since one person's intelligence was not sufficient to shed light on all things within the [Four] Seas, the Three Dukes and the Nine Ministers were established to aid and assist him.

Since inaccessible states with varied customs and remote and secluded locales could not receive and be enriched by the ruler's virtue, Lords of the Land were established to instruct and admonish them.

This made it so that
no land was untended,
no season was not [met with its proper] response,
no official concealed his activities,
no state neglected to benefit [the people].
By these means, they clothed the cold and fed the hungry, nourished the old and infirm, and gave respite to those wearied from their labors.

[Moreover,] if you look at the sages from the perspective of the common man,[7] then
[the cook] Yi Yin, with cauldron on his back, sought to serve Tang;
[the butcher] Lü Wang, with carving knife in hand, entered Zhou [to serve as a high official];[8]
Baili Xi was sold back to [Duke Mu of] Qin;[9]
Guan Zhong was tied and fettered [and taken to the court of Duke Huan of Qi].

---

6. Contrast this passage with the idyllic view of archaic society found in 8.6.

There are numerous references in the *Mozi* to the concept of "establishing the Son of Heaven." See, for example, MoZ 1.3/3/13, 1.4/5/2, 2.2/12/22, 2.3/14/20, 3.1/16/16–17, 3.2/17/22, 3.3/21/17, 7.3/48/16, and 12.2/107/25.

7. *Bu yi tu bu zhi ren* 布衣徒步之人, "people who wear plain clothing and go on foot." All the following examples are of individuals who found themselves in very humble circumstances but went on to have powerful ministerial careers. See *Shiji* 124, "Biographies of the Wandering Knights."

8. Lü Wang sold meat by the roadside before coming to the attention of King Wen; he eventually rose to become prime minister and Grand Duke.

9. Baili Xi was prime minister of Qin in the time of Duke Mu (ca. 660–621 B.C.E.). He was captured by Jin forces in Yu and escaped to Chu. Duke Mu told the ruler of Chu that Baili Xi had abandoned his office and offered five sheepskins for his return for prosecution. He thus secured the return of his valuable minister for a trifling amount.

Confucius's stove was not black,
and Mozi's mat was not warm.[10]

Thus it is that sages
do not consider mountains high,
do not consider rivers wide.

They withstand insult and humiliation in order to seek to serve a ruler of their age. They do not crave high salaries or covet official posts but instead want to work to advance the world's benefits and eradicate the common people's hardships. In a work that has been transmitted to us it is written:

"The Divine Farmer was haggard and downcast;
Yao was emaciated and forlorn;
Shun was weather-beaten and dark;
and Yu had calloused hands and feet."

Looking at it from this perspective, the sages' anxious toiling for the common people is profound indeed. Thus from the Son of Heaven down to the common people, when
the four limbs are not exercised
and thought and forethought [are] not applied,
yet the tasks of governance are addressed and resolved—such a thing has never been heard of. [19/203/1–10]

19.2

The propensity of terrain [is such that] water flows east, but people must work on it so that the floodwaters flow through the valleys.

Grain and crops grow in the spring, but people must apply their efforts to them so that the five grains can reach maturity.

If they had let the water flow naturally or waited for the plants to grow by themselves, the accomplishments of Gun and Yu would not have been established, and the wisdom of Lord Millet would not have been employed.

What I call non-action [means]
not allowing private ambitions to interfere with the public Way,
not allowing lustful desires to distort upright techniques.

[It means]
complying with the inherent patterns of things when initiating undertakings,
according with the natural endowments of things when establishing accomplishments,
and advancing the natural propensities of things so that misguided precedents are not able to dominate.

Thus,

10. Confucius's stove was not black with soot, and Mozi's mat was not warm from the heat of his body, because they were away from home so often.

the undertakings of government will succeed,
but [you] personally will not be glorified.[11]
[Your] accomplishments will be established,
but your reputation will not obtain.
[Non-action] does not mean that
a stimulus will not produce a response
or that a push will not move [something].
If you
use fire to dry out a well
or use the Huai [River] to irrigate a mountain,
these are cases of using personal [effort] in contradiction of the natural course [of things]. Thus I would call such [activities] "taking deliberate action." But if
on the water you use a boat,
in the sand you use a *shu*,
in the mud you use a *chun*,
in the mountains you use a *lei*,[12]
in the summer you dig [ditches],
in the winter you pile up [dikes],
in accordance with a high place you make a mound,
and following a low one you dig a pond,
these [activities] are not what I would call "deliberate action." [19/203/12–18]

19.3

As sages carry out their affairs, they differ in specific [details] but agree on matters of principle; they start out along different paths but return to the same place.[13] In preserving [their states] against danger and stabilizing them against collapse, they are as one, and their wills never deviate from the desire to bring benefit to others. How might I illuminate this point?

Long ago, Chu wanted to attack Song. Mozi heard about it and was deeply grieved over it, so he left Lu and hurried off [toward Chu], traveling for ten days and ten nights. [Although] his feet swelled with blisters, he did not stop; he tore his clothes into shreds to bandage his feet [instead]. Arriving at Ying, he had an audience with the king of Chu and said, "I[14] have heard that the great king is raising troops in preparation for an attack on Song. Do you attack Song because you are certain to get it? Or do you attack Song despite making life bitter for the masses, overworking the

11. Taking *fa* 伐 as equivalent to *fa* 閥.
12. For the conveyances *shu*, *chun* 輴, and *lei* 蔂, see n. 5. The character *shu* is unusual. See *Morohashi*, no. 41134.
13. This statement is found in nearly the same words in 8.6.
14. Literally, "your subject," a conventionally humble way to refer to oneself when addressing a ruler.

people, exhausting your army, and destroying their weaponry, thereby shouldering a reputation for being unjust in the world, even though you gain not a single inch of territory?"

The king replied, "If I were certain not to get Song and, moreover, I would be considered unjust, why would I attack it?"

Mozi said, "Splendid! I will show you that the great king will certainly harm [his reputation of being] just and not get Song."

The king responded, "[But] Gongshu Ban, the most skilled artisan in the world, is making a 'Cloud Ladder'[15] device in preparation for the attack on Song. How could I not take [Song]?"

Mozi replied, "I request that if you should allow Gongshu to prepare the attack, you give me permission to defend Song."

Subsequently, Gongshu Ban prepared the device to attack Song, and Mozi prepared the provisions to defend Song. [Gongshu Ban made] nine attacks and Mozi nine times repelled him. Chu could not enter Song. Finally Chu' s troops retreated and called off the attack on Song.[16]

Duangan Mu declined an official salary and remained at home. When Marquis Wen of Wei passed by his village gate, he bowed from his chariot. His driver asked, "My Lord, why did you bow from your chariot?"

Marquis Wen said, "Duangan Mu is here. This is why I bowed."

The driver said, "Duangan Mu is a scholar who wears simple attire. For my lord to bow at his village gate—is this not excessive?"

Marquis Wen replied, "Duangan Mu does not chase after power and profit. He embraces the Way of the Superior Man; secluding himself in an impoverished lane, his reputation spreads a thousand *li*. How could I presume not to bow?

> Duangan Mu is resplendent because of his virtue;
> I am resplendent because of my power.
> Duangan Mu is rich in Rightness;
> I am rich in wealth.
> Power is not as honorable as virtue;
> wealth is not as lofty as Rightness.

Even if Duangan Mu could change places with me, he would not do so. All day long I am saddened and embarrassed by my shadow.[17] How could I scorn him?"

Some time later, Qin raised troops to attack Wei, but Sima Yu[18] admonished the ruler of Qin, saying, "Duangan Mu is a worthy, and his ruler has treated him with

15. *Yunti* 雲梯, "cloud ladders," were scaling ladders used to attack walled cities.

16. This contest between Mozi and Gongshu Ban was a tabletop war game, not an actual invasion of Song by Chu. *Mozi*, chap. 50 (*zhuan* 13.2), is entitled "Gongshu Ban" and recounts many tales of the legendary craftsman. For this anecdote, see MoZ 13.2/116/13–19.

17. Compare 10.31: "Now when he examined his evening gait, the Duke of Zhou was embarrassed by his shadow. Thus the Superior Man scrutinizes [himself] in solitude."

18. Sima Yu 司馬庾 was a grandee of Qin during the Warring States period. He is identified in the *Zhanguoce* as Sima Geng 庚 or Sima Tang 唐.

propriety. There is no one in the world who does not recognize this. None among the Lords of the Land has failed to hear of this. If you raise troops and attack [his state], does not this amount to hindering Rightness?" Thereupon Qin demobilized its troops and did not attack Wei.

Now Mozi, tripping and stumbling, hastened ten thousand *li* to preserve Chu and Song, but Duangan Mu, [by] shutting his gate and refusing to come out, brought peace to Qin and Wei. As for going or staying, their propensities opposed each other, but both could preserve a state. This is what I mean by "[They start out along] different paths but return to the same place."

Now, those who extinguish a fire draw water from the well and hasten to the fire.

> Some use a jug or a bottle,
> while others use a tub or a basin.

Their squareness or roundness, angularity or smoothness, is not alike. In how much water they hold, they are all different; but for extinguishing a fire, they are all equal. Thus,

> the singing of Qin, Chu, Yan, and Wei have different traditions, but all are joyful.
> The wailing of the nine Yi and the eight Di tribes have different sounds, but all are sorrowful.

Now singing is evidence of joy,[19] and wailing is the product of grief. An ardent feeling internally is manifested as a response externally. The cause [of the response] lies in the feeling itself.[20] Thus the hearts of sages never deviate, day and night, from the desire to benefit others. The scope of their beneficence reaching so far, the results are correspondingly great. [19/203/20–19/204/11]

19.4

When the customary usages of an age fall into disuse and decline and those who repudiate learning become numerous, [they say]: "People's natures possess strengths and weaknesses, just as fish are swift and cranes are particolored. This is something natural that cannot be diminished or enhanced."[21] I believe this is not so. That fish are swift and cranes are particolored is analogous to

> what makes people people
> and what makes horses horses,

insofar as their muscles, bones, frame, and body, which they receive from Heaven, cannot be altered. Judging the issue from this perspective, they are not the same in kind.

19. The Chinese character 樂 means both "joy" (read *le*) and "music" (read *yue*).

20. Compare 10.53: "What was the same was that there were voices, but the beliefs derived from them were different; they were inherent in the [respective] feelings [of the singers]."

21. A statement similar to this appears in 1.8.

Now when a horse is a young colt, it jumps and kicks, raises its tail and runs, and people cannot control it.

Its bite is strong enough to pierce flesh and break bones,
and its kick is hard enough to break a skull or crush a chest.

But

when a groom tames it
or a fine charioteer trains it,
he restrains it with bridle and harness
and leads it with rein and bit,

so that even if it must cross a precipice or leap a ditch, it would not dare to shy away. Thus, its form makes it a horse, and a horse cannot be transformed [into anything else.] That the horse can be mounted and ridden is achieved through training. A horse is a dumb brute, and yet it is possible to penetrate its vital energy and will by relying on training to perfect the horse. How much more is this true of people! [19/204/13–18]

Moreover, those whose persons were upright and whose natures were good,

who radiated their ardor to perfect their Humaneness,[22]
who relied on their discontent to act with Rightness,

whose nature and destiny could be a source of pleasure, and who did not need to rely on study and inquiry to tally with the Way, were Yao, Shun, and King Wen.

Those who indulged deeply in wine and sex, whose conduct was unrestrained,

who could not be instructed by means of the Way
or taught by the example of virtue,
whom a stern father could not correct,
whom a worthy teacher could not transform,

were Dan Zhu and Shang Jun.[23]

Those with delicate, tender faces and brilliant white teeth, whose figures were beautiful and whose bone structure was elegant, who did not need to rely on cream and powder or perfume and unguents, [and] who by nature could please others, were Xi Shi and Yang Wen.

Those who were ugly and grotesque, whose mouths were large, and whose teeth were crooked, whose bellies were fat and whose backs were hunched, [and] who applied white powder and black mascara but could not be made beautiful were Mo Mu and Bi Sui.

Now those who

in loftiness do not reach Yao and Shun,
in baseness do not compare with Shang Jun,
who in beauty do not reach Xi Shi,
and who in ugliness do not compare with Mo Mu,

22. Supplying the character *ren* 仁, as suggested by Wang Niansun. See Zhang Shuangdi 1997, 2:1968n.10.

23. Dan Zhu 丹朱 was the son of the sage-ruler Yao, and Shang Jun 商均 was the son of the sage-ruler Shun. Both were judged unworthy by their fathers. See 10.64 and, more fully, 20.11.

are those to whom education and instruction are conveyed and to whom perfume and unguents are applied.

Furthermore, a son may kill his father, but the fathers of the world do not cast away their sons [as a result]. Why? It is because most sons love their fathers. A Confucian may be wicked and corrupt, but [people] do not abandon the Way of the Former Kings [as a result]. Why? [It is because] most [Confucians] put it into practice.

Now, rejecting study because those who study have faults is like

taking one instance of choking to refuse grain and not eat
or taking one problem with stumbling to stop walking and not go [anywhere].

This is deluded. [19/204/20–27]

Now a fine horse needs no whips or spurs to go. A poor-quality horse, even if whips and spurs were doubled, would not proceed. But never to use whips and spurs for this reason would be foolish. Now a coward may wield a sharp sword, but if he struck, he could not cut, and if he stabbed, he could not pierce. In the case of a brave warrior, with one blow he could rend the flesh and wound the body. If on account of this, you were to abandon [the blades of legendary swordsmiths] Gan Jiang and Mo Ye and use your fists to fight instead—this would be perverse. What I mean to say is: abide by the majority and conform to the customary. When you are not praising the heights of the Nine Heavens, you are speaking of the depths of the Yellow Springs; this amounts to discussing the limits of two extremes. How can these [extremes] be [the basis for] general assessments? [19/205/1–5]

Oranges and pomelos[24] grow in winter, but people say winter brings death, for most things die in winter.
Shepherd's purse and wheat die in the summer, but people say summer brings growth because most things grow in summer.
The twists and turns of the Yangzi and the Yellow rivers sometimes flow north and sometimes flow south, but people say that they flow eastward.
Jupiter and Saturn move eastward day by day and month by month, but people say that the stars and planets shift westward day by day and month by month;

they take the majority as their basis.

Among the Hu people are those who are knowledgeable and principled, but people call them stupid;
Among the Yue people are those who are dull-witted and slow, but people call them clever;

they consider the majority when naming them.

Now, Yao' s eyebrows were of eight colors, and his [body's] nine apertures all flowed into one another.[25] He was public minded, upright, and devoid of personal preferences. With one pronouncement, the multitudes were united.

Shun had two pupils in each eye. This was called "Double Discernment." What he did became laws, and what he said became statutes.

---

24. Rejecting the emendation proposed by Lau, HNZ, 205, line 7.
25. *Tong dong* 通洞, "were interconnected."

Yu's ears had three openings. This was called "Great Penetration." He increased benefits and eradicated harms, clearing the waterways and dredging the rivers.

King Wen had four nipples. This was called "Great Humaneness." The world returned home to him, and the common people grew close to him.

Gao Yao[26] had a horselike mouth. This was called "Utter Trustworthiness." He judged cases with clarity and brilliance as he judiciously examined human emotions.

> Xie[27] was born from an egg;
> Qi[28] was born from a stone;

Shi Huang[29] was born and could write; Yi was born with a long left[30] arm and was an outstanding archer. Nine such worthies as these appeared only once in a thousand years, yet it was as if they followed on one another's heels. Nowadays we are bereft of the heavenly blessings of these five sages or the flourishing talent of these four worthies. [Under such circumstances,] wanting to abandon study and follow nature is like abandoning a boat in the hopes that you will walk on water.

When [precious swords like] Chun'gou and Yuchang were first taken from their molds,

> if you sliced with them, they would not cut;
> if you stabbed with them, they would not pierce.

But once enhanced by polishing and grinding and rubbed until their points were sharp, in water they could cut through a dragon boat, and on land they could slash through rhinoceros-hide armor.[31]

When a mirror is first taken from its mold, it is hazy and does not yet reflect form or shape. When it is coated with dark tin [powder] and rubbed with a clean felt cloth, you can distinguish clearly the fine hair of the temples and eyebrows. Now, learning is a person's whetstone and tin. To say that learning does not enhance a person is a statement that refutes itself. [19/205/7–20]

---

26. Gao Yao was the minister of justice for the sage-ruler Shun.

27. Xie 契 (pronounced *qi* in most other usages) is identified in 11.3 as the minister of war for the sage-ruler Yao. His mother, Jian Di, supposedly became pregnant after eating a swallow's egg sent to her by the sage-emperor Di Ku. Xie is regarded as the founding ancestor of the ruling house of the Shang dynasty. See *Odes* 303 (Waley/Allen 1996, 320); and Hawkes 1985, 340.

28. Qi 啓, mythical son of Yu the Great, succeeded his father as king of the Xia dynasty. Qi's mother, the lady of Tushan, turned to stone but later split open to deliver her son. See Hawkes 1985, 333.

29. Not, as might be supposed, Qin Shihuangdi, but Shi huang 史皇, "Exalted Scribe," another name for Cang Jie, the supposed grand historian for the Yellow Emperor and the inventor of Chinese characters.

30. Rejecting the argument of Liu Wendian, based on the *Taiping yulan*, that this should be "right" rather than "left." See Lau, HNZ, 205n.9. The original text's reading of "left" is probably correct: it would be advantageous for an archer to have a long left arm (the arm that actually holds the bow), because that would allow the bow to be bent more deeply.

31. This phrase, which seems to be a cliché for describing the sharpness of a sword, recurs in 19.7.

19.5

The weakness of a wise person [in some field] makes him not as good [in that field] as a foolish person who is strong [in it].

The deficits of a worthy [in some field] make him not as good [in that field] as an ordinary person who surpasses [in it].[32]

How do I know this is so? With Song painting and Wu smelting, the carving of molds and the engraving of patterns are complex and intricate. Their creation of such subtle mysteries, [even] the sages Yao and Shun could not achieve. The young girls of Cai and the talented youth of Wey

in weaving their red waistbands,
in blending their marvelous colors,
in forming their black backgrounds,
and displaying their crimson patterns

[do what even] the wisdom of Yu and Tang could not attain! [19/205/22–24]

What Heaven covers,
what Earth supports,
is contained within the six coordinates;
is embraced within the universe.[33]

What yin and yang produce [from] the essence of blood and *qi* [are] creatures that have

a mouthful of teeth or a head bearing horns,[34]
front claws or rear hooves,
soaring wings or clutching talons

that advance by wriggling or move by crawling.

When happy, they are harmonious;
when angry, they are quarrelsome;
seeing benefit, they pursue it;
avoiding harm, they withdraw from it;

their instinctive responses in this respect are one. Although in their likes and dislikes they do not differ from people, nonetheless,

though their claws and teeth are sharp,
though their muscles and bones are strong,

they cannot avoid being controlled by people [because]

they cannot communicate their intelligence to one another,
and their abilities and strength cannot be made to act as one.

Each has its natural propensity that is not endowed or received from the outside. Thus their strengths have boundaries, and their accomplishments have limits.

---

32. A similar point is made in 9.11.

33. These lines echo the opening passage of chap. 4. For *liu he* 六合, the "six coordinates," see Major 1993, 146.

34. This description of animals echoes a similar passage in 15.1.

Now the wild goose follows the wind to fly in order to preserve its energy and strength. It holds straw in its mouth while soaring in order to fend off tethered arrows. Ants know how to build hills; badgers[35] make their winding tunnels; tigers and leopards have lairs of grass. Wild boars have grassy nests, rows of felled trees, and burrowed holes that join one another in the manner of palaces and rooms; they provide protection to guard them from the rain and shield them from the hot sun. Thus even birds and beasts know ways to seek out and accord with what brings them benefit.

Now [suppose] a person were born in a secluded and remote state and grew up in a leaking room in a poor house, was reared without older and younger brothers, and from childhood was bereft of father and mother. If [in addition] his eyes never witnessed proper rites, his ears never heard of former or ancient times, and he lived alone in his own home without going beyond his gate—even if by nature he was not stupid, nonetheless his knowledge would certainly be wanting. [19/205/26–19/206/8]

Long ago
Cang Jie invented writing;
Rong Cheng created the calendar;
Hu Cao[36] made clothing;
Lord Millet introduced agriculture;
Yi Di invented wine;
and Xi Zhong made carts.
These six men all had
the Way of spirit illumination
and [left behind] footprints of sagely wisdom.[37]

Thus [each] person invented something and bequeathed it to posterity. It is not the case that a single person alone would have been able to do all of them. Each fully applied his knowledge, prizing what he hoped to achieve so that subsequently each provided something for the world. Now if you had made these six men exchange their tasks, their brilliance would not have been apparent. Why? [It is because] the myriad things of the world are utterly numerous and knowledge is not sufficient to encompass them all. From the Zhou era onward, there have been no worthies like these six, and yet people have pursued all their callings. Among the people of the current age, there is not a single person of that caliber, yet people have come to know the Way of the Six Worthies. Education and training extended and continued [their work] so that their knowledge could flow forth and communicate with [later ages]. From this perspective, it is clear that learning can never cease. [19/206/10–14]

Now in the case of a blind person, his eyes cannot distinguish day from night or differentiate white from black; nevertheless when he grasps the *qin* and plucks the strings, triply plucking and doubly pressing,[38] touching and plucking, pulling and

35. *Huanhe* 貛貉. On the terms for "badger," see also chap. 1, n. 33.
36. Hu Cao 胡曹 was a (mythical) minister of the Yellow Emperor.
37. A similar argument is made in 12.10.
38. *Cantan* 參弾, "triply plucking (the strings)," and *fuhui*, 復徽, "doubly pressing (the frets)," refer to the movements of the player's right and left hands, respectively. We are grateful to Bo Lawergren

releasing, his hands are like a blur, and he never misses a string. If we tried to get someone who had never played the *qin* to do this, though possessing the clear sight of Li Zhu or the nimble fingers of Jue Duo,[39] it would be as if he could neither contract nor extend a finger. What is the reason for this? Such things are made possible only through repeated practice so they become habitual.

Thus,

the bow must await the stringing frame before it can be strung,
and the sword must await the whetstone before it can be sharpened.

Jade is harder than anything else, but it can be carved into the shape of beasts, the heads and the tails taking their true forms; this is the achievement of the abrasive stone.[40] Wood may be as straight as a marking cord, but if it is shaped to make a wheel, its bending will match the compass. This is the power of the bending frame. Things as hard as Tang jade can still be carved; it can be formed and made into useful things. How much more so is this the case with the human heart and mind! [19/206/16–20]

Moreover, the Quintessential Spirit is saturating and soaking, subtle and fine.[41]

Suddenly and quickly it alters and transforms
in accordance with things it moves and shifts

like the clouds rising and the winds drifting; it establishes and applies itself where it is most useful.

Among Superior Men are those who can

arouse the essence and examine the infinitesimal,
polish and grind their talents,
spontaneously exercise their spirit illumination,[42]
observe the broad spectrum of things,
penetrate the obstructions of things,
observe the clues to beginning and end,
perceive the realm that has no exterior,
wander freely within the limitless,
meander beyond the dust of the world.
Splendidly, they stand alone;
loftily, they leave the world.

Such are the means by which the mind of the sage wanders. However, people of later ages did not have the leisure to sit and still their thoughts, playing the *qin* and reading books, reflecting on observations of high antiquity, befriending worthies and great men, studying and debating, daily gaining self-mastery, delving into and

and Yuan Jung-ping (private communications) for their help with the technical terminology of this passage.

39. Jue Duo 攫掇, "Grabbing-Grasping," was a legendary figure known for manual adeptness. See 18.16.

40. *Jian* 礛 is a type of abrasive stone that is pulverized into grit and used in shaping jade. See similar comments in 16.81 and 17.28.

41. Lau, HNZ, 206n.7. Similar language appears in 1.1 and 15.4 to describe the Way.

42. Rejecting Yang Shuda's proposed emendation of *cheng* 誠 for *shi* 試. See Lau, HNZ, 206n.8.

analyzing the affairs of their age, distinguishing and differentiating white from black, estimating successes and losses, foretelling disasters and blessings, setting up norms and establishing rules to serve as laws and regulations, investigating thoroughly the roots and branches of the Way, studying deeply the essential qualities of things, establishing what is so and eradicating what is not so, illuminating and instructing later generations,

in death, leaving a legacy,
in life, possessing a glorious reputation.

Things like this are what human talent can achieve. But if no one can accomplish such things, it is because people are lazy and lax and have many idle days.

Now,

[among] people who come from regions where the soil is barren, there are many who have [good] minds. This is because their lives are laborious.

[Among] people who come from places where the soil is rich, there are many who are devoid of talents. This is because their lives are easy.

Looking at it from this perspective, a wise person who makes no effort does not compare with a foolish person who loves to learn. From the rulers, dukes, and ministers on down to the common people, there has never been a case of someone succeeding without exerting himself to the utmost. The *Odes* says,

"The days pass and the months proceed;
through study of brightness and brilliance, I gain radiance and light."[43]

This is what is referred to here. [19/206/22–19/207/6]

19.6

Reputation can be established through effort;
merit can be achieved through fortitude.

Thus the Superior Man

musters his will and commits himself to uprightness, hastening toward brilliant teachers;

encourages moderation and exalts loftiness, separating himself from the conventions of his age.

How might I illuminate this point?

Formerly, Nanrong Chou[44] was ashamed that he alone lacked the sagely Way. [Therefore,]

immersing himself in frost and dew,
arranging his sandals and hastening his steps,
he climbed mountains and forded rivers,
shielding his eyes from brambles and thorns,

43. *Odes* 288 (modified from Waley/Allen 1996, 302).
44. Nanrong Chou 南榮疇 features in a long narrative in *Zhuangzi* 23 (ZZ 23/64/25–23/65/24).

going a hundred stages[45] [with] his feet covered with blisters, not daring to rest.

[He reached] the south and met Lao Dan. Having received his instruction with a single word,

his Quintessential Spirit was suddenly enlightened;
his [formerly] obtuse and sad [heart became] orderly and lucid.

He was so pleased that for seven days he did not eat, although it was as if he had feasted on the *tailao*.[46]

Thus,

his brilliance illuminated all within the Four Seas,
and his reputation passed down to later generations.
He could summarily comprehend Heaven and Earth
and analyze something [as fine as] autumn floss.

Recognition and praise [of his merits] have not ceased to this day. This is what is meant by "Reputation can be established through effort."

When Wu and Chu[47] fought each other, the Chu undersecretary [Cheng] Daxin[48] grasped his charioteer's hand and said: "Today we confront a powerful enemy. We will

repel the glistening blades
and shield ourselves from arrows and stones.

If I die in battle, I still will win victory by [preserving] the people whole, [so that] our altars of soil and grain will be able to remain intact." Subsequently he pressed forward but did not retreat, for he was stabbed in the abdomen and beheaded [in battle]. Never turning his heels to reverse course, he died.

Shen Baoxu[49] declared: "If I give my all and fight this terrible enemy and fall as a bleeding corpse, I will show only the ability of an ordinary soldier. This is not so good as humbling myself and speaking self-deprecatingly and seeking aid from the Lords of the Land." Thereupon,

he packed his grain on his back and traveled barefoot,
fording streams and treading valleys,
ascending to the highest peaks
descending to the deepest gullies,
crossing rivers and streams,
defying rapids and mountain passes,
striding past hidden snares,
stumbling through sand and stone

until the whole area from his feet to his knees was swollen and covered with many large blisters. He journeyed for seven days and seven nights before he reached the court of Qin.

---

45. A "stage" (*she* 舍) is a day's march. See 17.182.
46. *Tailao* 太牢 was a sacrificial feast of beef, mutton, and pork.
47. The battle took place in 506 B.C.E.
48. Cheng Daxin 成大心 was a Chu grandee during the Spring and Autumn period.
49. Shen Baoxu 申包胥 was a scion of the royal house and high minister of Chu.

Standing [on one leg] like a crane and refusing sustenance,
by day he moaned and by night he wailed,
his face as if dead ashes,
his coloring swarthy and dark,
his tears ran down his face to collect in a pool.

When he met the king of Qin, he declared, "Wu is [like] Mound Pig or Long Snake.[50] It wants to gobble up the Upper States.[51] The disaster began in Chu. Our ruler has lost his altars of soil and grain. He has fled [to live amid] the grasses and reeds. The population has fled and dispersed; and husbands and wives, men and women, do not have a moment to inform [others] of their whereabouts. I was sent to report the emergency." The king of Qin thereupon raised a force of a thousand chariots and seventy thousand foot soldiers and appointed Zihu to command them. They crossed the pass to the east and attacked Wu at the Zhuo River, defeating Wu handily and thereby preserving Chu. Shen Baoxu's accomplishment was recorded in the court and among the official laws and proclamations. This is an example of merit attained through fortitude. [19/207/8–22]

For those with a frame seven feet tall,[52]
a heart that has borne anxiety, sadness, toil, and hardship,
and skin that has felt pain, illness, heat, and cold,

the instinctive responses of [all] people are the same. Sages know

the difficulty of attaining the opportune time
and that effort must be rendered quickly,

so they

mortify their bodies and belabor their forms;
weary their hearts and vex their livers;
never avoiding trouble and hardship;
never abandoning danger and peril.

In fact, I have heard that when Zifa battled,

he advanced like a flying arrow,
met [the enemy] like thunder and lightning,
and dispersed them like rain and wind.
He was round as a compass
and square as a carpenter's square.

He defeated his enemies and broke through their formations; none could withstand him.

When fighting in the wetlands, he was always victorious;
when attacking a city, it was sure to fall.

It is not that he looked lightly on his person or rejoiced in death. Rather, he placed responsibility in front and left [considerations of] benefit behind. Thus his reputa-

50. Mound Pig and Long Snake were two legendary monsters. See 8.6.

51. That is, the central states of the North China plain.

52. One Han dynasty "foot" (*chi* 尺) measured about nine English inches, so seven "feet" is equal to five feet, three inches.

tion was established and never faltered. This is an example of achieving merit through one's own fortitude.

For this reason,

if the tillers are not strong, the granaries and storerooms will not be full.

If the officials and attendants are not disciplined, their hearts and minds will not achieve the essence.

If generals and officers are not strong, their merit and fierceness will not succeed.

If princes and kings are lazy, in later ages they will have no reputation.

The *Odes* says,

"My horses are dappled;
the reins soft as silk;
I ride, I press on,
everywhere seeking wise counsel."[53]

This is to say that people have something to which they can apply their effort. [19/207/24–19/208/2]

19.7

Those who fully comprehend things cannot be startled by the unusual;
those who are versed in the Way cannot be moved by the strange;
those who examine words cannot be dazzled by their designations;
those who investigate into forms cannot be misled by their appearances.

People who follow the conventions of the present age mostly revere the ancient and scorn the present. Thus those who formulate [teachings of] the Way necessarily ascribe them to the Divine Farmer or the Yellow Emperor; only then will they proceed with their discussion. Muddled rulers of chaotic eras venerate what is remote and what proceeds therefrom, so they value such things. Those who study are blinded by their theories and respect [only] what they have heard. Facing one another,

seated with a dignified air[54] they praise [the ancients];
stiff-necked they recite [the ancient texts].

This shows that the distinction between what is true and what is false is not clear.

Now,

without a square and a compass, even Xi Zhong could not determine square and round;

without a level and a marking cord, even Lu Ban[55] could not straighten the crooked.

Thus,

53. *Odes*, 163 (Waley/Allen 1996, 135).

54. The same phrase occurs in 8.6.

55. Lu Ban was famously ingenious craftsman, also known as Gongshu Ban. See 19.3; and chap. 11, n. 81.

when Zhongzi Qi died, Bo Ya broke the strings and destroyed his *qin*, knowing that in his times no one could appreciate his playing.
When Hui Shi died, Zhuangzi ceased to talk, perceiving that there was no one else with whom he could converse. [19/208/4–9]

At the age of seven, Xiang Tuo became Confucius's teacher. From time to time, Confucius listened to his words. If someone this young were to offer a persuasion to a village elder, though, the child would not have time to duck a blow on the head. How would he be able to illuminate the Way [under such circumstances]?

In the past, Xiezi[56] had an audience with King Hui of Qin,[57] and the king was pleased with him. He asked Tang Guliang[58] about him. Tang Guliang said, "Xiezi is a debater from Shandong who uses clever persuasions to gain the confidence of young princes." King Hui accordingly hid his anger and awaited Xiezi. The next day when Xiezi had a second audience, the king rejected him and would not heed him. It is not that [Xiezi's] persuasion differed but that the way in which the king heard it changed.

If you mistake [the note] *zhi* for [the note] *yu*, it is not the fault of the string;
if you mistake a sweet taste for a bitter one, it is not the mistake of the flavor.

A man from Chu had some boiled monkey meat that he gave to his neighbors. They thought it was dog meat and found its flavor pleasing. Later, when they heard it was monkey, they knelt down and vomited all they had eaten. This was a case of not even beginning to know about flavor.

A music master from Handan made up a new tune and said it was composed by Li Qi.[59] All the people vied to learn it. Later when they discovered it was not written by Li Qi, they all abandoned the tune. This was a case of not even beginning to know about music.

A country fellow found a rough piece of jade. Being pleased by its appearance, he considered it to be precious and hid it away. When he showed it to others, people considered that it was just a stone, so he threw it away. This was a case of not even beginning to know about jade.

Thus when your [views] tally with what is essential, you will value what is true and [give] equal [consideration to] the present and the ancient. If you do not have the means to heed persuasions, then you will value what has come down from the past, [simply] because it is remote. This is why [Bian] He cried so hard that he bled at the foot of Mount Jing.[60]

Now,

---

56. See the account in LSCQ 16.7/96/30–32. Lau (HNZ, 208n.4) identifies Xiezi in this passage with Qi Shezi 祁射子 from *Shuo yuan* 17/3b.

57. King Hui of Qin 秦惠王 (r. 337–311 B.C.E.) was an aggressive ruler who expanded the power of Qin during his tenure as monarch. After taking the throne, he executed the reformer Shang Yang but carried on his progressive policies.

58. Tang Guliang 唐姑梁 was a minister of Qin.

59. According to Tao Fangqi, Li Qi 李奇 was a famous musician of Zhao. See Zhang Shuangdi 1997, 2:2013n.17.

60. For the story of Bian He and his attempt to present a piece of raw jade to successive kings of Chu, see chap. 14, n. 57.

a sword may be broken off and bent, thin and scratched, chipped and broken, and warped and twisted, but if it said to have been the sword of King Qingxiang of Chu, then it is prized, and the people will compete to wear it.

A *qin* may be twangy and sharp, crooked and bent, with its resonance gone and its aftertones excessive, but if it is said to have been the *qin* of King Zhuang of Chu,[61] then it is [prized], and the favored[62] will contend to play it.

Although the short-handled spears from Mount Miao and the [cast-iron] spear points of Sheepshead [Mountain] can cut through a dragon boat in the water and pierce armor of rhinoceros hide on land, no one wears them on his belt.

Although *qins* made of mountain *tong* wood with sounding boards of river-valley catalpa wood may sound as pure, lingering and clear as [the music of] Master Tang[63] or Bo Ya, no one plays them.

Those with penetrating discernment are not like this.

The swordsman hopes for a sharp blade; he does not hope for [the perfection of] Moyang or a Moye;
the horseman hopes for a thousand *li* [steed]; he does not hope for [the perfection of] Hualiu or Lü'er;
the *qin* player hopes for a pure, lingering, and clear sound; he does not hope for [the perfection of] Lanxie or Haozhong.[64]

One who [studies by] reciting the *Odes* and the *Documents* hopes to achieve a comprehensive understanding of the Way and a general knowledge of things; he does not hope for [the perfection of] a "Great Plan" or an "Ode of Shang."[65]

Sages perceive what is true and what is false, just as
what is white and black is distinguished by the eye
and what is high pitched and low pitched is differentiated by the ears.

But most people are not like this. Within themselves they lack a master [by means of which] to make [such] discernments. It is like a man who is born after his father dies. When [in later years] he climbs the tomb mound, he will wail and cry as ceremony demands, but nothing makes [those feelings] cleave to his heart. [19/208/11–28]

Thus,
when a boy and his twin look alike, only their mother can distinguish them.
When jade and [ordinary] stone are of the same sort, only a fine craftsman can identify them.
When texts and chronicles record strange things, only sages can discuss them.

Now, if we should get a new text from a sage and attribute it to Confucius or Mozi, then those disciples who point to every sentence and accept the text [as genuine] will certainly be numerous. Thus

61. King Zhuang of Chu reigned from 613 to 591 B.C.E.

62. Literally, "those in the anterooms"—that is, the ruler's favorites.

63. Master Tang 唐; according to Gao You and later commentators, this is a lexical variant for Music Master Tang 師堂, who is said to have instructed Confucius himself.

64. Moyang and Moye were famous swords; Hualiu and Lü'er, famous horses; and Lanxie and Haozhong, famous *qin*—in each case, exemplars of perfection.

65. These are key sections of the *Documents* and the *Odes*, respectively.

a beauty need not be of the same type as Xi Shi;
a knowledgeable scholar need not be of the same sort as Confucius or Mozi.

If his mind has the perspicacious capacity to penetrate things, then he will write books to illustrate matters, and they will be taken up by the learned. A scholar who truly attains clear-minded understanding, who grasps the profound mirror in his mind, illuminating things brilliantly and not changing his mind on account of [whether something is] ancient or current, will accordingly propound his writings and clearly point out [his views]. Then, even though his coffin might close, he would have no regrets. [19/209/1–5]

Formerly Duke Ping of Jin ordered his officials to make [a set of] bells. When they were finished and presented to Music Master Kuang, the latter said, "The bells are not in tune."

Duke Ping said, "I have shown them to skilled persons,[66] and they all think they are in tune. Yet you think they are not. Why?"

Music Master Kuang said, "If they are for those of later generations who have no knowledge of the notes, then they will do; but for those who know the notes, they will certainly know they are not in tune." Thus Music Master Kuang's wish for well-tuned bells was for those of later generations who knew the notes.[67]

The [people of the] Three Dynasties acted the same as we do, and the Five Hegemons had the same level of intelligence as we. [But] they alone had the reality of sagely knowledge, while we lack even

the reputation of a country village
or the common knowledge of a poor lane.

Why? [It is because] they set themselves straight and established their integrity, while we are rude idlers and lazy layabouts. [19/209/7–11]

Now Mao Qiang and Xi Shi were recognized by the world as beauties, but if they were made to

carry putrid rats in their mouths
and be wrapped in hedgehog skins,
and dress in leopard fur,[68]
with waist sashes of dead snakes,

---

66. *Gong* 工, "skilled workers"; it is not clear whether the reference here is to bronze founders or to professional musicians.

67. There is an implied criticism here that no one in his time understood sounds, but Music Master Kuang was looking at the set of bells from a long perspective. The passage also reflects the idea that bells and other expensive bronze ritual objects were explicitly intended (as their inscriptions show) to be handed down as heirlooms to later generations. Music Master Kuang is protecting the duke's reputation by insisting on well-tuned bells to be handed down and appreciated by the music connoisseurs of later times.

This anecdote seems to imply a concept of absolute pitch (see app. B, "Music and Mathematical Harmonics") and apparently reflects a belief that some of Music Master Kuang's legendary skill was attributable to his having the gift of perfect pitch. See also 20.21. We thank Dan Lusthaus (private communication) for sharing these insights with us.

68. In this context, the connotation is of masculinity and perhaps barbarism, not of luxury or feminine elegance.

even cloth-wearing, leather-belted [ordinary] people passing by all would look off to the left or right and hold their noses. But if we were to let them

wear perfume and unguents,
adjust their moth eyebrows,[69]
put on hair clasps and earrings,
dress in fine silk,
and trail [sleeves of] Qi silk gauze,
with white face powder and black mascara,
wearing jade sash-bangles,
walking with gliding steps,
wearing sprigs of fragrant angelica,
with enticing looks,
bewitching smiles,
haunting glances,
speaking delicately and softly,
exposing their beautiful teeth,
twitching the dimples in their cheeks,

then even among the great statesmen of the royal court, whose conduct displays a stern will and haughty air, there would be none who would not court these beauties, long for them, and desire to have sex with them.

Nowadays a person of average talent, benighted by ignorant and deluded wisdom, cloaked in insulting and shameful conduct, who has no training in his own calling or in the techniques that are his responsibility—how could he not make people look askance at him and hold their noses? [19/209/13–18]

Now dancers twirl their bodies like rings of jade. They bend and touch the ground and turn quickly and nimbly. As they move, they twist and turn, lithe and beautiful, imitating spirits.

Their bodies seem as light as wind-borne autumn floss,
their hair like banners flapping in the wind,
their steps are quick as those of a racehorse.

Acrobats, raising poles of *wu* [*tong*] or catalpa[70] wood and grasping crooked tree branches, are as uninhibited as monkeys. Laughing, they pull the leaves toward them; crouching and stretching like dragons, they perch on the branches like swallows. Holding thick tree limbs, they raise them effortlessly. As they dance, they rise like dragons or birds as they gather. They grasp and release; how fast they move!

There is no one among the spectators who does not grow faint at heart and weak in the knees. Meanwhile, the performers continue their act with a smile and then put on the costumes for the feather dance.

The dancers do not [inherently] have such supple and nimble [bodies];
the acrobats do not [inherently] have such keenness and strength.

It was the gradual, long-term practice and training that made them so. Thus,

69. Artificial eyebrows applied with makeup.
70. Equating *jia* 檟 with *zi* 梓, following Gao You's commentary.

when a tree grows, no one sees its progress; at a certain point, we realize that it has grown tall.

If a hard object is continually [sharpened] on a whetstone, no one sees it diminishing, but at some point we realize that it is thinner.

Pigweed and hyssop grow by leaps and bounds, each day adding several inches. But they cannot be used for the crossbeams of a building. With hardwoods [like] lindera, southernwood, or camphor, only after seven years can their growth be recognized. Then they can be used to make coffins and boats.

Thus, matters

that can be accomplished easily gain small fame for the one who does them;
[those] that are difficult to accomplish gain great merit.

The Superior Man cultivates his good points. Even though there might not be an [immediate] advantage, good fortune will come later. Thus the *Odes* says,

"The days pass and the months proceed;
through study of brightness and brilliance,
I gain radiance and light."[71]

This is what is referred to here. [19/209/20–28]

Translated by Sarah A. Queen and John S. Major

---

71. *Odes* 288 (modified from Waley/Allen 1996, 302). The same poem was quoted earlier in this chapter. See n. 43.

Twenty

THE EXALTED LINEAGE

WITH NINETEEN chapters behind him and his royal curriculum nearly complete, the young monarch who is the ideal reader of the *Huainanzi* is now invited to "knot the net of the Way of Governance and weave the web of the True King," thus rounding off his education. This chapter, "The Exalted Lineage," reminds the monarch, who has been trained to aspire to sagely rule, that the "Moral Potency that takes shape within is the great foundation of governance."[1] Moreover, this chapter makes clear that such internally generated Moral Potency has far-reaching cosmopolitical implications affecting both Heaven above and the people below. As this chapter returns to the theme of sagely governance, it does so with an eye to reiterating those attributes essential to its realization. It identifies for the reader a number of exemplary rulers of the recent and remote past who embodied these ideals and thereby brought order and harmony to the wider world. Not surprisingly, a number of the themes and concepts associated with the sage and his governance found in this chapter reiterate claims made in earlier chapters of the *Huainanzi*, drawing this great didactic oeuvre to a close.

1. 故德行於內治之大本 (21/226/21). Note that the phrase "Moral Potency taking shape within" occurs repeatedly in this chapter, recalling a central theme of the Mawangdui manuscript *Wuxing* (*Five Conducts*). See Csikszentmihalyi 2004.

The Chapter Title

We have translated the title "Tai zu" 泰族 as "The Exalted Lineage."[2] *Tai* is associated with all things that take the qualities of goodness and abundance to the extreme; thus the word denotes something that is exalted, honorable, extensive, and prosperous. *Zu* is a kinship term describing those associated by a blood relationship, such as a family, clan, or lineage. "The Exalted Lineage" carries a double meaning here. On the one hand, it refers to the illustrious line of rulers who have practiced sagely government since the beginning of historical time, beginning with the Five Thearchs and the Three Kings and continuing (at least in aspiration) to the sage-in-training of Liu An's own time, Emperor Wu. Collectively, those rulers comprise a fictive kinship lineage of sages. On the other hand, the title also refers implicitly to the Liu clan, the imperial house of the Han dynasty, and to the potential of members of that clan to bring honor and prosperity to their lineage by perpetuating the tradition of virtuous rule established by the dynastic founder. The *Huainanzi* was presented to the newly enthroned Emperor Wu in 139 B.C.E. and apparently was compiled under the supervision of and with the active participation of the emperor's uncle Liu An as a manifesto of Han imperial rule. The *Huainanzi* is thus self-described as the means for ensuring the prosperity, security, and longevity of the imperial house of Han. "The Exalted Lineage" implies that the Liu clan is uniquely positioned to perpetuate into the indefinite future a history of sagely governance extending back to the farthest roots of Chinese civilization.

Summary and Key Themes

Chapter 20 restates and brings into sharper focus the lessons of the preceding nineteen chapters. A summary of "The Exalted Lineage" is therefore, to some extent, a summary of the *Huainanzi* as a whole. But this chapter is more than just a recapitulation. It has an important message of its own, which is to define the psychological qualities needed by a sage-ruler.

The chapter opens with several sections emphasizing the "thus-of-itself" (*ziran* 自然) character of the natural world, recalling the cosmogonic and naturalist themes in chapters 1 through 6 used in the *Huainanzi* to set the stage for an inquiry into the human realm and its proper governance. The reader is reminded that the universe operates by its own principles and not for the benefit of any particular creatures among the "myriad things." To understand this is to possess "spirit illumination" (*shenming* 神明), and to activate spirit illumination by means of one's "Heavenly

2. This title can have many interpretations. Ames 1994, 100, translates it as "The Great Family," and Csikszentmihalyi, 2004, 158, understands it as "The Great Gathering." Le Blanc and Mathieu 2003 take a different interpretive tack altogether and render it as "De la synthèse ultime."

Heart" allows the sage-ruler to conform to the principles of the Way in all things. Thus the message of chapter 6 is reiterated: resonance (*ganying* 感應) links everything in the cosmos in constant interaction, and the ruler serves to modulate those interactions. Having achieved inner cultivation, as described in chapter 7, "The Quintessential Spirit," the ruler in his interactions with the external world is

> boundless and formless,
> quiet and voiceless. (20.8)

After a series of reminders from the worlds of craft and skill (such as woodworking and metal casting) that useful things are accomplished by following the natural propensities of things, the middle sections of the chapter hold up for emulation the great models of antiquity: the Five Thearchs and the Three Kings. Those worthies also succeeded in creating perfect governance by following the natural order of things. They understood that different circumstances require different approaches, that different problems require different solutions. They did not confine themselves to a single policy, and even in applying the classics, they practiced moderation and avoided going to extremes (20.13).

The sages of antiquity were broad-minded and farsighted (20.15). The people respond to the personal qualities of the sage, not to externalities. They stir in response to the ruler's Quintessential *qi*, are transformed by his Heavenly Heart, and are moved by his Quintessential Sincerity (20.17). In order to achieve this, the sages first governed themselves and thus were able to govern the state (20.18). Although the sages did not hesitate to use law in governance, they knew that law alone was not sufficient to create order: "Though laws exist, they must await a sage, and only then can there be good government" (20.21). An essential quality of the sage is that he is able to transform the people; thus laws exist, but they do not need to be relied on:

> [W]hen the ruler called, the people harmonized;
> when the ruler moved, the lowly followed. (20.23)

How does one cultivate the qualities of a sage? In part by understanding and embodying the virtues: Propriety and Wisdom (20.22–23) and Humaneness and Rightness (20.26–27). Collectively, these constitute one's Moral Potency. Here, again, one path to successful practice is to emulate model figures from the past: the Duke of Zhou, Confucius, the recluse Duangan Mu, the vigorous minister Li Ke, and many others—"These were men whose actions differed but who [alike] turned their steps toward goodness" (20.26).

Finally, how can one emulate the sages? Through education, so "The Exalted Lineage" turns (in sections 20.30 through 20.34) to the importance of education and the limitless joy and benefit that it brings. In contrast, ignorance is misery, whereas learning liberates even the meanest person from that miserable state. To neglect study is to impose on oneself an unnecessary handicap: "Thus when we compare failure to study with studying, it is like comparing the deaf and dumb with unimpaired people" (20.32). One might be tempted to take shortcuts when in power—such as Shang Yang's reliance on excessively harsh laws to maintain order or King Fuchai of Wu's reliance on the arrogance of military prowess to achieve security—but such techniques are of no avail in the long run.

The qualities of a sage can be reduced to two essentials: Humaneness and Wisdom. Accordingly, the chapter concludes on a note that is both cautionary and hopeful: cautionary because the ruler will be tempted to find an easy path, even though such paths lead only to ruin; hopeful because the essential qualities of a sage can be achieved:

> [T]here is no Humaneness greater than loving others;
> there is no Wisdom greater than understanding others.
>
> If you have neither of these, even if you are perceptive and smart, clever and skillful, and work hard and untiringly, you will not avoid disorder. (20.39)

Sources

Whereas previous chapters of the *Huainanzi* often drew extensively on other works of Warring States and Han literature, history, and political philosophy, representing a variety of perspectives, chapter 20 borrows primarily from the book's own content, along with the fund of historical anecdotes and political lore that was the common heritage of every educated person of the age. The work closes with a few reminders to its reader, a monarch in training to become a sage.

What are the lessons that the *Huainanzi* authors chose? They can be characterized as a series of complementary polarities: draw your lessons from human history, seeking inspiration from and emulating the greatest sages of the past, the Five Thearchs and the Three Kings;[3] but also become familiar with and correlate your governance

---

3. According to the summary in *Huainanzi* 21, this chapter

provides the means to observe how the Five Thearchs and the Three Kings
embraced the heavenly *qi*,
cherished the Heavenly Heart,
and grasped centrality and savored harmony.
Their Moral Potency having taken shape within [them],
it then cohered Heaven and Earth,
issued forth and aroused yin and yang,
ordered the four seasons,
rectified the changeable directions,
calmed things with its tranquillity,
and extended them with its efficaciousness.
[Their Moral Potency] then thereby
fired and smelted the myriad things,
buoyed up and transformed the innumerable life forms,
singing forth, they harmonized,
moving about, they followed along,

with the constant patterns and cycles inherent in Heaven, Earth, and the seasons.[4] Likewise, follow the inherent qualities of the myriad things and the inherent natural tendencies of your people, and you will be able to bring perfection to the world.[5] Be ever mindful of communing with Heaven above by means of your Heavenly Heart,[6] but be equally vigilant in transforming like a spirit[7] the habits and customs of the people below by means of your Quintessential Sincerity.[8] Heaven will respond in kind, repaying goodness with auspicious anomalies and evil with baleful occurrences.[9] So, too, will the people, as they did with the Great King Danfu: when he left Bin with staff and whip in hand, "the common people followed him, carrying their young, supporting their old, and shouldering their axes and earthenware [pots], they

---

so that all things within the Four Seas with a single mind unanimously offered their allegiance. (21.2)

Many chapters of the *Huainanzi* use various historical examples to present their arguments. The Five Thearchs and the Three Kings figure prominently throughout much of the text. They are cited as exemplary models of sagely governance in chaps. 6, 8, 10, 11, 13, 15, 20, and 21, although the specific rulers constituting these groups vary.

4. As explained in 20.4:

Thus the Great Man
conforms in Potency with Heaven and Earth,
conforms in brightness with the sun and moon,
conforms in numinous efficacy with the ghosts and spirits,
and conforms in trustworthiness with the four seasons.

See also 20.12. For a discussion of the ways in which the ruler should correlate his governance with Heaven, Earth, and the seasons, see chaps. 3–5.

5. See, especially, 20.10.

6. See 20.3, where the notions of the Heavenly Heart (*tianxin* 天心), Quintessential Sincerity, and spirit illumination are discussed together. Note that chap. 20 uses the terms "Heavenly Heart" and "Quintessential Sincerity" synonymously. The term *tianxin* appears in the *Huainanzi* only in chap. 20 (five times) and chap. 21 (once, in that chapter's summary of chap. 20). The text usually identifies the Utmost Essence or Quintessential Spirit as the medium through which humans move Heaven above and the Quintessential Sincerity as the means by which the ruler moves his people below. See, especially, chap. 6, "Surveying Obscurities," chap. 7, "The Quintessential Spirit," and chap. 10, "Profound Precepts."

7. See 20.4 and 20.18. Note that chap. 9 claims: "The loftiest [of rulers] transforms by means of his spirit" (9.8). References to the "spirit transformation" (*shen hua* 神化) of the populace and "transforming [the people] like a spirit" (*hua ru shen* 化如神) appear in chaps. 9, 10, 15, and 20.

8. For example, 20.9 concludes: "Thus if the ruler applies the Way to the people and they do not follow him, he has not exercised a sincere heart." "Sincerity" used as a noun or the related terms "Quintessential Sincerity," "Utmost Sincerity," the "sincere heart," and "the heart that is sincere" occur in chaps. 6, 9, 10, 11, 12, 15, 17, 18, and 20. The most extensive discussions of the concept are found in chaps. 10 and 20.

9. Heaven's responses, for example, are explained in 20.3:

Heaven and humanity are mutually in communication with each other. Thus
when a state is endangered and perishes, the pattern of Heaven changes.
When an age is deluded and chaotic, rainbows appear.

In 3.3: "The feelings of the rulers of men penetrate to Heaven on high." Resonance (*ganying*) is the principal subject of chap. 6.

traversed the Liang Mountains and established a state in Qizhou." In this way, they were drawn to his Quintessential Sincerity.[10] Turn inward to cultivate the insights that only spirit illumination[11] can provide, but look outward to the classics and to other great traditions of learning and inquiry, sources of both intellectual support and unsurpassed joy.[12] Make use of the law[13] but recognize its limitations, and make sure that it is administered by worthy men and supplemented with the appropriate panoply of virtues.[14] Never cease in your aspirations to sagely rule, but remember that no ruler can hope to ascend such lofty heights without worthy and virtuous assistants by his side. Establish a humane, trustworthy, and awe-inspiring presence by relying on both nonverbal and verbal forms of communication.[15] Remember these cardinal principles, aspire to them constantly, and you will become a sage.

The Chapter in the Context of the *Huainanzi* as a Whole

The fabric nearly complete, the weaver pauses to reflect on the warp and weft threads that, with every pass of the shuttle, combine to form this richly variegated tapestry of sagely governance. Casting one last glance over the intricate design of his fine production, he removes the fabric from the loom and prepares to add its final embellishment of embroidery, highlighting its essential themes.

If a young monarch-in-training has been diligent in working his way through the *Huainanzi*'s previous nineteen chapters, his education as an aspiring sage-ruler is nearly complete. It remains for him only to review and reflect on what he has learned. To that end, here, in this chapter, the reader is reminded of the complementary polarities running through much of the text, like the warp and weft threads of a great tapestry. Taken together, they constitute the web of a surpassingly comprehensive description of the Great Way.

Sarah A. Queen and John S. Major

---

10. See 20.9.

11. The term "spirit illumination" (*shenming* 神明) pervades the *Huainanzi*, appearing in thirteen of the text's twenty-one chapters: 1, 2, 4, 7, 8, 11, 12, 13, 15, 17, 19, 20, and 21. The term "spirit" or "spirits" (*shen*) appears in every chapter of the text.

12. For the joys of enlightenment fostered by learning and inquiry, see, especially, 20.30. For the most impassioned arguments that the ruler should exert himself to study, see chap. 19, "Cultivating Effort," esp. 19.5.

13. For discussions of the role and limits of law, see 20.21–24. For earlier discussions of the role of law in sagely governance, see esp. chap. 9, "The Ruler's Techniques."

14. Chap. 20 pairs Propriety and Rightness (20.22 and 20.23), Humaneness and Rightness (20.26 and 20.27), and Humaneness and Wisdom (20.39). These virtues also are discussed in many other chapters of the text.

15. For other discussions of the various forms of verbal and nonverbal forms of communication between the ruler and his people, see, for example, chaps. 6, 10, and 12.

Twenty

20.1

Heaven
established the sun and moon,
arranged the stars and planets,
harmonized the yin and yang,
and displayed the four seasons.
The day serves to blaze things with sunlight;
the evening serves to give them respite;
the wind serves to dry things out,
and the rain and dew serve to moisten them.
In giving life to things, no one sees the means by which it nurtures them and yet things reach maturity.
In taking life away from things, no one sees the means by which it sends them off to death and yet things cease to exist.

This is called "spirit illumination." Sages take it as their model. Thus,
when they initiate good fortune, no one sees from whence it originates and yet it arises.
When they eradicate calamity, no one sees the means by which they do so and yet it disappears.
Move away from it; it nears.
Approach it; it recedes.
Search for it; it will not be obtained.

Examine into it; it is not insubstantial.
Reckon it by days; it is incalculable.
Reckon it by years; there is surplus. [20/210/3–6]

20.2

When moisture comes, no one sees its form, yet the charcoal has already grown heavier.
When the wind blows, no one sees its image, yet the trees have already been set in motion.

The sun moves, but we do not see its movements. [The great horse] Qiji gallops with his back to the sun, and the grasses and trees are crushed under his hooves. Before there is enough time to set out the warning lights to announce his arrival,[1] the sun is already in front of him.

When Heaven is about to send forth a strong wind, before the grasses and trees have moved, birds have already begun to soar.
When it is about to send forth rain, before the dark clouds have gathered, the fish have already begun to gasp for air,[2]

for the *qi* of yin and yang move each other. Thus

cold and heat, dryness and moistness, follow one another in accordance with their kind.
Sounds and echoes reply to each other in accordance with their tone.

Thus the *Changes* says,

"When the crane calls in the treetop,
its babies respond to it."[3] [20/210/8–12]

20.3

When the High Ancestors went into mourning, for three years they did not speak and all within the Four Seas were silent and voiceless. [But] as soon as a single word was uttered, [they] greatly moved the world. This is because they relied on their Heavenly Heart when opening and closing their mouths. Thus, as soon as you stimulate the root, the hundred branches all respond. It is like the spring rains watering the myriad things;

turbulently they flow,
copiously they spread out;
there is no place that is not moistened

1. A reference to a system of watchtowers in border areas that make warning fires to signal the approach of mounted enemies.
2. This image also occurs in 9.4, 10.97, and 16.59.
3. *Zhouyi* 37/61/1.

and no plant that does not thrive. [20/210/14–16]

Thus, when the sage embraces his Heavenly Heart, his voice can move and transform the world. Thus, when his Quintessential Sincerity is stimulated within, an embodied *qi* responds in Heaven:

Lucky stars appear,
yellow dragons descend,
auspicious winds arrive,
sweet springs appear,
excellent grains thrive,
rivers do not fill and overflow,
and the seas do not churn and roil.

Thus the *Odes* says,

"Nurturing and yielding are the hundred spirits
even to the rivers and mountain peaks."[4]

When you oppose heaven and oppress the myriad things,

the sun and moon [suffer] partial eclipses;
the five planets lose their proper orbits;
the four seasons overstep one another.
In the day it is dark and at night it is light;
mountains crumble and rivers flood;
in winter there are thunderstorms, and in summer there are frosts.

The *Odes* says,

"In the first month, frost is abundant;
my heart is anxious and grieved."[5]

Heaven and humanity are mutually in communication with each other. Thus

when a state is endangered and perishes, the pattern of Heaven changes.
When an age is deluded and chaotic, rainbows appear.

The myriad things are mutually linked; Quintessence and baleful energy are mutually in conflict. Thus matters of spirit illumination

cannot be created by wisdom and cunning,
and cannot be achieved by agility and strength.
What Heaven and Earth embrace,
what yin and yang nurture,
what rain and dew moisten

are the myriad things that are born and live.

Kingfisher [feathers] and sea turtle [shell],
pearls and jade,
are colorful and bright,
glistening and glossy.
When rubbed, they are not scratched;
kept for a long time, they do not change.

---

4. *Odes* 273.
5. *Odes* 192.

Xi Zhong could not fashion them;
Lu Ban could not make them—
this is what is called the "great skill." [20/210/18–25]

20.4

A person of Song used ivory to make a mulberry leaf for the ruler.[6] It took three years for him to finish it.

Stem and veins, downy hairs and indentations,
tenuous points and lustrous color—

When it was mixed in among real mulberry leaves, one could not tell [which it was]. Liezi heard this and said, "If Heaven and Earth took three years to make a leaf, then among the myriad things, very few would have had leaves! Now when Heaven and Earth carry out their transformations,

they blow and [leaves] emerge;
they puff and [leaves] drop.

Why does [this person of Song] expend so much effort?" Thus

anything that can be measured is small,
and any [quantity] that can be counted is few.
No measurement can encompass the supremely great;
no enumeration can count the supremely numerous.

Thus

the realm of the nine provinces[7] cannot be measured in *qing* and *mu*;[8]
the eight cardinal points cannot be measured in circuits and *li*.
Mount Tai cannot be calculated in fathoms and feet;[9]
the rivers and seas cannot be measured in pecks and bushels.[10]

Thus the Great Man

conforms in Potency with Heaven and Earth,
conforms in brightness with the sun and moon,
conforms in numinous efficacy with the ghosts and spirits,
and conforms in trustworthiness with the four seasons.

Thus sages

embrace the *qi* of Heaven and enfold the heart of Heaven,
grasp centrality and embody harmony.

---

6. The same story appears in LieZ 8/45/13, where, however, the material is said to have been jade.

7. For the nine provinces (*jiu zhou* 九洲), see 4.1. For an extended discussion of the meanings of *jiu zhou* as both "nine provinces" and "nine continents," see John S. Major, "The Five Phases, Magic Squares, and Schematic Cosmography," in *Explorations in Early Chinese Cosmology: Papers Presented at the Workshop on Classical Chinese Thought Held at Harvard University, August 1976*, ed. Henry Rosemont Jr., Journal of the American Academy of Religion Studies, vol. 50, no. 2 (1984; repr., Charleston, S.C.: Booksurge, 2006), 134–45.

8. A *mu* 畝 is about one-sixth of an acre, and a *qing* 頃 is a hundred *mu*.

9. *Zhang* 丈 and *chi* 尺, roughly, "fathoms and feet"; a *zhang* is ten Chinese feet.

10. A *dou* 斗 is a dry measure, sometimes translated as a "peck"; a *hu* 斛 is five *dou*.

They do not descend from the ancestral temple, yet they journey to the Four Seas. [Everywhere] they alter habits and change customs, so that the people transform and become good as if it were their own natures. This is because [the sages] are capable of transforming [others] like a spirit.

The *Odes* says,

> "The spirits hear
> if in the end we are in harmony and peace."[11] [20/210/27–20/211/5]

20.5

Now with regard to ghosts and spirits,

> we look for them, but they are without form;
> we listen for them, but they are without voice;

yet we perform the Suburban Sacrifice to Heaven and the [appropriate] observances to the mountain and river [spirits].

> With prayer and sacrifice we seek prosperity;
> with invocations and charms we seek rain;
> with tortoise shell and milfoil we decide matters.

The *Odes* says,

> "When the spirits might descend
> cannot be calculated.
> How can you treat them with disdain?"[12] [20/211/5–7]

20.6

> Heaven extends to the highest;
> Earth extends to the thickest.
> The moon illuminates the nights;
> the sun illuminates the days.
> The arrayed stars are bright and clear;
> yin and yang transform.

There is no purposeful activity in this.[13] If you rectify their Ways, things will be thus-of-themselves. Therefore,

---

11. *Odes* 165, stanza 2. Zhang Shuangdi 1997, 2:2043n.14, refers to the *Erh Ya*, which gives *shen* 慎, "carefully," as a reading for the *shen* 神 in the text. Thus the original meaning of the poem is

> "Carefully we listen [to the song of the bird]
> so that in the end there may be harmony and peace."

In the context in which the *Huainanzi* cites the poem, however, it appears to follow an alternative reading that was accepted by many traditional scholars, so it is that version we give here. Waley/Allen 1996, 137, also follows the reading with *shen*, "spirits."

12. *Odes* 256.

13. Compare the opening lines of 20.10.

yin and the yang [cycle through] four seasons, but not [in order to] generate the myriad things.
Rain and dew fall in season, but not [in order to] nurture grasses and trees.
Spirit and illumination join,
yin and yang harmonize,
and the myriad things are born.
Thus,
tall mountains and deep forests
are not [for the benefit of] tigers and leopards.
Massive trees and leafy branches
are not [for the benefit of] flying birds.
Springs flow a thousand *li*,
and pools plunge a hundred *ren*,[14]
but not [for the benefit of] flood dragons.
Things reach their height and loftiness,
achieve their girth and massiveness;
mountains for residing and trees for perching,
nests for sheltering and caves for hiding,
water for soaking and land for traveling.
Each reaches its state of equipoise.
Now,
what is large generates what is small;
what is numerous generates what is scarce.
This is the Way of Heaven. Thus,
a small mound of earth cannot produce clouds and rain,
and a small stream cannot produce fish and turtles
because it is too small.
The steamy vapor [rising from] cattle and horses produces maggots and lice,
but the steamy vapor from maggots and lice cannot produce cattle and horses.
Thus
transformation is engendered from without;
it is not engendered from within. [20/211/9–15]

20.7

Now flood dragons crouch in deep pools, but their eggs hatch in earthen mounds. The male cloud-dragon sings in a high voice, and the female sings in a low voice; through transformation they achieve [their] form. This is the Utmost Essence. Thus when the sage nurtures his heart, nothing is better than sincerity. With Utmost Sincerity, he can move and transform [others].

14. One *ren* is eight Chinese feet (*chi* 尺).

Now those who possess the Way
amass essence inside themselves
and lodge spirit within their hearts.
[They] are quiet and indifferent, tranquil and undisturbed,
with pleasure and profundity in their breasts.[15]
Thus the *qi* of depravity has no place to tarry or obstruct.
The joints of [their] four limbs are well articulated;
their hairs' vapor vents away in an orderly fashion.
Thus the main axes of their bodies are harmonious and advantageous, so that none of the hundred channels and the nine apertures fail to flow freely. Thus where the spirit dwells, it is sure to attain its proper place. How could we say that this is just [a matter of] soothing the joints or arranging the hair? [20/211/17–21]

20.8

When a sagely ruler is in power, he is
boundless and formless,
quiet and voiceless.
The officials are as if devoid of tasks;
the court is as if devoid of people.
There are
no scholars in seclusion,
no people in exile,
none doing forced labor,
and none wrongfully mutilated.
Within the Four Seas, none fails to
look up to the ruler's Moral Potency
or imitate the ruler's directives.
The ["barbarian"] states of the Yi and the Di arrive with their respective interpreters,[16] [but] the sagely ruler declines to engage in disputations with their [various] households and persuasions with their [various] families. He extends the sincerity in [his] heart and applies it to the world, that is all.[17]

The *Odes* says,

"Let there be kindness in the Central States,
bringing tranquillity to the four quarters."[18]

When the interior is compliant, the exterior is peaceful. [20/211/23–26]

15. Reading *mu* 穆 for *mu* 繆.

16. On the use of multiple interpreters to communicate with the "barbarian" tribes, see 11.5.

17. In other words, the Yi and Di peoples arrive expecting to deal with issues of mutual interest through verbal communication—hence the interpreters—but the sage-ruler acts through nonverbal Quintessential Sincerity instead.

18. *Odes* 253.

20.9

When the Great King Danfu dwelled in Bin, the Dee tribes attacked him. He left with his staff and whip. The common people [followed Danfu]. Carrying their young, supporting their old, and shouldering their axes and earthenware [pots], they traversed the Liang Mountains and established a state in Qizhou. This is not something an order could summon.[19]

Duke Mu of Qin suffered the affront of having some local rustics eat the meat of his fine steeds.[20] [In response] he gave them fine liquor to drink. [Later], at the battle of Hann[yuan], [the rustics] fought to the death to repay Duke Mu. This is not something a written contract could have bound them to do.

Mizi was ruling in [the land of] Danfu. Wuma Qi went to see how he had transformed the people. He observed that when people fished at night, if they caught a small fish, they let it go. This was not something that restrictive laws could prohibit.[21]

When Confucius was minister of justice in Lu, no one threw litter on the roads, nor were prices raised in the marketplace. In tilling the fields and in fishing, people ceded to the elderly, and those with grizzled hair did not carry things. These are not things that laws could achieve.

Now the reason why an arrow

can be shot for a long distance and penetrate a hard substance is because the bow is strong, but the reason it can hit the tiny center of a target is due to the human heart.

Rewarding goodness and punishing wickedness is for government decrees, but the reason they can be carried out depends on Quintessential Sincerity.

Thus, though a bow may be strong, it cannot hit the target on its own.

Though a decree may be enlightened, it cannot be carried out on its own.

They must be grounded in Quintessential Sincerity[22] in order to be effective. Thus if the ruler applies the Way to the people and they do not follow him, he has not exercised a sincere heart. [20/211/26–20/212/5]

20.10

Heaven, Earth, and the four seasons do not [purposefully] produce the ten thousand things.[23]

19. Danfu was the (legendary) grandfather of King Wen, founder of the Zhou dynasty. The story is told more fully in 12.15, which in turn is almost identical to the version in *Zhuangzi* 28 (ZZ 28/81/23–28; Mair 1997, 285–86); another, abbreviated, version appears in 14.14. See also LSCQ 21.4/141/11–17; and Knoblock and Riegel 2000, 557–58.

20. A fuller version of this story appears in 13.18. See also LSCQ 5; and Knoblock and Riegel 2000, 202–3.

21. For the story of Mizi and the small fish, see 12.43.

22. Reading *jing cheng* 精誠 in place of *jing qi* 精氣.

23. Compare 20.6.

Spirit and illumination join,
yin and yang harmonize,

and the myriad things are born. When a sage rules the world, he does not change the people's nature but soothes and facilitates the nature that is already present and purifies and cleanses it. Thus following [the nature of things] may be considered great, whereas making [things] may be considered minor.

Yu dredged the Dragon Gate, broke through Yique, demarcated the Yangzi River, and channeled the Yellow River [so that] they ran eastward into the sea, by following the [natural] flow of water.

Lord Millet reclaimed the grasslands and introduced tillage, fertilized the soil and planted grain, enabling each of the five grains to grow appropriately, by following the propensity of the soil.

Tang and Wu, with three hundred armored chariots and three thousand soldiers in armor, quelled the violent and rebellious and brought Xia and Shang under control, by following the people's desire.

Thus if you can follow [the nature of things], you will be matchless in the world.

Now if things first have what is natural to them, afterward human affairs can be governed.

Thus,

a fine carpenter cannot carve metal,
and a skillful blacksmith cannot melt wood.
The propensity of metal is that it cannot be carved,
and the nature of wood is that it cannot be melted.

You can

mold clay into a vessel,
gouge out wood and make a boat,
forge iron and make a blade,
cast metal and make a bell.

By following their [inherent] possibilities,

you can

drive a horse and lead an ox,
use a rooster to announce night's end,
and tell a dog to guard the gate—

because it follows their natures.

People have a nature that is fond of sex, so there is the ceremony of marriage.

They have a nature that [requires] food and drink, so there is the suitability of a great banquet.

They have a nature that delights in music, so there are the sounds of bells, drums, pipes, and strings.

They have a nature to grieve and be melancholy, so there are the customs of wearing mourning clothes, crying, and jumping about [at funerals].

Therefore, the institutions and laws of the former kings followed what the people liked but [also] established controls and civilizing [restrictions] for them.

Following along with people's fondness for sex, they set up the rites of marriage so men and women could be [properly] separated.

Following along with their delight in music, they rectified the sounds of the "Ya" and "Song"[24] so that habits and customs would not be unrestrained.

Following along with their preference to live as families and find joy in their wives and children, they taught filial piety[25] so that fathers and sons would be affectionate.

Following along with their delight in friendship, they taught brotherly love so that older and younger would be in proper standing with each other.

Only after this did they

use court ceremonies to clarify high rank and low

and use rural libations[26] and archery contests to clarify adulthood and youth.

In season, [the youths] held exercises to practice using weapons or entered school according to their station to learn to cultivate the arts of human relations.

These all are cases in which people already possessed [qualities] by nature, which sages fashioned and completed. [20/212/7–19]

Thus if the nature is not there, it is not possible to educate or train [a person]. If the nature is there but has not been nurtured, he cannot follow the Way.

It is the nature of the silkworm to make silk, but unless you have a skilled female worker to boil the cocoon in hot water and draw its filaments, there can be no silk.

An egg transforms into a chick, but unless you have a mother hen to sit on and warm the egg and brood it for several days, it cannot produce a chick.

Human nature is endowed with Humaneness and Rightness, but unless you have a sage to institute laws and standards to teach and guide them, people will not be able to find the correct path.

Thus the teaching of the former kings was

to follow what people delight in so as to encourage goodness and

to follow what people hate so as to prohibit wickedness. Thus,

punishments and penalties were not used, but awe-inspiring conduct seemed to flow forth [everywhere].

Policies and ordinances were limited, but their transforming brilliance [pervaded] as if they were spiritlike.

Thus if you follow nature, the whole world will come along with you. If you go against nature, even if you were to publish the laws, it would be of no use. [20/212/21–25]

---

24. These are sections of the *Odes*.

25. Reading *xiao* 孝 for *shun* 順. See Lau, HNZ, 212n.6.

26. *Xiang yin* 鄉飲, "rural libations," was a village festival in which participants drank in order of seniority.

20.11

In former times, when the Five Thearchs and the Three Kings established their policies and instituted their teachings, they inevitably used the [procedures of] threes and fives.[27] What are the [procedures of] threes and fives?

Looking upward, they selected images from Heaven;
looking downward, they selected standards from Earth.
In the middle, they selected models from people.

Thereupon they established the Mingtang audiences and carried out the Mingtang edicts.

[Looking upward, they]
regulated the *qi* of yin and yang
and harmonized the nodes[28] of the four seasons,
[thereby] avoiding the calamities of illness and fever.

Looking downward, they observed Earth's patterns in order to devise standards and measures. They investigated the suitability of mountains and plains, rivers and water-meadows, rich and poor land, and high and low areas, setting tasks to generate wealth [and] to eradicate the disasters of hunger and cold. In the middle, they investigated human virtues to devise rites and music and implement the Way of Humaneness and Rightness in order to govern human relations and eradicate the calamities of violence and disorder.

Thereupon they clarified and outlined the [respective] natures of metal, wood, water, fire, and earth in order to establish the affection [that should prevail] between fathers and sons so as to perfect the family. They distinguished the high and low sounds of the five tones and the numerology of the mutual production of the six double pitch-pipe notes[29] in order to establish the Rightness [that should prevail between] rulers and minister so as to perfect the state. They studied the successive order of the four seasons in order to establish the propriety [that should prevail between] elders and the young so as to perfect bureaucratic rank. This all is called "threes."

To regulate the Rightness of ruler and ministers, the affection of fathers and sons, the distinction of husbands and wives, the precedence of elder and younger, the intimacy of friends—this is called "fives."

Thereupon [sage-kings]
parceled out the land and made provinces for them [i.e., the people],
divided up official duties and governed them,
built walled cities and [made] residences for them,
partitioned neighborhoods and differentiated them,
divided up wealth and clothed and fed them,
set up academies and taught and instructed them,
woke them up early and rested them late, to employ and exert them.

27. For *canwu* 參五, "(procedures of) threes and fives," see also 9.19 and 21.2.

28. *Jie* 節 are nodes on the stem of a plant (such as bamboo); by extension, they refer to regular periodicities of various sorts, such as calendrical intervals of time. See app. B.

29. For the twelve *lü* 律 and their mutual transformations, see 3.27.

These are the cords and netting of government. That being so, if they obtain the right people they will succeed; if they fail to obtain them, they will lose.

Thus when [the sage] Yao ruled the world, his governance and instruction were fair, and his Moral Potency was saturating and enriching. He was on the throne for seventy years and then sought a successor to rule the world. He sent orders to [all within] the four [sacred] mountains to recommend those who were low ranking but promising. [All within] the four [sacred] mountains selected Shun and introduced him to Yao. Yao married his two daughters to Shun to see how he would [manage] his inner [household]. Then he put him in charge of a hundred officials to see how he would manage external [affairs]. [Once] when Shun went into a thick forest, there were fierce winds with thunder and rain, but Shun did not lose his way. Then Yao entrusted his nine sons to Shun, gave him the Zhaohua jade, and turned over the world to him. He considered that even though there were laws and regulations, [Dan] Zhu[30] was not capable of being his successor. [20/212/27–20/213/10]

20.12

Now there are no things that
 only grow and never diminish,
 only succeed and never fail.
Only sages can
 flourish and not decline and
 be full and not insufficient.

When the Divine Farmer first made a *qin* [stringed instrument], it was in order to make people return to their spirits, suppress lewdness, and revert to their Heavenly Heart. By the age of decline, [their excesses] flowed, and they did not revert [to their Heavenly Heart]. People became lewd and [too] fond of sex, so that the state perished.

When Kui[31] first made music, he harmonized the six double pitch pipes and tuned the pentatonic notes in order to conduct the eight winds [from all directions]. By the age of decline, [people indulged in] drunkenness and lewdness. No one paid attention to government, so that the state was wiped out.

When Cang Jie first created writing, it was to admonish and govern all the officials and bring order to the myriad affairs. Foolish people took advantage of writing to not forget things, and the wise took advantage of it to record the affairs [of state]. By the age of decline, the wicked used it to inscribe falsehoods in order to free those who deserved punishment and in order to execute those who were not guilty.

When Tang first built hunting parks, it was so he might furnish himself with rare viands to sacrifice in the ancestral temple, as well as to drill his officers and nobles in practicing archery and charioteering so as to guard against the unexpected [i.e., inva-

30. Yao's unworthy son. See also 10.64 and 19.4.

31. A mythical figure, said to be the music master of Yao and Shun.

sions]. By the age of decline, people careened about [in chariots] chasing [game] and shooting arrows, wasting the common people's time and exhausting their energy.

When Yao elevated Yu, Xie, Lord Millet, and Gao Yao,
government and education became equitable;
wickedness and villainy abated;
punishments and lawsuits ceased;
and clothing and food sufficed.

Worthies exerted themselves to do good, and the untalented embraced their Moral Potency. When [the age] came to an end, [officials] formed factions and cabals. Each [supported] only his own kind. They abandoned the common good and chased after personal gain. [People] outside [the court] and within [the palace] promoted one another. Wicked people occupied the court, and worthies went to live in seclusion. [20/213/12–20][32]

The Way of Heaven and Earth [is such that]
when [things reach an extreme], then there is a reversal.[33]
When [something becomes] full, then there is an emptying.

The five colors, however bright, in time will fade. Flourishing trees and abundant grasses in time will decay. Things have [both] abundance and extinction; they cannot always stay the same.

Thus sages,
when affairs reach their limits, modify actions;
when laws grow corrupt, modify regulations.

It is not as if it gives them joy to alter ancient [practices] or to change constant rules, but [they do it] to save [their state] from defeat and ward off decline. They do away with lewdness and put a stop to wrongdoing in order to synchronize with the *qi* of Heaven and Earth and comply with what is appropriate for the ten thousand things. [20/213/22–25]

20.13

The sage
covers like Heaven, upholds like Earth,
illuminates like the sun and moon,

32. Following this passage are six sentences (20/213/21–22) that are repeated almost verbatim from 20.13. Following Wang Niansun, Lau (HNZ, 213n.9) notes that the six sentences beginning with "Thus, the shortcoming of the *Changes*" probably were inserted here erroneously some time after the text had been written. Accordingly, we have deleted them from the main text of our translation. They read as follows:

> Thus, the shortcoming of the *Changes* is divination.
> The shortcoming of the *Documents* is verbosity.
> The shortcoming of the *Music* is lewdness.
> The shortcoming of the *Odes* is falsity.
> The shortcoming of the *Rites* is censoriousness.
> The shortcoming of the *Spring and Autumn Annals* is [excessive] criticism.

33. *Laozi* 40.

harmonizes like yin and yang,
transforms like the four seasons,
[treats] the myriad things all differently,
is without precedent or novelty,
is without stranger or kin.
Thus [the sage] takes Heaven as his model.
Heaven does not have [only] a single season;
Earth does not have [only] a single benefit;
humankind does not have [only] a single affair.
Therefore,
various undertakings cannot but have multiple origins;
hurried steps cannot but take different directions.
The Five Phases are of different *qi*, but all are harmonious.
The Six Arts are of different categories, but all are connected.
Warmth and kindness, gentleness and goodness, are the influences of the *Odes*;
purity and grandeur, nobility and generosity, are the teachings of the *Documents*;
clarity and brilliance, perception and penetration, are the norms of the *Changes*;
deference and self-control, respect and humility, are the behaviors of the *Rites*;
broad-mindedness and magnanimity, simplicity and easiness, are the transforming [qualities] of the *Music*;[34]
reprimands and critiques, blame and appraisal, are the polishing cloths of the *Spring and Autumn* [*Annals*].
Thus [if relied on exclusively],
the shortcoming of the *Changes* is superstition;
the shortcoming of the *Music* is lewdness;
the shortcoming of the *Odes* is foolishness;
the shortcoming of the *Documents* is rigidity,
the shortcoming of the *Rites* is stubbornness, and
the shortcoming of the *Spring and Autumn* is censoriousness.[35]
The sage uses [all] six in conjunction and both prizes and institutes them.
If [the sage] loses their root, there will be disorder;
if he acquires their root, there will be order.
The beauty [of these classics] lies in harmony;
their shortcomings lie in expediency.
Water, fire, metal, wood, earth, and grain differ as things, but all are used.

34. A Confucian canonical text lost since ancient times.

35. The argument here is that overrelying or, even worse, relying exclusively on any one of these classics turns its strengths into shortcomings through exaggeration; each of the six has to be used in conjunction with the other five to allow their strengths to moderate and balance one another.

The compass, the square, the weight, the balance beam, the level, and the marking cord differ in shape, but all are applied.
Cinnabar, verdigris, glue, and lac[36] are not identical, but all are used.
Everything has something for which it is appropriate; each thing is suitable for something.
Wheels are round; carriage boxes are square;
their shafts are parallel; their axles are crosswise—
their propensities function to make them convenient.
The horses at the side of a team want to gallop;
the ones in the middle want to walk.[37]
The sash can never be new enough;
the belt hook can never be old enough;
if each is properly placed, they are suitable. [20/214/1–10]

[The poem] "Guan ju"[38] originated from [the cry of] a bird. The Superior Man praises it because it advocates that the female and the male should not leave their nest.

[The poem] "Lu ming"[39] originated from [the cry of] an animal. The Superior Man exalts it because it describes how deer, having found food, call to one another [to share it].

At the battle of Hong, [Song's] army was defeated and its prince captured. The *Spring and Autumn Annals* exalts him because he did not attack the enemy before they had set up their formations.

Bo Yi of Song sat in the fire [of a burning palace] and died. The *Spring and Autumn Annals* exalts her because she would not leave if it meant violating propriety.

For perfecting endeavors and establishing affairs, how can these examples be considered excessive? [Each] points in a single direction and discusses it, but you can derive a general outline from them. [20/214/10–13]

20.14

Wang Qiao and Chi Song
removed themselves from the milieu of polluting filth
and left the dust of the world behind.
They
inhaled the harmony of yin and yang,
imbibed the essence of Heaven and Earth,
breathing out and expelling the stale,

36. All these are ingredients used in making lacquerware.
37. The inside pair of a quadriga pulls more of the weight of the load.
38. The first poem in the *Odes*; it begins with the cry of birds traditionally identified as ospreys.
39. *Odes* 161; it begins with the cry of the deer.

breathing in and inhaling the new.
Dancing in the void they lightly rose up,
riding on clouds and floating on fog.

You could say they nurtured their natures, but you could not call them filial sons.

The Duke of Zhou executed Guan Shu and Cai Shu[40] to bring peace to the country and end their rebellion. You could call him a loyal minister, but you could not call him a good brother.

Tang banished [the tyrant] Jie and King Wu of Zhou executed [the tyrant] Djou so as to rid the world of cruelty and do away with evil. You could call them kind rulers, but you could not call them loyal officials.

Yue Yang[41] attacked the state of Zhongshan but could not enter it. The rulers of Zhongshan boiled Yue's son, but Yue Yang ate [the soup] to demonstrate his awesomeness. You could call him a fine general, but you could not call him a loving father.

Thus,

if [the sage] can do [something], he does it;
if he cannot do it, he does not do it.
If he cannot do it, he does not do it;
[but] if he can do it, he does it.[42] [20/214/15–20]
Shun and Xu You differed in their actions, but both were sages.
Yi Yin and Bo Yi differed in their Ways, but both were Humane.
Jizi and Bi Gan differed in their inclinations, but both were worthies.

Thus when using troops,

some are light,
some are heavy,[43]
some are greedy,
some are honest.

These four are opposites, yet none can be dispensed with.

Light troops want to advance;
heavy troops want to halt.
Greedy troops want to acquire;

honest troops do not take advantage of what is not theirs.

Thus,

courageous [troops][44] can be ordered to attack but cannot be ordered just to hold a position.

40. A reference to the Duke of Zhou's own brothers, who turned against him when he became regent for King Cheng. See 11.18 and 20.25; and chap. 21, n. 31.

41. See 18.4; and *Shiji* 44/4b, 71/4b, and 80/1a.

42. ZZ 2/4/25–26.

43. There is a pun here: some troops are lightly armed and highly mobile, and some are heavily armed and less mobile. But also some are brave and take life and death lightly; some are less brave and look upon life and death as weighty matters.

44. That is, those that take death lightly.

Heavy [troops] can be ordered to hold a position but cannot be ordered to press an attack.
Greedy [troops] can be ordered to advance and seize [a position] but cannot be ordered to defend their post.
Honest [troops] can be ordered to defend their post but cannot be ordered to advance and seize [a position].
Trustworthy [troops] can be ordered to hold fast to their duties but cannot be ordered to respond to alterations.[45]

These four kinds are opposites. Sages use them all, depending on which is best in [a given] situation. Now,

Heaven and Earth do not embrace just one thing;
yin and yang do not give birth to just one kind.
The sea does not reject rivers and floodwaters and so becomes great.
A mountain does not reject dirt and stones and so becomes high.
If you hold on to one corner but lose the myriad things;
if you select one thing but reject everything else;

then what you gain is little, and what you can control is shallow. [20/214/22–20/215/2]

20.15

The Way of a person who governs a great state cannot be small;
the regulations of a person whose realm is broad cannot be narrow.
The concerns of a person in a high position cannot be troublesome;
the teachings of a person whose people are numerous cannot be vexatious.

Now,

when matters are trifling, it is difficult to control them;
when laws are complex, it is difficult to implement them;
when demands are numerous, it is difficult to satisfy them.
If you measure something by inches, by the time you reach a fathom[46] there is bound to be a discrepancy.
If you weigh things by the *zhu*,[47] by the time you reach a *dan* there is sure to be an error.

If you weigh by the *dan* and measure by the fathom, it is fast and there will be fewer mistakes. If you inspect by the strand and count by the grains, it is troublesome and there will be no accuracy. Thus,

45. This line breaks the symmetry of the discussion of the four kinds of troops and may be a later intrusion.

46. A *zhang* 丈 is ten Chinese feet.

47. A *zhu* 銖 is a very tiny amount; a *dan* 石 (sometimes translated "picul") is 120 *jin* 斤 (catties). At about 250 grams to the catty in the early Han period, a *dan* weighed about 65 pounds.

if you stay on the main track, it is easy to seem wise;
if you get tangled up in tortuous debates, it is hard to seem intelligent.

Thus,

what contributes nothing to government but merely contributes to troublesome detail, the sage will not do.
What contributes nothing to usefulness but merely contributes to expense, the wise refrains from implementing.

Thus,

tasks can never be too specific;
affairs can never be too frugal;
demands can never be too few.
When tasks are specific, they are easy to accomplish;
when affairs are frugal, they are easy to control;
when demands are few, they are easy to satisfy.

If everyone considers them easy, then using them to employ others is easy indeed!

Confucius said,

"Petty disputes destroy discourse;
petty advantage destroys Rightness;
petty Rightness destroys the Way.

If the Way [itself] is petty, then it cannot prevail. If it prevails, it is necessarily simple." [20/215/4–10]

20.16

Rivers, because they twist and turn like a snake, can be far-reaching;
mountains, because they rise in stages, can be high;
yin and yang, because they do not act purposefully, can be harmonious;
the Way, because it floats aimlessly, can transform.

Now if you

understand [only] one matter,
investigate [only] one proposition,
or master [only] one skill,

you will be able to give a partial explanation, but you will not be able to give a comprehensive response.

If you [can]

arrange the knotweed and smartweed [spices] in rows,
provide the *bian* and *ou* [vessels] with trays,[48]
weigh firewood to kindle a fire,
measure out grain and steam it,

48. *Bian* 甂 and *ou* 甌 were two types of vessels used on the ancestral altar. This paragraph describes petty details of sacrificial rites.

you can manage small [matters], but you will not yet be able to manage large ones.

If you,

in circling, match the compass;
in squaring, match the [carpenter's] square;
in moving, become bestial;
in stillness, become refined;

you can enjoy dancing, but you cannot yet maneuver an army.

If you

clean the bowls and eat,
wash the goblets and drink,
clean your hands and offer food,

you can nourish the few but not feed the multitudes.

In sacrifices,

the one who slaughters and cooks and skins the dog and roasts the pig, adjusting the five flavors, is the slaughterer.

The one who sets out the vessels of rice and millet, goblets for wine and plates for meat, the bowls of fruit and sweetmeats, is the invoker.[49]

The one who is uniformly brilliant and splendidly attired, the one who is deeply silent and does not speak, the one on whom the spirits depend, is the impersonator of the dead.[50]

Even if the slaughterer or the invoker is incompetent, the impersonator of the dead does not step over the beakers and meat stands to replace him.[51]

Thus,

in stringing the *se*, the shorter strings are tight and the longer strings are loose.[52]
In attending to affairs, the lowly toil and the noble remain idle.

When Shun was the Son of Heaven, he plucked the five-stringed *qin* and chanted the poems of the "Southern Airs,"[53] and thereby governed the world.

Before the Duke of Zhou had gathered provisions or taken the bells and drums from their suspension cords, the four Yi tribes submitted.[54]

Zheng of Zhao [Qin Shihuangdi] by day decided lawsuits and by night arranged documents. Law clerks covered and connected the prefectures and counties to investigate and spy, overturning plots and detaining miscreants. He

fortified the five peaks to defend against the Yue [people]
and built the Great Wall to protect against the Hu [tribes].

---

49. This is the person who acts as an intermediary between the world of the spirits and that of the living during the sacrificial ceremony.

50. This is the person who represents the spirits receiving the sacrifice.

51. This is an allusion to ZZ 1/2/11.

52. *Ji* 急 and *huan* 緩 usually mean "fast" and "slow," respectively, but in reference to stringed instruments, they refer to string tension, "tight" and "loose," respectively. We are grateful to *qin* player Jung-Ping Yuan and musicologist Bo Lawergren for helping us with the terminology of Chinese stringed-instrument playing.

53. This is a section of the *Odes*.

54. The same image appears in 14.54.

But

wickedness and lewdness arose,

and robbers and bandits dwelt together in hordes.

The more trouble [he took with] matters, the greater the disorder became. Thus the law is an instrument of government, but it is not [the end] for which one governs. It is as with bows and arrows: they are tools for hitting the bull's-eye, but they are not the reason one hits the bull's-eye. [20/215/12–23]

20.17

The Yellow Emperor said,

"Broad and infinite,

[I] follow Heaven's Way,

and my *qi* is identical with the Origin."[55]

Thus,

those who identify their *qi* [with the Origin] are emperors;

those who identify their Rightness [with the Origin] are kings;

those who identify their strength [with the Origin] are hegemons,

those who lack even one of these attributes are lost.

Thus when a ruler has a firm intention of attacking [another state],

village dogs bark in packs,

roosters crow at night,

weapons in the storehouse stir,

and the war horses are alarmed.

If now the anger dissipates and the troops are demobilized,

the elderly sleep sweetly in their homes;

the lanes are devoid of [disgruntled] crowds;

and no calamity arises.

Such things are not responses to the law but are stirrings of the Quintessential *qi*.

Thus if you

do not speak, yet you are trustworthy,

do not act, yet you are Humane,

do not feel anger, yet you are awe-inspiring,

this is a case of your Heavenly Heart having moved and transformed [others].

If you

act and you are Humane,

speak and you are trustworthy,

feel angry and you are awe-inspiring,

this is a case of your Quintessential Sincerity having moved [others].

If you

55. The same statement attributed to the Yellow Emperor appears in 10.3 and in LSCQ 13.2/64/23–24; and Knoblock and Riegel 2000, 284.

act but you are not Humane,
speak but you are not trustworthy,
feel angry but you are not awe-inspiring,
this is a case of something external having caused it.

Thus,

If you rule by having the Way, although the laws be few, they will be enough to transform [the people];

if you act without the Way, though the laws be many, they will be [only] enough to cause disorder. [20/215/25–20/216/3]

20.18

In governing the self,
it is best to nurture the spirit.
The next best is to nurture the body.
In governing the state,
it is best to nurture transformation.
The next best is to correct the laws.
A clear spirit and a balanced will,
the hundred joints all in good order,
constitute the root of nurturing vitality.
To fatten the muscles and skin,
to fill the bowel and belly,
to satiate the lusts and desires,
constitute the branches of nurturing vitality.

If the people
yield to one another and compete to dwell humbly;
delegate benefit and compete to receive scantily,
work at tasks and compete to follow arduously,
daily transformed by their superiors and moved to goodness without realizing the means by which they came to be so, this is the root of government.

With beneficial rewards to encourage goodness
and fearful punishments to prevent misdeeds,
laws and ordinances corrected above
and the common people submitting below:
these are the branches of government.

Earlier generations nurtured the root, but later generations served the branches. This is why Great Peace does not arise. Now a ruler who desires to govern well does not appear in every age, and a minister who can accompany a ruler in initiating good government does not appear once in ten thousand [officials]. To rely on a minister who does not appear once in ten thousand to seek out a ruler who does not appear in every age is the reason why they do not meet once in ten thousand years! [20/216/5–10]

20.19

The nature of water
is to be saturating and clear.
In valleys where it is stagnant
and gives birth to green algae,

[that results from] not controlling it [according to] its nature. If you make channels where it flows and deepen the flow or build up where it [threatens to] flood through and raise [its level], you will enable it to move in compliance with its natural propensity, moving along and flowing onward. Though carrion and rotten bones flow and mix with the water, they cannot pollute it. The nature [of water] is not different; it is just a matter of whether it can flow through [a channel] or not flow through.

Customs and habits are like this. If [the ruler's] sincerity
floods through to goodness of will,
builds embankments against depravity of heart,
opens up the road to goodness
and blocks the path to wickedness,

then likewise [sincerity] emerges into a single Way, [so that] the people's nature can become good and customs and habits can be beautified. [20/216/12–15]

20.20

The reason why we respect Bian Que is not because he could prescribe medicines in accordance with the illnesses but because he could lay a hand on the breath and feel the pulse of the blood and understand from where illness derives.

The reason why we respect sages is not because they set punishments in accordance with the nature of the crime but because they know from where disorder arises.

If you do not cultivate [the people's] customs and habits yet give them free rein to fall into excess and depravity, and then you pursue them with punishments and restrain them with laws, though you maim and plunder [everyone in] the world, you will not be able to stop them.

Yu arose, Xia reigned;
Jie arose, Xia was lost.
Tang arose, Yin reigned;
Djou arose, Yin was lost.

It was not that laws and measures did not exist. [Rather], the cord and netting of [good order] were not extended, and so customs and habits deteriorated. [20/216/17–21]

20.21

The laws of the Three Dynasties are not lost. If an age is not well governed, it is because [rulers] lack the wisdom of the Three Dynasties.

The six double pitch pipes all exist. If no one hears them, it is because they lack the ear of Music Master Kuang.

Thus

though laws exist, they must await a sage and only then can there be good government.

Though pitch pipes are complete, they must await an ear and only then can they be heard.

Thus,

the reason why a state survives is not because it has laws but because it has worthies.

The reason why a state perishes is not because it has no laws but because it has no sages.

Duke Xian of Jin wanted to attack Yu, but Gong Zhiqi[56] was there. Because of this, Duke Xian could not sleep at night and found his food tasteless, yet he still dared not send in his soldiers. He made gifts of precious jades and fine horses. Gong Zhiqi remonstrated [with the ruler of Yu] but was not heeded. When his words were not put into practice, Gong Zhiqi crossed the border and left the state. Xun Xi attacked, and his soldiers, without bloodying their blades, seized the treasures and led the horses back to Jin. Thus

preserving a state does not depend on whether the moats and walls are firm and strong;

the success of an attack does not depend on a vehicle with a battering ram that can break down walls.

Rather, it is a matter of having a worthy or losing him.

Thus,

Zang Wuzhong[57] used his wisdom to preserve Lu, and no one in the world could cause it to fall.

Qu Boyu used his Humaneness to keep Wey intact, and no one in the world could threaten it.

The *Changes* says,

"Luxuriant is the mansion,
impoverished the family.
Peer through the gate:
The solitude of no one there."[58]

"No one there" does not refer to the multitudes of the common people. It means that there is no sage to govern the inherent patterns of things. [20/216/23–20/217/2]

---

56. Gong Zhiqi 宫之奇 was a grandee of Yu during the Spring and Autumn period. Duke Xian offered horses to the prince of Yu, saying he wanted to cross Yu to attack the small state of Guo. Gong Zhiqi advised the prince not to accept them, for he knew that after annexing Guo, Jin would attack Yu. Another account of this incident is given in 18.5. See chap. 18, n. 33.

57. Zang Wuzhong 臧武仲 was a grandee and minister of Lu during the Spring and Autumn period.

58. *Changes* 34/55.

20.22

If the people have no honesty and shame, they cannot be governed well.
If they do not cultivate Propriety and Rightness, honesty and shame will not be established.
If the people do not know Propriety and Rightness, the laws cannot rectify [them].
If they do not esteem the good and reject the wicked, they cannot incline toward Propriety and Rightness.
Without laws, you cannot create good government,
and without knowing Propriety and Rightness, you cannot implement laws.
The laws can execute the unfilial, but they cannot inspire people to achieve the conduct of Confucius and Zengzi.
The laws can punish robbers, but they cannot inspire people to achieve the honesty of Bo Yi.

Confucius's disciples numbered seventy, and they supported three thousand followers. All were filial when inside their households and brotherly when outside their households. Their speech was refined and elegant, and their conduct was ceremonious and exemplary. This was accomplished through education.

Those who served Mozi numbered one hundred and eighty. He could send them all to walk through fire and tread on blades, face death, and not turn their heels [to flee]. This was brought about by [the process of] transformation.

Now,
to slice through muscle and flesh
and puncture skin and hide,
making wounds so that blood flows, is extremely difficult [to bear]. But the people of Yue do it to seek glory.[59]

When a sage king is in power, he
clarifies likes and dislikes to instruct the people;
sets out criticism and praise to guide the people;
admires the worthy and promotes them;
derides the unworthy and demotes them.
He does not suffer the hardship of being wounded and bleeding yet enjoys a lofty reputation that is respected and manifest [through the ages]. Who among the people would not follow him? [20/217/4–11]

59. This is presumably a reference to the customs of scarification (i.e., creating decorative patterns of scars on the body) and tattooing.

20.23

In ancient times,

laws were established, but they were not violated;

punishments were elaborated, but they were not used.

It is not the case that they could punish but did not punish.

The hundred kinds of artisans adhered to the seasons, and their many achievements were, without exception, brilliant. Propriety and Rightness were cultivated, and the worthy and the virtuous were employed. Thus they promoted

the loftiest in the world to become the Three Dukes,[60]

the loftiest in the state to become the Nine Ministers,[61]

the loftiest in the counties to become the twenty-seven grandees,

and the loftiest in the prefectures to become the eighty-one functionaries.

Those whose knowledge surpassed ten thousand men were called "talented";

those whose knowledge surpassed a thousand men were called "eminent";

those whose knowledge surpassed a hundred men were called "brave";

those whose knowledge surpassed ten men were called "prominent."

Those who

understood the Way of Heaven,

investigated the patterns of Earth,

penetrated human feelings,

whose greatness sufficed to accommodate the multitudes,

whose Moral Potency sufficed to embrace the distant,

whose trustworthiness sufficed to unify heterogeneity,

and whose knowledge sufficed to understand alteration

were the "talented" among men.

Those whose

Moral Potency sufficed to transform [the people] through education,

conduct sufficed to accord with Rightness,

Humaneness sufficed to win the multitudes,

and brilliance sufficed to illuminate those below

were the "eminent" among men.

Those whose

conduct sufficed to be ceremonious and exemplary,

knowledge sufficed to resolve deceptive resemblances,

honesty enabled them to distribute resources,

trustworthiness enabled them to inspire [others] to honor their commitments,

60. Under the Zhou dynasty, as described in the *Zhouli*, or *Rites of Zhou*, these were the *taishi* 太師, or grand tutor; the *taifu* 太傅, or grand preceptor; and the *taibao* 太保, or grand guardian.

61. The nine ministers under the Zhou, as described in the *Zhouli*, were the prime minister, minister of instruction, minister of religious ceremonies, minister of war, minister of crime, minister of public works, junior tutor, junior preceptor, and junior guardian.

accomplished deeds could be emulated,
and spoken words could be used for guidance
were the "brave " among men.

Those who
held to their duties and did not abandon them,
dwelled in Rightness and were not partisan,
encountered hardships and did not illicitly avoid them,
and perceived advantages and did not illicitly gain from them
were the "prominent" among men.

The "talented," "eminent," "brave," and "prominent" each in accordance with their degree of ability occupied their official position and attained what was appropriate to each.

From the root flowing to the branches, using the heavy to control the light,
when the ruler called, the people harmonized;
when the ruler moved, the lowly followed.
Within the Four Seas, all submitted with a single mind, turning their backs on greed and avarice and turning toward Humaneness and Rightness. In transforming the people, they resembled the wind stirring the grasses and trees, leaving nothing unaffected.[62] [20/217/13–22]

20.24

Now,
if the foolish educate the wise
and the unworthy lead the worthy,
even if punishments and penalties are made harsher, the people will not follow them.

The small cannot prevail over the great;
the weak cannot dominate the strong.
Thus, the sagely ruler promotes the worthy in order to establish merit, [while] the unworthy ruler promotes those whose views are the same as his own.

King Wen promoted Grand Duke Wang[63] and Duke Shi of Zhao and became king.

Duke Huan of Qi appointed Guan Zhong and Xi Peng[64] and became hegemon.

These are examples of elevating worthies in order to establish merit.

62. This is a reference to *Analects* 12.19.

63. Lü Shang, spotted by the king fishing in a creek and elevated to high office.

64. Xi Peng 隰朋 (d. 645 B.C.E.), a grandee of Qi recruited into the government of Duke Huan by Guan Zhong, served as chief messenger to the court. Guan Zhong recommended that Xi Peng succeed him as prime minister on his death.

Fuchai of Wu employed Great Steward Pi and was destroyed.
Qin employed Li Si[65] and Zhao Gao[66] and perished.

These are cases of promoting those whose views are the same as his own.

Thus,

by observing who is being promoted, order and disorder can be observed;
by examining with whom one forms a faction, the worthy and unworthy can be assessed. [20/217/24–28]

20.25

When a sage coils, it is because he seeks to extend.
When he bends, it is because he seeks to straighten.

Thus,

though he travels along a crooked road
and journeys along a dark path,

it is because he wishes to elevate the Great Way and achieve great merit.

Similarly,

if you emerge from [the depths of] a forest, you will not be able to follow a straight course;
if you rescue a drowning person, you will not be able to avoid wetting your feet.

Yi Yin was anxious that the world was not well governed, so blending and harmonizing the five flavors, with cauldron and cutting board on his back, he journeyed

five times to Jie,
five times to Tang,

hoping to

make the turbid clear
and the endangered secure.

The Duke of Zhou was the arms and legs of the house of Zhou and the props and shelter of King Cheng. Guan Shu and Cai Shu supported Prince Lufu,[67] wanting to carry out a rebellion, but the Duke of Zhou executed them to stabilize the world. Fate left him no alternative.

---

65. Li Si 李斯 (d. 208 B.C.E.), a disciple of Xunzi and fellow student of Han Feizi, entered the government of Qin under the patronage of Lü Buwei and ultimately rose to be prime minister to the First Emperor. He was the driving force behind key policies such as a comprehensive ban on much of pre-Qin literature and the annihilation of local hereditary power. His biography is in *Shiji* 27.

66. Zhao Gao 趙高 (d. 207 B.C.E.) was a powerful eunuch official at the court of the First Emperor. When the emperor died on an imperial tour, Zhao and Li Si conspired to forge orders commanding the suicide of the heir apparent and placing the ineffectual Prince Huhai on the throne in his place.

67. Prince Lufu 公子祿父 was a son of the tyrant Djou enfeoffed by King Wu to carry on the sacrificial rites of the Shang royal house. When King Cheng acceded to the throne, with the Duke of Zhou as his regent, the prince rose in rebellion with the support of Guan Shu and Cai Shu. See 11.18 and 20.14; and chap. 21, n. 31.

Guanzi was anxious over the decline of the house of Zhou and the forceful aggressions of the Lords of the Land. The Yi and Di [tribes] attacked the Central States. The people could not secure a peaceful place to live. Thus he bore shame and insult to remain alive because, anxious about the Yi and Di calamities, he hoped to pacify the chaos of the Yi and Di.

Confucius hoped to implement the Way of the True Kings. East and west, south and north, despite [making] seventy persuasions, there was no place where he could find [a ruler] to match [his teachings]. Thus he went along with the lady of Wey[68] and Mi Zixia[69] in the hopes that [by their intervention] he could carry through the Way. These all are cases of [sages] desiring to bring peace and eradicate decadence. [They tried] from deep darkness to proceed to brilliant light, to act through expediency to bring about goodness. [20/218/1–8]

20.26

Evaluate those who pursue by what they bring back;
evaluate those who flee by where they end up.
Thus
Shun banished his younger brother;
the Duke of Zhou executed his older brothers,
but they both alike were considered humane.
Duke Wen [of Jin] planted rice,
Zengzi yoked a goat,
but they both alike were considered wise.
In the present age,
evil inevitably poses as goodness in order to explain itself;
depravity inevitably cloaks itself in uprightness to make excuses for itself.
When wandering [i.e., serving as a freelance political adviser], to not assess [your host] state;
when serving, to not choose [your own] office;
when acting, to not avoid defilement:
[people] call this the "Way of Yi Yin."
When there is division, differentiation, and competition for resources;
when relatives and brothers hold grudges against one another;
when bone and flesh rob each other,
[people] call this the "Rightness of the Duke of Zhou."
When actions are devoid of integrity or shame,
when disgrace does not result in death,[70]

68. Nanzi, the wife of Duke Ling. See LY 11/6/28.
69. Mi Zixia was a favorite of Duke Ling of Wey.
70. As it should, according to an earlier code of conduct.

[people] call this the "Subservience of Guanzi."

[When there is]

circulation of gifts and bribes,

hastening to the gates of the powerful,

establishment of the private and abandonment of the public,

forming of cabals to solicit [the ruler's] favor,

[people] call this the "Techniques of Confucius."

Such practices cause the distinction between the Superior Man and the petty man to become confused, so that no one knows whether something is right or wrong.

Thus,

a hundred streams may flow at once, but those that do not flow to the sea are not considered "river valleys."

[Some people] hasten, [some] amble, but those that do not turn their steps toward goodness will not become Superior Men.

Thus,

good speech comes down to what can be carried out;

good action comes down to Humaneness and Rightness.

Tian Zifang and Duangan Mu scorned rank and salary and valued their persons.

They did not allow desire to harm their lives;

they did not allow profit to ensnare their bodies.

Li Ke exhausted the strength of his arms and legs in order to direct and arrange the hundred officials and to be on good terms with the myriad people, enabling his ruler

in life to be free of wasteful endeavors,

in death to be free of a legacy of anxiety.

These were men whose actions differed but who [alike] turned their steps toward goodness.

Zhang Yi and Su Qin

had no permanent homes in which to dwell

and personally did not serve any particular ruler,

but they

negotiated the Vertical and Horizontal Alliances

and made plans that overturned and toppled the states,

confusing and disordering the world, disturbing and deceiving the Lords of the Land, causing the one hundred surnames to have no leisure to report their whereabouts.[71]

Sometimes following the Vertical Alliance;

sometimes following the Horizontal Alliance;

sometimes uniting the numerous and weak;

sometimes supporting the wealthy and powerful;

71. That is, the people became homeless refugees. A very similar phrase appears in 19.6.

these were men who differed in their conduct but who [alike] turned their steps toward depravity.

Thus the errors of the Superior Man are like solar or lunar eclipses.[72] What harm do they do to their brilliance? The approbations of the petty man are like a dog barking at the sunrise or an owl appearing at sunset. In what way do they augment their excellence? [20/218/10–21]

20.27

Now,

> the wise man does not behave recklessly;
> the brave man does not act rashly.
> He selects what is good and does it;
> he calculates what is right and practices it.

Thus

> when his endeavors end, his merit suffices to be relied on;
> when his body expires, his reputation suffices to be praised.

Though you possess wisdom and ability, you must take Humaneness and Rightness as their basis; only then is it possible to establish [your rule]. Wise and capable, hasty or slow, when a hundred situations arise simultaneously, the sage uniformly uses Humaneness and Rightness as his level and his marking cord.

> One who takes this to be central is called a Superior Man;
> one who does not take this to be central is called a petty man.
> Though the Superior Man dies, his reputation does not perish.
> Though the petty man attains power, his transgressions do not dissipate.

To get someone with his left hand to take a writ for the world and with his right hand to cut his own throat—this is something even a fool would not do, because his person is more precious than the world.[73]

If he should die in a disaster affecting his ruler or his loved ones, the Superior Man would look upon death merely as a return, because Rightness is weightier than his person. [Obtaining the whole] world is a great benefit, but compared to your person, it is trifling. Yet the weightiness of your person, compared to Rightness, is insubstantial. Rightness is what [must be kept] intact.

The *Odes* states,

> "Kind and gracious is the Superior Man,
> in seeking prosperity he has no regrets."[74]

---

72. This is an allusion to *Analects* 19.21: "Zigong said, 'The Superior Man's errors are like an eclipse of the sun or the moon; when he errs, everyone notices it; but when he makes amends, everyone looks up to him.'"

73. The same phrase appears in 7.11.

74. *Odes* 239; Waley translates these lines as "Happiness to our lord! / In quest of blessings may he never fail" (Waley/Allen 1996, 234–35). See LSCQ 20.3/131/16.

This refers to taking Humaneness[75] and Rightness as his level and his marking cord. [20/218/23–29]

20.28

Those who have the ability to accomplish the work of hegemon or king are invariably those who gain victory;
those who have the ability to gain victory are invariably those who are powerful;
those who have the ability to be powerful are invariably those who employ the people's strength;
those who have the ability to employ the people's strength are invariably those who gain the people's hearts;
those who have the ability to gain the people's hearts are invariably those who gain mastery over the self.

Thus,
the heart is the root of the self;
the self is the root of the state.
There has never been a person who gained "the self" and lost the people;
there has never been a person who lost "the self" and gained the people.

Thus, to establish the basis of order, you must exert yourself to secure the people.
The root of securing the people lies in sufficiency of use;
the root of sufficiency of use lies in not taking them from their seasonal [work];
the root of not taking them from their seasonal [work] lies in reducing endeavors;
the root of reducing endeavors lies in regulating desires;
the root of regulating desires lies in reverting back to nature.

It has never been possible
to agitate the root yet calm the branches;
to pollute the source yet purify the flow. [20/219/1–6]

Thus,
those who know the essential qualities of nature do not endeavor to make nature do what it cannot do.
Those who know the essential qualities of fate are not anxious about what fate cannot control.

Thus,
those who do not [erect] lofty palaces and terraces do not do so because they cherish trees;
those who do not [cast] massive bells and tripods do not do so because they cherish metal.

75. Reading *xin* 信 as *ren* 仁. See Lau, HNZ, 218n.10.

They straightforwardly put into practice the essential qualities of nature and fate so that their regulations and measures can be taken to constitute a standard for the myriad people.

Now when

the eyes delight in the five colors,
the mouth relishes enticing flavors,
the ears are enraptured by the five sounds,

the seven orifices struggle with one another and harm [your] nature, daily attracting wicked desires and disturbing its heavenly harmony. If you cannot govern "the self," how can you govern the world? Thus if in nurturing the self you achieve regulation, then in nurturing the people you will win their hearts. [20/219/8–11]

The expression "taking possession of the world" does not refer to holding power and position, accepting hereditary rank, or being referred to by a respectful title. It means

linking up with the strength of the world
and winning the hearts of the world.

The territory of [the tyrant] Djou to the left reached the Eastern Sea and to the right reached to the Sea of Sands. Before him lay Jiaozhi and behind him lay Youdu.[76] His armies climbed Rong Pass and reached the Pu River. Their warriors numbered in the tens and hundreds of thousands, but they all shot their arrows backward and fought with their halberds turned [toward the tyrant]. King Wu of Zhou with his left hand held a yellow battle-ax and with his right grasped a white banner[77] to direct his armies, and the enemy were shattered like broken tiles and fled, collapsing like a pile of earth.

[The tyrant] Djou had the title of "the one who faces south" [i.e., the ruler] but lacked the praise of even a single man. This is how he lost the world. Thus Jie and Djou cannot be considered [to have been true] kings, and [Kings] Tang and Wu cannot be considered to have banished them.

The Zhou people dwelled in the lands of Feng and Hao. Their territory did not exceed a hundred *li*, yet they swore an oath against [the tyrant] Djou at Mulberry Field and attacked and occupied the Yin state. They

held a memorial service at the ancestral temple of Tang the Victorious,
conferred a plaque at the gates of the village where Shang Rong lived,
built up the tomb of Bi Gan,
and released the imprisoned Jizi.

Only then did they

snap the drumsticks and destroy the drums of war,[78]
retire the five kinds of weapons,[79]

---

76. This description reflects the orientation of Chinese maps, with south at the top of the page. The places named correspond approximately to the Yellow Sea, the Gobi Desert, Vietnam, and the Inner Asian frontier grasslands. This passage echoes the description of the Divine Farmer's realm in 9.3.

77. This image of King Wu at war appears also in 6.1.

78. Used for signaling on the battlefield.

79. According to chap. 5, these are *mao* 矛, "spear"; *ji* 戟, "glaive"; *jian* 劍, "sword"; *ge* 戈, "hal-

release the oxen and the horses,
gather up the jade insignia tablets,[80]
and accept the fealty of the world.

The people [lit. the "hundred surnames"] sang ballads to celebrate them while the Lords of the Land, grasping gifts of exotic birds, came calling at their court, for the hearts of the people had been won. [20/219/13–20]

20.29

[King] Helü [of Wu][81] attacked Chu and, after five battles, entered [the capital] Ying. He

burned the grain in the tall granaries,
destroyed the Nine Dragon [Array of] Bells,
flogged King Ping's tomb,
and occupied King Zhao's[82] palace.

King Zhao escaped to Sui. With fathers and elder brothers carrying the young and supporting the old, the one hundred surnames followed him.

They roused one another to courage and directed it at the enemy;
committing their lives, they raised their [bare] arms and fought with them.

At this time, without a general to lead them, they still fell into formation, each man risking his life, and forced the Wu armies to retreat, regaining their Chu territory.

King Ling [of Chu]

built the Zhanghua tower
and initiated the Ganqi expedition.

Inside and outside the state, [everyone] was disturbed and agitated. The common people were wearied and exhausted. Qiji, availing himself of popular resentment, set up Prince Bi [as king],[83] [but] the common people cast him aside and abandoned him so that, suffering starvation in Ganqi, with only weeds to eat and water to drink, he pillowed [his head] on a mound of earth and died.

The mountains and rivers of the state of Chu had not altered;
the land and its territory had not changed;
the people and their nature were no different.

---

berd"; and *sha* 鎩, "partisan" (long-handled sword). Other lists of five weapons exist; all are products of late Warring States and Han environments and do not reflect the realities of early Zhou warfare.

80. The jade tablets were conferred on vassals as badges of office by the king. The Zhou's gathering up the jade insignia tablets of the vassals of the Shang was a final sign of their triumph.

81. King Helü of Wu 吳王闔閭 (r. 514–496 B.C.E.) was the father of King Fuchai. He usurped the throne of King Liao and went on to greatly increase the power of Wu, by some accounts becoming one of the Five Hegemons of the Zhou.

82. King Zhao of Chu 楚昭王 (r. 515–489 B.C.E.), the son of King Ping.

83. Qiji was an earlier name of King Ping, the younger brother of King Ling. In 529 B.C.E., taking advantage of the absence of King Ling, he conspired with Prince Bi 公子比 to murder the crown prince and set up Prince Bi as king. Later, he forced Prince Bi to commit suicide and set himself as up as King Ping.

[but]

with King Zhao, the people led one another and sacrificed for him;
with King Ling, the people turned their backs in rebellion and abandoned him.

[This is the difference between] winning the people and losing them.

Thus when the Son of Heaven attains the Way, he is secure [even] among the four Yi [tribes of "barbarians"];
when the Son of Heaven loses the Way, he is secure [only] among the Lords of the Land.
When the Lords of the Land attain the Way, they are secure [even] among the four neighboring states.
When the Lords of the Land lose the Way, they are secure [only] within the four boundaries [of their own states].

Thus Tang began with the seventy-*li* area of Bo, and King Wen originally governed the hundred *li* of Feng, but they both could have their decrees enforced, and what they forbade was eradicated all over the world. When the Zhou [dynasty] fell into decay, the Rong attacked Earl Fan[84] at Chuchou, seized him, and carried him off.

Thus,

he who attains the Way can command the Lords of the Land, though he may have only a hundred *li* of territory.
He who loses the Way, though he may rule the world, is still greatly frightened within his core domain.

Thus it is said, "Do not rely on the fact that others do not seize you, but rely on the fact that you cannot be seized." If you implement the Way of someone who could be seized, even if you do not conduct yourself like someone who might be usurped or murdered, it would be of no use in gaining control of the world. [20/219/22–20/220/3]

20.30

As a general rule, people survive by means of clothing and food. Now if you lock them in a dark room,

though you nourish them with fine delicacies,
though you clothe them with embroidered garments,

they will be incapable of joy because

their eyes have nothing to look upon,
and their ears having nothing to listen to.

If they were to peek through a narrow crack and see [even] rain or fog, they would laugh happily. How much more so if they were to open the door and fling apart the shutters so that from total darkness they could see bright light.

84. Earl of Fan 凡伯, a grandee of Zhou, was kidnapped by the Rong "barbarians" while on an embassy to Lu. See *Zuozhuan*, Yin 7.

If from total darkness they were to see bright light so that they were extremely happy, how much more so if they were to leave the room and take a seat in the hall where they could see the light of the sun and moon.

Seeing the light of the sun and moon, they would be boundlessly joyful! How much more so if they were to ascend Mount Tai, stride the stony peak, and gaze toward the Eight Extremities, observing [the constellation] Tiandu[85] as if it were their canopy and the Yangzi and Yellow rivers as if they were their belts, with the myriad things between them. Would not their joy be indescribably great? [20/220/5–9]

Moreover,

with a deaf person, the form of the ears is complete, but he is incapable of hearing.
With a blind person, the form of the eyes exists, but he is incapable of sight.

Now,

with speech, we communicate ourselves to others;
with hearing, others communicate themselves to us.
A dumb person cannot speak;
a deaf person cannot hear.

If one is deaf and dumb, the human Way cannot be communicated. Thus those who are afflicted with both deafness and dumbness, though they may impoverish their families seeking a cure, will not begrudge the cost. Do only the form and body suffer from deafness and dumbness? The heart and mind also suffer such ailments. Now if a finger is crooked, no one would fail to try to straighten it, [but] if the heart is obstructed, no one knows [enough] to strive to unblock it. This is to be confused about the [relative] categories of things.

[Suppose you were]

to comprehend the breadth and loftiness of the Six Arts,
to penetrate the depth and profundity of the Way and its Potency,
to reach where there is nothing above,
to go where there is nothing below,
to join with what has no limit,
to soar where there are no forms,
to be more expansive than the Four Seas,
to be loftier than Mount Tai,
to be richer than the Yangzi and Yellow rivers,
to penetrate boundlessly,
to shine brilliantly,

so that between Heaven and Earth there would be nothing to deter you. If you possessed the means to inspect and observe [the world like this]—would not that be indescribably great? [20/220/11–16]

85. Tiandu 天都, the "Celestial Capital," a constellation surrounding the celestial north pole.

20.31

What people know is superficial, yet things change ceaselessly. If previously you did not know something and now you know it, it is not that your [capacity to] know has increased but that there has been an augmentation of inquiry and learning.

Things that are frequently seen become known.
Things that are frequently done become doable.

Thus

if you have suffered calamities, you will take precautions.
If you have endured hardships, you will achieve solutions.

Now if you were to rely on the longevity of a single lifetime to survey

a thousand years' knowledge
and the theories of past and present,

even if they did not increase [as you were studying them] and their Way and patterns were all plainly apparent, it cannot be said that there is a technique [for doing so]. [20/220/18–20]

If someone wants to know the height of something but is unable [to do so], if you instruct him in the use of the sighting tube[86] and the level, he will be pleased.

If someone wants to know the weight of something but cannot, if you teach[87] him to employ the weight and balance beam, he will be happy.

If someone wants to know the distance of something but is unable [to do so], if you teach him to use "metal eyes,"[88] he will be delighted.

How much more [would a person be pleased] to understand how to respond to all things limitlessly?

To face great hardships and not become fearful,
to see many errors yet not become confused,
to be at ease and self-possessed—

how can such joy as this really be just the happiness derived from a single pleasure?

Now as for the Way,

those that have form are engendered by it; is it not their closest of kin?

---

86. A sighting tube, or aledade (*guan* 管), is a thin tube (like a gun sight but without lenses) used to aim surveying instruments or astronomical instruments. See, for example, Joseph Needham, *Mathematics and the Sciences of the Heavens and the Earth,* vol. 3 of *Science and Civilisation in China* (Cambridge: Cambridge University Press, 1959), 262. Using a level and a sighting tube, one can easily find the height of something (e.g., a tree or a wall) by means of triangulation.

This line and the two following lines echo *Mencius* 1A:7: "If you weigh [something], then its weight can be known; if you measure [something], then its length can be known."

87. *Yu* 予 is probably an error for *jiao* 教; in seal-script orthography, *yu* 予 and *xiao* 孝 (an alternative form of *jiao* 教) are very similar; hence the translation "teach."

88. "Metal eyes" must refer to some sort of sighting device; *guan* and *zhun* 管 準 and *quan* and *heng* 權 衡 are real devices, so *jinmu* 金目 also should be a real instrument of some sort. The phrase *jinmu* appears, however, to be otherwise unknown. Needham does not mention it in his section on surveying techniques in *Mathematics and the Sciences*, 569–79. Possibly, it refers to a rudimentary theodolite used to find distances by means of triangulation.

Those who eat grain and ingest *qi* receive them from it; is it not the most gracious of rulers?
Those who possess every kind of wisdom all learn from it; is it not the broadest of teachers?

If an archer shoots many times without hitting the target, if someone then instructs him in how to use an aiming device,[89] he will be happy. How much more so if someone instructs him in what gives rise to the aiming device! [20/220/22–26]

20.32

Now there is no one who does not know that study is good for you, but some cannot study because they have been harmed by amusements and pastimes. People all often harm what is useful with what is useless. Thus their knowledge is not broad, and their days are not sufficient.

If you use the power expended to make a man-made lake to plow [instead], then the fields will certainly be open to cultivation.
If you use earth piled up high as mountains to build dikes instead, then the water will certainly be enough for our uses.[90]
If you use the cost of feeding dogs and horses and swans and geese to nourish scholars instead, then your reputation will certainly be glorious.
If you use the days you might spend shooting and hunting and gambling at *liubo* to recite the *Odes* and read the *Documents* instead, then your understanding and knowledge will certainly be vast.

Thus when we compare failure to study with studying, it is like comparing the deaf and dumb with unimpaired people. [20/220/28–20/221/2]

20.33

As a general rule, those who study
can understand the distinction between the heavenly and the human
and can comprehend the root of order and disorder.

With a calm heart and clear mind to sustain them, observing the ends and beginnings of things, it can be said that their knowledge is all-embracing.

What Heaven creates includes birds, beasts, plants, and trees.
What humankind creates includes rites, ceremonies, regulations, and measures.
By building, people create palaces and rooms;

89. A sighting device of some kind for a crossbow. Compare 15.5: "In archery, if the calibration of the sights is not correct, the target will not be hit."

90. The "man-made lake" and "earth piled up high as mountains" refer to rulers' fondness for making ornamental projects that waste the labor of the common people. Compare the five kinds of "profligate indolence" in 8.9.

by fabricating, people create boats and carts.
The roots of the means to create order are Humaneness and Rightness;
the branches of the means to create order are laws and measures.
What people use to serve the living is the root;
what people use to serve the dead is the branches.

Roots and branches constitute a single body. What both of them cherish is a single nature.

One who places the root first and the branches behind is called a Superior Man.
One who uses the branches to harm the root is called a petty man.

The natures of the Superior Man and the petty man are not different; rather, it is a question of their priorities.

What is rich and flourishing about plants and trees is their roots, and what can die is their branches.

According to the nature of animals, the head is big and the tail is small.

If the branches are larger than the root, they will snap.
If the tail is larger than the middle, it will not wag.

Thus,

feed the mouth and the one hundred joints will be plump;
water the roots and the branches and leaves will be beautiful.

It is the nature of Heaven and Earth that things have roots and branches. In nurturing things there are priorities. When it comes to ordering humankind, how can there not be a beginning and an end? Thus Humaneness and Rightness are the root of order. Now if you do not know to try to cultivate the root and strive to order the branches, this amounts to neglecting the root yet watering the branches. [20/221/4–12]

Moreover, the genesis of law was as something to support[91] Humaneness and Rightness. Now if you emphasize law and abandon Humaneness and Rightness, this is prizing the hat and shoes yet forgetting the head and feet. Thus Humaneness and Rightness are meant to reinforce the foundation.

If you extend a structure's length without increasing its thickness, it will collapse;
if you increase a structure's height without expanding its foundation, it will topple.
Zhao Zheng [Qin Shihuangdi] did not add to his Moral Potency but piled up his eminence, so he was destroyed.
Earl Zhi did not practice Humaneness and Rightness but strove to expand his territory, so he was lost.

The *Discourses of the States* says,

"If we do not use a large beam, it cannot bear the weight.
Nothing is so heavy as a country,
and no beam can be compared to Moral Potency."[92]

---

91. LY 24/12/24.
92. *Guoyu* 4/11a/127.

If the ruler of a state has his people behind him, it is like a wall having a foundation and a tree having roots.

If the roots are deep, the tree will be stable;
if the foundation is excellent, then the top [of the wall] will be secure. [20/221/14–18]

20.34

The Way of the Five Thearchs and the Three Kings constitutes the warp and weft of the world and the rules and standards of order. Now Shang Yang's "Opening and Closing,"[93] Shenzi's "Three Tests,"[94] Han Feizi's "Solitary Indignation,"[95] and Zhang Yi's and Su Qin's "Horizontal and Vertical" [Alliance System][96] all were selective expediencies, one slice of the arts [of governance]. They are not

the great root of order
or the constant norm of service

that can be heard widely and transmitted through the ages.

[The Chu prime minister] Zinang[97] retreated and kept Chu intact, but retreating cannot be taken as a universal principle.
Xian Gao used deceit to preserve Zheng,[98] but deceit cannot be taken as a constant principle.

Now the sounds of the "Ya" and "Song"[99] all originated as verbal expressions and are rooted in human emotion; thus they serve to establish harmony between ruler and minister and affection between father and son. The music of "Shao" and "Xia"[100] penetrates metal and stone and infuses plants and trees.

---

93. *Zuozhuan*, Xi 20/1. Originally a reference to decisions about opening or closing gates, bridges and roads, walls and moats, to be made according to the requirements of a given point in time. Shang Yang used this term to refer to rewards and punishments, respectively.

94. Shen Buhai was a legalist philosopher and prime minister of Han. These "three tests" are alluded to in a commentary by Gao You but are not explicitly discussed in the surviving fragments of Shen's writings.

95. The title of part 4, chap. 11, of the *Hanfeizi* (HFZ 11/19/19–11/21/11). It alludes to Han Feizi's indignation over a situation in which influential men who curry favor by pandering to the ruler's likes and dislikes prevail at court, but worthy and disinterested men are passed over for appointment to official posts. For a discussion of this chapter of the *Hanfeizi*, see Bertil Lundhal, *Han Fei Zi: The Man and the Work* (Stockholm: Institute of Oriental Studies, Stockholm University, 1992), 142–43.

96. Mentioned also in 21.4. During this era, Qin and Chu were the most powerful states vying through warfare to unite the Central States. The Vertical Alliance refers to an alliance against the state of Qin in the west by six eastern states whose territory stretched vertically from south to north. The Horizontal Alliance was an alliance of six states whose territory stretched from east to west, organized by the Qin state to oppose the state of Chu.

97. Zinang 子囊 (d. 559 B.C.E.) was a son of King Zhuang who served as prime minister under King Kang of Chu. He is often cited as a paragon of loyalty. See LSCQ 19.2/120/22ff.

98. See 12.40, 13.10, and 18.11.

99. These are sections of the *Odes*.

100. Said to have been written by Shun and Yu, respectively.

Now if you appropriate the sounds of remorse and longing and express them with strings and woodwinds, then those who hear these tones will be lustful or sorrowful.

If lustful, they will disorder the distinction between male and female.
If sorrowful, they will stir the *qi* of remorse and longing.

How can this be called "music/joy"?[101]

When King [Youmu] of Zhao[102] wandered in exile in Fangling, he longed for his home town and wrote the poem "Mountains and Trees." None who heard it could hold back their tears.

When Jing Ke went west to [try to] stab to death the king of Qin,[103] Gao Jianli and Song Yi struck the *zhu*[104] and sang on the banks of the Yi River. Of those who heard this music there were none who did not stare angrily with wide open eyes and with hair standing on end under their caps.

If in response, one were to use sounds of that sort to create music to be brought into the ancestral hall, how could that be the music/joy referred to by the ancients? Thus ceremonial caps and carriages of state[105] are things that can be used but not enjoyed. The mixture of flavors in the *taigeng*[106] can be eaten but not savored.

[Instruments of] vermilion [lacquer] and [silk] strings that drip and surge [with emotion], so that for every note there are three sighs: such music can be heard but does not bring happiness.

Thus,

what has no sound sets the standard for what can be heard;
what has no taste sets the standard for what can be tasted.
Lustful sounds are clear to the ear,
and full flavors are pleasing to the mouth,

but these are not to be prized. [20/221/20–30]

Thus,

matters that do not have their basis in the Way and its Potency cannot be taken as models.

Words that do not accord with those of former [sage-]kings cannot be taken as the Way.

---

101. There is a play on words here, because the character 樂 means "music" when pronounced *yue* but means "joy" when pronounced *le*.

102. King [Youmu] of Zhao 趙幽穆王 (r. 235–229 B.C.E.) was the penultimate ruler of Zhao before its destruction. He was captured by the army of Qin in 229 B.C.E. and released into penal exile inside the victor's territory.

103. The assassination attempt took place in 227 B.C.E. Jing Ke tried to stab the king with a poisoned dagger but was thwarted and later was put to death. Jing Ke's friend Gao Jianli, a noted musician, later also tried to assassinate the same monarch (by then known as the First Emperor of Qin) by striking him with his *zhu* while playing a recital; that attempt also failed, and Gao was executed.

104. *Zhu* 筑, a five-stringed instrument.

105. According to commentators, the former refers to caps worn by high officials at court; the latter, to the royal carriage.

106. *Taigeng* 大羹 was a meat broth used at sacrifices to the spirits.

Tones [i.e., sung poetry] that are not [grounded in] the verbal expressions of the "Ya" and the "Song" cannot be taken as [proper] music.

Thus one may pick and choose among the sayings of these five masters[107] as a means to facilitate persuasions, but they are not the pervading principles of the world. [20/222/1–2]

20.35

When the sage-kings established governance and implemented education, they invariably examined their ends and beginnings. When they publicly posted laws and set up standards, they invariably traced their roots and branches to their source. They did not simply prepare one policy to address one thing at a time and leave it at that.

Seeing the beginnings, they would ponder the outcomes.
Observing the sources, they would know the currents.

Thus,

they implemented [policies] widely without exhausting themselves;
they long endured without defiling themselves.

Now,

water emerges from the mountains but flows into the sea.
Crops are born in the field but are stored in the granaries.

Sages, by seeing where things are born, know where they will end up. Thus,

Shun buried gold deep under the dangerous mountain cliffs to thwart the hearts of those who were covetous and greedy.

Yi Di made wine. Yu drank it and found it tasty, so he exiled Yi Di and forbade wine making so as to prevent dissolute conduct.

Master Yan[108] played for Duke Ping the music of the northern border area, but Music Master Kuang said, "This is the [kind of] music that can destroy a state." [The duke] sighed loudly and forbade it in order to stop the tide of lewdness and disorder.

Thus,

when the people became aware of writing, Potency declined;
when the people became aware of counting, generosity declined.
When the people became aware of bonds and contracts, trustworthiness declined;
when the people became aware of tricks and skills, unself-consciousness[109] declined.

---

107. That is, Shang Yang, Shenzi, Han Feizi, Su Qin, and Zhang Yi, as mentioned at the beginning of 20.35.

108. Master Yan 延; but most accounts list this as Master Juan 涓. See LSCQ 11.5/57/7; and Zhang Shuangdi 1997, 2:2111n.7. The latter points out that the historical person referred to here lived long after this incident is supposed to have occurred.

109. Reading *kong* 空. See Zhang Shuangdi 1997, 2:2112n.9. Note ZZ 8/4/7; LSCQ 15.3/82/30; and

When craftiness and deceit hide in your breast,
innocence and purity will not be complete,
and your spirit-engendered Potency will not be intact. [20/222/4–10]

20.36

The *se* does not make a sound, but each of its twenty-five strings responds to its own [respective] tone.
The axle of a cart does not revolve, but each of its thirty spokes contributes its respective strength to the turning [of the wheel].
Only when [all] strings have their [appropriate] tension and size is it possible to create a tune.[110]
Only through [appropriately] hard or easy pulling and [appropriate] moving and stopping is it possible for a cart to travel far.
What causes things to sound has no sound.
What enables things to journey a thousand *li* does not move.
Thus, when high and low
follow different Ways, there is order.
When they follow the same Way, there is disorder.
When those in high position take the Great Way, things go smoothly;
when matters are great but the Way is small, things go badly.
Thus,
trifling pleasures harm Rightness;
trifling cleverness harms the Way;
trifling debates harm order;
unwarranted harshness injures Moral Potency.
Great administration is not precipitous, thus the people are easy to lead.
Supreme government is magnanimous, thus those below do not plunder one another.[111]

Supreme Moral Potency[112] reverts to simplicity; thus the people have no vices. [20/222/12–16]

LY 16/9/8. Arthur Waley translates the *kung* as "in all sincerity," in *The Analects of Confucius* (London: Allen & Unwin, 1938), 140.

110. We are grateful to Jung-Ping Yuan and Bo Lawergren for advice on the proper translation of this sentence. The paired words *huanji* 緩急 and *xiaoda* 小大 function as nouns, "tension" and "size," both of them objects of the verb *you* 有. See also 20.16.

111. Retaining *xiang* 相 in this line, contrary to Lau's (HNZ 20/222/16) emendation.

112. Reading *de* 德 for *zhong* 中. See Lau, HNZ, 222n.9.

20.37

Shang Yang, on behalf of [the state of] Qin, established laws of collective responsibility, and the common people hated them.
Wu Qi, on behalf of [the state of] Chu, extended [rules] abolishing ranks and salaries, and meritorious officials rebelled.

Shang Yang's setting up laws and Wu Qi's use of military power are things the world approved of. But Shang Yang's use of laws destroyed Qin. He investigated the traces of knives and brushes [i.e., writings] but did not know the root of government or disorder. Wu Qi's use of military power weakened Chu. He was familiar with matters of military formations but did not understand the expediency of "fighting from the temple" [i.e., advance planning].[113]

Duke Xian of Jin attacking the Li [Rong] and taking their princess was not a bad thing [in itself], but Historian Su[114] sighed about it when he saw that it would bring disaster to four generations [of the duke's clan].

King Fuchai of Wu defeated Qi at Ailing and defeated Jin at Huang Chi.[115] He did not fail to win victories, yet [Wu] Zishu[116] was saddened by them because he foresaw that [his ruler] would certainly be taken prisoner in Yue.

[Gongzi] Xiao Bo[117] fled to Ju, and Chong'er[118] fled to Cao. They were not unbeleaguered, but Bao Shu[ya] and Maternal Uncle Fan followed and assisted them, knowing they [i.e., their rulers Xiao Bo and Chong'er] would rise to become hegemons.

King Goujian of Yue ensconced himself in Guiji, working on political matters without limit and making plans without rest, knowing that calamity could be turned into good fortune.

Marquis Xiang [of Zhao] won successive victories but had a mournful countenance, fearing that good fortune would become calamity.

Duke Huan of Qi lost the fields of Wenyang but became hegemon.

Earl Zhi seized the land of the three states of Jin but was destroyed.

Sages
perceive good fortune [though hidden] within multiple screens,
perceive bad fortune [though obscured] beyond ninefold curtains. [20/222/18–26]

113. See 15.4 and 15.9; and chap. 15, n. 13.

114. Historian Su 史蘇 was an official of the Jin court who divined the calamitous outcome of the duke's marriage. See *Zuozhuan*, Xi 15. For Lady Li, see 7.16 and 17.145.

115. He did this by forming an alliance with the lords of the states to resist the hegemony of Jin.

116. Wu Zishu 伍子胥 (d. 484 B.C.E.) was a refugee from Chu who took up service in Wu with the hope of avenging his father's death. He employed the general Sun Wu and led Wu to victory over Chu but foresaw the downfall of King Fuchai. His story is recorded in *Shiji* 68.

117. He later ruled as Duke Huan of Qi.

118. Later Duke Wen of Jin. See 12.22 and 18.18.

20.38

The *yuantian* silkworm[119] in one year [can be] harvested twice. It is not that this is not profitable, but the royal laws prohibit it because of the harm it does to the mulberry trees.

Stalks of rice resulting from scattered seeds of the previous year ripen first, but the farmer weeds them out because he would not, for the sake of this small benefit, harm the great harvest.

With family elders,

different rice is used to feed them;

different utensils are used to prepare food for them.

Children and wives ascend the hall barefoot, kneel, and pour the broth [for the elders]. It is not that [these practices] are without cost, but they are not things on which one can economize because that would injure Rightness.

Awaiting the marriage maker to seal the marriage contract;

exchanging the wedding presents to select a wife;

donning wedding attire to escort the bride home to your relations:

it is not that [these practices] are without annoyances, but they are not things that can be changed because they serve to hinder licentiousness.

[One can] get the people in their residences to watch one another and, when there are crimes, to report on one another. As a method for exposing traitors, this is not without efficacy, but such methods are not practiced as they injure [an atmosphere of] peaceful and harmonious hearts and give rise to hateful and revengeful resentments. Thus with endeavors,

though you bore only one hole, you open up one hundred fissures;

though you plant only one tree, you engender ten thousand leaves.

What you have bored is not enough to be considered useful, but what you have opened up is enough to bring ruin.

What you have planted is not enough to bring a profit, but what you have produced is enough to make a mess.[120]

The fool is beguiled by petty benefits and forgets their great harm. This cannot be considered exemplary.

Calamus deters fleas and lice, but people do not make mats out of it because it attracts centipedes.[121]

Foxes catch mice, but they cannot be turned loose in the courtyard because they will seize chickens.

Thus there are some endeavors that

bring small benefit but great harm,

gain something here but lose something there.

Thus in playing chess,

119. *Yuantian* 螈蚕 silkworm, also called *yuancan* 螈蠶.

120. Taking *hui* (or *huo*) 濊 as equivalent to *hui* 穢.

121. Centipedes were said to bore into the ear. See 17.26; and Zhang Shuangdi 1997, 1:1039n.3.

one may capture two pieces yet experience defeat;
one may give up a piece yet win victory. [20/222/28–20/223/9]

20.39

Stealing advantage cannot be practiced;
understanding technique cannot be taken as a model.

Thus Humaneness and Wisdom are the splendid aspects of human talent.

"Humaneness" means to love others;
"Wisdom" means to understand others.
If you love others, you will refrain from cruel punishments;
if you know others, you will refrain from chaotic governance.
When [political] order derives from culture and principles, there will be no perverse or erroneous endeavors.
When punishments are not excessive, there will be no violent and cruel conduct.

If

above there is no troublesome and disorderly governance,
below there will be no resentful and expectant hearts,

so that the one hundred forms of cruelty will be eradicated and centrality and harmony will be created. This is the means by which the Three Dynasties flourished.

Thus the *Documents* says,

"If [the ruler] is wise and kind,
the black-haired people will cherish him.
Why fear Huan Dou?
Why banish the Miao?"[122]

Earl Zhi possessed five talents that surpassed others, but he could not avoid dying by another's hand, for he did not love others.
The king of Qi had skills in three areas that surpassed those of others, but he was taken prisoner in Qin, for he did not understand worthy men.

Thus,

there is no Humaneness greater than loving others;
there is no Wisdom greater than understanding others.

If you have neither of these, even if you are perceptive and smart, clever and skillful, and work hard and untiringly, you will not avoid disorder. [20/223/11–17]

Translated by Sarah A. Queen and John S. Major

122. Similar language appears in the *Documents*, "Gao Yao." As Lau (HNZ, 223n.9) notes, the wording of the passage here differs from that in the received text of the *Documents*. See also Qu Wanli, *Shangshu jinzhu jinyi* (Taibei: Shangwu yinshuguan, 1970), 21–22.

Twenty-One

AN OVERVIEW OF THE ESSENTIALS

"YAO LÜE," or "An Overview of the Essentials," brings the *Huainanzi* to its close. Although "Yao lüe" appears at the end of the work (following the established convention of Chinese works of the late Warring States and early Han periods),[1] it is in effect an introduction because it orients readers to the contents of the text. We believe that the chapter was originally written by Liu An himself for oral recitation at the imperial court as a way of introducing the *Huainanzi* when it was first presented to Emperor Wu.[2] Having been recited at court, the "overview" would then have been appended in written form to the twenty substantive chapters of the *Huainanzi*, serving as a postscript to review and summarize its content. The chapter consists of four complementary sections. The first introduces the work as a whole and provides a rhymed list of the twenty chapter titles. The second gives a thoughtful and illuminating summary of each chapter in turn. The next section links the twenty chapters together in a grand design, showing that each chapter builds on those that precede it. The final section argues for the cogency and significance of the work as a whole by placing it in a comparative and historical framework.

1. See, for example, the similar concluding summaries in *Zhuangzi* 33 and *Shiji* 130.

2. We are very grateful to Martin Kern (private communication) for sharing his seminal views on the literary form of the "Yao lüe." See also Martin Kern, "Western Han Aesthetics and the Genesis of the *Fu*," *Harvard Journal of Asiatic Studies* 63 (2003): 383–437, and "Language, Argument, and Southern Culture in the *Huainanzi*: A Look at the 'Yaolüe'" (paper presented at the conference "Liu An's Vision of Empire: New Perspectives on the *Huainanzi*," Harvard University, Cambridge, Mass., May 31, 2008).

The Chapter Title

We have translated the chapter title "Yao lüe" 要略 as "An Overview of the Essentials."[3] As the title suggests, this chapter introduces readers to the most important aspects of both the individual chapters and the work as a whole. *Yao,* meaning "essential" or "main," is conveniently ambiguous—referring to the author's interest in capturing the text's most distinctive elements while suggesting the author's ambition to provide the emperor with all the knowledge "essential" to establishing efficacious and enlightened rulership. *Lüe,* meaning "outline," "summary," or "sketch," with the related meaning of "to put in order," indicates the synoptic and orderly approach adopted in the chapter's various sections. An intriguing idea, as Martin Kern has suggested, is that one could assign this chapter the alternative title "Liu An's *fu* 賦 on Presenting the *Huainanzi* to the Emperor."

Summary and Key Themes

The most conspicuous feature of this chapter is its literary form. It is a *fu,* a "poetic exposition," a form of oratory that was both very popular and highly admired in the Western Han period. *Fu* were intended above all for oral presentation, but the person reciting the *fu* would in most cases have been reading from a prepared written script. Although the Han imperial library catalog in the *Han shu* lists more than a thousand *fu,* only a few dozen examples now survive. *Fu* were polished literary pieces, but they often were written specifically as works of political and moral argumentation; their literary brilliance added credibility to the points they made. *Fu* are in that sense akin to the "persuasions" that appear in many Warring States and Han works, including some chapters of the *Huainanzi.*[4]

Typically of the genre, the "Overview of the Essentials" is characterized by the intense use of rhyme, metrical variety, deft shifts from one metrical form to another (for example, from classical tetrameter as found in the *Odes* to more complex meters echoing some of the poems of the *Chuci*), frequent use of syntactic parallelism, occasional passages of prose demarcating stages of the poetical argument, rich vocabulary, and an overall air of linguistic and literary virtuosity. The "Yao lüe" would have been recited at the court of Emperor Wu, perhaps by Liu An himself or perhaps by a skilled performer reciting on his behalf, in the course of presenting a copy of the *Huainanzi* to the throne; the dexterity of the oral presentation would have been understood as part of the argument for the validity of the work.

An example of the ingenuity that went into the composition of this expository piece is the list of chapter titles at the end of 21.1, which turns out to be not simply a

3. Le Blanc and Mathieu 2003, chap. 21, translate "Yao lüe" as "Sommaire."

4. Kern, "Western Han Aesthetics," 389–407.

series of titles, but a passage of rhymed trisyllabic verse. (Note that words that rhymed in Han dynasty Chinese do not necessarily rhyme in modern Mandarin.) Here is the list, with rhymes noted by numbers in parentheses:

You yuan dao 有原道	It has "Originating in the Way,"
you chu zhen 有俶真 (1)	it has "Activating the Genuine,"
you tian wen 有天文 (1)	it has "Celestial Patterns,"
you di xing 有墬形 (1)	it has "Terrestrial Forms,"
you shi ze 有時則	it has "Seasonal Rules,"
you lan ming 有覽冥 (1)	it has "Surveying Obscurities,"
you jing shen 有精神 (1)	it has "Quintessential Spirit,"
you ben jing 有本經 (1)	it has "The Basic Warp,"
you zhu shu 有主術	it has "The Ruler's Techniques,"
you mou cheng 有繆稱 (2)	it has "Profound Precepts,"
you qi su 有齊俗	it has "Integrating Customs,"
you dao ying 有道應 (2)	it has "Responses of the Way,"
you fan lun 有氾論	it has "Boundless Discourses,"
you quan yan 有詮言 (3)	it has "Sayings Explained,"
you bing lüe 有兵略	it has "An Overview of the Military,"
you shui shan 有說山 (3)	it has "A Mountain of Persuasions,"
you shui lin 有說林	it has "A Forest of Persuasions,"
you ren jian 有人間 (3)	it has "Among Others,"
you xiu wu 有脩務 (4)	it has "Cultivating Effort,"
you tai zu 有泰族 (4)	[and] it has "The Exalted Lineage."[5]

From this, a number of interesting conclusions follow: the chapters of the *Huainanzi* were assembled in a deliberate order; the chapter titles were added during or after the compilation of the text, and were worded so as to rhyme; and there are an even number of chapters in order to allow chapter titles to follow the standard *fu* scheme of rhyming on even lines (with optional rhymes on a few odd lines as well). One can even gain insight into fine-grained editorial decisions affecting the compilation of the text. For example, one can see that if based on content alone, "Shui shan" (A Mountain of Persuasions) and "Shui lin" (A Forest of Persuasions) could easily have been a single chapter. But it was necessary to divide their content between two chapters in order to have an even number of chapters in the book (excluding the final twenty-first chapter) and to have an unrhymed odd line, in the list of chapter titles, between the rhymed even lines "Shui shan" and "Ren jian" (Among Others). Clearly, this evidence of deliberate editorial care shows the old view of the *Huainanzi* as a miscellaneous compilation, lacking order or coherence, to be completely untenable.

5. Again, we are grateful to Martin Kern (private communication) for sharing his insights into the rhyme-scheme of this passage. The rhymes are (1) *zhen* 真 and *geng* 耕 (a "combined rhyme"), (2) *zheng* 蒸, (3) *yuan* 元, and (4) *hou* 侯 and *wu* 屋 (a "combined rhyme").

In keeping with the rhetorical strategy of the *lüe*, "overview," this *fu* surveys the entire *Huainanzi*—not once, but four times, each with a different approach. "An Overview of the Essentials" begins by outlining the chapter's aims and giving a rhymed list of the twenty chapter names. It next summarizes the twenty preceding chapters, then shows how the chapters are linked together in an organizational chain, and concludes with a review of previous writings on related subjects, declaring the *Huainanzi* to have surpassed them all.

In the chapter's introductory paragraph, the author lays out his broad philosophical claims about the text and identifies the contents of each chapter. The opening lines explain that the *Huainanzi* contains all the knowledge and techniques needed to govern the Chinese empire both effectively and virtuously. The author states that the *Huainanzi* provides an account of the Way and its Potency and describes their relationship to human beings and their affairs. Arguing that previous and contemporaneous works had failed to make this connection explicit, the author's most important task, according to the account of the text given in "Yao lüe," is to demonstrate the critical link between cosmic and political order. Thus both the beginning and the end of this introduction emphasize the interrelationship between the Way and human affairs, asserting that such knowledge will enable the ruler to adapt to the times and so will ensure the efficacy and longevity of his reign. This short introductory section ends by listing the twenty chapter titles.

The second and largest section of "An Overview of the Essentials" comprises the individual chapter summaries. It introduces the main topics of each chapter as well as the categories, concepts, and vocabulary pertaining to them. Most important, it outlines both the practical applications and the benefits of the knowledge derived from mastering the contents of each chapter. This link between the theoretical and the practical, or the descriptive and prescriptive, qualities of the chapters is evident in the semantic and syntactic structures of the chapter summaries. Here, again, we see the author's effort to harmonize the "Way" (*dao*) and "human affairs" (*shi*)—that is, the cosmological and political dimensions of the work—which the author claims is one of the principal and distinctive contributions of the *Huainanzi*'s twenty chapters.

In contrast to the second section, which treats chapters separately, the third section of "An Overview of the Essentials" summarizes the chapters in relation to one another. The *Huainanzi* is a systematic, coherent, and exhaustive arrangement of topics, intended to be read and studied from beginning to end. Accordingly, this section demonstrates that comprehending the content of each succeeding chapter is predicated on successfully mastering the principles presented in the preceding one. Both this summary and the text as a whole move from cosmogony to cosmology to ontology; from the metaphenomenal Way as utter nondifferentiation to the phenomenal world of differentiated things that it generates and sustains; from the Way's macrocosmic aspects visible in Heaven, Earth, and the four seasons to its microcosmic manifestations in human beings; from cosmogony to human genesis; from the motions of the celestial bodies to the movements of human history; and from the cultivation of oneself to the virtuous and efficacious rulership of the world. Hence, this summary describes the text's authority as a compendium encapsulating everything worth knowing and using in governing the world.

The conclusion to the third section once again highlights the *Huainanzi*'s unique adeptness at clarifying the inherent connections between the Way and human affairs, by drawing analogies from history, culture, and the arts. The theme of each analogy is incompleteness. Yet each deficiency noted can be remedied by supplying the missing component, thereby achieving a synthesis. Similarly, the author asserts that discussions of the Way are incomplete, and so the distinctive contribution of the *Huainanzi* is that it speaks of the Way not in isolation but in relation to concrete things and that it speaks of techniques (*shu*) not in isolation but in relation to concrete affairs. By elucidating the links between both the "Way" and "things" and "techniques" and "affairs," only the *Huainanzi*, the author explains, expands the discussion of their interrelation until "it will leave no empty spaces"—in other words, until nothing more can be said. Its contribution, therefore, lies in its capacity to relate them, a quality of the text that is emphasized throughout the different sections of "An Overview of the Essentials."

The fourth section deepens the author's claim for comprehensiveness by situating the *Huainanzi* at the culmination of an evolution of practices and texts stretching from King Wen of the Zhou dynasty through innovations in Warring States times and during the Qin dynasty. The author summarizes several noteworthy events during these diverse periods by recounting both their particular historical circumstances and the technical and textual contributions made by key advisers and thinkers who figured prominently in each era. Nonetheless, the creation of the *Huainanzi* is different from the time- and context-bound nature of these earlier innovations because of its purported timelessness and comprehensiveness. This polemical claim is reinforced in the concluding passage of this narrative, in which the author summarizes the "book of the Liu clan" itself and characterizes the *Huainanzi* as an exhaustive repository of knowledge concerning matters both theoretical and practical.

Sources

The most obvious and important influence of "An Overview of the Essentials" is the long-standing genre of inventories or taxonomies that originated with such well-known Warring States exemplars as the "Fei Ru" (Opposing the Confucians) section of the *Mozi*, the "Xianxue" (Eminent Learning) section of the *Hanfeizi*, and the "Fei shi er zi" (Opposing the Twelve Masters) chapter of the *Xunzi*. The "Tianxia" (The World) chapter of the *Zhuangzi* may also have been a source for the author of "An Overview of the Essentials"; these two chapters appear to reflect a common literary and intellectual milieu. In this regard, the *Huainanzi*'s postscript and the taxonomy it contains are not unique, and undoubtedly the author is not the first to include them in a work. However, with the different examples of this genre in mind, the author of "An Overview of the Essentials" used various methods of categorization to construct his rationale for depicting early China's intellectual landscape so as to highlight the uniqueness of his own literary production. For example, unlike earlier examples of this genre, the taxonomy included in "An Overview of the Essentials" explicitly links past innovations to specific historical events and circumstances, thereby serving one of the overarching rhetorical purposes of the postface—to demonstrate that the *Huainanzi* both completely subsumes and surpasses all that came before it by virtue of its innovativeness, timelessness, and comprehensiveness. And by couching the postface in the performative *fu* genre, Liu An achieved the considerable feat of using an aesthetic act to reinforce the chapter's intellectual argument.

The Chapter in the Context of the *Huainanzi* as a Whole

"An Overview of the Essentials" stands out from the rest of the chapters in the *Huainanzi* on several accounts. Its form sets it apart; whereas the other chapters of the text are by no means lacking in literary sophistication, and some even contain extended passages in the *fu* style (for example, 5.15, 8.9, and 19.1), this is the only chapter that is a *fu* in its entirety. The chapter's literary style is dense and sometimes difficult; it includes some of the most arcane terminology in the entire text and clearly was intended to dazzle its audience. The unique literary qualities of this chapter are matched by an equally striking originality of ideas. Whereas the novelty of most chapters derives from a combination of selection, arrangement, and topical comment, "An Overview of the Essentials" is far less indebted to and dependent on received sources to argue its main points. This is all the more striking when this feature of the chapter is considered in conjunction with its distinctly uniform voice, which in turn derives from the essentially performative character of the *fu* genre. Rather than the deliberate diversity of viewpoints characteristic of the body of the work, this chapter employs a singular and consistent voice to survey the content of the text and explain its indispensable contribution to rulership. Moreover, this voice explicitly identifies the *Huainanzi* as the "book of the Liu clan" and tries to persuade the reader (that is, the ruler) that one imperial relative is willing and able to make a substantial contribution to the cause of empire. In this chapter, we seem to hear the voice of Liu An himself, who used the occasion of his visit to the imperial court to recite this *fu* (or have it recited on his behalf) in the course of formally presenting the *Huainanzi* to Emperor Wu and who then added its written script as a postface to the book itself to preserve it for posterity. In this poetic exposition, Liu An recounts the vision that inspired him to attract to his court the best minds of his day to create this literary monument to a syncretic and pluralistic vision of empire. The *Huainanzi*'s authors deliberately used the elastic and malleable terms *dao* and *de*, with their multiplicity of conceptual and practical resonances, as universal subjects of debate and discussion shared by all the traditions across the empire and spanning the earlier dynasties and generations. With such a conception of the Way and its Potency, therefore, the *Huainanzi* was not limited to one perspective or interpretation, or one application of its meaning, but tried to harmonize these different resonances and thereby provide a new account of the Way in all its multiplicity, which would encapsulate and surpass all preceding literary endeavors and ensure that this illustrious work would stand the test of time.[6]

Sarah A. Queen, Judson Murray, and John S. Major

---

6. For detailed analyses of these and other important aspects of the *Huainanzi*'s postscript, see Sarah A. Queen, "Inventories of the Past: Rethinking the 'School' Affiliation of the *Huainanzi*," *Asia Major*, 3rd ser., 14, no. 1 (2001): 51–72; and Judson B. Murray, "A Study of 'Yao lue' 要略, 'A Summary of the Essentials': Understanding the *Huainanzi* Through the Point of View of the Author of the Postface," *Early China* 29 (2004): 45–108, and "The Consummate *Dao*: The 'Way' (*Dao*) and 'Human Affairs' (*shi*) in the *Huainanzi*" (Ph.D. diss., Brown University, 2007), esp. 58–121.

Twenty-One

21.1

We have created and composed these writings and discourses as a means to

knot the net of the Way and its Potency
and weave the web of humankind and its affairs,[1]
above investigating them in Heaven,
below examining them on Earth,
and in the middle comprehending them through patterns.[2]

Although they are not yet able to draw out fully the core of the Profound Mystery, they are abundantly sufficient to observe its ends and beginnings.[3] If we [only] summarized the essentials or provided an overview and our words did not discriminate the Pure, Uncarved Block and differentiate the Great Ancestor, then it would cause people in their confusion to fail to understand them. Thus,

numerous are the words we have composed
and extensive are the illustrations we have provided,

yet we still fear that people will depart from the root and follow the branches.

Thus,

1. For *jigang* 紀綱 and *jingwei* 經緯 as verbs, see the related description of the Grand One as one who "knots the net of the eight directional end points and weaves the web of the six coordinates" in 8.7.

2. For the various usages and meanings of *li* 理, see app. A.

3. *Zhongshi* 終始.

if we speak of the Way but do not speak of affairs,
there would be no means to shift with[4] the times.
[Conversely],
if we speak of affairs but do not speak of the Way,
there would be no means to move with[5] [the processes of] transformation.

Therefore we composed [the book's] twenty essays [as follows]:
It has "Originating in the Way,"
it has "Activating the Genuine,"
it has "Celestial Patterns,"
it has "Terrestrial Forms,"
it has "Seasonal Rules,"
it has "Surveying Obscurities,"
it has "Quintessential Spirit,"
it has "The Basic Warp,"
it has "The Ruler's Techniques,"
it has "Profound Precepts,"
it has "Integrating Customs,"
it has "Responses of the Way,"
it has "Boundless Discourses,"
it has "Sayings Explained,"
it has "An Overview of the Military,"
it has "A Mountain of Persuasions,"
it has "A Forest of Persuasions,"
it has "Among Others,"
it has "Cultivating Effort,"
[and] it has "The Exalted Lineage."[6] [21/223/21–28]

21.2

"Originating in the Way"
[begins with] the six coordinates contracted[7] and compressed
and the myriad things chaotic and confused.
[It then] diagrams the features of the Grand One
and fathoms the depths of the Dark Unseen,

4. Literally, "float and sink."

5. Literally, "go and stop."

6. This list of chapters is in rhymed trisyllabic verse. For its rhyme-scheme, see the introduction to this chapter.

7. The phrase *lu mou* 盧牟 is rather obscure. Most commentators take it as equivalent to *lu mou* 矑眸, "pupil of the eye"; the implication is that the six coordinates (i.e., the three dimensions: up–down, front–back, left–right) are compressed to the size of the pupil of an eye.

thereby soaring beyond the frame[8] of Empty Nothingness.
By relying on the small, it embraces the great;
by guarding the contracted, it orders the expansive.
It enables you to understand
the bad or good fortune of taking the lead or following behind
and the benefit or harm of taking action or remaining still.
If you sincerely comprehend its import, floodlike, you can achieve a grand vision.
If you desire a single expression to awaken to it:
"Revere the heavenly and preserve your genuineness."
If you desire a second expression to comprehend it:
"Devalue things and honor your person."
If you desire a third expression to fathom it:
"Externalize desires and return to your genuine dispositions."
If you grasp its main tenets,
inwardly you will harmonize the Five Orbs
and enrich the flesh and skin.
If you adhere to its models and standards
and partake of them to the end of your days,
they will provide the means
to respond and attend to the myriad aspects of the world
and observe and accompany its manifold alterations,
as if rolling a ball in the palm of your hand.
Surely it will suffice to make you joyous! [21/224/1–5]

"Activating the Genuine" exhaustively traces the transformation [of things] from their ends to their beginnings;
infuses and fills the essence of Something and Nothing;
distinguishes and differentiates the alterations of the myriad things;
unifies and equates the forms of death and life.
It enables you to
know to disregard things and return to the self;
investigate the distinctions between Humaneness and Rightness;
comprehend the patterns of identity and difference;
observe the guiding thread of Utmost Potency;
and know the binding cords of alterations and transformations.
Its explanations tally with the core of the Profound Mystery
and comprehend[9] the mother of creation and transformation.
[21/224/7–9]

---

8. The term *zhen* 軫 literally means "carriage crossbar" but also is a synecdoche for "chariot frame" and, by extension, for a framework of any kind.

9. Deleting *hui* 迴 as an erroneous intrusion, and rejecting Lau's (HNZ 21/224/9) emendation of *hui* to *dong* 迵.

"Celestial Patterns" provides the means by which to
harmonize the *qi* of yin and yang,
order the radiances of the sun and moon,
regulate the seasons of opening [spring/summer] and closing [fall/winter],
tabulate the movements of the stars and planets,
know the permutations of [their] retrograde and proper motion,
avoid the misfortunes associated with prohibitions and taboos,
follow the responses of the seasonal cycles,
and imitate the constancy of the Five Gods.
It enables you to
possess the means to gaze upward to Heaven and uphold what to follow
and thereby avoid disordering Heaven's regularities. [21/224/11–12]

"Terrestrial Forms" provides the means by which to
encompass the length from north to south,
reach the breadth from east to west,
survey the topography of the mountains and hillocks,
demarcate the locations of the rivers and valleys,
illuminate the master of the myriad things,
know the multitude of categories of living things,
tabulate the enumerations of mountains and chasms,
and chart the roadways far and near.
It enables you to
circulate comprehensively and prepare exhaustively,
so that you cannot be roused by things
or startled by oddities. [21/224/14–16]

"Seasonal Rules" provides the means by which to
follow Heaven's seasons above,
use Earth's resources below,
determine standards and implement correspondences,
aligning them with human norms.
It is formed into twelve sections to serve as models and guides.
Ending and beginning anew,
they repeat limitlessly,
adapting, complying, imitating, and according
in predicting bad and good fortune.
Taking and giving, opening and closing,
each has its prohibited days,
issuing commands and administering orders,
instructing and warning according to the season.
[It] enables the ruler of humankind to know the means by which to manage affairs. [21/224/18–20]

"Surveying Obscurities" provides the means by which to discuss
Utmost Essence penetrating the Nine Heavens,
Utmost Subtlety sinking into the Formless,
Unblemished Purity entering Utmost Clarity,
and Luminous Brightness penetrating Dark Obscurity.
It begins by
grasping things and deducing their categories,
observing them, taking hold of them,
lifting them up, and arranging them,
and pervasively positing them as categories of similarity,
by which things can be understood as ideas and visualized as forms.
It then
penetrates various obstructions,
bursts open various blockages,
to guide your awareness,
to connect it to the Limitless.
[It] then thereby illuminates
the stimuli of the various categories of things,
the responses of identical *qi*,
the unions of yin and yang,
and the intricacies of forms and shapes.
It is what leads you to observe and discern in a far-reaching and expansive way. [21/224/22–25]

"Quintessential Spirit" provides the means by which to
trace to the source the root from which human life arises
and understand what animates humans' form, frame, and nine orifices.
Taking its images from Heaven,
it coordinates and identifies humans' blood and *qi*
with thunder and lightning, wind and rain;
correlates and categorizes humans' happiness and anger
with dawn and dusk, cold and heat.
Judging the distinctions between life and death,
distinguishing the traces of identity and difference,
regulating the workings of movement and stillness,
it thereby returns to the Ancestor of nature and destiny.
It is what enables you to
cherish and nourish the essence and spirit,
pacify and still the ethereal and earthly souls,
not change the self on account of things,
and fortify and preserve the abode of Emptiness and Nothingness. [21/224/27–21/225/2]

"The Basic Warp" provides the means by which to
illuminate the Potency of the great sages
and penetrate the Way of the Unique Inception.[10]
Delineating and summarizing the devolution of decadent eras from past to present,
it thereby praises the flourishing prosperity of earlier ages[11]
and criticizes the corrupt governments of later ages.
It is what enables you to
dispense with the acuity and keenness of hearing and sight,
still the responses and movements of the essence and spirit,
restrain effusive and ephemeral viewpoints,
temper the harmony of nourishing your nature,
distinguish the conduct of [the Five] Thearchs and [Three] Kings,
and set out the differences between small and great. [21/225/4–6]

"The Ruler's Techniques" [addresses] the affairs of the ruler of humankind. It provides the means by which to adapt tasks [to individuals] and scrutinize responsibilities so as to ensure that each of the numerous officials exerts his abilities exhaustively.
[It] illuminates
how to wield authority and manage the handles of governance
and thereby regulate the multitudes below;
how to match official titles with actual performance
and investigate them [with the techniques of] threes and fives.[12]
It is what enables the ruler of men to
grasp techniques and sustain essentials
and not act recklessly based on happiness or anger.
Its techniques
straighten the bent and correct the crooked,
set aside self-interest and establish the public good,
enabling the one hundred officials to communicate in an orderly fashion
and gather around the ruler like the spokes of a wheel,
each exerting his utmost in his respective task,
while the people succeed in their accomplishments.
Such is the brilliance of the ruler's techniques. [21/225/8–11]

"Profound Precepts"
parses and analyzes [various] assessments of the Way and its Potency,
ranks and puts in sequence [diverse] differentiations of Humaneness and Rightness,

10. *Wei chu* 維初, taking *wei* here as a modifier implying a singular inception of the cosmos.
11. Reading *sheng* 聖 as *shi* 世. See Zhang Shuangdi 1997, 2:2136n.29.
12. *Canwu* 參五, "(correlations of) threes and fives," is a system for analyzing problems; "threes" refers to the triad of Heaven, Earth, and Man; "fives," to the Five Phases. See 9.19 and 20.11.

summarizes and juxtaposes the affairs of the human realm,
generally bringing them into conformity with the Potency of spirit illumination.
It proposes similes and selects appositions
to match them with analogies and illustrations;
it divides into segments and forms sections
to respond to brief aphorisms.
It is what makes it possible to find fault with persuasions and attack arguments, responding to provocations without error. [21/225/13–14]

"Integrating Customs" provides the means by which to
unify the weaknesses and strengths of the various living things,
equate the customs and habits of the nine Yi [tribes],
comprehend past and present discourses,
and thread together the patterns of the myriad things.
[It]
manages and regulates the suitability of Ritual and Rightness
and demarcates and delineates the ends and beginnings of human affairs. [21/225/16–17]

"Responses of the Way"
picks out and draws together the relics of past affairs,
pursues and surveys the traces of bygone antiquity,
and investigates the reversals of bad and good fortune, benefit and harm.
It tests and verifies them according to the techniques of Lao and Zhuang,[13]
thus matching them to the trajectories of gain and loss. [21/225/19–20]

"Boundless Discourses" provides the means by which to
stitch up the spaces in ragged seams and hems
and plug up the gaps in crooked and chattering teeth.[14]
It welcomes the straightforward and straightens out the devious,
in order to extend the Original Unhewn[15] and thereby anticipate
the alternations of success and failure
and the reversals of benefit and harm.[16]
It is what enables you to
not be foolishly immersed in the advantages of political power,

13. That is, Laozi and Zhuangzi.

14. "Ragged seams and hems" and "gaps in crooked and chattering teeth" are metaphors for the various shortcomings of the age, the consequences of persistent decline from the primordial era of sage-rulership.

15. This is a reference to both the primordial age's radical reliance on the Way and the inherent nature of the sage-ruler.

16. *Bing* 病, literally, "illness," but here used in a more general sense to mean "harm" or "misfortune."

not be seductively confused by the exigencies of affairs,
and so tally with constancy and change[17]
to link up and discern timely and generational alterations,
and extend and adjust [your policies] in accordance with transformations. [21/225/22–24]

"Sayings Explained" provides the means by which to
compare through analogy the tenets of human affairs
and elucidate through illustration the substance of order and disorder.
It ranks the hidden meanings of subtle sayings,
explaining them with literary expressions that reflect ultimate principles.
Thus it patches up and mends deficiencies due to errors and oversights. [21/225/26–27]

"An Overview of the Military" provides the means by which to illuminate
the techniques of battle, victory, assault, and capture;
the force of formations and movements;
and the variations of deception and subterfuge
embodying the Way of Adaptation and Compliance
and upholding the Theory of Holding Back;
it is what [enables you] to
know that when you form for battle or deploy to fight contrary to the Way, it will not work;
know that when you assault and capture or fortify and defend contrary to Moral Potency, it will not be formidable.
If you truly realize its implications,
whether advancing or retreating, moving right or left,
there will be no place to be attacked or endangered.
It takes relying on force as its substance
and clarity and stillness as its constant.
It avoids fullness and follows emptiness,
as if driving forward a flock of sheep.
Such are the means to discuss military affairs. [21/225/29–31]

"A Mountain of Persuasions" and "A Forest of Persuasions" demonstrate how to
skillfully and elegantly penetrate and bore open the blockages and obstructions of the many affairs
and thoroughly and comprehensively penetrate and pierce the barriers and hindrances of the myriad things,

17. *Yan ni* 曮晲, metaphorically, "constancy and change," but literally, "the path of the sun across the sky"—which is constant in the sense of being entirely predictable but also ever-changing as the position of sunrise and sunset on the horizon and the height of the sun's arc across the sky shift every day throughout the seasons of the year.

proposing analogies and selecting similes,
distinguishing categories and differentiating forms,
it thereby
leads and orders your awareness,
loosens and unties what is knotted up,
and unravels and unwinds what is wound up,
so as to illuminate the boundaries of affairs. [21/226/1–3]

"Among Others" provides the means by which to
observe the alterations of bad and good fortune,
discern the reversals of benefit and harm,
diagnose[18] the symptoms of success and failure,
and mark out and hold up to view the boundaries of ends and beginnings.[19]
[It]
differentiates and distinguishes the subtleties of the one hundred affairs
and discloses and reveals the mechanisms of preservation and loss,
enabling you to know
bad fortune as good fortune,
loss as gain,
success as failure,
and benefit as harm.
If you truly grasp [its] utmost implications, you will possess the means to move to and fro and up and down among the vulgar of the age, while remaining unharmed by slander, abuse, venom, or poison. [21/226/5–7]

"Cultivating Effort" provides the means by which those
whose entry into the Way is not profound
and whose appreciation of argumentation is not deep
can, by observing these literary expressions, turn themselves around
to take clarity and purity as constants
and mildness and serenity as roots.
[But those who]
idly and lazily set aside their studies,
give free rein to their desires and indulge their feelings.
and wish to misappropriate what they lack,
will be obstructed from the Great Way.
Now,

---

18. The term we translate as "diagnose," *zuanmai* 鑽脈, means "needle and pulse," both used as verbs: to insert an acupuncture needle (into someone) and to take (someone's) pulse.

19. That is, it allows you to investigate these things from their faint, almost archaeological, traces (metaphorically, footprints and eroded boundary markers).

madmen have no anxiety,
and sages, too, have no anxiety.
Sages have no anxiety
because they harmonize by means of Potency,
whereas madmen have no anxiety
because they do not know [the difference between] bad and good fortune.

Thus,

the non-action of those who fully comprehend [the Way]
and the non-action of those who are obstructed from [the Way]
are alike with regard to their non-action
but differ with regard to the means by which they are non-active.

Thus, on their behalf, what can be heeded has been brought to the surface, declared, circulated, and explained, thereby inspiring scholars to diligently appropriate [these principles] for themselves. [21/226/9–13]

"The Exalted Lineage"

traverses the eight end points,
extends to the highest heights,
illuminates the three luminaries above,
and harmonizes water and earth below.
It aligns the Way of past and present,
orders the hierarchy of human relationships and patterns,
summarizes the tenets of the myriad regions,
and returns them home to a single root,

thereby

knotting the net of the Way of Governance
and weaving the web of the affairs of the True King.[20]

[It] then

traces to the source the techniques of the mind,
sets in order instinct and nature,

and thereby

provides a lodging place for the numen of Clarity and Equanimity.
It clarifies and purifies the quintessence of spirit illumination,
thereby enfolding and cleaving to the harmony of Heaven.

It provides the means to observe how the Five Thearchs and the Three Kings

embraced the heavenly *qi*,
cherished the Heavenly Heart,
and grasped centrality and savored harmony.
Their Moral Potency having taken shape within [them],

20. These two lines reiterate the knotting and weaving metaphors (*jigang* 紀綱 and *jingwei* 經緯) found in the opening paragraph of this chapter.

it then cohered Heaven and Earth,
issued forth and aroused yin and yang,
ordered the four seasons,
rectified the changeable directions,
calmed things with its tranquillity,
and extended them with its efficaciousness.

[Their Moral Potency] then thereby
fired and smelted the myriad things,[21]
buoyed up and transformed the innumerable life forms,
singing forth, they harmonized,
moving about, they followed along,

so that all things within the Four Seas with a single mind unanimously offered their allegiance.

Thus,
lucky stars appeared,
auspicious winds arrived,
the Yellow Dragon descended,
phoenix nests lined the trees,
and the *qilin* tarried in the open fields.
Had Moral Potency not taken shape within [them],
yet their laws and tributes were implemented,
and their regulations and measures were employed exclusively,
then the spirits and divinities would not have responded to them;
good fortune and blessings would not have returned home to them;
all things within the Four Seas would not have submitted to them;
and subjects would not have been transformed by them.

Thus,
Moral Potency that takes shape within
is the great foundation of governance.

This is [the message of] "The Exalted Lineage" of the *Profoundly Illustrious*.[22] [21/226/15–21]

21.3

In all, these interconnected writings are the means to focus on the Way and remove obstructions, enabling succeeding generations to know what is appropriate to uphold or abandon and what is suitable to endorse or reject.

Externally, when they interact with things, they will not be bewildered;
internally, they will possess the means to lodge their spirit and nourish their *qi*.

21. That is, the myriad things are fired (*tao*) like ceramics and smelted (*ye*) like metal.

22. *Profoundly Illustrious* (*Honglie* 鴻烈) was an early alternative title for the *Huainanzi*.

They will take ease in and merge with utmost harmony, delighting themselves in what they have received from Heaven and Earth.

Therefore,

Had we discussed the Way ["Originating in the Way"][23] and not illuminated ends and beginnings ["Activating the Genuine"],
you would not know the models to follow.
Had we discussed ends and beginnings and not illuminated Heaven, Earth, and the four seasons ["Celestial Patterns," "Terrestrial Forms," and "Seasonal Rules," respectively],
you would not know the taboos to avoid.
Had we discussed Heaven, Earth, and the four seasons and not introduced examples and elucidated categories,
you would not recognize the subtleties of the Quintessential *qi* ["Surveying Obscurities"].
Had we discussed the Utmost Essence and not traced to its source the spiritlike *qi* of human beings,
you would not know the mechanism by which to nourish your vitality ["Quintessential Spirit"].
Had we traced to their source the genuine dispositions of human beings and not discussed the Potency of the great sages,
you would not know the [human] shortcomings associated with the Five Phases ["The Basic Warp"].
Had we discussed the Way of the [Five] Thearchs and not discussed the affairs of the ruler,
you would not know the proper order distinguishing the small from the great ["The Ruler's Techniques"].
Had we discussed the affairs of the ruler and not provided precepts and illustrations,
you would not know the times for taking action or remaining still ["Profound Precepts"].
Had we discussed precepts and illustrations and not discussed alterations in customs,
you would not know how to coordinate and equate their main tenets. ["Integrating Customs"].
Had we discussed alterations in customs and not discussed past events,
you would not know the responses of the Way and its Potency ["Responses of the Way"].
To know the Way and its Potency but not know the perversions of the age,
you would lack the means to accommodate yourself to the myriad aspects of the world ["Boundless Discourses"].
To know "Boundless Discourses" but not know "Sayings Explained,"

23. For clarity, the corresponding chapter titles are in brackets.

you would lack the means to take your ease.
To comprehend writings and compositions but not know the tenets of military affairs,
you would lack the means to respond to [enemy] troops ["An Overview of the Military"].
To know grand overviews but not know analogies and illustrations,
you would lack the means to clarify affairs by elaboration ["A Mountain of Persuasions" and "A Forest of Persuasions"].
To know the Public Way but not know interpersonal relations,
you would lack the means to respond to ill and good fortune ["Among Others"].
To know interpersonal relations but not know "Cultivating Effort,"
you would lack the means to inspire scholars to exert their utmost strength.

Should you desire
to forcibly abridge this composition
by observing and summarizing only its essentials

without traveling its winding paths and entering its subtle domains, this will not suffice to exhaust the meanings of the Way and its Potency.

Therefore, we composed [these] writings in twenty chapters. Thereby
the patterns of Heaven and Earth are thoroughly examined;
the affairs of the human realm are comprehensively engaged;
and the Way of [the Five] Thearchs and [Three] Kings is fully described.

Their discussions are
sometimes detailed and sometimes general,
sometimes subtle and sometimes obvious.
The tenets advanced in each chapter are different,
and each has a reason for being expressed.

Now, if we spoke exclusively of the Way, there would be nothing that is not contained in it. Nevertheless, only sages are capable of grasping its root and thereby knowing its branches. At this time, scholars lack the capabilities of sages, and if we do not provide them with detailed explanations,
then to the end of their days they will flounder in the midst of darkness and obscurity
without knowing the great awakening brought about by these writings' luminous and brilliant techniques. [21/226/23–21/227/4]

Now, the "Qian" and "Kun" [trigrams] of the *Changes* suffice to comprehend the Way and disclose its meanings. With the eight trigrams you can understand the inauspicious and auspicious and know bad and good fortune. Nevertheless, Fu Xi made them into the sixty-four permutations[24] [i.e., hexagrams], and the house of Zhou added six line-texts to each of the hexagrams, and these are the means to

24. *Bian* 變.

trace to the source and fathom the Way of Purity and Clarity
and grasp and follow the Ancestor of the myriad things.

The number of the five notes does not exceed *gong, shang, jue, zhi,* and *yu*. Nevertheless, you cannot play them all on the [unstopped] five strings of a *qin*. You must control and harmonize the fine and thick strings, and only then can you produce a melody.

Now, if you draw only the head of a dragon, those observing it will not be able to identify what animal it is. But if you add the body, there will be no confusion as to the animal's identity.

Now,

if our references to the "Way" were numerous,
[but] if our references to "things" were few;
if our references to "techniques" were extensive,
[but] if our references to "affairs" were superficial,
and we extended this [throughout] our discussions,
we would be left speechless.
Anyone who intended to study this

and who firmly wished to build on it, would [also] find himself with nothing to say. [21/227/6–11]

Now,

discussions about the Way are surpassingly profound;
therefore, we have written many compositions on it [i.e., the Way] to reveal its true qualities.
The myriad things are surpassingly numerous;
therefore we have broadly offered explanations of them to communicate their significance.

Though these compositions may be

winding and endless,
complicated and slow going,
intertwined and numerous,
and distant and dawdling,

in order to distill and purify their utmost meaning and ensure that they are neither opaque nor impenetrable, we have retained them and not discarded them.

Now, although the debris and putrid carcasses floating in the Yangzi and Yellow rivers cannot be surpassed in number, nevertheless those who offer sacrifices draw water from them. [This is because] the rivers are so large.

Although a cup of wine may be sweet, if a fly is immersed in it, even commoners will not drink it. [This is because] the cup is so small.

If you sincerely comprehend the discussions in these twenty chapters, you will thereby

observe their general patterns and grasp their essentials,
penetrate the Nine Fields,
pass through the Ten Gates,
externalize Heaven and Earth,

and extend beyond the mountains and rivers.
Wandering and ambling through the span of a single age,
governing and fashioning the forms of the Myriad Things,
surely this is an excellent journey! This being the case,
you will clasp the sun and the moon without being burned,
and you will anoint the myriad things without drying up.

How ample! How lucid!
It is enough to read this [alone]!
How far-reaching and vast! How boundless!
Here you may wander! [21/227/13–18]

21.4

In the age of King Wen,
[the Shang tyrant] Djou became the Son of Heaven.
Taxes and levies had no measures,
and executions and killings had no end.
[Djou] indulged himself in sensual pleasures
and drowned himself in intoxicating liquors.
Inside his palace compound, he constructed a public market
and created the punishment of the roasting beam.
[He] dismembered one who remonstrated with him[25]
and cut out the fetus from a pregnant woman.
The world shared the same mind in condemning him.

King Wen, however, with the accumulated goodness of four generations, cultivated Moral Potency and practiced Rightness as he dwelled in the region of Qizhou. Though his territory was no more than one hundred *li* square, two-thirds[26] of the world gave allegiance to him. King Wen hoped that by means of humility and softness, he would restrain the powerful and violent and thereby rid the world of brutality and cleanse it of tyranny and plundering to establish the Kingly Way. Thus, the *Strategies of the Grand Duke*[27] were born. [21/227/20–23]

When King Wen's work was left unfinished,
King Wu continued his efforts.

25. Bi Gan is the most famous example of a person executed for remonstrating with the vicious King Djou of the Shang dynasty.

26. The expression *er chui* 二垂, which also occurs in 12.35, is variously interpreted as meaning "two-thirds" or "one-half." See Zhang Shuangdi 1997, 2:1273n.1.

27. The tutor to Kings Wen and Wu, the Grand Duke (*taigong* 太公, also known as Grand Duke Wang of Lü) was said to have assisted the Zhou in their conquest of the Shang. In the *Lüshi chunqiu*, he is cited on numerous occasions for the good influence he had on these kings. See, for example, Knoblock and Riegel 2000, 2/4.2A, 4/3.1, 24/2.1. Several works attributed to him are listed in *Han shu* 30 under the rubric *dao jia*, or "Daoist school." See *Han shu* 30/1729.

Employing the strategies of the Grand Duke,
he mobilized a small contingent of troops[28]
and personally donned battle armor and helmet

to chastise the impious and punish the unjust. He vanquished the enemy troops at Muye[29] and thereby ascended to the position of Son of Heaven. At that time,

the world was not yet settled,
and the lands within the seas were not yet calmed.

Yet King Wu hoped that by illuminating the exceptional Moral Potency of King Wen, he might inspire the Yi and Di [tribes][30] each to come and pay tribute with their respective riches. Since those from the most distant lands had not yet arrived, King Wu decreed three years of mourning and entombed King Wen in a state chamber where his remains awaited those from these distant regions.

King Wu was on the throne for three years and then expired. His son King Cheng was still in his infancy [when his father died], and he was not yet able to attend to the affairs [of governance]. Cai Shu and Guan Shu[31] backed Prince Lufu [heir of the tyrant Djou], and they wanted to foment a rebellion. The Duke of Zhou,[32] however, continued the efforts of King Wen. He preserved the governance of the Son of Heaven by aiding and supporting the Zhou household and assisting King Cheng.

Fearing that if the path of war were not quelled,
then ministers and subjects might imperil the sovereign,

he consequently

retired his war horses to Mount Hua,
pastured his war oxen in Peach Grove,
destroyed his war drums and snapped his war drumsticks,[33]
and taking up the tablet of a minister, he held forth in audience,
thereby placating and settling the royal household
and calming and comforting the Lords of the Land.

When King Cheng came of age and could attend to the affairs of governance, the Duke of Zhou was enfeoffed in [the state of] Lu where he modified the prevailing habits and changed the local customs.

Confucius

28. Following Xu Shen's reading of the character *fu* 賦 "tax" as *bing* 兵, "soldiers." See Zhang Shuangdi 1997, 2:2153n.7.

29. Muye was the location of the decisive battle in the Zhou conquest of the Shang.

30. The Yi and Di tribes were people living beyond the Central States. The people of the Central States considered their customs barbarous and uncivilized.

31. Cai Shu and Guan Shu were the two eldest of the younger brothers (*shu*) of King Wu; they were deputed to govern parts of the former Shang territory after King Wu conquered the Shang. When King Wu died, his heir, King Cheng, was still a minor, and the youngest brother of King Wu (Dan, the Duke of Zhou) became his regent. Cai Shu and Guan Shu, apparently dissatisfied with that arrangement, rebelled against the Zhou house. They supported an attempted restoration of the Shang under Prince Lufu but were defeated by the Duke of Zhou in the ensuing civil war. See 11.18, 20.14, and 20.25.

32. The youngest brother of King Wu of Zhou, the Duke of Zhou acted as regent to King Cheng when he was a minor; he is regarded as a paragon of good government and filial piety.

33. This was in order that the drum signal to retreat could not be given.

cultivated the Way of [Kings] Cheng and Kang,
and transmitted the teachings of the Duke of Zhou,

thereby

instructing his seventy disciples
and inspiring them to don the robes and caps [of officialdom]

and administer the documents and records. Thus, the learning of the Confucians was born. [21/227/25–21/228/2]

Master Mo

studied the work of the Confucians[34]
and received the techniques of Confucius.

[However,] he regarded

their rituals to be worrisome and inappropriate,
their lavish funerals to be wasteful of resources, impoverishing the people,

while their lengthy mourning periods harmed life and impeded undertakings. Thus, Master Mo rejected the Way of the Zhou dynasty and used the regulations of the Xia dynasty.[35]

In the age of Yu,[36] when the world was engulfed by a great flood, Yu personally

took up basket and spade, and putting [the interests of] the people first, he
dredged the Yellow River and channeled its nine tributaries;
bored out the Yangzi River and opened up its nine channels;
scooped out the five lakes and settled [the boundaries of] the Eastern Sea.

At that time,

since the burning heat was unrelenting,
and since the inundating dampness was unabsorbed,
those who died in the highlands were buried in the highlands;
[whereas] those who died in the marshes were buried in the marshes.[37]

Thus, economizing expenditures, frugal burials, and brief mourning periods were born. [21/228/4–7]

In the age of Duke Huan of Qi,[38]

the Son of Heaven was debased and weak;
the Lords of the Land were violent and aggressive.
The Southern Yi and Northern Di [tribes]

34. That is, the *ru*. See the discussion of this term in the general introduction to this book.

35. Although still not securely historically attested, the Xia dynasty was believed to have preceded the Shang dynasty. Its dates are thought to have been approximately 1950 to 1550 B.C.E. In Mozi's time, any knowledge of Xia rituals would have been highly speculative.

36. Yu, the legendary tamer of China's version of the Great Flood, was also considered the founder of the Xia dynasty.

37. That is, no special effort was made to find auspicious sites for tombs.

38. Duke Huan of Qi (r. 685–643 B.C.E.) was the first of the Lords of the Land to be named a hegemon (*ba* 霸).

in succession invaded the Central States,
and the continuity of the Central States hung by a thread.
The territory of the Qi kingdom was
sustained by the sea to the east
and barricaded by the Yellow River to the north.
Though its territory was narrow and its cultivated fields were sparse,
the people were very intelligent and resourceful.

Duke Huan was
vexed by the calamities of the Central States
and embittered by the rebellions of the Yi and Di [tribes].

He hoped that by preserving those whose kingdoms had perished and by continuing those whose bloodlines had been cut off,
the prestige of the Son of Heaven would be restored,
and the efforts of Kings Wen and Wu would be expanded.

Thus the writings of Master Guan[39] were born. [21/228/9–11]

Duke Jing of Qi[40]
enjoyed music and sex while inside his palace
and enjoyed dogs and horses while outside his palace.
When hunting and shooting, he would forget to return home.
When enjoying sex, he did so indiscriminately.
He built a terrace with a magnificent bedroom
and cast a grand bell.
When it was struck in the audience hall,
the sound [was so thunderous that] all the pheasants outside the city walls cried out.

In a single morning [session of court] he distributed three thousand bushels [of grain] as largesse. Liangqiu Ju and Zijia Kuai[41] led him about from the left and the right.[42] Thus, the admonitions of Master Yan were born.[43] [21/228/13–14]

In the twilight of the [Zhou] era, with the lords of the six states
the gorges were differentiated and the valleys were set apart,
the rivers were divided up and the mountains parceled out.

Each

---

39. These writings have likely come down to us as the work entitled *Guanzi*, named for Guan Zhong, the most famous (but possibly legendary) minister to Duke Huan of Qi. He is often credited with reforming his state and assisting the duke in his rise to become the first of the Five Hegemons of the Central States.

40. Duke Jing of Qi (r. 547–509 B.C.E.) reigned as a hegemon.

41. Liangqiu Ju 梁丘據 is depicted in the *Yanzi chunqiu* as a sycophant who had a deleterious influence on Duke Jing. The identity of Zijia Kuai 子家噲 is unclear; he may be Hui Qian 會譴 (also known as Yi Kuan 裔款), a minister often depicted as being in cahoots with Liangqiu Ju.

42. That is, in their capacity as his civil and military ministers.

43. The admonitions of Master Yan has likely come down to us as the work entitled *Yanzi Chunqiu* (*The Spring and Autumn Annals of Master Yan*), a collection of admonitions delivered by Yan Ying (ca. 589–500 B.C.E.) principally to Duke Jing of Qi. The admonitions and other anecdotes about Yanzi depict and convey his virtuous character.

governed his own realm
and defended his allotted territory
by seizing the handles of power
and by enforcing his governmental ordinances.
Below there were no regional governors,
while above there was no Son of Heaven.
They launched violent military campaigns in their struggles for power,
and the victor became the most honored.

They
relied on alliances with states,
bound themselves through important exchanges,
divided pledge tallies,
and established relations with distant regions,

thereby
preserving their principalities
and maintaining their ancestral altars.

Thus, the Vertical and Horizontal[44] Alliances and the Long- and Short-Term Coalitions were born. [21/228/16–18]

Master Shen[45] was the assistant of Marquis Zhaoxi of Hann[46] when the state of Hann broke off from the state of Jin. The land of these states was barren and their subjects were hostile, being wedged between powerful states.

The ancient rituals of the Jin state had not yet been destroyed,
while the new laws of the Hann state were repeatedly promulgated.
Ordinances of the previous rulers had not yet been rescinded,
while the ordinances of the later rulers were also being handed down.
Since new and old contradicted each other
and before and after undermined each other,
the various officials [of the state of Hann] were at cross-purposes and in confusion;
they did not know what [practices] to employ.
Thus, the writings on performance and title[47] were born. [21/228/20–22]

The customs of the kingdom of Qin were covetous and wolfish, forceful and violent.

They diminished Rightness and pursued profit.
Though they could awe others through punishments,

44. See chap. 20, n. 95.

45. Master Shen, or Shen Buhai, served Marquis Zhao of Hann and, in that capacity, advocated government by strict laws. He particularly emphasized administrative techniques—the devices by which a ruler can examine and test his bureaucracy. In particular, he advocated that officials were to act in strict accordance with the prescriptive titles of their posts. This technique was intended to consolidate the ruler's power.

46. Marquis Zhaoxi of Hann reigned from 362 to 333 B.C.E.

47. H. G. Creel, "The Meaning of Hsing-ming," in *What Is Taoism? And Other Studies in Chinese Cultural History* (Chicago: University of Chicago Press, 1970), 79–91.

they could not transform them through goodness.
Though they could encourage others through rewards,
they could not restrain them by [appeals to] their reputations.
Shielded by precipices and encircled by the Yellow River,
the Qin's four borders were thereby fortified.
The land was fertile and the topography advantageous
so that the Qin stockpiled reserves and burgeoned wealth.

Duke Xiao of Qin[48] wanted to swallow up the Lords of the Land with the ferocity of a tiger or wolf. Thus, the laws of Shang Yang[49] were born. [21/228/24–26]

In this book of the Liu clan [i.e., the *Huainanzi*], [we have]
observed the phenomena of Heaven and Earth,
penetrated past and present discussions,
weighed affairs and established regulations,
measured forms and applied what is suitable,
traced to its source the heart of the Way and its Potency,
and united the customs of the Three Kings,[50]
collecting them and alloying them.
At the core of the Profound Mystery,
the infinitesimal movements of the essence have been revealed.
By casting aside limits and boundaries
and by drawing on the pure and the tranquil,

[We have] thereby
unified the world,
brought order to the myriad things,
responded to alterations and transformations,
and comprehended their distinctions and categories.

We have not
followed a path made by a solitary footprint
or adhered to instructions from a single perspective
or allowed ourselves to be entrapped or fettered by things so that we would not advance or shift according to the age.
Thus,
situate [this book] in the narrowest of circumstances and nothing will obstruct it;
extend it to the whole world and it will leave no empty spaces.
[21/228/28–31]

Translated by Sarah A. Queen and Judson Murray

48. Duke Xiao of Qin died in 338 B.C.E.
49. Shang Yang helped carry out a series of reforms in the Qin state when he served Duke Xiao.
50. The Three Kings were Yu of the Xia, Tang of the Shang, and Wen or Wu of the Zhou.

Appendix A

KEY CHINESE TERMS AND THEIR TRANSLATIONS

THIS APPENDIX explains the translation decisions that we as a team made concerning the most significant terms in the conceptual framework of the *Huainanzi*. Most of the following entries address both translational and interpretive issues, partly because the two are inextricably intertwined. The *Huainanzi* is such a sophisticated and unusual text that many terms require unconventional or flexible translations, and these decisions cannot be justified without discussing how each term is used in the larger perspective of the text as a whole. Beyond this, however, we felt that a detailed discussion of both the background and the contextual usage of the central concepts of the *Huainanzi* would be helpful. Readers may encounter some repetition of themes or ideas both in this appendix and between these entries and the general and chapter introductions earlier in this volume, but we hope that such redundancies are excusable in the interest of making them more convenient to use. At the end of this appendix is a list to help track the Chinese transliterations of terms from their English equivalents. We have tried to translate key terms consistently, but in a work this large there will undoubtedly be some inconsistencies. Thus certain translations of common terms that appear in the body of the translation may not appear here, even though a synonym that serves as an alternative translation of the term may offer the same information.

ba 霸 hegemon

The *ba* was an office created during the Spring and Autumn period (770–481 B.C.E.) to authorize the ruler of one or another of the states that made up the Chinese polity to act as *primus inter pares* of state rulers on behalf of the Zhou king. The invention of the office is credited to Guan Zhong, the prime minister of Qi; the ruler whom Guan served, Duke Huan of Qi, was the first to hold the office. The office of hegemon was created in response to the declining power of the Zhou kings. Duke Huan (and subsequent hegemons) held a commission from the Zhou Son of Heaven to summon the other Lords of the Land to council, where he would adjudicate interstate disputes and organize the defense of the Zhou realm against non-Sinic peoples. The legitimacy of the hegemon as an institution became a hotly contested issue in pre-Han literature, with texts such as the *Mencius* decrying it as an aberrant devolution from the moral authority of the sage-kings, and other texts such as the *Guanzi* celebrating its progressive efficacy. The *Huainanzi* generally agrees with earlier texts like the *Xunzi*, which take a medial position. It views the office of hegemon as a provisionally efficacious response to a particular time but ranks the legitimacy and excellence of such a figure far below that of a true king or emperor.

ben 本 root, basis, foundation, fundamental, basic

Throughout the *Huainanzi*, the "root" signifies the fundamental organic principle of all cosmic, cognitive, physiological, personal, historical, and political realms. All things are conceived as having emerged from an undifferentiated yet dynamically generative root and to have achieved a progressively elaborate form through a process of ramification and individuation. Thus the cosmos progressed from the Grand One (that is, the Way) to yin and yang, the Five Phases, and the myriad things. The mind progresses from unified tranquillity and vacuity to ever more complex states of perception, emotion, and cognition. The human body develops from a protean embryo to an intricate structure of organs, limbs, and extremities. The person evolves from unself-conscious infant through increasingly sophisticated stages of self-awareness and maturity. History moves from the earliest eras of unalloyed simplicity through eras of successively more sophisticated and complex forms of economic, political, and social organization. Finally, the political realm begins with the simple apophatic self-cultivation of the ruler but extends through increasingly differentiated moral and cultural realms until it arrives at the minute contingencies of standards, measures, methods, and procedures. Intrinsic to the *Huainanzi*'s conceptualization of the root is the principle that the root is not consumed or dissipated by the process by which it differentiates into posterior phenomena. Rather, it persists and continues to pervade and control the ramified structure that it generated. For example, even in a latter age of intense elaboration, the Way remains the initiating and motive force at the basis of all processes and the single root that must be accessed if one hopes to influence or control events.

benmo 本末 root and branch, fundamental and peripheral

"Root and branch" designates the basic structural relationship informing all cosmic and human realms. In all domains, "root" and "branch" constituents may be identified. For example, in the cosmos the Way is the root, and Heaven, Earth, yin, and yang are branches; in the mind, tranquillity is the root, and perceptions, feelings, and thoughts are branches. In all root–branch relations, the root stands in a position of both diachronic, temporal priority and synchronic, normative priority to the branches. Thus the Way is prior to Heaven and Earth in that it existed first and continues to impel and control the latter phenomena even after they come into existence. In the same way, the mind's basic tranquillity precedes all perception, emotion, and thought and normatively should control and regulate all the operations of the mind even after its tranquillity has been stimulated to motion by external phenomena. Other root–branch structural relationships described by the *Huainanzi* likewise stand in the same position of relative temporal/normative priority and posteriority to one another (see *ben*).

bian 變 to alter, to vary, to change; permutations
Several words for "change" are used throughout the *Huainanzi*, and in our translation we have tried to distinguish among them consistently. *Bian* has the sense of alteration among states of being (for example, from a yin to a yang state, or vice versa) or of variation within defined parameters. It differs from *hua* 化, "transformation," in implying alternation or variation rather than fundamental and lasting change. The change from a caterpillar to a butterfly, for example, which is both substantive and irreversible, is a frequently cited instance of *hua* in the earlier literature. By contrast, a change that involves the realignment of constituent parts in a dynamic system (and that may be or is regularly reversed), such as that from day to night and back again, would be considered an instance of *bian*. In a few instances, we translate *bian* simply as "to change." See also *hua* 化, *yi* 易, and *yi* 移.

cheng 誠 sincerity
"Sincerity" denotes complete, uninhibited integration between a person's most basic, spontaneous impulses and his or her expressed words and actions. In the *Huainanzi*'s conception of human psychology, the baseline energy of human consciousness (that is, the *shen*, "spirit") is merged with the Way and partakes of its extreme potency and dynamism. When stimulated by external phenomena, consciousness moves within the mind–body matrix as a wave of *qi* that culminates in feeling or thought or sound or motion or some combination of them. Most of these expressions emerge depleted of the potency and dynamism intrinsic to the field from which they have arisen, because they are refracted through the prisms of self-consciousness, preconception, and insecurity that obstruct the ordinary human mind. In the rare instances that (or among the rare individuals for whom) an internal response evolves from baseline to full expression totally unimpeded, it produces a moment imbued with extraordinary power. Such sincerity can evoke a response in the minds and bodies of others or paranormal phenomena such as telekinesis. For these aspects of *cheng*, see chapters 6, 9, and 10. For the related term "Quintessential Sincerity" (*jing cheng* 精誠), see chapter 20.

chunqiu 春秋 spring and autumn, one year; *Spring and Autumn Annals*
"Spring and autumn" is a conventional synecdoche for a single year and is used occasionally in the text of the *Huainanzi*. From this connection is derived the name of the *Chunqiu* (*Spring and Autumn Annals*), which is a yearly chronicle of the state of

Lu from 770 to 476 B.C.E. By the Han period, the tradition attributing the authorship of the *Chunqiu* to Confucius himself had been long established. The *Huainanzi* affirms this tradition as well as the prevalent Confucian notion that when composing the *Chunqiu*, Confucius used subtle language to "praise and blame" the rulers of the era he chronicled, thus restoring moral rectitude to an age that in its own time was utterly corrupt and personally assuming the status of an "uncrowned king" (*suwang* 素王). The authors of the *Huainanzi* appropriated many themes and tropes from the Confucian exegetical tradition surrounding the *Chunqiu* to construct their own theories of political and especially military affairs.

dao 道 the Way

The "Way" is the *Huainanzi's* most basic signifier of ultimacy, and as such it is difficult to describe definitively in words. To say that it is the origin, totality, and animating impulse of all that is, ever was, and ever shall be is inadequate, for this would exclude what is not, never was, and never shall be. To say that the Way pervades and controls all existence and transformation distorts it, as this would imply that it is separable from all existence and transformation (even if only analytically). The text itself insists that the Way is ultimately ineffable and thus cannot be "understood" cognitively. Even though it cannot be known intellectually, because the Way is fundamental to all being, it can be experienced and embodied. This concept of the Way is not original to the *Huainanzi;* it is derivative of earlier texts such as the *Zhuangzi* and the *Daodejing*.

Occasionally, the *Huainanzi* uses "the Way" in the more limited sense in which it is used in early texts such as the *Analects*, in which the Way is not a cosmic entity but a cultural construct (for example, "the Way of the sage-kings," "the Way of Yao and Shun"). The word *dao* is sometimes employed in an even more limited sense as a particular "teaching" (for example, "the Way of archery"). Such usages always operate within a particular context, however. The default reading of the "Way" in any passage in which it is not clearly marked as denoting a more limited meaning is as the cosmic ultimate. Moreover, in many places where the Way is not used specifically, the concept is signified by metaphoric sobriquets such as "the Grand One" and "Grand Beginning." The *Huainanzi's* most detailed discussion of the Way is in chapter 1, although the concept figures prominently throughout the text.

de 德 Potency, Moral Potency

In the *Huainanzi*, as in the *Daodejing*, "Potency" is consistently conceptualized in terms of a fixed relationship with the Way. Whereas the Way is the root of all existence, Potency is the manifestation of the generative, transformative, and destructive dynamism of the Way in the phenomenal realm. Wherever the unimpeded operation of the Way may be perceived in the universe, Potency is manifest, and whenever a particular phenomenon perfectly embodies the Way in space and time, its unique Potency is on display. Thus in the movement of the stars and the change of the seasons, we see the Potency of Heaven, and in the ripening of the grain and the loftiness of mountains, we see the Potency of Earth. For human beings, Potency derives from perfectly embodying the Way in the workings of their minds and bodies, a state that for most people is consistently achievable only through self-cultivation. In this way, individuals may develop vast funds of Potency that can influence the human and cosmic realms in mysterious ways that transcend the ordinary limitations of time and space. For example, an individual of abundant Potency can calm the minds of rebellious subjects without leaving the palace hall or can make the harvest plentiful without issuing any commands. The *Huainanzi*'s most detailed discussion of Potency is in chapter 2, although the concept figures prominently throughout the text.

The *Huainanzi* occasionally uses the term *de* in contexts that accord with its usage in earlier Confucian texts such as the *Analects*. Here *de* represents a form of Potency that derives from exemplary moral action, and in these instances we translate *de* as "Moral Potency." Moral Potency has a discrete efficacy that can be discursively identified with values such as "Humaneness" (*ren*) and "Rightness" (*yi*) and contrasted with coercive force (as in the conventional formula *xingde*, "punishment and Moral Potency"). This does not mean that Potency and Moral Potency are two distinct phenomena, however. Moral Potency remains an expression of the dynamism of the Way in the phenomenal realm, forming a continuum with other more primordial and undifferentiated forms of Potency.

di 地 Earth, earthly

Earth was long venerated in the religious traditions of ancient China and remains so today. Every local potentate of ancient times maintained an altar to the soil, and a similar shrine may still be found in almost every rural Chinese village. In classical cosmological thought, Earth was a force that ranked alongside and just subordinate to Heaven (see *tian*). In the *Huainanzi*, Earth is given fourth place among the primal entities discussed on a chapter-by-chapter basis (see chapter 4). It was among the first phenomena to emerge from the undifferentiated Way. Although Heaven is usually cited as the force responsible for conditions beyond the control of humankind, Earth is also accorded great power within the phenomenal realm that houses human society. The *Huainanzi* generally views Heaven as more powerful because it encompasses forms of *qi* that are more rarefied and thus (within the conceptual framework of the text) more primordial and dynamic. Earth encompasses all those forms of *qi* that are more turbid and inert, but this still gives Earth a very significant role. For example, although the rarefied forms of *qi* that constitute the mind and spirit are said to come from Heaven, the grosser *qi* that forms our flesh, bones, and sinews is said to come from Earth (see chapter 7). Earth is thus instrumental in determining the material constitution of each individual's mind–body system, and characteristic differences between distinct groups of people are attributed to the unique *qi* of their respective native Earth.

dong 動 movement, disturbance; to move, to disturb; action, active

"Movement" or "action" is an important conceptual category in the *Huainanzi*, as it is the progeny and defining opposite of stillness (*jing*). Stillness is generally understood as the original and normative state of both the cosmos and human consciousness, but movement is acknowledged as an inevitable and indispensable product of cosmogenesis and sentience. Without both movement and stillness, time would not exist, as only by the contrast between the two can moments be differentiated from each other and the flow of time be made accessible to human perception. All phenomena begin in and are generated from stillness, but the process of differentiation that produces the phenomenal world is contingent on movement.

du 度 measure, standard, degree

"Standards" and "measures" are vital components of the *Huainanzi*'s political lexicon. These two meanings of *du* are inseparable and largely interchangeable in a Han cultural context. For example, the Han court issued a uniform cast-metal weight to serve as the standard for determining a single *jin*, and the same weight could be placed on a scale opposite some object or substance (say, one *jin* of tax grain) to measure it. The creation and dissemination of such standards was understood as a central and defining function of imperial power, for both its value in facilitating social intercourse and cohesion and its role in coordinating the relationship of local society and the imperial state. In the *Huainanzi*, the significance of standards has another dimension, as the text proposes that in any given age appropriate standards can be derived from a survey of the basic patterns of the cosmos. An example of this is the derivation of a perfect calendar year through careful astronomical observation. This operation ties in the third meaning of "degree," as the standard course of celestial bodies was measured in such units. (In this usage, *du* has the precise meaning of 1/365.25 of a circle; in such instances, we indicate Chinese "degrees" by a superscript "d" [for example, 11^{d}].) Standards thus give a sage-ruler a versatile mechanism to coordinate not only the state and society but also the entire human community and the cosmos at large.

fan 反 return, to revert, reversion, on the contrary, oppose, contradict

"Return" or "reversion" is a key concept in the *Huainanzi*. In the basic root–branches framework through which the text conceives all cosmic and human realms (see *ben* and *benmo*), any move from a "branch" state back toward a "root" state is marked as a "return" or "reversion." On a cosmic level, reversion is characteristic of the Way itself, as contingent phenomena tend over time (through death, decay, or destruction) to revert to the undifferentiated root from which they emerged. On a human level, reversion or return can be a process that unlocks great potential power, as in the "return to one's nature" (*fanxing*), "return to the self" (*fanji* 反己), or "return to one's spirit" (*fanshen*) achieved by the adept of apophatic personal cultivation. In general, any reversion or return to the root is normatively privileged by the *Huainanzi*, although the text asserts that certain forms of reversion are not possible. For example, the text insists that the progressive elaboration of human social and political institutions over time is not ultimately reversible, but it does concede that the effective operation of institutions in a latter age depends on a return to the root by political leaders through personal cultivation.

In some contexts, the *Huainanzi* uses the term *fan* in a more strictly logical or grammatical sense, meaning "on the contrary" or "conversely." This often reflects a conventional usage dating back to the Warring States period, marking an idea, a fact, or an argument that directly contradicts a particular persuasion (*shui*) or discourse (*lun*). In this sense, *fan* may also be used verbally and in such cases is translated as "to oppose" or "to contradict."

ganying 感應 resonance, stimulus and response

"Resonance" is a central operative principle of the cosmos as conceived by the *Huainanzi*. The phrase itself means "stimulus" (*gan* 感) and "response" (*ying* 應), which is how we have translated it when the *Huainanzi* refers specifically to the discrete component processes that the term denotes. Fundamentally, "resonance" is a process of dynamic interaction that transcends the limits of time, space, and ordinary linear causality. Through the mechanism of resonance, an event in one location (the "stimulus") produces simultaneous effects in another location (the "response"), even though the two phenomena have no direct spatial or mechanical contact. They may indeed be separated by vast gulfs of space. For example, connections between celestial events (eclipses, planetary motions) and events in the human community were understood as examples of "resonance."

For the authors of the *Huainanzi*, such connections were not coincidence or mere correspondence but dynamic influences exchanged through the energetic medium of *qi*. All phenomena are both composed of and impelled by *qi*, and since all currently differentiated *qi* emerged from an originally undifferentiated Grand One, all *qi* remains mutually resonantly linked. The pathways of resonance are not random, however. Objects are most sensitive to resonant influences emanating from other objects that share the same constituent form of *qi*.

The best example of this is an empirically observable phenomenon often cited by ancient authors to illustrate the concept of resonance itself: the harmonic resonance observable among musical instruments. If a string tuned to the pentatonic note *gong* on one *qin* is plucked, for example, the corresponding string on a separate *qin* will be perceived to vibrate. This was thought to occur because of the presence of Earth *qi*, which is responsible for the note *gong* in both instruments. When the Earth *qi* in the first instrument is activated (the stimulus), the corresponding Earth *qi* note in the other resonates (the response).

Such interactions were thought to be operative in the universe at all times. Someone who understood the patterns of these interactions could manipulate them to produce marvelous and beneficial effects across space-time. For example, during the summer, when Fire *qi* is ascendant (according to the Five-Phase understanding of seasonal influences), the ruler can wear red clothes (red being the color produced by Fire *qi*) so as to send out harmonizing resonances through the general matrix of cosmic *qi* and bring cosmic forces into line with the needs of the human community. The *Huainanzi*'s most thorough discussion of resonance is found in chapter 6.

he 和 harmony

"Harmony" is a key concept in the political lexicon of the *Huainanzi*. As was true for many other early Chinese texts, "harmony" is the single word that most perfectly expresses the *Huainanzi*'s normatively ideal state of human government and society. Among different traditions in ancient Chinese thought, there was no great variation in how harmony was conceived. For most, if not all, writers, harmony was generally marked by an absence of strife between ruler and ruled and among all the constituent elements of state and society. Where ancient authors differed was in articulating the means by which harmony was to be achieved. The *Huainanzi*'s vision of harmony is like that of most ancient texts, although it stresses the importance of harmony simultaneously suffusing and interconnecting both the human and cosmic realms. It is never enough in the *Huainanzi* for human beings to be in harmony with one another. Such a state can never be achieved or endure if human society is not dynamically coordinated with Heaven, Earth, and the larger forces of the cosmos.

Because the cosmic vision of the *Huainanzi* centers on the notion of the Way derived from texts like the *Daodejing* (*Laozi*), it frequently acknowledges that ultimate harmony may occasionally incorporate elements of destruction that are jarring to human sensibilities. Just as the spontaneous operations of the cosmos naturally include periods of dormancy and contraction (such as the cold of the winter months), the harmonious operations of the human polity may necessarily include destructive activities like punishment and warfare. In an ultimate sense, harmony does not depend on a total absence of violence but on the timeliness of all activities undertaken in the human realm and the persistence of all elements of the dynamic system that make up the human–cosmic matrix in their normatively correct relationship to one another.

Music is an important metaphor on which the concept of harmony is constructed, in both the *Huainanzi* and other early texts. The timely sounding of each note in a musical performance and their melodious relationship to one another exemplified the dynamic harmony that ideally should prevail in the human and cosmic realms. It is important, however, to refrain from anachronistically overreading modern notions of "musical harmony" into ancient Chinese texts. Many authorities insist that harmony in the strict technical sense of "an ordered progression of simultaneous sounds blended into musical chords" was a much later invention, but of course no one really knows what early Chinese music sounded like. With this cautionary note in mind, when applied to music we use the word "harmony" in a looser sense of "a pleasing consonant arrangement of musical notes."

hua 化 transformation, to transform, metamorphosis, to turn into

Transformation is key to the total conceptual framework of the *Huainanzi*, as the text pictures all cosmic and human reality as pervaded on all levels by constant transformation. In this view, it is the inherent disposition of all cosmic *qi* to transform continually. Such ceaseless transformation instantiates the intrinsic dynamism of the Way that brought the phenomenal world into being and that continues to impel it to evolve. This constant flow of transformation cannot be resisted; human beings can hope only to align themselves harmoniously with its ongoing course.

Collectively, such an alignment is achieved by organizing the human community within political and cultural structures, like those outlined in the *Huainanzi*, that are versatile enough to respond to the flow of cosmic change. Collective structures will never work effectively, however, unless individual leaders personally tap into and immerse themselves in the larger flow of transformation. The human mind–body system is a microcosm of the universe, so a person who harnesses and regulates the flow of energetic transformation within himself or herself (through the kinds of personal cultivation the *Huainanzi* advocates) becomes an agent who can direct cosmic transformation to channels that are harmonious and conducive to human flourishing.

Transformation also occurs naturally in the nonhuman world—for example, in chapter 5, where mice are said to turn into quail in the third month of spring. In such cases, we translate *hua* as "metamorphosis" or "to turn into."

ji 機 crux; fulcral moment, activation, mechanism

Ji originally referred to the trigger mechanism of a crossbow. Then in the *Huainanzi* and other early texts, it came to signify the unique moment or condition that activated a dramatic shift from one state to another. The ability to recognize and actualize the potential of such fulcral moments is cited throughout the *Huainanzi* as a hallmark of the Genuine Person and the sage. Another related meaning that uses the image of the crossbow is "mechanism" or "dynamism"; that is, *ji* may signify any complex system imbued with intrinsic motive power (for example, *tian ji*, the "Mechanism of Heaven").

jing 精 vital essence, essence, quintessence

Jing, or "essence," denotes a form of *qi* that is more rarefied, potent, and dynamic than the coarse *qi* constituting gross tangible matter. The character itself originally signified the seed kernel of a grain plant and later came to stand for human semen. As an adjective, *jing* may mean "essential" or "excellent." When used to describe troops, for example, *jing* denotes those soldiers that are most selectively recruited and highly trained: the elite.

In its most common nominal form, however, "essence" is a form of vitalizing energy. Like all *qi*, it has material substance, but it is not generally perceptible to the ordinary sense organs. Only its effects may be detected by ordinary perception. Essence is responsible for all the distinctive properties of animate beings—for example, the growth of plants and the awareness and mobility of animals. Certain inanimate objects are imbued with special properties by the presence of essence. It gives rise to the luster of jade and the potencies inherent in certain medicines. In human beings, essence impels all the gross motor skills and basic nervous responses.

jing 靜 tranquillity, quiescence, stillness, at rest

"Stillness" denotes both a cosmic and an existential state. On the cosmic level, stillness is the original state prior to all change and transformation; all things begin in and return to stillness. Even in the universe of differentiated phenomena, stillness is a primal force, for it is only by contrast with stillness that motion and thus time may be perceived. In this sense, stillness is closely related to Nothingness (*wu* 無). It is, in fact, the temporal embodiment of Nothingness, whose spatial counterpart is vacuity (*xu* 虛). Stillness is the opposite of movement (*dong*).

Existentially, stillness (along with vacuity) is the original state of the mind and the root of all cognitive processes. The mind's normative condition is stillness; it is moved only by external stimuli. When still, the mind retains and nurtures its vitalizing energies. If the stillness of the mind is chronically disturbed, its energies become depleted, sometimes leading to derangement, illness, or death. "Stilling the mind" through sustained meditative practice is thus a core element of the personal cultivation program advocated by the *Huainanzi* and a key route to the attainment of sagehood.

jingshen 精神 essence and spirit, Quintessential Spirit

The binome *jingshen* occurs frequently in the *Huainanzi*. Where parallelism or other factors indicate that the text is treating these concepts separately, we have translated it as "essence and spirit" (see *jing* 精 and *shen* 神). In some places, however, the *Huainanzi* clearly uses this binome to denote a particular substance: "Quintessential Spirit." Like *jing*, or "essence," *jingshen* also is a form of *qi*, one even more rarefied, potent, and dynamic than essence itself. When essence is responsible for basic animation, Quintessential Spirit is the intensely potent energy that constitutes the mind and gives rise to consciousness and illumination. Quintessential spirit circulates throughout the body, coordinating the body's activities under the control of the mind. All thoughts and emotions occur within a matrix composed of Quintessential Spirit, and violent feelings or fixation on externalities can cause *jingshen* to dissipate from the mind–body system. The apophatic self-cultivation of the sage is often conceptualized in terms of preserving and nurturing one's fund of Quintessential Spirit. Greater concentrations of Quintessential Spirit lead to progressively advanced levels of consciousness and awareness, sometimes developing into the realm of paranormal or what is today called "extrasensory perception." The *Huainanzi*'s most thorough discussion of *jingshen* is in chapter 7.

junzi 君子 Superior Man

Junzi originally meant "aristocrat" (literally, "the son of a lord"), and Confucius redefined it to denote a person of extraordinary moral merit rather than high birth. The *Huainanzi* generally uses the term as Confucius defined it, to mean a person who has acquired qualities of moral excellence, such as Humaneness and Rightness, through extensive study and education. The *Huainanzi* accords the Superior Man a role in maintaining communal harmony in the latter ages, and some of the "branch" chapters of the text, notably chapter 10, exalt "the Way of the Superior Man." But the

Superior Man is usually seen in the work as a whole as being surpassed by the sage (*sheng*), the Genuine Person (*zhenren*), and the Perfected Person (*zhiren*), whose attainments have reached a higher level.

li 理 pattern, principle, to put in order; to regulate
"Pattern" denotes the basic tendency of the cosmos to embody and express harmonious order. Originally the word signified the striations that could be seen in a piece of jade. Later it evolved to mean any sort of visual, dynamic, or logical pattern. The *Huainanzi* conceives of the cosmos as imbued with patterns that may be discerned by the most highly refined and sensitive human observers. For example, both the cycles of the moon and the changes of the seasons were understood as grand and broadly evident cosmic patterns. One of the chief benefits of the personal cultivation of the sage is gaining insight into the patterns of the cosmos, enabling him to construct institutions perfectly suited to the circumstances of the age. Chapter 5 offers an example in which all the seasonal ordinances are presented as human cultural institutions derived from underlying cosmic patterns.

li 利 profit, (material) benefit, advantage
"Profit" was an extraordinarily important and versatile category in the philosophical writings of the Warring States period. The character itself depicts a stalk of grain and a knife, indicating that it was meant to be understood in strictly material terms: harvested grain. Profit thus denotes material necessities like food, clothing, and shelter that are the mainstays of life. The Warring States thinker Mozi proposed that all moral and political imperatives be quantified and prioritized in terms of profit. Although his position was far from universally adopted, it was broadly influential. The *Huainanzi* does not give profit such an elevated status but insists, in contrast to Mozi and others, that states of being can be reached through personal cultivation that put the adept beyond the control of or desire for profit. The *Huainanzi* does concede, however, that profit is a useful and versatile measure by which to gauge the efficiency and utility of political institutions. The term is occasionally used verbally, as in the phrase *li min* 利民, "benefiting the people." See also *lihai* 利害.

li 禮 propriety, ritual, the rites, protocol
"Ritual" is a fundamental concept in the writings of Confucius and his later disciples. As such, it denotes all forms of symbolic action, ranging from the grandest ceremonies of the state cult to common courtesies such as bowing. Confucians asserted that ritual was the ideal instrument of social organization in that participation in ritual could coordinate human activity without recourse to bribery or threats. They conceived of a utopian community in which all social interaction would unfold with the same harmonious spontaneity of a ceremonial dance. Moreover, Confucians exalted ritual as among the essential instruments of personal transformation, because (according to them) sincere participation in ritual refined the energies and capacities of the mind–body system and cultivated the moral disposition of the individual.

The *Huainanzi* does not assign ritual such primal value. According to the *Huainanzi*, ritual did not exist in the earliest ideal societies, and at one time it was possible to order both the person and society at large in the complete absence of ritual. The text does agree with contemporary Confucians, however, that ritual has become an indispensable tool of state power in the current latter age. The *Huainanzi* also basically agrees that ritual can have beneficial effects for those who have not been improved by personal cultivation, although it would not accept (as Confucians insist) that learning or participating in ritual is a necessary path to the highest levels of personal attainment. Finally, the *Huainanzi* differs with Confucians over the normatively correct origins of ritual. Confucians insisted that correct rituals were the creations of the ancient sage-kings and that current-day rituals must be painstakingly reconstructed from the evidence of ancient practice. In contrast, the *Huainanzi* asserts that ritual must be made appropriate to the age and that correct ritual can be created in the current day only by a sage-ruler who can fathom the patterns of the cosmos and human history, thereby creating rituals perfectly suited to the circumstances of his own day. The *Huainanzi*'s views on ritual are detailed in chapter 11.

lihai 利害 benefit and harm, advantage and disadvantage

"Benefit" and "harm" are a matched pair in the statecraft theory of the Warring States period. The desire for benefit and the avoidance of harm were adduced as the two poles that conditioned and controlled human action, and so many early thinkers regarded the state's ability to dispense both forces (in the form of rewards and punishments) as the seminal instrument of state power and the structural foundation on which all order and prosperity could be built. The *Huainanzi* does not share the enthusiasm of such early statecraft thinkers as Mozi and Han Feizi for benefit and harm as instruments of state control, but it does acknowledge their utility to the efficient operation of certain institutions indispensable to government in latter ages. The *Huainanzi* insists, however, that benefit and harm are truly effective as instruments of state power only when they are wielded by rulers and officials who, because of their elevated levels of personal cultivation, are themselves beyond the controlling effects of benefit and harm. Only such rulers can use the instruments of benefit and harm completely dispassionately and with perfect insight into the appropriateness of their application from situation to situation. See also *xingde* 刑德.

ling 靈 numinous, divine

Ling denotes a quality of marvelous or extraordinary power that may exist in an object or a person. The ability to foretell the future or perceive current events from great distances, for example, are qualities described as "numinous." Numinous phenomena are assumed to display the same capacities as spirits, as they are able to transcend the ordinary limits of time and space, albeit within discrete contexts. Although numinous qualities might be colloquially described as "magical," the *Huainanzi* does not view such phenomena as supernatural. Rather, an object or a person is made "numinous" by possessing the same types of highly rarefied, potent, and dynamic *qi* (*jingshen*, "Quintessential Spirit") of which spirits are composed and which forms the material basis of their marvelous powers and properties.

liuhe 六合 the six coordinates

The "six coordinates" refer to the spatial realm encompassing what might be called "the known world." The six consist of the four cardinal directions (probably in practice conceived of as "front and back" and "left and right") combined with the dimensional planes of "up" and "down." Although in principle the vectors of the six coordinates extend without limit in all directions, as used in the text "the expanse within the six coordinates" is usually synonymous with "the known world." The whole universe of human habitation (both civilized and not), in contrast, is sometimes referred to as "the Nine Continents" (*jiu zhou* 九洲), and the farthest distance one can travel is denoted as "the Eight End Points" (*ba ji* 八極). The entire cosmos is encompassed by the very expansive term "space-time" (*yuzhou* 宇宙).

lun 論 to reason, to assess; assessment, argument, discourse

Lun denotes logical speech in various forms and contexts. Any instance of reasoned argumentation may be called *lun*, as may an argument or the task of reasoned argumentation in the abstract. Beyond this, *lun* may be used verbally in the sense of "to assess," or in the related nominal sense of "an assessment." A loosely defined genre of polemical writing known as *lun* was quite popular during the age of the *Huainanzi*'s composition, and the text contains many discussions and examples of it (most prominently, chapter 13). When *lun* is used in this sense, we have translated it as "discourse."

ming 命 life span, life circumstances, fate, destiny, to order, a decree

The base meaning of *ming* is "order" or "decree," from which came its alternative significance of "fate." The *Huainanzi* conceives of many contingencies affecting the human condition that are beyond individual control and are thus attributed to fate—for example, whether or not one is born in an orderly or a chaotic age. From this meaning comes that of "life span," as people were understood to have a certain fixed span of years mandated by their physiology at birth. An individual could generally do nothing to exceed his or her mandated life span, but it was possible to fall short of it by inviting harm or ruining one's physical constitution by overindulgence. One of the benefits of apophatic self-cultivation is refining both the energies of the mind–body system and personal conduct so that an individual's fated life span can be fulfilled.

ming 名 name, reputation, (official) title

The question of naming became a central controversy in the philosophical discourse of the Warring States period, which influenced the *Huainanzi*'s use of this term. There was general agreement that name should correspond to reality (*shi* 實, with which *ming* was frequently paired in the binome *mingshi*, "name and reality"). But whether particular realities required certain names or whether the initial pairing of name and reality was a matter of convention and, if so, by what mechanism such conventions were legitimately established, were contested issues. The *Huainanzi* generally holds that "naming" is a matter of human convention, although it asserts that the relation of name to reality cannot be completely arbitrary. Language as a system of names must have an organic integrity if the harmony of the human community and its alignment with the cosmos are to be maintained. For this reason, names should ideally be selected and assigned by a sage, as his comprehension of human and cosmic conditions empowers him to find the most appropriate name for each thing or affair. Above all, the *Huainanzi* asserts that ultimate truth cannot be captured in names. The Nameless (*wuming* 無名) is another sobriquet for the Way that generated, contains, and controls the cosmos. The sage's unique naming ability comes about because his consciousness is merged with the Nameless.

Throughout the ancient literature, the same term is used to denote "name" and "reputation." This was not a case of metonymy but arose from the particular understanding of how "reputation" was constituted: it hinged on whether a particular "name" (for example, "loyal," "humane") could be legitimately applied to the "reality" of a person's conduct and character. The *Huainanzi* frequently uses *ming* in this regard, and we have translated it accordingly. The text does not treat the question of personal reputation as completely inconsequential, and it expresses concern that distortion of reputation and reality can cause disharmony in the social and political realms. As in the case with "names," the *Huainanzi* insists that the ultimate power to rectify misalignments of reputation and reality lies in a domain transcending all moral and ethical distinctions. An individual's reputation is therefore never, even in ideal social and political circumstances, an infallible gauge of his or her worth, and the nurturing or preservation of one's reputation is not an ultimately efficacious path of personal development.

ming 明 to clarify, clarity; to discern, discernment; to illuminate, illumination, bright, brightness

The basic meaning of *ming* is "bright." The character combines the pictographs of the sun and the moon, a visual image of brightness. From that basis come the meanings "to clarify/clarity" and "to discern/discernment." The *Huainanzi* uses the term in all these senses. Beyond these basic meanings, the *Huainanzi* follows earlier texts like the *Zhuangzi* in using *ming* to denote the state of elevated consciousness that can be achieved through personal cultivation and is characteristic of the sage and the Genuine Person. In this sense, the term signifies a state of mind marked by exceptional cognitive and perceptual sensitivity and incisiveness, and we have generally translated it in these contexts as "clarity" or "illumination."

Mingtang 明堂 "Hall of Light" (generally not translated)

The Mingtang is a special structure mentioned in much of the early literature on ritual and sacrifice. Throughout imperial history, debates about the precise design and function of the Mingtang were frequent and heated. Generally it was agreed that whatever its function or design, the construction and use of a Mingtang was the exclusive prerogative of the Son of Heaven. Confucian canonical texts describe the Mingtang as a temple in which sacrifices were conducted. In the *Huainanzi*, the Mingtang is a multichambered palace building of simple construction and austere appearance in which the ruler holds court in a prescribed pattern of shifting from room to room in order to carry out the seasonal ordinances.

qi	氣	vital energy, vital breath (paired with *jing* 精 or in inner-cultivation contexts); otherwise *qi* (not translated)

Qi is both matter and energy, the basic substance out of which the entire universe is composed. The original meaning of the character was "steam" or "vapor," and in later cosmological thought, a vapor or gas was understood to be the original and pristine state of *qi*. Before time and space came into being, all *qi* was one and undifferentiated, existing in its primordial gaseous form. In that state, *qi* displays maximum dynamism and potential, and so it can (and does) transform into any shape or substance. During cosmogenesis, *qi* differentiated, combined, and transformed, acquiring the characteristics that produce the diversity of the phenomenal world. The most basic transformation was the division of *qi* into yin and yang polarities, and from that state *qi* further differentiated into the Five Phases of Earth, Fire, Water, Metal, and Wood. These five remain the most elementally perceptible forms of *qi* in the phenomenal universe, and most of the observable qualities and activities of matter are a product of one or more of these forms of *qi*. No quantum of *qi* remains perpetually in one form. All *qi* cycles continuously between the two poles of yin and yang and the stations of the Five Phases, returning periodically to its original, undifferentiated state. All the observable motions of the cosmos and all the organic processes of living beings are produced by this perennial movement of *qi* between different states and forms.

Qi is a central concept to virtually all the cosmological, cultural, and political concerns of the *Huainanzi*. It is especially important to the text's theory of personal cultivation. Following a venerable body of cultivation and medical lore, the *Huainanzi* conceptualizes the human body as a dynamic system engineered to accumulate, refine, and circulate different forms of *qi*. Cultivation thus centers on facilitating and perfecting the mind–body system's faculties for collecting and refining *qi*, a process in which breathing and breath control figure prominently. When *qi* is being used in a context of personal cultivation, we have translated it as "vital energy" or "vital breath" (when it refers literally to the intake of breath during meditation). Otherwise, we have left it untranslated.

qing	情	feelings, emotional responses, dispositional responsiveness, genuine responses, instinctive responses, disposition, true or genuine or essential qualities

Qing is a profoundly multivalent and versatile term that is featured prominently in a wide range of early texts. Its most basic meaning in the *Huainanzi* is "feeling": the emotional responses of joy, anger, desire, grief, and fear all are exemplary *qing*. In accordance with older texts (such as the text *Xing zi ming chu* 性自命出,

archaeologically recovered at Guodian), the *Huainanzi* conceives of these emotional responses as inherent dispositions originally present in human beings as a product of nature. In its pristine state, our mind is still; when we are stimulated by external events, our mind responds with a *qing*. This "feeling" is understood as a wave of *qi* in the originally placid matrix of the mind–body system. As it evolves, this wave of *qi* creates motions and sounds, such as laughing and dancing in the case of joy or screaming and fleeing in the case of fear. Such reactions are not learned but are built into the dynamic structure of the mind–body system and become manifest when the conditions are right. It is important to note that the *Huainanzi* (along with other earlier texts) does not clearly distinguish between a particular instance of emotional response and the inborn disposition from which it arises; for example, both a particular moment of joy and the ability to feel joy are labeled *qing*. "Feeling" is thus often inadequate as a translation of *qing*, since in the *Huainanzi*'s theory of human psychology this concept encompasses both what in English would be called "feeling" and what would be termed "instinct" or "disposition."

A related meaning of *qing* denotes any condition or quality of a thing or person that is genuine or authentic. Just as emotional responses are considered irreducible elements of the human condition from birth, any characteristic that is original to and inseparable from a particular phenomenon may be described as *qing*. When *qing* is used in the text in this sense, we have translated it as "genuine qualities" or "essential qualities."

Throughout the text, we have varied our translations of the term in accordance with its meaning in context.

qingxing 情性 disposition and nature, dispositional nature

Qing and *xing* are closely linked concepts in the *Huainanzi*, as the text conceives of emotional responses as constituent components of nature. Whereas *xing*, "nature," denotes the totality of all the potentials and inherent dispositions present in the human being at birth, *qing* denotes the particular affective dispositions subsumed within *xing*. *Qingxing* often appears as a binome in the *Huainanzi*, denoting the inborn capacities of human beings in their particular and global aspects. Where the text enumerates them separately, we have translated *qingxing* as "disposition and nature" or "feelings and nature." And where the text uses *qing* to modify *xing*, we have translated it as "dispositional nature."

quan 權 expediency, heft, weight

The *quan* is the weight used in conjunction with a steelyard or a set of balanced scales or, by extension, the entire weighing apparatus. From this meaning evolved the usage of the character in the *Huainanzi* and other ancient philosophical prose to denote "expediency." *Quan* entails weighing the exigencies of the moment against the imperatives of morality, and it refers to an act that violates a moral precept yet ultimately serves the greater good. Another technical usage of *quan* occurs in the *Huainanzi*'s discussion of military affairs (especially in chapter 15). There *quan* denotes a form of potential power that is intrinsic to a combatant before going into battle, an advantage that can "tip the scales" and lead to victory after the combat has begun. Examples are the training of the troops or the education of the commander. In these contexts, we have translated *quan* as "heft." In its literal meaning of "weight," *quan* is one of the six exemplary tools (along with the compass, square, marking cord, level, and the beam of a steelyard or scale) posited as standards (*du*) to guide the ruler's conduct under various circumstances (see 5.15).

ren 仁 Humaneness, humane

Humaneness is the cardinal virtue of Confucius and his later disciples. It generally refers to an ability to empathize with others and treat them with compassion. For most ancient Confucians, personal perfection could be understood in terms of this virtue: the path to sagehood was one of ever-deepening and expansive Humaneness. The *Huainanzi* does not generally assign Humaneness such exalted status but agrees with the *Daodejing* that neither the Way nor the sage is ultimately humane. The *Huainanzi* does state, though, that Humaneness is an indispensable principle for organizing human relations and human society in the current age. Humaneness is often paired with Rightness (*yi*), as the Way (*dao*) is often paired with Potency (*de*).

ru 儒 Confucian

Ru is an archaic term that originally referred to a ceremonial office at the royal court. During the Warring States period, it was adopted as the self-identifying sobriquet of Confucius's followers. In accordance with conventional English usage, we have translated this term as "Confucian." During the Han period, the parameters of the "Confucian" community were quite fluid. Those who considered themselves *ru* generally shared an esteem for Confucius as the greatest teacher of the classical age and a reverence for those texts identified by Confucius and his disciples as canonical (most often including, but not necessarily limited to, the "Five Classics": the *Changes*, *Odes*, *Documents*, *Rites*, and *Spring and Autumn Annals*). The *Huainanzi* is generally very critical of the Confucians as being too narrowly focused on cultural contingencies and phenomenal concerns. There were reportedly Confucians at the court of Liu An, however, and their influence can be seen in the prevalence of quotations from and allusions to the texts of the Five Classics throughout the *Huainanzi*. Although the *Huainanzi* denies that Confucian values embody ultimate truth or are universally efficacious, it does acknowledge the limited validity of Confucian moral teachings as essential to social harmony in latter ages.

shen 神 the spirit, spirits, spiritlike, divine, god

"Spirit" is a versatile word with many meanings and subtleties of meaning. In the ancient ancestral religion, spirits were powerful deities and the shades of departed ancestors who wielded power over the living world and had to be propitiated and appeased by sacrifice. The *Huainanzi* frequently uses "spirit" to signify this meaning, providing a detailed discussion of various spirits and their cults. However, throughout the *Huainanzi*, "spirit" also means an integral aspect of all living human beings, the "ghost in the machine" that is the site of all awareness and cognition. There is no contradiction in these usages, as the *Huainanzi* assumes that spirits may exist in embodied and disembodied forms. The spirit that today animates an individual's living body may become an object of the ancestral cult tomorrow after that person's death.

It is important to note that whether the *Huainanzi* is discussing embodied or disembodied spirits, it does not distinguish between a "spiritual" and a "material" realm. All spirits are thought to be a part of the same energetic system of *qi* from which all matter is composed. Spirits are not tangible or visible, but this does not mean that they lack material substance. They are merely composed of *qi* in a highly ethereal and dynamic state that is nonetheless equivalent to the *qi* from which all grosser matter is formed.

During a person's lifetime, the spirit is the animating impulse of the body and the energetic structure in which the mind is housed. Spirit and body form a single organic system of *qi;* they are thus pragmatically inseparable but analytically distinct. In the same way that one may have an injured hand but a healthy eye, one may have a sound body but a disordered spirit, and vice versa. Despite occupying autonomous realms of activity, spirit and body interpenetrate through the medium of *qi* and remain mutually influential. The techniques of personal cultivation discussed in the *Huainanzi* thus engage both poles of this spectrum, encompassing contemplative meditations focused on the spirit and dietary and yogic regimens targeting the physiological processes of the body.

Spirit and mind are likewise analytically distinct. The thoughts, memories, and emotional dispositions that constitute the mind are comparable to the ridges and figures of a seal pressed into the "wax" of the spirit. Although our mind embodies our ordinary experience of consciousness, our spirit is always present as the basic substrate of awareness. This is where the spirit is merged with and partakes of the impulsive dynamism of the Way itself; thus the goals of apophatic personal cultivation are often described in the *Huainanzi* as an effort to escape "mind" in favor of the unmediated experience of "spirit." The more the ordinary contents of consciousness are stripped away, the closer one approaches fusion with the cosmic ultimate and embodiment of its unlimited potential.

Like many ancient Chinese words, *shen* has both nominal and adjectival uses. When *shen* is used adjectivally in association with the ancestral spirits or other deities, we have translated it as "divine." However, the implication of spirit in the energetic matrix of *qi* also gives rise to a particular modifying use of *shen* that is related to, but not identical with, this meaning of "divine."

The remarkable properties of consciousness—its incredible sensitivity and speed—were understood to be products of the highly dynamic form of *qi* from which spirit was composed (see *jingshen*). The same was true for the extraordinary powers displayed by disembodied spirits like the departed ancestors. They could know conditions thousands of miles away, for example, because they could transverse such distances at the speed of thought (that is, in no time at all). The same type of highly rarefied and dynamic *qi* that composed human and ancestral spirits was thought to be present elsewhere in nature and to give rise to correspondingly marvelous phenomena. Lightning, magnetism, and the mechanism of cosmic resonance by which events separated by vast gulfs of space simultaneously influence one another (see *ganying*) were thought to evince the presence and operation of "spirit *qi*" (that is, the same type of *qi* of which spirits are composed) and are described as *shen*. When the *Huainanzi* uses *shen* in this mode, we have translated it as "spiritlike."

shen 身 person, the self

Shen denotes the individual person in all his or her physiological, psychological, and social aspects. It encompasses what in English would be identified as the body as well as the intellect and the personality. The *shen* therefore is the locus of individual personhood, but in many usages of the term, what in modern European and American culture might be deemed "externalities"—such as manner of speech, dress, and deportment, as well as acquired or inherited status—were also understood as component aspects of the "person." The *Huainanzi* generally agrees with the long tradition of self-cultivation theory in focusing on the "person," but distinguishes between more and less fundamental aspects of the person in the formulation of its cultivation regime.

Two related terms are "return to the self" (*fanji* 反己) and "return to one's nature" (*fanxing* 反性) (see *fan*).

sheng or *shengren* 聖, 聖人 the sage

Following many texts of the classical period, the *Huainanzi* uses the term "the sage" to denote the highest attainable level of human perfection. Sages have ultimate insight and are ingeniously creative. They have power not only to bring harmony to their own personal lives and environment but also to fashion standards and institutions on behalf of humanity at large. Indeed, sages in the *Huainanzi* are conceived of as a cosmic force unto themselves, as they exert a beneficent influence on the universe as a whole.

Like the Confucian Five Classics, the *Huainanzi* credits great sages of high antiquity, like Fuxi, with creating the seminal fundaments of human civilization. Unlike the Confucian canon, however, the *Huainanzi* does not locate the chief efficacy of the sage in the past. It is not enough to preserve and transmit the achievements of antiquity; the maintenance and harmonious operation of effective political and cultural institutions requires the guiding hand of a sage in the present day. The *Huainanzi* underscores the present-day political role of the sage as the ruler at the apex of the empire's political structure who is charged with becoming a sage and/or enlisting the aid of sage-ministers.

This emphasis on the political role of the sage stems partly from the *Huainanzi*'s conception of how sagehood is achieved and the relationship of the sage to the cosmic Way. The sage of the *Huainanzi* is much closer to that of the *Daodejing* than that of the Confucian classics, as he is not only a moral or an ethical paragon or a repository of knowledge. The sage does not achieve sagehood only through study of the phenomenal world or the imparted wisdom of past ages but especially through a program of apophatic personal cultivation centered on practices of contemplative meditation and yogic regimens. He thereby nurtures and purifies the energies of the mind–body system and brings consciousness into perfect alignment with the cosmic Way, effectively becoming an embodiment of the Way. In mind, body, speech, and deed, the sage perfectly embodies the potent dynamism of the Way, and all his responses to emerging circumstances have the same spontaneous efficacy.

Without such a leader, the *Huainanzi* asserts, human government cannot work. Both the cosmos and human society evolve so rapidly that it is never enough to reproduce the practices of the past. Each age requires a sage who embodies the Way in his person and can thus perceive through his penetrating insight how standards and institutions must be configured in the present day to bring the human community into harmony, both internally and with the underlying patterns of the cosmos.

The achievement of sagehood is thus the ultimate hallmark of political legitimacy, as the role of the sage is the cornerstone on which the entire imperial edifice envisioned by the *Huainanzi* is built. This would seem to create the potential for profound instability, as in a vast empire it is more likely for a sage to arise among the ruler's myriad subjects than for the ruler himself to achieve this lofty goal. The *Huainanzi* is aware of this problem and thus states that even a sage is incapable of overthrowing an established imperial government unless it has already descended into chaos. A sitting ruler thus does not have to perfectly embody the sage-ideal in order to secure his dynasty's throne; it is enough that he recognize the "sage-imperative" and strive toward becoming a sage, thereby staving off the disorder that would make his dynasty prone to usurpation.

shenhua 神化 spiritlike transformation, spirit transformation
Shenhua denotes a transformational effect that transcends the ordinary physical limits of time and space. This phrase is most often employed in reference to the sage, who is able to exert a pacifying and edifying influence on his subjects from even a vast distance. This is not regarded as a function of moral example but as a marvelous dynamism operating through the physical medium of *qi*. In this sense, it is called "spirit transformation" because it displays the same qualities as the activities of spirits and is driven by the radiating influence of the sage's own highly refined and potent spirit. Chapter 9 discusses spirit transformation at length, equating it with the transformational effect that spring and summer have on the living world during the calendar year.

shenming 神明 spirit illumination, spiritlike illumination
"Spirit illumination" denotes an aspect of both the Way and the sage throughout the text of the *Huainanzi*. At one point, the text asks rhetorically whether spirit illumination is comparable to sunlight (see 12.44) and answers that although like sunlight it is all-pervading, unlike sunlight spirit illumination cannot be blocked by window shutters or doors. Spirit illumination thus signifies the faculty by which both the Way and the sage (who perfectly embodies the Way in his person [see *shengren*]) comprehend and coordinate the entire phenomenal universe. Although when making a comparison between *shenming* and sunlight the text may be speaking figuratively, it seems

likely that the *Huainanzi* envisions spirit illumination as having an actual physical substrate, a form of *qi* that is even more subtle, suffusive, potent, and dynamic than light (see *jingshen*). This is why one of the most often cited characteristics of the sage is that he "communicates with spirit illumination." In other words, the abundant and highly refined *qi* of the sage's spirit (see *shen* 神) is seamlessly merged with the vast field of spirit illumination that pervades the entire universe. Through this medium, therefore, the sage can be aware of distant conditions and influence far-off events.

shi 事 affair, task, event, phenomenon, effort, practicalities, management

Shi has a wide range of meanings. In its most common usage, we translate it as "affair," referring to all the discrete undertakings that must be accomplished and all the various contingencies that may be encountered in the conduct of government. One of the *Huainanzi*'s main goals is to demonstrate how the Way finds expression in affairs. In this sense, *shi* has a broader significance, in that it need not be confined to the political or even the human realm. Almost any contingent occurrence or fact may be described as a *shi*, and in places where it is clearly being used in this broader sense, we have translated it as "event" or "phenomenon."

Shi is also used verbally, meaning "to work at," "to manage," or "to put forth effort," and even occasionally as a modifier meaning "effortful." In this context, *shi* denotes a mode of activity that is the converse of *wu wei* (non-action or effortless action), and when it appears as such, we have translated it accordingly.

shi 勢 propensity, trajectory, positional advantage, force, power

Shi is a very rich term that has no close equivalent in English. Its origin seems to have been in the military literature of the Warring States period, when it was devised as a conceptual gauge by which conditions on the battlefield could be measured and compared. The *shi* of a unit, position, or formation is derived from all the intrinsic (for example, the soldiers' weapons and training) and extrinsic (for example, the possession of the high ground, the achievement of surprise) factors, taken together, that contribute to its combat effectiveness. For example, all else being equal, well-trained archers have more *shi* than do poorly trained archers. The difference might be reversed, however, if the former were positioned in a defile and the latter were perched on a high hill. We have thus chosen to translate *shi* as "force" when it is used in the discussion of military affairs, as it combines two different dimensions of calculation in the same way that, in physics, "force" is a function of intrinsic (mass) and extrinsic (acceleration) factors.

From this military usage, *shi* was later imported into other realms of discourse such as politics, cosmology, and logic. One of the most common of these expanded meanings comes into the *Huainanzi* from early statecraft theory. In a political or social structure, an individual is said to have *shi* contingent on the systemic powers of the office or station that he or she occupies and the actual functioning of the system as a whole. Ideally, the *shi* of the prime minister, for example, should be less than that of the sovereign and more than that of the palace eunuchs, but this ideal situation could (and often was) distorted when individuals were able to accrue and exercise powers beyond the normative parameters of their station. When *shi* appears in these contexts, we have rendered it as "positional advantage."

From its seminal applications in military and statecraft theory, *shi* acquired a versatile general utility for discussing cosmic processes and human affairs. In its original usages, *shi* always implies both potency and directionality, never indiscriminate power but power tending toward specific effects. Thus it ultimately became common for ancient authors to write of the *shi* of a given situation or set of conditions, meaning its intrinsic tendency to evolve along a particular course. For example, it is the *shi* of a round object to roll; it is the *shi* of a poorly led state to become chaotic. When *shi* occurs in this context, we have translated it as "propensity" or "trajectory."

shi 詩 poetry; the *Odes*

Poetry, like music, was celebrated by Confucians as one of the defining excellences of humanity and seminal to our capacity for ethical self-improvement. In this regard, an entire text, the *Shijing* (*Classic of Odes*), composed of the collected poetry of the ancient sages, was included in the Five Classics. When the character *shi* appears in the *Huainanzi,* it sometimes refers to the generic phenomenon of poetry, but more often it refers specifically to the text of the *Odes.* The *Huainanzi* generally rejects the Confucian position on the ultimate importance of poetry but grants canonical status to the *Odes.*

The *Huainanzi* quotes the *Odes* as a source of wisdom but consistently regards it as a lesser manifestation characteristic of the latter age that does not channel the Potency of the ineffable Way. Likewise, the *Huainanzi* denigrates poetry as a pursuit that cannot lead to the highest levels of human perfectibility. Nonetheless, the *Huainanzi* evinces appreciation for the composers of lyrical verse. The text periodically shifts into verse for stylistic effect, even though it tends to express a heretical (from the Confucian perspective) preference for the baroque adornment of the *Chuci* (*Elegies of Chu*) over the more spartan style of the *Odes.* The *Huainanzi* authors were literati and aesthetes, and at several points the text admits that even though poetry may be a lesser attainment, it is an indispensable skill for leaders in the latter ages.

shouyi 守一 to preserve/to guard the One, to hold fast to the One

Shouyi signifies an aspect of the program of personal cultivation advocated throughout the *Huainanzi,* and "guarding the One" is often a metaphor for the process of personal cultivation itself. The ultimate goal of cultivation is to perfectly embody the Way in one's person. Just as "the One" is often a metaphor for the Way, "guarding the One" is used for the orientation of personal cultivation toward the Way. "Guarding the One" also expresses the *Huainanzi*'s conception of both the Way and the process of personal cultivation as possessing a physical substrate. The Way is most pristinely manifest in the phenomenal realm in the most rarefied and dynamic forms of *qi,* and the personal experience of the Way entails and arises from suffusion of the mind–body system with those same forms of *qi*. "Guarding the One" thus implies the actual psychophysiological process of nurturing and preserving the mind–body system's funds of highly rarefied *qi* through meditation and yogic exercise, a course that, if maintained to its ultimate end, may lead to sagehood.

shu 數 (cf. *shu* 術), enumerate, norms

The basic meaning of *shu* is "number." The *Huainanzi* frequently uses this term in reference to various forms of human and cosmic order, and throughout the text *shu* works in tandem with the concept of "pattern" (see *li* 理). Various mathematical properties and relationships are cited as intrinsic to the fundamental "pattern" of objects, organisms, or processes (for example, the division of the calendar year into twelve months). In human beings' interaction with the larger cosmos, counting and ordering things may be indispensable to the realization of their potential inherent pattern or harmony. From this sense comes the related meaning of "norm," as we have translated the character when used in this context. This character *shu* is often used in the *Huainanzi* as a loan for the character *shu* 術, "technique."

shu 書 writing, prose; the *Documents*

Shu denotes the act of writing in general. As a verb it means "to write," in the sense of literally picking up a brush and beginning to write characters on a solid medium. Nominally *shu* signifies prose writing. In this sense, it forms the name of the *Shujing* (or *Shang shu*; *Classic of Documents*), which was one of the Five Classics of the Confucian canon. For Confucians, the *Documents* was both a source of binding ethical principles and normative political injunctions and a timeless model for the correct composition of elegant prose. The *Huainanzi* cites the *Documents* as a source of ancient wisdom but does not accord it the ultimate authority that Confucians ascribe to it. Nor does it accept that prose composition is as important as Confucians view it to be or, if it were, that the *Documents* could stand as a particularly good model for how to do it. That being the case, the authors of the *Huainanzi* nevertheless are engaged with the concerns of prose composition. In chapter 21 and elsewhere, they note that parts of the text were designed as models for aspiring prose stylists of the age.

shu 術 techniques, arts

Shu denotes any set of routines, protocols, or procedures that may be used to a particular effect. The craft of a carpenter, the assessment protocols that a ruler may use to survey and control his ministers, and the forms of breath-control meditation that may lead to higher states of consciousness (and that are among the special procedures known as *dao shu* 道術, "techniques of the Way") are examples of what the *Huainanzi* refers to as "techniques." "Techniques" are an especially urgent concern in the *Huainanzi*. In many respects, the text conceptualizes the central task of rulership as identifying those techniques indispensable to the production of harmony and order, and deploying and integrating them in a hierarchical system that will realize these effects.

shuo (*shui*) 說 to speak, to describe, to persuade, persuasion
Shuo is the most common word used for the act of speaking in modern vernacular Chinese, and in the *Huainanzi* it occasionally appears in this or related contexts. Most often, however, *shuo* has the connotation of "persuasion," and the term is frequently used to denote specifically persuasive instances of speech or the rhetorical aspects of speech more generally. As a matter of word choice, *lun* refers to speech more grounded in logic, whereas *shuo* usually refers to speech that is more grounded in rhetoric. *Shuo* (often pronounced *shui* in this context) in fact became the name for a genre of persuasive speech/oral performance that sometimes combined rhetorical formulas with anecdotal illustrations, and where it is used in this way we have translated it as "persuasion." The *Huainanzi's* most detailed treatment of this form of speech is found in chapters 16 and 17.

su 俗 customs, conventions, vulgar
Su is a general term that encompasses all the constituent elements of "culture." All modes of dress, speech, behavior, or religious observance may be denoted as "customs." The most salient connotation of *su* is something that is widely shared or common; thus classical usage frequently distinguished between those forms of culture that were *ya* 雅 (refined, elegant), implying elite exclusivity, and those that were *su* (common, vulgar). (Unlike *su, ya* cannot be used nominally to refer to "customs" generically.) This sense of the term is generally confined to its use as a modifier, although *su* is occasionally used nominally to refer to the "vulgar (people)" (that is, the masses). The authors of the *Huainanzi* followed colloquial convention in occasionally using *su* in this way, and where it appears in this context, we have translated it accordingly. It is a hallmark of the *Huainanzi,* however, that it generally embraces the term *su* to mean any and all customs, expressing its conviction that conventional distinctions between "refined" and "vulgar" or "barbarian" and "civilized" are ultimately arbitrary. This point of view is found throughout the work but is argued most cogently in chapter 11.

tai chu 太初 Grand Beginning
"Grand Beginning" and the closely related term "Grand Inception" (*tai shi* 太始) are metaphors for the Way, expressing its status as the cosmogonic root of the phenomenal universe. Although it obviously connotes the moment of the cosmic origin, this image does not fully encompass the term's significance. The Way remains the "Grand Beginning" even during the time of differentiated cosmic maturity, as it is the root source from which all phenomenal transformations spring and to which all phenomena repeatedly return.

tai qing 太清 Grand Purity
"Grand Purity" appears at several points in the text. Most commonly, it is another sobriquet for the Way. As such, it expresses the idea that the Way began in pristine undifferentiated purity and that it remains pure despite any degree of differentiation.

The Way is never diminished or blemished by decay or corruption in the phenomenal world, as its potential for dynamic transformation remains infinitely elastic.

At other points in the text, Grand Purity is used figuratively, although its association with the Way is always implicit. In chapter 12, for example, Grand Purity is personified in dialogue with other anthropomorphized qualities of the Way, such as "Inexhaustible." Chapter 8 discusses the "reign of Grand Purity," an era in which none of the diverse techniques of rulership of latter ages were necessary and social harmony could be maintained by the ruler's embodiment of the Way alone.

tai yi 太一 Grand One

"Grand One" is another metaphor for the Way. The Way suffuses and encompasses all things. No matter what level of individuation or seeming durability an object or a phenomenon achieves, it remains wholly integral to the Way and is indissolubly implicated in its dynamic transformation.

Tai yi was also the name of a star, a stellar embodiment of a deity. Emperor Wu instituted the worship of Tai yi at the winter solstice of 113 B.C.E., barely a generation after the *Huainanzi* was written, as a major cult under the patronage of the imperial throne.

tian 天 Heaven, heavenly

The *Huainanzi* follows a venerable tradition of ancient Chinese religious and political thought by identifying Heaven as the supreme power among those in the phenomenal world. The physical locus of Heaven was literally understood to be the sky, and all the grand transformations most closely associated with the sky were viewed as manifestations of Heaven's power: the cyclical movement of the stars and planets, the tempestuous movements of wind and rain, the changing of the seasons. It is not difficult to imagine why a thoroughly agrarian society like that of ancient China would accord such primacy of place to Heaven thus conceived. Heaven's agency was not reducible to celestial events, however. Phenomena like the innate instincts of a living organism are often identified by such terms as "Heaven[-born] nature" (*tianxing* 天性).

In the *Huainanzi*'s cosmology, Heaven takes second place as a cosmic force after the all-encompassing Way. Heaven was generated from the Way and continues to be contained within and controlled by it. Nonetheless, Heaven occupies a significant place in the *Huainanzi*'s cosmogony and cosmology. Heaven is one of the first of the phenomena to emerge from the undifferentiated primal Way (preceded only by the polarities of yin and yang) and as such is one of the fundamental structures of the cosmos. In the "root–branch" schema according to which the text is laid out, Heaven is treated third (see chapter 3), before all the constituent elements of the human and political realms. Heaven is not a moral force for the *Huainanzi*, as it is in much of Confucian literature, but it is an essential model to which human sages must look when fashioning techniques and institutions that will harmonize the human community and bring it into alignment with the greater cosmic order.

tianming 天命 decree of Heaven, Heaven's decree (for nonruler), Mandate of Heaven (for ruler)

Two meanings of "Heaven's decree" were prevalent in the classical literature before the *Huainanzi.* In a more limited sense, *tianming* could refer to the Heaven-mandated life span that was an individual's bequest. For Confucians, this had both biological and moral dimensions, as it could be an individual's fate to die in fulfillment of a moral imperative before his or her biological life span had expired. The *Huainanzi* generally accepts this notion of *tianming,* although it almost always refers to the concept of a fated life span with the single character *ming* rather than the binome *tianming.* This reflects the tendency of the *Huainanzi*'s authors to deemphasize the moral dimensions of fate, contending that a truly illuminated individual will avoid entrapment in a fatal moral dilemma.

The more expansive meaning of *tianming* is generally rendered in English as "the Mandate of Heaven." This is a venerable concept dating back to the pre-Confucian political tradition, signifying the legitimating moral mandate that a ruling dynasty receives from Heaven, charging it to rule the world as Heaven's proxy. The Mandate of Heaven was the central political principle of much preimperial and Han political thought, and it was the precept on which successive dynasties and dynastic pretenders based their claims to imperial power. In this context, the *Huainanzi* is remarkable for virtually eliminating this notion from its political lexicon. The sage of the *Huainanzi* does not rule on the basis of the Mandate of Heaven. Instead, his claim to authority is rooted in his perfect embodiment of the Way through personal cultivation, which empowers him not only to rule the human realm with perfect impartiality and efficiency but also to perceive how the human community may best be brought into alignment with the cosmos.

tian xia 天下 the world, the empire; under Heaven

Tianxia literally means "(all)-under-Heaven." It denotes a geographic area, but precisely which area is somewhat ambiguous. The literal meaning of "all-under-Heaven" would include cosmographic realms assumed by the *Huainanzi*'s authors to lie beyond the scope of human habitation. In the contexts in which *tianxia* is used, however, it is clear that this is not what the term implies. *Tianxia* is almost always used for an implicit political geography to denote the domain within which the Son of Heaven holds sway or within which the question of who is to be the Son of Heaven is contested. Thus the salient meaning of "under Heaven" is political and does not literally refer to all spaces under the sky, but to all domains that are under the sovereign authority of Heaven's Son. For this reason, we have usually translated *tianxia* as "the world" (as the Son of Heaven was theoretically ruler of the world) or occasionally, when its specific designation of a political entity is clear, "the empire."

wen 文 patterns, culture, writings, civil (vs. military), text, decorative elegance

Wen is an exceptionally multivalent term that was accorded profound and increasing significance in the writings of the classical and imperial eras. Its root meaning is "pattern," but it is distinct from *li* 理 in that when it is used as such, *wen* almost always denotes a visual pattern (such as those made by the stars in the sky or the embroidery on a garment), whereas *li* may include an array of nonvisual patterns (for example, a drumbeat).

From this sense of visual pattern evolved the meanings "writing" and "text." Every form of written expression may be described as *wen*, including the *Huainanzi* itself. The centrality of the written word to all forms of cultural production helped give *wen* the expanded meaning of "culture" more generally. Thus ritual, music, song, and dance all were considered examples of *wen* in this broader sense. On this basis, *wen* acquired the connotation of "civil" versus "military," as ruling or effecting policy through cultural suasion was considered the complementary opposite of exercising power through military coercion. The *Huainanzi* uses *wen* in all these senses, as was universally conventional during the Former Han. We have translated the term variously as appropriate to the context of each use.

Confucians revered *wen* as one of the highest expressions of human potential, and the production and appreciation of *wen* as one of the chief paths to human fulfillment and perfection. The *Huainanzi* is less radically exalting of *wen*. Here, the line between human and cosmic *wen* was highly permeable, as the most valid and efficacious forms of human culture were based on perceived cosmic patterns. Many early Confucian writers (for example, Xunzi) agreed with this concept. Where the *Huainanzi* parts ways with such Confucians was in its insistence that even the cosmic phenomena on which human *wen* was patterned (for example, Heaven and Earth) were lesser and contingent devolutions from the undifferentiated and ineffable (and therefore impossible to capture in *wen*) Way. Thus no *wen* could ever be a carrier of truly ultimate value in the way that Confucian thinkers proposed. It is striking that of the 166 instances of the word *wen* in the *Huainanzi*, only 18, slightly less than 11 percent, occur in the "root" portion of the book (chapters 1–8).

The *Huainanzi* authors were consummate literati, however, and as such they were absorbed in and engaged with all the many concerns of literary production. Indeed, as we state in our general introduction, chapters 9 through 20 may effectively be read as an extended discourse on *wen* in all its various aspects and permutations. Each chapter is both an exploration and an exemplar of a discrete form of *wen* and its operation as part of a larger edifice of culture. Moreover, chapter 21, written entirely in the *fu* (poetic expression) style, is a superlative example of *wen*. Thus for the *Huainanzi*, although *wen* may not be regarded as a source of ultimate value, it is treated as an endeavor of profound (if not quite ultimate) significance.

wu 無 without, nothing, non-being, nonexistence, Nothingness

Wu is a common grammatical term of negation in classical Chinese, meaning "without" or "having no . . ." It is used throughout the *Huainanzi* in this common sense. However, following earlier texts such as the *Zhuangzi* and the *Daodejing*, the *Huainanzi* also constructs *wu* as a highly charged nominal category of profound philosophical significance. In this sense, *wu* is contrasted with *you* 有 (something or being). These two words are simple grammatical antonyms, but the *Huainanzi* uses them for the two penultimately fundamental parameters of cosmic reality.

Wu and *you* are often translated as "non-being" and "being," and we have done so at points in the text where such a translation is required for comprehensibility in English. Conceptually, however, these terms refer to notions closer to "absence" and "presence." A concrete example is a house. The walls, roof, and floor all constitute the aspects of the house that are *you*. The spaces for the windows and doors, and the open area in which people move and live, constitute that aspect of the house that is *wu*. Two points are of axiomatic significance to the *Huainanzi* (and earlier texts that it draws from). In this example, (1) *wu* is as determinative as *you* of the identity of the house (that is, a house becomes a house as much because of what is absent as what is present), and (2) *wu* is in fact superior to *you*, in that it is unitary, primal, and more replete with potential.

The sense in which *wu* is unitary may be self-evident. *You* realities are characterized as such principally by being distinguishable from one another. *Wu*, by contrast, is singular and indivisible; all *wu* forms a boundless unity and thus stands as a reality less contingent and thereby more substantive than that of *you*. The sense in which *wu* is more primal and potent than *you* is less obvious to those who do not share the *Huainanzi*'s grounding assumptions. One reason that "non-being" is a distortional translation of *wu* is that no space is ever considered completely devoid of any material substance whatsoever. Even completely "empty" space is permeated by highly rarefied *qi* in its most primordial and dynamic state, which in fact constitutes the material substrate of *wu*. As the cosmogonies described in chapter 2 make clear, *wu* was the original state of the entire cosmos before the appearance of any *you* phenomena. In that moment before time, the potential for the entire cascade of generation and transformation that would follow was latently contained; thus *wu* is a state imbued with virtually unlimited power. The *you* aspects of present-day phenomena therefore manifest a degraded and devolved state of cosmic senescence, whereas the *wu* aspects preserve the pristine potency of the cosmic origin.

Several other points must be mentioned with respect to the concept of *wu* as it is used in the *Huainanzi*. The preceding example of the house refers to the spatial dimension of *wu*, which is frequently specified in the text as *xu* 虛 (emptiness or vacuity). *Wu* also has a temporal dimension, which is identified as *jing* 靜 (stillness). Just as different objects cannot be distinguished without the gaps of empty space between them, discrete events cannot be differentiated unless they are punctuated by (or contrasted with) moments of stillness and inertness.

Both these spatial and temporal dimensions of *wu* are implicated in the *Huainanzi*'s discussion of its role in human consciousness. Like a house, the functional processes of the mind are conditioned by both *wu* and *you* aspects. Thoughts, feelings, and memories are *you*, but they are differentiated and made coherent only by the mind's capacity for and continual return to a state of emptiness and stillness. These moments of *wu*, in fact, are the baseline state of consciousness. The mind is normally empty and still and becomes stirred by thoughts and feelings only on contact with the external world. Much of the *Huainanzi*'s program of personal cultivation is thus centered on inducing a controlled experience of this original mind, emptying and stilling consciousness through focused meditation and yogic exercise. This is a key step on the path to sagehood demarcated by the text.

Finally, it is important to note that the text does not completely identify *wu* with the source of ultimate value; instead, that place is held by the Way. Although *wu* precedes *you*, the Way precedes *wu*; it is an ultimate that transcends even the distinction between "something" and "nothing." In the quest for human perfection, *wu* is thus a vital juncture, but it is not a goal in itself. As section 12.45 asserts, being "without something" is an admirable attainment, but being "without nothing" is an even higher level of attainment—the point at which the distinction between *wu* and *you* dissolves and one is wholly merged with the Way.

wu 物 object, thing

Any differentiable phenomenon may be termed an "object" in the *Huainanzi*. The status of object is of normative significance, as the source of ultimate value (the Way) encompasses all objects and can never be an object itself. Anything that may be termed an object thus represents a devolution from the ultimate and has diminished normative value.

Nonetheless, the status of object is not absolute but is subject to differing levels of degree. One extent to which a phenomenon is an object is contingent on how many comparable objects it may be contrasted with. Therefore, Heaven is less an object than is an ordinary stone because a stone is one among millions, but Heaven may be truly contrasted only with Earth.

Another plane along which the "objectness" of a phenomenon may be measured is its degree of agency. The more that any object may autonomously act on and influence other objects, the less an object it is. Here, again, Heaven compares favorably with a stone in this regard. Related to this sense of the word is the text's occasional use of *wu* as a verb (for example, in 10.107). If the English word "to thing" existed, it would be an appropriate translation. Lacking that verb in English, we translate *wu* in its verbal sense as "to differentiate."

These conceptual principles inform the *Huainanzi*'s discussion of the human existential condition. Human beings are likewise less like objects than are rocks, but only as a matter of degree. Moreover, this degree varies from human being to human being. The more that human beings are controlled by their attachments and responses to external objects, the more like objects they become. One way in which the *Huainanzi* conceptualizes the process of personal cultivation is as a path toward becoming more an agent and less an object. The final goal of that process is to become a sage, whom the text describes as "treating objects as objects, not being made an object by objects."

wu wei 無為 non-action, non-deliberative action, non-intentional action, non-purposive action, non-striving, without striving, inaction, do nothing, without effort, effortless action

Wu wei is a central concept to the cosmological, political, and ethical thought of the *Huainanzi*, but its use is informed by earlier texts, especially the *Daodejing* and the *Zhuangzi*. In all these writings, *wu wei* denotes a mode of activity that is common to both the Way and the sage. It is thus a potent means of articulating how ultimate value is instantiated in the phenomenal realm.

Wu wei presents a bevy of translational and interpretive problems, as its layers of accrued association, meaning, and implication are exceptionally rich. The phrase literally means "inaction" or "doing nothing," and in the *Huainanzi* it frequently is used in this sense. This is indeed the meaning with which it first appears in the early philosophical literature: the *Analects* describes Shun as a ruler who was so morally elevated that he could "order [the world] by doing nothing" (that is, rule by moral example alone). The *Huainanzi* and its antecedent texts appropriated the original implication of the term and fashioned new meanings from that figurative template. In this new mode, *wu wei* can apply to behavior that is to all appearances quite active, but even in such kinetic instances, a genuine moment of *wu wei* is not wholly unrelated to "doing nothing."

For the *Huainanzi*, these affinities are explicable in terms of the text's understanding of human psychology. The baseline of consciousness for all people is the original stillness and emptiness of the mind; thoughts, feelings, and actions arise only on contact with external stimuli. What distinguishes ordinary people from the sage is that they self-identify with (and are thus controlled by) these latter active products of consciousness. Thus the only time that ordinary people instantiate *wu wei* is when they are literally doing nothing. Only then are they grounded in the original stillness and emptiness of the mind. In contrast, the sage is always grounded in the original stillness and emptiness of the mind, even when he is responding actively and thoughtfully to external stimuli. His subjective, existential state when he is engaged in deliberation, combat, or any other activity is thus indistinguishable from that when he is doing nothing. In this sense, he is always engaged in *wu wei*.

Wu wei does not imply a state of unconsciousness, but it does indicate a total transcendence of self-consciousness. For the *Huainanzi*, the implications of this fact are both psychological and cosmological. When the Way impels some change (for example, the shift from spring to summer), it likewise does not do so self-consciously or through any prism of preconception or bias. *Wu wei* is thus the constant mode of activity of the Way itself, and when the sage engages in *wu wei*, he embodies the basic motive dynamism of the cosmic source. The difference between the activity of the sage and that of ordinary people is therefore not merely subjective. Because the sage channels the cosmic source through *wu wei*, his actions are infused with the same spontaneous power and efficacy as those of the Way itself and (despite occasionally appearing otherwise to ordinary perception) are just as conducive to cosmic and human harmony.

The *Huainanzi* uses *wu wei* in many different contexts, with a flexibility as to part of speech or shades of meaning that is very difficult to capture in English. We have tried to translate it in each instance using English phraseology that will be comprehensible in context but still will give some sense of the larger conceptual discourse informing the text's use of the term. This has required using different English phrases chosen to match the inflection of the term in the particular context in which it appears.

wu xing 五行 Five Phases, Five Conducts (Mencian contexts)
The binome *wu xing* became increasingly common and significant during the Han and subsequent eras. The basic meaning of *xing* is "to walk," although it also could mean "action" or "conduct." There was, in fact, a particular context in which *wu xing* meant "the Five Conducts," and this sometimes appears in the text of the *Huainanzi*. The more prevalent Han-era usage of *wu xing* is for the five basic forms in which *qi* appears in the material world: Earth, Water, Wood, Metal, and Fire. In the Warring States text *Lüshi chunqiu*, these five forms of *qi* were referred to as the *wu de*, or "Five Powers." By the Han period, it had become more common to refer to them as *wu xing*, a construction reflecting the fact that no *qi* was thought to remain in a single form permanently but to cycle perpetually through different forms in sequence. For this reason, it has become conventional to translate the binome as "Five Phases," and we have followed this convention. Here the word "phase" is borrowed from the vocabulary of modern chemistry; for example, ice, liquid water, and water vapor have quite different properties, but all are phases of H_2O. Wood, Fire, Earth, Metal, and Water have different properties, but all are phases of *qi*.

Originally *qi* was uniformly undifferentiated. With cosmogenesis, it first was differentiated into yin and yang polarities and then into the Five Phases. All perceptible matter is a manifestation of one or more of these Five Phases in various combinations and degrees of rarefaction. At their most rarefied, none of the Five Phases can be completely identified with the concrete materials from which they take their names. Rather, each may exist in a highly essential form that is more akin to energy than matter. Moreover, all *qi* is intrinsically volatile and dynamic, and it not only cycles perpetually among different phases and yin–yang polarities but also occasionally returns to its undifferentiated original state.

Yin, yang, and the Five Phases are the basic categories of all traditional correlative cosmology, and much of the cosmological thought of the *Huainanzi* is constructed around the elaboration of various systems of Five Phases correlations. Since almost all tangible material properties were thought to arise from the essential qualities of the Five Phases, many correlative links could be forged on the basis of Five-Phase affinities. For example, since Wood *qi* was thought to both suffuse the spleen and give rise to the flavor of sour, eating sour foods was asserted to be beneficial to the spleen. Wood was further correlated with the color (blue)green, the spring season, the direction east, the musical note *jue*, and so forth, creating an unlimited range of permutations of cross-correlation among spatial, temporal, physiological, cultural, and material dimensions. Such Five-Phase correlations are most prevalent in chapters 3, 4, and 5, but they appear prominently throughout the *Huainanzi* and constitute a conceptual template informing the text's discussion of the physical world.

As mentioned earlier, another usage of *wu xing* is "Five Conducts" rather than "Five Phases," and that sense of the term also appears in the *Huainanzi*. The "Five Conducts" are mentioned in the *Xunzi* as a doctrine attributed to Zisi and his latter-day disciple, Mencius. The exact referent of this phrase was a mystery until the discovery of a text entitled *Wu xing pian* among the writings recovered at Mawangdui. That text enumerates the Five Conducts as Humanity, Rightness, Propriety, Wisdom (the virtues that grow from Mencius's "Four Buds"), and Sageliness. Textual parallels—for example, in chapters 10 and 20—suggest that the *Huainanzi*'s authors were familiar with the *Wu xing pian*, and where *wu xing* appears to refer to the "Five Conducts," that is how we have translated it.

wu zang 五藏 Five Orbs

The term *wu zang* is not original to the *Huainanzi* but comes to the text from what by Han times had already become a rich literature on medicine and human physiology. *Wu zang* corresponds to the five organs of the human physiology that were thought to be critical generative and coordinating junctures for the dynamic matrix of *qi* that composed the mind–body system: the lungs, liver, spleen, gall bladder, and kidneys. As a noun, *zang* literally means "storehouse" or "repository," but in the physiological model built on these constructs, no one of the *wu zang* was envisioned as exclusively active or situated in the particular organ from which it takes its name. Each organ was thought to be the central coordinating point of a distinct ramified network of *qi* that pervaded the entire body, and it is to these five networks rather than to the specific organs themselves that the term *wu zang* refers. Thus (following the lead of the historian of Chinese medicine Manfred Porkert) we have translated the term as "Five Orbs," reflecting the expanded scope of each orb throughout the mind–body system.

The Five Orbs are important to the *Huainanzi* because they provide a conceptual bridge among the cosmic, physiological, and cognitive realms. In medical theory, each of the Five Orbs was correlated with one of the Five Phases of *qi* and was understood to be responsible for the generation and circulation of its particular form of *qi* throughout the mind–body system. The Five Orbs thus provide, through the extended network of Five-Phases cosmological correlations (see *wu xing*), an analytical scheme of relationships between the inner workings of the body and the external structures and transformations of the physical world. Moreover, the Five Orbs were thought to be the governing faculties of the five organs of sense perception, which were in turn the five gateways by which external stimuli gave rise to the *qing* 情 (emotional responses) of the mind–body system. The Five Orbs were thus conceived to be the material locus in which emotional responses were experienced, setting up a mutual feedback mechanism between physiology and consciousness. If the emotions were overstimulated or erratic, *qi* would hemorrhage from the Five Orbs; if the Five Orbs were well nourished and replete with *qi*, it would help regulate the mind's emotional responses to external events.

xin 心 mind, heart

Xin denotes both "heart," in the sense of the physical organ located in the chest, and "mind." These meanings are related in more than a metonymic sense. The heart is conceived of as the generative and coordinating point of a larger matrix of *qi* in the same way that the lungs, liver, spleen, kidneys, and gall bladder are coordinating points of their respective orbs (see *wu zang*). The heart is distinguished by two aspects. First, it is the controlling mechanism of the total system of which it and the Five Orbs are part; all Five Orbs normally operate under the coordinating regulation of the heart. Here again, as with each of the Five Orbs, "the heart" does not refer to the organ alone but to the matrix of *qi*, whose coordinating point is the heart. Second, it is the exclusive seat of discursive intelligence and self-awareness. Whereas the Five Orbs are the locus of discrete emotional responses and thus in some sense may "feel," the heart is the only component of this dynamic system that may think and thus perceive its own activity.

In English, the historical background of "heart" in literary and philosophical movements such as Romanticism creates unnecessarily false impressions if *xin* is consistently rendered as "heart." For example, when the *Huainanzi* declares that an individual's "*xin* does not understand," such a statement has none of the many and weighty implications of declaring in English that one's "heart does not understand." For these reasons, we have most frequently translated *xin* where it occurs in the text as "mind," the only exceptions being where the term clearly refers either to the physical organ or to the locus of feelings, a component of the mind–body system alongside the Five Orbs. Another special case is the phrase "the Heavenly Heart" (*tian xin* 天心), a profoundly empathetic state characteristic of the sage, emphasized in chapter 20.

The choice for "mind" is well justified and unavoidable, but it remains the lesser of two evils. The English word "mind" fails to match the semantic range and conceptual content of *xin* in certain important respects. The first relates to the deep-rooted heart–mind distinction in English. Translated as "heart," *xin* does not denote the romantic emotional center of English usage, but neither does *xin* translated as "mind" denote a purely rational faculty. The emotional responses are seated in the Five Orbs, but the experience of them penetrates and implicates the *xin*. Chapter 7 discusses how the emotional responses of the Five Orbs should ideally be regulated by the mind. They may become so intense as to "overthrow" the mind's regulating function and thus become the controlling impulses of cognition and behavior, resulting in a loss of *qi* affecting both the orbs and the *xin*. This raises questions about the exact structural relationship between the orbs and the heart–mind that the *Huainanzi* never explicitly answers. It would seem, in aggregate, that the mind is a structural matrix of *qi* analytically distinguishable from, but pragmatically forming a seamless continuum with, those of the Five Orbs. Thus whatever is experienced by any of the orbs coterminously occurs in the "mind."

Another problem that makes "mind" an inadequate translation for *xin* involves the latent Cartesian implication in classical English-language thought that "mind" constitutes an entity distinct from both "body" and "spirit." Any superficial perusal of the

Huainanzi will demonstrate that this is a conceptual model alien to the text. In the *Huainanzi*'s conceptual framework, the mind and the spirit are likewise analytically distinct but pragmatically inseparable: the spirit (see *shen* 神) is the matrix of super-rarefied *qi* (see *jingshen*) constituting the physiological substrate of the mind. The mind is effectively made up of thoughts, memories, skills, and dispositions (learned and unlearned) suspended in the matrix of the spirit like impressions in a wax seal, or the "software" programmed into the "hardware" of the spirit.

This analytical divide is the root cause of the most perilous human vulnerability. Although by nature (see *xing* 性) the spirit is tranquil and facilitates the mind's control of the Five Orbs, the structural edifice of the mind itself is unstable and prone to being drawn along aberrant and self-destructive paths. The learned attitudes, dispositions, and biases that help constitute the mind occlude the spirit's stabilizing power, making the mind susceptible to chronic flights of delusion and emotional excess that expend the *qi* reserves of the mind–body system. The attitudes, dispositions, and biases in question need not be extreme or extraordinary to create such vulnerability. They include fundamental distinctions acquired in the normal maturation process of almost any ordinary mind, such as that between self and other or life and death. For this reason, one of the chief personal cultivation prescriptions of the text centers on the "Techniques of the Mind" (see *xinshu*), aimed at "unlearning" cognitive impediments like the distinction between life and death, thereby penetrating beyond the level of the ordinary mind to an unmediated experience of spirit (and thus of the Way, which likewise transcends distinctions such as life and death, self and other).

In the same way that mind and spirit pragmatically form a seamless whole, this same mind–spirit complex is suffused throughout the bodily physiology and implicated in the same system of *qi* that animates the entire frame. Once again, an analytical distinction can be made, as the text notes many examples of people whose mind–spirit is ill, even though their physical body is well (and vice versa). Nonetheless, it consistently asserts that the interpenetration of these realms is so thorough that a harmful or beneficial effect in one sphere will produce congruent influences in the other. Any regimen whose goal is to refine consciousness thus cannot neglect the physical well-being of the body.

xing 形 shape, physical form, military formation

"Shape" or "form" is an important conceptual category in the *Huainanzi*, as it is a definitive aspect of the realm of "Something" (*you* 有). Form is contingent on differentiation, and thus any phenomenon that is at all identifiable belongs to the realm of form. The "Formless" (*wu xing* 無形) therefore denotes states of both cosmic development and human consciousness that are prior to and more replete with potential power (and thus closer to the embodiment of the Way) than the contingent realities of form.

In military parlance, "form" literally referred to the shapes into which troops were deployed on the field of battle to produce particular tactical effects; thus when the *Huainanzi* uses *xing* in this context, we have translated it as "military formation." As is common in these cases of homonymic affinity, the *Huainanzi* makes maximum use of the double entendres that may be derived from the dual significance of *xing* as both "form" and "formation," declaring, for example, that although the tactics of the military rely on "form/formation," military victory is nonetheless rooted in the "formless."

xing 性 nature, natural tendencies

"Nature" was a current and extraordinarily controversial concept in the philosophical literature of the Warring States period, and it became an almost ubiquitous fixture in the lexicon of ancient thinkers across the whole intellectual spectrum. The question of what constituted human "nature" was perceived as basic to the urgent task of determining what types of political and social institutions were best suited to controlling and harmonizing people, both collectively and individually. Although by the third century B.C.E., almost all authors used the term, few defined it in the same way.

The *Huainanzi* defines "nature" as all the inborn propensities, capacities, and dispositions that both guide the long-term growth and maturation of the human being and inform a person's cognition and behavior from moment to moment. Thus the fact that we grow two sets of teeth, that we have the ability to develop language skills, and that we are disposed to feel emotions like anger and joy all are "nature." The *Huainanzi* does not distinguish between material and metaphysical aspects of nature, as became common in late imperial Neo-Confucian philosophy. All aspects of nature are treated as instantiated in the matrix of *qi* that constitutes the human being from birth

The *Huainanzi* does not generally concern itself with the question (much debated in the intellectual lineage of Confucianism) of whether human nature is "good" or "evil." Instead, the text emphasizes the role of nature in instilling and impelling vitality, health, and longevity to the near exclusion of any discussion of nature as a moralizing agent. According to the *Huainanzi*, it is human beings' nature to grow and live long, although how long varies from person to person. In this latter regard, nature is closely allied to "fate" (see *ming* 命). At birth, a certain maximum life span is hard-wired into an individual's physiological bequest as a matter of nature.

Because one of the functions of nature is to sustain an individual in fulfilling his or her "fated" life span, the normative dynamic workings of nature provide a guide to the forms of behavior and mental states that will be most conducive to vitality and longevity. For example, it is natural for our minds to be still unless stimulated by external stimuli, and thus the maintenance of the stillness of the mind (through avoiding overstimulation, indulgence, excess, and the like) is conducive to health and vitality. The cultivation of the ability to deliberately sustain and/or return to stillness on encountering external things (see *yang xing*) is even more beneficial to the long-term flourishing of the mind–body system.

Although it may serve as a guide to preserving vitality, nature is fraught with vulnerability. Responsiveness to external stimuli is inherent to nature (see *qing*), but nature does not foreordain how such responses will translate into behavior. Dysfunctional learned attitudes, preconceptions, or dispositions fixed in the mind (see *xin*) can cause emotional responses to be manifested in behavior that destroys health and vitality. Long-term persistence in and habituation to such behavior can cause these aberrant responses to become "second nature," creating a vicious cycle in which the individual becomes more and more inclined to self-destructive behavior even while shortening his or her potential life span.

This inherent vulnerability of nature is matched by countervailing potential. All the workings of nature come from and express the dynamic impulses of the Way itself. Therefore, the more one strips away the impediments to the free and unobstructed operation of nature, the closer one comes to embodying the Way. In ultimate terms, nature thus contains not only the template for vitality and longevity but also the potential that, if unlocked, may transform the human being into a sage.

xingde 刑德 harm and benefit, recision and accretion, punishment and reward (when context clearly demands this sense)

The binome *xingde* became a standard trope in the statecraft and cosmological writings of the Warring States and Han periods. Its earlier meaning was two fundamental modes of state power. *Xing* literally means "punishment," and *de* (德) literally means "Moral Potency." These two terms signify the basic choice between rule by coercion or by moral suasion or, more broadly, the state's power to inflict harm or bestow benefits on its subjects collectively or individually. In practical terms, *xingde* were most often not treated as opposites but as complementary components of a single program of rule. Therefore, rather than "coercion and moral suasion," they colloquially refer to the more mundane state functions of punishment and reward (what in today's parlance might be called "hard" and "soft" power).

The term was adopted by cosmological theorists to denote opposing processes of harm and benefit observable in the workings of the natural world. Its most common use in this context in the *Huainanzi* is to denote the "recision and accretion" of yang throughout the calendar year. From the winter solstice to the summer solstice, yang energy accretes, figuratively likened to the cosmic dispensation of "rewards" to the living world in the form of light and warmth. From the summer solstice to the winter solstice, yang energy recedes, figuratively likened to the cosmic dispensation of "punishments" to the living world in the form of darkness and cold. This cycle of recision and accretion can be charted (for example, for astrological purposes), especially through the movement of the sun but also through observations of the moon, the planets, and the constellations. Accordingly, many astronomical phenomena are identified for astrological purposes in terms of their place in a "recision and accretion" model of celestial mechanics.

xingming 形名 form and name

The basic significance of "form and name" was found in ancient linguistic theory: a language was held to maintain functionality to the degree that the names of phenomena (see *ming* 名) consistently matched their actual form. This idea lent its name to a prescribed technique in statecraft theory. Within the newly routinized systems of authority designed by ancient Chinese statecraft theorists, the smooth functioning of a bureaucratized governmental structure depended on the ruler's consistent matching of each official's "name" (that is, the title of his office) with his "form" (that is, the systemic powers and responsibilities delegated to his office). For example, if an official bore the title of "minister of waterworks," the ruler was to periodically check to make sure that he was neither falling short of the entailed duties of his title (by, say, allowing dikes to fall into disrepair) nor exceeding them (by trespassing on the authority of the minister of roads). "Form and name" became shorthand for this basic principle of routinized governmental functionality, and it is mentioned frequently in the *Huainanzi* as one of the indispensable technologies of statecraft in the latter age.

xingming 性命 nature and life circumstances, nature and fate

Xing and *ming* are closely related concepts in the *Huainanzi* and antecedent texts, principally because both denote forces that affect the individual from birth. "Nature" refers to all natal factors that are intrinsic to the genetic makeup of the human being and that continue to operate throughout the human lifetime (see *xing* 性). "Fate" may also be intrinsic (for example, it includes one's predetermined maximum life span, which is hard-wired into the physiological constitution of one's mind–body system) but includes extrinsic factors such as one's inherited status at birth or the political climate of the age into which one is born (see *ming*命).

xing ming zhi qing 性命之情 the instinctive responses evoked by one's nature and life circumstances, the innate tendencies of nature and destiny, the emotional responses evoked by nature and fate, the dispositional responsiveness evoked by one's nature and life circumstances, the essential qualities of one's nature and life circumstances

Xing ming zhi qing is a phrase that occurs frequently in the *Huainanzi* and that presents unique difficulties for translation. It is not original to the *Huainanzi* but appears in earlier texts such as the *Lüshi chunqiu* and the "outer chapters" of the *Zhuangzi*. *Xing ming zhi qing* has two related meanings, neither of which is amenable to elegant phrasing in English, and both of which make sense only with a particular understanding of emotional or dispositional responses (see *qing*) and nature (see *xing* 性).

In the *Huainanzi*'s conceptual framework, all emotions are understood as responses to external stimuli. The basic template of an emotional response is hard-wired into our nature, but the actual real-time expression of an emotional response is subject to the distortional influence of many factors. For example, an innately appropriate fear response to a fatal threat is encoded in your nature, but your actual feelings and behavior in the face of such a threat are informed by the attitudes, values, and dispositions that you acquire during your lifetime. If your learned values and acquired habits had conditioned you to love life too dearly, your response to such a threat might be expressed as paralyzing cowardice rather than healthy fear. In this example, the latter response of "healthy fear" would exemplify what the *Huainanzi* refers to as *xing ming zhi qing*, the emotional response that arises from nature and fate rather than the emotional response (in this case, paralyzing fear) that arises from dysfunctional attitudes, values, and habits. "Fate" is implicated in this conceptual construct in two ways. First, the innately appropriate responses that are hard-wired into one's nature are part of the "mandated" (see *ming* 命) bequest that forms one's genetic makeup at birth. Second, the same responses are most conducive to the fulfillment of a person's fated life span (as in the preceding example, you will live longer if you take flight from healthy fear than if you freeze from paralyzing cowardice).

The second sense of *xing ming zhi qing* arises from both the theory of *qing* that informs the text and the general semantic range of the term itself. *Qing* is often used to denote "an essential quality [of a thing]," and in the *Huainanzi*'s understanding of nature, the inborn disposition to particular emotional responses are among nature's most definitive and essential qualities. Occasionally when the *Huainanzi* uses the term *xing ming zhi qing*, it is referring to *qing* in this more abstract sense (a usage that, as explained earlier, is nonetheless consistent with the more particular meaning of *qing* as "emotional response"). Where this occurs, we have translated it as "the essential quality of one's nature and life circumstances."

In either sense, *xing ming zhi qing* denotes a key conceptual concern in the *Huainanzi* as a whole. The text frequently exhorts the practitioner of personal cultivation to "penetrate the innate tendencies of nature and destiny." This is one of the paramount goals of the *Huainanzi*'s program of self-transformation: to jettison the dysfunctional tendencies acquired through learning or habit and to actualize the spontaneously efficacious responsiveness that is innate in the mind–body system.

Occasionally, the text shortens this phrase to *xing zhi qing* rather than *xing ming zhi qing*. We have rendered these occurrences as the "emotional responses of nature," or the "essential qualities of nature" as appropriate to each case. In practical terms, however, the longer and shorter forms of this phrase signify the same concept.

xinshu 心術 Techniques of the Mind

The *Huainanzi* focuses on "techniques" as an essential instrument of rulership (see *shu* 術). Among the techniques it discusses, the "Techniques of the Mind" are given very high priority. The text emphasizes the apophatic personal cultivation of the sage and his ministers as the root from which all normatively functional political processes grow, and within that crucial program of personal cultivation, the Techniques of the Mind are crucial. The *Huainanzi* does not give detailed descriptions of what these techniques entailed, but they obviously included forms of meditation aimed at stilling and emptying the mind so as to induce the experience of unmediated unity with the Way that might be accessed at the root of consciousness.

xu 虛 emptiness, vacuity

Emptiness is both a spatial and an existential manifestation of Nothingness (see *wu* 無). Within the cosmos, all spaces devoid of tangible, differentiable objects are empty, although, as indicated in our discussion of *qi* 氣, no space is ever absolutely empty, as *qi* itself is all-pervasive. Such spaces are prized in the *Huainanzi* because they embody the state of the cosmos at its origin and so retain the potential power and dynamism of that seminal moment. The human mind is empty when it is devoid of thoughts and feelings. Such a state is prized because it affords an experience of the Way that forms the original baseline of consciousness. Accordingly, many of the prescriptions of the *Huainanzi* focus on emptying the mind.

xun li 循理 to act in accordance with, to accord with patterns or principles

Xun li denotes a mode of activity of both the Way and the sage. The motions of the Way are not totally random. When observed carefully, they may reveal complex and consistent patterns. One of the hallmarks of the sage is that he is able to perceive these patterns and act in accordance with them. Thus every policy he advocates and every institution he builds conforms to the basic patterns structuring the phenomenal universe and derives maximum efficacy from operating in harmony with the cosmos.

yang xing 養性 to nourish the/one's nature

Yang xing is one formula by which the *Huainanzi* denotes its prescribed program of personal cultivation. The inborn capacities and tendencies that constitute nature come from the Way and express its potency and efficacy. Thus any program that amplifies and actualizes the potential of nature brings human beings closer to embodying the Way. "Nourishing one's nature" exemplifies the *Huainanzi*'s concept of the human organism as an integrated mind–body system. Since nature is the controlling mechanism of both consciousness and vitality, "nourishing one's nature" produces both elevated states of consciousness and beneficial conditions of bodily health and longevity. Techniques such as dietary regimens, breathing meditation, and macrobiotic yoga are what the *Huainanzi* terms "nourishing nature."

yi 一 unity, to unify; one, the One

Unification is a key theme in the *Huainanzi* for obvious reasons, as the text conceives of the ideal political realm as an empire uniting the entire world. This political concern is echoed in the text's cosmological thought. The "One" is another sobriquet for the Way, as the Way is the one reality outside which there may be nothing else (see *taiyi*). The text self-consciously uses the parallels between the unification of the phenomenal universe in the Way and the unification of the world under the sage (or, less abstractly, the Han dynasty).

yi 宜 suitability, suitable, appropriate

"Suitability" is an important concept in the *Huainanzi*. The cosmos is filled with intrinsic patterns, so the policies and institutions that are "suitable" in response to any cosmic condition match those underlying patterns. In the same vein, human beings have various capacities and tendencies as a function of the dynamic nature they receive at birth (see *xing* 性). A hallmark of the sage is that he is able to assign roles to people and place them into stations suited to their innate dispositions and potential.

yi 意 awareness, thought, intention

Awareness or thought (often with connotations of intentionality) is a natural product of the conscious mind arising in response to interaction with the external world. The *Huainanzi* exhorts the practitioner to dispel (or transcend) awareness and seek grounding in a prior and less contingent level of consciousness.

yi 易 change; the *Changes*

Yi denotes "change," although in its generic sense it signifies forms of change less fundamentally intrinsic than "transformation" (see *hua*). To "change" something is to swap one thing for another, whereas a "transformation" entails a complete and substantial metamorphosis (as from a caterpillar to a butterfly). As a proper noun, however, *Yi* denotes the *Yijing* (*Classic of Changes*), one of the Five Classics of the Confucian canon. The *Huainanzi* quotes and ascribes great authority to the *Changes* as a powerful tool for discerning and modeling cosmic patterns. It denies that the *Changes* is a text of ultimate wisdom, however, because the Way is ultimately beyond all form and cannot be captured in any pattern that depends on differentiation.

yi 移 to shift, to adapt, to modify, to adjust

Yi is another term in the *Huainanzi*'s rich lexicon of change. It generally is indicative of subtle, minor, or temporary changes, often with connotations of spatial location: a movement of an object's position or a slight modification of a person's mode of activity. A frequent use of the term is in injunctions to "shift with the times," to adjust the methods and procedures that will accommodate the changing conditions of the cosmos and human society. In our attempt to distinguish among these different forms of change, we have usually translated *yi* as "to shift," "to adapt," "to modify," or "to adjust."

yi 義 Rightness

"Rightness" is a fundamental ethical concept throughout the philosophical writings of the Warring States and Han periods. Despite some variation from text to text, "Rightness" almost always refers to an ethical imperative that constrains people according to the social and political context in which they live. Serving one's ruler to the best of one's ability or resisting the temptation of corruption are typical examples of Rightness. The *Huainanzi* generally does not give Rightness ultimate value but insists that Rightness acquired substance and relevance only when human society declined from its state of primordial harmony. The text acknowledges, however, that human history has reached a juncture at which Rightness (often paired with Humaneness [see *ren*]) is indispensable to effective political and social organization and that as an instrument of state power, the teaching and practice of Rightness is superior to the use of force or "rewards and punishments."

yin 因 to follow the natural course of things, to adapt to the natural pattern of things

Yin is often used to characterize the activity of the sage or the Genuine Person. Because the sage is not grounded in the duality of self and other, he does not try to impose preconceived conditions on the world but achieves efficacious ends by following along with the spontaneous tendency of the cosmos from moment to moment.

yin–yang 陰陽 yin–yang (not translated)

In their earliest uses, these characters referred to the shady and sunny parts of a hill and later came to signify the two fundamental polarities of *qi*. In the *Huainanzi*'s cosmogenic scheme, *qi* at first was unitary and undifferentiated. As the phenomenal world came into being, *qi* polarized into two modes: yin and yang. In its yin state, *qi* is inert, dark, cold, soft, and feminine. In its yang state, *qi* is kinetic, bright, warm, hard, and masculine. No tangible thing is made exclusively of yin or yang; all phenomena contain both yin and yang, and all *qi* is perpetually in motion from one polarity to the other. Yin and yang are the two most basic categories in the *Huainanzi*'s correlative cosmology. The "recision and accretion" of yin and yang, for example, provide a basic template by which the entire calendar year may be periodized according to the ascendancy of one type of *qi* or the other. Yin–yang affinities are thus one of the basic structural principles of the operation of cosmic resonance (see *ganying*), although the further division of *qi* into the Five Phases (see *wu xing*) is the template for much more intricate systems of correlation.

you 有 something, being, existence

The basic meaning of *you* is "to have," but the *Huainanzi* frequently uses this term nominally to denote "Something," the cosmological complementary opposite and progeny of "Nothing" (see *wu* 無). All differentiable things combine both *you* and *wu* aspects. For example, the hard wooden form of a bowl is Something, and the empty cavity that provides the utility of the bowl is Nothing, but the bowl would not be a bowl without both these aspects. Ordinary perception privileges Something as the most relevant realm of activity, but the *Huainanzi* asserts that Something is both inferior to and derivative of the realm of Nothing.

yuan 元 origin, source, to get to the source of; to find one's source in, *yuan* X = trace X to its source

Origins have a privileged status in the *Huainanzi* because of the basic root–branch cosmology that informs the text as a whole (see *ben* and *benmo*). The moment of origin is filled with dynamic potential, and the presence of the origin continues to pervade and impel a structure or phenomenon even as it matures and differentiates. When something is marked as an "origin," the *Huainanzi* accords it both temporal and normative priority. For example, one metaphor commonly used for the Way itself is the "Origin."

Yuan is also used as a verb throughout the text to mean "get to the source of" or "find (one's) origin." This meaning operates on many levels because in any domain there is great efficacy in accessing and actualizing the power of the origin. For example, in personal cultivation, the goal is to penetrate beyond posterior and contingent fixtures of mind, such as thought and memory, to arrive at the Way that is the origin of all consciousness.

yuan 原 source, origin, to originate in

Yuan is largely synonymous with its homophone *yuan* 元 and has most of the same nominal and verbal meanings. In general, the latter *yuan* is more often chosen to denote grand cosmic origins, and this *yuan* most frequently refers to the particular source of contingent phenomena. This is by no means a rigid rule, however, and in fact the first chapter of the text is entitled "Yuan dao," which we translate as "Originating in the Way" but which may also be understood to mean "The Dao as Origin."

yue 樂 music

Music was highly valued in Confucian discourse as an expression of humanity's most elevated and sublimely humanizing qualities. The *Huainanzi* does not similarly view human culture as a source of ultimate value and so does not see music as equally significant. It does, however, regard music as deeply rooted in human beings' spontaneous impulses. Music is thus privileged as a cultural form that, although of human origin, can embody and express the dynamic power of underlying cosmic forces.

Note that the same character 樂 can also be pronounced *le*, in which case it has the related but distinct meaning of "joy." We consistently translate *le* as "joy" or "delight," distinguishing it from *xi* 喜, "happiness, pleasure."

In some instances, the text uses a double entendre linking the two senses of the character *yue/le* (see, for example, 19.3: "Now singing is evidence of joy"). The Chinese, of course, means both "singing is evidence of joy" and "singing is evidence of music." Because it is impossible to convey the pun in English, in such cases we have added an explanatory footnote.

yuzhou 宇宙 eaves and roof beams; the cosmos, space-time

"Eaves and roof beams" is a synecdoche that may stand for the entire space of a domicile, as together these structural elements comprise its total area and volume. The *Huainanzi* (following earlier texts) appropriates this image as a metaphor for the cosmos, taking "eaves" and "roof beams" to represent the dimensions of space and time that compose the entire phenomenal universe.

zhen 真 genuine, authentic

The *Huainanzi* often uses "Genuine" in a figurative sense to denote the embodiment of the Way in a person or thing. A Genuine phenomenon is thus replete with Potency (see *de*), and, indeed, the *Huainanzi* frequently uses *zhen* and *de* as synonyms.

zheng 正 to align, to correct, to rectify, rectitude, upright

Zheng is an important term in the *Huainanzi*'s normative lexicon. Much of the ruler's task is described as bringing affairs into "alignment" or "rectifying" aberrant conditions. More often than not, however, such "rectification" is not described in moral terms (as it would be, for example, in Confucian discourse) but as bringing human and cosmic structures into integral alignment with one another. *Zheng* is, moreover, a resonant concept in the text's discussion of personal cultivation, in that it simultaneously implies both the rectification of aberrant forms of consciousness and the alignment of the body into the proper upright posture for meditation.

zhenren 真人 Genuine Person, Authentic Person, Realized Person

A genuine person is an adept who has reached a high level of attainment along the path of personal cultivation advocated by the *Huainanzi*. The Genuine Person has discarded the dysfunctional fixtures of the ordinary mind–body system that hinder the experience of the Way and is thus able to embody the Way in cognition, word, and deed. The *Huainanzi* distinguishes among the Superior Man (*junzi*), the sage (*sheng*), the Genuine Person, and the Perfected Person (*zhiren*). The Superior Man is generally portrayed as a person of lesser attainments than the other three, but chapter 10 accords the *junzi* an ultimately efficacious role in the social order. The terms "the sage," "the Genuine Person," and "the Perfected Person" appear to be used with slightly varying nuances in different chapters of the text, and their domains overlap. The sage is usually seen as playing a more direct and dynamic role in the social order than the others. In chapter 2, the sage is explicitly described as superior in attainments to the Genuine Person; in the same chapter, the Perfected Person is presented as the epitome of human development. In all cases, the exact implications of these terms are strongly dependent on context.

zhi 志 will, purpose, attention

Zhi denotes the characteristic tendency of consciousness to focus on an object, whether some abstract future goal or some physical object of immediate perception. In *Huainanzi*'s conceptual framework, once *zhi* attaches to an object, it reorients all the energies of the mind–body system toward it. This operation is ordinarily very routine and is intrinsic to the normal functioning of everyday consciousness (for example, when we are hungry, *zhi* orients us toward the acquisition of food until that need is satisfied), but it is vulnerable to intensifying into fixation or obsession, resulting in harmful or self-destructive cognition and behavior. The *Huainanzi* advances an ideal in which consciousness can operate in the absence of *zhi*. The sage has no "will" in the ordinary sense outlined earlier. His cognition and actions are driven entirely by the intrinsic impulses of the mind–body system itself, without needing the energetic link of *zhi* to some external object of volition.

zhi 治 to put in order, to regulate, to govern

Order is an ideal advocated in the *Huainanzi*, as in earlier texts. It expresses the goal of the integral system of techniques (see *shu* 術) prescribed by the text for efficacious rule. The *Huainanzi* also follows earlier traditions in drawing parallels between the internal ordering of the mind–body system and the holistic ordering of the body politic, portraying the latter as dependent on and flowing from the former.

zhi 智 knowledge, cleverness, crafty knowledge; wisdom, intelligence

Zhi denotes any mental faculty that can produce tangible results in the world, encompassing both quickness of wit and breadth of knowledge. The *Huainanzi* cites many positive examples of cleverness and erudition and generally acknowledges that *zhi* may be a powerful and efficacious quality. However, the text generally asserts that cleverness and knowledge are inferior to the deeper potentials that may be unlocked by apophatic personal cultivation. For every positive exemplar of cleverness in the *Huainanzi*, there is an example of someone whose reliance on such abilities resulted in defeat, self-subversion, or death.

zhi 知 to know, knowledge; wisdom, intelligence

All the faculties of mind that are rooted in its capacities for self-awareness and discrimination come under the compass of *zhi*, so *zhi* is variously used to mean "to know," "to understand," or "to recognize," and we have translated it as appropriate to each context. In addition, someone whose faculties of knowledge and understanding are particularly acute may be described as *zhi*, and in these contexts we have translated *zhi* as "wise" or "intelligent;" or as "wisdom" and "intelligence" when these qualities are being discussed in the abstract.

As in the case of the closely related term "cleverness" (see *zhi* 智), the *Huainanzi* acknowledges the validity and utility of wisdom or intelligence in discrete contexts. It likewise insists, however, that the mind's ultimate potential can be found only in levels of consciousness that precede the subject–object dualism on which wisdom and intelligence are contingent. The Genuine Person and the sage are thus often described as having "discarded wisdom" to arrive at their level of personal attainment.

zhigu 知故 intelligence and precedent, intelligence and acting on precedent

Whereas *zhi* denotes the mind's faculty of intelligence and wisdom, *gu* refers to discrete facts that may be assimilated by the mind and stored in memory. Together they describe the basic components of a decision-making process commonly undertaken by an ordinary mind. We act on both what we apprehend in the present moment and what we know about the past. The *Huainanzi* usually marks this as an inferior mode of engagement with the phenomenal world. The sage "discards wisdom and precedent," and so he does not undertake the kind of parsing that exemplifies the ordinary mind. Rather, his responses are grounded in a total comprehension of the situation at hand that does not distinguish between internal and external, subject and object, past and present.

zhilu 知慮 intelligence and forethought

"Intelligence and forethought" represents a basic operation of ordinary consciousness that is complementary to "intelligence and precedent" (see *zhigu*). Whereas "intelligence and precedent" represents the tendency of the mind to recall facts about the past when responding to the current moment, "intelligence and forethought" denotes the tendency of the ordinary mind to use the present conditions to imagine future outcomes. In contrast, the sage does not distinguish between present and future but responds with spontaneous and unself-conscious efficacy to the comprehensive cosmic context of any situation he encounters.

zhiren 至人 Perfected Person, Accomplished Person, the Perfected
Zhiren is a figurative term used throughout the *Huainanzi* to describe a person who has achieved the highest levels of human perfection delineated by the text. A Perfected Person completely embodies the Way in all cognition, word, and deed without any obstruction or distortion. The *zhiren* thus has achieved levels of self-cultivation more advanced than those of the Genuine Person (see *zhenren*). The terms "the sage" and "the Perfected" overlap in meaning, and they receive different emphasis and have different nuances of meaning in various chapters the *Huainanzi*. The distinctions between the two often must be inferred from the contexts in which they appear.

ziran 自然 spontaneously, naturally
Literally "so of itself," *ziran* describes the perfect spontaneity of all the activities of the Way and those cosmic phenomena (such as Heaven and Earth) that channel its Potency without obstruction. *Ziran* thus also denotes a state of action that can be achieved by human beings who embody the Way in their own persons. Whereas ordinary people are controlled by their attachment or responsiveness to external things, the activities of a sage or a Genuine Person are grounded in the most authentic root of their being (the Way) and are thus "so of themselves."

zong 宗 origins, ancestor
The "Ancestor" is used by the *Huainanzi* as a metaphor for the Way. Because all things emerged from the Way, the Way is literally the ancestor of all things. The text further exploits the suggestive parallels between the Way as "Ancestor" and the Liu clan as a kinship group united by common descent from a single sage-ancestor, Liu Bang, the founding emperor of the Han dynasty. Just as the diversified universe operates harmoniously under the control of the Ancestor, the extended Liu clan can embody the same spontaneous harmony in support of the ancestral throne.

Andrew Meyer

English-Language Finding List for Chinese Terms

Accomplished Person	*zhiren*
accord with patterns	*xun li*
action	*dong*

activation	*ji*
active	*dong*
adapt	*yi*
adapt to natural patterns of things	*yin*
adjust	*yi*
advantage	*li*
advantage and disadvantage	*lihai*
affair	*shi*
align	*zheng*
alter	*bian*
Ancestor	*zong*
appropriate	*yi*
argument	*lun*
arts	*shu*
assess, assessment	*lun*
attention	*zhi*
authentic	*zhen*
Authentic Person	*zhenren*
awareness	*yi*
basic	*ben*
basis	*ben*
being	*you*
benefit	*li*
benefit and harm	*lihai*
bright, brightness	*ming*
change	*yi, bian*
Changes, the	*Yi*
clarify, clarity	*ming*
cleverness	*zhi*
Confucian	*ru*
contradict, on the contrary	*fan*
convention	*su*
correct	*zheng*
cosmos	*yuzhou*
crafty knowledge	*zhi*
crux	*ji*
culture	*wen*
custom	*su*
decorative elegance	*wen*
decree	*ming*
Decree of Heaven	*tianming*
degree	*du*
describe	*shuo*
destiny	*ming*

discern, discernment	*ming*
discourse	*lun*
disposition	*qing*
disposition and nature	*qingxing*
dispositional nature	*qingxing*
dispositional responsiveness	*qing*
dispositional responsiveness evoked by nature and life circumstances	*xingming zhi qing*
disturbance, to disturb	*dong*
divine	*ling, shen*
do nothing	*wuwei*
Documents, the	*Shu*
Earth, earthly	*di*
eaves and roof beams	*yuzhou*
effort	*shi*
emotional responses	*qing*
emotional responses evoked by nature and fate	*xingming zhi qing*
empire	*tianxia*
emptiness	*xu*
enumerate	*shu*
essence	*jing*
essence and spirit	*jingshen*
essential qualities	*qing*
essential qualities of nature and life circumstances	*xingming zhi qing*
event	*shi*
existence	*you*
expediency	*quan*
fate	*ming*
feelings	*qing*
find one's source in	*yuan*
Five Conducts	*wu xing*
Five Orbs	*wu zang*
Five Phases	*wu xing*
follow the natural course of things	*yin*
force	*shi*
form and name	*xingming*
foundation	*ben*
fulcral moment	*ji*
fundamental	*ben*
fundamental and peripheral	*benmo*
genuine	*zhen*
Genuine Person	*zhenren*

genuine qualities	*qing*
genuine responses	*qing*
get to the source of	*yuan*
god	*shen*
govern	*zhi*
Grand Beginning, Grand Inception	*taichu*
Grand One	*taiyi*
Grand Purity	*taiqing*
guard the One	*shouyi*
Hall of Light	Mingtang
harm and benefit	*xingde*
harmony	*he*
heart	*xin*
Heaven, heavenly	*tian*
Heaven, under	*tianxia*
Heavenly Heart	*xin*
Heaven's Decree	*tianming*
hegemon	*ba*
heft	*quan*
hold fast to the One	*shouyi*
Humaneness, humane	*ren*
illuminate, illumination	*ming*
inaction	*wuwei*
innate tendencies of nature and destiny	*xing ming zhi qing*
instinctive responses	*qing*
instinctive responses evoked by nature and life circumstances	*xing ming zhi qing*
intelligence	*zhi*
intelligence and forethought	*zhilu*
intelligence and precedent	*zhigu*
intention	*yi*
know, knowledge	*zhi*
life circumstances	*ming*
life span	*ming*
Mandate of Heaven	*tianming*
measure	*du*
mechanism	*ji*
military formation	*xing*
mind	*xin*
modify	*yi*
Moral Potency	*de*
movement, to move	*dong*
music	*yue*
name	*ming*

naturally	*ziran*
nature	*xing*
nature and fate	*xing ming*
nature and life circumstances	*xing ming*
non-action	*wu wei*
non-being	*wu*
non-deliberative action	*wuwei*
nonexistence	*wu*
non-intentional action	*wuwei*
non-purposive action	*wuwei*
non-striving	*wuwei*
norms	*shu*
nothing, Nothingness	*wu*
nourish one's nature	*yangxing*
numinous	*ling*
object	*wu*
Odes, the	*Shi*
One	*yi*
one year	*chunqiu*
oppose	*fan*
order (v.)	*ming*
origin	*yuan*
origins	*zong*
Pattern	*li*
patterns	*wen*
Perfected Person	*zhiren*
person	*shen*
persuade, persuasion	*shuo (shui)*
phenomenon	*shi*
physical form	*xing*
poetry	*shi*
positional advantage	*shi*
Potency	*de*
preserve the One	*shouyi*
principle	*li*
profit	*li*
propensity	*shi*
propriety	*li*
prose	*shu*
protocol	*li*
punishment and reward	*xingde*
purpose	*zhi*
put in order	*li*
put in order	*zhi*

qi	*qi*
Quintessential Sincerity	*cheng*
Quintessential Spirit	*jingshen*
Realized Person	*zhenren*
reason (v.)	*lun*
recision and accretion	*xingde*
rectify, rectitude	*zheng*
regulate	*li*
regulate	*zhi*
reputation	*ming*
resonance	*ganying*
return	*fan*
reversion	*fan*
revert	*fan*
Rightness	*yi*
rites	*li*
ritual	*li*
root	*ben*
root and branch	*benmo*
sage	*shengren*
self	*shen*
shape	*xing*
shift	*yi*
sincerity	*cheng*
six coordinates	*liuhe*
Something	*you*
source	*yuan*
space-time	*yuzhou*
speak	*shuo*
spirit	*shen*
spirit illumination	*shenming*
spirit transformation	*shenhua*
spiritlike	*shen*
spiritlike illumination	*shenming*
spiritlike transformation	*shenhua*
spontaneously	*ziran*
spring and autumn	*chunqiu*
Spring and Autumn Annals	*Chunqiu*
standard	*du*
stimulus and response	*ganying*
suitability, suitable	*yi*
Superior Man	*junzi*
task	*shi*
techniques	*shu*

Techniques of the Mind	*xinshu*
text	*wen*
thing	*wu*
thought	*yi*
trace X to its source	*yuan*
trajectory	*shi*
transformation	*hua*
unity, unify	*yi*
upright	*zheng*
vacuity	*xu*
vary	*bian*
vital breath	*qi*
vital energy	*qi*
vital essence	*jing*
vulgar	*su*
weight	*quan*
will	*zhi*
wisdom	*zhi*
without	*wu*
without striving	*wuwei*
world	*tianxia*
writing	*shu*
writings	*wen*
yin–yang	*yin–yang*

Appendix B

CATEGORICAL TERMS

Astronomical Terms

In early China, as in other ancient societies, no distinction was made between astronomy and astrology. The task of locating periodical phenomena (the sun, moon, and planets that could be seen with the naked eye) and occasional portents (such as comets and meteors) was directed at ascertaining their astrological significance. Special attention was paid to the location of Jupiter, which was invested with particular astrological potency. The principal means of determining the location of heavenly bodies was with reference to the twenty-eight lunar lodges.

The Twenty-eight Lunar Lodges, with Angular Extensions

The twenty-eight lunar lodges (*xiu* 宿) are a set of constellations denoting unequal segments of a celestial circle approximating the ecliptic and the celestial equator. The system is very ancient, attested in full from the early fifth century B.C.E. and possibly dating back as far as the late third millennium B.C.E. The lunar lodge system provides a means of locating the sun, moon, and visible planets among the fixed stars (table 1). For example, the location of heavenly bodies in the portion of the sky below the horizon can be calculated using the lunar lodges. The list of lodges begins in the east with Horn (*jue* 角), whose determinative star is Alpha Virginis, and proceeds westerly around the celestial circle (table 2).

TABLE 1 The Five Visible Planets

Sui xing 歲星	Year Star	Jupiter
Ying huo 熒惑	Sparkling Deluder	Mars
Zhen xing 鎮星	Quelling Star	Saturn
Tai bo 太白	Great White	Venus
Chen xing 辰星	Chronograph Star	Mercury

TABLE 2 The Twenty-eight Lunar Lodges

1. *jue* 角	Horn 12^d	15. *kui* 奎	Stride 16^d
2. *kang* 亢	Neck 9^d	16. *lou* 婁	Bond 12^d
3. *di* 氐	Root 15^d	17. *wei* 胃	Stomach 14^d
4. *fang* 房	Room 5^d	18. *mao* 昴	Pleiades 11^d
5. *xin* 心	Heart 5^d	19. *bi* 畢	Net 16^d
6. *wei* 尾	Tail 18^d	20. *zui* 觜	Turtle Beak 2^d
7. *ji* 箕	Winnowing Basket 11.25^d	21. *shen* 參	Alignment 9^d
8. *nan dou* 南斗	Southern Dipper 26^d	22. [*dong*] *jing* 東井	[Eastern] Well 30^d
9. *qian niu* 牽牛	Ox Leader 8^d	23. *yu gui* 輿鬼	Ghost Bearer 4^d
10. *xu nü* 須女	Serving Maid 12^d	24. *liu* 柳	Willow 15^d
11. *xu* 虛	Emptiness 10^d	25. [*qi*] *xing* 七星	Seven Stars 7^d
12. *wei* 危	Rooftop 17^d	26. *zhang* 張	Extension 18^d
13. *ying shi* 營室	Encampment 16^d	27. *yi* 翼	Wings 18^d
14. *dong bi* 東壁	Eastern Wall 9^d	28. *zhen* 軫	Chariot Platform 17^d

The Jupiter Cycle

The planet Jupiter takes approximately twelve years to complete a single orbit around the sun. The twelve years of Jupiter's cycle had particular astrological significance. The names of the years apparently are from some unidentified non-Sinitic language; their origin is an unsolved mystery of the history of Chinese astrology. The Jupiter years also were correlated with the twelve earthly branches (table 3). At some time, perhaps as early as the fourth century B.C.E., the earthly-branch designations came to be associated with twelve animal names. These animal names do not appear in the *Huainanzi*, but subsequently became the usual way to refer to cyclical years. These names, too, have an unknown and mysterious origin.

TABLE 3 The Jupiter Cycle

Year Name	Cyclical Character (branch, *zhi* 支)	Animal (not in HNZ)
Shetige 攝提格	*zi* 子	Rat
Ming'e 單閼	*chou* 丑	Ox
Zhixu 執徐	*yin* 寅	Tiger
Dahuangluo 大荒落	*mao* 茂	Rabbit
Dunzang 敦牂	*chen* 辰	Dragon
Xiexia 協洽	*si* 巳	Snake
Tuntan 涒灘	*wu* 午	Horse
Zuo'e 作鄂	*wei* 危	Sheep
Yanmao 掩茂	*shen* 申	Monkey
Dayuanxian 大淵獻	*you* 酉	Rooster
Kundun 困敦	*xu* 虛	Dog
Chifenruo 赤奮若	*hai* 亥	Pig

Calendrical Terms

The ancient Chinese kept track of periodic time by means of a cycle of sixty quasi-numerals, the *ganzhi* sexagenary cycle. This cycle was calculated from two sets of ordinals: the ten heavenly stems (*gan* 干) and the twelve earthly branches (*zhi* 支). In very ancient times, these two sets were probably used separately for different purposes. During the Shang period (ca. 1550–1046 B.C.E.), the ten stems denoted a ten-day "week" used primarily to keep track of which royal ancestors were to receive sacrifices on which days. From very early times, the twelve branches were probably used to keep track of the lunar months and perhaps also of the twelve years of the Jupiter cycle. At some point, at least as early as the Shang and perhaps many centuries before that, the two sets began to be combined in the form 1, i; 2, ii; . . . 10, x; 1, xi; 2, xii; 3, i. . . . This system produced a sequence of sixty binomes, which was used to keep a continuous count of days. Much later, during the early imperial period, the sexagenary cycle also began to be used to keep track of years repeating at sixty-year intervals. Table 4 shows the heavenly stems, the earthly branches, and the sexagenary binomes.

TABLE 4 Stems, Branches, and the Sexagenary Cycle

Heavenly Stems (*tian gan* 天干)	Earthly Branches (*di zhi* 地支)
1. *jia* 甲	1. *zi* 子
2. *yi* 巳	2. *chou* 丑
3. *bing* 丙	3. *yin* 寅
4. *ding* 丁	4. *mao* 卯
5. *wu* 戊	5. *chen* 辰
6. *ji* 己	6. *si* 巳
7. *geng* 庚	7. *wu* 午
8. *xin* 辛	8. *wei* 未
9. *ren* 壬	9. *shen* 申
10. *gui* 癸	10. *you* 酉
	11. *xu* 戌
	12. *hai* 亥

The Sexagenary Cycle

1. *jiazi* 甲子	17. *gengchen* 庚辰	33. *bingshen* 丙申
2. *yichou* 乙丑	18. *xinsi* 辛巳	34. *dingyou* 丁酉
3. *bingyin* 丙寅	19. *renwu* 壬午	35. *wuxu* 戊戌
4. *dingmao* 丁卯	20. *guiwei* 癸未	36. *jihai* 己亥
5. *wuchen* 戊辰	21. *jiaxin* 甲辛	37. *gengzi* 庚子
6. *jisi* 己巳	22. *yiyou* 乙酉	38. *xinchou* 辛丑
7. *gengwu* 庚午	23. *bingxu* 丙戌	39. *renyin* 壬寅
8. *xinwei* 辛未	24. *dinghai* 丁亥	40. *guimao* 癸卯
9. *renshen* 壬申	25. *wuzi* 戊子	41. *jiachen* 甲辰
10. *guiyou* 癸酉	26. *jichou* 己丑	42. *yisi* 巳巳
11. *jiaxu* 甲戌	27. *gengyin* 庚寅	43. *bingwu* 丙午
12. *yihai* 乙亥	28. *xinmao* 辛卯	44. *dingwei* 丁未
13. *bingzi* 丙子	29. *renchen* 壬辰	45. *wushen* 戊申
14. *dingchou* 丁丑	30. *guisi* 癸巳	46. *jiyou* 己酉
15. *wuyin* 戊寅	31. *jiawu* 甲午	47. *gengxu* 庚戌
16. *jimao* 己卯	32. *yiwei* 巳未	48. *xinhai* 辛亥

49. *renzi* 壬子	53. *bingchen* 丙辰	57. *gengshen* 庚申
50. *guichou* 癸丑	54. *dingsi* 丁巳	58. *xinyou* 辛酉
51. *jiayin* 甲寅	55. *wuwu* 戊午	59. *renxu* 任戌
52. *yimao* 已卯	56. *jiwei* 己未	60. *guihai* 癸亥

Calendars

The task, and the fundamental problem, of calendars in early China, as elsewhere in the ancient world, was to keep track of and attempt to reconcile two incommensurable periods: the (approximately) 354-day lunar year of twelve lunar months, and the 365.25-day solar year. The basic technique for reconciling the lunar and solar years was the so-called Metonic cycle (named for its Greek discoverer in the Western world), according to which seven additional (intercalary) months were added at intervals during each nineteen-year period. Other adjustments were built into the calendar to take account of various anomalies that accumulated during repeated Metonic cycles. The main goal of the calendar reforms that were undertaken by imperial regimes from time to time was to identify and deal with such anomalies.

Both the government and ordinary people used the resulting lunar–solar calendar for ritual purposes. In practice, especially in making decisions about the times of planting and harvesting crops, people also used a separate solar calendar, keyed to the solstices, equinoxes, and the regular annual round of meteorological phenomena and agricultural activities (table 5).

TABLE 5 The Solar Year Agricultural Calendar

Name	Translation	Approximate Date
1. Lichun 立春	Spring Begins	February 4 or 5 (winter solstice, plus forty-six days)
2. Yushui 雨水	Rainwater	February 19 or 20
3. Jingzhe 驚蟄	Insects Awaken	March 6 or 7
4. Chunfen 春分	Spring Equinox	March 20 or 21
5. Qingming 清明	Clear and Bright	April 5 or 6
6. Guyu 穀雨	Grain Rain	April 20 or 21
7. Lixia 立夏	Summer Begins	May 6 or 7
8. Xiaoman 小滿	Small Grain	May 21 or 22

TABLE 5 (*continued*)

Name	Translation	Approximate Date
9. Mangzhong 芒種	Grain in Ear	June 6 or 7
10. Xiazhi 夏至	Summer Solstice	June 20 or 21
11. Xiaoshu 小暑	Lesser Heat	July 7 or 8
12. Dashu 大暑	Great Heat	July 23 or 24
13. Liqiu 立秋	Fall Begins	August 8 or 9
14. Chushu 處暑	Abiding Heat	August 23 or 24
15. Bailu 白露	White Dew	September 8 or 9
16. Qiufen 秋分	Autumn Equinox	September 22 or 23
17. Hanlu 寒露	Cold Dew	October 9 or 10
18. Shuangjiang 霜降	Frost Descends	October 24 or 25
19. Lidong 立冬	Winter Begins	November 8 or 9
20. Xiaoxue 小雪	Slight Snow	November 23 or 24
21. Daxue 大雪	Great Snow	December 7 or 8
22. Dongzhi 冬至	Winter Solstice	December 21 or 22
23. Xiaohan 小寒	Slight Cold	January 6 or 7
24. Dahan 大寒	Great Cold	January 21 or 22

The calendar was composed of twenty-four "nodes" (*jie* 節), or fortnights.

Reconciling Three Calendars

Three calendars were being used at the time the *Huainanzi* was written and throughout the imperial period: (1) the astronomical calendar, in which the months were denoted by the twelve earthly branches and the year (defined, for example, by the reciprocal waxing and waning of yin and yang) began with the month (designated *zi*) in which the winter solstice occurred; (2) the agricultural calendar of twenty-four "solar nodes" outlined in table 5; and (3) the civil calendar (also called the Xia calendar), in which the months were numbered (*zheng yue* 正月, *er yue* 二月, etc. [that is, "beginning month," "second month," and so on]) and the year began in the third astronomical month (designated *yin*), that is, at the second new moon following the month in which the winter solstice occurred. The first civil month was undoubtedly designated so as to keep the civil calendar and the agricultural calendar in approximate alignment. The astronomical months and the civil months are, of course, the same except for their designations. Both are correlated in the same way (for astrological purposes) with the twelve pitch-pipe notes of the duodecatonic scale and the same compass directions plotted around the horizon. Table 6 shows approximately how the three calendars relate to one another.

Correlative Cosmological Terms

The *Huainanzi*'s cosmology is based on the idea that all things in the world are made of *qi* and that those things sharing similar *qi* are likely to respond strongly to one another through the principle of resonance (*ganying*, "stimulus and response" [see appendix A]). Correlative categories therefore became important as a way both to classify phenomena and to predict which phenomena would be likely to be in strongly resonant relationships with one another. The two most important correlative categories are yin–yang and the Five Phases (*wuxing*). Tables 7 and 8 are lists (not exhaustive) of yin–yang and Five-Phase correlates that appear in the *Huainanzi*; other categories could be added on the basis of other texts. Note that some of the Five-Phase correlates (for example, directions and colors) were standardized, whereas others (for example, visceral orbs) often varied among different textual traditions.

In addition to yin–yang dualism and the Five Phases were other numerical correlative categories. For example, the twelve earthly branches correlated with months, directions, musical notes, the years of the Jupiter cycle, and other cosmological phenomena. Less important categories were based on ten (the heavenly stems) and eight (directions, winds). Interestingly, the *Huainanzi* does not use the eight trigrams of the *Changes* as a correlative category, although the *Changes* itself is frequently quoted as a canonical text.[1]

Music and Mathematical Harmonics

The *Huainanzi* cites the two ancient Chinese sequences of notes: the pentatonic scale (seen as correlated with the Five Phases) and the duodecatonic scale (seen as correlated with the earthly branches, months, and so on). The names of the pentatonic notes—*gong*, *zhi*, *shang*, *yu*, and *jue*—are customarily not translated, although they could be, because they seem to have been understood as sound words on the order of "do, re, mi." The names of the notes of the duodecatonic scale usually are translated, however, although at least some of them probably should not be (as they may be transcriptions of non-Sinitic words). The twelve notes are defined by the sounds of a set of twelve pitch pipes (*lü* 律) of standard lengths.

1. For diagrams of the various correlative systems found in the cosmological chapters of the *Huainanzi*, see Major 1993.

TABLE 6 Relationship of the Three Calendars

Astronomical Calendar	Common Months	Civil Calendar	Pitch Pipe Notes	Agricultural Calendar (range)	Direction	Characteristics
zi (1)	November–December	11	Yellow Bell	20–22	N	Winter solstice / Maximum yin
chou (2)	December–January	12	Great Regulator	22–24	NNE	Yang accretion begins
yin (3)	January–February	1	Great Budding	24–2	ENE	Civil year begins
mao (4)	February–March	2	Pinched Bell	1–3	E	Spring equinox
chen (5)	March–April	3	Maiden Purity	3–6	ESE	
si (6)	April–May	4	Median Regulator	6–8	SSE	
wu (7)	May–June	5	Luxuriant	8–10	S	Summer solstice / Maximum yang
wei (8)	June–July	6	Forest Bell	10–12	SSW	Yin accretion begins
shen (9)	July–August	7	Tranquil Pattern	12–14	WSW	
you (10)	August–September	8	Southern Regulator	14–16	W	Autumn equinox
xu (11)	September–October	9	Tireless	16–18	WNW	
hai (12)	October–November	10	Responsive Bell	18–20	NNW	

TABLE 7 Yin–Yang Correlates

Yin	Shady	Dark	Black	Cool	Cold	Square	Earth	Moon	Water	Metal
Yang	Sunny	Light	Red	Warm	Hot	Round	Heaven	Sun	Fire	Wood
Yin	Female	Damp	Cloudy	Rain	Internal	Frost	Autumn	Winter	Low	
Yang	Male	Dry	Clear	Wind	External	Dew	Spring	Summer	High	
Yin	Crawling	Passivity	Valleys	Recision						
Yang	Flying	Vigor	Hills	Accretion						

TABLE 8 Five-Phase Correlates

	Wood	**Fire**	**Earth**	**Metal**	**Water**
Direction	East	South	Center	West	North
Color	Bluegreen	Red	Yellow	White	Black
Symbol	Bluegreen Dragon	Vermilion Bird	Yellow Dragon	White Tiger	Dark Warrior
Season	Spring	Summer	Midsummer	Autumn	Winter
Planet	Jupiter	Mars	Saturn	Venus	Mercury
Tool	Compass	Balance beam	Marking cord	Square	Weight
Note	*jue*	*zhi*	*gong*	*shang*	*yu*
Heavenly Stems	*jia, yi*	*bing, ding*	*wu, ji*	*geng, xin*	*ren, gui*
Number	8	7	5	9	6
Species	Scaly	Feathered	Naked	Hairy	Armored
Flavor	Sour	Bitter	Sweet	Pungent	Salty
Smell	Musty	Burned	Fragrant	Rank	Putrid
Crop	Wheat	Rice	Millet	Legumes	Grain
Structural system	*qi* system	Blood system	Skin	Bones	Flesh
Visceral orb	Splenic	Pulmonary	Hepatic	Choleric	Renal
Organ of communication	Eyes	Nose	Mouth	Ears	Tongue

The two scales correlate with each other because their fundamental notes (*gong* and Yellow Bell) are defined as having the same pitch. In turn, that pitch is defined as the sound of a pitch pipe nine inches (*chi*) long. But because the length of an inch in ancient China varied from place to place and over time, it is no longer possible to say with any confidence what the pitch value of that tone might have been. The following two lists arbitrarily assign a hypothetical value of C to the fundamental, but this is an artificial value for illustrative purposes only and should not be assumed as corresponding to the actual pitch value of *gong*/Yellow Bell in ancient China. (Evidence from inscribed bell-sets from the middle Zhou period suggests, however, that the Chinese of that era did have the concept of absolute pitch and that their fundamental note was rather close to the value of C.)

The twelve notes of the pitch-pipe scale were generated from the fundamental by means of a procedure known as "ascending and descending thirds." The numerical value of each of the notes is multiplied by either ⅔ or 4⁄3, beginning with 81 (the square of the length of the Yellow Bell pitch pipe). Thus 81 × ⅔ = 54; 54 × 4⁄3 = 72; 72 × ⅔ = 48; and so on. There is one break in the sequence (both Responsive Bell and Luxuriant are multiplied by 4⁄3), allowing the notes generated to stay within a single octave. The sequence thus produced is as follows:

Yellow Bell (× ⅔ =)
Forest Bell (× 4⁄3 =)
Great Budding (× ⅔ =)
Southern Regulator (× 4⁄3 =)
Maiden Purity (× ⅔ =)
Responsive Bell (× 4⁄3 =)
Luxuriant (× 4⁄3 =)
Great Regulator (× ⅔ =)
Tranquil Pattern (× 4⁄3 =)
Pinched Bell (× ⅔ =)
Tireless (× 4⁄3 =)
Median Regulator

The difficulty with this procedure is that because of small increments of flatness at each step, after twelve steps the scale has gone flat by a half tone. That is, taking the fundamental note as a hypothetical C, Median Regulator (the twelfth step in the ascending and descending thirds sequence) winds up as F. If the next step were taken (Median Regulator × ⅔), the resulting note would be about a half tone short of completing the octave at C. The ascending and descending thirds method, in other words, produces an untempered scale. Whether the ancient Chinese also had a tempered scale is a matter of some dispute, and we will touch on this again later.

Rearranging the twelve pitch-pipe notes into an ascending scale, again with the fundamental set arbitrarily and hypothetically at C, we can see the relationship between the duodecatonic and pentatonic scales:

Yellow Bell	C	*gong*
Great Regulator	C-sharp	
Great Budding	D	*shang*
Pinched Bell	D-sharp	
Maiden Purity	E	*jue*
Median Regulator	F	
Luxuriant	F-sharp	
Forest Bell	G	*zhi*
Tranquil Pattern	G-sharp	
Southern Regulator	A	*yu*
Tireless	A-sharp	
Responsive Bell	B	
Yellow Bell	C	*gong*

In the terminology of early Chinese music, some notes (or scales or tuning systems) are sometimes described as *qing* 清, "clear," and others as *zhuo* 濁, "muddy" or "turbid." It is not at all obvious, and much disputed, what these terms mean when applied to music. (The same terms also are used to describe different grades or qualities of *qi* [see appendix A].) Sometimes *qing* and *zhuo* seem to refer to high notes and low notes; sometimes to tonic and flattened notes (or scales or tunings); sometimes perhaps to notes played on an open or a stopped string. As some musicologists have pointed out, these terms also suggest the intriguing possibility of a tempered scale in early Chinese music. That would mean that the pitch-pipe notes derived from the ascending and descending thirds method would subsequently and systematically be altered (tempered) to be slightly sharp, so the numerical value of the last note of the series of twelve could be multiplied by ⅔ to produce a note one octave above the fundamental note (C above middle C, in the hypothetical values we are using here), thus completing the octave. In other words, the meaning (or a meaning) of *qing* and *zhuo* might be "notes of a tempered scale" and "notes of an untempered scale." The two would sound quite different from each other, and that difference could account for some of the debates in Warring States and Han times about moral, proper, antique ritual music versus licentious popular music.

Weights and Measures

Weights and measures were standardized by the regime of Qin Shihuangdi as part of the Qin dynasty's program of nationalizing reforms. The Han dynasty adopted the Qin standards, but they were changed again during the Wang Mang interregnum. Over the long course of imperial history, the values of weights and measures changed greatly. For example, the Han "foot" (*chi*) measured about nine English inches, but in the twentieth century, under the Republic of China, it had grown to thirteen

TABLE 9 Weights and Measures

Weight	
1 *fen* 分	Weight of 12 millet grains: ~ 0.05 gram
12 *fen* = 1 *shu* 銖	Approximately 0.6 gram
12 *shu* = 1 *ban liang* 半兩	"Half ounce" (the weight of a standard Han coin): approximately 7.5 grams, or ¼ ounce
2 *ban liang* = 1 *liang* 兩	"Ounce": approximately 15 grams, or ½ ounce
16 *liang* = 1 *jin* 斤	"Catty": approximately 245 grams, or a bit more than ½ pound
30 *jin* = 1 *jun* 鈞	Approximately 7.4 kilograms, or 16 pounds
4 *jun* = 1 *dan* 石 (note special pronunciation of 石, usually pronounced *shi*)	Approximately 29.5 kilograms, or 65 pounds
Volume	
1 *ge* 合	Approximately 20 cubic centimeters, or 4 teaspoons
10 *ge* = 1 *sheng* 升	Approximately 200 cubic centimeters, or ⅞ cup
10 *sheng* = 1 *dou* 斗	Approximately 2 liters, or ½ gallon
10 *dou* = 1 *hu* 斛	"Bushel": approximately 20 liters, or 5 gallons
Length	
1 *fen* 分	Approximately 0.23 centimeter, or 1⁄10 inch
10 *fen* = 1 *cun* 寸	"Inch": approximately 2.3 centimeters, or 29⁄32 inch
10 *cun* = 1 *chi* 尺	"Foot": approximately 23 centimeters, or 9 inches
6 *chi* = 1 *bu* 步	"Double-pace": approximately 140 centimeters, or 54 inches
8 *chi* = 1 *xun* 尋 (or *ren* 仞)	"Fathom": approximately 185 centimeters, or 6 feet
10 *chi* = 1 *zhang* 丈	Sometimes (loosely) "fathom": Approximately 230 centimeters, or 7½ feet
2 *xun* = 1 *chang* 常	Approximately 370 centimeters, or 12 feet
4 *zhang* = 1 *pi* 匹	Approximately 920 centimeters, or 30 feet (the length of a standard [2 *chi*-wide] bolt of silk for tax purposes)
1 *li* 里	Approximately 0.4 kilometer, or ⅓ mile
Area	
1 *mu* (or *mou*) 畝	Approximately 67 square meters, or ⅙ acre (7,300 square feet)
100 *mu* = 1 *qing* 頃	Approximately 6,700 square meters (6.7 hectares), or 16.7 acres

inches. Table 9 gives rough approximations of the value of weights and measures in the early Han period. Many such tables give conversion figures specified to two or three decimal places.[2] Aside from the practical difficulties of computing values with such precision on the basis of textual records and archaeological artifacts, such spurious accuracy can be confusing rather than enlightening. The real utility of tables like these, we feel, is to create a practical mental image of the values of weights and measures mentioned in the text.

John S. Major

2. See, for example, Denis Twitchett and Michael Loewe, eds., *The Ch'in and Han Empires, 221 B.C.–A.D. 220*, vol. 1 of *The Cambridge History of China* (Cambridge: Cambridge University Press, 1986).

Appendix C

A CONCISE TEXTUAL HISTORY OF THE *HUAINANZI* AND A BIBLIOGRAPHY OF *HUAINANZI* STUDIES

A NUMBER of observations about the textual history of the *Huainanzi* can be made with relative certainty.[1] The first is that the surviving evidence testifies to a continuous transmission of the text from the time of its creation and presentation to Han emperor Wu in 139 B.C.E. Prior to the evidence provided by the many editions from the early Ming period (1368–1644), the testimony to this transmission comes principally from historical sources such as the *Shiji* and *Han shu* and the bibliographical monographs (*yiwenzhi* 藝文志) of the dynastic histories. These sources mention a work in twenty-one chapters being produced at the court of Huainan during the decade of the 140s B.C.E. as one of a trilogy of philosophical works ("inner," "middle," and "outer" books) written at Huainan and the only one to have been presented to the imperial court in Chang'an. Early copies of the work included this imperial recension and others recovered and taken to the imperial library by Liu De 劉德, father of the famous bibliographer Liu Xiang 劉向, after the fall of Huainan in 122 B.C.E. Liu Xiang is said to have combined the extant copies into one recension that undoubtedly was the one transmitted through the Han and into later periods. Earlier scholarly debate on whether or not the entire work was written by one person, Liu An, or by the team of eight scholars mentioned in the Gao You preface under the direction of Liu An, has now been resolved in favor of the latter

1. The following is a very short overview of the history of the text of the *Huainanzi*. This is discussed is much greater detail in Roth 1992. For a review article, see David Honey, "Philology, Filiation, and Bibliography in the Textual Criticism of the *Huai-nan Tzu*," *Early China* 19 (1994): 161–92.

position.[2] After our many years of working on the *Huainanzi*, we also agree with this conclusion, although we think it likely that the last chapter, the postface, was written by Liu.

Early commentaries attest to the popularity of the work among Han intellectuals, including Ma Rong 馬融 (77–166); Lu Zhi 盧植 (d. 192); Xu Shen 許慎 (58–148?), who wrote the etymological dictionary *Shuowen jiezi* 說文解字; and Gao You 高誘 (fl. 160–220), who also wrote a commentary on the *Lüshi chunqiu*. The latter two commentaries are the only ones that survived and only in fragmentary form. The original title of the Xu recension was *Huainan honglie jiangu* 淮南鴻烈間詁 (*The Vast and Luminous* [*Book*] *of Huainan, with Inserted Explanations*), suggesting that it contained commentaries interspersed throughout the text, either within or above the lines on the page.[3] The original title of the Gao recension was *Huainan honglie jiejing* 淮南鴻烈解經 (*The Vast and Luminous* [*Book*] *of Huainan, with Classical Explanations*), indicating that Gao had explained the meaning of the text using ideas from the Confucian classics.[4] In addition, each chapter title of the Gao recension was followed by the character *xun* 訓 (to explicate), as in, for example, 原道訓, "Originating in the Way, Explicated." With this, Gao was paying homage to his teacher Lu Zhi, from whom, he says, he received the explications of the text.[5] This character is not, as some have thought, part of the chapter titles in Liu An's original work or those of the other recensions of the text.

The two independent commentarial traditions (each with its own recension of the text and commentary) were conflated at some point, perhaps as early as the fourth century C.E. or even earlier.[6] To the best of our knowledge, by the end of the Northern Song dynasty, all editions contained this conflated commentary and recension of the text. Thirteen chapters were from the Gao recension (which itself contained some comments by Xu), and eight chapters were from the Xu recension. In all the extant editions, the Gao commentary is found in chapters 1–9, 13, 16, 17, and 19, and the Xu commentary is now found in chapters 10–12, 14, 15, 18, 20, and 21. In some editions, seven of the longest chapters are divided in half (chapters 1–5, 9, and 13), making a redaction of twenty-eight rather than twenty-one chapters. All these are Gao recension chapters, whose additional length is partly caused by the comparative

2. Roth 1992, 18–25.

3. Roth 1992, 36–39.

4. Roth 1992, 42–43.

5. In his preface, now found in most editions of the *Huainanzi*, Gao states that in his youth he studied the text with his teacher Lu Zhi and from him received the proper punctuation and meanings. In the year 205, after the Yellow Turban rebellion subsided and he was posted to the district of Puyang (now in Hebei), he returned to work on this text because he feared that few in his times were studying it any more. In doing this, he "deeply pondered the explications of his former master [Lu Zhi]" (深思先師之訓).

6. Roth 1992, 80–112, explores the question of the completeness of the original Gao commentary. In his preface, Gao notes that he lent eight chapters of his own original commentary to a friend who then suddenly died, and Gao never got them back. He rather vaguely states that he "later supplemented his losses," which has led several scholars to suggest that he did so by adding eight chapters from the Xu recension. The evidence that he did this is vexed, but it is clear that within two centuries the conflated recension of thirteen Gao and eight Xu chapters had already been created.

length and frequency of the Gao commentary. Some extant editions still follow this division, as discussed later. Only a few editions survive from these earlier periods (only one complete and one fragmentary). But by the early Ming dynasty, with its flourishing printing trade, the number of editions of the *Huainanzi* proliferated. Accordingly, the textual history of the work now is the history and filiation of its many editions.

Main Editions of the Text

The more than eighty-seven complete editions of the *Huainanzi* can be organized into six distinct lineages, with an "ancestral redaction" at the head of each one.[7] These redactions, the oldest extant editions in each of these lineages, are the following.

The Northern Song Redaction of 1050

The Northern Song redaction is a twenty-one-chapter edition that was originally printed around 1050. It remained in private collections and thus had little or no influence on the textual transmission of the *Huainanzi* until the nineteenth century, during which several traced facsimile copies were made. Unfortunately, in the copying, random errors were introduced into the text that were not in the original.[8] One of these copies, made in 1872 by Liu Maosheng 劉泖生, was the edition reprinted in the *Sibu congkan* 四部總刊, and it is known to us today in this edition and several facsimiles. The original exemplar was in the rare book collection of the Library of the Southern Manchuria Railroad Company when the Russian army entered Dalian at the close of World War II in 1945 and has not been seen since then. The Northern Song redaction is one of the most important editions of the text because it preserves so many early and accurate readings, yet it is not without errors.

The *Daozang* 道藏 Redaction of 1445

The very long history of the inclusion of the *Huainanzi* among the canonical works of the *Daozang* (*Daoist Patrology*) goes back to the Southern Song recension of 1121, the Northern Song recension of 1019, and possibly earlier.[9] In 1923, the Hanfenlou and Commercial Press in Shanghai began a three-year project to make a photolithographic reproduction of the one extant complete exemplar of the *Daozang*

7. For a complete analysis of the editions of the *Huainanzi*, see Roth 1992, 113–342.

8. Roth 1992, 137–41.

9. Roth 1992, 145–48. Chen Guofu, a renowned Daoist Patrology scholar, states that many of the taboo characters from this Southern Song recension are preserved in the 1445 recension. Earlier recensions of the patrology were made in 1019 and around 725. Roth lists four characters in the 1445 *Daozang* edition of the *Huainanzi* that preserves Northern Song taboos, thereby indicating a possible provenance in the 1019 recension.

recension of 1445, the one that is still preserved in the White Cloud Temple in Beijing. A number of exemplars of the 1445 *Daozang* were given to Daoist monasteries and temples throughout the land, but their circulation among non-Daoist literati was limited. Thus this twenty-eight-chapter recension of the *Huainanzi* had only limited influence during the Ming dynasty and even less influence during the Qing. Four editions based completely on this *Daozang Huainanzi* were published during the Ming and only one during the Qing.[10] Because of the *Daozang Huainanzi* redaction's superior readings, probably attributable to its Song or even Tang ancestry, this is one of the most reliable of the ancestral redactions. Nonetheless, it too is not without errors.

The Liu Ji 劉績 Redaction of 1501

The Liu Ji redaction in twenty-eight chapters, published in 1501, is in some ways the most interesting edition of the *Huainanzi*. Liu, a scholar and official from Jiangxia in Hubei Province who passed the metropolitan exam in 1490, was a brilliant textual scholar who was interested in Chinese science and produced a new edition of the *Guanzi*.[11] The significance of his *Huainanzi* redaction comes in large part from his subcommentary in which he discussed both the meaning of passages and the text-critical decisions he was making. His redaction has caused considerable scholarly controversy about its provenance.[12] Liu mentions that he used three earlier editions to make his new one: an "old edition," an "other edition," and a "different edition." The first shows affinities with the 1445 *Daozang* redaction but probably was closer to the redaction in the *Daoist Patrology* recension of 1019. The second is distinctly different from both the Northern Song and *Daozang* redactions but otherwise cannot be identified. The third edition varies significantly from the other two editions and shares meanings with the quotations from the Xu recension of the *Huainanzi* preserved in the encyclopedia *Taiping yulan* (published in 983); it thus appears to be quite old.[13] This redaction has had a regrettably minor influence on later editions, with only seven descendants, none of which is later than 1670. It now is available only on microfilm from an exemplar in the National Central Library in Taibei. Its lack of popularity may well be due to the sheer size and complexity of the Liu subcommentary.

The *Zhongli siziji* 中立四子集 Redaction of 1579

The *Zhongli siziji*, a twenty-eight-chapter redaction of the *Huainanzi*, is one of four works published in this collection, along with the *Laozi*, *Zhuangzi*, and *Guanzi*. This

10. Roth 1992, 148–62.

11. Roth 1992, 163–65.

12. For details, see Roth 1992, 165–73. Note that D. C. Lau believes that the Liu Ji redaction is largely derived from the *Daozang* redaction and that its unique textual variants were caused by Liu's unindicated emendation and conflation. Roth, however, disagrees with him.

13. For details about the research leading to these conclusions, see Roth 1992, 173–87.

collection was compiled after a change in districting under the first Ming emperor in 1373, in which the ancestral homes of these four famous philosophers were included in the same prefecture of Anhui Province, whose capital city had briefly been named Zhongli at that time. Although construction of a Ming "central capital" was begun there in 1370, it was abandoned five years later, and its name was changed to Fengyang 鳳陽 in 1375. The supervising editor for the project was a scholar and official named Zhu Dongguang 朱東光 (fl. ca. 1540–1585). Careful research has demonstrated that this redaction, which has no descendants, was created by conflating readings in two earlier editions: the Wang Ying 王鎣 edition of 1536 from the Liu Ji lineage and the Anzheng tang 安正堂 edition of 1533 from the *Daozang* lineage.[14] Because it is completely derived from two earlier ancestral redactions, it does not have to be consulted when creating a modern critical edition.

The Mao Yigui 茅一桂 Redaction of 1580

The Mao Yigui redaction was extremely prolific, with thirty descendants, and is thus one of the most influential editions of the *Huainanzi*.[15] Its descendants include the Mao Kun 茅坤 edition of 1590, the beautifully executed Wang Yiluan 汪一鸞 edition of 1591, and the *Siku quanshu* 四庫全書 edition of 1781. It is the ultimate source of all the extant twenty-one-chapter editions of the text that are not reprints of the Northern Song redaction, which means most of them. Its own provenance is rather complicated. Mao (fl. ca. 1555–1615) was the nephew of the famous statesman and philosopher Mao Kun (1512–1601); both hailed from Gui'an 歸安 in northern Zhejiang Province. Mao Yigui passed the provincial exams in 1588 but failed to rise any higher and held a succession of minor official posts in far-off districts during his career. Along with his senior collaborator, Wen Bo 溫博 from Wucheng 烏程 in Zhejiang Province, Mao established an edition with a unique arrangement of text and abridged commentary that was a conflation of three earlier editions.[16] One of these was the *Daozang* redaction, and another was the Wang Ying edition of the Liu Ji redaction, both of which have twenty-eight chapters. The identity of the third edition is significant because it must have had the twenty-one-chapter arrangement that Mao adopted and must have been his basic text. There is reason to believe that this third edition was the actual exemplar of the Northern Song redaction that was transmitted into the twentieth century, which was likely in a private collection in Wucheng at that time.[17] If it was not, then it must be from an edition closely related to the Northern Song redaction, given its distinct textual variants. Because the Mao Yigui redaction is likely to have been derived completely from older extant ancestral redactions, its independent testimony to the text of the *Huainanzi* is minimal.

14. For details about these editions, see Roth 1992, 194–200, 154–55, respectively. The provenance of the *Zhongli* edition is presented on 212–24.

15. These editions are identified and affiliated in Roth 1992, 235–70.

16. Details about the creation and provenance of this redaction can be found in Roth 1992, 225–35.

17. For this intriguing possibility, see Roth 1992, 234.

The Zhuang Kuiji 莊逵吉 Redaction of 1788

The twenty-one-chapter Zhuang Kuiji redaction greatly influenced twentieth-century editions and studies of the *Huainanzi* because of its relatively late creation during the Qing period and its eighteen descendants. Among these were several widely circulated collections and editions, including the Zhejiang Publishing Company's 1876 *Ershierzi* 二十二子 edition, the 1923 critical edition of Liu Wendian 劉文典, and the 1935 steel-movable-type edition in the collection *Sibu beiyao* 四部備要. The editor of the Zhuang Kuiji redaction, Zhuang Kuiji (1760–1813), was a young scholar who was born into an important family in the district of Wujin in Jiangsu Province. He was a student of the famous textual scholar Bi Yuan (1730–1797) and served under him in the Shenxi provincial capital of Xi'an when Bi was governor.[18] While governor, Bi assembled in his office some of the luminaries of the Han Learning textual movement, and Zhuang undoubtedly benefited from his position as a junior scholar among them.[19] In addition to establishing a new edition of the text, Zhuang wrote a subcommentary in which he cited variant readings, gave textual emendations, and explained some difficult passages in the text.[20]

The provenance of Zhuang's edition is complex, but it appears to have been based directly on a hand-collated exemplar of the Mao Kun edition of 1590 produced by his mentor, the Han Learning scholar Qian Dian 錢坫 (1744–1806). Qian added emendations from a number of other Ming editions: the Mao Yigui redaction, the *Zhongli* redaction, the *Yejinshan* 葉近山 edition of 1582 (a poor-quality reprint of the *Daozang* redaction), and perhaps the *Daozang* redaction itself. Using this method, Qian supplemented the abridged commentary in the Mao lineage until it was almost complete.[21] Unfortunately, Zhuang's redaction, although influential, is, in the last analysis, rather poor compared with the early Ming editions. It is based on a mediocre edition that contains textual errors and adds many hidden emendations and conflations.[22] Since Zhuang's redaction seems wholly derived from still extant editions and since it introduces many new errors into them, the possibility that it contains any accurate readings not in the other ancestral redactions is almost nonexistent. Thus despite its wide circulation, it need not be consulted to make a modern critical edition of the *Huainanzi*.

Because the *Zhongli* and the extremely prolific Mao Yigui and Zhuang Kuiji redactions and their descendants are derived from other extant redactions, none of these more than fifty editions are likely to contain possibly accurate variant readings not

18. Roth 1992, 271–74.

19. For an interesting study of the significance of the challenging of traditional readings and attributions of texts made by the Han Learning movement, see Benjamin Elman, *From Philosophy to Philology: Intellectual and Social Aspects of Change in Late Imperial China* (Cambridge, Mass.: Harvard University Press, 1985).

20. Roth 1992, 274–77.

21. Roth 1992, 277–83.

22. Roth 1992, 283–86.

already present in the Northern Song, *Daozang*, and Liu Ji redactions. Thus only these three need be consulted for a new critical edition.

Modern Critical Editions

In addition to using the three oldest ancestral redactions of the *Huainanzi*, a modern critical edition should include the emendations of the major textual scholars of the nineteenth and twentieth centuries.[23] Using a variety of scholarly techniques but often working on the inferior later editions of the *Huainanzi*—those in the Mao Yigui and Zhuang Kuiji lineages—Qing and Republican scholars nonetheless provided invaluable emendations that go well beyond corrections based on collations with the superior editions that were rare during their time but that are now well known, such as the Northern Song and *Daozang* redactions. The first published attempts to collect nineteenth-century textual critics of the *Huainanzi* were made in Japan in 1914 by Hattori Unokichi 服部宇之吉. Less than a decade later, more complete critical editions were compiled almost simultaneously in China by two scholars, Liu Wendian 劉文典 and Liu Jiali 劉家立. The Hattori edition was based on the 1798 Kubo Chikusui 久保筑水 edition from the Mao Yigui lineage, and it was combined with the *Daozang* redaction and one of its later editions in the *Daozang jiyao* 輯要 collection of 1796.[24] The Hattori edition includes the textual notes of Tokugawa scholars from the Kubo edition but not the Kubo edition's detailed comparisons with other editions. The textual emendations of the major Qing critics Wang Niansun 王念孫, and Yu Yue 俞樾 are included in this edition.

Liu Wendian's *Huainan honglie jijie* 淮南鴻烈集解 was completed in 1921 and published in 1923. It includes textual emendations by twenty-two of the most important Qing-dynasty textual critics, including Wang Niansun and his son Wang Yinzhi 王引之, Gu Guangqi 顧廣圻, and Yu Yue.[25] Liu Jiali's *Huainan jizheng* 淮南集證 was completed in 1921 and published in 1924 and seems to have been written independently. It cites sixteen Qing critics, many of the most important of whom are also found in Liu Wendian's work.[26] Both critical editions were likely based on the Zhejiang Publishing Company's edition of the Zhuang Kuiji redaction published in the *Ershierzi* (*Twenty-two Philosophers*) collection in 1876. Because Liu Wendian's work included more Qing textual scholars, it became much more widely circulated

23. Complete bibliographical data on all these modern critical editions are presented later in a separate section. For a discussion of the principles of establishing a modern critical edition, see Harold D. Roth, "Text and Edition in Early Chinese Philosophical Literature," *Journal of the American Oriental Society* 113, no. 2 (1993): 214–27.

24. Roth 1992, 311. The Kubo edition is on 267–68.

25. Roth 1992, 296–302, presents the provenance and assessment of this extremely widespread and thus influential edition.

26. Roth 1992, 302–8, discusses the provenance and assessment of this early critical edition. Between them, the two Lius offer a total of twenty-eight Qing textual critics in their editions. Unfortunately Liu Jiali's has, to my knowledge, never been reprinted, so it is difficult to consult today.

than Liu Jiali's, and it has been reprinted a number of times in different collections. It has also been quite popular with Western translators, serving as the basic text for the translations by Evan Morgan, Roger Ames, John Major, Claude Larre, Isabelle Robinet, and most other modern Western scholars, including Charles Le Blanc, Rémi Mathieu, and colleagues. Unfortunately, the original Zhuang Kuiji redaction had many textual errors, only some of which were corrected in later editions. Despite the convenience of its inclusion of so many Qing textual critics, since it was based on a derivative and flawed edition, there are better editions to use as the basis for translation.

The political and social upheavals in China and Japan undoubtedly influenced the fact that no new critical editions of note were published for half a century after the works of Liu Wendian and Liu Jiali. In 1974, Tokyo University professors Togawa Yoshiro 戸川芳郎, Kiyama Hideo 木山英雄, and Sawaya Harutsugu 澤谷昭次 produced a critical edition derived from the Northern Song and *Daozang* redactions and the Liu Wendian edition. Major Qing textual scholars from Liu are included. Waseda University professor Kusuyama Haruki 楠山春樹 compiled a three-volume critical edition published between 1979 and 1988. It is based on Liu Wendian's edition with emendations from the Northern Song and *Daozang* redactions and Liu's assembled textual scholars. Both editions contain modern Japanese translations.[27]

Three modern critical editions were published in China during the next decade:

1. Chen Yiping's 陈一平 *Huainanzi jiao zhu yi* 淮南子校・注・译, published in 1994, is based on Liu Wendian's edition and collated with nine other editions, including the Northern Song redaction. Chen also includes text critical comments by twenty-two Qing, Republican, and modern scholars, including Wang Niansun, Yu Yue, and Tao Fangqi.
2. Zhang Shuangdi's 張雙棣 *Huainanzi jiaoshi* 淮南校釋 was published in 1997. Zhang's base edition is the *Daozang* redaction, and it is collated with twelve other editions, including all the other ancestral redactions and the Liu Wendian critical edition. Zhang also made emendations drawing on the work of eighty-four textual scholars, including Wang Shumin 王叔岷, the dean of twentieth-century textual critics, and his younger followers Zheng Liangshu 鄭良樹 and Yu Dacheng 于大成.
3. He Ning's 何寧 *Huainanzi jishi* 淮南子集釋, published in 1998, uses the Zhejiang reprint of the Zhuang Kuiji redaction as the base text and corrects its readings by comparing them with the Northern Song, *Daozang*, *Zhongli*, and Mao Yigui redactions. He made further emendations based on a long list of Ming, Qing, and twentieth-century scholars given in a very useful bibliographical appendix. He Ning also includes the same major modern scholars as Zhang Shuangdi does.

Of the three Chinese editions, Zhang's is the most reliable because it is based on the high-quality *Daozang* redaction and presents its material in a clear and reader-

27. These two important Japanese critical editions are discussed in Roth 1992, 311–12.

friendly format. He's and Zhang's critical editions are superb because of the breadth of the editions cited and the wide variety of textual scholars included. Along with Kusuyama's work, these were the editions we most often consulted for our translation when we had difficulty understanding our basic edition.

The modern critical edition we used as the basis of our translation was D. C. Lau's *Huainanzi zhuzi suoyin* 淮南子逐字索引 of 1992, included in the Chinese University of Hong Kong's Institute of Chinese Studies Ancient Chinese Text Concordance Series. This Lau edition has all the basic elements of a modern critical text: it is based on the *Sibu congkan* edition of the Northern Song redaction but is collated with the other major ancestral redactions, the *Daozang* and the Liu Ji. Lau also consulted all the major nineteenth- and twentieth-century textual critics and a wide variety of other works. Added to that, of course, is the fact that Lau and his research team created a concordance to every character in the text—133,827, to be exact. The main drawbacks to Lau's work are the absence of the Gao and Xu commentaries and its sometimes questionable punctuation and sectioning. But this invaluable work will be the standard for the foreseeable future.

The following bibliography includes all translations of the *Huainanzi* into Western languages and many of the recent modern Chinese translations. These are followed by a list of the modern critical editions just discussed. Next comes a bibliography of publications on the philosophy of the *Huainanzi*, whose number has increased dramatically in the past several decades as more scholars have turned their attention to this too-long-overlooked masterpiece. The bibliography concludes with a list of the major pre-1960 textual and historical studies of the *Huainanzi* and a bibliography of such works since 1960. Studies published in the past fifty years are likely to be the most accessible for scholars wishing to pursue further research. These bibliographies are fairly complete but by no means exhaustive. For a full bibliography of textual and historical works as of 1990, see Harold D. Roth, *The Textual History of the Huai-nan Tzu*.

Translations into Western Languages

Ames, Roger T. *The Art of Rulership: A Study of Ancient Chinese Political Thought*. Honolulu: University of Hawai'i Press, 1983. Reprint, Albany: State University of New York Press, 1994. [Chap. 9]

Ames, Roger T., and D. C Lau. *Yuan Dao: Tracing Dao to Its Source*. Classics of Ancient China. New York: Ballantine Books, 1998. [Chap. 1]

Balfour, Frederic Henry. "The Principles of Nature; a Chapter from the 'History of Great Light' by Huai-nan-Tze, Prince of Kiang-Ling." *China Review*, no. 9 (1880–1881): 281–97. [Chap. 1]

——. *Taoist Texts: Ethical, Political and Speculative*. London: Trubner, 1884; Shanghai: Kelly & Walsh, 1884. [Includes chap. 1]

Birdwhistell, [Jo] Anne [née Joanne Letitia Davison]. "A Translation of Chapter 17 (Shuolin) of the *Huainanzi*." Master's thesis, Stanford University, 1968.

Chatley, Herbert. "*Huai-nan-tsu* Chapter Three." Draft translation, ca. 1939. Original typescript in the Needham Research Institute Library, Cambridge, England.

Erkes, Eduard. "Das Weltbild des *Huai-nan-Tze*." *Ostasiens Zeitschrift*, no. 5 (1916–1917): 27–80. [Chap. 4]

Harper, Donald. "*Huai-nan Tzu* Chapter 10: Translation and Prolegomena." Master's thesis, University of California, Berkeley, 1978.

Kraft, Eva. "Zum *Huai-nan-Tzu*. Enfürung, Übersetzung (Kapitel I und II) und Interpretation." *Monumenta Serica*, no. 16 (1957): 191–286; no. 17 (1958): 128–207.

Larre, Claude. *Le Traité VII du Houai Nan Tseu: Les ésprits légers et subtils animateurs de l'essence: Analyse des structures d'expression et traduction, avec notes et commentaires, de la partie doctrinale du traité VII du Houai Nan Tseu (HNT VII, 1a–7a)*. Variétés sinologiques, vol. 67. Taibei: Institut Ricci, 1982.

Larre, Claude, Isabelle Robinet, and Elisabeth Rochat de la Vallée. *Les Grands Traités du Huainanzi*. Variétés sinologiques, vol. 75. Paris: Institut Ricci, 1993. [Chaps. 1, 7, 11, 13, 18]

Le Blanc, Charles. *Huai-nan Tzu: Philosophical Synthesis in Early Han Thought: The Idea of Resonance (Kan-ying) with a Translation and Analysis of Chapter Six*. Hong Kong: Hong Kong University Press, 1985.

Le Blanc, Charles, and Rémi Mathieu, eds. *Philosophes taoïstes*. Vol. 2, *Huainan zi: Texte traduit, présenté et annoté*. Bibliothèque de la Pléiade. Paris: Éditions Gallimard, 2003. [Complete translation]

Major, John S. *Heaven and Earth in Early Han Thought: Chapters Three, Four and Five of the Huainanzi*. SUNY Series in Chinese Philosophy and Culture. Albany: State University of New York Press, 1993.

——. "Topography and Cosmology in Early Han Thought: Chapter Four of the *Huai-nan Tzu*." Ph.D. diss., Harvard University, 1973.

Morgan, Evan S. "The Operations and Manifestations of the Tao Exemplified in History." *Journal of the North China Branch of the Royal Asiatic Society*, no. 52 (1921): 1–39. [Chap. 12]

——. *Tao, the Great Luminant: Essays from Huai-nan Tzu*. 1933. Reprint, Taibei: Cheng Wen, 1974. [Chaps. 1, 2, 7, 8, 12 ,13, 15, 19]

Pomeranceva, Larisa E. *Pozdnie daosy o prirode obscestve i iskustve "Huainan'czy."* Moscow: University of Moscow, 1979. [Chaps. 1, 2, 6, 9, 21]

Ryden, Edmund. *Philosophy of Peace in Han China: A Study of the Huainanzi Ch. 15 on Military Strategy*. Taibei: Ricci Institute, 1998.

Sailey, Jay. "An Annotated Translation of *Huai Nan Tzu* Chapter XVI." Master's thesis, Stanford University, 1971.

Wallacker, Benjamin. *The Huai-nan-tzu, Book Eleven: Behavior, Culture and the Cosmos*. American Oriental Series, vol. 48. New Haven, Conn.: American Oriental Society, 1962.

Modern Chinese Translations

Chen Guangzhong 陈广忠. *Huainanzi yizhu* 淮南子译注. Zhongguo gudai mingzhu jinyi congshu 中國古代名著今譯叢書. Changchun: Jilin wenshi chubanshe, 1990.

Liu Kangde 劉康德. *Huainanzi zhijie* 淮南子直解. Shanghai: Fudan daxue, 2001.

Wang Ning 王宁, comp., and Wang Guiyuan 王贵元 and Ye Guigang 叶桂刚, eds. *Huainanzi* 淮南子. In *Pingxiben baihua Lüshi chunqiu, Huainanzi* 评析本白话吕氏春秋, 淮南子, 303–645. Beijing: Beijing guangbo xueyuan chubanshe, 1993.

Wu Guangping 吳广平 and Liu Wensheng 刘文生. *Baihua Huainanzi* 白话淮南子. Changsha: Yuelu shushe, 1998. [*Huainanzi* preface by Mao Dun 茅盾, 1925]
Xiong Lihui 熊禮匯. *Xinyi Huainanzi* 新譯淮南子. Taibei: Sanmin shuju, 1997.

Critical Editions

Chen Yiping 陈一平. *Huainanzi jiao zhu yi* 淮南子校・注・译. Guangzhou: Guangdong renmin chuban she, 1994. [Includes modern Chinese translation]
Hattori Unokichi 服部宇之吉. *Enanji* 淮南子. Kanbun taikei 漢文大系, vol. 20. Tokyo: Fuji Bookstore, 1914.
He Ning 何寧. *Huainanzi jishi* 淮南子集釋. Beijing: Zhonghua shuju, 1998.
Kusuyama Haruki 楠山春樹. *Enanji* 淮南子. Vols. 54, 55, 62. In *Shinshaku kanbun taikei* 新釋漢文大系. Tokyo: Meiji shōin, 1979–1988. [Includes modern Japanese translation]
Lau, D. C. *Huainanzi zhuzi suoyin* 淮南子逐字索引. Institute for Chinese Studies Chinese Text Concordance Series. Hong Kong: Commercial Press, 1992.
Liu Jiali 劉家立. *Huainan jizheng* 淮南集證. Shanghai: Zhonghua shuju, 1924.
Liu Wendian 劉文典. *Huainan honglie jijie* 淮南鴻烈集解. Shanghai: Commercial Press, 1923. Reprint, Feng Yi 馮逸 and Qiao Hua 喬華, eds. *Xinbian zhuzi jicheng* 新編諸子集成. Beijing : Zhonghua shuju, 1989. [Appends Liu Wendian's text-critical comments and lost *Huainanzi* passages from his work *Sanyu zhaji*, along with Qian Tang's *Huainan tianwenxun buzhu*]
Togawa Yoshirō 戸川芳郎, Kiyama Hideo 木山英雄, and Sawaya Harutsugu 澤谷昭次. *Enanji* 淮南子. In *Chūgoku koten bungaku taikei* 中國古典文學大系, vol. 6. 1974. Reprint, Tokyo: Heibonsha, 1978. [Includes modern Japanese translation]
Zhang Shuangdi 張雙棣. *Huainanzi jiaoshi* 淮南子校釋. Beijing: Beijing University Press, 1997.

Philosophy of the *Huainanzi*

Alt, Wayne. "The *Huai-nan Tzu* Alteration." *Journal of Chinese Philosophy* 20, no. 1 (1993): 73–86.
Ames, Roger T. "Wu-Wei in the 'Art of Rulership' Chapter of *Huai-nan Tzu*: Its Sources and Philosophical Orientation." *Philosophy East and West* 31, no. 2 (1981): 193–213.
Arima Takuya 有馬卓也. *Enanji no seiji shisō* 淮南子の政治思想. Tokyo: Kyūko shoin, 1998.
Bai Guanghua 白光華. "Wo dui *Huainanzi* de yixie kanfa" 我對 «淮南子» 的一些看法. *Daojia wenhua yanjiu* 道家文化研究, no. 6 (1995): 192–99.
Chen Dehe 陳德和. *Huainanzi de zhexue* 淮南子的哲學. Renwen congshu, vol. 9, 945–46. Jiayi Xian, Dalinzhen: Nanhua guanli xueyuan, 1999.
Chen Jing 陈静. *Ziyou yu zhixu de kunhuo: "Huainanzi" yanjiu* 自由与秩序的困惑:「淮南子」研究. Kunming: Yunnan daxue chubanshe, 2004.
Chen Ligui 陳麗桂. "Cong chutu zhujian *Wenzi* kan gu, jinben *Wenzi* yu *Huainanzi* zhijiande xianhou guanxi ji jige sixiang lunti" 從出土竹簡《文子》看古、今本《文子》與《淮南子》之間的先後關系及幾個思想論題. *Zhexue yu Wenhua* 哲學與文化 23, no. 8 (1996): 1871–84.
——. "Daojia yangsheng guan zai Handai de yanbian yu zhuanhua—yi *Huainanzi, Laozi zhigui, Laozi He Shang gong zhangju, Laozi Xiang'er zhu* wei hexin" 道家養生觀在

漢代的演變與轉化—以《淮 南 子》、《老子指歸》、《老子河上公章句》、《老子想爾注》為核心. *Guowen xuebao* 國文學報, no. 39 (2006): 35–80.

——. "Huainan duo Chuyu: Lun *Huainanzi* de wenzi" 淮南多楚語—論淮南子的文字. *Hanxue yanjiu* 漢學研究 2, no. 1 (1984): 167–83.

——. "Shi jiu jin ben *Wenzi* yu *Huainanzi* de buchongxi neirong tuice guben *Wenzi* de ji ge sixiang lunti" 試就今本 «文子» 與 «淮南子» 的不重襲內容推測古本 «文子» 的幾個思想論題. *Daojia wenhua yanjiu* 道家文化研究, no. 18 (2000): 200–31.

Chen Yiping 陈一平. *Huiji gejia xueshuo de juzhu: "Huainanzi."* 汇集各家学说的巨著: 《淮南子》. Beijing: Zhongguo wenlian chuban gongsi, 1997.

Cullen, Christopher. "A Chinese Eratosthenes of the Flat Earth: A Study of a Fragment of Cosmology in *Huai Nan Tzu*." *Bulletin of the School of Oriental and African Studies* 39, no. 1 (1976): 106–27. [Revised and expanded version in John S. Major, *Heaven and Earth in Early Han Thought: Chapters Three, Four, and Five of the Huainanzi*. SUNY Series in Chinese Philosophy and Culture (Albany: State University of New York Press, 1993), 269–90]

Dai Shu 戴黍. *"Huainanzi" zhidao sixiang yanjiu* 《淮南子》 治道思想研究. Guangzhou: Zhongshan daxue chubanshe, 2005.

Davis, Tenney L. "The Dualistic Cosmogony of *Huai-Nan-Tzu* and Its Relations to the Background of Chinese and of European Alchemy." *Isis* 25, no. 2 (1936): 327–40.

Duan Qiuguan 段秋关. *"Huainanzi" yu Liu An de falü sixiang* "淮南子" 与刘安的法律思想. Beijing: Qunzhong chubanshe, 1986.

Fang Zushen 方祖燊. "*Huainanzi* yu qi zuozhe" 淮南子與其作者. *Zhongyang* 中央 1973.10:141–47.

Goldin, Paul Rakita. "Insidious Syncretism in the Political Philosophy of *Huai-Nan-Tzu*." *Asian Philosophy* 9, no. 3 (1999): 165–91.

Harlez, Charles Joseph de. "Textes taoistes." *Annales du Musée Guimet*, no. 20 (1891): 171–212.

Howard, Jeffrey A. "Concepts of Comprehensiveness and Historical Change in the *Huai-Nan-Tzu*." In *Explorations in Early Chinese Cosmology: Papers Presented at the Workshop on Classical Chinese Thought Held at Harvard University, August 1976*, edited by Henry Rosemont Jr., 119–32. Journal of the American Academy of Religion Studies, vol. 50, no. 2. 1984. Reprint, Charleston, S.C.: Booksurge, 2006

Hu Shi 胡適. *Huainanwang shu* 淮南王書. 1931. Reprint, Taibei: Taiwan shangwu yinshuguan, 1962.

Kanaya Osamu 金谷治. *Rōsō teki sekai: Enanji no shisō* 老莊的世界: 淮南子の思想. 1959. Reprint, Tokyo: Kōdansha, 1992.

Kandel, Barbara. "Der Versüch einer politischen Restauration: Liu An, der König von Huai-Nan." *Nachrichten der Gesellschaft für Natur- und Völkerkunde Ostasiens*, no. 113 (1973): 33–96.

Kohn, Livia. "Cosmology, Myth, and Philosophy in Ancient China: New Studies on the 'Huainan Zi.'" *Asian Folklore Studies* 53, no. 2 (1994): 319–36.

Kusuyama Haruki 楠山春樹. "*Enanji* yori mitaru *Sōshi* no seiritsu" 淮南子より見たる莊子の成立. *Filosofia*, no. 41 (1961): 41–68.

——. "Enanō '*Sōshi* ryakuyō' *Sōshi* kōkai' kō" 淮南王莊子略要莊子后解考. *Filosofia*, no. 38 (1960): 52–70.

Kuttner, Fritz A. "The 749-Temperament of *Huai Nan Tzu* (+ 123 B.C.)." *Asian Music* 6, nos. 1–2: (1975): 88–112. [Special issue: *Perspectives on Asian Music: Essays in Honor of Dr. Laurence E. R. Picken*]

Laloy, Louis. "Hoaî-Nân Tzè et la musique." *T'oung Pao* 15, nos. 1–5 (1914): 501–30.

Le Blanc, Charles. "From Cosmology to Ontology Through Resonance: A Chinese Interpretation of Reality." In *Beyond Textuality: Asceticism and Violence in Anthropological Interpretation*, edited by Gilles Bibeau and Ellen Corin, 57–77. Paris: Mouton de Bruyter, 1995.

——. "From Ontology to Cosmogony: Notes on Chuang Tzu and Huai-nan Tzu." In *Chinese Ideas About Nature and Society: Studies in Honour of Derk Bodde*, edited by Charles LeBlanc and Susan Blader, 117–29. Hong Kong: Hong Kong University Press, 1987.

——. *Huai-nan Tzu*. In *Early Chinese Texts: A Bibliographical Guide*, edited by Michael Loewe, 189–95. Early China Special Monograph, no. 2. Berkeley, Calif.: Society for the Study of Early China and Institute of East Asian Studies, 1993.

——. *Huai-nan Tzu: Philosophical Synthesis in Early Han Thought: The Idea of Resonance (Kan-ying) with a Translation and Analysis of Chapter Six*. Hong Kong: Hong Kong University Press, 1985.

Le Blanc, Charles, and Rémi Mathieu. *Mythe et philosophie à l'aube de la Chine impériale: Études sur Le Huainanzi*. Montréal: Presses de l'Université de Montréal, 1992; Paris: De Boccard, 1992.

Li Zeng 李增. *Huainanzi zhexue sixiang yanjiu* 淮南子哲學思想研究 [original title: *Huainanzi sixiang zhi yanjiu lunwen ji* 淮南子思想之研究論文集]. Taibei: Hongxie wenhua shiye, 1997.

Liu Dehan 劉德漢. *Huainanzi yu Laozi canzheng* 淮南子與老子参證. Taibei: Lexue shuju, 2001.

Liu Xiaogan 劉笑敢. "*Huainanzi* and Wu-Wei (Non-Action)." In *Contacts Between Cultures*. Vol. 3, *Eastern Asia: Literature and Humanities*, edited by Bernard Hung-Kay Luk and Barry D. Steben, 28–30. Lewiston, N.Y.: Edwin Mellen, 1992.

——. "Wuwei (Non-Action): From *Laozi* to *Huainanzi*." *Taoist Resources* 3 (1991): 41–56.

Loewe, Michael. "Huang Lao Thought and the *Huainanzi*." *Journal of the Royal Asiatic Society*, 3rd ser., 4, no. 3 (1994): 377–95.

Major, John S. "Animals and Animal Metaphors in *Huainanzi*." *Asia Major*, 3rd ser., 21, no. 1 (2008): 133–51.

——. "Astrology in the *Huai-nan Tzu* and Some Related Texts." *Society for the Study of Chinese Religions Bulletin*, no. 8 (1980): 20–31.

——. "Celestial Cycles and Mathematical Harmonics in the *Huainanzi*." *Extrême-orient / Extrême-occident* 16 (1994): 121–34 .

——. "The Five Phases, Magic Squares, and Schematic Cosmography." In *Explorations in Early Chinese Cosmology: Papers Presented at the Workshop on Classical Chinese Thought Held at Harvard University, August 1976*, edited by Henry Rosemont Jr., 133–66. Journal of the American Academy of Religion Studies, vol. 50, no. 2. 1984. Reprint, Charleston, S.C.: Booksurge, 2006

——. "Numerology in the *Huai-nan Tzu*." In *Sagehood and Systematizing Thought in Warring States and Han China*, ed. Kidder Smith, 3–10. Brunswick, Maine: Bowdoin College Asian Studies Program, 1990.

——. "Substance, Process, Phase: *Wuxing* in the *Huainanzi*." In *Chinese Texts and Philosophical Contexts: Essays Dedicated to Angus C. Graham*, edited by Henry Rosemont Jr., 67–78. La Salle, Ill.: Open Court Press, 1991.

Mou Zhongjian 牟鐘鑒. "*Huainanzi* dui *Lüshi chunqiu* de jicheng he fahui" «淮南子» 對 «呂氏春秋» 的繼承和發揮. *Daojia wenhua yanjiu* 道家文化研究, no. 14 (1998): 338–52.

Murray, Judson. "The Consummate Dao: The 'Way' (Dao) and 'Human Affairs' (*shi*) in the *Huainanzi*." Ph.D. diss., Brown University, 2007.

——. "A Study of 'Yaolüe' 要略, 'A Summary of the Essentials': Understanding the *Huainanzi* Through the Point of View of the Author of the Postface." *Early China* 29 (2004): 45–110.

Pan Yuting 潘雨廷. "Lun shang Huanglao yu *Huainanzi*" 論尚黃老與«淮南子». *Daojia wenhua yanjiu* 道家文化研究, no. 1 (1992): 214–29.

Parker, E. H. "Hwai-Nan-Tsz, Philosopher and Prince." *New China Review*, no. 1 (1919): 505–21.

——. "Some More of Hwai-Nan-Tsz's Ideas." *New China Review*, no. 2 (1920): 551–62.

Pfizmaier, August. "Die Könige von Hoai-Nan aus dem Hause Han." *Sitzungsberichte der Akademie der Wissenschaften Wien, Philosophisch-Historische Klasse*, no. 39 (1862): 575–618.

Pokora, Timoteus. "The Notion of Coldness in *Huai-Nan-Tzu*." *Nachrichten der Gesellschaft für Natur- und Völkerkunde Ostasiens*, no. 125 (1979): 69–74.

Puett, Michael. "Aligning and Orienting the Cosmos: Anthropomorphic Gods and Theomorphic Humans in the *Huainanzi*." Chapter 7 in *To Become a God: Cosmology, Sacrifice, and Self-Divination in Early China*. Cambridge, Mass.: Harvard University Press, 2002.

——. "Violent Misreadings: The Hermeneutics of Cosmology in the *Huainanzi*." *Bulletin of the Museum of Far Eastern Antiquities* 72 (2000): 29–47.

Queen, Sarah A. "The Creation and Domestication of the Techniques of Lao-Zhuang: Anecdotal Narrative and Philosophical Argumentation in *Huainanzi* Chapter 12, 'Reponses of the Way' (Dao Ying 道 應)." *Asia Major*, 3rd ser., 21, no. 1 (2008): 201–47.

——. "Inventories of the Past: Re-Thinking the 'School' Affiliation of the *Huainanzi*." *Asia Major*, 3rd ser., 14, no. 1 (2001): 51–72.

Rosemont, Henry, Jr. *Explorations in Early Chinese Cosmology: Papers Presented at the Workshop on Classical Chinese Thought Held at Harvard University, August 1976*. Journal of the American Academy of Religion Studies, vol. 50, no. 2. 1984. Reprint, Charleston, S.C.: Booksurge, 2006.

Roth, Harold D. "The Early Taoist Concept of *Shen:* A Ghost in the Machine?" In *Sagehood and Systematizing Thought in Warring States and Han China*, edited by Kidder Smith, 11–32. Brunswick, Maine: Bowdoin College Asian Studies Program, 1990.

——. "Evidence for Stages of Meditation in Early Taoism." *Bulletin of the School of Oriental and African Studies* 60, no. 2 (1997): 295–314.

——. "Nature and Self-Cultivation in *Huainanzi*'s "Original Way." In *Polishing the Chinese Mirror: Essays in Honor of Henry Rosemont Jr.*, edited by Marthe Chandler and Ronnie Littlejohn, 270–92. New York: Global Scholarly Publications, 2008.

——. "Psychology and Self-Cultivation in Early Taoistic Thought." *Harvard Journal of Asiatic Studies* 51, no. 2 (1991): 599–650.

——. "Who Compiled the *Chuang Tzu*?" In *Chinese Texts and Philosophical Contexts: Essays Dedicated to Angus C. Graham*, edited by Henry Rosemont Jr., 79–128. La Salle, Ill.: Open Court Press, 1991.

Shen Jinhua 沈晋华. *Huainanzi jianyan lu* 淮南子箴言录. Beijing: Beijing guangbo xueyuan chubanshe, 1992.

Van Ess, Hans. "Argument and Persuasion in the First Chapter of *Huainanzi* and Its Use of Particles." *Oriens Extremus* 45 (2005–2006): 255–70.

Vankeerberghen, Griet. "Een Vertaling en Studie van Hoofdstuk 21 'Yao Lüeh' van *Huai Nan Tzu*" [A Translation and Study of Chapter 21 'Yaolüe' of *Huainanzi*]. Master's thesis, University of Leuven, 1990.
——. "Emotions and the Actions of the Sage: Recommendations for an Orderly Heart in the 'Huainanzi.'" *Philosophy East and West* 45, no. 4 (1995): 527–44. [Special issue: *Comparative Philosophy in the Low Countries*]
——. *The Huainanzi and Liu An's Claim to Moral Authority.* SUNY Series in Chinese Philosophy and Culture. Albany: State University of New York Press, 2001.
Xu Fuguan 徐復觀. "Liu An de shidai yu *Huainanzi*" 劉安的時代與淮南子. *Dalu zazhi* 大陸雜誌 47, no. 6 (1973): 1–38.
Yang Youli 杨有礼. *Xin Daojia honglie ji: "Huainanzi" yu Zhongguo wenhua* 新道家鸿烈集:《淮南子》与中国文化. Kaifeng: Henan University Press, 2001.
Zhang Guohua 張國華. "*Huainan honglie* yu *Chunqiu fanlu*" «淮南鴻烈» 與 «春秋繁露». *Daojia wenhua yanjiu* 道家文化研究, no. 6 (1995): 200–16.

Essential Textual and Historical Studies Before 1960

Centre Franco-Chinoise d'études sinologiques. *Huainanzi tongjian* 淮南子通檢. Beijing: Zhongfa hanxue yanjiusuo, 1944.
Kimura Eiichi 木村英一. "Koshohon *Enanji* 'Heiryakuhen' ni tsuite" 古鈔本淮南子兵略篇に就いて. *Shinagaku* 支那學 10, no. 2 (1940): 127–37; no. 3 (1941): 181–212.
Kuraishi Takeshiro 倉石武四郎. "*Enanji* no rekishi" 淮南子の歷史. *Shinagaku* 支那學 3 (1923): 334–68, 421–51.
Lao Ge 勞格 (1820–1864). *Dushu zazhi* 讀書雜識. 1878. Reprint, Taibei: Guangwen, 1970.
Liu Wendian 劉文典. *Sanyu zhaji* 三餘札集. 1935–1939. Reprint, Taibei: Shijie, 1963.
Lu Xinyuan 陸心源. *Yigutang ji* 儀顧堂集. 1862 [reprinted in the collection *Qianyuan congji* 潛園叢集]. Facsimile reprint of 1898 edition. Taibei: Taibei gufeng chubanshe, 1970.
Qian Tang 錢塘 (1735–1790). *Huainan "Tianwen" xun buzhu* 淮南天文訓補注. 1828; preface, 1788. Reprint, Hubei: Chongwen, 1877. [Included as an appendix in the *Xinbianzhuzi jicheng* reprint of the Liu Wendian critical edition]
Shimada Kan 島田翰. *Kobun kyūsho kō* 古文舊書考. 1905. Reprint, Beijing: Zaoyu tang, 1927.
Su Song 蘇頌 (1020–1101). *Su Weigong wenji* 蘇魏公文集. Compiled by Su Xi 蘇攜 (1065–1140). Preface to 1st ed., 1139. *Siku quanshu* edition, 1781. Facsimile reprint of the Wenyuange 文源閣 manuscript. Taibei: Commercial Press, 1973.
——. *Su Weigong wenji*. Edited by Su Tingyu 蘇廷玉 from the Wenlange 文瀾閣 manuscript of the *Siku quanshu* edition, 1842. Facsimile reprint of 1865 edition. Taibei: Qingyou chubanshe, 1960.
Tao Fangqi 陶方琦 (1845–1884). *Hanzishi wenchao* 漢孳室文鈔. Compiled by Ma Yongxi 馬用錫 and printed by Xu Youlan 徐友蘭, 1894.
——. *Huainan xuzhu yitong gu* 淮南許注異同詁. 1881. 2nd ed., including two supplements, *buyi* 補遺 and *xubu* 續補, 1884. Facsimile reprint of 2nd ed. Taibei: Wenhai chubanshe, n.d.
Wang Niansun 王念孫 and Wang Yinzhi 王引之. *Dushu zazhi* 讀書雜志. 1832. Reprint of 1870 edition. Taibei: Shijie, 1963.

Wu Chengshi 吳承仕. *Huainan jiuzhu jiaoli* 淮南舊注校理. Shexin (Anhui), 1924. In *Wu Jianzhai Yishu* 吳檢齋遺書. Beijing: Beijing shifan daxue chubanshe, 1985.

Yang Shuda 楊樹達. "Du Liu Wendian-jun *Huainan honglie jijie*" 讀劉文典君淮南鴻烈集解. In *Huainanzi lunwen ji* 淮南子論文集, edited and compiled by Chen Xinxiong 陳新雄 and Yü Dacheng 于大成, 133–43. Taibei: Muyi chubanshe, 1976.

——. *Huainanzi zhengwen* 淮南子證聞. Beijing: Zhongguo gexue yuan, 1953. In *Yang Shuda wenji* 楊樹達文集, vol. 11, compiled by Yang Bojun 楊伯峻. Shanghai: Guji chubanshe, 1983.

Ye Dehui 葉德輝 (1864–1927). *Huainan honglie jiangu* 淮南鴻烈閒詁. Changsha, 1895.

Yu Xingwu 于省吾. "*Huainanzi* xinzheng" 淮南子新證. In *Shuangjianchi zhuzi xinzheng* 雙劍誃諸子新證. Taibei: Yiwen, 1957.

Yu Yue 俞樾. "Huainan Neipian pingyi" 淮南內篇評議. In *Zhuzi pingyi* 諸子評議. 1870. Reprint, Shanghai: Commercial Press, 1935.

Textual and Historical Studies Since 1960

Akatsuka Kiyoshi 赤塚忠. "Ryūan" 劉安. In *Chūgoku no Shisōka* 中國の思想家, 147–61. Tokyo: Keisō Bookstore, 1963.

Chen Guangzhong 陈廣忠. *Huainanzi gushi xuanbian* 淮南子故事选编. Hefei: Huangshan shu she, 1985.

Chen Ligui 陳麗桂. "Baishi nian laide *Huainanzi* yanjiu mulu" 八十年來的淮南子研究目錄. *Zhongguo shumu jikan* 中國書目季刊 25, no. 3 (1991): 48–67.

Chen Xinxiong 陳新雄 and Yu Dacheng 于大成, comps. and eds. *Huainanzi lunwen ji* 淮南子論文集. Taibei: Muyi chubanshe, 1976.

Chen Yiping 陈一平. *Huiji gejia xueshuo de juzhu: "Huainanzi"* 汇集各家学说的巨著:《淮南子》. Beijing: Zhongguo wenlian chubangongsi, 1997.

Ding Yuanzhi 丁原植. *Huainanzi yu Wenzi kaobian* 淮南子與文子考辯. Taibei: Wanjuanlou, 1999.

Guo Cuigan 郭翠軒. "*Huainanzi* zhuben kaolüe" 淮南子注本考略. In *Huainanzi lunwen ji* 淮南子論文集, edited and compiled by Chen Xinxiong 陳新雄 and Yu Dacheng 于大成, 125–29. Taibei: Muyi chubanshe, 1976.

He Zhihua 何志華 and Zhu Guofan 朱國藩. *Tang Song leishu zhengyin "Huainanzi" ziliao huibian* 唐宋類書徵引《淮南子》資料彙編. Hong Kong: Zhongwen daxue chubanshe, 2005.

Honey, David. "Philology, Filiation, and Bibliography in the Textual Criticism of the *Huainan Tzu*." *Early China* 19 (1994): 161–92.

Ikeda Tomohisa 池田知久. "*Enanji* no seiritsu: *Shiki* to *Kanjo* no kentō" 淮南子の成立一史記と漢書の檢討. *Tōhōgaku* 東方學, no. 59 (1980): 18–31.

——. "*Enanji* 'Yōryakuhen' ni tsuite" 淮南子要略篇について. In *Ikeda Suetoshi hakushi koki kinen Tōyōgaku ronshū* 池田末利博士古稀記念東洋學論集, 401–9. Hiroshima, 1980.

Jin Qiyuan 金其源. "*Huainanzi* guanjian" 淮南子管見. In *Zhuzi guanjian* 諸子管見. Taibei: Shijie, 1963.

Jin Sheng 金生. "*Huainanzi* pianming de chengwei wenti" 淮南子篇名的稱謂問題. *Zhongguo zhexue* 中國哲學, no. 9 (1983): 256.

Lau, D. C. [Liu Dianjue 劉殿爵]. "Du *Huainan honglie jie* zhaji" 讀淮南子鴻烈解札記. *United College Journal* 6 (1967–1968): 139–88.

Li Jiansheng 李建胜. *Shengxian zhimou: "Huainanzi" pian* 圣贤智谋:《淮南子》篇. Beijing: Hualing chubanshe, 1996.

Ma Zonghuo 馬宗霍 (1897–1976). *Huainan Gaozhu canzheng* 淮南高注参正. Jinan: Qi Lu shushe, 1984.

Roth, Harold D. "Filiation Analysis and the Textual History of the *Huai-Nan Tzu*." *Transactions of the International Conference of Orientalists in Japan*, no. 28 (1982): 60–81.

——. "The Strange Case of the Overdue Book: A Study in the Fortuity of Textual Transmission." In *From Benares to Beijing: Essays in Honour of Professor Yun-Hua Jan*, edited by Gregory Schopen and Koichi Shinohara, 177–208. Oakville, Ont.: Mosaic Press, 1992.

——. "Text and Edition in Early Chinese Philosophical Literature." *Journal of the American Oriental Society* 113, no. 2 (1993): 214–27.

——. *The Textual History of the Huai-nan Tzu*. Monographs of the Association for Asian Studies, vol. 46. Ann Arbor, Mich.: Association for Asian Studies, 1992.

Ruan Tingzhuo 阮廷焯. "*Huainanzi* yinyong xian Qin zhuzi yiwen kao" 淮南子引用先秦諸子佚文考. In *Rao Zongyi jiaoshou nanyou zengbie lunwenji* 饒宗頤教授南遊贈別論文集, edited by Yan Gengwang 嚴耕望, 67–84. Taibei: Rao Zongyi *Festschrift* Publishing Committee, 1970.

——. "*Huainanzi* zhayi" 淮南子札迻. *Lianhe shuyuan xuebao* 聯合書院學報, no. 6 (1967): 127–33.

Sun Jiwen 孙纪文. *Huainanzi yanjiu* 淮南子研究. Beijing: Xueyuan chubanshe, 2005.

Tao Lei 陶磊. *Huainanzi "Tianwen" yanjiu: cong shushushi de jiaodu* 淮南子《天文》研究: 从数术史的角度. Jinan: Qilu shushe, 2003.

Wallacker, Benjamin E. "Liu An, Second King of Huai-nan (180?–122 B.C.)." *Journal of the American Oriental Society* 92 (1972): 36–49.

Wang Jinguan 王錦觀. "Liu Dianjue '*Du Huainan honglie zhaji*' kanwu biao" 劉殿爵 '讀淮南鴻烈札記' 勘誤表. *United College Journal* 7 (1968–1969): 179–82.

Wang Shumin 王叔岷. "Ba Riben guchao juanzi ben *Huainan honglie* 'Binglüe' *jiangu dinian*" 跋日本古鈔卷子本淮南鴻烈兵略閒詁第廿. In *Zhuzi jiaozheng* 諸子斠證, 493–540. Taibei: Shijie, 1963.

——. "*Huainanzi* jiaozheng, buyi, xubu" 淮南子斠證, 補遺, 續補. In *Zhuzi jiaozheng* 諸子斠證, 327–492. Taibei: Shijie, 1963.

——. "*Huainanzi* yin *Zhuang* ju ou" «淮南子» 引 «莊» 舉偶. *Daojia wenhua yanjiu* 道家文化研究, no. 14 (1998): 364–400.

——. "*Huainanzi* yu *Zhuangzi*" 淮南子與莊子. In *Huainanzi lunwen ji* 淮南子論文集, edited and compiled by Chen Xinxiong 陳新雄 and Yu Dacheng 于大成, 27–40. Taibei: Muyi chubanshe, 1976.

Wang Yundu 王云度. *Liu An pingzhuan* 刘安评传. Nanjing: Nanjing daxue chubanshe, 1997.

Wu Liancheng 吳連城. "*Huainanzi* cunjuan jiaokanji" 淮南子存雋校勘記. *Jinyang xuekan* 晉陽學刊, no. 3 (1982): 58–61.

Wu Zeyu 吳則虞. "*Huainanzi* shulu" 淮南子書錄. *Wenshi* 2 (1963): 291–314.

Xi Zezong 席澤宗. "*Huainanzi* 'Tianwen' xun shulue" 淮南子天文訓述略. *Kexue tongbao* 科學通報, 1963.6:35–39.

Xu Kuangyi 许匡一. *Huainanzi quanyi* 淮南子全译. Guiyang: Guizhou renmin chubanshe, 1993.

Yu Dacheng 于大成. *Huainan lunwen sanzhong* 淮南論文三種. Taibei: Wenshizhe chubanshe, 1975.

——. "Huainan wang shukao" 淮南王書考. *Zhongshan xueshu wenhua jikan* 中山學術文化集刊, no. 4 (1969): 61–100. [Reprinted in *Huainan lunwen sanzhong* 淮南論文三種 (Taibei: Wenshizhe chubanshe, 1975), 1–56]
——. "*Huainan zazhi* buzheng" 淮南雜志補正. *Zhongshan xueshu wenhua jikan* 中山學術文化集刊, no. 5 (1970): 9–72. [Reprinted in *Huainan lunwen sanzhong* (Taibei: Wenshizhe chubanshe, 1975), 95–199]
——. *Huainanzi jiaoshi* 淮南子校釋. 2 vols. Taibei: National Taiwan Normal University, 1969.
——. "*Huainanzi jiaoshi* zixu" 淮南子校釋自序. *Guangxing* 光星, no. 8 (1970): 6–17; (1971): 3–35.
——. "*Huainanzi* jinshi yuyi" 淮南子今釋語譯. In *Zhongguo xueshu mingzhu jinshi yuyi* 中國學術名著今釋語譯, vol. 3. Taibei: Xinan shuzhu, 1978.
——. *Huainanzi jinzhu jinyi* 淮南子今注今譯. Taibei: Xinan shuzhu, 1977.
——. "Liu Ji ben *Huainanzi* chuyu *Zang* ben kao" 劉績本淮南子出於藏本考. *Guoli Zhengzhi daxue xuebao*, no. 32 (1975): 41–73.
——. "Minguo yilai de *Huainan* xue" 民國以來的淮南學. *Chuangxin* 創新 no. 48 (1972): 5–7; no. 50 (1972): 3–4; no. 52 (1972): 4–5; no. 55 (1972): 6–8; no. 58 (1972): 5–6. [Reprinted as "Liushi nianlai zhi *Huainanzi* xue" 六十年來之淮南子學, in *Huainan lunwen sanzhong* (Taibei: Wenshizhe chubanshe, 1975), 79–123]
Zhang Xiaohu 張嘯虎. "Lun *Huainanzi* de wencai" 論淮南子的文采. *Beifang luncong* 北方論叢, no. 62 (1983): 43–47.
Zhang Yan 張嚴. "*Huainanzi* ershiyi juan lunci deshi pingyi" 淮南子二十一卷論次得失平議. *Dalu zazhi* 大陸雜志 31, no. 6 (1965): 15–18.
——. "*Huainanzi* zhujia yisi ji banben deshi pingyi" 淮南子注家疑似及版本得失平議. *Dalu zazhi* 大陸雜志 30, no. 8 (1965): 5–10.
Zheng Liangshu 鄭良樹. *Huainanzi jiaoli* 淮南子斠理. Taibei: Jiaxin Cement Co. Cultural Foundation, 1969.
——. *Huainanzi tonglun* 淮南子通論. Taibei: Haiyang shishe, 1964.
——. "*Huainanzi* chuanben zhijian ji" 淮南子傳本知見記. *Guoli Zhongyang tushuguan guankan* 國立中央圖書館館刊 1, no. 1 (1967): 27–39.
——. "*Huainanzi* zhujiao zhujia shuping" 淮南子注校諸家述評. *Guoli Zhongyang tushuguan guankan* 國立中央圖書館館刊 2, no. 2 (1968): 47–58.
——. "Liu Ji ben *Huainanzi* jiaoji" 劉績本淮南子斠記. *Youshi xuezhi* 幼師學誌 6, no. 3 (1967): 1–33.
——. "Qufu yu *Huainanzi*" 屈賦與淮南子. *Dalu zazhi* 大陸雜志 52, no. 6 (1976).
Zhou Lisheng 周立升. "*Huainanzi* de Yi dao guan" «淮南子» 的易道關. *Daojia wenhua yanjiu* 道家文化研究, no. 2 (1992): 223–35.
Zhu Rong 祝融. Huainanzi "*Binglüe xun*" *yizhu* 淮南子《兵略训》译注. Beijing: Junshi kexue chubanshe, 1993.

Harold D. Roth, with Matthew Duperon

INDEX

TRANSLATIONS FROM THE ASIAN CLASSICS

Major Plays of Chikamatsu, tr. Donald Keene 1961

Four Major Plays of Chikamatsu, tr. Donald Keene. Paperback ed. only. 1961; rev. ed. 1997

Records of the Grand Historian of China, translated from the Shih chi of Ssu-ma Ch'ien, tr. Burton Watson, 2 vols. 1961

Instructions for Practical Living and Other Neo-Confucian Writings by Wang Yang-ming, tr. Wing-tsit Chan 1963

Hsün Tzu: Basic Writings, tr. Burton Watson, paperback ed. only. 1963; rev. ed. 1996

Chuang Tzu: Basic Writings, tr. Burton Watson, paperback ed. only. 1964; rev. ed. 1996

The Mahābhārata, tr. Chakravarthi V. Narasimhan. Also in paperback ed. 1965; rev. ed. 1997

The Manyōshū, Nippon Gakujutsu Shinkōkai edition 1965

Su Tung-p'o: Selections from a Sung Dynasty Poet, tr. Burton Watson. Also in paperback ed. 1965

Bhartrihari: Poems, tr. Barbara Stoler Miller. Also in paperback ed. 1967

Basic Writings of Mo Tzu, Hsün Tzu, and Han Fei Tzu, tr. Burton Watson. Also in separate paperback eds. 1967

The Awakening of Faith, Attributed to Aśvaghosha, tr. Yoshito S. Hakeda. Also in paperback ed. 1967

Reflections on Things at Hand: The Neo-Confucian Anthology, comp. Chu Hsi and Lü Tsu-ch'ien, tr. Wing-tsit Chan 1967

The Platform Sutra of the Sixth Patriarch, tr. Philip B. Yampolsky. Also in paperback ed. 1967

Essays in Idleness: The Tsurezuregusa of Kenkō, tr. Donald Keene. Also in paperback ed. 1967

The Pillow Book of Sei Shōnagon, tr. Ivan Morris, 2 vols. 1967

Two Plays of Ancient India: The Little Clay Cart and the Minister's Seal, tr. J. A. B. van Buitenen 1968

The Complete Works of Chuang Tzu, tr. Burton Watson 1968

The Romance of the Western Chamber (Hsi Hsiang chi), tr. S. I. Hsiung. Also in paperback ed. 1968

The Manyōshū, Nippon Gakujutsu Shinkōkai edition. Paperback ed. only. 1969

Records of the Historian: Chapters from the Shih chi of Ssu-ma Ch'ien, tr. Burton Watson. Paperback ed. only. 1969

Cold Mountain: 100 Poems by the T'ang Poet Han-shan, tr. Burton Watson. Also in paperback ed. 1970

Twenty Plays of the Nō Theatre, ed. Donald Keene. Also in paperback ed. 1970

Chūshingura: The Treasury of Loyal Retainers, tr. Donald Keene. Also in paperback ed. 1971; rev. ed. 1997

The Zen Master Hakuin: Selected Writings, tr. Philip B. Yampolsky 1971

Chinese Rhyme-Prose: Poems in the Fu Form from the Han and Six Dynasties Periods, tr. Burton Watson. Also in paperback ed. 1971

Kūkai: Major Works, tr. Yoshito S. Hakeda. Also in paperback ed. 1972

The Old Man Who Does as He Pleases: Selections from the Poetry and Prose of Lu Yu, tr. Burton Watson 1973

The Lion's Roar of Queen Śrīmālā, tr. Alex and Hideko Wayman 1974

Courtier and Commoner in Ancient China: Selections from the History of the Former Han by Pan Ku, tr. Burton Watson. Also in paperback ed. 1974

Japanese Literature in Chinese, vol. 1: *Poetry and Prose in Chinese by Japanese Writers of the Early Period*, tr. Burton Watson 1975

Japanese Literature in Chinese, vol. 2: *Poetry and Prose in Chinese by Japanese Writers of the Later Period*, tr. Burton Watson 1976

Love Song of the Dark Lord: Jayadeva's Gītagovinda, tr. Barbara Stoler Miller. Also in paperback ed. Cloth ed. includes critical text of the Sanskrit. 1977; rev. ed. 1997

Ryōkan: Zen Monk-Poet of Japan, tr. Burton Watson 1977

Calming the Mind and Discerning the Real: From the Lam rim chen mo of Tsoṇ-kha-pa, tr. Alex Wayman 1978

The Hermit and the Love-Thief: Sanskrit Poems of Bhartrihari and Bilhaṇa, tr. Barbara Stoler Miller 1978

The Lute: Kao Ming's P'i-p'a chi, tr. Jean Mulligan. Also in paperback ed. 1980

A Chronicle of Gods and Sovereigns: Jinnō Shōtōki of Kitabatake Chikafusa, tr. H. Paul Varley 1980

Among the Flowers: The Hua-chien chi, tr. Lois Fusek 1982

Grass Hill: Poems and Prose by the Japanese Monk Gensei, tr. Burton Watson 1983

Doctors, Diviners, and Magicians of Ancient China: Biographies of Fang-shih, tr. Kenneth J. DeWoskin. Also in paperback ed. 1983

Theater of Memory: The Plays of Kālidāsa, ed. Barbara Stoler Miller. Also in paperback ed. 1984

The Columbia Book of Chinese Poetry: From Early Times to the Thirteenth Century, ed. and tr. Burton Watson. Also in paperback ed. 1984

Poems of Love and War: From the Eight Anthologies and the Ten Long Poems of Classical Tamil, tr. A. K. Ramanujan. Also in paperback ed. 1985

The Bhagavad Gita: Krishna's Counsel in Time of War, tr. Barbara Stoler Miller 1986

The Columbia Book of Later Chinese Poetry, ed. and tr. Jonathan Chaves. Also in paperback ed. 1986

The Tso Chuan: Selections from China's Oldest Narrative History, tr. Burton Watson 1989

Waiting for the Wind: Thirty-six Poets of Japan's Late Medieval Age, tr. Steven Carter 1989
Selected Writings of Nichiren, ed. Philip B. Yampolsky 1990
Saigyō, Poems of a Mountain Home, tr. Burton Watson 1990
The Book of Lieh Tzu: A Classic of the Tao, tr. A. C. Graham. Morningside ed. 1990
The Tale of an Anklet: An Epic of South India—The Cilappatikāram of Iḷaṅkō Aṭikaḷ, tr. R. Parthasarathy 1993
Waiting for the Dawn: A Plan for the Prince, tr. with introduction by Wm. Theodore de Bary 1993
Yoshitsune and the Thousand Cherry Trees: A Masterpiece of the Eighteenth-Century Japanese Puppet Theater, tr., annotated, and with introduction by Stanleigh H. Jones, Jr. 1993
The Lotus Sutra, tr. Burton Watson. Also in paperback ed. 1993
The Classic of Changes: A New Translation of the I Ching *as Interpreted by Wang Bi*, tr. Richard John Lynn 1994
Beyond Spring: Tz'u Poems of the Sung Dynasty, tr. Julie Landau 1994
The Columbia Anthology of Traditional Chinese Literature, ed. Victor H. Mair 1994
Scenes for Mandarins: The Elite Theater of the Ming, tr. Cyril Birch 1995
Letters of Nichiren, ed. Philip B. Yampolsky; tr. Burton Watson et al. 1996
Unforgotten Dreams: Poems by the Zen Monk Shōtetsu, tr. Steven D. Carter 1997
The Vimalakirti Sutra, tr. Burton Watson 1997
Japanese and Chinese Poems to Sing: The Wakan rōei shū, tr. J. Thomas Rimer and Jonathan Chaves 1997
Breeze Through Bamboo: Kanshi of Ema Saikō, tr. Hiroaki Sato 1998
A Tower for the Summer Heat, by Li Yu, tr. Patrick Hanan 1998
Traditional Japanese Theater: An Anthology of Plays, by Karen Brazell 1998
The Original Analects: Sayings of Confucius and His Successors (0479–0249), by E. Bruce Brooks and A. Taeko Brooks 1998
The Classic of the Way and Virtue: A New Translation of the Tao-te ching *of Laozi as Interpreted by Wang Bi*, tr. Richard John Lynn 1999
The Four Hundred Songs of War and Wisdom: An Anthology of Poems from Classical Tamil, The Puṛanāṇūṛu, ed. and tr. George L. Hart and Hank Heifetz 1999
Original Tao: Inward Training (Nei-yeh) *and the Foundations of Taoist Mysticism*, by Harold D. Roth 1999
Lao Tzu's Tao Te Ching: *A Translation of the Startling New Documents Found at Guodian*, by Robert G. Henricks 2000
The Shorter Columbia Anthology of Traditional Chinese Literature, ed. Victor H. Mair 2000
Mistress and Maid (Jiaohongji), by Meng Chengshun, tr. Cyril Birch 2001
Chikamatsu: Five Late Plays, tr. and ed. C. Andrew Gerstle 2001
The Essential Lotus: Selections from the Lotus Sutra, tr. Burton Watson 2002
Early Modern Japanese Literature: An Anthology, 1600–1900, ed. Haruo Shirane 2002; abridged 2008
The Columbia Anthology of Traditional Korean Poetry, ed. Peter H. Lee 2002
The Sound of the Kiss, or The Story That Must Never Be Told: Pingali Suranna's Kalapurnodayamu, tr. Vecheru Narayana Rao and David Shulman 2003
The Selected Poems of Du Fu, tr. Burton Watson 2003
Far Beyond the Field: Haiku by Japanese Women, tr. Makoto Ueda 2003
Just Living: Poems and Prose by the Japanese Monk Tonna, ed. and tr. Steven D. Carter 2003
Han Feizi: Basic Writings, tr. Burton Watson 2003
Mozi: Basic Writings, tr. Burton Watson 2003
Xunzi: Basic Writings, tr. Burton Watson 2003
Zhuangzi: Basic Writings, tr. Burton Watson 2003
The Awakening of Faith, Attributed to Aśvaghosha, tr. Yoshito S. Hakeda, introduction by Ryuichi Abe 2005
The Tales of the Heike, tr. Burton Watson, ed. Haruo Shirane 2006
Tales of Moonlight and Rain, by Ueda Akinari, tr. with introduction by Anthony H. Chambers 2007
Traditional Japanese Literature: An Anthology, Beginnings to 1600, ed. Haruo Shirane 2007
The Philosophy of Qi, by Kaibara Ekken, tr. Mary Evelyn Tucker 2007
The Analects of Confucius, tr. Burton Watson 2007
The Art of War: Sun Zi's Military Methods, tr. Victor Mair 2007
One Hundred Poets: One Poem Each: A Translation of the Ogura Hyakunin Isshu, tr. Peter McMillan 2008
Zeami: Performance Notes, tr. Tom Hare 2008
Zongmi on Chan, tr. Jeffrey Lyle Broughton 2009
Scripture of the Lotus Blossom of the Fine Dharma, rev. ed., tr. Leon Hurvitz, preface and introduction by Stephen R. Teiser 2009
Mencius, tr. Irene Bloom, ed. with an introduction by Philip J. Ivanhoe 2009
Clouds Thick, Whereabouts Unknown: Poems by Zen Monks of China, Charles Egan 2010
The Mozi: A Complete Translation, tr. Ian Johnston 2010